ACCOUNTING
TEXT AND CASES

ROBERT N. ANTHONY, D.B.A.

Professor Emeritus
Graduate School of
Business Administration
Harvard University

JAMES S. REECE, D.B.A., C.M.A.

Professor
School of
Business Administration
The University of Michigan

JULIE H. HERTENSTEIN, D.B.A.

Associate Professor
College of Business Administration
Northeastern University

NINTH EDITION 1995

IRWIN

Chicago • Bogotá • Boston • Buenos Aires • Caracas
London • Madrid • Mexico City • Sydney • Toronto

Senior sponsoring editor: *Jeff Shelstad*
Developmental editor: *Jackie Scruggs*
Marketing manager: *Heather L. Woods*
Project editor: Stephanie M. Britt
Production supervisor: *Bette Ittersagen*
Designer: *Heidi J. Baughman*
Cover designer: Tim Goldman
Art coordinator: *Heather Burbridge*
Compositor: *Carlisle Communications, Ltd.*
Typeface: *10/12 Melior*
Printer: *R. R. Donnelley & Sons Company*

3 2280 00776 7049

Library of Congress Cataloging-in-Publication Data

Anthony, Robert Newton
  Accounting, text and cases / Robert N. Anthony, James S. Reece, Julie H. Hertenstein.--9th ed.
    p.   cm.
  Includes bibliographical references and index.
  ISBN 0-256-12372-1   International edition ISBN 0-256-16551-3
  1. Accounting.   2. Accounting—Case studies.   I. Reece, James S.
II. Hertenstein, Julie Huffman.   III. Title.
HF5635.A69   1995
658.15'11—dc20   94—21933

Printed in the United States of America
1 2 3 4 5 6 7 8 9 0 DO 1 0 9 8 7 6 5 4

Preface

An accounting text can be written with an emphasis on either of two viewpoints: (1) what the user of accounting information needs to know about accounting or (2) what the preparer of accounting reports needs to know about accounting. This book focuses on the user of accounting information. Because such a person needs to know enough about the preparation of accounting reports to use them intelligently, this text includes the technical material needed for this purpose. The book is aimed primarily, however, at the person who wants to be a knowledgeable user of accounting information. This focus is reinforced in the book's case studies, which help the student learn that accounting is not a cut-and-dried subject with all of its "answers" clearly indicated by the application of rules.

The focus of the book makes it particularly appropriate for required core courses in accounting, in which many of the students are not planning to take further elective accounting courses. First, we believe that if a core course stresses the more analytical uses of accounting information by managers and outside analysts rather than the procedural details that the practicing accountant needs to know, then those students who do not take further accounting courses will be left with a positive view of the importance of accounting rather than with the negative "bean counter" stereotype. Second, we feel that a user orientation in the core course actually is likely to generate a greater number of accounting majors from the class than if the course is oriented more toward the person who has already decided to major in accounting. Similarly, in our experience the required accounting module in a management development program will generate little participant interest unless the module is oriented toward the nonaccountant user of accounting information. In sum, we think the book conveys the fact that accounting is interesting and fun, not dull and tedious.

Specifically, this book is used in at least the following four ways:

1. As an introductory course where most (if not all) of the students have no prior training in accounting. In many schools this introduction comprises two separate courses, one dealing with financial accounting and the other with management accounting. Many schools use this book for both such courses, whereas some use it only for financial accounting (Chapter 1 and Chapters 2–14) or for management accounting (Chapter 1 and Chapters 15–28). It is used in such introductory courses at both the upper under graduate level and in graduate programs. In addition to its widespread use in schools of business and management, it is also used in introductory accounting courses in some law schools, education schools, and schools of public health.

2. As an elective course that builds on a required introductory course in accounting—particularly where the introductory course had more of a procedural orientation and the elective is intended to be more conceptual, analytical, and user-oriented.

3. As the accounting module in a management development program where the participants represent a variety of functional and technical backgrounds.

4. As a nontechnical accounting reference book for nonaccountants in business and other organizations.

Although designed for beginning students, the book does not contain enough "pencil-pushing" material to meet the needs of some instructors of introductory courses. Such instructors may wish to use the companion volume, *Accounting Principles Workbook*,[1] which, in addition to key terms and discussion questions, has more problem material (10–15 problems per chapter), a short practice set, and some cases that are not in this volume.

Many instructors also assign or recommend the programmed text *Essentials of Accounting*,[2] either as preliminary to study of the subject (it is often sent in advance to participants in M.B.A. and management development programs) or as a review device. It is a self-study introductory treatment of financial accounting, geared to Part 1 of this text.

The Cases As in previous editions the cases have been selected because of their interest and educational value as a basis for class discussion. They are not

---

[1] *Accounting Principles Workbook*, 8th ed. (Homewood, Ill.: Richard D. Irwin, 1995).
[2] Robert N. Anthony, *Essentials of Accounting*, 5th ed. (Reading, Mass.: Addison-Wesley, 1993). This material is also available in the form of computer software for IBM-compatible and Apple computers, titled *Teach Yourself Essentials of Accounting*.

necessarily intended to illustrate either correct or incorrect handling of management problems. Skill in the management use of accounting information can be acquired, we believe, only through experience. Thinking about a case and discussing it in informal discussion groups and in the classroom require the student to do something—to analyze a problem, to weigh various factors involved in it, to make some calculations, to take a position, and so on. In class the student is required to explain her or his point of view, to defend it, to understand and appraise the arguments of colleagues, and to decide what arguments are the strongest. Practice in doing these things helps to increase skill and understanding; in fact, many educators believe that the really important parts of a subject can be learned only by experience of some sort, as opposed to merely hearing or reading about them. Thus, although the case material comprises less than half the pages in this book, the discussion of these cases is by far the more important part of the educational process. Of course, such discussions contribute to the students' communication skills as well as to their understanding of accounting.

This edition has a total of 121 cases. Some of these are new, and the majority of them that were carried over from the previous edition have been updated (in some instances with a change in case name).

Occasionally, a student or instructor questions our use of small business settings for many of the cases. Such cases often avoid certain complexities at a point when the student is not yet prepared to deal with them. We also would note that studies have reported that small businesses (those employing fewer than 500 people) represent over 99 percent of all U.S. businesses, provide about 50 percent of all private-sector jobs, generate almost 40 percent of the GNP, and contribute two out of three newly created jobs. We therefore feel that exposure to some small business cases is beneficial to students, many of whom will eventually work in such firms or work with them as auditors or consultants.

Changes in the Ninth Edition

Developments in accounting, particularly financial accounting, have continued to be rapid in the last five years. These have resulted in many updating changes in the text. (Part 1 reflects Financial Accounting Standards Board [FASB] pronouncements through mid-1994, as well as the 1993 tax act.) More specifically, Chapters 2–12 reflect evolutionary and updating changes, including the additions of sections on executory contracts in Chapter 8, ESOPs and nonprofit organizations' equity in Chapter 9, other postretirement benefits in Chapter 10, and ethical problems in Chapter 14. For simplification the T-account method of preparing a cash flow statement has been deleted from Chapter 11.

The structure of Part 2 on management accounting has been changed in recognition of some students' confusing different cost *constructs* with different cost *systems*. The new structure stresses that there is *one* management accounting system, which uses full cost information (as well as information on revenues and assets) for various measurement purposes, and uses responsibility cost information for management control purposes. In addition to the two purposes of measurement and control, management accounting has a third purpose—to aid in choosing from among alternative courses of action; but information for this purpose cannot come directly from the management accounting *system* because each alternative choice problem requires its own arrangement of accounting information.

Chapter 15 presents this new structure. The cost behavior coverage in Chapter 16 has been expanded to place far more emphasis on step-function costs and on the importance of being explicit about the relevant time period when characterizing a cost's behavior. Activity-based costing has been added to Chapter 18, and a brief discussion of quality costs is included in Chapter 19.

With this new structure the analysis of nonproduction variances appears in Chapter 21, immediately following coverage of production cost variances in Chapter 20. (Formerly, the two aspects of variance analysis were separated by several chapters, which some instructors found undesirable.) This unified treatment of variance analysis provides a natural transition into the other management control topics in Chapters 22–25, which include expanded treatment of control reports and incentive compensation in a new Chapter 25. Then short-run and long-term alternative choice decisions are described in Chapters 26 and 27, with Chapter 28 providing a summary of Part 2.

Acknowledgments

We are grateful to the many instructors and students who have made suggestions for improving this book. Included among those people are our colleagues at the Harvard Business School and the schools of business administration at The University of Michigan and Northeastern University, as well as the anonymous reviewers who commented on the previous edition.

Robert N. Anthony
James S. Reece
Julie H. Hertenstein

Contents

ix

Index and Source of Cases

The 121 cases included in this book are listed below in alphabetical order, together with their authors' names and the institution with which each author was affiliated at the time the case was written. Cases with no name shown were written by, or under the supervision of, Robert N. Anthony, James S. Reece, or Julie H. Hertenstein. Unless otherwise indicated on the first page of a case, the copyright on all cases herein is held by Osceola Institute. No case may be reproduced in any form or by any means without the permission of its copyright holder. Information on requesting permission to reproduce Harvard Business School or Osceola Institute cases is included on the copyright page of this book. We regret that we are unable to provide permission information for cases not copyrighted by Harvard or Osceola.

Comments on the text, cases, or instructor's manual, or new ideas for teaching the cases, would be welcomed and should be sent to Professor Reece at the School of Business Administration, The University of Michigan, Ann Arbor, MI 48109-1234.

PART 1

FINANCIAL ACCOUNTING

1

The Nature and Purpose
of Accounting

Most of the world's work is done through organizations—groups of people who work together to accomplish one or more objectives. In doing its work, an organization uses resources—labor, materials, various services, buildings, and equipment. These resources need to be financed, or paid for. To work effectively, the people in an organization need information about the amounts of these resources, the means of financing them, and the results achieved through using them. Parties outside the organization need similar information to make judgments about the organization. **Accounting** is a system that provides such information.

Organizations can be classified broadly as either for-profit or nonprofit. As these names suggest, a dominant purpose of organizations in the former category is to earn a profit, whereas organizations in the latter category have other objectives, such as governing, providing social services, providing education, and so on. Of the employed persons in the United States, approximately two-thirds work in for-profit organizations and one-third in government and other nonprofit organizations. Accounting is basically similar in both types of organizations.

THE NEED FOR INFORMATION

In its details information differs greatly among organizations of various types. But viewed broadly, the information needs of most organizations are

ILLUSTRATION 1–1
TYPES OF INFORMATION

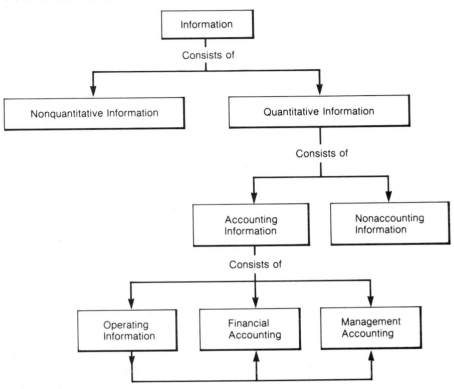

similar. We shall outline and illustrate these general information needs by referring to Varsity Motors, Inc., an automobile dealership.

Varsity Motors seeks to earn a profit by selling new and used automobiles and parts and accessories, and by providing repair service. It is an organization of 52 people headed by Pat Voss, its president. It owns a building that contains the showroom, service shop, a storeroom for parts and accessories, and office space. It also owns a number of new and used automobiles, which it offers for sale; a stock of spare parts, accessories, and supplies; and cash in the bank. These are examples of the resources the company needs to conduct its business.

Illustration 1–1 depicts the different types of information that might be useful to people interested in Varsity Motors. As shown in the illustration, information can be either quantitative or nonquantitative. Quantitative information is information that is expressed in numbers. Examples of nonquantitative information are visual impressions, conversations, television programs, and newspaper stories. Accounting is primarily concerned with quantitative information.

Accounting is one of several types of quantitive information. Accounting information is distinguished from the other types in that it usually is expressed in *monetary* amounts. Data on employees' ages and years of experience are quantitative, but they are not usually considered to be accounting information. The line here is not sharply drawn, however; nonmonetary information is often included in accounting reports when it will help the reader understand the report. For example, an accounting sales report for Varsity Motors would show not only the monetary amount of sales revenue, but also the number of automobiles sold, which is nonmonetary information.

What information is needed about the amounts and financing of the resources used in Varsity Motors and the results achieved by the use of these resources? This information can be classified into three categories: (1) operating information, (2) financial accounting information, and (3) management accounting information. Each is shown in the bottom section of Illustration 1–1.

Operating Information

A considerable amount of **operating information** is required to conduct an organization's day-to-day activities. For example, Varsity Motors' employees must be paid exactly the amounts owed them, and the government requires that records be maintained for each employee showing amounts earned and paid, as well as various deductions. The sales force needs to know what automobiles are available for sale and each one's cost and selling price. When an automobile is sold, a record must be made of that fact. The person in the stockroom needs to know what parts and accessories are on hand; and if the stock of a certain part becomes depleted, this fact needs to be known so that an additional quantity can be ordered. Amounts owed by the company's customers need to be known; and if a customer does not pay a bill on time, this fact needs to be known so that appropriate action can be taken. The company needs to know the amounts it owes to others, when these amounts should be paid, and how much money it has in the bank.

Operating information constitutes by far the largest quantity of accounting information. As suggested by the arrows at the bottom of Illustration 1–1, this operating information provides the basic data for both management accounting and financial accounting.

Financial Accounting

Financial accounting information is intended both for managers and also for the use of parties external to the organization, including shareholders (and trustees in nonprofit organizations), banks and other creditors, government agencies, investment advisers, and the general public. Shareholders who have furnished capital to Varsity Motors want information on how well the company is doing. If they should decide to sell their shares, they need information that helps them judge how much their investment is worth.

Prospective buyers of these shares need similar information. If the company wants to borrow money, the lender wants information that will show that the company is sound and that there is a high probability that the loan will be repaid.

Only in rare instances can outside parties insist that an organization furnish information tailor-made to their specifications. In most cases, they must accept the information that the organization chooses to supply. They could not conceivably understand this information without knowing the ground rules that governed its preparation. Moreover, they cannot be expected to learn a new set of ground rules for each organization of interest to them, nor can they compare information about two organizations unless both sets of information are prepared according to common ground rules. These ground rules are the subject matter of financial accounting (also called **financial reporting**).

Management Accounting

Varsity Motors' president, vice president of sales, service manager, and other managers do not have the time to examine the details of the operating information. Instead, they rely on summaries of this information. They use these summaries, together with other information, to carry out their management responsibilities. The accounting information specifically prepared to aid managers is called **management accounting information.** This information is used in three management functions: (1) planning, (2) implementation, and (3) control.

Planning. Performed by managers at all levels, in all organizations, **planning** is the process of deciding what actions should be taken in the future. A plan may be made for any segment of the organization or for the entire organization. When Varsity Motors' service manager decides the order in which automobiles will be repaired and which mechanic will work on each of them, the service manager is engaged in planning in the same sense as, but on a smaller scale than, the president when the latter decides to build a new showroom and service facility.

An important form of planning is called **budgeting.** Budgeting is the process of planning the overall activities of the organization for a specified period of time, usually a year. A primary objective of budgeting is to *coordinate* the separate plans made for various segments of the organization so as to assure that these plans harmonize with one another. For example, Varsity's sales plans and service department capacity plans must be consistent. Also, budgeting helps managers determine whether the coming year's activities are likely to produce satisfactory results and, if not, what should be done. Even tiny organizations find budgeting useful; many persons prepare a budget for their household.

Planning involves making decisions. Decisions are arrived at by (1) recognizing that a problem or an opportunity exists, (2) identifying alternative ways of addressing the problem or opportunity, (3) analyzing the consequences of each alternative, and (4) comparing these consequences so as to decide which is best. Accounting information is useful especially in the analysis step of the decision-making process.

Implementation. Making plans does not itself ensure that the plans will be implemented. In the case of the annual budget, each manager must take actions to provide the human and other resources that will be needed to achieve the planned results. Each manager must also make more detailed implementation plans than are encompassed in the budget; specific actions to be taken on a week-to-week and even day-to-day basis must be planned in advance.

The **implementation** of these very specific plans requires supervision on the part of the manager. Although much of this activity is routine, the manager also must react to events that were not anticipated when the budget was prepared. Indeed, a key managerial responsibility is to change previous plans appropriately to adjust for new conditions. If an unexpected situation impacts more than one part of the organization, the managers affected must coordinate their responses, just as their original plans were coordinated.

Control. In Varsity Motors most automobile sales are made by salespersons and most service work is done by mechanics. It is not the responsibility of Pat Voss and the other managers to do this work themselves. Rather, it is their responsibility to see that it is done, and done properly, by the employees of the organization. The process they use to assure that employees perform properly is called **control.** Accounting information is used in the control process as a means of communication, motivation, attention-getting, and appraisal.

As a means of *communication,* accounting reports (especially budgets) can assist in informing employees about management's plans and in general about the types of action management wishes the organization to take. As a means of *motivation,* accounting reports can induce members of the organization to act in a way that is consistent with the organization's overall goals and objectives. As a means of *attention-getting,* accounting information signals that problems may exist that require investigation and possibly action; this process is called **feedback.** As a means of *appraisal,* accounting helps show how well managers of the organization have performed, particularly with respect to the budgeted performance of the departments for which they are responsible. This provides a basis for a salary increase, promotion, corrective action of various kinds, or (in extreme cases) dismissal.

The relationship among the management functions of planning, implementation, and control is shown in Illustration 1–2. Chapter 15 will further introduce management accounting and contrast it with financial reporting.

Definition of Accounting

Accounting is related to all of the activities described above, and in all of them the emphasis is on using accounting information in the process of *making decisions.* Both managers within an organization and interested

ILLUSTRATION 1–2
RELATIONSHIP OF MANAGEMENT FUNCTIONS

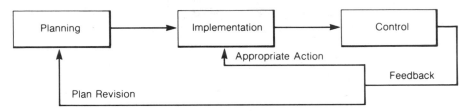

outside parties use accounting information in making decisions that affect the organization. Thus, of the several available definitions of accounting, the one developed by an American Accounting Association committee is perhaps the best because of its focus on accounting as an aid to decision making. This committee defined accounting as *"the process of identifying, measuring, and communicating economic information to permit informed judgments and decisions by users of the information."*[1]

THE PROFESSION OF ACCOUNTING

In most organizations the accounting group is the largest staff unit, that is, the largest group other than the "line" activities of production and marketing. The accounting group consists essentially of two types of people: (1) bookkeepers and other data-entry employees who maintain the detailed operating records and (2) professional accountants who decide how items should be reported, prepare the reports, interpret these reports, prepare special analyses, design and operate the systems through which information flows, and ensure that the information is accurate. In 1992 there were 1,365,000 accountants and 1,841,000 bookkeepers and accounting clerks in the United States.[2]

All publicly owned companies and many other organizations have their accounting reports audited by a public accounting firm. These firms also perform other services for clients. Some of these firms are very large: the six largest (colloquially called the Big Six) each have tens of thousands of employees and hundreds of offices around the world, with annual revenues totaling billions of dollars. They are far larger than any law firm, medical group practice, or other professional firm. At the other extreme, thousands of public accountants practice as individuals. All told, in 1991 a total of 68,000 accounting and auditing firms employed about 525,000 people and generated $34 billion of revenues.[3]

---

[1]American Accounting Association, *A Statement of Basic Accounting Theory* (Sarasota, Fla.: 1966), p. 1.

[2]U.S. Bureau of the Census, *Statistical Abstract of the United States: 1993,* 113th ed. (Washington, D.C.: 1993).

[3]Ibid.

Most public accountants are licensed by their state and are designated as Certified Public Accountants (CPAs). The professional organization of CPAs is the American Institute of Certified Public Accountants (AICPA). Many accountants employed by industry belong to the Institute of Management Accountants (IMA), formerly the National Association of Accountants. The IMA administers the Certified Management Accountant (CMA) program. Some accountants in industry also are Certified Internal Auditors (CIA). Many college and university accounting faculty members belong to the American Accounting Association (AAA).

Although accounting is a staff function performed by accounting professionals within an organization, the ultimate responsibility for the generation of accounting information—whether financial or managerial—rests with *management.* Management's responsibility for accounting is the reason that one of the top officers of many businesses is the **controller.** Within the division of top management's duties, the controller is the person responsible for satisfying other managers' needs for management accounting information and for complying with the requirements of financial reporting. To these ends the controller's office employs accounting professionals in both management and financial accounting. These accountants design, install, and operate the information systems required to generate financial and managerial reports.

OUR APPROACH TO ACCOUNTING

Accounting can be approached from either of two directions: from the viewpoint of the accountant or from the viewpoint of the user of accounting information. The former approach emphasizes the concepts and techniques that are involved in collecting, summarizing, and reporting accounting information; the latter emphasizes what the user needs to know about accounting. We focus on the latter approach. The difference between these two approaches is only one of emphasis. Accountants need to know how information is to be used because they should collect and report information in a form that is most helpful to those who use it. Users need to know what the accountant does; otherwise, they are unlikely to understand the real meaning of the information that is provided.

The approach to accounting taken here is something like that used by an airplane pilot in learning to use flight instruments. The pilot needs to know the meaning of the message conveyed by each of the instruments—for example, that a needle on a certain gauge going above a given point probably means that a certain component is not functioning properly. The word *probably* is used because, for one reason or another, an instrument may not always give the reading that it is supposed to give. As the user of the instrument, the pilot must realize this and must also understand something of the likelihood of, and the reason for, these abnormalities. On the other hand, the pilot does not need to know how to design, construct, calibrate, or repair airplane instruments. Specialists are available for these important functions.

Similarly, those who use accounting information must understand what a given accounting figure probably means, what its limitations are, and the circumstances in which it may mean something different from the apparent "signal" that it gives. They do not, however, need to know how to design, construct, operate, or check on the accuracy of an accounting system. They can rely on accountants for these important functions.

Preconceptions about Accounting

Readers of this book have already been exposed to a great deal of accounting information. Cash register or credit card receipts, checks written or (preferably) received, bank statements, merchants' and utilities' bills—all these are parts of accounting systems. One reads in the newspaper about the profit (or losses) of a company or an industry, about dividends, or about money being spent to build new buildings; this information comes from accounting systems. Even before beginning a formal study of the subject, therefore, the reader has accumulated a number of ideas about accounting.

The trouble is that some of these ideas probably are incorrect. For example, it seems intuitively reasonable that accounting should report what a business is "worth." But accounting does not, in fact, do this, nor does it even attempt to do so. As another example, there is a general notion that the word *asset* refers to valuable things, good things to have. But the skills and abilities of an organization's employees are not assets in the accounting sense, even though they may be a key determinant of the organization's success.

Thus, as with many other subjects, students of accounting must be wary of preconceptions. They will discover that accounting *as it really is* may be different in important respects from what they had surmised it to be. They will find that there are sound reasons for these differences, and it is important that they understand these reasons. To achieve such an understanding, users need to know enough about accounting concepts and techniques to understand the nature and limitations of the accounting information. They do not, however, need the detailed knowledge that the accountant must have.

Plan of the Book

We described above three types of accounting information: operating information, financial accounting information, and management accounting information. Since our viewpoint is that of the current and potential *users* (as opposed to preparers) of accounting information, we shall not describe operating information in any great detail. The book is therefore divided into two approximately equal parts, the first on financial accounting and the second on management accounting.

The discussion of financial accounting comes first because the structure of financial accounting underlies *all* accounting. This structure consists of a few basic principles and concepts, a set of relationships among the elements comprising the accounting system, a terminology, and a number of rules and guidelines for the application of the principles and concepts to specific situations. We shall describe the financial accounting structure in a general way in Chapters 2, 3, and 4; and we shall then go over the same ground again in more detail in Chapters 5 through 14.

The second half of the book discusses the nature and use of management accounting information. The management of an organization can establish whatever ground rules it wishes for the accounting information collected for its own use. Thus, although the principles of financial accounting are applicable to all organizations, the rules of management accounting are tailor-made to meet the needs of the management of a specific organization.

Nevertheless, a similarity exists in both financial accounting practices and management accounting practices in most organizations. There are obvious economies in using financial accounting information wherever possible for management accounting purposes rather than devising two completely different systems for the two purposes.

THE FINANCIAL ACCOUNTING FRAMEWORK

Suppose you were asked to keep track of what was going on in an organization so as to provide useful information for management. One way of carrying out this assignment would be to write down a narrative of important events in a log similar to that kept by the captain of a ship.

After some experience with your log, you would gradually develop a set of rules to guide your efforts. For example, since it would be impossible to write down every action of every person in the organization, you would develop rules to guide you in choosing between those events that were important enough to record and those that should be omitted. You would also find that your log would be more valuable if you standardized certain terms. People who studied it would then have a clearer understanding of what you meant. Furthermore, if you standardized terms and their definitions, you could turn the job of keeping the log over to someone else and have some assurance that this person's report of events would convey the same information that you would have conveyed had you been keeping the log yourself.

In devising these rules of keeping a log, you would necessarily be somewhat arbitrary. There might be several ways of describing a certain event, all equally good. But in order to have a common basis of understanding, you would select just one of these for use in your recordkeeping system.

All these considerations were actually involved in the development of the accounting process. As is described below, accounting has evolved over a period of many centuries, and during this time certain terminology, rules, and conventions have come to be accepted as useful. If you are to understand accounting reports—the end products of an accounting system—you must be familiar with the rules and conventions lying behind these reports.

Accounting's Historical Antecedents

Accounting has existed for many centuries. We cannot know, of course, when humans began keeping accounting records in their heads, but symbols recording transactions between tribes have been found to date back to 5000 BC. The Sumerian civilization in Mesopotamia kept such records on clay tablets beginning about 3200 BC, and more than 3,000 years ago scribes in Babylonia and Egypt actually received what in effect was formal accounting training in schools. Persia under Darius (521–486 BC) had government scribes who performed "surprise audits" of the accounts of the provinces, and similar audits were made in the Hebrew civilization, in which the chief scribe was the second highest position in government. However, in ancient Greece (c. 1400 BC) it became customary to use slaves as scribes and auditors; it was assumed that statements from slaves, who could be tortured, would be more reliable than those from freemen, whom the law protected from such drastic verification techniques.

Accounting later became more prestigious in Greece, however, and records of construction costs of government buildings were carved on the structures. (One such tablet indicates that the Parthenon cost 469 silver talents, or about $2 million at today's prices. By comparison the Pyramid of Cheops in Egypt cost 1,500 talents, according to accounting records inscribed on the pyramid and reported by Herodotus.) In the Roman Empire in about 200 BC, quaestors in the territories were responsible for supervising the local government accountants. The quaestors' reports to Rome were given in person and heard by an examiner, a practice that gives us our modern-day term *auditor* (from Latin *audire,* to hear). In the Byzantine Empire Constantine (early fourth century AD) founded a public administration school in which accounting was taught. The Holy Roman Empire under Charlemagne (642–814 AD) continued the Roman and Persian examples of government accountants and auditors; after his death this group was disbanded, and the disintegration of the empire soon followed.

Accounting declined in the Middle Ages but was revived in Italy during the Crusades. Full-blown double-entry bookkeeping appears in Genoese records of 1340, and the Office of Exchequer (from an Old French word meaning a counting table covered with a checkered cloth) developed in England. In the 15th century branches of the Medici Bank were required to submit annual balance sheets to the main office in Florence. In 1631 an accountant was sent from Holland by the financial backers of the settlement at Plymouth, Massachusetts, to investigate the colony's increasing debt; the new Americans thus experienced their first audit.[4]

Accounting and Managers.   Although for centuries accounting on any large scale was primarily associated with governmental activities (particularly tax collection), the Industrial Revolution brought additional accounting needs. Large-scale enterprises required vast amounts of money to finance them and increasing numbers of people to direct their operations. Thus the owner-manager combination, which in small businesses was (and

---

[4]Information in these three paragraphs was drawn from Willard E. Stone, "Antecedents of the Accounting Profession," *Accounting Review,* April 1969, pp. 284–91.

often still is) personified in one individual, gave way to two distinct groups: investors and managers. The former group put demands on the latter to know how the firm was protecting and using the resources entrusted to it; that is, the investors wanted "an accounting" from the managers. (Today the primary manifestation of this "stewardship" accounting is the corporate annual report.) At the same time, managers of these larger, multilocation enterprises had to supplement management by personal observation with more formal internal accounting information; thus began the development of management accounting.

Accounting as a Language

Accounting is aptly called the language of business. The task of learning accounting, very similar to the task of learning a new language, is complicated by the fact that many words used in accounting mean almost but not quite the same thing as the identical words mean in everyday, nonaccounting usage. Accounting is not exactly a foreign language; the problem of learning it is more like that of an American learning to speak English as it is spoken in Great Britain. For example, the grain that Americans call wheat is called corn by the British; and the British use the word *maize* for what Americans call corn. Unless they are careful, Americans will fail to recognize that some words are used in Great Britain in a different sense from that used in America.

Similarly, some words are used in a different sense in accounting from their colloquial meanings. For example, an amount labeled "net worth" appears on many accounting reports. The commonsense interpretation is that this amount refers to what something is worth, what its value is. However, such an interpretation is incorrect, and misunderstandings can arise if the user of an accounting statement does not understand what accountants mean by net worth. (The correct meaning, somewhat technical in nature, will be given in Chapter 2.)

Accounting also resembles a language in that some of its rules are definite whereas others are not. There are differences of opinion among accountants as to how a given event should be reported, just as grammarians differ as to many matters of sentence structure, punctuation, and word choice. Nevertheless, just as many practices are clearly poor English, many practices are definitely poor accounting. In these chapters an attempt is made to describe the elements of good accounting and to indicate areas in which there are differences of opinion as to what constitutes good practice.

Finally, languages evolve in response to the changing needs of society, and so does accounting. The rules described here are currently in use, but some of them will probably be modified to meet the changing needs of organizations and their constituencies.

Nature of Principles

The rules and conventions of accounting are commonly referred to as "principles." The word **principle** is here used to mean "a general law or rule adopted or professed as a guide to action; a settled ground or basis of conduct or practice."[5] Note that this definition describes a principle as a general law or rule that is to be used as a guide to action. This means that accounting principles do not prescribe exactly how each event occurring in an organization should be recorded. Consequently, there are many matters in accounting practice that differ from one organization to another. In part, these differences are inevitable because a single detailed set of rules could not conceivably apply to every organization. In part, the differences reflect that within "generally accepted accounting principles" accountants have considerable latitude in which to express their own ideas as to the best way of recording and reporting a specific event.

Readers should realize, therefore, that they cannot know the precise meaning of many of the items in an accounting report unless they know which of several equally acceptable possibilities has been selected by the person who prepared the report. The meaning intended in a specific situation requires knowledge of the context.

Criteria

Accounting principles are established by humans. Unlike the principles of physics, chemistry, and the other natural sciences, accounting principles were not deduced from basic axioms, nor can they be verified by observation and experiment. Instead, they have evolved. This evolutionary process is going on constantly; accounting principles are not eternal truths.

The general acceptance of an accounting principle usually depends on how well it meets three criteria: relevance, objectivity, and feasibility. A principle has **relevance** to the extent that it results in information that is meaningful and useful to those who need to know something about a certain organization. A principle has **objectivity** to the extent that the information is not influenced by the personal bias or judgment of those who furnish it. Objectivity connotes reliability, trustworthiness. It also connotes verifiability, which means that there is some way of finding out whether the information is correct. A principle has **feasibility** to the extent that it can be implemented without undue complexity or cost.

These criteria often conflict with one another. The most relevant solution is likely to be the least objective and the least feasible.

> **Example.** The development of a new product may have a significant effect on a company's real value—"miracle" drugs and personal computer chips being spectacular examples. Information about the value of new products is most useful to the investor; it is indeed relevant. But the best estimate of the value of a new product is likely to be that made by management, and this is a highly subjective estimate. Accounting therefore does not attempt to record such values. Accounting sacrifices relevance in the interests of objectivity.

---

[5]Committee on Terminology, American Institute of Certified Public Accountants, "Review and Résumé," *Accounting Terminilogy Bulletin No. 1* (New York: 1953), p. 9.

The measure of the value of the owners' interest in Genentech, Inc., obtained from the stock market quotations (i.e., multiplying the price per share of stock times the number of shares outstanding) is a much more accurate reflection of the true value than the amount at which this item appears in the corporation's accounting records. As of January 1, 1994, the marketplace gave this value as $4.38 billion; the accounting records gave it as $1.12 billion. The difference does not indicate an error in the accounting records. It merely illustrates the fact that accounting does not attempt to report market values.

In developing new principles the essential problem is to strike the right balance between relevance on the one hand and objectivity and feasibility on the other. Failure to appreciate this problem often leads to unwarranted criticism of accounting principles. It is easy to criticize accounting on the grounds that accounting information is not as relevant as it might be; but the critic often overlooks the fact that proposals to increase relevance almost always involve a sacrifice of objectivity and feasibility. On balance, such a sacrifice may not be worthwhile.

Source of Accounting Principles

The foundation of accounting consists of a set of what are called **generally accepted accounting principles,** or **GAAP** for short. Currently, these principles are established by the Financial Accounting Standards Board (FASB). Created in 1973, the FASB consists of seven leading accountants with diverse backgrounds who work full time on developing new or modified principles. The board is supported by a professional staff that does research and prepares a discussion memorandum on each problem that the board addresses. The board acts only after interested parties have been given an opportunity to suggest solutions to problems and to comment on proposed pronouncements. The FASB is a nongovernmental organization financed by contributions from business firms and the accounting profession; its annual budget is in excess of $10 million.[6]

Each of the *Standards* of the FASB and *Opinions* of the Accounting Principles Board (APB, predecessor to the FASB) deals with a specific topic. Collectively, they do not cover all the important topics in accounting. If an authoritative pronouncement has not been made on a given topic, accountants can treat that topic in the way they believe most fairly presents the situation.

Companies are not legally required to adhere to GAAP as established by the FASB. As a practical matter, however, there are strong pressures for them to do so. The accounting reports of most companies are audited by certified public accountants who are members of the AICPA. Although the AICPA does not require its members to force companies to adhere to FASB

---

[6]The FASB accepts as authoritative the pronouncements of two earlier bodies: *Opinions* of the Accounting Principles Board and *Accounting Research Bulletins* of the Committee on Accounting Research. We shall refer to both of these in this book.

standards, it does require that if the CPA finds that the company has not followed FASB standards, the difference must be called to public attention. Since companies usually do not like to go counter to the FASB—even though they may feel strongly that the FASB principle is not appropriate in their particular situation—they almost always conform to the FASB pronouncements.

Another source of pressure to conform to GAAP is the U.S. Securities and Exchange Commission (SEC). This agency, which exists to protect the interests of investors, has jurisdiction over any corporation with 500 or more shareholders and $5 million or more total assets. The SEC requires these companies to file accounting reports prepared in accordance with GAAP. In its *Regulation S–X,* its *Financial Reporting Series Releases,* and its *Staff Accounting Bulletins,* the SEC spells out acceptable accounting principles in more detail than, but generally consistent with, the pronouncements of the FASB. Legally, the Securities Exchange Act of 1934 gave the SEC the authority to promulgate GAAP; but over the years, for the most part the SEC has relied on the FASB and its predecessors for carrying out the standard-setting process.

The AICPA has issued pronouncements for accounting in several industries, including finance companies, government contractors, and real estate investment trusts. Formerly, these were called *Audit Guides,* but recent ones are called *Statements of Position.* An Emerging Issues Task Force, organized under the auspices of the FASB, develops "consensus positions" on the accounting treatment of new types of events, principally those involving new financial instruments. Although these pronouncements do not have the force of FASB *Standards,* most organizations follow them. (Those organizations that deviate from them must demonstrate that they have adequate reason for doing so.) The Governmental Accounting Standards Board, established in 1984, sets standards for state and municipal governments.

Various regulatory bodies also prescribe accounting rules for the companies they regulate. Among those subjected to such rules are banks and other financial institutions, insurance companies, railroads, airlines, pipelines, radio and television companies, and electric and gas companies. These rules are not necessarily consistent with the principles of the FASB, although there has been a tendency in recent years for regulatory agencies to change their accounting rules so that they do conform.

The authority of the FASB and other agencies exists, of course, only in the United States of America. Accounting principles in other countries differ in some respects from American GAAP, but there is a basic similarity throughout the world. In 1973 efforts were begun to codify a set of accounting principles that would apply internationally, and several statements have been published since then by the International Accounting Standards Committee (IASC). They are generally consistent with the principles described in this book.

A convenient source of data about the various accounting practices used by American companies is *Accounting Trends & Techniques,* published annually by the AICPA. It summarizes the practices of 600 companies. Since these are relatively large companies, the summaries do not necessarily reflect the practices of all companies. This qualification should be kept in mind when data from this report are given in this text.

FINANCIAL STATEMENTS

The end product of the financial accounting process is a set of reports that are called **financial statements.** GAAP require that three such reports be prepared: (1) a balance sheet, (2) an income statement, and (3) a statement of cash flows. As we examine the details of the financial accounting process, it is important to keep in mind the objective toward which the process is aimed: the preparation of these three financial statements.

Most reports, in any field, can be classified into one of two categories called (1) **stock,** or **status, reports** and (2) **flow reports.** The amount of water in a reservoir at a given moment of time is a measure of stock, whereas the amount of water that moves through the reservoir in a day is a measure of flow. Reports of stocks are always as of a specified *instant* in time; reports of flow always cover a specified *period* of time. Reports of stocks are like snapshots; reports of flows are more like motion pictures. One of the accounting reports, the balance sheet, is a report of stocks. It shows information about the resources of an organization at a specified moment of time. The other two reports, the income statement and the cash flow statement, are reports of flow. They report activities of the organization for a period of time, such as a quarter or a year.

The next nine chapters describe the balance sheet and income statement. We shall defer a description of the cash flow statement until Chapter 11. Because this report is derived from data originally collected for the other two reports, it is inappropriate to discuss the cash flow statement until the balance sheet and income statement have been thoroughly explained.

Financial Statement Objectives

We indicated earlier that financial accounting statements, while also of use to management, are intended primarily to provide relevant information to parties external to the business. In 1978 the FASB issued a formal statement of financial reporting objectives.[7] The entire statement contains 63 paragraphs and thus is too lengthy to describe here in detail. We will simply highlight the key objectives. (The numbering is ours, not that of the FASB.)

Financial reporting should provide information:

1. Useful to present and potential investors and creditors in making rational investment and credit decisions.

---

[7]Financial Accounting Standards Board, "Objectives of Financial Reporting by Business Enterprises," *Statement of Financial Accounting Concepts No. 1* (Norwalk, Conn.: November 1978).

2. Comprehensible to those who have a reasonable understanding of business and economic activities and are willing to study the information with reasonable diligence.

3. About the economic resources of an enterprise, the claims to those resources, and the effects of transactions and events that change resources and claims to those resources.

4. About an enterprise's financial performance during a period.

5. To help users assess the amounts, timing, and uncertainty of prospective cash receipts from dividends or interest and the proceeds from the sale or redemption of securities or loans.

Objectives 1 and 2 apply to all financial accounting information. Note that the intended users are expected to have attained a reasonable level of sophistication in using the statements; the statements are not prepared for uninformed persons. Objective 3 is related to the balance sheet, objective 4 to the income statement, and objective 5 to the cash flow statement. As the five objectives collectively suggest, financial statements provide information about the *past* to aid users in making predictions and decisions related to the *future* financial status and flows of the business.

Income Tax Reporting

The Internal Revenue Service (IRS) specifies the ways in which taxable income is calculated for the purpose of assessing income taxes. Because the tax laws' purposes differ from the objectives of financial reporting, the IRS regulations differ in some respects from GAAP. These differences mean that the amount of pretax income or loss shown on the taxpayer's income statement prepared according to GAAP will probably not be equal to the taxable income or loss shown on the taxpayer's income tax return.

Thus, in the United States, financial accounting, management accounting, and income tax accounting are essentially separate processes. GAAP provides the principles for financial accounting; top management for management accounting; and the IRS and Congress for income tax accounting. The underlying operating information that is the basic data for all three processes is the same. The pieces or building blocks of operating information simply are put together in different ways for these three different processes. Thus, companies do not in any literal (or cynical) sense "keep three different sets of books," as is sometimes asserted. Also, though differences among the three processes do exist, in practice the similarities are greater than the differences.

SUMMARY

An organization has three types of accounting information: (1) operating information, which has to do with the details of operations; (2) management accounting information, which is used internally for planning, implementation, and control; and (3) financial accounting information, which is used both by management and by external parties.

Financial accounting is governed by ground rules that are referred to as generally accepted accounting principles (GAAP). These ground rules may be different than the reader believes them to be, based on previous exposure to accounting information. They are prescribed by the Financial Accounting Standards Board. They attempt to strike a balance between the criterion of relevance on the one hand and the criteria of objectivity and feasibility on the other.

The end products of the financial accounting process are three financial statements: the balance sheet, the income statement, and the cash flow statement. The balance sheet is a report of status or stocks as of a moment of time, whereas the other two statements summarize flows over a period of time.

In the United States, calculating taxable income for income tax purposes differs from the process of calculating income for the financial accounting income statement.

Cases

CASE 1–1 Kim Brooks

In the early fall of 1993, Kim Brooks was employed as a district sales engineer for a large chemical firm. During a routine discussion with plant chemists, Brooks learned that the company had developed a use for the recycled material, in pulverized form, from which plastic sodapop bottles are made. Because the state had mandatory deposits on all beverage bottles, Brooks realized that a ready supply of this material was available. All that was needed was an organization to tap that bottle supply, grind the bottles, and deliver the pulverized plastic to the chemical company. It was an opportunity Brooks had long awaited—a chance to start a business.

In November 1993 Brooks began checking into the costs involved in setting up a plastic bottle grinding business. A used truck and three trailers were acquired to pick up the empty bottles. Brooks purchased one used grinding machine but had to buy a second one new; supplies and parts necessary to run and maintain the machines were also purchased. These items used most of the $75,000 Brooks had saved.

A warehouse costing $162,000 was found in an excellent location for the business. Brooks was able to interest family members enough in this project that three of them, two sisters and a brother, invested $30,000 each. These funds gave Brooks more than enough money to put a down payment on the warehouse. The bank approved a mortgage for the balance on the building. In granting the mortgage, however, the bank official suggested that Brooks start from the beginning with proper accounting records. He said these records would help not only with future bank dealings but also with tax returns and general management of the company. He suggested Brooks find a good accountant to provide assistance from the start, to get things going on the right foot.

Brooks's neighbor, Marion Zimmer, was an accountant with a local firm. When they sat down to talk about the new business, Brooks explained, "I know little about keeping proper records." Zimmer suggested, "Start by listing all of the items purchased for the business and all the debts incurred. You should also start a daybook of transactions." Zimmer offered to find an accountant experienced in dealing with start-up businesses who would be willing to take Brooks on as a client and who would build a set of accounts for the firm as soon as regular business was underway.

Confident now that the venture was starting on solid ground, Kim Brooks opened the warehouse, signed contracts with two local bottling companies, and hired two grinding machine workers and a truck driver. By February 1994 the new firm was making regular deliveries to Brooks's former employer.

Questions

1. Why did Brooks need any records? What records were needed?

2. See what you can do to draw up a list of the assets and liabilities of Brooks's company, as the accountant suggested, making any assumptions you consider useful. How should Brooks go about putting a value on the company's assets?

3. Now that Brooks has started to make sales, what information is needed to determine "profit and loss"? What should be the general construction of a profit and loss analysis for Brooks's business? How frequently should Brooks do such an analysis?

4. What other kinds of changes in assets, liabilities, and owners' claims will need careful recording and reporting if Brooks is to keep in control of the business?

CASE 1–2 Baron Coburg*

Once upon a time many, many years ago, there lived a feudal landlord in a small province of Western Europe. The landlord, Baron Coburg, lived in a castle high on a hill. He was responsible for the well-being of many peasants who occupied the lands surrounding his castle. Each spring, as the snow began to melt, the Baron would decide how to provide for all his peasants during the coming year.

One spring, the Baron was thinking about the wheat crop of the coming growing season. "I believe that 30 acres of my land, being worth five bushels of wheat per acre, will produce enough wheat for next winter," he mused, "but who should do the farming? I believe I'll give Ivan and Frederick the responsibility of growing the wheat." Whereupon Ivan and Frederick were summoned for an audience with Baron Coburg.

"Ivan, you will farm on the 20-acre plot of ground and Frederick will farm the 10-acre plot," the Baron began. "I will give Ivan 20 bushels of wheat for seed and 20 pounds of fertilizer. (Twenty pounds of fertilizer are worth two bushels of wheat.) Frederick will get 10 bushels of wheat for seed and 10 pounds of fertilizer. I will give each of you an ox to pull a plow, but you will have to make arrangements with Feyador the Plowmaker for a plow. The oxen, incidentally, are only

three years old and have never been used for farming, so they should have a good 10 years of farming ahead of them. Take good care of them because an ox is worth 40 bushels of wheat. Come back next fall and return the oxen and the plows along with your harvest."

Ivan and Frederick genuflected and withdrew from the Great Hall, taking with them the things provided by the Baron.

The summer came and went, and after the harvest Ivan and Frederick returned to the Great Hall to account to their master for the things given them in the spring. Ivan said, "My Lord, I present you with a slightly used ox, a plow, broken beyond repair, and 223 bushels of wheat. I, unfortunately, owe Feyador the Plowmaker three bushels of wheat for the plow I got from him last spring. And, as you might expect, I used all the fertilizer and seed you have me last spring. You will also remember, my Lord, that you took 20 bushels of my harvest for your own personal use."

Frederick spoke next. "Here, my Lord, is a partially used ox, the plow, for which I gave Feyador the Plowmaker 3 bushels of wheat from my harvest, and 105 bushels of wheat. I, too, used all my seed and fertilizer last spring. Also, my Lord, you took 30 bushels of wheat several days ago for your own table. I believe the plow is good for two more seasons."

---

*Copyright © by *The Accounting Review*.

"You did well," said the Baron. Blessed with this benediction, the two peasants departed.

After they had taken their leave, the Baron began to contemplate what had happened. "Yes," he thought, "they did well, but I wonder which one did better?"

Questions

1. For each farm, prepare balance sheets as of the beginning and end of the growing season and an income statement for the season. (Do not be concerned that you do not have much understanding of what a balance sheet and income statement are; just use your intuition as best you can.)

2. Which peasant was the better farmer?

2

Basic Accounting Concepts:
The Balance Sheet

This chapter describes 5 of the 11 basic concepts from which principles of accounting are derived. Also described, in a preliminary way, are the nature of the balance sheet and the principal categories of items that appear in it. Finally, the chapter shows how amounts that appear in the balance sheet are changed to reflect events that affect an organization's resources.

The material presented here should be regarded as an overview. Each of the topics introduced will be discussed in more depth in later chapters.

BASIC CONCEPTS

Accounting principles are built on a foundation of a few basic concepts. These concepts are so basic that most accountants do not consciously think of them; they are regarded as self-evident. Nonaccountants will not find these concepts to be self-evident, however. Accounting could be constructed on a foundation of quite different concepts; indeed, some accounting theorists argue that certain of the present concepts are wrong and should be changed. Nevertheless, in order to understand accounting as it now exists, one must understand the underlying concepts currently used.

The Financial Accounting Standard Board (FASB) completed its project "Conceptual Framework" in 1985 with the publication of the sixth *State-*

ment of Financial Accounting Concepts.[1] These statements are intended to provide the FASB with explicit conceptual criteria to help resolve future accounting issues, rather than trying to deal with each issue on an ad hoc basis. The concept statements themselves do not establish generally accepted accounting principles (GAAP). Prior to the FASB's effort, other groups had addressed the task of identifying basic accounting concepts. These earlier efforts resulted in specific lists of basic concepts.[2]

The concepts we shall use in this book, while not identical to those listed by other authors or groups, reflect concepts that are widely accepted and applied in practice by accountants in North America. These 11 concepts are as follows:

1. Money measurement.
2. Entity.
3. Going concern.
4. Cost.
5. Dual aspect.
6. Accounting period.
7. Conservatism.
8. Realization.
9. Matching.
10. Consistency.
11. Materiality.

The first five are discussed below, and the other six are discussed in Chapter 3.

1. The Money Measurement Concept

In financial accounting, a record is made only of information that can be expressed in monetary terms. The advantage of such a record is that money provides a common denominator by means of which heterogeneous facts about an entity can be expressed as numbers that can be added and subtracted.

> **Example.** Although it may be a fact that a business owns $30,000 of cash; 6,000 pounds of raw material; six trucks; 50,000 square feet of building space; and so on, these amounts cannot be added together to produce a meaningful total of what the business owns. Expressing these items in monetary terms—$30,000 of cash; $9,000 of raw material; $150,000 of trucks; and $4,000,000 of buildings—makes such an addition possible. Thus, despite the old cliché about not adding apples and oranges, it *is* easy to add them if both the apples and the oranges are expressed in terms of their respective monetary values.

Despite its advantage, the money measurement concept imposes a severe limitation on the scope of an accounting report. Accounting does not report

---

[1] *No. 1,* "Objectives of Financial Reporting by Business Enterprises" (November 1978); *No. 2,* "Qualitative Characteristics of Accounting Information" (May 1980); *No. 3,* "Elements of Financial Statements of Business Enterprises" (December 1980); *No. 4,* "Objectives of Financial Reporting by Nonbusiness Organizations" (December 1980); *No. 5,* "Recognition and Measurement in Financial Statements of Business Enterprises" (December 1984); and *No. 6,* "Elements of Financial Statements" (December 1985), replacing *No. 3.*

[2] AAA, *A Statement of Basic Accounting Theory* (Sarasota, Fla.: 1966), lists four "basic standards" and five "guidelines." AICPA, "Basic Concepts and Accounting Principles Underlying Financial Statements of Business Enterprises," *APB Statement No. 4* (New York: October 1970), lists 13 "basic features."

the state of the president's health, that the sales manager is not on speaking terms with the production manager, that a strike is beginning, or that a competitor has placed a better product on the market. Accounting therefore does not give a complete account of the happenings in an organization or a full picture of its condition. It follows, then, that the reader of an accounting report should not expect to find therein all of the, or perhaps even the most important, facts about an organization.

Money is expressed in terms of its value at the time an event is recorded in the accounts. Subsequent changes in the purchasing power of money do not affect this amount. Thus, a machine purchased in 1994 for $200,000 and land purchased in 1979 for $200,000 are each listed in the 1994 accounting records at $200,000, although the purchasing power of the dollar in 1994 was much less than it was in 1979. It is sometimes said that accounting assumes that money is an unvarying yardstick of value, but this statement is inaccurate. Accountants know full well that the purchasing power of the dollar changes. They do not, however, attempt to reflect such changes in the accounts.

2. The Entity Concept

Accounts are kept for entities, as distinguished from the persons who are associated with these entities. In recording events in accounting, the important question is, How do these events affect the entity? How they affect the persons who own, operate, or otherwise are associated with the entity is irrelevant. For example, suppose that the owner of a clothing store removes $100 from the store's cash register for his or her personal use. The real effect of this event on the owner as a person may be negligible; although the cash has been taken out of the business's "pocket" and put into the owner's pocket, in either pocket the cash belongs to the owner. Nevertheless, because of the entity concept, the accounting records show that the business has less cash than it had previously.

It is sometimes difficult to define with precision the entity for which a set of accounts is kept. Consider the case of a married couple who own and operate an unincorporated retail store. In *law* there is no distinction between the financial affairs of the store and those of its owners. A creditor of the store can sue and, if successful, collect from the owners' personal resources as well as from the resources of the business. In *accounting,* by contrast, a set of accounts is kept for the store as a separate business entity, and the events reflected in these accounts must be those of the store. The nonbusiness events that affect the couple must not be included in these accounts. In accounting the *business* owns the resources of the store, even though the resources are legally owned by the couple. In accounting debts owed by the business are kept separate from personal debts owed by the couple. The expenses of operating the store are kept separate from the couple's personal expenses for food, clothing, housing, and the like.

The necessity for making such a distinction between the entity and its owners can create problems. Suppose, for example, that the couple lives on the same premises as the business. How much of the rent, electric bill, and property taxes associated with these premises is properly an expense of the business, and how much is personal expense of the family? Answers to questions like these are often difficult to ascertain, and are indeed somewhat arbitrary.

For a *corporation* the distinction is often quite easily made. A corporation is a legal entity, separate from the persons who own it, and the accounts of many corporations correspond exactly to the scope of the legal entity. There may be complications, however. In the case of a group of legally separate corporations that are related to one another by shareholdings, the whole group may be treated as a single entity for financial reporting purposes, giving rise to what are called *consolidated* accounting statements. Conversely, within a single corporation, a separate set of accounts may be maintained for each of its principal operating units. For example, General Electric Company maintains separate accounts for each of its several business units (appliances, motors, plastics, lighting, aircraft engines, and others).

An **entity** is any organization or activity for which accounting reports are prepared. Although our examples tend to be drawn from business companies, accounting entities include governments, churches, universities, and other nonbusiness organizations.

One entity may be part of a larger entity. Thus, a set of accounts may be maintained for an individual elementary school, another set for the whole school district, and still another set for all the schools in a particular state. There even exists a set of accounts, called the national income accounts, for the entire economic activity of the United States. In general, detailed accounting records are maintained for entities at the lowest level in the hierarchy, and reports for higher levels are prepared by summarizing the detailed data of these low-level entities.

3. The Going-Concern Concept

Unless there is good evidence to the contrary, accounting assumes that an entity is a **going concern**—that it will continue to operate for an indefinitely long period in the future. The significance of this assumption can be indicated by contrasting it with a possible alternative, namely, that the entity is about to be liquidated. Under the latter assumption, accounting would attempt to measure at all times what the entity's resources are currently worth to potential buyers. Under the going-concern concept, by contrast, there is no need to constantly measure an entity's worth to potential buyers, and it is not done. Instead, it is assumed that the resources currently available to the entity will be used in its future operations. In a manufacturing company, for example, resources will be used to create goods that will eventually be sold to customers. At the time such a sale takes place, accounting recognizes the value of the goods as evidenced by their selling price. The current resale values of the individual machines, supplies, and other resources used in the manufacturing process are irrelevant because there is no intention of selling them individually. Rather, they will be used as part of the manufacturing process, and it is the resulting goods that will be sold.

> **Example.** At any given moment, a blue jeans manufacturer has jeans in various stages of the production process. If the business were liquidated today, these partially completed jeans would have little if any value. Accounting does not attempt to value these jeans at what they are currently worth. Instead, accounting assumes that the manufacturing process will be carried through to completion, and therefore that the amount for which the partially completed jeans could be sold if the company were liquidated today is irrelevant.

If, however, the accountant has good reason to believe that an entity *is* going to be liquidated, then its resources would be reported at their liquidation value. Such circumstances are uncommon.

4. The Cost Concept

The economic resources of an entity are called its **assets.** They consist of money, land, buildings, machinery, and other property and property rights, as will be described in a subsequent section. A fundamental concept of accounting, closely related to the going-concern concept, is that an asset is ordinarily entered in the accounting records at the price paid to acquire it—at its **cost.**[3] This cost is the basis for all subsequent accounting for the asset.

Since, for a variety of reasons, the real worth of an asset may change with the passage of time, the accounting measurement of assets does not necessarily—indeed, does not ordinarily—reflect what assets are worth, except at the moment they are acquired. There is therefore a considerable difference between the way in which assets are measured in accounting and the everyday, nonaccounting notion that assets are measured at what they are worth. In accounting, assets are initially recorded at their cost. (For emphasis, this is also referred to as an asset's *historical* cost.) This amount is ordinarily unaffected by subsequent changes in the value of the asset. By contrast, in ordinary usage the "value" of an asset usually means the amount for which it currently could be sold.

> **Example.** If a business buys a plot of land, paying $250,000 for it, this asset would be recorded in the accounts of the business at the amount of $250,000. If a year later the land could be sold for $275,000, or if it could be sold for only $220,000, no change would ordinarily be made in the accounting records to reflect this fact.

Thus, the amounts at which assets are shown in an entity's accounts do *not* indicate sales values of the assets. Probably the most common mistake made by uninformed persons reading accounting reports is that of believing

---

[3] *APB Opinion No. 29* (May 1973) requires that donated assets be entered at their fair value at the date of receipt.

there is a close correspondence between the amount at which an asset appears in these reports and the actual value of the asset. The amount reported as cash *is,* of course, the value of the cash the entity owns. However, the amounts reported for land, buildings, equipment, and similar assets have no necessary relationship to what these items are currently worth. In general, it is safe to say that the longer an asset has been owned by an entity, the less likely it is that the amount at which the asset appears on the accounting records corresponds to its current market value.

The cost concept does not mean that all assets remain on the accounting records at their original purchase price for as long as the entity owns them. The cost of an asset that has a long but nevertheless limited life is systematically reduced over that life by the process called **depreciation,** as discussed in Chapter 7. The purpose of the depreciation process is to remove systematically the cost of the asset from the asset accounts and to show it as a cost of operations. Depreciation has no necessary relationship to changes in market value or in the real worth of the asset.

Goodwill.   It follows from the cost concept that if an entity pays *nothing* for an item it acquires (other than as a donation), this item will usually *not* appear on the accounting records as an asset. Thus, such factors as the knowledge and skills that are built up as a business operates, the teamwork that grows up within the organization, the increasing importance of a favorable location as time goes on, the good reputation a company builds with its customers, the trade names developed by the company—*none of these* appears as an asset in the accounts of the company.

On some accounting reports the term *goodwill* appears. Reasoning from the everyday definition of this word, one might conclude that it represents the accountant's appraisal of what the company's name and reputation are worth. This is not so. Goodwill appears in the accounts of a company only when the company has *purchased* some intangible and valuable economic resource. A common case is when one company buys another company and pays more than the fair value of its individual assets. The amount by which the purchase price exceeds the value of these assets is called **goodwill,** representing the value of the name, reputation, clientele, or similar intangible resources of the purchased company. Unless a business has actually purchased such intangibles, however, no item for goodwill is shown in its accounts. If the item does appear, the amount shown initially is the purchase price, even though the management may believe that the real value is considerably higher.

> **Example.**   When Philip Morris Incorporated paid $5.8 billion to acquire the General Foods Corporation, $2.8 billion was for the value of the General Foods organization and its various brand names (e.g., Jell-O, Good Seasons, Kool-Aid, Maxwell House). This $2.8 billion was recorded in the Philip Morris accounts as goodwill.

To emphasize the distinction between the accounting concept and the ordinary meaning of value, the term **book value** is used for the historical cost amounts as shown in the accounting records and the term **market value** for the actual value of the asset as reflected in the marketplace.

Rationale for the Cost Concept. The cost concept provides an excellent illustration of the problem of applying the three basic criteria discussed in Chapter 1: relevance, objectivity, and feasibility. If the only criterion were relevance, then the cost concept would not be defensible. Clearly, investors and other financial statement users are more interested in what the business is actually worth today than in what the assets cost originally.

But who knows what a business is worth today? Any estimate of current value is just that—an estimate—and informed people will disagree on what the estimate should be. For example, on the same day, some people believe that the shares of stock of a given company are overpriced and they should therefore sell the stock; others believe that the shares are underpriced and they buy. Furthermore, accounting reports are prepared by an organization's management. If these reports contained estimates of what the entity is actually worth, these would be management's estimates. It is quite possible that such estimates would be biased.

The cost concept, by contrast, provides a relatively objective foundation for accounting. It is not *purely* objective, as we shall see, for judgments are necessary in applying it. It is much more objective, however, than the alternative of attempting to estimate current values. Essentially, readers of an accounting report must recognize that it is based on the cost concept, and they must arrive at their own estimate of current value partly by analyzing the information in the report and partly by using nonaccounting information.

Furthermore, a "market value" or "current worth" concept would be difficult to apply because it would require that the accountant attempt to keep track of the ups and downs of the market price of each asset. The cost concept leads to a much more feasible system.

In summary, adherence to the cost concept indicates a willingness on the part of the accounting profession to sacrifice some degree of relevance in exchange for greater objectivity and greater feasibility.

5. The Dual-Aspect Concept

The economic resources of an entity are called assets. The claims of various parties against these assets are called **equities.** There are two types of equities: (1) **liabilities,** which are the claims of creditors (that is, everyone other than the owners of the business) and (2) **owners' equity,** which is the claims of the owners of the business. (Owners' equity for an incorporated business is commonly called **shareholders' equity.**) Since all of the assets of a business are claimed by someone (either by its owners or by its creditors) and since the total of these claims cannot exceed the amount of assets to be claimed, it follows that

$$\text{ASSETS} = \text{EQUITIES}$$

This is the **fundamental accounting equation,** which is the formal expression of the dual-aspect concept. As we shall see, all accounting procedures are derived from this equation. To reflect the two types of equities, the equation is

$$\text{ASSETS} = \text{LIABILITIES} + \text{OWNERS' EQUITY}$$

Events that affect the numbers in an entity's accounting records are called **transactions.** Although it is certainly not self-evident to someone just beginning to study accounting, every transaction has a *dual impact* on the accounting records. Accounting systems are set up so as to record both of these aspects of a transaction; this is why accounting is called a **double-entry system.**

To illustrate the dual-aspect concept, suppose that Ms. Jones starts a business and that her first act is to open a bank account in which she deposits $40,000 of her own money. The dual aspect of this transaction is that the business now has an asset, cash, of $40,000, and Ms. Jones, the owner,[4] has a claim, also of $40,000, against this asset. In other words,

$$\text{Assets (cash), \$40,000} = \text{Equities (owner's), \$40,000}$$

If as its next transaction, the business borrowed $15,000 from a bank, the business's accounting records would change in two ways: (1) they would show a $15,000 increase in cash, making the amount $55,000, and (2) they would show a new claim against the assets, the bank's claim, in the amount of $15,000. At this point, the accounting records of the business would show the following:

Cash	$55,000	Owed to bank	$15,000
		Owner's equity	40,000
Total assets	$55,000	Total equities	$55,000

To repeat, every transaction recorded in the accounts affects at least two items. There is no conceivable way that a transaction can result in only a single change in the accounts.

THE BALANCE SHEET

The financial position of an accounting entity as of a specified moment in time is shown by a **balance sheet.** Its more formal name is a **statement of financial position.** More specifically, the balance sheet reports the assets and equities (liabilities and owners' equity) of the entity at the specified moment in time.[5] Because the balance sheet is a snapshot as of an instant in time, it is a status report (rather than a flow report).

---

[4]Recall from the entity concept that the accounts of the business are kept separate from those of Ms. Jones as an individual.

[5]A balance sheet dated December 31 is implicitly understood to mean "at the close of business on December 31." Sometimes the identical balance sheet may be dated January 1,

A simplified balance sheet for a corporation is shown in Illustration 2-1. Before considering its details, first examine this balance sheet in terms of the basic concepts already described. Note that the amounts are *expressed in money* and reflect only those matters that can be measured in monetary terms. The *entity* involved is the Garsden Corporation, and the balance sheet pertains to that entity rather than to any of the individuals associated with it. The statement assumes that Garsden Corporation is a *going concern.* The asset amounts stated are governed by the *cost concept.* The *dual-aspect concept* is evident from the fact that the assets listed on the left-hand side of this balance sheet are equal in total to the liabilities and shareholders' equity listed on the right-hand side.

Because of the dual-aspect concept, the two sides necessarily add up to the same total. This equality does not tell anything about the company's financial health. The label "balance sheet" can give the impression that there is something significant about the fact that the two sides balance. This is not so; the two sides always balance.

In the Garsden Corporation balance sheet, assets are listed on the left and equities on the right. An alternative practice is to list assets at the top of the page and to list equities beneath them. The former format is called the **account form,** and the latter is called the **report form** of balance sheet.

An Overall View

The balance sheet is the fundamental accounting statement in the sense that *every* accounting transaction can be analyzed in terms of its dual impact on the balance sheet. To understand the information a balance sheet conveys and how economic events affect the balance sheet, the reader must be absolutely clear as to the meaning of its two sides. They can be interpreted in either of two ways, both of which are correct.

Resources and Claims View. One interpretation has already been indicated. The items listed on the asset side are the economic resources of the entity as of the date of the balance sheet. The amounts stated for each asset are recorded in accordance with the basic concepts described above. Liabilities and owners' equity are claims against the entity as of the balance sheet date. Liabilities are the claims of outside parties—amounts that the entity owes to banks, vendors, employees, and other creditors. Owners' equity shows the claims of the owners.

However, an entity's owners do not have a claim in the same sense that the creditors do. In the Garsden Corporation illustration, it can be said with assurance that governmental taxing authorities had a claim of $1,672,000 as of December 31, 1993—that the corporation owed them $1,672,000, neither

---

meaning "at the beginning of business on January 1." From the standpoint of accounting these two dates are the *same* moment of time. Ordinarily the "close of business" connotation is the correct one because the balance sheet is ordinarily dated as of the end of the year or other period for which accounting reports are prepared.

ILLUSTRATION 2–1

GARSDEN CORPORATION ← Name of entity

Balance Sheet ← Name of statement

As of December 31, 1993 ← Moment of time

Assets

Current assets:

Cash	$ 3,448,891	
Marketable securities	246,221	
Accounts receivable	5,954,588	
Inventories	12,623,412	
Prepaid expenses	377,960	
Total current assets		$22,651,072

Property, plant, and equipment:

Land		642,367
Buildings and equipment, at cost	26,303,481	
Less: Accumulated depreciation	13,534,069	
Net property, plant, and equipment		12,769,412

Other assets:

Investments	110,000	
Intangible assets	63,214	
		173,214
Total assets		$36,236,065

Liabilities and Shareholders' Equity

Current liabilities:

Accounts payable	$ 6,301,442	
Taxes payable	1,672,000	
Accrued expenses	640,407	
Deferred revenues	205,240	
Current portion of long-term debt	300,000	
Total current liabilities		$ 9,119,089

Long-term debt		3,000,000
Total liabilities		12,119,089

Shareholders' equity:

Paid-in capital	5,000,000	
Retained earnings	19,116,976	
Total shareholders' equity		24,116,976
Total liabilities and shareholders' equity		$36,236,065

more nor less. It is more difficult to interpret as a claim the amount shown as shareholders' equity, $24,116,976. *If* the corporation were liquidated as of December 31, 1993, *if* the assets were sold for their book value, and *if* the creditors were paid the $12,119,089 owed them, then the shareholders would get what was left, which would be $24,116,976. However, these "if" conditions are obviously unrealistic. According to the going-concern concept, the corporation is not going to be liquidated; and according to the cost concept, the assets are not shown at their liquidation values.

The shareholders' equity might be worth considerably more or less than $24,116,976. The shareholders' equity of a healthy, growing company is usually worth considerably more than its "book value"—the amount shown on the balance sheet. On the other hand, if a company is not salable as a going concern and is liquidated with the assets being sold piecemeal, the owners' proceeds are often only a small fraction of the amount stated for shareholders' equity on the balance sheet. Often when a bankrupt company's assets are liquidated, the proceeds are inadequate to satisfy 100 percent of the creditors' claims, in which case the owners receive nothing.

The resources and claims view of the balance sheet has some shortcomings. We have already pointed out the difficulty of interpreting shareholders' equity as a claim. Also, the notion of "claiming" assets is rather legalistic, and has the most meaning if a company is being liquidated in bankruptcy—which is inconsistent with the going-concern concept. Therefore, the second way of interpreting the balance sheet has considerable appeal.

Sources and Uses of Funds View.   In this alternative view, the left-hand side of the balance sheet is said to show the forms in which the entity has used, or *invested,* the funds provided to it as of the balance sheet date. These investments have been made in order to help the entity achieve its objectives, which in a business organization include earning a satisfactory profit. The right-hand side shows the *sources of the funds* that are invested in the assets—it shows how the assets were *financed.* The several liability items describe how much of that financing was obtained from trade creditors (accounts payable), from lenders (long-term debt), and from other creditors. The owners' equity section shows the financing supplied by the owners. (The two ways in which the owners of a business corporation provide it with funds—paid-in capital and retained earnings—will be explained later in the chapter.)

Thus, with the sources and uses of funds view, the fundamental accounting equation, Assets = Liabilities + Owners' Equity, has this interpretation: Every dollar invested in the entity's assets was supplied either by the entity's creditors or by its owners; and every dollar thus supplied is invested in some asset.

Both ways of interpreting the balance sheet are correct. In certain circumstances, the resources and claims view is easier to understand. In analyzing the balance sheet of a going concern, however, the sources and uses of funds view usually provides a more meaningful interpretation.

**Account
Categories**

Although each individual asset or equity—each building, piece of equipment, bank loan, and so on—could conceivably be listed separately on the
balance sheet, it is more practicable and more informative to summarize and
group related items into classifications or **account categories.** There is no
fixed pattern as to the number of such categories or the amount of detail
reported. Rather, the format is governed by management's opinion as to the
most useful way of presenting significant information about the status of the
entity.

As in any classification scheme, the categories are defined so that (1) the
individual items included in a category resemble one another in significant
respects and (2) the items in one category are essentially different from
those in all other categories. Although the items included in a category are
similar to one another, they are not identical.

> **Example.** The category labeled *cash* usually includes money on deposit in
> savings accounts as well as money on deposit in checking accounts. These two
> types of money are *similar* in that they are both in highly liquid form, but they
> are not *identical* because certain restrictions may apply to withdrawals from
> savings accounts that do not apply to checking accounts.

The balance sheet in Illustration 2–1 gives a minimum amount of detail.
The terms used on this balance sheet are common ones, and they are
described briefly below. More detailed descriptions are given in Chapters 5
through 9.

Note that the amounts in Illustration 2–1 are rounded to the nearest
dollar. Cents are rarely shown; and in a large company, the amounts are
usually rounded to thousands or even millions of dollars. Although rounding is done in preparing financial statements, the underlying detailed
records are maintained to the cent.

Assets

We shall now supersede the short definition of an asset given in the
preceding section by the following more exact statement: **Assets** are economic resources that are controlled by an entity and whose cost (or fair
value) at the time of acquisition could be objectively measured. The three
key points in this definition are that (1) an asset must be an *economic
resource,* (2) the resource must be *controlled* by the entity, and (3) its cost (or
fair value) at the time of acquisition must be *objectively measurable.*

A resource is an *economic* resource if it provides *future benefits* to the
entity. Resources provide future benefits under any of three conditions: (1)
they are cash or can be converted to cash, (2) they are goods that are
expected to be sold and cash received for them, or (3) they are items
expected to be used in future activities that will generate cash inflows to the
entity. Thus, economic resources either are cash or items that will eventually result in cash inflows.

> **Example.** Garsden Corporation is a manufacturing company. The cash that
> it has on deposit in banks is an asset because it is money that can be used to

acquire other resources. Amounts owed by customers are assets that when collected will generate cash. The goods Garsden has manufactured and still has on hand are assets because they are expected to be sold. The equipment and other manufacturing facilities it owns are assets because it is expected that they will be used to produce additional goods. However, merchandise that cannot be sold because it is damaged or obsolete is not an asset, even though it is owned by the business, because it will not generate cash.

Control is an accounting concept similar to, but not quite the same as, the legal concept of ownership. When a business buys an automobile on an installment loan (e.g., it pays $575 a month for 36 months), the business may not own the car in the legal sense because title to the car does not pass to the buyer until the last installment has been paid. Nevertheless, if the business is responsible for maintaining and insuring the car, the automobile is regarded as being fully controlled by the business and is an asset. Possession or temporary control is not enough to qualify the item as an asset, however.

> **Example.** Office space leased on an annual basis is not an asset, nor is an automobile or other piece of equipment that is leased for a relatively short time. In both cases, the entity's control over the use of the item is only temporary. On the other hand, if a business leases a building or an item of equipment for a period of time that equals or almost equals its useful life, such an item is an asset even though the entity does not own it.

The *objective measurability* test is usually clear-cut; but in some instances it is difficult to apply. If the resource was purchased for cash or for the promise to pay cash, it is an asset. If the resource was manufactured or constructed by the business, then money was paid for the costs of manufacture or construction, and it is an asset. If the resource was acquired by trading in some other asset or by issuing shares of the company's stock, it is an asset. If the resource was donated and it has future benefit, then the resource is an asset. On the other hand, as already pointed out, a valuable reputation is not an asset if it arose gradually over a period of time rather than being acquired at an objectively measurable cost.

On most business balance sheets, assets are listed in decreasing order of their liquidity, that is, in order of the promptness with which they are expected to be converted into cash. On some balance sheets, notably those of public utilities, the order is reversed and the least liquid assets are listed first.

Assets are customarily grouped into categories. Current assets are almost always reported in a separate category. All noncurrent assets may be grouped together or in various groupings such as "property, plant, and equipment" and "other assets," as shown on the Garsden Corporation balance sheet.

Current Assets. Cash and other assets that are expected to be realized in cash or sold or consumed during the normal operating cycle of the entity or within one year, whichever is longer, are called **current assets.** The distinction between current assets and noncurrent assets is important because lenders and others pay close attention to the total of current assets. The essence of the distinction is *time*. Current assets are those resources that are held only for a short period of time. Although the usual time limit is one year, exceptions occur in companies whose normal operating cycle is longer than one year. Tobacco companies and distilleries, for example, include their inventories as current assets even though tobacco and liquor remain in inventory for an aging process that lasts two years or more.

Cash consists of funds that are readily available for disbursement. Most of these funds are on deposit in checking accounts in banks, and the remainder is in cash registers or petty cash boxes on the entity's premises.

Marketable securities are investments that are both readily marketable and expected to be converted into cash within a year. These investments are made in order to earn some return on cash that otherwise would be temporarily idle.

Accounts receivable are amounts owed to the entity by its customers. Accounts receivable are reported on the balance sheet as the amount owed less an allowance for that portion that probably will not be collected. (Methods of estimating this "allowance for doubtful accounts" are described in Chapter 5.) Amounts owed the entity by parties other than customers would appear under the heading **notes receivable** or **other receivables** rather than as accounts receivable. If the amounts owed are evidenced by written promises to pay, they are listed as notes receivable.

Inventories are the aggregate of those items that are either (1) held for sale in the ordinary course of business, (2) in process of production for such sale, or (3) are soon to be consumed in the production of goods or services that will be available for sale. Note that inventory relates to goods that will be sold in the ordinary course of business. A truck offered for sale by a truck dealer is inventory. A truck used by the dealer to make service calls is not inventory; it is an item of equipment, which is a noncurrent asset.

Prepaid expenses represent certain assets, usually of an intangible nature, whose usefulness will expire in the near future. An example is an insurance policy. A business pays for insurance protection in advance. Its right to this protection is an asset—an economic resource that will provide future benefits. Since this right will expire within a fairly short period of time, it is a current asset. The amount on the balance sheet is the future amount of the benefit.

> **Example.**   If on January 1, 1993, Garsden Corporation paid $250,000 for insurance protection for two years, the amount of prepaid insurance expense on the December 31, 1993, balance sheet would be $125,000, which is the cost of the one year of protection then remaining.

Property, Plant, and Equipment.   This category consists of assets that are tangible and relatively long-lived. The term **fixed assets** is also used for this category. The entity has acquired these assets in order to use them to produce goods and services that will generate future cash inflows. If such assets are instead held for resale, they are classified as inventory, even though in a sense they are long-lived assets. (They will be long-lived to their purchaser, but they are not expected to be held long-term by their seller.)

In the balance sheet shown in Illustration 2–1, the first item of property, plant, and equipment is land, which is reported at its cost, $642,367. Land is shown separately because it is not depreciated, as are buildings and equipment. The first amount shown for buildings and equipment, $26,303,481, is the *original cost* of all the items of tangible long-lived property other than land—the amounts paid to acquire these items. The next item, accumulated depreciation, means that a portion of the original cost of the buildings and equipment, amounting to $13,534,069, has been written off, allocated as a cost of doing business. Depreciation will be discussed in detail in Chapter 7.

Other Assets. Another type of noncurrent asset is **investments.** These are securities of one company owned by another in order either to control the other company or in anticipation of earning a long-term return from the investment. They are therefore to be distinguished from marketable securities, which are a current asset reflecting the short-run use of excess cash.

Intangible assets include goodwill (briefly described earlier), patents, copyrights, trademarks, franchises, and similar valuable but nonphysical things controlled by the business. They are distinguished from prepaid expenses (intangible *current* assets) in that they have a longer life span than prepaid expenses.

Liabilities

In general, **liabilities** are obligations to outside parties arising from events that have already happened. (A few complicated items that may appear in the liabilities section of the balance sheet do not fit this definition; they will be discussed in later chapters.) Liability obligations exist as a result of *past* transactions or events. Thus, on December 31, wages not yet paid to an employee who worked from December 27 to December 31 are a liability; but that person's wages to be earned next week (the first week in January) are not a liability as of December 31.[6]

Liabilities are claims against the entity's assets. Unless otherwise noted, an individual liability is not a claim against any *specific* asset or group of assets. Thus, although accounts payable typically arise from the purchase of items for inventory, accounts payable are claims against the assets in general and not specifically against inventories. If a liability *is* a claim against a specific asset, its title indicates that fact, as in a *mortgage* loan or *secured* long-term debt.

With minor exceptions, a liability is reported at the amount that would be required to satisfy the obligation as of the balance sheet date.[7] For a loan

---

[6]Although, in a sense, employees are not outside parties, in accounting they are considered such to the extent that they are not owners of the entity. Only owners of the entity are "inside parties."

[7]We shall describe an alternative interpretation of the amount of a liability in Chapter 8.

this includes the "principal" that is owed as well as any interest earned by the lender but unpaid as of the balance sheet date. (Often this interest payable or "accrued" interest is shown separately from the principal owed.) Thus, if the December 31 balance sheet showed $100,000 for a loan payable and $1,000 interest payable on that loan, a $101,000 payment to the lender would be required to satisfy the loan liability obligation as of December 31. Note that the total amount needed to satisfy the obligation is reported, not just the portion of that total that is due and payable as of the balance sheet date. The $100,000 loan is a liability even though there may be no principal payment due for another five years.

Current Liabilities. These are obligations that are expected to be satisfied either by the use of current assets or by the creation of other current liabilities. The one-year time interval or current operating cycle criterion that applies to classifying current assets also applies to current liabilities.

Accounts payable represent the claims of suppliers arising from their furnishing goods or services to the entity for which they have not yet been paid. (Such suppliers often are called **vendors.**) Usually these claims are unsecured. Amounts owed to financial institutions (which are suppliers of funds rather than of goods or services) are called **notes payable** or **short-term loans** (or some other name that describes the nature of the debt instrument) rather than accounts payable.

Taxes payable shows the amount that the entity owes government agencies for taxes. It is shown separately from other obligations both because of its size and because the amount owed may not be precisely known as of the date of the balance sheet. Often the liability for federal and state income taxes is shown separately from other tax liabilities, such as property taxes.

Accrued expenses represent amounts that have been earned by outside parties but have not yet been paid by the entity. Usually there is no invoice or similar document submitted by the party to whom the money is owed. Interest earned by a lender but not yet paid by the entity is an accrued expense. Another example is the wages and salaries owed to employees for work they have performed but for which they have not yet been paid. The term *accrued expenses,* although frequently used as a balance sheet category, is not as descriptive as the names used in the detailed records for specific accrued expenses, such as **interest payable** and **wages payable.**

Deferred revenues (also called **unearned revenues** or **precollected revenues**) represent the liability that arises because the entity has received advance payment for a service it has agreed to render in the future. An example is unearned subscription revenues, which represent magazine subscription payments received in advance, for which the publishing company agrees to deliver issues of its magazine during some future period.

Current portion of long-term debt represents that part of a long-term loan that is due within the next year. It is reported separately from the noncurrent portion so that current liabilities will give a complete picture of the entity's short-term obligations.

Other Liabilities. Those obligations that do not meet the criteria for being classified as current liabilities are simply called **other liabilities.** They are also sometimes called **noncurrent liabilities** or **long-term debt.**

> **Example.** Garsden Corporation has a $3,300,000 loan outstanding. Of this amount, $300,000 is due within the next year and is therefore a current liability. The remaining $3 million is due in some future period (or periods) beyond the next year (i.e., after December 31, 1993) and is thus shown as long-term debt.

Owners' Equity

The **owners' equity** section of the balance sheet shows the amount the owners have invested in the entity. The terminology used in this section varies with different forms of organization. In a corporation the ownership interest is evidenced by shares of stock, and the owners' equity section of its balance sheet is therefore usually labeled **shareholders' equity** or **stockholders' equity.**

Paid-In Capital. The shareholders' equity is divided into two main categories. The first category, called **paid-in capital** or **contributed capital,** is the amount the owners have invested directly in the business by purchasing shares of stock as these shares were issued by the corporation. Paid-in capital in most corporations is further subdivided into **capital stock** and **additional paid-in capital.** Each share of stock has a stated or "par" value; capital stock shows this value per share times the number of shares outstanding. If investors actually paid more into the corporation than the stated value (as is almost always the case), the excess is shown separately as additional paid-in capital.

> **Example.** Garsden Corporation has outstanding 1 million shares of common stock with a par value of $1 per share. Investors actually paid into the corporation $5 million for these shares. The balance sheet in Illustration 2–1 could be modified to show:

Paid-in capital:		
Common stock at par	$1,000,000	
Additional paid-in capital	4,000,000	
Total paid-in capital		$5,000,000

Retained Earnings. The second category of shareholders' equity is labeled retained earnings. The owners' equity increases through *earnings* (i.e., the results of profitable operations) and decreases when earnings are paid out in the form of dividends. **Retained earnings** is the difference between the *total* earnings of the entity *from its inception* to date and the *total* amount of dividends paid out to its shareholders *over its the entire life.* That is, the difference represents that part of the total earnings that have been retained for use in—*reinvested* in—the business.[8] If the difference is negative, the item usually is labeled **deficit** rather than retained earnings.

Note that the amount of retained earnings on a given date is the *cumulative* amount that has been retained in the business from the beginning of the corporation's existence up to that date. The amount shown for Garsden Corporation means that *since the company began operations,* the total amount it has paid out in dividends is $19,116,976 less than the total amount of its earnings.

Note also that the amount of retained earnings does not indicate the *form* in which the retained earnings have been reinvested. They may be invested in *any* of the resources that appear on the assets side of the balance sheet. (This is true of all liabilities and items of owners' equity, not just retained earnings.) There is a common misconception that there is some connection between the amount of a company's retained earnings and the amount of cash it holds. That no such connection exists should be apparent from the fact that the Garsden Corporation balance sheet shows over $19 million of retained earnings but only $3.4 million of cash.

> **Example.** In a magazine article[9] Philip Moore wrote: "It [General Motors Corporation] has $8 billion of cash surplus on deposit in some 380 banks around the world." When a reader pointed out that the GM balance sheet showed only $550 million of cash as an asset, Moore replied, "The $8 billion figure refers to what I understand to be General Motors' current capital surplus, which I assumed to be either in cash or highly liquid form such as Treasury bills, most of which would be on deposit either in cash or as nominee in the 380 banks."[10] If Mr. Moore had taken a course in accounting, he would have realized that "earned surplus" on the equities side of the balance sheet (which was GM's terminology for retained earnings) has no relationship whatsoever to any specific asset, such as cash, or to "highly liquid assets."

Other Terms. Instead of retained earnings, the term *earned surplus* or simply *surplus* was formerly used and is still used by some companies. The term is misleading, since it connotes something tangible, something left over. There is, in fact, nothing tangible about retained earnings. All the tangible things owned by the business appear as assets on the balance sheet. Because of this misleading connotation (illustrated in the previous example), the use of *surplus* is no longer recommended.[11] (GM now uses the cumbersome but descriptive caption, "Net income retained for use in the business," but still uses "capital surplus" for additional paid-in capital.)

---

[8]Shareholders' equity can also be affected by events other than the accumulation of earnings and the distribution of these earnings as dividends. Examples are donations of capital, revaluation of stock, and the creation of special reserves. Some of these events will be discussed in Chapter 9.

[9]"What's Good for the Country Is Good for GM," *Washington Monthly,* December 1970, pp. 10–18.

[10]*Washington Monthly,* March 1971, p. 4.

[11]The word *surplus* is also sometimes used with other modifiers (capital surplus, paid-in surplus) to label the item that is more appropriately called *additional paid-in capital.*

Net worth is another term whose use in financial statements is frowned upon. It is a synonym for the term *owners' equity*. Net worth can be a misleading term because it implies that the amount indicates what the owners' interest is "worth," which, as has been emphasized, is erroneous. Nevertheless, the term is frequently used in articles and conversation.

Owners' equity is also sometimes called **net assets,** since the amount shown for owners' equity is always equal to assets net of (i.e., minus) liabilities. Similarly, the FASB defines owners' equity simply as "the residual interest in the assets of an entity that remains after deducting its liabilities."[12] The use of the word *residual* reflects the fact that in law, owners' claims rank below creditors' claims. For the same reason, common stock is sometimes referred to as a "residual security."

Unincorporated Businesses.   In unincorporated businesses different terminology is used in the owners' equity section. In a **proprietorship**—a business owned by one person—the owner's equity is customarily shown as a single number with a title such as "Lee Jones, capital," rather than making a distinction between the owner's initial investment and the accumulated earnings retained in the business.

In a **partnership,** which is an unincorporated business owned jointly by several persons, there is a capital account for each partner, thus:

Jane Davis, capital	$75,432	
Wayne Smith, capital	75,432	
Total partners' equity		$150,864

A proprietorship or partnership balance sheet also may show a reconciliation of the beginning and ending balance in each owner's capital account. An owner's capital is increased by her or his share of the entity's earnings during the period, and is decreased by the owner's **drawings.** (Drawings in an unincorporated firm are analogous to a corporation's dividends.) For example, a proprietorship's 1993 year-end balance sheet might show the following:

Lee Jones, capital, as of January 1, 1993	$180,000
Add: 1993 earnings	45,000
Deduct: 1993 drawings	(40,000)
Lee Jones, capital, as of December 31, 1993	$185,000

The reader may have heard the terms *partnership accounting* and *corporation accounting* and thus may have formed the impression that different accounting systems are used for different forms of business organizations. This is not so. The treatment of assets and liabilities is generally the

---

[12]FASB, *Statement of Financial Accounting Concepts No. 6* (December 1985), par. 49.

same in all forms of business organizations: differences occur principally in the owners' equity section, as noted above. Nonbusiness organizations do treat certain items differently than businesses, but these differences are beyond the scope of this book.

Having explained the two components of owners' equity in a corporation, we can now expand the fundamental accounting equation to read:

ASSETS = LIABILITIES + PAID-IN CAPITAL + RETAINED EARNINGS

RATIOS

In using financial statement information it often is helpful to express certain important relationships as ratios or percentages. Some of these ratios will be introduced at appropriate places throughout the book and they will be summarized in Chapter 13. A **ratio** is simply one number expressed in terms of another. It is found by dividing one number, the base, into the other. Since Garsden Corporation (Illustration 2–1) had current assets of $22,651,072 and current liabilities of $9,119,089, the ratio of its current assets to its current liabilities was $22,651,072 ÷ $9,119,089, or 2.5 to 1.

Current Ratio.   The ratio of current assets to current liabilities is called the **current ratio.** It is an important indication of an entity's ability to meet its current obligations because if current assets do not exceed current liabilities by a comfortable margin, the entity may be unable to pay its current bills. This is because most current assets are expected to be converted into cash within a year or less, whereas most current liabilities are obligations expected to use cash within a year or less. As a rough rule of thumb, a current ratio of at least 2 to 1 is believed to be desirable in a typical manufacturing company. Garsden's current ratio of 2.5 to 1 is therefore satisfactory. (The "to 1" part of the ratio is usually not explicitly stated; Garsden's current ratio is simply 2.5.)

BALANCE SHEET CHANGES

At the moment an entity begins, its financial status can be recorded on a balance sheet. From that time on, events occur that change the numbers on this first balance sheet, and the accountant records these transactions in accordance with the concepts given earlier in this chapter. Accounting systems accumulate and summarize these changes as a basis for preparing new balance sheets at prescribed intervals, such as the end of a quarter or a year. Each balance sheet shows the financial condition of the entity as of the date it was prepared, after giving effect to all of these changes.

Although in practice a balance sheet is prepared only at prescribed intervals, in learning the accounting process it is useful to consider the changes one by one. This makes it possible to study the effect of individual events without getting entangled with the mechanisms used to record these transactions. The following examples show the effects of a few transactions on the balance sheet. For simplicity, they are assumed to occur on successive days.

Original Capital Contribution

Jan. 1   John Smith starts an incorporated CD and tape store called Music Mart, Inc. He does this by depositing $25,000 of his own funds in a bank account that he has opened in the name of the business entity and taking $25,000 of stock certificates in return. He is thus the sole owner of the corporation. The balance sheet of Music Mart, Inc., will then be as follows:

MUSIC MART
Balance Sheet
As of January 1

Assets		Liabilities and Owner's Equity	
Cash..........................	$25,000	Paid-in capital..................	$25,000

Bank Loan

Jan. 2   Music Mart borrows $12,500 from a bank; the loan is evidenced by a legal document called a note. This transaction increases the asset, cash, and the business incurs a liability to the bank called notes payable. The balance sheet after this transaction will appear thus:

MUSIC MART
Balance Sheet
As of January 2

Assets		Liabilities and Owner's Equity	
Cash..........................	$37,500	Notes payable	$12,500
		Paid-in capital..................	25,000
Total	$37,500	Total	$37,500

Purchase of Merchandise

Jan. 3   The business buys inventory (merchandise it intends to sell) in the amount of $5,000, paying cash. This transaction decreases cash and increases another asset, inventory. The balance sheet will now be as follows:

MUSIC MART
Balance Sheet
As of January 3

Assets		Liabilities and Owner's Equity	
Cash..........................	$32,500	Notes payable	$12,500
Inventory	5,000	Paid-in capital..................	25,000
Total	$37,500	Total	$37,500

Sale of Merchandise

Jan. 4   For $750 cash the store sells merchandise that costs $500. The effect of this transaction is to decrease inventory by $500, increase cash by $750, and increase owner's equity by the difference, or $250. The $250 is the profit on this sale. To distinguish it from the paid-in capital portion of owner's equity it is recorded as retained earnings. The balance sheet will then look like this:

MUSIC MART
Balance Sheet
As of January 4

Assets		Liabilities and Owner's Equity	
Cash	$33,250	Notes payable	$12,500
Inventory	4,500	Paid-in capital	25,000
		Retained earnings	250
Total	$37,750	Total	$37,750

CONCLUDING COMMENT

At this point readers should not be alarmed if they do not yet fully understand some of the topics in this chapter. In subsequent chapters we shall expand considerably on the concepts, categorizations, and terms introduced here. We shall describe modifications and qualifications to some of the basic concepts, and we shall introduce many additional terms that are used on balance sheets. We shall not, however, discard the basic structure that was introduced in this chapter; it was based on the equation Assets = Liabilities + Owners' Equity. Furthermore, it is important to remember that *every* accounting transaction can be recorded in terms of its effect on the balance sheet. The reader should be able to relate all the new material to this basic structure.

SUMMARY

The basic concepts discussed in this chapter may be briefly summarized as follows:

1.   *Money measurement.* Accounting records only those facts that can be expressed in monetary terms.

2.   *Entity.* Accounts are kept for entities as distinguished from the persons associated with those entities.

3.   *Going-concern.* Accounting assumes that an entity will continue to exist indefinitely and that it is not about to be liquidated.

4.   *Cost.* An asset is ordinarily entered in the accounts at the amount paid to acquire it. This cost, rather than current market value, is the basis for subsequent accounting for the asset.

5.   *Dual-aspect.* Every transaction affects at least two items and preserves the fundamental equation: Assets = Liabilities + Owners' Equity.

The balance sheet shows the financial condition of an entity as of a specified moment in time. It consists of two sides. The assets side shows the economic resources controlled by the entity that are expected to provide future benefits to it and that were acquired at objectively measurable amounts. The equities side shows the liabilities, which are obligations of the entity, and the owners' equity, which is the amount invested by the owners. In a corporation, owners' equity is subdivided into paid-in capital and retained earnings.

Cases

CASE 2–1 Maynard Company (A)

Diane Maynard made the following request of a friend:

> My bookkeeper has quit, and I need to see the balance sheets of my company. He has left behind a book with the numbers already entered in it. Would you be willing to prepare balance sheets for me? Also, any comments you care to make about the numbers would be appreciated. The Cash account is healthy, which is a good sign, and he has told me that the net income in June was $19,635.

The book contained a detailed record of transactions, and from it the friend was able to copy off the balances at the beginning of the month and at the end of the month as shown in Exhibit 1. Diane Maynard owned all the stock of Maynard Company.

Questions

1. Prepare balance sheets as of June 1 and as of June 30, in proper format.

2. Make comments about how the financial condition as of the end of June compared with that at the beginning of June.

3. Why do retained earnings not increase by the amount of June net income?

4. As of June 30, do you feel that Maynard Company is worth the amount in Shareholder's Equity, $619,446? Explain.

EXHIBIT 1

Account Balances

	June 1	June 30
Accounts payable.	$ 8,517	$ 21,315
Accounts receivable.	21,798	26,505
Accrued wages payable	1,974	2,202
Accumulated depreciation on building	156,000	157,950
Accumulated depreciation on equipment	5,304	5,928
Bank notes payable	8,385	29,250
Building.	585,000	585,000
Capital stock	390,000	390,000
Cash	34,983	66,660
Equipment (at cost)	13,260	36,660
Land	89,700	89,700
Merchandise inventory.	29,835	26,520
Note receivable, Diane Maynard.	11,700	0
Other noncurrent assets	4,857	5,265
Other noncurrent liabilities	2,451	2,451
Prepaid insurance.	3,150	2,826
Retained earnings.	221,511	229,446
Supplies on hand	5,559	6,630
Taxes payable	5,700	7,224

CASE 2–2   Music Mart, Inc.

On a sheet of paper, set up in pencil the balance sheet of Music Mart, Inc., as it appears after the last transaction described in the text (January 4), leaving considerable space between each item. Record the effect, if any, of the following events on the balance sheet, either by revising existing figures (cross out, rather than erase) or by adding new items as necessary. At least one of these events does not affect the balance sheet. The basic equation, Assets = Liabilities + Owners' Equity, must be preserved at all times. Errors will be minimized if you make a separate list of the balance sheet items affected by each transaction and the amount (+ or –) by which each is to be changed.

After you have recorded these events, prepare a balance sheet in proper form. Assume that all these transactions occurred in January and that there were no other transactions in January.

1. The store purchased and received merchandise for inventory for $5,000, agreeing to pay within 30 days.

2. Merchandise costing $1,500 was sold for $2,300, which was received in cash.

3. Merchandise costing $1,700 was sold for $2,620, the customers agreeing to pay $2,620 within 30 days.

4. The store purchased a three-year fire insurance policy for $1,224, paying cash.

5. The store purchased two lots of land of equal size for a total of $24,000. It paid $6,000 in cash and gave a 10-year mortgage for $18,000.

6. The store sold one of the two lots of land for $12,000. It received $3,000 cash, and in addition, the buyer assumed $9,000 of the mortgage; that is, Music Mart, Inc., became no longer responsible for this half.

7. Smith received a bona fide offer of $33,000 for the business; although his equity was then only $26,970, he rejected the offer. It was evident that the store had already acquired goodwill of $6,030.

8. Smith withdrew $1,000 cash from the store's bank account for his personal use.

9. Smith took merchandise costing $750 from the store's inventory for his personal use.

10. Smith learned that the individual who purchased the land (No. 6 above) subsequently sold it for $14,000. The lot still owned by Music Mart, Inc., was identical in value with this other plot.

11. The store paid off $6,000 of its note payable (disregard interest).

12. Smith sold one-third of the stock he owned in Music Mart, Inc., for $11,000 cash.

13. Merchandise costing $850 was sold for $1,310, which was received in cash.

CASE 2–3   Redwood Cafe (A)*

On March 31, 1991, the partnership that had been organized to operate the Redwood Cafe was dissolved under unusual circumstances, and in connection with its dissolution, preparation of a balance sheet became necessary.

The partnership was formed by Mr. and Mrs. Henry Antoine and Mrs. Sandra

---

* Based on a case decided by the Supreme Court of the State of Oregon (216 P2d 1005).

Landers, who had become acquainted while working in a Portland, Oregon, restaurant. On November 1, 1990, each of the three partners contributed $16,000 cash to the partnership. The Antoines' contribution represented practically all of their savings. Mrs. Landers' payment was the proceeds of her late husband's insurance policy.

On that day also the partnership signed a one-year lease to the Redwood Cafe, located in a nearby recreational area. The monthly rent on the cafe was $1,500. This facility attracted the partners in part because there were living accommodations on the floor above the restaurant. One room was occupied by the Antoines and another by Mrs. Landers.

The partners borrowed $21,000 from a local bank and used this plus $35,000 of partnership funds to buy out the previous operator of the cafe. Of this amount, $53,200 was for equipment and $2,800 was for the food and beverages then on hand. The partnership paid $1,428 for local operating licenses, good for one year beginning November 1, and paid $1,400 for a new cash register. The remainder of the $69,000 was deposited in a checking account.

Shortly after November 1, the partners opened the restaurant. Mr. Antoine was the cook, and Mrs. Antoine and Mrs. Landers waited on customers. Mrs. Antoine also ordered the food, beverages, and supplies, operated the cash register, and was responsible for the checking account.

The restaurant operated throughout the winter season of 1990–91. It was not very successful. On the morning of March 31, 1991, Mrs. Antoine discovered that Mr. Antoine and Mrs. Landers had disappeared. Mrs. Landers had taken all her possessions, but Mr. Antoine had left behind most of his clothing, presumably because he could not remove it without warning Mrs. Antoine. The new cash register and its contents were also missing. Mrs. Antoine concluded that the partnership was dissolved. (The court subsequently affirmed that the partnership was dissolved as of March 30.)

Mrs. Antoine decided to continue operating the Redwood Cafe. She realized that an accounting would have to be made as of March 30 and called in Donald Simpson, an acquaintance who was knowledgeable about accounting.

In response to Mr. Simpson's questions, Mrs. Antoine said that the cash register had contained $311 and that the checking account balance was $1,030. Ski instructors who were permitted to charge their meals had run up accounts totaling $870. (These accounts subsequently were paid in full.) Redwood Cafe owed suppliers amounts totaling $1,583. Mr. Simpson estimated that depreciation on the assets amounted to $2,445. Food and beverages on hand were estimated to be worth $2,430. During the period of its operation, the partners drew salaries at agreed-upon amounts, and these payments were up to date. The clothing that Mr. Antoine left behind was estimated to be worth $750. The partnership had also repaid $2,100 of the bank loan.

Mr. Simpson explained that in order to account for the partners' equity, he would prepare a balance sheet. He would list the items that the partnership owned as of March 30, subtract the amounts that it owed to outside parties, and the balance would be the equity of the three partners. Each partner would be entitled to one third of this amount.

Questions

1. Prepare a balance sheet for the Redwood Cafe as of November 2, 1990.

2. Prepare a balance sheet as of March 30, 1991.

3. Disregarding the marital complications, do you suppose that the partners received the equity determined in Question 2? Why?

CASE 2–4   Los Niños Day Care Center

After six months of operations, Consuelo Gonzalez wanted to analyze the performance of Los Niños Day Care Center. She wanted to know where the company stood as of December 31, 1993, and what its future prospects were.

Los Niños Day Care Center was a company organized by Ms. Gonzalez in 1993 to provide supervised care, preschool education, a snack, and a noonday meal primarily for children of working mothers. To provide for the center's initial capital, Ms. Gonzalez took out a $42,000 mortgage on her own house. She invested $36,000 of this in common stock of the center. Friends of hers invested $18,000 in cash, receiving stock in return. A government agency made a one-year loan of $11,930 to the center.

With these funds, the center purchased property for $67,200, of which $13,400 was for land and $53,800 was for a building on the land. The purchase was financed in part with a $45,400 mortgage, the remainder being paid in cash. Interest on the mortgage was to be paid quarterly, but no principal repayment was required until the company had become established. The center also purchased $23,400 of furniture and equipment for cash.

During the first six months of operation, which ended December 31, 1993, the center paid out the following additional amounts in cash:

Salary* to Ms. Gonzalez	$13,500
Salaries* of part-time employees	8,842
Insurance (one-year policy)	2,650
Utilities	1,710
Food and supplies	7,340
Interest and miscellaneous	5,750
Total paid out	$39,792

*Includes payroll taxes.

The center received $28,660 in student fees in cash. In addition, parents owed the center $1,100 for student fees. As of December 31, 1993, Ms. Gonzalez estimated that $660 of supplies were still on hand. The center owed food suppliers $1,140.

In thinking about the future, Ms. Gonzalez estimated that for the next six months, ending June 30, student fees received (in addition to the $1,100 student fees that applied to the first six months) would be $43,100. This was higher than the amount for the first six months because enrollments were higher.

She estimated that the center would pay $22,030 in salaries, $2,150 cash for utilities (which was higher than the first six months because of expected colder weather), $9,400 for additional food and supplies (higher because of the higher enrollment), and $4,560 for interest and miscellaneous (lower than the first six months because certain start-up costs were paid for during the first six months). She also expected to pay back the government loan.

She estimated that supplies on hand as of June 30 would be $660 and that nothing would be owed suppliers. She did not include any additional amount for insurance because the amount paid in the first six months covered this cost for the whole year.

She knew that many companies recorded depreciation on buildings, furniture, and equipment; however, she had a firm offer of $95,000 cash for these assets from someone who wanted to buy the center, so she thought that under these circumstances depreciation was inappropriate.

Questions

1. Prepare a balance sheet for Los Niños Day Care Center as of December 31, 1993. (In order to minimize errors, it is suggested that you

treat each event separately; show the items that are affected and the amount of increase or decrease in each item. For events that affect shareholders' equity, other than the initial investment, increase or decrease the Retained Earnings item. This item will have a negative amount, which should be indicated by enclosing it in parentheses. Show noncurrent assets at their original cost.)

2. Prepare an estimated balance sheet as of June 30, 1994.

3. Should the noncurrent assets be reported on the December 31, 1993, balance sheet at their cost, at $95,000, or at some other amount? (The amount need not be calculated.) If at some amount other than cost, how would the balance sheet prepared in Question 1 be changed?

4. Does it appear likely that Los Niños Day Care Center will become a viable company; that is, is it likely to be profitable if Ms. Gonzalez's estimates are correct?

3

Basic Accounting Concepts: The Income Statement

This chapter introduces the idea of income as used in financial accounting and describes the income statement, the financial statement that reports income and its determinants.

In the course of this discussion, we shall explain the last 6 of the 11 basic concepts listed in Chapter 2:

6. Accounting period.	9. Matching.
7. Conservatism.	10. Consistency.
8. Realization.	11. Materiality.

As was the case in Chapter 2, the discussion of topics in this chapter is introductory. Each will be explained in more depth in later chapters.

THE NATURE OF INCOME

Chapter 2 described the balance sheet, which reports the financial condition of an entity as of one moment in time. Chapter 3 describes a second financial statement, the income statement, which summarizes the results of operations for a period of time. It is therefore a *flow* report, as contrasted with the balance sheet, which is a *status* report. These two financial statements illustrate the only two ways in which any entity—whether it be a business, a human body, or the universe—can be described:

ILLUSTRATION 3–1
BASIC BUSINESS FINANCIAL FLOWS

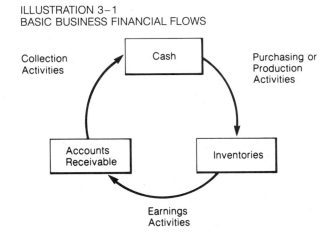

(1) in terms of flows through time and (2) in terms of its status or state as of one moment in time.

Flows in a business are continuous. Their essential nature, in many businesses, is indicated by the simplified diagram in Illustration 3–1. The business has a pool of cash that it has obtained from investors or from past profitable operations. It uses this cash to acquire inventories, either by purchasing goods from others or by producing them itself. It also incurs other costs. (Accounts payable and various other assets and liability accounts may intervene between the incurrence of these costs and the cash outflow to pay for them.) It sells the goods to customers. The customers either pay cash or agree to pay later, thus creating accounts receivable. When the customer pays, the pool of cash is replenished.

For most types of businesses, the income statement focuses on the section of the flow diagram that is labeled "earnings activities"—also commonly called the business's operating activities or simply its operations. The income statement reports the nature and magnitude of these activities for a specified period of time.

Essentially, this report consists of two elements. One reports the inflows (creation) of assets—cash or accounts receivable—that result from the sale of goods and services to customers; these amounts are called **revenues.** The other reports the outflows (consumption) of resources that were required in order to generate these revenues; these amounts are called **expenses.** Profit (more formally, **income**) is the amount by which revenues exceed expenses. Since the word *income* is often used with various qualifying adjectives, the term **net income** is used to refer to the net excess of all the revenues over all the expenses. Some companies use the term **net earnings** rather than net income. If total expenses exceed total revenues, the difference is a **net loss.**

THE ACCOUNTING PERIOD CONCEPT

Net income for the entire life of an organization is relatively easy to measure. This is simply the difference between the money that comes in and the money that goes out (excluding, of course, money invested by the owners or paid to the owners).

> **Example.** Michael and Judith Lincoln operated a children's camp for one summer, renting all the necessary facilities and equipment. Before the camp opened, they invested $24,000 for food, the initial rental payment, and certain other costs. The camp received $122,400 in fees from parents. At the end of the summer, after all affairs were wound up, the Lincolns had the $24,000 back and $15,237 additional. This $15,237 was the net income of the camp business. It was the difference between the revenues they received from parents and the expenses incurred for food, wages, and other costs. The income statement for the business looked like this:

Revenues		$122,400
Less expenses:		
Food	$42,756	
Wages	46,935	
Rental	12,000	
Other costs	5,472	
Total expenses		107,163
Net income		$ 15,237

Relatively few business ventures have a life of only a few months, as was the case with the Lincolns' summer camp. Most of them operate for many years. Indeed, in accordance with the going-concern concept, it is usually assumed that the life of a business is indefinitely long. Management and other interested parties are unwilling to wait until the business has ended before obtaining information on how much income has been earned. They need to know at frequent intervals "how things are going."

This need leads to the **accounting period concept:** accounting measures activities for a specified interval of time, called the *accounting period.* For the purpose of reporting to outsiders, one year is the usual accounting period. Pacioli, the first author of an accounting text, wrote in 1494: "Books should be closed each year, especially in a partnership, because frequent accounting makes for long friendship."[1] Most corporate bylaws require an annual report to the shareholders, and income tax reporting is also on an annual basis.

In the majority of businesses, the accounting year, or **fiscal year,** corresponds to the calendar year; but many businesses use the *natural business*

---

[1] Lucas Pacioli, *Summa de Arithmetica Geometria Proportioni et Proportionalita,* from the translation by John B. Geijsbeck.

year instead of the calendar year. For example, nearly all department stores end their fiscal year on January 31, which is after the Christmas rush and its repercussions in the form of returns and clearance sales.

Interim Reports

Management needs information more often than once a year. Income statements for management are therefore prepared more frequently. The most common period is a month, but the period may be as short as a week or even a day. The Securities and Exchange Commission (SEC) requires quarterly income statements from companies over which it has jurisdiction. These reports are called **interim reports** to distinguish them from the annual reports.

Businesses are living, ongoing organisms. The act of chopping the continuous stream of business events into time periods is therefore somewhat arbitrary, since business activities do not stop or change significantly as one accounting period ends and another begins. This fact makes the problem of measuring income for an accounting period the most difficult problem in accounting.

> **Example.** If the Lincolns operated a year-round hotel instead of a summer camp, their income for a year could not be measured simply as the difference between the money taken in and the money paid out. As of the end of the year, some of the guests would not have paid their bills. Yet these unpaid bills are an asset, accounts receivable, that surely increases the "well-offness" of the business even though the cash has not yet been received. Conversely, some of the cash paid out may have been for the purchase of an asset, such as the hotel itself, that will benefit the business beyond the end of this accounting period. It would be incorrect to conclude that the hotel's income has been decreased by the amount of such payments.

Relation between Income and Owners' Equity

As explained in Chapter 2, the net income of an accounting period increases owners' equity. More specifically for a corporation, net income increases retained earnings. In order to understand the implication of this relationship, let us refer to the January 4 transaction of Music Mart, Inc. (page 44). On that day, merchandise costing $500 was sold for $750 cash. Looking first at the effect of this transaction on assets, we note that although inventory decreased by $500, cash increased by $750, so that the total assets increased by the difference, $250. From the dual-aspect concept, which states that the total of the assets must always equal the total of the liabilities and owners' equity, we know that the liabilities and owner's equity side of the balance sheet must also have increased by $250. Since no liabilities were affected, the increase must have occurred in owner's equity. In summary, because assets were sold for more than was paid for them, the owner's equity increased. Since owners' equity is made up of paid-in capital and retained earnings and since the owner did not contribute more capital, the increase must have been in retained earnings. Such net increases in retained earnings are called **income.**

In understanding how this income came about, let us consider separately two aspects of this event: the $750 received from the sale and the $500 decrease in inventory. If we look only at the $750, we see that it is an increase in cash and a corresponding *increase* in retained earnings. The $500, taken by itself, is a decrease in the asset, inventory, and a corresponding *decrease* in retained earnings. These two aspects illustrate the only two ways in which earnings activities—that is, operations—can affect retained earnings: they can increase it or they can decrease it.

Revenues and Expenses.   It follows that revenues and expenses can also be defined in terms of their effect on retained earnings: a **revenue** is an increase in retained earnings resulting from the operations of the entity, and an **expense** is a decrease.[2]

Restating the transactions described above in these terms, there was revenue of $750, expense of $500, and income of $250. The basic equation is:

$$\text{REVENUES} - \text{EXPENSES} = \text{NET INCOME}$$

This equation clearly indicates that income is a *difference.* Sometimes the word *income* is used improperly as a synonym for *revenue.* This is because the approved definitions as given above are of relatively recent origin and some companies have not kept up with the latest developments. Also, some nonprofit entities such as churches refer to their "income and outgo" or "income and expenses" rather than to revenues and expenses.

On an income statement no misunderstanding is caused by such an error because revenues, however labeled, appear at the top and income at the bottom. But in other contexts confusion can be created. For example, if one reads that Company X had income of $1 million, a completely false impression of the size of the company is given if the intended meaning was that Company X had *revenues* of $1 million.[3]

Income Not the Same as Increase in Cash

It is extremely important to understand that the income of a period is associated with changes in *retained earnings* and that it has no necessary relation to changes in *cash* during that period. Income connotes "well-offness": roughly speaking, the bigger the income is, the better off the owners are. An increase in cash, however, does not necessarily mean that

---

[2]As pointed out in Chapter 2, unincorporated businesses ordinarily do not subdivide owners' equity into paid-in capital and retained earnings. Nevertheless, conceptually the distinction between changes in owners' equity related to paid-in capital and those related to retained earnings is both valid and useful in an unincorporated business.

[3]The income tax Form 1040 still contains the phrases "dividend income" and "interest income" for items that actually are revenues.

the owners are any better off—that the retained earnings portion of their equity has increased. The increase in cash may merely be offset by a decrease in some other asset or by an increase in a liability, with no effect on retained earnings at all.

Again, reference to the transactions of Music Mart, Inc., may help to clarify this point. When Music Mart borrowed $12,500 from the bank on January 2 (page 43), its increase in cash was exactly matched by an increase in the liability to the bank. There was no change in retained earnings; no income resulted from this transaction. The $12,500 was not revenue; it was the proceeds of a borrowing transaction, whereas revenues are related to earnings transactions. Similarly, the purchase of inventory for $5,000 cash on January 3 resulted in a decrease in cash, but there was an exactly corresponding increase in another asset, inventory. Owner's equity was not changed. This was an asset purchase transaction, not an earnings transaction.

As we have already seen, the sale for $750 of inventory costing $500 *did* result in income. But note that the income was $250, whereas cash increased by $750; even here, the income is different from the amount by which the cash increased. In short, although individuals typically measure their *personal income* by the amount of money they receive, this concept of income is not correct when applied to a *business* entity.

THE CONSERVATISM CONCEPT

Managers are human beings. Like most humans, they would like to give a favorable report on how well the entity for which they are responsible has performed. Yet, as the FASB says, "prudent reporting based on a healthy skepticism builds confidence in the results and, in the long run, best serves all of the divergent interests [of financial statement users]."[4] This long-standing philosophy of prudent reporting leads to the **conservatism concept.**

This concept is often articulated as a preference for understatement rather than overstatement of net income and net assets (i.e., owners' equity) when dealing with measurement uncertainties. Thus, if two estimates of some future amount are about equally likely, there is a preference for using the smaller number when measuring assets or revenues, and the larger for liabilities or expenses. For decades the concept was stated informally as "anticipate no profits but anticipate all losses."

We state the conservatism concept's two aspects somewhat more formally:

1. Recognize *revenues* (increases in retained earnings) only when they are *reasonably certain.*

---

[4]"Qualitative Characteristics of Accounting Information," *FASB Statement of Accounting Concepts No. 2* (May 1980), par. 97.

2. Recognize *expenses* (decreases in retained earnings) as soon as they are *reasonably possible.*

> **Examples.** In December 1993 Lynn Jones agrees to buy an automobile from Varsity Motors, Inc., for delivery in January 1994. Although this is good news to Varsity Motors, it is possible that something will go wrong and the sale will not be consummated. Therefore, the conservatism concept requires that the revenue not be recorded, that is, *recognized,* until the automobile is actually delivered. Thus, Varsity Motors does not recognize revenue from this transaction in 1993 because the revenue is not *reasonably certain* in 1993, even though it is *reasonably possible.* Rather, if the automobile is actually delivered in 1994, revenue is recognized in 1994.
>
> As another example, an uninsured automobile disappears from Varsity Motors' premises in December 1993. Possibly, it will be recovered; possibly, it has been stolen and is gone forever. In the latter case Varsity Motors' retained earnings has decreased; the company has incurred an expense. Suppose that Varsity Motors is not reasonably certain that the auto is gone forever until early 1994. Nevertheless, the conservatism concept requires that the expense be recognized in 1993, the year in which it became *reasonably possible* that there was an expense, rather than in 1994, the year in which the expense became *reasonably certain.*
>
> As a final example, consider the amount reported as inventory. If late in 1993 an entity learns that the selling price of certain goods in its inventory has declined to less than the cost of these goods, a loss (i.e., an expense) is recognized in 1993, even though in actual fact prices may rise again and the goods may be sold in 1994 at a profit. This is because it is *reasonably possible* that owners' equity has been reduced in 1993. (This "lower of cost or market" rule, probably the most well-known application of the conservatism concept, is described in Chapter 5.)

Obviously, in various situations there are problems in deciding what is meant by such imprecise phrases as *about equally likely, reasonably certain,* and *reasonably possible.* For some specific problems accounting principles give guidance—for example, the inventory principle just described. However, as with many accounting matters, judgment is often involved, and there is only a fine line between "prudently" reporting net income and owners' equity on the one hand and misleadingly understating them on the other.

Application to Revenue Recognition   In general, revenue from the sale of goods is recognized in the period in which goods were delivered to customers. Revenue from the performance of services is recognized in the period in which the services were performed. For many events, cash is received at the time of delivery or performance, and this is excellent evidence that the revenue has been earned. This is the case with most supermarkets and for many transactions in other retail stores and service firms. It can happen, however, that the cash is received in either

ILLUSTRATION 3–2

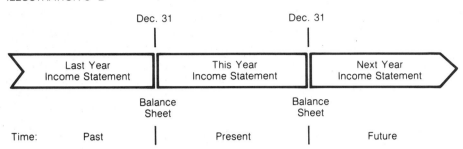

an earlier period or a later period than that in which the revenue is recognized. Examples of each are given below.

Precollected Revenue. Magazine publishing companies sell subscriptions that the subscriber pays for in advance; the company receives the cash *before* it renders the service of providing the magazine. Referring to Illustration 3–2, if subscription money is received this year for magazines to be delivered next year, the revenue belongs in next year. The money received is therefore recorded, not as revenue for this year, but rather as a liability on the balance sheet as of the end of this year. The liability, **precollected** (or **unearned**) **revenue,** represents the company's obligation to provide its subscribers the future issues of the magazine for which they have already paid. Similarly, rent on property is often paid in advance. When this happens, the revenue is properly recognized in the period in which the services of the rented property are provided, not the period in which the rent payment is received. In sum, precollected revenues have been *paid* to the entity, but have not as yet been *earned* by the entity.

Accounts Receivable. The converse of the above situation is illustrated by sales made on credit: the customer agrees to pay for the goods or services sometime *after* the date on which they are actually received. The revenue is recognized in the period in which the sale is made. If the payment is not due until the following period, an asset—**accounts receivable**—is shown on the balance sheet as of the end of the current period. When the bill is paid by the customer (i.e., the account receivable is collected), the amount received is not revenue. Rather, it reduces the amount of accounts receivable outstanding and increases cash, leaving retained earnings unchanged. The *sale* is the earnings transaction that affects retained earnings; collection of the account receivable is the conversion of a noncash asset into cash, which is not an earnings transaction.

The distinction between revenue and receipts is illustrated in the following tabulation, which shows various types of sales transactions and classifies the effect of each on cash receipts and sales revenue for "this year":

		This Year	
	Amount	Cash Receipts	Sales Revenue
1. Cash sales made this year	$200	$200	$200
2. Credit sales made last year; cash received this year	300	300	0
3. Credit sales made this year; cash received this year	400	400	400
4. Credit sales made this year; cash received next year	100	0	0
Total		$900	$700

In this illustration this year's total cash receipts do not equal this year's total sales revenue. The totals would be equal in a given accounting period only if (1) the company made all its sales for cash or (2) the amount of cash collected from credit customers in the accounting period happened by chance to equal the amount of credit sales made during that period.

Accrued Revenue. When a bank lends money, it is providing a service to the borrower, namely, the use of the bank's money. The bank's charge for this service is called **interest,** and the amount the bank earns is **interest revenue.** The bank earns interest revenue on each day that the borrower is permitted to use the money. For some loan transactions the borrower does not actually pay the interest in the year in which the money was used but rather pays it next year. Even if this interest payment is not made until next year, the bank has *earned* revenue this year for a loan outstanding during the year. The amount earned but unpaid as of the end of this year is an asset on the bank's balance sheet called **accrued interest revenue** or **interest receivable.** It is similar to an account receivable. In sum, accrued revenue is the reverse of precollected revenue: accrued revenues have been *earned by* the entity but have not as yet been *paid to* the entity.

THE REALIZATION CONCEPT

The conservatism concept suggests the period *when* revenue should be recognized. Another concept, the **realization concept,** indicates the *amount* of revenue that should be recognized from a given sale.

Realization refers to inflows of cash or claims to cash (e.g., accounts receivable) arising from the sale of goods or services. Thus, if a customer buys $50 worth of items at a grocery store, paying cash, the store realizes $50 from the sale. If a clothing store sells a suit for $300, the purchaser agreeing to pay within 30 days, the store realizes $300 (in receivables) from the sale, *provided* that the purchaser has a good credit record so that payment is reasonably certain (conservatism concept).

The realization concept states that the amount recognized as revenue is the amount that is reasonably certain to be realized—that is, that customers are reasonably certain to pay. Of course, there is room for differences in judgment as to how certain "reasonably certain" is. However, the concept does clearly allow for the amount of revenue recognized to be less than the selling price of the goods and services sold. One obvious situation is the sale of merchandise at a discount—at an amount less than its normal selling price. In such cases, revenue is recorded at the lower amount, not the normal price.

> **Example.** In many instances, the sale of a new car is made at a negotiated price that is lower than the manufacturer's list ("sticker") price for the automobile. In these circumstances, revenue is the amount at which the sale is made, rather than the list price. If the list price is $25,000 and the car is actually sold for $23,500, then the revenue is $23,500.

A less obvious situation arises with the sale of merchandise on credit. When a company makes a credit sale, it expects that the customer will pay the bill. Experience may indicate, however, that not all customers do pay their bills. In measuring the revenue for a period, the amount of sales made on credit should be reduced by the estimated amount of credit sales that will never be realized—that is, by the estimated amount of bad debts.

> **Example.** If a store makes credit sales of $100,000 during a period and if experience indicates that 3 percent of credit sales will eventually become bad debts, the amount of revenue for the period is $97,000, not $100,000.

Although conceptually the estimated amount of bad debts is part of the calculation of revenue, in practice this amount is often treated as an expense. Thus, revenue is often reported as $100,000, and there is an expense—bad debt expense—of $3,000. The effect on net income is the same as if the revenue were reported as $97,000.

THE MATCHING CONCEPT

As noted earlier, the sale of merchandise has two aspects: (1) a revenue aspect, reflecting an increase in retained earnings equal to the amount of revenue realized, and (2) an expense aspect, reflecting the decrease in retained earnings because the merchandise (an asset) has left the business. In order to measure correctly this sale's *net* effect on retained earnings in a period, both of these aspects must be recognized in the same accounting period. This leads to the **matching concept:** when a given event affects both revenues and expenses, the effect on each should be recognized in the *same* accounting period.

Usually, the matching concept is applied by first determining the items of revenue to recognize for the period and their amounts (in accordance with the conservatism and realization concepts), and then matching items of cost to these revenues. For example, if goods costing $1,000 are sold for $1,500, it is first determined when the $1,500 is reasonably certain to be realized;

then the $1,000 cost of sales is matched with those revenues as an expense, resulting in $500 income from the sale. However, as we shall see in later chapters, in some situations the applicable expenses are identified first, and then revenues are matched to them. Here we shall assume that applicable revenues of a period have been identified; the problem is to determine the costs that match with these revenues. These matched costs are expenses of the period.

RECOGNITION OF EXPENSES

In discussing the period in which an expense is recognized (i.e., recorded), we shall use four terms—*cost, expenditure, expense,* and *disbursement*—whose meanings must be kept clear. Although these terms tend to be used interchangeably in everyday conversation, in accounting they are not synonyms.

Terminology   **Cost** is a monetary measurement of the amount of resources used for some purpose. An **expenditure** is a decrease in an asset (usually cash) or an increase in a liability (often accounts payable) associated with the incurrence of a cost. The expenditures in an accounting period equal the cost of all the goods and services acquired in that period. An **expense** is an item of cost applicable to the current accounting period. An expense represents resources consumed by the entity's *earnings activities* during the current period. When an expenditure is made, the related cost is either an asset or an expense. If the cost benefits future periods, it is an increase in an asset. If not, it is an expense—a reduction in retained earnings—of the current period. A **disbursement** is the payment of cash. A cash expenditure is a disbursement; but so is any cash payment, such as paying an account payable, repaying a loan, or paying a cash dividend to shareholders.

> **Example.**   An item of inventory costing $1,000 is received in March, the vendor is paid in April, and the item is shipped to a customer in May. In March there is a cost of $1,000 (acquisition of a good) and an expenditure of $1,000 (increase in accounts payable). In April there is a disbursement of $1,000 (cash payment). In May there is an expense of $1,000 (consumption of inventory).

Criteria for Expense Recognition   The matching concept provides one criterion for deciding what costs are expenses in an accounting period: the revenue and expense effects of a given event should be recognized in the same accounting period. There are two other related criteria: (1) costs associated with activities of the period are expenses of the period; and (2) costs that cannot be associated with revenues of future periods are expenses of the current period. An example of each criterion is given below.

Direct Matching.   The association of cost of sales with revenues for the same goods or services has already been mentioned. Similarly, if a salesperson is paid a commission, the commission is reported as an expense in the same period in which the revenue arising from these sales is recognized. The period in which the commission is recognized as an expense may be different from the period in which the salesperson receives the commission in cash.

> **Example.**   Ms. A was paid $2,000 cash in 1993 as a commission on an order she booked late in 1993. But the goods were not shipped, and thus the sales revenue was not recognized until early 1994. Thus, the $2,000 is an expense of 1994. Mr. B was paid $1,000 cash in early 1994 as a commission on goods that were shipped in late 1993. The $1,000 is an expense of 1993. Note that in both cases the cash disbursement took place in a different period from the period in which the expense was recognized.

Period Costs.   Some items of expense are associated with a certain accounting period, even though they cannot be traced to any specific revenue transactions occurring in that period. In general, these expenses are the costs of being in business. In a retail store they include the costs of operating the store during the period, even though these costs cannot be traced directly to the specific merchandise sold. In a manufacturing firm they include all of the nonproduction costs—all the costs incurred "outside the factory walls." These expenses are called **period costs.**

> **Example.**   If a salesperson is paid a salary rather than a commission as in the previous example, the salary is reported as an expense in the period in which the employee works. The amount of the salary is not affected by the volume of sales, and hence there is no direct relationship between the salary cost and revenue. The salary is one of the costs of operating the business during the period and hence is related only in an *indirect* way to the revenue of the period.

Costs Not Associated with Future Revenue.   Even if a cost item is not associated with the operations of a period, it is reported as an expense of that period if it cannot be associated with the revenue of some *future* period. An item of cost must be either an asset or an expense. For a cost of this period to be an asset, it must, by definition, be expected to provide a benefit in some future period. If it does not qualify as an asset by this test, it must be an expense of the current period. Even if the item of cost benefits the future in some general way, but there is no feasible or objective way of associating these benefit with specific future periods, the item is an expense.

> **Example.**   Employee training programs are intended to provide benefits to future periods in that the participants are expected to perform better as a result of the training. The future benefits of this training cannot be objectively measured, however. So training costs are charged as an expense of the current period, rather than being treated as an asset.

Under this general principle many items of cost are charged as expenses in the current period even though they have no connection with the revenues of the period or even with the ongoing operations of the period. If assets are destroyed by fire or lost by theft, for example, the amount of the loss is an expense of the current period. In general, if a cost is incurred and there is no reasonable basis for classifying the cost as an asset, it is reported as an expense.

If during the period an item that once was classified as an asset is found to have no value for future periods, the asset amount is removed from the balance sheet and becomes an expense of the period. This can happen, for example, when goods held in inventory are found to have deteriorated, become obsolete, or otherwise become unsalable.

Expenses and Expenditures

Expenditures take place when an entity acquires goods or services. An expenditure may be made by cash, by incurring a liability (such as an account payable), by the exchange of another asset (such as a trade-in vehicle), or by some combination of these. As already noted, these expenditures can be either assets or expenses. Over the entire life of an entity, most expenditures become expenses. (The exception would be assets that are liquidated as the business closes down its operations at the end of its life.) In any time segment *shorter* than the life of an entity, however, there is no necessary correspondence between expenses and expenditures.

> **Example.** Late in 1993 $5,000 of fuel oil was purchased for cash. This was an *expenditure* of $5,000, which was the exchange of cash for another asset. If none of this fuel oil was consumed in 1993, there was no *expense* in 1993. Rather, the fuel oil was an asset as of the end of 1993. If the fuel oil was consumed in 1994, there was an *expense* of $5,000 in 1994.

Four types of transactions need to be considered in distinguishing between amounts that are properly considered as expenses of a given accounting period and the expenditures made in connection with these items. Focusing on "this year" in Illustration 3–2, these are as follows:

1. Expenditures made this year that are also expenses of this year.
2. Expenditures made prior to this year that become expenses during this year. These appeared as assets on the balance sheet at the beginning of this year.
3. Expenditures made this year that will become expenses in future years. These will appear as assets on the balance sheet at the end of this year.
4. Expenses of this year that will be paid for in a future year. On the balance sheet at the end of this year, these appear as liabilities.

1. Expenditures that Are Also Expenses. This is the simplest and most common type of transaction, and the least troublesome to account for. If an item is acquired during the year, it is an expenditure. If it is consumed during the same year, it is an expense of the year. "Consumed," as used here, means more precisely that the item provides its intended benefit. For example, raw materials that are converted into salable goods are not considered to be consumed until the goods are sold. At that time the raw materials cost is a part of the expense, cost of goods sold.

2. Beginning Assets that Become Expenses. On January 1 the balance sheet shows the entity's assets. Assets are resources that provide future benefits to the entity. The expenditures for the beginning-of-the-period assets were made in some earlier period. These expenditures were recorded as assets rather than as expenses because the future benefit test was met when the resources were acquired. During this year some of these benefits are "released" and "used up" (i.e., some assets are consumed); hence, the expenditures are transformed into expenses. The three principal types of such assets are described below.

First, there are *inventories* of salable goods. These become expenses when the goods are sold.

Second, there are *prepaid expenses* (sometimes called *deferred charges*). These represent services or other assets (usually intangible) purchased prior to this year but whose benefits have not been fully used up when the year begins. They become expenses in the year in which the benefits are received—that is, when the services are used or the assets are consumed. Prepaid insurance protection, prepaid lawyers' retainer fees, and prepaid rent are such items.

> **Example.** On December 31, 1993 a company purchased for $90,000 an insurance policy providing three years of protection. The $90,000 appears as an asset on the balance sheet of December 31, 1993. In 1994 $30,000 (one third) becomes an expense and $60,000 remains as an asset on the balance sheet of December 31, 1994. In 1995 $30,000 more becomes an expense, and the remaining $30,000 is an expense in 1996.

The third category of assets that will become expenses is *long-lived (noncurrent) assets.* With the exception of land, assets have a limited useful life; they do not last forever. They are purchased with the expectation that they will be used in the operation of the entity in future periods, and they will become expenses in these future periods. The principle is exactly the same as that of the insurance policy previously mentioned, which also was purchased for the benefit of future periods. An important practical differ- ence between a long-lived asset, such as a building, and an insurance policy, however, is that the life of a building is usually difficult to estimate whereas the life of an insurance policy is known precisely. Thus, estimating what portion of a building's cost is an expense of a given accounting period is a more difficult task than that of determining the insurance expense of a period. The mechanism used to convert the cost of fixed assets to expense is called **depreciation;** it is described in Chapter 7.

3. Expenditures that Are Not Yet Expenses. As the preceding examples show, some expenditures made to acquire assets are not expenses of this year because the assets' benefits have not yet been used up as of the year's end. These include not only the purchase of long-lived assets but also expenditures incurred in connection with the *production* of goods that are to be sold in some future year. Thus, wages and salaries earned by production personnel and all other costs associated with producing goods become part of the cost of the goods produced and remain as an asset, *inventory,* until the goods are sold. Chapter 6 discusses in more detail the distinction between production costs (also called product costs), which initially are added to inventory amounts, and other operating costs (period costs), which are expenses of the current period.

4. Expenses Not Yet Paid.   Some expenses of this year are not paid for by the end of the year. The parties who furnished services during the year have a claim against the entity for the amounts owed them. These amounts are therefore liabilities (called **accrued expenses**) of the entity as of December 31. The liability for wages earned but not yet paid, **accrued wages** (or wages payable), is an example already mentioned. The cost of using borrowed money during a period is interest expense of that period. If this interest expense has not been paid, the end-of-period balance sheet will show a liability, **accrued interest expense** (or interest payable). Several other types of obligations have the same characteristic: although services were rendered prior to the date for which the balance sheet is prepared, these services have not yet been paid for. The *recognition* of these expenses reduces retained earnings; the subsequent *payment* of the obligation (i.e., the disbursement) does not affect retained earnings.[5]

For all obligations of this type, the transaction involved is essentially the same: the expense is recognized in the period in which the services were used, and the obligation that results from these services is shown in the liability section of the balance sheet as of the end of the period.

> **Example.**   In the final days of 1993, Aneel Prahalad earned $300 that was not paid him. This is an expense of $300 in 1993, and there is a corresponding liability of $300 (accrued wages) on his employer's balance sheet as of December 31, 1993. In 1994 when Prahalad is paid, the liability is eliminated and there is a $300 decrease in cash. Accrued wages liability will always occur for an entity whose last payday of the year (for example, the fourth Friday in December) does not fall on the last day of the year.

In this example the basic equality, Assets = Liabilities + Owners' Equity, is always maintained. The earning of wages resulted in an expense of $300, which was a decrease in owners' equity (retained earnings), and there was an equal increase in the liability, accrued wages. Thus the total of the equities—liabilities and owners' equity—was unchanged. The payment of the $300 resulted in a decrease in cash and a decrease in the liability, accrued wages, so both assets and liabilities were reduced by $300.

---

[5]Strictly speaking, this fourth category is conceptually the same as the first: The creation of the accrued expense liability is an expenditure associated with the cost of acquiring the labor services or of using the borrowed funds. However, unlike transactions in the first category, this type of transaction is neither simple nor common; thus, pedagogically it is useful to treat it as a separate category.

Dividends   Dividends that a corporation pays to its shareholders are *not* expenses. Dividends are a *distribution* of net income, rather than an item in the calculation of net income. Cash dividends reduce the asset, cash, and reduce retained earnings by an equal amount. This is the only common transaction in business entities in which a reduction in retained earnings is not an expense. Similarly, in an unincorporated business, owner's or partners' drawings are not treated as expenses.

Summary of Expense Measurement   The proper classification of expenditures as either assets or expenses is one of the most difficult problems in accounting. As an aid in this process and as a summary of the preceding discussion, Illustration 3–3 gives a decision diagram that should be helpful. It shows that an entity starts an accounting period with certain assets and that during the period it makes expenditures. If these costs are not paid for in cash or by an exchange of another asset, they result in liabilities on the year-end balance sheet. In preparing the end-of-period balance sheet and the period's income statement, the accountant must classify these assets and expenditures either as expenses, which will appear on the income statement, or as assets, which will appear on the end-of-period balance sheet. In order to do this classification, the three questions shown on the diagram must be addressed.

GAINS AND LOSSES

Throughout this chapter, revenue, which increases retained earnings, has been associated with the sale of a company's goods and services. Retained earnings can increase for other reasons. For example, if a company sells marketable securities for more than it paid for them, retained earnings has increased, but this is not sales revenue (unless the company is in the business of selling securities). Technically, such increases in retained earnings are called **gains,** to distinguish them from revenues from the sale of goods and services.

Similarly, decreases in retained earnings (except dividends) for reasons not associated with operations are referred to as **losses,** and these are sometimes distinguished from expenses. Loss of assets by fire or theft has already been mentioned. Sale of marketable securities at an amount less than was paid for them is another example.

As a practical matter, no sharp distinction is made between sales revenues and gains; they both increase retained earnings. Similarly, expenses and losses both decrease retained earnings, so again in practice no sharp distinction is made between them.

THE CONSISTENCY CONCEPT

The nine concepts that have been described in this and the preceding chapter are so broad that in practice there are several different methods in

ILLUSTRATION 3–3
DECISION DIAGRAM: ASSETS AND EXPENSES

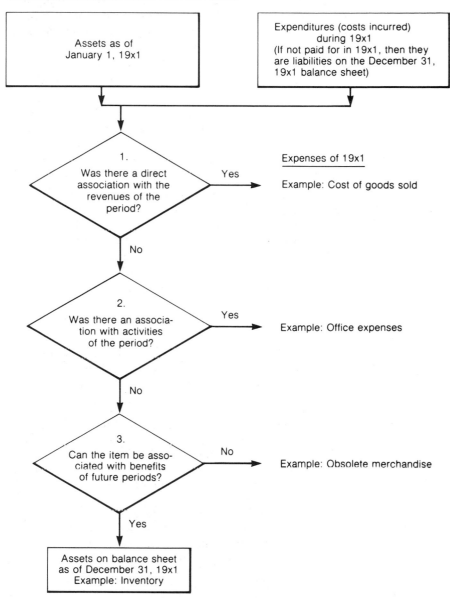

which a given event may be recorded. As mentioned above, for example, bad debts may be recognized either as a reduction in revenue or as an expense. The **consistency concept** states that once an entity has decided on one method it should use the *same* method for all subsequent events of the same character unless it has a sound reason to change methods. If an entity frequently changed the manner of handling a given class of events in the accounting records—for example, frequently changing between the straight-line method and an accelerated method for depreciating its building—comparison of its financial statements for one period with those of another period would be difficult.

Because of this concept, changes in the method of keeping accounts are not made lightly. If a company changes an accounting method from the method used in the preceding year, the company's outside auditors must report this in their opinion letter—the auditors' report that accompanies the annual financial statements distributed to shareholders. (Auditors' opinion letters will be described more fully in Chapter 14.)

Consistency, as used here, has a narrow meaning. It refers only to consistency *over time,* not to *logical* consistency at a given moment of time. For example, long-lived assets are recorded at cost, but inventories are recorded at the lower of their cost or market value. Some people argue that this is inconsistent. Whatever the merits of this argument may be, it does not involve the *accounting* concept of consistency. This concept does not mean that the treatment of different categories of transactions must be consistent with one another, but only that transactions in a given category must be treated consistently from one accounting period to the next.

THE MATERIALITY CONCEPT

In law there is a doctrine called *de minimis non curat lex,* which means that the court will not consider trivial matters. Similarly, the accountant does not attempt to record events so insignificant that the work of recording them is not justified by the usefulness of the results.

> **Example.**   Conceptually, a brand-new pad of paper is an asset of the entity. Every time someone writes on a page of the pad, part of this asset is used up, and retained earnings decreases correspondingly. Theoretically, it would be possible to ascertain the number of partly used pads that are owned by the entity at the end of the accounting period and to show this amount as an asset. But the cost of such an effort would obviously be unwarranted, and no accountant would attempt to do this. Accountants take the simpler, even though less exact, course of action and treat the asset as being used up either at the time the pads were purchased or at the time they were issued from supplies inventory to the user.

Unfortunately, there is no agreement as to the exact line separating material events from immaterial events. The decision depends on judgment and common sense. It is natural for the beginning student, who does not have an appreciation of the cost of collecting accounting information, to expect an accountant to be more meticulous in recording events in the accounts than the practicing accountant actually would be.

The materiality concept is important in the process of determining the expenses and revenue for a given accounting period. Many of the expense items are necessarily estimates, and in some cases they are not very close estimates. Beyond a certain point it is not worthwhile to attempt to refine these estimates.

> **Example.** Telephone bills, although rendered monthly, often do not coincide with a calendar month. It would be possible to analyze each bill and classify all the toll calls according to the month in which they were made. This would be following the matching concept precisely. Few companies bother to do this, however. On the grounds that a procedure to determine the actual expense would not be justified by the accuracy gained, they simply consider the telephone bill as an expense of the month in which the bill is received. Since the amount of the bill is likely to be relatively stable from one month to another, no significant error is introduced.

Materiality is also used in another sense in accounting. The principle of **full disclosure** requires that all important information about the financial condition and activities of an entity must be disclosed in reports prepared for outside parties. In this sense, also, there is no definitive rule that separates material from immaterial information. (This topic is discussed further in Chapter 14.) In sum the **materiality concept** states that insignificant events may be disregarded, but there must be full disclosure of all important information.

THE INCOME STATEMENT

The accounting report that summarizes the revenues and the expenses of an accounting period is called the **income statement** (or the **profit and loss statement, statement of earnings,** or **statement of operations**). In a technical sense the income statement is subordinate to the balance sheet. This is because it shows in some detail the items that collectively account for most of the period's net change in *only one* balance sheet item, retained earnings. ("Most" excludes dividends as well as a few relatively unusual retained earnings changes that are described in later chapters.) Nevertheless, the information on the income statement is regarded by many to be more important than information on the balance sheet. This is because the income statement reports the results of operations and indicates reasons for the entity's profitability (or lack thereof). The importance of the income statement is illustrated by this fact: in situations where accountants in recording an event must choose between a procedure that distorts the balance sheet or one that distorts the income statement, they usually choose not to distort the income statement.

In practice, there is considerable variety in the formats and degree of detail used in income statements. Illustration 3–4 shows an income statement for Garsden Corporation (whose balance sheet was shown in Illustration 2–1). It is representative of the income statements published in corporations' annual reports to their shareholders (with the exception of a few complex items that are discussed in later chapters). Income statements

ILLUSTRATION 3–4

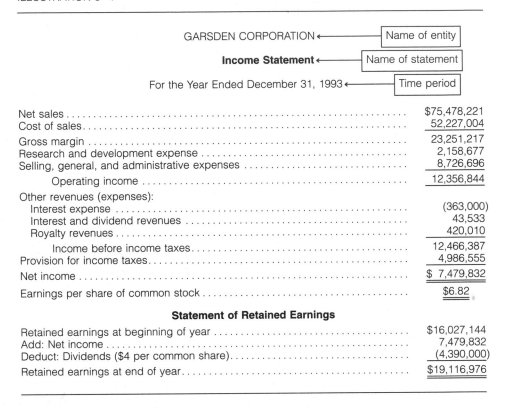

GARSDEN CORPORATION — Name of entity

Income Statement — Name of statement

For the Year Ended December 31, 1993 — Time period

Net sales	$75,478,221
Cost of sales	52,227,004
Gross margin	23,251,217
Research and development expense	2,158,677
Selling, general, and administrative expenses	8,726,696
Operating income	12,356,844
Other revenues (expenses):	
Interest expense	(363,000)
Interest and dividend revenues	43,533
Royalty revenues	420,010
Income before income taxes	12,466,387
Provision for income taxes	4,986,555
Net income	$ 7,479,832
Earnings per share of common stock	$6.82

Statement of Retained Earnings

Retained earnings at beginning of year	$16,027,144
Add: Net income	7,479,832
Deduct: Dividends ($4 per common share)	(4,390,000)
Retained earnings at end of year	$19,116,976

prepared for use by the managers of an entity usually contain more detailed information than that shown in Illustration 3–4.

The heading of the income statement must show (1) the entity to which it relates (Garsden Corporation), (2) the name of the statement (income statement), and (3) the time period covered (year ended December 31, 1993). The balance sheet in Illustration 2–1 and the income statement in Illustration 3–4 give information for only one year. To provide a basis for comparison, the SEC requires that corporate annual reports contain income statements for the most recent three years and balance sheets as of the end of the most recent two years.

Comments about the items listed on this income statement and variations often found in practice are given in the following paragraphs.

Revenues

An income statement sometimes reports several separate items in the sales revenue section, the net of which is the **net sales** (or **net sales revenue**) figure. For example, Garsden's income statement might have shown:

Gross sales		$77,157,525
Less: Returns and allowances	$ 528,348	
Sales discounts	1,150,956	
Net sales.		$75,478,221

Gross sales is the total invoice price of the goods shipped or services rendered during the period. It usually does not include sales taxes or excise taxes that may be charged the customer. Such taxes are not revenues but rather represent collections that the business makes on behalf of the government. They are a liability to the government until paid. Similarly, postage, freight, or other items billed to the customer at cost are not revenues. These items usually do not appear in the sales figure but instead are an offset to the costs the company incurs for them. However, exceptions are made to these rules when it is not feasible to disentangle the revenue and nonrevenue portions of the items in question.

Sales returns and allowances represent the sales value of goods that were returned by customers and allowances that were made to customers because the goods were defective or for some other reason. The amount can be subtracted from the sales figure directly, without showing it as a separate item on the income statement. However, it is often considered as being important enough information to warrant reporting it separately. **Sales discounts** are the amount of discounts taken by customers for prompt payment. (These are sometimes called **cash discounts.**)

> **Example.** Assume that a business offers a 2 percent discount to customers who pay within 10 days from the date of the invoice. The business sells $1,000 of merchandise to a customer who takes advantage of this discount. The business receives only $980 cash and records the other $20 as a sales discount.

Trade discounts, which are formulas used in figuring the actual selling price from published catalogs or price lists (e.g., "list less 40 percent"), do not appear in the accounting records at all.

Other revenues are revenues earned from activities not associated with the sale of the company's goods and services. Interest and dividends earned on marketable securities owned by the company are examples. Garsden also had revenues from royalties paid by other companies that Garsden has licensed to use its patented manufacturing process. Although it is preferable to show such peripheral revenues separately from sales revenues, as in Illustration 3–4, many companies add them to net sales and report a total revenue amount.

Cost of Sales

Because of the matching concept, at the same time that income is increased by the sales value of goods or services sold, it is also decreased by the cost of those goods or services. Indeed, it would be possible to record only the net increase in retained earnings that results from a sale. However, reporting the separate amounts for sales revenue and the cost of sales provides information useful to both management and outside users of income statements.

The cost of goods or services sold is called the **cost of sales.** In manufacturing firms and retailing businesses, it is often called the **cost of goods sold.** In most businesses, the cost of sales amount is associated with a decrease in the asset, inventory, which has been consumed in generating the sales revenues. (The principal exception is personal-services businesses such as barber or beauty shops, which have no significant inventories.) Procedures for measuring the cost of sales are described in Chapter 6.

Gross Margin

The difference between net sales revenue and cost of sales is the **gross margin** (or **gross profit**). On most income statements, as in Illustration 3–4, this amount appears as a separate item. It does not appear separately on some companies' income statements but can be calculated as the difference between net sales and cost of sales if the company has disclosed the cost of sales amount.

Some companies do not show cost of sales as one item on the income statement. Instead, they list individual expenses by *object,* such as salaries and wages, usage of goods and services, and interest. In such an income statement it is impossible to calculate the gross margin because the broad objects (e.g., salaries and wages) intermingle *product* costs (e.g., factory labor) with *period* costs (e.g., administrative salaries). Gross margin is the difference between the revenues generated from selling products (goods or services) and the related *product* costs.

Expenses

The classifications given in Illustration 3–4 are a minimum. In many income statements, especially those prepared for internal use, the "selling, general, and administrative expense" category is broken down so as to show separately the principal items of which it is composed.

The separate disclosure of **research and development expense** is a relatively recent requirement. Formerly, most companies included this expense as part of general and administrative expenses. Because the amount spent on research and development can provide an important clue as to how aggressive the company is in keeping its products and processes up to date, the FASB requires that this amount be reported separately if it is material.

The FASB also requires separate disclosure of the amount of **interest expense** in a period. In some instances, to be discussed in Chapter 7, the interest *expense* of a period is not the same as the interest *cost* incurred during the period.

Many companies' income statements show an amount for **operating income,** as in Illustration 3–4. To operating income are added other revenue items, and other expenses are subtracted (indicated by parentheses in Illustration 3–4); the result is **income before income taxes.** A company that shows an operating income amount wants to distinguish the income generated by its primary operating activities from its nonoperating revenues and expenses. Many companies reject this distinction. They say, for example, that interest expense reflects the cost of financing assets used in operations and therefore should not be presented in a way that suggests it is a "nonoperating" item. Nearly all companies report a pretax income amount before subtracting the **provision for income taxes** (also called **income tax expense**).

Net Income

Net income is colloquially referred to as "the bottom line" of the income statement (for obvious reasons). The bottom line must be labeled **net income** or **net earnings,** with no qualification or modification. (If negative, it is labeled **net loss.**) For corporations not only is total net income reported but also the **net income per share** of stock. The per-share amount is obtained by dividing the dollar amount of net income by the number of shares of stock that were outstanding during the year.

Statement of Retained Earnings

Strictly speaking, the income statement ends with the item "earnings per share." Illustration 3–4 goes beyond this to show other changes in retained earnings that have occurred during the period. This final section links the period's income statement to the beginning-of-the-period and end-of-the-period balance sheets by completing the explanation of the net change in retained earnings between those two balance sheet snapshots. For Garsden, this section shows that (1) at the start of 1993, retained earnings was $16,027,144; (2) during 1993, retained earnings was increased by the amount of 1993 net income, $7,479,832, and was decreased by the amount of 1993 dividends, $4,390,000; and thus (3) at the end of 1993, retained earnings was $19,116,976. This calculation, whether shown on a separate page or included at the bottom of the income statement, is called a **statement of retained earnings** (or sometimes a **reconciliation of retained earnings**).

Relation between Balance Sheet and Income Statement

The balance sheet and income statement are said to **articulate** because there is a definite relationship between them. More specifically, as shown in the statement of retained earnings, the amount of net income reported on the income statement, together with the amount of dividends, explains the change in retained earnings between the two balance sheets prepared as of the beginning and the end of the accounting period. This relationship was shown schematically in Illustration 3–2 and is shown more specifically in Illustration 3–5. The latter uses the Garsden Corporation December 31,

ILLUSTRATION 3–5
A "PACKAGE" OF ACCOUNTING REPORTS

GARSDEN CORPORATION

Balance Sheet
As of December 31, 1992

Assets

Current assets	$23,839,904
Plant and equipment	14,255,720
Other assets	180,535
Total assets	$38,276,159

Liabilities and Shareholders' Equity

Current liabilities	$12,891,570
Other liabilities	4,357,445
Common stock	5,000,000
Retained earnings	16,027,144
Total liabilities and equity	$38,276,159

Income Statement
For the Year 1993

Net sales	$75,478,221
Less: Cost of sales	52,227,004
Gross margin	23,251,217
Less: Expenses	10,784,830
Income before taxes	12,466,387
Provision for income taxes	4,986,555
Net income	7,479,832
Retained earnings, beginning	16,027,144
	23,506,976
Less: Dividends	(4,390,000)
Retained earnings, ending	$19,116,976

Balance Sheet
As of December 31, 1993

Assets

Current assets	$22,651,072
Plant and equipment	13,411,779
Other assets	173,214
Total assets	$36,236,065

Liabilities and Shareholders' Equity

Current liabilities	$ 9,119,089
Other liabilities	3,000,000
Common stock	5,000,000
Retained earnings	19,116,976
Total liabilities and equity	$36,236,065

1993, balance sheet that was shown in more detail in Illustration 2–1 and a condensed version of Garsden's income statement from Illustration 3–4, together with the beginning-of-1993 balance sheet. (Recall that the end of 1992 and the beginning of 1993 are the same moment in time.) Note how the income statement and related statement of retained earnings, a flow report, reconciles the retained earnings amounts from the beginning and ending balance sheets, which are status reports.

Income Statement Percentages

In analyzing an income statement, percentage relationships are often calculated. Usually, the net sales amount is taken as 100 percent. Each income statement item is then expressed as a percentage of net sales. The most important are the gross margin percentage and the profit margin.

The **gross margin percentage** is gross margin divided by net sales. In Illustration 3–5 this is $23,251,217 ÷ $75,478,221 = 30.8 percent. It indicates the average margin obtained on products (goods or services) sold. The percentage varies widely among industries, but healthy companies in the same industry tend to have similar gross margin percentages.

The **profit margin** is net income divided by net sales. For Garsden this is $7,479,832 ÷ $75,478,221 = 9.9 percent. Profit margins also vary widely among industries. A successful supermarket may have a profit margin of about 1.5 percent, whereas the typical profit margin in healthy manufacturing companies tends to be closer to 8 percent.[6]

OTHER CONCEPTS OF INCOME

We have described how income is measured and reported in accordance with generally accepted accounting principles (GAAP). Not all income statements are prepared in accordance with these principles, however. As noted in Chapter 1, some regulatory bodies require the use of different principles by companies within their jurisdiction. Three other variations of the income concept are described below: cash-basis accounting, income tax accounting, and the economic concept of income.

Accrual versus Cash-Basis Accounting

The measurement of income described in this chapter is based on what is called accrual accounting. Central to accrual accounting are the realization concept and the matching concept. **Accrual accounting** measures income for a period as the difference between the revenues recognized in that period and the expenses that are matched with those revenues. As noted previously, the period's revenues generally are not the same as the period's

---

[6]Surveys indicate that most Americans believe that corporate profit margins average 25 percent or more. The 1993 median profit margin for the Fortune 500 industrial firms was only 2.9 percent.

cash receipts from customers, and the period's expenses generally are not the same as the period's cash disbursements.

An alternative way of measuring income is called **cash-basis accounting.** With this method sales are not recorded until the period in which they are received in cash. Similarly, costs are subtracted from sales in the period in which they are paid for by cash disbursements. Thus, neither the realization nor matching concept applies in cash-basis accounting.

In practice "pure" cash-basis accounting is rare. This is because a pure cash-basis approach would require treating the acquisition of inventories as a reduction in profit when the acquisition costs are paid rather than when the inventories are sold. Similarly, costs of acquiring items of plant and equipment would be treated as profit reductions when paid in cash rather than in the later periods when these long-lived items are used. Clearly, such a pure cash-basis approach would result in balance sheets and income statements that would be of limited usefulness. Thus, what is commonly called cash-basis accounting essentially is actually a mixture of cash basis for some items (especially sales and period costs) and accrual basis for other items (especially product costs and long-lived assets). This mixture is also sometimes called **modified cash-basis accounting** to distinguish it from a pure cash-basis method.

Cash-basis accounting is seen most often in small firms that provide services and therefore do not have significant amounts of inventories. Examples include restaurants, beauty parlors and barber shops, and income-tax preparation firms. Since most of these establishments do not extend credit to their customers, cash-basis profit may not differ dramatically from accrual-basis income. Nevertheless, cash-basis accounting is *not* permitted by GAAP for any type of business entity.

Income Tax Accounting

Most business entities must calculate their taxable income and pay a federal tax (and in some cases, a state or local tax) based on this income. The amounts of revenues and expenses used to determine federal taxable income are usually similar to, but not identical with, amounts measured in accordance with GAAP. The differences are sufficiently significant so that it is unwise to rely on income tax regulations as a basis for solving business accounting problems, or vice versa. For example, tax regulations permit certain kinds of businesses to report income using the modified cash basis, which, as noted above, is not in accordance with GAAP.

Unless tax rates applicable to the business are expected to increase in the future, a business usually reports the *minimum* possible amount of taxable income in the current year, thus postponing tax payments as much as possible to future years. It does this generally by recognizing expenses as soon as legally possible, but postponing the recognition of revenue for as long as possible. Note that this is a process of shifting revenue and expense from one period to another. Over the long run in most businesses there is little difference between the total expenses and revenues computed for tax purposes and the total expenses and revenues computed for financial accounting. The objective of minimizing current taxes is, as the Supreme Court has pointed out, entirely legal and ethical, provided it is done in accordance with the tax regulations. It is also legal and proper under most circumstances to calculate income one way for tax purposes and another way for financial accounting purposes (a fact that comes as a surprise to many newcomers to accounting).

> **Example.** Income tax regulations permit the cost of most fixed assets to be charged as expenses (i.e., depreciated) over a shorter time period than the estimated useful life of these assets and at amounts in the early years that are greater than the cost of the asset benefits consumed in those years (so-called accelerated depreciation). These practices result in higher tax-deductible expenses and correspondingly lower taxable income in the early years of an asset's life, and therefore encourage businesses to invest in new fixed assets. Most businesses use these practices in calculating their taxable income, but they use different practices for financial accounting.

Although tax regulations are not described in detail in this book, references are made to accounting practices that are or are not consistent with them. The manager learns early the importance of becoming thoroughly familiar with the principal tax rules that affect the business and also the importance of consulting tax experts when unusual situations arise.

Economic Income

Economic theory is not constrained by the practical need of reporting an income amount annually to an entity's owners or other interested parties. Thus, in economic theory income is defined as the difference between the value of a business at the end of an accounting period and its value at the beginning of the period, after proper adjustments for transactions with owners (i.e., additional paid-in capital and dividends). Both economists and accountants recognize that this **economic income** cannot be feasibly measured for a given accounting period. Measuring economic income would involve estimating unrealized changes in value, including changes in the value of such intangibles as a company's patents and brand names, whereas accounting income focuses on actual *transactions* that have taken place. Also, economists regard interest on all equities—both interest-bearing liabilities and owners' equity—as an element of cost. Accountants treat only the interest on borrowings as a cost on the grounds that interest on the use of owners' capital cannot be objectively measured. Consequently, accounting net income to an economist is a mixture of "true" income and the cost of using shareholders' capital. To an economist accounting net income is an attempt to measure the income accruing to the entity's *owners;* but it is an overstatement of the income earned by the *entity itself* because the cost of using owners' funds has not been subtracted.

SUMMARY

This chapter described the remaining basic accounting concepts:

6. *Accounting period.* Accounting measures activities for a specified interval of time, which is usually one year.

7. *Conservatism.* Revenues are recognized only when they are reasonably certain, whereas expenses are recognized as soon as they are reasonably possible.

8. *Realization.* The amount recognized as revenue is the amount that customers are reasonably certain to pay.

9. *Matching.* When a given event affects both revenues and expenses, the effect on each should be recognized in the same accounting period. Related to the matching concept are two expense recognition criteria: (1) costs associated with activities of the period are expenses of the period; and (2) costs that cannot be associated with revenues of future periods are expenses of the current period.

10. *Consistency.* Once an entity has decided on a certain accounting method, it will use the same method for all subsequent events of the same character unless it has a sound reason to change methods.

11. *Materiality.* Insignificant events may be disregarded, but there must be full disclosure of all important information.

The income statement summarizes the revenues and expenses of an entity for an accounting period. The usual accounting period is one year, but many companies prepare interim income statements on a monthly or quarterly basis. The income statement and balance sheet articulate in that a period's income statement (and related statement of retained earnings) explains the change in retained earnings between the balance sheets prepared as of the beginning and the end of the period.

Only accrual-basis accounting, which employs the realization and matching concepts, is permitted under GAAP. Income tax accounting regulations differ in some important respects from GAAP, including permitting certain types of businesses to calculate income using modified cash-basis accounting. Economic income is a theoretical concept rather than a practical approach to measuring income.

Cases

CASE 3–1 Maynard Company (B)

Diane Maynard was grateful for the balance sheets that her friend prepared (see Maynard Company (A)). In going over the numbers, she remarked, "It's sort of surprising that cash increased by $31,677, but net income was only $19,635. Why was that?"

Her friend replied, "A partial answer to that question is to look at an income statement for June. I think I can find the data I need to prepare one for you."

In addition to the data given in the (A) case, her friend found a record of cash receipts and disbursements, which is summarized in Exhibit 1. She also learned that all accounts payable were to vendors for purchase of merchandise inventory and that cost of sales was $39,345 in June.

Questions

1. Prepare an income statement for June in proper format. Explain the derivation of each item on this statement, including cost of sales.

2. Explain why the change in the cash balance was greater than the net income.

3. Explain why the following amounts are *incorrect* cost of sales amounts for June: (a) $14,715 and (b) $36,030. Under what circumstances would these amounts be correct cost of sales amounts?

EXHIBIT 1

Cash Receipts and Disbursements
Month of June

Cash Receipts		Cash Disbursements	
Cash sales	$ 44,420	Equipment purchased	$23,400
Credit customers	21,798	Other assets purchased	408
Diane Maynard	11,700	Payments on accounts payable	8,517
Bank loan	20,865	Cash purchases of merchandise	14,715
Total receipts	$ 98,783	Cash purchase of supplies	1,671
		Dividends	11,700
		Wages paid	5,660
		Utilities paid	900
		Miscellaneous payments	135
		Total disbursements	$67,106

Reconciliation:

Cash balance, June 1	$ 34,983
Receipts	98,783
Subtotal	133,766
Disbursements	67,106
Cash balance, June 30	$ 66,660

CASE 3–2   Santa Fe Art Gallery

Pat Green opened the Santa Fe Art Gallery, choosing an approach to this business that differed from many other art galleries in the area. Whereas many of the other galleries took works of art on commission, Pat chose to purchase selected works from the artists and then to resell them to the public. This approach, plus Pat's expertise at identifying promising but unknown artists, enabled Pat to earn a higher margin than other galleries. However, a substantial financial investment was required to purchase the inventory of works of art that were offered for sale; fortunately, Pat had a sizable inheritance to invest in this business.

Artists in the Santa Fe area liked to do business with the Santa Fe Art Gallery, not only because they felt it was a prestigious place to have their work offered for sale, but also because they could receive cash immediately for their work (which could be very important to struggling young artists) rather than wait a longer, unpredictable time until the piece was purchased by the public.

A partial inventory of works held for sale at the Santa Fe Art Gallery at the beginning of September is shown in Exhibit 1.

During the months of September and October, the events listed in Exhibit 2 occurred.

Questions

1. Determine the effect of each of these events on cash. For example, the event on September 2 decreases cash by $3,000.

2. Identify which events affect the income statement and which do not. For those events that you determine do not affect the income statement, explain why they do not.

3. Prepare income statements for September and for October.

4. Compare the performance of the Santa Fe Art Gallery in September with that in October. In which month do you think the gallery did better?

EXHIBIT 1
PARTIAL INVENTORY OF WORKS HELD FOR SALE

Category	Item No.	Cost
Painting	1307	$ 400
Painting	1308	400
Painting	1309	400
Painting	1325	2,000
Painting	1327	3,500
Painting	1351	750
Painting	1363	4,200
Pottery	1327	300
Pottery	1333	100
Pottery	1358	500
Pottery	1372	750
Pottery	1423	600
Sculpture	1299	3,000
Sculpture	1302	8,000
Sculpture	1321	2,000
Sculpture	1328	2,500
Sculpture	1369	3,800
Sculpture	1417	6,700
Sculpture	1420	7,800

EXHIBIT 2

	Date	Event
September	2	Pat purchased 3 pieces, Paintings 1478, 1479, and 1480, from a promising new artist for a total of $3,000.
	5	Pat sold Painting 1479 for $2,500 to a couple from Boston who were planning a wedding in Santa Fe.
	9	Randy, a part-time employee of the Santa Fe Art Gallery, sold Pottery 1423 for $1,200. Randy received a 5 percent commission on sales in addition to a small salary.
	16	Pat sold Sculpture 1302 to a customer from New York City for $15,750.
	22	Pat purchased additional display cabinets for sculptures for $3,250 cash.
	27	Randy sold Painting 1325 to a customer from Chicago for $5,500.
	28	Randy received a $200 deposit from a Florida customer who wanted to purchase Sculpture 1299. The price of Sculpture 1299 was $6,700. The customer wanted to reflect on this purchase before completing it. Sometimes customers would return and negotiate for a lower price. In such cases the Santa Fe Art Gallery might or might not agree to lower the price. All but $50 of the deposit would be refundable if the customer decided within a week not to complete the purchase. If the customer failed to complete the purchase or request a refund within one week, the entire $200 was forfeited.
	29	Pat paid general expenses of $810, which included Randy's salary, rent, utilities, and other miscellaneous expenses that were paid in cash. Depreciation of showcases and furniture in the gallery was the gallery's only noncash expense; with the new sculpture cases this amounted to $200 per month.
	30	Pat wrote Randy a check for September's commissions.
October	2	The Florida customer returned to purchase Sculpture 1299. Randy agreed to sell it for $6,500, which was well within the range Pat had approved. The full $200 deposit was applied to the purchase price.
	5	Pat purchased two pieces of sculpture from one of the gallery's best-selling artists. Sculptures 1481 and 1482 cost $5,500 and $6,200, respectively.
	8	Pat sold Pottery 1327 for $750 and Painting 1308 for $870.
	12	Randy sold Pottery 1358 for $1,200 to a couple vacationing from New Jersey. Randy remembered the couple, who had purchased a piece of art from the Santa Fe Gallery the previous year.
	16	Pat purchased Pottery 1483 and 1484 for $250 and $450, respectively, from Jean, an artist whose works had recently been sold by Santa Fe Art Gallery. In addition, Jean introduced Pat to a new potter who had just begun working in Santa Fe, from whom Pat purchased two more items, Pottery 1485 and 1486 for $100 and $150, respectively.
	18	Pat sold Sculpture 1328 for $6,200.
	22	Pat sold Pottery 1486 for $375.
	23	Pat sold Pottery 1485 for $500.
	26	Pat received a $500 deposit from a man from San Francisco who wished to purchase Sculpture 1420, which was priced at $17,000. All but $125 would be refundable if the customer decided within one week not to purchase the sculpture.
	27	Randy received a deposit of $400, of which $100 was not refundable, on Sculpture 1482, which was priced at $14,000.
	29	Pat paid general expenses of $825 in cash. Depreciation expense was still $200.
	30	Pat sold Sculpture 1321 for $4,200.
	31	Pat wrote Randy a check for October's commissions.

CASE 3–3 Redwood Cafe (B)

In addition to preparing the balance sheet described in Redwood Cafe (A), Mr. Simpson, the accountant, agreed to prepare an income statement. He said that such a financial statement would show Mrs. Antoine how profitable operations had been, and thus help her to judge whether it was worthwhile to continue operating the restaurant.

In addition to the information given in the (A) case, Mr. Simpson learned that cash received from customers through March 30 amounted to $43,480 and that cash payments were as follows:

Monthly payments to partners	$23,150
Wages to part-time employees	5,480
Interest	540
Food and beverage suppliers	10,016
Telephone and electricity	3,270
Miscellaneous	255
Rent payments	7,500

Questions

1. Prepare an income statement for the period of the cafe's operations through March 30, 1991.

2. What does this income statement tell Mrs. Antoine?

CASE 3–4 John Bartlett*

John Bartlett invented an inexpensive surge protector that protected personal computers against voltage surges caused by lightning or by power plants activating a new generator during a peak demand period. He expected a patent, with a legal life of 17 years, for the protector soon. With confidence in the protector's commercial value but no excess funds of his own, he sought the necessary capital to put the protector on the market from his friends and acquaintances. The proposition that he placed before possible associates was that a corporation, Bartlett Products Company, should be formed with capital stock of $100,000 par value.

The project looked attractive to a number of the individuals to whom the inventor presented it, but the most promising among them—a retired businessman—said he would be unwilling to invest his capital without knowing what uses were intended for the cash to be received from the proposed sale of stock. He suggested that the inventor determine the probable costs of experimentation and special machinery and prepare a statement of the estimated assets and liabilities of the proposed company when ready to begin actual operation. He also asked for a statement of the estimated transactions for the first year of operations, to be based on studies the inventor had made of probable markets and costs of labor and materials. Mr. Bartlett consented to supply this information to the best of his ability.

After consulting the engineer who had helped him construct his patent models, Mr. Bartlett drew up the following list of data relating to the transactions of the proposed corporation during its period of organization and development:

1. The retired businessman would pay the corporation $40,000 cash for which he would receive stock with a par value of $40,000. The remaining stock (par value,

*Copyright © by the President and Fellows of Harvard College. Harvard Business School case 146–004.

EXHIBIT 1

BARTLETT PRODUCTS COMPANY
Estimated Balance Sheet
As of Date Company Begins Operations

Assets		*Liabilities and Owners' Equity*	
Cash	$ 11,400	Liabilities.............................	$ 0
Inventory...........................	800	Capital stock	100,000
Machinery..........................	20,000	Retained earnings.....................	0
Organization costs	6,600		
Experimental costs....................	1,200		
Patent	60,000		
Total assets	$100,000	Total liabilities and owners' equity.........	$100,000

$60,000) would be given to Mr. Bartlett in exchange for the patent on the protector.

2. Probable cost of incorporation and organization, including estimated officers' salaries during developmental period, $6,600.

3. Probable cost of developing special machinery, $20,000. This sum includes the cost of expert services, materials, rent of a small shop, and the cost of power, light, and miscellaneous expenditures.

4. Probable cost of raw materials, $2,000, of which $1,200 is to be used in experimental production.

On the basis of the above information, Mr. Bartlett prepared the estimated balance sheet shown in Exhibit 1. Mr. Bartlett then set down the following estimates as a beginning step in furnishing the rest of the information desired:

1. Expected sales, all to be received in cash by the end of the first year of operation, $336,000.

2. Expected additional purchases of raw materials and supplies during the course of this operating year, all paid for in cash by end of year, $106,000.

3. Expected borrowing from the bank during year (loans to be repaid before close of year), $8,000. Interest on these loans, $650.

4. Expected payroll and other cash expenses and manufacturing costs for the operating year, $127,000 of manufacturing costs (excluding raw materials and supplies) plus $21,000 for selling and administrative expenses for a total of $148,000.

5. Expected inventory of raw materials and supplies at close of period, at cost, $18,000.

6. No inventory of unsold protectors expected as of the end of the period. All products to be manufactured on the basis of firm orders received; none to be produced for inventory.

7. New equipment to be purchased for cash, $4,000.

8. All experimental and organization costs, previously capitalized, to be charged against income of the operating year.

9. Estimated depreciation of machinery, $2,400.

10. Dividends paid in cash, $11,000.

11. Estimated income tax expense for the year, $16,960. Ten percent of this amount would not be due until early in the following year.

It should be noted that the transactions summarized above would not necessarily take place in the sequence indicated. In practice, a considerable number of separate events, or transactions, would occur throughout the year, and many of them would be dependent on one another. For example, operations were begun with an initial cash balance and inventory of raw materials, products were manufactured, and sales of these products provided funds for financing subsequent operations. Then, in turn, sales of the product subsequently manufactured yielded more funds.

Questions

1. Trace the effect on the balance sheet of each of the projected events appearing in Mr. Bartlett's list. Thus, item 1, taken alone, would mean that cash would be increased by $336,000 and that (subject to reductions for various costs covered in later items) retained earnings would be increased by $336,000. Notice that in this question you are asked to consider all items in terms of their effect on the balance sheet.

2. Prepare an income statement covering the first year of planned operations and a balance sheet as of the end of that year.

3. *Assume* that the retired manufacturer received capital stock with a par value of $30,000 for the $140,000 cash he paid to the corporation, John Bartlett still receiving stock with a par value of $60,000 in exchange for his patent. Under these circumstances, how would the balance sheet in Exhibit 1 appear?

4. *Assume* that the management is interested in what the results would be if no products were sold during the first year, even though production continued at the level indicated in the original plans. The following changes would be made in the 11 items listed above: items 1, 5, 6, 10, and 11 are to be disregarded. Instead of item 3, assume that a loan of $310,000 is obtained, and that the loan is not repaid, but that interest thereon of $38,000 is paid during the year. Prepare an income statement for the year and a balance sheet as of the end of the year. Contrast these financial statements with those prepared in Question 2.

CASE 3–5   Pinetree Motel

Mr. and Mrs. Ilyong Kim had purchased the Pinetree Motel in 1988 with their life savings, supplemented by a loan from a close personal friend. The motel consisted of 20 units (i.e., rentable rooms) and was located near a vacation area that was popular during both the summer and winter seasons. The Kims had entered the motel business because Mrs. Kim had long wanted to run a business of her own.

Both Mr. and Mrs. Kim felt that they had been successful. Each year saw a growth in revenue from room rentals. Furthermore, their bank balance had increased. They noted that many of their customers returned year after year. This was attributed to their location and their efforts to provide consistently clean rooms and up-to-date furnishings.

The Kims had no formal business training but felt their experience since acquiring the motel had alerted them to the management problems involved. Both Mr. and Mrs. Kim devoted their full time to operating the motel. In addition, they hired part-time help for daily room-cleaning work. They had no dining facilities but had installed vending machines to supplement room rentals. The vending machines posed no inventory or maintenance problems as the vending machine company provided servicing and maintenance.

EXHIBIT 1

Cash Register and Checkbook Summary during 1992

Receipts	
From rooms	$236,758
From vending machines	7,703
Total	$244,461
Checks Drawn	
Owners' drawings	$ 86,100
Wages and salaries	26,305
Paid to laundry	8,800
Replacement of glasses, bed linens, and towels	1,660
Advertising	2,335
Payroll taxes	2,894
Fuel for heating	12,205
Repairs and maintenance	8,980
Cleaning and other supplies	6,820
Telephone	2,789
Electricity	5,611
Property taxes	9,870
Insurance	11,584
Interest	10,605
Total	$196,558

A frequent guest at Pinetree Motel was Marcus Carter, controller of a large company. Mr. Carter visited a company branch plant near the motel several times a year. As he stayed at the motel during these trips, he became acquainted with the Kims.

In May 1993 Mrs. Kim showed Mr. Carter the current issue of a motel trade journal that contained operating data for motels with 40 or fewer units for the calendar year 1992. Mrs. Kim commented: "These figures show a profit of 21 percent. Our profit last year was $134,003 on sales of $244,461, or 55 percent. We think 1992 was our best year to date, but we can't make our figures jibe with those in the magazine, and we wonder if we really are 34 percent ahead of the industry average. Can you help us?"

Mr. Carter was interested and willing to help. He told Mrs. Kim to get the available figures for 1992 so that he could look them over that evening. The principal records the Kims kept to reflect the motel's financial transactions were a record of receipts taken from the cash register and a checkbook describing cash paid out. In addition, certain rough notations of other expenses incurred were available.

That evening Mrs. Kim showed Mr. Carter the cash summary for the year 1992, as given in Exhibit 1. Mr. Carter immediately noted that the difference between receipts and expenditures was $47,903 and asked Mrs. Kim to explain why she had stated the profit was $134,003. Mrs. Kim replied, "Oh, that's easy. Our drawings aren't expenses; after all, we are the owners. My husband and I have consistently taken only about $85,000 a year out because we want the rest of the profits to accumulate in the business. As I said, our bank balance has steadily risen. Furthermore, I have a local accountant make out the annual income tax statements so I don't have to

EXHIBIT 2

**1992 Operating Data for Motels
with 40 or Fewer Units**
(expressed as percentages of total revenues)

Revenues:	
Room rentals	98.7
Other revenue	1.3
Total revenues	100.0
Operating expenses:	
Payroll costs	22.5
Administrative and general	4.2
Direct operating expenses	5.9
Fees and commissions	3.3
Advertising and promotion	1.2
Repairs and maintenance	4.8
Utilities	7.5
Total	49.4
Fixed expenses:	
Property taxes, fees	4.4
Insurance	2.5
Depreciation	12.5
Interest	7.7
Rent	2.8
Total	29.9
Profit (pretax)	20.7

worry about them. That income tax stuff is so complicated that I avoid it."

Mr. Carter worked with the trade journal's figures (Exhibit 2) and the cash summary (Exhibit 1) that evening and quickly found he needed more information. He told Mrs. Kim that he was returning to the home office the next morning but would be back in two weeks for another visit to the branch plant. Meanwhile, he wanted Mrs. Kim to get together some additional information. Mr. Carter suggested to Mrs. Kim that an important noncash expense was depreciation. Mr. Carter also wanted to know about expenses that had been incurred in 1991 but not paid until 1992. He told Mrs. Kim to check up on wages and salaries, insurance, advertising, taxes, utilities, and any other items paid in 1992 but applicable to 1991.

In addition, Mr. Carter instructed Mrs. Kim to try to find items of expense properly chargeable to 1992 but not paid by December

31, 1992. Mrs. Kim told Mr. Carter the same types of expenses were involved, that is, wages and salaries, insurance, advertising, taxes, and so forth. Also Mr. Carter inquired about income from room rentals. He asked if any of the cash receipts during 1992 related to rentals during 1991 and if there were any rentals during 1992 that had not been collected.

During the two weeks Mr. Carter was back at the home office, Mrs. Kim checked the records and compiled the additional information requested by Mr. Carter. The evening Mr. Carter returned to the Pinetree Motel, Mrs. Kim gave him a summary of the information she had gathered (Exhibit 3). With all the additional information, Mr. Carter constructed an operating statement that matched in form the one appearing in the trade journal. He calculated both the dollar amounts and percentage composition of each expense for more useful comparison with the journal's figures.

EXHIBIT 3

Additional Information about the Business

Chargeable in 1991 but paid in January 1992:

Wages and salaries	$ 795
Advertising	600
Payroll taxes	84
Fuel for heating	933
Telephone	105
Electricity	360
Property taxes	1,005
Insurance	2,025
Interest	687

Chargeable in 1992 but not paid by December 31, 1992:

Wages and salaries	1,128
Advertising	996
Payroll taxes	126
Fuel for heating	840
Cleaning and other supplies	75
Telephone	153
Electricity	492
Property taxes	1,119
Interest	579

Also, 1992 depreciation charges of $30,280.

Also, 1992 cash receipts included a $1,660 payment from a company that had rented several units during December 1991 for a convention in the nearby city. There were no such uncollected rentals as of December 31, 1992.

Questions

1. Prepare an operating statement such as Mr. Carter prepared.

2. As Mr. Carter, what comments would you make to the Kims regarding the motel's progress to date?

CASE 3-6 National Helontogical Association

Each December the incoming members of the board of directors of the National Helontogical Association (NHA) met in joint session with the outgoing board as a means of smoothing the transition from one administration to another. At the meeting in December 1993, questions were raised about whether the 1993 board had adhered to the general policy of the association. The ensuing discussion became quite heated.

NHA was a nonprofit professional association whose 3,000 members were experts in helontology,[1] a specialized branch of engineering. The association represented the interest of its members before congressional committees and various scientific bodies, published two professional journals, arranged an annual meeting and several regional meetings, and appointed committees

---

[1]Disguised name.

EXHIBIT 1

Estimated Income Statement
Year Ending December 31, 1993

Revenues:	
Membership dues.....................................	$287,550
Journal subscriptions.................................	31,005
Publication sales.....................................	11,880
Foundation grant.....................................	54,000
Annual meeting, 1992 profit...........................	3,405
Total revenues..................................	387,840
Expenses:	
Printing and mailing publications	92,400
Committee meeting expense	49,200
Annual meeting advance	10,800
Desktop publishing system............................	27,000
Administrative salaries and expenses	171,465
Miscellaneous	25,050
Total expenses	375,915
Excess of revenues over expenses	$ 11,925

that developed positions on various topics of interest to the membership.

The operating activities of the association were managed by George Tremble, its executive secretary. Mr. Tremble reported to the board of directors. The board consisted of four officers and seven other members. Six members of the 1994 board (i.e., the board that assumed responsibility on January 1, 1994) were also on the 1993 board; the other five members were newly elected. The president served a one-year term.

The financial policy of the association was that each year should "stand on its own feet"; that is, expenses of the year should approximately equal the revenues of the year. At the meeting in December 1993, Mr. Tremble presented an estimated income statement for 1993 (Exhibit 1). Although some of the December transactions were necessarily estimated, Mr. Tremble assured the board that the actual totals for the year would closely approximate the numbers shown.

Wilma Fosdick, one of the newly elected board members, raised a question about the foundation grant of $54,000. She questioned whether this item should be counted as revenue. If it were excluded, there was a deficit; and this showed that the 1993 board had, in effect, eaten into reserves and thus made it more difficult to provide the level of service that the members had a right to expect in 1994. This led to detailed questions about items on the income statement, which brought forth the following information from Mr. Tremble:

1. In 1993 NHA received a $54,000 cash grant from the Workwood Foundation for the purpose of financing a symposium to be held in June 1994. During 1993 approximately $2,700 was spent in preliminary planning for this symposium and was included in Committee Meeting Expenses. When asked why the $54,000 had been recorded as revenue in 1993 rather than in 1994, Mr. Tremble said that the grant was obtained entirely by the initiative and persuasiveness of the 1993 president, so 1993 should be given credit for it. Further, although the grant was intended to finance the symposium, there was no legal

requirement that the symposium be held; if for any reason it was not held, the money would be used for the general operations of the association.

2. In early December 1993 the association took delivery of, and paid for, a new desktop publishing system costing $27,000. This system would greatly simplify the work of preparing membership lists, correspondence, and manuscripts submitted for publication. Except for this new system, the typewriters, desks, and other equipment in the association office were quite old.

3. Ordinarily, members paid their dues during the first few months of the year. Because of the need to raise cash to finance the purchase of the desktop publishing system, in September 1993 the association announced that members who paid their 1994 dues before December 15, 1993, would receive a free copy of the book of papers presented at the special symposium to be held in June 1994. The approximate per copy cost of publishing this book was expected to be $16, and it was expected to be sold for $18. Consequently, $32,400 of 1994 dues were received by December 15, 1993.

4. In July 1993 the association sent a membership directory to members. Its long-standing practice was to publish such a directory every two years. The cost of preparing and printing this directory was $23,250. Of the 4,000 copies printed, 3,000 were mailed to members in 1993. The remaining 1,000 were held to meet the needs of new members who would join before the next directory came out; they would receive a free copy of the directory when they joined.

5. Members received the association's journals at no extra cost, as a part of the membership privileges. Some libraries and other nonmembers also subscribed to the journals. The $31,005 reported as subscription revenue was the cash received in 1993. Of this amount, about $8,100 was for journals that would be delivered in 1994. Offsetting this was $5,400 of subscription revenue received in 1992 for journals delivered in 1993; this $5,400 had been reported as 1992 revenue.

6. The association had advanced $10,800 to the committee responsible for planning the 1993 annual meeting held in late November. This amount was used for preliminary expenses. Registration fees at the annual meeting were set so as to cover all conventional costs, so that it was expected that the $10,800, plus any profit, would be returned to the association after the committee had finished paying the convention bills. The 1992 convention had resulted in a $3,405 profit, but the results of the 1993 convention were not known, although the attendance was about as anticipated.

Question

Did the association have an excess or a deficit in 1993?

4

Accounting Records and Systems

As we emphasized in Chapter 2, each individual accounting transaction can be recorded in terms of its effect on the balance sheet. For example, the Music Mart illustration in Chapter 2 starts with the item "Cash, $25,000" on the January 1 balance sheet and then records the transaction on January 2 involving an increase of $12,500 in cash in effect by erasing the $25,000 and entering the new number, $37,500. Although this procedure was appropriate as an explanatory device, it is not a practical way of handling the many transactions that occur in the actual operations of an organization.

This chapter describes some of the accounting procedures that are used in practice. *No new accounting concepts are introduced.* The procedures described here provide the mechanical means for making it easier to record and summarize transactions. Although many organizations use computer-based accounting systems, we describe the procedures used in a manual system because the basic steps in either type of system are the same and it is easier to visualize these steps in a manual system.

RECORDKEEPING FUNDAMENTALS

We are not concerned here with recordkeeping procedures for the purpose of training bookkeepers. Nevertheless, some knowledge of these procedures is useful for at least two reasons. First, as is the case with many

ILLUSTRATION 4–1
EXAMPLE OF A T ACCOUNT

Cash

(*Increases*)	(*Decreases*)
Beginning balance -0-	
5,000	750
4,000	7,200
200	4,800
12,000	3,000
21,200	15,750
New balance 5,450	

subjects, accounting is something that is best learned by doing—by solving problems. Although any accounting problem can be solved without the aid of the tools discussed in this chapter, using these tools will often speed up the problem-solving process considerably. Second, the debit-and-credit mechanism, which is the principal technique discussed here, provides an analytical framework that is similar in function to and offers the same advantages as the symbols and equations used in algebra.

The Account

Assume that the item "Cash, $10,000" appears on a balance sheet. Subsequent cash transactions can affect this amount in only one of two ways: they can increase it or they can decrease it. Instead of increasing or decreasing the item by erasing the old amount and entering the new amount for each transaction, considerable effort can be saved by collecting all the increases together and all the decreases together and then periodically calculating the *net* change resulting from all of them. This can be done by adding the sum of the increases to the beginning amount and then subtracting the sum of the decreases. The difference is the new cash balance.

In accounting the device called an **account** is used for calculating the net change. The simplest form of account, called a **T account,** looks like the account shown in Illustration 4–1. Because this account is for a brand-new entity (to be described later in this chapter) its beginning balance is zero. All increases are listed on one side, and all decreases are listed on the other. Fundamentally this account is no different from the register in the reader's checkbook, where increases in cash (deposits) are recorded in one column and decreases (checks written) are recorded in another column. However, whereas a checkbook register contains a third column to show a running balance in the account, a T account is balanced only periodically. (Note that the dollar sign is omitted in the T account; this is the usual bookkeeping procedure.)

The saving in effort made possible by T accounts can be seen even from this brief illustration. If the balance were changed for each of the eight items listed, four additions and four subtractions would be required. By using the account device, the new balance is obtained by only two additions (to find the 21,200 and 15,750) and one subtraction (21,200 − 15,750).

In actual accounting systems the account form is set up so that other useful information in addition to the amount of each increase or decrease can be recorded. A common arrangement of the columns is the following:

Cash

August 1993

Date	Explanation	(R)	Amount	Date	Explanation	(R)	Amount
1	Balance		–0–	1	Prepaid Rent	6	750
1	Paid-In Cap.	1	5,000	2	Equipment	3	7,200
1	Note Payable	2	4,000	26	Accts. Pay.	6	4,800
29	Accts. Rec.	5	200	31	Wages	4	3,000
31	Cash Sales	5	12,000				

The essence of this form of the account is the same as that of the T account; in fact, the T can be observed in the double-ruled lines. Its headings are self-explanatory except that of "R" (standing for "reference"), under which is entered a simple code showing the source of the information recorded. This is useful if one needs to check back to the source of the entry at some future time.

Permanent Accounts and Temporary Accounts

The accounts maintained for the various items on the balance sheet are called **permanent** (or **real**) accounts. At the end of each accounting period the balance of each permanent account is determined—each account is "balanced." These balances are the numbers reported in the balance sheet as of the end of the period. The period-ending balance in a permanent account is carried forward into the next accounting period as that period's beginning balance.

Recall that revenues and expenses are respectively increases and decreases in retained earnings arising from the entity's earnings activities. Although revenue and expense transactions could be entered directly in the Retained Earnings account, this is not done in practice. Entering revenue and expense items directly to Retained Earnings would result in an intermingling of the many specific items that are required to prepare the income statement. All of these items would have to be "sorted out"—classified by income statement categories—if they were intermingled. Also, because so many of an entity's transactions are earnings transactions, the Retained Earnings account could have several pages of entries every period.

To avoid cluttering the Retained Earnings account a **temporary account** is established for each revenue and expense item that will appear on the income statement. Thus, there are temporary accounts for sales revenues, cost of sales, selling expenses, and so on. Revenue and expense transactions are recorded in their respective temporary accounts as the period progresses. This procedure creates a "sort as you go" routine for these transactions instead of leaving them to be sorted at the end of the period. For example, all of the entries to the Sales Revenue account can be added at the end of the period to arrive at the amount of net sales for the income statement. All of the income statement temporary account sums are combined into one *net income* amount, which is then entered in the Retained Earnings account. Thus, in practice Retained Earnings has *fewer* entries made to it than almost any other permanent account. (The process of combining the temporary account sums into one amount for the net change in retained earnings will be illustrated later in the chapter.)

The Ledger

A **ledger** is a group of accounts. In a manual system it may be a bound book with the title "general ledger" printed on the cover. Inside are pages, one (or more) for each account; the Cash account shown above is an example of the top of a ledger page. All the accounts of a small business could be maintained in such a book. The ledger is not necessarily a bound book, however. It may consist of a set of loose-leaf pages, or, with computers, a set of impulses on a magnetic disk or tape.

The Chart of Accounts

Prior to setting up an accounting system, a list is prepared showing each item for which a ledger account is to be maintained. This list is called the **chart of accounts.** The accounts on the list are numbered in a way that facilitates summarization of detailed accounts into account categories for the financial statements. For example, the beginning of a chart of accounts might appear as follows:

> 1 – –   Current assets
> 1 1 –   Cash
> 1 1 1   Cash, First National Bank
> 1 1 2   Cash, Second National Bank

The actual accounting entries are made in the lowest-level accounts, which are 111 and 112 in the example.

There are at least as many separate accounts as there are items on the balance sheet and income statement. Usually there are many more accounts than this minimum number so that detailed information useful to management can be collected. For example, although only the single item "accounts receivable" appears on the balance sheet, a separate account for each customer is maintained in a ledger. Management's desire to have small account "building blocks" so that information can be built up and summarized in any of several ways can lead to a proliferation of accounts. With a manual system, the sheer bulk of the number of ledger pages limits the proliferation. In a computer-based system the constraints are much less severe.

Debit and Credit

The left-hand side of any account is arbitrarily called the **debit side,** and the right-hand side is called the **credit side.** Amounts entered on the left-hand side are called **debits,** and amounts entered on the right-hand side are called **credits.** The verb *to debit* means to make an entry in the left-hand side of an account, and the verb *to credit* means to make an entry in the right-hand side of an account. *The words* debit *and* credit *have no other meaning in accounting.*

In ordinary usage these words do have other meanings. *Credit* has a favorable connotation (such as, "she is a credit to her family") and *debit* has an unfavorable connotation (such as, "chalk up a debit against him"). In accounting these words do not imply any sort of value judgment; they mean simply "left" and "right." Debit and credit are usually abbreviated as **dr.** and **cr.**[1]

If each account were considered by itself without regard to its relationship to other accounts, it would make no difference whether increases were recorded on the debit side or on the credit side. In the 15th century a Franciscan monk, Lucas Pacioli, described a method of arranging accounts so that the *dual aspect* present in every accounting transaction would be expressed by a debit amount and an equal and offsetting credit amount.

This method made possible the following rule, to which there is absolutely no exception: *for each transaction the debit amount* (or the sum of all the debit amounts, if there are more than one) *must equal the credit amount* (or the sum of all the credit amounts). This is why bookkeeping is called *double-entry* bookkeeping. It follows that the recording of a transaction in which debits do not equal credits is incorrect. For all the accounts combined the sum of the debit balances must equal the sum of the credit balances; otherwise something has been done incorrectly. Thus, the debit and credit arrangement used in accounting provides a useful means of checking the accuracy with which the transactions have been recorded.

Pacioli based his procedures on the fundamental equation, Assets = Liabilities + Owners' Equity. He arbitrarily decided that *asset* accounts

---

[1]The noun *debit* is derived from the Latin *debitur,* which means debtor. Credit is derived from the Latin *creditor,* which means lender. Apparently the dr. and cr. abbreviations came from the first and last letters of these Latin words. In accounting, debit and credit do *not* mean debtor and creditor.

should *increase* on the left-hand, or *debit,* side. That decision immediately led to the rule that *asset* accounts must *decrease* on the right-hand, or *credit,* side. Given those rules for asset accounts, it followed that (1) in order for debits to equal credits and (2) in order to maintain the fundamental accounting equation, then the rules for liability and owners' equity accounts had to be the opposite from those for assets. *Liability and owners' equity* accounts *increase* on the right-hand—*credit*—side, and they *decrease* on the left-hand—*debit*—side. Schematically, these rules are:

Assets		=	Liabilities		+	Owners' Equity	
Debit	Credit		Debit	Credit		Debit	Credit
+	−		−	+		−	+

The rules for recording revenues and expenses are derived from the rules for owners' equity. By definition a revenue increases owners' equity (more specifically, retained earnings in a corporation), and owners' equity increases on the credit side. It necessarily follows that *revenues are credits.* If revenues decrease, such as for a sales return, the *decrease in revenues* must therefore be a *debit.*

Expenses are the opposite of revenues in that expenses decrease owners' equity. Therefore, the rule for expenses must be the following: *expenses are debits.* It is also commonly said that an expense account has been **charged** when it has been debited. If an expense needs to be reversed (such as when returned goods are put back into inventory, thus reversing the cost of sales entry that was made when the goods were originally sold), the *decrease in expenses* is a *credit.*

Mastering these rules requires practice in using them rather than sheer memorization. We will therefore begin that practice by recording a simple set of transactions.

TRANSACTION ANALYSIS

In order to record a transaction it must be analyzed to determine its dual effect on the entity's accounts. This analysis results in a decision as to which account is to be debited and which is to be credited. The result of the transaction analysis must preserve the two basic identities: (1) Assets = Liabilities + Owners' Equity; and (2) Debits = Credits. The beginner often finds that half of the accounting entry—particularly a change in cash—is relatively obvious, but that the other half—often a change in retained earnings—is less obvious. Our advice is to first record whichever half of the entry is more obvious, whether it is the debit or the credit portion, and then figure out the less obvious half.

Example: Campus Pizzeria, Inc.

Meredith Snelson started Campus Pizzeria, Inc., on August 1. Snelson was the sole owner of the corporation. The following transactions all took place in August. Revenue and expense transactions represent *summaries* of sales and expenses for the entire month; in practice such entries could be made every day. We will present each transaction, analyze it, and show how it would be entered in the accounts. Each transaction is numbered and its number is shown parenthetically beside the entry in the account. (This is a good practice for the reader to employ when working on similar problems.)

1. On August 1, Snelson invested $5,000 in the business as owner.

Analysis: This transaction increased **Cash** (a debit). Liabilities were not affected because the $5,000 was not a loan; rather, it was contributed capital. Thus, the owner's equity account, **Paid-In Capital,** increased (a credit). This is an equity financing transaction.	**Cash** (1) 5,000 **Paid-In Capital** (1) 5,000

2. On August 1, the firm paid $750 rent for the month of August.

Analysis: **Cash** decreased (a credit). The rent has been paid in advance; thus, it is an asset, because the benefits of using the rented space have not yet been received. **Prepaid Expenses** is increased (a debit). This is an asset acquisition transaction: prepaid rent was acquired in exchange for cash.	**Cash** (1) 5,000 (2) 750 **Prepaid Expenses** (2) 750

3. The firm borrowed $4,000 from a bank on a 9 percent note payable, with interest payable quarterly and the principal due in full at the end of two years.

Analysis: This was a debt financing transaction. **Cash** increased (a debit) by the $4,000 proceeds of the loan. The liability, **Notes Payable,** increased by an equal amount (a credit).	**Cash** (1) 5,000 (2) 750 (3) 4,000 **Notes Payable** (3) 4,000

4. Equipment costing $7,200 was purchased for cash. The expected life of the equipment was 10 years.

Analysis: **Cash** decreased by $7,200 (a credit). The equipment will provide benefits for several years, so it is an asset. The account **Equipment, at cost,** is increased by $7,200 (a debit). This was an asset acquisition transaction: The equipment was acquired in exchange for cash.	**Cash** (1) 5,000 (2) 750 (3) 4,000 (4) 7,200 **Equipment, at cost** (4) 7,200

5. An initial inventory of pizza ingredients and boxes was purchased on credit for $800.

Analysis: These items will be used in the future, so they are an asset. **Inventory** is increased by $800 (a debit). The firm has not yet paid for these items but is obligated to do so at some future time. Thus, the liability, **Accounts Payable,** is increased by $800 (a credit).

Inventory	
(5) 800	

Accounts Payable	
	(5) 800

6. In August pizza sales were $12,000, all for cash.

Analysis: **Cash** increased by $12,000. This cash increase did not arise from a liability; nor did the owner make an additional investment. The cash was earned by selling pizzas to customers. This is an earnings transaction, which increases retained earnings. Rather than directly increasing Retained Earnings (a credit), we will increase **Sales Revenues**, a temporary account.

Cash			
(1)	5,000	(2)	750
(3)	4,000	(4)	7,200
(6)	12,000		

Sales Revenues	
	(6) 12,000

7. During August the pizzeria's employees were paid $3,000 in wages.*

Analysis: **Cash** was decreased (a credit) by $3,000. Wages represent labor resources consumed in providing the pizzeria's services to its customers. This is therefore an earnings transaction that reduces retained earnings. Rather than directly decreasing Retained Earnings (a debit), we will enter the expense in a temporary account, **Wage Expense.**

Cash			
(1)	5,000	(2)	750
(3)	4,000	(4)	7,200
(6)	12,000	(7)	3,000

Wage Expense	
(7) 3,000	

8. During the month an additional $5,750 of ingredients and boxes was purchased on credit.

Analysis: Except for the amount, this transaction is identical to transaction 5 above. Thus, **Inventory** is increased (debited) and **Accounts Payable** is increased (credited) by $5,750.

Inventory	
(5) 800	
(8) 5,750	

Accounts Payable	
	(5) 800
	(8) 5,750

---

* Because this is an introductory example, we are disregarding certain real-world complications such as payroll taxes.

9. August sales consumed $6,000 of ingredients and boxes.

Analysis: These items have been removed from **Inventory,** so that asset account is reduced (credited). Resources consumed in generating sales revenues are expenses. Again, rather than directly reducing Retained Earnings, the $6,000 debit is made to a temporary account, **Cost of Sales.** This is an earnings transaction.

Inventory			
(5)	800	(9)	6,000
(8)	5,750		

Cost of Sales		
(9)	6,000	

10. At the end of the month, bills for various utilities used in August were received, totaling $450.

Analysis: The bills have not yet been paid, so **Accounts Payable** is increased by $450 (a credit). This liability is an expenditure for the utilities that were used (consumed) in August's earnings activities. These resources are thus an expense of August, and are debited to **Utilities Expense,** a temporary account.

Accounts Payable			
		(5)	800
		(8)	5,750
		(10)	450

Utilities Expense		
(10)	450	

11. During the month $4,800 of accounts payable was paid.

Analysis: Paying bills obviously decreases **Cash** (a credit). It also reduces the obligation the entity has to its vendors, so **Accounts Payable** is also reduced (a debit).

Cash			
(1)	5,000	(2)	750
(3)	4,000	(4)	7,200
(6)	12,000	(7)	3,000
		(11)	4,800

Accounts Payable			
(11)	4,800	(5)	800
		(8)	5,750
		(10)	450

12. On August 13, the firm catered a party for a fee of $200. Because the customer was a friend of Snelson's, the customer was told that payment could be made some time later in the month.

Analysis: Because services have been rendered, revenues have been earned. Thus, increase (credit) the temporary **Sales Revenues** account by $200. Since this was not a cash sale, the asset increased (debited) is **Accounts Receivable.** This is an earnings transaction.

Sales Revenues			
		(6)	12,000
		(12)	200

Accounts Receivable		
(12)	200	

13. On August 29, a check was received from Snelson's friend for the party of August 13.

Analysis: Payment (collection) of a receivable increases **Cash** (a debit). It also eliminates the receivable asset, so **Accounts Receivable** is decreased by $200 (a credit).			
		Cash	
(1)	5,000	(2)	750
(3)	4,000	(4)	7,200
(6)	12,000	(7)	3,000
(13)	**200**	(11)	4,800
		Accounts Receivable	
(12)	200	**(13)**	**200**

This completes—for the moment—the August transactions for Campus Pizzeria, Inc.

Balancing Accounts

The transactions we recorded above are called **original entries.** Such entries are those that obviously need to be made because a check has been written, an invoice has been received, sales have been made, and so on. After recording these original entries a balance is taken in each account.

An asset account is balanced as illustrated earlier in the chapter for Cash: the entries on each side are added up; then the sum of the credits is subtracted from the sum of the debits to get the new balance. An asset account's balance is a debit amount. (Asset accounts are thus called **debit-balance accounts.**) The balance in Cash is $5,450. (Because Cash is an asset account, it is understood that the balance is a debit amount.)

Illustration 4–2 shows the formal procedure for **ruling and balancing** an asset account. This is similar to what was shown in Illustration 4–1, except that there the line "To Balance   5,450" was omitted because we were just introducing the idea of an account. The "To Balance" entry goes with the new "Balance" entry, thus preserving the rule that no debit (here, for the new balance) is made without making an equal credit (here, "To Balance"). The double rules under the two $21,200 totals indicate that all of the information appearing above the double rules has been captured in the new balance that appears below the double rules. The procedure for ruling and balancing a liability account is completely analogous to that just described for an asset account.

The formal procedure for the temporary revenue and expense accounts differs slightly from that for the permanent accounts, as will be described below. At this point all that is necessary is to find the sum of the credits in the Sales Revenues account and the sum of the debits in each expense account (which is trivial here because no expense account had more than one debit).

ILLUSTRATION 4–2
BALANCING AN ACCOUNT

Cash

Balance	–0–		750
	5,000		7,200
	4,000		4,800
	200		3,000
	12,000	To Balance	5,450
	21,200		21,200
Balance	5,450		

**The Trial
Balance**

After determining the balance of each account a trial balance is taken. A **trial balance** is simply a list of the account names and the balances in each account as of a given moment of time, with debit balances shown in one column and credit balances in another column. The preparation of a trial balance serves two principal purposes: (1) it shows whether the equality of debits and credits has been maintained, and (2) it provides a convenient summary transcript of the ledger records as a basis for making the adjusting and closing entries (described in the next section) that precede the preparation of the period's financial statements.

Campus Pizzeria's trial balance is shown in Illustration 4–3. Because Campus Pizzeria was a new entity as of August 1, all the permanent (balance sheet) accounts had a zero beginning balance. As a result, the August 31 balances are based entirely on the 13 entries thus far recorded. In successive accounting periods the entity's permanent accounts will have non-zero beginning balances. (We suggest, as practice, that the reader verify each amount in Illustration 4–3.)

Although the trial balance shows that total debits equal total credits and thus indicates that the integrity of the basic accounting equation has been maintained, it does not prove that errors have not been made. Entries may have been omitted entirely, or they may have been posted to the wrong account. Offsetting errors may have been made, or a transaction may have been analyzed incorrectly. For example, if the debit for the purchase of a piece of equipment were made incorrectly to an expense account rather than correctly to an asset account, the totals of the trial balance would not be affected.

ILLUSTRATION 4–3
A TRIAL BALANCE

CAMPUS PIZZERIA, INC.
Trial Balance
As of August 31

Account	Balance Debit	Balance Credit
Cash	$ 5,450	
Accounts receivable.....................................	–0–	
Inventory..	550	
Prepaid expenses.......................................	750	
Equipment, at cost.....................................	7,200	
Accounts payable.......................................		$ 2,200
Notes payable...		4,000
Paid-in capital..		5,000
Sales revenues..		12,200
Cost of sales	6,000	
Wage expense	3,000	
Utilities expense	450	
Totals..	$23,400	$23,400

THE ADJUSTING AND CLOSING PROCESS

Adjusting Entries

Most entries to be made in the accounts are original entries. However, some events that affect the accounts are not evidenced by the obvious documents associated with original entries. The effects of these events are recorded at the end of the accounting period by means of **adjusting entries.** The purpose of the adjusting entries is to modify account balances so that they will reflect fairly the situation as of the end of the period.

Continuous Transactions. Most adjusting entries are made in connection with events that are, in effect, continuous transactions. Consider a tankful of fuel oil purchased for $1,000. On the day of delivery the $1,000 of fuel oil was an asset. But each day thereafter some fuel oil was consumed in the furnace, whereupon part of the $1,000 became an expense. Rather than record this consumption daily, a single adjusting entry is made at the end of the accounting period to show how much of the fuel oil is still an asset at that time and how much has become expense during the period. For example, if $600 was consumed and hence became an expense, $400 remains as an asset.

There are two ways of handling these events, both of which give the same result. Under one method, the $1,000 expenditure is originally recorded as an asset, Fuel Oil Inventory, as in the following entry:

Fuel Oil Inventory		**Accounts Payable**	
1,000			1,000

At the end of the accounting period the asset account is adjusted by subtracting the cost of fuel oil consumed, thus:

Fuel Expense		Fuel Oil Inventory	
600			600

Under the other method, the $1,000 expenditure for fuel oil is originally recorded in an expense account (instead of an inventory account). Then the fuel oil remaining at the end of the period is subtracted from expense and shown as an asset, thus:

Fuel Oil Inventory		Fuel Expense	
400			400

Although neither method reflects the correct facts *within* the period (with the trivial exception that the first method does reflect the facts on the day the oil was delivered), both reflect a correct statement of the facts as of the *end* of the accounting period. Because accounting focuses on deriving the proper amounts for the statements that are prepared at the end of the accounting period, the choice between these methods depends solely on which is more convenient.

Types of Adjusting Entries. Events that require adjusting entries essentially relate to the difference between expense and expenditure and between revenue and receipts, discussed in Chapter 3. Four types of such events, together with examples of each, are given below:

1. *Recorded costs to be apportioned among two or more accounting periods.* The fuel oil transaction given above is one example. Another is insurance protection, originally recorded as Prepaid Insurance (an asset), $800 of which becomes an expense in the current period:

Insurance Expense		Prepaid Insurance	
800			800

When an asset is reduced, as prepaid insurance was here, it is said that there has been a **write-off** of part (or all) of the asset.

2. *Unrecorded expenses.* These expenses were incurred during the period, but no record of them has yet been made. Example: For $150 of wages earned by an employee during the period but not yet paid to the employee:

Wage Expense		Accrued Wages	
150			150

3.   *Recorded revenues to be apportioned among two or more accounting periods.* As was the case with recorded costs, these amounts were initially recorded in one account, and at the end of the accounting period must be properly divided between a revenue account and a liability account. For example, rent collected during the period and recorded as rent revenue, $600 of which is applicable to the next period and hence is a liability at the end of the current period:

Rent Revenue			Unearned Rent Revenue	
600				600

4.   *Unrecorded revenues.* These revenues were earned during the period, but no record of them has yet been made. For example, $120 of interest earned by the entity during the period but not yet received:

Accrued Interest Receivable			Interest Revenue	
120				120

Depreciation.   Most long-lived assets give up their benefits to the entity in a continuous stream. Thus, the cost of these assets is continuously being converted to an expense (written off) in the same manner as the current assets—fuel oil and prepaid insurance—that were discussed above. The item that shows the portion of such long-lived asset costs that has become expense *during an accounting period* is called **depreciation expense.** Instead of subtracting the depreciation expense for the period directly from the asset amount—instead of crediting depreciation to the account for the asset being depreciated—the credit is made to a separate account, **Accumulated Depreciation.** The adjusting entry to record the depreciation expense for a period is therefore in the following form:

Depreciation Expense			Accumulated Depreciation	
2,000				2,000

There is a reason for crediting depreciation to Accumulated Depreciation rather than directly to the asset. Generally accepted accounting principles (GAAP) require separate disclosure of (1) the original cost of the entity's depreciable assets and (2) the depreciation that has been accumulated on these assets from the time they were acquired until the date of the balance sheet. Keeping these two items separate in the accounts facilitates the necessary disclosure, which appears on the balance sheet as the following:

Equipment, at cost...............................	$10,000
Less: Accumulated depreciation......................	4,000
Net equipment......................................	$6,000

Accumulated depreciation is called a **contra asset account** because it is subtracted from some other asset account. Another contra asset account is Allowance for Doubtful Accounts, described below.

Other Adjustments. Accountants make a variety of other adjusting entries in order to make the accounts reflect fairly the results of the entity's operations during the period and its status as of the end of the period. An example, discussed in more detail in Chapter 5, is **bad debt expense.** This is an adjustment made in order to recognize the likelihood that not all credit customers will pay their bills, and, thus, the Accounts Receivable account may overstate the *realizable* amount of those bills. An adjusting entry that records the write-off of receivables for the estimated amount of bad debts is as follows:

Bad Debt Expense		**Allowance for Doubtful Accounts**	
300			300

On the balance sheet the accumulated allowance for doubtful accounts is subtracted from accounts receivable, thus:

Accounts receivable, gross	$10,000
Less: Allowance for doubtful accounts.................	400
Net accounts receivable	$9.600

A Caution. When the student is given a problem involving the preparation of accounting statements, the precise nature of the original entries must be described, since the student has no other way of finding out about them. Information about the *adjusting* entries will not necessarily be given, however. Students, like practicing accountants, are expected to be on the lookout for situations that require adjustment.

Campus Pizzeria Adjusting Entries. A review of Campus Pizzeria's trial balance indicates three items that will generate adjusting entries: the write-off of prepaid expenses (rent), depreciation on the equipment, and accrued interest on the note payable.

14. Adjusting entry for rent expense.

Analysis: As of the end of August, the benefits from the $750 prepaid rent have all been received. Thus, the asset, **Prepaid Expenses,** is reduced by $750 (a credit). This rent applied to August operations, so it is an expense of August: debit **Rent Expense** for $750. This is an earnings transaction.	**Prepaid Expenses**			
	(2)	750	**(14)**	750
	Rent Expense			
	(14)	750		

15. Adjusting entry for depreciation expense.

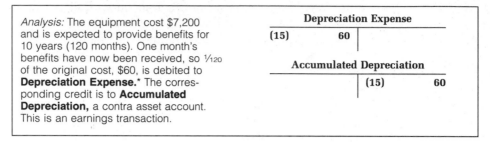

	Depreciation Expense	
(15)	60	

Accumulated Depreciation		
	(15)	60

Analysis: The equipment cost $7,200 and is expected to provide benefits for 10 years (120 months). One month's benefits have now been received, so $\frac{1}{120}$ of the original cost, $60, is debited to **Depreciation Expense.*** The corresponding credit is to **Accumulated Depreciation,** a contra asset account. This is an earnings transaction.

16. Adjusting entry for accrued interest expense (interest payable).

	Interest Expense	
(16)	30	

Accrued Expenses		
	(16)	30

Analysis: The bank has earned one month's interest on the note. The interest rate is 9 percent a year, so one month's interest on $4,000 will be ¾ percent, or $30. This amount is debited to **Interest Expense.** Because the interest has not yet been paid, the credit is to the liability account, **Accrued Expenses** (or Interest Payable). This is an earnings transaction because the interest is in the nature of "rent" on the borrowed funds used this month.

Closing Entries

The temporary revenue and expense accounts are actually subdivisions of owners' equity (retained earnings). At the end of the period the temporary accounts are *closed* to Retained Earnings in order to determine the net effect of all the revenue and expense transactions—the net income or loss. Rather than closing each temporary account directly to Retained Earnings, however, each is first closed to an intermediate account whose purpose is to summarize the revenue and expense transactions. This account is variously called **Income Summary, Profit and Loss,** or **Expense and Revenue Summary.** This account reflects the net income or loss for a given accounting period. Income Summary is a *clearing* account that in turn is closed to Retained Earnings to complete the closing process.

The **closing** process consists of transferring the balance of each temporary account to the clearing account. To close a revenue account, the sum of the credits is found, and then this sum is debited to the revenue account and credited to Income Summary. This gives the revenue account a balance of zero, and transfers its former credit balance to Income Summary. The result is as though the credit balance in the revenue account were "picked

*This method of charging the cost of an asset to expense in a level stream over the asset's life is called straight-line depreciation. Other methods will be described in Chapter 7.

up and moved" to the credit side of Income Summary without making any entry. But in an accounting system such informality is not permitted, and the transfer of the revenue balance to Income Summary must be accomplished with an equal debit and credit. For Campus Pizzeria this is done as follows (we use letters to label the closing entries to distinguish them from the original and adjusting entries):

A. Closing the Sales Revenues account.

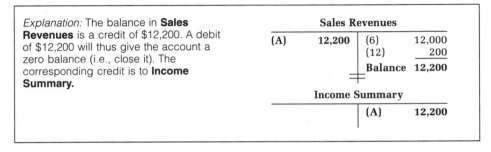

Explanation: The balance in **Sales Revenues** is a credit of $12,200. A debit of $12,200 will thus give the account a zero balance (i.e., close it). The corresponding credit is to **Income Summary.**

	Sales Revenues		
(A)	12,200	(6)	12,000
		(12)	200
		Balance	12,200

	Income Summary		
		(A)	12,200

The double rule intersecting the stem of the T account designates that it has been closed. All the information it contained is now residing, in summary form, in Income Summary. As far as preparing the financial statements is concerned, the Sales Revenue page of the ledger could now be thrown away—that is the sense in which this is a temporary account. (Of course, in practice such an accounting record would not be destroyed.)

Closing an expense account is the mirror image of closing a revenue account. There are six expense accounts to be closed (the letters continue the labeling of the closing entries): (B) Cost of Sales, (C) Wage Expense, (D) Utilities Expense, (E) Rent Expense, (F) Depreciation Expense, and (G) Interest Expense.[2] Since all of these closing entries are the same in substance, we will illustrate only one of them:

B. Closing the Cost of Sales account.

Explanation: The balance in **Cost of Sales** is a debit of $6,000; a credit of $6,000 will thus close this account. The corresponding debit is to **Income Summary.**

	Cost of Sales		
(9)	6,000	(B)	6,000

	Income Summary		
(B)	6,000	(A)	12,200

At this stage the only accounts remaining open are the permanent accounts (which are always balanced at the end of the period, but are never closed) and Income Summary (which is a temporary account). Income

---

[2]In actual accounting practice another trial balance would be taken after the adjusting entries were made and before the closing entries commence.

Summary is closed in exactly the same manner as other temporary accounts, except that first the debits and credits have to be summed and netted (as in balancing a permanent account). This net amount, which is the period's *income before income taxes,* is $1,910 (explained below). It generates one more adjusting entry—the entry needed to record the estimated income tax liability arising from the period's income. Assuming that the applicable income tax rate is 20 percent, the amount of estimated tax liability is $382 (= $1,910 * 0.20). This amount is debited to Income Tax Expense (a temporary account created for recording this final adjusting entry), and is credited to Income Tax Liability. Income Tax Expense is then closed to Income Summary, which completes the closing of all the expense accounts. (For simplicity we will make the income tax expense debit directly to Income Summary so that we do not have to illustrate creating and closing another expense account that has only one entry made to it.)

To complete the closing process, Income Summary is closed. Its balance is credited (if a net profit) or debited (if a net loss) to Retained Earnings, which can then be balanced to complete the balancing of the permanent accounts.

H. Closing the Income Summary account to Retained Earnings.

	Income Summary		
Explanation: After closing all of the temporary accounts (except Income Tax Expense) to Income Summary, the sum of its debits, $10,290, is netted against the sum of its credits, $12,200. This leaves a net credit balance in the account of $1,910, which is the pretax income for August. After the income tax adjusting entry for $382 is made, **Income Summary** is closed by debiting it for $1,528; the corresponding credit is to **Retained Earnings.** Since this was a new entity as of August 1, Retained Earnings had a zero beginning balance. To complete the process, Retained Earnings is balanced in the same manner as other balance sheet accounts. Next month, any profit (or loss) for September will be added to (subtracted from) this $1,528 new beginning balance.	(B) 6,000 (C) 3,000 (D) 450 (E) 750 (F) 60 (G) 30 ——— 10,290 (17) 382 (H) 1,528	(A)	12,200 ——— 12,200

	Income Tax Liability	
	(17)	382

	Retained Earnings	
	Balance	−0−
To Balance 1,528	(H)	1,528
	Balance	1,528

Statement Preparation

After the adjusting and closing entries have been made, the period's financial statements can be prepared. The numbers for the income statement can be thought of as coming from either of two equivalent sources: (1) the balances in the temporary accounts just prior to their closing or (2) the credit (revenue) and debit (expense) entries to the Income Summary account. Amounts for the balance sheet are the balances in the permanent

ILLUSTRATION 4–4
FINANCIAL STATEMENTS

CAMPUS PIZZERIA, INC.
Balance Sheet
As of August 31

*Assets**		*Liabilities and Owner's Equity*	
Cash	$ 5,450	Accounts payable..........................	$ 2,200
Accounts receivable.......................	0	Notes payable............................	4,000
Inventory..................................	550	Accrued expenses........................	30
Prepaid expenses.........................	0	Income tax liability	382
Total current assets	6,000	Total liabilities............................	6,612
Equipment, at cost........................	7,200	Paid-in capital	5,000
Less: Accumulated depreciation...........	60	Retained earnings.........................	1,528
Equipment, net	7,140	Total owner's equity	6,528
Total assets	$13,140	Total liabilities and owner's equity...........	$13,140

*Ordinarily, accounts with zero balances are not shown. Two are included here for completeness, since both did have entries made to them during the period.

Income Statement
For the Month of August

Sales revenues		$12,200
Cost of sales		6,000
Gross margin................................		6,200
Operating expenses:		
Wages..........................	$3,000	
Rent............................	750	
Utilities..........................	450	
Depreciation......................	60	
Interest	30	4,290
Income before income taxes		1,910
Income tax expense.........................		382
Net income.................................		$ 1,528

accounts. In most companies the accounts reported in the financial statements are summaries of more detailed accounts in the ledger.

The August financial statements for Campus Pizzeria, Inc., are shown in Illustration 4–4. Since the accounting period was one month, these are interim statements. It is also important to remember that the August net income and the August 31 retained earnings amounts are the same in this case only because (1) this is the first accounting period for a new entity and (2) the entity did not pay any dividends in this period.

The Journal

In the preceding illustration of the accounting process we recorded transactions directly in T accounts. In practice transactions are initially recorded in a journal and then T account entries are made at the end of the period based on the transactions recorded in the journal.

A **journal** is a chronological record of accounting transactions showing the names of accounts that are to be debited or credited, the amounts of the debits and credits, and any useful supplementary information about the transaction. A journal is analogous to a diary.

The traditional format for writing a **journal entry** is as follows:

```
dr.   Cash............................................  5,000
     cr.    Paid-In Capital ............................         5,000
```

In practice the notations dr. and cr. are not used because the accountant distinguishes debits from credits on the basis of the order (debits first) and indentation (credits indented) of the accounts. We will use the dr. and cr. in this chapter and Chapter 5 as a reminder to the reader but will follow common practice in subsequent chapters.

ILLUSTRATION 4–5

JOURNAL

Date		Accounts	LF	Debit	Credit
Aug.	1	Cash	10	5,000.00	
		Paid–In Capital	30		5,000.00
	1	Prepaid Expenses	14	750.00	
		Cash	10		750.00
	1	Cash	10	4,000.00	
		Notes Payable	21		4,000.00
	2	Equipment	15	7,200.00	
		Cash	10		7,200.00
	2	Inventory	13	800.00	
		Accounts Payable	20		800.00

Illustration 4–5 shows a journal that records the first few transactions for Campus Pizzeria. With respect to format, note the following: (1) the debit entry is listed first, (2) the debit amounts appear in the left-hand money column, (3) the account to be credited appears below the debit entry and is indented, and (4) the credit amounts appear in the right-hand money column. "LF" is an abbreviation for "ledger folio," which is the page reference to the ledger account where the entry is to be made. This reference is inserted at the time the entry is **posted** to (i.e., entered in) the appropriate T account in the ledger. Thus, the presence of numbers in the LF column indicates that the entries have been posted to the appropriate T accounts. They also provide an **audit trail,** a way of tracing the amounts in the ledger back to their sources. In some bookkeeping systems a brief explanation is written beneath each journal entry.

The *journal* thus contains explicit instructions on the revenue and expense items to be recorded in the temporary accounts and the changes to be made to the balances in the permanent accounts. No account balance is ever changed except on the basis of a journal entry. The *ledger* is a device for *reclassifying* and *summarizing,* by accounts, information originally listed in chronological order in the journal. Entries are first made in the journal and are later posted to ledger accounts.

Summary of the Accounting Process

1.   The first and most important part of the accounting process is the *analysis of transactions.* This is the process of deciding which account or accounts should be debited, which should be credited, and in what amounts, in order to reflect events in the accounting records. This requires both a knowledge of accounting concepts and judgment.

2.   Next comes the purely mechanical step of *journalizing original entries*—recording the results of the transaction analysis in the journal.

3.   *Posting* is the process of recording changes in the ledger accounts exactly as specified by the journal entries. This is also purely mechanical.

4.   At the ending of the accounting period judgment is involved in deciding on the *adjusting entries.* These are journalized and posted in the same way as original entries.

5.   The *closing entries* are journalized and posted. This is a purely mechanical step.

6.   *Financial statements* are prepared. This requires judgment as to the best arrangement and terminology, but the numbers that are used result from the judgments made in steps 1 and 4.

These six steps are taken sequentially during an accounting period and are repeated in each subsequent period. The steps are therefore commonly referred to as the **accounting cycle.** Illustration 4–6 depicts the accounting cycle schematically. Note that the ending balance sheet account balances from step 6 became the beginning balances for the next repetition of the cycle. Some accountants use a *worksheet* in the latter steps of the accounting cycle. Worksheets are described in the appendix to this chapter.

ACCOUNTING SYSTEMS

The simple journals and ledgers described in the preceding pages, together with the rules for using them, constitute an accounting system. But this particular system would not usually be the best system for a given organization. The best system is that one that best achieves the following objectives:

1.   To process the information efficiently—at low cost.

2.   To obtain reports quickly.

3.   To ensure a high degree of accuracy.

4.   To minimize the possibility of theft or fraud.

Designing a good accounting system is a specialized job requiring a high degree of skill. Only a few of the principles are noted here.

ILLUSTRATION 4–6
THE ACCOUNTING CYCLE

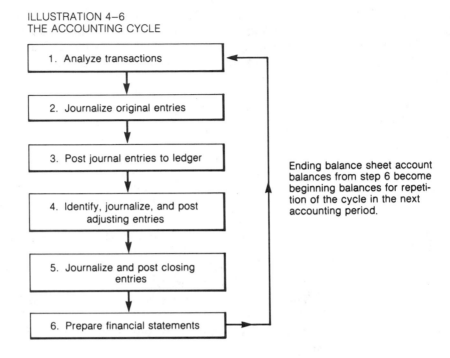

1. Analyze transactions

2. Journalize original entries

3. Post journal entries to ledger

4. Identify, journalize, and post adjusting entries

5. Journalize and post closing entries

6. Prepare financial statements

Ending balance sheet account balances from step 6 become beginning balances for repetition of the cycle in the next accounting period.

Special Journals

The journal form shown in Illustration 4–5 is called a **general journal.** This form requires that the title of each account affected by each entry be written down. If many entries are made to a single account, efficiency can be increased by using a **special journal,** or **register.** A special journal has several columns, each headed with the name of an account to be debited or credited, plus (usually) a Miscellaneous column in which entries to other accounts may be recorded. Entries to the accounts indicated by column headings are made simply by entering the proper amount in these columns. At the end of the accounting period all the amounts in each column are added and the total is posted as one amount to the appropriate account. Entries in the Miscellaneous column are posted individually.

Illustration 4–7 gives an example of a special journal used to record debits to Cash and credits to various accounts. This is called a **cash receipts journal.** Columns are provided for the accounts in which entries are likely to be made frequently (here, Accounts Receivable for collections, and Sales for cash sales). A column is also provided for credits to other accounts. To illustrate the use of this journal, on May 31, Mary Able made a $300 payment on her account. Fred Black and Henry Cheng also made payments. The check marks in the LF (ledger folio) column indicate that these payments also have been credited to each customer's account in the accounts receivable subsidiary ledger (described in the next section). Also on May 31, $56 interest revenue from a savings account at Peoples Bank was

ILLUSTRATION 4–7

CASH RECEIPTS JOURNAL

Date		Received from	LF	Accounts Receivable Cr.	Sales Cr.	Other Cr.		Cash Dr.
						Account	Amount	
May	31	Brought forward*		4,200.00	2,000.00		940.00	7,140.00
	31	Mary Able	✓	300.00				300.00
	31	Fred Black	✓	650.00				650.00
	31	Henry Cheng	✓	210.00				210.00
	31	Cash Sales			430.00			430.00
	31	Peoples Bank	561			Interest Revenue	56.00	56.00
		Totals		5,360.00	2,430.00		996.00	8,786.00
		(Account No.)		(120)	(511)			(111)

* These are totals from the preceding journal page.

received in cash. The number 561 in the LF column indicates that this transaction has been posted in account 561, Interest Revenue. The total credits in the Accounts Receivable column, $5,360, will be credited as a single entry to Accounts Receivable (account 120). Similarly, $2,430 will be credited to Sales (account 511), and $8,786 will be debited to Cash (account 111).

Control Accounts and Subsidiary Ledgers

Most organizations use one or more **subsidiary ledgers,** which are groups of related accounts taken out of the general ledger. For example, all the separate accounts for individual customers may be kept in an accounts receivable ledger. One advantage of this practice is that several bookkeepers can be working on the ledger accounts simultaneously.

In order to keep the general ledger in balance, a **control account** takes the place of the individual accounts removed to the subsidiary ledger. A control account shows in summary form the debits and credits shown in detail in a subsidiary ledger. When subsidiary ledgers are used, each amount is, in effect, posted twice. It is posted, often daily, to the proper account in the subsidiary ledger. It also becomes a part of the total that is posted at the end of the period to the control account in the general ledger. In a large business most if not all of the general ledger accounts are control accounts.

Imprest Funds

Another work-saving device is the **imprest fund,** which consists of cash advanced to a responsible person and periodically replenished by additional cash equal to the amount expended by this person. The operation of an imprest fund is illustrated by its most common version, the **petty cash**

fund. The fund is established by drawing a check on the entity's bank account. The person responsible for the fund cashes the check and puts the money in a petty cash box. This transaction is recorded by the following entry:

dr.	Petty Cash	50	
cr.	Cash		50

The petty cash is used to pay small bills until it is nearly exhausted. At that time, these bills are summarized and a check is drawn for the amount they total. A journal entry is made debiting the various expense or asset accounts represented by the bills; for example:

dr.	Office Supplies	21	
	Miscellaneous Expense	25	
cr.	Cash		46

Note that the credit is to the regular Cash account. Once established, the Petty Cash account in the ledger is not changed unless the size of the fund is changed.

This procedure saves the effort involved in drawing checks and making separate journal entries for small bills. It also provides a safeguard, since the petty cash box should at all times contain cash and receipted bills that together total the amount shown in the Petty Cash account.

The imprest device is by no means limited to petty cash. Many government disbursing agencies operate on the same principle, but in amounts that run into millions of dollars. These agencies are advanced funds by the U.S. Treasury Department, they disburse these funds to pay authorized bills, and they submit these bills to the Treasury Department as a basis for replenishing the fund. The accounting entries are essentially the same as those given above for petty cash.

Internal Accounting Controls

Two objectives of an accounting system stated above—accuracy and protection against theft or fraud—cannot be attained absolutely without conflicting with the other two—speed and economy. A system that can't be "beaten" would be prohibitively expensive and time-consuming. A basic principle of internal accounting control, therefore, is that the system should make it *as difficult as is practical* for people to be dishonest or careless. Such a principle is based not on a cynical view of people in general but rather on the realistic assumption that a few people will be dishonest or careless if it is easy for them to do so.

Some of the devices used to ensure reasonable accuracy have been touched on already; for example, the idea of verifying one set of figures against another. The idea of divided responsibility is another important one. Whenever feasible, one person should not be responsible for recording all aspects of a transaction, nor should the custodian of assets (e.g., the storekeeper or the cashier) be permitted to do the accounting for these assets. Thus, one person's work is a check on another's. Although this does not eliminate the possibility that two people will steal through collusion, the likelihood of dishonesty is greatly reduced.

These brief comments indicate only the nature of the problem of internal accounting control, which is a big subject. Furthermore, a book that focuses on accounting *principles,* as this one does, cannot detail the complexities involved in the *operation* of accounting systems. For example, cash transactions are very easy to analyze, whereas some textbooks on auditing contain a dozen pages of questions that should be considered in connection with the internal accounting control of the single item, cash.

Significant Recordkeeping Ideas

At least two significant ideas should emerge from this description of the recordkeeping process and of accounting systems.

The first is the idea of *debit and credit equality:* "every debit must have an equal credit." Much more than a mechanical bookkeeping requirement, this idea is a way of thinking that is extremely useful in analyzing what is going on in an organization. There is a natural human tendency to think about only part of the consequences of a decision and to overlook some equally important part. For example, although a growing cash balance looks good superficially, this is only half of the story. It makes considerable difference whether the credits offsetting these debits to cash reflect revenues from profitable operations or whether they reflect emergency bank loans.

The second significant idea is that of *balancing:* one total should always equal some other total. Four balancing techniques have been described: (1) the fundamental debit-credit structure; (2) the trial balance; (3) the control-subsidiary relationship, in which the total of the subsidiary account items must always equal a control account total; and (4) the imprest technique, in which the sum of cash and paid bills must always equal a predetermined total. As noted above, these devices provide a check on arithmetic accuracy, they lessen the risk of loss through dishonesty, and they lessen the chance that some part of a transaction will be overlooked.

COMPUTER-BASED ACCOUNTING SYSTEMS

Most organizations now do their accounting work with an electronic computer rather than with the manual methods described above. We initially explained the process in terms of manual methods because the forms and records used in manual systems are visible whereas the operations that go on inside a computer are invisible. Also, in solving problems of the type encountered in an introductory accounting course, students often find it more convenient to use manual methods, even if they have access to a computer. In this section we give a brief overview of computer-based accounting systems.

**What a
Computer-
Based System
Does**

As noted above, some steps in the accounting cycle involve judgment, whereas others are primarily mechanical. These mechanical steps are usually referred to as **bookkeeping.** A computer-based system performs some or all of the bookkeeping steps—that is, it records and stores data, performs arithmetic operations on data, sorts and summarizes data, and prepares reports. These functions are described below as inputs, processing, and outputs.

Inputs.   In some computer systems data are entered by a data-entry clerk (using a keyboard) who copies them from a paper record such as a sales order or purchase order. In other systems the computer accepts input data from equipment located at the point of origin. Examples are factory time records; inventory counts, when the person counting uses a hand-held recording device; and receiving records, when a similar device is used.

An especially striking and familiar example of direct computer data input is the scanning device used at the supermarket or department store check-out stand. The scanner reads a bar code printed on the item (or on a tag attached to the item); this code specifically identifies the item. The computer to which the scanner is connected then uses stored information on each item's selling price to calculate an itemized list of the amount owed by the customer. A summary of sales revenue, cost of goods sold (also stored for each item in the computer), and gross margin by items or categories of items, is available for use by store management at the end of each day.

The inputs to one business's computer may be the outputs of the computer of another business. For example, a factory computer may generate purchase orders for parts to be supplied by a vendor. These outputs are transmitted electronically to the vendor, where they become sales orders inputs, without a paper purchase order ever being produced. Similarly, a wholesaler's salesperson may record orders placed by a retail store on a hand-held device; the information is then transmitted to a central computer by telephone lines.

Processing.   Once data are in machine-readable form, they can be used in a number of ways. Such data provide a rapid and accurate source of information. For example, an airline reservation system has a record of the availability of seats in each of several fare categories for every flight the airline will operate over the next several months. Any travel agent connected to the system by a terminal can request information about flight availability and price; the computer can process hundreds of such inquiries every minute. If the agent wishes to book a seat, the computer decreases availability on the flight and sends information to the travel agency's printer, which prepares a ticket, boarding pass, itinerary, and customer invoice. Computer systems also sort data in ways that may be of interest and use to management.

Outputs.   Computer-based systems can prepare reports that include either tables of numbers or graphs. These can be generated at regular intervals in a prescribed format or prepared in a form specified by an individual user. In some systems the user produces customized reports locally by using a personal computer or terminal that can retrieve data from a central computer-based system.

Relation to Manual Systems

Computer-based accounting systems are usually operated by several interconnected software programs, each of which is called a *module.* There may be a module for any of the following: sales orders, shipments, and the related accounts receivable (often called an *order-entry module*); manufacturing costs; purchase orders, inventory, and related accounts payable (a *purchasing module*); payroll and other personnel records; fixed asset acquisitions, location, and depreciation; income taxes; cash; and the general ledger. These modules are, in fact, special journals and subsidiary ledgers, as described earlier in this chapter. The subsidiary ledgers are related to the general ledger by control accounts, as was described above.

Hundreds of software programs are available. Some provide a complete set of modules for a small enterprise for a few hundred dollars; for a larger company the cost may be several thousand dollars. Some programs are designed for a specific industry (for example, time-intensive professional service businesses such as law, accounting, and architectural firms). These software programs can handle quantitative nonmonetary data as well as monetary data. Manual accounting systems, by contrast, are limited primarily to monetary data.

Problems with Computer Systems

Despite their many advantages, computer-based systems are not without their problems. Although a small company can purchase "off-the-shelf" software and have its system up and running in a few days, system development and installation in a larger, more complex organization may take many months and cost millions of dollars. Such systems usually require an outside consultant for their design and implementation. (The Big Six accounting firm, Arthur Andersen & Co., has a systems consulting arm, Andersen Consulting, that is the largest consulting firm in the world.) Moreover, technological advances make existing systems obsolete within a few years, and much time and money must be spent to update them. Nevertheless, the advantages of a computer-based system are so great that almost every organization needs one.

Unlike a manual system, a computer-based system does not leave a paper trail that can be readily audited. The system must therefore rely on the internal controls described above. In a few spectacular instances the lack (or circumvention) of such controls has resulted in business frauds and resultant failure; but the number of such events is very small relative to the number of computer-based systems in use.

Finally, a computer-based system will not be fully effective until its developers learn to design reports that the system's users need and can understand. This job of education, for both developers and users, can be substantial. If it is not done properly the system will spew out reports that no one uses, and the potential users will not appreciate the information that they could receive if only they knew how to ask for it.

SUMMARY

The account is a device for collecting information about each item that is to be accounted for. It has two sides: the left-hand, or debit, side and the right-hand, or credit, side. The rules are such that asset and expense accounts increase on the debit side, whereas liabilities, owners' equity, and revenue accounts increase on the credit side. This maintains both the equation: Assets = Liabilities + Owners' Equity, and the equation: Debits = Credits.

A ledger is a group of accounts. Entries are made to ledger accounts on the basis of instructions given in a journal, which is a chronological record of transactions.

At the end of an accounting period, adjusting entries are made so that after adjustment the revenue and expense accounts will show the appropriate amounts for the period. These temporary accounts are then closed to the Income Summary account, which in turn is closed to Retained Earnings.

In manual accounting systems, special journals, subsidiary ledgers, and other devices facilitate the process of recording accounting data. A computer-based system performs the same functions more rapidly, and it can provide a variety of useful management reports if it has been designed thoughtfully and its users have been properly trained.

APPENDIX: ADDITIONAL ACCOUNTING CYCLE PROCEDURES

Errors Revealed by the Trial Balance

Following are four suggested aids in detecting errors revealed by differences between the debit and credit totals of the trial balance in a manual system. (Computerized systems are usually programmed to reject entries that would create a debit–credit imbalance.)

1. If the difference between the totals is 0.01, 1.00, 100, 1,000, and so forth, the error is probably in addition. Such an error is usually detected by re-adding the columns of the trial balance, or, if necessary, the columns in the ledger accounts.

2. When the discrepancy is an even number, the error may be the result of making a debit entry in a credit column or vice versa. Divide the difference in totals by 2 and look through first the trial balance and then the ledger accounts for an amount corresponding to this quotient. The difference is divided by 2 because an item placed in the wrong column results in a difference of twice its amount.

3. If the difference is divisible by 9, the error is probably either a transposition or a transplacement, and the search can be narrowed down to

numbers where these errors might have been made. A **transposition** occurs when 79 is written for 97, 318 for 813, and so on. A **transplacement,** or **slide,** occurs when the digits of the number are moved to the left or right, as when $6,328.00 is written as $632.80 or $63.28.

4.   When the source of error is not readily discernible, it is advisable to check the trial balance against the ledger to determine whether all the account balances have been copied properly. This check may reveal that certain accounts have been omitted. As a last resort it may be necessary to check all of the numbers in the ledger with the journal and to check all additions and subtractions in the several accounts.

Care in making the entries—such as writing legibly, double-checking additions and subtractions as journalizing and posting proceed, and making sure all entries are entered properly—will save much time otherwise spent in hunting for errors.

The Worksheet

A worksheet is a preliminary compilation of figures that facilitates recording or analysis. A worksheet is often used prior to the formal journalizing and posting of the adjusting and closing entries. Its use permits the accountant to make a dry run of the whole process. Since a pencil is ordinarily used, any errors detected on the worksheet can be easily corrected, whereas alterations to the formal records are to be avoided. The worksheet also classifies account balances according to the financial statements in which they are to appear.

A worksheet is often used instead of, rather than preliminary to, the adjusting and closing process. Many entities formally close their books only once a year but nevertheless prepare monthly financial statements. These interim statements are prepared from a worksheet listing the account balances at the end of the month together with the adjustments necessary to reflect revenue and expense in that month. Statements are prepared from the adjusted account balances developed on this worksheet. The income statement figures on such a worksheet would be cumulative for the year to date. An income statement for the current month can be derived from the cumulative figures simply by subtracting the corresponding figures on the preceding month's worksheet.

Illustration 4–8 shows a worksheet for Campus Pizzeria, Inc. The four adjustments shown thereon reflect the preclosing adjusting entries for prepaid expenses, depreciation, and accrued interest and the final adjusting entry for income taxes. Note that additional accounts are added as needed at the bottom of the worksheet.

The last item on this worksheet, $1,528, is the net income for the period. It is found by subtracting the sum of the other debits to Income Statement from the sum of the credits to Income Statement. Showing the same amount in the Balance Sheet credit column has the effect of closing the net income to Retained Earnings. After this amount has been entered, each column of a

ILLUSTRATION 4–8
A WORKSHEET

	Trial Balance August 31		Adjustments		Income Statement		Balance Sheet	
	Dr.	Cr.	Dr.	Cr.	Dr.	Cr.	Dr.	Cr.
Cash	5,450						5,450	
Accounts receivable	—0—						—0—	
Inventory	550						550	
Prepaid expenses	750			750			—0—	
Equipment, at cost	7,200						7,200	
Accounts payable		2,200						2,200
Notes payable		4,400						4,400
Paid-in capital		5,000						5,000
Retained earnings		—0—						—0—
Sales revenues		12,000				12,000		12,000
Cost of sales	6,000				6,000			
Wage expense	3,000				3,000			
Utilities	450				450			
	23,400	23,400						
Rent expense			750		750			
Depreciation expense			60		60			
Accumulated depreciation				60				60
Interest expense			30		30			
Accrued expenses				30				30
Income tax expense			382		382			
Income tax liability				382				382
Net income					1,528			1,528
			1,222	1,222	12,200	12,200	13,200	13,200

pair should add to the same total; this is a check on the arithmetic accuracy of the whole closing process.

Cases

CASE 4-1 PC Depot

PC Depot was a retail store for personal computers and hand-held calculators, selling several national brands in each product line. The store was opened in early September by Barbara Thompson, a young woman previously employed in direct computer sales for a national firm specializing in business computers.

Thompson knew the importance of adequate records. One of her first decisions, therefore, was to hire Chris Jarrard, a local accountant, to set up her bookkeeping system.

Jarrard wrote up the store's preopening financial transactions in journal form to serve as an example (Exhibit 1). Thompson agreed to write up the remainder of the store's September financial transactions for Jarrard's later review.

At the end of September, Thompson had the following items to record:

EXHIBIT 1
GENERAL JOURNAL

Entry Number	Account	Amount Dr.	Amount Cr.
(1)	Cash...	165,000	
	Bank Loan Payable (15%)............................		100,000
	Proprietor's Capital		65,000
(2)	Rent Expense (September).............................	1,485	
	Cash...		1,485
(3)	Merchandise Inventory................................	137,500	
	Accounts Payable		137,500
(4)	Furniture and Fixtures (10-year life)...................	15,500	
	Cash...		15,500
(5)	Advertising Expense...................................	1,320	
	Cash...		1,320
(6)	Wages Expense..	935	
	Cash...		935
(7)	Office Supplies Expense	1,100	
	Cash...		1,100
(8)	Utilities Expense.......................................	275	
	Cash...		275

(9)	Cash sales for September	$38,000
(10)	Credit sales for September	14,850
(11)	Cash received from credit customers	3,614
(12)	Bills paid to merchandise suppliers.	96,195
(13)	New merchandise received on credit from supplier	49,940
(14)	Ms. Thompson ascertained the cost of merchandise sold was	38,140
(15)	Wages paid to assistant.	688
(16)	Wages earned but unpaid at the end of September	440
(17)	Rent paid for October.	1,485
(18)	Insurance bill paid for one year (September 1–August 31)	2,310
(19)	Bills received, but unpaid, from electric company	226
(20)	Purchased sign, paying $660 cash and agreeing to pay the $1,100 balance by December 31	1,760

Questions

1. Explain the events that probably gave rise to journal entries 1 through 8 of Exhibit 1.

2. Set up a ledger account (in T account form) for each account named in the general journal. Post entries 1 through 8 to these accounts, using the entry number as a cross-referenco.

3. Analyze the facts listed as 9 through 20, resolving them into their debit and credit elements. Prepare journal entries and post to the ledger accounts. (Do not prepare closing entries.)

4. Consider any other transactions that should be recorded. Why are these adjusting entries required? Prepare journal entries for them and post to ledger accounts.

5. Prepare closing entries and post to ledger accounts. What new ledger accounts are required? Why?

6. Prepare an income statement for September and a balance sheet as of September 30.

CASE 4–2   Save-Mart

Save-Mart was a retail store. Its account balances on February 28 (the end of its fiscal year), before adjustments, were as shown below.

Debit Balances			Credit Balances		
Cash	$	88,860	Accumulated depreciation on store		
Accounts receivable.		127,430	equipment	$	11,420
Merchandise inventory.		903,130	Notes payable.		88,500
Store equipment		70,970	Accounts payable.		88,970
Supplies inventory		17,480	Common stock		100,000
Prepaid insurance.		12,430	Retained earnings.		33,500
Selling expense.		10,880	Sales		988,700
Sales salaries.		47,140			
Miscellaneous general expense		18,930			
Sales discounts.		3,340			
Interest expense		7,100			
Social security tax expense		3,400			
Total		$1,311,090	Total		$1,311,090

The data for the adjustments are:

1. Cost of merchandise sold, $604,783.

2. Store equipment had a useful life of 7 years. (All equipment was less than 7 years old.)

3. Supplies inventory, February 28, $3,877. (Purchases of supplies during the year were debited to the Supplies Inventory account.)

4. Expired insurance, $7,125.

5. The note payable was at an interest rate of 9 percent, payable monthly. It had been outstanding throughout the year.

6. Sales salaries earned but not paid to employees, $2,340.

7. The statement sent by the bank, adjusted for checks outstanding, showed a balance of $88,110. The difference represented bank service charges.

Questions

1. Set up T accounts with the balances given above.

2. Journalize and post adjusting entries, adding other T accounts as necessary.

3. Journalize and post closing entries.

4. Prepare an income statement for the year and a balance sheet as of February 28.

Case 4–3   Copies Express

Copies Express was incorporated on November 20, 1992, and began operating on January 2, 1993. The balance sheet as of the beginning of operations is shown in Exhibit 1.

In preparing financial statements for the first year of operations, the accountant reviewed the record of cash receipts and cash disbursements for Copies Express. This information appears in Exhibit 2.

In addition the accountant examined certain other information relative to operations. These additional items appear in Exhibit 3.

Questions

1. Prepare an income statement for 1993 and a balance sheet as of December 31, 1993.

2. Be prepared to explain the derivation of each number on these financial statements.

EXHIBIT 1
COPIES EXPRESS, INC.

Balance Sheet
As of January 2, 1993

Assets

Cash	$ 2,000
Supplies	24,400
Building and equipment	300,000
Land	12,000
Total	$338,400

Liabilities and Owners' Equity

Accounts payable	$ 10,400
Bank loan	24,000
Capital stock	304,000
Total	$338,400

EXHIBIT 2
COPIES EXPRESS, INC.

Cash Receipts and Disbursements: 1993

Cash Receipts

Cash sales	$176,450
Collect accounts receivable	64,750
Total	$241,200

Cash Disbursements

Wages and salaries....................	$ 85,750
Heat, light, power	15,000
Additional supplies	52,600
Selling and administration	28,375
Interest (Note 1)......................	2,880
Payment—bank loan (12/31).............	12,000
Payment—accounts payable.............	10,400
Total	$207,005

Note 1. Interest at 12 percent per annum on the bank loan was payable June 30 and December 31 [($24,000 * .12) = $2880]. Interest payments for 1993 were made when due.

EXHIBIT 3
OTHER INFORMATION RELATIVE TO OPERATIONS

1. At the end of 1993 Copies Express owed $9,875 to suppliers for the purchase of photocopy supplies for which it had not yet paid.

2. The yearly depreciation expense on the buildings and equipment was $15,000.

3. At the end of 1993 Copies Express was owed $11,000 for copying services by customers who had not yet paid. Copies Express expected that all of these customers would pay within 30 days.

4. An inventory taken of the supplies at year-end revealed that the year's cost of supplies was $60,250.

5. Income taxes for 1993 were expected to be $11,593. They were unpaid as of December 31, 1993.

CASE 4–4   Trevino's Service Station[*]

On March 15, Julio Trevino signed a lease agreement to operate a gasoline service station that was owned by the Octane Oil Company (hereafter, simply "Octane"). Trevino had contacted the regional sales manager of Octane in response to an advertisement that solicited applicants "with $25,000 to invest" to lease and operate a newly erected Octane gasoline service station. Trevino had been able to accumulate approximately $32,000 for investment purposes as a result of a $25,000 inheritance and savings on the salary of $865 per week he earned as manager of a service station operated as a separate department of a J. C. Penney store. Most of this $32,000 was held in government bonds.

The regional sales manager for Octane was impressed with Trevino's personal and financial qualifications, and after several interviews, a lease agreement was signed. During one of these meetings the sales manager informed Trevino that the new station would be ready for occupancy on May 1 at a total investment cost of $300,000. Of this amount, $100,000 had already been paid for land, and a total of $200,000 would be spent for a building that would be "good for about 40 years." In discussing profit potential, the sales manager pointed out that Octane's national advertising program and the consumer appeal generated by the attractive station "will be worth at least $30,000 a year to you in consumer goodwill."

The lease agreement stipulated that Trevino pay a rental of $1,250 per month for the station plus $0.04 for each gallon of gasoline delivered to the station by Octane.[1] A sepa-

[1] The lease, which covered a period of one year beginning May 1, was automatically renewable unless notice of cancellation was given by either party at least 30 days prior to an anniversary date. The regional sales manager of the Octane Oil Company estimated that approximately 150,000 gallons of gasoline would be delivered to Trevino's Service Station during the first 12 months

---

[*] Copyright © by the President and Fellows of Harvard College. Harvard Business School case 114–010.

rate agreement was also signed whereby Octane agreed to sell and Trevino agreed to buy certain minimum quantities of gasoline and other automotive products for the service station operation.

As both an evidence of good faith and as a prepayment on certain obligations that he would shortly incur to Octane, Trevino was required to deposit $20,000 with Octane at the time the lease was signed. Trevino raised the cash for this deposit by liquidating government bonds. Octane used most of this money to defray certain obligations incurred by Trevino to the oil company prior to the opening of the new station. The deductions from the $20,000 deposit were applied as follows:

1. Opening inventories of gasoline, oil, grease, tires, batteries, and accessories..	$13,250
2. Rental fee ($1,250 flat rental for the month of May and $170 figured as $0.04 per gallon for the gasoline delivered in the opening inventory)................	1,420
3. Down payment (on Trevino's behalf) on equipment costing $12,875	2,575
	$17,245

The equipment, including floor and hydraulic jacks, a battery charger, tune-up sets, and oil and grease guns, became Trevino's property. A representative of the oil company stated that this equipment would last about five years. The unpaid, noninterest-bearing balance of $10,300 Trevino owed Octane for equipment was to be paid in five semiannual installments of $2,060 each. The first such payment was due November 1. The $2,755 remaining from the $20,000 originally deposited with Octane was returned to Trevino on April 30. He deposited this money in a special checking account he had set up for his service station venture.

Just before opening for business on May 1, Trevino converted some additional government bonds into $7,000 cash which he also placed in the service station checking account. Prior to May 1, he wrote the following checks: $1,650 for office furniture that had an expected life of 10 years, and $900 for a fire and casualty insurance policy providing coverage for a 1-year period beginning May 1. On April 30, Trevino transferred $200 from the service station checking account to the cash drawer at the service station. It was Trevino's intention to deposit in the bank all but $200 of the cash on hand at the close of each business day. The balance in the service station checking account at the start of business was, therefore, $7,005. In addition, Trevino had $2,700 in a savings account.

On May 1, the service station was opened for business. In his effort to build up a clientele, Trevino worked approximately 60 hours per week compared with 40 in his previous job. In addition, three other people were employed on either a full- or part-time basis. Trevino was reasonably well satisfied with the patronage he was able to build up during the first two months the station was open. At the end of June, however, he felt it would be desirable to take a more careful look at how he was making out in his new business venture. Trevino felt that he should record his progress and present position in a form that would be useful not only at the present time but also for comparative purposes in the future, perhaps at six-month intervals ending on June 30 and December 31.

Trevino maintained a simple recordkeeping system in which cash receipts and cash payments were itemized daily in a loose-leaf notebook. Separate pages were reserved for specific items in this notebook. During the months of May and June, the following cash receipts and payments had been recorded:

---

of operation. Subsequently, Trevino's records revealed that 27,000 gallons (including the initial inventory) were actually delivered during the first two months of operation.

Cash receipts (May and June):

Sales of gasoline, motor oil, tires batteries, and accessories and the revenue from lubrications, washing and polishing, and miscellaneous sales and services	$69,510
Rental from parking area on service station land	500
	$70,010

Cash payments (May and June):

Purchases (includes gasoline, motor oil, grease, tires, batteries, and accessories)	$44,694
Rent (does not include $1,420 deduction from $20,000 deposit)	2,018
Payroll (does not include any payments to Trevino)	9,450
Utilities	445
Advertising	690
Miscellaneous	355
Withdrawals by Trevino (June 1 and June 19)	6,750
	$64,402

The $500 listed in cash receipts as rental from parking area had been received from an adjacent business establishment that used one portion of the service station site as a parking space for certain of its employees. The rental received covered a period extending from May 15 to July 15.

In addition to the record of cash receipts and payments, a detailed listing was kept of the amounts of money that were due from, or owed to, other individuals or companies. An analysis of these records revealed that $143 was due the business for gas, oil, and car servicing from a wealthy widow friend of the Trevino family who preferred to deal on a credit basis. Also, on the evening of June 30, one of the employees completed waxing a car for a regular customer who was out of town and would be unable to call for his car until July 3. Trevino had quoted a price of $56 for this job. Trevino recalled that when he once worked at an automobile agency, he had heard that setting up a reserve for bad debts equal to 2 percent of all outstanding accounts was a good idea. Trevino had also jotted

down the fact that he and his family had used gas and oil from the service station worth $101 at retail prices, for which no payment had been made. Approximately $79 had been paid to Octane Oil Company for this merchandise.

A further summary of his records revealed the following unpaid bills resulting from operations in June:

Octane Oil Company for merchandise	$1,804
Rent payable (figured at $0.04 per gallon on most recent delivery of gasoline)	75
Utilities for the month of June	425
	$2,304

The service station's employees had last been paid on Saturday, June 28, for services rendered through Saturday evening. Wages earned on June 29 and 30 would amount to $232 in the following Saturday's payroll.

Trevino took a physical inventory on the evening of June 30, and he found gasoline, motor oil, grease, tires, batteries, and accessorizes on hand that had cost $10,018. While Trevino was figuring his inventory position, he compared his recorded gallonage sales of gasoline on hand at the end of the period against the volume of gasoline in the beginning inventory plus deliveries. In this manner, Trevino ascertained that shrinkage due to evaporation, temperature changes, waste, and other causes amounted to 302 gallons of gasoline that he estimated had cost $360.

Late in June, Trevino's married son realized that he would be unable, because of a prolonged illness, to make payment of $192 for interest expense and $800 for principal repayment on a $2,400 bank loan. Trevino, who had acted as cosigner on the note, would be obliged to meet this payment on July 1.

Questions

1. Prepare a May 1 and a June 30 balance sheet for Julio Trevino's service station and an income statement for the intervening period.

2. Has Julio Trevino's investment in the gasoline station been a good one for him? Has his return on his investment been greater or less than he would have received had he invested his funds at 15 percent elsewhere?

CASE 4–5 Olympic Lumber Company*

Jason Cornfield reread the letter that his new boss had given him that morning:

> As your agent, I am indeed happy that you agreed to insure Olympic Lumber's building and inventory with a $1,250,000 fire insurance policy. The policy, which was effective November 1, 1987, will cover the loss from the untimely fire, and will continue to provide coverage through the end of 1991. While I am of course sincerely sorry that you incurred the loss, I am sure you will agree that the expenditure of $50,000 for the policy was one of Olympic's more prudent decisions. Please call me when you have reconstructed your financial statements.

Jason Cornfield had been hired to replace Olympic's accountant, who had been fired for incompetence in early January 1988. Jason gazed out at the bleak winter day and reviewed the events that had led up to his predecessor's dismissal. Until early 1988, Jason had operated a small but successful accounting practice. Shortly after the first of the year, he had been offered the job of accountant for Olympic by Bill Woodstock, president of Olympic Lumber Company. Woodstock explained to him that the company had been doing very well, and in fact had had a record sales and profit performance in 1987. To celebrate the success, the company had hosted a party for its suppliers and customers on New Year's Eve. The guests became overly festive in their celebrations and began lighting firecrackers. Unfortunately, a skyrocket landed in the rough two-by-four inventory and burned Olympic's entire inventory and building. Because of the suddenness of the fire, all financial records had been lost.

Woodstock informed Jason that his accountant, Leonard Firebird, had been unable to reconstruct financial statements for the fiscal year that had just ended. He said, "Firebird was OK for the routine stuff, but this assignment, and the challenge of rebuilding Olympic, requires real creative talent. That's why I'm counting on you."

Investigating the background of Olympic, Cornfield learned that the company had been formed in early 1983 and that the building had been purchased and occupied on May 1 of that year. Cornfield next came across a letter to Woodstock from a major supplier, who wrote, "I certainly enjoyed your party and was sorry it ended so abruptly. I appreciated receiving the first installment on the note with which you financed your initial inventory purchase from us late last May. Since we agreed that you will make payments every six months, unless I hear otherwise, I will expect your second payment of $62,500 on June 1 plus the 12 percent per annum interest over the six-month period."

Cornfield next asked Woodstock if he had any records that would help him in his work. The latter searched his briefcase and finally found a balance sheet (Exhibit 1). Woodstock observed that expenditures for administrative salaries and licenses in 1987 had been a

* Reprinted from *Stanford Business Cases* with the permission of the publishers, Stanford University Graduate School of Business. © by the Board of Trustees of the Leland Stanford Junior University.

EXHIBIT 1

OLYMPIC LUMBER COMPANY
Balance Sheet
As of June 30, 1987

Assets

Cash and short-term investments........	$	51,639
Accounts receivable..................		266,465
Supplies............................		18,034
Inventory—lumber....................		363,124
Land...............................		110,000
Building.................. $600,000		
Less accumulated		
depreciation............... 90,000		510,000
Total assets.........................		$1,319,262

Liabilities

Accounts payable.....................	$	90,059
Accrued interest payable..............		2,500
Notes payable		250,000
Total liabilities..................		342,559

Owners' Equity

Capital stock........................		500,000
Retained earnings....................		476,703
Total owners' equity.............		976,703
Total liabilities and owners' equity		$1,319,262

---

third higher than their 1986 levels of $75,000 and $900, respectively. He commented that over the years freight expense had averaged $1,250 per month, that advertising had been 6 percent of sales, and selling expenses (including salespersons' compensation) had been 20 percent of sales. Utilities had been some 15 percent higher than the previous year's $3,600 total.

As Cornfield turned to leave, Woodstock remarked, "One more thing. I found a scrap of paper among the ashes, and it said, 'Closing entries to be made: Sales, DR 1,151,250; Supplies Expense, CR 10,263.' The rest was unintelligible. I don't know what that means but maybe it will be helpful to you."

The new accountant then learned that the company had had a physical inventory on December 31, and Cornfield called the auditors who informed him that the lumber inventory on that date had been $332,000. They were also able to supply him with a list of all of Olympic's customers and suppliers. Calling the suppliers, he learned that all of the monies previously owed them had been paid in cash (except for the note referred to above) and that a third of the inventory acquired over the last six months of the year was still owed on account. Cornfield next discovered that total purchases of inventory in the second half of 1987 had been $200,000 more than the amount of the June 30 inventory level. Then he found out that no supplies had been purchased during 1987.

After considerable pencil pushing, Cornfield was still unable to calculate his cash balance. He knew Woodstock was growing impatient for the statements and consequently was startled to see the latter charge brusquely into his cluttered cubicle and drop an envelope on the desk. Opening it, Cornfield realized to his relief that it was Olympic's bank statement, dated December 31, with a balance in cash and short-term investments of $64,820.

Cornfield's phone rang and he heard Woodstock's secretary ask him when he would complete the financial statements. He replied, "I realize my answer is due, and I will have the statements ready in a few minutes."

Question

Assuming that the fire took place early on January 1, 1988, prepare an income statement for the six months ended December 31, 1987, and a balance sheet as of December 31, 1987. (Ignore income taxes. Assume that the sales and supplies figures are for the last six months of 1987 only and that straight-line depreciation was used for the building.)

5

Revenue and
Monetary Assets

This and the next four chapters discuss more thoroughly certain balance sheet and income statement items that were treated in an introductory fashion in Chapters 2 and 3. This chapter discusses the two problems in revenue recognition: (1) *When*—in which accounting period—should revenue be recognized? and (2) *How much* revenue should be recognized? A closely related matter, the measurement of monetary assets, especially accounts receivable, is also discussed.

TIMING OF REVENUE RECOGNITION

Presumably, most activities in a company are intended to contribute to its profit-seeking objective. These activities may include a fairly long chain of events. Illustration 5–1 depicts this sequence, called the **operating cycle,** for a typical manufacturing firm. (The reader should consider how to modify the diagram for other types of businesses.) In accounting, revenue is recognized at a single point in this cycle. The basic reason for choosing a single point rather than attempting to measure the separate profit contribution of each part of the cycle stems from the criterion of *objectivity*. There is no objective way of measuring the amount of profit that is earned in each step of the operating cycle.

ILLUSTRATION 5–1
THE BUSINESS OPERATING CYCLE

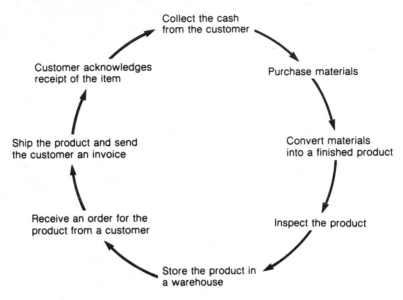

Basic Recognition Criteria

The conservatism concept and the realization concept, described in Chapter 3, suggest the following revenue recognition criteria: Revenue should be recognized in the earliest period in which (1) the entity has *substantially performed* what is required in order to earn income and (2) the amount of income can be *reliably measured.*

The criteria are expressed in terms of earning and measuring income rather than revenue because both the revenue and expense components of a transaction need to be reliably measurable in order to recognize the revenue. Because of the matching concept, both components are recognized in the same period, and thus income is recognized. Applications of this general idea to certain types of revenues are summarized in Illustration 5–2 and discussed in more detail below.

As this and later chapters will increasingly make clear, the measurement of a period's income is an approximation because it incorporates estimates of such things as bad debts, future warranty costs, useful lives of fixed assets, and other items. Although GAAP provides guidance that enhances objectivity, the fact inevitably remains that the desire to measure the operating performance of an entity for some relatively short period of time results in an estimate, not a precise determination, of that period's income.

Delivery Method

The typical business earns revenue by selling goods or services to customers. The business has performed substantially what is required in

ILLUSTRATION 5–2
TIMING OF REVENUE RECOGNITION

Event	Conditions for Revenue Recognition at This Time	Revenue Recognition Method
1. Sales order received	Never	None
2. Deposit or advance payment received	Never	None
3. Goods being produced	Certain long-term contracts	Percentage of completion
4. Production completed; goods stored	Precious metals; certain agricultural products	Production
5. Goods shipped or services provided	Usually	Delivery
6. Customer pays account receivable	Collection is uncertain	Installment

order to earn income when it delivers these goods or provides these services to customers. Thus, the most common approach, called the **delivery method,** is to recognize the revenue in the period in which goods are delivered or services are provided.

Revenues for goods are *not* recognized when sales orders are received. Even though in some businesses the amount of income that will be earned can be reliably estimated at that time, there has been no performance until the goods have been shipped. For services, providing the service is the act of performance. Revenues from renting hotel rooms are recognized each day the room is rented. Revenues from maintenance contracts are recognized in each month covered by the contract. Revenue from repairing an automobile is recognized when the repairs have been completed (not when the repairs are only partially completed because the service is to provide a completed repair job).

In the usual situation the amount of income that will be earned can be reliably estimated when goods are delivered or services provided. The test of the marketplace, a price agreed to by the customer minus the appropriate cost of sales, is usually excellent evidence of the amount of income earned. Even though some customers may not pay their bills, allowances can be made for this in estimating the amount of revenue.

When goods are delivered, title usually is transferred from the seller to the buyer, but transfer of title is *not* a necessary condition for revenue recognition. When goods are sold on the installment credit basis, for example, the buyer does not have a clear title until the installment payments have been completed. (Automobile sales are a common example.) If, however, there is a reasonable certainty that these payments will be made, revenue is recognized at the time of delivery.

Consignment Shipments. In a consignment shipment the supplier, or **consignor,** ships goods to the **consignee,** who attempts to sell them. The consignor retains title to the goods until they are sold. The consignee can return any unsold goods to the consignor. In these circumstances performance has not been substantially completed until the goods are sold by the consignee. Thus, the consignor does not recognize revenue until that time.[1] A consignment shipment therefore represents only the movement of the supplier's asset, inventory, from one place to another. The amount of merchandise out on consignment can be shown by a journal entry, at cost:

dr.	Inventory on Consignment	1,000	
cr.	Merchandise Inventory		1,000

In the period in which these goods are sold by the consignee, the effect on the accounts of the consignor would be as in the following entries:

dr.	Cost of Goods Sold	1,000	
cr.	Inventory on Consignment		1,000
	To record the cost of consigned goods sold.		
dr.	Accounts Receivable	1,400	
cr.	Sales Revenue		1,400
	To record the consignor's sales value.		

Franchises.   Some companies, called **franchisors,** sell franchises that permit the **franchisee** to use a well-known name (e.g., Taco Bell, Days Inn, Avis). The franchisor may also agree to provide advice and other services in return for the franchise fee. A franchisor recognizes revenue during the period in which it provides the services, rather than when the fee is received. In particular, a franchisor often receives a large initial fee for which it agrees to provide site selection, personnel training, advice on equipment selection, and other services. It cannot recognize revenue until these services have been provided; normally, this is after the franchisee commences operations.[2]

Percentage-of-Completion Method

High-rise buildings, bridges, aircraft, ships, space exploration hardware, and certain other items involve a design/development and construction/production period that extends over several years. Such projects are performed under contracts in which the customer provides the product specifications. The contract also stipulates either (1) predetermined amounts the customer must pay at various points during the project, called a **fixed-price contract** or (2) some sort of formula that will determine customer payments as a function of actual project costs plus a reasonable profit, called a **cost-reimbursement contract.**

---

[1]"Revenue Recognition When Right of Return Exists," *FASB Statement No. 48* (June 1981). This *Statement* also describes circumstances when revenue may not be recognized even if title to the goods has passed from the consignor to the consignee.

[2]"Accounting for Franchise Fee Revenue," *FASB Statement No. 45* (March 1981).

ILLUSTRATION 5–3
LONG-TERM CONTRACT ACCOUNTING METHODS

Year	Customer Payments Received	Project Costs Incurred	Year-End Percent Complete	Completed-Contract Method			Percentage-of-Completion Method		
				Revenues	Expenses	Income	Revenues*	Expenses	Income
1....	$120,000	$160,000	20	$ 0	$ 0	0	$180,000	$160,000	$ 20,000
2....	410,000	400,000	70	0	0	0	450,000	400,000	50,000
3....	370,000	240,000	100	900,000	800,000	100,000	270,000	240,000	30,000
Total..	$900,000	$800,000		$900,000	$800,000	$100,000	$900,000	$800,000	$100,000

*This amount for a year is the percent of completion *accomplished that year* times total project revenues. In this example, 20 percent, 50 percent, and 30 percent of the work was accomplished in years 1, 2, and 3, respectively.

During each accounting period in which the contractor works on the contract, there has been performance. If the income earned by the work done in the period can be reliably estimated, then revenue is appropriately recognized in each such period. This method of revenue recognition is called the **percentage-of-completion method** because the amount of revenue is related to the percentage of the total project work that was performed in the period.

If the amount of income earned in a period cannot be reliably estimated, then the revenue is recognized only when the project has been completed. This is the **completed-contract method.** Costs incurred on the project are held as an asset, Contract Work in Progress, until the period in which revenue is recognized.[3]

On a cost-reimbursement contract, the amount of income earned in each period often can be reliably estimated. If the owner agrees to pay cost plus 10 percent and if the work proceeds as planned, the revenue is 110 percent of the costs incurred in the period. A fixed-price contract usually specifies how the satisfactory completion of each phase of the project is to be determined; such points in the project are called *milestones*. If good project plans exist, the number of milestones reached enables the contractor to reliably estimate the percent complete and hence the revenue earned on the contract.

Illustration 5–3 shows the application of these two methods to a three-year project. Note that both methods report the same total project income over the entire three-year period, but only the percentage-of-completion method allocates this total to each of the three years. Also note that the customer payments (cash inflows) are irrelevant in determining the amount of revenue recognized each year under either method.[4]

---

[3]"Contractor Accounting," *FASB Statement No. 56* (February 1982).
[4]For income tax accounting purposes, most long-term contracts entered into after July 10, 1989, must be accounted for under the percentage-of-completion method.

Production Method

For certain grains and other crops the government sets price supports and assures the farmer that the products can be sold for at least these prices. The minimum amount of income that will be earned can therefore be reliably measured as soon as the crops have been harvested, even though they have not been sold at that time. Furthermore, the farmer's performance has been substantially completed. In these circumstances a case can be made for recognizing revenue at the time of harvest. This **production method** is permitted but not required by generally accepted accounting principles. GAAP also permits revenue recognition when gold, silver, and similar precious metals have been produced from the mine, even though the metals have not yet been sold. In recent years, however, fluctuations in the sales value of these metals have been large, and the rationale for the production method is therefore weaker. Relatively few mining companies now use the production method.

Installment Method

Many retail stores sell merchandise on an installment basis, in which the customer pays a certain amount per week or per month. If the customers are good credit risks, then the payments are likely to be received and the store can reliably measure its income at the time the sale is made. In other circumstances a significant number of customers may not complete their payments, and the merchandise is repossessed (if it can be located).

In these latter circumstances the amount of income that is realized cannot be reliably measured at the time the sale is made, so revenue is not recorded at that time. Instead, revenue is recognized when the installment payments are received. In the pure **installment method,** the installment payment is counted as revenue, and a proportional part of the cost of sales is counted as a cost in the same period.

In a more conservative variation, the **cost-recovery method,** cost of sales is recorded at an amount equal to the installment payment. The result is that no income is reported until the installment payments have recouped the total cost of sales.

The FASB states that sales revenue should "ordinarily" be recognized when the sale is made and that an installment method is acceptable only when "the circumstances are such that the collection of the sales price is not reasonably assured."[5]

The effect of the installment method is to postpone the recognition of revenue and income to later periods as compared with the delivery method. If a company wants to report as much income as it legitimately can in the current period, it will therefore prefer to report in its income statement the full amount of the transaction at the time of sale. If it wants to postpone the recognition of taxable income for income tax purposes, it will use the installment method in calculating its taxable income.

---

[5] *APB Opinion No. 10* (December 1966), par. 12.

Example. A jeweler sells a watch in 1993 for $400, and the customer agrees to make payments totaling $200 in 1993 and $200 in 1994. (The customer would ordinarily pay interest in addition to the payments for the watch itself, but this is a separate revenue item that is disregarded here.) The watch cost the jeweler $220. Alternative ways of accounting for this transaction are as follows:

	Effect on Income Statements			
	Delivery Method		*Installment Method*	
	1993	*1994*	*1993*	*1994*
Sales revenue	$400	$0	$200	$200
Cost of goods sold	220	0	110	110
Gross margin	$180	$0	$ 90	$ 90

Although the total gross margin for the transaction is the same under either method, the jeweler can report a lower gross margin and hence a lower taxable income for 1993 by using the installment method.[6]

Real Estate Sales. Some developers sell land to customers who make a small down payment and pay the balance of the purchase price over a number of years. In some cases the buyer later becomes disenchanted with the deal or becomes unable to continue with the payments. Because of the consequent uncertainty as to the amount of income that will be realized, three conditions must be met in order for revenue to be recognized: (1) the period of cancellation of the contract with a refund to the buyer has expired; (2) the buyer has made cumulative payments equal to at least 10 percent of the purchase price; *and* (3) the seller has completed improvements (roads, utility connections, and so on) or is making progress on these improvements and is clearly capable of eventually completing them. If the improvements have been completed and the receivable from the buyer is probably collectible, then the full sales price is recognized as revenue, and appropriate costs are matched against the revenue. If the improvements are in progress, the percentage-of-completion method is used to recognize the revenue. If there is doubt as to the collectibility of the receivables, the installment method is used. If any of the three above-mentioned criteria for revenue recognition is not met, the seller records any payments received as a liability, deposits on land sales.[7]

Similar but more complex criteria govern the recognition of revenue on the sale of land for commercial use (office buildings, hotels, and other commercial property) and residential property. The required down payments range from 5 percent to 25 percent, depending on the nature of the property, and certain other requirements must be met.[8]

---

[6]Income tax regulations do not permit the use of the installment method for sales on "revolving credit" accounts. These are *charge accounts* where a certain minimum percentage of the account balance must be paid each month, as opposed to installment sales *contracts,* which are related to a specific purchase such as a major appliance.

[7]"Accounting for Sales of Real Estate," *FASB Statement No. 66* (October 1982).

[8]Ibid.

AMOUNT OF REVENUE RECOGNIZED

In Chapter 3 we stated that the amount recorded as revenue is the amount that customers are reasonably certain to pay. This concept requires that certain adjustments be made to the gross sales value of the goods or services sold. These adjustments are discussed in this section.

Bad Debts

The main source of revenue in many businesses is the sale of goods or services to customers on credit, or "on account." These sales may involve a single payment or they may involve a series of payments, as in the installment sales transactions discussed above. They give rise to the sales revenue and also to the asset, accounts receivable. These accounts, in turn, give rise to losses when customers do not pay the amounts they owe.

Assume that Essel Company began operations in 1992 and that the company made sales of $262,250, all on credit, during the year. In the interest of simplicity, further assume that no money had been received from customers in 1992. The records made of these transactions would result in accounts receivable of $262,250 and sales revenue of $262,250. It would be correct to report $262,250 as an asset on the balance sheet as of the end of 1992 and $262,250 as sales revenue on the income statement for 1992 if, *but only if,* it is believed that all customers eventually will pay the full amount of their obligations to Essel Company. Unfortunately, some of these customers may never pay their bills. If they do not, their accounts become **bad debts.**

Consider first the extreme case. A person makes a purchase with no intention of paying for it and in fact does not pay for it. In this case the company has not actually made a sale at all. No revenue was actually earned, and nothing valuable was added to the asset, accounts receivable, as a result of this transaction. If this event were recorded as an increase in Sales Revenue and as an increase in Accounts Receivable, both of these accounts would be overstated, and income for the period and owners' equity at the end of the period also would be overstated.

In the more usual bad debt situation, the customer fully intends to pay but for one reason or another never actually makes payment. The effect is the same as that in the extreme case. Such a sale is also recorded initially by debiting Accounts Receivable and crediting Sales Revenue at the sales value of the customer's purchase. In these situations another entry must be made to show that the amount debited to Accounts Receivable does not represent the amount of the additional asset and that owners' equity has not in fact increased by the amount of the sale.

Accounting Recognition of Bad Debts. When a company makes a sale, the fact that the customer will never pay the bill is, of course, not known; otherwise, the sale would not have been made. Even at the end of the accounting period, the company may not know specifically *which* of its accounts receivable will never be collected. An estimate of the amount of bad debts can nevertheless be made, and the accounting records are adjusted at the end of each accounting period to reflect this estimate.

One way of making this adjustment is by a **direct write-off method.** Accounts that are believed to be uncollectible are simply eliminated from the records by subtracting the amount of the bad debt from Accounts Receivable and showing the same amount as an expense item on the income statement. The entry to accomplish this would be as follows:

```
dr.   Bad Debt Expense.............................. 200
   cr.    Accounts Receivable ........................       200
```

The direct write-off method, however, requires that the specific uncollectible accounts be identified, whereas this usually is not possible.

With an alternative procedure, the **allowance method,** the *total* amount of uncollectible accounts is estimated. This estimated amount is shown as a deduction from accounts receivable on the balance sheet and as an expense on the income statement. Instead of reducing the accounts receivable amount directly, the estimate is often shown as a separate contra asset number on the balance sheet so that the reader can observe both the total amount owed by customers and that portion of the amount that the company believes will not be collected.[9]

Accounts Involved. The balance sheet contra asset account for Accounts Receivable is called **Allowance for Doubtful** (or **Uncollectible**) **Accounts.** (In a bank, the title is Allowance for Uncollectible Loans.) At one time, it was often labeled Reserve for Bad Debts, but this caused confusion since the word *reserve* connotes to many people that a sum of money has been set aside and such is not the case. The Allowance for Doubtful Accounts is in the nature of a decrease in Accounts Receivable for specific, *but as yet unknown,* customers. The corresponding income statement account is called **Bad Debt Expense.**

Making the Estimate. In those situations in which using the direct write-off method is not feasible, any one of several methods may be used to estimate the amount of bad debt expense in an accounting period. The most common method is to estimate bad debt expense as a percentage of *credit* sales. (The percentage is applied to credit sales since, of course, cash sales do not result in bad debts.) The percentage used depends in part on past experience and in part on management's judgment as to whether past experience reflects the current situation. The allowance for doubtful accounts should be sufficient at all times to absorb the accounts that prove to be uncollectible. Because business conditions fluctuate, the amount may turn out to be too large in some periods and too small in others. In practice, because of the concept of conservatism, it is common to find that the

---

[9]Income tax regulations do not permit use of the allowance method (except by small banks and thrift institutions for loans receivable). Rather, the direct write-off method must be used for each specific account that becomes partially or totally worthless.

ILLUSTRATION 5–4
AGING SCHEDULE FOR ESTIMATING BAD DEBTS

Status as of December 31, 1992	Amount Outstanding	Estimated Percent Uncollectible	Allowance for Doubtful Accounts
Current.	$207,605	1	$2,076
Overdue:			
Less than 1 month	26,003	1	260
1 up to 2 months.	10,228	5	511
2 up to 3 months.	7,685	10	769
3 up to 6 months.	3,876	20	775
6 months and over	6,853	40	2,741
Total	$262,250		$7,132

allowance is too large rather than too small. On the other hand, there have been some cases in which the allowance for doubtful accounts turned out to be woefully inadequate.

Aging Accounts Receivable. Sometimes different percentages are applied to accounts outstanding for various lengths of time. This requires the preparation of an **aging schedule,** which is also a useful device for analyzing the quality of the asset, accounts receivable. An example for Essel Company is shown in Illustration 5–4.

The Adjusting Entry. Once the amount of the allowance has been determined, it is recorded as one of the adjusting entries made at the end of the accounting period. If Essel Company management estimated the allowance for doubtful accounts on the basis of the above aging schedule, the entry would be:

dr.	Bad Debt Expense.	7,132	
cr.	Allowance for Doubtful Accounts		7,132

The accounts receivable section of the December 31, 1992, balance sheet would then appear as follows:

Accounts receivable.	$262,250
Less: Allowance for doubtful accounts.	7,132
Accounts receivable, net	$255,118

The 1992 income statement would show $7,132 of bad debt expense.

The contra asset account, Allowance for Doubtful Accounts, usually will have a balance even before the adjusting entry is made. In these circumstances the amount reported as bad debt expense on the income statement will be different from the amount reported as allowance for doubtful accounts on the balance sheet. (In the Essel Company example just given, this did not occur because the company was organized in 1992, and the above entry was the first one made to Allowance for Doubtful Accounts.)

Write-Off of an Uncollectible Account. When a company decides that a specific customer is never going to pay the amount owed, Accounts Receivable is reduced by the amount owed and a corresponding reduction is made in the Allowance for Doubtful Accounts. This entry has *no effect* on Bad Debt Expense or on income of the period in which the account is written off.

Example. If sometime in 1993 the Essel Company decided that James Johnson was never going to pay his bill of $250, the following entry would be made:

    dr. Allowance for Doubtful Accounts............... 250
        cr. Accounts Receivable.........................   250

A balance sheet prepared immediately after this transaction had been recorded (assuming no other changes since December 31, 1992) would appear as follows:

Accounts receivable..................................	$262,000
Less: Allowance for doubtful accounts.................	6,882
Accounts receivable, net	$255,118

Note that the *net* amount of accounts receivable is unchanged by this write-off.

Collection of a Bad Debt Written Off. If, by some unexpected stroke of good fortune, James Johnson should subsequently pay all or part of the amount he owed, Cash would be increased (i.e., debited) and a corresponding credit would be recorded, usually to add back the amount to Allowance for Doubtful Accounts on the balance sheet.

Sales Discounts

As mentioned in Chapter 3, sales revenue is recorded at not more than the sales value of the actual transaction. Trade discounts and other deductions that may be made from list or catalog prices are disregarded.

Some businesses offer a so-called **cash discount** to induce customers to pay bills quickly. For example, if a business sells goods on terms of "2/10, n/30," it permits customers to deduct 2 percent from the invoice amount if they pay within 10 days; otherwise, the full (net) amount is due within 30 days.[10] The cash discount can be recorded in any of three ways:

---

[10]This is a powerful inducement because by forgoing the 2 percent the customer has the use of the money only for an additional 20 days. Since there are about 18 20-day periods in a year, this amounts to an annual interest rate of 18 * 2 percent = 36 percent.

1. The discount can be recorded as a reduction from gross sales.

2. The discount can be recorded as an expense of the period.

3. Sales revenue can be initially recorded at the *net* amount after deduction of the discount. Amounts received from customers who do *not* take the discount would then be recorded as additional revenue. Thus, a $1,000 sale subject to a 2 percent cash discount would be recorded at the time of sale as:

```
dr.   Accounts Receivable ...........................   980
    cr.    Sales Revenue..............................        980
```

If the discount were not taken by the customer, the entry upon receipt of the customer's payment would be:

```
dr.   Cash.........................................   1,000
    cr.    Discounts Not Taken ......................         20
           Accounts Receivable........................        980
```

Credit Card Sales

Millions of retailers and service establishments who sell on credit have contracted with an outside agency to handle some or all of their accounts receivable. There are two types of these credit card plans.

The first type is a bank plan, called MasterCard or Visa. In this plan, merchants send their credit slips to the bank along with other bank deposits. The bank arranges to have the charges collected from the customers. If a customer's account is with another bank, the sales slip is sent to that bank for collection. So far as the merchant is concerned, this type of transaction is not a credit sale. No accounts receivable appear in the merchant's accounts. The sales slip is the same as cash and is credited to the merchant's account by the bank as soon as it is deposited, just like a check. The only difference between a credit card sales slip and a check is that in the former case the bank deducts a fee for the service of handling the accounts receivable paperwork and assuming the risk of bad debts. This fee is in the nature of a sales discount and is recorded as such in the merchant's accounts thus:

```
dr.   Cash..........................................   970
           Sales Discount (Credit Cards)..................   30
    cr.    Sales Revenue..............................        1,000
```

In the other type of plan, the merchant sends the sales slips to a credit card company and receives reimbursement from this company within 30 days or whatever period is agreed upon. American Express and Discover are examples. Because of the interval that elapses between the submission of sales slips and the receipt of cash, in this plan the merchant *does* have accounts receivable. These receivables are due the merchant from the credit card company, not from the merchant's customers. There are no bad debts, however, because the credit card company assumes the risk of loss, provided the merchant follows instructions in making out and approving the sales slip. When the slips are sent in, the entry is:

```
dr.   Accounts Receivable .......................... 970
        Sales Discount (Credit Cards) .................. 30
      cr.   Sales Revenue.............................         1,000
```

When cash is received from the credit card company, Cash is debited and Accounts Receivable is credited.

Sales Returns and Allowances

When customers are dissatisfied with goods or services sold to them, the company may permit them to return the goods for full credit, or it may refund part or all of the sales price. In these circumstances, the amount originally recorded as revenue turns out to be an overstatement of the true amount of the sale. Sales returns and allowances are conceptually similar to bad debts.

Some companies treat sales returns and allowances in the same way that they treat bad debt expense. They estimate the percentage of revenues that will eventually result in returns and allowances, and set up an account for this amount. The offsetting credit is to a liability account, thus:

```
dr.  Sales Returns and Allowances .................. 1,000
     cr.   Provision for Returns and Allowances .......        1,000
```

The Sales Returns and Allowances account is analogous to Bad Debt Expense. The Provision for Returns and Allowances account is analogous to Allowance for Doubtful Accounts, except the former is treated as a liability rather than as a contra asset. When goods are returned or allowances made, Provision for Returns and Allowances is debited; the credit is to the customer's account receivable or to Cash (if a refund is made).

Other companies do not attempt to estimate the amount of returns and allowances associated with sales revenue of the current period. Instead, they simply debit Sales Returns and Allowances whenever a sales return or allowance occurs, with an offsetting credit to Accounts Receivable (or to Cash, if the returned goods had already been paid for). When this practice is followed, the sales returns and allowances deducted from revenue of a period do not relate to the actual goods included in the sales revenue of that period. The justification for this apparent departure from the matching concept is that the amounts are difficult to estimate in advance, are likely to be relatively constant from one period to the next, and are relatively small. Under these circumstances, the practice is consistent with the materiality concept.

Revenue Adjustment versus Expense

The need for recognizing bad debts, sales discounts, and sales returns and allowances arises because of one aspect of the realization concept— namely, that revenues should be reported at the amount that is reasonably certain to be collected. This concept would seem to require that these amounts be subtracted from gross revenues in order to determine the net revenue of the period. The effect of some of the practices described above, however, is to report the amounts as expenses rather than as adjustments to revenues.

Whether companies report these amounts as expenses or as adjustments to revenues, the effect on income is exactly the same. The difference between the two methods is in the way they affect revenue and gross margin. The consistency concept requires that a company follow the same method from one year to the next; thus, comparisons within a company are not affected by these differences in practice. They may have a significant effect when the income statements of companies that use different methods are being compared, however.

> **Example.** Following are income statements for Company A, which treats the items of the type discussed in this section as adjustments to revenue, and Company B, which treats them as expenses. Otherwise, the firms are identical.

Income Statements

(000s)

	Company A		Company B	
	Amount	*Percent*	*Amount*	*Percent*
Gross sales............................	$1,000	110.0	$1,000	100.0
Less: Sales discounts....................	20	2.2	0	
Bad debts........................	40	4.4	0	
Returns	30	3.3	0	
Net sales...............................	910	100.0	1,000	100.0
Cost of sales...........................	600	65.9	600	60.0
Gross margin	310	34.1	400	40.0
Other expenses	210	23.1	210	21.0
Discounts, bad debts, returns.............	0		90	9.0
Income................................	$ 100	11.1	$ 100	10.0

Note the differences between the two income statements, not only in the dollar amounts of net sales and gross margin but also, more importantly, in the percentages. (In reporting percentage relationships on an income statement, net sales is customarily taken as 100 percent, and the percentages for other items are calculated by dividing each by the amount of net sales.) Various combinations of these alternatives would produce still different amounts and percentages.

Warranty Costs

Companies usually have an obligation to repair or replace defective goods. This obligation arises either because it is an explicit part of the sales contract or because there is an implicit legal doctrine that says that customers have a right to receive satisfactory products. In either case the obligation is called a **warranty.**

If it is likely that a material amount of costs will be incurred in future periods in replacing or repairing goods sold in the current period, both the conservatism and matching concepts require that income in the current period be adjusted accordingly.[11] The amount of the adjustment is usually estimated as a percentage of sales revenue. This adjustment is recorded as an expense with an entry such as the following:

dr.   Estimated Warranty Expense 2,000
     cr.   Allowance for Warranties   2,000

When costs are incurred in the future in repairing or replacing the goods, Allowance for Warranties, a liability account, is debited, and Cash, Parts Inventory, or some other balance sheet account is credited. Analogous to the write-off of an uncollectible receivable, this warranty repair or replacement transaction affects neither the estimated warranty expense nor the income of the period in which it takes place.

Conceptually, Estimated Warranty Expense is an upward adjustment of Cost of Sales rather than a downward adjustment of Sales Revenue. We nevertheless have included the topic here because the accounting procedures for warranty costs are so similar to those for bad debts and sales returns and allowances. Both types of adjustment reduce the period's reported income.

Interest Revenue

A principal source of revenue to a bank or other lending institution is interest on the money that it lends.[12] Industrial and commercial companies also may earn interest revenue. Under the realization concept the amount of revenue for a period is the amount the lender earned on the money the borrower had available for use during that period. Accounting for this amount depends on whether interest is paid at **maturity**—that is, when the loan is repaid—or whether it is in effect paid when the money is borrowed. In the latter case, the loan is said to be **discounted.** Examples of each are given below.

Example. *Interest Paid at Maturity.* On September 1, 1993, a bank loaned $10,000 for one year at 9 percent interest, the interest and principal to be paid on August 31, 1994. The bank's entry on September 1, 1993, is:

dr.   Loans Receivable 10,000
     cr.   Cash   10,000

On December 31, 1993, an adjusting entry is made to record the fact that interest for one-third of a year, $300, was earned in 1993:

---

[11]Income tax regulations do not permit recognizing warranty costs until they are actually incurred.

[12]In practice this amount is often called interest *income* rather than interest *revenue.* Conceptually, it is revenue.

```
dr.   Interest Receivable ........................... 300
     cr.   Interest Revenue............................           300
```

On August 31, 1994, when the loan is repaid, the entry is:

```
dr.   Cash......................................... 10,900
     cr.   Loans Receivable...........................         10,000
           Interest Receivable.........................            300
           Interest Revenue...........................            600
```

Corresponding entries are made on the books of the borrower to record interest expense.

Example. *Discounted Loan.* On September 1, 1993, a bank loaned $10,000 for one year at 9 percent discounted. The borrower received $10,000 less the $900 prepaid interest, or $9,100.[13] On that day the bank has a liability of $900 because it has not yet performed the service of permitting the use of the money. The bank's entry on September 1, 1993, is:

```
dr.   Loans Receivable ........................... 10,000
     cr.   Cash ...................................          9,100
           Unearned Interest Revenue ................           900
```

The borrower records a $9,100 increase in Cash, a $900 increase in Prepaid Interest Expense, and a $10,000 increase in Notes Payablo.

On December 31, 1993, the bank makes an adjusting entry to record the fact that $300 interest (one-third of a year) was earned in 1993 and is therefore no longer a liability:

```
dr.   Unearned Interest Revenue .................... 300
     cr.   Interest Revenue...........................           300
```

On August 31, 1994, when the loan is repaid, the entry is:

```
dr.   Cash......................................... 10,000
     cr.   Loans Receivable...........................         10,000
```

After repayment by the borrower, an adjusting entry is also made by the bank to record the fact that $600 interest (two-thirds of a year) was earned in 1994:

```
dr.   Unearned Interest Revenue .................... 600
     cr.   Interest Revenue...........................           600
```

Interest Component of a Sale. When buyers purchase goods on an installment plan, they pay both for the goods themselves and for the interest that the seller charges on the amount of the unpaid balance. Revenue from the sales value of the goods should be recorded separately from interest revenue. In most sales to consumers, this separation is easy to recognize since federal regulations require that the amount of interest be specified in the sales contract. Although the goods' sales value may be recognized at the time of the sale (unless the installment method is used), the interest revenue is recognized in the period or periods in which it is earned; that is, it is spread over the life of the installment contract.

---

[13]The *effective* interest rate on this loan is more than 9 percent, since the borrower pays $900 *interest* for the use of only $9,100 for one year.

In some sales agreements the buyer gives a note promising to pay several months or even years in the future; but the note does not explicitly indicate that an interest charge is involved. Since any rational merchant expects to receive more money for a sale that is not completed for many months in the future than for a cash sale, it is apparent that the amount of the note includes both the sales value of the goods and an interest charge. In recording the transaction these two components must be shown separately. If the full amount of the note were recognized as revenue in the period in which the transaction took place, revenue for that period would be overstated by the amount of the interest component. The interest implicit in such a transaction is calculated by applying the going rate of interest for transactions of this general type.[14] The same principle is used for notes that state a rate of interest significantly below the going rate.

> **Example.** On September 1, 1993, a customer purchased a piece of equipment and gave in payment a note promising to pay $10,000 one year later, with no interest stated. The going rate of interest was 8 percent. The entry on September 1, 1993, would be:

> dr. Notes Receivable............................... 10,000
>   cr.   Sales Revenue...............................   9,259
>   Unearned Interest Revenue.................   741

> The adjusting entry on December 31, 1993, and the entry recording payment of the note on August 31, 1994, would be similar to those given above for a discounted loan.

MONETARY ASSETS

Monetary assets are money or claims to receive fixed sums of money (e.g., accounts receivable or notes receivable). By contrast, most **nonmonetary assets** are items that will be used in the future in the production and sale of goods and services. No separate classification for monetary assets appears on the balance sheet. The traditional distinction on the balance sheet is between current assets and noncurrent assets. The reason for calling attention to the distinction between monetary and nonmonetary assets is that the concepts governing the amounts at which they appear on the balance sheet differ for these two categories.

Difference in Reporting Monetary and Nonmonetary Assets

In general and with the notable exception of inventories (discussed in Chapter 6), *nonmonetary* assets appear on the balance sheet at *unexpired cost*. When acquired, they were recorded at cost. The amount shown on the balance sheet at any time thereafter is the amount not yet written off as an expense. If a building was acquired in 1978 at a cost of $1 million and if

---

[14]"Interest on Receivables and Payables," *APB Opinion No. 21* (August 1971), specifies the details as to how the rate of interest is determined. The interest revenue amount is found by using present value techniques described in Chapter 8, *not* by discounting the face amount of the note.

$375,000 of its cost has been written off as depreciation expense in the intervening 15 years, the balance sheet for December 31, 1993, will report the asset amount of this building at $625,000, *regardless* of its market value at that time.

For *monetary* assets the idea of unexpired cost is not appropriate. As we have seen above, the accounts receivable item is reported at its *estimated realizable value.* This is the effect of the adjustment for the estimated amount of bad debts included in the accounts receivable. Cash, of course, is reported at its face amount, whether on hand or deposited in banks.

Cash

Cash consists of funds that are immediately available for disbursement. Cash is usually held in checking accounts on which little or no interest is earned. If an entity has a temporary excess of cash, it may loan the excess to a bank and receive interest on it. The evidence of such a loan is called a **certificate of deposit.** A certificate of deposit has a maturity date, and a penalty is involved if the entity cashes it prior to that date. Therefore, these funds are not as liquid as cash in a checking account. Some companies include certificates of deposit in the amount reported for cash, whereas other companies disclose separately an amount for these certificates.

Receivables

The **accounts receivable** discussed in the preceding section were amounts due from customers. For nonfinancial institutions these are often called **trade receivables.** As already explained, financial institutions have loans receivable and interest receivable. Also, an entity may advance funds to employees for various reasons, a principal one being to provide for travel expenses. Such receivables are reported separately from trade receivables in an account with a title such as Due from Employees.

Marketable Securities

If an entity has a temporary excess of cash, rather than—or in addition to—investing it in certificates of deposit, the entity may invest it in **marketable securities.** Marketable securities are of several types. **Commercial paper** is a colloquial name for short-term, interest-bearing promissory notes issued by large companies with high credit ratings and a temporary need for more cash. **Treasury bills** are short-term obligations of the U.S. Treasury; that is, the investor in a Treasury bill is making a short-term loan to the federal government. Stocks of companies as well as bonds of companies and government entities are also marketable securities if they are, in fact, marketable—that is, if they can be readily sold.

Most companies report marketable securities as a separate line on the balance sheet, some of them preferring the caption "temporary investments." Some companies include certificates of deposit in the marketable securities or investments total rather than as a separate item or as a part of cash. Capital stock of other companies held for the purpose of exercising some control over those companies, or stocks and bonds not traded on a securities market, are reported as **investments** rather than as marketable securities. (Investments are discussed in Chapter 12.)

Security Categories. Because of the short-term nature of most marketable securities, their original cost is approximately equal to their market value as of the balance sheet date. Thus, until recently, most companies reported the total of these securities at cost and explained parenthetically on the balance sheet or in a note that "cost approximates market."[15] However, *FASB Statement No. 115*[16] sets out explicit rules for the balance sheet valuation of marketable securities. Application of the rules involves classifying such securities into three categories:

1. **Held-to-maturity securities** are debt securities that the entity intends to hold to maturity. They are reported on the balance sheet at cost.

2. **Trading securities** are debt and equity securities that are held for current resale. They are reported at market value, with any unrealized gains or losses of the period included in the calculation of the period's income. The entry for an unrealized gain of $5,000 would be:

   ```
   dr.   Marketable Securities..........................  5,000
      cr.    Gain on Marketable Securities ..............           5,000
   ```

   This would increase the period's pretax income by $5,000. An analogous entry would be made for a loss, which would decrease the period's reported income.

3. **Available-for-sale securities** are debt and equity securities that do not fit either of the other two categories. They are reported at market value, and any unrealized gains (or losses) of the period are directly credited (or debited) to an owner's equity account; that is, the write-up (or write-down) does not "flow through" the income statement as it does in the case of trading securities.

These rules, which apply both to financial institutions and other companies, took effect in 1994.

ANALYSIS OF MONETARY ASSETS

Some relationships that are helpful in analyzing a company's monetary assets are described below. They include the current ratio, the acid-test

---

[15]Of the companies' statements analyzed in the AICPA's *Accounting Trends & Techniques* (1993), 68 percent reported that "cost approximates market value."

[16]"Accounting for Certain Investments in Debt and Equity Securities," *FASB Statement No. 115* (May 1993).

ILLUSTRATION 5–5
CONDENSED FINANCIAL STATEMENTS

KELLOGG COMPANY
Balance Sheet
As of December 31, 1993
(millions)

Assets

Current assets:	
Cash and temporary investments	$ 98.1
Accounts receivable (less allowances)	536.8
Inventories	403.1
Prepaid expenses	207.1
Total current assets	1,245.1
All other assets	2,992.0
Total assets	4,237.1

Liabilities and Shareholders' Equity

Current liabilities	$1,214.6
All other liabilities and stockholders' equity	3,022.5
Total liabilities and stockholders' equity	$4,237.1

Income Statement
For the Year Ended December 31, 1993
(in millions)

Net sales and revenues	$6,293.9
Expenses*	5,613.2
Net earnings	$ 680.7

*Includes depreciation expense of $265.2 million.

ratio, days' cash, and days' receivables. These ratios will be illustrated using the information given for Kellogg Company in Illustration 5–5.

Current Ratio

As explained in Chapter 2, the current ratio is:

$$\text{Current ratio} = \frac{\text{Current assets}}{\text{Current liabilities}} = \frac{\$1,245.1}{\$1,214.6} = 1.03$$

The current ratio is the most commonly used of all balance sheet ratios. It not only is a measure of the company's liquidity but also is a measure of the margin of safety that management maintains in order to allow for the inevitable unevenness in the flow of funds through the current asset and current liability accounts. If this flow were absolutely smooth and uniform (so that, for example, money coming in from customers each day exactly equaled that day's maturing obligations), the requirements for such a safety margin would be small. Since a company rarely can count on such an even flow, it needs a supply of liquid funds to be assured of being able to pay its bills when they come due. The current ratio indicates the size of this buffer.

In interpreting the current ratio, consideration of the proportion of various types of current assets is important. Even if two companies have the same current ratio, a company with a high percentage of its current assets in the form of monetary assets is more liquid than one with a high percentage in inventory. Also, the nature of the business must be considered. For example, a manufacturer that makes high-fashion clothing needs a relatively high current ratio, since there is high risk involved in both this firm's accounts receivable and its inventory. On the other hand, a metals distributor may safely have a lower current ratio than the clothing manufacturer's, since the distributor's primary current asset would be inventories of steel, copper, and aluminum shapes, which do not become obsolete and whose prices may be increasing because of inflation.

Acid-Test Ratio

Some of the current assets are nonmonetary assets. A ratio that focuses on the relationship of *monetary assets* to current liabilities is called the **acid-test ratio,** or **quick ratio.** Quick assets are those current assets that are also monetary assets; they therefore exclude inventories and prepaid items. The formula is:

$$\text{Acid-test ratio} = \frac{\text{Monetary current assets}}{\text{Current liabilities}} = \frac{\$634.9}{\$1,214.6} = 0.52$$

Days' Cash

Although cash is a necessary asset, it earns little or no return. Thus, although too little cash is an obvious signal of difficulty, too much cash is a sign that management has not taken advantage of opportunities to put cash to work in, say, certificates of deposit or marketable securities.

One way to judge how well the company is managing its cash is to calculate roughly how many days' bills the cash on hand would pay. The first step is to use the income statement to estimate cash expenses: a rough approximation would be to take total expenses and subtract noncash expenses such as depreciation. This total is then divided by 365 to arrive at daily cash needs:

$$\text{Cash costs per day} = \frac{\$5,348.0}{365} = \$14.65 \text{ per day}$$

This amount can then be divided into the cash balance to determine approximately the "days' cash" on hand:

$$\frac{\text{Cash}}{\text{Cash costs per day}} = \frac{\$98.1}{\$14.65 \text{ per day}} = 7 \text{ days}[17]$$

---

[17]This result needs to be interpreted in light of the fact that Kellogg Company reports cash and highly liquid temporary investments as a single combined amount. For companies that separately report cash and marketable securities, basing the calculation on "pure" cash typically will give a result of only two or three days.

Combining these two steps, the formula for **days' cash** is:

$$\text{Days' cash} = \frac{\text{Cash}}{\text{Cash expenses} \div 365}$$

It must be emphasized that this is a rough approximation. The calculation focuses on routine operating expenses; it does not take account of cash needed for major asset purchases or loan repayments. Thus, a firm might appear to have too much cash on hand because it has just received cash from bonds issued to finance construction of a new facility. On the other hand, firms with good cash management procedures would not let even that cash sit idle; they would invest it in short-term securities for as long as possible, even if that is only one or two days. In companies that manage their cash well, the days' cash will usually be only a few days. (Some analysts calculate this ratio using in the numerator cash plus marketable securities rather than just "pure" cash. The ratio then indicates short-term liquidity, rather than cash management.)

Days' Receivables

A calculation similar to that used in days' cash can be used to see how many days' worth of sales are represented in accounts receivable. The formula is:

$$\text{Days' receivables} = \frac{\text{Receivables}}{\text{Sales} \div 365} = \frac{\$536.8}{\$6,293.9 \div 365} = 31 \text{ days}$$

The result is also called the average **collection period** for the receivables. If available, the amount of sales in the denominator should be *credit* sales, which is more closely related to receivables than is total sales.

The collection period can be related roughly to the credit terms offered by the company. A rule of thumb is that the collection period should not exceed 1⅓ times the regular payment period; that is, if the company's typical terms call for payment in 30 days, it is said that the average collection period should not exceed 40 days. Like all rules of thumb, this one has a great many exceptions. Changes in the ratio indicate changes in the company's credit policy or changes in its ability to collect its receivables.

As with other ratios, comparisons should be made with the collection period of other firms in the same industry and also with a firm's own ratio for previous years. For example, in industries with excess capacity, looser credit policies are sometimes used as a competitive marketing tool, thus increasing the days' receivables. If a firm's collection period is significantly longer than its competitors', this suggests inadequate collection procedures.

The aging schedule in Illustration 5–4 also provides useful information in analyzing the quality of the accounts receivable. An increase in the proportion of overdue amounts is a serious danger signal. Although aging schedules frequently are used within corporations, they are not disclosed in corporate annual reports to shareholders.

SUMMARY

Although a business earns income continuously, accounting recognizes revenue only in the period in which the entity has performed substantially what is required in order to earn income and in which the amount of income can be reliably measured. In the usual case of the sale of goods or services, this is the period in which goods are delivered or services performed. If income cannot be reliably measured at this time, as in certain types of installment sales, revenue recognition is postponed. If the earning process takes place over several accounting periods, the percentage-of-completion method recognizes revenue in each of these periods, provided that reliable measurement of accomplishment is possible.

The realization concept states that the amount of revenue recognized in a period is the amount that is reasonably certain to be collected from customers. Accordingly, the gross sales revenue is reduced by the estimated amount of bad debts that are hidden in credit sales. A corresponding reduction is made in the asset, accounts receivable. Similar reductions may be made for warranty costs and for sales returns and allowances.

Monetary assets are money or claims to receive fixed sums of money. Cash, certificates of deposit, and accounts receivable are reported at realizable amounts (which, in the case of cash and certificates of deposit, is the same as the face amount). Marketable equity securities are reported at either cost or current market value, depending on the company's intentions regarding holding the securities.

The current ratio, the acid-test ratio, days' cash, and days' receivables are useful tools in analyzing a company's monetary assets.

Cases

CASE 5–1 Moyer Corporation (A)

On December 31, 1992, before the yearly financial statements were prepared, the controller of the Moyer Corporation reviewed certain transactions that affected accounts receivable and the allowance for doubtful accounts. The controller first examined the December 31, 1991, balance sheet (Exhibit 1). A subsequent review of the year's transactions applicable to accounts receivable revealed the items listed below:

1. Sales on account during 1992 amounted to $9,965,575.

2. Payment received on accounts receivable during 1992 totaled $9,685,420.

3. During the year accounts receivable totaling $26,854 were deemed uncollectible and were written off.

4. Two accounts that had been written off as uncollectible in 1991 were collected in 1992. One account for $2,108 was paid in full. A partial payment of $1,566 was made by the Hollowell Company on another account that originally had amounted to $2,486. The controller was reasonably sure this account would be paid in full because reliable reports were circulating that the trustee in bankruptcy for the Hollowell Company would pay all obligations 100 cents on the dollar.

5. The allowance for bad debts was adjusted to equal 3 percent of the balance in accounts receivable at the end of the year.

Questions

1. Analyze the effect of each of these transactions in terms of its effect on accounts receivable, allowance for doubtful accounts, and any other account that may be involved, and prepare necessary journal entries.

2. Give the correct totals for accounts receivable and the allowance for doubtful accounts as of December 31, 1992, after the transactions affecting them had been recorded.

3. Calculate the ratios described in the text as of December 31, 1992. Assume that amounts for items other than those described in the case are the same as on December 31, 1991.

EXHIBIT 1

MOYER CORPORATION
Balance Sheet
As of December 31, 1991

Assets

Current assets:

Cash		$ 671,344
Accounts receivable	$ 988,257	
Less: Allowance for doubtful accounts	29,648	958,609
U.S. Treasury securities at cost		274,060
Inventories		1,734,405
Total current assets		3,638,418

Other assets:

Investments		412,294
Land		186,563
Building	2,405,259	
Less: Accumulated depreciation	663,379	1,741,880
Factory machinery	3,425,585	
Less: Accumulated depreciation	1,642,358	1,783,227
Furniture and fixtures	56,484	
Less: Accumulated depreciation	40,400	16,084
Automotive equipment	58,298	
Less: Accumulated depreciation	37,156	21,142
Office machines	42,534	
Less: Accumulated depreciation	28,005	14,529
Tools		61,294
Patent		56,250
Prepaid expenses		100,190
Total assets		$8,031,871

Liabilities and Shareholders' Equity

Current liabilities:

Accounts payable		$ 510,000
Taxes payable		709,354
Accrued salaries, wages, and interest		141,478
Long-term debt, due within one year		69,300
Total current liabilities		1,430,132

Noncurrent liabilities:

Long-term debt		1,247,368

Shareholders' equity:

Common stock		2,503,275
Retained earnings		2,851,096
Total shareholders' equity		5,354,371
Total liabilities and shareholders' equity		$8,031,871

CASE 5–2   MacDonald's Farm*

Early in 1994, Denise Grey was notified by a lawyer that her recently deceased uncle had willed her the ownership of a 2,000-acre wheat farm in Iowa. The lawyer asked whether Grey wanted to keep the farm or sell it.

Grey was an assistant vice president in the consumer credit department of a large New York bank. Despite the distance between New York and Iowa, Grey was interested in retaining ownership of the farm if she could determine its profitability. During the last 10 years of his life, Jeremiah MacDonald had hired professional managers to run his farm while he remained in semiretirement in Florida.

Keeping the farm as an investment was particularly interesting to Grey for the following reasons:

1. Recent grain deals with foreign countries had begun to increase present farm commodity prices, and many experts believed these prices would remain high for the next several years.

2. Although the number of small farms had decreased markedly in the last 20 years, large farms such as MacDonald's using mechanization and new hybrid seed varieties could be very profitable.

3. After some downward movement in the 1980s, the value of good farmland in Iowa was beginning to appreciate at about 10 percent a year.

Included in the lawyer's letter were data on revenues and expenses for 1993 and certain information on balance sheet items, which are summarized below:

Beginning inventory	0 bushels
1993 wheat production	210,000 bushels
Shipped to grain elevator	180,000 bushels
Grain stored at farm at end of 1993 . .	30,000 bushels

Prices:

The average price per bushel which the elevator operator had agreed to pay for wheat shipped to the grain elevator in 1993 was $2.90. The price per bushel at the time of the wheat harvest was $2.80. The closing price per bushel on December 31, 1993, was $3.07.

Accounts receivable:

At year-end the proceeds from 20,000 bushels shipped to the grain elevator had not yet been received from the elevator operator. The average sales price of these 20,000 bushels of wheat had been $2.98 per bushel. There were no uncollected proceeds on December 31, 1992.

Cash:

The farm had a checking account balance of $7,700 and a savings account balance of $23,200.

Land:

The original cost of the land was $375,000. It was appraised for estate tax purposes at $1,050 per acre.

Buildings and machinery:

Buildings and machinery with an original cost of $412,500 and accumulated depreciation of $300,000 are employed on the farm. The equipment was appraised at net book value.

Current liabilities:

The farm has notes payable and accounts payable totaling $33,000.

Owner's equity:

Common stock has a par value of $7,500 plus an additional paid-in capital of $450,000. There was no record of retained

---

* Copyright © by the President and Fellows of Harvard College. Harvard Business School case 173–226.

1993 Expenses for the MacDonald Farm

A. Production costs per bushel:

Seed	$0.053
Fertilizer and chemicals................................	0.295
Machinery costs, fuel and repairs........................	0.107
Part-time labor and other costs	0.058
Total production cost per bushel......................	$0.513

B. Annual costs not related to the volume of production:

Salaries and wages...................................	$ 72,500
Insurance...	4,500
Taxes*..	32,500
Depreciation	28,500
Other expenses	45,000
Total costs not related to production volume	$ 183,000

*This figure excludes income taxes since the corporation was taxed as a sole proprietorship.

earnings, although it was known that Jeremiah MacDonald withdrew most of the earnings in the last few years in order to continue the lifestyle to which he had become accustomed in Florida.

Looking over the data on revenues and expenses, Grey discovered that there were no monetary numbers for 1993's total revenues or ending inventory. The lawyer's letter explained that there was some doubt in his mind about when revenue for the farm should be recognized and about the appropriate way to value the grain inventory. The lawyer's understanding was that there are at least three alternative stages in the wheat growing cycle at which revenue could be counted.

First, the *production method* could be used. Since wheat has a daily valuation on the Chicago Commodity Exchange, any unsold inventory as of December 31 could be valued at market price very objectively. In this way revenue can be counted for all wheat produced in a given year, regardless of whether it is sold or not. A decision not to sell this wheat before December 31 is based on speculation about future wheat price increases.

Second, the *sales method* (also called the *delivery method*) could be used. This would recognize revenue when the grain is purchased from the farm by the grain elevator operator in the neighboring town. In this instance the owner of the grain elevator had just sold control to a Kansas City company with no previous experience in running such a facility. The manager of the MacDonald Farm had expressed some concern about selling to an unknown operator.

Third, the *collection method* could be used. Under this approach, revenue is counted when the cash is actually received by the farm from the grain elevator operator. Full collection often took several months because a grain elevator operator might keep wheat for a considerable time in the hope that prices would rise so he could sell at a greater profit.

Questions

1. Prepare the 1993 income statement and the related ending balance sheet for the MacDonald Farm recognizing revenue by the:
   a. Sales (delivery) method.
   b. Collection method.
   c. Production method.
   Which method would you recommend?

2. Assume that the MacDonald Farm had received a firm offer of $225,000 for 100 acres of the farm that would be used as the site of a new housing development. This development would have no effect on the use of the remaining acreage as a farm, and Ms. Grey planned to accept it. How would you account in the 1993 financial statements for the economic gain represented by this appreciation in land values?

3. Should Grey retain ownership of the farm?

CASE 5–3 Middleburg Realty Company

Middleburg Realty Company was incorporated July 1, 1992, for the purpose of buying eight houses in a bankrupt housing development and then selling these houses. Two persons were involved in the company. Angie Hausner was to be responsible for the day-to-day affairs of the company and for selling the houses. Darryl Brown invested $250,000 in cash in return for all the common stock in the company.

The understanding between the two was the Ms. Hausner would receive a sales commission of 25 percent of the gross margin on the houses and a bonus at the end of the year. Mr. Brown would be entitled to a $5,880 cash dividend in 1992, plus one half the income (before income taxes) of the company, after deducting the $5,880. Ms. Hausner would receive shares of stock equal in value to the remainder of the pretax income (after the $5,880 and the additional payments to Mr. Brown).

This arrangement would be continued in succeeding years, except that each stockholder would be entitled to a cash dividend of 5 percent of his or her equity, and the remainder would be divided equally. In this way, Ms. Hausner would build up a stock ownership without having to invest cash.

The housing development consisted of 25 houses, of which 17 had been sold before the project went bankrupt. The bank that had taken over the property sold the eight houses to Middleburg Realty Company for $1,281,000 on July 1, 1992. Middleburg Realty paid $175,000 cash and took out a five-year 11 percent loan for $1,106,000 with the bank; this loan was secured by the inventory of unsold homes that Middleburg Realty might have at any point in the next five years. Semi-annual payments of $110,600 plus interest were to be made on December 31 and June 30.

By the end of 1992, five of the houses had been sold for a total of $945,000; they had cost $820,452. Also, during the year the company had incurred costs of $5,895 for incorporation fees and miscellaneous expenses, about which there were no questions. Questions arose, however, with regard to certain other events that affected the calculation of income. These events are listed below.

1. Because few vacant houses remained, because the neighborhood had acquired a good reputation, and because economic conditions in the area had improved, Ms. Hausner judged that the value of the unsold houses had increased by at least 5 percent since July 1. She increased the asking prices accordingly. She recommended that 90 percent of this increase be added to the inventory cost of the houses (the other 10 percent, or 0.5 percent of the original cost, would be recorded as profit when the houses were sold). Mr. Brown agreed that the value of the houses had increased 5 percent.

2. Ms. Hausner disliked the wallpaper in certain rooms in House No. 23, and with

Mr. Brown's concurrence, she had the rooms repapered at a cost of $2,050. She did not increase the asking price of this house to reflect the repapering (the asking price was raised 5 percent, as explained above), although she felt the new paper definitely improved the house's appearance.

3. A maintenance company was hired to mow lawns, rake leaves, and otherwise keep the unsold properties in attractive condition; $4,840 was paid for this work in 1992. No records were kept of the amount attributable to each house, but since this work stopped as soon as a house was sold, it seemed reasonable to Ms. Hausner to attribute half to the five sold houses and half to the three unsold houses.

4. For all intents and purposes, House No. 24 was sold. The buyer had executed an agreement to purchase and had made an "earnest" payment of $2,000, which was not returnable so long as Middleburg Realty acted in good faith. Ms. Hausner thought she was entitled to $500 of this amount as commission. The selling price

of the house was $189,600 and its cost from the bank was $160,000.

5. During 1992 advertising expense on the three unsold homes amounted to $4,620, which was attributed equally to each house. The other five houses had been sold without placing advertisements.

6. During November 1992 a water pipe broke in House No. 25 (an unsold home), causing $2,725 worth of damage. The company's insurance policy covered all but $500 of the damage.

Questions

1. What should Ms. Hausner's commission be for the period July 1, 1992, to December 31, 1992?

2. Prepare an income statement for the six months ended December 31, 1992, and a balance sheet as of that date. Be certain that your income statement differentiates between gross margin and income. (Ignore income taxes.) For the balance sheet assume that the company has no office space or equipment; Ms. Hausner runs the business "from her home, phone, and automobile." She has been paid her commission on the five sold houses.

CASE 5–4   Jean Coffin (A)

"Your course unfortunately doesn't give me the answer to a great many real-life problems," said Jean Coffin to an accounting professor. "I've read the text and listened to you attentively, but every once in a while I run across something that doesn't seem to fit the rules."

"Not all of life's complications can be covered in a first course," the professor replied. "As is the case with law, medicine, or indeed any of the professions, many matters are dealt with in advanced courses, and others are not settled in any classroom. Never-

theless, some problems that are not specifically discussed can be solved satisfactorily by relating them to principles that you already have learned. Let's take revenue recognition as a particularly difficult case in point. If you will write down some of the matters about which you are now uncomfortable, I'd be glad to discuss them with you—that is, after you have given some thought as to the most reasonable solution."

A week later, Coffin returned with the list given below.

1. **Electric Utility Bills.** When an electric utility customer uses electricity, the electric company has earned revenues. It is obviously impossible, however, for the company to read all of its customers' meters on the evening of December 31. How does the electric company know its revenue for a given year?

2. **Retainer Fee.** A law firm received a "retainer" of $10,000 on July 1, 19x1, from a client. In return, it agreed to furnish general legal advice upon request for one year. In addition, the client would be billed for regular legal services such as representation in litigation. There was no way of knowing how often, or when, the client would request advice, and it was quite possible that no such advice would be requested. How much of the $10,000 should be counted as revenue in 19x1?

3. **Cruise.** Raymond's, a travel agency, chartered a cruise ship for two weeks beginning January 23, 19x2, for $200,000. In return, the ship's owner agreed to pay all costs of the cruise. In 19x1, Raymond's sold all available space on the ship for $260,000. It incurred $40,000 in selling and other costs in doing so. All the $260,000 was received in cash from passengers in 19x1. Raymond's paid $50,000 as an advance payment to the ship owner in 19x1. How much, if any, of the $260,000 was revenue to Raymond's in 19x1? Does the question of whether passengers were entitled to a refund in 19x2 if they canceled their reservations make any difference in the answer?

4. **Accretion.** A nursery owner had one plot of land containing Christmas trees that were four years old on November 1, 19x1. The owner had incurred costs of $3 per tree up to that time. A wholesaler offered to buy the trees for $4 each and to pay in addition all costs of cutting and bundling, and transporting them to market. The nursery owner declined this offer, deciding that it would more profitable to let the trees grow for one more year. Only a trivial amount of additional cost would be involved. The price of Christmas trees varies with their height. Should the nursery owner recognize any revenue from these trees in 19x1?

5. **"Unbilled" Receivables.** The balance sheet of an architectural firm shows a significant asset labeled Unbilled Receivables. The firm says this represents in-process projects, valued at the rates at which the customers will be charged for the architects' time. Why would a firm do this instead of valuing projects in process at their cost, the same as a manufacturing firm would value its in-process inventory? Does it make any difference in the reported owners' equity for the architectural firm to report such in-process work as receivables rather than as inventory?

6. **Premium Coupons.** A manufacturer of coffee enclosed a premium coupon with each $2.50 (at wholesale) jar of coffee that it sold to retailers. Customers could use this coupon to apply to $0.50 of the price of a new type of instant tea that the manufacturer was introducing and that it sold for $2.00 wholesale. The manufacturer reimbursed retail stores $0.60 for each such coupon they submitted. (The extra $0.10 was to pay the grocer for coupon handling costs.) Past experience with similar premium offers indicated that approximately 20 percent of such coupons are eventually redeemed. At the end of 19x1, however, only about 10 percent of the coupons issued in 19x1 had been redeemed. In recording the revenues for the company for 19x1, what allowance, if any, should be made for these coupons? If an allowance should be made, should it apply to the sales revenue of coffee or to the sales revenue of tea?

7. **Travelers Checks.** A bank sells a customer $500 of American Express travelers checks, for which the bank collects from the customer $505. (The bank chargers a 1 percent fee for this service.) How does the bank record this transaction? How does the transaction affect American Express's balance sheet?

8. **Product Repurchase Agreement.** In December 19x1 Manufacturer A sold merchandise to Wholesaler B. B used this inven-

tory as collateral for a bank loan of $100,000 and sent the $100,000 to A. Manufacturer A agreed to repurchase the goods on or before July 1, 19x2, for $112,000, the difference representing interest on the loan and compensation for B's services. Does Manufacturer A have revenue in 19x1?

9. Franchises. A national real estate brokerage firm has become highly successful by selling franchises to local real estate brokers. It charges $10,000 for the initial franchise fee and a service fee of 6 percent of the broker's revenue thereafter. For this it permits use of its well-known name, and provides a one-week initial training course, a nationwide referral system, and various marketing and management aids. Currently, the franchise fee accounts for 25 percent of the national firm's receipts, but it expects that the United States market will be saturated within the next three years, and thereafter the firm will have to depend on the service fee and new sources of revenue that it may develop. Should it recognize the $10,000 as revenue in the year in which the franchise agreement is signed? If it does, what will happen to its profits after the market has become saturated?

10. Computer Systems. In early 1993 the sales vice president of Tech-Logic reached agreement to deliver several computer systems with a total price of $570,000 to an organization in one of the newly independent countries established following the dissolution of the former Soviet Union. Tech-Logic management was very excited about this contract. The countries that were part of the former Soviet Union represented a major new market that was just opening up for trade, and these countries especially needed the kinds of high-technology products that Tech-Logic sold. Tech-Logic manufactured and shipped the entire $570,000 order during 1993. Tech-Logic normally recognized revenue on the sale of its products when they were shipped. However, Tech-Logic's controller wondered whether the same revenue recognition policy should apply to this contract. First, contract law in these countries was evolving and it was hard to know if certain laws existed or what they were. In addition, the controller was uncertain when Tech-Logic would receive the $570,000 in cash. He had heard that in many of these countries it was difficult to obtain currencies needed for foreign exchange, although the customer kept assuring Tech-Logic that they would receive cash shortly. The controller pondered whether to recognize the entire $570,000 as revenue in 1993. If not, then when should this revenue be recognized?

6

Cost of Sales and Inventories

This chapter describes principles and procedures for measuring cost of sales as reported on the income statement and for the related measurement of inventory on the balance sheet. These costs may be accounted for either by the periodic inventory method or the perpetual inventory method; each method is described. The cost of individual units of inventory and of individual goods sold can be measured by any of several methods, including specific identification; average cost; first-in, first-out (FIFO); and last-in, first-out (LIFO). All of these methods are described and compared later in the chapter.

We begin with a brief overview of accounting for inventory and cost of sales in three types of companies: merchandising, manufacturing, and service. Next, we describe in detail the procedures in merchandising companies. The procedures in manufacturing companies start with the same steps used in merchandising companies and incorporate additional aspects associated with the manufacturing process. We therefore limit the discussion of manufacturing companies to these additional matters. Service companies are also discussed.

Types of Companies

A single company may conduct merchandising, service, and/or manufacturing activities. For convenience, we shall assume that each company described here conducts only one type. If a company does conduct more than one type of activity, it will use the accounting method appropriate for each type.

Retail stores, wholesalers, distributors, and similar companies that sell tangible goods are merchandising companies.[1] A **merchandising company** sells goods in substantially the same physical form as that in which it acquires them. Its cost of sales is therefore the acquisition cost of the goods that are sold. On the balance sheet a current asset, merchandise inventory, shows the cost of goods that have been acquired but not yet sold as of the balance sheet date.

A **manufacturing company** converts raw materials and purchased parts into finished goods. Its cost of sales includes the conversion costs as well as the raw material and parts costs of the goods that it sells. A manufacturing company has three types of inventory accounts: materials, work in process, and finished goods.

Because both merchandising and manufacturing companies sell tangible goods, their income statements sometimes use the term **cost of goods sold** rather than cost of sales. We shall use the two terms interchangeably for merchandising and manufacturing companies, but use only cost of sales for service organizations.

Service organizations furnish intangible services rather than tangible goods. They include hotels, beauty parlors and other personal-service organizations, hospitals and other health care organizations, educational organizations, banks and other financial institutions, and governmental units. Service organizations may have materials inventories—for example, the pipes and fittings of a plumbing company. Professional service firms, such as law, consulting, accounting, and architectural firms, may have intangible inventories consisting of costs that have been incurred on behalf of clients but that have not yet been billed to clients. These inventories, often called **jobs in progress** or **unbilled costs,** correspond to work in process inventories in a manufacturing company. Service organizations do not have finished goods inventories.

In the United States about 21 percent of the civilian work force is employed in merchandising companies, 17 percent in manufacturing companies, 41 percent in nongovernmental service organizations, and 5 percent in governmental entities. (The other 16 percent are in mining, construction, transportation, communication, public utilities, and agriculture.)[2]

Supplies

In addition to inventory accounts for goods directly involved in the merchandising or manufacturing process, a company may have one or more inventory accounts for supplies. **Supplies** are tangible items that will be consumed in the course of normal operations. Examples include office and

---

[1]The word *products* is often used when *goods* is intended. For clarity, throughout this book, we use *goods* for tangible items, *services* for intangibles, and *products* for the sum of goods and services. In other words, the outputs of an entity, whether tangible or intangible, are its products.

[2]U.S. Bureau of Labor Statistics data.

janitorial supplies, and lubricants and repair parts for equipment. Supplies are distinguished from merchandise in that they are not sold as such, and they are distinguished from materials in that supplies are not accounted for separately as an element of the cost of goods manufactured. Paper offered for sale is merchandise inventory in a stationery store; paper is materials inventory in a company that manufactures books; and paper intended for use in the office is supplies inventory in any organization. Supplies will not be discussed further in this chapter.

MERCHANDISING COMPANIES

We shall now describe in detail the principles and procedures related to accounting for inventories and cost of goods sold in merchandising companies.

Acquisition Cost

Merchandise is added to inventory at its cost, in accordance with the basic cost concept. Cost includes both the cost of acquiring the merchandise and also any expenditures made to make the goods ready for sale. Thus, merchandise cost includes not only the invoice cost of the goods purchased, but also freight and other shipping costs of bringing the goods to the point of sale and the cost of unpacking the goods and marking prices on them. Since the recordkeeping task of attaching these latter elements of cost to individual units of merchandise may be considerable, some or all of them may be excluded from merchandise product costs and reported as general operating expenses of the period in which they are incurred.

The purchase cost is also adjusted for returns and allowances and for cash discounts given by the suppliers of the merchandise. As was the case with sales discounts (see Chapter 5), purchase discounts can be accounted for either by recording the purchase amount as net of the discount or by recording the purchase amount at the invoice price and recording the discount when it is taken. If the purchase is originally recorded at the net amount, and if the discount is not subsequently taken, the amount of the lost discount is debited to an account, Purchase Discounts Not Taken. This account provides useful information to management.

Example. If merchandise costing $1,000 is purchased on terms of 2 percent discount if the invoice is paid within 10 days, this acquisition is recorded thus:

Merchandise Inventory	980	
Accounts Payable		980

If the company lost the discount by not paying the invoice within 10 days, the entry would be:

Accounts Payable	980	
Purchase Discounts Not Taken	20	
Cash		1,000

In accounting the word *purchase* refers not to the placing of a purchase order but rather to the *receipt* of the merchandise that was ordered. No accounting entry is made when merchandise is ordered. The entry is made only when the merchandise becomes the property of the buyer. Under commercial law goods in transit usually belong to the buyer as soon as they are delivered to the transportation company if the terms are "FOB shipping point" (if the buyer pays the transportation costs). If the seller pays the transportation costs ("FOB destination"), title does not pass until the goods arrive at the buyer's warehouse.

The Basic Measurement Problem

Think of merchandise inventory as a tank or a reservoir, as in Illustration 6–1. At the beginning of an accounting period there is a certain amount of goods in the reservoir; this is the beginning inventory. During the period additional merchandise is purchased and added to the reservoir. Also during the period merchandise sold is withdrawn from the reservoir. At the end of the accounting period the amount of goods remaining in the reservoir is the ending inventory.

The amount of **goods available for sale** during the period is the sum of the beginning inventory plus the purchases during the period. This sum is $11,400 in Illustration 6–1. The problem to be discussed in this section,

ILLUSTRATION 6–1
MERCHANDISE INVENTORY AND FLOWS

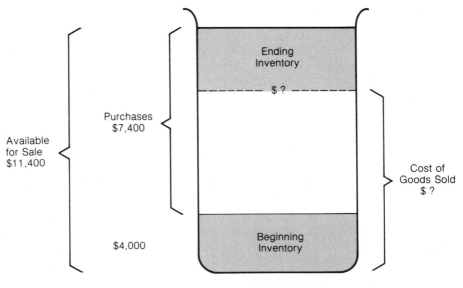

Inventory Reservoir

and indeed in most of the chapter, is how to divide the amount of goods available for sale between (1) the ending inventory and (2) cost of goods sold. How much of the $11,400 is still on hand at the end of the period, and how much was sold during the period? This is a significant problem because its resolution affects both the amount of inventory reported on the balance sheet and (perhaps more importantly) the amount of profit reported on the income statement for the period.

There are two approaches to this problem:

1.   We can determine the amount of ending inventory (i.e., the amount in the reservoir at the end of the period) and *deduce cost of goods sold* by subtracting the ending inventory from the goods available for sale. This is the periodic inventory method.

2.   We can measure the amount actually delivered to customers and *deduce the ending inventory* by subtracting cost of goods sold from the goods available for sale. This is the perpetual inventory method.

Periodic Inventory Method

In the **periodic inventory method** a physical count is made of merchandise in the ending inventory, and the cost of this inventory is determined. This process is called *taking a physical inventory*. Assume that the physical inventory shows the cost of the merchandise remaining at the end of the period to be $2,000. Cost of goods sold is deduced by subtracting the ending inventory from the amount of goods available for sale, thus:

Beginning inventory	$ 4,000
Plus: Purchases	7,400
Equals: Goods available for sale	11,400
Less: Ending inventory	2,000
Cost of goods sold	$ 9,400

The amount of beginning inventory in the above calculation is the amount found by the physical inventory taken at the end of the *preceding* period. (Recall that in accounting the end of one period and the beginning of the next period are the same instant in time, even though the dates—say, June 30 and July 1—may make them appear to be different.)

Some companies show such a calculation in the cost of goods sold section of the income statement itself. Most firms that deduce cost of goods sold by the method shown above do not present the details. Still others report additional detail, particularly on internal reports to management (as opposed to reports for shareholders). For example, if there are freight charges and the return of purchased merchandise, the internal income statement might show:

Beginning inventory		$ 4,000
Plus: Purchases, gross	$7,000	
Freight-in	600	
	7,600	
Less: Purchase returns	200	
Net purchases		7,400
Goods available for sale		11,400
Less: Ending inventory		2,000
Cost of goods sold		$ 9,400

Accounts. When the cost of goods sold is deduced by the method described above, a separate account is established for each element in the calculation. Thus, a **Purchases** account is established and the invoice cost of merchandise purchased is debited to this account rather than directly to Merchandise Inventory. Accounts are also established for Freight-In, Purchase Returns, and any other items involved in the calculation.

Rules for debiting and crediting these accounts can be deduced from their relationship to other accounts. Since Purchases shows *additions* to the asset account, Merchandise Inventory, it increases on the *debit* side. Purchase Returns is a *reduction* in Purchases and hence must have the opposite rule; return of goods to suppliers are thus recorded as *credits* to the Purchase Returns account. The Freight-In account adds to the cost of purchases and therefore increases on the debit side. The rules can also be deduced by thinking of the offsetting part of the transaction. Whenever possible it is simplest to assume that the other account is Cash. Thus, a cash purchase involves a decrease in Cash, which is a credit; therefore, the entry to Purchases must be a debit.

As of the end of the period, these accounts are closed to Cost of Goods Sold. First, the balance in the Merchandise Inventory account is closed. (Recall that no entries were made to this account during the period, so the amount in the account is the *beginning* balance.) The entry is:

Cost of Goods Sold	4,000	
Merchandise Inventory		4,000

Next, the temporary Purchases, Purchase Returns, and Freight-In accounts are closed to Cost of Goods Sold by entries that can be summarized as follows:

Cost of Goods Sold	7,400	
Purchase Returns	200	
Purchases		7,000
Freight-In		600

The new balance (from the physical inventory) is entered in Merchandise Inventory:

ILLUSTRATION 6–2
PERPETUAL INVENTORY CARD

Item: Cassette Deck, Model S150   Unit: Each

Date	Receipts			Shipments			Balance		
	Unit Cost	Total	Units	Unit Cost	Total	Units	Unit Cost	Total	
Jan. 2							40	100	4,000
12				32	100	3,200	8	100	800
14	70	100	7,000				78	100	7,800
25				56	100	5,600	22	100	2,200
27				2	100	200*	20	100	2,000

*This entry is a purchase return to the manufacturer.

Merchandise Inventory 2,000		
Cost of Goods Sold		2,000

Finally, Cost of Goods Sold is closed:

Income Summary 9,400		
Cost of Goods Sold		9,400

Perpetual Inventory Method

In the **perpetual inventory method** a record is maintained of each item carried in the inventory. In a manual system this record is a card similar to the sample shown in Illustration 6–2. In essence this record is a subsidiary ledger account, and Merchandise Inventory is its control account. Purchases are entered directly on this record and also debited to Merchandise Inventory; the offsetting credit is to Accounts Payable or Cash. Deliveries of goods to customers are entered on this record and are credited to Merchandise Inventory; the offsetting debit is to Cost of Goods Sold. The balance of the inventory record at the end of the period is the amount of that particular item in the ending inventory. The sum of the balances for all the items is the ending inventory for the entity.

Assuming for simplicity that a company had only the one item shown in Illustration 6–2, the journal entries for the transactions listed there would be:

For purchases:

(1)

Merchandise Inventory 7,000		
Accounts Payable		7,000

For shipments to customers:

(2)

Cost of Goods Sold...................................	8,800	
Merchandise Inventory...........................		8,800

For purchase returns:

(3)

Accounts Payable	200	
Merchandise Inventory...........................		200

In many perpetual inventory systems freight-in is not entered on the perpetual inventory cards. Instead, it is accumulated in a separate account. Assuming the same $600 freight-in as in the previous example, the closing entry for this account would be:

(4)

Cost of Goods Sold...................................	600	
Freight-In		600

Cost of Goods Sold is closed to Income Summary, as in the periodic inventory method; that is:

(5)

Income Summary	9,400	
Cost of Goods Sold		9,400

These entries would be posted to ledger accounts as shown below:

Merchandise Inventory				**Cost of Goods Sold**	
Balance	4,000	(2) Shipments	8,800 ⟶ 8,800	(5) To Income	
(1) Purchases	7,000	(3) Returns	200 (4) Freight 600	Summary	9,400
		To balance	2,000		
	11,000		11,000	9,400	9,400
Balance	2,000				

In the perpetual inventory method no separate Purchases account is needed; purchases are debited directly to Merchandise Inventory.

Comparison of Periodic and Perpetual Methods

Both inventory methods match the cost of goods sold with the sales revenue for those same goods. Thus, either method is in accord with the matching concept. Without this matching, the gross margin amount for a period would not be meaningful.

The perpetual inventory method requires that a record be maintained for each item carried in inventory and therefore requires additional recordkeeping. This recordkeeping is not likely to be burdensome for a store offering at most a few hundred, relatively high-cost, items, such as a jewelry or an appliance store. Such recordkeeping may not be worthwhile in stores that stock many low-cost items, such as grocery stores and drugstores. (A large supermarket may stock 10,000 or more different items.) However, the development of electronic point-of-sale terminals, which have scanners that identify each item sold by reading a bar code on the item's package, has led many such stores to change to the perpetual inventory method.

The perpetual inventory method has three important advantages. First, the detailed record maintained for each item is useful in deciding when and how much to reorder and in analyzing customer demand for the item. In many stores using point-of-sale terminals with scanners, sales data are used as input to computer models that automatically prepare orders in a central warehouse to replenish the store's inventory. This helps avoid both stock-outs and excess inventories of the various items carried by the store.

Second, the perpetual inventory record has a built-in check that is not possible with the periodic method. In the latter, the physical inventory at the end of the period is a necessary part of the calculation of cost of goods sold. The difference between the goods available for sale and the goods on hand is *assumed* to be the cost of goods sold. This assumption is not necessarily correct because some of the goods may have been pilfered, lost, thrown away, or overlooked when the physical inventory was taken. Collectively, these goods that are not in inventory but were not sold make up the period's **inventory shrinkage.** In the perpetual inventory system an actual count of the goods on hand can be used as a check on the accuracy of the inventory records. Shrinkage thus can be identified separately rather than being buried in cost of goods sold.

Third, with a perpetual inventory system an income statement can be prepared without taking a physical inventory. Thus, an income statement can be prepared every month, with the accuracy of the underlying perpetual inventory records being checked by an annual or semiannual physical inventory.

Retail Method

A store that does not maintain perpetual inventory records can nevertheless prepare reasonably accurate monthly income statements without taking a physical inventory by using the **retail method.** In this method purchases are recorded at both their cost and their retail selling price. The gross margin percentage of the goods available for sale is calculated from these records. The *complement* of this percentage is applied to sales for the month (obtained from sales register records) to find the approximate cost of goods sold.

Example. Assume the following:

	At Cost	At Retail
Beginning inventory	$ 4,000	$ 6,000
Purchases	7,000	10,000
Goods available for sale	$11,000	$16,000

The gross margin percentage is ($16,000 − $11,000) ÷ $16,000 = 31 percent. The complement of this is 100 percent − 31 percent = 69 percent. If sales for the month were $13,000, it is assumed that cost of goods sold was 69 percent of this amount, or $8,970. In applying the retail method in practice, adjustments must be made for markdowns that are made from initial retail prices (e.g., in clearance sales).

A variation of this method, the **gross profit method,** simply applies a "normal" gross margin percentage to the amount of sales in order to arrive at an approximation of cost of goods sold. Records are not kept of the retail value of goods available for sale. With this method a "normal" margin is determined for each department in the store, and the salesperson or checkout clerk records the department number of each item the customer purchases. A department's sales for the month are multiplied by the complement of the department's gross margin percentage to approximate the department's cost of goods sold. Sales and cost of goods sold amounts are then summed across all departments to determine the store's gross margin.

The retail and gross profit methods are not methods in addition to the periodic and perpetual methods. Rather, they can be viewed as variations of the perpetual method in that cost of goods sold is determined without taking a physical inventory.

MANUFACTURING COMPANIES

A manufacturing company has as a major function the conversion of raw materials and purchased parts into finished goods. In any company cost of sales is the total of the acquisition cost plus conversion costs (if any) of the products that are sold. The manufacturer therefore includes in cost of goods sold the cost of materials and parts used, the cost of labor, and other costs incurred in the manufacture of the goods that are sold. The difference between accounting for the cost of sales in a merchandising company and in a manufacturing company arises because the merchandising company usually has no conversion costs. Its cost of goods sold is practically the same as the purchase price of these goods.

The measurement of cost of goods sold is therefore more complicated in a manufacturing company than in a merchandising company. In a manufacturing company this cost must be obtained by collecting and aggregating the several elements of manufacturing cost.

Inventory Accounts

A manufacturing company has three types of inventory accounts. Their names and the nature of their content are as follows:

1. Materials Inventory: Items of material that are to become a part of the ultimately salable goods that result from the manufacturing process. They are costed at acquisition cost, with the same types of adjustments for freight-in and returns as those made in calculating the net purchase cost of merchandise inventory, described above.

2. Work in Process Inventory: Goods that have started through the manufacturing process but have not yet been finished. They are costed as the sum of (1) the materials thus far issued for them plus (2) the labor and other manufacturing costs incurred on these items up to the end of the accounting period.

3. Finished Goods Inventory: Goods that have been manufactured but have not yet been shipped to customers. They are costed at the total cost incurred in manufacturing them. This account is essentially the same as Merchandise Inventory in a merchandising company, except that the items are recorded at the cost of manufacturing them rather than at their acquisition cost.

There are wide variations in the relative size of the three types of inventories among companies. Those companies with a short production cycle may have so little work in process at the end of the accounting period that they do not have a separate Work in Process Inventory account. At the end of the period they charge all manufacturing costs to Finished Goods Inventory (or to Cost of Goods Sold if there is no Finished Goods Inventory account). This process is called **back flushing.** Companies that produce items to customer order and ship to the customer as soon as the order is completed have little or no finished goods inventory.

A diagram of these accounts and the flow of costs from one to another is shown in Illustration 6-3. Using the periodic inventory method, we shall trace the flow of costs through these accounts. Each step is described by giving the relevant journal entries. The effect on ledger accounts is shown in Illustration 6-4.

ILLUSTRATION 6-3
MANUFACTURING INVENTORIES AND FLOWS

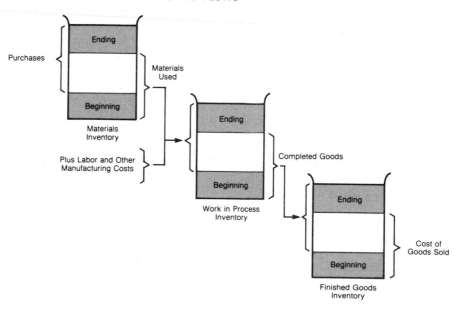

ILLUSTRATION 6–4
FLOW OF COSTS THROUGH INVENTORIES (000 omitted)

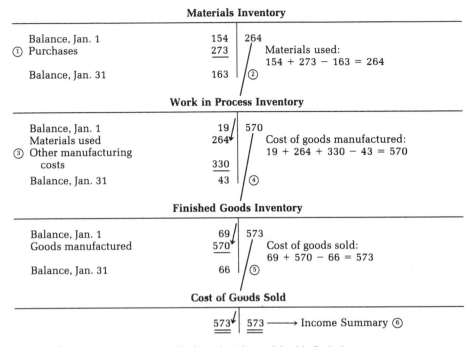

Note: Circled numbers correspond to journal entries explained in the text.

In the merchandising company we established a separate account to show the calculation of cost of goods sold. We could use similar accounts in a manufacturing company to show separately the calculation of materials used, cost of goods manufactured, and cost of goods sold. In the following description, however, we have not used these accounts. Instead, we arrive at the amounts by calculations made outside the accounts. There is no substantive difference between the two methods.

Materials Used   During an accounting period various items of material are issued from a storage area to the production facilities for conversion into goods. The term **materials used** means the sum of all materials issued during the period. Such materials range in their degree of refinement from truly raw materials, such as crude oil or iron ore, to sophisticated components, such as motors or miniature circuit chips. Traditionally, all such purchased items were referred to as raw materials. However, there is nothing very "raw" about a motor or circuit chip. We shall use the term **materials inventory** to include the entire range of purchased items that are intended to become a part of salable goods during the production process.

In determining the cost of materials used, the periodic method may be used. That is, the assumption is made that the amount of materials used is the difference between the materials available for use during the period (which is the total of the beginning inventory and the period's net purchases) and the ending inventory. This assumption does not take into account any waste or spoilage of materials that might have occurred. In practice, waste and spoilage are either disregarded or collected separately and removed from material costs by crediting Materials Inventory and debiting a separate manufacturing cost account.

We shall make this calculation in the Materials Inventory account. First, the amount of purchases made during the period, which includes $266,000 as the invoice cost of materials received plus $7,000 of freight charges on these materials, is added to Materials Inventory. These amounts would have first been debited to the temporary accounts, Purchases and Freight-In, and would have been credited to Accounts Payable. The $273,000 cost is then transferred to Materials Inventory by closing the two temporary accounts with this entry:

(1)

Materials Inventory.................................	273,000	
Purchases.......................................		266,000
Freight-In.......................................		7,000

A physical inventory shows the amount of materials on hand as of the end of the period to be $163,000. Since $154,000 was on hand at the beginning of the period and $273,000 was added by the above entry, the total amount available was $427,000. By subtracting $163,000 from $427,000, we determine the amount of materials used: $264,000. It is subtracted from Materials Inventory and added to Work in Process Inventory by the following entry:

(2)

Work in Process Inventory..........................	264,000	
Materials Inventory.............................		264,000

Cost of Goods Manufactured

The sum of materials used, direct labor, and other manufacturing costs is the total amount of cost added to Work in Process Inventory during the period. Given the amount in Work in Process Inventory at the beginning of the period and the amount remaining at the end of the period, the **cost of goods manufactured** (the goods completed and transferred to Finished Goods Inventory) can be deduced.

The cost of materials used was added by the preceding entry. Other manufacturing costs incurred during the period are accumulated in various temporary accounts. For example, if employees directly involved in the conversion process earned $151,000 during the period, this amount would have been debited to a temporary Direct Labor account and credited to Wages Payable. The costs of direct labor and other resources used in the conversion process are added to Work in Process Inventory by closing the temporary accounts, as in the following entry:

```
                                    (3)
Work in Process Inventory .......................... 330,000
    Direct Labor .....................................          151,000
    Indirect Labor....................................           24,000
    Factory Heat, Light, and Power ..................           90,000
    Factory Supplies Used............................           22,000
    Factory Insurance and Taxes......................            8,000
    Depreciation, Plant and Equipment...............           35,000
```

A physical inventory shows the amount of work in process at the end of the period to be $43,000. Since $19,000 was on hand at the beginning of the period and $264,000 of materials and $330,000 of other manufacturing costs were added by entries 2 and 3, the total amount available was $613,000. By subtracting $43,000 from $613,000, we determine the cost of goods manufactured during the period to be $570,000. This figure is subtracted from Work in Process Inventory and added to Finished Goods Inventory by the following entry:

```
                                    (4)
Finished Goods Inventory ......................... 570,000
    Work in Process Inventory.......................          570,000
```

Cost of Goods Sold

Having determined the cost of goods manufactured, the cost of goods sold is found by (1) adding the cost of goods manufactured to the beginning finished goods inventory so as to find the total amount available for sale and then (2) subtracting the ending finished goods inventory. As with the periodic method in a merchandising company, the assumption is that if the merchandise is not in inventory, it has been sold.

A physical inventory shows the amount of finished goods at the end of the period to be $66,000. Since $69,000 was on hand at the beginning of the period and $570,000 of manufactured goods were completed during the period and added to finished goods inventory, the total amount available was $639,000. Subtracting $66,000 from $639,000 yields the cost of goods sold: $573,000. It is subtracted from Finished Goods Inventory and recorded as Cost of Goods Sold by the following entry:

```
                                    (5)
Cost of Goods Sold................................... 573,000
    Finished Goods Inventory........................          573,000
```

The balance in the Cost of Goods Sold account is then closed to Income Summary by the following entry:

```
                                    (6)
Income Summary .................................... 573,000
    Cost of Goods Sold .............................          573,000
```

ILLUSTRATION 6–5

ALFMAN MANUFACTURING COMPANY

Income Statement
January

Net sales			$669,000
Cost of goods sold:			
Materials cost:			
Materials inventory, Jan. 1		$154,000	
Purchases	$266,000		
Plus: Freight-in	7,000		
Total purchases		273,000	
Material available.................		427,000	
Less: Materials inventory, Jan. 31		163,000	
Cost of materials used		$264,000	
Direct labor cost		151,000	
Manufacturing overhead cost:			
Indirect labor	24,000		
Factory heat, light, and power	90,000		
Factory supplies used	22,000		
Insurance and taxes..................	8,000		
Depreciation—plant and equipment	35,000		
Total manufacturing overhead cost		179,000	
Total manufacturing costs		594,000	
Add: Work in process inventory, Jan. 1		19,000	
Total		613,000	
Less: Work in process inventory, Jan. 31...		43,000	
Cost of goods manufactured.............		570,000	
Add: Finished goods inventory, Jan. 1		69,000	
Cost of goods available for sale...........		639,000	
Less: Finished goods inventory, Jan. 31....		66,000	
Cost of goods sold			573,000
Gross margin			96,000
Selling and administrative expenses:			
Selling expense		39,000	
Administrative expense		3,000	
Depreciation—nonmanufacturing facilities..		32,000	74,000
Operating profit			22,000
Other revenue...........................			15,000
Income before income taxes...............			37,000
Provision for income taxes.................			13,000
Net income			$ 24,000

A detailed income statement derived from these six entries is shown in Illustration 6–5. The format of this statement matches the accounting procedures described above for the periodic method. In practice, this amount of detail is seldom seen. At the other extreme, most published income statements show only a one-line disclosure of cost of sales; Illustration 6–5's gross margin line would be the third line in such income statements (after net sales revenues and cost of goods sold). Various levels of detail between these two extremes can be found, particularly in internal income statements prepared for managers.

Product Costing Systems

The foregoing entries assumed the use of the periodic inventory method. The same transactions could be accounted for using the perpetual inventory method. In a manufacturing company the perpetual inventory method is called a **product costing system.** In such a system the cost of each product is accumulated as it flows through the production process. The amounts involved in the journal entries are obtained directly from the cost records rather than being deduced in the manner described above. The mechanisms used for collecting this information are described in Chapters 17–19.

Product Costs and Period Costs

In the accounting process described above items of cost included in the cost of producing goods are called **product costs.** Because these product costs "flow through" inventory accounts (see Illustration 6–3), they are also referred to as **inventory costs** or **inventoriable costs.** To arrive at gross margin, product costs are matched with, and subtracted from, the sales revenues in the period in which the goods are sold. Other items of cost that are matched with revenue in a given accounting period are called **period costs.** They are reported on the income statement of the period under a caption such as "selling, general, and administrative expense."

In accordance with generally accepted accounting principles (GAAP), the cost of each product includes (1) materials cost, (2) labor costs incurred directly in producing the product, and (3) a fair share of the other production costs. These other costs are called **indirect production costs** or **production overhead.** Collectively, the materials, labor, and production overhead costs comprise the **full production cost** of a product.

Companies differ in their opinions on whether specific items should be treated as product costs or period costs. Some companies include the cost of such support functions as production administration, human resource management, industrial engineering, plant protection, and product cost accounting as production overhead and hence as product costs. Other companies include the cost of some or all of these functions as period costs.[3]

The way in which a manufacturing company classifies its costs into period costs and product costs can have an important effect on its reported net income. Period costs are expenses in the accounting period in which they are incurred, whereas product costs initially add to the total amount of the entity's assets. *Product costs do not have an impact on income until the*

---

[3]Effective in 1987, the Internal Revenue Service published detailed rules regarding the types of support costs that should be treated as production overhead (inventory) costs rather than as period costs. These **Uniform Capitalization ("UNICAP") rules** have had the effect of greatly decreasing the variations in practice among companies.

product has been sold, which may be in a later accounting period than the period in which the costs were incurred. The larger the inventory in relation to sales, the longer the time interval that elapses between the incurrence of a product cost and its impact on income.[4]

All costs of a merchandising company, except the acquisition cost of its merchandise inventory (and other assets such as fixtures), are period costs. Thus, all labor and other operating costs incurred in a given period affect the income of that period. In a manufacturing company, on the other hand, those labor and other costs associated with the manufacturing process affect, initially, the value of inventory. These manufacturing (product) costs affect income only in the accounting period in which the goods containing these costs are sold.

> **Example.** Consider a wage increase amounting to $100,000 per year. In a merchandising company income is reduced $100,000 in the year in which the increase becomes effective, other things being equal. In a manufacturing company, however, that part of the increase paid to manufacturing employees first goes to increase the inventory value of the goods they worked on, and income is not affected until these goods are sold.

SERVICE COMPANIES

In principle, product costing in service firms is the same as in manufacturing firms. Application of these principles is described below for three types of service organization.

Personal services organizations such as barber shops, beauty parlors, and medical and dental practices have no inventories other than supplies inventory. Although these organizations may estimate the average cost of a haircut, a wash and set, or a routine office visit to aid them in pricing these services, these costs do not flow through inventory accounts as do product costs in a merchandising or manufacturing firm. A personal services organization may identify the labor costs of the people directly providing the service (e.g., a dental hygienist) and supplies costs (X-ray film) as elements of cost of sales, to distinguish them from "office overhead" costs (receptionist, rent, utilities, and so on).

Another category of service organization includes **building trade firms** (e.g., plumbing and electrical firms) and **repair businesses** that repair or maintain such items as appliances and automobiles. The inventories of repair parts and building materials carried by these firms are analogous to materials inventories in a manufacturing firm. Thus, the accounting for

---

[4]*FASB Statement No. 34* (October 1979) requires that interest costs related to items produced as "discrete projects" (such as ships) be treated as product costs. (The accounting procedures for this are the same as for capitalized interest on assets produced for an enterprise's own use, described in Chapter 7.) "However, interest cost shall not be capitalized for inventories that are routinely manufactured or otherwise produced in large quantities on a repetitive basis" (*Statement No. 34*, par. 10).

these inventories is conceptually the same as materials inventory ac-counting in a manufacturing firm. When materials are issued, they are recorded on some sort of cost sheet for the job. The labor costs of tradespersons or repairpersons are also recorded on this sheet, which in effect is a subsidiary work in process inventory record for the job.

In the third type of service company, **professional service firms** such as law and accounting firms, there are labor product costs but no materials costs. The accounting procedures are similar to those for building trade and repair businesses. Each project that the firm works on is given a job number and a subsidiary account is set up for the job. Time spent by professionals on a job, and any related travel costs and long-distance telephone charges, are charged to that job's account. Collectively, these job costs constitute the firm's work in process inventory, which is the only inventory (other than supplies) that such firms have. When a point is reached in the project where the agreement with the client permits these job costs to be billed, a *markup* is added for office overhead and profit, and the client is billed. The related accounting entries record the revenues—usually called **billings**—and trans-fer the costs from the Jobs in Progress account to expense, as in this example:

Accounts Receivable	10,000	
Billings (or Revenues)		10,000
Project Expenses	4,000	
Jobs in Progress		4,000

INVENTORY COSTING METHODS

One important topic remains to be discussed: the measurement of inventory and cost of goods sold when the per-unit cost of one or more items in inventory changes during the accounting period. The basic problem is that shown in Illustration 6–1: How should the cost of goods available for sale be divided between (1) cost of goods sold and (2) ending inventory? Note that the goods available for sale are assumed to be either sold or still on hand in inventory. It follows that the higher the amount assigned to cost of goods sold, the lower the amount of ending inventory, and vice versa. Several acceptable methods of handling this problem exist and the choice of method can have a significant effect on reported income. We shall discuss four widely used methods:

1. Specific identification.
2. Average cost.
3. First-in, first-out (FIFO).
4. Last-in, first-out (LIFO).

We shall illustrate these methods with an example from a merchandising company, but the same principles apply to a manufacturing company. As an illustration we shall assume the following for a year:

	Units	Unit Cost	Total Cost
Inventory, January 1	100	$ 8	$ 800
Purchased June 1	60	9	540
Purchased October 1	80	10	800
Goods available for sale	240	8.917	$2,140
Goods sold during the year	150	?	?
Ending inventory	90	?	?

Specific Identification Method

When there is a means of keeping track of the purchase cost of each item, such as with a code affixed to the item, it is possible to ascertain the actual cost of each item sold. This **specific identification method** is common practice with certain big-ticket items such as automobiles and with unique items such as paintings, expensive jewelry, and custom-made furniture; and bar codes and scanners are making it feasible with lower-cost items. In many cases, however, when a substantial number of physically similar items are sold, this method can be unsatisfactory because the cost of goods sold depends on what specific items happen to be sold. Indeed, a merchant can deliberately manipulate the cost of goods sold by selecting items that have a relatively high cost or a relatively low cost.

Example. In the illustration above, 150 units were sold. If the merchant selected the 100 units with a unit cost of $8 and 50 of the units having a unit cost of $9, the cost of goods sold would be (100 * $8) + (50 * $9) = $1,250. If the 150 units with the highest cost were selected, the cost of goods sold would be (80 * $10) + (60 * $9) + (10 * $8) = $1,420.

Average Cost Method

With the **average cost method** the average cost of the goods available for sale is computed, and the units in both cost of goods sold and ending inventory are costed at this average cost. In the periodic inventory method this average is computed for the whole period. It is a weighted average: each unit cost is weighted by the number of units with that cost. In the perpetual inventory method a new average unit cost is sometimes calculated after each purchase. In either case the average cost is representative of the cost of all of the items that were available for sale during the period.

Example. Assuming the periodic inventory method, the 240 units available for sale have a total cost of $2,140; hence, the average cost is $2,140 ÷ 240 = $8.917. The calculations of cost of goods sold and ending inventory are as follows:

	Units	Unit Cost	Total*
Cost of goods sold	150	$8.917	$1,338
Ending inventory	90	8.917	802
Total	240		$2,140

* Rounded.

Some companies use a predetermined unit cost for all transactions during the period. This is a **standard cost system** and is discussed in Chapter 19. It is essentially a variation of the average cost method.

The average cost method gives results that are in between the next two methods to be described, FIFO and LIFO. It is therefore a compromise for those who do not find the arguments for one or the other of these methods to be compelling.

First-In, First-Out Method

The FIFO method assumes that the oldest goods are sold first and that the most recently purchased goods are in the ending inventory. In the illustration, for the 150 units sold it is assumed that the 100 units in beginning inventory were sold first and that the other 50 units sold were from the purchase made on June 1.

	Units	Unit Cost	Total Cost
Cost of goods sold:			
From beginning inventory	100	$ 8	$ 800
From purchase of June 1	50	9	450
Cost of goods sold	150		$1,250
Ending inventory:			
From purchase of June 1	10	$ 9	$ 90
From purchase of October 1	80	10	800
Ending inventory	90		$ 890

We shall contrast the LIFO and FIFO methods below. For the moment, it is sufficient to note that with FIFO (1) cost of goods sold is likely to approximate the *physical* flow of the goods because most companies sell their oldest merchandise first and (2) the ending inventory approximates the *current cost* of the goods, since it is costed at the amounts of most recent purchases.

Last-In, First-Out Method

The LIFO method is the opposite of FIFO. Cost of goods sold is based on the most recent purchases, and ending inventory is costed at the cost of the oldest units available.

	Units	Unit Cost	Total Cost
Cost of goods sold:			
From purchase of October 1	80	$10	$ 800
From purchase of June 1	60	9	540
From beginning inventory	10	8	80
Cost of goods sold	150		$1,420
Ending inventory:			
From beginning inventory	90	$ 8	$ 720

Note that with LIFO (1) cost of goods sold does *not* reflect the usual physical flow of merchandise and (2) the ending inventory may be costed at amounts prevailing several years ago, which in an era of rapid inflation are *far below* current costs.

LIFO Dollar Value Method.   Originally LIFO was used only by companies whose inventory consisted of fungible products, such as wheat, each unit of which is physically like every other unit. Other companies, however, successfully argued that this was unfair to them. Thus, LIFO may now be used for almost any kind of inventory. It is applied to an inventory of physically unlike items by the so-called **LIFO dollar value method.** In this method items whose prices tend to move together are grouped into an *inventory pool.* For example, a pool may consist of all the items in the inventory of the housewares department in a store. The calculations required to determine cost of goods sold and inventory amounts with this method are beyond the scope of this book. Compared with the unit-by-unit LIFO method, dollar value LIFO saves a considerable amount of recordkeeping effort.

Changes in Inventory.   In a year when the *physical* size of the inventory *increases* above the amount on hand at the beginning of the year, with LIFO the inventory account is increased by the additional quantity valued at the costs existing during that year. During a period of growth the inventory account will therefore consist of a number of *layers,* a new layer being added each year. If subsequently the physical inventory should *decrease* in size, these layers are, in effect, stripped off, taking the most recently added layer first in accordance with the basic LIFO rule. This process can have a peculiar effect on the income statement. If inventory is decreased to the extent that several LIFO layers are stripped off, then inventory items will be moving into cost of goods sold at costs established several years previously. If there has been constant inflation during the interim, such a decrease in inventory can result in a significant increase in reported income. Some people assert that in a recession, some companies deliberately eat into their LIFO inventories in order to increase reported income in a lean year.

> **Example.**   Illustration 6–6 depicts a situation in which the unit cost of an item of inventory was $10.00 in the year in which LIFO was adopted (the "base" year, 19x0). In each of the next five years, in anticipation of continuing sales increases, the company increased inventory by 50 units a year. In 19x6, inflation increased and sales fell dramatically. The company therefore reduced its inventory significantly by purchasing 300 fewer units than the number of units sold. This action caused all five of the LIFO layers to be stripped off (amounting to 250 units), as well as 50 units of the base layer. The 19x6 cost of goods sold using LIFO was $10,020. By contrast, if 19x6 purchases had equaled or exceeded sales (in physical units), then cost of goods sold would have been based entirely on the 19x6 acquisition cost of $13.50 per unit: 800 * $13.50 = $10,800. This is $780 (7.8 percent) higher than the cost of goods sold with the LIFO layers being stripped.

ILLUSTRATION 6–6

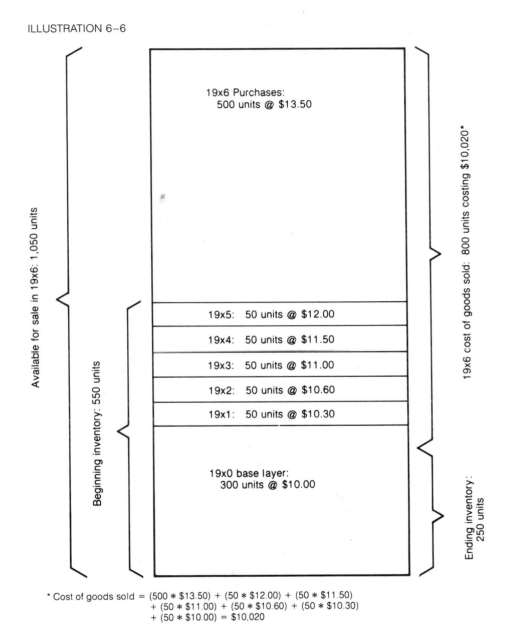

Available for sale in 19x6: 1,050 units

Beginning inventory: 550 units

19x6 Purchases:
500 units @ $13.50

19x5: 50 units @ $12.00

19x4: 50 units @ $11.50

19x3: 50 units @ $11.00

19x2: 50 units @ $10.60

19x1: 50 units @ $10.30

19x0 base layer:
300 units @ $10.00

19x6 cost of goods sold: 800 units costing $10,020*

Ending inventory:
250 units

* Cost of goods sold = (500 ∗ $13.50) + (50 ∗ $12.00) + (50 ∗ $11.50)
+ (50 ∗ $11.00) + (50 ∗ $10.60) + (50 ∗ $10.30)
+ (50 ∗ $10.00) = $10,020

LIFO Reserve. Some companies that use LIFO for determining their balance sheet valuation of inventory nevertheless keep their detailed inventory records on a FIFO or average cost basis. The inventory amounts on these other bases usually will be higher than the LIFO valuation shown on the balance sheet. The difference between the LIFO valuation and the FIFO or average cost valuation is sometimes called the **LIFO Reserve.** The terminology is unfortunate because "reserve" suggests something set aside or saved for some special future purpose. The LIFO Reserve is nothing more than the mathematical difference between two inventory amounts, one based on LIFO and the other one based on a different method of valuing inventory.

Comparison of Methods

The following table summarizes the illustrative results of three of the four methods described above (the specific identification method depends on the specific items selected):

	Cost of Goods Sold	Ending Inventory	Total
FIFO........................	$1,250	$890	$2,140
Average cost.................	1,338	802	2,140
LIFO........................	1,420	720	2,140

All of the methods described are in accordance with United States GAAP, and all are acceptable by the Internal Revenue Service (IRS) for calculating taxable income.[5] However, most other countries do not permit the use of LIFO.

Arguments for FIFO. A primary conceptual argument for using FIFO is that it matches the costs of the goods that are *physically* sold with the revenues generated by selling those goods. Also, many companies set selling prices by adding a gross margin to the cost of the actual goods to be sold. Conceptually, such a price results in the company's recovering the funds it had invested in the particular item to be sold, plus a margin to provide for recovery of selling and administrative costs and a reasonable profit. For example, this pricing philosophy is commonly applied in retailing companies such as grocery and department stores.

> **Example.** This brief item from *The Wall Street Journal* reflects the idea of pricing based on the cost of the goods actually (physically) sold: "Retail coffee prices are being cut by supermarket chains around the nation. The reductions are selective because of lingering high-priced inventories; when these are gone, wholesale-price cuts can be passed on to the public."

Thus, it is argued, if a company's management thinks of gross margin as the difference between selling prices and the cost of the goods physically sold, then it should use FIFO, which will report this same margin in the company's income statement.

The other primary argument for FIFO reflects a balance sheet orientation. Many people feel that the amount shown for inventory on the balance sheet should be approximately equal to the current cost of that inventory. The

---

[5]*Accounting Trends & Techniques* (1993) reports that of the 1,011 mentions of inventory methods in the 600 companies surveyed, 415 used FIFO, 193 used average cost, and 358 used LIFO. (The 600 companies had 1,011 inventories because many companies use different methods for different categories of inventory.) Only 23 companies used LIFO for *all* inventories; another 189 used it for 50 percent or more of their inventories.

mechanics of FIFO, which assume that the goods in inventory are those most recently acquired, result in an inventory valuation that is closer to current costs than would result if LIFO or average cost were used. (This is true irrespective of the rate of inflation.)

A final argument for FIFO is more practical than conceptual. Many companies select accounting methods with the objective of maximizing in the near term the amount of income that is reported to their shareholders. Since for several decades in this country the costs of the items in most companies' inventories have been increasing and since FIFO reports a lower cost of goods sold amount than average cost or LIFO does under such inflationary conditions, many companies have preferred FIFO because of its characteristic of increasing reported income.

Arguments for LIFO. Proponents of LIFO also base their primary conceptual argument on the matching concept. They argue that gross margin should reflect the difference between sales revenues, which are necessarily current amounts, and the current cost of the goods sold. Although seldom made explicit, this LIFO matching argument assumes that a company's management sets selling prices by adding a margin to current costs rather than to historical costs. If this is indeed the case, then the gross margin reported using LIFO will reflect management's thinking as to the nature of gross margin.

It should be pointed out that although this conceptual argument for LIFO involves the notion of the current cost of goods sold, LIFO only approximates these current costs. Generally, **current cost of goods sold** means the cost of acquiring items identical in type and number to those sold to *replenish the inventory* immediately after a sale. This is also called **replacement cost inventory accounting,** or, more jocularly, *NIFO* (for next-in, first-out). True replacement cost accounting is not permitted either by GAAP or the income tax code.

While focusing on income statement matching, LIFO proponents downplay the impact of LIFO on balance sheet inventory valuation. Because the base layer of inventory is valued forever in terms of price levels prevailing when LIFO was adopted, the LIFO inventory valuation departs further and further from reality as time goes on, thus reflecting neither actual purchase costs nor replacement costs. In periods of prolonged inflation, such as the 1970s and early 1980s, this LIFO valuation may be far below current costs, making the inventory figure of dubious usefulness. Thus, whereas FIFO leads to a cost of goods sold amount of questionable usefulness and thus casts doubt on the usefulness of the income statement, LIFO casts a similar doubt in the usefulness of the balance sheet amount for inventory and, thus, on the amounts for current assets, total assets, and owners' equity.

This problem with LIFO can be mitigated, however. Although the amount reported as inventory on the balance sheet may be unrealistically low, the company can provide explanations in the notes to the financial statements that permit the reader to convert the inventory to a FIFO basis.

Income Tax Considerations. FIFO, average cost, and LIFO are all permitted for U.S. income tax calculations—although once a method is chosen, a company cannot change it without seeking permission from the IRS. If a company chooses the LIFO method for tax purposes, it must also use LIFO in its published financial statements. This **LIFO conformity rule** is the only significant instance in which the IRS requires use of the same accounting method for income tax and "book" (financial reporting) purposes.

In periods of inflation LIFO results in lower income than FIFO or average costs, and thus results in lower income taxes. If the physical size of inventory remains constant or grows, LIFO reduces taxable income indefinitely. Only if LIFO layers are stripped off in future years might taxable income under LIFO exceed taxable income under FIFO; and even in that case, LIFO will have postponed some income tax payments. These tax advantages of LIFO, which improve a company's cash flow, lead many companies to select the LIFO method, outweighing any conceptual pros and cons of the various alternatives.

Why Not More LIFO? Since LIFO improves a company's cash flow, why don't *all* companies use it for *all* of their inventories? At least three reasons can be given.

First, many large U.S. corporations have operations in countries where LIFO is not permitted. For such a company, the non-LIFO foreign inventories cannot be changed to a LIFO basis when they are added to domestic inventories. Thus, even if all of its domestic inventories are on LIFO, the company is precluded from reporting 100 percent of its inventories on a LIFO basis.

Second, although the economy as a whole may be experiencing inflation, the prices of the specific items in a company's inventory are not necessarily increasing. In some instances, particularly in the electronics industry, specific prices fall even while general inflation continues. For example, in 1970 the retail price of a four-function, hand-held calculator was $395; today, a similar item retails for under $10. Companies whose inventory replacement costs are trending downward will pay lower taxes by using FIFO rather than LIFO.

Third, and probably most important, in a company for which LIFO will reduce taxable income and thus lower income tax payments, the company also must report the lower LIFO income to its shareholders because of the LIFO conformity rule. This means that the cash flow improvement from LIFO will be accompanied by a decrease in reported earnings per share (relative to cash flows and earnings if FIFO were used). Although academic research studies suggest that the stock market does not penalize a company whose earnings drop because of a change to LIFO, many top managers of U.S. companies have long held the view that lower reported earnings per share are associated with lower stock prices, whatever the cause of the lower earnings. Thus, in considering LIFO, many managers see a dilemma: increasing cash flow through lower tax payments is clearly good for the corporation, but they believe that the accompanying decrease in reported earnings is bad for the shareholders. Since top management serves at the pleasure of the board of directors and since the board is supposed to protect shareholders' interests, often the decision is to opt for FIFO and higher reported earnings rather than LIFO and improved cash flows.

LOWER OF COST OR MARKET

All the foregoing had to do with measuring the *cost* of inventory. The LIFO and FIFO methods are alternative ways of measuring cost. The general inventory valuation principle, deriving from the conservatism concept, is that inventory is reported on the balance sheet at the *lower of its cost or its market value.*

In the ordinary situation inventory is reported at its cost. It is reduced below cost (i.e., written down) only when there is evidence that the value of the items, when eventually sold or otherwise disposed of, will be less than their cost. Such evidence may include physical deterioration, obsolescence, drops in price level, or other causes. When this evidence exists inventory is stated at market.

Since the goods in inventory have not in fact been sold, their true market value is not ordinarily known and must therefore be estimated. The FASB states that this estimate should be the current *replacement* cost of the item; that is, what it would cost currently to purchase or manufacture the item.[6] The FASB further sets upper and lower boundaries on "market":

1. It should not be higher than the estimated selling price of the item less the costs associated with selling it. This amount is called the **net realizable value.**

2. It should not be lower than the net realizable value less a normal profit margin.

These principles can be compressed into the following rule: Use historical cost if that cost is lowest; otherwise, use the next-to-lowest of the other three possibilities.

Example. Assume four items with amounts as in the table shown below. The inventory amount to be used for each is starred.

	Item			
	1	*2*	*3*	*4*
a. Historical cost	$7*	$9	$9	$10
b. Current replacement cost	8	8*	7	9
c. Net realizable value (ceiling)	10	9	9	8*
d. Net realizable value less profit margin (floor)	9	7	8*	7

[6]*Accounting Research Bulletin No. 43,* Chapter 4.

As is true for the rules for marketable securities, which are applied to the individual securities in a portfolio, the rule for inventory is applied to each item in inventory (i.e., each unique part number or product number).

ANALYSIS OF INVENTORY

Inventory Turnover

The ratio most commonly used in analyzing the size of the inventory item is **inventory turnover:**

$$\text{Inventory turnover} = \frac{\text{Cost of goods sold}}{\text{Inventory}}$$

If the cost of goods sold for a year is $1 million and inventory is $250,000, then the inventory turnover is 4.0 times. This is equivalent to saying that the inventory turns over once every three months (quarter of a year).

Some companies calculate this ratio on the basis of the ending inventory, others on the basis of the average inventory. The average may be simply one-half the sum of beginning and ending inventories for the year, or it may be an average of monthly inventory levels. The end-of-period basis is more representative of the current state of the inventory if volume is expected to continue at previous levels. The average basis is a better reflection of events that occurred during the period because it measures the amount of inventory that supported the sales activity of that period.

Inventory turnover varies greatly with the nature of the business. It should be high for a store that sells fresh produce; otherwise spoilage is likely to be a problem. A supermarket may have an inventory turnover close to 50, a petroleum refinery 20. On the other hand, a jewelry store with a wide selection of expensive and unusual items may not turn its inventory as often as once a year, and most art galleries have a turnover much lower than 1.

One must also consider the seasonality of sales. For example, college book stores have high inventories before the start of each new term, with lower inventories in between. In such entities an annual calculation of inventory turnover has little meaning, and inventory measured at various seasonal high and low points is of more significance.

Inventory turnover indicates the velocity with which merchandise moves through a business. Turnover may fall either because of inventory buildup in anticipation of increased sales or because sales volume has declined, leaving excess merchandise on hand. The first is a favorable event; the second is unfavorable. The turnover number itself does not indicate which is the cause.

Days' Inventory. The same relationship can be expressed as the number of days' inventory on hand. If one has already calculated inventory turnover, then days' inventory is simply 365 ÷ inventory turnover. Days' inventory can be calculated directly as follows:

$$\text{Days' inventory} = \frac{\text{Inventory}}{\text{Cost of goods sold} \div 365} = \frac{\$250,000}{\$1,000,000 \div 365} = 91 \text{ days}$$

Of course, both the inventory turnover and days' inventory calculations are affected by the company's inventory costing method. Because, relative to FIFO, the LIFO method results in lower reported inventory value on the balance sheet and higher cost of goods sold, a company using LIFO will have a higher indicated inventory turnover ratio and a lower indicated number of days' inventory than if it were using FIFO. Such differences must be taken into account when comparing ratios for different entities.

SUMMARY

The objectives of inventory accounting are (1) to match the cost of goods sold, an expense, with the revenue earned from the sale of those goods in an accounting period and (2) to measure the cost of inventory on hand at the end of the period, which is an asset.

A merchandising company has one inventory account. The separation of the cost of the goods available for sale into the amount determined to be cost of goods sold and the amount determined to be ending merchandise inventory can be accomplished either by the periodic inventory method or the perpetual inventory method. In the former, ending inventory is obtained by a physical count, and cost of goods sold is obtained by deduction. In the latter, both amounts are obtained directly from inventory records.

A manufacturing company has three inventory accounts: materials, work in process, and finished goods. In the periodic inventory method the amount in each account is determined by taking a physical inventory and then deducing the cost of materials used, the cost of goods manufactured, and the cost of goods sold. In a perpetual inventory system, also called a product costing system, these costs are obtained directly from the accounting records.

Inventory is ordinarily measured at its cost. In a merchandising company cost is essentially the amount expended to acquire the goods. In a manufacturing company product costs include, in addition to materials costs, the labor cost and other production costs incurred in converting the materials into finished goods. Other operating costs, in either type of company, are called period costs; they are expenses of the current period.

The flow of costs can be measured by any of several methods, including specific identification; average costs; first-in, first-out (FIFO); and last-in, first-out (LIFO). Although the LIFO method usually results in lower income taxes, many companies do not use it because the LIFO conformity rule would result in their reporting lower net income to their shareholders.

If the market value of an inventory item is below cost, the item is reported at its market value.

Two ratios helpful in analyzing inventories are inventory turnover and days' inventory.

Cases

CASE 6–1 Riechel Company

Listed below in alphabetical order are certain accounts of the Riechel Company with balances for the year ended December 31.

Questions

1. Prepare a detailed income statement for the year ended December 31.

2. Assume that inventories on December 31 were the same amounts as on January 1. How would an income statement prepared under this assumption differ from that requested in Question 1? Explain the reasons for these changes. (Assume that income tax expense is the same percentage of income before income taxes.)

Administrative expense	$ 43,730
Customer returns and allowances	46,060
Depreciation—nonfactory	4,050
Depreciation—plant and equipment	44,500
Direct labor cost	221,830
Dividends	20,000
Factory heat, light, and power	100,100
Factory supplies cost	28,350
Finished goods inventory, 1/1	84,160
Finished goods inventory, 12/31	87,880
Freight-in	10,530
Gain on disposal of machinery	7,920
Goods in process inventory, 1/1	33,140
Goods in process inventory, 12/31	34,160
Income tax expense	28,560
Indirect labor	27,980
Insurance and taxes (factory)	15,160
Interest expenses	11,710
Purchases	323,480
Raw materials inventory, 1/1	198,680
Raw materials inventory, 12/31	176,660
Sales	1,010,200
Selling expense	51,960

CASE 6-2   Fahning Manufacturing Company*

The management of Fahning Manufacturing Company annually prepared a budget of expected financial operations for the ensuing calendar year. The completed budget provided information on all aspects of the coming year's operations. It included a projected balance sheet as of the end of the year and a projected income statement.

The final preparation of statements was accomplished only after careful integration of detailed computations submitted by each department. This was done to ensure that the operations of all departments were in balance with one another. For example, the finance department needed to base its schedules of loan transactions and of collections and disbursements on numbers that were dependent on manufacturing, purchasing, and selling expectations. The level of production would be geared to the forecasts of the sales department, and purchasing would be geared to the proposed manufacturing schedule.

In short, it was necessary to integrate the estimates of each department and to revise them in terms of the overall effect on operations to arrive at a coordinated and profitable plan of operations for the coming year. The budget statements ultimately derived from the adjusted estimated transactions would then serve the company as a reliable guide and measure of the coming year's operations.

At the time the 1993 budget was being prepared, in November of 1992, projected 1992 financial statements were compiled for use as a comparison with the budgeted figures. These 1992 statements were based on ten months' actual and two months' projected transactions. They appear as Exhibits 1, 2, and 3.

---

*Copyright © by the President and Fellows of Harvard College. Harvard Business School case 195-147.

Below is the summary of expected operations for the budget year 1993 as finally accepted:

1. *Sales:* All on credit, $2,562,000; sales returns and allowances, $19,200; sales discounts taken by customers (for prompt payment), $49,200. (The sales figure is net of expected bad debts.)

2. *Purchases of goods and services:*
   a. New assets:
      Purchased for cash: manufacturing plant and equipment, $144,000; prepaid manufacturing taxes and insurance, $78,000. Purchased on accounts payable: materials, $825,000; supplies, $66,000.
   b. Services used to convert materials into work in process, all purchased for cash: direct manufacturing labor, $492,000; indirect manufacturing labor, $198,000; social security taxes on labor, $49,200; power, heat, and light, $135,600.
   c. Selling and administrative services, purchased for cash: $522,000.

3. *Conversion of assets into work in process:* This appears as an increase in the cost of work in process and a decrease in the appropriate asset accounts. Depreciation of manufacturing building and equipment, $140,400; expiration of prepaid taxes and insurance, $52,800; supplies used in manufacturing, $61,200; materials put into process, $811,800.

4. *Transfer of work in process to finished goods:* This appears as an increase in finished goods and a decrease in work in process. Total cost accumulated on goods that have been completed and transferred to finished goods, $1,901,952.

5. *Cost of finished goods sold to customers:* $1,806,624.

EXHIBIT 1

FAHNING MANUFACTURING COMPANY
Projected Balance Sheet
December 31, 1992

Assets

Current assets:

Cash and marketable securities		$ 118,440
Accounts receivable (net of allowance for doubtful accounts)		311,760
Inventories:		
Materials	$ 110,520	
Work in process	172,200	
Finished goods	257,040	
Supplies	17,280	557,040
Prepaid taxes and insurance		66,720
Total current assets		1,053,960
Other assets:		
Manufacturing plant at cost	2,678,400	
Less: Accumulated depreciation	907,200	1,771,200
Total assets		$2,825,160

Liabilities and Shareholders' Equity

Current liabilities:

Accounts payable	$ 185,760	
Notes payable	288,840	
Income taxes payable	9,000	
Total current liabilities		$ 483,600
Shareholders' equity:		
Capital stock	1,512,000	
Retained earnings	829,560	2,341,560
Total liabilities and shareholders' equity		$2,825,160

---

6. *Financial transactions:*
   a. $264,000, borrowed on notes payable to bank.
   b. Notes payable repaid, $300,000.
   c. Cash payment to bank of $38,400 for interest on loans.

7. *Cash receipts from customers on accounts receivable: $2,604,000.*

8. *Cash payments of liabilities:*
   a. Payment of accounts payable, $788,400.
   b. Payment of 1992 income tax, $9,000.

9. *Estimated federal income tax on 1993 income: $58,000, of which $5,800 is estimated to be unpaid as of December 31, 1993.*

10. *Dividends declared for year and paid in cash: $36,000.*

This summary presents the complete cycle of the Fahning Manufacturing Company's budgeted yearly operations from the purchase of goods and services through their various stages of conversion to completion of the finished product to the sale of this product. All costs and cash receipts and disbursements involved in this cycle are presented, including the provision for federal income taxes and the payment of dividends.

Questions

1. Journalize each of the projected transactions. Set up T accounts with balances as shown on

EXHIBIT 2

FAHNING MANUFACTURING COMPANY
Projected 1992 Statement of Cost of Goods Sold

Finished goods inventory, 1/1/92			$ 218,820
Work in process inventory, 1/1/92		$ 137,760	
Materials used		663,120	
Plus: Factory expenses:			
Direct manufacturing labor		419,040	
Factory overhead:			
Indirect manufacturing labor	$170,640		
Power, heat, and light	116,760		
Depreciation of plant	126,600		
Social security taxes	42,120		
Taxes and insurance, factory	46,320		
Supplies	56,880	559,320	
		1,779,240	
Less: Work in process inventory, 12/31/92		172,200	
Cost of goods manufactured (i.e., completed)			1,607,040
			1,825,320
Less: Finished goods inventory, 12/31/92			257,040
Cost of goods sold			$1,568,280

EXHIBIT 3

FAHNING MANUFACTURING COMPANY
Projected 1992 Income Statement

Sales		$2,295,600
Less: Sales returns and allowances	$17,640	
Sales discounts allowed	43,920	61,560
Net sales		2,234,040
Less: Cost of goods sold (per schedule)		1,568,280
Gross margin		665,760
Less: Selling and administrative expense		437,160
Operating income		228,600
Less: Interest expense		34,080
Income before federal income tax		194,520
Less: Estimated income tax expense		89,520
Net income		$ 105,000

the balance sheet for December 31, 1992, and post the journal entries to these accounts.

2. Prepare a projected statement of cost of goods sold for 1993, a projected income statement for 1993, and a projected balance sheet as of December 31, 1993.

3. Describe the principal differences between the 1993 estimates and the 1992 figures as shown in Exhibits 1, 2, and 3. In what respects is 1993 performance expected to be better than 1992 performance, and in what respects is it expected to be worse?

CASE 6–3 Medfield Corporation

Medfield Corporation had traditionally used the FIFO method of inventory valuation. You are given the information shown below on transactions affecting Medfield's inventory account.

Questions

1. Calculate the cost of goods sold and year-end inventory amounts for 1991, 1992, and 1993 using the *(a)* FIFO, *(b)* LIFO, and *(c)* average cost methods.

2. Medfield Corporation is considering switching from FIFO to LIFO to reduce its income tax expense. Assuming a corporate income tax rate of 40 percent, calculate the tax savings this would have made for 1991 to 1993. Would you recommend that Medfield Corporation make this change?

3. Dollar sales for 1994 are expected to drop by approximately 8 percent, as a recession in Medfield's market is forecasted to continue at least through the first three quarters of the year. Total sales are forecasted to be 2,700 cartons. Medfield Corporation will be unable to raise its selling price from the 1993 level of $35.75. However, costs are expected to increase to $24 per carton for the whole year. Due to these cost/price pressures, the corporation wishes to lower its investment in inventory by holding only the essential inventory of 400 cartons at any time during the year. What is the effect of remaining on FIFO, assuming Medfield had adopted FIFO in 1991? What is the effect of remaining on LIFO, assuming Medfield adopted LIFO in 1991? What method would you recommend now?

4. What is the LIFO reserve in 1991? What is the LIFO reserve in 1992? What is the significance of the LIFO reserve number? How much did the LIFO reserve increase in 1992? What is the significance of this increase?

5. Despite continuing inflation in the United States in the 1980s and the early 1990s, many companies continue to use FIFO for all or part of their inventories. Why is this the case?

1991	
Beginning balance	1,840 cartons @ $20.00
Purchases	600 cartons @ 20.25
	800 cartons @ 21.00
	400 cartons @ 21.25
	200 cartons @ 21.50
Sales	2,820 cartons @ 34.00
1992	
Beginning balance	1,020 cartons
Purchases	700 cartons @ $21.50
	700 cartons @ 21.50
	700 cartons @ 22.00
	1,000 cartons @ 22.25
Sales	3,080 cartons @ 35.75
1993	
Beginning balance	1,040 cartons
Purchases	1,000 cartons @ $22.50
	700 cartons @ 22.75
	700 cartons @ 23.00
	700 cartons @ 23.50
Sales	2,950 cartons @ 35.75

CASE 6–4   Morgan Manufacturing

Charles Crutchfield, manager of manufacturing operations at Morgan Manufacturing, was evaluating the performance of the company. Given his position, he was primarily interested in the health of the operating aspects of the business. At Morgan, the gross margin percentage was considered to be a key measure of operating performance; other measures considered to provide essential information on the health of business operations were pretax return on sales and pretax return on assets. Crutchfield considered the after-tax versions of these measures less relevant for his purposes because they combined information reflecting the health of operations with information reflecting the

effectiveness of the tax accounting department, which was not under his control.

From Morgan Manufacturing's 1991 income statements and balance sheets, shown in Exhibit 1, Crutchfield computed Morgan Manufacturing's gross margin percentage (44.5%), pretax return on sales (14.5%), and pretax return on assets (13.4%). Crutchfield was especially interested in comparing his firm's performance against that of its major competitor, Westwood, Inc. Crutchfield felt that Morgan had recently made significant productivity improvements over Westwood that would be reflected in the financial statements. When he looked at Westwood's 1991 financial statements (Exhibit 2), he was quite

EXHIBIT 1
MORGAN MANUFACTURING FINANCIAL STATEMENTS ($ millions)

Income Statement, for the year ended December 31	1990	1991
Sales	$1,500	$2,000
Cost of goods sold	810	1,110
Gross margin	690	890
Selling, general, and administrative expenses	450	600
Income before taxes	240	290
Income tax expense	96	116
Net income	$ 144	$ 174

Balance Sheet, as of December 31	1990	1991
Cash	$ 100	$ 140
Accounts receivable	250	350
Inventory	120	100
Plant, property, and equipment (net)	1,385	1,580
Total assets	$1,855	$2,170
Current liabilities	$ 250	$ 325
Long-term liabilities	500	675
Common stock	400	400
Retained earnings	705	770
Total liabilities and owners' equity	$1,855	$2,170
LIFO reserve	$10	$70

EXHIBIT 2
WESTWOOD, INC. FINANCIAL STATEMENTS ($ millions)

Income Statement, for the year ended December 31	1990	1991
Sales	$1,500	$2,000
Cost of goods sold	800	1,100
Gross margin	700	900
Selling, general, and administrative expenses	450	600
Income before taxes	250	300
Income tax expense	100	120
Net income	$ 150	$ 180

Balance Sheet, as of December 31	1990	1991
Cash	$ 100	$ 140
Accounts receivable	250	350
Inventory	140	170
Plant, property, and equipment (net)	1,385	1,580
Total assets	$1,875	$2,240
Current liabilities	$ 250	$ 330
Long-term liabilities	500	675
Common stock	400	400
Retained earnings	725	835
Total liabilities and owners' equity	$1,875	$2,240

disappointed. Despite the similarities between the two companies based on the three key measures, he concluded that Westwood's financial performance was better.

Distraught, Crutchfield sought the advice of Edward Drewery, controller. "How can Westwood's results be better than ours, when I know that our operations are more efficient?" The controller responded, "I'm not sure about the relative efficiency of the two firms' operations, but I do know that we use a different method to account for inventory than Westwood uses. Have you taken that into account?" "Not really," replied Crutchfield. "Well, all you need to know," continued Drewery, "is that we use LIFO; Westwood uses FIFO; and our LIFO reserve was $10 million in 1990 and $70 million in 1991."

Crutchfield wondered how the reported results could be adjusted so that the comparison could be done on a comparable basis.

Questions

1. What are Westwood's gross margin percentage, pretax return on sales (pretax income ÷ sales), and pretax return on assets (pretax income ÷ total assets)?

2. Which accounts and financial measures that appear on the income statement or balance sheet are affected by the differing choices of inventory accounting method? Explain how the choice of different inventory accounting methods affects one's ability to directly compare the results of these two companies.

3. Using the information available in the exhibits, make the necessary adjustments to the 1991 results so that you can better compare the performance of the two companies on the three key measures.

4. Which of the two companies do you believe is performing better? Why?

CASE 6–5   R. J. Reynolds Tobacco Company*

On September 13, 1989, Louis V. Gerstner, in his fifth month as chief executive officer (CEO) of RJR Nabisco Holding Corp., received a call from James W. Johnston, the executive he had recruited in June to head the R. J. Reynolds Tobacco Company (RJRT), RJR Nabisco's U.S. tobacco division. Johnston had been investigating the buildup of excess cigarette inventories in the warehouses of RJRT's independent distributors.

Johnston's opposition to this practice of "trade loading" had been a factor in his departure from the company five years earlier and now he was in a position to put an end to it. In 1988 the company had instituted, and then abandoned, a three-year plan to eliminate trade loading gradually, but Johnston now proposed to do it immediately. It would be, he said, "a real statement of change in emphasis and direction," and "there's probably no single thing . . . that would [energize] the place as much" as this action.[1] He asked for Gerstner's approval.

Company Background. Chewing tobacco was the first product manufactured by RJRT, a firm founded in 1875 in Winston-Salem, North Carolina, by Richard Joshua Reynolds. By the early 1900s the company was the largest employer in North Carolina, having purchased many competing local firms.

In 1913 RJRT was the first company to market a national brand of ready-to-smoke cigarettes. At the time most smokers preferred to roll their own, as the regional brands had a reputation for poor taste. With a clever advertising campaign and prices half those of rival brands, Camel cigarettes swamped the competitors and became the first cigarette to be sold by the carton. RJRT lost its number one market position to American Tobacco Company's Lucky Strikes in 1929, but regained it in the next decade through aggressive advertising. RJRT again lost its lead position to American Tobacco in the 1940s, when management's attention was diverted to breaking a union formed by workers.

Early reports about the dangers of cigarette smoking led to RJRT's 1954 introduction of Winston, the first major filtered cigarette, followed soon by Salem, the first mass-marketed menthol cigarette. With these two new products, RJRT's sales again passed those of American Tobacco in 1959. In the 1960s RJRT diversified into transportation, energy, and food. In the late 1970s and early 1980s it focused on consumer products, acquiring Del Monte, Heublein, Inc., and Nabisco (including Planters and LifeSavers). During the 1980s RJR divested many businesses, retaining only its tobacco and food products operations. In 1983 a new rival, Philip Morris, overtook RJRT's leading position in the industry with its popular Marlboro brand.

The Buyout. In November 1988 RJR Nabisco agreed to be purchased by the investment firm of Kohlberg Kravis Roberts & Company (KKR) in a leveraged buyout agreement worth approximately $25 billion. F. Ross Johnson, RJR Nabisco's flamboyant chairman, originated the idea for a buyout. Johnson had risen to his position through a series of victories in corporate power struggles and company mergers and acquisitions. As CEO of Standard Brands, he negotiated a merger with Nabisco in 1981 through a $1.9 billion stock swap. Johnson became

*Copyright © by the President and Fellows of Harvard College. Harvard Business School case 194–074.
[1]Carol J. Loomis, "The $600 Million Cigarette Scam," *Fortune,* Dec. 4, 1989, p. 100.

CEO of the new Nabisco Brands in 1984, and in 1985 he helped to engineer the merger with RJRT. Through careful cultivation of board members, Johnson developed the support he needed to become chairman of RJR Nabisco in 1986.

As chairman, Johnson was dissatisfied with the $50–$60 market value of the company's stock. Johnson was sure the company was worth much more. Accordingly, in the fall of 1988, he proposed to the board that he lead a management buyout of the giant corporation at $75 per share, a transaction valued at an unprecedented $17 billion. In response, the surprised board formed a special committee to put RJR Nabisco up for auction. This led to a multi-round bidding war involving most of the major Wall Street takeover specialists. Johnson and his backers at the Shearson Lehman Hutton brokerage unit of American Express ultimately lost to KKR, whose winning bid of $109 per share, $25 billion in total, was financed by high-yield, unsecured junk bonds. On February 9, 1989, RJR Holdings Corporation, an entity set up by KKR, officially acquired ownership of RJR Nabisco, and Johnson resigned. KKR quickly hired Gerstner, formerly a top executive at American Express, to take over as CEO in April.

When Gerstner assumed control the company had a very different financial profile from the one run by Johnson. In the second quarter of 1989, RJR Holdings Corporation had over $1 billion of interest expense and long-term debt of $22.3 billion. In comparison, in the second quarter of 1988, RJR Nabisco incurred only $145 million in interest expense and its total long-term debt at the end of 1988 was $4.9 billion.

Current Position. In 1988 RJRT was the second largest cigarette manufacturer in the United States, with a 31.8 percent share (see Exhibit 1). Together with RJR Nabisco's international tobacco operations, tobacco product

EXHIBIT 1
1988 RJRT MARKET SHARE AND POSITION[1]

Brand	Market Share*	Market Position*
Winston	10.7%	2
Salem	7.3	3
Camel	4.3	6
Doral	3.4	9
Vantage	2.9	11
RJRT overall	31.8%	2

*Based on independent estimated 1988 shipments to wholesalers.
[1]Source: RJR Nabisco, Form 10-K (1988), p. F-6.

sales of $7.1 billion generated operating income of $1.9 billion, compared to $6.3 billion and $1.8 billion, respectively, in 1987. (See Exhibit 2 for RJR Nabisco financial statements.) RJRT sold its cigarettes primarily to chain stores, other large retail outlets, and through distributors to retail and wholesale outlets. No customer accounted for more than 5 percent of sales in 1988. RJRT's marketing efforts were aimed at its ultimate consumer—the general public. Image-oriented advertising techniques utilized newspapers and magazines, billboards, coupons, point-of-sale displays, and sponsorship of recreational events.

Smoking and Society. U.S. cigarette sales peaked in the early 1980s and have since declined. Although tobacco companies once marketed their products as actually promoting health, research studies were published in the 1950s linking cigarette smoking and lung cancer. In 1964 a report by the Surgeon General of the United States condemned smoking as carcinogenic. Despite tobacco industry claims that the studies showed at best a correlation between smoking and disease rather than a causal connection, laws were passed requiring warnings about smoking's health effects to be printed on all cigarette packages and advertising. In

EXHIBIT 2
RJR NABISCO, INC., 1988 FINANCIAL STATEMENTS ($ millions)

Consolidated Statements of Income (condensed)[2]

	For the Years Ended December 31	
	1988	1987
Net sales[3]	$16,956	$15,766
Costs and expenses:		
Cost of products sold	8,786	8,221
Selling, advertising, administrative, and general expenses	5,322	4,991
Restructuring expense, net	—	250
Operating income	2,848	2,304
Interest expense	(579)	(489)
Other income, net	17	1
Income from continuing operations before taxes	2,286	1,816
Provision for income taxes	893	735
Income from continuing operations	1,393	1,081
All other items[4]	—	288
Net income	$ 1,393	$ 1,209

Consolidated Balance Sheets (condensed)[5]

	As of December 31	
Assets	1988	1987
Current assets:		
Cash and cash equivalents	$ 1,425	$ 1,088
Accounts and notes receivable (less allowances of $84 and $61, respectively)	1,920	1,745
Inventories	2,571	2,678
Prepaid expenses and excise taxes	265	329
Total current assets	6,181	5,840
Net property, plant, and equipment	6,149	5,847
Goodwill and trademarks, net	4,555	4,525
Other assets and deferred charges	866	649
Total assets	$17,751	$16,861
Liabilities and Stockholders' Equity		
Current liabilities:		
Accounts payable and accrued accounts	$ 3,220	$ 3,187
Other current liabilities	1,060	936
Total current liabilities	4,280	4,123
Long-term debt	4,975	3,884
Other noncurrent liabilities	1,617	1,797
Deferred income taxes	1,060	846
Redeemable preferred stock	125	173
Total common stockholders' equity	5,694	6,038
Total liabilities and stockholders' equity	$17,751	$16,861

[2]Source: RJR Nabisco Form 10-K (1988), p. F-3.
[3]Excludes excise taxes of $3,448 and $3,314 for 1988 and 1987, respectively.
[4]Includes income (loss) from discontinued operations, gain (loss) on sale of discontinued operations, and extraordinary loss from early extinguishment of debt, net of taxes.
[5]Source: RJR Nabisco Form 10-K (1988), p. F-5.

EXHIBIT 2 *(concluded)*

Consolidated Statements of Cash Flows[6]

| | For the years Ended December 31 | |
	1988	1987
Cash flows from operating activities	$ 1,840	$ 1,769
Cash flows from investing activities:		
Capital expenditures	(1,142)	(936)
Deposits on fresh fruit vessels	(126)	—
Proceeds from sale of capital assets	52	48
Proceeds from dispositions of businesses	489	1,597
Acquisitions of businesses and minority interests	(189)	(72)
Collections of notes receivable	19	92
Net cash flows from (used in) investing activities	(897)	729
Cash flows from financing activities:		
Dividends paid	(494)	(474)
Proceeds from issuing long-term debt	1,435	1,288
Payments to retire long-term debt	(236)	(2,680)
Increase (decrease) in notes payable	9	(89)
Proceeds from issuance of stock	22	11
Repurchase of stock	(1,380)	(317)
Net cash flows from (used in) financing activities	(644)	(2,261)
Effect of exchange rate changes on cash and cash equivalents	38	24
Net change in cash and cash equivalents	337	261
Cash and cash equivalents at beginning of year	1,088	827
Cash and cash equivalents at end of year	$ 1,425	$ 1,088

[6]Source: RJR Nabisco Form 10-K (1988), p. F-4.

1971 radio and television advertising of tobacco products was banned.

During the 1980s, movements to ban smoking in public places grew. The Surgeon General called for a "smoke-free society" by the year 2000. Cigarette smoke inhaled by nonsmokers was recommended for the EPA's list of "Group A" carcinogens, which included the most dangerous compounds such as asbestos. The cigarette industry continued to question the link between smoking and disease, spending massive amounts on lobbying and election campaign contributions. A Philip Morris spokesperson offered this diagnosis of the situation: "It's part of the whole antibusiness movement, the Green Movement ... People have more time to think these days, and so they're more and more critical of everything. Look how critical they are of governments. And there's this health-consciousness movement running through the world."[2]

Nevertheless, the tide had clearly turned against the tobacco industry. Smoking, which in 1960 was the socially accepted habit of 58 percent of men and 34 percent of women, was rapidly becoming the socially unacceptable "vice" of a minority. The Surgeon General reported that a 1987 survey

[2]Maggie Mahar, "Going Up in Smoke?" *Barron's,* July 9, 1990, p. 21.

indicated that the incidence of smoking varied inversely with level of education, ranging from 36 percent of those who never finished high school to 16 percent of college graduates.

The Tobacco Industry's Response. Cigarette manufacturers offset the 2½ percent to 3 percent annual decline in the population of U.S. cigarette smokers by increasing their prices by about 10 percent per year. Company executives had long held that cigarette demand by brand-loyal smokers was little affected by price increases, but the rise of the "savings segment" in the cigarette market had cast doubt on this view. This segment, which included generic cigarettes and discount brands priced $.30 to $.55 below regular branded products, reached 15 percent market share by 1989, double its 1985 level.

Cigarette manufacturers had two options to maintain profitability: expand the world market or diversify into other businesses. Both options faced the same problem: no other business generated the extraordinary operating margins of the domestic cigarette trade. RJRT's 1989 operating margin on its U.S. cigarette business was over 42 percent, whereas the Nabisco operations returned only 12 percent. Profits on foreign sales of cigarettes were much lower than domestic sales largely due to tax differences; combined federal and state taxes averaged 28 percent of the cost of a package of cigarettes in the United States, whereas the worldwide average was 66 percent.

The world cigarette market was growing at an annual rate of 1 percent. Growth was greatest (over 2 percent per year) in the less-developed countries, but smokers there could not afford the more expensive imported brands; in the richer countries, however, cigarette consumption was growing more slowly or actually declining. Cigarette marketing in less-developed countries was often unregulated and unopposed due to lack of governmental resources, while advertising restrictions and public health education campaigns like those in the United States lessened smoking's popularity in the more-developed countries.

All large tobacco companies had diversified their operations, to the extent that most of their sales revenue came from nontobacco sources. Due to the profitability of cigarettes, however, more than one-half of each company's operating income came from cigarette sales. In particular, cigarettes represented 73 percent of RJR Nabisco's income, and this situation was expected to continue for some time (see Exhibit 3).

Trade Loading. Trade loading was fueled by "push"—inducements by the manufacturer to wholesalers to buy more product than they needed, and by "pull"—manufacturer-financed retail promotions. In both push and pull, price discounts were a major tactic.

Trade loading produced problems for three reasons. First, pull was difficult because unit sales of cigarettes in the United States were falling. Second, manufacturers had to pay a $.16 per-pack federal excise tax on all cigarettes shipped to wholesalers. Third, the tobacco industry had a full return policy for cigarettes more than six months old, regarded as too stale to sell. (Exhibit 4 shows current FASB standards for revenue recognition when a right of return exists.) Although manufacturers received an excise tax credit for returned cigarettes, the costs of producing these cigarettes had been wasted.

By its nature, trade loading tended to perpetuate itself. Reporting steady or increasing results would be difficult without continuing trade loading. Gerald H. Long, retired RJRT senior executive, remembered the corporate philosophy under F. Ross Johnson in this way: "My friend Ross said, 'Jerry, you have one great big major objective, and that's producing over $300 million a quarter in operat-

EXHIBIT 3
SELECTED EXCERPTS FROM CONSOLIDATED FINANCIAL STATEMENTS[7] ($ millions)

Summary of Significant Accounting Policies: Inventories

In all of the Company's businesses, inventories are stated at the lower of cost or market. Various methods are used for determining cost. The cost of domestic inventories is determined principally under the LIFO method. The cost of remaining inventories is determined under the FIFO, specific lot, and weighted-average methods. In accordance with recognized trade practice, stocks of tobacco, which must be cured for more than one year, are classified as current assets.

Segment Information: Lines of Business Data

	1988	1987
Net sales:		
Tobacco	$ 7,068	$ 6,346
Food	9,888	9,420
Consolidated net sales	$16,956	$15,766
Operating income:		
Tobacco	$ 1,924	$ 1,822
Food	1,215	1,035
Corporate[8]	(291)	(553)
Consolidated operating income	$ 2,848	$ 2,304
Assets at December 31:		
Tobacco	$ 5,393	$ 5,208
Food	10,382	10,117
Corporate[9]	1,976	1,536
Consolidated assets	$17,751	$16,861

Quarterly Results of Operations (Unaudited)

	First	Second	Third	Fourth
1988				
Net sales	$3,792	$4,286	$4,160	$4,718
Net income	273	354	355	411
1987				
Net sales	$3,489	$4,023	$3,835	$4,419
Net income	220	299	320	370

[7]Source: RJR Nabisco Form 10-K, pp. F-2, F-19, and F-21.
[8]Includes amortization of intangibles and restructuring expense.
[9]All cash and cash equivalents are included in corporate assets.

ing profits.' "[3] RJRT's reliance on trade loading was also increasing because it was losing ground to its competitor, Philip Morris.

Company executives estimated that RJRT's 1984 wholesaler inventory was 5 billion

[3]Loomis, p. 96.

cigarettes, rising to 14 billion at the beginning of 1988. At the beginning of 1989 there was an excess of 18.5 billion RJRT cigarettes in customer warehouses, a 42-day surplus over the ideal wholesale stock of 4½ days of supply or 2 billion cigarettes. Inventory runoff, reduction in shipments, and unusually large numbers of returned cigarettes reduced

EXHIBIT 4
CRITERIA FOR RECOGNIZING REVENUE WHEN RIGHT OF RETURN EXISTS[10]

---

6. If an enterprise sells its product but gives the buyer the right to return the product, revenue from the sales transaction shall be recognized at time of sale only if *all* of the following conditions are met:

   a. The seller's price to the buyer is substantially fixed or determinable at the date of sale.

   b. The buyer has paid the seller, or the buyer is obligated to pay the seller and the obligation is not contingent on resale of the product.

   c. The buyer's obligation to the seller would not be changed in the event of theft or physical destruction or damage of the product.

   d. The buyer acquiring the product for resale has economic substance apart from that provided by the seller. [Note: This condition relates primarily to buyers that exist "on paper," that is, buyers that have little or no physical facilities or employees. It prevents enterprises from recognizing sales revenue on transactions with parties that the sellers have established primarily for the purpose of recognizing such sales revenue.]

   e. The seller does not have significant obligations for future performance to directly bring about resale of the product by the buyer.

   f. The amount of future returns can be reasonably estimated . . .

   Sales revenue and cost of sales that are not recognized at time of sale because the foregoing conditions are not met shall be recognized either when the return privilege has substantially expired or if those conditions subsequently are met, whichever occurs first.

7. If sales revenue is recognized because the conditions of paragraph 6 are met, any costs or losses that may be expected in connection with any returns shall be accrued. . . . Sales revenue and cost of sales reported in the income statement shall be reduced to reflect estimated returns.

---

[10]"Revenue Recognition When Right of Return Exists," *FASB Statement No. 48* (June 1981), paras. 6 and 7.

---

the excess to 1 billion cigarettes by September 1989, but continued trade loading would produce another inflated inventory, perhaps even larger than before, by early 1990.

Although RJRT's trade load was the largest, all tobacco industry firms practiced trade loading. *Fortune* magazine estimated that wholesalers had excess inventory of 30 billion cigarettes of other brands in addition to the 18.5 billion excess RJRT cigarettes.[4] Cigarette manufacturers lacked good data on retail sales because a large proportion of cigarettes was sold through retail outlets such as newspaper stands and convenience stores that lacked scanner technology to count sales. Thus, manufacturers relied on sales to wholesalers as a proxy for shares of the consumer market.

Price discounts for large-volume purchases provided one incentive for wholesalers to participate in trade loading. The prospect of price increases also encouraged

wholesalers to purchase more product than usual for inventory. In 1983 cigarette manufacturers adopted a policy of regular June and December price increases, whereas price increases had previously followed no fixed schedule. Wholesalers responded by making large semiannual cigarette purchases, boosting manufacturers' reported earnings in the June and December quarters (see Exhibit 3). Manufacturer price discounts and favorable payment terms also motivated smaller peaks in April and September. In fact, wholesaler profits in some cases had become dependent upon artificial end-of-quarter increases resulting from trade loading. Eliminating the practice would transform them into breakeven or money-losing operations.

In 1988, RJRT adopted a three-year plan designed to eliminate trade loading gradually such that projected semiannual cigarette price increases would offset unit sales reductions from decreasing trade inventories. By limiting shipments to wholesalers at the end of the second quarter, RJRT brought excess

---

[4]Ibid., p. 94.

inventories down to 10 billion cigarettes. However, as management focused its attention on the negotiations leading to the November 1988 buyout of RJR Nabisco, the plan was neglected, thus producing the high excess wholesaler inventories in early 1989.

Trade loading also contributed to the return of 2.5 billion cigarettes to RJRT in 1988, 1.4 percent of the 177 billion sold in that year. Some data indicated that RJRT's return problem was worse than its competitors'. One of Johnston's greatest concerns was that returns were only the tip of an iceberg: Because of the difficulty in keeping track of massive cigarette inventories, stale cigarettes could end up in stores, resulting in consumer dissatisfaction and further market share erosion.

Soon after he became CEO, Johnston sought more information about the scope of the trade loading problem. He commissioned a wholesaler inventory count, a task complicated by the fact that wholesalers, having run out of space in their own warehouses, were renting additional space to store excess inventories. Johnston's analysis showed that while trade loading was propping up reported income, its effects on cash flow were negative. Excessive end-of-quarter demand disrupted production schedules and increased production costs, and the manufacturer's need to "push" trade loading through price discounts also drained cash from the company. By eliminating trade loading, the company would increase its net cash flow by a small amount, probably less than $20 million.

The end of the third quarter of 1989 was fast approaching. Wholesalers would add yet another layer to their cigarette inventories unless the company took action to restrain them. Gerstner had to make a decision about trade loading soon.

Questions

1. Estimate the effect of trade loading on RJRT's and RJR Nabisco's reported income. Is it material?

2. Does RJRT's (and the industry's) practice of recognizing revenue on sales to wholesalers seem like a reasonable interpretation of generally accepted accounting principles?

3. Who was helped and who was hurt by trade loading?

4. What are Gerstner's alternatives in deciding what to do about trade loading? What would you do?

CASE 6–6 Jean Coffin (B)

Because an earlier visit with the accounting instructor (see Jean Coffin (A)) had cleared up some puzzling matters, Jean Coffin decided to prepare a new list of problems as a basis for a second discussion. As before, Coffin knew that the instructor expected that tentative answers to these questions be worked out prior to the meeting. The list follows:

1. Evidently, there are three ways of handling purchase discounts: they can be deducted from the cost of the purchased goods, they can be reported as other income, or purchase discounts not taken can be reported as an expense of the period. But isn't the effect on net income the same under all these methods? If so, why argue about which is preferable?

2. Calculating cost of goods sold by adjusting total production costs by the changes in work in process and finished goods inventories seems to me to be much simpler than the lengthy calculation shown in Illustration 6–5. It would appear to be even simpler to adjust for the change in materials inventory also, so that cost of goods sold would equal

total production costs adjusted for the net change in inventories. Would this give the same result as that in Illustration 6–5?

3. It is said that the perpetual inventory method identifies the amount of inventory shrinkage from pilferage, spoilage, and the like, an amount which is not revealed by the periodic inventory method. Having identified this amount, however, how should it be recorded in the accounts?

4. People have said that the LIFO method assumes that the goods purchased last are sold first. If this is so, the assumption is clearly unrealistic because companies ordinarily sell their oldest merchandise first. Can a method based on such an unrealistic assumption be supported, other than as a tax gimmick?

5. A certain automobile dealer bases its selling prices on the actual invoice cost of each automobile. In a given model year, the invoice cost for similar automobiles may be increased once or twice to reflect increased manufacturing costs. Would this automobile dealer be wrong if it used the LIFO method? By contrast, a certain hardware dealer changes its selling prices whenever the wholesale price of its goods changes as reported in wholesalers' price lists. Would this hardware dealer be wrong if it used the FIFO method?

6. Are the following generalizations valid?

   a. The difference between LIFO and FIFO is relatively small if inventory turnover is relatively high.
   b. The average cost method will result in net income that is somewhere between that produced by the LIFO method and that produced by the FIFO method.
   c. If prices rise in one year and fall by an equal amount the next year, the total income for the two years is the same under the FIFO method as under the LIFO method.

7. If the LIFO method is used and prices are rising, ending inventory will normally be significantly below prevailing market prices. Therefore, what justification is there for applying the lower-of-cost-or-market rule to LIFO inventories?

8. A certain distillery manufactured bourbon whiskey, which it aged in charred, white oak barrels for four years before bottling and selling it. Whiskey was carried in inventory at approximately $1 per gallon, which was the cost of ingredients, labor, and factory overhead of the manufacturing process. Barrels, which could not be reused, cost $0.70 per gallon. The distillery incurred $0.20 of warehousing costs per gallon per year, including costs involved in moving and testing the barrels. It also incurred $0.10 per gallon of interest costs per year. The costs of barrels, warehousing, and interest were charged directly to expense. If the distillery had consistently earned pretax profit of $600,000 per year on annual production and sale of 1 million gallons, what would happen to profits if it increased production to 1.2 million gallons per year? At what amounts should it carry its whiskey in inventory?

9. A company produced a "made for TV" movie at a total cost of $1 million. It sold the rights to the initial showing to a network for $1 million, and fully expected to sell the rights for a repeat showing the following year for $300,000. It thought that in future years, additional reruns would generate at least another $300,000 of revenue. How much should the company report as cost of sales for the first year? Would the answer be different if in the first year the producing company agreed to pay $100,000 for advertising and promoting the initial showing?

7

Long-Lived Assets
and Their Amortization

Chapters 5 and 6 discussed monetary assets and inventories. Investments are discussed in Chapter 12. This chapter describes other categories of assets. The common characteristic of these assets is that they have long lives; they provide benefits to the entity for several future years. We describe the accounting principles involved in recording the acquisition of long-lived assets, the conversion of acquisition costs to expenses, and the disposition of such assets when they no longer provide service.

NATURE OF LONG-LIVED ASSETS

When an entity makes an expenditure, the benefits from the goods or services acquired either are obtained in the current period or are expected to be obtained in future periods. If the benefits are obtained in the current period, the costs of the goods or services are *expenses*. If benefits are expected in future periods, the costs are *assets* in the current period and the expenditures are said to be **capitalized.** Although inventory and prepaid expenses also are assets because they benefit future periods, the term **capital assets** is usually taken to mean long-lived assets—assets that provide service for several future years.

A capital asset can usefully be thought of as a bundle of services. When a company buys a truck that is intended to last for 200,000 miles, it is in effect

ILLUSTRATION 7–1
EXPENDITURES AND EXPENSES

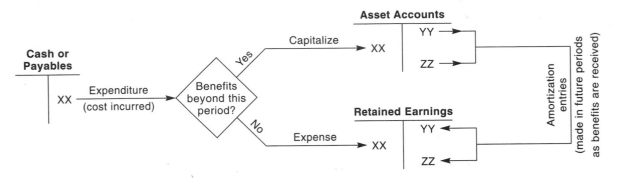

buying transportation services that will benefit the company over several future years. The cost of these services, that is, the cost of the truck, should be matched with the revenues that are obtained from its use in these future periods. The general name for this matching process is **amortization,** but other names are used for various types of capital assets, as will be described. The portion of the asset's cost that is charged to a given period is an expense of that period. A capital asset is therefore essentially similar to a prepaid insurance policy or other prepaid expense. It is initially recorded as an asset and is converted to an expense in one or more future periods. The difference is that the life of most capital assets is longer than that of most prepaid expenses.

Illustration 7–1 uses T accounts to depict how expenditures either are expensed in the current period (period costs) or are capitalized in an asset account and amortized (expensed) in later periods. Note that all costs *eventually* become expenses, but capital assets' costs do so over a period of several years, whereas period costs become expenses as they are incurred.

Types of Long-Lived Assets

Illustration 7–2 lists principal types of long-lived assets and the terminology used for the process of amortizing the cost of each type. The principal distinction is between tangible assets and intangible assets. A **tangible asset** is an asset that has physical substance, such as a building or a machine. An **intangible asset,** such as patent rights or copyrights, has no physical substance. Many such assets are referred to as **intellectual property.**

Long-lived tangible assets are usually listed on the balance sheet under the heading "property, plant, and equipment." The term **fixed assets** is often used in informal discussion and appears in several balance sheets in this book simply because it is shorter. Property includes *land,* which ordinarily is not amortized because its useful life is assumed to be indefinitely long.

ILLUSTRATION 7–2
TYPES OF LONG-LIVED ASSETS AND AMORTIZATION METHODS

Type of Asset	Method of Converting to Expense
Tangible assets:	
Land	Not amortized
Plant and equipment	Depreciation
Natural resources	Depletion
Intangible assets:	
Goodwill	Amortization
Patents, copyrights, etc.	Amortization
Leasehold improvements	Amortization
Deferred charges	Amortization
Research and development costs	Not capitalized
Marketable securities	None (see Chapter 5)
Investments	None (see Chapter 12)

Plant and equipment includes buildings, machinery, office equipment, and other types of long-lived capital assets. The accounting process of converting the original cost of plant and equipment assets to expense is called **depreciation.** Natural resources, such as petroleum and natural gas in the ground (but *not* after they have been taken out of the ground and become inventory), are usually reported as a separate category. The accounting process of converting the cost of these natural resource assets to expense is called **depletion.**

The several categories of intangible assets will be discussed separately in later sections of this chapter. When intangible assets are converted to expenses, the accounting process has no specific name (as in the case of fixed assets and natural resources); it is just called **amortization.**

PLANT AND EQUIPMENT: ACQUISITION

Distinction between Asset and Expense

The distinction between expenditures that are capitalized and expenditures that are expensed as period costs is not entirely clear-cut. Some borderline cases are described in the following paragraphs.

Low-Cost Items. In accordance with the materiality concept, items that have a low unit cost, such as calculators and hand tools, are charged immediately as expenses, even though they may have a long life. Each company sets its own criteria for items that are to be capitalized. Generally, the line is drawn in terms of the cost of an item, which may be anywhere from $25 to $1,000, or even more. Items costing less are expensed.

Nevertheless, the capitalized cost of a new facility may include the cost of the initial outfit of small items that do not individually meet the criteria for capitalization. Examples are the initial outfit of small tools in a factory, the books in a library, and the tableware and kitchen utensils in a restaurant.

When these items are replaced, the cost of the replacement items is charged as an expense, not capitalized.

Betterments.   Repair and maintenance is work done to keep an asset in good operating condition or to bring it back to good operating condition if it has broken down. Repair and maintenance costs are ordinarily period costs; they are not added to the capitalized cost of the asset. A **betterment** is added to the cost of the asset. The distinction between maintenance expenses and betterments is this: maintenance keeps the asset in good condition but in no better condition than when it was purchased; a betterment makes the asset better than it was when it was purchased or extends its useful life beyond the original estimate of useful life.

In practice the line between the two is difficult to draw. A new accessory designed to make a machine operate more efficiently or perform new functions is a betterment; an overhaul during which worn-out parts are replaced with new ones is maintenance. In the interest of conservatism, some work that strictly speaking should be considered as a betterment is charged as an expense of the current period.

Replacements.   Replacements may be either assets or expenses, depending on how the asset unit is defined. The replacement of an entire asset results in the writing off of the old asset and the recording of the new asset. The replacement of a component part of an asset is maintenance expense. For example, some companies treat a building as a single asset unit, whereas others treat each major component (structure, plumbing, elevators, heating and air-conditioning system) as a separate asset. The replacement of an elevator would result in a maintenance charge in the former case and in a new asset in the latter. In general, the broader the definition of the asset unit, the greater will be the amount of costs charged as maintenance and, hence, expensed in the year the replacement parts are installed.

Items Included in Cost

The governing principle is that the cost of an item of property, plant, or equipment includes *all expenditures that are necessary to make the asset ready for its intended use.* In many cases the amount can be determined easily. For example, the cost of a truck purchased for cash is simply the amount of cash paid. In other cases the problem is more complicated. The cost of a parcel of land includes the purchase price, broker's commission, legal fees, and the cost of grading or of tearing down existing structures so as to make the land ready for its intended use. The cost of machinery includes the purchase price, sales tax, transportation costs to where the machinery is to be used, and installation costs.

Despite the principle stated above, many organizations do not capitalize all the costs incurred to make the asset ready to provide service. Some capitalize only the purchase price. They do this both because it is simpler and also in order to minimize property taxes, which may be calculated on the basis of the capitalized amount.

Self-Constructed Assets. When a company constructs a building or item of equipment for its own use, the amount of capitalized cost includes all the costs incurred in construction. As in the case of product costs, these costs include the materials and labor directly associated with the project, as well as a fair share of the company's indirect costs incurred during the construction period. The FASB requires that these capitalized costs also include interest.[1] The amount of interest capitalized is the amount related to borrowings made to finance the project (construction loans) if these are identifiable. If not, the company must estimate the interest cost that could have been avoided if the asset in question had not been constructed. The total amount of interest capitalized cannot exceed the company's total interest cost for the period. The interest capitalization period ends when the asset is substantially complete and ready for its intended use. If the company contracts with an outside party to build the asset and makes deposits or progress payments to the contractor, then interest costs associated with these funds are included in the capitalized cost.

As is the case with other items of cost, if interest cost is capitalized rather than expensed, this has the effect of increasing the income of the current period and decreasing income during the years of the asset's useful life. This decrease occurs because each year's depreciation expense for the asset is larger than it would have been had the interest cost not been capitalized.

Noncash Costs. In the great majority of cases, a capital asset is acquired for cash or for a note or other obligation whose cash equivalent is easily determined. When some other consideration, such as common stock, is given, there may be problems in determining the amount to be capitalized. The general principle is this: first, the fair market value of the consideration given for the asset should be determined; and, second, if it is not feasible to determine this value, then the fair market value of the new capital asset itself is used. (Special rules apply when one capital asset is traded in as part payment for a new asset, as described in a following section.)

Acquisitions Recorded at Other than Cost

There are a few exceptions to the basic rule that asset acquisitions are recorded in the accounts at cost. If the entity acquires an asset by donation or pays substantially less than the market value of the asset, the asset is recorded at its fair market value.[2] This happens, for example, when a community donates land or a building in order to induce a company to locate there. As another example, if property suddenly increases in value shortly after its acquisition (for instance, because of the discovery of oil or of a mineral deposit), the amount originally recorded for this **fortunate acquisition** may be increased to reflect its current value.

---

[1]"Capitalization of Interest Cost," *FASB Statement No. 34* (October 1979).
[2]"Accounting for Nonmonetary Transactions," *APB Opinion No. 29* (May 1973), par. 18.

Such exceptions to the general rule are relatively rare, and their rarity emphasizes the importance of the general rule that *assets are recorded at cost.* Furthermore, as will be seen in the next section, increases in market value do not affect the accounting records for capital assets. Competent investors acquire or build apartment houses or shopping centers with the expectation that part of the profit from this investment will be derived from the appreciation of the property. This appreciation may in fact occur year after year, but it is not recorded in the accounts. The rule is: "Property, plant and equipment should not be written up by an entity to reflect appraisal, market or current values which are above cost to the entity."[3]

The reason for the supremacy of the cost concept over a system geared to changes in current value is the importance of the basic criterion of objectivity. We may know in a general way that the value of an apartment house is increasing, but there is no objective way of measuring the amount of increase until a sale takes place. When this happens, a new cost is established, and the asset is recorded at this cost in the accounts of the new owner.

Basket Purchases

Sometimes an entity acquires in one transaction several capital assets that are to appear in more than one balance sheet category. This is called a **basket purchase.** The company must divide the basket's cost between the categories on some reasonable basis. Usually this requires an appraisal of the relative value of each asset included in the basket purchase.

Such a separation is always required when land and a building are purchased in a single transaction; this is because the building will subsequently be depreciated, whereas the land will remain on the books at its cost. A separation may also be necessary if the capital assets in the basket have different useful lives, because they will then be depreciated at different rates.

> **Example.** A parcel of land with a building thereon is purchased for $800,000. An appraiser states that the land is worth $90,000 and the building is worth $810,000, a total of $900,000. Since the appraised value of the land is 10 percent of the total appraised value of the basket, the land is entered in the accounts at 10 percent of the total cost, or $80,000. The building is entered at 90 percent of the cost, or $720,000. Note that it would *not* be correct to use the appraised value of one asset as the amount to be capitalized and to capitalize the other asset at the remainder of the purchase price. Thus, it would not be correct to record the land at $90,000 and the building at $710,000.

PLANT AND EQUIPMENT: DEPRECIATION

Unless otherwise indicated, the discussion of depreciation accounting in this section will relate to *financial reporting* (i.e., generally accepted

---

[3]"Status of Accounting Research Bulletins," *APB Opinion No. 6* (October 1965), par. 17.

accounting principles, or GAAP), as distinguished from income tax reporting. Depreciation in financial reporting is based on the matching concept, whereas the Economic Recovery Tax Act of 1981 essentially eliminated the matching concept as the basis of income tax depreciation calculations. (Depreciation for income tax purposes is described in a later section.)

With the exception of land, most items of plant and equipment have a limited useful life; that is, they will provide service to the entity over a limited number of future accounting periods. A fraction of the cost of the asset is therefore properly chargeable as an expense in each of the accounting periods in which the asset provides service to the entity. The accounting process for this gradual conversion of plant and equipment capitalized cost into expense is called **depreciation.**[4]

Why is depreciation an expense? The answer is that the costs of *all* goods and services consumed by an entity during an accounting period are expenses. The cost of insurance protection provided in a year is an expense of that year even though the insurance premium was paid two or three years previously. Depreciation expense is conceptually just like insurance expense. The principal difference is that the fraction of total cost of an item of plant and equipment that is an expense in a given year is difficult to estimate, whereas the fraction of the total cost of an insurance policy that is an expense in a given year can be easily calculated. This difference does not change the fundamental fact that both insurance policies and plant and equipment provide benefits to the entity over a finite number of accounting periods, and a fraction of their original cost must therefore be charged as an expense of each of these periods.

The useful life of a tangible long-lived asset is limited by either deterioration or obsolescence. **Deterioration** is the physical process of wearing out. **Obsolescence** refers to loss of usefulness because of the development of improved equipment or processes, changes in style, or other causes not related to the physical condition of the asset. We will refer to the time until an asset wears out as its **physical life,** and the time until it becomes obsolete or is expected to be disposed of as its **service life.** Although the word *depreciation* is sometimes used as referring only to physical deterioration ("wear and tear"), this usage is incorrect. In many cases a piece of equipment's service life is shorter than its physical life; computers are a good example.

Judgments Required

In order to determine the depreciation expense for an accounting period, three judgments or estimates must be made for each depreciable asset:

---

[4]If the asset is used in the production process, its depreciation is properly chargeable as an item of product cost that is initially added to Work in Process Inventory, then flows through Finished Goods Inventory, and becomes an expense (cost of goods sold) in the period in which the product is sold, as described in Chapter 6. In the interests of simplicity, in this chapter we shall not distinguish between the depreciation that is a product cost and the depreciation that is a period expense.

1.   The *service life* of the asset—the number of accounting periods over which the asset will be useful to the specific entity that owns it.

2.   The asset's **residual value** at the end of its service life—any amount eventually recovered through sale, trade-in, or salvage. The **net cost** of the asset to the entity is its original cost less its residual value. It is this net cost that should be charged as an expense over the asset's life, not its original cost. In a great many situations, however, the estimated residual value is so small or uncertain that it is disregarded.

3.   The *method of depreciation*—the method that will be used to allocate a fraction of the asset's net cost to each of the accounting periods in which it is expected to be used.

Accountants, not being clairvoyant, cannot know in advance how long the asset will be used or what its residual value will be. Often they have no scientific or strictly logical way of deciding the best depreciation method. The amount of depreciation expense that results from these judgments is therefore an *estimate*—yet another estimate that affects the amount of each period's reported income. Because of the arithmetic precision of the calculations that take place *after* these judgments are made, the inexact nature of depreciation expense is sometimes overlooked.

Service Life   The service life of an asset is the period of time over which it is expected to provide service (i.e., benefits) to the entity that controls it. As mentioned above, the service life may be shorter than the physical life because of obsolescence or because the entity may plan to dispose of an asset before its physical life ends. For example, although automobiles typically have a useful physical life of about 10 years, many companies trade in their automobiles every two years and buy new ones. In these companies the service life is two years. If the asset's service life to a particular entity is clearly less than the asset's useful physical life, then the estimated residual value of the asset at the end of its service life should be greater than zero.

Estimating the service life of an asset is a difficult problem. Formerly, the Internal Revenue Service published **guideline lives** for various categories of assets; these lives were allowed for income tax depreciation calculations. Many companies also used these guideline lives for financial reporting purposes, since the guidelines were based on actual corporate asset holding periods. However, tax law changes during the 1980s eliminated these guideline lives and substituted "cost recovery periods" that generally are shorter than the assets' useful lives. (For example, a new apartment house has a cost recovery period of 27½ years.) Since GAAP clearly indicates that depreciation is to be based on realistic service lives, companies should make their own estimates of the useful lives of their various categories of depreciable assets for financial reporting purposes rather than relying on income tax lives.

Depreciation Methods

Consider a piece of equipment purchased for $1,000 with an estimated service life of 10 years and estimated residual value of zero. The objective of depreciation accounting is to charge this net cost of $1,000 as an expense over the 10-year period. How much should be charged as an expense each year?

This question cannot be answered directly by observing the amount of asset value physically consumed in a given year. Physically the equipment continues to be equipment; usually, there is no observable indication of its decline in usefulness. Nor can the question be answered in terms of changes in the equipment's market value during the year, because accounting is concerned with the amortization of cost, not with changes in market values. An indirect approach must therefore be used. Any method that is "systematic and rational" is permitted.[5] Three conceptual ways of looking at the depreciation process are described below, together with the methods that follow from each.

Straight-Line Method.   One concept views a fixed asset as providing its services in a level stream. That is, the service provided (benefit received) is equal in each year of the asset's life, just as a three-year insurance policy provides equal insurance protection in each of its three years. This concept leads to the **straight-line method,** which charges as an expense an equal fraction of the net cost of the asset each year. For a piece of equipment whose net cost is $1,000 with an estimated service life of 10 years, $1/10$ of $1,000 (= $100) is the depreciation expense of the first year, another $1/10$ is the depreciation expense of the second year, and so on. Expressed another way, the equipment is said to have a **depreciation rate** of 10 percent per year, the rate being the reciprocal of the estimated service life.

Accelerated Methods.   A second concept recognizes that the stream of benefits provided by a fixed asset may not be level. Rather, the benefits provided may be greatest in the first year of the asset's service life and least in the last year. This pattern may occur because the asset's mechanical efficiency tends to decline with age, because maintenance costs tend to increase with age, or because of the increasing likelihood that better equipment will become available and make it obsolete. Often, when a facility is not working at capacity, it is the older equipment that is not used. It is argued, therefore, that when an asset was purchased, the probability that the earlier periods would benefit more than the later periods was taken into account and that the depreciation method should reflect this. Such a line of reasoning leads to an **accelerated method** that charges a larger fraction of the cost as an expense of the early years than of the later years.[6]

Accelerated methods have been used in financial reporting by some companies since 1954 when their use was first permitted for income tax

[5]AICPA, *Accounting Research Bulletin No. 43* (June 1953), Chap. 9, Sec. C, par. 5.

[6]An argument can also be made for an opposite approach: charging a smaller fraction of the cost in the early years and a larger fraction in the later years. This leads to an **annuity method.** It is rarely used in published financial statements.

purposes. Two methods, the double-declining-balance method and sum-of-the-years'-digits (or simply years'-digits) method, are described below. The effect of either of these methods is to write off approximately two-thirds of the asset's cost in the first half of its estimated life, as contrasted with the straight-line method under which, of course, half the cost is written off in each half of the asset's estimated life. Thus, if an accelerated method is used, depreciation expense is greater in the early years and less in the later years as compared with the straight-line method.

In a **declining-balance method** each year's depreciation is found by applying a rate to the net book value of the asset as of the beginning of that year. (In the straight-line method the depreciation rate is applied to original cost net of residual value, not to each year's net book value.) The **net book value** of an asset at a point in time is the original acquisition cost less total depreciation accumulated up to that time. With a declining-balance method, the asset's estimated residual value, if any, has no effect on the annual depreciation charges because residual value is not included in the calculation of an asset's net book value.

The declining-balance rate is a stated percentage of the straight-line rate. Thus, for an asset with a useful life of 10 years (straight-line rate = 10 percent), 200 percent declining balance would use a rate of 20 percent (= 200 percent * 10 percent). Similarly, 150 percent declining balance would use a rate of 15 percent. The 200 percent declining-balance method is also called the **double-declining-balance method** because the depreciation rate is double the straight-line rate.

After several years the annual depreciation charge with a declining-balance method will be lower than the annual charge with the straight-line method. The usual practice is to change at that time from declining-balance to straight-line depreciation for the remainder of the asset's life.

In the **years'-digits method,** the numbers 1, 2, 3, . . . , n are added, where n is the estimated years of useful life. This sum can be found by the equation (using 10 years for the example):

$$SYD = n\left(\frac{n+1}{2}\right) = 10\left(\frac{10+1}{2}\right) = 55$$

The depreciation rate each year is a fraction in which the denominator is the sum of these digits and the numerator is, for the first year, n; for the second year, $n - 1$; for the third year, $n - 2$; and so on. Thus, for a 10-year asset, the rate is $10/55$ the first year, $9/55$ the second year, $8/55$ the third year, and so on. As with the straight-line method, the rate is applied to the net cost—cost less residual value—of the asset.

Comparison of Methods. Illustration 7–3 is an example of the way these three methods work out for a piece of equipment costing $1,000 with an estimated service life of 10 years and no residual value. Illustration 7–4 shows the same depreciation patterns graphically.

Units-of-Production Method. A third concept of depreciation also treats the asset as consisting of a bundle of service units; but it does not assume

ILLUSTRATION 7–3
COMPARISON OF DEPRECIATION METHODS

Year	Straight-Line (10 percent rate)		Double-Declining-Balance (20 percent rate)		Years'-Digits		
	Annual Depre-ciation	Net Book Value, 12/31	Annual Depre-ciation	Net Book Value, 12/31	Rate	Annual Depre-ciation	Net Book Value, 12/31
0.....................		$1,000		$1,000.00			$1,000.00
1.....................	$ 100	900	$ 200.00	800.00	10/55	$ 181.82	818.18
2.....................	100	800	160.00	640.00	9/55	163.64	654.54
3.....................	100	700	128.00	512.00	8/55	145.45	509.09
4.....................	100	600	102.40	409.60	7/55	127.27	381.82
5.....................	100	500	81.92	327.68	6/55	109.09	272.73
6.....................	100	400	65.54	262.14	5/55	90.91	181.82
7.....................	100	300	65.54	196.60	4/55	72.73	109.09
8.....................	100	200	65.54	131.06	3/55	54.55	54.54
9.....................	100	100	65.54	65.52	2/55	36.36	18.18
10....................	100	0	65.52	0	1/55	18.18	0
	$1,000		$1,000.00			$1,000.00	

that these service units will be provided in a mathematical *time-phased pattern,* as is assumed by the straight-line and accelerated methods. Rather, with this concept a period's depreciation is related to the *number of service units* provided by the asset during the period.

This view leads to the **units-of-production method,** in which the cost of each service unit is the net cost of the asset divided by the total number of such units. The depreciation charge for a period is then the number of units consumed in that period multiplied by the net cost of one unit. For example, if a truck has an estimated net cost of $60,000 and is expected to give service for 300,000 miles, depreciation would be charged at a rate of 20 cents per mile (= $60,000 ÷ 300,000). The depreciation expense in a year in which the truck traveled 50,000 miles would be $10,000.

Choice of a Depreciation Method

Later in this chapter depreciation methods allowed in computing taxable income for the IRS are described. In deciding on a depreciation method for *financial reporting* purposes, income tax considerations are kept entirely separate. For tax purposes corporations in most instances use the tax code's accelerated depreciation rules, thereby receiving as quickly as possible the tax savings related to depreciation.

With respect to financial reporting, we have previously indicated that each type of method—straight line, accelerated, and units of production—has its own conceptual basis as to the pattern in which an asset provides its bundle of services. In theory GAAP allows a choice of methods so that a company can match the method to the pattern that obtains for an asset in

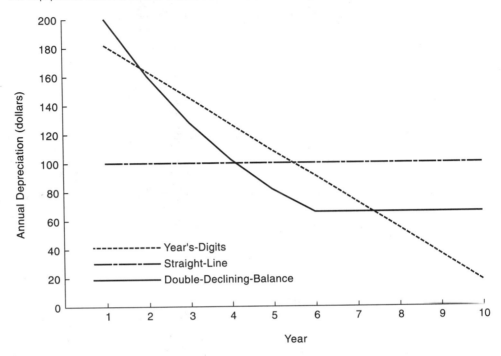

ILLUSTRATION 7–4
ANNUAL DEPRECIATION CHARGES
For Equipment with Net Cost of $1,000 and 10-Year Service Life

that particular company. Strictly speaking, this means that different methods would apply to different types of assets in a given company. However, there is little evidence that companies think about service benefit patterns when selecting depreciation methods for their financial accounting. In most cases a single method is applied to all of a company's depreciable assets. The method usually chosen is straight line.[7]

ACCOUNTING FOR DEPRECIATION

Assume that on January 1, 1986, Trantor Company purchased for $1 million a building with an estimated service life of 40 years and zero

---

[7] *Accounting Trends & Techniques* (1993) reports the following usage of methods by the 600 companies in its survey (the percentages add to more than 100 percent because some companies used more than one method):

Straight-line	94%
Declining-balance	4
Years'-digits	2
Unspecified accelerated	10
Units-of-production	8

residual value. Trantor decided to depreciate this building on a straight-line basis, $25,000 per year. Now consider how to record this depreciation in the *financial* accounting records.

It would be possible to reduce the asset value by $25,000 a year and to show on the balance sheet only the remaining amount, which at the end of 1986 would be $975,000. However, this is not ordinarily done. Instead, a separate contra-asset account is maintained for the cumulative amount of depreciation. This account is usually called **accumulated depreciation**, or it may have some other name such as *allowance for depreciation*. GAAP requires disclosure of the amount of accumulated depreciation, either on the balance sheet or in a note thereto.[8] Usually, both the original cost and the accumulated depreciation amounts appear on the balance sheet itself. For Trantor the figures as of December 31, 1986, would look like this:

Building, at cost	$1,000,000	
Less: Accumulated depreciation	25,000	
Building, net		$975,000

As of December 31, 1987, another year's depreciation would be added, and the balance sheet would then show:

Building at cost	$1,000,000	
Less: Accumulated depreciation	50,000	
Building, net		$950,000

The foregoing amounts can be interpreted as follows:

Original cost of the building	$1,000,000
That portion of the original cost charged as expense for all periods to date	50,000
That portion of original cost remaining to be charged as expense of future periods	$ 950,000

The $950,000 is the **book value** of the asset. This is often labeled **net book value** to distinguish it from original cost, which is called the **gross book value**. The term *book* value is intended to highlight the fact that the amount is not an appraisal or market value.

On the income statement the expense item is usually labeled **depreciation expense**. In the income statement for 1986, this item for Trantor Company would be $25,000 (disregarding depreciation on assets other than

---

[8]"Disclosure of Depreciable Assets and Depreciation," *APB Opinion No. 12* (December 1967), par. 5.

this building); and $25,000 would also appear in the income statements for 1987, for 1988, and for following years until the building was either disposed of or fully depreciated.

The annual journal entry for depreciation on Trantor's building, which is one of the adjusting entries, would be as follows:

```
Depreciation Expense ............................... 25,000
        Accumulated Depreciation ....................... 25,000
```

Change in Depreciation Rates

Suppose that in the year 2005 Trantor Company decides that the building is likely to last until 2030, which is 5 years longer than the 40 years originally estimated. In theory, Trantor should change the depreciation rate so that the book value remaining in 2005 would be charged off over the newly estimated *remaining* service life of 25 years. Because of all the uncertainties and estimates inherent in the depreciation process, however, such changes in the depreciation rate usually are not made in practice.

Fully Depreciated Assets. Even if Trantor Company should use its building for more than 40 years, depreciation would cease to be accumulated at the end of the 40th year, since by then the total original cost of the building would have been charged to expense. Until the asset is disposed of, it is customary to continue to show the asset on the balance sheet. Thus, as of December 31, 2025, and for as long thereafter as Trantor owned the building, the balance sheet would show the following:

Building, at cost	$1,000,000	
Less: Accumulated depreciation	1,000,000	
Building, net		$0

Partial Year Depreciation

Often, half a year's depreciation is recorded in the year of acquisition and half a year's depreciation in the year of disposal, no matter what the actual date of acquisition or disposal is. This **half-year convention** is justified on the grounds that if the entity is acquiring and disposing of assets throughout the year, the inaccuracies in this procedure as regards specific assets will "wash out" over the course of the year. Other companies use an analogous half-quarter or half-month convention.

Disclosure

The amount of the depreciation charged off in the year must be disclosed in the financial statements. In a merchandising company this can be done by reporting depreciation expense as a separate item on the income statement. In many manufacturing companies a separate income statement item may not be feasible; this is because depreciation of production plant and equipment is part of cost of goods sold (product costs), whereas the depreciation of other assets is part of general and administrative expenses, which are period costs. In these circumstances the total amount of depreciation expense is reported in a note accompanying the financial statements. The balance sheet, or a note thereto, must disclose the original cost of major classes of depreciable assets, the amount of accumulated depreciation, and the depreciation method or methods used.

PLANT AND EQUIPMENT: DISPOSAL

Suppose that at the end of 10 years (December 31, 1995) Trantor Company sells its building. At that time $10/40$ of the original cost, or $250,000, will have been built up in the Accumulated Depreciation account, and the net book value of the building will be $750,000. If the building is sold for $750,000 cash, the accounts are changed as follows:

```
Cash...............................................  750,000
Accumulated Depreciation..........................  250,000
    Building........................................            1,000,000
```

Since the building is no longer an asset of Trantor, both its original cost and its accumulated depreciation must be removed from the accounts. This is exactly what the preceding entry accomplishes.

If the building were sold for less than $750,000—for $650,000—the $100,000 difference is recorded as a loss, as in the following entry:

```
Cash...............................................  650,000
Accumulated Depreciation..........................  250,000
Loss on Sale of Building...........................  100,000
    Building........................................            1,000,000
```

Note that the effect on the Building and the Accumulated Depreciation accounts is identical with that in the previous illustration: the amounts relating to this building disappear. The loss is a decrease in Retained Earnings, reflecting the fact that the total depreciation expense recorded for the preceding 10 years was less than what Trantor now knows to have been the actual net cost of the building over that period of time. The actual net cost turns out to have been $350,000, whereas the total depreciation expense charged has amounted to only $250,000.

Since the depreciation expense as originally recorded turns out to have been incorrect, the Retained Earnings account, which reflects the net of all revenue and expenses to date, is also incorrect. There is therefore some logic in closing the Loss on Sale of Building account directly to Retained Earnings, thus correcting the error contained therein. Nevertheless, the matching concept requires that this loss be shown as an expense on the income statement of the current period. An asset cost amount that no longer benefits future periods is an expense of the current period.

If an asset is sold for *more* than its book value, the entries are analogous to those described above. The account Gain on the Sale of Building (or other category of long-lived asset) is credited for the excess of the selling price over net book value. This account (as well as Loss on Sale of . . .) is usually included in "other income" on the income statement, rather than being shown as a separate line item.

The *objective* of depreciation accounting is to charge as depreciation expense over the service life of the asset the exact difference between its original cost and its ultimate residual value. If this objective were attained, there would be no gain or loss reported when the asset is disposed of, which is consistent with the view that an enterprise earns income by using its fixed assets, not by disposing of them. However, since an asset's ultimate service life and residual value cannot be perfectly forecasted when the asset is acquired, asset disposals usually involve some reported gain or loss.

Market Values.   The net book value of an asset usually is not the same as its market value. However, if Trantor's building was sold at the end of 1995 for $650,000, this was by definition its market value at that time. Also, the $1 million original cost was presumably its market value on January 1, 1986, when it was acquired. Thus, the first and the last transactions for the building take account of market values. In the intervening periods, changes in market values are disregarded in the financial statements and underlying accounting records.

Impaired Assets.   An exception to this general rule is made in the case of an **impaired asset**—an asset for which the value of its remaining benefits, as measured by the future cash flows the asset's use will generate, is less than its net book value. If the entity expects to hold such an asset, it is written down to its fair value. If the entity plans to dispose of an impaired asset, it is valued at the lower of cost or fair value, less the cost of disposal. Any write-down is reported as an element of the period's income.[9] This is analogous to the lower-of-cost-or-market rule for inventories.

> **Example.**   On January 1, 19x1, a company paid $1 million for a specialized machine, expecting to use it to produce a specific item for 6 years. The equipment was depreciated using the straight-line method. By January 19x4 demand for the item had dropped so much that the company expected that the cash flows the item would generate over the remainder of its product life cycle would be less than the equipment's net book value ($500,000). The equipment was therefore written down to $300,000, its estimated market value on January 1, 19x4. This write-down reduced 19x4 reported income.

Exchanges and Trade-Ins

Some items of property and equipment are disposed of by trading them in or exchanging them for new assets. When this is done, the value of the old asset is used in calculating the acquisition cost of the new asset. The

---

[9]As of late 1994, the FASB was completing development of a *Statement* on this topic.

amount used in this calculation depends on whether or not the asset traded is similar to the new asset. If the trade-in is similar—of the same general type or performing the same function—its value is assumed to be its net book value. If the asset traded is dissimilar, its value is its estimated fair market value.[10]

> **Example.** Assume a company trades in two automobiles, each of which originally cost $20,000, of which $15,000 has been depreciated; thus, each has a net book value of $5,000. Each has a fair market value of $7,000 as a used car.
>
> The first automobile is traded for another automobile with a list price of $30,000, and $18,000 cash is given to the dealer in addition to the trade-in. In this case the cost of the new automobile is recorded as $23,000, the sum of the $18,000 cash and the $5,000 *net book value* of the trade-in.
>
> The second automobile is traded for a piece of equipment that also has a list price of $30,000, and $18,000 cash is given in addition to the trade-in. In this case the cost of the new equipment is recorded as $25,000—the sum of the $18,000 cash and the $7,000 *market value* of the trade-in.

Journal entries for these two transactions are as follows:

1. For an exchange of similar assets:

Automobile (New)...................................	23,000	
Accumulated Depreciation (Automobile)..............	15,000	
Cash		18,000
Automobile (Old)		20,000

2. For other exchanges:

Equipment (New)	25,000	
Accumulated Depreciation (Automobile)..............	15,000	
Cash		18,000
Automobile (Old)		20,000
Gain on Disposal of Automobile...................		2,000

In both cases the cost and accumulated depreciation of the old asset are removed from the accounts. Also in both cases the list price of the new asset is disregarded. In the case of an exchange of similar assets, no gain or loss is recognized; in other exchanges the gain or loss is recognized. These rules are required for both financial reporting and income tax purposes. (Tax regulations use the term *like-kind exchange* where similar assets are involved.)

The rationale behind these rules is that an exchange of similar assets does not result in the culmination of an earnings process, whereas an exchange of dissimilar assets does. For example, if a professional football team exchanges the contract of one of its players for cash and the contract of a player from another team, the team's process of generating earnings is not materially affected. On the other hand, if a farm owner exchanges a plot of

---

[10]"Accounting for Nonmonetary Transactions," *APB Opinion No. 29* (May 1973).

tilled acreage for a new tractor, then the earnings process has ended on that portion of the farm that was exchanged.

Group Depreciation

The procedures described above related to a single fixed asset, such as one building or one automobile. To find the total depreciation expense for a whole category of assets, this procedure could be repeated for each single asset, and the total depreciation for all the assets in the category would then be recorded by one journal entry. This is **unit depreciation,** also called **item depreciation.**

An alternative procedure is to treat all similar assets (such as all automobiles or all office chairs) as a "pool" or group rather than making the calculation for each one separately. The process is called **group depreciation.** Annual depreciation expense under group depreciation is computed in a manner similar to that described above for an individual asset. If the straight-line method is used, for example, the depreciation rate is applied to the total original cost of the entire group of assets.

If the group method is used, no gain or loss is recognized when an individual asset is sold or otherwise disposed of. Upon disposal the asset account is credited for the asset's original cost, as in the entries given above. However, the difference between cost and the sales proceeds is debited or credited to Accumulated Depreciation rather than to a gain or loss account. This procedure assumes that gains on some sales in the group are offset by losses on others. This assumption is reasonable if the group contains a relatively large number of similar assets.

> **Example.** A used microcomputer with original cost of $3,000 is disposed of for $400 cash. Assuming group depreciation is used, the journal entry for this transaction is:
>
> | | | |
> |---|---:|---:|
> | Cash . . . . | 400 | |
> | Accumulated Deprecation, Microcomputers . . . . | 2,600 | |
> | Microcomputers . . . . | | 3,000 |

SIGNIFICANCE OF DEPRECIATION

The amount shown as accumulated depreciation on the balance sheet does *not* represent the "accumulation" of any tangible thing. It is merely that portion of the depreciable assets' original cost that already has been matched as expense against revenue.

Occasionally, an entity does set aside money for the specific purpose of purchasing new assets, a process sometimes called **funding depreciation.** This is a *financing* transaction, which is completely separate from the accounting process of *recording* depreciation—the operating expense associated with the use of fixed assets. If depreciation is funded, cash or securities are set aside in such a way that they cannot be used in the regular operation of the entity (e.g., a special bank account may be created). This practice is not common. It is mentioned here only to emphasize, by contrast, the point that the depreciation process itself is *not* a means of automatically creating a fund for the replacement of assets.

There is a widespread belief that in some mysterious way depreciation does represent money, specifically, money that can be used to purchase new assets. Sometimes this erroneous belief is reinforced by an entity's using the term "reserve for depreciation" to mean accumulated depreciation. Depreciation is *not* money; the money that the entity has is shown by the balance in its Cash account.

> **Example.** This quotation is from a well-known publication: "Most large companies draw much of the cash flow they employ for expanding and modernizing their operations from their depreciation reserves." This statement is not true in anything remotely approaching a literal sense.

A widespread belief that the net book value of assets is related to their real value is equally erroneous.

> **Example.** An auditor's report included the following statement: "Our inspection of insurance policies in force at the close of the year disclosed that the plant assets on the basis of book values were amply protected against fire." Such a statement has little if any significance. What investors want to know is whether the insurance protection equals the *replacement cost* of the assets, and this is unlikely to correspond to their book value.

The key to a practical understanding of depreciation is a sentence from *Accounting Research Bulletin No. 43:*[11] "Depreciation is a process of allocation, not of valuation." Depreciation expense does *not* represent the shrinkage in assets' market value during an accounting period. Particularly during periods of inflation, a depreciable asset's market value may be even higher at the end of the period than it was at the beginning. Neither does the net book value represent the market value of the depreciable assets. *Depreciation expense is the systematic allocation of the original cost of an asset to the periods in which the asset provides benefits to the entity.* It follows that the net book value of fixed assets reported on the balance sheet represents only that portion of the assets' original cost that has *not yet* been charged to expense through this systematic allocation process.

No one really knows how long an asset will last or what its residual value will be at the end of its life. Without this knowledge each year's depreciation expense is necessarily an estimate, one of several estimates we have now discussed that affect the period's reported income.

INCOME TAX CONSIDERATIONS

For several decades Congress has used the income tax laws as a device to encourage corporations to invest in new productive assets. The two key

---

[11]AICPA, *Accounting Research Bulletin No. 43* (June 1953), Chap. 9, Sec. C, par. 5.

ILLUSTRATION 7–5
INCOME TAX DEPRECIABLE ASSET CLASSES
By Length of Recovery Period

Recovery Period (Years)	Recovery Method	Examples of Items in This Class
3	200% declining-balance	Special tooling, certain horses
5	200% declining-balance	Automobiles and trucks; computers; equipment for construction, oil drilling, timber cutting, and manufacturing of chemicals, apparel, and electronic products
7	200% declining-balance	Office furniture and most other machinery and equipment
10	200% declining-balance	Barges and tugboats; equipment for manufacturing grain, sugar, and vegetable oil products
15	150% declining-balance	Gas pipelines; cement plants; industrial steam and electricity plants; land improvements; telephone central offices
20	150% declining-balance	Railroad structures, municipal sewers, farm buildings
27½	Straight-line	Residential rental property; elevators and escalators
31½	Straight-line	Other buildings

mechanisms to encourage this capital formation have been depreciation allowances and the investment tax credit.[12]

Income Tax Depreciation

Background. From 1954 until 1981, an incentive to invest in capital assets was provided by allowing the use of accelerated depreciation in calculating taxable income for federal income tax purposes. The Economic Recovery Tax Act of 1981 was intended (in part) to increase this incentive by shortening asset lives for tax purposes to periods substantially shorter than the assets' actual service lives. The 1981 act even dropped the use of the term *depreciation* and instead called the specified approach the **accelerated cost recovery system (ACRS).** Subsequent tax laws changed the details and the formal name—now **modified accelerated cost recovery system (MACRS)**—but the general approach has continued.

The ACRS approach provides for a series of asset classes, each class having its own depreciation life (called *recovery period* in the regulations) and method. These are shown in Illustration 7–5 for assets placed in service after 1986.[13] As with financial accounting declining-balance depreciation calculations, ACRS calculations ignore the estimated residual value of the asset.

---

[12]Our description of income tax matters throughout this text is intended to give general principles only. Details are spelled out in thousands of pages of Internal Revenue Service Regulations.

[13]The tax laws also permit the use of straight-line depreciation over longer (realistic) asset lives. However, it is usually to a company's benefit to use the accelerated cost-recovery provisions.

Half-Year Convention. The tax rules also incorporate the **half-year convention.** Under this convention property acquired or disposed of at any point during the year is assumed to have been acquired or disposed of at the *midpoint* of that year. Thus, an asset in, say, the five-year class is actually depreciated over six years, with half a year's depreciation taken in both the first and sixth years and a full year's taken in each of the intervening four years.[14]

> **Example.** Assume that a machine in the five-year class is acquired at some point in 19x1 for $100,000. This asset would have the following cost recovery schedule, based on the double-declining-balance method for this class and the half-year convention:

Year	Cost Recovery Deduction	Computation
19x1........	$ 20,000	½ * 40% * $100,000
19x2........	32,000	40% * ($100,000 – $20,000)
19x3........	19,200	40% * ($80,000 – $32,000)
19x4........	11,520	40% * ($48,000 – $19,200)
19x5........	11,520	Net book value at end of 19x4 is $17,280; this is allocated
19x6........	5,760	to the remaining 1½ years, using the straight-line method.
Total........	$100,000	

As a practical matter ACRS's complex combination of a declining-balance method, the half-year convention, and the change to straight-line depreciation for the latter portion of the recovery period has made income tax depreciation calculations a "look-up" procedure. Instead of doing the calculations as illustrated above, the accountant uses an IRS table to look up the percentage of an asset's cost that can be depreciated in each year and applies this percentage to the asset's original cost. Thus, in the above example for the years 19x1–19x6 the accountant would find in a table the percentages 20.00, 32.00, 19.20, 11.52, 11.52, and 5.76, and would then multiply each year's percentage by the $100,000 original cost to arrive at that year's ACRS depreciation charge.

Investment Tax Credit

In most years since 1962, the tax laws have permitted a reduction in the year's income taxes equal to a percentage—often 10 percent—of the cost of any business machinery and equipment (but not buildings) acquired by a company during the year. This is called the **investment tax credit (ITC).** The

---

[14]As an illustration of the complexity of actual tax regulations, the four pages of fine print on the half-year convention include the following exceptions: (1) the convention does not apply to buildings—instead, first-year and last-year depreciation is based on the number of *months* the property was owned during those respective years; and (2) if more than 40 percent of the depreciable asset additions occurred in the last quarter of the year, then the *mid-quarter convention* applies, under which assets acquired in a given quarter are assumed to have been acquired in the middle of that quarter.

credit is a direct reduction in the company's income tax bill (as contrasted with an item deducted from revenues in arriving at the amount of taxable income). In effect, it is a *rebate* to the company acquiring a new fixed asset, except the rebate comes from the government rather than from the seller of the asset. For example, if a company acquired a $100,000 machine in 1985, it could deduct $10,000 from the federal income tax it would otherwise pay for 1985.

The 1986 Tax Act repealed the ITC for any assets placed in service on or after January 1, 1986. (The ITC was also suspended from 1966–67 and 1969–71.) Nevertheless, we describe accounting for the ITC here because history shows a pattern of the Congress reinstating the ITC to counteract economic downturns.

Either of two methods of accounting for the ITC is permitted for financial reporting purposes. The **flow-through method** reduces reported income tax expense by the amount of the ITC in the year in which the credit is taken. Conceptually, this method treats the ITC rebate as a tax reduction that is "earned" as a result of acquiring assets that qualify for the ITC.

The **deferral method** treats the ITC rebate as a reduction in the original cost of the asset (which, of course, is what a true rebate is). The deferral method spreads the tax credit over the years of the asset's useful life by reducing reported income tax expense in each of those years. This reduction in each year's income tax expense increases the year's net income; this is the same effect that reducing the asset's original cost, and hence its annual depreciation expense, would have on net income. Conceptually, the deferral method rejects the notion that the act of *acquiring* an asset should increase net income, which is the effect of the flow-through method. Rather, the credit is matched with the time periods in which the company is *using* the asset. Nevertheless, when the ITC was last in effect, almost 90 percent of large companies used the flow-through method.[15]

The accounting entries for the two methods are shown in the following example.

> **Example.**   In late December 19x1 a company purchased a $200,000 machine that qualified for a $20,000 investment tax credit. Regardless of which *financial reporting* treatment of the ITC the company chooses, its 19x1 tax liability will be decreased by $20,000. For financial reporting purposes the machine's useful life is 10 years, and straight-line depreciation is used.
>
> With the flow-through method the ITC would be recorded in 19x1 as follows:
>
> Income Tax Liability 20,000
> Income Tax Expense   20,000
>
> This has the effect of decreasing 19x1 income tax expense, and hence increasing 19x1 net income, by $20,000. The act of *acquiring* the asset has increased reported income.

---

[15]*Accounting Trends & Techniques* (1987).

With the deferral method the ITC would initially be recorded as a deferred credit (a liability), analogous to unearned revenues:

```
Income Tax Liability .................................  20,000
     Deferred Investment Tax Credits .................         20,000
```

Note that this entry has no effect on the 19x1 income statement. In 19x2 and the subsequent nine years, income tax expense would be decreased by $2,000 per year. The entry is:

```
Deferred Investment Tax Credits....................  2,000
     Income Tax Expense............................         2,000
```

This has the effect of increasing net income by $2,000 in each of the next 10 years, as compared with what the net income would have been if there were no investment tax credit. The ITC rebate is thus matched with the *use* of the asset, not with the act of acquiring it.

The income tax rules also permit special treatment of low-income housing, research expenditures, and restoration of historically important buildings, among other things. These provisions are beyond the scope of this introductory treatment.

A Caution. Especially since 1980, the tax code has been subject to frequent change. The rules described above are those in effect as of 1994.[16]

LEASED ASSETS

In a **lease** agreement the owner of property, the **lessor,** conveys to another party, the **lessee,** the right to use property, plant, or equipment for a stated period of time. For many leases this period of time is short relative to the total life of the asset. Agencies lease—or **rent,** which is another term for lease—automobiles for a few hours or days, and space in an office building may be leased on an annual basis. These leases are called **operating leases.** The lease payments are expenses of the accounting period to which they apply. The entry to record a period's operating lease payments of, say, $10,000 is thus:

```
Rental Expense .....................................  10,000
     Cash ...........................................         10,000
```

---

[16]As of 1994 corporate federal income tax rates were 15 percent for the first $50,000 of taxable income, 25 percent for the next $25,000, 34 percent for all income in excess of $75,000 up to $10 million, and 35 percent over $10 million. An additional 5 percent tax is imposed on taxable income between $100,000 and $335,000; the result is that corporations with taxable income of $335,000 or more have an average rate of 34 percent on all of their taxable income up to $10 million (including the first $75,000). Moreover, an additional 3 percent not to exceed $100,000 is imposed on income over $15 million; this phases out the benefits of the 34 percent rate and gives a company with income in excess of $18⅓ million a flat rate of 35 percent. Remember that many states also levy corporate income taxes; as a result, this book uses a 40 percent rate in illustrations.

Capital Leases   Other leases cover a period of time that is substantially equal to the estimated life of the asset, or they contain other provisions that give the lessee almost as many rights to the use of the asset as if the lessee owned it. Such leases are called **capital leases** or **financial leases.** Assets acquired under a capital lease are treated *as if they had been purchased.* The lease obligation is a liability, which is treated in the same manner as long-term debt. (Accounting for this liability is discussed further in the next chapter.)

The FASB has ruled that a lease is a capital lease if one or more of the following criteria are met: (1) ownership is transferred to the lessee at the end of the term of the lease, (2) the lessee has an option to purchase the asset at a "bargain" price, (3) the term of the lease is 75 percent or more of the economic life of the asset, or (4) the present value of the lease payments is 90 percent or more of the fair market value of the property (subject to certain detailed adjustments).[17] The idea of these criteria is to establish the substance (as opposed to the form) of the lease transaction. Even if only one of the four criteria is met, the transaction is viewed in substance as a sale of the asset to the lessee, with the lessor acting both as a seller of assets and as a finance company. In sum, a capital lease is, in effect, just another name for an installment loan.

The lease payments in a capital lease are usually set so that over the life of the lease the lessor will recover (1) the cost of the asset and (2) interest and a profit on the lessor's capital that is tied up in the asset. The amount debited as the cost of the asset acquired with a capital lease, and the offsetting liability for lease payments, is the *smaller* of (1) the fair value of the asset or (2) the present value of the stream of minimum lease payments required by the lease agreement. Fair value means the cash price that the acquirer of the leased item would have to pay for it if the seller were not providing financing to the acquirer in the form of a lease. The method of calculating the present value of the lease payments is described in the Appendix to Chapter 8. These two amounts are approximately the same in most lease transactions.

The asset amount is depreciated just as any item of plant or equipment owned by the organization would be. When lease payments are made to the lessor, part of the payment reduces the liability, and the remainder is interest expense of the period.

> **Example.**   A company leases an item of equipment whose useful life is 10 years. Lease payments are $1,558 per year payable at the end of each of the next 10 years. This is a capital lease because the lease term exceeds 75 percent of the asset's life. The fair value of the equipment is $10,000 (as is the present value of the lease payments). When the equipment is acquired, the entry is:
>
> Equipment 10,000
>   Capital Lease Obligations   10,000

---

[17]"Accounting for Leases," *FASB Statement No. 13* (November 1976).

Assume that the first annual lease payment consists of $900 of interest expense and $658 to reduce the liability. The entry for this payment is as follows:

```
Interest Expense....................................    900
Capital Lease Obligations...........................    658
    Cash............................................          1,558
```

Also, depreciation on the asset would be charged as an expense each year, just as if the entity had bought the asset for cash. Assuming the straight-line method is used, the entry is:

```
Depreciation Expense...............................  1,000
    Accumulated Depreciation.......................          1,000
```

At the end of the 10 years, all of the $10,000 asset cost will have been charged to expense via the depreciation mechanism. Also, the capital lease obligation will have been reduced to zero, and the annual interest expense will have been recognized in each of the 10 years via entries such as the one shown above. Note that once the leased item is acquired and the initial equipment asset and lease obligation liability entry is made, accounting for the leased asset and for the lease obligation are separate, unrelated processes.

Most assets of an entity are legally owned by that entity. Assets acquired by a capital lease are an exception to this general rule. They are legally owned by the lessor, but they are accounted for as if they were owned by the lessee. In this way the lease obligation, which is in substance a long-term loan, is disclosed as a liability. Before *FASB Statement No. 13,* many companies preferred leasing assets to purchasing them outright because the lease obligation was, in effect, hidden from the view of financial statement users. Such "off-balance-sheet financing" was seriously curtailed by *Statement No. 13.*

NATURAL RESOURCES

Natural resources (such as unextracted coal, oil, other minerals, and gas) are assets of the company that owns the right to extract them. The general principles for measuring the acquisition cost of these **wasting assets** are the same as those for other tangible assets. If purchased, the cost is the purchase price and related acquisition costs. Many companies acquire these assets as a consequence of exploring for them. There are two strongly held views as to how these exploration costs should be accounted for, particularly for oil and gas companies.

A petroleum company, in a given year, may be exploring in many different locations; it probably will discover oil and gas reserves in only a few of them. Some people argue that *all* the exploration costs of a year should be capitalized as the asset value of the reserves that are discovered during the year; this is the **full cost method.** Others argue that only the costs incurred at locations in which reserves are discovered should be capitalized as the cost of these reserves and that the "dry-hole" costs should be immediately expensed; this is the **successful efforts method.**

> **Example.** A petroleum company explores 10 locations, incurring costs of $10 million at each. It discovers oil and gas reserves at three of these locations. If it uses the full cost method, the asset amount of the newly discovered reserves will be recorded as $100 million. If it uses the successful efforts method, the asset amount will be recorded as $30 million and the other $70 million will be charged to expense.

In its *Statement No. 19* (December 1977) the FASB required the use of the successful efforts method. In August 1978, however, the SEC ruled that either method would continue to be acceptable for SEC filings. This SEC action led the FASB to issue *Statement No. 25* (February 1979), which amended *Statement No. 19* to permit either method. (This reversal by the FASB serves as a reminder that determining GAAP is formally the SEC's legislated responsibility, even though in most cases the SEC accepts the FASB's accounting standards.)

Depletion

The process of amortizing the cost of natural resources in the accounting periods benefitted is called **depletion.** The objective is the same as that for depreciation: to allocate the cost in some systematic manner to the years of the asset's useful life. The units-of-production method is ordinarily used.

> **Example.** If an oil property cost $250 million and is estimated to contain 50 million barrels of oil, the depletion rate is $5 per barrel. The total depletion for a year in which 8 million barrels of oil were produced would be $40 million.

For income tax purposes, however, the depletion allowance may bear no relation to cost. Rather, it is a percentage of revenue. The permitted percentage varies with the type of asset and, like other provisions of the tax law, is subject to change. Depletion is an example of an income tax provision that is inconsistent with GAAP. Advocates of the tax law treatment of depletion claim that it stimulates exploration for and development of new supplies of natural resources and is therefore in the national interest.

Accretion and Appreciation

For timberland, cattle, tobacco, wine, and other agricultural products, the increase in value that arises through the natural process of growth or aging is called **accretion.** Since accretion does not represent realized revenue, it is ordinarily not recognized in the accounts. However, the costs incurred in the growing or aging process are added to the asset value, just as is done in the case of costs incurred in the manufacture of goods.

Appreciation is also an increase in the *value* of an asset. It is *not* the opposite of depreciation, which is a write-off of cost. Appreciation of assets is recognized in the accounts only under highly unusual circumstances. For example, if a business is purchased by a new owner and an appraisal discloses that the current market value of certain assets is substantially above their book value, in some instances (described below) these assets' values are written up to their current value. Generally, however, increases in value are recognized in the accounts only when revenue is realized, whereas expiration of cost is recognized when it occurs.

INTANGIBLE ASSETS

Intangible long-lived assets—such as goodwill, organization costs (i.e., costs incurred to get a company started), trademarks, and patents—are usually converted to expenses over a number of accounting periods. The systematic allocation of the costs of these assets to the periods in which they provide benefits is called **amortization.** (There is no specialized term for the process of amortizing these assets, as there is for fixed assets and natural resources.)

The amortization of intangible assets is essentially the same process as the depreciation of tangible assets. However, the straight-line method must be used for amortization of intangibles unless "a company demonstrates that another systematic method is more appropriate."[18] Also, amortization of an intangible asset is usually credited directly to the asset account rather than being accumulated in a separate contra asset account, as is the case with accumulated depreciation. Thus, the entry recording one year's amortization of a five-year license that originally cost $50,000 would be:

```
Amortization Expense ............................  10,000
    Licenses .......................................       10,000
```

Intangible assets are sometimes classified as being either "identifiable" or "unidentifiable." Patents, licenses, and trademarks are **identifiable intangibles;** they can be sold individually (although, of course, they are not sold in the ordinary course of business). By contrast, customer loyalty and a reputation for quality are **unidentifiable intangibles;** they cannot be realized without selling the entire enterprise.

Goodwill

When one company buys another company, the purchasing company may pay more for the acquired company than the fair market value of its **net identifiable assets**—tangible assets plus identifiable intangibles, net of any liabilities assumed by the purchaser. The amount by which the purchase price exceeds the fair value of the net identifiable assets is recorded as an asset of the acquiring company. Although sometimes reported on the balance sheet with a descriptive title such as "excess of acquisition cost over net assets acquired," the amount is customarily called **goodwill.**

---

[18]"Intangible Assets," *APB Opinion No. 17* (August 1970), par. 30.

It is important to note that goodwill arises only as part of a *purchase* transaction. In most cases this is a transaction in which one company acquires all the assets of another company for some consideration *other than* an exchange of common stock. (More details are given in Chapter 12.) The buying company is willing to pay more than the fair value of the identifiable assets because the acquired company has a strong management team, a favorable reputation in the marketplace, superior production methods, or other unidentifiable intangibles.

The acquisition cost of the identifiable assets acquired is their fair market value at the time of acquisition. Usually, these values are determined by appraisal, but in some cases the net book value of these assets is accepted as being their fair value. If there is evidence that the fair market value differs from net book value, either higher or lower, the market value governs.

Example. Company A acquires all the assets of Company B, giving Company B $1,500,000 cash. Company B has cash of $50,000, accounts receivable that are believed to have a realizable value of $60,000, and other identifiable assets that are estimated to have a current market value of $1,100,000. The amount of goodwill is calculated as follows:

Total purchase price		$1,500,000
Less		
Cash acquired	$ 50,000	
Accounts receivable	60,000	
Other identifiable assets (estimated)	1,100,000	1,210,000
Goodwill		$ 290,000

Amortization. In most cases there is no way of estimating the useful life of goodwill and hence no reliable way of deciding what fraction of the cost should be amortized as an expense in a given year. A company may select whatever period it believes to be reasonable, but in no event can the amortization period exceed 40 years.[19]

For income tax purposes, however, goodwill cannot be amortized at all. Therefore, for income tax purposes the acquiring company wants to value the depreciable assets as high as it legitimately can, leaving the minimum possible amount to be recorded as goodwill. The amount can nevertheless be significant. For example, General Electric's 1986 purchase of RCA for $6.4 billion resulted in $3.7 billion of goodwill. Amortized over the maximum 40 years, this is $92.5 million annual expense, which is not tax deductible.

Patents, Copyrights, Franchise Rights

Patents, copyrights, franchise rights, and similar intangible assets are initially recorded at their cost. If they are purchased, the cost is the amount paid. If a patented invention is developed within the company, however, the costs involved ordinarily are not capitalized. These are considered to be

---

[19]Ibid., par. 29. For financial institutions the maximum period is 25 years. (Source: SEC, *Staff Accounting Bulletin No. 42* [December 31, 1981].)

research and development costs, which are discussed separately in a following section.

The cost of any of these intangible assets is amortized over the useful life of the asset. If the useful life is limited by agreement or by law (e.g., 17 years for a patent), the amortization period cannot be longer. It may be shorter if the company believes that because of technological advances or other reasons, the practical life will be shorter than the legal life. In no case may the period exceed 40 years.

Leasehold Improvements

Leased property reverts to the owner at the end of the period of the lease. Any improvements made to the property belong to the owner; the lessee loses the use of them when the leased property is returned. Therefore, the useful life of such improvements corresponds to the period of the lease. The lease agreement may contain renewal options that effectively extend the life beyond the period of the original lease agreement. It follows that although improvements which otherwise meet the criteria for capitalization are capitalized, the useful life of these improvements is not determined by the physical characteristics of the improvements themselves but rather by the terms of the lease agreement.

> **Example.**   A company leases office space and spends $90,000 for remodeling to suit its needs. The lease is for an original period of three years with an option to renew for another three years. The physical life of the improvements is 10 years. The leasehold improvements are amortized over a period of six years, or $15,000 a year, if the lessee believes it likely that the lease will be renewed. Otherwise, they are amortized over three years, at $30,000 a year. In any event they are not amortized over 10 years.

Deferred Charges

Deferred charges are conceptually the same as prepaid expenses, a current asset discussed in Chapter 2. They are included as long-lived assets only if they have a relatively long useful life—that is, if they benefit several future years. Goodwill, patents, copyrights, and indeed all long-lived assets subject to amortization are deferred charges in the literal sense. However, the term is usually restricted to long-lived intangibles other than those listed in the preceding paragraphs. They may include the cost of organizing a company and the related preoperating or start-up costs of preparing the company or some part thereof, such as a new store, to generate revenue. During the preoperating period, no revenue is being earned, and thus there is nothing against which to match these costs.

Practice varies greatly with respect to these items. Some companies charge them off as expenses as the costs are incurred, even though there is no offsetting revenue. This reflects the conservatism concept. Other companies capitalize them. If capitalized, they are usually amortized over a relatively short period of time, often in the next year in the case of the preoperating costs of a new store, but rarely more than five years.

Research and Development Costs

Research and development (R&D) costs are costs incurred for the purpose of developing new or improved goods, processes, or services. The fruits of R&D efforts are increased revenues or lower costs. Since these fruits will not be picked until future periods, often five years or more after a research project is started, a good case can be made for capitalizing R&D costs and amortizing them over the periods benefitted. This practice was common at one time, but the FASB no longer permits it. Instead, it requires that R&D costs be treated as period costs—that is, charged off as an expense of the current period.[20]

The reason given by the FASB for its requirement is that by their very nature, the future benefits to be derived from current R&D efforts are highly uncertain. The efforts that are eventually unsuccessful cannot be identified in advance; otherwise, they would not have been undertaken. Although near the end of the development stage the success of certain projects seems reasonably assured, the FASB has concluded that there is no objective way of distinguishing between these projects and the unsuccessful ones.

The FASB decision is a particularly interesting example of the inherent conflict between certain concepts. Capitalizing R&D costs and then amortizing them over the future periods likely to benefit is consistent with the matching concept. However, it is inconsistent with the criterion that accounting should be reasonably objective, and it is not in accord with the conservatism concept. The FASB decided that the latter considerations were more important than the matching concept in this instance.

If a company does R&D work for a customer (i.e., another company or a government agency) and is paid for this work, these payments constitute revenue. The related costs are held as an asset in Work in Process Inventory. They are matched against revenue and therefore are charged as expenses in the period in which the revenue is earned.

Software Development.   The costs of developing computer software to be sold, leased, or licensed are a type of R&D cost. These costs must be expensed as incurred up until the point that the technological feasibility of the software product has been established. Technological feasibility is established upon completion of a detailed program design or completion of a working model. Thereafter, the costs of bringing the software to market, such as producing product masters, can be capitalized. Capitalization of such costs ceases when the product is available for release to customers. Annual amortization of such costs is the greater of (1) the straight-line method amount or (2) the amount determined by the ratio of the year's revenues to the total anticipated revenues for the product. Thus, a product with an estimated market life of four years and with half of its estimated lifetime revenues coming in the first year would have half (not one-fourth) of its capitalized costs amortized in the first year.[21]

---

[20]"Accounting for Research and Development Costs," *FASB Statement No. 2* (October 1974).

[21]"Accounting for the Costs of Computer Software," *FASB Statement No. 86* (August 1985).

SUMMARY

Items of property, plant, and equipment are capitalized at their acquisition cost, which includes all elements of cost involved in making them ready to provide service. Except for land, a portion of this cost (less residual value, if any) is charged as depreciation expense to each of the accounting periods in which the asset provides service. A corresponding reduction is made each period in the net book value of the asset account. Any systematic method may be used for depreciation. The straight-line method is ordinarily used for financial accounting purposes, but declining-balance methods are the basis for the cost recovery deductions allowed for income tax purposes.

When an asset is disposed of, its cost and accumulated depreciation are removed from the accounts, and any gain or loss appears on the income statement (unless group depreciation is used).

Assets acquired with capital leases are accounted for as if they were owned, and the lease obligation is separately accounted for as long-term debt. Natural resources are accounted for in the same way as fixed assets, except that the expense item is called depletion rather than depreciation.

Intangible assets are also recorded at cost. In the case of goodwill, this cost is the difference between the price paid for a company and the fair market value of the identifiable assets acquired (net of any liabilities assumed by the purchaser). If intangible assets have a determinable service life, their cost is amortized over that life, using the straight-line method. For assets with no determinable service life, the amortization period must not exceed 40 years. R&D costs are expensed as incurred; this includes most of the costs of developing marketable computer software.

Accounting for long-lived assets involves making estimates that result in each year's depreciation and amortization expense amounts being approximations. Since these amounts affect income in each year of an asset's life, reported income itself is an estimate. (Similar comments apply to the estimates described in earlier chapters for such assets as receivables and inventories and for the related expense amounts for bad debts and cost of sales.)

Cases

CASE 7-1 Moyer Corporation (B)

After the controller of Moyer Corporation had ascertained the changes in accounts receivable and the allowance for doubtful accounts in 1992, a similar analysis was made of property, plant, and equipment and accumulated depreciation accounts. Again the controller examined the December 31, 1991, balance sheet (see Exhibit 1 of Moyer Corporation (A), Case 5-1). Also reviewed were the following company transactions that were found to be applicable to these accounts:

1. On January 2, 1992, one of the factory machines was sold for its book value, $3,866. This machine was recorded on the books at $31,233 with accumulated depreciation of $27,367.

2. Tools were carried on the books at cost, and at the end of each year a physical inventory was taken to determine what tools still remained. The account was written down to the extent of the decrease in tools as ascertained by the year-end inventory. At the end of 1992, it was determined that there had been a decrease in the tool inventory amounting to $7,850.

3. On March 1, 1992, the company sold for $2,336 cash an automobile that was recorded on the books at a cost of $8,354 and had an accumulated depreciation of $5,180, giving a net book value of $3,174 as of January 1, 1992. In this and other cases of the sale of long-lived assets during the year, the accumulated deprecia-

tion and depreciation expense items were both increased by an amount that reflected the depreciation chargeable for the months in 1992 in which the asset was held prior to the sale, at rates listed in item 7 below.

4. The patent listed on the balance sheet had been purchased by the Moyer Corporation on December 31, 1981, for $168,750. This patent had been granted on December 31, 1979. The cost of the patent was to be written off as an expense over the remainder of its legal life. (The legal life of a patent is 17 years from the date granted.)

5. On July 1, 1992, a typewriter that had cost $1,027 and had been fully depreciated on December 31, 1991, was sold for $75.

6. On October 1, 1992, the company sold a desk for $80. This piece of furniture was recorded on the books at a cost of $490 with an accumulated depreciation of $395 as of January 1, 1992.

7. Depreciation was calculated at the following rates:

Buildings...........................	2%
Factory machinery	10*
Furniture and fixtures	10
Automotive equipment...................	20
Office machines	10

*Included in the factory machinery cost of $3,425,585 was a machine costing $85,000 that had been fully depreciated on December 31, 1991, and that was still in use.

Questions

1. In a manner similar to that used in Moyer Corporation (A), analyze the effect of each of these transactions on the property, plant, and equipment accounts, accumulated depreciation, and any other accounts that may be involved; prepare journal entries for these transactions.

2. Give the correct totals for property, plant, and equipment, and the amount of accumulated depreciation as of December 31, 1992, after the transactions affecting them had been recorded.

CASE 7–2 Jean Coffin (C)*

Jean Coffin said to the accounting instructor, "The general principle for arriving at the amount of a fixed asset that is to be capitalized is reasonably clear, but there certainly are a great many problems in applying this principle to specific situations." Following are some of the problems Jean Coffin presented:

1. Suppose that the Bruce Manufacturing Company used its own maintenance crew to build an additional wing on its existing factory building. What would be the proper accounting treatment of the following items:

    a. Architects' fees.

    b. The cost of snow removal during construction.

    c. Cash discounts earned for prompt payment on materials purchased for construction.

    d. The cost of building a combined construction office and toolshed that would be torn down once the factory wing had been completed.

    e. Interest on money borrowed to finance construction.

    f. Local real estate taxes for the period of construction on the portion of land to be occupied by the new wing.

    g. The cost of mistakes made during construction.

    h. The overhead costs of the maintenance department that include supervision; depreciation on buildings and equipment of maintenance department shops; heat, light, and power for these shops; and allocations of cost for such items as the cafeteria, medical office, and personnel department.

    i. The cost of insurance during construction and the cost of damages or losses on any injuries or losses not covered by insurance.

2. Assume that the Archer Company bought a large piece of land, including the buildings thereon, with the intent of razing the buildings and constructing a combined hotel and office building in their place. The existing buildings consisted of a theater and several stores and small apartment buildings, all in active use at the time of the purchase.

    a. What accounting treatment should be accorded that portion of the purchase price considered to be the amount paid for the buildings that were subsequently razed?

    b. How should the costs of demolishing the old buildings be treated?

    c. Suppose that a single company had owned this large piece of land, including the buildings thereon, and instead of selling to the Archer Company had decided to have the buildings razed and to have a combined hotel and office building

*Copyright © by the President and Fellows of Harvard College. Harvard Business School case 105–033.

constructed on the site for its own benefit. In what respects, if any, should the accounting treatment of the old buildings and the cost of demolishing them differ from your recommendations with respect to (*a*) and (*b*) above?

3. Midland Manufacturing Company purchased a new machine. It is clear that the invoice price of the new machine should be capitalized, and it also seems reasonable to capitalize the transportation cost to bring the machine to the Midland plant. I'm not so clear, however, on the following items.

a. The new machine is heavier than the old machine it replaced; consequently, the foundation under the machine has had to be strengthened by the installation of additional steel beams. Should this cost be charged to the building, added to the cost of the machine, or be expensed?

b. The installation of the machine took longer and was more costly than anticipated. In addition to time spent by the regular maintenance crew on installation, it became necessary to hire an outside engineer to assist in the installation and in "working out the bugs" to get the machine running properly. His costs included not only his fee but also his transportation, hotel expense, and meals. Moreover, the foreman of the department and the plant superintendent both spent a considerable amount of time assisting in the installation work. Before the new machine was working properly, a large amount of material had been spoiled during trial runs. How should all of these costs be treated?

c. In addition to the invoice price and transportation, it was necessary to pay a state sales tax on purchasing the machine. Is this part of the machine's cost?

d. In connection with payment for the new machine, the machine manufacturer was willing to accept the Midland Company's old machine as partial payment. The amount allowed as a trade-in was larger than the depreciated value at which the old machine was being carried in the books of the Midland Company. Should the difference have been treated as a reduction in the cost of the new machine or a gain on disposal of the old one?

4. A computer manufacturing company sold outright about 25 percent of its products (in terms of dollar volume) and leased 75 percent. On average, a given computer was leased for four years. The cost of leased computers was initially recorded as an asset and was depreciated over four years. The company assisted new customers in installing the computer and in designing the related systems. These "applications engineering" services were furnished without charge, and the company's cost was reported as part of its marketing expense. Applications engineering costs averaged about 5 percent of the sales value of a computer, but about 20 percent of the first-year rental revenue of a leased computer. Recently, the company's installation of computers grew rapidly. Because the applications engineering cost was such a high percentage of lease revenue, reported income did not increase at all. Research and development costs must be expensed as incurred. Does the same principle apply to applications engineering costs, or could these costs be added to the asset value of leased computers and amortized over the lease period? If so, could other marketing costs related to leased computers be treated in the same way?

5. Using the deferral method of accounting for the investment tax credit in effect

reduces the capitalized cost of the asset that gave rise to the credit, whereas the flow-through method reduces reported income tax expense for the period in which the asset was acquired. While I can understand permitting accounting alternatives such as FIFO versus LIFO and straight-line versus accelerated depreciation, I cannot understand the rationale for permitting two different treatments for the investment tax credit. What is the rationale?

6. An electronics component manufacturer announced a new product that would soon be available. This product, a new generation component, had features highly sought by customers for their next generation of electronics products. To meet the demands of its customers, many of whom had begun to impose quality standards on suppliers, the electronics component manufacturer would have to achieve a quality standard of 65 ppm, that is, 65 or fewer defective parts per million parts delivered to the customer.

The equipment intended to produce the new component at the 65 ppm quality standard was custom-built by the manufacturer. Once the equipment was physically installed in the plant, the company performed extensive testing and debugging efforts to assure that the components met the required standard. A couple of months after installation, the new equipment was producing components which, while commercially viable, did not quite meet the quality standard. A key customer was eager to purchase the new component for use in its own new product, however. The customer agreed to purchase the component now if the electronics com-

ponent manufacturer would continue to push to meet the quality standard.

Since the new manufacturing equipment was going to begin to generate revenue, the fixed asset accounting manager reviewed the costs capitalized as part of this asset. The costs of the material, labor, and overhead required to fabricate and install the equipment had been capitalized. In addition, the debugging and testing costs incurred to attempt to bring the new manufacturing equipment to the 65 ppm quality standard had also been capitalized, as these costs had been required to make the equipment ready for its intended use. The total costs were approximately one-half million dollars, and they would be amortized over the asset's productive life beginning with production for the eager first customer.

The engineers believed that at least $50,000 of additional debugging, fine tuning, and testing would be required for the new equipment to reach the 65 ppm quality standard. Should those costs continue to be capitalized, despite the fact that the equipment was producing components that were sold commercially? If so, once the quality standard was achieved and the full cost of the asset was known, should the amount of depreciation for the initial production periods be adjusted? The 65 ppm standard was an extremely tough standard; the engineers who had designed the equipment were confident they could achieve it, although a few skeptics had expressed the concern that the standard might never be achieved. What implications, if any, might this have for capitalizing the cost of the asset?

CASE 7–3   Stafford Press

Stafford Press was founded in 1983 as a one-man job printing firm in a small southwestern town. Shortly after its founding, Lucas Stafford, the owner, decided to concen-

trate on one specialty line of printing. Because of a high degree of technical proficiency, the company experienced a rapid growth.

EXHIBIT 1

STAFFORD PRESS
Condensed Balance Sheet
As of December 31, 1993

Assets			Liabilities and Owner's Equity	
Current assets:				
Cash		$395,868	Current liabilities	$160,223
Other current assets		251,790	Common stock	400,000
Total current assets		647,658	Retained earnings	358,648
Property and equipment:				
Land		34,034		
Buildings	$350,064			
Less: Accumulated depreciation	199,056	151,008		
Equipment	265,093			
Less: Accumulated depreciation	178,922	86,171		
Total assets		$918,871	Total liabilities and owner's equity	$918,871

However, Stafford Press suffered from a competitive disadvantage in that the major market for its specialized output was in a metropolitan area over 300 miles away from the company's plant. For this reason, in 1993, having accumulated some extra cash to finance a move, the owner decided to move nearer his primary market. He also decided to expand and modernize his facilities at the time of the move. After some investigation, an attractive site was found in a suburb of his primary market, and the move was made.

A balance sheet prepared just prior to the move is shown in Exhibit 1. The transactions that arose from this move are described in the following paragraphs:

1. The land at the old site, together with the building thereon, was sold for $149,860 cash.

2. Certain equipment was sold for $35,200 cash. This equipment appeared on the books at a cost of $73,645 less accumulated depreciation of $40,890 for a net book value of $32,755.

3. A new printing press was purchased. The invoice cost of this equipment was $112,110. A 2 percent cash discount was taken by Stafford Press so that only $109,868 was actually paid to the seller. Stafford Press also paid $450 to a trucker to have this equipment delivered. Installation of this equipment was made by Stafford Press employees who worked a total of 60 hours. These workers received $15 per hour in wages, but their time was ordinarily charged to printing jobs at $30.50 per hour, the difference representing an allowance for overhead ($12.15) and profit ($3.35).

4. Stafford Press paid $140,000 to purchase land on which the new plant was to be built. A rundown building, which Stafford's appraiser said had no value, was standing on the plot of land. Stafford Press paid $21,235 to have the old building on the plot of land torn down. In addition, the company paid $13,950 to have permanent drainage facilities installed on the new land.

5. A new composing machine with an invoice cost of $28,030 was purchased. The company paid $20,830 cash and received a trade-in allowance of $7,200 on a used piece of equipment. The used equipment could have been sold outright for not more than $6,050. It had cost $12,000 new, and accumulated depreciation on it was $5,200, making the net book value $6,800.

6. The company erected a building at the new site for $561,000. Of this amount, $136,000 was paid in cash, and $425,000 was borrowed on a mortgage.

7. Trucking and other costs associated with moving equipment from the old location to the new location and installing it were $8,440. In addition, Stafford Press employees worked an estimated 125 hours on that part of the move that related to equipment.

8. During the moving operation, a piece of equipment costing $10,000 was dropped and damaged; $3,220 was spent to repair it. Management believed, however, that the salvage value of this equipment had been reduced by $660 from the original estimate of $1,950 to $1,290. Up until that time, the equipment was being depreciated at $805 per year, representing a 10 percent rate after deduction of estimated salvage of $1,950. Accumulated depreciation was $3,220.

Questions

1. Analyze the effect of each of these transactions on the items in the balance sheet and income statement. For transactions that affect owner's equity, distinguish between those that affect the net income of the current year and those that do not. In most cases, the results of your analysis can be set forth most clearly in the form of journal entries.

2. Adjust the balance sheet in Exhibit 1 to show the effect of these transactions.

CASE 7–4 Digitrex Company

Digitrex Company had developed and successfully tested a computer system that the company believed had significant advantages over other computers in its price range. Digitrex was considering marketing the computer under any of three financial arrangements, at the customer's option: (1) outright sale at $30,000, (2) a capital lease at $7,200 per year for five years, and (3) an operating lease at $7,500 per year.

Before making a final decision on the terms for each option, John Ames, financial vice president, decided to estimate the options' relative attractiveness to typical potential customers. For this purpose he devised a hypothetical company, Gamma Company, with financial statements as summarized in Exhibit 1. He assumed that except for the acquisition of a Digitrex computer, the income statements would continue unchanged for the next five years.

John recognized that a company would presumably perform a net present value analysis as part of its evaluation of the alternatives. However, he knew that the impact of the alternative on the financial statements was also a relevant consideration in most decisions, as, for example, a company might have a loan covenant that required a minimum level of working capital or current ratio. Therefore, John asked an assistant to calculate the effect of each of the three pro-

EXHIBIT 1
GAMMA CORPORATION FINANCIAL STATEMENTS
(thousands of dollars)

Balance Sheet
As of June 30, 19x2

Assets			*Liabilities and Owners' Equity*	
Current assets................		$200	Current liabilities...............	$100
Plant and equipment	$600		Long-term debt................	100
Accumulated depreciation	300		Shareholders' equity............	300
Plant and equipment, net		300		
Total assets		$500	Total liabilities and equity	$500

Income Statement
For the Six Months Ending June 30, 19x2

Sales revenue...	$500
Expenses unrelated to computer	450
Pretax margin unrelated to computer	50
Computer depreciation.................................	0
Computer interest and lease expense	0
Income before income taxes............................	50
Provision for income taxes.............................	20
Net income	$ 30

posed financing methods on Gamma's balance sheets and income statements, using the following assumptions:

1. The computer would be acquired on July 1, 19x2 (i.e., in the middle of the year).

2. Gamma Company's effective income tax rate was 40 percent. For simplicity, it was assumed that income taxes were paid in cash in the year to which the income tax expense was applicable. There was no investment tax credit in effect as of 19x2.

3. If Gamma purchased the computer, it would depreciate the $30,000 cost using the income tax code's ACRS allowances over six calendar years (i.e., 19x2–19x7), both for income tax purposes and for its financial statements (see Exhibit 2). It would pay the $30,000 in cash on July 1, 19x2. (Mr. Ames decided not to complicate the calculations by including the

EXHIBIT 2
ACRS Depreciation Schedule for a
Computer Costing $30,000

Year	*ACRS Allowance* *(Percent of Original Cost)*	*Depreciation* *Amount*
19x2	20.0%	$6,000
19x3	32.0	9,600
19x4	19.2	5,760
19x5	11.52	3,456
19x6	11.52	3,456
19x7	5.76	1,728

possibility that Gamma would borrow part of the purchase price.)

4. If Gamma leased the computer on a capital lease, it would make five annual payments, each of $7,200, with the first on July 1, 19x2. These payments were assumed to be treated in the same way for both income tax purposes and financial reporting purposes. For income tax and financial reporting purposes, the interest

expense applicable to each of the six calendar years was as follows: 19x2, $1,145; 19x3, $2,044; 19x4, $1,526; 19x5, $956; 19x6, $329; and 19x7, $0.[1]

5. If Gamma leased the machine on an operating lease, it would make annual payments of $7,500 starting on July 1, 19x2. Gamma could return the computer to Digitrex without further obligation at the end of any year (i.e., on June 30).

---

[1]These amounts were determined using techniques that are described in the Appendix to Chapter 8.

Questions

1. For each of the three alternatives, estimate Gamma Company's balance sheet as of July 1, 19x2 (immediately after the acquisition of the computer) and its income statement for the second half of 19x2, for each of the years 19x3 through 19x6, and for the first half of 19x7. Round all numbers to the nearest $100. (Note that Exhibit 1 numbers are expressed in thousands of dollars.)

2. Are either or both of these lease alternatives so unattractive, as compared with outright purchase, that it would be a waste of effort for Digitrex to attempt to lease the computers?

CASE 7–5 Depreciation at Delta and Pan Am*

Property, plant, and equipment (PP&E) is a significant asset category of most airline companies. PP&E usually comprises more than half of the total assets of an airline, and depreciation and amortization of these assets is a major operating expense. Depreciation and amortization of PP&E at both Delta Air Lines, Inc., and Pan Am Corporation in 1988[1] amounted to approximately 5 percent of operating expenses.

Salary and wage expenses, fuel costs, and travel agent commissions are also significant airline operating expenses. However, depreciation of PP&E is different in that the methods and estimates used to determine the amount of this expense can vary widely among companies. The methods chosen for financial reporting can have a significant effect on a company's earnings. Furthermore, unless the user of the financial statements sifts through the footnotes to sort out the details, comparability among companies within an industry is difficult.

---

*Copyright © by the President and Fellows of Harvard College. Harvard Business School case 190–035.

[1]Delta's 1988 fiscal year end was June 30, 1988; Pan Am's was December 31, 1988.

Delta Air Lines, Inc.

We are pleased to report that fiscal 1988 was one of the most successful years in the history of Delta Air Lines. The Company established new earnings records for the second consecutive year and continued to strengthen its competitive position . . . We look forward to the coming year with confidence. While we expect competition to be no less challenging than in prior years, we believe that Delta has the resources to meet the competitive challenges, to continue its growth and development, and to maintain its position of leadership in the airline industry. *(Excerpt from the Report to Stockholders included in the 1988 Delta Air Lines, Inc., Annual Report.)*

As a major air carrier Delta served 131 U.S. cities as well as 24 destinations abroad. Delta operated from its primary "hub" in Atlanta, Georgia, and other major hubs throughout the country. While the majority of its revenues was derived from domestic operations, approximately 10 percent of Delta's 1988 revenues came from international routes (excluding Canada).

In fiscal 1988 Delta enplaned 58.6 million passengers, a 22 percent increase from 1987.

EXHIBIT 1
SELECTED OPERATING STATISTICS—
1988 (dollars in thousands)

	Delta	Pan Am
Operating revenues	$6,915,377	$3,359,151
Operating expenses	6,148,293	3,443,334
Operating income (loss)	497,084	(84,183)
Net income (loss)	306,826	(118,254)
Revenue passengers enplaned (000)	58,565	15,011
Revenue passenger miles (000,000)[a]	49,009	28,961
Available seat miles (000,000)[b]	85,834	45,343
Average yield per revenue passenger mile[c]	$0.1315	$0.1014
Passenger load factor[d]	57.1%	63.9%
Break-even passenger load factor[e]	52.7%	69.0%
Operating cost per available seat mile	$0.748	$0.751
Cargo ton miles (000,000)[f]	653[g]	721[g]
Average yield per cargo ton mile[g]	$0.5358	$0.2440
Average aircraft utilization (hours per day)	8.62	9.07
Average fuel price per gallon	$0.56	$0.60
Total gallons of fuel consumed (000)	1,753,538	914,832

[a]"Revenue passenger miles" are determined by multiplying the number of revenue passengers by the miles flown.

[b]"Available seat miles" are determined by multiplying the number of seats available for passengers by the number of miles those seats are flown.

[c]"Yield" represents the scheduled passenger or cargo revenue divided by revenue passenger miles or cargo ton miles.

[d]"Passenger load factor" is determined by dividing revenue passenger miles by available seat miles.

[e]"Break-even passenger load factor" represents the number of revenue passenger miles at which operating earnings would have been zero divided by available seat miles.

[f]"Cargo ton miles" are determined by multiplying the number of tons of cargo carried by the miles flown.

[g]The Delta amount includes freight and mail. The Pan Am amount includes freight only.

Revenue passenger miles (RPMs) were 49.0 billion in 1988, a 28 percent increase from 1987. Cargo ton miles were 653 million, up 36 percent from 1987. (See selected operating statistics in Exhibit 1.) Passenger service accounted for 93 percent of Delta's 1988 operating revenues, with cargo accounting for 5 percent and the remaining 2 percent coming from other sources. Total operating revenues for 1988 were $6.9 billion, an increase of $1.6 billion, or 30 percent, above fiscal 1987 amounts. Net earnings were a record $306.8 million in 1988, breaking the previous record of $263.7 million set in 1987 by 16 percent.

The increases in RPMs and cargo ton miles noted above were partly attributable to the acquisition of Western Air Lines, Inc., by Delta in the middle of fiscal 1987. Western was operated as a wholly owned subsidiary until it was merged into Delta on April 1, 1987. In 1988 Delta nearly completed the integration of the Western routes into the Delta route system. This restructuring would continue in 1989. Also in 1989 Delta would proceed with construction of a new 24-gate terminal in Orlando, Florida, scheduled to be completed by the end of fiscal 1990. The new terminal, along with additional nonstop service to nine new markets, was part of an effort to develop a regional hub in this growing market.

International expansion was a significant part of Delta's growth plans. In 1988 Delta added Dublin, Ireland, and Seoul, Korea, to

EXHIBIT 2
DELTA AIR LINES, INC. FLEET AT JUNE 30, 1988

Type of Aircraft	Seats	Owned	Leased	Total
L-1011-100/200	302	23	—	23
L-1011-250	269	6	—	6
L-1011-500	218/241	10	—	10
DC-10-10	284	3	3	6
DC-8-71	212	—	7	7
B-767-300	254	—	15	15
B-767-200	204	15	—	15
B-757-200	187	15	23	38
B-727-200	148	108	23	131
B-737-300	128	—	13	13
B-737-200	107/115	1	60	61
MD-82/88	142	—	22	22
DC-9-32	98	31	5	36
		212	171	383

its list of international destinations. Delta's presence in the Far East was further strengthened on July 1, 1988, when one-stop service to Taipei, Taiwan, was added.

Property and Equipment. Net property and equipment of $3.6 billion was recorded on Delta's balance sheet at June 30, 1988, and consisted of the following (in millions of dollars):

Flight equipment:	
Owned...........................	$ 4,625
Under capital leases	222
Ground property and equipment.........	1,222
Advance payments for new equipment....	226
Total........................	6,295
Less accumulated depreciation and amortization......................	(2,729)
Total............................	$ 3,566

Net property and equipment accounted for 62 percent of total assets at June 30, 1988, down from 69 percent a year earlier. Delta's fleet at June 30, 1988, consisted of 212 owned aircraft and 171 leased aircraft (Exhibit 2). Delta also had orders outstanding for 54 air-craft and options to purchase 88 aircraft. Delta claimed that its fleet was among the youngest and most modern in the industry, with good fuel economy and low operating costs.

Effective July 1, 1986, Delta began depreciating its aircraft on a straight-line basis over a 15-year period from dates placed in service (see excerpt from Delta's "Notes to Consolidated Financial Statements" in Exhibit 3). Residual value was computed as 10 percent of cost. Previous to this date, Delta's depreciable life for aircraft was 10 years.

Pan Am Corporation

During the past year, your Corporation has recorded modest—but measurable—improvement in its financial performance and position within the industry. . . . Believing strongly that radical actions were neither necessary nor prudent, we have instead pursued conservative, fundamental programs aimed at the kind of steady improvement which we did, in fact, achieve. . . . One of our early tasks was to provide greater stability in an organization that had for

EXHIBIT 3
EXCERPT FROM DELTA AIR LINES, INC., 1988 "NOTES TO
CONSOLIDATED FINANCIAL STATEMENTS"

Summary of Significant Accounting Policies:

Depreciation and Amortization—Prior to July 1, 1986, substantially all of the company's flight equipment was being depreciated on a straight-line basis to residual values (10% of cost) over a 10-year period from dates placed in service. As a result of a comprehensive review of its fleet plan, effective July 1, 1986, the company increased the estimated useful lives of substantially all of its flight equipment. Flight equipment that was not already fully depreciated is now depreciated on a straight-line basis to residual values (10% of cost) over a 15-year period from dates placed in service. The effect of this change was a $130 million decrease in depreciation expense, and a $69 million ($1.54 per share) increase in net income, for the year ended June 30, 1987. Ground property and equipment are depreciated on a straight-line basis over their estimated service lives, which range from 3 to 30 years.

some time lacked a clear focus and direction in many critical areas related to planning, scheduling and marketing. [*Excerpt from the Letter to Shareholders included in the 1988 Pan Am Corporation Annual Report.*]

Pan Am Corporation was the parent of Pan American World Airways, Inc., its principal subsidiary. Commercial air transportation operations were also conducted through two other wholly owned subsidiaries, Pan Am Express, Inc., and Pan Am Shuttle, Inc. (The comments here relate principally to Pan American World Airways, Inc., referred to as "Pan Am," except where otherwise noted.)

Pan Am served 31 U.S. cities and 68 destinations abroad. Main bases of flight operations were maintained in New York and Miami in the United States and in Berlin, Frankfurt, London, and Paris in Europe. The majority (87 percent) of Pan Am's operating revenues was derived from scheduled passenger revenue, of which international operations accounted for 80 percent and domestic service for the remaining 20 percent. Cargo accounted for 7 percent of operating revenues and charter and other revenues accounted for the remaining 6 percent.

Fifteen million passengers were enplaned in 1988, an increase of 11 percent from 1987. RPMs were 29.0 billion in 1988, up 12.2 percent from 1987. Freight ton miles were 721 million in 1988, an 18.8 percent increase

from the 1987 level. Total operating revenues for Pan Am in 1988 were $3.4 billion, an increase of approximately $447 million, or 15.3 percent, from 1987. (See selected operating statistics in Exhibit 1.)

The increases in RPMs and freight ton miles positively affected Pan Am's operations. However, the increases were not enough to allow Pan Am to show a profit. The net loss reported in 1988 was $118.3 million, $156.3 million less than the 1987 loss of $274.6 million. These losses brought Pan Am's negative net worth to $535.3 million at the end of 1988. In both 1987 and 1988 Pan Am Corporation's auditors issued qualified opinions. The Report of Independent Public Accountants in 1988 stated ". . . the Corporation has suffered recurring losses from operations and has a net working capital deficiency and a capital deficit that raise substantial doubt about its ability to continue as a going concern. . . . The consolidated financial statements do not include any adjustments that might result from the outcome of this uncertainty."

In an effort to improve the situation at Pan Am Corporation, the board of directors elected a new chairman and chief executive officer from outside the corporation in early 1988. Additional senior management changes were also made. To improve liquidity, various actions were taken that included the sale

EXHIBIT 4
PAN AMERICAN WORLD AIRWAYS, INC., FLEET AT DECEMBER
31, 1988

Type of Aircraft	Seats	Owned	Leased	Total
B-747-100	359 to 412	13	15	28
B-747-212	413	6	1	7
B-727-200	145 to 163	20	50	70
B-737-200	105	—	4	4
A300B4	254	—	12	12
A310-200	196 to 221	3	4	7
A310-300	192 to 196	—	12	12
Total		42	98	140

and leaseback of aircraft and the sale of rights to aircraft orders and options.

Despite these efforts and other marketing, yield-management, and service-enhancement programs, the company felt that in the longer term it must be part of a larger network with additional traffic to support its route structure. New aircraft, airport gates, and landing slots, along with better representation in computerized reservation systems, would be necessary to gain the needed additional traffic.

Property and Equipment. At December 31, 1988, property, plant, and equipment at Pan Am Corporation (including all subsidiaries) consisted of the following (in millions of dollars):

Flight equipment:	
Owned................................	$1,444
Under capital leases.....................	35
Ground and other property and equipment:	
Owned................................	629
Under capital leases.....................	10
Total................................	2,118
Less accumulated depreciation and amortization.......................	(995)
Total................................	$1,123

Net property and equipment at Pan Am Corporation represented approximately 52 percent of total assets at December 31, 1988.

This was down from about 54 percent at the end of 1987. Pan Am's fleet at year-end increased to 140 aircraft, up 15 from the previous year (see Exhibit 4). These aircraft were depreciated over periods ranging from 18 to 25 years, and a residual value of 15 percent was used. (See excerpts from Pan Am Corporation's "Notes to Consolidated Financial Statements" in Exhibit 5.)

Questions

1. The following are hypothetical events:
   - On January 1, 1989, the company purchases and takes delivery of a new Boeing 747 aircraft. The cost is $50 million.
   - On January 1, 1993, the company extends the estimated service life of this aircraft by five years.
   - On December 31, 1999, the plane is sold for $20 million.

   (a) Estimate how Delta and Pan Am would account for the above events. Compute depreciation expense for each year through 1999. Ignore the effect of income taxes.

   (b) Repeat (a) above assuming that both airlines use the double-declining-balance method of depreciation.

2. Are the differences between the way each airline accounts for depreciation significant? Why would companies depreciate the same aircraft using different

EXHIBIT 5
EXCERPT FROM PAN AM CORPORATION 1988, "NOTES TO
CONSOLIDATED FINANCIAL STATEMENTS"

Summary of Significant Accounting Policies

G. Property and Depreciation
  Operating property and equipment is depreciated to estimated residual value on a straight-
line basis over the estimated useful lives of the equipment as follows:

Aircraft Type	Useful Life	Residual Value
B-747-100	21–25 years	15%
B-747-200	22–25	15
B-727-200	24–25	15
A310-200	18	15

Other property and equipment, primarily of Pan American World Airways, Inc., is depreciated
over a period of four to twenty years without residual value. During 1987, the lives of B727-200
aircraft were extended by an average of five years, decreasing 1987 depreciation expense by
$12,914,000.
  Cost of additions to leased aircraft and facilities are amortized, principally over the remaining
life of the related lease. Expenditures which materially increase equipment values or extend
useful lives are capitalized. The costs of property and equipment disposed of and accumulated
depreciation thereon are removed from the related accounts and the gain or loss, if any, is
recorded in results of operations.
  Property under capital leases and the related obligations thereon are recorded at the present
value of future lease payments and are amortized over the life of the leases.

lives and residual values? What reasons could be given to support these differences? Is different treatment proper?

3. Both Delta and Pan Am extended the lives of certain aircraft in fiscal 1987. Under what circumstances do you believe that the extension of service lives is proper?

4. How would your answer to Question 1 change if the aircraft were leased instead of purchased? Assume that the transaction qualifies as a capital lease, and that the present value of future minimum lease payments is $50 million. Further assume that the length of the lease for each company is the same as the estimated useful life of the aircraft. (For this question ignore the second and third events described in Question 1.)

8

Sources of Capital: Debt

Chapter 8 begins a more detailed description of the liabilities and owners' equity portion of the balance sheet. In this chapter we discuss liabilities and the related interest expense, while Chapter 9 discusses owners' equity. As mentioned in Chapter 2, liabilities and owners' equity represent the sources of the funds that have been used to finance the entity's investments in assets.

Identifying the needs for new funds and acquiring these funds is part of the function known as *financial management*. The treasurer and financial executives in an organization need to have extensive knowledge about the various means of raising money and the legal and tax rules that relate to financing. Other members of management should have a general understanding of these matters even though they need not be familiar with all the details. This chapter discusses the accounting aspects of liabilities at a level that is intended to give the nonfinancial manager a general understanding of the subject.

In the typical organization, arranging new sources of long-term liabilities is an event that occurs infrequently; but when it does occur, it is likely to have a major impact on the financial statements. The Appendix to this chapter introduces the concept of present value, a fundamental concept in the balance sheet valuation of liabilities.

NATURE OF LIABILITIES

In Chapter 2 a liability was defined as an obligation to an outside party arising from a transaction or an event that has already happened. This definition is approximately correct. However, some accounting liabilities are not legally enforceable obligations, and some legal obligations are not liabilities in the accounting meaning of this word.

An estimated allowance for future costs under a warranty agreement is an example of a liability that is not a definite obligation at the time it is set up. When a warranty agreement applies, the liability account is set up in the period in which the revenue is recognized, the offsetting debit being charged to an expense account such as Estimated Warranty Expense. Later on, when repairs or replacements under warranty are made, the liability account will be debited and other balance sheet accounts such as Parts Inventory will be credited.

Executory Contracts

An example of a legal obligation that is not an accounting liability is an **executory contract**—a contract in which *neither* party has as yet performed. Understanding the nature of such agreements is important, not only in determining accounting liabilities but also in determining revenues and expenses. Five examples follow that illustrate the concept.

1.   A sales order is placed for the future delivery of certain goods to the buyer. If the goods are not shipped in the current period, neither party has performed: The buyer has not paid anything and the seller has not shipped the goods. Thus, in accounting the sales order is not recognized—neither party has a liability and no revenue is recognized.

2.   A baseball club signs a contract to pay a certain player $1 million per year for five years. The player works in the year in which the contract is signed; in this first year, the player has performed, so the contract is not an executory contract. If the baseball club has not paid all of the $1 million by the end of the first year, it has a liability for the unpaid amount. However, the agreement is currently an executory contract for the other four years; the remaining $4 million obligation is not recorded as a liability (or as anything) in the current year.

3.   A law firm signs a contract in which it agrees to provide legal services next year. This is an executory contract in the current year; signing the contract does not constitute performance. This is conceptually the same as the sales order example, except that future provision of services is involved rather than future delivery of goods.

4.   A law firm signs a contract in which it agrees to provide legal services next year on an as-needed basis; it receives a $50,000 retainer fee for so agreeing. This is not an executory contract because the client has performed by paying the $50,000. However, because the law firm has not yet performed, it records a liability of $50,000 in the current year; the $50,000 is not yet revenue. The law firm does earn $50,000 revenue in the following

year, whether or not it is actually called upon by the client to perform any services.

5. The seller of a house receives $10,000 as a nonrefundable deposit from the buyer of the house; subsequently, the would-be buyer decides not to purchase the house after all. This is not an executory contract because the buyer has performed to the extent of $10,000. This $10,000 is a liability to the seller at the time the deposit is made; subsequently, when the buyer does not consummate the purchase, the $10,000 becomes revenue to the seller.

Contingencies   A **contingency** is a set of circumstances involving uncertainty as to possible gain (a *gain contingency*) or loss (a *loss contingency*) that will ultimately be resolved when some future event occurs or fails to occur. Gain contingencies usually are not recorded because recording them would mean recognizing revenues before they are reasonably certain, which is not in accord with the conservatism concept. Accounting for loss contingencies is more judgmental. Examples of such contingencies include two items previously discussed—collectibility of receivables and future warranty costs—as well as threatened or pending litigation, guarantees of indebtedness to others, risk of damage or loss to property by fire, flood, earthquake, or other hazard, and actual or possible claims and assessments.

A loss contingency is recognized—recorded—as a liability (with an offsetting debit to an appropriate expense account to record the loss) only if *both* of the following conditions are met:

a. Information available prior to issuance of the financial statements indicates that it is probable that an asset had been impaired or a liability had been incurred . . . and

b. The amount of loss can be reasonably estimated. If one or both conditions are not met, the contingency must nevertheless be disclosed (but not recognized) if there is at least a reasonable possibility that a loss may have been incurred.[1]

For example, assume that during the period a lawsuit claiming damages has been filed against a company. If the company concludes that there is a reasonable possibility of losing the lawsuit *and* if the amount can be reasonably estimated, a liability is recognized. Even if a lawsuit has not actually been filed but the company believes it probable that one will be, there is a liability. If the amount of the probable loss can be estimated only within a range, the lower end of this range is the amount of the liability. The possible loss above this lower limit is disclosed in notes to the financial statements, but it is not recorded in the accounts.[2]

---

[1]"Accounting for Contingencies," *FASB Statement No. 5* (March 1975), par. 8.

[2]"Reasonable Estimation of the Amount of a Loss," *FASB Interpretation No. 14* (September 1976), par. 3.

Example. A company's internal auditor discovered that an employee had made errors in calculating the amount of customs duties due on imported merchandise, resulting in underpayments totaling $100,000. The company immediately paid the $100,000 to the government. The penalty would be at the court's discretion, with a maximum of 10 times the value of the merchandise; in this instance, the maximum penalty could be $30 million. On the other hand, there would be no penalty if the court decided that the error was not willful. Based on the experience of other companies with similar violations, the company decided that the lower limit of the probable range of penalties was $300,000 and recorded this amount as a liability and an expense. It disclosed the possibility of paying up to $30 million in a note accompanying its balance sheet.

A company is said to be "contingently liable" if it has guaranteed payment of a loan made to a third party. But this is not a liability in the accounting sense unless available information indicates that the borrower has defaulted or will probably default.[3] The possibility of loss from future earthquakes or other natural catastrophes is not a liability because the events have not yet happened.

There are often practical difficulties in accounting for contingencies. *Statement No. 5* distinguishes among three degrees of uncertainty—*probable* ("likely to occur"), *remote* ("slight" chance of occurring), and *reasonably possible* ("more than remote but less than likely"). In practice, judgment must often be exercised in deciding whether a contingency loss is probable, thus requiring its recognition, or only reasonably possible, thus requiring disclosure of the contingency but not its recognition. The company's reported income for the period is affected by how this judgment is made, which raises the possibility that the judgment will be biased. Moreover, in the case of a pending lawsuit, a company does not want to signal a presumption of its own guilt by recognizing the liability in its financial statements before a trial or other settlement has taken place.

Liabilities as a Source of Funds

As described in Chapter 2, current liabilities are those that are to be satisfied in the near future. One noteworthy aspect of current liabilities is that they often provide funds to the company at no cost. For example, if suppliers permit a company to pay for materials or supplies 30 days after delivery, this credit policy results in an interest-free, 30-day loan to the company. Similarly, unearned subscription revenue prepaid to a magazine publisher is, in effect, an interest-free loan from subscribers to the publisher.

With these exceptions, a company pays for the use of the capital that others furnish. Capital obtained from borrowing is called **debt capital.** Capital obtained from shareholders, either as a direct contribution (paid-in

---

[3]Even though such a guarantee may not create a liability, the nature and amount of the guarantee must be disclosed in a note to the balance sheet. See *FASB Statement No. 5* and "Disclosure of Indirect Guarantees of Indebtedness to Others," *FASB Interpretation No. 34* (March 1981).

capital) or indirectly as retained earnings, is called **equity capital.** The rest of this chapter deals with debt capital. (Equity capital is dealt with in Chapter 9.)

DEBT CAPITAL

The debt instruments that a firm uses to obtain capital can be classified generally as either term loans or bonds. We will describe these instruments in general terms; additional details can be found in texts on financial management.

Term Loans

A business loan repayable according to a specified schedule, usually with equal installments of principal and interest, is a **term loan.** The lender is usually a bank or an insurance company. Ordinarily a company's obligation to repay a term loan extends over a period of several years, making the loan a noncurrent liability. However, short-term loans can also be arranged, particularly for businesses with seasonal sales patterns that need cash to finance a buildup of inventories prior to the selling season (e.g., toy manufacturers). For major corporations term loans are a less significant source of debt capital than bonds.

Bonds

A **bond** is a certificate promising to pay its holder (1) a specified sum of money at a stated date, called the **maturity date,** and (2) interest at a stated rate until the maturity date. Although bonds are usually issued in units of $1,000, the *price* of a bond is usually quoted as a percentage of this face value; thus, a price of 98 means $980. The stated interest rate is usually constant for the life of the bond. However, for some bonds, called **variable rate bonds,** the rate may be expressed in terms such as "the prime rate plus 2 percent"; the rate thus varies each year with that year's prime rate. Bonds may be issued to the general public through the intermediary of an investment banker, or they may be privately placed with an insurance company or other financial institution.

Long-term creditors usually require the borrowing entity to maintain certain minimum financial ratios (e.g., current ratio) and to refrain from taking actions that might endanger the safety of the money loaned. These requirements, called **covenants,** are spelled out in the loan or bond **indenture** (usually a lengthy document). If any of these covenants is not lived up to, the loan is technically in **default,** and the creditors can demand immediate repayment. In the event of default, however, creditors are more likely to require changes in the management or take other corrective action rather than demand immediate repayment.

A **mortgage bond** (or simply **mortgage**) is a bond secured by designated pledged assets of the borrower, usually land, buildings, and equipment.

Should the firm default on the mortgage, the pledged assets may be sold to repay the mortgage. If the proceeds from the sale of the pledged assets are less than the amount of the mortgage, then the mortgage holder becomes a general creditor for the shortfall. If the bond is not secured by specific assets of the issuing entity it is referred to as a **debenture.**

Bond Redemption.   In an ordinary bond issue the principal amount is paid in one lump sum at the maturity date. This payment is said to **redeem** the bond. In order to accumulate cash for redemption, the borrower (bond issuer) may be required to deposit money regularly in an account restricted for this purpose. Bonds that have such a requirement are **sinking fund bonds.** Sinking funds may be used to redeem bonds at maturity, or to redeem outstanding bonds at regular intervals by buying them in the open market or by redeeming certain bonds that are randomly selected. Bond sinking funds are usually controlled by a trustee, such as a bank; they appear in the "investments" or "other assets" section of the balance sheet.

Serial bonds are also redeemed in installments, the redemption date for each bond in the bond issue being specified on the bond itself. The primary difference between a sinking fund bond and a serial bond is that holders of serial bonds know the date when their bonds will be redeemed, whereas holders of sinking fund bonds do not. The latter may end up holding their bonds to maturity, or their bonds may be randomly selected for redemption by the sinking fund at some earlier time.

A bond may also be **callable;** the issuing entity may, at its option, call the bonds for redemption before the maturity date. If this is done, the corporation usually must pay a premium for the privilege.

Other Features of Bonds.   Some bonds are **convertible;** they may be exchanged for a specified number of shares of the issuing corporation's common stock if the bondholder elects to do so. Sinking fund bonds and serial bonds may also be callable, convertible, or both.

Finally, some bonds (and also some term loans) are **subordinated.** In the event a company goes bankrupt and is liquidated, the claims of the subordinated debtholders are subordinate (i.e., inferior) to the claims of any general or secured creditors. However, subordinated creditors' claims take precedence over those of the company's shareholders (equity investors).

ACCOUNTING FOR BONDS

We will now describe how a bond is recorded in the accounts when it is issued, how bond interest expense is recorded while the bond is outstanding, and how the bond's redemption is recorded.

Recording a Bond Issue

To illustrate the entries typically made to record the proceeds from an issue of bonds, assume Mason Corporation issues 100 bonds, each with a **par value** (also called **principal** or **face value**) of $1,000. The bonds have a stated interest rate, called the **coupon rate**[4], of 10 percent. This means that the annual interest payment will be 10 percent of the par value—in this case, $100 per year.[5] The bonds will mature at the end of the 20th year after their issuance. They are not secured by any specific Mason Corporation assets. Such a bond would be called a "10 percent, 20-year debenture." If the corporation received $1,000 for each of these bonds, the following entry would be made:

```
Cash................................................. 100,000
    Bonds Payable ...................................          100,000
```

(In practice the liability account title describes the specific bond issue, with a separate account for each issue. The title is abbreviated here.)

Discount and Premium.   A fundamental concept in finance is the relationship between risk and return: The higher the risk an investment represents, the higher the return the investor expects to receive from making the investment. For example, if an investor can earn 8 percent interest on a $1,000 investment in a federally insured certificate of deposit, the investor will expect a bond to provide more than an 8 percent return because there is some risk that either the bond's interest payments or its principal redemption will not be received in full by the bondholder. Similarly, if bonds of a given risk are currently providing a 12 percent return to their holders, investors will not be willing to pay $1,000 for a newly issued bond of comparable risk that has only a 10 percent coupon rate. By the same token, they would be willing to pay *more* than $1,000 for a bond having comparable risk and a 14 percent coupon rate.

There is always some delay between the time a bond's coupon rate is decided upon and when the bond is actually available to be issued to the public. During this delay the prevailing rate of return on bonds of comparable risk may have changed. For this reason bonds often are issued for *less* than their par value—at a **discount.** This occurs when the prevailing market rate is *higher* than the bond's coupon rate. Recall that the bond's par value is fixed at $1,000, and the annual interest payment is fixed once the coupon rate is set (interest payment = par value * coupon rate). Thus, in order to earn a return higher than the coupon rate, the bondholder must invest less than $1,000 in the bond. Similarly, if prevailing rates are *lower* than the bond's coupon rate, bondholders will be willing to invest *more* than the bond's par value, and the bond will be issued at a **premium.**[6]

---

[4]Before computers were widely used for keeping bondholder records, a bondholder requested each periodic interest payment by mailing in a coupon, printed on sheets attached to the bond certificate, to the bond issuer. That is the origin of the term *coupon rate* and also of the expression "coupon clipper" to describe someone with substantial financial investments.

[5]In practice interest payments are usually made in semiannual installments, rather than annually—in this case, $50 every six months. For simplicity we will usually assume annual payments.

[6]Although it is colloquially said that an investor "pays" for a newly issued bond and that

Example. If the prevailing rate of interest in the bond market is more than 10 percent for bonds with a risk similar to those issued by Mason Corporation, potential investors will be unwilling to pay $1,000 for a Mason Corporation 10 percent bond. They would be willing to invest an amount such that the $100 annual interest payment on this bond would yield the market rate of interest. Assume that this market rate is 12 percent. The bond would therefore be sold at a price of $851, or at a discount of $149.[7]

The words *discount* and *premium* carry no connotation of bad or good. They reflect simply a difference between the coupon interest rate for the issue and the going market rate of interest at the time of issuance. The coupon rate is usually quite close to the market rate as of the date of issue. In recent years, however, some companies have issued bonds at an interest rate of zero. These **zero coupon bonds** are issued at a "deep discount" because the investor's entire return comes in the form of a gain that is the difference between the discounted price paid for the bond and the $1,000 par value received at maturity.

From the standpoint of the bond issuer, the discount or premium on a bond is a function only of the interest rates prevailing at the time of issuance of the bonds. Subsequent changes in the level of interest rates (and hence in bond prices) do not affect the amount recorded in the accounts. To emphasize this fact, the discount or premium recorded by the bond issuer is often called **original issue discount** or **premium.**

Issuance Costs. The offering of a bond issue to the public is usually undertaken by an investment banking firm that charges the issuer a fee for this service. In addition to this fee, the issuer also incurs printing, legal, and accounting costs in connection with the bond issue. These **bond issuance costs** are recorded as a deferred charge, which is an asset analogous to prepaid expenses. The issuance costs are *not* subtracted from the bond liability on the balance sheet, nor are they combined with any bond discount or premium.[8]

Example. Mason Corporation's bonds, for which investors paid $851 each, also had issue costs to Mason averaging $21 per bond, resulting in a net cash inflow to Mason of $830 per bond. The discount is $149 per bond, not $170 (= $149 + $21).

Accounting Entries. If the conditions of the preceding examples are assumed, and Mason Corporation received $83,000 net cash proceeds from the issuance of $100,000 face amount of bonds, the following entry would be made:

---

corporations "sell" their bonds, a bond is *not* an asset of the corporation that is sold, as are goods. Rather, bonds are evidence of a contribution of funds—a long-term loan—to the firm by investors. To the investor, the bond *is* an asset, and it can be sold to another investor. Such an exchange between investors has no impact on the flow of cash into or out of the firm, however. (Similar comments apply to shares of a corporation's common stock.)

[7]The $851 is formally called the **present value** of the bond; the method of calculating it is described in the Appendix to this chapter. The precise present value is $850.61. If the interest were received in $50 semiannual amounts, the present value would be $849.54.

[8]"Interest on Receivables and Payables," *APB Opinion No. 21* (August 1971), par. 16.

Cash	83,000	
Bond Discount	14,900	
Deferred Charges	2,100	
Bonds Payable		100,000

By contrast, if prevailing rates for similar bonds had been 9 percent, the bonds would have been issued at a premium of $91 per bond, and the entry would have been:

Cash	107,000	
Deferred Charges	2,100	
Bond Premium		9,100
Bonds Payable		100,000

Balance Sheet Presentation

Bonds payable are shown in the long-term liabilities section of the balance sheet until one year before they mature, when ordinarily they become current liabilities. The description should give the principal facts about the issue—for example, "10 percent debentures due 2014." When a bond issue is to be *refunded* with a new long-term liability, however, it is not shown as a current liability in the year of maturity since it will not require the use of current assets. If the bonds are to be retired in installments (as with serial bonds), the portion to be retired within a year is shown in the current liabilities section.

Bond discount or premium is shown on the balance sheet as a direct deduction from, or addition to, the face amount of the bond, as illustrated:

If a Discount:		*If a Premium:*	
Bonds payable:		Bonds payable:	
Face value	$100,000	Face value	$100,000
Less: Unamortized discount	14,900	Plus: Unamortized premium	9,100
	$ 85,100		$109,100

The principal amount less unamortized discount (or plus unamortized premium) is called the **book value** (or **net book value**) of the bond. It is the basis of calculating the bond's periodic interest expense, as described below. Note in the above two examples that the initial book value of a bond is equal to the proceeds from its issuance, ignoring any issuance costs. The book value less unamortized issuance costs (deferred charges) is called the **net carrying amount** of the bond.

Bond Interest Expense

To the *investor,* the return on a bond is made up of two components: (1) the periodic cash interest payments and (2) the difference between the bond's par value (received in cash at redemption) and the amount paid for the bond. The second component is a gain if the bond was purchased at a discount or a loss if purchased at a premium.

From the standpoint of the bond *issuer,* a bond's interest expense also has two components that are the mirror image of the investor's return components. **Bond interest expense** is made up of (1) the periodic cash interest payments to the bondholder and (2) amortization of original issue discount or premium. The amount of the issuer's interest expense when related to the initial proceeds from issuing the bond (ignoring issuance costs) determines the **effective rate of interest** on the bond. The effective rate is higher than the coupon rate for bonds issued at a discount; the effective rate is lower than the coupon rate for bonds issued at a premium.[9] (Calculation of the effective rate is described in the appendix to this chapter.)

Discount/Premium Amortization. Bond discount or premium is amortized using the **compound interest method**, also called the **effective interest method** or simply the **interest method.** (This method also is described in the Appendix). Straight-line amortization is not permitted unless the results would not differ materially from those obtained with the interest method.[10] With the interest method of amortization, the discount or premium is written off in such a way that each period's interest *expense* (as opposed to the cash interest payment) bears a constant ratio to the beginning-of-the-period book value of the bonds over the entire life of the issue. This ratio is the effective interest rate on the bonds. In the Mason example, if the bonds were issued for $851 each, this rate is 12 percent.[11]

Example. The first year's interest expense for the 10 percent Mason Corporation bonds that were assumed to have been issued for $851 each would be calculated as follows: *Interest expense is equal to the book value of the bonds at the start of the year* ($85,100) *times the effective interest rate* (12 percent), which equals $10,212. Of this total interest expense for the year, $10,000 is the fixed cash interest payment (based on the bonds' par value and coupon rate) and the remaining $212 is the amortization of original issue discount. The entry is:

```
Bond Interest Expense ............................. 10,212
     Bond Discount .................................        212
     Cash ..........................................     10,000
```

This entry reduces the unamortized bond discount by $212 to a new balance of $14,688 (= $14,900 − $212). Thus, at the beginning of the second year the bond's book value will be $85,312 (= $100,000 − $14,688). Next year's interest expense will be 12 percent of this book value, or $10,237; of this total, $237 is the second year's discount amortization and $10,000 is the fixed cash interest payment.

---

[9] *APB Opinion No. 21* also requires disclosure of this effective rate of interest on the bond.

[10] *APB Opinion No. 21,* par. 15.

[11] Readers checking our numbers with calculators may get slightly different results for our illustrative Mason bonds. Recall (from footnote 7) that the precise present value for a 12 percent return was $850.61 per bond, which we rounded to $851. This rounding changes the precise return to 11.994 percent, but we still use 12 percent.

Continuing this process for the entire 20 years will completely amortize the original bond discount. Over the 20 years, the bonds' book value will gradually increase up to the $100,000 par value that must be paid to Mason's bondholders at maturity. Thus, the effect of bond discount/premium accounting procedures is that (1) when the bond is issued, its book value equals the cash proceeds received by the issuer (ignoring issuance costs) and (2) at maturity, the book value equals the amount of cash that must be paid out to fulfill the bond payable liability obligation. In other words, there is a matching of the cash flows and liability amounts at bond issuance and maturity, which would not be the case without the systematic amortization of discount or premium.

Adjusting Entries. If the interest payment date does not coincide with the closing of the company's books, an adjusting entry is made to record accrued interest expense and the amortization of discount or premium.

> **Example.** Mason Corporation bonds are issued for $851 each on October 1. The interest date is September 30, and the fiscal year ends on December 31. The following entries would be made:

1. Adjustment on December 31 to record one-fourth year's interest accrued since October 1:

Bond Interest Expense	2,553	
Bond Discount		53
Accrued Interest Payable		2,500

2. Payment of annual interest on September 30; entry to record three-fourths of a year's interest expense and one year's payment:

Bond Interest Expense	7,659	
Accrued Interest Payable	2,500	
Bond Discount		159
Cash		10,000

Bond issuance costs, which are treated as a deferred charge, usually are amortized using the straight-line method. Thus, for Mason's bonds, the annual issuance cost amortization would be $105 (= $2,100 ÷ 20 years).

Retirement of Bonds

Bonds may be retired in total, or they may be retired in installments over a period of years (i.e., as with sinking fund or serial bonds). In either case the retirement is recorded by a debit to Bonds Payable and a credit to Cash (or to a sinking fund that has been set up for this purpose). The bond discount or premium will have been completely amortized by the maturity date, so no additional entry is required for discount or premium at that time.

Refunding a Bond Issue

Callable bonds can be paid off before their maturity dates by paying investors more than the bonds' par value. In periods when interest rates have declined, a company may consider it advantageous to **refund** a bond issue, that is, to call the old issue and issue a new one with a lower rate of interest. At that point the company must account for the **call premium** (the difference between the call price and par value), any other costs of the refunding, and any unamortized issue costs and discount (or premium) on the old bonds.

Recall that the bonds' face amount, adjusted for unamortized premium or discount and costs of issuance, is called the **net carrying amount** of the debt to be refunded. The amount paid on refunding, including the call premium and miscellaneous costs of refunding, is called the **reacquisition price.** The difference between these two amounts must be reported as a separate loss or gain on the income statement for the period in which the refunding takes place.[12]

Example.   Suppose that the 100 Mason Corporation bonds are called at the end of five years by paying the call price of the bonds at that time, $1,050 per bond, to each bondholder. Assume that miscellaneous refunding costs are $1,000 in total. Also, much of the bond discount and issuance costs will not have been amortized. The $13,553 of unamortized discount is determined using the compound interest method. Unamortized bond issuance costs after five years (one quarter of the bonds' scheduled life) would be: ¾ * $2,100 = $1,575. The loss is determined as follows:

Reacquisition price ($105,000 + $1,000).		$106,000
Net carrying amount:		
Face value	$100,000	
Less: Unamortized discount.	(13,553)	
Less: Unamortized issuance costs	(1,575)	84,872
Loss on retirement of bonds.		$ 21,128

The accounting entries are:

Bonds Payable	100,000	
Loss on Retirement of Bonds	21,128	
Cash		106,000
Bond Discount.		13,553
Deferred Charges (Issuance Costs)		1,575

OTHER LIABILITIES

This chapter thus far has focused on debt capital—long-term loans and bonds. For completeness, other liabilities will be discussed briefly.

---

[12]"Early Extinguishment of Debt," *APB Opinion No. 26* (October 1972), par. 20, as amended by "Extinguishment of Debt," *FASB Statement No. 76* (November 1983). *FASB Statement No. 4*, "Reporting Gains and Losses from Extinguishment of Debt" (March 1975), as amended by *FASB Statement No. 64*, "Extinguishment of Debt Made to Satisfy Sinking-Fund Requirements" (September 1982), requires that in most instances such a gain or loss be reported on the income statement as an *extraordinary* gain or loss, below income from operations. (Extraordinary items are discussed in Chapter 10.)

Current Liabilities. As explained in Chapter 2, these are obligations that are expected to be satisfied either by the use of current assets (usually by cash) or by the creation of other current liabilities within one year or less. The largest current liability for most entities is accounts payable, amounts owed to suppliers of goods and services. These amounts are recorded based on an invoice (i.e., a bill) from the supplier of the goods or services. Entries to other current liability accounts usually arise from adjusting entries: accrued wages payable, accrued interest payable, and estimated taxes payable are examples that have previously been described.

Leases. We explained capital leases in the preceding chapter when we described the acquisition of fixed assets other than through outright purchase. Recall that a capital lease is essentially an installment loan obligation. This obligation is initially recorded at an amount equal to the fair value of the asset acquired or the present value of the future stream of lease payments the lessor will make to the lessee. How these payments reduce the lease obligation in each period—called *amortizing the obligation*—is explained in this chapter's appendix.

Deferred Taxes. Another liability section item of significant size for many corporations is labeled *deferred income taxes.* This is a complicated topic and its mechanics are described in Chapter 10. Suffice it to say here that deferred taxes arise when a company uses a different method in preparing its corporate income tax return than is used in preparing its income statement for shareholder reporting purposes. For example, most corporations use straight-line depreciation for shareholder reporting but use the tax law's accelerated cost recovery provisions for income tax reporting.

ANALYSIS OF CAPITAL STRUCTURE

Debt Ratios   The relative amount of a company's capital that was obtained from various sources is a matter of great importance in analyzing the soundness of the company's financial position. In illustrating the ratios intended for this purpose, the following summary of the liabilities and owners' equity side of a company's balance sheet will be used:

	$ millions	Percent
Current liabilities	$1,600	23%
Long-term liabilities	1,800	26
Shareholders' equity	3,600	51
Total liabilities and owners' equity	$7,000	100%

Attention is often focused on the sources of **invested capital** (also called **permanent capital**): **debt capital** (long-term liabilities) and **equity capital** (owners' equity). From the point of view of the company, debt capital is risky because if bondholders and other creditors are not paid promptly, they can take legal action to obtain payment. Such action can, in extreme cases, force the company into bankruptcy. Equity capital is much less risky to the company because shareholders receive dividends only at the discretion of the directors and the shareholders cannot force bankruptcy.[13] Because the shareholders have less certainty of receiving dividends than the bondholders have of receiving interest, investors usually are unwilling to invest in a company's stock unless they see a reasonable expectation of making a higher return (dividends plus stock price appreciation) than they could obtain as bondholders. Investors would be unwilling to give up the relatively certain prospect of receiving 8 percent or 9 percent interest on bonds, unless the probable, but less certain, return on an equity investment were considerably higher, say, 12 percent or more.

Leverage.   From the company's standpoint the greater the proportion of its invested capital that is obtained from shareholders, the less worry the company has in meeting its fixed obligations. But in return for this lessened worry, the company must expect to pay a higher overall cost of obtaining its capital. Conversely, the more funds that are obtained from bonds, the more the company can use debt funds obtained at relatively low cost in the hopes of earning more on these funds for the shareholders.

The relatively low cost of debt capital arises not only from the fact that investors typically are willing to accept a lower return on bonds than on stocks but also because debt interest (including bond interest payments) is tax deductible to the corporation, whereas dividends are not. Assuming a 40 percent tax rate, for every $1 that a company pays out in interest, it receives a tax saving of $0.40. Thus, its net cost is only 60 percent of the stated interest rate. For example, debt capital obtained from a bond issue with a yield of 10 percent costs the company only about 6 percent. By contrast, if equity investors require a return of 12 percent, the cost of obtaining equity capital is the full 12 percent.

Debt/Equity Ratio.   A company with a high proportion of long-term debt is said to be highly **leveraged.** The **debt/equity ratio** shows the balance that the management of a particular company has struck between these forces of risk versus cost. This is often called simply the **debt ratio.** It may be calculated in several ways. Debt may be defined as total liabilities, as interest-bearing current liabilities plus noncurrent liabilities, or as only noncurrent liabilities. The user must always be careful to ascertain which method is used in a given situation. Including current liabilities, the debt/equity ratio for the illustrative company is:

$$\frac{\text{Total liabilities}}{\text{Shareholders' equity}} = \frac{\$3,400}{\$3,600} = 94 \text{ percent}$$

Excluding current liabilities, the ratio is:

---

[13]Note that risk is here viewed from the standpoint of the company. From the viewpoint of *investors,* the opposite situation prevails. Thus, bondholders have a relatively low risk of not receiving their payments, whereas stockholders have a relatively high risk. Based on this latter perspective, equity capital is called **risk capital.**

$$\frac{\text{Long-term liabilities}}{\text{Shareholders' equity}} = \frac{\$1,800}{\$3,600} = 50 \text{ percent}$$

Debt/Capitalization Ratio. The mix of debt and equity in the capital structure may also be expressed as the ratio of long-term debt to total invested capital (debt plus equity). This ratio is called the **debt/ capitalization ratio.** For our illustrative company, it is the ratio of $1,800 to $5,400, or 33 percent. Note that this ratio is based on the same data as is the debt/equity ratio; it is just another way of expressing the relationship. (As an analogy, one can say that the female/male ratio in a class is 100 percent, or that females make up 50 percent of the total enrollment in the class.) The debt/capitalization ratio varies widely among industries but is less than 50 percent in the majority of industrial companies.

Times Interest Earned

Another measure of a company's financial soundness is the **times interest earned,** or **interest coverage ratio.** This is the relationship of a company's income to its interest requirements. The numerator of this ratio is the company's *pretax* income *before* subtraction of interest expense. Assuming that for our illustrative company this amount was $1,000, and that interest expense was $200, the calculation is:

$$\text{Times interest earned} = \frac{\text{Income before interest}}{\text{Interest expense}} = \frac{\$1,000}{\$200} = 5.0 \text{ times}$$

Bond Ratings

Organizations such as Standard & Poor's and Moody's provide ratings on bonds to indicate their quality, meaning their relative level of risk. A number of factors are considered in rating a corporation's bonds, including various financial ratios and evaluation of the prospects of the company's industry and the company's market position in that industry. The debt/ capitalization ratio and interest coverage ratio are especially important. For example, as of late 1993 the typical industrial company meriting Standard & Poor's top "AAA" rating had a debt/capitalization ratio in the preceding three years of about 22 percent and interest coverage of about 17 times.[14] (Standard & Poor's debt/capitalization ratio definition includes interest-bearing current liabilities, as well as long-term debt.)

SUMMARY

Liabilities and owners' equity represents the sources of the funds that are invested in the firm's assets. Liabilities and owners' equity consists of current liabilities, other liabilities (primarily long-term debt), and owners' equity. Current liabilities are distinguished from other liabilities by their

---

[14]"Credit Comments," *Standard & Poor's CreditWeek,* November 8, 1993.

time horizon (one year or less). Liabilities are distinguished from owners' equity by their nature as obligations to outside parties. Executory contracts are not liabilities because neither party has performed. Loss contingencies create liabilities only if it is probable that a liability has been incurred and the amount of loss can be reasonably estimated.

The liability arising from the issuance of bonds is shown at its face amount (par value), adjusted for any difference between this face amount and the amount of cash actually paid by investors for the bonds; this difference is recorded as bond premium or discount. Premium or discount is amortized over the life of the issue using the interest method. This amortization plus the periodic cash interest payments equal the bonds' interest expense of each period. No gain or loss results when a bond is redeemed at maturity, but early retirement will lead to such a gain or loss.

If a company has leased equipment but the lease is, in effect, a vehicle to finance the purchase of the equipment, then this capital lease obligation is reported as a liability. Other liabilities include current liabilities and deferred income taxes.

Debt/equity ratios and interest coverage indicate the level of risk associated with the amount of a company's debt capital.

APPENDIX: PRESENT VALUE

The concept of present value underlies the valuation of many liabilities. The concept is also applied in valuing many monetary assets (which is the nature of most of a bank's assets). Related to these liability and asset valuations is the interest method, which is used to amortize discount, premium, and the principal amount of all long-term debt, including capital leases. Finally, the present value concept is used in analyzing proposals to acquire new long-lived assets. These asset acquisition proposals are called *capital investment decisions* and are described in detail in Chapter 27.

Concept of Present Value   Many people have difficulty understanding the present value concept because it differs from what we were taught as children—that it is a good thing to put money into a piggy bank. We are congratulated when the bank is finally opened and the accumulated coins are counted. Children are taught that it is better to have a given amount of money in the future than to use that money today. More formally, children are taught that a dollar received at some future time is more valuable than a dollar received today.

Business managers think differently, however. They expect a dollar invested today to *increase* in amount as time passes, because they expect to earn a profit on that investment. It follows that an amount of money available for investment today is *more* valuable to the manager than an equal amount that will not be available until some future time. Money available today can be invested to earn still more money, whereas money not yet received obviously cannot be invested today. To the manager, therefore, the value of a given amount of money today—its *present value*—is more than the value of the same amount received at some future time.

Compound Interest. To make the idea of present value more concrete, consider first the idea of **compound interest.** Suppose we invest $1,000 in a savings account that pays interest of 5 percent compounded annually. (Interest is invariably stated at an annual rate; thus, "5 percent" means 5 percent per year.) "Compounded annually" means that the interest earned the first year is retained in the account and, along with the initial $1,000, earns interest in the second year; and so on for future years. If we make no withdrawals from this account, over time the account balance will grow as shown below:

Year	Beginning-of-Year Balance	Interest Earned*	End-of-Year Balance
1	$1,000.00	$50.00	$1,050.00
2	1,050.00	52.50	1,102.50
3	1,102.50	55.13	1,157.63
4	1,157.63	57.88	1,215.51
5	1,215.51	60.78	1,276.28
.	.	.	.
10	1,551.33	77.57	1,628.89

*Some amounts may appear to be off by one cent, because the actual calculations were carried to 4 decimal places and then rounded.

Based on this table, one can make the following statement: "$1,000 invested today at 5 percent interest, compounded annually, will accumulate to $1,628.89 after 10 years." An equivalent statement is that the *future value* of $1,000 invested for 10 years at 5 percent interest is $1,628.89.

Rather than obtaining a future value (*FV*) from a table, it can be calculated using the compound interest formula:

$$FV = p(1 + i)^n$$

where

p = Principal (initial investment)
i = Interest rate
n = Number of periods

Thus, the future value of $1,000 invested at 5 percent for 10 years is given by:[15]

---

[15]Interest may be compounded more frequently than once a year. Interest on savings accounts, for example, may be compounded quarterly, monthly, or even daily. In such a case both the number of periods and the rate per period must be converted to the period used in compounding. For example, with quarterly compounding, the number of periods is 40 (i.e., 40 quarters in 10 years), and the interest rate *per quarter* would be 1.25 percent (= 5 percent

$FV = \$1,000(1 + 0.05)^{10} = \$1,628.89$

Discounting. To arrive at *present* values we reverse the future value concept. The reverse of interest compounding is called **discounting.** For example, if the future value of $1,000 at 5 percent interest for 10 years is $1,628.89, then we can also say that the *present value* of $1,628.89 *discounted* at 5 percent for 10 years is $1,000. The interest rate (5 percent in the example) in present value problems is commonly referred to as the **discount rate** or the **rate of return.** This illustration leads to a more formal definition of **present value:**

> The present value of an amount that is expected to be received at a specified time in the future is the amount that, if invested today at a designated rate of return, would cumulate to the specified amount.

Thus, assuming a 5 percent rate of return, the present value of $1,628.89 to be received 10 years hence is $1,000, because (as we have illustrated) if $1,000 were invested today at 5 percent, it would cumulate to $1,628.89 after 10 years.

Finding Present Values

The present value (*PV*) of an amount p to be received n years hence, discounted at a rate of i, is given by the formula:

$$PV = \frac{p}{(1 + i)^n}$$

Appendix Table A (at the back of the book) is a table of present values that were derived from this formula. The amounts in such a table are expressed as the present value of $1 to be received some number of years hence, discounted at some rate. To find the present value of an amount other than $1, we multiply the amount by the appropriate present value factor from Table A.

> **Example.** To find the *PV* of $400 to be received 10 years hence, discounted at a rate of 8 percent, we first find the 10 year/8 percent factor from Table A, which is 0.463. Hence the *PV* of $400 is $400 * 0.463 = $185.20. This means that $185.20 invested today at a return of 8 percent will cumulate to $400 by the end of 10 years.

Inspection of Table A reveals two basic points about present value:

1. Present value decreases as the number of years in the future in which the payment is to be received increases.
2. Present value decreases as the discount rate increases.

÷ 4). Thus, the future value of $1,000 invested for ten years at 5 percent compounded quarterly is $1,000(1.0125)^{40} = $1,643.62. The results of the formulas given in this chapter are available in published tables and are programmed into many calculators.

Present Value of a Series of Payments

In many business situations the entity expects to receive a series of annual payments over a period of several years, rather than simply receiving a single amount at some future point. The present value of a series of payments is found by summing the present values of the individual payments. Computational procedures generally assume that each payment in the series is to be received at the *end* of its respective period rather than in a continuous flow during the period.

> **Example.** Using a 10 percent discount rate, what is the present value of the following series of payments: year 1, $1,000; year 2, $1,500; year 3, $2,000; and year 4, $2,500?

Solution:

Year	Payment	Discount Factor (Table A)	Present Value
1	$1,000	0.909	$ 909
2	1,500	0.826	1,239
3	2,000	0.751	1,502
4	2,500	0.683	1,708
Present value of the series			$5,358

Equal Payments. In many situations, such as the repayment of loans, the series of payments is comprised of equal amounts each period. (Technically, such a series of equal payments is called an **annuity**.) If the payments are $1,750 per year for four years, then the present value of the series discounted at 10 percent would be:

Year	Payment	Discount Factor	Present Value
1	$1,750	0.909	$1,591
2	1,750	0.826	1,446
3	1,750	0.751	1,314
4	1,750	0.683	1,195
Present value of the series			$5,546

Rather than look up discount factors for each year in such a problem, one can use a table such as Appendix Table B. In that table the factor shown for four years at 10 percent is 3.170. This number is the same (except for rounding error) as the sum of the individual years' factors in the previous example: 0.909, 0.826, 0.751, and 0.683; and 3.170 * $1,750 = $5,548. This example illustrates that each factor in Table B was obtained by cumulating the factors for the corresponding year and all preceding years in the same interest rate column of Table A. Thus, the present value of a level series can be found in one step using Table B.

The values in Table B can also be used to find the present value of a series of equal payments between any two points in time. The procedure is to subtract the Table B factor for the year *preceding* the year of the first payment from the factor for the last year of payment.

> **Example.**   What is the present value of $1,000 a year to be received in years 6 through 10, assuming a 12 percent discount rate?

Solution:

Time Period	PV Factor (Table B)
Years 1–10................................	5.650
Years 1–5.................................	3.605
Difference (years 6–10)	2.045
PV = $1,000 * 2.045 =......................	$2,045

Present Values and Liabilities

The amount shown on the balance sheet for a liability such as a loan is often thought of as being the amount the borrower must repay to satisfy the obligation. This is only partly true. Certainly, the borrowing entity must repay the amount borrowed, called the **principal** in the case of a term loan or bond; and the amount shown on the balance sheet of the borrower *is* the amount of unpaid principal. However, the borrower's future payments to satisfy the obligation far exceed the amount of unpaid principal because interest must be paid on the amount of outstanding principal over the life of the loan.

In many cases the balance sheet liability is properly interpreted as meaning not the dollar amount of the principal but rather the *present value* of the series of future interest payments plus the *present value* of the future principal payments.

> **Example.**   Kinnear Company borrowed $25,000, with interest at 10 percent (i.e., $2,500) to be paid annually and the principal to be repaid in one lump sum at the end of five years. The balance sheet liability would be reported as $25,000. This can be interpreted as the sum of the present values, as follows:

	Present Value
Interest, $2,500 * 3.791 (Table B)	$ 9,478
Principal, $25,000 * 0.621 (Table A)	15,525
Total present value	$25,003*

*Does not add exactly to $25,000 because of rounding.

ILLUSTRATION 8–1
LOAN AMORTIZATION SCHEDULE*

Year	(a) Principal Owed at Beginning of Year	(b) Annual Payment	(c) Interest Portion of Payment (a) * 10%	(d) Reduction of Principal (b) – (c)	(e) Ending Principal (a) – (d)
1.............	$25,000	$ 6,595	$2,500	$ 4,095	$20,905
2.............	20,905	6,595	2,091	4,504	16,401
3.............	16,401	6,595	1,640	4,955	11,446
4.............	11,446	6,595	1,145	5,450	5,995
5.............	5,995	6,595	600	5,995	0
Totals........		$32,975	$7,976	$20,000	

*Some numbers may appear to be off by 1 owing to rounding.

If the annual repayments are of a constant amount, with each payment including both interest and a reduction of principal, Table B can be used to find the amount of these payments.

> **Example.** Kinnear Company borrowed $25,000 with interest at 10 percent to be repaid in equal annual amounts at the end of each of the next five years. The present value of this obligation is $25,000. The amount of the annual installments is $6,595. It is found by dividing $25,000 by the 5 year/10 percent factor in Table B, which is 3.791.

Each payment of $6,595 in the above example consists of two components: (1) interest on the amount of principal outstanding during the year and (2) reduction of that principal. These two components of each payment can be calculated as shown in Illustration 8–1, which is called a **loan amortization schedule.**

Column c of the schedule shows how much interest expense on this loan Kinnear Company should recognize each year. Column e shows the proper balance sheet valuation of the loan liability as of the end of each year (or, equivalently, as of the beginning of the next year, as shown in column a). The amounts in columns c and d represent the only conceptually correct way to divide each year's payment between interest expense and principal reduction (amortization). This approach is called the **compound interest method** (or **effective interest method** or simply **interest method**) of debt amortization.

Note how the amounts in column c decrease over time, whereas the amounts in column d increase. Someone not familiar with the compound interest method might assume that each year's $6,595 payment reflects a principal reduction of $5,000 (= $25,000 ÷ 5 years) and interest expense of $1,595 (= $6,595 – $5,000). Such an assumption is incorrect.

Note also that the compound interest method amounts are calculated such that the interest expense is always a constant *percentage* of the principal outstanding during the year (10 percent in the illustration). This means that Kinnear Company's interest expense on this loan is a true 10 percent in *every* year the loan is outstanding and that the true interest rate on the loan over its entire life is 10 percent. This is the same principle mentioned in the chapter text in the illustration of bond discount amortization. The interest expense, the sum of the cash interest costs and the discount amortization on Mason Corporation's 10 percent bonds issued for $851, will be a constant rate (12 percent) of the book value of the bonds for each of the 20 years they are outstanding, provided that the initial discount is amortized using the compound interest method.

Present Values and Assets

Accounting for interest-bearing receivables and similar monetary assets is the mirror image of accounting for monetary liabilities. For example, in the Kinnear Company loan illustration above, column *c* in Illustration 8–1 shows how much interest *revenue* Kinnear's lender should report each year on this loan. Similarly, column *e* shows the proper year-end valuation of the loan *receivable* asset on the lender's balance sheet. We can therefore conclude that the amount shown for a loan receivable or similar monetary asset is the present value of the future payments the asset holder will receive in satisfaction of the credit the asset holder has extended to the borrower (Kinnear Company in the illustration).

Calculating Bond Yields

The **yield** on a bond is the rate of return that the bondholder earns as a result of investing in the bond. The investor's return is made up of two parts: (1) the bond's interest payments and (2) any difference between what the investor paid for the bond and the proceeds she or he receives upon selling the bond. This difference is referred to as the investor's **capital gain** or **loss** on the bond. Both the interest stream and future proceeds must be adjusted to present values to be comparable with the current market price.

Current Yield. The yield to maturity on a bond (described below) should not be confused with the **current yield,** which is the annual interest payment divided by the current price.

> **Example.** If at a given point in time Mason Corporation's 10 percent bonds were selling on a bond market at a price of 94 (i.e., $940), then the current yield at that time would be $100 ÷ $940 = 10.6 percent.

Yield to Maturity. The yield on a bond actually is investor-specific because the capital gain (or loss) portion of the yield depends on what a specific investor paid for the bond and how much he or she sells it for. Thus, in calculating a bond's yield to maturity, it is assumed that (1) the bond will be purchased at the current market price and (2) the bond will then be held until maturity. Also, income tax effects are ignored in calculating bond yields. The **yield to maturity** of a bond is the discount rate that will make the sum of (1) the present value of the series of future interest payments plus (2) the present value of the bond redemption proceeds equal to the current *market price* of the bond.

> **Example.** Exactly 10 years before their maturity, Mason Corporation 10 percent bonds have a market price of $887. Mason makes the $100 per year interest payments in a lump sum at year-end. The yield to maturity is the discount rate that will make the present value of the 10-year series of future $100 annual interest payments plus the present value of the $1,000 bond redemption proceeds 10 years hence equal to the bond's current market price of $887. This rate is 12 percent, which can be demonstrated as follows:

PV of interest stream ($100 * 5.650*)	$565
PV of redemption proceeds ($1,000 * 0.322*)	322
Sum of PVs (market price)	$887

*Ten-year/12 percent factors from Tables B and A, respectively.

This 12 percent yield to maturity is also called the **effective rate of interest** on the bond.

The calculation of yield to maturity can be a fairly cumbersome trial-and-error procedure if present value tables are used. This procedure is programmed into relatively inexpensive business calculators, which can find the yield in a few seconds.

Bond Prices. A similar calculation can be used to determine the "rational" market price of a bond, given current yields on bonds of similar quality (or risk).

> **Example.** When Mason's 20-year, 10 percent bonds were *issued*, the prevailing market interest rate (yield) of similar bonds was 12 percent. The market price of Mason's bonds should be the price that would result in a yield of 12 percent to a Mason bondholder. This price will be the present value of the 20-year interest stream and the proceeds at maturity (20 years hence):

PV of interest stream ($100 * 7.469*)	$747
PV of redemption proceeds ($1,000 * 0.104*)	104
Market price for 12% yield	$851

*Twenty-year/12 percent factors from Tables B and A, respectively.

This $851 is the amount that was given in the text in the Mason Corporation example of 10 percent bonds that were issued at a discount because the prevailing market rate for comparable bonds was 12 percent.

Cases

CASE 8–1 Martin Corporation (A)

Until 1993, Martin Corporation, a young manufacturer of specialty consumer products, had not had its financial statements audited. It had, however, relied on the auditing firm of Kline & Burrows to prepare its income tax returns. Because it was considering borrowing on a long-term note and the lender surely would require audited statements, Martin decided to have its 1993 financial statements attested by Kline & Burrows.

Kline & Burrows assigned Jennifer Warshaw to do preliminary work on the engagement, under the direction of Allen Burrows. Martin's financial vice president had prepared the preliminary financial statements shown in Exhibit 1. In examining the information on which these financial statements were based, Ms. Warshaw discovered the facts listed below. She referred these to Mr. Burrows.

1. In 1993 a group of female employees sued the company, asserting that their salaries were unjustifiably lower than salaries of men doing comparable work. They asked back pay of $250,000. A large number of similar suits had been filed in other companies, but results were extremely varied. Martin's outside counsel thought that the company probably would win the suit but pointed out that the decisions thus far were divided, and it was difficult to forecast the outcome. In any event, it was unlikely that the suit would come to trial in 1994. No provision for this loss had been made in the financial statements.

2. The company had a second lawsuit outstanding. It involved a customer who was injured by one of the company's products. The customer asked for $500,000 damages. Based on discussions with the customer's attorney, Martin's attorney believed that the suit probably could be settled for $50,000. There was no guarantee of this, of course. On the other hand, if the suit went to trial, Martin might win it. Martin did not carry product liability insurance. Martin reported $50,000 as a Reserve for Contingencies, with a corresponding debit to Retained Earnings.

3. In 1993 plant maintenance expenditures were $44,000. Normally, plant maintenance expense was about $60,000 a year, and $60,000 had indeed been budgeted for 1993. Management decided, however, to economize in 1993, even though it was recognized that the amount would probably have to be made up in future years. In view of this, the estimated income statement included an item of $60,000 for plant maintenance expense, with an offsetting credit of $16,000 to a reserve account included as a noncurrent liability.

4. In early January 1993 the company issued a 5 percent $100,000 bond to one of its stockholders in return for $80,000 cash. The discount of $20,000 arose because the 5 percent interest rate was below the going interest rate at the time; the stockholder thought that this arrangement provided a personal income tax advantage as compared with an $80,000 bond at the market rate of interest.

EXHIBIT 1

MARTIN CORPORATION
Proposed Income Statement (condensed)
For the Year 1993

Net sales	$1,658,130
Cost of sales	1,071,690
Gross margin	586,440
Operating expenses	329,100
Operating income	257,340
Nonoperating income and expense (net)	9,360
Pretax income	247,980
Provision for income taxes	99,300
Net income	$ 148,680

Proposed Balance Sheet (condensed)
As of December 31, 1993

Assets

Current assets:		
Cash and short-term investments		$ 107,026
Accounts receivable, gross	$262,904	
Less: Allowance for doubtful accounts	5,250	257,654
Inventories		376,006
Prepaid expenses		10,814
Total current assets		751,500
Plant and equipment, at cost	310,996	
Less: Accumulated depreciation	139,830	171,166
Goodwill		101,084
Development costs		124,648
Other deferred charges		166,878
Total assets		$1,315,276

Liabilities and Shareholders' Equity

Current liabilities	$ 421,770
Noncurrent liabilities	228,704
Total liabilities	650,474
Common stock (100,000 shares)	100,000
Capital surplus	82,500
Retained earnings	432,302
Reserve for contingencies	50,000
Total liabilities and shareholders' equity	$1,315,276

The company included the $20,000 discount as one of the components of the asset "other deferred charges" on the balance sheet and included the $100,000 as a noncurrent liability. When questioned about this treatment, the financial vice president said, "I know that other companies may record such a transaction differently, but after all we do owe $100,000. And anyway, what does it matter where the discount appears?"

5. The $20,000 bond discount was reduced by $784 in 1993, and Ms. Warshaw

calculated that this was the correct amount of amortization. However, the $784 was included as an item of nonoperating expense on the income statement, rather than being charged directly to Retained Earnings.

6.   In connection with the issuance of the $100,000 bond, the company had incurred legal fees amounting to $500. These costs were included in nonoperating expenses in the income statement because, according to the financial vice president, "issuing bonds is an unusual financial transaction for us, not a routine operating transaction."

7.   On January 2, 1993, the company had leased a new Lincoln Town Car, valued at $35,000, to be used for various official company purposes. After three years of $13,581 annual year-end lease payments, title to the car would pass to Martin, which expected to use the car through at least year-end 1997. The $13,581 lease payment for 1993 was included in operating expenses in the income statement.

Although Mr. Burrows recognized that some of these transactions might affect the provision for income taxes, he decided not to consider the possible tax implications until after he had thought through the appropriate financial accounting treatment.

Questions

1.   How should each of the above seven items be reported in the 1993 income statement and balance sheet?

2.   (Optional—requires knowledge of Appendix material.) The bond described in item 4 above has a 15-year maturity date. What is the yield rate to the investor who paid $80,000 for this bond? Is the $784 discount amortization cited in item 5 indeed the correct first-year amount? (Assume that the $5,000 annual interest payment is made in a lump sum at year-end.)

3.   (Optional) If the lease in item 7 is determined to be a capital lease, what is its effective interest rate?

CASE 8–2   Stybel Industries, Inc.*

Larry Stybel sat at his desk, feeling less than content. This was a direct result of Stybel Industries' poor results for the third quarter of 19x2 and the even gloomier outlook for the final quarter.

Picking up *The Wall Street Journal,* Larry turned to the stock exchange listings. "Oh no!" he groaned. "We've slipped yet another 50 cents; that's $2 in the last month." Despondently he picked up his telephone and was just about to make a call when the name Stybel caught his eye. This time it was in the bond listings. "That has lost us money as well," thought Larry, "They're only worth $750 each now, and we are going to have to pay $1,000 to redeem them."

For the rest of the morning Larry worried about the bond value. The more he thought about it, the less he felt it was Stybel Industries that had lost. Suddenly Larry hit on a brilliant idea to generate additional income for Stybel Industries. He hurriedly called in his assistant, Keith Edwards, and described his idea, which was to buy back all the bonds at $750, thus making $250 on each bond.

Keith returned to his desk and began to calculate the expected cash availability of Stybel Industries as of late December, the date Larry wanted to repurchase the bonds. Very quickly it became obvious that $3 million was not available for the repurchase; in fact, $300,000 would have been difficult.

Walking into Larry's office, Keith informed him of the cash position and waited for the explosion. Instead, Larry smiled at his assis-

---

EXHIBIT 1

STYBEL INDUSTRIES, INC.
Liabilities and Stockholders' Equity
As of December 31
(thousands of dollars)

	19x0	19x1
Current liabilities:		
Notes payable—banks	$ 0	$ 2,037
Accounts payable—trade	6,662	5,565
Accrued and other liabilities	1,811	1,894
Federal income and other taxes	2,122	2,010
Total current liabilities	10,595	11,506
Long-term debt (Note 1)	3,725	3,749
Shareholders' equity:		
Capital stock—par value $7.50 per share	9,305	9,305
Capital in excess of par value	7,464	7,464
Retained earnings	26,085	25,063
	42,854	41,832
Less: Treasury stock	1,416	1,416
Total shareholders' equity	41,438	40,416
Total liabilities and shareholders' equity	$55,758	$55,671

Note 1: Long-term debt. On January 1, 19x0, the company issued 4,000 5-percent bonds payable that mature December 31, 19x9 (ten years after issuance). Interest of $25 per $1,000 bond is paid semiannually. The effective interest rate at issuance was 6 percent. As of December 31, 19x0, and 19x1, respectively, $275,000 and $251,000 of discount remained unamortized. These bonds are reflected on the accompanying balance sheets as follows:

	19x0	19x1
Bonds payable	$4,000	$4,000
Less: Unamortized discount	275	251
Bonds payable, net	3,725	3,749

---

tant and said, "I wondered how long it would take you to realize that; but I've already decided we can achieve my objective by selling some new bonds to buy back the old ones. In fact, we're going to sell $4 million worth so we can make that plant expansion I've been planning for the last two years."

Keith felt obliged to point out that the new issue would sell at the same price as the old issue. "No, no," said Larry. "I've already talked with the bank and they suggested we issue a 10 percent coupon bond issue[1] for late

December, when the expected interest rate will still be 10 percent. That will net us $4,000,000 exactly. Funny thing was, they said that if we made them 12 percent bonds, we would get $4,498,000. That would mean an additional $498,000 profit, so, all in all, we could make over $1.5 million on that issue. That's not bad for one morning's work, is it?"

"Sounds OK to me" said Keith. "The only thing that's bothering me is that the figure on the balance sheet for the existing bonds is not $4,000,000 but about $3,749,000. There is a footnote, but that didn't help me understand the balance sheet number at all." (See Exhibit 1.) "I don't understand why it's not

---

[1] Semiannual payments of $50 interest per $1,000 face value bond. Full payment of principal after 10 years.

the full $4 million; after all, that's what we have to pay back, isn't it?"

"Let me have a look," said Larry. "Yes, you are right; I know these accountants have funny ways of doing things, but this really seems way out to me."

"Yes," said Keith, "and that's going to cut our profit down to $749,000 on the repurchase."

"Oh well, I guess we have to go with the 12 percent issue and make do with nearly $1.2 million in profit," chuckled Larry.

"Yes, I reckon we can get by on that," laughingly agreed Keith.

Questions

1. *a.* How would you explain to Larry and Keith the $3,749,000 on the balance sheet?
    b. How would you explain the $4,000,000 issue price of the 10 percent bond and the $4,498,000 issue price of the 12 percent bond? (No detailed calculations are necessary.)

2. *a.* If they choose to issue the 10 percent bonds, what amount would you treat as gain on the repurchase? Why?
    b. If they choose to issue the 12 percent bonds, what amount would you treat as gain? Why?
    c. How would you account for the purchase of the existing bonds and the issuance of the 12 percent bonds? Give the journal entries and the long-term debt portion of the balance sheets for Stybel Industries as of December 31, 19x2, and 19x3. Assume that the old bonds were repurchased for $3,000,000 and the new bonds (12 percent coupon rate) were issued for $4,498,000 on January 1, 19x3. Ignore income taxes.

3. What will be the effect on the Cash account for the years 19x3, 19x4, and 19x5?

Case 8-3   Megashye Engineering Company

Megashye Engineering Company was founded by two partners, Meredith Gale and Shelley Yeaton, shortly after they had graduated from engineering school. Within five years the partners had built a thriving business, primarily through the development of a product line of measuring instruments based on the laser principle. Success brought with it the need for new permanent capital. After careful calculation, the partners placed the amount of this need at $1.2 million. This would replace a term loan that was about to mature and provide for plant expansion and related working capital.

At first, they sought a wealthy investor, or group of investors, who would provide the $1.2 million in return for an interest in the partnership. They soon discovered, however, that although some investors were interested in participating in new ventures, none of them was willing to participate as partner in an industrial company because of the risks to their personal fortunes that were inherent in such an arrangement. Gale and Yeaton therefore planned to incorporate the Megashye Engineering Company, in which they would own all the stock.

After further investigation, they learned that Arbor Capital Corporation, a venture capital firm, might be interested in providing permanent financing. In thinking about what they should propose to Arbor, their first idea was that Arbor would be asked to provide $1.2 million, of which $1.1 million would be a long-term loan. For the other $100,000, Arbor would receive 10 percent of the Megashye common stock as a "sweetener." If Arbor would pay $100,000 for 10 percent of the stock, this would mean that the 90 percent that would be owned by Gale and Yeaton would have a value of $900,000. Although this was considerably higher than Megashye's net assets, they thought that this amount was appropriate in view of the profitability of the product line that they had successfully developed.

A little calculation convinced them, however, that this idea (hereafter, proposal A) was too risky. The resulting ratio of debt to equity would be greater than 100 percent, which was considered unsound for an industrial company.

Their next idea was to change the debt/equity ratio by using preferred stock in lieu of most of the debt. Specifically, they thought of a package consisting of $200,000 debt, $900,000 preferred stock, and $100,000 common stock (proposal B). They learned, however, that Arbor Capital Corporation was not interested in accepting preferred stock, even at a dividend that exceeded the interest rate on debt. Thereupon, they approached Arbor with a proposal of $600,000 debt and $600,000 equity (proposal C). For the $600,000 equity, Arbor would receive 6/15 (i.e., 40 percent) of the common stock.

The Arbor representative was considerably interested in the company and its prospects but explained that Arbor ordinarily did not participate in a major financing of a relatively new company unless it obtained at least 50 percent equity as part of the deal. They were interested only in a proposal for $300,000 debt and $900,000 for half of the equity (proposal D). The debt/equity ratio in this proposal was attractive, but Gale and Yeaton were not happy about sharing control of the company equally with an outside party.

Before proceeding further, they decided to see if they could locate another venture capital investor who might be interested in one of the other proposals. In calculating the impli-

cations of these proposals, Gale and Yeaton assumed an interest cost of debt of 8 percent, which seemed to be the rate for companies similar to Megashye, and a dividend rate for preferred stock of 10 percent. They assumed, as a best guess, that Megashye would earn $300,000 a year after income taxes on operating income but before interest costs and the tax savings thereon. They included their own common stock equity at $900,000.

They also made pessimistic calculations based on income of $100,000 (instead of $300,000) per year and optimistic calculations based on income of $500,000 a year. They realized, of course, that the $100,000 pessimistic calculations were not necessarily the minimum amount of income; it was possible that the company would lose money. On the other hand, $500,000 was about the maximum amount of income that could be expected with the plant that could be financed with the $1.2 million. The applicable income tax rate was 34 percent.

Questions

1. For each of the four proposals, calculate the return on common shareholders' equity (= net income after preferred dividends ÷ common shareholders' equity) that would be earned under each of the three income assumptions. Round calculations to the nearest $1,000 and 1/10 percent.

2. Calculate the pretax earnings and return on its $1.2 million investment to Arbor Capital Corporation under each of the four proposals. Assume that Arbor receives a dividend equal to its portion of common stock ownership times Megashye's net income after preferred dividends (if any); assume a "negative dividend" if Megashye has a net loss.

3. Were the partners correct in rejecting proposals A and B?

4. Comment on the likelihood that Megashye Engineering Company could find a more attractive financing proposal than proposal D.

5. Assume that proposal D is accepted, that the net assets (total assets minus liabilities) of the partnership are $700,000, and that upon incorporation 180,000 shares of $1 par value stock are issued, 90,000 to the original partners and 90,000 to Arbor. Give journal entries for two ways of recording these transactions, one recognizing goodwill and the other not recognizing goodwill. Which way is preferable?

CASE 8–4   Paul Murray

Paul Murray would soon graduate from business school with his MBA. He had accepted a fine job offer. Paul's wife, Nancy, was an attorney with a local firm specializing in corporate law. Paul and Nancy were expecting their first child a few months after Paul's graduation. With the experience of paying for their own graduate educations fresh in their minds, Paul and Nancy recognized that they would have to plan early to accumulate enough money to send their child through four years of college.

Paul wanted to accumulate a fund equal to four times the first year's tuition, room, and board by the time his child entered college. Paul and Nancy assumed that these fees might increase, perhaps annually, through the four years of college. However, if they invested the funds appropriately, the investments would yield enough to cover the increase in fees through the four years of college.

Ideally, Paul and Nancy wanted their child to be able to choose among an array of public or private colleges with good academic reputations. A recent *Wall Street Journal* article had indicated that the average tuition, room, and board at private four-year institutions was about $15,000.[1] They felt that if their child were entering college this coming fall, $18,000 per year for tuition, room, and board would provide the range of choice they sought.

Questions

1. In the recent past college fees had been increasing at about 8 percent per year.[2] Because this rate of increase exceeded the general inflation rate, Paul and Nancy felt it would decline to a level closer to measures of general inflation, such as the Consumer Price Index. Thus, they decided to assume that college fees would increase 6 percent per year. At this rate, how much will one year of college cost 18 years from this fall?

2. Assume the Murrays want to accumulate a fund equal to four times the first year's tuition by the end of year 18. Assume further that they make a single payment into this fund at the end of each year, including the 18th year. How much would they have to contribute to this fund each year, assuming that their investments earn 6 percent per year?

3. How would their annual contributions differ if their investments earned 8 percent? 10 percent? 4 percent?

---

[1] *The Wall Street Journal,* January 5, 1994, page B-1.
[2] Ibid.

CASE 8–5   Jean Coffin (D)

Having recently studied liabilities and the concept of present value, Jean Coffin was interested in discussing with the accounting professor several matters that had recently come to Jean's attention in the newspaper and on television. Each of these matters is described below.

1. On a late-night talk show a guest described having found a bond in the attic of his home in a small Missouri town. The bond had been issued in 1871 by the town, apparently to finance a municipal water system. The bond was payable to the bearer (whoever happened to have the bond in his or her possession), rather than to a specifically named individual. The face amount of the bond was $100, and the stated interest rate was 10 percent. According to the terms of the bond, it could be redeemed at any future time of the bearer's choosing for its face value plus accumulated *compound* interest. Jean was anxious to use the professor's calculator to determine what this bond was worth because only the amount "several million dollars" was mentioned during the show.

2. Jean also had read about "zero-coupon" bonds, which are bonds that pay no interest. Therefore, they are offered at a substantial discount from par value, since the investor's entire return is the difference between the discounted offering price and the par value. In particular, Jean had read that one company had issued eight-year, zero-coupon bonds at a price of $327 per $1,000 par value. Jean wanted to discuss the following with the accounting professor: (*a*) Was the yield on these bonds 15 percent, as Jean had calculated? (*b*) Assuming that bond discount amortization is tax deductible by the issuing corporation, that the issuer has a 40 percent income tax rate, and that for tax purposes a straight-line amortization of original discount is permissible, what is the effective or "true" after-tax interest rate to the issuer of this bond? And (*c*), if instead of issuing these zero-coupon bonds, the company had issued 15 percent coupon bonds with issue proceeds of $1,000 per bond (i.e., par value), what would the issuer's effective after-tax interest rate have been on these alternative bonds?

3. Jean had also read about a new financing gimmick called a "debt-for-equity swap."

The technique works as follows: A company's bonds are currently trading on the New York Bond Exchange at a sizable discount because their coupon rate is well below current market interest rates. The company arranges with an investment banking firm to buy up these bonds on the open market. The company then issues new shares of common stock to the investment banker in exchange for the bonds (which are then retired). The shares issued have a value about 4 percent higher than the amount the investment banker has spent acquiring the bonds. Finally, the investment banker sells these shares on the open market, realizing the 4 percent profit. According to the article Jean had read, Exxon Corporation had swapped 1.4 million common shares valued at $43 million for bonds with a face value of $72 million, thereby realizing a tax-free gain of $29 million. Jean wondered two things about such a transaction: (*a*) Why doesn't the company issue the shares directly and use the proceeds to buy back the bonds on the open market, instead of using an investment banker as an intermediary? And (*b*), should the gain on such a swap be treated as income for financial reporting purposes since, in a sense, the company has done nothing of substance to earn it?

4. Jean was aware that major airlines had "frequent flyer" plans, through which a traveler could earn upgrades from coach to first class, or tickets for free travel. Jean wondered how the airlines should account for upgrade and free travel coupons that had been issued to travelers but had not as yet been redeemed. Were they a liability? If so, how would the amount be determined, and what would be the offsetting debit?

5. Jean Coffin had noticed that many retailers, especially those dealing in high-ticket consumer goods like stereos, computers, and VCRs, offered to sell customers extended warranty contracts when they purchased the product. Jean had heard that retailers earned a much higher margin on an

extended warranty contract than on the product it covered. For example, for a projection TV that cost $2,000, the customer might be offered the option to purchase a three-year warranty contract for $180. The margin on the projection TV might be 8 percent, or $160; the margin on the extended warranty contract might be 75 percent, or $135. Hence, when a customer purchased both the projection TV and the warranty, the margin on the total purchase was $295 or 13.5 percent. The proportion of customers purchasing extended warranty contracts depended on the product but, because consumers wanted to protect their investment in high-ticket items, the vast majority purchased extended warranty contracts, and the proportion was very predictable.

Jean Coffin wondered how to account for this combined purchase. One alternative, which Jean called Alternative A, was to treat the purchase of the projection TV and the purchase of the warranty contract completely separately. For the projection TV, revenue of $2,000 and cost of goods sold of $1,840 would be recognized immediately. For the three-year warranty, the payment received would be treated as deferred revenue, and one-third of the revenue ($60) and one-third of the cost of the service ($15) would be recognized each year for three years. Under this alternative, the accounting would reflect the immediate sale of a low-margin product followed by three years' sale of a high-margin service.

Jean Coffin was not satisfied with this alternative. She figured that the purchase of the projection TV and the service contract was really a single purchase, not two separate purchases, and thus the margin earned on the sale was really the 13.5 percent combined margin. Using this reasoning, Jean saw two alternative ways to treat the sale. First, all of the revenue from the sale of the projection TV and the three-year warranty ($2,180) as well as all of the cost associated with both ($1,885 = $1,840 + $45) could be recognized immediately (Alternative B). Retailers had reasonably accurate information regarding historical service costs to predict the $45 future service cost. However, if actual service costs differed from those estimated, a subsequent adjustment could be made.

Another approach (Alternative C) was to defer recognition of some proportion of the revenue until the warranty period expired. The proportion of the revenue to be recognized immediately would depend on the proportion of the costs associated with the product versus the proportion associated with the service contract. In this example, $1,840 ÷ $1,885 = 97.6 percent of the revenue (or $2,128) would be recognized immediately, with a cost of goods sold of $1,840, and a margin of 13.5 percent; similarly, $45 ÷ $1,885 = 2.4 percent of the revenue (or $52) would be deferred and recognized over the three-year life of the service contract, with an associated cost of $15 per year and a margin of 13.5 percent.

Jean wondered which alternative provided the most appropriate representation of the profitability of the sales of such retailers. She also wondered how the different choices would affect both the balance sheet and the income statement.

9

Sources of Capital: Owners' Equity

This chapter continues our more detailed description of the liabilities and owners' equity portion of the balance sheet. A company obtains its permanent capital (also called invested capital) from two sources: debt and equity. Debt capital consists principally of bonds and long-term loans, as discussed in Chapter 8. This chapter discusses equity capital, the capital supplied by the entity's owners.

The chapter begins with a discussion of the characteristics of the several legal forms of business organizations—proprietorships, partnerships, and corporations. This is followed by a description of the accounting for owners' equity in each form. The primary emphasis is on the ownership interests of a corporation as evidenced by its common and preferred stock. The final section deals with some relatively new financial instruments that blur the traditional line between debt and equity.

FORMS OF BUSINESS ORGANIZATION

The three principal legal forms of business ownership are the sole proprietorship, the partnership, and the corporation.

Sole Proprietorship
A business entity owned by an individual is a **sole proprietorship.** This is a simple form for a business organization. Essentially all that one does to

form a proprietorship is to begin selling goods or one's services. There are no incorporation fees to pay, no special reports to file (except an additional schedule on the proprietor's personal income tax return), and no co-owners with whom to disagree, to share liability for their actions, or to share the profits of the business. The profits of a proprietorship, whether withdrawn by the proprietor or retained in the firm, are taxed at the proprietor's personal income tax rate, which may be lower than the corporate tax rate.

On the other hand, sole proprietorships cannot issue stock or bonds, so it is difficult for them to raise large amounts of capital. They can borrow money from banks or individuals, but they cannot obtain outside equity capital because, by definition, investors who provide equity capital have an ownership interest. Moreover, the proprietor is personally responsible for the entity's debts. In the event of the firm's failure, creditors have claims not only against the assets of the proprietorship but also against the *personal* assets of the proprietor.

Partnership

A **partnership** is a business with the same features as a proprietorship, except that it is owned jointly by two or more persons, called the **partners.** A partnership also is a relatively simple and inexpensive kind of organization to form. In a partnership each partner is personally liable for all debts incurred by the business; in the event of the firm's failure, each partner's personal assets are jeopardized. Also, each partner is responsible for the business actions of the other partners. For example, if one partner in an architectural firm makes a mistake in designing a building that ultimately results in a lawsuit, the potential liability extends to *all* the partners. Each partner pays a personal income tax on his or her share of the partnership's taxable income whether or not the profits are actually distributed to the partners in cash.

Some partnerships are **limited partnerships.** They are managed by a general partner, who receives a larger share of the income in exchange for shouldering all potential liability of the partnership. The limited partners provide capital but have little say about operations. Such partnerships are common in oil exploration and real estate investment ventures.

Corporation

A **corporation** is a legal entity with essentially perpetual existence. It comes into being under the auspices of a state, which grants it a *charter* to operate. The corporation is an artificial person in the sense that it is taxed on its net income as an *entity,* and legal liability accrues to the corporation itself rather than to its owners.

Compared with a proprietorship or a partnership, the corporate form of organization has several disadvantages:

1.   There may be significant legal and other fees involved in its formation.

2. The corporation's activities are limited to those specifically granted in its charter.

3. It is subject to numerous regulations and requirements.

4. It must secure permission from each state in which it wishes to operate.

5. Its income is subject to *double taxation.* The corporation's income is taxed, and distributions of any net income to shareholders in the form of dividends are taxed again, this time at the shareholder's personal income tax rate.[1]

On the other hand, in addition to its limited liability and indefinite existence, a corporation has the advantage of being able to raise capital from a large number of investors through issuing bonds and stock. Moreover, corporate shareholders can usually liquidate their ownership by selling their shares to others, and organized securities exchanges exist to facilitate such sales. A corporation whose shares are traded on a securities exchange is called a **public corporation,** in contrast with a private or "tightly held" corporation, whose shares are owned by an individual or by a relatively few individuals and their families. The financial reports and certain other activities of larger public corporations are regulated by the Securities and Exchange Commission (SEC).

As of 1989, 73 percent of the 19.6 million U.S. business firms were proprietorships, 8 percent were partnerships, and 19 percent were corporations. However, the great bulk of business activity in the United States is performed by corporations. Using net sales figures as a measure of activity, in 1989 corporations accounted for 90 percent of total $11.6 trillion U.S. business sales, whereas proprietorships accounted for 6 percent and partnerships for only 4 percent. Of the total 1989 pretax income of $536 billion, proprietorships accounted for 25 percent, partnerships for 2.6 percent, and corporations for 73 percent.[2]

ACCOUNTING FOR PROPRIETOR'S AND PARTNERS' EQUITY

Proprietorship Equity

Not much more need be said about the owner's equity accounts in a sole proprietorship than the comments made in Chapter 2. There may be one capital account in which all entries affecting the owner's equity are recorded. A separate **drawing account** may be set up for recording periodic withdrawals made by the owner. The drawing account may be closed into the capital account at the end of the accounting period, or it may be kept

---

[1]An exception is an **S corporation** (formerly a "Subchapter S" corporation). If certain conditions are met, including having no more than 35 shareholders, these firms pay no corporate income tax. Instead, as in a partnership, the owners are taxed on their respective shares of taxable income at their personal tax rates.

[2]U.S. Bureau of the Census, *Statistical Abstract of the United States: 1993,* 113th ed. (Washington, D.C.: 1993).

separate so as to show the owner's original contribution of capital separate from the effect on owner's equity of operating transactions.

As far as the ultimate effect is concerned, it is immaterial whether the owner regards withdrawals as salary or as a return of profit. However, if a proprietor wishes to compare the proprietorship's income statement with that of a corporation, a certain part of the owner's drawings must be viewed as being salary expense and only the remainder as equivalent to corporate dividends. Consistent with this quasi-corporate approach to proprietorship accounting, some proprietorships maintain a separate owner's equity account that is analogous to Retained Earnings in a corporation. Whatever the *format* chosen for reporting proprietorship equity, in *substance* it is the same as owners' equity in a corporation.

Partnership Equity

A partnership has an owner's equity account for each partner. The amounts credited to each account depend on the terms of the partnership agreement. In the absence of a specific agreement, the law assumes that net income is to be divided equally among the partners. This is also common in written partnership agreements. If such is the case, in a three-person partnership the capital account, or the drawing account, of each partner is credited with one-third of net income. It is debited with the actual amount of the partner's withdrawals.

Partnership agreements may also provide that the partners receive stated salaries and a stated share of residual profits after salaries, or a stated percentage of interest on the capital they have invested and a stated share of residual profits, or a combination of salary and interest. The accounting required in connection with such arrangements depends on the specific terms of the agreement.

> **Example.** The partnership agreement of Jackson and Curtin provided that Jackson (who worked half-time) would receive a salary of $20,000 and Curtin a salary of $40,000; that each would receive 8 percent interest on their invested capital; and that they would share equally in the remainder of net income. In 1993 the average balance in Jackson's capital account was $30,000 and in Curtin's was $70,000. The partnership net income (before partners' salaries) was $80,000.
>
> The amount to be credited to each partner's equity account would be computed as follows:

	Total	Jackson	Curtin
Salary	$60,000	$20,000	$40,000
Interest on capital.	8,000	2,400	5,600
Remainder	12,000	6,000	6,000
Total.	$80,000	$28,400	$51,600

Whatever the partnership arrangement, the law does not regard salaries or interest payments to the partners as being different from any other type of withdrawal, since the partnership is not an entity legally separate from the individual partners. Nevertheless, some partnerships prepare income statements that include partners' salaries as an expense, and balance sheets with equity accounts analogous to paid-in capital and retained earnings. This enables the partners to compare their statements with those of similar businesses that are incorporated.

Ownership in a Corporation

Ownership in a corporation is evidenced by a **stock certificate.** This capital stock may be either *common* or *preferred*. Each corporation is authorized in its charter to issue a maximum number of **shares** of each class of stock. Each stock certificate shows how many shares of ownership it represents. Because a corporation's owners hold stock certificates that indicate their shares of ownership, owners' equity in a corporation is called **shareholders' equity** or **stockholders' equity.**

Preferred Stock

Preferred stock pays a stated dividend, much like the interest payment on bonds. However, the dividend is not a legal liability until it has been declared by the directors, nor is it a tax-deductible expense to the corporation. Preferred stock has preference, or priority, over common as to the receipt of dividends, distribution of assets in the event of liquidation, and other specified matters. Preferred stock may be cumulative or noncumulative. With **cumulative preferred stock,** if the corporation is unable to pay the dividend, the unpaid dividends accumulate and must be paid before the firm can resume payment of common stock dividends. The undeclared dividends are not, however, recorded as a liability.

> **Example.** In 1993 Cotting Corporation did not pay the $9 dividend on each share of its $9 cumulative preferred stock. Hence, no dividend could be paid on the common stock in 1993. In 1994 holders of Cotting's common stock cannot be paid any dividend unless $18 is paid on the $9 cumulative preferred (1994's $9 dividend plus the $9 from 1993).

Preferred stock is usually issued with a face, or par, value of $100 per share. The dividend rate (9 percent in the above example) is analogous to the coupon rate on a bond, although in practice the dividend is usually stated at its dollar amount rather than as a percentage of par value. Also, like bonds, a preferred stock may be convertible into a specified number of shares of common stock; this is called a **convertible preferred.** Although preferred stock is usually outstanding indefinitely, some issues of preferred stock are redeemable on a specified date or at the holder's option. These **redeemable preferreds** are further discussed later in this chapter.

If a corporation is liquidated, preferred stockholders are entitled to receive par value for their shares, provided that assets exist after all liabilities have been settled. Also, whereas bondholders can force the firm into bankruptcy if an interest payment on the bonds is missed, preferred stockholders have no such recourse if their dividend is not paid. Interest on bonds is an expense, both for financial accounting purposes and for income tax purposes, whereas a dividend on stock, including preferred stock, is not an expense. Accounting treatment of preferred stock is substantially the same as for common stock, described below.

Contrary to many persons' preconception, issuance of bonds is a much larger source of funds for corporations than is issuance of either common or preferred stock. For example, in 1991 corporations raised over $465 billion by issuing one of these three types of securities. Of this amount 84 percent was raised by issuing bonds, 12.5 percent by common stock, and only 3.7 percent by preferred stock.[3] The principal reason for the unpopularity of preferred stock is that its dividends are not a deductible expense for income tax purposes, whereas interest on bonds is.

Common Stock

Every corporation has **common stock.** Common shareholders have a residual interest in profits and assets, below that of all other creditors and preferred stockholders. Common stock may have a par value, or it may be no-par stock. No-par stock usually has a stated value analogous to par value. In the following description, statements about par value apply also to stated value.

The **par value** of a share of stock[4] is usually a nominal amount, such as $1. Whereas par value on a bond or on preferred stock has meaning, par value for common stock amount is an essentially meaningless amount. Many years ago shareholders had an obligation to a corporation's creditors if they had purchased their shares (when issued by the corporation) at an amount less than par. This is not the case today because most states' corporation laws forbid issuing stock at a price below its par value. The important thing to remember about par value is that in isolation it is meaningless and tells us *nothing* about the proceeds received by the corporation upon issuance of the stock.

The **book value** of common stock is the total common shareholders' equity as reported on the balance sheet.[5] This section of the balance sheet consists of two parts: (1) the amount invested in the firm by its shareholders, called **paid-in capital** and (2) retained earnings. The amount of paid-in capital can be reported as a single amount. Nevertheless, most corporations report this amount in two pieces: (1) the par or stated value of the

---

[3]Ibid.

[4]Henceforth, the word *stock* unmodified by *common* or *preferred* will mean common stock.

[5]The book value of a *corporation* is a term sometimes used to mean the amount of owners' equity. If a corporation has no preferred stock, then the book value of the corporation equals the book value of its common stock plus its retained earnings. The book value of a corporation is also called its net assets because book value equals owners' equity, and owners' equity equals assets minus (net of) liabilities.

outstanding shares of capital stock, usually called **common stock at par,** and (2) the amount by which the proceeds from issuing common stock have exceeded the par value of the shares issued, usually called **additional paid-in capital** or **other paid-in capital.** (The FASB suggests the more descriptive but cumbersome title, "capital contributed in excess of the par or stated value of shares.") If both components of paid-in capital are reported separately, the reader of the balance sheet must add them together to arrive at the amount that investors have paid into the corporation when shares of stock have been issued. This is a nuisance, and generally accepted accounting principles (GAAP) do not require that the two components be separately reported. The practice started decades ago when par value *did* mean something, and certain old accounting habits die hard.

Recording a Common Stock Issue. To illustrate the issuance of stock, let us consider Kuick Corporation, which received a charter from the state authorizing the issuance of 200,000 shares of $1 par value common stock. If 100,000 shares of this stock were issued at a price of $7 per share and the proceeds were received by Kuick immediately, this financing transaction could be recorded in either of two ways. The most useful way from the standpoint of statement users would be:

Cash	700,000	
Common Stock		700,000

However, in practice most corporations record the transaction this way:

Cash	700,000	
Common Stock at Par		100,000
Additional Paid-In Capital		600,000

Issuance Costs. The offering of an issue of stock is often handled by an investment banking firm that receives a fee, or "spread," for this service. Usually the corporation records only the net amount received from the investment banker (the amount remitted by shareholders less the banker's spread).

In addition to this spread, the corporation incurs legal, auditing, and printing costs. These issuance costs are usually also deducted from the amount received from the issue. (The entry would debit Additional Paid-In Capital and credit Cash or Accounts Payable.) Note that because of the spread and other issuance costs, the amount actually remitted by the shareholders is greater than the amount by which paid-in capital (par value plus additional paid-in capital) increases on the balance sheet. Note also that there is a paid-in capital transaction between the company and its shareholders only when the shares are issued. When a shareholder sells stock to another party, the amounts in the company's accounts are not affected in any way; the only change is in the company's detailed record of the identity of its shareholders.

Treasury Stock   **Treasury stock** is a corporation's own stock that has been issued and subsequently reacquired by purchase. The firm may reacquire its shares for a number of reasons: to obtain shares that can be used in the future for acquisitions, bonus plans, exercise of warrants, and conversion of convertible bonds or preferred stocks; to increase the earnings per share; to thwart an attempt by an outsider to accumulate shares in anticipation of a takeover attempt; or to increase the market price of each share of the stock.

Treasury stock is clearly not an "economic resource" of an entity. A corporation cannot own part of itself. Therefore, treasury stock is not an asset, and it has no voting, dividend, or other shareholder rights. Rather, it is reported on the balance sheet as a reduction in shareholders' equity—as a reduction in the number and book value of the shares outstanding.

Two methods of accounting for treasury stock are permitted. For a given situation either method has the same effect on total owners' equity. With the simpler method, called the **cost method,** when treasury stock is purchased, the amount debited to Treasury Stock (contra equity account) is its reacquisition cost, regardless of its par value. It continues to be shown at this reacquisition cost until it is canceled or reissued, at which time adjustments are made in shareholders' equity to dispose of any differences between this cost, the paid-in value (i.e., the net proceeds at the time the stock was originally issued), and, in the event of reissuance, the amount then received.[b]

If treasury shares are reissued, any excess of selling price above cost is credited to a paid-in capital account (such as Paid-In Capital from Treasury Stock Transactions). If treasury stock is sold at a price below its reacquisition cost, the loss may be deducted from the related paid-in capital account if such an account already exists from prior transactions; otherwise the loss is debited to Retained Earnings. Any gain or loss on the resale of treasury stock is *not* shown on the income statement, nor is it recognized for income tax purposes.[7]

Reserves   Some shareholders do not understand that there is no connection between the amount shown as retained earnings and the corporation's ability to pay cash dividends to the shareholders. In an attempt to lower these shareholders' dividend aspiration levels, a corporation may show on

---

[6]An exception occurs if stock is reacquired at an amount significantly in excess of its fair value. This may occur when the company wants to buy out a stockholder who is contemplating an "unfriendly" takeover attempt or who is otherwise viewed by the corporation's board of directors as being problematical. (General Motors' buyout of H. Ross Perot's shares in 1986 was a notable example.) When such a so-called "greenmail" transaction takes place, only the fair value is recorded as the cost of the treasury shares, and the excess of the price paid over the fair value is recorded as an expense. (Source: *FASB Technical Bulletin No. 85-6* [December 31, 1985].)

[7]The other permissable method is the *par value method.* It is more complicated and is described in advanced texts.

its balance sheet an appropriation, or **reserve,** as a separate item that is subtracted from Retained Earnings. For example, a *reserve for future expansion* signals to shareholders the corporation's intention to use internally generated funds (rather than a new bond or stock issue) to finance the acquisition of new assets. Also, if some contingency does not meet the criteria (described in Chapter 8) for recording it as a liability, then a *reserve for contingencies* may be shown.

None of these reserves represents money, or anything tangible; the assets of a business are reported on the assets side of the balance sheet, not in the shareholders' equity section. The accounting entry creating the reserve involves a debit to Retained Earnings and a credit to the reserve account. This entry simply moves an amount from one owners' equity account to another. It does not affect any asset account, nor does the reserve represent anything more than a segregated portion of Retained Earnings. Because the use of the word *reserve* tends to be misleading to unsophisticated readers of financial statements (it connotes something stashed away), such usage fortunately is on the decline.

Retained Earnings

The remaining owners' equity account is Retained Earnings. As pointed out in previous chapters, the amount of **retained earnings** represents the *cumulative* net income of the firm since its beginning, less the total dividends (or drawings, in the case of unincorporated businesses) that have been paid to owners over the entire life of the entity. Stated from more of a financial management point of view, retained earnings shows the amount of assets that have been financed by "plowing profits back into the business," rather than paying all of the company's net income out as dividends. The importance to owners (and others) of understanding in some detail *why* the amount of retained earnings has changed between two balance sheet dates is the essential underlying reason that the income statement is prepared.

Dividends

Dividends are ordinarily paid to shareholders in cash, but they occasionally are paid in other assets. Dividends are debited to Retained Earnings on the date they are declared (i.e., voted) by the board of directors, even though payment is made at a later date. On the date of declaration, the dividends become a legal liability.

> **Example.** If Kuick Corporation declared a $6,000 dividend on December 15 to be paid on January 15 to holders of record as of January 1, the entries would be as follows:
>
> 1. Declaration of dividend on December 15:
>
> Retained Earnings 6,000
>   Dividends Payable (a liability account)............   6,000

2. Payment of dividend on January 15:

```
Dividends Payable .................................. 6,000
    Cash............................................          6,000
```

Stock Dividends.   Sometimes a company wants to retain funds in the business to finance expansion, and this precludes paying a cash dividend; yet the company still wants its shareholders to receive a dividend of some kind. Such a company may declare a **stock dividend,** which increases every shareholder's number of shares by the same percentage. For example, if a 5 percent stock dividend were declared, the holder of 100 shares would receive 5 more shares from the corporation (either newly issued or from treasury stock). Since each shareholder's holdings are increased by the same proportion, every shareholder's equity in the corporation remains unchanged.

Although a stock dividend does not change either the corporation's earnings, its assets, or each shareholder's proportionate equity, it does increase the number of outstanding shares. In theory, therefore, such a dividend should reduce the market price per share of the stock. For the 5 percent stock dividend example, if the price before the dividend was $10.50 per share, theoretically it should drop to $10 (= $10.50 ÷ 105%) after the stock dividend. However, studies indicate that shareholders do perceive a stock dividend as having some value because, in some cases, the price per share does not drop as much as theory would predict.

To record a stock dividend, Retained Earnings is debited with the *fair* value of the additional shares issued, with the credit being to the paid-in capital accounts.

> **Example.**   If Kuick Corporation declared a 5 percent stock dividend to the holders of its 100,000 outstanding shares (par value of $1) when the market price of a share was $10.50, the entry would be:
>
> ```
> Retained Earnings .................................. 52,500
>     Common Stock at Par ...........................          5,000
>     Additional Paid-In Capital .......................         47,500
> ```

The $52,500 is the fair value, at $10.50 per share, of the 5,000 additional shares issued as a dividend. The $47,500 is the difference between the $52,500 fair value and the par value of the newly issued shares. Note that the total amount of owners' equity is *not* changed by this transaction; there is just a shift of $52,500 out of Retained Earnings and into the paid-in capital accounts.

Stock Splits.   In a **stock split** each shareholder receives a multiple of the number of shares previously held. For example, in a two-for-one split, the holder of 100 shares would receive 100 additional shares, doubling the total held before the split. Thus, like a stock dividend, a stock split merely increases the number of shares of stock outstanding with no change in each shareholder's portion of total owners' equity. Such a split has no effect on the amount of shareholders' equity; its effect is solely to repackage the evidence of ownership in smaller units. No transfer is made from Retained Earnings to Paid-In Capital when a stock split is effected. However, the par value *per share* is reduced proportionately; if the stock was $1 par prior to a two-for-one split, it would automatically become $0.50 par after the split. Since the number of outstanding shares doubled and the par value per share halved, the total of Common Stock at Par remains unchanged, as does the amount in Additional Paid-In Capital.

Stock splits are usually effected to reduce the price of a share of stock, thus allegedly making the stock appealing to a wider range of investors (including those who prefer to trade only in round lots of 100 shares). Theoretically, a stock split should automatically reduce the market price of a share of stock in inverse proportion to the split: A two-for-one split should exactly halve the market price. In practice, however, the price reduction sometimes is less than proportional to the split, indicating that the split may add value in the eyes of shareholders.

The difference between a stock dividend and a stock split is a matter of intent. The intent of a stock dividend is to give shareholders "ostensibly separate evidence" of their interests in the firm without having to distribute cash. The intent of a stock split is to reduce the market price of the shares to improve their marketability. The presumption is that any increase in shares smaller than 20 to 25 percent is *not* a stock split.[8]

Spin-Offs. The stock referred to in the preceding paragraphs is the company's own stock. If the company owns shares of some *other* corporation's stock that it distributes to its shareholders, this distribution is called a **spin-off.** It is essentially similar to a cash dividend, and it is recorded in the same manner except that the credit is to the Investments asset account rather than to Cash. Most spin-offs are of the stock of a company's wholly owned subsidiary, as opposed to stock that was being held as an investment.

Warrants and Stock Options

Warrants. The right to purchase shares of common stock at a stated price within a given time period is called a **warrant.** For example, a warrant could give its holder the right to buy 100 shares of Sterling Company common stock for $25 per share anytime between January 1, 1995, and December 31, 1999. If during this period the market price of Sterling's common stock rises to $31, the holder of the option can *exercise* it by paying Sterling $25. The share of stock received can then be sold for $31, so the warrant holder gains $6. Warrants are negotiable; they can be bought and sold. Some companies have warrants that are traded on stock exchanges, just like other corporate securities. In this case the warrant holder can sell the warrant and realize its value without actually exercising it.

Some corporations issue warrants in conjunction with the issuance of bonds, putting an exercise price on the warrants of about 15 to 20 percent above the current market price of the common stock. If the investor expects

---

[8]*Accounting Research Bulletin No. 43* (June 1953), Chapter 7B.

the firm to prosper and expects this prosperity to be reflected in the market price of the common stock, then the warrant has value. The investor will then accept a correspondingly lower interest rate on the bond, thus reducing the interest cost of the bond to the issuer. Also, some small firms that investors regard as being very risky would not be able to attract investors to their bonds without using warrants as a "sweetener."

The value of a warrant at the time it is issued is a matter of opinion. This value sometimes can be approximated by estimating the higher interest rate that would have been required for the bonds if there were no warrants; the warrant's value is then assumed to be the difference between the present value of the bonds using this higher rate and the actual bond proceeds. Whatever the value is judged to be, the warrants are recorded separately from the bond liability by an entry such as:[9]

```
Cash ............................................... 210,000
    Bonds Payable .................................          200,000
    Bond Premium ..................................            6,000
    Warrants Outstanding ..........................            4,000
```

Warrants Outstanding is a shareholders' equity account.

Stock Options. A **stock option** is essentially the same as a warrant except that it is not negotiable. Many corporations grant options to certain officers and employees, either to obtain widespread ownership among employees or as a form of compensation. If the options are intended as compensation, their fair value at the time they are granted is estimated using an option pricing model (described in advanced finance courses). This value is then charged ratably to Salaries Expense over the vesting period of the option. (Vesting means that the option can be exercised even if the employee leaves the company.)[10]

> **Example.** An employee is granted an option to buy 5,000 shares of her company's common stock at a stated price, and the estimated fair value of this option is $150,000. The option vests at the rate of 1,000 shares per year. The company will charge $30,000 per year to Salaries Expense over each of the next five years to account for this option.

Employee Stock Ownership Plans

Some corporations have a program of setting aside stock for the benefit of employees as a group (as distinguished from options, which are granted to certain employees as individuals). This is called an **Employee Stock Ownership Plan (ESOP).** Such a plan can have important income tax benefits to the corporation. (Contributions to the plan are tax-deductible employee compensation.) The plan's manager can vote the ESOP's shares,

---

[9]"Accounting for Convertible Debt and Debt Issued with Stock Purchase Warrants," *APB Opinion No. 14* (March 1969), par. 16.

[10]As this book goes to press in late 1994, the FASB has proposed the treatment described here, but has not issued a final *Statement*.

ILLUSTRATION 9–1
PRESENTATION OF OWNERS' EQUITY

KELLOGG COMPANY AND SUBSIDIARIES
Consolidated Balance Sheet
At December 31
(millions)

	1993	1992
Shareholders' equity		
Common stock, $.25 par value	$ **77.6**	$ 77.5
Capital in excess of par value	**72.0**	69.2
Retained earnings	**3,409.4**	3,033.9
Treasury stock, at cost	**(1,653.1)**	(1,105.0)
Currency translation and pension adjustments	**(192.5)**	130.4
Total shareholders' equity	**$ 1,713.4**	$ 1,945.2

and the plan receives dividends. The plan is a separate entity whose assets (i.e., the stock that it holds and reinvested dividends) do not appear on the balance sheet of the corporation (just as the accounting records of other shareholders do not appear). However, the ESOP amounts are disclosed in notes to the financial statements.

Balance Sheet Presentation   In sum, the shareholders' equity section of the balance sheet maintains a distinct separation between capital invested by the shareholders and equity resulting from the retention of earnings in the business. There is a separation between paid-in capital—which in turn is usually subdivided into par value and additional paid-in capital—and retained earnings. If a company has more than one class of stock, a note to the balance sheet provides details on each class. As an example Illustration 9–1 shows the owners' equity section of an actual corporation's balance sheet.

EARNINGS PER SHARE

In analyzing the financial statements of a corporation, investors pay particular attention to the amount called **earnings per share.** This is computed by dividing net income *applicable to the common stock* (explained below) by the number of shares of common stock outstanding. (Recall that treasury stock is not considered to be stock outstanding.) The FASB requires that earnings per share be reported on the income statement and has provided detailed guidelines for making the calculation.[11]

If the corporation has a simple capital structure with only one class of common stock, the net income used in this calculation is the same as the net income shown on the income statement.

---

[11]"Earnings per Share," *APB Opinion No. 15* (May 1969); and "Reporting the Results of Operations," *APB Opinion No. 30* (June 1973).

Example.   The 1993 income statement of McLean Corporation showed net income of $7 million. The corporation had 1 million shares of common stock outstanding in 1993. It therefore earned $7 per share.

The various classes of stock that a corporation might issue can be divided into one of two categories: (1) senior securities and (2) common stock and its equivalent. **Senior securities,** usually preferred stock, are those that have a claim on net income ahead of the claim of the common shareholders. The income figure used in the calculation of earnings per share is the amount that remains *after* the claims of the senior securities have been deducted from net income.

Example.   Nugent Corporation in 1993 had net income of $7 million. It had outstanding 100,000 shares of $8 preferred stock (i.e., preferred stock whose annual dividend is $8 per share) and 1 million shares of common stock. The preferred stock dividend of $800,000 must be subtracted from net income to arrive at net income applicable to common stock. Nugent's earnings per share were therefore ($7,000,000 − $800,000) ÷ 1,000,000 shares = $6.20 per share.

If the number of shares of common stock outstanding fluctuates within a year, then the *weighted-average* number of shares outstanding is computed.

Example.   Optel Corporation in 1993 had net income of $7 million. On January 1 it had outstanding 1 million shares of common stock. On July 1 it issued an additional 500,000 shares, which were therefore outstanding for half of the year. Its weighted-average number of common shares outstanding was 1,000,000 + (500,000 * ½) = 1,250,000. Its earnings per share were $7,000,000 ÷ 1,250,000 = $5.60.

Common Stock Equivalents

A security that is not *in form* a common stock but contains provisions that enable its holder to become a common shareholder and, because of its terms or the circumstances under which it was issued, is *in substance* equivalent to a common stock is called a **common stock equivalent.** The value of a common stock equivalent is derived in large part from the value of the common stock to which it is related. Convertible bonds and convertible preferreds may be common stock equivalents (depending on whether specific criteria are met at a given point in time), and stock options and warrants always are common stock equivalents.[12]

When a corporation has securities that are common stock equivalents, the FASB requires that the amount of such securities be taken into account in calculating earnings per share. The detailed criteria for deciding whether a security is a common stock equivalent and, if so, how the equivalent number of shares should be calculated are too lengthy to be given here. *APB Opinion No. 15* is the longest of the 31 *Opinions* of the Accounting Principles Board, and it is so complex that the American Institute of CPAs issued an "interpretation" that is over twice as long as the *Opinion* itself.

---

[12]*APB Opinion No. 15,* as amended by *FASB Statements No. 55* (February 1982) and *No. 85* (March 1985).

APB Opinion No. 15 also states that if a corporation has securities that *may* under certain circumstances have a claim on common earnings—even though these securities are not equivalent common shares—then the corporation should report two numbers for earnings per share: (1) **primary earnings per share,** net income divided by the number of common and common equivalent shares, as above, and (2) **fully diluted earnings per share,** in which it is assumed that the maximum amount of potential conversion, exercise of warrants, and the like has taken place.

THE LINE BETWEEN DEBT AND EQUITY

Chapter 8 described the trade-off between the lower after-tax cost of debt capital (relative to equity capital) and the risk that financial leverage adds to the shareholders' investment. In general, corporate financial managers favor leverage and the tax-deductible interest associated with debt capital *up to a point,* but they are concerned about the exposure to risk beyond that point. Although they like the lower risk of equity capital, they also realize that equity capital is inherently more expensive than debt capital. Thus, they want as much debt in the capital structure as is practicable without alarming investors by having an excessively high debt/equity (or equivalently, debt/capitalization) ratio.

In recent years investment banking firms have developed a variety of financial instruments that are intended both to suit the needs of various types of investors and also to provide the corporation with securities of different risk characteristics. Some of these instruments tend to blur the line between debt and equity, and their existence requires that caution be exercised in using the debt/equity or debt/capitalization ratio to analyze capital structure. Two examples, each previously mentioned in passing, will be described.

Zero-Coupon Bonds

A company may issue bonds that pay no interest but whose face value is payable in, say, five years. These are called **zero-coupon bonds.** They may be issued by a start-up corporation that anticipates having little cash flow in the near future with which to make interest payments. Because there are no interest payments, zero-coupon bonds are sold at a deep discount from their par value. As described in the preceding chapter, this discount is determined by finding the present value of the bonds' future principal redemption payment at maturity. If investors view the issuing corporation's prospects as somewhat shaky, they will use a high discount rate in arriving at this present value.

> **Example.** If investors discount a five-year, zero-coupon bond at 14 percent, at the date of issuance they will pay only $519 for each $1,000 par value bond (using Table A, as explained in the Appendix to Chapter 8).

Although no cash interest is paid, the annual amortization of the $481 discount is reported as interest expense by the corporation. This noncash interest expense resulting from the discount amortization is tax deductible to the corporation (and, usually, is taxable interest revenue to the investor). However, the corporation has no cash interest payments to worry about for the five-year period. Thus, a zero-coupon bond meets the traditional definition of a debt security, but its burden may be less onerous to the corporation than that of cumulative preferred stock, which is not debt but whose dividends are expected to be declared and paid annually.

Redeemable Preferred Stock

A corporation may issue preferred stock that not only pays annual dividends but may also be redeemed by the investor on or after a certain date, say five years hence. This **redeemable preferred stock** may be issued, for example, as part of the payment made to the owner of a small company when it is acquired by a larger one. The redemption price may be considerably higher than its par value. Redeemable preferred stock is evidence of ownership in the company and is therefore an equity security; yet the company's obligation to pay the redemption price may be fully as certain as that for the redemption of bonds when they mature, which is a liability.

The Securities and Exchange Commission (SEC) requires that redeemable preferred stock be listed as a separate item on the balance sheet at its redemption price. This item must be listed between the liability and owners' equity sections and not included in the total of either liabilities or owners' equity. This indicates that the SEC is not willing to decide whether redeemable preferred stock is debt or whether it is equity.

EQUITY IN NONPROFIT ORGANIZATIONS

Nonprofit organizations do not receive equity capital from shareholders; however, they do receive equity capital from contributions. These capital contributions are usually in the form of endowment or contributed "plant." **Endowment** consists of contributions whose principal is to be kept intact indefinitely, with the earnings on that principal being available to finance current operations. **Contributed plant** consists of contributed buildings, works of art and other museum objects, or the funds to acquire these or similar assets. Endowment and plant contributions are distinguished from contributions intended for operating purposes, such as contributions to an annual alumni/alumnae fund; operating contributions are revenues, not contributed capital.

In both for-profit and nonprofit organizations, equity is increased by earning net income. In a nonprofit organization the cumulative net income amount is usually labeled "operating equity" rather than "retained earnings." Since nonprofit organizations do not pay dividends, their equity does not decrease as does a dividend-paying entity's equity when it declares a dividend. However, a nonprofit organization's equity does decrease in any year in which its operations were unprofitable.

This difference in the source of equity funds is the only substantive difference in accounting for the two types of organization. Many other differences are found in practice, but these result from nonprofit accounting traditions and terminology differences rather than from actual differences in substance.

SUMMARY

Although the legal forms of organization—proprietorship, partnership, and corporation—differ, all three conceptually have paid-in capital and retained earnings as components of owners' equity. Most corporations report two separate components of paid-in capital: par value and additional paid-in capital. Neither number is meaningful in isolation; their sum shows the proceeds the corporation received when the stock was issued.

Preferred stock pays a stated dividend, which may be cumulative. Although this dividend is analogous to bond interest, it is not a liability. Preferred shareholders have precedence over common shareholders in matters of dividend payments and distribution of proceeds of a corporate liquidation.

Treasury stock is stock that a corporation has reacquired by purchase. It is not an asset and is not counted as either paid-in capital or as outstanding shares. Ordinarily, it is recorded at its reacquisition cost; subsequent reissuance of the stock may lead to a reported loss or gain.

Retained earnings is the cumulative amount of net income an entity has earned since its inception, less the cumulative amount of dividends it has paid to its owners. Stock dividends and stock splits do not affect the relative holdings of shareholders nor the total amount of owners' equity. Creation of a reserve account also does not affect the total of owners' equity; a reserve is simply a reclassification of a portion of retained earnings. The calculation of earnings per share is based on the amount of net income applicable to common stock (net income less preferred stock dividends) and the number of outstanding shares, including common stock equivalents.

Securities such as zero-coupon bonds and redeemable preferreds have blurred the distinction between debt capital and equity capital, and thus complicate the ratio analysis of capital structure.

The nature of nonprofit organizations' equity capital differs from that of for-profit organizations, but otherwise accounting for the two types of entities is substantively similar.

Cases

CASE 9–1   Xytech, Inc.

Xytech was a high-tech company that had been started by three partners in early 19x0. Their successful product designs led to rapid growth of the company, with resulting needs for additional capital to support the growth. This case describes the major financing transactions entered into by Xytech in its first ten years of existence. The firm's earnings history is also given.

You are to write a journal entry for each transaction as it is described. You should be explicit about what noncurrent liability and owners' equity—that is, invested capital—accounts are affected by the transactions; but effects on assets (including cash) and current liabilities can be recorded in a single account, "A&CL."

19x0: The firm began as a partnership on January 10, with the three equal partners, Able, Baker, and Cabot, each contributing $100,000 capital. The accountant set up a capital account for each of the three partners. On April 1 the partners arranged with a bank a $100,000, 8 percent, five-year "balloon" note, which meant that only quarterly interest was payable for five years, with the principal due in full as a lump sum at the end of the fifth year. The firm's net loss for 19x0 was $54,000. A salary for each partner was included in the calculation of net loss; no other payments were made to the partners.

19x1: To help the firm deal with a short-term liquidity problem, on April 26, Cabot liquidated some personal securities and loaned the firm the $50,000 proceeds. Cabot

expected to be repaid these funds in no more than one year. In October Baker's ownership interest in the firm was sold out equally to Able and Cabot, with Baker receiving a total of $110,000 in notes and cash from Able and Cabot. The firm had $12,000 net income for the year. Able and Cabot planned to incorporate the firm as of January 1, 19x2. Prepare a statement of invested capital for the partnership as of December 31, 19x1.

19x2: The firm was incorporated on January 1, as planned. The articles of incorporation authorized 500 shares of $100 par value common stock, but only 100 shares were issued, 50 each to Able and Cabot. On March 21 the bank agreed to increase the $100,000 balloon note to $150,000; the $50,000 proceeds were used to repay Cabot's $50,000 loan. The net income for the year was $26,000.

19x3: In anticipation of a public offering of Xytech, Inc. stock, the firm effected a 1,000-for-1 stock split in November. The year's net income was $43,000. Calculate the 19x3 earnings per share amount.

19x4: In January the firm went public. An investment banker sold 100,000 newly issued shares at $7.75 per share. The banker's fee and other issuance costs amounted to $55,000. The year's net income (after stock issuance costs) was $68,000. Prepare a statement of invested capital as of December 31, 19x4.

19x5: In January the company issued 500 twenty-year bonds with a face value of

$1,000 each and a coupon rate of 6 percent. Although the bonds were issued at par, because of issuance costs the proceeds were only $950 per bond. Part of the proceeds was used to repay the firm's prior long-term debt. The year's net income was $85,000.

19x6: In April Able and Cabot each sold 25,000 of their common shares, receiving proceeds of $11 per share. The company earned net income of $111,000. On December 31, the firm declared a dividend of $0.15 per share, payable January 31, 19x7, to holders of record as of January 15. Prepare a statement of invested capital as of December 31, 19x6.

19x7: Feeling that the market was undervaluing the company's stock, in June the management decided to purchase 20,000 shares on the open market. The purchase was effected July 1 at a price of $10 per share. The shares were held as treasury stock, available for possible reissuance. The year's net income was $152,000. In December a $0.20 per share dividend was declared, payable the following month. Calculate the year's earnings per share.

19x8: In January the company issued 4,000 shares of convertible cumulative preferred stock with an annual dividend rate of $5 per share. Proceeds of the issuance were $200,000. Each share was convertible upon the holder's demand into two shares of Xytech common stock. Net income before preferred dividends was $186,000. In December a dividend of $0.25 per common share was declared, payable the following month. Calculate the primary and fully diluted earnings per share of common stock in 19x8.

19x9: Net income before preferred stock dividends was $252,000. Instead of paying a cash dividend to common stock shareholders, on December 31, the firm declared a 5 percent stock dividend. The market price of the common stock on December 31 was $17 per share. No shares of preferred stock were converted during the year. Calculate the primary and fully diluted earnings per share for 19x9 and prepare a statement of invested capital as of December 31. What is the company's debt/capitalization ratio at year-end?

CASE 9–2   FMC Corporation Recapitalization (A)*

FMC Corporation, a diversified industrial company based in Chicago, Illinois, was considering the reorganization of its financial structure through a major recapitalization. Through selective divesting, cost-cutting measures, and productivity enhancements, FMC had realized a return on equity exceeding 18 percent and a return on capital employed exceeding 15 percent for the years 1984 and 1985. (See Exhibit 1 for consolidated financial statements.)

*Copyright © by the President and Fellows of Harvard College. Harvard Business School case 194–075.

Robert Malott, FMC's chief executive officer (CEO), had seen his company eliminate debt and increase earnings substantially during 1984 and 1985. Since Malott had become CEO in 1973, he had reduced the diversity of FMC's portfolio of businesses, focused on its core competencies, and observed the company throwing off more and more cash from operations. In fact, cash provided from continuing operations had risen from $200 million in 1977 to $403 million in 1986. The company was by any standard a "cash machine" and was considered by many analysts to be in an enviable position.

EXHIBIT 1
FMC CORPORATION—CONSOLIDATED BALANCE SHEETS
($ thousands)

	Year Ended December 31	
	1985	*1984*
ASSETS		
Current Assets		
Cash.	$ 6,794	$ 7,220
Marketable securities	155,124	186,758
Trade receivables, net	454,373	384,776
Inventories	232,444	244,528
Other current assets.	96,818	60,649
Deferred income taxes.	158,949	191,351
Total current assets.	1,104,502	1,075,282
Investments	179,054	188,073
Property, plant, and equipment, net	1,327,625	1,108,409
Patents and deferred charges	59,802	18,434
Intangibles of acquired companies.	19,739	9,788
Total assets.	$2,690,722	$2,399,986
LIABILITIES AND STOCKHOLDERS' EQUITY		
Current Liabilities		
Short-term debt	$ 37,475	$ 31,116
Accounts payable, trade and other.	465,740	404,743
Accrued payroll.	92,536	88,045
Accrued and other liabilities	225,452	199,214
Reserve for discontinued operations.	117,291	117,244
Current portion of long-term debt	30,209	14,107
Income taxes payable	45,284	77,024
Total current liabilities.	1,013,987	931,493
Long-term debt, less current portion.	303,210	292,173
Deferred income taxes.	243,146	210,895
Minority interests in consolidated companies	7,279	5,665
Stockholders' Equity		
Preferred stock, no par value, authorized 5,000,000 shares;		
$2.25 cumulative convertible; preference value $24,553	3,069	3,843
Common stock, $5 par value, authorized 60,000,000 shares	178,948	177,710
Capital in excess of par value of capital stock.	105,354	101,152
Retained earnings.	1,440,204	1,301,222
Foreign currency translation adjustment	(90,684)	(106,095)
Treasury stock, common, at cost.	(513,791)	(518,072)
Total stockholders' equity	1,123,100	959,760
Total liabilities and stockholders' equity	$2,690,722	$2,399,986

(continued)

However, in early 1986 FMC's strong cash position forced Malott to make a decision regarding the financial structure of the corporation. With so much cash and with a stock price that was only at nine times earnings, management feared a takeover bid by potential raiders.[1] One option Malott considered

---

[1]G. Slutsker, *Forbes,* April 7, 1986.

EXHIBIT 1 *(concluded)*
FMC CORPORATION—CONSOLIDATED STATEMENTS OF INCOME
(in thousands, except per-share data)

	Year Ended December 31		
	1985	*1984*	*1983*
Revenue			
Sales.	$3,260,847	$3,337,839	$3,246,758
Equity in net earnings of affiliates	15,445	16,573	17,027
Interest income.	32,108	69,352	48,082
Other income	20,049	6,025	8,906
Total revenue	3,328,449	3,429,789	3,320,773
Costs and expenses			
Cost of sales.	2,448,544	2,521,576	2,520,056
Selling, general and administrative expenses	424,209	395,452	387,777
Research and development	149,361	120,578	102,366
Interest expense.	35,490	42,020	48,991
Minority interests	1,768	1,518	1,421
Total costs and expenses	3,059,372	3,081,144	3,060,611
Income before income taxes.	269,077	348,645	260,162
Provision for income taxes.	72,524	122,782	71,762
Income from continuing operations	196,553	225,863	188,400
Loss from discontinued operations	—	(187,895)	(19,616)
Net income	$ 196,553	$ 37,968	$ 168,784

was taking the company private in a leveraged buyout. However, initiating a leveraged buyout would mean potentially competing with corporate raiders who might top any bid he would make. Instead, Malott decided to recapitalize the company. Malott explained:

> In many cases leveraged buyouts tend to take advantage of the public shareholders. Management is benefitted out of proportion to the contribution they are making, [but] the public shareholders are not allowed to participate in the results of the leveraging procedure.[2]

The recapitalization plan had three main goals: eliminate a takeover attempt, give FMC employees a greater stake in the company and its future by expanding employee own-

ership, and invest aggressively in existing businesses and concentrate on current and related businesses. Malott realized that the plan involved considerable risk and that earnings would be more sensitive to short-term operating fluctuations, but he expressed confidence that the company's history showed that its debt could be repaid with the cash generated from its operations.

The provisions of the final recapitalization plan that was approved at FMC's annual meeting on May 22, 1986, were as follows:

> *Public Shareholders:* All public shareholders would receive $80 in cash and one share of the recapitalized company for each common share held.
>
> *Management and Employee Benefit Plans:* Management and holders of stock in employee benefit plans would receive 5.67 shares for each share held.

---

[2]Ibid.

Employee Thrift Plan Shareholders: These shareholders would receive 4.209 new shares and $25 per share for each share held.

In addition, 11.3 million shares held by the company's pension plan would be retired in early 1986 to ensure that they could not be seized by anyone seeking control of the company. As a result, employee ownership of FMC would rise from 19 percent to 41 percent and the proportion of stock held by the public would decline from 81 percent to 59 percent. Exhibit 2 shows how the income statement might have appeared if the restructuring had taken place on January 1, 1985, and how the balance sheet would have appeared if the restructuring had taken place on December 31, 1985.

This recapitalization program, dubbed a "leveraged cash-out," resembled a stock split in which only the insiders' shares were split. The public shareholders' equity was diluted by the increase in insiders' shares, but the former were compensated for this dilution with a substantial cash payment and highly favorable tax treatment. (The $80 per share cash-out received capital gains tax treatment for public shareholders.) To finance the sweetened plan, FMC secured a total of $1.4 billion in bank debt and a total of $625 million in subordinated debt from Goldman Sachs. This debt increased FMC's total debt burden from $370 million to $2.2 billion.

The plan approved by shareholders was actually the second plan proposed. The provisions of the preliminary plan closely resembled the final plan, except that public shareholders would have received only $70 cash and one new share for each common share held, and FMC would have incurred only $1.7 billion in new debt to finance the plan ($1.3 billion bank debt and $0.4 billion subordinated debentures). FMC's prelimi-

nary plan had been criticized by some shareholders, most notably, Ivan Boesky. Boesky, along with a group of companies he controlled, had bought a 7.5 percent stake in the corporation.[3] In his filing with the Securities and Exchange Commission (SEC), Boesky had stated that the preliminary recapitalization plan unfairly rewarded management at the expense of public shareholders, and had hinted that he would vote against the proposal at FMC's annual meeting. FMC responded with the final recapitalization plan described above, in which they "sweetened the plan in response to current economic and market conditions."

Though initial word of the recapitalization raised FMC's stock price from $70 to $85 within days, the move met with criticism from some securities analysts. One analyst pointed to "negative stockholders' equity," and noted that FMC's interest payment would be about $250 million in the first year, yet the company had earned only $270 million in pretax income in 1985. Others expressed concern that FMC could not find better uses for its money. These critics felt that the burden of so much debt would diminish the company's ability to make acquisitions and develop internally.

Later Developments. In 1986 the SEC charged that Ivan Boesky and others had engaged in various acts of insider trading of securities. Among the incidents cited in SEC documents was Boesky's purchase of about 95,300 shares of FMC stock between February 18 and 21, 1986, during which period the price per share rose from $73.75 to $85.625. Ultimately, Mr. Boesky sold these shares for a profit of approximately $975,000.

On December 18, 1986, FMC filed a lawsuit against Boesky and others alleging that

---

[3]*Wall Street Journal,* April 29, 1986.

EXHIBIT 2
PRO FORMA FINANCIAL INFORMATION

The Pro Forma Consolidated Income Statement for the year ended December 31, 1985, and the Pro Forma Consolidated Balance Sheet as of December 31, 1985, have been prepared to reflect the Recapitalization, the conversion of the company's outstanding Convertible Securities, the incurrence of obligations under the Bank Agreements, the issuance of the Senior Subordinated Debentures and the Subordinated Debentures, the repayment of certain existing indebtedness, and the payment of costs related to the Recapitalization. The Recapitalization has been accounted for as a redemption of Shares not subject to purchase accounting.

The Pro Forma Consolidated Income Statement was prepared as if the Recapitalization had occurred on January 1, 1985. The Pro Forma Consolidated Balance Sheet was prepared as if the Recapitalization had occurred on December 31, 1985.

No changes in revenues and expenses have been made to reflect the results of any modification to operations that might have been made had the Recapitalization been consummated on the assumed effective dates of the Recapitalization for presenting pro forma results. The pro forma expenses include the recurring costs that are directly attributed to the Recapitalization, such as interest expense arising from the Financing and the related tax effects thereof. The pro forma financial information does not purport to be indicative of the results that would actually have been obtained had such transactions been completed as of the date and for the periods presented or that may be obtained in the future.

PRO FORMA CONSOLIDATED INCOME STATEMENT
(in thousands, except per-share data)

	Year Ended December 31, 1985	
	Actual	*Pro Forma*
	(unaudited)	
Revenue		
Sales	$ 3,260,847	$ 3,260,847
Equity in net earnings of affiliates	15,445	15,445
Interest income	32,108	17,328
Other income	20,049	20,049
Total revenue	3,328,449	3,313,669
Costs and expenses		
Cost of sales	2,448,544	2,452,777
Selling, general and administrative expenses	424,209	424,209
Research and development	149,361	149,361
Interest expense	35,490	255,342
Minority interests	1,768	1,768
Total costs and expenses	3,059,372	3,283,457
Income before income taxes	269,077	30,212
Provision for income taxes (benefit)	72,524	(33,387)
Net income	$ 196,553	$ 63,599
Ratio of earnings to fixed charges	5.3	1.1

(continued)

EXHIBIT 2 *(continued)*
PRO FORMA CONSOLIDATED BALANCE SHEET
(in thousands)

	Year Ended December 31, 1985	
	Actual	*Pro forma*
	(unaudited)	
ASSETS		
Current Assets		
Cash	$ 6,794	$ 6,794
Marketable securities.	155,124	75,724
Trade receivables, net.	454,373	154,373
Inventories	232,444	232,444
Other current assets.	96,818	96,818
Deferred income taxes	158,949	158,949
Total current assets	1,104,502	725,102
Investments	179,054	179,054
Property, plant, and equipment, net	1,327,625	1,327,625
Patents and deferred charges.	59,802	119,802
Intangibles of acquired companies.	19,739	19,739
Total assets	$2,690,722	$2,371,322
LIABILITIES AND STOCKHOLDERS' EQUITY (Deficit)		
Current Liabilities		
Short-term debt.	$ 37,475	—
Accounts payable, trade and other	465,740	$ 465,740
Accrued payroll.	92,536	92,536
Accrued and other liabilities.	225,452	225,452
Reserve for discontinued operations	117,291	57,291
Current portion of long-term debt	30,209	—
Income taxes payable	45,284	45,284
Total current liabilities.	1,013,987	886,303
Long-term debt, less current portion	303,210	1,900,310
Deferred income taxes	243,146	243,146
Minority interests in consolidated companies.	7,279	7,279
Stockholders' Equity (Deficit)		
Preferred stock, no par value, authorized 5,000,000 shares; $2.25 cumulative convertible; preference value $24,553 .	3,069	—
Common stock, $5 par value, authorized 60,000,000 shares.	178,948	—
Common stock, $.10 par value		4,531
Capital in excess of par value of capital stock.	105,354	—
Retained earnings.	1,440,204	(579,563)
Foreign currency translation adjustment	(90,684)	(90,684)
Treasury stock, common, at cost	(513,791)	—
Total stockholders' equity (deficit).	1,123,100	(665,716)
Total liabilities and stockholders' equity.	$2,690,722	$2,371,322
Book value per common share	$42.75	($19.60)

(continued)

EXHIBIT 2 *(concluded)*
PRO FORMA CHANGEs IN CASH DUE TO THE RECAPITALIZATION
(in millions)

Accounts receivable facility	$ 300.0*
Revolving credit facility	1,000.0
Senior subordinated debentures	225.0
Subordinated debentures	400.0
Cash payment of $80.00 per share to public stockholders (assumes conversion of all outstanding convertible securities)	(1,735.6)
Cash payment of $25.00 per share for shares held by the stock fund of thrift plan	(59.6)
Retirement of debt outstanding at December 31, 1985	(89.2)
Construction equipment receivables reacquired from FMC Finance and deducted from reserve for discontinued operations	(60.0)
Estimated fees and expenses	(60.0)
Net change in cash	$ (79.4)

Sources: Proxy Statement/Prospectus, May 2, 1986.
*The $300.0 million reduction in trade receivables reflects the sale of accounts receivable pursuant to the Accounts Receivable Facility.

their illegal insider trading added to the cost of the company's recapitalization plan. The lawsuits charged that the insider trading meant that FMC had to sweeten the plan by $10 per share, adding approximately $225 million to the cost of the plan for FMC. The suit also named Drexel, Burnham, Lambert; Goldman Sachs; Shearson Lehman Brothers; David Brown; Dennis Levine; and Ira Sokolow. FMC sought total damages of $260 million, including $225 million to cover its additional recapitalization costs, recovery of the $975,000 profit made by Boesky, and a $17.5 million fee paid by FMC to Goldman Sachs, its financial adviser. In announcing the lawsuit Mr. Malott stated, "The freedoms and obligations of the free market system have been jeopardized by Wall Street players caught in the grip of takeover fever and get-rich-quick schemes."[4]

---

[4]*Boston Globe,* April 14, 1987.

Questions

1. What are the implications of the different "deals" for the three different categories of common stockholders under the recapitalization?

2. Using the historical and pro forma information in Exhibits 1 and 2, explain as specifically as you can how the proposed restructuring was to be accomplished and how the financial condition and performance of FMC would be affected. Try to reconstruct the journal entries that the restructuring required. The following hints may be helpful as you attempt this reconstruction:

   a. Figure out which balance sheet accounts change or are affected by the restructuring transactions; set up T accounts for these accounts.

   b. Treat *all* of stockholders' equity as a single T account; that is, you are only concerned with *total* stockholders' equity.

   c. Treat the actual 1985 balance sheet like a beginning balance sheet. Post the beginning balances to the selected T accounts.

d. Post the pro forma changes in cash (from Exhibit 2) to your T accounts. The resultant ending balance sheet should be (or should closely resemble) the pro forma 1985 balance sheet, because this is what you are trying to explain.

3. What is meant by "negative stockholders' equity"? What do you think the implications of this will be?

4. Do you believe that the lenders knew that FMC would give so much cash to the stockholders? Did they know that the stockholders' equity account would be negative? Did FMC's lenders truly believe that FMC's equity had a negative value? If not, why not?

5. If you were an employee of FMC, how would you feel about the recapitalization? If you were an FMC plant manager and the plant needed new equipment, would you submit a new equipment proposal for corporate headquarters' approval following the recapitalization?

CASE 9–3 Trelease Industries, Inc.*

Trelease Industries, Inc., was a diversified firm whose stock was traded on a regional stock exchange. Information related to the firm's capital structure and income is given below.

Market Price of Common Stock. The following table reflects the average market price of Trelease's common stock over a three-year period:

	19x2	19x1	19x0
	Average Price		
First quarter	50	45	40
Second quarter	60	52	41
Third quarter	70	50	40
Fourth quarter	70	50	45
December 31 closing price . .	72	51	44

Cash Dividends. Cash dividends of $0.375 per common share were declared and paid for each quarter of 19x0 and 19x1. Cash dividends of $0.75 per common share were declared and paid for each quarter of 19x2.

Convertible Debentures. Seven percent convertible debentures with a principal amount of $10,000,000 due in 20 years were issued for cash at a price of $100 in the last quarter of 19x0. Each $100 par value debenture was convertible into two shares of common stock. No debentures were converted during 19x0 or 19x1. The entire issue was converted at the beginning of the third quarter of 19x2 because the issue was called by the company. These convertible debentures were *not* common stock equivalents under the terms of *Opinion No. 15*. The Aa bond[1] rate at the time the debentures were issued was 10 percent. The debentures carried a coupon interest rate of 7 percent and had a market value of $100 at issuance. The effective yield of 7 percent was not less than 66⅔ percent of the Aa bond rate. Effective yield is the same as the coupon interest rate in this case only because the market value at issuance was $100.

Convertible Preferred Stock. At the beginning of the second quarter of 19x1, 600,000 shares of convertible preferred stock were issued for assets in a purchase transaction. The annual dividend on each share of this convertible preferred stock is $0.70. Each share is convertible into one share of

---

*This case is based on the illustrative example given in *APB Opinion No. 15* (May 1969), as amended by *FASB Statements No. 55* (February 1982) and *No. 85* (March 1985).

[1]"Aa" is the next-to-highest quality rating given bonds by the two major rating services, Moody's and Standard & Poor's. ("Aaa" is the highest rating.)

common stock. This convertible stock had a market value of $53 at the time of issuance and *was* therefore a common stock equivalent under the terms of *Opinion No. 15* at the time of its issuance because the effective yield on market value was only 1.3 percent and the Aa bond rate was 12 percent. Holders of 500,000 shares of this convertible preferred stock converted their preferred stock into common stock during 19x2 because the cash dividend on the common stock exceeded the cash dividend on the preferred stock.

Warrants. Warrants to buy 500,000 shares of common stock at $60 per share for a period of five years were issued along with the convertible preferred stock mentioned above. No warrants have been exercised.

The number of common shares represented by the warrants was 71,428 for each of the third and fourth quarters of 19x2 ($60 exercise price * 500,000 warrants = $30,000,000; $30,000,000 ÷ $70 per share market price = 428,572 shares; 500,000 shares − 428,572 shares = 71,428 shares). No shares were deemed to be represented by the warrants for the second quarter of 19x2 or for any preceding quarter because the market price of the stock did not exceed the exercise price for substantially all of three consecutive months until the third quarter of 19x2.

Common Stock. The number of shares of common stock outstanding was as follows:

	19x2	19x1
Beginning of year	3,300,000	3,300,000
Conversion of preferred stock	500,000	—
Conversion of debentures	200,000	—
End of year	4,000,000	3,300,000

Weighted-Average Number of Shares. The weighted-average number of shares of common stock equivalents was determined as follows:

	19x2	19x1
Common stock:		
Shares outstanding from beginning of period	3,300,000	3,300,000
500,000 shares issued on conversion of preferred stock; assume issuance evenly during year	250,000	—
200,000 shares issued on conversion of convertible debentures at beginning of third quarter of 19x2	100,000	—
	3,650,000	3,300,000
Common stock equivalents:		
600,000 shares convertible preferred stock issued at the beginning of the second quarter of 19x1, excluding 250,000 shares included under common stock in 19x2	350,000	450,000
Warrants: 71,428 common share equivalents outstanding for third and fourth quarters of 19x2, i.e., one-half year	35,714	—
	385,714	450,000
Weighted-average number of shares	4,035,714	3,750,000

The weighted-average number of shares would be adjusted to calculate fully diluted earnings per share, as is shown in this table:

	19x2	19x1
Weighted-average number of shares......................	4,035,714	3,750,000
Shares applicable to convertible debentures converted at the beginning of the third quarter of 19x2, excluding 100,000 shares included under common stock for 19x2..	100,000	200,000
Shares applicable to warrants included above	(35,714)	—
Shares applicable to warrants based on year-end price of $72...	83,333	—
	4,183,333	3,950,000

Net Income. Income before extraordinary item and net income would be adjusted for interest expense on the debentures in calculating fully diluted earnings per share. Taxes in 19x1 and 19x2 were 46 percent. Trelease's net income (before preferred stock dividends) was as follows:

19x2:	Income before extra-	
	ordinary item.............	$12,900,000
	Net income................	13,800,000
19x1:	Net income................	10,300,000

Questions

1. Be prepared to explain the calculations shown above for arriving at the weighted-average number of common shares, common stock equivalents, and fully diluted shares.

2. Starting with the item "Income before extraordinary item," complete the remainder of the 19x2 and 19x1 income statements.

3. Compute Trelease's primary and fully diluted earnings per share for 19x2 and 19x1.

10

Other Items That Affect Net Income

The preceding chapters discussed the accounting treatment of many of the items that affect net income. This chapter discusses additional items—personnel costs, income taxes, extraordinary items, discontinued operations, accounting changes, and foreign currency accounting problems—and completes the more detailed discussion of income statement and balance sheet items that began with Chapter 5.

PERSONNEL COSTS

Personnel costs include wages and salaries earned by employees and other costs related to their services. (Customarily, the word *wages* refers to the compensation of employees who are paid on a piece-rate, hourly, daily, or weekly basis, whereas the word *salaries* refers to compensation expressed in longer terms; we use *wages* to denote either category.) The effect on the accounting records of earning and paying wages is more complicated than merely debiting Wages Expense and crediting Cash. This is because when wages are earned or paid, certain other transactions occur almost automatically.

Employees are rarely paid the gross amount of wages they earn, since from their gross earnings the following must be deducted:

1. An amount representing the employee's FICA (for Federal Insurance

Contribution Act) contributions for Social Security and Medicare coverage. In 1994 Social Security tax was 6.2 percent of the first $60,600 of wages earned each year; the Medicare tax was 1.45 percent of wages, without limit.

2. An amount withheld from gross earnings to apply toward the employee's personal state and federal income taxes.

3. Deductions for charitable contributions, savings plans, union dues, and a variety of other items.

None of these deductions represents a cost *to the employer.* In the case of the tax deductions, the employer is acting as a collection agent for the state and federal governments. The withholding of these amounts and their subsequent transfer to the government does not affect net income or owners' equity. Rather, the withholding creates a liability, and the subsequent transfer to the government pays off this liability. Similarly, the employer is acting as a collection agent in the case of the other deductions. The employee is paid the net amount after these deductions have been taken.

When wages are earned, certain other costs are automatically created. The employer must pay a tax equal in amount to the employee's FICA tax, and the employer must also pay an additional percentage of the employee's pay for the *unemployment insurance tax.* The *employer's* share of these taxes *is* an element of cost.

> **Example.** If an employee with three dependents earned $600 for work in a certain week in 1994, $45.90 for FICA tax contribution and $63.00 for withholding tax would be deducted from this $600, and the employee's take-home pay would be $491.10. (Other possible deductions are omitted.) The *employer* would incur an expense of $45.90 for FICA and an additional expense of, say, $54 for federal and state unemployment insurance taxes, or a total of $99.90 for employment taxes.
>
> The journal entries for these transactions are as follows:

1. When wages are earned:

Wages Cost[1]	600.00	
Wages Payable		600.00

Employment Tax Cost	99.90	
FICA Taxes Payable		45.90
Unemployment Taxes Payable		54.00

2. When the employee is paid:

Wages Payable	600.00	
Cash		491.10
FICA Taxes Payable		45.90
Withholding Taxes Payable		63.00

---

[1]As pointed out previously, manufacturing labor costs are a product cost debited to Work in Process Inventory. Other labor costs are period costs debited to Wage and Salary Expense. We use the account Wages Cost here to include either of these.

3. When the government is paid:

```
FICA Taxes Payable (45.90 + 45.90) . . . . . . . . . .  91.80
Unemployment Taxes Payable. . . . . . . . . . . . . . . .  54.00
Withholding Taxes Payable. . . . . . . . . . . . . . . . . .  63.00
    Cash. . . . . . . . . . . . . . . . . . . . . . . . . . . . . . . . . . . . . .           208.80
```

In practice the above entries would be made for all employees as a group. The government does require, however, that a record be kept of the amount of FICA tax and withholding tax accumulated for each employee.

In addition to cash wages or salaries, most organizations provide **fringe benefits** to their employees. Among these are pensions, life insurance, health care, and vacations. Such fringe benefits may amount to as much as 40 percent of payroll. These amounts are costs of the period in which the employee worked, just as are the cash earnings. Accounting for many of these fringe benefits is relatively straightforward. However, that is not the case with pensions.

Pensions

Payments that employees will receive after they retire are called **pensions.** Pension costs are typically in the range of 5 to 10 percent of payroll. In some organizations employees contribute part of their pension cost, and this cost is a payroll deduction that is treated just like the other deductions mentioned above. It does not involve a cost to the organization. The employer's contribution for pension benefits *is* a cost to the employer, just as are other fringe benefits.

Pension plans are regulated under the Employee Retirement Income Security Act of 1974 (ERISA). The provisions of this act are such that in most cases pension plans must be **funded.** This means that the company must make pension plan contributions in cash to a bank, insurance company, or other trustee for the pension fund. However, the law does not require that a plan be *fully* funded. That is, at a given point in time, the plan assets do not have to be sufficient to provide all future plan benefits that have already been earned by employees if no further contributions were made to the plan. For example, as of 1993 General Motors' pension plan was underfunded by $1.2 billion, almost double GM's shareholders' equity.

The trustee invests the contributions and pays pension benefits directly to employees after they retire. The pension fund is therefore a separate entity, with its own set of accounts. As an indication of the significance of pension plans in the United States, as of 1993 the total assets of such plans totaled nearly $2.5 *trillion,* which was almost 40 percent of the country's total financial assets.[2]

Types of Pension Plans. There are two general types of pension plans: (1) defined contribution plans and (2) defined benefit plans.

---

[2]Source: Pension and Welfare Benefits Administration.

In a **defined contribution plan,** the employer contributes to the pension fund an agreed amount each year for each employee, often determined as a percentage of the employee's salary. The employee's pension benefits thus depend on how much has been accumulated (contributions plus gains on the investments of those contributions) for her or him as of the date of retirement. There is no promise as to how much those benefits (*outputs* of the plan) will be; the agreement relates only to plan contributions (*inputs*). Thus, by definition, a defined contribution plan is never underfunded or overfunded. In such plans, common in educational institutions but less so in other organizations, the organization's pension cost for a year is simply the agreed-upon contribution. The entry recording this cost is:

```
Pension Cost ........................................ 100,000
     Cash ...........................................          100,000
```

In a **defined benefit plan** the employer agrees to contribute to the pension fund an amount large enough so that employees will receive a specified amount of monthly benefits after retirement. This amount depends upon the employee's years of service before retirement, the employee's average earnings during some period immediately preceding retirement, and possibly upon other factors. Thus, this plan's benefits (outputs) are agreed upon and the company must determine the amount of contributions (inputs) necessary to provide these benefits.

Pension Cost.   The determination of the amount of annual pension cost for a defined benefit plan is extremely complicated. *FASB Statement No. 87*[3] is 132 pages long, including 11 pages of definitions. We will provide only a conceptual overview of these matters.

To calculate its pension contribution in a given year, the company must first make a number of estimates: how many years employees will work until they retire; employee turnover; average earnings on which the pension benefits will be calculated; how many years the employee will live after retirement; probable increases in benefit payments due to inflation, new union contracts, or other factors; and the amount that the pension fund will earn on funds invested in it. The pension calculations incorporating these estimates are based on the present value concept.

The year's **service cost** is the present value of the future benefits employees have earned during the year. The year's **interest cost** is the amount by which the present value of the plan's beginning-of-the-year obligations has increased during the year. Offsetting these two cost elements is the **actual return on plan assets,** which is the gain in the fair value of the plan's assets during the year, adjusted for plan contributions and benefit payments made during the year. (If a loss, it is *added* to the service cost and interest cost elements.)

---

[3]"Employers' Accounting for Pensions," *FASB Statement No. 87* (December 1985).

The fourth element of pension cost relates to the amortization of several other pension-related items. One of these is **prior service cost.** This cost arises if a new pension plan is instituted and it takes into account employees' service prior to the initiation of the new plan. Prior service cost can also arise if a plan is amended or "sweetened"— the terms are made more generous with the result that the contributions to date are inadequate to meet the amended obligations. Rather than having the cost of such a "sweetening" impact only the year in which the plan is amended, the present value of the added benefits is amortized over the expected service life of the employees affected by the amendment.

The year's **net pension cost** is the algebraic sum of the four elements just described: service cost plus interest cost minus actual return (or plus actual loss) plus amortization. Not surprisingly, most companies engage an **actuary,** a professional who specializes in such matters, to make all of the estimates and calculations that eventually boil down to this one amount for net pension cost.[4]

Accounting Entries.   The year's pension cost for a defined benefit plan is an adjusting entry, analogous to the entry for accrued interest expense payable. If the net pension cost for the year were $500,000, the entry would be:

```
Net Pension Cost....................................  500,000
     Unfunded Accrued Pension Cost (a liability)......           500,000
```

If a subsequent contribution of $450,000 were made to the plan by the employer, the entry would be:

```
Unfunded Accrued Pension Cost.....................  450,000
     Cash.............................................           450,000
```

Note that this liability is related to how much of the employer's accrued pension cost has not as yet been contributed to the separate pension plan entity. If the employer has contributed *more* than the amount of its accrued pension cost, then the excess is recorded as Prepaid Pension Cost, an asset.

Disclosure.   In addition to reporting the period's net pension cost and unfunded plan position, for each of its defined benefit plans a company must disclose a number of detailed items, such as each of the four components of net pension cost and the elements of the calculation of a plan's funding position. These details are reported in a note to the financial statements. Also, the plan itself must make certain disclosures as an entity.[5]

---

[4]The FASB uses the term *net pension cost* rather than *net pension expense* for the same reason we used Wages Cost rather than Wages Expense in the previous section: Pension costs for manufacturing employees may be capitalized as part of the cost of inventory rather than treated as a period expense.

[5]"Accounting and Reporting by Defined Benefit Pension Plans," *FASB Statement No. 35* (March 1980).

Other Postretirement Benefits

Beginning no later than 1993, companies are also required by *FASB Statement No. 106* to make disclosures of **nonpension postretirement benefits,** such as health care and life insurance benefits.[6] Formerly, such expenses were recognized on a pay-as-you-go basis. Now, the substance of accounting for these benefits is similar to that for pensions: The total costs that will be incurred by retirees is estimated and a portion of the present value of these costs is charged as an expense in each year that an employee works. For health care costs, this requires estimating employees' needs for postretirement health care services as well as the future cost of such services. These are even more difficult and uncertain estimates than those required for pensions.

For many companies this requirement resulted in identification of a huge obligation for previously unfunded and unrecognized future nonpension postretirement benefits that employees already had earned. Companies were given the choice of treating this obligation either as (1) a change in accounting principle (described later in this chapter), with the entire obligation treated as an expense of the period in which the change was made; or (2) on a delayed basis, amortizing the obligation on a straight-line basis over the average remaining service period of active plan participants or 20 years, whichever is longer. Many companies elected the first, "one-big-hit" approach; as an extreme case, for General Motors this approach reduced 1992 net earnings by $20.8 billion ($33.38 per share).

Until they were required to do so by *FASB 106,* many companies had not estimated the overhanging burden of future health care benefits. This led some companies to reduce such benefits, which in some cases led to labor disputes.

Compensated Absences

In some organizations any vacation and sick leave days that were *earned* this year but *not used* this year can be carried forward and used at some future time. If the amount can be reasonably estimated, the cost of these **future compensated absences** is treated as an expense of the period in which the future absence time is *earned.* The offsetting credit is to an accrued liability account. When the employee is later compensated, the liability account is debited and Cash is credited.[7]

INCOME TAXES

To the beginning accounting student, accounting for income taxes might seem to be straightforward. One might think that all that is involved is calculating the year's income tax liability—the year's tax bill—and then

---

[6]"Employers' Accounting for Postretirement Benefits Other Than Pensions," *FASB Statement No. 106* (December 1990).
[7]"Accounting for Compensated Absences," *FASB Statement No. 43* (November 1980).

debiting this amount to Income Tax Expense and crediting it to Income Tax Liability. (Some companies call the tax expense account **Provision for Income Taxes.** Also, the liability account may be called **Taxes Payable.**) Unfortunately, income tax accounting is not so simple.

Book-to-Tax Differences

For most revenue and expense transactions the amount used in calculating taxable income for income tax purposes is the same as the amount used in calculating pretax income in the income statement as prepared for shareholders. (The term **taxable income** always means income as reported to the taxing authorities; **pretax accounting income,** or **pretax book income,** refers to the amount reported in the income statement that is prepared in accordance with GAAP.) Taxable income and pretax book income are affected in the same way by most revenue and expense transactions. However, *most* is not the same as *all* transactions. Those transactions that are *not* reported in the same way for book and tax purposes cause a difference between pretax book income and taxable income. It is these **book-to-tax differences** that create the complications in accounting for income taxes.

Why the Difference? Before further explaining these complications we should consider why the difference between taxable income and book income arises. The answer essentially is that the process of income taxation has little to do with the reporting of financial information to shareholders and other interested outside parties. Income tax laws are formulated, in part, to encourage certain kinds of behavior by taxpayers on the premise that such behavior is good for the economy as a whole. For example, the accelerated depreciation provisions of the corporate tax law are intended to encourage investment in fixed assets. By contrast, GAAP is formulated to accomplish the objectives of financial reporting (described in Chapter 1), including providing information that is useful to investors and creditors in making rational investment and credit decisions.

As a specific example of the different perspectives of taxation and financial reporting, consider depreciation. If a corporation acquires an asset that qualifies for accelerated depreciation over six years for tax purposes, the corporation should take advantage of that provision of the law; it should depreciate the asset as rapidly as the law permits. Assuming nonincreasing tax rates over time, the present value of the tax savings associated with reporting a dollar of depreciation expense now is greater than the present value of the savings if the expense is reported in the future. On the other hand, if the corporation believes that the asset will give up its benefits in a *level stream* over an *eight-year* period, the depreciation method customarily used in financial reporting is the straight-line method, which, for an eight-year life, would have an annual rate of 12.5 percent. Over the useful life of the asset, this method will provide the appropriate *matching* of the asset's original cost with the benefits received from using the asset. Thus, the company would be completely justified in using straight-line depreciation for book purposes while at the same time using accelerated depreciation for tax purposes.

Some critics of business like to suggest that there is something cynical or evil about these book versus tax differences. But there is nothing wrong with a corporation's (or an individual's) doing everything legally permitted to reduce income taxes. As Supreme Court Justice Learned Hand wrote in 1947 in *Commissioner* vs. *Newman:*

> Over and over again courts have said there is nothing sinister in so arranging one's affairs as to keep taxes as low as possible. Everybody does so, rich or poor, and all do right, for nobody owes any public duty to pay more than the law demands; taxes are enforced exactions, not voluntary contributions. To demand more in the name of morals is mere cant.

Permanent and Temporary Differences. There are two important classes of book-to-tax differences. First, the income tax regulations prohibit certain deductions from taxable income that are expenses under GAAP, and they permit certain revenue items to be excluded from taxable income. For example, fines are not tax deductible, and interest revenue on municipal bonds is not taxable. These exceptions create **permanent differences** between pretax book income and tax income. The differences are permanent in the sense that they will not reverse or "turn around" in some subsequent year.

In other situations the income tax regulations permit or require revenues or expenses to be recognized in a *different period* than the recognition method used in financial reporting. For example, the tax law permits certain types of business to use the installment method for recognizing revenues, even though the company may use the sales method for financial reporting. Another example is estimated warranty expense; GAAP requires that this be accrued in the period in which the warranted items are sold, whereas the tax law does not permit a deduction until the period in which warranty costs are actually incurred. These book-to-tax accounting recognition differences lead to **temporary differences** (also called **timing differences**). These differences *do* reverse or "turn around" in later periods. For example, for a given installment sale contract, the total amount of revenue recognized for book (delivery method) and tax (installment method) purposes is the same over the *entire life* of the contract; but the amount recognized in *any one year* will differ if the installment contract collections span more than one year.

No special accounting problem arises in the case of permanent differences. For a "tax preference," such as the municipal bond interest exclusion, the amount reported to shareholders as income tax expense of the current period is simply lower than it would be if the preferential treatment did not exist. Permanent differences lower the effective tax rate that is applied to pretax book income. For an unallowable deduction, such as a fine, the reported income tax expense will be higher than if the expense could be also deducted for tax purposes.

By contrast, temporary differences do create complications in accounting for income tax expense. The reason has to do with the matching concept. The FASB feels that in each period a current or deferred tax consequence should be recognized for all events that have been recognized in the financial statements. This means that, ignoring permanent differences, the amount of reported income tax expense is the amount of tax that would be due *if* the amount of pretax book income had also been reported to the government as taxable income. For example, assuming a 34 percent tax rate, if in some year a corporation reports $1 million pretax income, then it should also report $340,000 income tax expense, *irrespective of the amount of the company's actual tax obligation for that year.* The FASB believes that it would be misleading or confusing to users of the income statement if an amount of income tax expense other than $340,000 were reported when $1 million pretax income is reported and the tax rate is 34 percent.

Deferred Taxes   It might occur to the reader that if Income Tax Expense is debited without regard to the company's *actual* tax bill but Cash must be credited based on the payment of that actual bill, then the dual aspect principle of accounting will be violated—less formally, "the books won't balance."

> **Example.** Because of temporary differences, in 19x1 a corporation reported $1 million pretax income to its shareholders but only $800,000 taxable income to the IRS. Thus, its income tax expense was $340,000, but its actual income taxes were only $272,000 (= $800,000 * 0.34). Assume that these taxes have been paid (i.e., the taxes have all been credited to Cash; none is still a credit in Taxes Payable). Since an expense reduces Retained Earnings, we can think of these transactions solely in terms of their impact on the balance sheet:

Assets	= Liabilities +	Owners' Equity
Cash −272,000		Retained Earnings −340,000
(reflecting actual		(reflecting tax rate applied
tax bill payments)		to pretax book income)

> *Question:* Is the missing $68,000 (= $340,000 − $272,000) credit entry a further reduction in assets, or is it an increase in a liability account or an owners' equity account?

The answer is that the credit is an increase in a liability account called **Deferred Income Taxes.** In journal entry form, the combined income tax expense and income tax payment transaction is:

```
Income Tax Expense ................................ 340,000
     Cash............................................      272,000
     Deferred Income Taxes .........................       68,000
```

Rationale for Deferred Taxes. The meaning of, and rationale for, deferred taxes is best introduced with an example. The example will illustrate temporary differences created by the use of different depreciation methods for book and tax purposes, which is the most common source of timing differences in practice. Assume that a company purchased for $1,000,000 a single asset that fell into the five-year class for income tax purposes. The income tax cost recovery (depreciation) allowances for such an asset are $200,000, $320,000, $192,000, $115,200, $115,200, and $57,600 for years one through six respectively. (Recall from Chapter 7 that, owing to the half-year convention, a "five-year" asset's depreciation is actually spread out over six years.) Assume that for financial reporting purposes, the company will use the straight-line method over eight years, the estimated useful life of the asset; assuming no residual value for the asset, this results in depreciation expense of $125,000 per year. There are no other differences between the company's book and tax accounting methods; the amount of income for book and tax purposes, *before* subtracting depreciation expense, is $1 million per year. Finally, assume that the applicable tax rate is 40 percent (to include both federal and state income taxes).

Part A of Illustration 10–1 shows how the company would calculate its *income taxes* in each of these eight years. Note that by the end of 19x6, the asset is fully depreciated for *tax* purposes even though it has two remaining years of actual service life.

Part B shows the calculation of income tax expense for *financial reporting* purposes. Note that over the entire eight-year life span of the asset, the same total amount of depreciation ($1 million) is reported for both tax and book purposes. Thus, the eight-year totals for taxable income and pretax book income are equal ($7 million), as are the totals for income taxes paid and income tax expense ($2.8 million). However, the different depreciation methods result in temporary (timing) differences as to how these totals are distributed across the eight years.

Part C shows how the difference between a year's income tax expense and taxes paid affects the Deferred Income Taxes account. Positive amounts shown in the column labeled Income Tax Deferred are credits to Deferred Income Taxes; negative amounts (shown in parentheses) are debits. This account increases to a balance of $134,800 before it begins to decrease. The decreases beginning in 19x4 reflect *timing difference reversals.* These reversals are caused by the fact that, starting in 19x4, the straight-line depreciation charge of $125,000 for pretax book income calculations exceeds the cost recovery allowance used in determining taxable income. Because the total amount of depreciation expense over the eight-year useful life of the asset is the same ($1 million) for book and tax purposes, the timing difference reversals completely eliminate the balance in Deferred Income Taxes by the end of 19x8.

For any year during the eight-year period, the balance in Deferred Income Taxes can be thought of as an interest-free loan from the government that has resulted from the Congress passing a tax law that allows accelerated depreciation for calculating taxable income rather than allowing only straight-line depreciation. For example, the deferred tax balance at the end of 19x3 means that the company has been able to *postpone* (or defer) paying income taxes of $134,800 by taking advantage of the tax law's accelerated

ILLUSTRATION 10–1
DEFERRED TAXES RELATED TO A SINGLE ASSET
(thousands of dollars)

Part A. Calculation of Income Taxes

Year	Income before Depreciation and Taxes	Cost Recovery Allowance	Taxable Income	Income Tax (at 40 percent)
19x1	$1,000.0	$ 200.0	$ 800.0	$ 320.0
19x2	1,000.0	320.0	680.0	272.0
19x3	1,000.0	192.0	808.0	323.2
19x4	1,000.0	115.2	884.8	353.9
19x5	1,000.0	115.2	884.8	353.9
19x6	1,000.0	57.6	942.4	377.0
19x7	1,000.0	—	1,000.0	400.0
19x8	1,000.0	—	1,000.0	400.0
	$8,000.0	$1,000.0	$7,000.0	$2,800.0

Part B. Calculation of Income Tax Expense

Year	Income before Depreciation and Taxes	Depreciation Allowance	Pretax Income	Income Tax Expense (at 40 percent)
19x1	$1,000.0	$ 125.0	$ 875.0	$ 350.0
19x2	1,000.0	125.0	875.0	350.0
19x3	1,000.0	125.0	875.0	350.0
19x4	1,000.0	125.0	875.0	350.0
19x5	1,000.0	125.0	875.0	350.0
19x6	1,000.0	125.0	875.0	350.0
19x7	1,000.0	125.0	875.0	350.0
19x8	1,000.0	125.0	875.0	350.0
	$8,000.0	$1,000.0	$7,000.0	$2,800.0

Part C. Deferred Income Taxes Account

Year	(1) Income Tax Expense (Part B)	(2) Income Taxes (Part A)	Income Tax Deferred (1) − (2)	Year-End Balance in Deferred Income Taxes*
19x1	$ 350.0	$ 320.0	$ 30.0	$ 30.0
19x2	350.0	272.0	78.0	108.0
19x3	350.0	323.2	26.8	134.8
19x4	350.0	353.9	(3.9)	130.9
19x5	350.0	353.9	(3.9)	127.0
19x6	350.0	377.0	(27.0)	100.0
19x7	350.0	400.0	(50.0)	50.0
19x8	350.0	400.0	(50.0)	0.0

*The beginning balance is assumed to be zero.

depreciation provision. This is like having an interest-free $134,800 loan, compared with what would be the case if straight-line depreciation had to be used for tax purposes.

Accounting Entries

The actual income tax due for a year is calculated as in Part A and is recorded in the following journal entry (for 19x1):

```
Income Tax Expense ............................... 320,000
    Income Taxes Payable .......................        320,000
```

The income tax expense amount is then adjusted to reflect the income tax that should be matched with pretax accounting income. For 19x1, this requires an addition of $30,000 (= $350,000 − $320,000) to Income Tax Expense, so the entry is:

```
Income Tax Expense ............................... 30,000
    Deferred Income Taxes .........................        30,000
```

After this entry Income Tax Expense totals $350,000, which is the amount reported on the income statement for 19x1.

When the taxes are paid, the entry is:[8]

```
Income Taxes Payable ............................. 320,000
    Cash ...........................................        320,000
```

Combining all three entries, the *net* effect is as shown in this single entry:

```
Income Tax Expense ............................... 350,000
    Cash ...........................................        320,000
    Deferred Income Taxes .........................         30,000
```

Nature of Deferred Income Taxes Liability.   Deferred Income Taxes is a liability account. It is shown separately from Income Tax Liability (or Taxes Payable), which is the amount actually owed the government at the time. Deferred Income Taxes is not a liability in the sense that the amount is an obligation owed to the government as of the date of the balance sheet. It is a liability only in the sense of a deferred credit to income. It is an amount that will reduce income tax expense in the years in which income tax actually paid exceeds the amount of financial accounting income tax expense (19x4–x8 in the example).

As was shown in Part C, column 4, the $134,800 by which reported income tax expense exceeded actual taxes paid in the early years (19x1–x3) exactly equaled the $134,800 by which income taxes paid exceeded income tax expense in the later years (19x4–x8). Thus, at the end of the life of the asset, the balance in the Deferred Income Tax account was zero. This is always the case with respect to a single asset. If, however, we drop the assumption that the company operates with only a single asset and make instead the more realistic assumption that a company acquires additional assets each year, a strange situation develops in the Deferred Income Taxes liability account. This is shown in Illustration 10–2.

---

[8]In practice, corporations must make estimated payments throughout the year, just as individuals do.

ILLUSTRATION 10–2
BEHAVIOR OF DEFERRED TAX ACCOUNT
(thousands of dollars)

	Changes in Deferred Income Taxes Account								
	19x1	*19x2*	*19x3*	*19x4*	*19x5*	*19x6*	*19x7*	*19x8*	*19x9*
Beginning balance ..	0.0	30.0	138.0	272.8	403.7	530.7	630.7	680.7	680.7
For asset added in:									
19x1	30.0	78.0	26.8	−3.9	−3.9	−27.0	−50.0	−50.0	
19x2		30.0	78.0	26.8	−3.9	−3.9	−27.0	−50.0	−50.0
19x3			30.0	78.0	26.8	−3.9	−3.9	−27.0	−50.0
19x4				30.0	78.0	26.8	−3.9	−3.9	−27.0
19x5					30.0	78.0	26.8	−3.9	−3.9
19x6						30.0	78.0	26.8	−3.9
19x7							30.0	78.0	26.8
19x8								30.0	78.0
19x9 (replaces 19x1 asset)									30.0
Ending balance	30.0	138.0	272.8	403.7	530.7	630.7	680.7	680.7	680.7

The illustration assumes that the situation described for Illustration 10–1 is repeated each year. Each year the company acquires an identical $1 million asset, using the accelerated cost recovery deductions for tax purposes, while depreciating the asset on a straight-line basis over eight years for calculating reported income. For the first eight years (19x1–x8), these acquisitions make the company grow in size. Thereafter, each year's acquisition only replaces the asset acquired eight years previously, whose service life has just ended.

In 19x1 Deferred Income Taxes increases by the $30,000 shown in Part C of Illustration 10–1. In 19x2 it increases another $78,000 for the asset acquired in 19x1, plus $30,000 for the additional asset acquired in 19x2. From 19x3 to 19x7 the balance in Deferred Income Taxes increases still further. In 19x4 the timing differences from the 19x1 asset start to reverse; this reversal is $3,900 in 19x4. But this 19x4 reversal is more than offset by the 19x4 credits for the 19x2–x4 assets, so the balance in Deferred Income Taxes continues to increase. By year-end 19x7, the balance stabilizes at $680,700 because from 19x8 on, each year's total $134,800 reversals (debits) equal each year's $134,800 credits. Under the assumed conditions, then, from year-end 19x7 on there would be a "permanent" deferred tax liability of $680,700.

"Permanent" Deferrals. As long as the company grows in size, the credit balance in Deferred Income Taxes continues to increase. Even if the company stops growing in size, as is assumed in 19x9, a sizable credit balance remains in the account. This balance remains permanently; there will always be a credit balance in the Deferred Income Taxes account unless the company stops acquiring assets (i.e., it begins to shrink).

Furthermore, since replacement costs of assets increase in periods of inflation, the credit balance will continue to grow even if the physical size of the company remains constant. For these reasons many companies report a large deferred income taxes liability on their balance sheet. This is not an obligation owed to some outside party, and it is unlikely that the balance in the account ever will be eliminated, or even that it will decrease. The effective permanency of this increasing credit balance has led many companies to argue against deferred tax accounting since it became a requirement for GAAP in 1967.

Deferrals are not necessarily permanent, however. For example, for professional service firms such as architectural and consulting firms, the IRS has generally permitted recognizing revenues when clients pay their bills (the collection method), as opposed to when the firm has performed the services for the client. If a firm's revenues are growing, this results in an increasing balance of deferred taxes, because collections always lag behind the performance of work. However, if a firm were to cease operations, the full amount of the deferred taxes would come due as the clients for whom work had already been performed sent in their cash payments. (A similar but less extreme effect occurs if the firm's revenues decrease, rather than the firm completely ceasing operations.) This phenomenon causes the FASB to believe that deferred taxes are indeed a liability. The FASB draws an analogy with an item that is clearly a liability—accounts payable. Even though the balance in Accounts Payable increases as a firm grows, there is turnover within the account—that is, old payables are paid (debits) as new ones are recorded (credits). Similarly, as Illustration 10–2 demonstrates, the fact that the balance in Deferred Income Taxes is growing (or constant) does not mean that reversals of old deferrals are not taking place.

Deferred Tax Assets. In some circumstances book-to-tax differences result in a deferred tax asset. For example, GAAP requires a company to charge estimated future warranty costs as an expense of the period in which the warranted goods are sold; but tax law does not permit deducting such costs until they actually are incurred. This means that an appliance manufacturer with increasing sales (assuming corresponding increasing warranty costs) will show an increasing balance in a deferred income taxes asset account; this happens because (other things being equal) each period's lower warranty costs on its tax return will result in higher taxable income than its pretax book income. Similarly, a magazine publisher is required for income tax purposes to recognize subscription payments when they are received, whereas GAAP requires that these prepayments be treated as a liability (Deferred Subscription Revenues). With a growing subscription base (or a constant base but increasing subscription prices), the publisher will also experience an increasing balance in a deferred income tax asset account, because each year's taxable income will be greater than its pretax book income.

Also giving rise to a deferred tax asset are **tax-loss carryforwards.** These are deductions or credits that a company cannot make use of on its current tax return that may be carried forward to reduce taxable income in a future year. However, the amount of the deferred tax asset cannot exceed the amount of future tax benefits that the company actually expects to receive. If the company believes that "it is more likely than not (a likelihood of more than 50 percent) that some portion or all of the deferred tax assets will not be realized," a *valuation allowance* must be established to reduce the nominal amount of the deferred tax asset to its estimated realizable amount.[9]

Tax Rate Changes. The discussion of deferred taxes thus far has assumed that the tax rate would indefinitely remain constant. This assumption masked an issue in deferred tax accounting. We will state the issue in the form of two questions: (1) Should the amount of tax deferral caused by a temporary difference be based on the tax rate in effect when the difference arose or on the rate expected to be in effect when the difference reverses? (2) If corporate tax rates change, should deferred income taxes assets and liabilities be restated, based on the new rates?

The FASB's answer to these questions is that new deferrals are entered in the accounts based on the tax rates that currently enacted tax laws state will be in effect when the temporary differences will reverse. The balance in a deferred income taxes account is adjusted if a later change in the tax law changes the rates from those that were expected to apply. This adjustment affects reported (book) net income in the year in which the tax rate change is enacted; the adjustment is a component of income tax expense.[10]

> **Example.** A new tax law is passed in 19x7 that reduces the corporate income tax rate from 40 percent to 35 percent. This change requires that the balance in Deferred Income Taxes (Illustration 10–2) be reduced from $680,700, which was calculated based on a 40 percent rate, to $595,613, a reduction of $85,087. The journal entry is:

> Deferred Income Taxes (liability) 85,087
>   Income Tax Expense 85,087

Financial Statement Disclosure. The FASB requires that deferred tax asset and liability amounts be reported separately; they cannot be combined into a single net asset or net liability amount. Also, deferred tax assets and liabilities must be classified as current or noncurrent based on the classification of the related asset or liability for financial reporting. Thus, for example, a deferred tax liability related to fixed asset depreciation timing differences would be classified as noncurrent because the depreciable asset

---

[9]"Accounting for Income Taxes," *FASB Statement No. 109* (February 1992).
[10]Ibid.

ILLUSTRATION 10–3
SEPARATION OF OPERATING INCOME FROM OTHER ITEMS

BASEL CORPORATION
Condensed Statement of Income and Retained Earnings
Year Ended December 31, 1993
(in thousands)

Net sales and other revenue		$60,281
Expenses		46,157
Income from continuing operations before income taxes		14,124
Provision for income taxes		5,650
Income from continuing operations		8,474
Extraordinary loss (less applicable income taxes of $400)		(600)
Discontinued operations (Note A):		
Loss from operations of Division X (less applicable income taxes of $320)	$480	
Loss on disposal of Division X (less applicable income taxes of $640)	960	(1,440)
Cumulative effect of change in accounting principle (Note B)		(400)
Net income		$ 6,034
Retained earnings at beginning of year:		
As previously reported		$41,400
Adjustments (Note C)		(1,200)
As restated		40,200
Add net income		6,034
Deduct dividends		(2,000)
Retained earnings at end of year		$44,234

is noncurrent. On the other hand, a deferred tax liability relating to using the installment method for tax purposes would be classified as current (assuming the related installment receivables were classified as current).

NONOPERATING ITEMS

To the extent feasible, the income statement should show the results of the year's normal operations separately from special and presumably nonrecurring events that affected net income and retained earnings. This permits the reader to see more clearly the profitability of normal activities. This section describes four types of transactions that are reported separately from the revenues and expenses of recurring operations: extraordinary items, discontinued operations, changes in accounting principles, and adjustments to retained earnings. The first three of these affect net income for the period, whereas the fourth does not. The method of reporting these four types of transactions on the income statement is shown in Illustration 10–3. (Notes A, B, and C are not given here. They would explain the three items in some detail.)

Extraordinary Items

At one time companies had considerable latitude in deciding on the types of transactions that should be classified as nonrecurring. The publication of *APB Opinion No. 30* in 1973 greatly reduced this discretion.[11] The basic reason for this change was to correct abuses that sometimes occurred under the former practice. For example, formerly a company might charge certain nonrecurring costs directly to Retained Earnings, so that these costs would not appear on any income statement. In a few companies the direct debits to Retained Earnings over a period of years almost equaled the sum of the net income amounts reported for these years. Other companies reported a variety of losses as "extraordinary" in the hope that readers would regard them as abnormal and not likely to recur.

APB Opinion No. 30 requires that in order to qualify as an extraordinary item, an event must satisfy two criteria:

1. The event must be *unusual;* it should be highly abnormal and unrelated to, or only incidentally related to, the ordinary activities of the entity.

2. The event must occur *infrequently;* it should be of a type that would not reasonably be expected to recur in the foreseeable future.

The words of these criteria do not convey their narrowness as clearly as do the illustrations that are used to explain it. The following gains and losses are specifically *not* extraordinary:

1. Write-down or write-off of accounts receivable, inventory, or intangible assets.

2. Gains or losses from changes in the value of foreign currency.

3. Gains or losses on disposal of a segment of a business (discussed in the next section).

4. Gains or losses from the disposal of fixed assets.

5. Effects of a strike.

The few items that may be extraordinary include major casualties (such as earthquakes), the loss when a foreign government expropriates assets, a major loss resulting from the enactment of a new law (such as a pollution-control law), and gains and losses from refunding certain bond issues.[12]

Accounting Treatment. In those rare cases in which extraordinary gains or losses can be identified, they are reported separately on the income statement below "income from continuing operations," as shown in Illustration 10–3. The amount reported is the net amount after the income tax effect of the item has been taken into account.

---

[11]"Reporting the Results of Operations," *APB Opinion No. 30* (June 1973). See also, "Reporting the Results of Operations," *APB Opinion No. 9* (December 1966).

[12]"Reporting Gains and Losses from Extinguishment of Debt," *FASB Statement No. 4* (March 1975); and "Extinguishments of Debt Made to Satisfy Sinking-Fund Requirements," *FASB Statement No. 64* (September 1982).

Example.   If a company had an extraordinary loss of $1 million, its taxable income presumably would be reduced by $1 million. At an income tax rate of 40 percent, its income tax would be reduced by $400,000, and the ultimate effect on net income would therefore be only $600,000.

Discontinued Operations

Another type of transaction that, if material, is reported separately on the income statement is the gain or loss from the discontinuance of a division or other identifiable segment of the company.[13] The transaction must involve a whole business unit, as contrasted with the disposition of an individual asset or discontinuance of one product in a product line. Discontinuance may occur by abandoning the segment and selling off the remaining assets or by selling the whole segment as a unit to some other company. In the former case, a loss is likely; in the latter case, there may be either a gain or a loss, depending on how attractive the segment is to the other company.

If a loss is expected from discontinuing a segment, the loss is recorded in the period in which the *decision* to discontinue is made, which may be earlier than the period in which the actual transaction is consummated. Usually, the amount of this loss is an estimate. This estimate may be quite complicated, for it must take into account (1) the estimated revenues and expenses of the discontinued segment during the period in which it continues to be operated by the company; (2) the estimated proceeds of the sale; and (3) the book value of the assets that will be written off when the segment is disposed of. If a gain is expected, it is not recognized until it is realized, which ordinarily is the disposal date.

Accounting Treatment.   As is the case with extraordinary items, the amounts related to discontinued operations are reported after their income tax effect has been taken into account. As shown in Illustration 10–3, two amounts are reported:

1. The net income or loss attributable to the operations of the segment until it is sold.

2. The estimated net gain or loss on disposal after taking account of all aspects of the sale, including the amount received and the write-off of assets that are not sold.

Change in Accounting Principles

The third type of nonrecurring item reported on the income statement is the effect of a change in accounting principles. Sometimes a change is required by a new FASB *Statement.* In most other circumstances the consistency concept requires that a company use the same accounting principles from one year to the next. But if a company has a sound reason for doing so, it may occasionally shift from one generally accepted principle to another one. For example, several methods of depreciation are

---

[13]*APB Opinion No. 30,* pars. 8, 9, 13–18.

acceptable; if a company has a sound reason for doing so, it may shift from one method to another.

If the company had used the new method in earlier years, its net income in those years would have been different, and this would have affected the balance in Retained Earnings. Retained Earnings therefore needs to be adjusted to reflect the *cumulative* effect of the change in all prior periods' net income. (For a change in depreciation methods, this would involve all prior years in which the depreciable assets currently on hand were in use.) The cumulative effect of the change is not recorded by changing Retained Earnings directly, however. Instead, it is reported as one of the nonrecurring items on the income statement of the year in which the change is made, as shown in Illustration 10–3.[14]

Adjustments to Retained Earnings

At one time companies were permitted to make entries directly to Retained Earnings for **prior period adjustments.** Such adjustments were made to take account of the effect of events that (1) had occurred in earlier years but that had been inadvertently omitted from the income statements of those years or (2) had been included in these statements at amounts that turned out to be incorrect. Examples included the effect of settlement of lawsuits or the amount of income taxes finally paid. In 1977 the FASB severely limited prior period adjustments to Retained Earnings.[15] Only two types are now permitted. One is a technical aspect of income taxes, and the other is the correction of errors.

Errors are defined as "mathematical mistakes, mistakes in the application of accounting principles, or oversight or misuse of facts that existed at the time the financial statements were prepared." Also, "a change from an accounting principle that is not generally accepted to one that is generally accepted is a correction of an error."[16] By contrast, corrections of *estimates,* such as estimated useful lives of assets or estimated allowances for bad debts or warranty expense, are not prior period adjustments.

In addition, as noted in Chapter 5, a period's unrealized gain or loss in "available-for-sale" marketable securities is charged directly to a separate component of owners' equity. Similarly, a period's foreign currency translation adjustments (described later in this chapter) are charged directly to a special owners' equity account, rather than being flowed through the income statement.[17]

With these exceptions, *FASB Statement No. 16* requires that "all items of profit and loss recognized during a period, including accruals of estimated losses from loss contingencies, shall be included in the determination of net income for that period."

---

[14]"Accounting Changes," *APB Opinion No. 20* (July 1971).
[15]"Prior Period Adjustments," *FASB Statement No. 16* (June 1977).
[16]*APB Opinion No. 20,* par. 13.
[17]"Accounting for Certain Investments in Debt and Equity Securities," *FASB Statement No. 115* (May 1993); and "Foreign Currency Translation," *FASB Statement No. 52* (December 1981).

FOREIGN CURRENCY ACCOUNTING

Changes in the price of a foreign currency vis-à-vis the dollar—that is, fluctuating **exchange rates**—cause problems in preparing financial statements involving a foreign subsidiary.[18] These problems are foreign currency *translation* accounting problems. Also, whether or not a company has a foreign subsidiary, the company may engage in transactions with foreign entities; these transactions lead to foreign currency *transaction* accounting problems. Both types of problems are discussed below.

Foreign Currency Transactions

If an American firm buys or sells goods abroad or borrows from, or grants credit to, a foreign entity, the firm may experience a **foreign currency transaction** gain or loss as a result of exchange rate fluctuations between the date the transaction was entered into and the date cash is transmitted.

> **Example.** Shipley Shoe Store received from an Italian manufacturer a shipment of shoes with an invoice for 10 million lire. On the date the invoice was received and the transaction journalized, the exchange rate was $0.00060 per lira, giving a $6,000 account payable for the shoes received. Thirty days later, when Shipley paid its bill in lire, the exchange rate had increased to $0.00061 per lira. Thus, Shipley had to pay $6,100 to buy the required lire, and a currency exchange loss of $100 was realized. This would be accounted for as follows:
>
> | | | |
> |---|---:|---:|
> | Accounts Payable | 6,000 | |
> | Loss on Foreign Exchange | 100 | |
> | Cash | | 6,100 |

Note that this transaction loss occurred because the transaction was denominated in a currency other than the dollar. If Shipley had originally agreed to pay $6,000 rather than 10 million lire for the shipment, no transaction loss would have occurred.

Transaction gains and losses are included in the calculation of net income for the period in which the exchange rate changes. This is true whether or not the gain or loss has been realized. For example, if Shipley had still owed the 10 million lire as of December 31, 1993, and if at that time the exchange rate was anything other than $0.00060 per lira, then Shipley would have recognized a transaction gain or loss in its 1993 income statement. If the payment were then made on January 12, 1994, another gain or loss would have been recognized if the exchange rate were different on January 12, 1994, than it was on December 31, 1993.[19] The sum of these two

---

[18]As will be explained in Chapter 12, a subsidiary is an entity controlled by another entity, called its parent. Consolidated financial statements report on the parent and all of its subsidiaries as if they were a single entity.

[19]"Foreign Currency Translation," *FASB Statement No. 52* (December 1981), par. 15.

recognized transaction gains or losses would equal whatever gain or loss was ultimately *realized*.

Foreign Currency Translation

Usually the accounts of a foreign subsidiary are kept in the currency of the country in which the subsidiary operates, which is called the subsidiary's **functional currency.** In preparing consolidated statements, the American parent must translate these foreign currency amounts into dollars (called more generally the **reporting currency**). Because exchange rates fluctuate, the question arises as to the date or dates that should be used to determine the exchange rates used in this **foreign currency translation** process.

FASB 52. There are various possible answers to this question, and at one time GAAP was sufficiently broad enough that a company could use any of several different methods to make these translations. In 1981 *FASB Statement No. 52* limited the choices to one—the **net investment,** or **current rate, method.** With this method the parent's investment in a foreign subsidiary is considered to be an investment in the subsidiary's net assets (i.e., assets minus liabilities). Accordingly, *all* of the foreign entity's assets and liabilities are translated at the *current* exchange rate as of the balance sheet date. All revenue and expense items are translated at the *average* rate for the period.

> **Example.** The Franco Company, a French subsidiary of its U.S. parent, Americo, Inc., was formed on January 1, 19x1. Americo's initial investment in Franco was $850,000, which at the time was equivalent to 5,000,000 francs because the January 1, 19x1, exchange rate was $0.170 per franc. Franco's 19x1 financial statements are shown in Illustration 10–4. All year-end assets and liabilities are translated at the $0.160 per franc exchange rate as of December 31, 19x1. All income statement items are translated at the average 19x1 exchange rate, which was $0.165. Franco's capital stock is translated at the rate in effect when it was issued to Americo, $0.170. The dollar amount for retained earnings is simply the beginning balance (zero) plus net income ($165,000) less dividends (zero).

Collectively, these translation calculations leave the dollar balance sheet's sum of liabilities and owners' equity $55,000 greater than the total assets. The negative $55,000 translation adjustment restores the dollar balance sheet's equality. But this $55,000 downward adjustment can be viewed as more than just a "plug" figure. Since Americo held French franc net assets while the value of the franc fell relative to the dollar, Americo sustained a holding loss in the dollar value of this net assets investment. The calculation of this loss is shown at the bottom of Illustration 10–4. The translation loss (or gain) does *not* appear on the translated income statement. Rather, *FASB 52* requires that this amount be disclosed and accumulated in a separate account in the owners' equity portion of the translated

ILLUSTRATION 10–4
FOREIGN STATEMENT TRANSLATIONS

FRANCO COMPANY
Balance Sheet
As of December 31, 19x1
(in thousands except exchange rate)

Assets	Francs	Exchange Rate	Dollars
Cash	Fr 1,000	$0.160	$ 160
Receivables	5,000	0.160	800
Inventories	3,000	0.160	480
Equipment (net)	4,000	0.160	640
	Fr 13,000		$2,080

Liabilities and Owners' Equity	Francs	Exchange Rate	Dollars
Liabilities	Fr 7,000	0.160	$1,120
Capital stock	5,000	0.170*	850
Retained earnings	1,000		165
Accumulated translation adjustment†	—		(55)
	Fr 13,000		$2,080

Income Statement
For the Year Ended December 31, 19x1
(In thousands except exchange rate)

	Francs	Exchange Rate	Dollars
Revenues	Fr 20,000	$0.165	$3,300
Cost of sales	12,000	0.165	1,980
Other expenses	7,000	0.165	1,155
Net income	Fr 1,000		$ 165

*Exchange rate as of the date the capital stock was issued.
†Calculation of translation loss:

Jan. 1, 19x1, net assets = Fr 5,000:
Translated at Dec. 31, 19x1, rate = 5,000 * $0.160 = $800
Translated at Jan. 1, 19x1, rate = 5,000 * $0.170 = 850
Loss on beginning-of-year net assets (50)

Increment in net assets during 19x1 = Fr 1,000:
Translated at Dec. 31, 19x1, rate = 1,000 * $0.160 = 160
Translated at average 19x1 rate = 1,000 * $0.165 = 165
Loss on increment in net assets (5)
Total loss in dollar value of net assets $ (55)

balance sheet. This account usually appears below retained earnings, with a name such as "Cumulative foreign currency translation adjustments." The translated foreign subsidiary's statements are then consolidated with the parent's statements, as described in Chapter 12.

NET INCOME

The bottom line on the income statement is labeled **net income** or **net earnings** (or **loss**), without any qualifying phrase. The term *net income* never appears as a label for any other item on the income statement. Note that in Illustration 10–3 the label is "Income from continuing operations," not "Net income from continuing operations."

Net income therefore means, *almost* unambiguously, the net addition to Retained Earnings during the accounting period, regardless of whether it arises from ordinary operations or from other events and regardless of whether the transactions entering into its determination are recurring or are highly unusual. We say "almost" because, as described above, direct adjustments to Retained Earnings are permitted to correct errors; and, in effect, Retained Earnings can be further adjusted via special owners' equity accounts for foreign currency translations and for unrealized gains or losses on "available-for-sale" marketable securities.

ACCOUNTING AND CHANGING PRICES

In this final section of the chapter, we discuss a proposal which is *not* currently a part of GAAP, but which is advocated by many people and which may be accepted in the future if the rate of inflation again becomes high. The proposal is that changing prices be given explicit recognition in financial statements that are *supplementary* to the financial statements we have previously discussed.

Nature of the Problem

Financial accounting essentially measures historical costs—that is, costs incurred at the time a transaction took place. The problem with this approach is illustrated by the following.

Suppose that in 1985 you purchased a parcel of land for $20,000. In 1990 an identical parcel adjoining the first one became available, and you purchased it for $28,000. In June 1994 you received an offer to sell either parcel or both for $32,000 each, but decided to continue holding the land. At that point a balance sheet including your two identical assets would show a total land cost of $48,000; yet you did not pay half of this amount ($24,000) for *either* parcel, and their total *value* in June 1994 was $64,000.

Suppose further that a farmer paid you $1,000 per parcel for the right to grow crops on your land during 1994. Ignoring costs such as property taxes, historical cost accounting indicates a return of 5.0 percent (= $1,000 ÷ $20,000) on the first parcel, 3.6 percent on the second, and 4.2 percent on the combined parcels. Yet, in terms of their physical characteristics and market values, the parcels are identical. Moreover, if you had sold them both for $32,000 each, and the *new* owner had been paid $1,000 per parcel by the farmer, the new owner's return on either parcel (or the combined parcels) would have been only 3.1 percent (= $1,000 ÷ $32,000 or $2,000 ÷ $64,000).

In the 1980s the FASB required large companies, as an experiment, to prepare supplementary financial statements that recognized the effect of changing prices on a company's purchasing power—its ability to acquire a given physical quantity of goods and services.[20] Two approaches were required; they were referred to as constant dollar accounting and current cost accounting.

Constant Dollar Accounting.   With **constant dollar accounting,** all balance sheet and income statement items are adjusted by a general price index such as the Gross National Product Implicit Deflator, which measures changes in the prices of a "market basket" of all goods and services.

> **Example.**   If a company had $100,000 cash as of December 31, 19x1, when the price index was 300, and this amount was to be restated in units of purchasing power as of December 31, 19x2, when the index was 330 (i.e., there was 10 percent inflation during the year), then the restated amount would be:
>
> $$\$100,000 \text{ (as of Dec. 19x1)} * \frac{330 \text{ (Dec. 19x2 index)}}{300 \text{ (Dec. 19x1 index)}} = \text{C}\$110,000$$
>
> The C$ sign stands for constant dollars, to emphasize that the amount is expressed in units of purchasing power, not nominal dollars.

This requirement met with widespread criticism, and it was discontinued in 1984.[21]

Current Cost Accounting.   In **current cost accounting** a company determines the cost of replacing specific assets—their **replacement cost** or *specific prices.* For inventories, current cost is the cost as of the balance sheet date for purchasing goods of the same kind and quantity as those in inventory, or for acquiring the resources needed to produce such goods.

For property, plant, and equipment, current cost means the cost of acquiring the same **service potential** as embodied in the assets owned. The replacement cost of a plant, for example, is not necessarily the cost of exactly replicating all the specific assets of the plant. Rather, the replacement cost can be based on replicating the plant's *capacity,* using current technology and know-how. If a beer company owned several small breweries but current technology and production economies were such that only much larger breweries were now being built, the replacement cost would relate to a single larger-scale, more efficient brewery. In such a case, asset-specific price indexes can be used to aid in making the current cost

---

[20]"Financial Reporting and Changing Prices," *FASB Statement No. 33* (September 1979).
[21]"Financial Reporting and Changing Prices: Elimination of Certain Disclosures," *FASB Statement No. 82* (November 1984).

estimates; such indexes (e.g., construction cost per barrel of capacity) are maintained by many industry associations.

Only inventories and fixed assets are subject to adjustments to a current cost basis. The historical cost amounts for other assets and for all liabilities are presumed to reflect adequately their current costs. Current cost owners' equity (net assets) is found by subtracting liabilities from adjusted total assets.

The requirement to report supplementary current cost information, and thus the whole experiment, was discontinued in December 1986.[22]

Related Developments

Although currently there are no efforts to reinstate supplementary disclosures of the type described above, there are several proposals to adjust monetary items to their current values rather than reporting the traditional historical cost amounts. Such adjustments can have a significant effect on the financial statements of banks and similar financial institutions, most of whose assets are monetary. These are referred to as **mark to market adjustments,** and the adjusted numbers would be included in the financial statements themselves rather than disclosed as supplementary information, as was the case with the experiment conducted in the 1980s.

SUMMARY

In analyzing transactions regarding wages costs, a careful distinction must be made between the amount earned by the employee, the additional cost that the employer incurs for payroll taxes, and the amount collected from employees that is to be transmitted to the government. Pension and other postretirement benefit costs are costs associated with work done in the current period, although the actual pension payments and provision of other benefits may not begin until many years later. Accounting for defined contribution plans is straightforward, but accounting for defined benefit plans and other postretirement benefits requires complicated estimates and computations.

A period's income tax expense is calculated based on the amount of financial accounting pretax income, as opposed to the taxable income reported to the government. The resulting difference between reported income tax expense and the income tax actually payable is recorded in Deferred Income Taxes. This account does not represent an amount due the government; Taxes Payable shows the amount that is currently due.

A few unusual items are reported on the income statement separately from revenues and expenses of recurring operations. These include extraordinary losses or gains, gain or loss from discontinued operations, and the adjustment that results from changing accounting principles.

---

[22]"Financial Reporting and Changing Prices," *FASB Statement No. 89* (December 1986).

Foreign currency *transaction* gains or losses arise from transactions between a domestic company and a foreign entity, where the transaction is denominated in the foreign entity's currency; they are included in net income. Foreign currency *translation* gains or losses arise from a domestic parent's holding an investment in the net assets of a foreign subsidiary; they are accumulated in the owners' equity section of the parent's consolidated balance sheet.

Although the experiment to report supplementary financial information on the impact of inflation was abandoned, there have been recent proposals to state certain monetary items at their current values rather than on a historical cost basis.

Cases

CASE 10–1 Martin Corporation (B)

In addition to the transactions listed in Martin Corporation (A), Case 8–1, several other matters were referred to Allen Burrows for his opinion as to how they should be reported on the 1993 income statement and balance sheet.

1. Martin had purchased advertising brochures costing $125,000 in 1993. At the end of 1993, one-fifth of these brochures were on hand; they would be mailed in 1994 to prospective customers who sent in a coupon request for them. As of March 1, 1994, almost all the brochures had been mailed. Martin had charged $100,000 of the cost of these brochures as an expense in 1993, and showed $25,000 as a deferred charge as of December 31, 1993.

2. In 1993 the company had placed magazine advertisements, costing $75,000, offering these brochures. The advertisements had appeared in 1993. Because the sales generated by the brochures would not occur until after prospective customers had received the brochures and placed orders, which would primarily be in 1994, Martin had recorded the full $75,000 as a deferred charge on its December 31, 1993, balance sheet.

3. Martin's long-standing practice was to capitalize the costs of development projects if they were likely to result in successful new products. Upon introduction of the product, these amounts were written off to cost of sales over a five-year period. During 1993 $55,000 had been added to the asset account and $36,000 had been charged off as an expense. Preliminary research efforts were charged to expense, so the amount capitalized was an amount that related to products added to Martin's line. In the majority of instances, these products at least produced some gross profit, and some of them were highly successful.

4. In 1993 the financial vice president decided to capitalize, as a deferred charge, the costs of the company's employee training program, which amounted to $35,000. He had read several books and articles on "human resource accounting" that advocated such treatment because the value of these training programs would certainly benefit operations in future years.

5. For many years, Martin's practice had been to set its allowance for doubtful accounts at 2 percent of accounts receivable. This amount had been satisfactory. In 1993, however, a customer who owed $19,040 went bankrupt. From inquiries made at local banks, Martin Corporation could obtain no reliable estimate of the amount that eventually could be recovered. The loss might be negligible, and it might be the entire $19,040. The $19,040 was included as an account receivable on the proposed balance sheet.

6. Martin did not carry fire or theft insurance on its automobiles and trucks. Instead, it followed the practice of self-insurance. It charged $5,000 as an expense in 1993, which was the approximate cost of fire and theft insurance policies, and credited this amount

to an insurance reserve, a noncurrent liability. During 1993 only one charge, for $3,750, was made to this reserve account, representing the cost of repairing a truck that had been stolen and later recovered. The balance in the reserve account as of January 1, 1993, was $20,900.

7. In 1993 the board of directors voted to sell a parking lot that the company had operated for several years. Another company had expressed an interest in buying the lot for approximately $125,000. In 1993 the pretax income generated by this lot was $19,000. The book value of the assets that would be sold was $50,000 as of the end of 1993. Martin did not reflect this transaction in its financial statements because no final agreement had been reached with the proposed buyer and because the sale would not take place until well into 1994, even if a final agreement were reached in the near future.

8. During 1993 the president of Martin exercised a stock option and the corporation used treasury stock for this purpose. The treasury stock had been acquired several years earlier at a cost of $10,000 and was carried in the shareholders' equity section of the balance sheet at this amount. In accordance with the terms of the option agreement, the president paid $13,000 for it. He immediately sold this stock, however, for $25,000. Martin disregarded the fact that the stock was clearly worth $25,000 and recorded the transaction as:

Cash	13,000	
Gain on Treasury Stock		3,000
Treasury Stock		10,000

The $3,000 gain was included as a nonoperating income item on the income statement.

9. Martin's long-standing practice was to declare an annual cash dividend of $50,000 in December and to pay it in January. When the dividend was paid, the following entry was made:

Retained Earnings	50,000	
Cash		50,000

Questions

1. What changes in the financial statements (see Martin Corporation (A)) is Martin required to make in accordance with generally accepted accounting principles? Ignore income taxes and assume that all the transactions are material.

2. As Mr. Burrows, what additional changes, if any, would you recommend be made in the proposed income statement in order to present the results more fairly?

CASE 10–2   Silver Appliance Company

Silver Appliance Company operated a large retail appliance store in San Diego. The store sold all sorts of household appliances, plus auto and home sound equipment. The company's owner, Brian Silver (known by his customers as "Big Brian" because of his rather ample proportions), had for many years been an extremely productive salesman in a San Diego store of the Highland Appliance chain. Having built up a large personal clientele during those years, Mr. Silver felt he could easily shift customers to a new store, were he to open one. In 1986, he did just that, and the store had rapidly achieved an annual sales volume of over $5 million.

In 1989 Mr. Silver decided he could increase the store's volume, plus earn interest revenue, if he established an installment credit program to assist customers in financing their major purchases. The program was

EXHIBIT 1
INSTALLMENT SALES DATA
(thousands of dollars)

	1989	1990	1991	1992	1993
Installment receivables as of December 31	$190.1	$351.9	$526.2	$559.4	$489.1
Pretax profit as reported..............................	332.6	415.3	478.2	492.5	461.3
Gross margin percentage.............................	34.6%	35.1%	34.2%	33.4%	32.2%

Notes:
1. All installment sales contracts were for periods of one year or less.
2. The company's effective federal income tax rate in each year was approximately 34 percent.

a success, with the amount of installment receivables growing in each successive year (except for 1993).

In early 1994 Mr. Silver decided the firm had outgrown its sole-practitioner accounting firm. He therefore retained a national public accounting firm to provide Silver Appliance with various auditing, tax, and consulting services. The accounting firm's partner assigned to the Silver account was Suzi Chung. After reviewing Silver's accounting practices, Ms. Chung met with Mr. Silver to review these practices. Of particular interest to Ms. Chung was the fact that Silver used the typical accrual method (formally, the "delivery method") to recognize sales—and hence cost of sales and gross margin—on all sales, irrespective of whether the sales were for cash, were charged to a Visa or Master-Card account, or were financed on Silver's installment credit plan. Although she felt this made good sense for preparing income statements for Mr. Silver's use, Ms. Chung pointed out that the federal income tax laws permit the use of the installment method of revenue and gross margin recognition on installment plan sales.

With the installment method, the retailer recognizes revenues as installment payments are made and then applies the store's normal gross margin percentage to these payments to determine the gross margin for tax purposes.

For example, suppose a customer bought a $700 refrigerator having a cost of $490; then the gross margin percentage is 30 percent (= $210 ÷ $700). If the customer's first installment payment were $50 (ignoring interest), the store would at that time recognize $15 (= 30% * $50) gross margin for tax purposes.[1] The effect of using this method for calculating taxable income is that it delays, relative to the delivery basis, the reporting of gross margin, and hence defers the taxes on that margin until the margin is realized through the customer's cash installment payments.

After Ms. Chung's explanation of the installment method, Mr. Silver expressed a definite interest in changing to this method for tax purposes. "However," he said, "I want to keep using the regular basis for our monthly and annual income statements because I really feel we earn the margin when the customer signs the installment agreement and we deliver the appliances. But before we change, I'd like to see how much we've been overpaying in taxes the past few years by not using the installment method." To address this question, Ms. Chung gathered the data shown in Exhibit 1.

---

[1] The formal accounting treatment is to recognize $50 of revenues, match with that $35 cost of goods sold, and thus recognize $15 gross margin, as explained in Chapter 5.

Mr. Silver raised several other questions with Ms. Chung. "I understand in general the impact that this method would have on our tax payments; but it's not clear to me what the impact would be on our balance sheet, given that I don't want to change methods on our income statement. I've seen an item called 'deferred taxes' on balance sheets in the annual reports of some companies that I own stock in. I know this is somehow related to reporting income on different bases for shareholder and income tax reporting. Would we have such an account if we make this change? If so, you will have to explain to me how I should interpret the balance in that account.

"Also, I have a friend who owns an architectural firm that reports on the cash basis for tax purposes. She was telling me the other day that her billings have really dropped this year because of the downturn of local construction activity, and yet she is still having to make tax payments as big as last year's. Could this happen to us if we change our method for reporting installment sales for tax purposes?

"Finally, it occurs to me that we have already paid taxes on the installment sales profits we recognized in 1993, even though many of those sales have not yet been collected. If we change methods for 1994, are we going to end up paying taxes twice on those uncollected 1993 installment sales—once in 1993 and again in 1994?"

Questions

1. If Silver Appliance Company had used the installment method for tax purposes in the years 1989–93, how different would its tax payments have been in each of those years? What would the year-end balance in deferred taxes have been in each of those years? (Round calculations to the nearest $10.)

2. How would you respond to Mr. Silver's questions concerning (a) interpretation of the amount of deferred taxes, (b) tax payments in a period of declining sales, and (c) double taxation of installment sales made in 1993?

CASE 10–3 Union Carbide Corporation

The front page of *The Wall Street Journal* on June 20, 1980, carried an article with the headline, "Slick Accounting Ploys Help Many Companies Improve Their Income," and the subhead, "By Proper or Improper Means, They 'Manage' Earnings for the Desired Effect." Highlighted in the article were certain accounting principle changes that Union Carbide Corporation had adopted starting with the first quarter of 1980. The article quoted a prominent securities analyst as saying, "Carbide's changes . . . are merely an accounting mirage that greatly exaggerates reported earnings," and a well-known accounting professor who said, "It appears to me that Carbide is merely polishing its 1980 profits to make them look a lot better." The rest of this case consists of excerpts from Union Carbide's 1979 and 1980 annual reports related to the company's 1980 accounting changes.

The changes were announced in a special section of the chairman's and president's letter to stockholders at the front of the 1979 annual report:

> In order to improve its financial reporting, Union Carbide is making several accounting changes effective in 1980 . . . [that] will lead to an increase in reported net income and earnings per share in 1980 and subsequent years.

To depreciate the cost of machinery and equipment, Union Carbide will be using revised estimated useful lives rather than the shorter Internal Revenue Service guideline lives. . . . [This change] will result in more realistic historical depreciation costs. . . . On the whole, asset lives will be extended by about 35 percent over those used before the change. That extension will provide management and others with a better matching of depreciation cost with the revenue-producing capabilities of assets; and it will bring our asset depreciation lives more in line with those used by competitors.

Following a new requirement of the Financial Accounting Standards Board, the corporation will capitalize, rather than charge as expense, interest costs attributable to major capital projects in progress. The capitalized interest will be amortized over the average useful life of the assets.

Beginning in 1980, Union Carbide will include investment tax credits in income in the year earned (the flow-through method), rather than deferring them and taking them into income over the average life of the assets earning the credit (the deferral method). The flow-through method will alleviate the decreasing impact of the investment tax credit which results from use of the deferral method during periods of continuing inflation. The large majority of industry utilizes the flow-through method.

We estimate that changes in accounting for the items described above will have the following effects on the results we report for 1980:

	Net Income ($ million)	Earnings per Share ($)
Depreciation.	+ $ 92	+ $ 1.37
Capitalization of Interest	+ 20	+ 0.30
Investment Tax Credit (ITC)	+ 17	+ 0.26
	+ 129	+ 1.93
Cumulative Prior ITC Effect.	+ 217	+ 3.27
	+ $ 346	+ $ 5.20

The 1980 annual report included as part of a summary of 1976–80 financial data the information shown in Exhibit 1. The data in Exhibit 1 relating to the years 1978–80 were also included in the annual report's comparative income statements. The disclosures shown in Exhibit 1 were required by *APB Opinion No. 20*, "Accounting Changes" (July 1971). The adjustments shown in Exhibit 1 relate only to the change in accounting for the investment tax credit (ITC). A footnote to the 1980 statements disclosed that the effect of the ITC change on 1980 net income (before the cumulative retroactive effect through 1979 of $217 million, or $3.28 per share) was to increase 1980 net income by $24 million, or $0.36 per share.

The change in depreciation useful lives estimates did not require retroactive income statement disclosures because it was a change in accounting *estimates* rather than in an accounting *principle* (*APB 20*, par. 31). The change involving capitalization of interest costs did not result in any retroactive restatements of income because *FASB Statement No. 34*, "Capitalization of Interest Cost" (October 1979), expressly prohibited such retroactive restatements (par. 23). However, as required by *FASB 34*, Union Carbide disclosed in a footnote to its 1980 statements

EXHIBIT 1

UNION CARBIDE CORPORATION
Selected Financial Data
For the Years Ending December 31, 1976–1980
($ millions, except per-share figures)

	1980	1979	1978	1977	1976
Income before cumulative effect of change in accounting principle	**$ 673**	$ 556	$ 394	$ 385	$ 441
Cumulative effect of change in accounting for the ITC	**$ 217**	—	—	—	—
Net income.	**$ 890**	$ 556	$ 394	$ 385	$ 441
Income per share before cumulative effect of change in accounting principle	**$10.08**	$8.47	$6.09	$6.05	$7.15
Cumulative effect per share of change in accounting for the ITC	**$ 3.28**	—	—	—	—
Net income per share	**$13.36**	$8.47	$6.09	$6.05	$7.15
Pro forma net income with 1980 change in accounting for the ITC applied retro- actively.	**$ 673**	$ 573	$ 448	$ 431	$ 487
Pro forma net income per share	**$10.08**	$8.73	$6.92	$6.78	$7.89

that the effect of capitalizing interest costs attributable to major capital projects in process was to increase 1980 net income by $24 million, or $0.36 per share.

In the 1980 report's "Financial Review" section, the effect of the retroactive application of the 1980 change in depreciation lives on 1979 results was disclosed as follows:[1]

1979 Data (millions, except per-share figures)

	As Reported	As Restated
Depreciation.	$470	$315
Net income.	556	671
Net income per share	$8.47	$10.23

A footnote to the 1980 statements disclosed that the revision of estimated useful lives increased 1980 net income by $94 million, or $1.41 per share.

Also, in 1980, Union Carbide increased the estimated future return on pension plan assets used in calculating the actuarial

present value of accumulated plan benefits from 7 percent to 8 percent. This revised estimate was not mentioned in the footnote on accounting changes or elsewhere in the annual report, but rather was disclosed in the footnote entitled "Retirement Program." That footnote also included the following table:

Millions of dollars as of January 1*	**1980**	1979
Actuarial present value of accumulated plan benefits:		
Vested	**$1,233**	$1,241
Non-Vested	**121**	133
	$1,354	$1,374
Net Assets Available for Benefits . .	**$1,385**	$1,156

* *Casewriter's note: FASB 36 requires that these disclosures be made as of the pension plan's "most recent benefit information date for which the data are available." It is not unusual for this date to be earlier than the fiscal year ending date, as is the case here.*

As a postscript to the above 1980 accounting change information, the reader may be interested to know that for 1981, Union Carbide reported net income of $649 million (comparable with $673 million for 1980) or

---

[1] The report contained these data by quarter of 1979, as well as the total 1979 amounts shown here.

$9.56 per share (comparable with $10.08 for 1980). Also, in 1981 the company further increased the estimated rate of return used to determine the actuarial present value of ac-

cumulated pension plan benefits from 8 percent to 9 percent. The 1981 retirement plan footnote table comparable with the table shown above was as follows:

Millions of dollars as of January 1	**1981**	1980
Actuarial present value of accumulated plan benefits:		
Vested	**$1,239**	$1,233
Non-Vested	**108**	121
	$1,347	$1,354
Net Assets Available for Benefits	**$1,683**	$1,385

Questions

1. Compare the estimated earnings impacts of the 1980 accounting changes that were given in the 1979 annual report with the actual impacts on 1980 earnings as reported in the 1980 annual report. Why are there differences between the estimated and actual amounts? Why are the estimated and actual cumulative prior ITC *total* amounts identical ($217 million)? Why, then, aren't the cumulative prior ITC *per share* amounts identical ($3.27 estimated versus $3.28 actual)?

2. What was the impact on 1980 and 1981 reported earnings of the increases in the estimated rate of return used in pension plan calculations? (Give a general answer; far more data than are given are necessary to develop a precise numerical answer.) What other impacts did these increases have?

3. Evaluate the company's stated reasons for making the various accounting changes in 1980. Also evaluate the adequacy of the company's disclosures concerning the impacts on reported earnings of these changes.

4. If you were writing a report that included a comparison of Union Carbide's 1979 and 1980 net income and earnings per share, what net income and earnings per share amounts would you use for each year?

5. Do you feel *The Wall Street Journal*'s headline and subhead were appropriate in regard to Union Carbide's 1980 changes? Do you agree with the quoted comments of the securities analyst and the accounting professor?

CASE 10–4 Major League Baseball (B)*

In May 1985 the accounting firm of Ernst & Whinney submitted its compilation of the profitability of major league baseball teams

* This case is copyrighted by its authors, Professor George H. Sorter, New York University, and Professor Thomas I. Selling, Amos Tuck School of Dartmouth College, and is used here with their permission.

for the 1984 season. The reported total loss from operations for the 24 teams included in the report was $36,112,000 (see Schedule A). Other estimates of the results ranged from a $65 million loss announced by the baseball club owners to a $9 million profit claimed by the Baseball Players' Association.

MAJOR LEAGUE BASEBALL, 1984 SEASON
Combined Summary of Operations
(before income taxes, unaudited)
(000s omitted)

	Top Eight	Percent	Middle Eight	Percent	Bottom Eight	Percent	Total	Percent
Operating revenues, including receipts of Major Leagues Central Fund (Schedule B)	$222,519		$185,308		$175,696		$583,523	
Operating expenses:								
Spring training	3,707	1.8%	3,367	1.7%	3,419	1.6%	10,493	1.7%
Team (Schedule C)	93,623	45.8	103,100	52.5	104,844	48.0	301,567	48.7
Player development (Schedule D)	18,794	9.2	17,763	9.0	21,576	9.9	58,133	9.4
Team replacement (Schedule E)	14,354	7.0	16,228	8.3	27,629	12.6	58,211	9.4
Stadium operations	29,778	14.6	21,873	11.1	20,942	9.6	72,593	11.7
Ticket department, and publicity and promotion	15,282	7.5	12,769	6.5	16,066	7.4	44,117	7.1
General and administrative	27,322	13.4	19,646	10.0	22,294	10.2	69,262	11.2
Major Leagues Central Fund Player Relations	930	0.5	930	0.5	930	0.4	2,790	0.4
Committee expenses	823	0.4	823	0.4	823	0.4	2,469	0.4
	204,613	100.0%	196,499	100.0%	218,523	100.0%	619,635	100.0%
Profit (loss) from operations	17,906		(11,191)		(42,827)		(36,112)	
Other income (expense):								
Stadium income from non-baseball activities—net	2,346		441				2,787	
Investment income	4,852		1,993		1,519		8,364	
Interest expense	(4,427)		(9,585)		(9,996)		(24,008)	
Charitable contributions	(724)		(69)		(942)		(1,735)	
Miscellaneous—net	(2,602)		(138)		694		(2,046)	
	(555)		(7,358)		(8,725)		(16,638)	
Profit (loss) before income taxes	$ 17,351		$ (18,549)		$ (51,552)		$ (52,750)	

MAJOR LEAGUE BASEBALL, 1984 SEASON
Combined Operating Revenues
(unaudited, 000s omitted)

	Top Eight	Percent	Middle Eight	Percent	Bottom Eight	Percent	Total	Percent
Game receipts:								
Regular season home game receipts—net of admission taxes, visiting club's share, and leagues' shares	$ 83,802	37.6%	$ 70,741	38.2%	$ 61,410	35.0%	$215,953	37.0%
Regular season "away" game receipts	13,761	6.2	11,441	6.2	10,414	5.9	35,616	6.1
Receipts from exhibition games	2,610	1.2	1,563	0.8	1,470	0.8	5,643	1.0
Unredeemed tickets, rain checks, etc.	441	0.2	823	0.4	1,226	0.7	2,490	0.4
All-Star game	460	0.2	460	0.2	460	0.3	1,380	0.2
	101,074	45.4	85,028	45.8	74,980	42.7	261,082	44.7
Broadcasting and television:								
Games of the Week—regular season	14,422	6.5	14,422	7.8	15,096	8.6	43,940	7.5
World Series	13,401	6.0	13,401	7.2	13,400	7.6	40,202	6.9
League Championship Series	9,852	4.4	9,252	5.0	8,952	5.1	28,056	4.8
Copyright Royalty Tribunal	1,337	0.6	1,311	0.7	1,197	0.7	3,845	0.7
All-Star game	2,467	1.1	2,467	1.3	2,467	1.4	7,401	1.3
Amortization of amounts received in 1983 relating to new network telecasting agreements	691	0.3	2,456	1.3	1,540	0.9	4,687	0.8
Local and regional television	26,819	12.1	21,733	11.8	27,880	15.8	76,432	13.1
Local and regional radio	7,710	3.5	6,544	3.5	9,788	5.6	24,042	4.1
Foreign	182	0.1	182	0.1	182	0.1	546	0.1
	76,881	34.6	71,768	38.7	80,502	45.8	229,151	39.3
Advertising	4,534	2.0	4,984	2.7	3,328	1.9	12,846	2.2
Concessions—net	20,602	9.2	16,969	9.2	10,535	6.1	48,106	8.3
Parking—net	5,588	2.5	1,593	0.9	419	0.2	7,600	1.3
Restaurant, suites, and stadium clubs—net	7,083	3.2	2,239	1.2	3,170	1.8	12,492	2.1
Royalties and licensing fees	562	0.3	548	0.3	782	0.4	1,892	0.3
	38,369	17.2	26,333	14.3	18,234	10.4	82,936	14.2
League Championship and World Series:								
Ticket sales—net	1,364	0.6	1,187	0.6			2,551	0.5
Concessions, etc.	2,046	0.9	447	0.3			2,493	0.4
	3,410	1.5	1,634	0.9			5,044	0.9
Other operating revenues	2,785	1.3	545	0.3	1,980	1.1	5,310	0.9
Total combined operating revenues	$222,519	100.0%	$185,308	100.0%	$175,696	100.0%	$583,523	100.0%

SCHEDULE C

MAJOR LEAGUE BASEBALL, 1984 SEASON
Combined Team Operating Expenses
(unaudited, 000s omitted)

	Top Eight	Percent*	Middle Eight	Percent*	Bottom Eight	Percent*	Total	Percent*
Salaries:								
Players	$70,929	34.7%	$ 79,396	40.4%	$ 81,986	37.5%	$232,311	37.5%
Manager, coaches, and trainers	4,345	2.1	4,662	2.4	4,597	2.1	13,604	2.2
Other salaries	797	0.4	707	0.4	1,341	0.6	2,845	0.5
	76,071	37.2	84,765	43.1	87,924	40.2	248,760	40.1
Workers' compensation and payroll taxes	505	0.2	558	0.3	594	0.3	1,657	0.3
Players' Benefit Trust	4,769	2.3	4,769	2.4	4,769	2.2	14,307	2.3
Hotels and meals	2,111	1.0	2,226	1.1	2,400	1.1	6,737	1.1
Transportation and road trip expense	4,372	2.1	3,885	2.0	4,788	2.2	13,045	2.1
Uniforms and playing equipment	472	0.2	309	0.2	319	0.1	1,100	0.2
Clubhouse expenses	306	0.1	395	0.2	244	0.1	945	0.2
Bats	120	0.1	102	0.1	130	0.1	352	0.1
Baseballs	383	0.2	362	0.2	381	0.2	1,126	0.2
Medical expenses—including team physician, supplies, hospital costs, etc.	501	0.2	388	0.2	345	0.2	1,234	0.2
Players' moving allowances and expenses	153	0.1	160	0.1	204	0.1	517	0.1
Insurance (life, accident, team travel, disaster, etc.)	404	0.2	1,011	0.5	1,406	0.6	2,821	0.5
Other	3,456	1.7	4,170	2.1	1,340	0.6	8,966	1.4
Total combined team operating expenses	$93,623	45.8%	$103,100	52.5%	$104,844	48.0%	$301,567	48.7%

* Represents the percentage of each item to total opeating expenses (as shown on Schedule A).

SCHEDULE D

MAJOR LEAGUE BASEBALL, 1984 SEASON
Combined Player Development Expenses
(unaudited, 000s omitted)

	Top Eight	Middle Eight	Bottom Eight	Total
Salaries of farm director, player development director, assistants, and other administrative personnel	$ 890	$ 1,410	$ 1,552	$ 3,852
Salaries of minor league managers, pitching and batting coaches, and other instructors	1,874	1,927	2,340	6,141
Other salaries	73	174	187	434
Expenses of minor league managers, pitching and batting coaches, and other instructors	276	275	256	807
	3,113	3,786	4,335	11,234
Player development contract expenses:				
Salaries (including Major League players on option)	7,059	6,370	7,435	20,864
Payroll taxes.	47 I	468	773	1,712
Bonuses	164	181	658	1,003
Transportation home and assignments	995	964	1,175	3,134
Selection rights and payment.	128	127	113	368
Uniforms and equipment.	241	305	227	773
Medical expenses.	178	234	201	613
Makeup and rookie clubs	326	588	315	1,229
Hotels and meals	580	590	412	1,582
Travel and entertainment.	486	613	880	1,979
	10,628	10,440	12,189	33,257
Operating (profits) losses of owned clubs.	663	(549)	609	723
National Association fees	127	133	64	324
Winter Instructional League	825	845	699	2,369
Spring training (other than Major League team)	1,948	2,069	2,033	6,050
Other	1,490	1,039	1,647	4,176
	5,053	3,537	5,052	13,642
Total combined player development expenses	$18,794	$17,763	$21,576	$58,133

Background

The Major League of Professional Baseball Clubs consisted of 26 teams divided into two leagues, the American League (14 teams), and the National League. Each league was further divided into two divisions, East and West. Each club played a 162-game, intraleague, regular season schedule that began in early April and ended in early October. League champions were determined in a best-of-five-games League Championship Series between the East and West division teams with the best won-lost record over the regular season. The two league champions competed in a best-of-seven games World Series.

In 1984, attendance at regular season games totaled 44.7 million, a record high and more than 50 percent higher than attendance in 1970. Total gross revenues in 1984 for the 26 clubs exceeded $600 million. The two largest sources of revenue were ticket sales and sales of radio and television broadcasting rights.

The Major League Baseball Players' Association was formed in 1953; it became a union in 1966. Each team carried 25 players on its roster. From 1976 (when the courts

SCHEDULE E

MAJOR LEAGUE BASEBALL, 1984 SEASON
Combined Team Replacement Costs and Expenses
(unaudited, 000s omitted)

	Top Eight	Middle Eight	Bottom Eight	Total
Player acquisition costs:				
Amortization of initial roster cost	$ 1,461	$ 1,365	$ 7,401	$10,227
Amortization of players' contracts:				
First year players' bonuses (high school, college, or minor league players who are not on a major league contract)	2,985	2,731	7,013	12,729
Contracts acquired from other clubs	426	190	44	660
Signing bonuses.	738	2,308	2,876	5,922
Unamortized cost of players' contracts—players released or retired.	296	441	960	1,697
Drafts and returns—(gain) loss on contracts acquired and disposed of during year	(20)	1,663	(26)	1,617
Net (gain) loss on outright contract sales	(68)	(190)	844	586
College scholarship plan cost	47	66	23	136
Total player acquisition costs	5,865	8,574	19,135	33,574
Scouting expenses:				
Salaries.	4,249	3,742	4,291	12,282
Travel.	3,170	3,100	3,083	9,353
Major League Scouting Bureau.	550	718	557	1,825
Tryout camps.	229	66	103	398
Other.	291	28	460	779
Total scouting expenses	8,489	7,654	8,494	24,637
Total combined team replacement costs and expenses	$14,354	$16,228	$27,629	$58,211

struck down the ownership clauses binding players to teams) to 1984, salaries increased 700 percent. The average salary in 1984 was approximately $363,000 and 40 players earned in excess of $1 million per year. The agreement with the owners and the Players' Association provided that, after playing six years of major league baseball, a player could become a free agent, that is, sell his services to the highest bidder.

The growth in the importance of broadcasting as a source of revenues had encouraged some broadcasters to gain ownership of baseball clubs to insure permanent access to broadcast rights. Similarly, advertisers such as breweries sought synergism through promotion of their product at low rates or the association of their product with major league baseball.

The major difference in the taxation of professional sports franchises and other business enterprises was the treatment of the excess of the club's purchase price over the fair market value of the identifiable assets acquired. Under 1985 tax law, 50 percent of this excess was normally allocated to player contracts and could be amortized over the expected future playing career of a player. The annual amortization was termed "initial-roster depreciation." The other 50 percent was allocated to other identifiable assets and to "goodwill"; goodwill was not a deduction for income tax purposes.

As partnerships, the clubs themselves were not taxable entities. Instead, each partner's share of the club's profit or loss was reflected in his or her taxable income. Distribution of cash from the club to the partners was tax free. Given a seven- to ten-year average turnover of club ownership, a partnership interest in a baseball club often constituted a tax shelter: the club could be unprofitable for tax purposes due to the initial-roster depreciation, but it might also generate positive cash flows from operations.

Financial Reporting Issues

A players' strike in 1980 caused the cancellation of approximately one-third of the regular season. The strike ended in a five-year agreement between owners and players concerning many issues, most important of which were the terms of free agency and the amount of money owners would contribute to the players' pension fund. Throughout the protracted negotiations, the owners refused to disclose their clubs' financial statements.

In an effort to avert the potentially disastrous consequences of another long strike, the owners agreed to full disclosure of their financial statements in the course of contract negotiations during the 1985 season. Indeed, only a few years earlier, then-Commissioner of Major League Baseball, Bowie Kuhn, mandated that all clubs prepare and submit audited financial statements.

The accounting firm of Ernst & Whinney had been engaged for the previous six years by Major League Baseball to prepare a summary report from the financial statements submitted by the clubs. This report was supposed to contain summary information grouped by (1) the 8 most financially successful, (2) the 8 least financially successful, and (3) the remaining 10 clubs. However, only 24 clubs reported in time to be included in the 1984 report. The schedules included in this case are taken from that report. In submitting its report, Ernst & Whinney pointed out that "although certain reclassifications and combinations have been made to various revenue and expense categories as submitted by the individual clubs, other inconsistencies in account classifications may

still exist." Because of these uncertainties and because the underlying financial statements were not audited by Ernst & Whinney, the firm stated, "we are unable to and do not express an opinion or any other form of assurance on them."

There was general agreement that a club's profit from operations should be measured before interest expense (because interest varied with the amount of borrowing), investment income, charitable contributions, and the miscellaneous income listed on Schedule A. There was also agreement that stadium income from nonbaseball activities should be excluded, but there was disagreement as to what constituted "nonbaseball activities." The principal areas of disagreement were: initial-roster depreciation, deferred compensation, and related-party transactions. An independent accounting expert had been hired by the owners' group. This expert's views on these issues are presented below.

Initial-Roster Depreciation. The owners' expert reported:

> Initial-roster depreciation is a proper and required charge under generally accepted accounting principles (GAAP). Once the asset is set up, it clearly must be amortized because baseball players don't play forever. Nevertheless, in my opinion it should not be included as a cost of baseball operations.
>
> For one thing, this charge arises *only* when ownership changes. Therefore, two clubs with identical baseball operations would report different GAAP results if one was sold and the other was not. This expense properly should be associated with ownership changes and therefore should be excluded from operating results.
>
> Moreover, player development expenditures are not capitalized unless a club is sold, at which time they are capitalized in the initial roster. Thus, the club that has been sold recognizes both past and current player development expenditures as an expense, and the operating income of a club that has been sold will be less over its

lifetime than the operating income of one that has not been. It seems that operating expenditures should include either past or current player development expenditures—but not both.

Tracing the amount of initial-roster depreciation was somewhat difficult. It was included in various line items for different clubs and under different circumstances—if, for instance, the player on the initial roster was subsequently sold or released. After a diligent search I concluded that the proper initial-roster depreciation amount in 1984 was approximately $12 million, and I reduced the loss accordingly.

Deferred Compensation. Most players had compensation that was deferred for extensive periods, well beyond the players' contractual obligations. Basically, three types of deferred compensation contracts existed.

One type stated that a player, in addition to his current compensation, would receive, say, $100,000 in the year 2000. In a sense this represented a defined-benefit pension plan, and it was discounted and its present value reported as the expense.

A second type of contract stated that a player would receive, say, $500,000 a year, of which $100,000 was deferred at an interest rate of 10 percent to the year 2000. In this contract the $100,000 accretes and compounds by the stated interest rate each year. As long as the stated interest rate approximated market, which it generally did, no discounting was required.

It was the third type of contract that posed the major problem. This type, now rare, stated that a player would receive, say, $500,000 a year, of which $100,000 was deferred to the year 2000. No interest rate was stated or implied by the contract and, thus, only $100,000 would be received in the year 2000. Most, if not all, clubs in this circumstance did not calculate the present value of the $100,000 in figuring player compensation expense.

With respect to the third type of contract, the owners' expert reported:

There is no real question, despite widespread misunderstanding, that deferred compensation (under GAAP and common sense) must be considered an expense of the period during which the player plays and not of the period in which he gets paid. There is also no question—or should be none—that the proper amount to be expensed is the present value of such compensation.

"Should," however, is the operative word here. Inquiry soon disclosed that those keeping the clubs' books shared the usual confusion about present value and that a diversity of practice existed, depending on how the contract was worded.

To determine which contract types existed and how much they amounted to, I queried each club about contract type and accounting method. This was not an easy task because of the confusion noted above. I also had to determine whether the yearly interest accretions under the first and third types of contracts were appropriately reported as interest rather than as operating expense and thus excluded from baseball operating losses. The final adjustment I made was not significant, amounting to approximately $700,000.

Related-Party Transactions. One type of related-party transaction was parking and concession revenue. With respect to this item, the owners' expert reported:

Until recently the parking and concession revenue of one baseball club was realized by a municipal corporation and thus did not affect the operating results of the club. A year or so ago, however, the club's parent company purchased the municipal corporation's parking and concession rights, but the income of this now-related entity continued not to be reflected in the club's operations. For the purpose of my analysis, I consolidated the two entities and made an adjustment that further reduced the loss by $1.8 million.

Other related-party problems were more difficult. Examples of these are given in the following paragraphs, paraphrased from the report of the owners' expert:

Atlanta Braves. The Atlanta Braves are part of Ted Turner's holdings that include the Turner Broadcasting System (WTBS), a national cable television network. WTBS holds the television broadcasting rights to Braves games. The total revenues from local radio, television, and cable rights received by the Braves in 1984 was $1,884,000. For television alone, the Braves received $1 million.

St. Louis Cardinals. The St. Louis Cardinals are part of the corporate structure of Anheuser-Busch, maker of the number-one-selling beer in the United States. It has been conjectured that Busch acquired the Cardinals because it was the only means available for acquiring the sponsorship of Cardinal games for Budweiser. The Cardinals show below-average local radio, television, and cable revenues of $2,930,000. Perhaps more important, however, is the accounting for use of the stadium in which the Cardinals play their home games. The Cardinals pay stadium rent to the Civic Center Redevelopment Corporation (CCRC), which is also owned by Anheuser-Busch. Cardinal stadium costs in 1984 were $2,099,000, compared to a league-wide average of $2,755,000. CCRC also keeps essentially all of the revenues from concessions and parking. CCRC reported estimated revenues from baseball operations of $5,780,000 and expenses of $3,230,000, which includes $757,000 of stadium depreciation.

Chicago Cubs. The Cubs are affiliated in ownership with the Chicago Tribune and WGN, a superstation like WTBS; but the team is also in a larger local media market and hence derives large local profits. The Cubs report revenues from local radio, television, and cable of $6,410,000. However, the club gave back $810,000 to its parent corporation in advertising.

Chicago White Sox. The owners of the White Sox used the team as a vehicle to establish Sportsvision, a pay television operation. The White Sox formed Sportsvision by investing $3.4 million. About $3 million of this was then paid back to the club as payment for a loan the club had guaranteed to the team. The latter obligates the White Sox to pay Sportsvision approximately $130,000 a year in interest. On its part, Sportsvision must pay a fee to broadcast White Sox games only if the company becomes profitable. In 1984, the White Sox were entitled to $475,000 for these rights; however, nothing was paid since Sportsvision was not profitable. Finally, the White Sox are obligated to pay the production costs for certain Sportsvision broadcasts, which amounted to $567,000 in 1984. Thus, in interest and production costs the White Sox paid Sportsvision almost $700,000 in 1984, but received nothing in return.

Los Angeles Dodgers. The Dodgers are probably the most successful sports franchise that has ever been fielded. Operating income is well over $5 million and net income is over $6 million. However, the Dodgers' general and administrative expenses are $8.4 million, principally because salaries of front office personnel, including benefits, total $4.4 million, approximately four times the average for baseball.

The owners' expert's views regarding related-party transactions of the sort just described were as follows:

> In each case we have one buyer and one seller in a unique national market. I found no way to determine what an independently bargained price might be. An extensive economic and marketing analysis would be required to determine what the appropriate fee arrangement might be, and it would be open to question and challenge even then. I believed that, given these circumstances, no reasonable adjustment could be made, and I contented myself with noting and disclosing

the relationship and the problem in my report.

Questions

1. In what respects, if any, were generally accepted accounting principles not followed in the reports summarized in Schedule A?

2. What overall approach to measuring profitability is appropriate in measuring the size of the "pie" involved in this controversy?

3. How should the issues described in the case be resolved? If feasible, indicate the approximate effect of your recommendations on profit from operations. If this is not feasible, indicate what principles should be followed in arriving at the amount.

4. What, if any, other types of adjustments should be explored?

CASE 10–5   Freedom Technology Company

Freedom Technology Company produced various types of household electronic equipment, which it sold primarily through two large retail store chains in the United States. On October 1, 19x1, Freedom established a wholly owned subsidiary in South Korea, called Freedom-Korea, for the purpose of assembling a small home version of a video arcade game that Freedom had been licensed to produce. The Korean subsidiary sold its output directly to the U.S. retailers that carried the game (as opposed to selling its output to its U.S. parent for resale to U.S. retailers).

Exhibit 1 shows the subsidiary's condensed balance sheet as of September 30, 19x2 (fiscal year-end) and an income statement for its first year of operations. Freedom's controller, Marion Rosenblum, asked a member of the accounting staff to translate

EXHIBIT 1

FREEDOM-KOREA
Balance Sheet
As of September 30, 19x2
(millions of won)

Assets		Liabilities and Owners' Equity	
Cash	W 591	Current liabilities	W 624
Receivables	1,182		
Inventories	552	Capital stock	1,000
Fixed assets	575	Retained earnings	1,276
	W2,900		W2,900

Income Statement
For the Year Ended September 30, 19x2
(millions of won)

Revenues	W7,090
Cost of sales	4,415
Other expenses	1,399
Net income	W1,276

these statements into dollars, following the standards of *FASB Statement No. 52*. The controller also was interested in how the statements translated in accord with *FASB 52* might differ from those prepared using the method formerly required by *FASB 8*.

The accounting staff person assembled the following information to assist in preparing the two sets of translated statements:

1. The South Korean unit of currency is the won (abbreviated W). As of October 1, 19x1, the exchange rate was one won = $0.00140; as of September 30, 19x2, the rate was one won = $0.00124.

2. As of October 1, 19x1, Freedom-Korea's assets were W400 million cash and W600 million fixed assets. No additional fixed assets were acquired during the first year of operations. On average, the year end inventories had been on hand 1½ months; the exchange rate on August 15, 19x2, was one won – $0.00126.

3. The capital stock of Freedom-Korea had been issued to Freedom-Technology on October 1, 19x1; no additional capital stock transactions had taken place during the fiscal year.

Questions

1. Prepare translated year-end statements for Freedom-Korea using the net investment method, as required by *FASB 52*.

2. Prior to issuance of *FASB 52, FASB 8* required use of the monetary/nonmonetary method. With this method, monetary assets and liabilities are translated at the rate prevailing as of the balance sheet date; and nonmonetary items are translated at the rates existing when the transactions occurred, called *historical rates*. Income statement items are translated at the average rate prevailing during the period, except for those expenses related to asset costs that are translated at historical rates— e.g., depreciation expense.

    Prepare translated statements using *FASB 8*'s monetary/nonmonetary method. (Note: Under *FASB 8*, any translation gain or loss was included as an item in the translated income statement. You may treat any such gain or loss as a "plug" figure; i.e., you are not expected to calculate it in detail.)

3. Compare your two sets of translated statements and comment on any differences between them. If the company were permitted a choice as to which method to use, which method do you think they would prefer?

11

The Statement of Cash Flows

Our attention thus far has been focused on the analysis of transactions in terms of their effect on the balance sheet and the income statement. In this chapter we describe the third accounting report that a company must prepare, the **statement of cash flows** (or **cash flow statement**).

The discussion of the cash flow statement was deferred to this point because this statement does not affect the way in which transactions are recorded in the accounts. The accounts provide information that is summarized in the balance sheet and the income statement. Information used in preparing the cash flow statement is derived from data reported in the other financial statements and therefore does not require any new accounts to be added to the recordkeeping system.

THE CONCEPT OF FLOW STATEMENTS

A balance sheet is a snapshot of the status of a firm's funds at one instant of time. The liabilities and owners' equity side of the balance sheet shows the *sources* from which the funds that the firm is currently using were obtained—so much from accounts payable, from long-term creditors, from shareholders, from retained earnings, and so on. The assets side shows the *uses* that the firm currently is making of these funds—so much is tied up in cash, in inventories, in plant and equipment, and so on.

A flow statement explains the *changes* that took place in a balance sheet account or group of accounts during the period *between* the dates of two balance sheet snapshots. The income statement (and related statement of retained earnings) is a flow statement: It explains changes that occurred in the Retained Earnings account by summarizing the increases (revenues) and decreases (expenses and dividends) in Retained Earnings during the accounting period.

Purpose of the Cash Flow Statement

The income statement focuses on the economic results of the entity's *operating* activities during a period. Key concepts in the measurement of the period's income are revenue recognition and the matching of expenses. Revenue is recognized in the period in which the entity performs its revenue-generating tasks (e.g., delivering goods or providing services), irrespective of whether the customer pays cash at that time or agrees to pay later. Expenses measure the resources consumed in generating the period's revenue and in administering the entity during the period, irrespective of when cash was used to pay for those resources. Thus, the period's income bears no direct relationship to the cash flows associated with the period's operations. Also, because of its focus on the results of operations, the income statement does not provide information about the entity's investing or financing activities during the period.

The purpose of the cash flow statement is to provide information about the *cash flows associated with the period's operations* and also about the entity's *investing and financing activities* during the period. This information is important both to shareholders, part of whose investment return (dividends) is dependent on cash flows, and also to lenders, whose interest payments and principal repayment require the use of cash. The welfare of other constituencies of a company—including its employees, its suppliers, and the local communities that may levy taxes on it—depends to varying degrees on the company's ability to generate adequate cash flows to fulfill its financial obligations.

The numbers on the cash flow statement are objective: *Cash is cash,* and the amounts of cash flows are not influenced by the judgments and estimates that are made in arriving at revenues, expenses, and other accruals. Because of this objectivity, many analysts pay considerable attention to the cash flow statement. It must be remembered that despite the judgments and estimates that influence balance sheet and income statement amounts, the numbers in those statements provide better information about an entity's financial status and operating performance than do cash flow statement numbers.

Sources and Uses of Cash

The activities that the cash flow statement describes can be classified in two categories: (1) activities that generate cash, called *sources* and (2) activities that involve spending cash, called *uses.* Of course, an entity's operations routinely generate cash (especially from sales to customers) and use cash (for most operating expenses). The user of a cash flow statement is interested primarily in the *net* amount of cash generated by operations rather than in the detailed operating cash inflows and outflows. Thus, rather than separately showing operating cash inflows as sources and outflows as uses, this net amount is shown. Operations ordinarily are a net source of cash; however, operations are a net use of cash if they use more cash than they generate. A net use of cash is common in start-up companies and in companies that are expanding rapidly.

Treating this net of operating inflows and outflows as a single number, here are the following major types of cash sources and uses:

Sources	*Uses*
1. Operations	1. Cash dividends
2. New borrowings	2. Repayment of borrowings
3. New stock issues	3. Repurchase of stock
4. Sale of property, plant, and equipment	4. Purchase of property, plant, and equipment
5. Sale of other noncurrent assets	5. Purchase of other noncurrent assets

Inspection of the above lists suggests why cash flow statements are felt to be useful. They help the user answer questions such as the following:

- How much cash was provided by the normal, ongoing operations of the company?
- In what other ways were significant amounts of cash raised?
- Is the company investing enough in new plant and equipment to maintain or increase capacity and to replace old facilities with more efficient ones?
- Is the company reinvesting excess cash in productive assets, or is it using the cash to retire stock?
- To what extent are the company's investments being financed by internally generated cash and to what extent by borrowing or other external sources?
- For the cash obtained externally, what proportion was from debt and what from equity?
- Is the company having to borrow cash in order to maintain its cash dividend payments?

Although the cash flow statement cannot provide complete answers to all of these questions, it can at least suggest answers and highlight areas where it would be desirable to gather more information before deciding, for example, whether to buy, sell, or hold one's investment in the company's common stock.

Meaning of "Cash." Companies using modern cash management techniques invest any temporary excess amounts of cash in highly liquid, short-term investments (e.g., money market funds and Treasury bills) for periods as short as one or two days. As a result, for purposes of the cash flow statement, "cash" means the sum of actual cash and these short-term investments; the sum is formally called **cash and cash equivalents.** The FASB defines cash equivalents as highly liquid investments that are readily convertible to known amounts of cash and which mature in no more than 90 days from the date of the financial statement.[1]

THE CASH FLOW STATEMENT

Imagine that you have a checking account in which amounts over some minimum balance, say $1,000, are automatically invested in highly liquid, interest-bearing securities. Instead of your account representing just cash, it constitutes the sum of cash and cash equivalents. In your checkbook register you record all deposits and other increases in the account (debits), and you also record all checks written and other withdrawals from the account (credits). Now assume that at the end of each year, you wish to prepare a summary of the sources of the items that you deposited in your account and a summary of the various uses you made of the cash in the account. For example, the sources categories might be wages, investment earnings, and gifts, and the uses categories might be housing costs, other living expenses, recreation/entertainment, health care, taxes, and major purchases (such as a new television set or a car). You could first classify each entry in your checkbook register according to one of these categories, and then add the amounts of all of the items in each category and report the totals of the various categories. The end result could reasonably be called a personal cash flow statement.

In substance, the cash flow statement for a business entity is analogous in that it summarizes a myriad of specific cash transactions into a few categories. However, in practice, the information for the statement of cash flows is not taken directly from the Cash and Cash Equivalents accounts but rather is derived from income statement and balance sheet data. This section describes these derivation techniques.

Statement Categories

FASB 95 does not use as many major categories for sources and uses as we listed above. Instead, those ten types of sources and uses are combined into

---

[1]"Statement of Cash Flows," *FASB Statement No. 95* (November 1987), as amended by "Statement of Cash Flows—Exemption of Certain Enterprises and Classification of Cash Flows from Certain Securities Acquired for Resale," *FASB Statement No. 102* (February 1989) and "Statement of Cash Flows—Net Reporting of Certain Cash Receipts and Cash Payments and Classification of Cash Flows from Hedging Transactions," *FASB Statement No. 104* (December 1989).

three major categories: operating activities, investing activities, and financing activities.

Operating activities are defined to be all transactions that are *not* investing or financing activities. These transactions include the cash inflows associated with sales revenues and the cash outflows associated with operating expenses, including payments to suppliers of goods or services and payments for wages, interest, and taxes.

Investing activities include acquiring long-lived assets such as property, plant, equipment, and investments in securities that are not cash equivalents; and lending money (i.e., loans receivable). Investing activities also include the opposites of these transactions: disinvesting activities such as disposing of long-lived assets, and collecting loans. Note that increases or decreases in accounts receivable and inventory are not treated as investment activities; the changes in these current assets are included in operating activities.

Financing activities include the borrowing of cash (notes payable, mortgages, bonds, and other noncurrent borrowings) and the issuance of equity securities (common or preferred stock). Repayments of borrowings are also financing activities, as are dividend payments to shareholders and the use of cash to retire stock. Changes in accounts payable, wages payable, interest payable, and taxes payable are not treated as financing activities; they are operating activities.

Because the procedures for developing the net cash flow from operations are more complex than those for developing cash flows related to investing and financing activities, we will describe the latter two cash flow statement categories first. The descriptions for all three categories are based on the financial statements shown in Illustrations 11–1 and 11–2.

Investing Activities

Illustration 11–1 shows that during 19x1 investment in plant and equipment (at cost) increased by $350,000 (from $2,000,000 to $2,350,000). This is the *net* increase in investment during the year: additional plant and equipment investments minus disposals amounted to a net increase (at cost) of $350,000. From the balance sheet alone one cannot determine whether there was $350,000 of new fixed assets acquired and no disposals or some combination of acquisitions and disposals that amounted to a net increase of $350,000. Thus, the preparer of the cash flow statement would need to examine the Plant and Equipment account to make this determination. In this instance it happens that the investment in new equipment was $500,000 and the original cost of equipment disposed of was $150,000, resulting in the $350,000 net increase.

Conceptually, this net amount should be broken down into the portion that represents a cash outflow and the portion that represents a cash inflow, and we do this in the description that follows. However, as a practical matter, flows that are not material in amount are often netted.

ILLUSTRATION 11–1

FAIRWAY CORPORATION
Balance Sheets
As of December 31, 19x0 and 19x1
(in thousands)

Assets	19x0	19x1	Change
Current assets:			
Cash and cash equivalents	$ 230	$ 326	$ 96
Accounts receivable.	586	673	87
Inventories	610	657	47
Total current assets	1,426	1,656	230
Noncurrent assets:			
Plant and equipment, at cost.	2,000	2,350	350
Accumulated depreciation	(1,000)	(970)	30
Plant and equipment, net	1,000	1,380	380
Investment securities	450	400	(50)
Total noncurrent assets	1,450	1,780	330
Total assets	$ 2,876	$3,436	$560
Liabilities and Shareholders' Equity			
Current liabilities:			
Accounts payable.	$ 332	$ 388	$ 56
Income taxes payable	9	10	1
Short-term borrowings	147	126	(21)
Total current liabilities.	488	524	36
Long-term debt.	500	835	335
Deferred taxes.	65	70	5
Total liabilities.	1,053	1,429	376
Shareholders' equity:			
Common stock ($1 par).	50	60	10
Additional paid-in capital	133	167	34
Retained earnings.	1,640	1,780	140
Total shareholders' equity	1,823	2,007	184
Total liabilities and shareholders' equity.	$ 2,876	$3,436	$560

If $500,000 cash was paid for the new assets and $20,000 cash received for the old assets, then the cash flow statement would report each of these investing transactions as follows:

Acquisition of plant and equipment	$(500,000)
Proceeds from disposals of plant and equipment.	20,000

Thus, inflows and outflows related to a specific type of asset are shown as separate gross amounts rather than as a single net amount (i.e., a $480,000 net outflow in the example just given).

ILLUSTRATION 11–2

FAIRWAY CORPORATION
Income Statement and Statement of Retained Earnings
For the Year Ended December 31, 19x1
(in thousands)

Sales revenues		$3,190
Cost of sales		2,290
Gross margin		900
Expenses:		
Depreciation	$120	
Other expenses	477*	
Income taxes	103	700
Net income		$ 200
Retained earnings, December 31, 19x0		$1,640
Add: 19x1 net income		200
Less: Cash dividends		(60)
Retained earnings, December 31, 19x1		$1,780

* Net of $20,000 gain on disposal of equipment.

A similar approach is applied to the 19x1 decrease of $50,000 in investment securities (from $450,000 to $400,000). If that decrease were the result of selling $50,000 of securities (at cost) during the year and receiving $50,000 cash, then one line on the cash flow statement would describe the transactions:

Proceeds from sales of investment securities	$50,000

On the other hand, if the $50,000 were the net of $75,000 cash inflows from securities sales and $25,000 outflows for purchases, then the cash flow statement would show:

Purchases of investment securities	$(25,000)
Proceeds from sales of investment securities	75,000

Finally, if the $50,000 net change in investment securities on the balance sheet were different from the associated net *cash flow*, then the cash flow would be reported. For example, if securities with a balance sheet carrying amount of $50,000 were sold for $53,000, the cash inflow reported would be $53,000, even though the balance sheet Investment Securities account decreased by $50,000.

ILLUSTRATION 11–3

FAIRWAY CORPORATION
Statement of Cash Flows
For the Year Ending December 31, 19x1
(in thousands)

Net cash flow from operating activities:

Net income...	$ 200
Noncash expenses, revenues, gains,and losses included in income:	
Depreciation...	120
Deferred taxes...	5
Increase in accounts receivable	(87)
Increase in inventories..	(47)
Increase in accounts payable	56
Increase in taxes payable......................................	1
Gain on sale of equipment	(20)
Net cash flow from operating activities	228

Cash flows from investing activities:

Acquisition of plant and equipment	(500)
Proceeds from disposals of plant and equipment.................	20
Purchase of investment securities..............................	(25)
Proceeds from sales of investment securities...................	75
Net cash used by investing activities......................	(430)

Cash flows from finanoing aotivities:

Proceeds of short-term debt....................................	15
Payments to settle short-term debt.............................	(36)
Proceeds of long-term debt	375
Payments on long-term debt	(40)
Proceeds from issuing common stock.............................	44
Dividends paid	(60)
Net cash provided by financing activities	298
Net increase (decrease) in cash and cash equivalents..........	96
Cash and cash equivalents at beginning of year	230
Cash and cash equivalents at end of year......................	$ 326

The company's investing activities are summarized in the middle section of the cash flow statement shown in Illustration 11–3. Note that all of the individual items are summarized to arrive at a single net amount of cash flow associated with investing activities, in this case an outflow (use) of $430,000.

Financing Activities

During 19x1 Fairway Corporation's short-term borrowings decreased by $21,000 (from $147,000 to $126,000). The underlying records reveal that this was the net effect of $15,000 of new borrowings and $36,000 repayments of old borrowings. Rather than reporting the net amount, the cash flow statement would show:

Proceeds of short-term debt	$ 15,000
Payments to settle short-term debt.	(36,000)

Similarly, analysis of the underlying transactions reveals that the $335,000 increase in long-term debt was the net of $375,000 new borrowings and $40,000 repayments of previous long-term debt. This would be reported as follows:

Proceeds of long-term debt.	$375,000
Payments on long-term debt.	(40,000)

The $40,000 cash payments are a reduction in the *principal* of the long-term debt; interest payments are treated as an operating transaction rather than as an investing activity.

Also during 19x1 Fairway issued 10,000 additional shares of $1 par value common stock resulting in cash proceeds to the corporation of $44,000. On the balance sheet this appears as a $10,000 increase in common stock at par and a $34,000 increase in additional paid-in capital. On the cash flow statement the following line would appear:

Proceeds from issuing common stock	$44,000

Finally, *FASB 95* treats dividend payments to shareholders as a financing activity. As shown at the bottom of Illustration 11–2, cash dividends amounted to $60,000. This would appear on the cash flow statement thus:

Dividends paid	$(60,000)

Note that it is the amount of cash dividends *paid* during the year, as opposed to the amount of dividends *declared* for the year, that appears on the cash flow statement. In this instance the amount paid was the same as the amount declared: $60,000. However, because the dividend declared for the last quarter of the year ordinarily is not paid until early in the following year, it is not unusual for the amount of dividends declared for the year to be different from the amount paid *during* that year.

The bottom section of the cash flow statement in Illustration 11–3 reports and summarizes all of the company's 19x1 financing activities. The net cash flow from these activities was a $298,000 inflow (source). We emphasize that although the level of detail we have shown is conceptually correct, certain immaterial flows would be netted in practice.

Noncash Transactions

Some significant investing and financing activities do not involve cash flows at all, such as the conversion of a convertible bond into common stock. Certain other investing and financing activities, although affecting cash, do not affect it in the full amount of the investment or financing transaction. For example, if an entity acquires a fixed asset costing $500,000 by making a $200,000 cash payment and giving the seller an equipment note payable for the other $300,000, *FASB 95* requires that the cash flow statement report only the $200,000 cash outflow associated with the fixed asset investment transaction.[2] However, *FASB 95* does require disclosure of the $300,000 noncash portion of the transaction in a narrative statement or supplemental schedule.

A transaction involving the conversion of $400,000 face value of bonds into common stock results in no cash inflows or outflows. Thus, it is not reported in the statement of cash flows. However, the substance of such a conversion is that stock is issued, resulting in a cash inflow, and then the proceeds of the issuance are used to retire the bonds, an equal and offsetting outflow. *FASB 95* requires that the conversion be reported in a supplemental disclosure, thus: "Additional stock was issued upon conversion of $400,000 of bonds payable."

Cash Flow from Operating Activities

As mentioned above, the cash flow statement reports the net cash flow generated by the period's operations. This net amount can be presented in two ways: the direct method and the indirect, or reconciliation, method.

Direct Method.   With the **direct method** of reporting cash flows from operating activities, summaries of operating inflows and outflows are shown and then combined to arrive at the net cash flow from operations. For Fairway Corporation in 19x1, the presentation would appear as follows:

Cash flows from operating activities:	
Cash received from customers	$3,103,000
Dividends and interest received	19,000
Cash provided by operating activities	3,122,000
Cash paid to suppliers and employees	2,729,000
Interest paid.	67,000
Income taxes paid	98,000
Cash disbursed for operating activities	2,894,000
Net cash flow from operating activities	$ 228,000

---

[2] In our view, the FASB's way of recording this transaction does not adequately capture its substance. In effect, there was a $300,000 *financing* transaction that momentarily increased cash, representing the note payable proceeds. Then this $300,000 plus another $200,000 cash was used to make the $500,000 investment in the fixed asset. Thus, in substance, there was an $300,000 financing activity inflow and a $500,000 investing activity outflow rather than a $200,000 investing activity outflow.

FASB 95 "encourages" companies to use this method. It results in a straightforward presentation that is intuitively understandable by users with little or no accounting training. However, it does not suggest why the year's net operating cash flow ($228,000) differed from the year's net income ($200,000).

Indirect Method. For this reason the direct method is not the one used by most companies.[3] They prefer a presentation that helps the user to understand the reasons for the difference between the period's net income and the period's net cash flow from operations—the **reconciliation,** or **indirect, method.** *FASB 95* permits either the direct or the reconciliation method. However, because one of the FASB's stated purposes of a statement of cash flows is to help users understand the differences between net income and the associated cash receipts and payments, if the direct method is used, then a reconciliation of net income and net cash flow from operating activities must be provided in a separate schedule.

Indirect Method Calculations

The indirect method is much harder to understand than the direct method. We will first illustrate the presentation and then explain the calculations on which the indirect method is based. The presentation is as shown in the top portion of Illustration 11–3, labeled "Net cash flow from operating activities."

The approach of the indirect method is to start with the net income amount and adjust it for differences between revenues (or gains) and operating cash inflows, and for differences between expenses (or losses) and operating cash outflows. For many companies, the largest adjustment relates to depreciation.

Depreciation. To understand the depreciation adjustment, consider the adjusting entry made to record depreciation expense:

Depreciation Expense 120,000
    Accumulated Depreciation. 120,000

Note that this entry reduces income by $120,000 but has *no effect* on Cash. (To affect Cash, the credit would have to be to Cash rather than to Accumulated Depreciation.) Now assume for the moment (contrary to fact) that (1) revenues were equal to operating cash inflows (Cash was debited whenever Sales Revenues was credited) and (2) total expenses *excluding* depreciation expense were equal to operating cash outflows (except for depreciation, Cash was credited whenever an expense account was debited). Then net income would be $120,000 lower than net operating cash flow because $120,000 depreciation expense was subtracted in the calculation of

[3]*Accounting Trends & Techniques* (1993) reports that only 15 of the 600 companies surveyed used the direct method.

net income, but this $120,000 expense did not reduce Cash. Thus, if we add $120,000 back to the amount of net income, then the resulting amount is the net cash flow from operations. Because of our assumptions, this is the only adjustment needed to take account of revenues that were not also cash inflows and expenses that were not also cash outflows. Note in the Illustration 11–3 reconciliation presentation that $120,000 is added to the net income of $200,000 as one of the adjustments.

Deferred Taxes.   To understand the adjustment labeled "Deferred taxes," we must review the nature of the Deferred Income Taxes account. This account will increase (be credited) if the period's income tax *expense* is larger than the period's income tax *payments*. Note in Illustration 11–1 that the balance in Deferred Taxes increased by $5,000 (from $65,000 to $70,000) during the year. Fairway's 19x1 tax expense was $5,000 larger than its 19x1 tax payments. Thus, the amount subtracted for income taxes in preparing Fairway's income statement overstated the *cash outflows* for taxes by $5,000. To adjust the income statement to a cash basis, therefore, requires that this $5,000 overstatement of cash outflows be added back to the net income figure. Note that in the indirect method presentation $5,000 is added to net income for this adjustment.

Analogously, if the balance in Deferred Income Taxes decreases during the year, then the amount of the decrease must be subtracted from net income. This is because the year's tax payments were greater than the amount of reported tax expense, and the income statement thus overstates operating cash flows. (An understatement of an outflow is equivalent to the overstatement of an inflow.)

Accounts Receivable.   To understand this adjustment, recall that the nature of the period's entries to Accounts Receivable is as follows:

Accounts Receivable

Beginning balance	Collections (debit to Cash)
Sales revenue	Ending balance
Beginning balance of next period	

The following equation describes these relationships:

Beginning balance + Sales revenues = Collections + Ending balance

For purposes of developing the operating cash flow amount, the amount of *collections* is of interest, because this is the amount of cash inflows that resulted from sales. Yet the period's net income is calculated based on the amount of revenues, not collections. The necessary adjustment can be calculated by a simple rearrangement of the above equation:

Collections = Sales revenues − (Ending balance − Beginning balance)

Thus, if the balance in Accounts Receivable *increased* during the year, collections can be deduced by *subtracting* the increase in receivables from sales revenues.

This was the case with Fairway Corporation in 19x1: collections = $3,190,000 − $87,000 = $3,103,000. (The $87,000 increase in receivables is the difference between the ending balance of $673,000 and the beginning balance of $586,000, as shown in Illustration 11–1.) Note that this result, $3,103,000, is the amount that was reported in the direct method as "Cash received from customers."[4]

In a similar manner it can be demonstrated that a *decrease* in the amount of accounts receivable during the period should be *added* to net income because such a decrease means that the period's cash inflows from customers (i.e., collections) exceeded the amount of sales revenue reported on the income statement.

Inventories. The adjustment related to inventories can also be developed by focusing on the T Account:

Inventories

Beginning balance	Cost of sales
Purchases (credit Cash)	Ending balance
Beginning balance of next period	

In this case the equation that is the basis of the adjustment is:

Purchases = Cost of sales + (Ending balance − Beginning balance)

If inventories increased during the period, cost of sales understates the cash outflows for purchases, and the inventory increase must therefore be added to cost of sales to deduce the cash outflows. But adding to cost of sales, an expense amount, is equivalent to subtracting from net income. Thus, if inventories *increased*, the amount of the increase is *subtracted* from net income to adjust income to a cash flow basis. For Fairway Corporation the inventories increase during 19x1 was $47,000 (= $657,000 − $610,000). Thus, $47,000 must be subtracted from 19x1 net income to adjust cost of sales from an expense amount to a cash outflow amount.

Similarly, a *decrease* in inventory would be *added* to net income, which is equivalent to subtracting the amount of the decrease from cost of sales. If inventory decreases during the period, then the cost of sales amount overstates the cash outflows for the period's inventory purchases, and this

---

[4]We are implicitly assuming that all sales are made on credit, which is the case with many nonretailing companies. The adjustment procedure is the same if some sales are made for cash. The reader can simply imagine that for a cash sale, Accounts Receivable is simultaneously debited for the sales revenue and credited for the collection of this revenue.

overstatement of outflows must be added back to net income to convert it to an operating cash flow amount.

Prepaid Expenses. Fairway Corporation had no prepaid expenses. If there are prepaid expenses, the adjustments related to them are the same as for inventories. An increase in the balance in Prepaid Expenses during the period is subtracted from the period's net income. A decrease in the balance of Prepaid Expenses is added to net income.

Accounts Payable. The adjustment related to changes in inventory converted the cost of sales expense item to a cash basis on the implicit assumption that all purchases for inventory were made for cash. The adjustment related to Accounts Payable relaxes this assumption and deals at the same time with purchases of resources that are expenses of the period, such as selling expenses, rather than assets. Since in a sense Accounts Payable is a mirror image of Accounts Receivable, the payables adjustment is algebraically the opposite of the receivables adjustment. Thus, if the balance in Accounts Payable *increases* during the period, the amount of the increase is *added* to net income to reflect the fact that the period's expenses overstate the cash outflows for payments to suppliers. If the balance in Accounts Payable declines during the period, then suppliers have been paid more than is reflected in expenses; thus, a *decrease* in Accounts Payable is *subtracted* from net income to adjust it to operating cash flows. For Fairway Corporation in 19x1, the $56,000 increase in Accounts Payable must be added to net income to adjust it to a cash flow amount.

Similar comments and the same rules apply to other payables related to operations—Interest Payable, Wages Payable, and Taxes Payable. However, there is no adjustment made for Notes Payable because that account relates to financing activities, not operating activities.

Gains and Losses. The final type of adjustment made to net income to convert it to cash flow from operations relates to gains or losses reported on the accrual-basis income statement. Such gains or losses ordinarily are related to the sale or disposal of property, plant, and equipment or of marketable securities. The income statement will report the difference between the proceeds (if any) from the asset's sale or disposal and the asset's carrying amount at the time of sale (net book value in the case of fixed assets). If the proceeds exceed the carrying amount, a gain will be reported; if the proceeds are less than the carrying amount, a loss will be reported.

However, from the standpoint of the cash flow statement, the write-off of the asset's carrying amount is not relevant; the cash outflow associated with that amount occurred in some earlier period when the asset was acquired. Only the cash proceeds from the sale are of concern. Thus, the carrying amount of the asset must be added back to net income, since it was a write-off of a capitalized cost, not a cash outflow. Moreover, any cash proceeds from the asset's disposal are treated as an investing activity inflow in that section of the cash flow statement. Therefore, if no adjustment was made, the disposal proceeds would get double-counted—once in the operating activities section and again in the investing section. Hence, the cash proceeds must be subtracted from net income to avoid this double counting. When both adjustments are taken into account—adding back the asset's carrying amount and subtracting the proceeds—the net effect simply reverses the reported gain or loss.

To illustrate such an adjustment, recall that Fairway Corporation sold a fixed asset in 19x1 for $20,000 cash. The original cost of the asset was $150,000, but it was fully depreciated, so its net book value was zero.[5] Thus, the sale resulted in a $20,000 gain that would have been recorded by this entry:

Cash...	20,000	
Accumulated Depreciation..........................	150,000	
Equipment, at Cost............................		150,000
Gain on Disposal of Equipment.................		20,000

In this case, because the carrying amount of the asset was zero, the gain and the cash proceeds are the same, $20,000. But recall that the $20,000 proceeds were treated as an inflow in the investing activities section of the cash flow statement. To report this $20,000 also as an inflow from operations would double-count it. Thus, the $20,000 gain must be subtracted in the cash flow from operating activities section to avoid this double-counting.

Book Value. Suppose instead that equipment with a net book value of $10,000 had been disposed of with no resultant cash proceeds. In this case the income statement would have reported a $10,000 loss; yet this would not have been associated with a $10,000 cash outflow. Thus, the adjustment to net income to convert it to net operating cash flow would be to add back the $10,000 loss; otherwise, net income would overstate cash outflows and thus understate net cash flow from operating activities.

As a final example, assume that property with a net book value of $10,000 was disposed of with cash proceeds of $15,000. The income statement would report a $5,000 gain. Since the sale of long-lived productive assets is treated as an investing activity, the $15,000 cash inflow from the disposal would be reported in that section of the cash flow statement. Thus, this $5,000 gain that is part of net income must be subtracted in the cash flow from operating activities section to preclude (1) double-counting the $15,000 proceeds and (2) counting the write-off of the $10,000 net book value as though it were a cash outflow when it is not.

In sum, the cash flow statement must accurately report the cash inflow (if any) associated with the sale or disposal of long-lived assets, not the

---

[5]Note in Illustrations 11−1 and 11−2 that Fairway's accumulated depreciation as of year-end 19x0 was $1,000,000 and 19x1 depreciation expense was $120,000, a sum of $1,120,000. Yet 19x1 year-end accumulated depreciation was $970,000, or $150,000 less than $1,120,000. Thus, the amount of accumulated depreciation associated with the asset disposed of during 19x1 was $150,000.

difference between cash proceeds and net book value which is reported in the income statement. Because the cash inflow proceeds are reported in the investing activities section of the statement and the write-off of the carrying amount of the asset does not involve a simultaneous cash outflow, any gain or loss reported in the income statement must be reversed in developing the amount for cash flow from operating activities.

Operating Activities: Summary. With the adjustment for gains or losses, the indirect method format for the operating activities section of the cash flow statement is complete. Collectively, the adjustments constitute a reconciliation of net income and net cash generated by operating activities. As seen in Illustration 11–3, the $228,000 net inflow is the same as would have been reported had the direct method been used. (Indeed, some of the adjustment techniques described for the indirect method can be used to obtain the numbers reported by the direct method; the direct method simply reports the results of the adjustments rather than showing the adjustments themselves.) Illustration 11–4 is presented as a summary of the adjustments we have described under the indirect method.

Summary of the Cash Flow Statement

The cash flow statement is divided into three major sections: operating, investing, and financing activities. Cash flow from operating activities can be prepared using the direct method or the indirect (reconciliation) method. Assuming use of the indirect method, the steps in preparing the statement of cash flows are as follows:

1. Find cash generated by operations by adjusting the net income as reported on the income statement using the procedures summarized in Illustration 11–4.

2. Identify any investing activities—for example, acquisition or sale of property, plant, and equipment or marketable securities. Report only the cash outflows associated with acquisitions; any portion of the cost of an

ILLUSTRATION 11–4
CALCULATING OPERATING CASH FLOW FROM NET INCOME

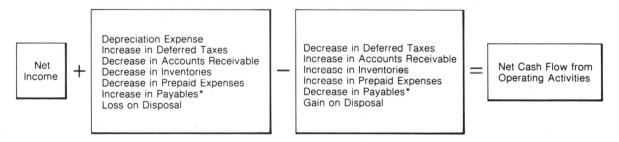

Net Income + [Depreciation Expense / Increase in Deferred Taxes / Decrease in Accounts Receivable / Decrease in Inventories / Decrease in Prepaid Expenses / Increase in Payables* / Loss on Disposal] − [Decrease in Deferred Taxes / Increase in Accounts Receivable / Increase in Inventories / Increase in Prepaid Expenses / Decrease in Payables* / Gain on Disposal] = Net Cash Flow from Operating Activities

* Includes accounts payable, wages payable (accrued wages), interest payable (accrued interest expense), and taxes payable; does not include notes payable or current portion of long-term debt.

acquisition that was financed by a directly related liability (e.g., a mortgage) must be subtracted in arriving at the cash outflow associated with the acquisition. Report only the cash proceeds from the sale of an asset.

3. Identify any financing activities, such as new borrowings or repayments on existing borrowings, issuance or retirement of stock, and cash dividend payments. If a convertible security was converted, do not report it in the cash flow statement, but disclose it in a supplementary narrative.

4. Sum the subtotals for the three sections of the statement to determine the increase or decrease in cash (and equivalents). This amount is then added to the beginning cash balance to arrive at the ending cash balance, as shown in the bottom portion of Illustration 11–3.

MISCONCEPTIONS ABOUT DEPRECIATION

The way in which cash generated by operations is determined in the indirect method can lead to confusion about the nature of depreciation. Hence, this calculation warrants further discussion. Instead of calculating net cash flow from operations by showing cash inflows from customers and other revenue sources and then subtracting cash outflows for operating costs (the direct method), the starting point in the indirect method (as shown in Illustration 11–3) was the net income figure, to which depreciation was added. This add-back of depreciation was done because depreciation was an expense in Fairway's accrual-basis income statement that did not represent an outflow of cash during the period. By contrast, as was shown by the journal entry to record depreciation expense, depreciation was neither a source nor a use of cash.

Unfortunately, many people misunderstand the nature of the calculation deriving operating cash flow from net income. They have the misconception that depreciation is a source of cash. Their misunderstanding is compounded by the failure of some companies to label the add-back of depreciation as an adjustment needed to convert net income to cash generated by operations. Instead, these companies simply list both net income and depreciation under the heading, "cash flow from operations." This confusion is exemplified by statements in the business press such as the following:

> Depreciation should not be considered as a part of cash flow which can be used to pay dividends; rather, it should be considered as a source of funds to replace plant.

> This kind of capital expenditure we write off fairly quickly ... so that it becomes part of the financing. It's the cash flow.

> The weaker airlines generally leased rather than bought their planes, thus forfeiting the chance to boost cash flow from depreciation. When ticket sales are an airline's only source of cash, a plunge in bookings can quickly put a carrier out of business.

The loan may be repaid . . . through cash generated from the gradual liquidation of a fixed asset (represented by depreciation) or the earnings of the borrower. . . . These two items—depreciation and earnings—constitute cash flow.

These statements are fallacious. *Depreciation is not a source of cash.*

Some people argue that depreciation is a source of cash because depreciation expense reduces taxable income and hence reduces the cash outflow in payment of taxes. For example, if Fairway Corporation acquires more equipment in 19x2, the additional depreciation expense will reduce its 19x2 taxable income from what it would be if the equipment were not acquired, and hence will reduce the cash outflow for tax payments. This does not mean, however, that depreciation is a source of cash. The cash transaction is the income tax payment, and depreciation merely enters into the calculation of taxable income and hence reduces the tax payment. By the same token Fairway could reduce its taxes in 19x2 by increasing *any* expense, such as by giving every employee a 25 percent wage increase. Would one then say that increased wages expense is a source of cash?

Cash Flow Earnings

Since in most companies depreciation is the principal expense item that does not involve the use of cash, the sum of net income plus depreciation is often a good *approximation* of the cash generated by operations. (This is presumably what the author of the final quotation had in mind.) This total is often called **cash flow earnings.** Although depreciation enters into the calculation of this amount, depreciation is not itself a source of cash. The cash is generated by earnings activities, not by an adjusting entry for depreciation. The FASB specifically prohibits reporting an item labeled *cash flow income* or *cash earnings per share.*

PREPARATION OF THE CASH FLOW STATEMENT

Unlike the balance sheet and income statement, which are prepared directly from the firm's accounts, the cash flow statement is derived *analytically* from those accounts. This statement explains changes in asset, liability, and owners' equity accounts between the beginning and ending balance sheets of the period. Therefore, a logical way to prepare a cash flow statement is to identify and analyze the causes of differences between account amounts in the beginning and ending balance sheets. This analysis can be done in one of three ways: (1) by directly analyzing differences calculated from the comparative balance sheets, (2) by using a worksheet, and (3) by using T accounts.

The first approach is essentially the same as we have already used in explaining the derivation of amounts shown in Illustration 11–3, based on amounts in Illustration 11–1. The worksheet and T account approaches are not conceptually different but are more methodical and hence reduce the chance of errors. We will demonstrate the worksheet method below.

We emphasize that these descriptions contain no new concepts. The two alternative approaches are merely mechanical devices for arriving at the amounts to be reported on the statement of cash flows.

Cash Flow Worksheet

Illustration 11–5 is the worksheet for preparation of Fairway Corporation's 19x1 cash flow statement. On it have been entered the beginning and ending account balances from Illustration 11–1, and changes in these account balances have been calculated in the final column. We must explain the $96,000 increase in Cash. For each of the other accounts, we will reconstruct the journal entries that caused the changes. Entries that affect the amount of cash will be classified as one of three types: cash from operations, cash from investing activities, and cash from financing activities. Because these classifications correspond to the format of the cash flow statement, using them will facilitate its final preparation. The numbers in the entries that follow correspond to those on the completed worksheet in Illustration 11–6.

Worksheet Entries

Retained Earnings. A good starting point for the analysis is the $140,000 change in Retained Earnings. Illustration 11–2 showed a condensed version of Fairway's income statement and a reconciliation of the beginning and ending balances of Retained Earnings. From these statements we can see that two things affected the level of retained earnings: net income ($200,000), a source of cash; and payment of cash dividends ($60,000), a use of cash. We thus can record these two entries on the worksheet:

(1)

Cash from Operations	200,000	
Retained Earnings		200,000

(2)

Retained Earnings	60,000	
Cash from Financing Activities		60,000

At this point note that these two entries result in a net credit to Retained Earnings of $140,000. The last column of the worksheet shows that a change of $140,000 cr. was the amount we needed to explain. Thus, the analysis of the change in Retained Earnings is complete.

Plant and Equipment. The changes in these accounts can be caused by acquisition or disposal of fixed assets and by changes in accumulated depreciation. As explained above, depreciation is an expense that is quite properly subtracted in arriving at net income but that, unlike most expenses, does not affect cash. Hence, we must add back the depreciation expense to net income; otherwise, Cash from Operations would be understated. The $120,000 depreciation expense for the period is shown in the income statement in Illustration 11–2. The entry for the worksheet is:

ILLUSTRATION 11–5

FAIRWAY CORPORATION
Worksheet to Develop the Cash Flow Statement
For the Year Ended December 31, 19x1

	Beginning Balances	Analytical Entries		Ending Balances	Net Change
		Debit	Credit		
Debit-balance accounts:					
Cash	230,000			326,000	96,000 dr.
Accounts receivable	586,000			673,000	87,000 dr.
Inventories	610,000			657,000	47,000 dr.
Plant and equipment, at cost	2,000,000			2,350,000	350,000 dr.
Accumulated depreciation	(1,000,000)			(970,000)	30,000 dr.
Investment securities	450,000			400,000	50,000 cr.
	2,876,000			3,436,000	560,000 dr.
Credit-balance accounts:					
Accounts payable	332,000			388,000	56,000 cr.
Income taxes payable	9,000			10,000	1,000 cr.
Short-term borrowings	147,000			126,000	21,000 dr.
Long-term debt	500,000			835,000	335,000 cr.
Deferred taxes	65,000			70,000	5,000 cr.
Common stock ($1 par)	50,000			60,000	10,000 cr.
Additional paid-in capital	133,000			167,000	34,000 cr.
Retained earnings	1,640,000			1,780,000	140,000 cr.
	2,876,000			3,436,000	560,000 cr.
		Sources	Uses		
Cash from operations:					
Cash from investing activities:					
Cash from financing activities:					

ILLUSTRATION 11–6

FAIRWAY CORPORATION
Completed Cash Flow Statement Worksheet
For the Year Ended December 31, 19x1

	Beginning Balances	Analytical Entries*		Ending Balances	Net Change
		Debit	Credit		
Debit-balance accounts:					
Cash	230,000	96,000		326,000	96,000 dr.
Accounts receivable	586,000	(7a) 87,000		673,000	87,000 dr.
Inventories	610,000	(7b) 47,000		657,000	47,000 dr.
Plant and equipment, at cost	2,000,000	(4) 500,000	(5) 150,000	2,350,000	350,000 dr.
Accumulated depreciation	(1,000,000)	(5) 150,000	(3) 120,000	(970,000)	30,000 dr.
Investment securities	450,000	(9a) 25,000	(9b) 75,000	400,000	50,000 cr.
	2,876,000			3,436,000	560,000 dr.
Credit-balance accounts:					
Accounts payable	332,000		(7c) 56,000	388,000	56,000 cr.
Income taxes payable	9,000		(7d) 1,000	10,000	1,000 cr.
Short-term borrowings	147,000	(10b) 36,000	(10a) 15,000	126,000	21,000 cr.
Long-term debt	500,000	(11b) 40,000	(11a) 375,000	835,000	335,000 cr.
Deferred taxes	65,000		(8) 5,000	70,000	5,000 cr.
Common stock ($1 par)	50,000		(12) 10,000	60,000	10,000 cr.
Additional paid-in capital	133,000		(12) 34,000	167,000	34,000 cr.
Retained earnings	1,640,000	(2) 60,000	(1) 200,000	1,780,000	140,000 cr.
	2,876,000	1,041,000	1,041,000	3,436,000	560,000 cr.

		Sources	Uses		
Cash from operations:					
Net income		(1) 200,000			
Depreciation expense		(3) 120,000			
Gain on disposal			(6) 20,000		
Increase in accounts receivable			(7a) 87,000		
Increase in inventories			(7b) 47,000		
Increase in accounts payable		(7c) 56,000			
Increase in taxes payable		(7d) 1,000			
Increase in deferred taxes		(8) 5,000			
Cash from investing activities:					
Equipment acquisition			(4) 500,000		
Proceeds from disposal		(6) 20,000			
Purchase of securities			(9a) 25,000		
Sale of securities		(9b) 75,000			
Cash from financing activities:					
Dividends paid			(2) 60,000		
Short-term debt proceeds		(10a) 15,000			
Short-term debt payments			(10b) 36,000		
Long-term debt proceeds		(11a) 375,000			
Long-term debt payments			(11b) 40,000		
Proceeds from stock issuance		(12) 44,000			
		911,000	815,000		96,000 dr.

* Numbers in parentheses correspond to entries described in the text.

(3)
Cash from Operations................................. 120,000
    Accumulated Depreciation........................   120,000

Other company records indicate that $500,000 of new equipment was purchased during the year. Thus, as another entry we have:

(4)
Plant and Equipment, at Cost 500,000
    Cash from Investing Activities   500,000

Entries 3 and 4 do not completely explain the net increase of $350,000 in Plant and Equipment, at Cost, nor the net increase of $30,000 in Accumulated Depreciation. (Since Accumulated Depreciation is a contra asset, its changing from $1,000,000 to $970,000 constitutes an increase in assets.) The disposal of a fully depreciated asset, having original cost of $150,000, needs to be included in the analysis:

(5)
Accumulated Depreciation............................ 150,000
    Plant and Equipment, at Cost   150,000

Entries 3, 4, and 5 now collectively explain the $350,000 increase in Plant and Equipment, at Cost, and the $30,000 increase in Accumulated Depreciation.

Note that the write-off transaction in entry 5 does not affect cash flow. However, we also know that there were $20,000 cash proceeds from the disposal, which must be shown as a source in the investing activities section of the cash flow statement. This $20,000 was treated as a gain on the income statement, since the net book value of the equipment disposed of was zero. But net income, including this $20,000, has already been reflected as a source of cash from operations in entry 1. Thus, we need to reclassify this $20,000 from an operating activity source to an investing activity source, as with this entry:

(6)
Cash from Investing Activities 20,000
    Cash from Operations............................   20,000

Other Adjustments to Net Income.   Entries 3 and 6 constitute two of several adjustments that must be made to convert the net income amount, $200,000 in entry 1, to the net cash flow from operations. Illustration 11−4 reminds us of the other adjustments, which are related to changes in receivables, inventories, and payables. These adjustments are made with the following entries:

(7a)
Accounts Receivable 87,000
    Cash from Operations............................   87,000

(7b)

Inventories	47,000	
Cash from Operations		47,000

(7c)

Cash from Operations	56,000	
Accounts Payable		56,000

(7d)

Cash from Operations	1,000	
Income Taxes Payable		1,000

Also, the $5,000 increase in deferred taxes, representing income tax expense that did not require a current outflow of cash, leads to this adjustment:

(8)

Cash from Operations	5,000	
Deferred Taxes		5,000

The analysis has now taken care of all items affecting cash from operations but is incomplete as to investing and financing activities.

Investment Securities. The one remaining unexplained asset change (other than Cash, which is what we are explaining overall) is the $50,000 decrease in Investment Securities. Underlying records show that this was the net effect of both new investments ($25,000) and of securities sales ($75,000). The FASB wants each component reflected separately in the cash flow statement, which will require these entries:

(9a)

Investment Securities	25,000	
Cash from Investing Activities		25,000

(9b)

Cash from Investing Activities	75,000	
Investment Securities		75,000

Debt Transactions. Short-Term Borrowings and Long-Term Debt both changed during 19x1. As with other balance sheet changes, the net amount of a change in debt is explained by reporting both the inflows and outflows contributing to the net change. For Short-Term Borrowings, underlying records reveal that the net decrease of $21,000 is explained by new short-term debt of $15,000 and repayments on earlier short-term debt of $36,000. This leads to the following entries:

(10a)

Cash from Financing Activities	15,000	
Short-Term Borrowings		15,000

(10b)

Short-Term Borrowings	36,000	
Cash from Financing Activities		36,000

Similarly, the net increase in Long-Term Debt of $335,000 is explained thus:

(11a)

Cash from Financing Activities......................	375,000	
Long-Term Debt..................................		375,000

(11b)

Long-Term Debt....................................	40,000	
Cash from Financing Activities..................		40,000

Paid-in Capital.   The remaining two account changes to be analyzed are those in Common Stock ($1 par) and Additional Paid-In Capital; that is, total paid-in capital. During the year 10,000 shares of Fairway Corporation $1 par common stock were issued, for which the firm received $44,000. This financing activity leads to this worksheet entry:

(12)

Cash from Financing Activities......................	44,000	
Common Stock ($1 par)..........................		10,000
Additional Paid-In Capital		34,000

This entry completes the analysis of changes on the worksheet (Illustration 11–6). The change of every noncash account has been explained, and the offsetting entries have been classified as sources of cash (debits in the lower portion of the worksheet) or as uses of cash (credits); and these sources and uses have been further classified as arising from operations, investing activities, or financing activities. As a check, the debits (sources) and credits (uses) below the double line are added and the net change compared with the top line of the worksheet. Both changes are $96,000 dr., showing the accuracy of the amounts of the analytical entries.

Statement Preparation

The actual preparation of the cash flow statement is now straightforward. All of the amounts needed for the statement of cash flows appear on the worksheet in Illustration 11–6. All that is necessary is to put these amounts in the proper format, as shown in Illustration 11–3. We have used the indirect method to develop the amount for cash from operating activities because it is illustrative of usual practice. The direct method is also permitted; but if it is used, a reconciliation of net income with net cash flow from operations must be presented in a separate schedule.

Summary of Preparation Procedures

To prepare a cash flow statement, the following steps are taken:

1.   From the company's balance sheets, enter the beginning and ending balances of each account and the change in each account's balance on a worksheet (such as in Illustration 11–6).

2.   For each account (other than Cash), analyze the nature of the transactions causing the amount of net change and classify the change from

ILLUSTRATION 11–7
LOCATING AMOUNTS FOR A CASH FLOW STATEMENT

Item	*Location on Financial Statements*
1. *Cash from operations:*	
a. Net income	Income statement
b. Plus: Depreciation expense	Income statement (or note thereto)
c. Plus: Amortization of prepaid expense, goodwill, and other intangibles	Income statement (or note) or change in balance sheet item
d. Plus: Increase (or Minus: Decrease) in deferred income taxes	Change in deferred tax liability
e. Minus: Increase in accounts receivable, inventories; Plus: Increase in payables.	Changes in balance sheet items
f. Plus: Loss (or Minus: Gain) on disposal of assets (Note 1).	Income statement
2. *Cash from investing activities:*	
a. Purchase of noncurrent assets.	Increase in asset account (Note 1), net of related financing
b. Proceeds from asset disposals	Decrease in net book value less loss (or plus gain) from income statement (Note 1)
c. Loans made to (or collected from) another entity. . .	Change in loans receivable account (Note 2)
3. *Cash from financing activities:*	
a. Borrowings or debt repayments.	Changes in liability accounts (Note 2)
b. Issuance or retirement of stock	Changes in paid-in capital accounts (Note 2)
c. Cash dividends	Retained earnings statement (Note 3)
d. Conversion of bonds and stock.	Balance sheet changes (Note 3)

Notes:
1. The change in the asset account is affected by depreciation, sale of assets, and purchase of assets. The amount of each is reported in a note accompanying the balance sheet and in detailed accounting records within the organization.
2. Only the net change can be determined from the balance sheet, whereas the FASB requires that any increases and decreases be reported separately.
3. The conversion of bonds or preferred stock to common stock does not affect the total amount of cash flow. Such transactions are not reported in the statement itself, but are disclosed supplementally.

each such transaction as either cash from operations, cash from investing activities, or cash from financing activities. This analysis will require reference to the income statement (e.g., to explain the change in Retained Earnings) and, in some cases, to other financial records of the company. Illustration 11–7 summarizes the nature of such transactions and the place where information about them is likely to be found.

3. After the account changes have been analyzed and classified, the debits and credits are totaled and then combined as a check to see that their net amount is equal to the amount of change in Cash.

4. The cash flow statement is prepared directly from the worksheet, using the format shown in Illustration 11–3.

ANALYSIS OF THE CASH FLOW STATEMENT

At the outset of this chapter, several questions were mentioned that analysis of the cash flow statement can help answer. In specifying the operating, investing, and financing activities classifications as the basic format for this statement, the FASB intended to aid in the analysis of the statement's contents. (Formerly a variety of formats was permitted, and investing and financing activities usually were intermingled in categories of sources and uses.)

For example, for Fairway Corporation the statement in Illustration 11–3 indicates that operations did not generate enough cash ($228,000) to fund the company's 19x1 investing activities ($430,000). The $202,000 difference was financed through borrowings and a common stock issue, which also provided funds for dividend payments and a $96,000 buildup in cash and cash equivalents. Given this relatively large increase in cash (42 percent higher than at the start of the year), the question is raised as to why Fairway borrowed the additional $375,000 in long-term debt rather than a lesser amount, or why the $44,000 stock issuance was undertaken. Perhaps the company plans to make some significant investments early in 19x2. (Statement analysis often raises as many questions as it answers.)

Ratios

In addition to the classification of the information into three categories, two specific analytic techniques will now be suggested.

Coverage Ratios. Two "coverage" ratios, *times interest earned* and *fixed charges coverage,* were described in Chapter 8. Both of these ratios would be conceptually sounder if the numerator were based on cash generated by operations rather than on income, because interest, lease payments, and similar fixed charges must be paid by using cash. The amount for cash generated by operations should be adjusted to a pretax, pre-fixed-charges basis (as was the case when these ratios were based on income in Chapter 8). These coverage ratios will ordinarily be higher when based on operating cash rather than on income because cash generated by operations is usually a larger amount than net income.

Source and Use Percentages. Despite the FASB's prescribed cash flow statement format, some analysts find it useful to reorganize the data into the previously popular sources and uses format, as is done in Illustration 11–8. As shown in that illustration, the amount of total sources of cash can be treated as 100 percent; then each cash flow statement item can be expressed as a percentage of total sources. For example, internally generated cash provided 30 percent (= $228,000 ÷ $757,000) of the total sources; equipment purchases used 66 percent (= $500,000 ÷ $757,000) of the total sources; and dividends used another 8 percent.

A ratio used by credit officers in evaluating corporations' creditworthiness for long-term debt is the **ratio of cash generated by operations to total debt** (both short- and long-term debt). For a corporate bond to qualify for an AAA rating from Standard & Poor's, this ratio must be at least 100 percent (that is, 1 to 1).

"Free" Cash Flow. Some analysts calculate the amount of **"free" cash flow,** which is cash from operations minus three items: (1) cash used by essential investing activities (e.g., fixed asset replacements necessary to

ILLUSTRATION 11–8
CASH FLOWS PRESENTED IN SOURCES AND USES FORMAT

FAIRWAY CORPORATION
Sources and Uses of Cash
For the Year Ended December 31, 19x1
(dollars in thousands)

	Amount	*Percent*
Sources of cash:		
Cash generated by operations	$228	30.1
Short-term borrowings	15	2.0
Long-term debt	375	49.5
Issuance of common stock	44	5.8
Proceeds from disposal of equipment	20	2.6
Sale of investment securities	75	9.9
Total sources of cash	757	100.0
Uses of cash		
Acquisition of plant and equipment	500	66.1
Purchase of investment securities	25	3.3
Dividends paid	60	7.9
Repayment of short-term debt	36	4.8
Repayment of long-term debt	40	5.3
Total uses of cash	661	87.3
Net increase in cash	$ 96	12.7

maintain existing capacity), (2) scheduled debt repayments, and (3) normal dividend payments. If positive, the amount indicates cash available to retire additional debt, increase dividends, or invest in new lines of business. If negative, it indicates the amount of financing needed just to support current operations and programs.

Cash Flow Projections

The purpose of analyzing cash flow statements is not solely to understand what has happened in the past. In addition, this analysis serves as a means of projecting what cash flows may look like in the future.

A projected cash flow statement is an essential device for planning the amount, timing, and character of new financing. These projections are important both to management in anticipating future cash needs and to prospective lenders for appraising a company's ability to repay debt on the proposed terms. Estimated uses of cash for new plant and equipment, for increased receivables and inventories, for dividends, and for the repayment of debt are made for each of the next several years. Estimates are also made of the cash to be provided by operations. The difference, if positive, represents the cash that must be obtained by borrowing or the issuance of new equity securities. If the indicated amount of new cash required is greater than management thinks it is feasible to raise, then the plans for new plant and equipment acquisitions and dividend policies are reexamined so that the uses of cash can be brought into balance with anticipated sources of financing them.

For shorter-term financial planning, cash flow projections are made for each of the next several months or several quarters. This **cash budget** is useful in anticipating seasonal financing needs; for example, toy manufacturers need short-term financing for inventories prior to the major holiday sales season. Similarly, the cash budget will indicate when excess cash will be available to invest in short-term marketable securities.

SUMMARY

A statement of cash flows provides information about an entity's investing and financing activities during the accounting period, as well as showing how much cash was generated by the period's operations.

The net amount of cash generated by operations is not the same as net income. Some expenses (notably depreciation) subtracted in arriving at net income for the period do not use cash. The net amount of cash generated by operations can be derived indirectly from the net income figure by making adjustments for those income statement amounts that were not accompanied by an equal amount of cash flow. These adjustments take account of changes in accounts receivable, inventories, payables, and deferred taxes. Also, depreciation is added back to net income because it is an expense that does not involve a corresponding use of cash. However, one must not infer from this calculation that depreciation is itself a source of cash, for it definitely is not. The net cash flow from operating activities can also be developed directly from cash receipts and payments related to operations.

The cash flow statement does not include certain financing and investing activities that do not cause a change in cash, such as the purchase of fixed assets with a long-term mortgage note or the conversion of a bond into common stock. However, these noncash transactions are supplementally disclosed so as to give a full picture of investing and financing activities.

Cash flow statements are also prepared prospectively so that an organization can anticipate both short-term and longer-term needs to raise additional cash through borrowing or by issuing additional shares of stock.

Cases

CASE 11–1 Medieval Adventures Company

Medieval Adventures Company was founded by Aaron Reinholz to produce a game marketed under the name "Castles and Unicorns." Each "Castles and Unicorns" cost the company $35 to produce. In addition to these production costs that varied in direct proportion to volume (so-called variable costs), the company also incurred $10,000 monthly "being in business" costs (so-called fixed costs) irrespective of the month's volume. The company sold its product for $55 each.

As of December 31, Reinholz had been producing "Castles and Unicorns" for three months using rented facilities. The balance sheet on that date was as follows:

MEDIEVAL ADVENTURES COMPANY
Balance Sheet
As of December 31

Assets

Cash	$146,250
Accounts receivable	68,750
Inventory	35,000
	$250,000

Equities

Common stock	$250,000
Retained earnings	0
	$250,000

Reinholz was very pleased to be operating at a profit in such a short time. December sales had been 750 units, up from 500 in November, enough to report a profit for the month and to eliminate the deficit accumulated in October and November. Sales were expected to be 1,000 units in January, and Reinholz's projections showed sales increases of 500 units per month after that. Thus, by May monthly sales were expected to be 3,000 units. By September that figure would be 5,000 units.

Reinholz was very conscious of developing good sales channel relationships in order to increase sales, so "Castles and Unicorns" deliveries were always prompt. This required production schedules 30 days in advance of predicted sales. For example, Medieval Adventures had produced 1,000 "Castles and Unicorns" in December for January sales, and would produce 1,500 in January for February's demand. The company billed its customers with stated terms of 30 days net, but did not strictly enforce these credit terms with the result that customers seemed to be taking an additional month to pay. All of the company's costs were paid in cash in the month in which they were incurred.

Reinholz's predictions came true. By March, sales had reached 2,000 "Castles and Unicorns," and 2,500 units were produced in March for April sale. Total profit for the year by March 31 had reached $60,000. In order to get a respite from the increasingly hectic activities of running the business, in mid-April Reinholz went on a family vacation.

Within the week the company's bookkeeper called. Medieval Adventures' bank balance was almost zero, so necessary materials could not be purchased. Unless Reinholz returned immediately to raise more cash, the entire operation would have to shut down within a few days.

Questions

1. Prepare monthly income statements, balance sheets, and cash budgets based on sales increases of 500 units per month and 30-day advance production for January through September. When will the company need extra funds? How much will be needed? When can a short-term loan to cover the need be repaid?

2. How is it possible that a company starts with $250,000 in capital and has profitable sales for a period of six months and still ends up with a zero bank balance? Why did Medieval Adventures need money in April? How could this need have been avoided?

3. From your calculations and financial statements for Question 1, *derive* cash flow statements for the months of March, May, and July from each month's beginning and ending balance sheets and income statement. Compare these derived cash flow statements with the cash budgets prepared directly in Question 1.

CASE 11–2   Amerbran Company (A)

Amerbran Company was a diversified company that sold various consumer products, including food, tobacco, distilled, and personal care products and financial services. Financial statements for the company are shown in Exhibit 1.

The 19x1 financial statements reflect the following transactions (dollar amounts are in thousands):

1. Depreciation and amortization expense was $115,974.

2. Net income included a loss of $66,046 resulting from the write-off of some obsolete equipment. The equipment had not yet been disposed of.

3. Net income included $59,610 from Amerbran's investment in a subsidiary; none of this income had been received in cash.

4. The year-end balance in Deferred Income Taxes was $17,548 lower than it was at the start of the year.

5. New property, plant, and equipment purchases totaled $260,075, all paid for with cash. Disposals of fixed assets generated $33,162 cash proceeds.

6. Acquisition of another company that was made for cash resulted in additional depreciable assets of $31,691 and goodwill of $102,030.

7. Cash dividends were paid in the amount of $216,158.

8. The firm declared and issued a 100 percent common stock dividend effective September 10, 19x1; that is, each shareholder received as a dividend a number of shares equal to his or her holdings prior to the dividend. The newly issued shares were valued at par in recording this transaction.

9. The firm spent $30,609 to purchase treasury stock on the open market. Some of the shares so acquired were reissued to certain employees as a bonus.

10. The firm increased its short-term debt as indicated on the balance sheet in Exhibit 1. Long-term borrowings decreased by $34,606.

Question

Prepare a statement of cash flows for the year 19x1. In order for your statement to show the correct increase in cash ($4,960), you will need to add a "miscellaneous activities" category; this will capture several transactions that were not described because they are more complicated than those covered in the text.

EXHIBIT 1

AMERBRAN COMPANY
Balance Sheets
As of December 31
(in thousands)

	19x1	19x0
Assets		
Cash	28,912	$ 23,952
Accounts receivable	756,152	687,325
Inventories	1,244,912	1,225,402
Prepaid expenses	76,140	77,167
Total current assets	2,106,116	2,013,846
Investments	1,116,534	1,058,637
Property, plant, and equipment, at cost	1,566,268	1,366,719
Less accumulated depreciation	723,442	645,734
Net property, plant, and equipment	842,826	720,985
Goodwill	645,210	577,606
Other assets	115,826	62,374
Total assets	$4,826,512	$4,433,448
Liabilities and Shareholders' Equity		
Accounts payable	$ 271,452	$ 238,377
Short-term debt	430,776	351,112
Accrued expenses payable	922,990	728,262
Total current liabilities	1,625,218	1,317,751
Long-term liabilities	880,674	932,828
Total liabilities	2,505,892	2,250,579
Convertible preferred stock	33,828	42,611
Common stock, at par	322,834	161,417
Additional paid-in capital	53,641	57,072
Treasury stock, at cost	(110,948)	(102,705)
Retained earnings	2,021,265	2,024,474
Total shareholders' equity	2,320,620	2,182,869
Total liabilities and shareholders' equity	$4,826,512	$4,433,448

Income Statement
For the year ended December 31, 19x1
(in thousands)

Sales revenues, net	$7,622,677
Cost of sales	2,803,623
Excise taxes on goods sold	2,887,616
Gross margin	1,931,438
Selling, general, and administrative expenses	1,328,107
Income before income taxes	603,331
Provision for income taxes	274,558
Net income	$ 328,773

CASE 11–3   Statements of Cash Flows: Three Examples*

John Stacey, a sales engineer for Aldhus Corporation, was worried. A flight delay had caused him to miss last week's accounting class in the evening MBA program in which he had enrolled at the suggestion of the personnel director at Aldhus, a growing manufacturer of computer peripherals. The class he had missed had been devoted to a lecture and discussion of the statement of cash flows, and he was sure the material he had missed would be covered in the weekly quiz that was part of each class session. A classmate had faxed Stacey some notes distributed by their instructor, but the notes were too cryptic to be understood by anyone who had missed the class.

In desperation, John called Lucille Barnes, the assistant controller at Aldhus, to ask if she could take a few minutes to point him in the right direction toward understanding the statement of cash flows. She was pleased to accommodate the request, and they agreed to meet within the hour.

After they had exchanged greetings, Lucille handed John three cash flow statements from the annual reports of other high-technology companies (Exhibits 1, 2, and 3). John was worried that Lucille would ask him to explain them, and that she would see how confused he still was about some aspects of accounting; instead, Lucille began explaining.

Barnes: The statement of cash flows is really a very useful part of the set of three statements companies are required to prepare. In some cases it tells more about what is actually happening in a business than either the balance sheet or income statement. The

statements of cash flows that I have given you are very revealing. Let me give you a brief overview of the statements, and then you take some time to study them. I've prepared some questions to guide your study. We can meet again tomorrow to discuss any questions that remain. I don't think you have to worry about your next quiz because if you understand how balance sheets and income statements are prepared, much about the statement of cash flows will seem pretty obvious.

Stacey: I hope you're right. I really like the accounting course, and I want to do well in it and really learn the material. That's why I panicked when I couldn't understand the notes our instructor passed out last week.

Barnes: Forget those notes for now and just concentrate on studying the statements I've given you. Notice that the statement is divided into three sections: operating activities, investing activities, and financing activities. Each section shows the cash inflows and the cash outflows associated with that type of activity.

Operating activities shows the inflows and outflows related to the fundamental operations of the basic line or lines of business that the company is in. For example, it would include cash receipts from the sale of goods or services and the cash outflows for purchasing inventory, and paying wages, taxes, and rent.

Investing activities shows cash flows for the purchase and sale of assets not generally held for resale and for the making and collecting of loans. (Maybe it should more appropriately be called the investing and disinvesting activities section.) Here is where you would see if the company sold a building, purchased equipment, made a loan to a

---

*Copyright © by the President and Fellows of Harvard College. Harvard Business School case 193–103.

subsidiary, or purchased a piece of equity in its supplier.

Finally, financing activities shows the cash flows associated with increasing or decreasing the firm's financing, for example, issuing or repurchasing stock and borrowing or repaying loans. It also includes dividends, which are cash flows associated with equity. However, ironically, it does not include interest payments; these are included in operating activities.

Stacey: That seems strange to me. Since loans are the reason interest payments are made, why are they not included in the financing activities section? You know, interest is to loans as dividends are to equity?

Barnes: Actually, in some countries, such as the United Kingdom, interest is included in the investing activities section! But in the United States the FASB decided that interest payments should be in the operating activities section instead. This is one of these situations where you might have to do some adjusting if you were trying to compare a U.K. company like British Petroleum to a U.S. company like Exxon.

Stacey: That is interesting! How can I use each section of the statement?

Barnes: The operating activity section is the cash flow engine of the company. When this engine is working effectively, it provides the cash flows to cover the cash needs of operations. In a healthy, growing company we would expect growth in operating working capital accounts, such as inventory and accounts receivable (uses of cash) as well as in accounts payable and other operating payables (sources of cash). Obviously there can be quite a bit of variability in working capital accounts from period to period but, on average, inventories, receivables, and accounts payable usually grow in growing companies. In addition, this operating cash flow engine provides cash for needed investments, to repay debt, and to pay dividends. There are

exceptions, of course. Start-up companies, for example, usually have negative cash flows from operations because they have not gotten their cash flow engines up to speed. Companies in cyclical industries may have negative operating cash flow in a "down" year; a company that has experienced an extensive strike could also be expected to have negative cash flow from operations. Although an occasional year of negative operating cash flow does not spell disaster, nonetheless, we should expect operating cash flow, on average, to be positive.

Investing activities are a different story. Whereas we expect positive operating cash flow, we also expect a healthy company to continually invest in more plant, equipment, land, and other fixed assets to replace the assets that have been used up or have become technologically obsolete, as well as to expand and grow. Although companies often sell assets that are no longer of use to them, we would normally expect them to purchase more capital assets than they sell. As a result, in general, we expect negative cash flows from investing activities. Like operating activities, exceptions occur, especially if the firm divests a business or subsidiary.

Cash flows from financing activities could as easily be positive as negative in a healthy company, and they are likely to change back and forth. If the company's need for cash to invest exceeds the cash flow generated by operating activities, this will require extra financing by debt or equity, therefore a positive financing cash flow. On the other hand, if cash flow from operating activities exceeds the investing needs, the firm will have excess cash to repay debt or pay more dividends, producing negative cash flows from financing.

Stacey: I am beginning to see why you said that the statement of cash flows is so useful. Where do you start your review and analysis?

EXHIBIT 1
ALPHA CORPORATION, CONSOLIDATED STATEMENTS OF CASH FLOWS ($ millions)

	Year Ended June 30,		
	1991	*1990*	*1989*
Operating Activities			
Loss from continuing operations	**$(377.9)**	$(623.5)	$(320.6)
Depreciation.	**168.4**	220.1	263.4
Amortization of capitalized software	**41.4**	58.2	39.1
Gain from sale of investments and other assets	**(16.6)**	(119.0)	—
Restructuring and other unusual items, net.	**135.5**	384.1	125.3
Changes in other accounts affecting operations			
Accounts receivable.	**160.8**	73.4	(45.2)
Inventory.	**80.2**	100.9	(3.0)
Other current assets.	**17.0**	(1.2)	(13.0)
Accounts payable and other current liabilities	**(91.3)**	(21.3)	41.0
Other	**2.8**	14.1	(10.5)
Net cash provided by continuing operations	**120.3**	85.8	76.5
Net cash provided by (used in) discontinued operations . . .	**4.9**	3.5	(29.7)
Net cash provided by operating activities	**125.2**	89.3	46.8
Investing Activities			
Investment in depreciable assets	**(129.7)**	(174.4)	(303.6)
Proceeds from disposal of depreciable and other assets .	**157.0**	242.0	94.1
Proceeds from the sale of discontinued operations	**25.3**	407.3	—
Investment in capitalized software	**(27.8)**	(43.1)	(59.5)
Other	**(6.0)**	(13.0)	14.2
Net cash provided by (used in) investing activities	**18.8**	418.8	(254.8)
Financing Activities			
(Decrease) increase in short-term borrowings	**(2.6)**	(222.6)	139.8
Proceeds from long-term debt.	**44.4**	167.7	305.0
Payments of long-term debt	**(126.5)**	(544.8)	(91.7)
Proceeds from sale of Class B common stock.	**5.0**	8.7	17.5
Purchase of treasury stock	**(.3)**	(.6)	(18.8)
Dividends paid	**—**	(7.2)	(26.0)
Net cash provided by (used in) financing activities	**(80.0)**	(598.8)	325.8
Effect of changes in foreign exchange rates	**.1**	1.1	(3.9)
Increase (decrease) in cash equivalents	**64.1**	(89.6)	113.9
Cash and equivalents at beginning of year	**169.1**	258.7	144.8
Cash and equivalents at end of year	**$ 233.2**	$ 169.1	$ 258.7

Barnes: A way to approach the cash flow statement is to begin with cash flows from operating activities. If this is the cash flow engine, then the first question is, "Is cash flow from operating activities greater, or less, than zero?" Also of interest is the trend: Is it increasing or decreasing?

Stacey: As you were talking, I glanced at the cash flows from operations sections of the first two statements you gave me (Exhibits 1 and 2). They look very different. On the first one, depreciation seems to provide cash flows, but there is no mention of depreciation on the second.

Barnes: I forgot to mention that there are two ways operating cash flows can be presented. Sometimes they are presented using the indirect method, as in the first statement

EXHIBIT 2
BETA CORPORATION, CONSOLIDATED STATEMENTS OF CASH FLOWS ($ thousands)

	Year Ended December 31,		
	1991	*1990*	*1989*
Cash Flows from Operating Activities:			
Cash received from customers	**$ 83,865**	$ 73,273	$ 51,110
Cash paid to suppliers and employees.	**(77,820)**	(65,480)	(46,589)
Interest received.	**643**	355	132
Interest paid.	**(536)**	(1,046)	(908)
Income taxes paid	**(2,233)**	(102)	(75)
Net cash generated by operating activities	**3,919**	7,000	3,670
Cash Flows from Investing Activities:			
Capital expenditures	**(6,031)**	(4,600)	(3,650)
Marketable securities purchases.	**(8,000)**	—	—
Net cash used in investing activities	**(14,031)**	(4,600)	(3,650)
Cash Flow from Financing Activities:			
Net payments under working capital line of credit	**—**	(2,000)	(860)
Net payments under equipment line of credit	**(985)**	(126)	(388)
Principal payments under capital lease obligations	**(169)**	(213)	(276)
Proceeds (payment) of subordinated debt	**(5,000)**	—	4,400
Proceeds from the issuance of common stock	**23,082**	141	639
Net cash provided by (used in) financing activities	**16,928**	(2,198)	3,515
Effect of exchange rate changes on cash.	**(4)**	14	
Net increase in cash and cash equivalents	**6,812**	216	3,535
Cash and cash equivalents at beginning of year	**5,375**	5,159	1,624
Cash and cash equivalents at end of year	**$ 12,187**	$ 5,375	$ 5,159
Reconciliation of Net Income to Net Cash **Generated by Operating Activities:**			
Net income.	**$ 6,323**	$ 5,201	$ 417
Adjustments to Reconcile Net Income to Net **Cash Consumed by Operating Activities:**			
Bad debt provision.	**99**	47	98
Depreciation and amortization.	**4,028**	2,701	2,231
Amortization of original issue discount.	**208**	324	68
Loss on disposition of assets.	**17**	9	58
Compensation expense related to stock grants.	**40**	85	
Changes in Assets and Liabilities:			
(Increase) in accounts receivable.	**(10,837)**	(613)	(1,550)
(Increase) decrease in inventory.	**(951)**	(810)	1,043
(Increase) decrease in deposits and other assets	**(665)**	366	(762)
Increase (decrease) in accounts payable and accrued expenses	**5,657**	(310)	2,067
Total adjustments	**(2,404)**	1,799	3,253
Net cash generated by operating activities	**$ 3,919**	$ 7,000	$ 3,670

I gave you (Exhibit 1). Using that method, net income is adjusted for all noncash revenues and expenses, one of which is depreciation. Depreciation is *never* a source of cash, but it *is* deducted to compute net income, so it must be added back. Likewise, operating cash flows not included in net income, such as purchases of inventory not sold, have to be added or subtracted.

When the direct method is used to present cash flows from operations, that section of the report looks much more like a summary from the operating cash account, as it does in the second report I gave you (Exhibit 2).

Stacey: Which of the methods is better?

Barnes: I think the direct statement of cash flows from operations is easier to understand, but relatively few companies present their operating cash flows that way. Most of the statements you'll see will use the indirect method. The reason for this is that if the direct method is used, a reconciliation of income to cash flows from operations is also required (see Exhibit 2), so most companies simply use the reconciliation as their summary of cash flows from operations.

But let's get back to how I approach the statement of cash flows.

Assuming operating cash flows are greater than zero, the next challenge is to decide whether they are adequate for important, routine expenditures. Again, our expectations are tempered by our understanding of the company and its situation. Just like we do not expect a start-up company to have positive operating cash flows, we also do not expect a company still in a very rapid growth phase to have enough cash flow from operations to finance all of its investments. However, for a mature company we expect operations to generate enough cash to "keep the company whole." This would include the amount of investment required to replace those fixed assets that are used up or technologically obsolete, as well as cash required to pay the annual dividend that the shareholders have come to expect. It's hard to know

precisely how much cash is required to keep the company's fixed assets "whole," and the cash flow statement does not separate investing cash flows for replacement and renewal from those investing cash flows for expansion and growth. However, the annual depreciation amount is a very rough surrogate for the amount of fixed assets that need to be replaced each year. In periods when prices are rising, we should expect that the cost to replace assets would be somewhat greater than the cost of older assets that are being depreciated. Thus, it is common to expect the portion of investing activities related to the purchase of fixed assets to exceed the annual depreciation.

After considering whether operating cash flows cover capital expenditures and dividends, I look to see whether there are other major cash needs such as acquisitions, stock repurchase, or debt repayment. If so, how do these cash needs fit with the availability of cash? Are these needs discretionary, like acquisitions?

If there are cash shortfalls, I investigate how they are being funded. Is it by issuing stock? By borrowing? By selling businesses or assets? In each case I consider whether the company is likely to be able to continue such funding and for how long. Will the funding source continue to be available, or are they likely nearing the limit? Will continuing to use this source hurt the company in any way?

Stacey: Do you always have to look at all of those things in every case?

Barnes: No. But if you stop short of a full review, you may miss an important part of the story.

In evaluating the cash flow statement, you are evaluating many pieces of evidence to produce an overall picture. However, it would be rare to find a company where all of the evidence is positive or where all of the evidence is negative. To do a balanced evaluation, you must search out both the good news and the bad news in each cash flow

EXHIBIT 3
GAMMA CORPORATION, CONSOLIDATED STATEMENTS OF CASH FLOWS ($ thousands)

	Year Ended		
	June 29, 1991	*June 30, 1990*	*July 1, 1989*
Cash Flows from Operating Activities:			
Net income/(loss)	**$ (617,427)**	$ 74,393	$ 1,072,610
Adjustments to Reconcile Net Income to Net Cash Provided by Operating Activities:			
Depreciation and amortization..........................	**828,560**	796,201	686,738
Other adjustments to income...........................	**189,077**	92,329	49,702
(Increase)/decrease in accounts receivable..............	**105,977**	(241,357)	(373,248)
(Increase)/decrease in inventories	**18,616**	99,743	(62,942)
(Increase)/decrease in prepaid expenses.................	**(47,239)**	(90,602)	18,965
Increase/(decrease) in accounts payable................	**(17,694)**	107,001	30,645
(Decrease) in taxes	**(105,614)**	(201,560)	(75,502)
Increase in deferred revenues and customer advances	**92,222**	69,207	105,847
Increase in restructuring reserve........................	**593,160**	443,544	—
Increase in other liabilities	**1,263**	285,175	26,576
Total adjustments	**1,658,328**	1,359,681	406,781
Net cash flows from operating activities	**1,040,901**	1,434,074	1,479,391
Cash Flows from Investing Activities:			
Purchase of plant, property, and equipment..............	**(737,548)**	(1,027,625)	(1,223,038)
(Increase) of other assets, net..........................	**(55,782)**	(75,489)	(67,624)
Purchase of Kienzle business	**(233,261)**	—	—
Net cash flows from investing activities..................	**(1,026,591)**	(1,103,144)	(1,290,662)
Net cash flows from operating and investing activities......	**14,310**	330,960	188,729
Net Flows from Financing Activities:			
Proceeds from issuance of debt........................	**14,249**	17,661	40,425
Payments to retire debt................................	**(112,426)**	(20,896)	(153,245)
Purchase of treasury shares...........................	**(240,719)**	(270,231)	(814,958)
Issuance of treasury shares, including tax benefits	**239,653**	296,225	230,733
Net cash flows from financing activities...................	**(99,243)**	22,759	(697,045)
Net increase/(decrease) in cash and cash equivalents.....	**(84,933)**	353,719	(508,316)
Cash and cash equivalents at beginning of year	**2,008,983**	1,655,264	2,163,580
Cash and cash equivalents at end of year...............	**$ 1,924,050**	$ 2,008,983	$ 1,655,264

statement. To reach an overall conclusion you need to judge the relative importance of each piece of evidence and assess its relationship to the overall picture. Like in a legal case, your conclusion needs to be based on the "weight of the evidence."

I think the best way to learn about statements of cash flow is to study some carefully. The statements I've given you are a place to start. I wrote out some questions to guide your study. Try to develop answers, and we can meet tomorrow to discuss them. By the time we finish, I think you'll be well prepared for the quiz in your next class.

Questions:

Exhibits 1, 2, and 3 contain cash flow statements from three companies. Each cash flow statement has three years of data. Examine the contents of these cash flow statements carefully. Answer the following questions about each of the three cash flow statements.

1. For each of the years on the statement of cash flows:

a. What were the firm's major sources of cash? Its major uses of cash?

b. Was cash flow from operations greater than or less than net income? Explain in detail the major reasons for the difference between these two figures.

c. Was the firm able to generate enough cash from operations to pay for all of its capital expenditures (also called investments in depreciable assets, or purchases of plant, property, and equipment)?

d. Did the cash flow from operations cover both the capital expenditures *and* the firm's dividend payments, if any?

e. If it did, how did the firm invest its excess cash?

f. If not, what were the sources of cash the firm used to pay for the capital expenditures and/or dividends?

g. Were the working capital (current asset and current liability) accounts other than cash and cash equivalents primarily sources of cash, or users of cash?

h. What other major items affected cash flows?

2. What was the trend in:
    a. Net income?
    b. Cash flow from (continuing) operations?
    c. Capital expenditures?
    d. Dividends?
    e. Net borrowing (proceeds less payments of short- and long-term debt)?
    f. Working capital accounts?

3. Based on the evidence in the statement of cash flows alone, what is your assessment of the financial strength of this business? Why?

CASE 11–4   FMC Corporation Recapitalization (B)*

The recapitalization plan approved at FMC Corporation's annual meeting on May 22, 1986, would significantly change the financial structure of the company. (See Case 9–3, FMC Corporation Recapitalization (A), for background information and details of the recapitalization.) One of the primary reasons given for undertaking the recapitalization was FMC's large cash flow from operations, a condition that some observers referred to as "excess cash flow." (See Exhibit 1, Consolidated Statements of Changes in Financial Position.)

FMC's cash flow situation would change following the recapitalization, however. In the first year, FMC's interest payment on debt would be about $255 million, compared to 1985's actual interest payments of $35 million and pretax income of $270 million.

These higher interest payments would clearly absorb much of the excess cash flow. In addition, cash would eventually be required to repay the more than $1.9 billion principal of the debt that was to be used to finance the recapitalization.

Some critics were concerned about FMC's future ability to finance the investments that would be needed to keep FMC's existing businesses competitive. Others, even more pessimistic, were concerned about FMC's ability to survive, given its large debt service requirements, its negative stockholders' equity, and its very limited potential to borrow additional funds following the recapitalization.

Questions

1. Study the Statements of Changes in Financial Position (Cash Flow Statements) in Exhibit 1. Is the evidence you find there consistent with the assertion that FMC has "excess cash flow" from operations? If so, what specific evidence would you cite to support this assertion?

EXHIBIT 1
FMC CORPORATION—CONSOLIDATED STATEMENTS OF CHANGES IN FINANCIAL POSITION
($ thousands)

	Year Ended December 31		
	1985	*1984*	*1983*
Cash provided (required) by continuing operations:			
Income from continuing operations	$ 196,553	$ 225,863	$ 188,400
Provision for depreciation	161,197	140,193	143,356
Provision for deferred income taxes	35,237	(6,830)	30,191
Dividends received from unconsolidated affiliates, net of equity in earnings	(435)	17,718	(1,290)
Other	(1,464)	(8,736)	(7,351)
Cash provided by continuing operations before working capital changes	$ 391,088	$ 368,208	$ 353,306
Decrease (increase) in working capital from selected items (detail below)	(13,909)	46,391	107,053
Cash provided by continuing operations	$ 377,179	$ 414,599	$ 460,959
Cash provided (required) by discontinued operations	$ 29,463	$ (10,760)	$ 13,464
Cash provided (required) by investing activities:			
Acquisition of Lithco and BS&B Engineering	($ 153,433)	—	—
Capital expenditures	(319,031)	(182,645)	(169,245)
Disposal of property, plant, and equipment	26,472	18,497	19,771
Decrease (increase) in investments	20,827	(239)	(49,163)
Cash required by investing activities	($ 425,165)	($ 164,387)	($ 198,637)
Cash provided (required) by financing activities:			
Increase in short-term debt	$ 8,591	$ 10,973	$ 5,753
Increase (decrease) in long-term debt	26,496	(66,003)	(43,351)
Issue (repurchase) of capital stock	8,947	(466,407)	31,799
Cash provided (required) by financing activities	$ 44,034	($ 521,437)	$ (5,799)
Cash required for dividends to stockholders	$ (57,571)	$ (56,907)	$ (61,980)
Increase (decrease) in cash and marketable securities	$ (32,060)	($ 338,892)	$ 208,007
Cash and marketable securities, beginning of year	$ 193,978	$ 532,870	$ 324,863
Cash and marketable securities, end of year	$ 161,918	$ 193,978	$ 532,870

Foreign currency translation effects have been eliminated from the above items.

Decrease (increase) in working capital from selected items:			
Trade receivables	$ (59,497)	$ (15,515)	$ 16,160
Inventories	37,484	(19,463)	152,283
Other current assets	(34,069)	(2,240)	2,540
Accounts payable and accruals	75,826	64,824	(51,950)
Income taxes payable	(31,740)	31,817	7,429
Net translation adjustment on working capital	(1,913)	(13,032)	(18,809)
Decrease (increase) in working capital from selected items	$ (13,909)	$ 46,391	$ 107,653

2. An important issue in determining whether FMC can survive is whether the cash flow from operations will be sufficient for FMC's post-recapitalization needs. Use the information contained in the cash flow statements (Exhibit 1), the consolidated financial statements in the (A) case, and reasonable assumptions about the future to project expected cash flows for a period of time to test the feasibility of FMC's position, and/or to try to understand

what actions FMC managers must take in order to ensure the firm's continued survival.

a. As a starting point for your analysis:

    i. Assume cash flow from continuing operations (before the payment of the additional interest required for the new debt) remains at the level it has been recently.

    ii. Assume FMC wants to continue reinvesting in existing businesses at levels similar to the recent past. This reinvestment in existing businesses is represented by the capital expenditures amount.

b. You must consider additional items such as:

    i. Will FMC have to pay additional interest on the new debt? How much?

    ii. Do you think the recapitalized FMC will be likely to pay dividends on the new stock?

    iii. Do you think the recapitalized FMC would want to acquire new businesses, or will they focus on managing the existing businesses and repaying the debt?

    iv. Will the recapitalized FMC be borrowing additional funds? Will lenders be eager to lend to them following the recapitalization?

c. Using the assumptions you have been given or have made above, plus your best judgment about what is likely to happen to the remaining cash flows following the recapitalization, project FMC's cash flows for at least five years in order to answer the following questions:

    i. Will FMC be able to cover necessary expenditures such as capital expenditures and interest payments?

    ii. Will FMC have any cash left over to repay the debt? If FMC repays some of the principal, what will happen to the interest payments? How will that affect the future cash flows?

3. How long will it take for the debt/equity ratio to reach a "reasonable" level?

4. How long will it take until stockholders' equity is positive?

5. Will FMC survive?

CASE 11–5 W. T. Grant Company*

In 1976 Sandy Johnson was a business school student enrolled in an accounting course. Johnson had grown up in a neighborhood close to a Grant's variety store. Johnson had become intrigued by the story of W. T. Grant when that local store closed in late 1975, and had followed the coverage in the popular business press very closely. The firm's bankruptcy proceedings and eventual store closings seemed to take many in the financial world by surprise. Johnson wanted to know if a study of the firm's financial statements would have shown the growing problems the company faced. With this in mind, Johnson went to the business school library and found the W. T. Grant Company income statement and balance sheet data for the period from 1965 to 1974 that are shown in Exhibit 1.

Sandy Johnson used these data to calculate ten ratios. The profitability picture of W. T. Grant was seen by calculating (1) the net profit margin, (2) the return on shareholders' equity, and (3) the return on assets for each year. Turnover information was derived from the (4) accounts receivable collection period (days' receivables), (5) inventory turnover, and (6) total assets turnover ratios. Insight into Grant's liquidity came from a look

*The casewriter wishes to acknowledge the cooperation of Professor Clyde P. Stickney in the preparation of this case.

EXHIBIT 1
SELECTED DATA FROM W. T. GRANT COMPANY FINANCIAL STATEMENTS FOR FISCAL YEARS 1965–1974*
(millions of dollars)

	1965	1966	1967	1968	1969	1970	1971	1972	1973	1974
Income statement data:										
Sales revenues	839.7	920.8	979.5	1,096.2	1,210.9	1,254.1	1,374.8	1,644.7	1,849.8	1,762.0
Cost of merchandise sold	578.1	631.6	669.6	741.2	817.7	843.2	931.2	1,125.3	1,282.9	1,303.3
Net income	31.5	31.6	33.0	38.2	41.8	36.4	31.6	35.0	10.9	(177.3)
Balance sheet data:										
Cash and marketable securities	22.6	39.0	25.1	25.6	33.0	34.0	49.9	30.9	46.0	79.6
Accounts receivable	173.1	230.4	272.5	312.8	368.3	358.4	408.3	468.6	540.8	431.2
Inventories	151.4	174.6	183.7	208.6	222.1	260.5	298.7	399.5	450.6	407.4
Other current assets	0.0	4.2	4.0	4.4	5.0	5.3	5.3	6.7	7.3	6.6
Current assets	347.1	448.2	485.3	551.4	628.4	658.2	762.2	905.7	1,044.7	924.8
Other assets	59.1	64.5	66.3	70.7	78.4	88.4	113.4	130.8	150.3	157.5
Total assets	406.2	512.7	551.6	622.1	706.8	746.6	875.6	1,036.5	1,195.0	1,082.3
Current liabilities	133.0	218.2	235.4	285.3	366.7	423.0	435.2	590.4	661.1	749.9
Long-term debt	70.0	70.0	62.6	43.3	35.4	32.3	128.4	126.7	220.3	216.3
Other liabilities	11.0	12.2	12.9	13.4	14.0	14.3	14.9	16.6	18.8	2.2
Total liabilities	214.0	300.4	310.9	342.0	416.1	469.6	578.5	733.7	900.2	968.4
Shareholders' equity	192.2	212.3	240.7	280.1	290.7	277.0	297.1	302.8	294.8	113.9
Total liabilities and equity	406.2	512.7	551.6	622.1	706.8	746.6	875.6	1,036.5	1,195.0	1,082.3
Other data:										
No. of stores (year-end)	1,088	1,104	1,086	1,092	1,095	1,116	1,168	1,208	1,189	1,152
Stock price, high	$31.13	$35.13	$37.38	$45.13	$59.00	$54.88	$70.63	$48.63	$41.00	$11.38
Stock price, low	$18.00	$20.50	$20.75	$30.00	$39.25	$26.88	$41.50	$34.75	$9.63	$1.50
Earnings per share	$2.39	$2.30	$2.39	$2.71	$2.99	$2.64	$2.25	$2.49	$0.76	($12.74)

* Note: Each fiscal year began on February 1 of the year shown at the top of the column, and ended January 31 of the following year. Data shown may not be as originally reported because of retroactive restatement for subsequent accounting method changes.

393

EXHIBIT 2
STATEMENTS OF CHANGES IN FINANCIAL POSITION FOR FISCAL YEARS 1965–1974
(millions of dollars)

	1965	1966	1967	1968	1969	1970	1971	1972	1973	1974
Sources of funds:										
Net income	31.5	31.6	33.0	38.2	41.8	36.4	31.6	35.0	10.9	(177.3)
Depreciation and amortization	6.9	7.5	8.2	8.4	9.0	9.6	10.6	12.0	13.6	14.6
Deferred income taxes	1.1	0.8	0.5	0.4	0.3	0.2	1.1	2.3	2.7	(14.6)
Undistributed earnings of unconsol. subsids.	(1.2)	(1.1)	(1.5)	(1.8)	(2.1)	(2.8)	(2.4)	(3.4)	(3.6)	(0.3)
Net increase (decrease) in other liabilities	0.5	0.4	0.1	0.2	0.2	0.2	(0.5)	(0.6)	(0.5)	(2.1)
Total funds provided by current operations	38.8	39.2	40.3	45.4	49.2	43.6	40.4	45.3	23.1	(179.7)
Proceeds from issuance of debt	35.0	—	—	—	—	—	100.0	—	100.0	—
Proceeds from sale of common stock	3.4	2.7	4.1	5.4	5.3	6.8	9.9	3.7	2.8	0.9
Proceeds from disposal of property	0.0	0.0	0.1	0.5	0.0	0.0	0.0	2.2	(0.6)	0.0
Total sources of funds	77.2	41.9	44.5	51.4	54.5	50.3	150.4	51.1	125.4	(178.9)
Applications of funds:										
Property and equipment	8.0	15.3	7.8	10.6	14.4	16.1	25.9	26.3	23.1	15.5
Dividends	10.2	14.1	14.4	17.7	19.7	20.8	21.1	21.1	21.1	4.5
Investments in unconsolidated subsidiaries	25.1	0.3	0.4	0.0	0.0	0.4	6.0	2.0	5.7	5.2
Long-term debt retirement	0.0	0.0	1.5	1.5	1.7	1.5	1.6	1.6	6.1	4.0
Purchase of common or preferred stock	0.2	0.4	0.9	4.8	23.1	14.2	0.3	11.7	0.8	0.0
Other applications	0.6	0.0	(0.4)	0.5	0.1	23.9	3.6	0.1	0.3	0.7
Total applications of funds	44.1	30.1	24.6	35.1	59.0	76.9	58.5	62.8	57.1	29.9
Increase (decrease) in working capital	33.1	11.8	19.9	16.3	(4.5)	(26.6)	91.9	(11.7)	68.3	(208.8)
Increase (decrease) in working capital by element:										
Cash and securities	(16.4)	16.4	(13.9)	0.5	7.4	1.0	15.9	(19.0)	15.1	33.6
Accounts receivable	53.7	57.3	42.1	40.3	55.5	(9.9)	49.9	60.3	72.2	(109.6)
Inventories	10.6	23.2	9.1	24.9	13.5	38.4	38.2	100.8	51.1	(43.2)
Other current assets	0.0	4.2	(0.2)	0.4	0.6	0.3	0.0	1.4	0.6	(0.7)
Accounts payable	2.5	1.4	(6.2)	(15.6)	(7.5)	(9.8)	(14.0)	15.9	2.8	8.1
Short-term debt	0.0	(60.3)	(1.6)	(18.9)	(64.0)	(64.3)	8.7	(152.3)	(63.1)	(147.9)
Other current liabilities	(17.6)	(26.3)	(9.4)	(15.4)	(9.9)	17.8	(6.9)	(18.8)	(10.4)	51.0
Increase (decrease) in working capital	33.1	11.8	19.9	16.3	(4.5)	(26.6)	91.9	(11.7)	68.3	(208.8)

394

at the firm's (7) current ratio and (8) quick (acid-test) ratio. Johnson also calculated solvency ratios such as (9) total liabilities/ owners' equity and (10) long-term debt/ capitalization (where capitalization is the sum of long-term debt and owners' equity).

The company's annual reports also provided other data that drew Johnson's curiosity. These were the W. T. Grant statements of changes in financial position, summarized in Exhibit 2. Johnson noted that these statements were actually what the textbook called funds flow statements prepared on the working capital basis. The statements showed that funds provided by current operations remained fairly stable until 1973. Johnson questioned how this could be in light of the rapid increases in long-term debt the company had experienced after 1970. If funds flow was stable, why the need for so much new debt? Could it be the company was desperately short of cash and had to borrow just to stay afloat? Johnson decided to look into an analysis of cash flows.

Johnson's accounting professor was happy to provide a diagram that showed how to convert certain working capital flow data to cash flow data (see Exhibit 3).

Questions

1. Calculate for yourself the 10 ratios mentioned in the case. Some needed formulas to which you have not yet been exposed are:

$$\text{Return on shareholders' equity} = \frac{\text{Net income}}{\text{Shareholders' equity}}$$

$$\text{Return on assets} = \frac{\text{Net income}}{\text{Total assets}}$$

$$\text{Total assets turnover} = \frac{\text{Sales}}{\text{Total assets}}$$

For simplicity, use year-end amounts (rather than averages) for balance sheet items in your calculations. What patterns do the ratios show? In what year does the seriousness of Grant's problems become apparent?

2. Following the method given in Exhibit 3, calculate the cash flow provided by operations for W. T. Grant for each year from 1965 to 1974. (Note: Each year's changes in each working capital component account are shown in the bottom portion of Exhibit 2.) Does the depth of Grant's problems show itself sooner with this analysis? Could careful analysis have predicted Grant's failure well in advance?

EXHIBIT 3
COMPUTING CASH FLOW PROVIDED BY OPERATIONS FROM PUBLISHED FINANCIAL STATEMENTS

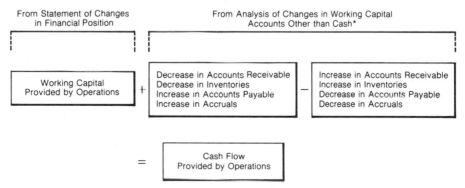

* "Accruals" means accrued liabilities. Accounts such as "Bank Loans" and "Current Portion of Long-Term Debt" must be excluded from the analysis. Even though treated as current liabilities, they represent neither cash provided nor cash used by *operations*.

12

Acquisitions and Consolidated Statements

Many corporations acquire an ownership interest in other corporations. Depending primarily on the percentage of ownership acquired, these investments in other corporations can be accounted for (1) at their fair value, (2) on an equity basis, or (3) on a consolidated basis. This chapter describes these three methods of accounting.

Because the most difficult problems arise in accounting for consolidated entities, most of the chapter deals with such entities. The chapter describes the two possible methods of recording the acquisition itself—the purchase method and the pooling method—and the subsequent preparation of consolidated financial statements for these entities.

ACCOUNTING FOR INVESTMENTS

If Company A owns securities of Company B, then A is the *investing* company and B is the *investee* company. A's holdings of B's securities are reported on A's balance sheet as an asset, Investments.

Fair-Value Method

If the investing company's holdings constitute only a small fraction of the common stock of the investee company, and if the stock's fair value is readily determinable, then *FASB 115* (described in Chapter 5) applies. Such stock is treated as an "available-for-sale" equity security and the **fair-value method** is used: The stock is reported on the balance sheet at fair value with unrealized gains or losses excluded from earnings and entered directly in a special owners' equity account.[1] Dividends received do not affect the carrying amount of the investment. Rather, they are treated as revenues:

```
Cash .............................................. 50,000
    Dividend Revenues ..............................        50,000
```

These revenues are usually included on the income statement under the caption "other income."

Equity Method   If the investing company's holdings constitute a large enough fraction of the ownership interest in the investee company so that the investing company can influence the actions of the investee, the investment is accounted for by the **equity method.** Unless the investing company can demonstrate that it does *not* "exercise significant influence" on the investee company, ownership of 20 percent or more of the investee company's common stock requires the use of the equity method.[2]

In the equity method the investment is initially recorded at its cost. Thereafter, the balance sheet investment amount is increased (debited) to reflect the investing company's share in the investee's net income; the offsetting credit is to a revenue account. If a dividend is received from the investee, the balance sheet investment amount is decreased (credited) and the offsetting debit is to Cash. Thus, in the fair-value method the income statement reports dividends; in the equity method the income statement reports the investing company's share of the investee's net income, irrespective of how much of that income is distributed in the form of dividends.

Recording the Acquisition.   To illustrate the entries made under the equity method, assume that Merkle Company acquired 25 percent of the common stock of Pentel Company on January 2, 19x1, for $250,000 cash. Merkle Company's entry for this transaction would be:

```
Investments ....................................... 250,000
    Cash ..........................................         250,000
```

Recording Earnings.   If Pentel Company's net income for 19x1 was $100,000, Merkle Company would increase the amount of its investment by its share (25 percent) of this amount, or $25,000. The following entry would be made on December 31, 19x1:

---

[1]"Accounting for Certain Investments in Debt and Equity Securities," *FASB Statement No. 115* (May 1993). If a stock's fair value is not readily determinable, then it is reported at its cost. *FASB 115* does not apply if the equity method (described in the next section) is used.

[2]"Equity Method for Investments in Common Stock," *APB Opinion No. 18* (March 1971); and "Criteria for Applying the Equity Method of Accounting for Investments in Common Stock," *FASB Interpretation No. 35* (May 1981).

```
Investments ....................................... 25,000
        Investment Revenue............................         25,000
```

Dividends. If Merkle Company received $10,000 in dividends from Pentel Company during 19x1, Merkle would make the following entry:

```
Cash............................................... 10,000
        Investments.....................................         10,000
```

Note that this dividend entry reduces the amount of investments on the balance sheet but does not affect the income statement. (Investment revenue is also usually a part of *other income* on the income statement.)

Consolidated Basis

If an investing company owns more than 50 percent of the stock of another company, it reports on a **consolidated basis.**[3] Such an acquisition is carried on the accounts of the investing company in accordance with the equity method. Consolidated financial statements are prepared by adjusting these accounts, as will be described in detail later in the chapter.

In summary, three methods of reporting an investment are possible, depending (with some qualifications) on the amount of stock that a company owns, as follows:

Amount of Ownership	Method of Reporting
Over 50%	Consolidated statements
20–50%	Equity method
Less than 20%	Fair-value method

BUSINESS COMBINATIONS

A business combination occurs when two companies are brought together in a single accounting entity. In some cases an acquiring company dissolves the acquired corporation and incorporates the latter's assets and liabilities with its own assets and liabilities. In other cases the acquired company continues to exist as a separate corporation. It then becomes a **subsidiary** of the acquiring company. The acquiring company is its **parent.**

The pace of business combinations—also called **mergers and acquisitions**—in the United States is cyclical. In 1988, a year of relatively low "M&A" activity, 1,889 deals were consummated at a total value of $44.3 billion. In 1990, there were 4,168 deals with a total value of $172 billion.[4]

---

[3]"Consolidation of All Majority-Owned Subsidiaries," *FASB Statement No. 94* (October 1987). Par. 4 of *FASB 94* describes the criteria for exclusion from the consolidation requirement; these exceptions are unusual in practice.

[4]U.S. Bureau of the Census, *Statistical Abstract of the United States: 1993,* 113th ed. (Washington, D.C.: 1993).

**Purchase
versus Pooling**

If the acquiring corporation pays cash for the acquired firm, the accounting method used to record the acquisition is called the **purchase method.** If the acquiring corporation issues its stock in exchange for the stock of the other firm, the acquisition may be accounted for by use of either the purchase method or the **pooling of interests** (or simply **pooling**) **method.** Prior to 1971, companies usually favored the pooling method because, as will be shown later, this method resulted in financial statement numbers that were believed to be more desirable than if the purchase method had been used.

Effective November 1, 1970, however, the use of the pooling of interests method was severely restricted by *APB Opinion No. 16.*[5] That opinion set up specific criteria that had to be met for a transaction to qualify as a pooling. These criteria are lengthy, complicated, and subject to various interpretations; only a summary of their general thrust is appropriate here. In general, to qualify for pooling treatment *all* of the following conditions must be met:

- The acquiring corporation issues only common stock with rights identical to the majority of its outstanding voting common stock in exchange for substantially all of the voting common stock of the acquired company. (This is the key criterion; if cash is involved, the transaction must be accounted for as a purchase.)
- Each combining company is autonomous and has not been a subsidiary or division of another corporation within the previous two years.
- The combination is effected in a single transaction or is completed according to a specific plan within one year.
- Within the previous two years neither company has reacquired shares of its voting common stock for purposes of using these shares for business combinations.
- The combined corporation does not agree to retire or reacquire any of the common stock issued to effect the combination.
- The combined corporation does not intend to dispose of a significant part of the assets of the combining companies within two years after the combination (other than disposals to eliminate duplicate facilities).

To illustrate accounting for the pooling and purchase methods, we will use the balance sheets for two hypothetical corporations, shown in Illustration 12–1. We assume that Corporation A plans to acquire all 100,000 shares of Corporation B stock and that it will pay for this stock with 200,000 shares of its own stock, which has a market value of $30 per share, a total of $6 million. We assume also that Corporation A can arrange the transaction in such a way that it can, at A's discretion, qualify either as a pooling or as a

---

[5]"Business Combinations," *APB Opinion No. 16* (August 1970).

ILLUSTRATION 12–1

Preacquisition Balance Sheets
As of Proposed Date of Acquisition
(in thousands)

	Corporation A	Corporation B
Assets		
Cash and marketable securities	$ 6,000	$1,000
Accounts receivable	5,000	1,400
Inventories	6,400	1,800
Total current assets	17,400	4,200
Plant and equipment (net of accumulated depreciation)	10,600	2,800
Total assets	$28,000	$7,000
Liabilities and Shareholders' Equity		
Accounts payable	$ 6,000	$1,700
Other current liabilities	1,500	300
Total current liabilities	7,500	2,000
Long-term debt	8,200	1,600
Total liabilities	15,700	3,600
Common stock (par plus paid-in capital)*	2,500	700
Retained earnings	9,800	2,700
Total shareholders' equity	12,300	3,400
Total liabilities and shareholders' equity	$28,000	$7,000
*Number of shares outstanding	1,000,000	100,000

purchase. One of the factors A's management will consider in deciding which way to arrange the combination is the impact that each treatment would have on its financial statements.

Accounting as a Pooling

The underlying premise of pooling accounting is that there is a "marriage" of the two entities, with the two shareholder groups agreeing to a simple merging of the two firms' resources, talents, risks, and earnings streams. Accordingly, under pooling treatment the balance sheets of A and B would simply be added together to arrive at the new consolidated balance sheet for A, which is the surviving entity. Any intercorporate obligations involved (for example, a receivable on A's balance sheet that was due from B) would be eliminated. With this exception the new enterprise (the A–B combination) is accounted for as the sum of its parts, as shown in the first column of Illustration 12–2.

The assets and liabilities of the combined firm are carried at the sum of their previous *book* values. Similarly, the Common Stock and Retained Earnings accounts of the combining firms are simply added to determine the combined firm's shareholders' equity. Note that when one compares A's preacquisition balance sheet in Illustration 12–1 with the *pro forma*

ILLUSTRATION 12–2

CORPORATION A
Pro Forma Consolidated Balance Sheets
As of Proposed Date of Acquisition
(in thousands)

	Pooling Accounting	Purchase Accounting
Assets		
Cash and marketable securities....................	$ 7,000	$ 7,000
Accounts receivable............................	6,400	6,400
Inventories	8,200	8,200
Total current assets.......................	21,600	21,600
Goodwill	—	1,500
Plant and equipment (net of accumulated depreciation)	13,400	14,500
Total assets................................	$35,000	$37,600
Liabilities and Shareholders' Equity		
Accounts payable..............................	$7,700	$7,700
Other current liabilities.......................	1,800	1,800
Total current liabilities....................	9,500	9,500
Long-term debt	9,800	9,800
Total liabilities.........................	19,300	19,300
Common stock (par plus paid-in capital)*............	3,200	8,500
Retained earnings.............................	12,500	9,800
Total shareholders' equity	15,700	18,300
Total liabilities and shareholders' equity..............	$35,000	$37,600
*Number of shares outstanding..................	1,200,000	1,200,000

(projected) pooling balance sheet in Illustration 12–2, there is no evidence of the fact that A paid stock worth $6 million for B's net assets, which had a book value of only $3.4 million (as indicated by its shareholders' equity). This $2.6 million difference appears nowhere on the balance sheet.

Accounting as a Purchase

The underlying premise of purchase accounting is that instead of a marriage of A and B, A is buying the *net* assets of B. A is buying B's assets and assuming B's liabilities, the equivalent to buying B's shareholders' equity. In accordance with the cost concept, the net assets of B go onto A's balance sheet at the amount that Corporation A paid for them: $6 million. This treatment involves two steps.

First, B's identifiable assets are revalued to their *fair* value. (Identifiable assets include all tangible assets plus "identifiable" intangibles, such as patents and licenses.) In Illustration 12–2 it is assumed that all of the assets on B's preacquisition balance sheet were reported at amounts approximately equal to their fair values, except for plant and equipment. Plant and equipment had a book value of $2.8 million but a fair value of $3.9 million, an increase of $1.1 million. Hence, with purchase accounting the consolidated plant and equipment account shows $14.5 million ($10.6 million for

A's preacquisition plant and equipment plus the acquired fixed assets of B, newly valued at $3.9 million).

Second, after the revaluation of B's identifiable assets, any excess of the purchase price over the total amount of B's revalued identifiable net assets is shown on the consolidated balance sheet as an asset called **goodwill**.[6] This amount is $1.5 million, as shown in the second column of Illustration 12–2. It is calculated as follows:

Purchase price	$6,000,000
Less: Book value of net assets acquired	3,400,000
	2,600,000
Less: Write-up of identifiable assets to fair value	1,100,000
Goodwill	$1,500,000

Hence, of the $2.6 million excess of the purchase price over the book value of Corporation B (which did not appear under pooling accounting), $1.1 million has been assigned to plant and equipment, and the remaining $1.5 million is shown on the balance sheet as goodwill. Goodwill is amortized using the straight-line method over a period not to exceed 40 years for financial accounting purposes. (For income tax purposes, goodwill acquired after August 10, 1993, is amortized on a straight-line basis over 15 years; goodwill acquired prior to that date is not tax deductible.)

If the purchase price is *less* than the book value of the assets purchased, the presumption is that the book values overstate the fair value of these assets. Otherwise, the acquired company would have been better off to sell the assets piecemeal rather than to sell the company as a unit. Therefore, these assets should be written down so that their total value equals the purchase price. Thus, with rare exceptions, there is no **negative goodwill**.[7]

Impact on Balance Sheet

Comparing the two balance sheets in Illustration 12–2, we can see that the pooling transaction will result in a more "attractive" balance sheet than will a purchase, in the sense that the asset costs that will be amortized and charged against income in future periods are lower. With pooling accounting the amount shown for plant and equipment is lower (though physically, these assets are identical regardless of accounting method), so future depreciation charges will be lower. Also, no goodwill appears under pooling, so there will be no goodwill amortization expense as a "drag" on future earnings.

Impact on Earnings

To fully understand the financial reporting impacts of the alternatives, the effect on reported earnings must also be considered. Assume that prior

---

[6]The preferred caption for this account is "Excess of cost over net assets of acquired companies."

[7]These rare exceptions are described in *APB Opinion No. 16,* par. 91.

ILLUSTRATION 12–3

Pro Forma Consolidated Income Results
For the First Year after Combination
(in thousands, except per share amounts)

	Corporation A	Corporation B
If independent corporations:		
Income before taxes..................................	$3,780	$945
Income tax expense (40%)............................	1,512	378
Net income...	$2,268	$567
Number of oustanding shares	1,000,000	100,000
Earnings per share	$2.27	$5.67
Combined A–B, pooling treatment:		
Income before taxes..................................		$4,725
Income tax expense (40%)............................		1,890
Net income...		$2,835
Number of outstanding shares..........................		1,200,000
Earnings per share		$2.36
Combined A–B, purchase treatment:		
Unadjusted income before taxes (as above)		$4,725
Less: Additional depreciation expense....................		110
Less: Amortization of goodwill		100
Income before taxes..................................		4,515
Income tax expense (40%)............................		1,806
Net income...		$2,709
Number of outstanding shares..........................		1,200,000
Earnings per share		$2.26

---

to the combination a pro forma income statement has been prepared for operations conducted in the first year after the acquisition. The projections assume that there are no benefits from "synergism"; thus, the pro forma combined A–B earnings are the same as the sum of what the projected earnings of the two firms would have been if they had remained independent. Assume also that there are no intercorporate transactions between A and B.

Illustration 12–3 shows that under *pooling* treatment of the combined firm's results, the net incomes of A and B are simply added to arrive at the consolidated figure. A's preacquisition stockholders presumably would benefit from the combination because net income per share would be $2.36, as compared with $2.27.

Under *purchase* accounting, arriving at the amount of consolidated income requires making two adjustments to the sum of the two firms' pretax incomes. First, the additional depreciation expense resulting from the acquisition must be taken into account. In other words, the consolidated depreciation expense is greater than the sum of the independent firms' depreciation because Corporation B's plant and equipment amount was written up from its book value of $2.8 million to its fair value of $3.9 million. Illustration 12–3 assumes that this difference will result in an additional $110,000 depreciation expense for each of the next 10 years. Second, the $1.5 million goodwill must be amortized. The illustration assumes the use of an amortization period of 15 years, or $100,000 per year. Thus, under the purchase treatment, net income is lower than with the pooling treatment.

Illustration 12–3 shows why Corporation A's management would prefer pooling treatment. If the combination were accounted for as a purchase, net income would be lower ($2,709,000 versus $2,835,000), but the number of outstanding shares would be the same (1,200,000). Hence, purchase-treatment net income would be $2.26 per share, compared to $2.36 with pooling. In this case first-year purchase-treatment earnings per share would be slightly lower than what A had planned to earn on its own without the acquisition ($2.27).

The accounting treatment when stock is exchanged in a combination is no longer a matter of management discretion. It is, however, a continuing matter of discussion among accountants, some of whom feel *APB Opinion No. 16* is too restrictive, whereas others feel pooling treatment should not be permitted under any circumstances.

CONSOLIDATED STATEMENTS

A "company," as it is thought of by its management, its employees, its competitors, and the general public, may actually consist of a number of different corporations created for various legal, tax, and financial reasons. The existence of a family of corporations is by no means peculiar to big business. A fairly small enterprise may consist of one corporation that owns its real estate and buildings, another that primarily handles production, another for marketing activities, and over them all a *parent corporation* as the locus of management and control. Each of these corporations is a legal entity, and each therefore has its own financial statements. Although the company itself may not be a separate legal entity, it is an important *economic* entity, and a set of financial statements for the whole business enterprise may be more useful than the statements of the separate corporations of which it consists.

Such statements are called **consolidated financial statements.** They are prepared by first adjusting and then combining the financial statements of the separate corporations. No separate journals or ledgers are kept for the consolidated entity. The adjustments are made on worksheets using data from the accounts of the separate corporations. Also, only legal entities are involved in the consolidation process. If an acquired corporation has been dissolved and as a result its assets have come under the legal ownership of the acquiring company, its assets and liabilities are already reflected in the acquiring company's accounts.

Basis for Consolidation

The legal tie that binds the other corporations, or *subsidiaries,* to the parent is the ownership of their stock. A subsidiary is not consolidated unless more than 50 percent of its voting common stock is owned by the parent. Until 1988 even a 100-percent owned subsidiary might not be consolidated if its business was so different from that of the other companies in the family that including it in the consolidation would result in financial statements that did not well describe the family as a whole.

> **Example.**   General Electric Company's 1993 consolidated financial statements showed a debt-to-equity ratio of 109 percent, which is unusually high for an industrial company. However, if the debt of its subsidiary General Electric Capital Services, Inc., were excluded, the ratio would drop to 9.3 percent.

Nevertheless, the FASB now requires that any majority-owned subsidiary be consolidated, irrespective of whether its activities are homogeneous with those of its parent. Also, foreign subsidiaries must be consolidated.

Consolidation Procedure

Illustration 12–4 shows the consolidation process in the simplest possible situation, consisting of the parent company and one subsidiary company, named Parent and Subsidiary, respectively. Parent owns 100 percent of Subsidiary's stock; this stock is an asset shown on Parent's balance sheet as Investment in Subsidiary. The investment is recorded at cost. It is assumed here that Parent purchased Subsidiary for $55,000, and this purchase price was equal to Subsidiary's book value (capital stock plus retained earnings) as of the time of acquisition.

The two companies have been operating for a year. At the end of that year their separate balance sheets are as summarized in the first two columns of Illustration 12–4. If the two columns were simply added together, the sum of the balance sheet amounts would contain some items that, so far as the consolidated entity is concerned, would be counted twice. To preclude this double counting, adjustments are made in the next two columns; these are explained below. Essentially, these adjustments eliminate the effect of transactions that have occurred between the two corporations as separate legal entities. Since the consolidated financial statements should report only assets owned by the consolidated entity and the liabilities and owners' equity of parties *outside* the consolidated entity, these internal transactions must be eliminated. The consolidated balance sheet that results from these adjustments appears in the last column. The adjustments are as follows:

1. Intercompany Financial Transactions.   The consolidated balance sheet must show as accounts receivable and accounts payable only amounts owed by and to parties outside the consolidated business. Therefore,

ILLUSTRATION 12-4
CONSOLIDATION WORKSHEET

	Separate Statements		Intercompany Eliminations*		Consolidated Balance Sheet
	Parent	Sub-sidiary	Dr.	Cr.	
Assets					
Cash	45,000	12,000			57,000
Accounts receivable	40,000	11,000		(1) 5,000	46,000
Inventory	30,000	15,000		(4) 2,000	43,000
Fixed assets, net	245,000	45,000			290,000
Investment in subsidiary	55,000	—		(2) 55,000	—
	415,000	83,000			436,000
Liabilities and Shareholders' Equity					
Accounts payable	20,000	13,000	(1) 5,000		28,000
Other current liabilities	25,000	9,000			34,000
Long-term liabilities	100,000	—			100,000
Capital stock	100,000	40,000	(2) 40,000		100,000
Retained earnings	170,000	21,000	(2) 15,000 (4) 2,000		174,000
	415,000	83,000			436,000

* Parenthetical numbers correspond with text description.

amounts that the companies owe *to one another* must be eliminated. Assuming that Parent owes Subsidiary $5,000, this amount is eliminated from their respective Accounts Payable and Accounts Receivable accounts. The effect is shown in the following hypothetical journal entry (remember that no journal entries actually are made in the books of either corporation):

Accounts Payable (Parent)........................... 5,000
    Accounts Receivable (Subsidiary).................   5,000

The payment of dividends by the subsidiary to the parent is a financial transaction that has no effect on the consolidated entity. In the separate statements this was recorded on Parent's books as a credit to Investment Revenue (which was closed to Parent's Retained Earnings) and on Subsidiary's books as a debit to Dividends (which was closed to Subsidiary's Retained Earnings). Since this transaction ultimately affected only the two retained earnings accounts, adding to one account the same amount that was subtracted from the other, the act of combining the two of them automatically eliminates its effect. Therefore, no further adjustment is necessary.

2. Elimination of the Investment. Parent company's investment in Subsidiary's stock is strictly an intrafamily matter and must therefore be eliminated from the consolidated balance sheet. Because it is assumed that the stock was purchased at book value, the $55,000 cost shown on Parent's books must have equaled Subsidiary's capital stock plus retained earnings at the time of purchase. We know that capital stock is $40,000; the difference, $15,000, must therefore be the amount of retained earnings at that time. To eliminate the investment, therefore, the entry is as follows:

```
Capital Stock (Subsidiary)........................... 40,000
Retained Earnings (Subsidiary) ...................... 15,000
    Investment in Subsidiary (Parent)...............          55,000
```

The additional $6,000 of retained earnings (= $21,000 − $15,000) now shown on Subsidiary's books has been earned by Subsidiary subsequent to its acquisition by Parent.

3. Intercompany Sales.   In accordance with the realization concept, the consolidated company does not earn revenue until sales are made to the outside world. The revenue, the related costs, and the resulting profit for sales made between companies in the consolidated entity must therefore be eliminated from the consolidated accounts.

The sales and cost of sales on intercompany transactions are subtracted from the total sales and cost of sales amounts on the consolidated income statement. If this were not done, the amounts would overstate the volume of business done by the consolidated entity with the outside world. To do this, records must be kept that show the sales revenue and the cost of sales of any sales made within the family.

> **Example.**   Subsidiary sold goods costing it $52,000 to Parent for $60,000. Parent then sold these goods to outside customers for $75,000. The consolidated entity's gross margin on these sales was $23,000 (= $75,000 − $52,000). Of this amount, $8,000 (= $60,000 − $52,000) appeared on Subsidiary's income statement, and $15,000 (= $75,000 − $60,000) appeared on Parent's income statement. Hence, the consolidated *income* amount would not be overstated. However, the correct consolidated sales revenue amount is $75,000, not $135,000 (= $60,000 + $75,000). Similarly, the correct consolidated cost of sales amount is $52,000, not $112,000. Thus, Subsidiary's sales and Parent's cost of sales must be reduced by the $60,000 intercompany transfer to avoid double counting:

```
Sales (Subsidiary) ................................... 60,000
    Cost of Sales (Parent)............................          60,000
```

These adjustments would be made on the worksheet for the consolidated income statement. (This worksheet is not illustrated here, but it is similar in nature to the worksheet for the consolidated balance sheet.) Also, as mentioned above, any accounts receivable and payable amounts arising from Subsidiary's sales to Parent would be eliminated.

4. Intercompany Profit.   If goods sold by Subsidiary to Parent have not been sold by Parent to the outside world, these intercompany sales transactions will affect the Inventory account of the buyer (Parent) and the Retained Earnings account of the seller (Subsidiary). Adjustments to these accounts are required. Assume that in the preceding example, Parent sold to outside customers only three-fourths of the products it acquired from Subsidiary and the other one-fourth remains in Parent's inventory at the end of the year at its cost to Parent of $15,000. The products sold to the outside world present no problem because they have disappeared from inventory and the revenue has been realized. The $15,000 remaining in Parent's inventory, however, is regarded by Subsidiary as a sale, and the $2,000 gross margin on that amount (one fourth of Subsidiary gross margin of $8,000) appears in Subsidiary's Retained Earnings. This portion of the profit must be eliminated from the consolidated balance sheet. This is done by reducing Subsidiary's Retained Earnings and Parent's Inventory by the amount of the gross margin, as in the following entry:

Retained Earnings (Subsidiary)	2,000	
Inventory (Parent)		2,000

(To avoid double counting, the entry shown in the example—eliminating Subsidiary's $60,000 sales to Parent and Parent's $60,000 cost of sales—must still be made, even though some of these goods remain in Parent's inventory.)

The necessary eliminations having been recorded, the amounts for the consolidated balance sheet can now be obtained by carrying each line across the worksheet, as shown in Illustration 12–4.

In the preceding example two of the most difficult problems in preparing consolidated statements did not arise because of simplifying assumptions that were made. These problems are described below.

Asset Valuation

In the example it was assumed that Parent purchased Subsidiary's stock at its *book* value. But a subsidiary's stock is often purchased at an amount higher than its book value. As explained earlier, purchase accounting for an acquisition requires that the book value of the acquired identifiable assets be adjusted to show their fair value and that any remaining excess of purchase price over the revalued net assets be shown as an asset called goodwill. In the above illustration, if Parent had paid $70,000 rather than $55,000 for Subsidiary's stock and if Subsidiary's assets were found to be recorded at their fair value, there would be goodwill of $15,000, and adjustment 2 (elimination of the investment) would have been:

Goodwill	15,000	
Capital Stock (Subsidiary)...........................	40,000	
Retained Earnings (Subsidiary)	15,000	
Investment in Subsidiary (Parent)...............		70,000

Furthermore, an adjustment to the consolidated financial statements is necessary to write off at least ¹⁄₄₀ of the goodwill as an expense of the consolidated company for the year. Assuming a 15-year amortization period and a 40 percent tax rate, the effect of this entry on the balance sheet would be:

Income Taxes Payable	400	
Retained Earnings	600	
Goodwill		1,000[8]

Minority Interest

If Parent had purchased less than 100 percent of Subsidiary's stock, then there would exist a **minority interest**—the equity of Subsidiary's other owners. On the consolidated balance sheet, this minority interest appears as a separate equity item, just above shareholders' equity. For example, if Parent owned 80 percent of Subsidiary's stock, for which it had paid 80 percent of Subsidiary's book value, or $44,000, adjustment 2 would have been as follows:

Capital Stock (Subsidiary)	32,000	
Retained Earnings (Subsidiary)	12,000	
Investment in Subsidiary (Parent)		44,000

As this elimination suggests, at the time Parent acquired 80 percent of Subsidiary's stock the minority interest amount was $11,000, the sum of the remaining 20 percent of Subsidiary's capital stock and retained earnings.

After the acquisition this minority interest would increase by 20 percent of the increase in Subsidiary's retained earnings, *after* elimination of Subsidiary's $2,000 profit on sales to Parent. This intercompany profit adjustment is prorated between Parent and the minority shareholders in proportion to their respective ownership. Hence, if Parent owned 80 percent of Subsidiary, on the consolidated balance sheet the following amounts would appear:

Minority interest	$ 11,800
Shareholders' equity:	
Capital stock	100,000
Retained earnings	173,200

---

[8]Actually, there would first be a $1,000 debit to Amortization Expense for the consolidated income statement; but when the tax adjusting entry was made and Income Summary closed to Retained Earnings, the net effect would be as shown here. Also, if the book and tax goodwill amortization periods were different (as often happens in practice), there would be an impact on Deferred Income Taxes.

The amount for minority interest is the net of four items:

20% of Subsidiary capital stock	$ 8,000
20% of Subsidiary retained earnings at time of acquisition	3,000
20% of the $6,000 increase in Subsidiary retained earnings since acquisition	1,200
Less 20% of the $2,000 intercompany profit	(400)
Total minority interest	$11,800

Similarly, the consolidated retained earnings amount, which was $174,000 when we assumed Parent owned 100 percent of Subsidiary, is now $800 less ($173,200), reflecting the $1,200 minority interest in the $6,000 postacquisition increase in Subsidiary's retained earnings, adjusted downward for the $400 minority interest share of the $2,000 intercompany profit elimination.

SUMMARY

Depending on the fraction of stock owned, a corporation reports an investment in other companies (1) at fair value, (2) on the equity basis, or (3) by the preparation of consolidated financial statements.

Acquisitions of other companies are reported on the basis of their purchase cost unless certain stringent criteria are met, in which case they are reported on a pooling of interests basis. If treated as a purchase, the acquisitions often give rise to an asset called goodwill, which is the excess of the acquisition cost over the fair value of the net identifiable assets acquired. Goodwill must be amortized over a period not to exceed 40 years.

Consolidated balance sheets and income statements are prepared by combining the accounts of the separate corporations in a corporate family. In combining these accounts the effects of transactions occurring within the family are eliminated so that the consolidated statements reflect only transactions between members of the family and the outside world.

Cases

CASE 12–1 Hardin Tool Company

The management of Pratt Engineering Company had agreed in principle to a proposal from Hardin Tool Company to acquire all its stock in exchange for Hardin securities. The two managements were in general agreement that Hardin would issue 100,000 shares of its authorized but unissued stock in exchange for the 40,000 shares of Pratt common stock. Hardin's investment banking firm had given an opinion that a new public offering of 100,000 shares of Hardin common stock could be made successfully at $8 per share.

Depending on how the details of the acquisition were structured, it could be accounted for either as a purchase or as a pooling of interests.

Condensed balance sheets for the two companies, projected to the date of the proposed acquisition, and condensed income statements estimated for the separate organizations, are given in Exhibit 1. The income statements reflect the best estimate of results of operations if the two firms were not to merge but were to continue to operate as separate companies. There were no intercompany receivables or payables, and no intercompany sales or other transactions were contemplated.

An appraiser had been retained by the two firms and had appraised Pratt's net assets (assets less liabilities) at $600,000. The difference between this amount and Pratt's $441,000 book value was wholly attributable to the appraiser's valuation of Pratt's plant and equipment.

EXHIBIT 1

Condensed Balance Sheets
As of the Proposed Acquisition Date
(thousands of dollars)

	Hardin	Pratt
Assets		
Current assets	$ 432	$ 246
Plant and equipment	690	312
Total assets	$1,122	$ 558
Liabilities and Equity		
Current liabilities	$ 263	$ 107
Long-term debt	195	10
Common stock ($1 par)	100	40
Additional paid-in capital	218	94
Retained earnings	346	307
Total liabilities and equity	$1,122	$ 558

Condensed Income Statements
For the First Year after Combination
(thousands of dollars)

	Hardin	Pratt
Sales	$2,100	$1,500
Expenses	1,620	1,120
Income	480	380
Income tax expense	168	133
Net income	$ 312	$ 247

Although an exchange of common stock was the most frequently talked about way of consummating the merger, one Pratt shareholder inquired about the possibility of a package consisting of 50,000 shares of Hardin common stock, and $400,000 of either cumulative preferred stock with a 10 percent dividend or debentures with a 10 percent interest rate. Under either of these possibilities, the transaction would be accounted for as a purchase.

Questions

1. Prepare consolidated balance sheets as of the proposed acquisition date, assuming the exchange of 100,000 shares of Hardin common stock, (a) on a pooling of interests basis and (b) on a purchase basis.

2. Assuming that in its first year of operations the combined company would achieve the same results of operations as the sum of the two firms' independent operations, what would be the combined company's net income and earnings per share on a pooling basis? On a purchase basis? (Assume a goodwill amortization period of 40 years, an average plant and equipment life of 10 years, straight-line depreciation, and an income tax rate of 35 percent. Round results—except earnings per share—to the nearest thousand dollars.)

3. As an adviser to Hardin, would you recommend that the transaction be consummated on a purchase basis or on a pooling basis?

4. What would be the combined net income and earnings per share under (a) the preferred stock package and (b) the debenture package? Is either of these proposals preferable to the all-common-stock proposal?

CASE 12–2   Carter Corporation

Early in 19x1, Carter Corporation acquired Diroff Corporation. Diroff continued to operate as a Carter subsidiary. At the end of 19x1, the president of Carter asked the company's public accounting firm to prepare consolidated financial statements. Data from the separate financial statements of the two corporations are given in Exhibit 1. (For the purpose of this case, these data have been condensed and rounded.)

The following additional information was provided:

1. During 19x1 Diroff delivered and billed to Carter goods amounting to $34,000. Diroff's cost for these goods was $25,500. Carter had paid Diroff invoices billed through November 30 that totaled $28,900. All of the Diroff goods were sold to outside customers in 19x1.

2. Late in December 19x1, Carter took a loan from Diroff for $32,300 cash. The loan was evidently a five-year note. (No interest on this loan was recorded in the accounts of either company because the transaction occurred so near the end of the year.)

The accountant proceeded to prepare consolidated financial statements. In discussing them with the president, however, the accountant discovered that he had made two assumptions:

1. He had assumed that Carter had acquired 100 percent of Diroff's stock, whereas in fact Carter had acquired only 75 percent.

2. He had assumed that Diroff's dividend was included in Carter's $37,400 of other income, whereas in fact Carter had not received the dividend in 19x1 and had made no entry to record the fact that the dividend had been declared and was owed to Carter as of December 31, 19x1.

The accountant thereupon prepared revised consolidated statements.

After these revised statements had been mailed, the accountant received a telephone call from Carter's president: "Sorry, but I was wrong about our sales of Diroff merchandise," he said. "Carter's sales were indeed $1,040,400 but only $20,400 was from sales of Diroff products. We discovered that $13,600 of Diroff products were in Carter's

EXHIBIT 1
FINANCIAL STATEMENT INFORMATION

Balance Sheet Data as of December 31, 19x1

	Carter	Diroff
Assets		
Cash	$ 57,800	$ 20,400
Accounts receivable	110,500	35,700
Inventory	120,700	54,400
Investment in subsidiary	142,800	—
Plant (net)	477,700	134,300
Loans receivable	—	32,300
Total assets	$ 909,500	$277,100
Liabilities and Equity		
Current liabilities	$ 88,400	$ 62,900
Noncurrent liabilities	170,000	54,400
Capital stock	255,000	102,000
Retained earnings	396,100	57,800
Total liabilities and equity	$ 909,500	$277,100

Income Statement Data, 19x1

	Carter	Diroff
Sales	$1,040,400	$408,000
Cost of sales	816,000	299,200
Gross margin	224,400	108,800
Expenses (including income taxes)	234,600	61,200
Operating income (loss)	(10,200)	47,600
Other income	37,400	—
Net income	27,200	47,600
Dividends	—	30,600
Added to retained earnings	$ 27,200	$ 17,000

inventory as of December 31, 19x1. Don't bother to prepare new statements, however. Tell me the changes, and I'll make them on the statements you sent me."

Questions

1. Reconstruct the consolidated financial statements that the accountant originally prepared.

2. Prepare revised consolidated financial statements based on the information that the accountant learned in his first conversation with the president.

3. What changes should be made in the financial statements as a result of the president's telephone conversation?

4. Contrast the financial performance and status of the company as reported in the original consolidated statements and as finally revised.

CASE 12–3   United States Steel and Marathon Oil

In October 1981 Mobil Corporation announced a tender offer to buy up to 40 million shares of Marathon Oil Company common stock at a price of $85 per share. Marathon had approximately 59 million shares outstanding at the time, which had traded the day before the offer at a price of $64. Mobil's offer stated that if more than 30 million shares were tendered, Mobil planned to acquire the remaining outstanding shares through merger, with the remaining shareholders receiving debentures (bonds) in exchange for their shares.

Marathon's board of directors opposed the Mobil offer, deeming it "grossly inadequate." The board hired First Boston Company to appraise Marathon's net assets (assets less liabilities). The appraisal, including goodwill, estimated the value at $11–$13 billion. Marathon also initiated a court action claiming that a Mobil-Marathon combination would lessen competition in the industry, a claim that was upheld in the courts.

With Marathon's support, on November 18, 1981, United States Steel Corporation (USS) made a tender offer for 30 million Marathon shares at $125 per share. The USS offer also contemplated acquiring remaining outstanding shares with debt if at least 30 million shares were tendered initially. The following week, Mobil increased its original offer to $126 per share. The board again rejected Mobil's offer, as well as one from Gulf Oil Corporation, on the basis that attempted merger with either oil company would be squelched on antitrust grounds. The board instead supported the USS offer. Enough shares were tendered to USS that it gained 51 percent control of Marathon. Marathon's fees to lawyers and investment bankers in fending off the Mobil offer and consummating the merger with USS were $38 million.

The information below was contained in a proxy statement to Marathon shareholders explaining the proposed merger. When consummated, the merger would be accounted for using the purchase method. Exhibit 1 shows income statements for USS and Marathon Oil for the year ended December 31, 1981. Exhibit 2 shows condensed balance sheets for the two firms as of December 31, 1981.

Several adjustments to these individual company statements were necessary to provide the stockholders with pro forma consolidated statements as of December 31, 1981, assuming the purchase had been consummated as of January 1, 1981. These changes relating to a hypothetical January 1, 1981, purchase were as follows:

a. USS's offer was to purchase Marathon Oil for $6.137 billion. The funds for the purchase were to be provided by additional bank loans and long-term notes for $4.467 billion, plus cash and liquidated marketable securities of $1.670 billion. This large USS debt increase would have caused 1981 consolidated interest and other financing costs to increase by $696 million. The use of cash and marketable securities for the purchase would have cost the consolidated operations $217 million in lost 1981 interest revenue, which affects the nonoperating income item.

b. Marathon Oil's 1981 year-end inventories were estimated to have a current value $1.244 billion greater than their LIFO book value.

c. Marathon's 1981 year-end property, plant, and equipment, including oil and gas property reserves, were estimated to have a current value of $7.786 billion.

d. Had USS purchased Marathon's property, plant, and equipment on January 1,

EXHIBIT 1

UNITED STATES STEEL CORPORATION
AND MARATHON OIL COMPANY
Income Statements
For the Year Ended December 31, 1981
(millions of dollars, except per share amounts)

	U.S. Steel	Marathon
Sales	$13,941	$9,733
Cost of sales and other operating costs (excludes items shown below).	12,439	6,816
Wear and exhaustion	571	283
Taxes other than income taxes	227	1,341
Total operating costs	13,237	8,440
Operating income.	704	1,293
Nonoperating income.	1,224	81
Interest and other financing costs.	(225)	(159)
Unusual items	40	—
Income before taxes on income	1,743	1,215
Provision for estimated U.S. and foreign income taxes	666	872
Net income.	$ 1,077	$ 343
Net income per common share:		
Primary	$ 12.07	$ 5.82
Fully diluted	11.47	—

1981, at the fair market value of those assets, amortization expense on those assets for 1981 would have been $154 million greater than the amount actually recorded by Marathon as "wear and exhaustion" ($283 million).

e. For tax purposes, Marathon would be treated as though the company were being liquidated. In this tax-basis liquidation, Marathon would be subject to "recapture" of former years' accelerated depreciation, with the result that 1981 year-end taxes payable, a current liability, would increase by $392 million. As a consequence of this liquidation treatment, the remaining $196 million of Marathon's $588 million deferred taxes would be eliminated.

f. The 1981 income tax expense savings from the interest and amortization adjustments mentioned above would have been $491 million.

g. The net effect on 1981 unadjusted consolidated net income from all of the above *pro forma* adjustments was to reduce it by $576 million.

Questions

1. Using the information given, prepare adjusting entries to the individual company 1981 financial statements and use these entries to prepare a pro forma consolidated balance sheet as of December 31, 1981, and a pro forma consolidated income statement for the year ended December 31, 1981, assuming the purchase had been consummated on January 1, 1981.

2. Be prepared to describe how you determined the amount of goodwill for the pro forma 1981 year-end consolidated balance sheet.

3. If one divides each company's 1981 net income, as shown in Exhibit 1, by its respective number of outstanding shares, shown in Exhibit 2, the results are not the $12.07 and

EXHIBIT 2

UNITED STATES STEEL CORPORATION
AND MARATHON OIL COMPANY
Condensed Balance Sheets
As of December 31, 1981
(millions of dollars)

	U.S. Steel	Marathon
Assets		
Current assets (excluding inventories)...................	$ 4,214	$ 907
Inventories	1,198	576
Property, plant, and equipment—net	6,676	4,233
Other assets	1,228	278
Total assets	$13,316	$5,994
Liabilities		
Current liabilities.....................................	$ 2,823	$1,475
Long-term debt......................................	2,340	1,368
Deferred income taxes	732	588
Redeemable preferred stock of consolidated subsidiary....	500	—
Other noncurrent liabilities	661	501
Total liabilities..................................	7,056	3,932
Shareholders' Equity		
Common stock*......................................	1,812	198
Additional paid-in capital	96	—
Retained earnings....................................	4,352	1,864
Total shareholders' equity	6,260	2,062
Total liabilities and shareholders' equity..................	$13,316	$5,994
* Number of shares outstanding	90,578,885	58,689,306

$5.82 shown in Exhibit 1. What could account for the apparent discrepancy?

4. Approximately what would have been the consolidated 1981 primary earnings per share had the purchase been consummated on January 1, 1981?

5. Calculate the following ratios for USS (without Marathon consolidated) for 1981: profit margin, current ratio, acid-test ratio, long-term debt/equity, times interest earned, and return on equity (= net income/owners' equity). Repeat the ratio calculations, based on your pro forma 1981 consolidated statements. What does a comparison of these two sets of ratios suggest about the short-run benefits to USS's shareholders arising from the purchase of Marathon?

13

Financial Statement Analysis

In previous chapters the principal focus has been on conveying an understanding of the information contained in the three basic financial statements: the balance sheet, the income statement, and the cash flow statement. This chapter describes how this information is analyzed, both by parties outside the firm and by the company's own management.

All analyses of accounting data involve comparisons. An absolute statement, such as "Company X earned $1 million profit," is by itself not useful. It becomes useful only when the $1 million is compared with something else. The comparison may be quite imprecise and intuitive. For example, if we know that Company X is an industrial giant with tens of thousands of employees, we know intuitively that $1 million profit is a poor showing because we have built up in our minds the impression that such companies should earn much more than that. Or, the comparison may be much more formal, explicit, and precise, as is the case when the $1 million profit this year is compared with last year's profit. In either case, the process of comparison makes the number meaningful.

BUSINESS OBJECTIVES

Comparisons are essentially intended to shed light on how well a company is achieving its objectives. In order to decide the types of comparisons that are useful, we need first to consider what a business is all about—what its objectives are. Let us say as a generalization that *the overall objective of a business is to create value for its shareholders while maintaining a sound financial position.*[1] Implicit in this statement is the assumption that value creation can be measured. But if a company's equity securities are not publicly traded and hence the total market valuation of its equity securities cannot be calculated, then shareholder value creation cannot be directly measured. Nevertheless, profit and return on investment, which are indicators of value creation, can be measured in all cases. Of course, employee satisfaction, social responsibility, ethical considerations, and other nonmeasurable objectives are also important and must be taken into account whenever possible in appraising the overall success of an enterprise. The measurement of profit has already been discussed; below we briefly discuss return on investment and maintaining a sound financial position.

Return on Investment

Return on investment (ROI) is broadly defined as net income divided by investment.[2] The term *investment* is used in three different senses in financial analysis, thus giving three different ROI ratios: return on assets, return on owners' equity, and return on invested capital.

Return on assets (ROA) reflects how much the firm has earned on the investment of *all* the financial resources committed to the firm. Thus, the ROA measure is appropriate if one considers the investment in the firm to include current liabilities, long-term liabilities, and owners' equity, which are the total sources of funds invested in the assets. It is a useful measure if one wants to evaluate how well an enterprise has used its funds, without regard to the relative magnitudes of the sources of those funds (short-term creditors, long-term creditors, bondholders, and shareholders). The ROA ratio often is used by top management to evaluate individual business units within a multidivisional firm (e.g., the laundry equipment division of a household appliance firm). The division manager has significant influence over the assets used in the division but has little control over how those assets are financed because the division does not arrange its own loans, issue its own bonds or capital stock, or in many cases pay its own bills (current liabilities).

Return on owners' equity (ROE) reflects how much the firm has earned on the funds invested by the shareholders (either directly or through retained earnings). This ROE ratio is obviously of interest to present or

---

[1]This statement is not necessarily consistent with the *profit maximization* assumption often made in economics. The techniques in this chapter are equally applicable under a profit maximization assumption, however, so there is no point in arguing here whether the profit maximization assumption is valid and useful. Discussion of this point is deferred until Chapter 26.

[2]As described later net income may be subject to an adjustment for interest expense when calculating ROI.

ILLUSTRATION 13−1
RATIOS FOR SELECTED INDUSTRIES, 1993

	Percent Return on Equity*	Percent Return on Sales†	Price/ Earnings Ratio‡
Aerospace and defense	14.1	3.6	13
Airlines	−11.2	−1.0	NM§
Apparel	11.7	3.7	20
Appliances and home furnishings	12.2	3.1	24
Automotive parts	15.7	3.5	19
Banks and bank holding companies	15.3	11.8	10
Beverages	28.2	7.9	23
Building materials	15.4	4.6	23
Cars and trucks	21.5	2.4	17
Chemicals	8.1	3.0	39
Computers and peripherals	−15.3	−4.8	NM
Computer software and services	18.4	8.4	35
Conglomerates	17.6	5.0	20
Containers and packaging	−2.3	−0.6	NM
Drugs and research	27.2	14.2	17
Food processing	21.9	4.2	18
Food retailing	14.4	0.7	20
General manufacturing	14.6	6.0	23
Health care services	18.6	4.9	21
Insurance	9.1	4.7	15
Leisure time industries	7.9	3.3	47
Metals and mining	−7.7	−2.1	NM
Oil and gas	10.5	3.7	20
Paper and forest products	6.3	2.1	33
Personal care products	16.2	4.4	33
Pollution control	6.1	2.7	48
Publishing and broadcasting	13.1	6.0	31
Railroads	13.5	7.1	20
Retailing (nonfood)	15.4	2.9	20
Semiconductors	23.3	12.5	14
Steel	−27.4	−3.2	NM
Telecommunications	12.4	6.1	25
Tobacco	18.3	5.5	16
Trucking	10.4	2.5	21
Utilities	9.8	8.1	15
All-industry composite	11.9	4.3	21

* Return on equity: Net income ÷ Ending common shareholders' equity.
† Return on sales: Net income (before extraordinary items) ÷ Sales.
‡ Price/earnings ratio: Closing price ÷ Primary earnings per share (before extraordinary items).
§ NM: Not meaningful.
Source: Calculated from Compustat data.

prospective shareholders, and is also of concern to management because this measure is viewed as an important indicator of shareholder value creation. The ratio is not generally of interest to division managers, however, because they are primarily concerned with the efficient use of assets rather than with the relative roles of creditors and shareholders in financing those assets. Illustration 13−1 shows average ROE for various industries. Note that the 1993 range is from −27.4 percent to 28.2 percent.

The third ROI ratio is **return on invested capital (ROIC).** Invested capital (also called **permanent capital**) is equal to noncurrent liabilities plus shareholders' equity and hence represents the funds entrusted to the firm for relatively long periods of time. ROIC focuses on the use of this permanent capital. It is presumed that the current liabilities will fluctuate more or less automatically with changes in current assets and that both will vary with the level of current operations.

Invested capital is also equal to working capital plus noncurrent assets. This equivalency points out that the owners and long-term creditors of the firm must in effect finance the plant and equipment, other long-term assets of the firm, and the portion of current assets not financed by current liabilities.

Some firms use ROIC to measure divisional performance, often labeling the ratio **return on capital employed (ROCE)** or **return on net assets (RONA).**[3] This measure is appropriate for those divisions whose managers have a significant influence on decisions regarding asset acquisitions, purchasing and production schedules (which determine inventory levels), credit policy (accounts receivable), and cash management and also on the level of their divisions' current liabilities.

Sound Financial Position

In addition to desiring a satisfactory return, investors expect their capital to be protected from more than a normal amount of risk. The return on the shareholders' investment could be increased if incremental investments in the assets for new projects were financed solely by liabilities, provided the return on these incremental investments exceeds the interest cost of the added debt. This "financial leverage" policy, however, would increase the shareholders' risk of losing their investment, because interest charges and principal repayments on the liabilities are fixed obligations and failure to make these payments could throw the company into bankruptcy. The degree of risk in a situation can be measured in part by the relative amounts of liabilities and owners' equity and by the funds available to discharge the liabilities. This analysis also involves the use of ratios.

Structure of the Analysis

Many ratios have been described in previous chapters. In this section these ratios and others are discussed in a sequence intended to facilitate an understanding of the total business. Thus, we shall assume here that one first looks at the firm's performance in the broadest terms and then works down through various levels of detail in order to identify the significant factors that accounted for the overall results. If the values of the ratios used in this analysis are compared with their values for other time periods, this comparison is called a **longitudinal,** or **trend, analysis.**

---

[3]In this context the companies are using "net assets" to mean assets less *current* liabilities, whereas the formal accounting meaning is assets minus *all* liabilities.

Dozens of ratios can be computed from a single set of financial statements. Each analyst tends to have a set of favorite ratios, selected from those described below and perhaps from some we do not describe. (Certain ratios that are useful only in a specific industry, such as banking, are not described here.) Although we describe many frequently used ratios, the best analytical procedure is not to compute all of them mechanically but rather to decide first which ratios might be relevant in the particular type of investigation being made.

Illustration 13–2 shows some of the important ratios and other relationships that aid in the analysis of how satisfactory a company's performance was.[4] These ratios can be grouped into four categories: overall measures, profitability measures, tests of investment utilization, and tests of financial condition. The ratios calculated below are based on the Kellogg Company's financial statements shown in Illustration 13–3.

OVERALL MEASURES

Return on Investment

As explained above, return on investment can be calculated in three different ways, depending on whether one views investment as being total assets, invested capital, or shareholders' equity. These ratios are calculated as follows:

$$\frac{\text{Return on}}{\text{assets}} = \frac{\text{Net income} + \text{Interest}(1 - \text{Tax rate})}{\text{Total assets}}$$

$$= \frac{\$680.7 + \$33.3(.66)}{\$4,237.1} = 16.6 \text{ percent}$$

$$\frac{\text{Return on}}{\text{invested capital}} = \frac{\text{Net income} + \text{Interest}(1 - \text{Tax rate})}{\text{Long-term liabilities} + \text{Shareholders' equity}}$$

$$= \frac{\$680.7 + \$33.3(.66)}{\$1,309.1 + \$1,713.4} = 23.2 \text{ percent}$$

$$\frac{\text{Return on share-}}{\text{holders' equity}} = \frac{\text{Net income}}{\text{Shareholders' equity}} = \frac{\$680.7}{\$1,713.4} = 39.7 \text{ percent}$$

Treatment of Interest. These formulas immediately raise a question: Why is aftertax interest expense added back to net income when figuring ROA or ROIC but not when calculating ROE? The answer is that in calculating these returns the analyst is attempting to determine how well management has used a pool of capital, whether that pool includes all equities (which equal total assets), invested capital, or just shareholders' equity. The analyst can then compare these returns with the cost of using the pools of funds. However, in arriving at the net income amount, *part* of

---

[4]Diagrams analogous to Illustration 13–2 can be drawn to show return on invested capital or return on assets, as alternative ROI measures.

ILLUSTRATION 13–2
FACTORS AFFECTING RETURN ON INVESTMENT*

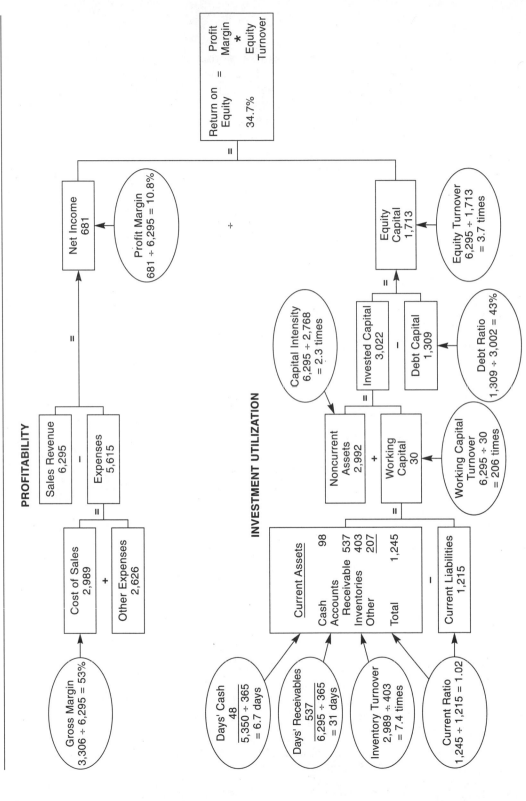

* Numbers based on Illustration 13–3, rounded.

ILLUSTRATION 13–3

KELLOGG COMPANY AND SUBSIDIARIES
Consolidated Balance Sheet
At December 31,

(Dollars in millions)	1993	1992
Current assets		
Cash and temporary investments	$ **98.1**	$ 126.3
Accounts receivable, less allowances of $6.0 and $6.2	**536.8**	519.1
Inventories	**403.1**	416.4
Deferred income taxes	**85.5**	66.2
Prepaid expenses	**121.6**	108.6
Total current assets	**1,245.1**	1,236.6
Property		
Land	**40.6**	40.5
Buildings	**1,065.7**	1,021.2
Machinery and equipment	**2,857.6**	2,629.4
Construction in progress	**308.6**	302.6
Accumulated depreciation	**(1,504.1)**	(1,331.0)
Property, net	**2,768.4**	2,662.7
Intangible assets	**59.1**	53.3
Other assets	**164.5**	62.4
Total assets	**$ 4,237.1**	$ 4,015.0
Current liabilities		
Current maturities of long-term debt	$ **1.5**	$ 1.9
Notes payable	**386.7**	210.0
Accounts payable	**308.8**	313.8
Accrued liabilities:		
Income taxes	**65.9**	104.1
Salaries and wages	**76.5**	78.0
Advertising and promotion	**233.8**	228.0
Other	**141.4**	135.2
Total current liabilities	**1,214.6**	1,071.0
Long-term debt	**521.6**	314.9
Nonpension postretirement benefits	**450.9**	407.6
Deferred income taxes	**188.9**	184.6
Other liabilities	**147.7**	91.7
Shareholders' equity		
Common stock, $.25 par value	**77.6**	77.5
Capital in excess of par value	**72.0**	69.2
Retained earnings	**3,409.4**	3,033.9
Treasury stock, at cost	**(1,653.1)**	(1,105.0)
Currency translation and pension adjustments	**(192.5)**	(130.4)
Total shareholders' equity	**1,713.4**	1,945.2
Total liabilities and shareholders' equity	**$ 4,237.1**	$ 4,015.0

ILLUSTRATION 13–3 *(concluded)*

KELLOGG COMPANY AND SUBSIDIARIES
Consolidated Earnings and Retained Earnings
Year ended December 31,

(Dollars in millions, except per share amounts)	1993	1992	1991
Net sales	$6,295.4	$6,190.6	$5,786.6
Cost of goods sold	2,989.0	2,987.7	2,828.7
Gross margin	3,306.4	3,202.9	2,957.9
Selling and administrative expense	2,237.5	2,140.1	1,930.0
Other expenses (revenue)	1.5	(36.8)	(14.6)
Interest expense	33.3	29.2	58.3
Earnings before income taxes and cumulative effect of accounting change	1,034.1	1,070.4	984.2
Income taxes	353.4	387.6	378.2
Earnings before cumulative effect of accounting change	680.7	682.8	606.0
Cumulative effect of change in method of accounting for nonpension postretirement benefits (net of income tax benefit of $144.6)		(251.6)	
Net earnings — $2.94, $1.81, $2.51 a share	680.7	431.2	606.0
Retained earnings, beginning of year	3,033.9	2,889.1	2,542.4
Dividends paid — $1.32, $1.20, $1.075 a share	(305.2)	(286.4)	(259.3)
Retained earnings, end of year	$3,409.4	$3,033.9	$2,889.1

Consolidated Statement of Cash Flows [condensed]
Year ended December 31,

(Dollars in millions)	1993	1992	1991
Operating activities			
Net earnings	$ 680.7	$ 431.2	$ 606.0
Depreciation	265.2	231.5	222.8
Net amount of other adjustments for noncash items included in calculation of net earnings	(145.7)	79.2	105.6
Cash provided by operating activities	800.2	741.9	934.4
Investing activities			
Additions to properties	(449.7)	(473.6)	(333.5)
Property disposals	114.6	133.8	25.2
Other	(25.1)	(10.6)	(11.6)
Cash used by investing activities	(360.2)	(350.4)	(319.9)
Financing activities			
New borrowings	676.5	504.0	186.4
Reduction of borrowings	(293.2)	(440.9)	(400.0)
Issuance of common stock	2.9	13.4	17.7
Purchase of treasury stock	(548.1)	(224.1)	(83.6)
Cash dividends	(305.2)	(286.4)	(259.3)
Other	2.9	11.4	1.1
Cash used by financing activities	(464.2)	(422.6)	(537.7)
Effect of exchange rate changes on cash	(4.0)	(20.6)	0.7
Increase (decrease) in cash and temporary investments	(28.2)	(51.7)	77.5
Cash and temporary investments at beginning of year	126.3	178.0	100.5
Cash and temporary investments at end of year	$ 98.1	$ 126.3	$ 178.0

Notes:

1. Earnings per share amounts are based on the weighted-average number of shares outstanding—231.5, 238.9, and 241.2 million shares respectively for 1993, 1992, and 1991.

2. The market price of Kellogg Company stock on December 31, 1993, 1992, and 1991 was respectively $56¾, $67, and $65⅜.

the cost of capital—the interest on the debt portion—was subtracted as an expense. The resulting net income therefore understates the earnings generated by using either the total equities pool or the invested capital pool.

Note that the amount of the adjustment is the *aftertax* interest cost of the firm. Because interest expense is tax deductible, the aftertax interest cost is the interest expense multiplied by the complement of the tax rate. Kellogg's tax rate in 1993 was 34 percent (= $353.4 ÷ $1,034.1).

On the other hand, in determining the return on the shareholders' investment, interest expense *should* be included in the earnings calculation, since the earnings accruing to the shareholders (i.e., net income) must reflect the fact that payments (in the form of interest) have been made to the creditors for the use of their funds.

Thus, the returns calculated using the above equations reflect the earnings generated by using a pool of funds, *excluding* the cost of the funds in the pool. This is the conceptually correct way to calculate the ratios. However, because making the interest adjustments adds complexity, some analysts ignore them in practice and simply use net income as the numerator in all three of the ROI ratios.

Average Investment. In many situations a more representative return percentage is arrived at by using the *average* investment during the period rather than the year-end investment. Ordinarily, the average investment is found by taking one-half the sum of the beginning and ending investment. If, however, a significant amount of new debt or equity funds was obtained near the end of the year, using the beginning-of-year amounts rather than the simple average would be more meaningful. Ending balance sheet amounts have been used in the examples so that they can be easily traced back to Illustration 13–3.

Tangible Assets. ROA is sometimes calculated on the basis of tangible assets rather than total assets—goodwill and other intangible assets are excluded. When so calculated, the return is clearly labeled **return on tangible assets.** A similar approach can be used for calculating ROIC or ROE.

Interest-Bearing Debt. The calculations above treated deferred income taxes as a liability. Many analysts exclude deferred taxes, as well as excluding minority interest as a component of owners' equity. (Kellogg has no minority interest.) Some analysts include as a part of invested capital any short-term notes and long-term debt maturing in one year, even though these are classified as current liabilities. These analysts maintain that debt capital includes all funds supplied by investors who expect a return in the form of interest. In any event the description of the ratio should make clear which approach is used.

Investment Turnover and Profit Margin

Return on investment is equal to net income divided by investment. As Illustration 13–2 suggests, ROI can also be looked at as the combined effect of two factors: profitability and investment utilization. A ratio can be associated with each of these factors. Algebraically, it is clear that the following is in fact an equality:

$$\frac{\text{Net income}}{\text{Investment}} = \frac{\text{Net income}}{\text{Sales}} * \frac{\text{Sales}}{\text{Investment}}$$

Each of the two terms on the right-hand side of the equation has meaning of its own. Net income divided by sales is called **profit margin** or **return on sales (ROS);** it is an overall ratio for profitability. Sales divided by investment is called **investment turnover;** it is an overall ratio for investment utilization. Investment turnover is called, more specifically, **asset turnover, invested capital turnover,** or **equity turnover,** depending on which definition of investment is being used.

These relationships suggest the two fundamental ways that the ROI can be improved. First, it can be improved by increasing the profit margin—by earning more profit per dollar of sales. Second, it can be improved by increasing the investment turnover. In turn, the investment turnover can be increased in either of two ways: (1) by generating more sales volume with the same amount of investment or (2) by reducing the amount of investment required for a given level of sales volume.

As shown in Illustration 13–2, these two factors can be further decomposed into elements that can be looked at individually. The point of this decomposition is that no one manager can significantly influence the overall ROI measure, simply because an overall measure reflects the combined effects of a number of factors. However, the items on the left side of Illustration 13–2 do correspond with the responsibilities of individual managers. For example, the manager who is responsible for the firm's credit policies and procedures influences the level of accounts receivable. Thus, the outside analyst, as well as the firm's management, can use the ROI chart to identify potential problem areas in the business, as described in the separate sections on profitability ratios and investment utilization ratios.

Price/Earnings Ratio

The broadest and most widely used overall measure of performance is the **price/earnings,** or **P/E, ratio:**

$$\frac{\text{Market price per share}}{\text{Net income per share}} = \frac{\$56.75}{\$2.94} = 19 \text{ times}$$

This measure involves an amount not directly controlled by the company: the market price of its common stock. Thus, the P/E ratio is the best indicator of how *investors* judge the firm's future performance.[5] (We say *future* performance because, conceptually, the market price indicates shareholders' expectations about future returns—dividends and share price increases—discounted to a present value at a rate reflecting the riskiness of these returns.) Management, of course, is interested in this market appraisal, and a decline in the company's P/E ratio not explainable by a general

---

[5]Major newspapers such as *The Wall Street Journal* print firms' P/E ratios along with the daily stock quotations.

decline in stock market prices is cause for concern. Also, management compares its P/E ratio with those of similar companies to determine the marketplace's relative rankings of the firms.

As Illustration 13–1 indicates, P/E ratios for industries vary, reflecting differing expectations about the relative rate of *growth in earnings* in those industries. At times, the P/E ratios for virtually all companies decline because predictions of general economic conditions suggest that corporate profits will decrease.

PROFITABILITY RATIOS

Each of the items on the income statement in Illustration 13–3 can be expressed as a percentage of sales. Examining relationships within a statement in this way is called a **vertical analysis.** As noted in Chapter 3, net sales is usually taken as 100 percent. Of the percentages that can be calculated, gross margin ($3,306.4 ÷ $6,295.4 = 52.5 percent), income before taxes ($1,034.1 ÷ $6,295.4 = 16.4 percent), and net income ($680.7 ÷ $6,295.4 = 10.8 percent) are all important. Retailing firms tend to pay particular attention to their gross margin percentage. A discount retailing strategy, for example, is based (in part) on the premise that selling goods at a lower gross margin percentage will generate more volume so that *total* gross margin will compare favorably with that of firms having a larger gross margin percentage but lower sales volume and lower asset turnover.

Profit Margin   As mentioned previously, the profit margin is a measure of overall profitability. Some people treat this measure as if it were the most important single measure of performance. Critics of the social performance of a company or an industry, for example, may base their criticism on its relatively high profit margin. This is erroneous. Net income, considered either by itself or as a percentage of sales, does not take into account the investment employed to produce that income. As Illustration 13–1 indicates, utilities have a relatively high ROS, but their ROE is below average, reflecting the very large fixed asset base that a utility must finance. On the other hand, food retailers (supermarkets) have only a 0.7 percent ROS, but their ROE is above average. This reflects the facts that (1) supermarkets do not have any accounts receivable to finance, (2) their inventory turnover is very rapid, and (3) many rent their premises, which therefore do not appear as balance sheet assets; i.e., their investment turnover is high.

Illustration 13–2 suggests the things top management needs to examine if the profit margin is unsatisfactory. Perhaps dollar sales volume has declined, either because fewer items are being sold or because they are being sold at lower prices, or both. Perhaps the gross margin is being squeezed because cost of sales increases cannot be passed along to customers in the form of higher prices. Cost of sales may be up because of production inefficiencies. Perhaps other expenses have gotten out of control: Maybe management has gotten lax about administrative expenses or is spending more for marketing costs than the sales results would seem to justify.

INVESTMENT UTILIZATION RATIOS

Ratios that deal with the lower branch of Illustration 13–2 represent tests of *investment utilization.* Whereas profitability measures focus on income statement figures, utilization tests involve both balance sheet and income statement amounts. We have already looked at the all-encompassing utilization ratio, return on investment (ROI). In this section less broad measures will be examined.

Investment Turnover

As with other ratios involving investment, three turnover ratios can be calculated:

$$\text{Asset turnover} = \frac{\text{Sales revenue}}{\text{Total assets}} = \frac{\$6{,}295.4}{\$4{,}237.1} = 1.5 \text{ times}$$

$$\text{Invested capital turnover} = \frac{\text{Sales revenue}}{\text{Invested capital}} = \frac{\$6{,}295.4}{\$3{,}022.5} = 2.1 \text{ times}$$

$$\text{Equity turnover} = \frac{\text{Sales revenue}}{\text{Shareholders' equity}} = \frac{\$6{,}295.4}{\$1{,}713.4} = 3.7 \text{ times}$$

Because of industry disparities in investment turnover, judgments about the adequacy of a firm's turnover must be made carefully. ROI is profit margin multiplied by investment turnover. Thus, if two firms have different turnover ratios, the firm with the lower turnover will need to earn a higher profit margin to achieve a given level of ROI, as is the case with utilities. Comparing the turnover ratios of two similar companies in the same industry is valid, of course, and may help explain why one achieves a higher ROI than the other. Similarly, comparing profit margins of companies in the same industry is valid, provided the companies are similar enough that the implicit assumption of their having equal investment turnover is valid. (Gap and Kmart are in the same industry—nonfood retailing—but it is not valid to compare them solely on the basis of either profit margin or investment turnover, because their different marketing strategies should cause these ratios to differ.)

Capital Intensity

Several investment utilization ratios that are less encompassing than investment turnover can be calculated. One of these is the **capital intensity ratio:**

$$\text{Capital intensity} = \frac{\text{Sales revenue}}{\text{Property, plant, and equipment}} = \frac{\$6{,}295.4}{\$2{,}768.4} = 2.3 \text{ times}$$

The capital intensity ratio (sometimes called **fixed asset turnover**) focuses only on the property, plant, and equipment item. Companies that have a high ratio of plant to sales revenue, such as steel companies, are particularly vulnerable to cyclical fluctuations in business activity. Because the costs associated with this plant are relatively fixed, when these companies' sales revenue drops in a recession, they are unable to cover these costs. Conversely, a company that is not capital intensive, as is the case with many service businesses, can reduce its costs as its revenues decline and therefore has less difficulty in a recession.

Working Capital Measures

Management is interested in the velocity with which funds move through the various current accounts. Ratios for days' cash, days' receivables, days' inventory, and inventory turnover (described near the ends of Chapters 5 and 6) provide the information on these flows. The reader can review the calculations of these ratios by referring to Illustration 13–2.

Days' Payables. An analogous ratio can be calculated for days' payables:

$$\text{Days' payables} = \frac{\text{Operating payables}}{\text{Pretax cash expenses} \div 365}$$

Pretax cash expenses can be approximated by adding all expenses except taxes and then subtracting noncash expenses such as depreciation. (This is the same procedure as for the days' cash ratio, except that taxes usually are included there.) Operating payables include accounts payable, accrued wages and payroll taxes, and other items that represent deferred payments for operating expenses. A note payable would be included if its proceeds financed accounts receivable or inventories; otherwise, short-term debt is excluded. For Kellogg, the ratio is:

$$\text{Days' payables} = \frac{\$308.8 + \$76.5 + \$233.8 + \$141.4}{\$4,996.1 \div 365} = 56 \text{ days}$$

Cash Conversion Cycle. Days' receivables, days' inventory, and days' payables can be combined to determine the **cash conversion cycle.** This is the length of time for cash to complete the operating cycle shown in Illustration 5–1, after incorporating payment deferrals. It is calculated as follows (using numbers for Kellogg):

	Days
Receivables conversion period (days' receivables)	31
Plus: Inventory conversion period (days' inventory)	49
Operating cycle.	80
Less: Payment deferral period (days' payables)	56
Cash conversion cycle	24

The result of this calculation is a measure of liquidity (discussed in the next section); it also indicates the time interval for which additional short-term financing might be needed to support a spurt in sales.

Working Capital Turnover. In addition to the ratios that focus on specific working capital items, it is often useful to look at the turnover of working capital as a whole:

$$\text{Working capital turnover} = \frac{\text{Sales revenue}}{\text{Working capital}} = \frac{\$6,295.4}{\$30.5} = 206 \text{ times}$$

Some analysts prefer to look at working capital as a percentage of sales. For Kellogg, this is 0.5 percent. Since this is simply the inverse of the working capital turnover ratio, it conveys the same information but in a slightly different way.

Each of these measures of turnover gives an indication of how well the firm is managing some particular subset of its assets. The investment turnover figures permit a comparison of similar firms' investment bases vis-à-vis the sales generated by those firms. The days' cash, receivables, and inventory ratios help identify whether a firm is tying up excessive amounts of funds in current assets. Excess levels of assets hurt performance because they require additional capital, and there is a cost associated with this capital. To the extent that debt could be reduced by cutting the level of assets, interest costs would fall, increasing net income, and the investment base would decrease, thus having a doubly favorable impact on ROI.

FINANCIAL CONDITION RATIOS

Liquidity and Solvency

Whereas the ratios previously discussed are indicators of the firm's success in marketing management and operations management, financial condition ratios are related to the firm's financial management. Financial condition ratios look at the company's liquidity and solvency. **Liquidity** refers to the company's ability to meet its current obligations. Thus, liquidity tests focus on the size of, and relationships between, current liabilities and current assets. (Current assets presumably will be converted into cash in order to pay the current liabilities.) **Solvency,** on the other hand, pertains to the company's ability to meet the interest costs and repayment schedules associated with its long-term obligations.

Most of the ratios used for this purpose have been discussed in previous chapters: current ratio, acid-test (or quick) ratio, debt/equity ratio, debt/capitalization ratio, times interest earned, and cash generated by operations/total debt. Also, the cash conversion cycle, described previously, is related to liquidity.

Dividend Policy

Two other ratios are not, strictly speaking, tests of financial condition. They are related to another aspect of financial management: dividend policy. These ratios are the **dividend yield** and **dividend payout:**

$$\text{Dividend yield} = \frac{\text{Dividends per share}}{\text{Market price per share}} = \frac{\$1.32}{\$56.75} = 2.3 \text{ percent}$$

$$\text{Dividend payout} = \frac{\text{Dividends}}{\text{Net income}} = \frac{\$305.2}{\$680.7} = 45 \text{ percent}$$

A company must reach decisions as to how its growth should be financed. Each company has a target debt/equity ratio it attempts to maintain. To do so, it must raise a certain fraction of additional capital from debt sources and the remainder from equity sources. Equity capital can be raised either by issuing new stock or by retaining earnings. If a company finds it expensive to raise new equity capital directly from investors, it can obtain its additional equity capital by retaining earnings. The more of the net income it retains in this fashion, the less it can pay out to shareholders as dividends. Of course, this applies only to a profitable company. If a company is in financial difficulty, it simply may not be able to afford to pay dividends.

The dividend yield on stocks is often compared with the yield (interest) on bonds, but such a comparison is not valid. The earnings of bondholders consist entirely of their interest (adjusted for amortization of discount or premium), whereas the earnings of shareholders consist not only of their dividends but also of retained earnings. Although shareholders do not receive retained earnings, the fact that part of the net income has been retained in the business (and presumably invested in income-producing assets) should enhance future earnings per share. This, in turn, should increase the market value of the shareholders' investment.

The ratios described in this book are summarized in Illustration 13–4 on p. 434.

GROWTH MEASURES

Analysts are also interested in the growth rate of certain key items such as sales, net income, and earnings per share. These rates are often compared with the rate of inflation to see if the company is keeping pace with inflation or experiencing real growth. Common growth rate calculations include average growth rate and compound growth rate. Both involve looking at information over a period of years, typically five or ten. The calculations will be illustrated using Kellogg's 1988–93 sales data (expressed in millions):

	1993	1992	1991	1990	1989	1988
Net sales..............	$6,295	$6,191	$5,787	$5,181	$4,652	$4,349

To calculate **average growth rate,** growth is first calculated on a year-to-year basis. From 1988 to 1989, this was 6.97 percent (= $4,652 ÷ $4,349 − 100 percent); from 1989 to 1990, 11.37 percent; and so on. These five year-to-year rates are then averaged; the result is an average growth rate in sales of 7.74 percent.

ILLUSTRATION 13–4
SUMMARY OF RATIOS

Name of Ratio	Formula	State Results as	Discussed in Chapter
Overall performance measures:			
1. Price/earnings ratio	$\dfrac{\text{Market price per share}}{\text{Net income per share}}$	Times	13
2. Return on assets	$\dfrac{\text{Net income} + \text{Interest}(1 - \text{Tax rate})}{\text{Total assets}}$	Percent	13
3. Return on invested capital	$\dfrac{\text{Net income} + \text{Interest}(1 - \text{Tax rate})}{\text{Long-term liabilities} + \text{Shareholders' equity}}$	Percent	13
4. Return on shareholders' equity	$\dfrac{\text{Net income}}{\text{Shareholders' equity}}$	Percent	13
Profitability measures:			
5. Gross margin percentage	$\dfrac{\text{Gross margin}}{\text{Net sales revenues}}$	Percent	3,13
6. Profit margin	$\dfrac{\text{Net income}}{\text{Net sales revenues}}$	Percent	3,13
7. Earnings per share	$\dfrac{\text{Net income}}{\text{No. shares outstanding}}$	Dollars	9
Tests of investment utilization:			
8. Asset turnover	$\dfrac{\text{Sales revenues}}{\text{Total assets}}$	Times	13
9. Invested capital turnover	$\dfrac{\text{Sales revenues}}{\text{Long-term liabilities} + \text{Shareholders' equity}}$	Times	13
10. Equity turnover	$\dfrac{\text{Sales revenues}}{\text{Shareholders' equity}}$	Times	13
11. Capital intensity	$\dfrac{\text{Sales revenues}}{\text{Property, plant, and equipment}}$	Times	13
12. Days' cash	$\dfrac{\text{Cash}}{\text{Cash expenses} \div 365}$	Days	5
13. Days' receivables (or collection period)	$\dfrac{\text{Accounts receivable}}{\text{Sales} \div 365}$	Days	5
14. Days' inventory	$\dfrac{\text{Inventory}}{\text{Cost of sales} \div 365}$	Days	6
15. Inventory turnover	$\dfrac{\text{Cost of sales}}{\text{Inventory}}$	Times	6
16. Working capital turnover	$\dfrac{\text{Sales revenues}}{\text{Working capital}}$	Times	13

ILLUSTRATION 13–4 *(concluded)*
SUMMARY OF RATIOS

Name of Ratio	Formula	State Results as	Discussed in Chapter
Tests of financial condition:			
17. Current ratio	$\dfrac{\text{Current assets}}{\text{Current liabilities}}$	Ratio	5
18. Acid-test (quick) ratio	$\dfrac{\text{Monetary current assets}}{\text{Current liabilities}}$	Ratio	5
19. Debt/equity ratio	$\dfrac{\text{Long-term liabilities}}{\text{Shareholders' equity}}$	Percent	8
	or $\dfrac{\text{Total liabilities}}{\text{Shareholders' equity}}$	Percent	8
20. Debt/capitalization	$\dfrac{\text{Long-term liabilities}}{\text{Long-term liabilities} + \text{Shareholders' equity}}$	Percent	8
21. Times interest earned	$\dfrac{\text{Pretax operating profit} + \text{Interest}}{\text{Interest}}$	Times	9
22. Cash flow/debt	$\dfrac{\text{Cash generated by operations}}{\text{Total debt}}$	Percent	11
23. Dividend yield	$\dfrac{\text{Dividends per share}}{\text{Market price per share}}$	Percent	13
24. Dividend payout	$\dfrac{\text{Dividends}}{\text{Net income}}$	Percent	13

Notes:
1. *Averaging.* When one term of a formula is an income statement item and the other term is a balance sheet item, it is often preferable to use the average of the beginning and ending balance sheet amounts rather than the ending balance sheet amounts.
2. *Tangible assets.* Ratios involving noncurrent assets or total assets often exclude intangible assets such as goodwill and trademarks. When this is done, the word *tangible* is usually used in identifying the ratio.
3. *Debt.* Debt ratios may exclude accounts payable, accrued liabilities, deferred income taxes and other noninterest-bearing liabilities. The reader often has no way of knowing whether this has been done, however. Conceptually, *debt* means interest-bearing liabilities.
4. *Coverage ratios.* Times interest earned and other coverage ratios can be calculated using pretax cash generated by operations instead of pretax operating profit.

The **compound growth rate** calculation uses the compound interest/ present value concepts described in the appendix to Chapter 8. In this instance the question is: At what rate would $4,349 have to grow to reach the amount of $6,295 after five years? (More formally: What rate of return gives a present value of $4,349 to a future value of $6,295 in five years?) Using Table A at the end of this book, this rate can be approximated as almost 8 percent (since $4,349 ÷ $6,295 = 0.691, which falls near the 0.681 factor for 8 percent on the five-year line); using a preprogrammed calculator, the rate can be calculated as 7.68 percent.

In some cases, the compound growth rate method can give misleading results because either the base year number (here, for 1988) or the final year number (for 1993) is abnormally high or low. In such a case, the average growth rate method is preferable.

MAKING COMPARISONS

Difficulties
An approximately accurate report of actual performance can be obtained from a company's financial statements. Finding an adequate standard with which these actual amounts can be compared, however, is often difficult. Some of the problems are described below. Financial statement analysis is used as an example, but the same problems arise in analyzing other types of quantitative data.

Deciding on the Proper Basis for Comparison.   In general, a youth who can high jump six feet is a better high jumper than a youth who can only jump five feet. In business, however, there are situations in which one cannot tell whether a higher number represents better performance than a lower number.

A high current ratio is not necessarily better than a low current ratio. For example, the current ratio for Kellogg on December 31, 1993, was 1.03 to 1. Suppose that on January 2, 1994, Kellogg borrowed $300 million of long-term debt and used these funds to pay down accounts payable. A balance sheet prepared subsequent to this transaction would show $1,245 million of current assets and $915 million of current liabilities, and the current ratio would accordingly be 1.36 to 1, 1⅓ times the ratio two days earlier. Yet, one could scarcely say that a company that had increased its long-term debt in order to pay current liabilities was in an improved financial condition.

In some comparisons the direction of change that represents "better" is reasonably apparent. Generally, a high profit margin is better than a low one, and a high ROI is better than a low one. Even these statements have qualifications, however. A high return may indicate that the company is only skimming the cream off the market; a more intensive marketing effort now could lead to a more sustained growth in the future.

Many standards can usefully be thought of as a *quality range* rather than as a single number. Actual performance that goes outside the range in *either* direction is an indication of an unsatisfactory situation. For a certain company the current ratio may be considered satisfactory if it is within the range 1.5:1 to 2.5:1. Below 1.5:1 there is the danger of being unable to meet maturing obligations. Above 2.5:1 there is an indication that funds are being left idle rather than being efficiently employed.

Differences in the Situations.   No reasonable person would expect a 12-year-old youth to run as fast as a 19-year-old athlete; the youth's performance should be compared to others of the same age, sex, and training. Differences in the factors that affect a company's performance this year as compared with last year are complex. Nevertheless, some attempt must be made to allow for these differences. The task is more difficult when we attempt to compare one company with another, even if both are of the same size and in the same industry. It becomes exceedingly difficult if the two companies are in different industries or if they are of substantially different size.

Changes in the Dollar Measuring Stick. Accounting amounts are expressed in historical dollars. A change in price levels may therefore seriously lessen the validity of comparisons of ratios computed for different time periods. Also, a ratio whose numerator and denominator are expressed in dollars of significantly different purchasing power (e.g., the capital intensity ratio when the fixed assets were acquired many years ago) may have no useful meaning. The fact that plant and equipment amounts are stated as unexpired historical dollar costs causes particular difficulty in making comparisons of ratios. Two companies, for example, might have physically identical facilities in all respects except age, and they might operate exactly the same way and earn exactly the same net income. If, however, the facilities of one company were purchased at a time when prices were low and the facilities are almost fully depreciated, and if the facilities of the other company were purchased at a time of higher prices and those facilities are relatively new, then the ROI of the company that carried its assets at a low book value would be much higher than the ROI of the other company.

Differences in Definition. The term *six feet* used to measure the high jumper's leap is precisely defined and easily measured. But the individual elements making up such terms as *current assets* and *current liabilities* are by no means precisely defined, and there is considerable diversity in practice as to how they should be measured. Similarly, profit may mean (1) net income as determined by using generally accepted accounting principles (which in turn can be a range of values, depending on the particular methods used for depreciation, inventory valuation, and so forth); (2) income after taxes, based on the firm's income tax return; (3) profit as determined by procedures required by a regulatory agency; or (4) profit as shown on a report intended for the use of management only.

Hidden Short-Run Changes. A balance sheet may not reflect the typical situation. It reports as of one moment in time and tells nothing about short-term fluctuations in assets and equities that have occurred within the period between two balance sheet dates. Many department stores, for example, publish annual balance sheets as of January 31. By that date Christmas inventories have been sold out, and payments of many of the Christmas receivables have been received; but Easter merchandise has not started to arrive, and payables for this merchandise have not yet been generated. Current assets (other than cash) and current liabilities as reported on the January 31 balance sheet are therefore likely to be lower than at other times of the year. As a result ratios such as inventory turnover and the average collection period may not be representative of the situation in other seasons.

Moreover, companies have been known to deliberately clean up their balance sheets just before the end of the year. They may reduce inventories, which increases the inventory turnover ratio, and then build up inventories again early in the next year. Such window dressing of the balance sheet is difficult for an outside analyst to discern.

The Past as an Indication of the Future. Financial statements are historical documents, and financial ratios show relationships that have existed in the past. Managers and analysts alike are primarily interested in what is happening now and what is likely to happen rather than what did happen. Often, outside analysts must rely on past data as an indication of the current situation. But they should not be misled into believing that the historical ratios necessarily reflect current conditions—much less that they reflect future conditions.

Possible Bases for Comparison

An actual financial statement amount or ratio can be compared against four types of standards: (1) experience, (2) a budget, (3) an historical amount, and (4) an external benchmark.

Experience.   Managers and analysts gradually build up their own ideas as to what constitutes good or poor performance. One important advantage that experienced people have is that they possess a feeling for what the "right" relationships are in a given situation. These subjective standards of a competent analyst or manager are more important than standards based on mechanical comparisons.

Budgets.   Almost all companies prepare budgets that show what performance is expected to be under the circumstances prevailing. If actual performance corresponds with budgeted performance, there is a reasonable inference that performance was good.

Two important qualifications affect this inference, however. First, the budgeted amounts may not have been developed very carefully. The comparison can, of course, be no more valid than the validity of the standards. Second, the budgeted amounts were necessarily arrived at on the basis of various assumptions as to the conditions that would be prevailing during the period. If these assumptions turn out to be incorrect, the amounts are also incorrect as a measure of results "under the circumstances prevailing." If, because of a recession or other economic phenomenon outside the control of management, net income is lower than the amount budgeted, it cannot fairly be said that the difference indicates poor management performance. Nevertheless, the budget is a type of standard that has fewer inherent difficulties than either historical or external standards. Of course, outside analysts frequently do not have access to a company's budget; but some overall budget parameters (such as earnings per share and return on investment) are publicly stated by top management as corporate financial goals.

Historical Standards.   A comparison of a company's current performance with its past performance raises relatively few comparison problems and is consistent with a management philosophy of continuous improvement. Such a comparison does not run into the problem of differences in accounting methods. If a method has changed, the change must be reported in the financial statements. Moreover, the analyst can also recollect or find out from supplementary data some of the circumstances that have changed between the two periods and thus allow for these changes in making the comparison. At best, however, a comparison between a current amount and a historical amount in the same company can show only that the current period is better or worse than the past. This may not provide a sound basis for judgment because the historical amount may not have represented an acceptable standard. A company that increases its ROE from 1 percent to 2 percent has doubled its ROE, but it nevertheless is not doing very well.

External Benchmarks.   When one company is compared with another, environmental and accounting differences may raise serious problems of comparability. If, however, the analyst is able to allow for these differences, then the outside data provide a performance check that has the advantage of being arrived at independently. Moreover, the two companies may have been affected by the same set of economic conditions, so this important cause of noncomparability may be neutralized.

Some companies use the results of a highly regarded competitor as a benchmark. Others identify the best performer among their various quasi-independent business units and use this unit's results as a benchmark against which to compare the other units' performance. Such comparisons may involve overall results or specific parameters such as inventory turnover or production efficiency.

Several organizations, including Dun & Bradstreet, various industry associations, and the Department of Commerce, publish average ratios for groups of companies in the same industry. Several on-line computer database services provide access to financial and statistical information for several thousand industrial companies and utilities in the United States and Canada; ratios can be calculated from these data. A reference librarian can assist in locating these various sources.

Use of industrywide ratios involves all the difficulties of using ratios derived from one other company plus the special problems that arise when the data for several companies are thrown together into a single average. Nevertheless, they may give some useful impressions about the average situation in an industry.

Use of Comparisons

The principal value of analyzing financial statement information is that it *suggests questions* that need to be answered. Such an analysis rarely provides the answers. A large unfavorable difference between actual performance and whatever standard is used indicates that something may be wrong, and this leads to an investigation. Even when the analysis indicates strongly that something *is* wrong (as when one company's income has declined while incomes of comparable companies have increased), the analysis rarely shows the underlying causes of the difficulty. Nevertheless, the ability to pick from thousands of potential questions those few that are really worth asking is an important one.

Keep in mind the basic relationships shown in Illustration 13–2, or some variation applicable to the situation being analyzed. The only number that encompasses all these relationships is an ROI ratio. A change in any less inclusive ratio may be misleading as an indication of better or worse performance, because it may have been offset by compensating changes in other ratios. An increase in dollars of net income indicates improved performance only if there was no offsetting increase in the investment required. An increase in the net profit margin indicates improved performance only if there was no offsetting decrease in sales volume or increase in investment. An increase in the gross margin percentage indicates improved performance only if there was no offsetting decrease in sales volume, increase in investment, or increase in selling and administrative expenses.

In short, the use of any ratio other than ROI, taken by itself, implies that all other things are equal. This *ceteris paribus* condition ordinarily does not prevail, and the validity of comparisons is lessened to the extent that it does not. Yet, the ROI ratio is so broad that it does not give a clue as to which of the underlying factors may be responsible for changes in it. It is to find these factors, which if unfavorable indicate possible trouble areas, that the subsidiary ratios of profitability are used. Furthermore, an ROI ratio tells nothing about the financial condition of the company; liquidity and solvency ratios are necessary for this purpose.

SUMMARY

The numbers on financial statements are usually most useful for analytical purposes when they are expressed in relative terms in the form of ratios. ROI measures overall performance, but other ratios help the analyst find more specific areas affecting ROI where investigation may be fruitful. Categories of ratios include those related to profitability, investment utilization, and financial condition. Although a great many ratios can be calculated, only a few are ordinarily necessary in connection with a given problem.

The essential task is to find a standard or norm with which actual performance can be compared. In general, there are four types of standards: (1) subjective standards, derived from the analyst's experience; (2) budgets, set in advance of the period under review; (3) historical data, showing performance of the same company in the past; and (4) the performance of other companies, as shown by their financial statements or by industry averages. None of these is perfect, but a rough allowance for the factors that cause noncomparability often can be made. The comparison may then suggest important questions that need to be investigated; it rarely indicates answers to the questions.

Cases

CASE 13–1   Genmo Corporation

On the night of February 27, 1994, certain records of the Genmo Corporation were accidentally destroyed by fire. Two days after that the principal owner had an appointment with an investor to discuss the possible sale of the company. The owner needed as much information as could be gathered for this purpose, recognizing that over a longer period of time a more complete reconstruction would be possible.

On the morning of February 28, the following were available: (1) A balance sheet as of December 31, 1992, and an income state-

ment for 1992 (Exhibit 1). (2) Certain fragmentary data and ratios that had been calculated from the current financial statements (Exhibit 2). The statements themselves had been destroyed in the fire. (In ratios involving balance sheet amounts, Genmo used year-end amounts rather than an average.) And (3) the following data (in thousands):

1993 revenues..............................	$10,281
Current liabilities, December 31, 1993........	2,285

EXHIBIT 1
GENMO CORPORATION FINANCIAL STATEMENTS
(thousands of dollars)

Balance Sheet
As of December 31, 1992

Assets

Current assets:

Cash..		$ 18
Marketable securities		494
Accounts receivable		728
Inventories......................................		972
Prepaid expenses		214
Total current assets		2,426
Investments.....................................		898
Real estate, plant, and equipment....................	$4,727	
Less: Accumulated depreciation.....................	2,433	2,294
Special tools		171
Goodwill..		594
Total assets		$6,383

EXHIBIT 1 *(concluded)*

Liabilities and Shareholders' Equity

Current liabilities:

Accounts payable		$ 732
Loans payable		266
Accrued liabilities		1,232
Total current liabilities		2,230
Long-term debt		250
Other noncurrent liabilities		951
Total liabilities		3,431

Shareholders' equity:

Preferred stock		25
Common stock		54
Additional paid-in capital		667
Retained earnings		2,206
Total shareholders' equity		2,952
Total liabilities and shareholders' equity		$6,383

Income Statement, 1992

Total revenues		$9,779
Cost of sales (excluding depreciation and amortization)	$8,165	
Depreciation	278	
Amortization of goodwill and special tools	343	
	8,786	
Selling, general, and administrative expenses	430	
Provision for income taxes	163	
Total costs and expenses		9,379
Net income		$ 400

EXHIBIT 2
SELECTED RATIOS

	1993	1992
Acid-test ratio	0.671	0.556
Current ratio	1.172	1.088
Inventory turnover (times)	10.005	8.400
Days' receivables	39.66	27.17
Gross margin percentage	15.12	16.50
Profit margin percentage	2.831	4.090
Invested capital turnover (times)	2.091	2.355
Debt/equity ratio (percentage)	62.15	40.68
Return on shareholders' equity	?	13.55

Questions

1. Prepare a balance sheet as of December 31, 1993, and the 1993 income statement.

2. What was the return on shareholders' equity for 1993?

CASE 13–2 Amerbran Company (B)

Using the 19x1 financial statements in Amerbran Company (A), Case 11–2, together with the 19x0 income statement shown in Exhibit 1 below, calculate the ratios listed below for 19x0 and 19x1. Use year-end amounts for ratios that involve balance sheet data. The company's interest expense in 19x0 and 19x1 was (in thousands) $105,165 and $102,791 respectively.

1. Return on assets.
2. Return on equity.
3. Gross margin percentage.
4. Return on sales.
5. Asset turnover.
6. Days' cash.
7. Days' receivables.
8. Days' inventories.
9. Inventory turnover.
10. Current ratio.
11. Acid-test ratio.
12. Debt/capitalization ratio.
13. Times interest earned.

EXHIBIT 1

AMERBRAN COMPANY
Income Statement
For the Year Ended December 31, 19x0
(in thousands)

Sales revenue, net.	$6,577,480
Cost of sales.	2,573,350
Excise taxes on goods sold	2,354,350
Gross margin	1,649,780
Selling, general, and administrative expenses.	974,121
Income before income taxes.	675,659
Provision for income taxes.	296,877
Net income	$ 378,782

Questions

1. Comment on Amerbran's treatment of excise taxes as part of the calculation of gross margin.

2. As an outside analyst, what questions would you want to ask Amerbran's management based on the ratios you have calculated?

CASE 13–3 The Financial Detective*

The financial statements of no two companies are alike. Industries differ, and each has a financial norm around which companies within the industry operate. An airline, for example, would naturally be expected to have high fixed assets (airplanes), whereas a consulting firm would not. A paper company would be expected to have a lower gross margin than an automobile manufacturer because its product is more likely a commodity.

Similarly, companies within industries have different financial characteristics, in part because of varied strategies. The following paragraphs describe two participants in each of a number of different industries. Their strategies and market niches provide clues as to the financial condition and performance one would expect of them. The companies' size-adjusted financial statements and operating data, which have been put in a standardized format, are shown in Exhibit 1 on pp. 444–45. It is up to you to match the financial data with the company descriptions.

*Copyright © 1988 by the Darden Graduate Business School Foundation, Charlottesville, VA.

EXHIBIT 1
SIZE-ADJUSTED FINANCIAL DATA

	Health Products		Appliances		Computers	
	"A"	"B"	"C"	"D"	"E"	"F"
Percentage of total assets:						
Cash and equivalents	11.3%	0.7%	1.8%	3.7%	15.4%	19.3%
Receivables	14.6	16.7	23.9	13.4	18.7	10.7
Inventory	17.8	16.7	30.5	25.8	22.7	21.4
Other current assets	6.3	2.0	4.9	2.8	9.1	0.6
Total current assets	50.0	36.1	61.1	45.7	65.9	52.0
Net property, plant, and equipment	34.4	23.3	31.0	32.3	23.1	42.2
Other assets	15.6	40.6	7.9	22.0	11.0	5.8
Total assets	100.0%	100.0%	100.0%	100.0%	100.0%	100.0%
Accounts payable	14.1%	15.1%	11.3%	12.1%	9.5%	2.1%
Other current liabilities	12.8	9.5	16.3	21.2	31.0	16.5
Total current liabilities	26.9	24.6	27.6	33.3	40.5	18.6
Long-term debt	11.2	21.5	16.5	6.8	14.6	12.0
Other liabilities	8.7	5.3	7.3	3.3	4.4	1.7
Total liabilities	46.8	51.4	51.4	43.4	59.5	32.3
Minority interest	0.0	0.0	0.0	2.7	0.8	0.0
Owners' equity	53.2	48.6	48.6	53.9	39.7	67.7
Total liabilities and owners' equity	100.0%	100.0%	100.0%	100.0%	100.0%	100.0%
Percentage of sales:						
Revenues	100.0%	100.0%	100.0%	100.0%	100.0%	100.0%
Cost of goods sold	36.9	64.0	72.8	79.3	69.7	35.7
Gross profit	63.1	36.0	27.2	20.7	30.3	64.3
SG&A (all operating expenses for firms H and O)	40.3	21.7	13.3	14.4	29.4	16.3
R&D expense	7.7	3.2	NAv.	NAv.	NAv.	15.8
Interest expense	1.4	3.4	0.6	0.6	1.9	1.3
Other expense (income)	(1.2)	0.5	(0.4)	(0.4)	(2.7)	0.0
Income before taxes	14.9	7.2	13.7	6.1	1.7	30.9
Income taxes	4.5	1.9	5.7	1.5	1.1	9.5
Net income	10.4%	5.3%	8.0%	4.6%	0.6%	21.4%
Selected ratios:						
Sales/assets	122%	82%	223%	173%	128%	76%
Return on assets	13%	4%	18%	8%	1%	16%
Return on equity	24%	12%	37%	15%	2%	24%
Quick ratio	0.96	0.71	0.93	0.51	0.84	0.162
Current ratio	1.86	1.47	2.21	1.37	1.63	2.80
Days' receivables	43	75	39	28	54	51
Inventory turnover (times)	6.88	4.87	7.32	6.69	5.62	3.56
Long-term debt/equity	21%	44%	34%	13%	37%	18%
Dividend payout	33%	49%	50%	43%	0%	0%
Price/earnings ratio	17.9	22.1	13.5	13.5	32.0	21.5
Market/book value	4.44	2.09	5.16	1.91	1.21	5.05

Note: NAv. = not available.

	Retailing		Electronics		Hotels		Newspapers		Transportation	
	"G"	"H"	"I"	"J"	"K"	"L"	"M"	"N"	"O"	"P"
	0.2%	15.6%	5.8%	15.6%	14.1%	0.3%	8.5%	4.4%	1.8%	0.9%
	1.9	34.7	20.7	19.9	7.3	9.2	8.7	9.0	6.5	18.7
	51.7	5.5	17.1	17.4	NAv.	3.5	4.5	2.1	1.5	3.9
	2.8	0.0	7.3	7.3	NAv.	4.1	2.6	3.1	0.9	1.3
	56.6	55.8	50.9	60.2	23.1	17.1	24.3	18.6	10.7	24.8
	41.8	6.4	45.9	35.7	49.5	48.0	14.0	56.2	82.3	73.3
	1.6	37.8	3.2	4.1	27.4	34.9	61.7	25.2	7.0	1.9
	100.0%	100.0%	100.0%	100.0%	100.0%	100.0%	100.0%	100.0%	100.0%	100.0%
	21.4%	8.6%	10.3%	25.0%	8.9%	9.5%	5.4%	6.2%	12.0%	5.1%
	12.6	31.1	21.0	4.3	0.9	11.4	9.7	11.9	1.4	21.0
	34.0	39.7	31.3	29.3	9.8	20.9	15.1	18.1	13.4	26.1
	3.6	12.8	6.5	11.4	21.6	46.5	25.6	19.6	14.5	13.7
	18.4	29.4	5.7	6.5	14.3	17.5	7.9	14.1	27.4	17.7
	56.0	81.9	43.5	47.2	45.7	84.9	48.6	51.8	55.3	57.5
	0.0	0.0	0.0	0.0	0.0	0.0	0.0	0.0	0.4	0.0
	44.0	18.1	56.5	52.8	54.3	15.1	51.4	48.2	44.3	42.5
	100.0%	100.0%	100.0%	100.0%	100.0%	100.0%	100.0%	100.0%	100.0%	100.0%
	100.0%	100.0%	100.0%	100.0%	100.0%	100.0%	100.0%	100.0%	100.0%	100.0%
	77.0	NAv.	60.5	78.3	41.0	92.1	45.9	54.2	NAv.	82.4
	23.0	100.0	39.5	21.7	59.0	7.9	54.1	45.8	100.0	17.6
	16.3	97.1	24.7	17.8	33.8	1.1	28.6	28.6	86.1	7.6
	NAv.	NAv.	NAv.	NAv.	NAv.	NAv.	NAv.	NAv.	NAv.	NAv.
	0.7	NAv.	1.2	0.4	6.5	1.4	2.3	1.4	2.5	0.5
	(0.7)	(1.1)	7.4	(3.9)	0.7	(0.7)	(11.8)	(0.1)	0.0	5.8
	6.7	4.0	6.2	7.4	18.0	6.1	35.0	15.9	11.4	3.7
	2.8	0.6	1.6	1.9	4.4	2.7	14.4	6.4	4.5	1.4
	3.9%	3.4%	4.6%	5.5%	13.6%	3.4%	20.6%	9.5%	6.9%	2.3%
	311%	65%	126%	131%	55%	121%	73%	99%	46%	191%
	12%	2%	6%	7%	8%	4%	15%	9%	3%	4%
	28%	12%	10%	18%	14%	28%	29%	19%	7%	11%
	0.6	1.27	0.81	1.21	2.18	0.45	1.14	0.74	0.62	0.75
	1.67	1.41	1.62	2.06	2.36	0.82	1.61	1.03	0.80	0.95
	2	196	60	55	49	28	43	33	52	36
	6.02	11.77	7.38	7.57	NAv.	13.21	16.24	47.28	30.97	49.22
	8%	70%	11%	22%	40%	308%	50%	41%	33%	32%
	11%	46%	27%	24%	21%	10%	33%	20%	42%	43%
	27.7	11.0	22.7	19.6	17.8	21.8	20.9	20.7	20.9	23.3
	8.02	1.11	2.15	2.43	2.53	5.13	4.58	3.98	1.52	2.42

Health Products. Of companies A and B, one manufactured pharmaceuticals and a variety of low-margin hospital supplies, and both product lines were marketed primarily through direct sales to doctors and hospitals. The firm had recently acquired a large hospital supply company and, therefore, had significant goodwill on its books. The other firm manufactured and nationally mass-marketed a broad line of name-brand toiletries, nonprescription drugs, and consumer and baby-care products through 165 decentralized subsidiaries.

Household Appliances. The two home-appliance manufacturers are companies C and D. One focused on marketing high-quality washers, dryers, dishwashers, and refrigerators under its own name. The other company attempted to segment the market for the same products by selling under its own name and under three other brand names. The second firm had a contract to sell one brand solely as a private-label item through a large department store chain.

Computers. Companies E and F manufactured computers. One had a highly focused product line: supercomputer systems for scientific applications. Most of these computers were used for physical research, such as that related to weather, energy, and defense. Although the output of these units was relatively small, the price tag was the highest in the industry. The other firm manufactured large mainframe computers and had an emerging position in the supercomputer segment; it also developed and marketed related software and provided financial and insurance services as well. Computer and software sales were responsible for about two-thirds of the company's revenues, and financial services for the remaining one-third.

Retailing. Companies G and H were two retailers with different market emphases. One company was a large, national chain of department stores that sold largely on credit everything from automotive equipment and services to clothing and household items, through its (primarily) leased properties. It also marketed its products through a catalog and provided a variety of financial services. Merchandise sales were responsible for about 60 percent of revenues, and insurance sales for about 32 percent. The other firm was a rapidly growing chain of discount department stores and wholesale clubs that owned a large portion of its outlets. As a discounter, it provided little or no credit to customers.

Electronics. Two electronics companies are shown as companies I and J. Both produced semiconductors, but one specialized in their manufacture and also produced small desktop and hand-held computing equipment. About half its electronic components were sold to the defense industry. The other firm was financially conservative. It specialized in radio and television equipment and made semiconductors as a secondary, but increasingly important, line of business (over 30 percent of revenues).

Hotels. Companies K and L were both large hotel/motel chains. In addition, one company owned one of the largest food-service contractors in the country, a large chain of family restaurants, and a large chain of fast-food restaurants. This firm financed its hotels via off-balance-sheet limited partnerships. The company had significant assets in the form of food service and hotel management contracts. Hotel revenues accounted for about 40 percent of the total and contract services for about 45 percent. The other firm operated a worldwide chain of high-quality hotels and motels in addition to a smaller line of casinos.

Newspapers. Companies M and N owned newspapers. One had a large flagship newspaper that was sold around the country and around the world. Because the company was centered largely around one product, it had strong central controls. This company's second most important line of business was periodicals (16 percent of revenues). The other firm owned a number of small newspapers throughout the Midwest. Broadcasting was its secondary line of business and accounted for about 27 percent of total revenues. This company had a significant amount of goodwill stemming from acquisitions.

Transportation. Of transportation companies O and P, one was a large national trucking and freight-forwarding company. The other was primarily a railroad, although 20 percent of its revenues were derived from real estate and exploitation of natural resources.

Questions

1. Decide which company is which in each industry pair, describing the rationale for your decision. (Also, feel free to guess what the name of each actual company is.)

2. We know that the mix of assets and the composition of liabilities and owners' equity differ *across* industries. What are the factors creating such differences between firms in the *same* industry?

CASE 13–4 Springfield National Bank*

John Dawson, Jr., president of Dawson Stores, Inc., had a discussion with Stefanie Anderson, a loan officer at Springfield National Bank. Both Mr. Dawson and Dawson Stores, Inc., were deposit customers of the bank and had been for several years. Dawson's comments were directly to the point:

> It appears that we are going to have some working capital needs during the next year at Dawson Stores, Inc. I would like to obtain a $1,000,000 line of credit, on an unsecured basis, to cover these short-term needs. Could you set up the line of credit for a year to be reviewed when next year's statements are available?
>
> I know from my friends that you need information about the company in order to grant this request, so I have brought a copy of the company's statements for the last four years for you. Could you let me know about the line of credit in a few days? We are having a board meeting in two weeks, and I

would like to get the appropriate paperwork for you at that time.

In reviewing the reports of previous contacts by bank personnel with Dawson Stores, Inc., Ms. Anderson found the information summarized below:

> Dawson Stores, Inc., had been incorporated in 1881. The stock had been widely dispersed upon the death of John Dawson, Sr., who had divided his share among his 5 children and 14 grandchildren.
>
> Dawson Stores, Inc., had maintained its deposit accounts with Springfield for many years, even during the years John Dawson, Sr., had managed the company. The accounts had varied over the past few years. Average balances of the accounts were $350,000 for the past year. The company had occasionally purchased certificates of deposits for short periods.
>
> Dawson Stores, Inc., had not used bank credit in the last 10 years. A recent Dun & Bradstreet report requested by a business development officer reported all trade accounts satisfactory and contained only satisfactory

*Copyright © by Ray G. Stephens.

EXHIBIT 1

DAWSON STORES, INC.
Comparative Balance Sheets
As of January 31
(amounts in thousands)

	1990	1991	1992	1993
Assets				
Current assets:				
Cash	$ 107	$ 141	$ 709	$ 916
Accounts receivable (net)	2,862	3,007	3,378	3,767
Inventories	2,600	2,383	2,821	3,090
Supplies and prepaid expenses	70	100	91	75
Total current assets	5,639	5,631	6,999	7,848
Investments and other assets	287	318	162	201
Property, plant, and equipment (net)	4,917	5,186	5,385	5,707
Total assets	$10,843	$11,135	$12,546	$13,756
Liabilities and Shareholders' Equity				
Current liabilities:				
Accounts payable	$ 1,153	$ 1,166	$ 1,767	$ 2,272
Taxes other than income taxes	379	389	414	418
Accrued liabilities	410	454	676	792
Income taxes, currently payable	221	229	491	480
Deferred income taxes, installment sales	374	401	484	589
Current portion of long-term debt	119	143	181	141
Total current liabilities	2,656	2,782	4,013	4,692
Long-term debt	3,494	3,430	3,136	2,942
Deferred credits	266	292	244	302
Shareholders' equity:				
Capital stock	130	130	130	130
Retained earnings	4,297	4,501	5,023	5,690
Total liabilities and shareholders' equity	$10,843	$11,135	$12,546	$13,756

information. The D&B report showed the officers were John as president and his brother Bill as vice president and treasurer. The directors were the officers, their two sisters, and two cousins, the latter four residing in other states. Credit terms included both revolving (30-day) accounts and installment sales.

Dawson Stores, Inc., has operated seven stores for the past six years. All store locations have been modernized frequently. One store location was moved during the past year to a new location two blocks from the previous location.

The call report from the business development officer reported the premises orderly and well located for this chain of small retail soft-goods and hard-goods stores (based upon visits to three of seven locations), all located in the Springfield trade area. The president was happy with his present bank services, but in the opinion of the business development officer there was little possibility for further business.

The audited financial statements left with Ms. Anderson by John Dawson are summarized in Exhibits 1, 2, and 3. Notes accompanying these financial statements gave the following additional information.

Accounts Receivable. Retail customer accounts receivable are written off in full when any portion of the unpaid balance is past due 12 months. The allowance for losses arising from uncollectible customer accounts receivable is based on historical bad debt experience and current aging of the accounts.

Accounts receivable (in thousands):	1990	1991	1992	1993
Thirty-day accounts	$ 68	$ 75	$ 40	$ 32
Deferred payment accounts	2,606	2,709	3,102	3,595
Other accounts	245	310	348	251
Less: Allowance for losses	(57)	(87)	(112)	(111)
	$2,862	$3,007	$3,378	$3,767

Thirty-day accounts are revolving charge accounts that are billed every 30 days. Deferred payment accounts are accounts requiring monthly principal payments of at least 10 percent of the outstanding balance plus interest at 15 percent. Other accounts are for sales contracts from three to five years from the sales of office properties. The following is an aging schedule of accounts receivable as of January 31, 1993:

(in thousands)	30 Days or Less	30 to 60 Days	Over 60 Days
Thirty-day	$ 29	$ 3	$ 1
Deferred payment	3,200	288	106
Other	228	23	–0–

Inventories. Substantially all inventories are recorded at cost on the last-in, first-out

EXHIBIT 2

DAWSON STORES, INC.
Comparative Statements of Income and Retained Earnings
For the Years Ending January 31
(amounts in thousands)

	1990	1991	1992	1993
Revenues	$18,297	$19,558	$21,976	$24,128
Cost of sales	12,816	13,884	15,163	16,527
	5,481	5,674	6,813	7,601
Operating expenses	4,789	5,023	5,422	5,830
Earnings before income taxes	692	651	1,391	1,771
Income taxes:				
Current	246	275	690	813
Deferred	91	48	34	104
	337	323	724	917
Net income	355	328	667	854
Retained earnings, beginning of the year	4,058	4,297	4,501	5,023
Less: Dividends	116	124	145	187
Retained earnings, end of year	$ 4,297	4,501	5,023	$ 5,690
Earnings per share (100,000 shares issued and outstanding)	$3.55	$3.28	$6.67	$8.54

EXHIBIT 3

DAWSON STORES, INC.
Statements of Cash Flows
For the Years Ending January 31
(amounts in thousands)

	1990	*1991*	*1992*	*1993*
Cash flows from operating activities:				
Net income..........	$ 355	$ 328	$ 667	$ 854
Adjustments for differences between net income and				
cash flows from operating activities:				
Depreciation and amortization expense..........	329	358	388	424
Equity in loss of joint venture..........	—	—	37	38
(Increases) Decreases in current assets:				
Accounts receivable (net)..........	(379)	(145)	(371)	(389)
Inventories..........	(28)	217	(438)	(269)
Supplies and prepaid expenses..........	(7)	(30)	9	16
Increases (Decreases) in current liabilities:				
Accounts payable..........	89	13	601	505
Accrued liabilities and others..........	157	54	247	120
Income taxes currently payable..........	(10)	8	262	(11)
Deferred income taxes..........	30	27	83	105
Cash provided by operations..........	536	830	1,485	1,393
Cash flow for investing activities:				
Additions to property, plant, and equipment..........	(725)	(656)	(416)	(933)
Receipts from disposals of property and equipment..........	126	138	29	287
Mortgages assumed by purchasers of office properties				
and prepayment on long-term debt..........	(103)	(168)	(209)	(102)
Investments..........	(17)	(27)	—	(46)
Other (net)..........	64	81	80	29
Cash used for investing activities..........	(655)	(632)	(516)	(765)
Cash flow for financing activities:				
Proceeds from long-term debt..........	229	104	97	218
Reductions of long-term debt..........	(119)	(144)	(353)	(452)
Cash dividends..........	(116)	(124)	(145)	(187)
Cash used for financing activities..........	(6)	(164)	(401)	(421)
Increase (Decrease) in cash..........	(125)	34	568	207
Cash at beginning of the year..........	232	107	141	709
Cash at end of the year..........	$ 107	$ 141	$ 709	$ 916

(LIFO) method. Inventories on January 31 are stated less the following amounts that would have been determined under the retail method without regard to last-in, first-out principles (Amounts in thousands):

1990	*1991*	*1992*	*1993*
$283	$519	$560	$660

Plant. Property, plant, and equipment is carried at cost less accumulated depreciation. Depreciation is computed using the straight-line method for financial reporting purposes and accelerated methods for tax purposes.

	1990	1991	1992	1993
Land	$ 1,128	$ 1,285	$ 948	$ 1,023
Building and improvements	4,643	5,050	5,760	5,969
Fixtures and equipment	1,311	1,426	1,427	1,602
Construction in progress	329	304	266	351
Accumulated depreciation	(2,494)	(2,879)	(3,016)	(3,238)
	$ 4,917	$ 5,186	$ 5,385	$ 5,707

Annual minimum rentals on long-term noncancellable leases are as follows:

1993	$ 245
1994	238
1995	226
1996	222
1997	219
Beyond 1997	1,848

Contingent rentals are based upon a percentage of sales. Most leases require additional payments for real estate taxes, insurance, and other expenses that are included in operating costs in the accompanying statement of income and retained earnings.

Income Taxes. Deferred income taxes are provided for income and expenses that are recognized in different accounting periods for financial reporting than for income tax purposes. The temporary differences and the related deferred taxes are as follows:

	1990	1991	1992	1993
Excess of tax over book depreciation	$28	$22	$ 25	$ 5
Deferred income on installment sales	66	23	77	104
Other	(3)	3	(68)	(5)
Total	$91	$48	$ 34	$104

Long-Term Debt. The long-term debt of Dawson Stores, Inc., is composed of mortgage loans from three savings institutions on the store properties that the company occupies. There is no debt agreement that places restrictions on the company's operations or financing.

Questions

1. Appraise the recent performance and financial position of Dawson Stores, Inc., using selected financial ratios as appropriate.

2. As Stefanie Anderson, would you conclude that the company is a good credit risk?

14

Understanding Financial Statements

The first section of this chapter describes certain information contained in corporate annual reports that has not yet been discussed. The next section reviews the criteria and concepts introduced in Chapters 1, 2, and 3, bringing together amplifications and qualifications to the concepts that have been developed in later chapters. Alternative treatments of accounting transactions that are possible within the framework of these concepts are described. Finally, this chapter discusses the meaning of information contained in financial reports, in view of all the above.

ADDITIONAL INFORMATION IN ANNUAL REPORTS

The annual report that a company prepares for the use of shareholders, financial analysts, and other outside parties contains important information in addition to the three financial statements. At its option, a company may include information about products, personnel, facilities, or any other topics. Often, this information is accompanied with colored photographs and diagrams of various kinds. A company is *required* to provide certain other types of information, including the auditors' opinion, notes to the financial statements, management's discussion and analysis (a narrative identification and explanation of financial highlights), business segment information, and certain comparative data for previous years.

Auditors'
Opinion

All companies whose securities are listed on an organized stock exchange, most other corporations, and a great many unincorporated businesses have their financial statements and the underlying accounting records examined by independent, outside public accountants called **auditors.** Usually, these are certified public accountants (CPAs) who meet prescribed professional standards and are licensed to practice by the state in which they do business. The auditors' examination relates only to the financial statements, including notes, not to nonfinancial material that may appear in a company's annual report.

The results of the auditors' examination are presented in a report commonly called the **auditors' opinion.** In 1988 the content of the opinion was expanded to clarify the auditors' responsibility, the work they do, and the assurance they give.[1] This 1988 change was the first modification to the auditors' standard report since 1948. The change in the auditors' opinion was one of nine new auditing standards issued in order to narrow the gap between what auditors believed their responsibilities were and the expectations of financial statement users and the general public. The paragraphs required by the AICPA for a standard report, and additional paragraphs required under certain circumstances, are shown in Illustration 14–1.

Scope. The first two paragraphs of the opinion discuss the scope of the auditors' work. Specifically noted is that it is management's responsibility, not the auditors', to prepare the financial statements. The scope section also stresses that the auditors are responsible for deciding what audit procedures are necessary to provide *reasonable assurance* that the financial statements do not include *material misstatements.* Management cannot ask the auditors, for example, to "perform as much of an audit as you can for $100,000."

In making their examination, auditors no longer rely primarily on a detailed rechecking of the analysis, journalizing, and posting of each transaction. Rather, they satisfy themselves that the accounting *system* is designed to ensure that the data are processed properly. The auditors (1) make test checks of how well the system is working, (2) verify the existence of assets (for example, they must observe the taking of physical inventory), (3) ask a sample of customers to confirm, or verify, the accuracy of the accounts receivable, (4) check bank balances and investment securities, and (5) make sure that especially important or nonroutine transactions are recorded in conformity with generally accepted accounting principles (GAAP).

These checks provide reasonable assurance that errors have not been committed through oversight or carelessness and that there has been no fraudulent activity. They do not provide absolute assurance, however; almost any system can be beaten by someone intent on doing so. Although spectacular frauds receive much publicity, they are infrequent relative to the number of companies audited every year.

---

[1]AICPA, "Reports on Audited Financial Statements," *Statement on Auditing Standards No. 58* (1988).

ILLUSTRATION 14–1
AUDITORS' REPORT

Standard Report:

We have audited the accompanying balance sheets of X Company as of December 31, 19x2 and 19x1, and the related statements of income, retained earnings, and cash flows for each of the three years in the period ended December 31, 19x2. These financial statements are the responsibility of the Company's management. Our responsibility is to express an opinion on these financial statements based on our audits.

We conducted our audits in accordance with generally accepting auditing standards. Those standards require that we plan and perform the audit to obtain reasonable assurance about whether the financial statements are free of material misstatement. An audit includes examining, on a test basis, evidence supporting the amounts and disclosures in the financial statements. An audit also includes assessing the accounting principles used and significant estimates made by management, as well as evaluating the overall financial statement presentation. We believe that our audits provide a reasonable basis for our opinion.

In our opinion, such financial statements present fairly, in all material respects, the financial position of X Company as of December 31, 19x2 and 19x1, and the results of its operations and its cash flows for each of the three years in the period ended December 31, 19x2, in conformity with generally accepted accounting principles.

Illustrative required paragraph to report an inconsistency:

As discussed in Note X to the financial statements, the Company changed its method of computing depreciation in 19x2.

Illustrative required paragraph to report an uncertainty:

As discussed in Note Y to the financial statements, the Company is a defendant in a lawsuit alleging infringement of certain patent rights and claiming royalties and punitive damages. The ultimate outcome of the litigation cannot presently be determined. Accordingly, no provision for any liability that may result upon adjudication has been made in the accompanying financial statements.

Illustrative required paragraph to report going-concern doubt:

The accompanying financial statements have been prepared assuming that the Company will continue as a going concern. As discussed in Note Z to the financial statements, the Company has suffered recurring losses from operations and has a net capital deficiency that raises substantial doubt about the entity's ability to continue as a going concern. Management's plans in regard to these matters are also described in Note Z. The financial statements do not include any adjustments that might result from the outcome of this uncertainty.

Opinion. The third paragraph is known as the **opinion paragraph.** The key phrases in this paragraph are *present fairly* and *in conformity with generally accepted accounting principles.*

Fairness. The word *fairly* should be contrasted with the word *accurately.* The auditors do not say that the reported net income is the only, or even the most accurate, number that could have been reported. Rather, they say that of the many alternative principles that could have been used, those actually selected by management do give a fair picture in the circumstances relevant to the particular company. This contrast between fairness and accuracy is further emphasized by the fact that the auditors' report is called an *opinion.* Auditors do not certify the accuracy of the statements; instead, they give their professional opinion that the presentation is fair.

When two or more alternative practices are permitted by GAAP and either is fair (which is an ambiguous criterion), management, not the auditors, decides which one to use. In the opinion letter, the auditors do not state that management has necessarily made the *best* choice among alternative principles but only that the choice made by management was an acceptable one.

Principles. The second phrase means that each of the accounting principles used in preparing the statements is "generally accepted." For many transactions there are several generally accepted alternative treatments, and the auditors' opinion merely states that management has selected one of these. If the Financial Accounting Standards Board (FASB), or one of its predecessor bodies, has issued a pronouncement on a certain point, this constitutes a generally accepted accounting principle. Rule 203 of the AICPA Code of Professional Ethics states that no departures from such pronouncements can be regarded as a generally accepted accounting principle "unless the member can demonstrate that due to unusual circumstances the financial statements would otherwise have been misleading." Such circumstances are exceedingly rare. If they do exist, the report must describe the departure, give the reasons for making it, and show its approximate effect on the reported results. For all practical purposes, generally accepted accounting principles are what the FASB says they are.

Qualified Opinions.   An auditors' report containing only the three paragraphs described above is informally called a **clean opinion.** Other reports are said to be **qualified opinions.** Qualification may occur for any of three reasons: (1) a lack of consistency, (2) existence of a major uncertainty, or (3) doubt as to the entity's ability to continue as a going concern.

Consistency.   If a company has changed an accounting method from the method used in the preceding year, the auditors' report must point this out in a paragraph following the opinion paragraph. Consistency here does not mean, for example, that the method used to measure plant and equipment is consistent with that used to measure inventory; nor does it mean that the company's practices are consistent with industry practices, or even that the several corporations within a consolidated enterprise have used the same methods. Rather, consistency refers solely to use of the same methods in successive years' financial statements. The details of any inconsistency are spelled out in a note to the financial statements cited in this additional report paragraph. (See Illustration 14–1 for an example.)

Uncertainty.   Sometimes a major uncertainty (such as a pending lawsuit) may ultimately have a material effect on the company's financial position. Auditors are required to call attention to such uncertainties in an additional report paragraph following the opinion paragraph, without making a prediction of the eventual outcome. The nature of the uncertainty is described in a statement note cited in this extra report paragraph. (An example is given in Illustration 14–1.)

Going-Concern Doubt.   A significant 1988 change in auditing standards was the new requirement that the auditors *in every audit* evaluate whether there is a substantial doubt about the company's ability to continue as a going concern over the next year. If the auditors conclude that there is substantial doubt, then this must be disclosed in a report paragraph following the opinion paragraph.[2] Again, a statement note cited in this additional report paragraph explains in some detail why the going-concern doubt exists. (See Illustration 14–1 for an example.)

In rare cases, the auditors' opinion may be a **disclaimer;** they report that they are unable to express an opinion. This may happen because limitations were placed on the scope of the audit by management. If the auditors conclude that the financial statements do *not* "present fairly" the situation, they write an **adverse opinion.** This may occur if the company has departed from GAAP or clearly is no longer a going concern. Adverse opinions and disclaimers are extremely serious matters. They usually result in a suspension of trading in the company's equity securities.

Notes to Financial Statements

We have discussed three required financial statements: the balance sheet, the income statement, and the statement of cash flows. A fourth type of required information is also important—the notes that accompany and are deemed to be an integral part of the financial statements themselves. The requirements for these **notes to financial statements** are becoming increasingly elaborate and detailed.

One of these notes, usually the first, summarizes the accounting policies the company has followed in preparing the statements. Among other topics, this note usually describes the basis of consolidation (if the statements are consolidated statements), depreciation methods, policies with respect to the amortization of intangible assets, inventory methods, and policies regarding the recognition of revenues.

Other notes give details on long-term debt (including the maturity date and interest rate of each bond issue), a description of stock option plans and other management incentive plans, a description of postretirement benefits, and the total rental expense and the minimum amount of rent that must be paid in the future under current lease commitments.[3] Additional detail on the composition of inventories and of depreciable assets is given. A note on income taxes explains the difference between the reported provision for income taxes and the amount of taxes that actually will be paid on the year's activities. (Timing differences in reporting depreciation expense are often the major cause of this difference.) Major contingencies must be discussed. Most annual reports have several pages of these notes.

---

[2]AICPA, "The Auditor's Consideration of an Entity's Ability to Continue as a Going Concern," *Statement on Auditing Standards No. 59* (1988). Formerly, major uncertainties, including doubt as to ability to continue as a going concern, were reported by inserting a phrase beginning "subject to [ultimate resolution of the uncertainty]" in the opinion paragraph, and such opinions were hence called **subject-to opinions.**

[3]This is required by "Accounting for Leases," *FASB Statement No. 13* (November 1976).

In addition to these notes, the Securities and Exchange Commission requires that the annual report include a discussion of the company's financial condition and results of operations written by senior management (usually the chief executive officer). Also required is a statement from management accepting responsibility for the financial statements (to counter the incorrect impression that the outside auditors have this responsibility)[4] and for the system of internal controls that is intended to ensure that the numbers are reliable.

Segment Reporting

Current economic and political forces affect different industries in different ways. Moreover, typical margins, return on assets, and other financial ratios vary widely among industries. Analysts therefore find it difficult to estimate the effect of these forces and to use typical ratios if the financial statements of a multiple-industry company report only the aggregate results.

For this reason, corporations (except small, privately owned corporations) are required to supplement the overall financial statements with additional information about the principal *industry segments* in which they operate. Each company can decide for itself the most useful way of dividing its operations into segments. In some cases, the nature of the product lines provides a natural basis for classification; in other cases, it is the nature of the production process or the marketing methods. No company is required to report on more than 10 segments.

For each segment, the company reports (1) revenues; (2) operating profit or loss; and (3) identifiable assets, usually including depreciation expense on these assets. Which expense items to include in the calculation of operating profit is open to some differences in interpretation. In general, these items include all the expenses that can be identified with the segment but not expenses of corporate headquarters, interest expense, or income tax expense.

In addition to this report on industry segments, corporations are also required to provide other information, including amounts of sales and profit in each major geographical area of the world and sales to government agencies or to single customers if these sales constitute a significant fraction of the total.[5]

Full Disclosure

A fundamental accounting principle is that the financial statements and the accompanying notes must contain a **full disclosure** of *material* financial information. This includes not only information known as of the balance

---

[4]Note that the first paragraph of the auditors' standard report also stresses that the statements are management's responsibility.

[5]"Financial Reporting for Segments of a Business Enterprise," *FASB Statement No. 14* (December 1976); and "Disclosure of Information about Major Customers," *FASB Statement No. 30* (August 1979).

sheet date but also information that comes to light after the end of the accounting period that may affect the information contained in the financial statements. For example, if in January 19x2 one of the company's plants was destroyed by fire, this fact should be disclosed in the company's 19x1 annual report, even though the amount of plant on the December 31, 19x1, balance sheet was properly reported as of that time.

Disagreement arises as to what constitutes full disclosure. In general, if an item of economic information would cause informed investors to appraise the company differently than would be the case without that item of information, it should be disclosed. Clearly, there is room for differences of opinion as to what such items are, but recent court decisions have taken an increasingly broad view of disclosure requirements.

Comparative Statements

In addition to the financial statements for the current year, the annual report must also contain the previous year's balance sheet and the preceding two years' income and cash flow statements. Many companies also include summaries of important financial statement items for a period of 5 or 10 years.

The information from prior years that is published in the current annual report is usually the same information as that originally published. Under some circumstances, however, information for prior years is restated. If the accounting entity is changed, either by the acquisition of other companies or by the disposition of segments of the business, the amounts for prior years are restated so as to show comparable data for the entity as it currently exists.

> **Example.** If the Cameron Company in 1994 acquired Subsidiary A and disposed of one of its own subsidiaries, B, the financial statements of 1994 and earlier years would be restated by adding the financial data for Subsidiary A and subtracting those of Subsidiary B.

The financial statements for prior years must also be restated to reflect certain changes in accounting principles.[6] These include (1) a change from the LIFO method of inventory to another method, (2) a change in the method of accounting for long-term contracts from the completed-contract method to the percentage-of-completion method, or vice versa, and (3) a change in certain accounting practices of extractive industries.

With these few exceptions, however, prior year statements are not restated. Instead, when a company makes a change in its accounting practices that affects the net income reported in prior periods, the *cumulative* effect of this change on the net income of all prior periods is calculated, and this amount is reported on the *current* year's income statement. If a company believes that estimates that affected the reported net income in

---

[6]"Accounting Changes," *APB Opinion No. 20* (July 1971).

prior years were incorrect (such as when subsequent events show that the estimated service life of depreciable assets was too long or too short), it does not go back and correct the financial statements for the prior years. These rather strict restrictions on recasting the data in prior year financial statements exist because of the belief that public confidence in the financial statements would be lessened if they were subject to frequent restatement.

Securities and Exchange Commission (SEC) Reports

In addition to the annual report to its shareholders, companies that are under the jurisdiction of the Securities and Exchange Commission must file an annual report with the SEC. This report is filed on SEC Form 10–K and is therefore known as the **10–K report.** In general the financial data in this report are consistent with, but in somewhat more detail than, the data in the annual report. Rules governing the preparation of Form 10–K are contained in SEC *Regulation S–X.* With few exceptions, they are consistent with the standards of the FASB.

The SEC also requires that certain financial data be included in the notice of annual meeting sent to all shareholders. These include the compensation of each top executive, the compensation of officers and directors as a group, a description of proposed changes in incentive compensation plans, and a description of any of the company's financial transactions that involved officers and directors as individuals (such as loans made by a bank whose president was a director of the company).

Interim Statements. Companies under the jurisdiction of the SEC also file quarterly reports on Form 10–Q. These interim statements contain a summary of financial statements for the current quarter and for the year to date. Although they are not audited in the strict sense, the auditors go over them to ensure that they appear to be reasonable. If significant events occur at any time, such as a major investment by one company in the stock of another or a decision to dispose of a division, the company must report these events to the SEC on Form 8–K, usually within a month of their occurrence. In certain circumstances, such as the discovery of a significant improper act, the 8–K report must be filed immediately.

All SEC reports are widely available. Because they often contain more detailed information than the company's annual report and because the data are set forth in a standard format, financial analysts use these reports more than reports published by the company.

REVIEW OF CRITERIA AND CONCEPTS

In Chapter 1 we listed three criteria that governed financial accounting concepts and principles; in Chapters 2 and 3 we described 11 basic concepts. It is appropriate here that we reconsider these criteria and concepts with the benefit of the additional material that has been discussed in the intervening chapters.

Criteria

There are three basic accounting criteria:

1. Accounting information should be **relevant.** Accounting reports should provide information that describes as accurately and completely as possible the status of assets, liabilities, and owners' equity, the results of operations, and cash flows.

2. Accounting information should be **objective.** The amounts reported should not be biased, particularly by the subjective judgments of management. (The FASB uses the term *reliable* in the same way we use *objective*.)

3. The reporting of accounting information should be **feasible.** Its value should exceed the cost of collecting and reporting it.

There is an inevitable conflict between the criterion of *relevance* on the one hand and the criteria of *objectivity* and *feasibility* on the other. Accounting concepts and principles reflect a workable compromise between these opposing forces. Failure to appreciate this fact is behind the feeling of many of the uninitiated that "accounting doesn't make sense."

Of the many examples of this conflict, perhaps the most clear-cut is that relating to the measurement of property, plant, and equipment. In general the most relevant rule for stating the amounts of these items—the rule that would provide readers of financial statements with what they really want to know—would be to state these assets at their current value, what they are really worth. But such a rule would be neither objective nor feasible in most situations.

Conceptually, the worth of an asset is measured by the present value of the future cash flows it will generate. However, there is no feasible way of making this calculation. In the first place, the subjective opinions of management as to future cash flows and the appropriate discount rate would have to be used. Second, for many assets, such as administrative offices, it is not really meaningful to think of the asset as generating cash flows (at least not *positive* cash flows). Although more feasible, even replacement cost numbers can have a high degree of subjectivity, especially if the asset is a specialized piece of equipment and is not, in fact, likely to be replaced at the end of its service life. Furthermore, an entity is more than the sum of its individual assets, and the financial statements cannot possibly report what the *total* resources, both physical and human, are actually worth.

At the other extreme, the most objective and feasible rules for measuring property, plant, and equipment would be either (1) to state these assets at acquisition cost and report them as an asset at cost until they are disposed of or (2) to write them off the books immediately. In most cases either rule would be perfectly simple to apply and would involve little, if any, subjective judgment. But with either rule, accounting could not report the depreciation expense that is properly charged to the operations of each accounting period. A net income figure that includes such an estimate of asset cost expiration is much more relevant for most purposes than one that omits depreciation altogether.

Accounting takes a middle ground. Assets are originally booked at cost, which is an objectively determined amount in most cases, and this cost then is systematically charged as an expense in the accounting periods over the useful life of the asset. The annual depreciation charge is an estimate, and several ways of making this estimate are permitted; but the number of permitted alternatives is small, and freedom to tamper with the estimates is further restricted by the concept of consistency.

Concepts

Eleven basic financial accounting concepts were stated in Chapters 2 and 3. Other persons might classify and describe basic concepts somewhat differently than we have. (The FASB has published five *Concepts Statements,* totaling more than 300 pages of small print; however, they contain no succinct list of basic concepts.) The 11 concepts are repeated below, with amplifications and qualifications given for certain of them.

1. Money Measurement. *Accounting records only those facts that can be expressed in monetary terms.* In the accounts there are no exceptions to this concept, although nonmonetary information is often provided as supplementary data. Assets are recorded at the number of dollars (or dollar equivalents) paid to acquire them. Although the purchasing power of the monetary unit changes because of inflation, accounting does not reflect these changes in purchasing power. Thus, the monetary unit used in accounting is *not* a unit of constant purchasing power.

2. Entity. *Accounts are kept for entities, as distinguished from the persons who are associated with those entities.* In small businesses, particularly unincorporated ones, some problems arise in distinguishing between transactions affecting the entity and transactions affecting the owners. In parent companies that have subsidiaries, a subsidiary is considered to be part of the consolidated entity if the parent owns more than 50 percent of its common stock. Because governments and other nonprofit organizations do not control subunits by stock ownership, there may be difficulties in defining the entity in many such organizations.

3. Going Concern. *Accounting assumes that an entity will continue to operate indefinitely and that it is not about to be liquidated.* The going-concern concept does not assume that the entity will exist forever. Rather, it assumes that the entity will continue to operate long enough to use up its long-lived assets and to pay off its long-term liabilities as they mature—that is, for the foreseeable future. This concept explains why accounting ordinarily does not attempt to keep track of the liquidation value or current market value of individual long-lived assets.

There is one important qualification to this statement. If there is strong evidence that the entity will *not* continue in existence, asset amounts are recorded at their estimated liquidation value.

4. Cost. *An asset is ordinarily entered in the accounts at the amount paid to acquire it, and this cost rather than current market value is the basis* *for subsequent accounting for the asset.* There are important qualifications to this concept. If the amount paid is obviously less than the fair market value of the asset (as in the case of donated assets), the asset is recorded at fair market value. There are differences of opinion as to how the cost of products manufactured by a company should be measured, as noted in Chapter 6.

Also, market value does affect the subsequent accounting for certain types of assets. Inventory is reported at the lower of its cost or market value. Trading securities and available-for-sale securities are reported at fair value. Certain investments are reported at the book value of the equity of the company whose stock is owned (i.e., the equity method), rather than at cost. These, however, are exceptions to the general rule.

Depreciation, depletion, and amortization are write-offs of an asset's cost as the asset gives up its benefits to the entity; these write-offs are not intended to reflect changes in market value.

5. Dual Aspect. *The total amount of assets equals the total amount of liabilities and owners' equity.* There are absolutely no exceptions to this concept. It is important not only because mechanically it lessens the possibility of making errors in recording transactions but also because conceptually it aids in understanding the effect of transactions on an accounting entity. The fact that "for every debit there must be a credit" helps one to remember to take account of both aspects of a transaction.

6. Accounting Period. *Accounting measures activities for a specified interval of time, usually one year.* Reporting on results at frequent intervals, both to management and to outside parties, is obviously necessary. The need for doing this, however, causes most of the difficult problems in accounting: the problems associated with accrual accounting. In measuring the net income of an accounting period, the revenues and expenses that properly belong to that period must be measured. These measurements depend in part on estimates of what is going to happen in future periods, which is unknown.

7. Conservatism. *Revenues are recognized only when they are reasonably certain, whereas expenses are recognized as soon as they are reasonably possible.* This concept explains why bad debt expense is recognized in the period in which the related sales revenues are recorded, rather than later when some customers actually default on their payments. Similarly, the concept is the basis for recognizing future warranty costs as an expense in the period in which the warranted goods are sold, rather than later when the warranty costs are paid.

The conservatism concept also explains why certain assets are recorded at the lower of cost or market value. It is also a reason behind certain FASB decisions, such as the one that most research and development (R&D) costs should be expensed as incurred rather than be capitalized. Although these R&D costs may benefit future periods, it is possible they will not. Also, the conservatism concept suggests that revenues should usually be recognized in the period in which goods were delivered to customers or services were rendered, since at that point it is reasonably certain that the revenues have been earned.

8. Realization.   *The amount recognized as revenue is the amount that is reasonably certain to be realized, that is, paid by customers.* Many problems arise in deciding on both the period in which the revenue for a given transaction should be recognized and the amount of such revenue. The conservatism concept suggests *when* to recognize revenue; the realization concept suggests *how much* to recognize. In unusual circumstances, the amount of revenue recognized may reflect a considerable amount of optimism as to future earnings, but the auditors will ordinarily detect and call attention to revenues whose realization is not reasonably certain. Chapter 5 is suggested as a refresher for exceptions and clarifications of this concept.

9. Matching.   *When a given event affects both revenues and expenses, the effect on each should be recognized in the same accounting period.* Costs are reported as expenses in the period when (1) there is a direct association between costs and revenues of the period, (2) costs are associated with activities of the period itself, or (3) costs cannot be associated with revenues of any future period.

Differences of opinion about the application of this concept and the realization concept are at the heart of most accounting controversies. We shall elaborate on these in connection with our discussion of the income statement.

10. Consistency.   *Once an entity has decided on a certain accounting method, it should use the same method for all subsequent events of the same character unless it has a sound reason to change methods.* This concept is always adhered to in theory, but the practical problem is to decide when a "sound reason" for a change exists. At the root of some changes in method is the desire to increase the amount of net income reported in the current period. This is definitely not an acceptable reason for making a change. Nevertheless, some companies make a change for this purpose and devise other reasons to justify it.

11. Materiality.   *Insignificant events may be disregarded, but there must be full disclosure of all important information.* This concept is probably the least precise of any. Although much has been written on the meaning of materiality, although auditing firms have their own (unpublished) rules of thumb on what constitutes a material item or difference, and although many attempts have been made to define specifically what the concept means, there is no authoritative, explicit statement in existence. In the absence of specific guidelines, accountants rely on their own judgment. The general notion is that an item is material if its disclosure is likely to lead the user of accounting information to make a different judgment or reach a different conclusion. Recent court cases have tended to lead to an increasingly strict interpretation of materiality.

The materiality concept can also be invoked as a reason to depart from the other concepts in the interest of simplicity, when the effect of such a departure is not material. For example, FASB *Statements* include as the last sentence of every standard: "The provisions of this Statement need not be applied to immaterial items."

Importance of the Concepts.   These 11 concepts govern the accounting in all business organizations. Governments and certain nonprofit organizations follow somewhat different accounting practices, which are not consistent with the conservatism, realization, and matching concepts. A discussion of these differences is outside the scope of this book.[7]

The many practices and procedures described in earlier chapters were amplifications and applications of these basic concepts rather than additions to them. As a matter of practice, for example, accumulated depreciation is shown in a separate account rather than being credited directly to the asset account. But the basic idea of depreciation accounting is nevertheless in accordance with the concepts that assets are recorded at cost and costs are matched with revenues.

Any conceivable transaction, provided it is clearly described, can be analyzed in terms of its effect on the assets, liabilities, and owners' equity of the entity in accordance with the basic accounting concepts. For an extremely large fraction of the transactions in a typical business, the analysis is simple: For a cash sale, debit Cash and credit Sales Revenue; for receipts from a credit customer, credit Accounts Receivable and debit Cash.

In a relatively small number of transactions, the analysis is difficult. For example, a number of transactions involve a credit to Cash or Accounts Payable for the purchase of goods or services. The question is whether the offsetting debit is to an asset account or to an expense account. The answer to this question depends on whether the entity has or has not acquired something that has beneficial value beyond the end of the accounting period, which is sometimes a matter of judgment.

Many of these difficult situations require judgment because of inevitable uncertainties about the future. How long will the building really last? Is a decline in the market value of inventory only temporary, or should the inventory be written down? There are no unequivocal answers to such questions and hence no way of arriving at a result with which everyone would agree.

Misconceptions about Concepts.   Some of the basic concepts are intuitively sensible—for example, the idea that accounting data are expressed in monetary terms. Certain concepts, however, are rather different from the impression that typical laypersons have about accounting information.

Undoubtedly, the greatest misconception relates to the cost concept. To those who do not understand accounting, it seems only reasonable that the accountant should report the *value* of assets—what they are really worth—

---

[7]For such a discussion, see Robert N. Anthony, *Should Business and Nonbusiness Accounting Be Different?* (Boston: Harvard Business School Press, 1989); "Objectives of Financial Reporting by Nonbusiness Organizations," *FASB Concepts Statement No. 4* (December 1980); and "Elements of Financial Statements," *FASB Concepts Statement No. 6* (December 1985).

rather than merely the flow of costs. They find it difficult to believe that the balance sheet is not, even approximately, a statement showing what the entity is worth, especially when they see or hear the owners' equity of an entity referred to as its "net worth." Even if they eventually recognize that the balance sheet does not report current values, they criticize accounting and accountants for not doing this.

A related misconception results from a failure to appreciate the significance of the going-concern concept. Only after accepting the idea that productive assets are held not for sale but for their future usefulness can there be an appreciation that the market value of these assets does not have enough significance to warrant using market value rather than the more objective historical cost data.

The matching concept is also a difficult one to comprehend. When people make a personal expenditure to the grocer, to the service station, and so on, they know that they are that much "out of pocket." They have difficulty understanding the fact that many business expenditures are merely the exchange of one asset for another, with the business getting as much as it gives up. Expenses occur in the time period when costs expire—when they are used up—and this time period is not necessarily the same as the time period in which the expenditure is made.

Those who do understand the basic concepts do not necessarily agree with all of them. The accounting profession is constantly involved in debates over one or another of the currently accepted principles. Since these principles are not laws of nature, they are subject to change and in recent years have been changing with increasing frequency. At the same time, although financial statement *users* may wish that certain principles were different, these users need to know how the statements *were* prepared, not how they *might have been* prepared.

ACCOUNTING ALTERNATIVES

Notwithstanding the basic concepts and generally accepted accounting principles, there are considerable differences in the way certain transactions may be recorded. These differences result from (1) requirements imposed by regulatory agencies in certain industries, (2) the latitude that exists within GAAP, and (3) judgments that must be made in applying a given principle.

Regulatory Requirements

Certain groups of companies are required to adhere to accounting principles that are not necessarily consistent with those required by the FASB. Railroads and other common carriers follow rules prescribed by the Interstate Commerce Commission; public utilities, by the Federal Energy Regulatory Commission and by state regulatory agencies. In approving the financial statements of such entities, if the statements are not prepared in accordance with GAAP, the auditors' opinion says the statements are "consistent with practice followed in the industry," or words to that effect. When regulatory requirements differ from GAAP, most organizations prepare two sets of financial statements, one consistent with GAAP and the other consistent with the requirements of the regulatory agency.

Income Tax Principles

Principles governing the calculation of income for federal income tax purposes are basically the same as the principles of financial accounting. However, there are important differences, some of which are described here.

Under certain conditions, taxpayers may elect to disregard the accrual concept and to be taxed on the difference between cash receipts and cash expenditures. Many personal-services businesses do this.

The depletion allowance computed for tax purposes bears no relation to the depletion principle of financial accounting. Tax accounting depletion is based on revenues; financial accounting depletion is based on costs.

In taxation a distinction is made between ordinary income and capital gains, with the latter sometimes being taxed less heavily than the former. In financial accounting the distinction, although present, is not so important, because both ordinary income and capital gains usually enter into the measurement of net income.

The accrual basis of accounting is not completely followed in income tax accounting. For example, in income tax accounting prepaid rent or subscriptions are counted as revenue when the cash is received; but these prepayments are a liability, deferred (or unearned) revenue, in financial accounting.

Finally, as already pointed out, although the principles are basically the same, a company usually applies them differently in its tax accounting and its financial accounting. It does this primarily by changing the *timing,* rather than the *amount,* of revenues and expenses. For tax purposes, a company usually reports costs as early as it legitimately can and defers revenue until as late as it legitimately can so as to postpone cash outlays for taxes as long as possible. For financial accounting purposes, by contrast, it tends to report costs in later time periods and revenues in earlier time periods.

Latitude in Methods

In his 1965 *Inventory,* Paul Grady listed some 35 topics on which alternative treatments are permitted within GAAP, and gave from two to eight alternatives for each.[8] These topics range in importance from cash discounts on sales, which may be accounted for either at the time the sale is made or the time the receivable is collected, to the question of how to account for exploration costs in the oil and gas industry.

Earlier chapters have listed some examples of topics on which alternative treatments are permitted within GAAP: Inventory can be recorded at LIFO,

---

[8]Paul Grady, "Inventory of Generally Accepted Accounting Principles," *Accounting Research Study No. 7* (AICPA, 1965), pp. 373–79.

at FIFO, or at average cost, or some parts of inventory may be handled one way and some another; inventory cost may or may not include inward transportation, storage costs, handling costs, or cash discounts on purchases. Assets may be depreciated by any systematic and rational method. Revenue on installment sales may be recognized either on the installment basis or on the delivery basis.

In recent years standards promulgated by the FASB have reduced the amount of latitude permitted. In some cases, such as the treatment of research and development costs, the FASB eliminated all but one alternative. In other cases, such as the treatment of an acquisition as a purchase or a pooling of interests and the capitalization of certain leases, the FASB has carefully spelled out the circumstances under which each alternative practice can be used. Nevertheless, many of the alternatives on Grady's list are still permitted as generally accepted accounting principles.

Basis of Choice   Given this latitude, how does the management of a company decide which of two or more alternative methods to use? In the case of companies whose common stock is traded on an exchange, a long-standing belief of many top managers has been that the stock price—and hence the shareholder value—will be maximized by choosing those methods that will maximize short-run reported earnings per share. This argument has been given by some companies in explaining why they have not changed from FIFO inventory accounting to LIFO, even when LIFO would improve their cash flows. (Recall that tax laws require a company to use LIFO for shareholder reporting in order to use it for income tax reporting.) Such companies seem to believe that the stock market values a company's stock by applying a price/earnings ratio to the earnings per share of companies in an industry, without regard to differences in accounting practices among those companies, and that it is therefore in a company's self-interest to report earnings as high as feasible.

In some cases a company chooses its methods to conform with the methods of other companies in the same industry. In other instances a company's loan agreements or bond indentures may contain minimum working capital or current ratio covenants, or ceilings on the debt/equity ratio. These may cause a company to retain a method if a change to an alternative would lower current assets or owners' equity, or they may cause the company to change to a method that would raise these items (e.g., a change from LIFO to FIFO).

Also, if the bonus of senior managers is calculated on the basis of reported earnings, then these managers may oppose a change that has the effect of reducing reported earnings. However, the board of directors should adjust the method of calculating the bonus in these circumstances.

On the other hand, a few companies have long believed that they can increase investor confidence and the market value of their stock by using the most "conservative" accounting principles (LIFO, accelerated depreciation, and so on) that tend to *minimize* short-run reported earnings. This "quality of earnings" philosophy assumes that investors are wary of companies that try to magnify their reported earnings by using "liberal" accounting principles. Some companies may also feel that the lower reported earnings, using conservative principles, will temper employee requests for higher wages or avoid media charges of profiteering.

Only in recent years have accounting researchers turned their attention to the issue of companies' accounting principle choices. At this point, the research provides a theory of accounting choice or **"positive accounting" theory,** but no concrete explanations as to how and why specific accounting policies are chosen.

Controversies over Principles

In many cases an accounting requirement described matter-of-factly in this text has evolved only after years of controversy; in some instances the requirement has not quelled the controversy. For example, the usefulness of reporting supplemental inflation-adjusted financial data was mentioned over 50 years ago by some academics, and the APB formally affirmed this usefulness in 1969 in its *Statement No. 3.*[9] However, not until 1979 did the FASB require supplemental inflation-adjusted disclosures, and then only of large companies.[10] Controversy arose over whether the required constant dollar amounts were very relevant and whether the replacement cost amounts were sufficiently objective. The FASB dropped the requirement in late 1986, during a period of very low inflation.[11] In this matter a clear consensus on what is "right" does not exist. In some instances the business community is unable to reach such a consensus. In others, businesspeople may be in general agreement, but security analysts, accounting academics, or even the chief accountant of the SEC may have differing views.

Efficient Markets Hypothesis. Many accounting academics and a few issuers and users of financial statements have been influenced in their views on accounting principles by research studies dealing with the **efficient markets hypothesis (EMH).** According to the EMH, a change in a company's accounting methods has no effect on the price of its stock; shareholders look behind the accounting change and recognize that there has been no actual change in the company's performance. Thus, a change in financial reporting depreciation methods (with the tax method left unchanged) is said to have no impact on the stock price because the price reflects real cash flows (which are unaffected since the method for income tax reporting was not changed) rather than "artificial" accounting numbers.

---

[9]"Financial Statements Restated for General Price-Level Changes," *APB Statement No. 3* (June 1969).

[10]"Financial Reporting and Changing Prices," *FASB Statement No. 33* (September 1979).

[11]"Financial Reporting and Changing Prices," *FASB Statement No. 89* (December 1986).

Other academics feel that studies whose results are used to support the EMH are inconclusive. They argue that the inability of the EMH research tools to *detect* an effect on stock prices is not the same as *proving* there has been no effect. Certainly, most nonacademics remain dubious about the EMH point of view. Evidence of this includes the great management uproar over the effect that proposed new accounting standards will have on reported earnings, even when corporate cash flows will not be affected by changing to the proposed method.

> **Example.** The following quotes are taken from a leading business periodical's stories reporting on proposed FASB standards, none of which would have impacted a company's cash flows:
>
> If the FASB approves the new rule, reported income would be sharply pared, worsening [affected companies'] debt-to-equity ratios and making it tougher for them to borrow more money.
>
> Companies might have to reduce reported profit to reflect executives' gains on incentive stock options. Because of tax rules, this new expense wouldn't even be deductible. Says a General Motors executive, "If we had to book an expense but got no tax deduction, it would discourage our use of incentive stock options."

Moreover, why do many companies that could save taxes and thus improve cash flow by changing to LIFO continue to use FIFO? In many instances, management feels that markets are not efficient and that the lower reported earnings will diminish shareholder wealth. Similarly, there is evidence that *FASB 2,* which requires that R&D costs be expensed in the year incurred, has influenced managers not to authorize otherwise worthwhile R&D projects.[12]

In sum, EMH research has added a new dimension to the ongoing controversies over accounting principles rather than eliminating controversy.

Implications of These Differences

The existence of diversity in accounting practice should not be considered as a reason for criticizing accountants or accounting. A business is a complex organism, and there is no conceivable way of prescribing a uniform set of rules for reducing the significant facts about that organism to a few pages of numbers any more than there is any way of formulating a standard set of rules for biographers. Standard procedures for listing physical characteristics, birth dates, marital status, and certain other information about a person can easily be specified, but these details do not really describe the person completely. The accuracy and usefulness of the picture of a person

---

[12]See Jean C. Cooper and Frank H. Selto, "An Experimental Examination of the Effects of SFAS No. 2 on R&D Investment Decisions," *Accounting Organizations and Society* 16, no. 3 (1991), pp. 227–42.

that emerges from a biography depends on the author's skill and judgment in the collection, analysis, and presentation of information about the subject. So it is with financial statements.

Nor should the existence of diversity lead to frustration on the part of the user. The consistency concept prevents diversity from becoming chaos. Although Company A may follow practices that differ from those of other companies, Company A ordinarily follows the same practices year after year; if it changes, the consistency concept requires that the change be disclosed. Thus, its statements are likely to be comparable with one another from year to year. Also, companies in a given industry tend to use the same methods in order to facilitate intercompany comparisons within the industry.

Inherent Limitations

In addition to the points noted above, it is important to remember that accounting has inherent limitations. The two most important—limitations that no foreseeable improvement in accounting practice can overcome—are that (1) accounting reports are necessarily monetary and (2) they are necessarily influenced by estimates of future events.

Accounting reports are limited to information that can be expressed in monetary terms. Nothing in the accounts explicitly describes the ability of the entity's personnel, the effectiveness of its organization, the impact of outside forces, or other nonmonetary information vital to the complete understanding of an entity.

Some accounting numbers are influenced by future events that cannot conceivably be foreseen, so these numbers are necessarily estimates. The depreciation expense of the current period, for example, depends partly on how long the assets will be used in the future. The real significance of accounts receivable and the related item of sales revenue cannot be assessed until the number of credit customers who will not pay their bills is known. The actual value of inventory depends on what the goods can be sold for in the future. The possible impacts of contingent future events—such as the results of pending litigation, retroactive agreements on wage rates, and redetermination of profits on contracts—are not shown in the financial statements, although if material they should appear in a footnote.

In accounting, one refers to the *measurement* of income rather than to the *determination* of income. According to the dictionary, to determine is "to fix conclusively and authoritatively," and accounting cannot do this. A measurement, on the other hand, is an approximation according to some agreed-upon measuring stick. This is what accounting sets out to do.

Ethical Problems

In dealing with the issues mentioned above, the controller, or other accountant responsible for preparing the financial statements, may face ethical problems. Potential problems involve transactions that fall at different points along a spectrum of legality.

At one extreme, there are transactions that may be illegal under the Foreign Corrupt Practices Act, but that the accountant believes are in the best interests of the shareholders and society in general. For example, bribing a government official is illegal, but in some countries business cannot be readily conducted without greasing palms. It can be argued that deciding not to do business in such a country not only may deny shareholders profit opportunities, but also may harm that country's citizens by denying access to worthwhile products or employment opportunities. What should the accountant do when she or he learns of such transactions?

Then there are transactions that management wants recorded in a way that, although legal, does not "fairly present" the company's performance. For example, booking revenues before goods are shipped (perhaps in order to increase a year-end bonus or to meet a strongly held earnings-per-share expectation of influential security analysts) is clearly contrary to GAAP.

At the other end of the spectrum are management judgments about recording transactions that are neither illegal nor contrary to GAAP but that the accountant nevertheless feels are unsound. An example is reducing the percentage of the bad debt allowance in order to increase reported profit. Another example is the "big bath" phenomenon when a new senior management team writes off substantial amounts of assets (particularly intangibles, such as goodwill) in the year it takes over, thereby reducing the amounts that will be charged off in future years and increasing the net income of those years. Such questionable transactions are collectively called *managing earnings.*

In all of these circumstances, ethical principles stated by professional organizations (e.g., the Institute of Management Accountants) require that the accountant take some action. If the matter is important and management is unwilling to change its opinion, then the accountant is required to notify the board of directors and, in some instances, the SEC. There are federal laws in place to protect these whistle-blowers from retribution.

The problem is that the accountant may not believe that the board or the courts will in fact provide this protection. Also, publicly challenging a superior's decision is, at a minimum, unsettling. Moreover, the accountant may fear being informally black-listed, which makes finding alternative employment much more difficult. No book can state how these ethical problems should be resolved. Each individual needs to be sensitized to these issues so that to the extent possible such problems can be avoided and unpleasant personal dilemmas minimized.

MEANING OF THE FINANCIAL STATEMENTS

Preceding chapters have discussed in detail the treatment of specific items that are reported on the financial statements. With this discussion as background, we shall now attempt to summarize the meaning of each statement as a whole.

**Income
Statement**

The income statement is the dominant financial statement in the sense that when it comes to a choice between a fair income statement presentation and a fair balance sheet presentation, the decision is usually made in favor of the former. For example, those who advocate the LIFO inventory method do so in the belief that it provides a better measure of income than does FIFO, although they know that it can result in unrealistically low inventory amounts on the balance sheet. Many balance sheet items are simply the offsetting debits or credits for entries that were designed to measure revenues or expenses properly on the income statement. The deferred income tax item is the most notable example: Although recorded as a liability, it does not represent an obligation comparable with, say, a note payable.

The income statement measures the changes in retained earnings that have occurred for whatever reason during the accounting period, except for the payment of dividends and infrequent other transactions. It does not necessarily reflect only the results of normal operations, since it also includes extraordinary transactions, the effect of accounting changes, the loss or gain on the disposal of assets, and even the loss or gain on the disposal of a major division.

In the majority of companies, the amount of revenues realized from the sale of goods and services can be measured within fairly close limits. Adjustments to gross revenue are necessary to provide for uncollectible accounts, warranty costs, and similar items; but the proper amount of such adjustments often can be estimated within a narrow range. In some companies, such as those that sell on an installment basis or that perform long-term contracts on a fixed-price basis, the amount of revenue that should be recognized is more difficult to estimate.

Usually, the appropriate amounts of expenses that should be deducted from revenues are more difficult to measure than are the revenue items. Judgments about these matters can have an important influence on net income.

Capitalization. One important source of difficulty is the distinction between capital costs, product costs, and expenses. The effect on current income of expenditures made during the current period depends significantly on how these expenditures are classified. The difference is diagrammed in Illustration 14−2.

Consider the expenditure of $1,000 for labor services. If the labor cost is incurred for selling, general, or administrative activities, it is an expense, and the entire $1,000 affects income of the current period. If the labor cost is incurred in manufacturing a product, it is a product cost, and the $1,000 affects income only in the period in which the product is sold. (The diagram assumes that 40 percent of these goods are sold in the current year.) If the labor cost is incurred in building a depreciable asset, it is capitalized as part of the cost of the asset, and it affects net income over a succession of future periods as the cost is depreciated. Wide latitude exists as to which

ILLUSTRATION 14–2
EFFECT ON INCOME OF ALTERNATIVE COST PRACTICES

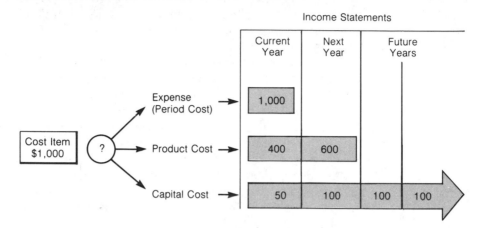

expenditures are to be capitalized and which are to be expensed. For those items that are capitalized, the amount to be charged as expense in a given period can vary widely, depending on the estimate of service life and the method of depreciation, depletion, or amortization that is used.

Quality of Earnings. The reliability of the income statement as a report of the company's performance differs widely among various types of companies. Analysts make judgments about the impact of these differences and refer to the *quality* of earnings as reported on a given income statement, as contrasted with the reported *amount* of earnings. The net income of a retail store that sells only for cash, has a high inventory turnover, and leases its building and equipment is of high quality because the reported amount is relatively uninfluenced by estimates. By contrast, an income statement is of lower quality if it contains large items that require estimates of future events (such as depreciation expense), significant nonrecurring gains or losses, or changes in accounting principles.

Balance Sheet   The balance sheet can be viewed as a statement of the resources controlled by an entity (assets) and of the sources of the funds used to acquire these resources (equities, or liabilities and owners' equity). No single overall characterization fits the individual balance sheet items. Rather, the balance sheet must be viewed as a collection of several types of items, with the amounts for each type being reported according to different concepts and the whole being tied together only in the mechanical sense that the sum of the debit balances equals the sum of the credit balances. The balance sheet is, therefore, literally a "sheet of balances." In terms of the method of measurement used, the principal types of balance sheet items are

(1) monetary assets and liabilities, (2) unexpired costs, (3) inventories, (4) investments, and (5) other liabilities and owners' equity.

Monetary Items. These items include cash and other assets that represent a specific monetary claim against some external party, and liabilities that represent a specific monetary obligation to some external party. Accounts receivable are a monetary asset. The amount that each customer owes is definite, and it is usually possible to estimate the amount of uncollectible accounts within fairly close limits. Marketable securities are usually considered to be monetary assets. Monetary assets are reported at essentially their current cash equivalent, and monetary liabilities (which include most liabilities) are reported at the current cash equivalent of the obligation.

Unexpired Costs. Property, plant, and equipment, intangible assets, prepaid expenses, and deferred charges are initially recorded at acquisition cost and (except for land) are charged off as expenses in a succession of future accounting periods. Amounts reported on a given balance sheet, therefore, are amounts that have not yet been charged off. The balance sheet is the "temporary home" of these costs until the time comes for them to appear as expenses on an income statement.

Inventories. These assets are reported at the lower of cost or market value. Except for the recognition of market value when it is below cost, inventories are reported in the same way as other unexpired costs.

Investments. Investments in securities other than those classified as trading or available-for-sale securities are usually owned in order to exercise control over another company. Special rules govern the way they are reported, as described in Chapter 12.

Other Liabilities and Owners' Equity. These include deferred income taxes, which arise as a consequence of the procedure that matches income tax expense with reported net income and which definitely are not a claim by the government against the business. Also, as described in Chapter 9, the precise borderline between liabilities and owners' equity is unclear. This is illustrated by the nature of zero-coupon bonds and redeemable preferred stock.

The amount reported in the owners' equity section does not show what the owners' stake in the company is worth, what the owners are entitled to, what can be paid to them as dividends, or what they will receive if the entity is liquidated. Basically, the paid-in capital amount is the amount of funds that the shareholders have "actively" furnished the company as new issues of stock have taken place, and retained earnings are the stockholders' "passive" investment of earnings that the company has not distributed to them as dividends.

Omissions. The balance sheet does not show all the valuable things that a business controls nor all of its obligations. It does not show the value of an entity's human resources, the value of new products or processes that result from research and development activities, or the value of future revenues that will result from current expenditures for advertising and sales promotion. The liabilities side obviously cannot report contingencies that the accountant does not know about, such as the costs involved in recalling a product subsequently found to be defective or the cost of complying with pollution-control regulations promulgated after a plant was built. In extreme cases, these unknowns can bankrupt a company when they come to light.

Statement of Cash Flows

The statement of cash flows is a derived statement in the sense that it is usually prepared from data originally collected for the balance sheet or income statement. It shows the sources of additional funds that the business obtained during the period and the purposes for which these funds were used. These sources and uses are categorized as being related to either operating activities, investing activities, or financing activities. The information on this statement is not affected as the income statement is by judgments about the capitalization of assets and the write-off of expenses. For example, the choices of depreciation method and service life can have a significant effect on net income, but they have no effect on the cash flow statement because the amount of depreciation charged is neither a source nor a use of cash. This is the principal reason that financial analysts like the cash flow statement. It is much more definite and is not influenced by the judgments and estimates that affect the other two financial statements. It does not, however, show how net income was earned. Since net income is the best overall measure of how well the business has performed during the period, a cash flow statement is therefore not a substitute for the income statement. Similarly, being a flow statement, the cash flow statement cannot provide the information on the financial position of the business that is given on the balance sheet, which is a status report.

SUMMARY

In addition to the financial statements, the annual report contains the auditors' opinion, which states that the underlying records have been examined and that the information is fair and conforms to generally accepted accounting principles. The annual report contains explanatory notes and may contain additional information about the company.

Although accounting principles are developed in accordance with three criteria and 11 basic concepts, these principles permit considerable latitude in the treatment of transactions. Also, accounting reports are necessarily influenced by judgments, some of which may cause ethical problems for the accountant. A business is a complicated organism, and no set of numbers can convey a completely accurate picture of its activities or its status.

The income statement reports revenues and expenses measured in accordance with accounting principles. It does not report the economic "well-offness" of the business, primarily because expenses are measured in terms of historical cost rather than current cost. Balance sheet items are reported under a variety of measurement concepts. The balance sheet does not report most items at their actual value, nor are all things of value to the entity reported. The cash flow statement is not affected by estimates and a company's practices with respect to the matching and realization concepts as are the other two financial statements.

Cases

CASE 14–1 Payson Lunch*

In mid-1993, Mr. and Mrs. Richard Bingham decided to go into the restaurant business. Mr. Bingham was dissatisfied with his job as cook in a restaurant where he earned $9.75 an hour. During July 1993, the Binghams found a business that seemed to be what they wanted. This was the Payson Lunch, a lunch counter located in Fisher's Department Store downtown. The Payson Lunch was operated under a lease with the department store; only the equipment was actually the property of the operator of the lunchroom. The equipment was old, but Mr. Bingham thought that it was in fairly good condition.

The couple opened negotiations with the current lunchroom operator and quickly reached an agreement to take over the lease and equipment on September 1, and to pay the operator a price of $10,300. Of this price, Mr. Bingham estimated that $4,600 represented the fair value of the equipment. The lease expired on August 31, 1994, and was renewable for three years if Fisher's consented. Under the terms of the lease, Fisher's furnished space, heat, light, and water, and the operators (i.e., the Binghams) paid Fisher's 15 percent of gross receipts as rent.

The Binghams paid the $10,300 from their personal savings account and also transferred $5,150 to a checking account that they opened in the name of Payson Lunch.

Shortly after they started operations, the cooking range broke down. The Binghams thereupon sold the range for $400 (which was approximately its estimated value as a part of the $4,600) and purchased a new range for $4,000. It was installed immediately, and they paid $600 for its installation. The coffee urn also broke down, but Mr. Bingham was able to repair it himself by working 16 hours one Sunday.

Early in 1994, the Binghams called in a firm that specialized in making out reports for small businesses and requested financial statements for Payson Lunch for the period ended December 31, 1993. From their cash register and checkbook, they had the following figures:

Cash receipts:	
Cash receipts from customers.............	$33,165
Sale of cooking range....................	400
Total cash receipts..................	$33,565

Cash disbursements:	
Food and supplies.......................	$14,275
City restaurant license, valid September 1, 1993, to August 31, 1994...................	225
15 percent rent paid to Fisher's for September, October, and November.........	3,460
New cooking range.........................	4,000
Installation of cooking range................	600
Other operating expenses..................	90
Withdrawals for personal use...............	3,800
Total cash disbursements...........	$26,450

Before going home on December 31, the Binghams had estimated the value of food

*Copyright © by the President and Fellows of Harvard College. Harvard Business School case 151-003.

and supplies then on hand to be about $750 at cost. Early in January, they paid two bills, the December meat bill of $890 and the December rent of $1,515.

The Binghams also explained to the accountant that the cash receipts of $33,165 included $3,850 received from the sale of 140 "coupon books" at $27.50 each. Each book contained coupons with a face value of $30, which could be used to pay for meals. As of December 31, coupons with a face value of $2,700 had been used to pay for meals; therefore, coupons with a face value of $1,500 were still outstanding.

Questions

1. Prepare a balance sheet as of December 31, 1993, and an income statement and cash flow statement for the four-month period ending December 31, 1993. Explain briefly your treatment of the coupon books and of anything else you believe needs comment.

2. Comment briefly on the significant information revealed by your financial statements.

CASE 14–2 Limited Editions, Inc.*

> If you haven't learned to love it by 1987, we'll buy it back at the original price.

The above statement appeared as the prominent headline in a Limited Editions, Inc., advertisement placed in a monthly magazine catering to a select, high-income readership. Its intent was to announce the company's new porcelain figurine, "Foxes in Spring," which would be offered in limited quantities at a price of $2,000. Limited Editions' idea was to offer literally "a beautiful investment opportunity" with capital gains potential to a wealthy investor. By guaranteeing that production would be limited, the figurines could immediately attain status similar to an antique.

The guarantee offered by Limited was quite simple:

> Subject to being in its original condition, we guarantee to repurchase any of our "Foxes in Spring" figurines at the original price of $2,000 at any time after five years from the date of purchase.

The guarantee was not restricted to the original purchaser and hence was transferable from one party to another. The only other return provision allowed a purchaser to receive an 80 percent refund of the purchase price if the figurine was returned within three months from the date of purchase.

The figurines were offered for sale in only one extremely reputable store in each of 10 large American cities. These stores were individually identified in the advertisement. Each of the 10 was provided with one "Foxes in Spring" figurine to be used for display. It was informally understood that Limited Editions would not ask for the return of the figurine. The stores otherwise had no inventory. When a customer signed a "subscription request," the store forwarded it to Limited Editions. The "subscription" was an indication of interest but carried no contractual obligation on the part of the buyer. Limited would fill the subscription by shipping directly to the customer. Upon notification of shipment, the retail store would then bill the customer. Upon collection, the store deducted its 10 percent commission and forwarded the net amount of $1,800 to Limited Editions. If a figurine was returned in the first

---

*Copyright © by the President and Fellows of Harvard College. Harvard Business School case 176-038.

three months, Limited Editions simply sent an 80 percent refund ($1,600) to the customer. Limited Editions did not request a refund of the 10 percent sales commission from the retail store.

Production of "Foxes in Spring" was strictly limited to 500 pieces. The design of the figurine and the mold from which it would be produced were created by an artist for a fee of $50,000. This fee was paid in 1982. Production was contracted out to a reputable company, which agreed to run batches of 100 pieces upon instructions from Limited Editions. When a batch was produced, each figurine was then hand painted and finished by skilled workers. Because of the extremely high-quality standards demanded by Limited Editions, the early batches cost substantially more to produce, paint, and finish than did the later batches. Figurine statistics for 1982 are shown in Exhibit 1. Production cost data are summarized in Exhibit 2.

Limited Editions, Inc., was incorporated in June 1982. The stock was sold for $10,000. One half of the stock was owned by a small, diversified, over-the-counter company engaged in a variety of businesses, and the other half was owned by a small number of venture capitalists who played an active role in managing the company. The venture capitalists' interest in Limited Editions, Inc., was in part nurtured by the widely publicized success stories of companies like the Franklin Mint[1] that capitalized on the public's recent interest in "collector items" as an investment hedge against inflation. Both the

---

[1]The Franklin Mint, traded on the New York Stock Exchange, was recognized as one of the leading producers of limited edition collectibles. Its issues included commemorative and art medals in silver and gold, sculptures in pewter and bronze, deluxe leatherbound books, and works of art in fine crystal.

EXHIBIT 1
STATISTICS FOR 1982

	Number
Figurines produced	400
Figurine subscriptions received	320
Figurines shipped to customers	290
Figurines sent to retailers for display	10
Figurines returned	0
Figurines in inventory	100
Figurines for which cash was collected by December 31, 1982	240
Figurines shipped but not paid for by December 31, 1982	50

management and the owners of Limited Editions hoped to build the company into a leader in this new, unexploited figurine market. Encouraged by the apparent success of the company's first figurine, management was already making plans for a number of future offerings.

Design and production began in July 1982, promotion in September, and sales in October. The bulk of 1982 sales appeared to be related to the year-end Christmas season. Of the 290 figurines shipped to customers in 1982, 100 were to shareholders (or members of their families). Since these sales were not made through a retail dealer, the full $2,000 purchase price was received in cash by Limited Editions. Of the 190 pieces shipped to nonrelated parties, cash had been received by year-end from the retailers for 140 pieces. None of the 190 pieces was returned in 1982, but 20 of them were returned early in 1983, some after the three-month period had expired. Each of the 20 customers was promptly paid the $1,600 refund.

Promotional and advertising costs of $25,000 were paid in 1982. Limited Editions planned to do no further advertising of "Foxes in Spring" in 1983. General and administrative expenses for 1982 were $50,000, and all these expenses were paid in cash

EXHIBIT 2
BATCH PRODUCTION DATA

Batch	Date	Units	Cost	Average Cost per Unit
1	July 1982	100	$100,000	$1,000
2	September 1982	100	80,000	800
3	October 1982	100	60,000	600
4	December 1982*	100	40,000	400
5	March 1983†	100	20,000	200

*The manufacturer was paid for the December shipment in January 1983.
†As of December 31, 1982, Limited Editions was not really sure what the last batch of 100 figurines would cost. The $20,000 ultimately paid would have been a reasonable estimate as of December 31, 1982.

before year-end. It was expected that these costs would continue at roughly the same level in future years.

Question

Prepare an income statement and cash flow statement for 1982, and a balance sheet as of December 31, 1982. You may ignore income taxes.

CASE 14–3 Royal Crest, Inc.*

The Houston office of Ogilby, McKinnon & Co., a large public accounting firm, had been engaged to review the 1976 financial statements of Royal Crest, Inc., a leading manufacturer and distributor of citizens' band radios and other communications equipment. The accounting firm had been the auditors for Royal Crest since January 1972.

Near the completion of the 1976 audit, a question was raised as to the proper valuation of the citizens' band radio inventory, a question that generated opposing views. The financial statements in question are shown in Exhibits 1 and 2.

The Citizens' Band. In 1958, the Federal Communications Commission (FCC) allocated part of the shortwave radio band as a "citizens' band" (CB) to be used for local, personal, and business communication. The FCC removed almost all legal barriers to access the CB airwaves. The only application requirements were that the applicant be at least 18 years of age and pay a $4 application fee.

Until 1974, the CB radio was used primarily by businesses that needed a method of communication between a home office and a vehicle. Also, many long-haul truckers used CBs to share information with each other. The oil embargo and resultant fuel shortage of 1974, however, changed the usage of the CB radio. Some motorists, noticing that truckers always seemed to know where to find fuel, learned about the truckers' secret weapon. The general public soon realized the usefulness of the CB in obtaining highway information in emergencies or simply for companionship.

*Copyright © by the President and Fellows of Harvard College. Harvard Business School case 178-114.

EXHIBIT 1

ROYAL CREST, INC.
Income Statements

	Year Ended August 31	
	1976 (unaudited)	1975
Net sales.	$72,143,451	$26,123,929
Cost of sales	43,411,164	16,198,173
Gross profit	28,732,287	9,925,756
Expenses:		
Selling and advertising	10,921,566	2,212,009
General and administrative.	4,442,103	2,247,801
Interest	522,722	565,712
	15,886,391	5,025,522
Earnings before income taxes	12,845,896	4,900,234
Income taxes.	1,764,360	2,047,713
Net earnings	$11,081,536	$ 2,852,521
Earnings per share.	$8.76	$2.57
Average common shares outstanding	1,265,367	1,110,386

The surge in consumer demand was evident in the number of CB applications received by the FCC, which in the first 8 months of 1974 equaled the total number filed in the previous 15 years. Requests for CB licenses hit an all-time high in January 1976, following the unprecedented Christmas sales the month before. As of November 1, 1976, approximately seven million CB licenses had been granted. This number understated the actual number of CB radios in use, because not all CB operators complied with the license requirement.

The Product. A CB radio is a transceiver, that is, it is equipped both to send and to receive messages. Various solid-state circuits and a speaker are required to receive the signal and make it audible. A microphone, additional circuits, and a transformer are needed to convert the human voice to a radio signal and transmit it. Finally, a tuner and 12 to 14 quartz crystals are necessary to allow selection of a desired channel. All of these parts were available from a number of suppliers. Also, the assembly of the CB radio was quite simple and required no elaborate equipment or skilled labor. Firms with small amounts of capital could therefore easily establish themselves in the CB business. Because of this ease of entry, from 1958 to 1974 several foreign firms entered the industry and soon dominated it, producing some 80 percent of the U.S. demand. Few U.S. firms remained in the production end of the CB industry.

When the demand for CBs spurted in 1974, many U.S. firms did not have adequate production facilities and thus had to rely heavily on Japanese firms for radios built to the U.S. companies' design specifications. It was impossible, though, for any CB manufacturer, foreign or domestic, to keep pace with the skyrocketing demand. Inventories of component parts—particularly the quartz

EXHIBIT 2

ROYAL CREST, INC.
Balance Sheets

	As of August 31	
	1976 (unaudited)	1975
Assets		
Current assets:		
Cash and temporary investments	$ 1,972,496	$ 313,861
Marketable equity securities (market value $771,500)	762,450	—
Accounts receivable (net).	12,434,941	6,072,787
Inventories (see Note A below)	18,411,680	6,283,383
Other	61,678	22,874
Total current assets	33,643,245	12,692,905
Property, plant, and equipment (at cost)	6,073,765	3,385,946
Less: Accumulated depreciation and amortization	(1,551,784)	(1,161,888)
Property, plant, and equipment (net)	4,521,981	2,224,058
Other assets and deferred charges	262,661	262,610
Total assets	$38,427,887	$15,179,573
Liabilities and Stockholders' Equity		
Current liabilities:		
Notes payable to bank	$ 7,398,619	$ 3,281,373
Current maturities on long-term debt	85,797	167,346
Accounts payable.	7,009,786	3,175,270
Accrued expenses.	1,300,231	763,766
Income taxes payable	182,634	2,001,420
Total current liabilities.	15,977,067	9,389,175
Long-term portion of long-term debt	1,000,291	1,640,901
Deferred income taxes	136,206	58,905
Total liabilities.	17,113,564	11,088,981
Stockholders' equity:		
Capital stock	7,615,254	825,572
Retained earnings.	13,699,069	3,265,020
Total liabilities and stockholders' equity	$38,427,887	$15,179,573

Note A:	Antennas and Accessories	CB Radios	
Inventories:			
Finished goods	$ 369,218	$ 8,025,641	
Work in process	966,596	2,701,010	
Raw materials	857,386	5,134,181	
	$2,193,200	$15,860,832	$18,054,032
Supplies			357,648
Total			$18,411,680

crystals—were insufficient. Also, production facilities, which had been geared to a much lower demand level, fell far short of total capacity required to meet demand. Thus, throughout 1974–75, there was a major shortage of CBs.

By 1976, new production facilities for both CB radios and components had started operations. More importantly, a technological breakthrough called "phase-locked-loop" design used semiconductors to replace all but three of the quartz crystals. These events eased the shortage. Also, since the United States was a leader in semiconductor technology, more CB production plants opened in the United States to capitalize on this new technology that significantly reduced the domestic manufacturing cost of CB radios.

Marketing. The marketing of CBs was probably least affected by the changes wrought in 1974. Most producers sold their products through some 20 manufacturers' representatives to hundreds of small dealers, many of whom carried several competing CB lines. All sales to dealers were made with the right to return goods to the manufacturer.

During the 1974–75 shortage, some CB manufacturers began to allocate their production to the representatives and let them assume the responsibility to distribute the radios to their dealers as they saw fit. The allocation formulas used by both manufacturers and representatives were complicated by the fact that many astute dealers had deliberately overordered and/or placed duplicate orders with different companies in anticipation of insufficient deliveries.

Sales to the ultimate consumer were almost always handled by the dealer. Most radios sold in the $100–$250 price range, with the price of a typical CB averaging $150. Installation and an antenna were extra. It was common practice for manufacturers to provide a 90-day warranty against malfunction of the radio, but some gave warranties of

up to one year's duration. Repairs under warranty were performed by local "factory-authorized" shops.

The Industry. The growth in the number of companies involved in the industry paralleled the increased popularity of the CB itself. The number of manufacturers or importers of CB radios stood at 15 by 1974, at 30 by 1975, and at anywhere from 45 to 60 by the end of 1976. Most of these companies were dependent on Japanese products, but a growing number were increasing their domestic manufacturing capability. Competition was keen, and products were differentiated on the bases of quality, price, service, technical features, "gadgets" (such as digital channel number readout), and duration of warranties.

Until 1975, most U.S. firms involved in CB production and/or distribution lacked substantial financial or technological resources. With the exception of Radio Shack, most companies were small, undercapitalized, and obviously beneficiaries of being "in the right place at the right time."

A number of the small firms took advantage of the soaring demand by making large common stock offerings to an eager Wall Street—some "going public" for the first time—to obtain capital needed for growth. By 1975, however, large, established companies with strong financial resources began to enter the CB industry, attracted by the smaller companies' soaring profits and the vast market potential. Some industry observers felt that the smaller firms might actually benefit because of the infusion of advertising and development money the larger companies would make. Although this would increase competition, it would also improve the quality of the product and further heighten public awareness of CBs. However, a number of financial analysts felt that several of the smaller companies would be unable to take the financial strain of this competition and that a "shakeout" of the industry would occur—particularly when supply caught up with demand.

Royal Crest, Inc. Royal Crest, Inc., was founded in Corpus Christi, Texas, in 1967 by two brothers, William and Robert Hopkins, who previously owned an electronic parts distributorship. Initially, the firm principally manufactured radio and television antennas in a Mexican plant. This strategy provided advantages of lower duties than those imposed on Japanese goods and lower transportation costs. Sales blossomed from $300,000 in the first year to $2.5 million by 1970, and 1970 profit was $500,000 before taxes.

At that time, William Hopkins proposed that Royal Crest expand its product line to include two-way communications equipment, principally CB radios. Not only would their Mexican production strategy be equally applicable to this endeavor, but because of the popularity of Royal Crest antennas, retailers would readily provide shelf space to other products carrying the Royal Crest brand name. After negotiation of a $1 million loan with Houston banks and some 18 months' work expanding the Mexican facility, Royal Crest CBs were on the shelves of U.S. dealers. Through 1972 and 1973, sales were somewhat lower than expected but were still encouraging. By 1974, however, the "boom" had begun and a second production shift had to be added to the Mexican plant in September. In 1975, though, two production shifts could no longer meet demand, and the Hopkins brothers were forced to contract with a major Japanese firm for part of their needs, at least until a major expansion could be made to the Mexican plant. They realized that this temporary strategy eliminated their cost advantage, but, given the "seller's market," they felt that this deviation was advisable.

These conditions prevailed until early 1976, when supply and demand began to equilibrate. At the same time the major expansion of the Mexican plant, which was partially financed by the firm's first public stock offering in August 1975, was completed. Soon dealers, finding themselves receiving full shipments of CB radios from several companies at once, began returning all or portions of the shipments to the manufacturers.

The FCC Decision. From the beginning of the CB craze, the industry had been petitioning the FCC for an increase in the number of CB channels. The industry feared that the 23 existing channels would become so congested that they would become virtually unusable, which could eventually lead to the industry's demise. On July 27, 1976, the FCC ruled that:

1. The number of CB channels would be increased from 23 to 40, effective January 1, 1977.

2. The new 40-channel CB radios could not be sold until January 1, 1977, and the FCC would not approve any 40-channel radio designs until November 1, 1976. Therefore, manufacturers who entered the models into production before that date ran the risk that the product would be unmarketable.

3. Current inventories of 23-channel CBs could be "retrofitted" to conform to the new 40-channel standards, but radios already sold to final users could not be remanufactured. After intense pressure by CB manufacturers, the FCC withdrew its decision prohibiting the remanufacture of previously sold radios. As a result, several manufacturers, including Royal Crest, offered CB purchasers the option of sending their radios back to the company for remanufacture at a cost of $25 to $30.

The FCC's decision sent shock waves through the industry because it had only three months to design and build workable prototypes of new 40-channel models. But public reaction to the announcement created an even bigger shock. Since new radios with expanded channel capacities were authorized by the FCC, there was a great deal of uncertainty among customers as to the purchase of 23-channel radios. Sales to consumers began to fall noticeably. Distributors, already canceling duplicate purchase orders because of oversupply, further canceled orders and returned merchandise to manufacturers. Also, some dealers and manufacturers panicked and slashed prices. In early October 1976, the following was reported:

> Prices on the once costly CB units have now come down well below the $100 mark, and some mass merchandisers have shocked old CBers with prices below $60. Profit margins for retailers that were once in the 35% area are now dissolving rapidly.[1]

The FCC decision could not have caught Royal Crest at a worse time. They were finishing production of 23-channel sets for the Christmas season ahead. Also, they had recently entered into an agreement with their Japanese supplier for an additional 2,000 sets. Technically, they could still cancel the shipment, but the Japanese manufacturers had made it clear to the entire CB industry that cancellation (which forced the supplier to take the loss) could result in permanently severing relations between that supplier and the U.S. buyer. The Hopkins brothers felt this risk was too great because a secondary source of supply might be necessary for 40-channel CB radios, especially if demand for them was equal to the 1975 demand for 23-channel CBs. Thus, a shipment of now-unwanted CBs came in from Japan to Royal Crest's central warehouse.

---

[1] "Some CB Marketers Buck the Trend," *Advertising Age,* October 4, 1976.

It was this situation that Royal Crest's auditors had to assess as they reviewed the annual financial statements for the fiscal year ending August 31, 1976.

The 1976 Audit. On October 10, Ogilby, McKinnon & Co. began the final steps in their annual audit. Within a few days, Mary Lynch, one of the senior accountants on the audit engagement, was alerted by one of the junior staff auditors to a potential trouble spot, namely, Royal Crest's inventory of 23-channel CBs. As of August 31, the company had accumulated $8 million worth of radios. This amount exceeded the cost of the radios they had sold in the entire fourth quarter (see Exhibit 3 for the fiscal 1976 quarterly results). Furthermore, unit sales had been dropping steadily since that date, even though Royal Crest had marked down their selling price some 30 percent. After performing some rough computations, Lynch determined that at current prices, a minor write-down of the ending inventory valuation might be necessary. (Approximate sales price and production cost breakdowns are provided in Exhibit 4.) However, given the tremendous competition in the market and the apparent glut of 23-channel CBs within the distribution channels, she doubted whether current prices were a realistic yardstick by which to measure the inventory's net realizable value.

Lynch soon realized that it would be quite difficult to convince Royal Crest management to go along with any write-down proposal. Not only would a write-down be based on subjective estimates of future events—which had often proved wrong in this flourishing industry—but management had two strong incentives to fight the proposal. First, because the capital needs for the planned 40-channel radio operations were made more critical by the slumping 23-channel radio sales, Royal Crest was currently negotiating a

EXHIBIT 3

ROYAL CREST, INC.
Fiscal 1976 Quarterly Results (unaudited)

	Quarter Ended			
	11/30/75	*2/28/76*	*5/31/76*	*8/31/76*
Net sales..........................	$13,991,415	$19,974,501	$26,474,981	$11,702,554
Cost of sales	7,731,410	11,580,922	15,555,017	8,543,815
Gross profit	6,260,005	8,393,579	10,919,964	3,158,739
Operating expenses................	2,244,285	3,410,236	4,829,304	5,402,566
Earnings (loss) before income taxes ...	4,015,720	4,983,343	6,090,660	(2,243,827)
Income taxes......................	515,531	252,698	762,668	233,463
Net earnings (loss).................	$ 3,500,189	$ 4,730,645	$ 5,327,992	$ (2,477,290)
Earnings (loss) per share	$2.96	$4.01	$3.95	($1,81)

EXHIBIT 4
SALES PRICE AND COST BREAKDOWNS

Retail selling price, average CB radio		$150–$160
Average dealer cost (manufacturer's selling price)......		$100
Gross margin (of manufacturer)......................		38%
Average manufacturing cost/unit.....................		$62
Materials and overhead........................	$45.50	
Labor....................... 5 hours @ $3.30 =	16.50	
	$62.00	

large increase in its unsecured line of credit with its Houston banks. In addition to the requirement that the company have an un-qualified auditors' report, the current bank agreement also required that Royal Crest maintain a current ratio of two to one. Second, the company was exploring the possibility of acquiring a small manufacturer of two-way office intercom systems through a swap of its common stock.

Lynch attempted to resolve the inventory write-down issue by investigating common industry practice. However, most other firms in the industry had December 31 year-ends,

well beyond the date by which Royal Crest's statements had to be prepared.

After discussions with her audit manager, Lynch decided that a write-down of the 23-channel CB radio inventory should be brought to the attention of management. Thus, on November 8, she approached William Hopkins to gain his views on a write-down and the following exchange occurred:

Lynch: We're tremendously concerned about your inventory of 23-channel CBs. By current valuation, on August 31 you had over $8 million in finished CBs in stock, and your margins on them had declined to about 15 percent above your cost. And the price deterioration has continued, as you well know. Even that $10 gross margin has just about evaporated. Frankly, with the intense competition in the industry and all those radios on the verge of becoming obsolete, I can see only one direction for the gross margin—down! We are beginning to think that a substantial write-down to realizable value may be necessary—on the order of $1 to $2 million—to state the inventory value fairly.

Hopkins: A write-down? Well, Mary, I think you've forgotten some important details. First, even though we've had some cancellations of Christmas orders, we don't think the holiday sales period will be all that bad at current price levels. The worst of the price deterioration is behind us.

Lynch: But what if one of the shakier companies dumps its inventory on the market to raise cash?

Hopkins: It's possible, but I doubt it. By now, any company with serious intentions of staying in the CB business has arranged credit to finance production of the 40s. Those companies that were strapped for cash would have dumped long ago, as some did. Besides, have you seen the sales figures we've put together on those 40s?

Lynch: Yes.

Hopkins: Well, then, you know we expect to sell the 40-channel rigs at about 25 percent more than the suggested retail on our current line—some $40 more than the 23-channel rigs were selling for before they were discounted! I have a feeling a lot of people will think twice before paying those higher prices. A lot of 23-channel rigs will sell, at current prices, on that basis. Besides, it's not like the 40-channel CBs are going to materialize magically on store shelves on January 1. We haven't begun building sets yet, and we're not going to until we get our design tested and accepted by the FCC. By the time we get the 40-channel rigs off the assembly line, catalogs printed for our sales reps, and the

CBs into the stores, it probably won't be earlier than February or maybe March. So there are going to be three additional months where the 23-channel rigs won't have competition from the 40s.

Also, we can remanufacture the 23s we have in stock to accommodate 40 channels for about $25. And, come to think of it, a lot of them aren't even going to need to be remanufactured. The only places where the 23 channels are congested are in the metropolitan areas which have high population densities. But in rural areas, folks don't need 40-channels! In fact, a lot of them in rural areas don't even need 23. And we sell a lot of sets in those areas. Why, the Midwest and South are our best sales territories! So, we fully expect to sell them off, either by remanufacture or as-is, quickly and without further price reductions.

Lynch: I doubt that you can sell remanufactured sets for the same price you could sell new 40-channel sets.

Hopkins: True, but we won't have to give them away, either. Don't forget that technology is on our side; that new phase-locked-loop design has lowered our material costs 40 percent.

Lynch: I understand what you're saying, but I still have a few problems. The 23-channel radios are the only CBs on the market now. Everyone knows the 40s can't be sold for another two months or so, and I'm sure some customers have been told by dealers, who are as anxious as you are to be rid of the 23s, that it'll be even longer than that. Nevertheless, the 23s don't seem to be selling. Also, why are customers going to buy 23s in January or February when the delivery date on the 40s is even closer? They're probably waiting for the higher-priced product if they haven't bought a CB by December 31. I just can't see margins on the 23s staying where they are, bad though they may be. I really believe that there has been a material economic loss on these sets and they should be written down.

Hopkins: Look, I'll grant you I'm speculating a little, but so are you. Neither of us can say with precision what the public's going to do. I just can't see that profit margins will decline so much further that we need to write the inventory down now.

Lynch: Well, you know my position. Let me look into this situation some more and discuss it with other members of my firm and I'll get back to you.

Hopkins: Well, that's fine as long as you communicate my position to them. Time is running short. In fact, I'm on my way over to Houston now to meet with the banks. They are really anxious to see the audited 1976 statements.

Two other brief discussions were held in the next few days, but neither position changed significantly. On November 15, Mary Lynch received a call from William Hopkins.

Hopkins: I thought I'd let you know about a couple of items that came to my attention in the last few days, Mary. First, I received a November 8 press release from Electronic Industries Association, our trade association, predicting that sales of 23s will rise in the next couple of months after our minidepression last summer. Also, there was a piece in the November 15 *Electronic News* about inventory write-downs in the CB industry. I'll admit I'm a bit surprised, because a few major companies are taking write-downs; but there's a pretty substantial amount of evidence that backs up my position too. In fact, there was something in the article I forgot to mention before. We have been looking into sales of our radios in Canada. Canada's stay-

ing with the 23-channel rigs, and we expect to work off a lot of our inventory there. So there's even less need for a write-down in my opinion.

Lynch: I've seen the EIA piece, but I haven't seen that article. Could you send me a copy?

Hopkins: Sure, I'll put it in the mail today!

As promised, the next day the article arrived in the mail. What William Hopkins had told Lynch over the phone was true. There was backing in the article for his position. But there was an equal amount of support for her own stand on the matter, as evidenced by several companies' substantial inventory write-downs. Also, the article raised a question as to whether even those were sufficient. Though the trade association had indeed predicted increased sales, there was little, if any, backing for their claims contained in the article. Neither article, in effect, settled anything, and Lynch was placed in even more of a quandary as to the proper course of action in the situation.

Questions

1. What additional steps should Mary Lynch take in completing the Royal Crest audit?
2. If you were William Hopkins, what additional steps would you take if the auditors insist on a write-down?
3. Should the value of the inventory be written down? How would you prepare the adjustment?
4. How would you phrase your auditors' opinion if the inventory were not written down?

CASE 14–4 SafeCard Services, Inc.

In 1981, SafeCard Services, Inc., had as its primary business a credit card loss notification service called Hot-Line. For an annual

fee of $12, SafeCard would immediately notify the customer's credit card issuers (i.e., American Express, Visa, oil companies, department stores, and so on) if the customer's credit cards were stolen or otherwise lost. This Hot-Line service was marketed through direct-mail advertising campaigns in conjunction with the credit card services of major oil companies (e.g., Gulf and ARCO), department stores (including Sears and J.C. Penney), banks, and others—about 75 credit card issuers in total.

SafeCard's marketing approach was as follows. First, the customer of a credit card issuer was sent a description of the Hot-Line service. This description explained that the Hot-Line customer would keep on file with SafeCard a list of all of his or her credit cards. SafeCard provided a toll-free number through which a customer could inform Safe-Card if the customer's credit cards became lost. SafeCard would then immediately notify the issuers of the lost cards to cease honoring them and would assist the customer in obtaining replacement cards. Second, the prospective Hot-Line customer was offered six months of free Hot-Line service. If this offer were accepted, at the end of the six months the credit card issuer (e.g., Gulf Oil) through which SafeCard had reached the prospect would bill the customer $12 to continue the service for another year. At this point, the customer could either cancel the service or could pay the $12 to continue it. About 50 percent paid to continue the service after their six-month free trial. Those who did subscribe in this way were automatically billed by the credit card issuer every 12 months to renew the service for another year. According to SafeCard, about 80 percent of a year's paid subscribers renewed the service for the following year.

SafeCard incurred substantial costs in obtaining new customers, primarily for direct-mail descriptive materials and postage. Until fiscal 1980, SafeCard capitalized (as a noncurrent asset) these costs of obtaining *new* subscribers and amortized them over three years. Beginning in fiscal 1980, SafeCard extended the amortization period to 10 years, using an accelerated amortization pattern that was essentially the same as 250 percent declining balance. Thus, after five years, each $100 of initially capitalized marketing cost would have been written down to about $24.

When a new subscriber signed up for a year's paid Hot-Line service, or when a subscriber renewed for another year, SafeCard debited Accounts Receivable for $12, credited about 80 percent of this amount to Customers' Advance Payments, and credited the remainder to Allowance for Cancellations.

SafeCard also paid an annual commission to the credit card issuing company through which SafeCard had secured the subscription. This commission compensated the issuing company for its services in billing and collecting the $12 annual fee. The commission was deducted by the credit card company from the subscription revenues it remitted to SafeCard. When SafeCard received a payment from a credit card company, it debited Cash for the actual cash proceeds and debited Prepaid Direct Marketing Costs for the commission (i.e., the two debits totaled $12 for each new or renewal subscription). The $12 credit was to Accounts Receivable. These commissions were amortized on a straight-line basis over 12 months, as were the prepaid revenues that had been credited to Customers' Advance Payments.

SafeCard's accounting practices were the subject of an article in *Barron's* on July 6, 1981, written by Professor Abraham J. Briloff, a well-known critic of certain corporate accounting practices. Briloff was critical of SafeCard's capitalization of marketing costs, particularly those related to generating new subscriptions. He pointed out that Safe-Card expensed these costs as incurred for tax

EXHIBIT 1

SAFECARD SERVICES, INC.
Consolidated Statements of Earnings
(millions of dollars)

	Year Ended October 31		Six Months Ended April 30,
	1979	*1980*	*1981*
Revenues:			
Direct-mail marketing revenues:			
Sales of service programs	$10.0	$15.3	$11.4
Sales of merchandise	1.9	*	—
Interest and other income.........................	0.6	0.8	0.8
Net revenues	12.5	16.1	12.2
Operating costs and expenses:			
Cost of service programs	5.1	7.8	6.3
Cost of merchandise	2.0	*	—
General and administrative expenses	1.5	2.3	1.4
Other expenses.....................................	0.2	0.2	—
	8.8	10.3	7.7
Earnings before income taxes:	3.7	5.8	4.5
Income taxes:			
Currently payable....................................	—	—	—
Deferred	1.7	2.7	2.2
Net earnings	$ 2.0	$ 3.1	$ 2.3

*Less than $0.1 ($100,000).

purposes, with the result that the company in fiscal 1980 reported a $4.3 million loss to the IRS while reporting pretax earnings of $5.8 million to its shareholders. Briloff noted that SafeCard had never had to pay income taxes and would not have to do so in the near future because of its $5.9 million operating loss tax carryforwards as of October 31, 1980. Briloff concluded that SafeCard's accounting practices left "room for serious doubt" as to whether the company was "as profitable as its reported results would seem to suggest."

SafeCard's financial statements related to its 1979 and 1980 fiscal years, and the first half of fiscal 1981, are shown in Exhibits 1 and 2. Exhibit 3 shows the company's marketing costs and the division of these costs between expense and assets (deferrals) for the same time frame. Professor Briloff felt that the costs incurred in getting new subscribers should be capitalized for 6 months (the free trial period), then written off evenly over the ensuing 12 months. Thus, for example, the $2.8 million incurred in the fourth quarter of fiscal 1978 (i.e., August 1–October 31, 1978) would be written off as a $700,000 expense in each of the quarters starting with the second quarter of fiscal 1979 (i.e., February 1–April 30, 1979) and ending with the first quarter of fiscal 1980 (i.e., November 1, 1979–January 31, 1980).

EXHIBIT 2

SAFECARD SERVICES, INC.
Consolidated Balance Sheets
(millions of dollars)

	As of October 31			As of April 30, 1981
	1978	1979	1980	
Assets				
Current assets:				
Cash	$ 3.9	$ 7.2	$ 7.1	$10.1
Accounts receivable (net)	2.5	2.3	6.6	1.6
Prepaid direct marketing costs	2.4	4.8	9.0	9.8
Total current assets	9.8	14.3	22.7	21.5
Property, equipment, and leasehold improvements (net)	0.4	0.4	0.6	0.7
Deferred direct marketing costs	3.9	4.9	11.4	15.2
	$14.1	$19.6	$34.7	$37.4
Liabilities and Stockholders' Equity				
Current liabilities:				
Accounts payable	$ 0.3	$ 0.6	$ 1.8	$ 0.6
Accrued expenses	0.1	*	0.1	*
Allowance for cancellations	1.1	1.6	4.7	3.6
Customers' advance payments	4.2	5.3	10.1	10.7
Deferred income taxes	0.3	1.6	1.2	1.5
Total current liabilities	6.0	9.1	17.9	16.4
Deferred income taxes	1.9	2.3	5.5	7.4
Shareholders' equity:				
Common stock[†]	3.9	3.9	3.9	3.9
Retained earnings	2.3	4.3	7.4	9.7
	$14.1	$19.6	$34.7	$37.4

*Less than $0.1 ($100,000).
[†]Approximately 5.2 million shares were outstanding in each period.

Questions

1. Write journal entries for: (a) the "sale" of a year's services for one customer; (b) Safe-Card's receipt from the selling agent; (c) the net effect of (a) and (b); and (d) cancellation of the service one year hence when the $12 renewal fee appears on a customer's credit card bill.

2. What would SafeCard's pretax income have been in fiscal 1979 and 1980 and the first half of fiscal 1981 if marketing costs were (a) expensed immediately as incurred? (b) expensed as proposed by Professor Briloff? (Not enough data are given in Exhibit 3 to calculate fiscal 1979 income using Briloff's approach.)

3. One of the FASB's objectives for financial reporting is to provide information that helps financial statement users assess an enterprise's prospective cash flows. From the information given in Exhibits 1, 2, and 3, prepare cash flow statements for fiscal 1979 and 1980 and the first half of fiscal 1981. (Note: Because the information in the exhibits is somewhat condensed and has been rounded to the nearest $0.1 million, you may need an "other" or "unexplained" item in your cash flow statements to make them reconcile with Safe-Card's reported cash balances.)

EXHIBIT 3

SAFECARD SERVICES, INC.
Marketing Costs
(millions of dollars)

Quarter*	Costs Incurred	Costs Expensed	Increase in Deferrals
1978–4	$ 2.8	$0.8	$ 2.0
1979–1	1.4	1.1	0.3
1979–2	1.4	1.2	0.2
1979–3	1.3	1.2	0.1
1979–4	3.4	1.6	1.8
Total 1979	7.5	5.1	2.4
1980–1	4.5	1.5	3.0
1980–2	3.9	I.7	2.2
1980–3	4.3	1.9	2.4
1980–4	5.8	2.7	3.1
Total 1980	18.5	7.8	10.7
1981–1	5.2	2.9	2.3
1981–2	5.7	3.4	2.3
First half, 1981	10.9	6.3	4.6

*These are quarters of SafeCard's fiscal years. Thus, for example, 1978–4 is the period from August 1–October 31, 1978.

4. Do you feel that SafeCard's accounting practices were misleading? If so, what alternative practices would you recommend?

5. Shortly after the *Barron's* article appeared, SafeCard's common stock (traded over the counter) dropped from $25 to $10 per share. Was this warranted? How does this price decrease relate to the efficient markets hypothesis?

CASE 14–5 U.S. Windpower, Inc.*

Early in January 1985, Gerald R. Alderson, President and Chief Executive Officer of U.S. Windpower, Inc. (USW), was preparing to meet with the Audit Committee of the Board of Directors of USW and with two partners of

*Copyright © by the President and Fellows of Harvard College. Harvard Business School case 186–123.

Coopers & Lybrand, the company's auditors, to discuss the audit for the year ending December 31, 1984. Alderson knew that the main issue was how the company should account for the notes it received as partial payment for the sale of windpower plants. In previous years, the company had deferred recognition of almost all the revenues represented by these notes until they were actually collected in cash. Several recent circumstances had raised the question of whether a less conservative method of revenue recognition might now be appropriate.

The first circumstance was an offer by a wealthy individual to purchase up to 25 percent of the outstanding equity of USW at a price equivalent to $25 per share of common stock. This offer had been solicited by Alderson to accommodate the desires of a number of shareholders who had invested in the expectation that USW would eventually "go public" and they would then be able to sell their shares at a profit. An initial public offering still seemed remote, however, and some of the early investors had asked Alderson to help them find another way to liquidate part of their holdings.

When this prospective purchaser reviewed the 1983 financial statements of USW (Exhibit 1), he questioned the accounting treatment of the notes. Specifically, he was worried that any existing investors who sold to him might later argue that they had been misled by the way the company reported the notes receivable; they might use this argument to seek to rescind the sale or to claim damages. The prospective purchaser had discussed his concerns with the auditors, who had reaffirmed their "clean" (unqualified) opinion on the 1983 financial statements.

The second circumstance was the performance during 1984 of the company's newest model windmill, the 56–100. Although earlier models had experienced significant operational difficulties, the 56–100 had so far exceeded its design specifications in actual operations.

Given the performance of the 56–100 and the fact that Coopers & Lybrand had been sensitized to the revenue recognition issue, Alderson thought it was likely that the auditors would want to see a different approach taken in reporting the notes for the year ending December 31, 1984. He wanted to be prepared with a position he could defend to the Audit Committee and the auditors.

Company Background.   USW was incorporated in 1979 to continue research and development into wind energy generation that had been begun in 1974 by Russell Wolfe and Stanley Charren. Following the 1973 Arab oil embargo, Wolfe had begun to investigate alternatives to the use of fossil fuel for electric power generation and had become convinced that wind energy had good potential. He persuaded Charren of the validity of his ideas. With the guidance of Charren and the financial help of some of their friends, Wolfe began to design and build prototype machines. These early operations were conducted initially under an informal organization and later under a limited partnership.[1]

By 1979, it was clear that the capital requirements to continue R&D and to begin commercial production required the corporate form of organization. Shortly after incorporation, USW successfully completed a private placement of $5.4 million of common stock, primarily to several venture capital groups. In June 1981, the company raised an additional $5.2 million through a private placement of convertible preferred stock. Additional private placements of convertible preferred stock in 1982 and 1983 raised $4.3 million and $2.9 million respectively, each offering at higher implicit valuations as the company neared its goal of a reliable product. Jerry Alderson joined USW in 1980 as Vice President for Finance to develop and implement a plan for financing the company. He became President and CEO about a year

---

[1]In a limited partnership, the limited partners are not personally liable for the partnership's debts. Such a partnership must have at least one general partner who is fully liable.

EXHIBIT 1

U.S. WINDPOWER, INC.
Consolidated Balance Sheet
December 31, 1983 and 1982
(in thousands)

Assets

	1983	1982
Cash	$ 589	$ 1,421
Accounts receivable (Note 2)	6,791	—
Unbilled receivables (Note 1)	223	2,217
Partnership notes and interest receivable (Notes 1 and 3)	2,843	523
Inventories (Note 1)	2,284	1,491
Property, plant and equipment (net) (Notes 1 and 4)	4,792	4,183
Other assets	1,214	656
Total assets	$ 18,736	$ 10,491

Liabilities and Stockholders' Equity

	1983	1982
Bank loan payable (Note 5)	$ 6,800	—
Accounts payable	3,093	$ 3,168
Accrued liabilities	1,311	732
Long-term liabilities (Note 6)	1,346	2,030
Commitments and contingencies (Note 10)		
Total liabilities	12,550	5,930
Capital stock (Notes 7, 8, and 9)	163	127
Capital in excess of par value	18,192	15,322
Retained earnings (deficit)	(12,169)	(10,888)
Total stockholders' equity	6,186	4,561
Total liabilities and stockholders' equity	$ 18,736	$ 10,491

Consolidated Statement of Income
For the Year Ended December 31, 1983
(in thousands, except per share amount)

Sales (Notes 1 and 3)	$29,665
Cost of sales	26,240
Gross profit	3,425
Operating expenses:	
General and administrative	3,440
Engineering, research and development	2,919
	6,359
Operating (loss)	(2,934)
Interest income, net	1,757
Net (loss)	$ (1,177)
Net (loss) per common share	$(1.96)

The accompanying notes are an integral part of the consolidated financial statements.

EXHIBIT 1 *(continued)*

Notes to Consolidated Financial Statements

1. Significant Accounting Policies

Principles of Consolidation: The consolidated financial statements include the accounts of U.S. Windpower, Inc., and its wholly owned subsidiaries after elimination of intercompany accounts and transactions between the companies.

Revenue: As consideration for sale of Windplants®, the Company receives both cash and interest-bearing notes from the purchasers. These notes require level annual payments (principal and interest) over ten- or fifteen-year periods and are secured by an interest in the underlying assets. The Company recognizes revenue from the cash portion of the sales price on the percentage-of-completion method of accounting (the ratio of actual costs incurred to estimated total costs of each project).

As each phase of a project becomes completed, the purchaser delivers a note to the Company for the noncash portion of the sales price. The Company recognizes revenue in the amount of principal and interest on these notes as payments accrue over the ten- or fifteen-year periods.

Revenue from management, maintenance, and other services is recognized as earned. For the year ended December 31, 1983, this revenue totaled $338,000.

Inventories: Inventories, valued at the lower of cost or market, on a first-in, first-out basis, consist mainly of raw materials, work in process, and spare parts.

Depreciation: Depreciation is recorded on a straight-line basis calculated to recover the cost of the assets, less estimated salvage value, over their estimated useful lives:

Substations and control buildings	10 years
Machinery and equipment....................	2 to 10 years
Furniture and fixtures	5 years
Leasehold improvements....................	Lesser of the life of the improvement or the lease, generally 5 years.

Maintenance: These costs are charged to expense as incurred.

Engineering Research and Development: These costs are charged to expense as incurred.

Federal Income Taxes: The Company and its subsidiaries file consolidated federal income tax returns. The tax benefit of any losses is not recognized until recovery from future earnings can be reasonably assured. At December 31, 1983, the Company had net operating loss and investment tax credit carryforwards of approximately $19,500,000 and $530,000, respectively, portions of which would expire in years 1994 through 1998.

2. Accounts Receivable

At December 31, 1983, accounts receivable consisted of the following (in thousands):

Sales of Windplants®	$5,889
Advances to partnerships..................	902
	$6,791

3. Notes Receivable and Deferred Income

In connection with the Company's policy for recognizing revenue from notes and related interest thereon (see Note 1–Revenue) the Statement of Income includes $1,584,000 principal amount in revenues and $2,159,000 in interest income. A summary of accounts by machine model is shown below:

	Machine Model		
	56–100	*56–50*	*Total*
Partnership notes and interest receivable	$ 6,094	$ 37,239	$ 43,333
Deferred income (net)	(6,082)	(34,408)	(40,490)
	$ 12	$ 2,831	$ 2,843

The deferred income and related interest income will be recognized as revenues during the accounting periods in which the payments accrue, as explained in Note 1.

EXHIBIT 1 *(continued)*

At December 31, 1983, notes receivable and interest receivable payments of $85,000 and $1,439,000, respectively, were past due. The Company believes that these amounts will be collected in future periods.

4. Property, Plant, and Equipment

At December 31, 1983, property, plant, and equipment consists of (in thousands):

Machinery and equipment	$ 3,067
Substations and control buildings.......................	2,617
Furniture and fixtures and leasehold improvements	274
	5,958
Less accumulated depreciation.........................	(1,166)
	$ 4,792

Depreciation expense included in the income statement for the year ending December 31, 1983, was $891,000.

5. Bank Loan Payable

In connection with the construction of a Windplant® for Windpower Partners 1983–1 (see Note 10) the Company entered into a $34,000,000 revolving credit arrangement with several banks. Borrowings bear interest at 1 percent above the prime rate and are secured by substantially all of the assets of the Company. In addition, there are commitment and agency fees totaling three quarters of 1 percent per annum.

Borrowings during the year averaged $3,035,000. The highest amount borrowed was $10,400,000 and the weighted average interest rate, including fees, was 14.7 percent.

6. Long-Term Liabilities

Long-term liabilities consist of (1) a note payable in the amount of $750,000 due in twenty equal quarterly installments of $37,500, commencing March 31, 1985, and bearing interest at 20 percent per annum (certain notes receivable from the sale of Windplants® are collateral for the note), and (2) liabilities, aggregating $596,000, under a capitalized lease; installment purchases of property, plant, and equipment at interest rates ranging from 7 to 19 percent; and deferred compensation arrangements with two former employees.

Long-term liabilities mature $190,000 in 1984 and $296,000, $274,000, $245,000, $191,000, and $150,000 in the years 1985 through 1989, respectively.

7. Common Stock

Common stock at December 31, 1983, consisted of the following:

		Shares	
	Par Value	Authorized	Outstanding
Common Stock	$.01	2,200,000	672,732
Series B Junior Common Stock..........................	.01	100,000	97,519
Series C Junior Common Stock..........................	.01	200,000	—
		2,500,000	770,251

Each share of Series B and C Junior Common Stock entitles the holder to one-tenth of the voting and liquidation rights of one share of common stock. The holder of the Series B and C Junior Common Stock are not entitled to dividends.

Shares of Series B and C Junior Common Stock are not transferable and are convertible into regular common stock on a 1-for-1 basis on the last day of any fiscal year in which revenues are $20 million for Series B and $40 million for Series C and in which income before taxes and extraordinary items is $1 million and $2 million, respectively, or upon a merger under certain conditions in which the company is not the surviving entity, or when shares representing more than 50 percent of the voting power are exchanged, or upon the sale of substantially all of the assets of the Company. If the circumstances under which Series C Junior Common Stock becomes convertible into common stock have not occurred prior to December 31, 1988, the conversion rights will expire.

EXHIBIT 1 *(continued)*

At December 31, 1983, a total of 1,235,574 shares of the Company's authorized common stock have been reserved for issuance as follows:

Conversion of:	
Series B and C Junior Common Stock..................	300,000
Preferred Stock......................................	659,574
Stock Options and Warrants..........................	276,000
	1,235,574

8. Preferred Stock and Warrants

Preferred stock at December 31, 1983, consisted of the following:

	Par Value	*Shares Outstanding*
Preferred stock, 250,000 shares authorized:		
Series A..	$1.00	65,000
Series B	1.00	54,000
Series C	1.00	36,250
		155,250

All series of stock have a $6.40 per share cumulative annual dividend payable quarterly. During 1983, dividends of $104,000 were paid on the Series A preferred stock. In December, 1983, all preferred stockholders approved a moratorium on dividend payments until the third quarter, 1985. The Company has no accrued or in-arrears dividends on preferred stock.

All preferred stock was issued at $80 per share and is convertible into common stock at the option of the holder at conversion prices of $16, $26, and $28.50 per share respectively for Series A, B, and C stock. The conversion prices are subject to adjustment if certain dilutive events were to occur and all preferred stockholders vote separately as a single class to elect a prescribed number of members to the Board of Directors.

All series of preferred stock are redeemable at the option of the Company in each twelve-month period ending June 25 as follows: 1984 at 112 percent, 1985 at 110 percent, and declining 2 percent each year until 1990 and thereafter at 100 percent of the respective original sales price.

On each June 30, 1987 through 1990 for Series A, and June 30, 1988 through 1991 for Series B and C, the Company is obligated to redeem one-fourth of the shares issued at a price of $80 per share, subject to adjustment for shares converted prior to such date.

In conjunction with the preferred stock issues, the company has issued warrants and at December 31, 1983, has outstanding 75,117 warrants to purchase common stock at $10 per share. The warrants can be exercised at any time but expire as follows: 26,000 on June 25, 1991, and 49,117 on December 29, 1993. No warrants were exercised during the year.

9. Stock Options

The Company has an incentive common stock option plan and a restricted common stock option plan. In addition, nonqualified common stock options have been issued to certain employees and consultants of the Company. Incentive stock options are exercisable in installments from the date of the grant, and in all cases any unexercised options expire 10 years from the date of grant.

10. Commitments and Contingencies

The Company leases facilities under long-term operating leases with annual lease costs of $507,000 in 1984, $483,000 in 1985, $370,000 in 1986, $304,000 in 1987, and $286,000 in 1988 and thereafter. Lease expense for the year ended December 31, 1983, totaled $427,000.

The Company has entered into agreements for easements on certain land which require payments to landowners for the use of the property. The easements generally require initial payments and subsequent payments that are dependent upon gross revenues realized or the number of windmills installed. These agreements would require payments of approximately $200,000 per year for the years 1984 through 1988 unless the Company assigns them to purchasers of Windplants® or unless the Company decides at any time not to develop such properties. In 1983 easement payments totaled approximately $325,000.

EXHIBIT 1 *(concluded)*

Separate subsidiaries of the Company act as a general partner for each partnership and generally hold a 1 percent interest in the respective partnership. As a general partner, together with the other general partners, each subsidiary is liable for all debts, liabilities, and obligations of its respective partnership to the extent not paid by such partnerships.

In June 1983, Windpower Partners 1983–1 was formed and as such, the Company entered into a contract to construct a Windplant® with a projected annual output under estimated wind conditions of approximately 103 million kwh of electricity. At December 31, 1983, the Windplant® was approximately 20 percent complete. The Company has guaranteed payment of the principal and interest of a term note between a bank and Windpower Partners 1983–1 in the amount of $3,518,000. The note is due in three installments of $1,366,000 on March 12, 1984, $208,000 on September 12, 1984, and $1,944,000 on March 12, 1985, with interest at 1 percent over prime.

The Company is obligated under certain maintenance agreements and a three-year warranty agreement to warrant operation of the Windplants® it has sold in accordance with original equipment specifications. In addition, at its option, the Company has elected to implement certain technological improvements that have been developed in the manufacture of the more recent windmills. A program has been prescribed that will involve the retrofit of a substantial number of units to conform with current specifications at a cost aggregating approximately $4.3 million over the next three years.

At December 31, 1983, the Company had outstanding purchase commitments of approximately $5,100,000.

---

later. A 1970 graduate of the Harvard Business School, Alderson had first worked on the audit staff of Arthur Andersen & Co. In 1972, he left to join the Itel Corporation, a financial services firm, where he held a variety of financial and administrative positions.

USW's first commercial windpower plant was completed in late 1980 on a site in Greenfield, New Hampshire. It consisted of 20 windmills, each with a 30 kilowatt (kw) generator driven by a blade assembly with a swept diameter of 40 feet. These windmills used a microprocessor control system, a pitch control mechanism,[2] and other design concepts that were subsequently incorporated into later-model machines. Based on early experience with these first machines, USW's engineers decided to increase the blade length to a swept diameter of 56 feet and to incorporate a 50 kw generator in a new model, called the 56–50.

By the time of the development of the Model 56–50, the company had concluded that the best domestic opportunities for windpower plant construction were in California. There were two main reasons. First, California is divided by the Coastal Range into a region bordering the Pacific Ocean and an inland Central Valley. During the summer months, nearly unlimited sunshine over the Central Valley causes the atmosphere to heat up, with afternoon temperatures often rising to in excess of 100°F. This causes the air over the valley to rise, allowing cold Pacific air to rush in through mountain passes in the Coastal Range. This condition occurs at precisely the time when California electric utilities face their peak demands for air conditioning and agricultural irrigation purposes.

Second, the regulatory environment also favored construction in California. In 1978, to encourage the development of alternative energy sources, the U.S. Congress passed the Public Utility Regulatory Policies Act (PURPA). PURPA had a number of features, of which the most significant were:

---

[2] The pitch of the blade is its orientation to the wind. The pitch control mechanism controls this orientation to provide relatively constant power output at varying wind speeds.

1. *Qualifying facilities,* defined in the act as small power-generating facilities generating electricity using cogeneration[3] or alternatives to fossil fuels, were exempted from rate regulation by federal or state authorities.

2. Public utilities were required to allow these qualifying facilities to connect to their power-distribution grids and to buy power from them at the utilities' *avoided costs.* Avoided cost was the legislative counterpart of the economic concept of "marginal cost." Under PURPA, the avoided costs of a utility consist of two parts: energy costs and capacity costs. Energy costs are the variable costs associated with the production of energy and represent primarily the cost of fuel and certain operating and maintenance expenses. Capacity costs are the costs associated with the capability to deliver energy and consist primarily of the capital costs of facilities.

Although PURPA was a federal statute, PURPA required implementation by state regulatory agencies. The California authorities were particularly sympathetic to the objectives of PURPA. Indeed, the California Public Utilities Commission (CPUC), believing that small alternative-energy producers needed protection against the risk of fluctuation in fossil fuel prices, had authorized California utilities to enter into long-term power purchase agreements with alternative energy producers (such as USW) under which the producers could elect to receive, instead of actual avoided costs, a fixed price based on an estimate of future avoided costs.

---

[3]Cogeneration is a process whereby electric power is generated as a by-product of other industrial activities. A manufacturing plant generating steam for its own use, for example, might also use the steam to operate a turbine to generate electric power for sale to a utility.

USW therefore began to negotiate with landowners in Altamont Pass for the rights to erect windmills on their property. It also negotiated the first of a series of long-term power purchase agreements, which included the fixed-price feature described above, with Pacific Gas & Electric Co. (PG&E). The fixed price called for in these agreements was typically around 9 cents per kilowatt-hour (kwh) of electricity. The first USW windpower plant in Altamont Pass was completed in late 1981. By December 31, 1983, over 700 Model 56−50 machines had been installed in Altamont.

Early versions of the 56−50 experienced significant operational problems. At first USW attempted to deal with each problem as it arose by repairing the damaged machines and incorporating design changes in subsequent production machines. By mid-1983, it had become apparent that both the repaired machines and those manufactured with design changes were continuing to fail at an unacceptable rate. As a result USW decided to discontinue operating most of these machines until a more permanent solution could be developed. It was the company's expectation that eventually all of these early 56−50 machines would either be substantially modified or replaced with improved machines.

At approximately the same time that USW reached this decision, its engineers had completed the design of a new windmill, the Model 56−100. This new model used the same blades as the 56−50 but incorporated a larger generator capable of a 100 kw output. Five prototypes of the 56−100 were installed in Altamont Pass in June 1983 and performed satisfactorily during the peak summer wind months. As a result, the 56−100 was ordered into production in September 1983. By December of that year a total of 99 were installed in Altamont Pass.

EXHIBIT 2
INSTALLATION OF MODEL 56–100 WINDMILLS DURING 1984

Month	No. of Windmills Installed at Month-End	Average Percentage Availability
January	99	85*
February	99	93
March	99	95
April	99	95
May	102	99
June	211	93
July	285	94
August	351	95
September	373	96
October	376	97
November	376	96
December	601	93

*The relatively low availability in January is attributable to temporary and unusual failure, in the second week of the month, of a communication cable needed to control several groups of windmills from the control building. Because of the inability to communicate, the affected windmills were unavailable for actual operations, although all were undamaged and became operational as soon as communications were reestablished.

By the end of December 1984, approximately 600 Model 56–100 windmills would be installed in Altamont Pass. Exhibit 2 shows the number of 56–100 windmills installed as of the end of each month of 1984 and the average percentage availability for each month. During 1984, these windmills met or exceeded their projected cumulative energy production throughout the year. For the year as a whole, actual and projected output were virtually identical at almost 45 million kwh.

Sale of Windpower Plants. USW sold complete Windplants® rather than individual, stand-alone windmills. Each Windplant® was an integrated power plant, consisting of an array of windmills interconnected by a system of transformers and transmission lines for generating, collecting, and delivering electricity in commercial quantities to an electric utility grid for sale to the utility.

The typical customer for a Windplant® was a limited partnership formed for the express purpose of investing in the Windplant®. For each Windplant®, USW incorporated a new subsidiary to act as the general partner. Investors interested in the tax attributes of the Windplant® purchased limited partnership interests. The partnership then contracted with USW for construction of the plant and in turn sold the power generated by the plant to the utility. (For this purpose, USW assigned its rights under the power purchase agreement to the partnership.) The partnership entered into management and maintenance agreements with USW and deployed windmills on sites selected by USW. Most of the capital of the partnership was supplied by the limited partners. Because the Windplant® was financed by the partnership, the utility was able to obtain energy without the necessity of a high front-end investment. USW believed that this helped to overcome the utility's reluctance to rely on a seemingly new and untried technology. Eventually, however, USW expected to sell Windplants® directly to public utilities.

USW sold the Windplant® to the partnership at a price dependent on the plant's Designed Projected Output (DPO). DPO was a measure, expressed in kwh, of the amount of electricity the plant was expected to produce during a 12-month period. The actual output of an individual windmill depends on: (1) its power output at various wind speeds; (2) its availability to produce electricity, after allowance for downtime for repairs and maintenance; and (3) the actual wind conditions to which it is subjected. USW estimated that the average Model 56–100 windmill under average wind conditions in Altamont Pass would produce 210,000 kwh per year. Hence, the expected DPO of an Altamont Pass Windplant® consisting entirely of Model 56–100 machines would be 210,000 kwh times the number of machines in the plant.

USW warranted to the partnership that for three years after completion of construction the Windplant® would be free from defects and would perform in accordance with specifications. In determining whether the plant was performing up to its DPO specification, the actual output during the warranty period would be adjusted to reflect the difference between the actual wind conditions experienced and the statistically projected average wind conditions assumed in determining DPO. That is, USW did not warrant that actual wind conditions would equal or better the projected average conditions.

The price currently being charged by USW for a Windplant® was approximately $0.70 per kwh of DPO. The price was divided into two portions: a cash portion and a noncash portion. The cash portion was paid by the

EXHIBIT 3
COST OF A MODEL 56–100 WINDMILL

Standard manufacturing cost*	$40,500
Installation and other site-related costs	23,640
Total	$64,140

*Includes one windmill, three blades, one downtower control box, and all related cables. Calculated using full absorption of manufacturing overhead.

partnership in installments during plant construction. The noncash portion was represented by notes payable by the partnership to USW in 15 equal annual installments following completion of construction, with interest at 9 percent per annum on the unpaid balance of the notes.[4] Generally the cash portion was about half of the total purchase price, sufficient to compensate USW for its cost of manufacturing and installing the Windplant® (see Exhibit 3). In 1984, USW delivered 499 completed and installed Model 56–100 windmills to five limited partnerships and received payment for them in the form indicated in Exhibit 4.

The partnership paid USW the cash portion of the price out of the capital contributions of the limited partners. It was anticipated that interest and principal on the notes would be paid by the partnership out of the proceeds from the sale of electric power to the utility. The notes were liabilities of the partnership, not of the partners. Because of their limited liability, the limited partners were not obligated to contribute additional

---

[4]The interest rate was prescribed by the Internal Revenue Service as the minimum rate below which the borrower would be presumed to be receiving a taxable interest subsidy. As indicated in Note 5 to USW's annual report, the company was currently borrowing at approximately 15 percent per annum.

EXHIBIT 4
SALES OF MODEL 56–100 WINDMILLS IN 1984

Partnership	Machines Delivered	Cash Portion	Note Portion	Total Price
A	274	$24,459,000	$20,890,000	$45,349,000
B	65	5,430,000	4,577,000	10,007,000
C	89	5,518,000	8,146,000	13,664,000
D	5	490,000	458,000	948,000
E	66	4,702,000	5,520,000	10,225,000
Total	499	$40,599,000	$39,591,000	$80,190,000

capital to repay the notes, even if the proceeds from the sale of electricity were insufficient to repay them.[5] USW did, however, retain a security interest in the Windplant® and would be entitled to repossess it if the notes were not paid.

The Wind Energy Industry in California. About a dozen other companies were developing windpower plants in Altamont Pass, and there were also developments in other parts of the state. USW had about one-third of the installed capacity in Altamont Pass, and Altamont Pass had about one-half of the installed capacity in the state.

The wind energy industry can be divided into three main sectors: manufacturers, developers, and operators. Manufacturers conducted research and development on windmill design and produced the machines. Developers identified and acquired promising sites for windmills, acquired machines from manufacturers, and constructed the windmills on the sites. Operators maintained and operated the machines and sold the power generated to electric utilities.

USW was unusual in that it was active in all three sectors (as an operator, it acted as agent for the limited partnerships that actually owned the Windplants®). This was an essential element of the company's strategy. Given the experimental character of wind energy generation, USW management felt that is was important to retain operational control of the machines in order to be able to feed back information about operational problems into the R&D and manufacturing phases.

Jerry Alderson believed that many of the other companies in the industry were in the business primarily to take advantage of the tax incentives. He expected that when these incentives were no longer available—the federal energy tax credits were due to expire at the end of 1985 and the California ones at the end of 1986—there would be a shakeout of the industry, with companies manufacturing or deploying machines of inferior design leaving the business. He believed that this would have an adverse impact on the financial markets' perception of the wind energy industry in general. This would make it difficult for USW to achieve its objective of

---

[5]Although the limited partners were not "at risk" with respect to the noncash portion of the purchase price, a special provision of the U.S. Internal Revenue Code allowed the limited partners to use the full purchase price in calculating the Investment Tax Credits and Accelerated Cost Recovery System deductions. This included not only the regular 10 percent Investment Tax Credit but also an additional 15 percent Business Energy Credit. Similar provisions applied to California investors under the state income tax system.

going public during the period of adverse publicity.

Even those companies that survived would, in Alderson's opinion, have to adapt their tactics to the changed environment. In particular, he believed that in the absence of the tax incentives it would be impossible to continue to finance new Windplant® construction through the sale of limited partnership interests. He also believed that the wind energy technology was still too new to expect electric utilities to be willing to buy windpower plants. This seemed to present USW with two alternatives: (1) cease construction of new Windplants® and continue in business solely as an operator (as agent for the existing partnerships) of the Windplants® already completed as of the end of 1985; or (2) find new sources of financing that would permit USW to continue to build and operate Windplants®, but for its own account rather than for that of other parties.

Previous Revenue Recognition Practice. As mentioned at the beginning of this case, the accounting treatment of the notes received in partial payment for the sale of Windplants® had been an issue in every preceding fiscal period. For fiscal periods ending on or before December 31, 1982, USW had recognized interest and principal on the notes as revenue on the collection basis, that is, only when payments were received in cash. On the company's balance sheet, this treatment was reflected by showing a contra-asset, Deferred Income, that was equal in magnitude to the asset against which it was offset, Partnership Notes Receivable.

There were two reasons for this decision, both related to the limited operating experience with the installed machines. First, the collectibility of the notes, which depended upon the machines' ability to produce electric energy, was highly uncertain. Second, the company's liability under its warranty

was also highly uncertain. It was considered that both these uncertain and potentially offsetting amounts were of about the same order of magnitude and that, in view of the relatively small number of installed machines, the difference between them was not material. Hence, in management's opinion, excluding both items from the financial statements would result in a "fair" presentation of the company's financial position and results of operations. The auditors had concurred.

For the fiscal year ending December 31, 1983, with over 700 machines installed, the argument about materiality had much less force. Also, USW had begun to accumulate some operating experience on the machines, and it seemed appropriate to reflect this experience in the revenue recognition policy. As noted earlier, the experience with the earlier versions of the Model 56-50 was not very good, but the full dimensions of the problem were not yet evident at the end of 1983.

Taking all this into consideration, USW decided to recognize revenue on the notes received for 1983 Windplant® sales as the payments of interest and principal on the notes came due, regardless of whether the cash payments were made on schedule. As explained in Note 3 to the 1983 financial statements (Exhibit 1), this had the effect of recognizing as revenue in 1983 a total of $1,524,000 ($85,000 in notes receivable and $1,439,000 in interest receivable) that had not been paid when due—revenue that would not have been recognized under the collection method employed in 1982 and before.

The Decision for 1984. Given the favorable operating experience of the Model 56-100 machines, which was the only model newly installed during 1984, Alderson believed that it would be difficult to defend the relatively conservative revenue recognition approach that had been used through 1983. At the same time, he doubted that it would be appropriate to go to the other extreme and recognize the full face value of the notes, along with the cash portion of the sales price, upon completion of each Windplant®.

Alderson knew that Coopers & Lybrand would again issue an unqualified opinion on the 1984 financial statements only if they were persuaded that USW's accounting for the notes "fairly presented" USW's results of operations and its financial position and that the accounting was consistent with that followed in earlier years. He also knew that the auditors would be concerned about the auditability, or verifiability, of the statements.

Questions

1. In addition to the sales of Model 56–100 windmills shown in Exhibit 4, during 1984, $2,194,000 of principal payments came due on partnership notes received in connection with deliveries of windmills made in earlier years. All of the $2,194,000 was collected as due. Assuming that USW follows the same approach in recognizing revenue on Windplant® sales in 1984 as it did in 1983, estimate the amount of gross profit it will report on Windplant® sales for 1984.

2. Using case information, prepare as best you can a cash flow statement for the year ending December 31, 1983. Using this statement, as well as the financial statements in Exhibit 1, be prepared to comment on USW's financial condition as of December 31, 1983.

3. As Jerry Alderson, what would you recommend to the Audit Committee and to the outside auditors regarding revenue recognition on 1984 Windplant® deliveries?

MANAGEMENT ACCOUNTING

15

The Nature of Management Accounting

Part 1 focused on financial accounting—information reported in financial statements prepared primarily for shareholders, creditors, and other interested parties *outside* the organization. Part 2, the remainder of the book, discusses accounting information intended for the use of the organization's management.

This chapter distinguishes management accounting information from other types of information. We compare and contrast management accounting information with information used for financial reporting. The three main uses of management accounting information are described. The chapter concludes with some general observations regarding the use of accounting information by management.

MANAGEMENT ACCOUNTING AS ONE TYPE OF INFORMATION

As explained in Chapter 1, **management accounting** is the process within an organization that provides information used by an organization's managers in planning, implementing, and controlling the organization's activities. This process includes the identification, measurement, accumulation, analysis, preparation, interpretation, and communication of the information needed by management to perform its functions.[1] Management accounting

---

[1] Adapted from "Definition of Management Accounting," *IMA Statement Number 1A* (March 1981).

is applicable to all organizations: It is used by profit-oriented manufacturing, merchandising, financial, and service businesses and also by government and other nonprofit organizations of all types.

Whereas financial accounting has been written about for over 400 years, little was written about management accounting until the 20th century. The actual practice of management accounting goes back much further, however. The need for a type of accounting not aimed primarily at the preparation of financial statements was set forth in this 1875 memorandum by Thomas Sutherland, a British business executive:

> The present system of bookkeeping . . . is admirably suited for . . . ascertaining once a year or oftener the profits upon the company's transactions; but it is evident that in a business of this kind much detailed information is necessary regarding the working of the Company, and this information should be obtainable in such a practical form as to enable the managers to see readily and clearly the causes at work in favor of or against the success of the Company's operations.

In North America early management accounting systems were developed by textile mills and railroads in the latter half of the 19th century. Later, producers of tobacco products, steel, detergents, photographic film, and flour adapted the railroads' systems to their own organizations' needs. By 1925 most aspects of today's management accounting systems had been developed.[2]

Although these systems were developed primarily in large companies (most of them manufacturing firms), management accounting is applicable to both profit-seeking and nonprofit organizations of all sizes. In this book we often illustrate these systems in manufacturing settings because the systems required for other settings tend to be simpler and less complete; for example, a fast-food restaurant does not need an elaborate system to value its inventories, but most manufacturing firms do.

Information

Information is a fact, datum, observation, perception, or any other thing that adds to knowledge. The number 1,000 taken by itself is not information; the statement that 1,000 students are enrolled in a certain school *is* information.

Management accounting is one type of information. Its place in the whole picture is shown in Illustration 15–1 (identical to Illustration 1–1). As was described in Chapter 1, an organization's day-to-day activities require (and also generate) a considerable amount of *operating* information. This information provides the raw material for the summarized information that is reported in the financial accounting and management accounting processes.

Managers want whatever type of information that will help them do their jobs, whether the information be accounting or nonaccounting, quantitative

---

[2]For a fuller description of the history of management accounting, see Robert S. Kaplan, "The Evolution of Management Accounting," *Accounting Review,* July 1984.

ILLUSTRATION 15–1
TYPES OF INFORMATION

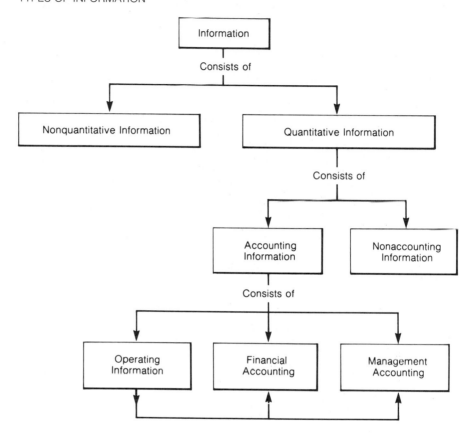

or nonquantitative. A rumor that an important customer is dissatisfied with a company's product and is about to change suppliers is neither accounting nor quantitative information, but is certainly important.[3]

Management Accounting

Part 1 focused on the three required financial statements: the balance sheet, income statement, and statement of cash flows. Although these financial statements are prepared for use by outside parties such as shareholders and creditors, they obviously are also useful to management. They provide an overall picture of an entity's financial condition and the results of its activities. Managerial uses of this information were described in Part 1.

---

[3]Books on organizational behavior discuss this nonquantitative information in depth. For example, in his classic study, *The Nature of Managerial Work* (New York: Harper & Row, 1973), p. 36, Henry Mintzberg reports that "gossip, speculation, and hearsay form a most important part of the manager's information diet."

Management, however, needs much more detailed financial information than that contained in the financial statements. In Part 2 we focus on this additional information.

Although operating information provides the raw data for management accounting, much of this information is not of direct interest to managers. In the normal course of events, a manager does not care about the amount of money an individual customer owes, the amount an individual employee earned last week, or the amount deposited in the bank yesterday. Records must be kept of these facts, but these records ordinarily are used by operating personnel rather than by managers. The manager is interested in summaries drawn from these records rather than in the underlying details.

In general, therefore, management accounting information is *summary* information. To understand it, one needs to know something about the source of raw data, but only enough to be able to understand the resulting summaries.

Management Accountants

Those employees of an organization who are responsible for the design and operation of the management accounting system are called **management accountants.** In many organizations the highest-level management accountant is called the **controller.** The controller in smaller organizations typically reports directly to the president. In larger organizations, the controller reports to an executive vice president or a vice president of finance, who in turn reports to the president. Many controllers are also responsible for their organization's financial reporting function. In larger organizations, however, the controller's responsibilities are primarily directed inward—the controller's job is to provide information that can be used within the organization by its managers. By contrast, more outward-directed tasks such as arranging loans and other external sources of funds are usually the responsibility of a separate financial manager, often called the **treasurer.**

Management accountants have a professional program that grants the designation of **Certified Management Accountant (CMA).** In order to become a CMA, the candidate must pass a four-part examination. Afterward, continuing education credits and adherence to a code of ethics are required to maintain the certification. Unlike the CPA (Certified Public Accountant) certification, which state laws require public accountants to hold as a condition for practicing, the CMA program is voluntary. Some organizations require the CMA for advancement within their controller's departments.[4]

The CMA program is administered by the Institute of Certified Management Accountants, which is affiliated with the professional organization of management accountants, the Institute of Management Accountants (IMA).

---

[4]For more information about the CMA program, write the Institute of Certified Management Accountants, 10 Paragon Drive, Montvale, NJ 07645-0405.

The IMA publishes a journal, *Management Accounting*, and through its various local chapters conducts educational programs for its members. (In Canada the Society of Management Accountants plays a similar role.) The IMA also issues *Statements on Management Accounting.* Although not binding on organizations, these statements provide useful guidance in the design of management accounting systems.

The role and status of management accountants have increased in recent years. Once viewed primarily as a cost accounting technician, the controller increasingly is a key member of the top management team, a member of the board of directors in some organizations. Similarly, the members of the controller's department are taking on tasks involving the analysis of information, whereas their job in earlier years was primarily to collect and report information for others to analyze.

CONTRAST BETWEEN MANAGEMENT ACCOUNTING AND FINANCIAL REPORTING

Management accounting differs in several ways from the financial reporting process that was the focus of Part 1. To facilitate the transition from the study of financial accounting to management accounting, it is useful to state these differences and also to point out similarities.

Differences

Twelve important differences between management and financial accounting are described here. They are summarized in Illustration 15–2.

1. Necessity. Financial accounting *must* be done. Enough effort must be expended to collect data in acceptable form and with an acceptable degree of accuracy to meet the requirements of the Financial Accounting Standards Board (FASB), the Securities and Exchange Commission (SEC), and other outside parties, whether or not the management regards this information as useful. Management accounting, by contrast, is entirely optional: No outside agencies specify what must be done or that *anything* need be done. Because it is optional, there is no point in collecting a piece of management accounting information unless its value to management is believed to exceed the cost of collecting it.

2. Purpose. The purpose of financial accounting is to produce financial statements for outside users. When the statements have been produced, this purpose has been accomplished. Management accounting information, on the other hand, is only a means to an end, the end being the planning, implementing, and controlling functions of management.

3. Users. The users of financial accounting information (other than management itself) often are essentially a faceless group. The managements of most companies do not personally know many shareholders, creditors, or others who use the information in the financial statements. Moreover, the information needs of most of these external users must be presumed; most external users do not individually request the information they would like

ILLUSTRATION 15–2
MANAGEMENT ACCOUNTING CONTRASTED WITH FINANCIAL REPORTING

Dimension	Management Accounting	Financial Reporting
1. Necessity	Optional	Required
2. Purpose	A means to the end of assisting management	Produce statements for outside users
3. Users	Relatively small group; known identity	Relatively large group; mostly unknown
4. Underlying structure	Varies according to use of the information	One basic equation: Assets = Liabilities + Owners' Equity
5. Source of principles	Whatever is useful to management	GAAP
6. Time orientation	Historical and estimates of the future	Historical
7. Information content	Monetary and nonmonetary	Primarily monetary
8. Information precision	Many approximations	Fewer approximations
9. Report frequency	Varies with purpose; monthly and weekly common	Quarterly and annually
10. Report timeliness	Reports issued promptly after end of period covered	Delay of weeks or even months
11. Report entity	Responsibility centers	Overall organization
12. Liability potential	Virtually none	Few lawsuits, but threat is always present

to receive. By contrast, the users of management accounting information are known managers plus the people who help these managers analyze the information. Internal users' information needs are relatively well known because the controller's office solicits these needs in designing or revising the management accounting system.

4. Underlying Structure. Financial accounting is built around one fundamental equation: Assets = Liabilities + Owners' Equity. In management accounting there are three primary purposes of accounting information, each with its own set of concepts and constructs. (These three will be described later in this chapter.)

5. Source of Principles. Financial accounting information must be reported in accordance with generally accepted accounting principles (GAAP). Outside users need assurance that the financial statements are prepared in accordance with a mutually understood set of ground rules; otherwise, they cannot understand what the numbers mean. GAAP provides these common ground rules.

An organization's management, by contrast, can employ whatever accounting rules it finds most useful for its own purposes. Thus, in management accounting, there may be information on unfilled sales orders (i.e., backlog), even though these are not financial accounting transactions; fixed assets may be stated at current values rather than historical cost; certain production overhead costs may be omitted from inventories; or revenues may be recorded before they are realized—even though each of these concepts is inconsistent with GAAP. Rather than asking whether it conforms to GAAP, the basic question in management accounting is pragmatic: Is the information useful?

6. Time Orientation. Financial accounting records and reports the financial *history* of an organization. Entries are made in the accounts only after transactions have occurred. Although financial accounting information is used as a basis for making future plans, the information itself is historical. Management accounting includes, in its *formal* structure, numbers that represent estimates and plans for the future as well as information about the past. The objective of financial accounting is to "tell it like it *was*," not like it *will be*.

7. Information Content. The financial statements that are the end product of financial accounting include primarily monetary information. Management accounting reports deal with nonmonetary as well as monetary information. These reports show quantities of material as well as its monetary cost, number of employees and hours worked as well as labor costs, units of products sold as well as dollar amounts of revenue, defect rates as well as scrap costs, and so on. Some of the information is strictly nonmonetary; examples include the percentage of shipments made on time, the number of customer complaints received, and major competitors' estimated market shares.

8. Information Precision. Management needs information rapidly and is often willing to sacrifice some precision to gain speed in reporting. Thus, in management accounting approximations are often as useful as, or even more useful than, numbers that are more precise. Although financial accounting cannot be absolutely precise either, the approximations used in management accounting are broader than those in financial accounting.

9. Report Frequency. Corporations issue detailed financial statements only annually and less detailed interim reports quarterly. By contrast, fairly detailed management accounting reports are issued monthly in most larger organizations, and reports on certain activities may be prepared weekly, daily, or even in real time.

10. Report Timeliness. Because of the need for precision and a review by outside auditors, plus the time requirements of printing and distribution, financial accounting reports are distributed several weeks after the close of the accounting period. Larger corporations' annual reports for a fiscal year ending December 31 generally are not received by shareholders until March or April. By contrast, because management accounting reports may contain information on which management needs to take prompt action, these reports are usually issued within a few days of the end of a month (or the next morning for a daily report).

11. Report Entity. Financial statements describe the organization as a whole. Although companies that do business in several industries are required to report revenues and income for each industry, these are large segments of the whole enterprise. Management accounting by contrast focuses mainly on relatively small parts of the entity—on individual products, individual activities, or individual divisions, departments, and other responsibility centers. As we shall see, the necessity for dividing the total costs of an organization among these individual parts creates important problems in management accounting that do not exist in financial accounting.

12. Liability Potential.   Although it happens infrequently, a company may be sued by its shareholders or creditors for allegedly reporting misleading financial information in its annual report or in SEC filings. By contrast, as previously stated, management accounting reports need not be in accord with GAAP and are not public documents. Although a manager may be held liable for some illegal or unethical action and management accounting information conceivably may have played some role in his or her taking that action, it is the action itself, not the management accounting documents, that gives rise to the liability.

Similarities

Although differences do exist, most elements of financial accounting are also found in management accounting. There are two reasons for this. First, the same considerations that make GAAP sensible for purposes of financial accounting are likely to be relevant for purposes of management accounting. For example, management cannot base its reporting system on unverifiable, subjective estimates of profits submitted by lower echelons; for the same reason, financial accounting adheres to the cost and realization concepts.

Second, operating information is used both in preparing the financial statements and in management accounting. There is a presumption, therefore, that the basic data will be collected in accordance with generally accepted financial accounting principles. To do otherwise would require duplication of data collection activities.

Perhaps the most important similarity between financial and management accounting information is that both are used in decision making. Financial accounting information assists investors in evaluating companies' prospects so that decisions can be made about supplying debt or equity funds to these companies. Management accounting information is used in a wider array of decisions made by managers, including (but by no means limited to) decisions about product pricing, whether to buy some good or service on the outside or produce it inside, whether to make major investments in long-lived assets, and whether a responsibility center manager is deserving of a promotion or bonus.

Source Disciplines

Accounting is an applied subject. All applied subjects are based on foundations and concepts developed in a basic science or discipline. Whereas financial accounting has a single source discipline, management accounting has two such source disciplines. Financial accounting and part of management accounting are related to *economics,* which deals with the principles governing decisions on the use of scarce resources. Another part of management accounting is related to *social psychology,* which deals with the principles governing human behavior in organizations.

These two disciplines are quite dissimilar, which causes problems in understanding the management accounting principles derived from them. For example, for the purpose of deciding whether to purchase a new long-lived asset, the relevant accounting information is that developed according to principles of economics; but for the purpose of preparing a budget for the responsibility center in which that same asset is used, the principles of social psychology are at least equally important. Economics is impersonal; social psychology focuses on how people react to the information.

Some economists and some social psychologists criticize management accounting. Much of this criticism arises because each group has the mistaken belief that management accounting relates solely to its discipline. One of the significant problems in the real world is to give the appropriate weight to each of these disciplines.

TYPES OF MANAGEMENT ACCOUNTING INFORMATION AND THEIR USES

As noted above, financial accounting is essentially a single process, governed by a single set of generally accepted accounting principles and unified by the basic equation: Assets = Liabilities + Owners' Equity. Management accounting is more complicated. It does make use of a single system, but information in that system is used for two quite different purposes: (1) the measurement of revenues, costs, and assets; and (2) control. Management accounting has an additional purpose: To aid in choosing among alternative courses of action (called *alternative choice problems*). The information used for this third purpose cannot come directly from the management accounting *system* because each alternative choice problem requires its own arrangement of accounting information, and the system cannot feasibly provide for these variations.

There is no single unifying equation similar to the equation that governs all financial accounting. Moreover, for each of the three management accounting purposes there is a set of principles and generalizations applicable to the use of information for that purpose, but not necessarily for the other purposes. If a generalization that is valid for one purpose is applied to a problem that has another purpose, a serious error may result.

The uses of information for each of the three purposes of management accounting are summarized in Illustration 15−3. Some of these uses relate to historical information and others to estimates of the future. The former is a record of what has happened, and the latter is an estimate of what is going to happen. In Herbert Simon's useful characterization, historical data tend to be *score-keeping* information (How are we doing?) or *attention-directing*

ILLUSTRATION 15–3
PURPOSES AND USES OF MANAGEMENT ACCOUNTING INFORMATION

	Uses	
Purpose	Historical Data	Future Estimates
Measurement	Basis for external reporting Analyzing economic performance Cost-type contract payments	Normal pricing decisions
Control	Analyzing managerial performance Motivating and rewarding managers	Strategic planning Budgeting
Alternative choices	None	Short-run decisions (including contribution pricing) Capital budgeting

information (What problems require looking into?); by contrast, future estimates tend to be *problem-solving* information (What is the best way to deal with the problem?).[5] We would add that the reporting of either historical information or future estimates has an *influencing* impact in the sense that the reporting of such information tends to influence the actions of managers as they perform their day-to-day activities (for the same reasons that report cards tend to influence students' behavior).

The accounting information used for each purpose can be revenues, costs, expenses, assets, and/or liabilities. For convenience, in the introductory description that follows we focus on costs. Examples of the use of each type of cost are given, drawn from the experience of Varsity Motors Company, the automobile dealership introduced in Chapter 1.

Measurement

For the measurement purpose the management accounting system focuses on the measurement of *full costs*. (Other cost constructs that can be derived from a system that measures full costs will be described in later chapters.)

Full cost accounting measures the resources used in performing some activity. The full cost of producing goods or providing services is the sum of (1) the costs directly traced to the goods or services, called **direct costs,** plus (2) a fair share of costs incurred jointly in producing these and other goods or services, called **indirect costs.** Full cost accounting measures not only the direct and indirect costs of producing goods or providing services but also the direct and indirect costs of any other activity of interest to management, such as performing a research project or operating an employee cafeteria. Thus, full cost accounting is not restricted solely to measuring the costs of manufactured goods, as some people assume.

---

[5]Herbert A. Simon et al., *Centralization vs. Decentralization in Organizing the Controller's Department* (New York: Controllership Foundation, 1954), p. 3.

Example. In Varsity Motors, the direct costs of an automobile repair job include the cost of the parts used in the job and the cost of the time of the technician who performed the job. The full cost of the job includes these direct costs plus a fair share of the indirect costs, such as heating and lighting the repair shop, the shop supervisor's salary, property taxes, insurance, and even the president's salary.

Historical full costs are used in financial reporting. We have already discussed this use, particularly in Chapter 6, which gave the journal entries that accumulated materials costs, direct labor costs, and other production costs for goods as these goods moved through the production process.[6]

In many sales contracts the buyer agrees to pay the seller the cost of the goods produced or of the services rendered, plus a profit margin. Cost, in this context, usually means full cost. Similarly, in deciding what price to charge for its goods or services, a company often uses estimates of full costs plus a profit margin as a guide. Nonprofit organizations whose operations are financed by fees charged, such as colleges and hospitals, base these fees on the estimated full cost of the services rendered.

Finally, estimates of full costs are used in some types of planning activities, particularly in the type of long-range planning called strategic planning.

In Chapters 17–19 we describe the measurement of full cost information and its uses.

Control

The management accounting system is structured so that it measures costs by responsibility centers. A **responsibility center** is an organization unit headed by a manager who is responsible for its operations and performance. Such a structure is necessary because control can be exercised only through people.

Estimates of future responsibility costs are used in the planning process, particularly in the annual planning process called budgeting. Historical records of actual costs incurred in the responsibility centers are used in reporting and analyzing their performance. Such reports are useful because they are aligned with the organizational structure of managers who are responsible for performance. Corrective action can be taken only by individuals; so if performance is unsatisfactory, the person responsible must be identified before corrective action can be taken.

Example. Varsity Motors' June service department income statement indicated that the cost of repair parts was higher than it usually was for a similar dollar volume of service department activity. In investigating this matter, Lee

---

[6]Generally accepted accounting principles do not require that *all* items of production cost be included in the valuation of inventory. *Accounting Research Bulletin No. 43* states that the *omission of all overheads* from inventory is prohibited; so, taken literally, it permits the inclusion of some, but fewer than all, elements of full production cost. Nevertheless, most companies value inventories at their full production cost; a few companies exclude depreciation on production facilities.

Carroll realized that the service department's statement did not distinguish between parts used for service department repair jobs and those sold to service stations and to people who repair their cars themselves. After careful consideration, Lee Carroll decided to divide the service department into two responsibility centers, one responsible for repair work and the other responsible for parts sales (whether sold to outsiders or "sold" to the repair work department). In the future separate reports would be prepared for each of these responsibility centers.

Chapters 20–25 describe the uses of cost information structured by responsibility centers.

Alternative Choice Decisions

Many decisions involve the comparison of the estimated costs to be incurred (and also the revenues to be realized and/or assets to be employed) for each of the alternatives being considered. This information cannot be obtained directly from the management accounting system because the relevant costs are specific to the alternatives being considered.

These costs are always estimates of future costs. As with estimates of all types, they are sometimes derived from historical cost records. Because these estimates describe how costs would be different in the alternatives being considered, they are often called **differential costs.**

> **Example.** Ford Motor Company has offered Varsity Motors the opportunity to sell and service Ford trucks in addition to Ford automobiles. In considering this offer, company president Lee Carroll and the dealership's accountant estimated the additional annual revenues that truck sales and service might provide, as well as the additional cost of sales, costs of a truck salesperson and truck mechanics, and additional asset costs for truck parts inventory and an expansion of the repair shop. These revenue, operating cost, and asset items are all differential to Varsity Motors' present mode of operations. Carroll decided to reject the offer because the estimated differential return on investment was unsatisfactory.

Many alternative choice decisions involve short-run problems that relate only to a specific part of the business. For these decisions only estimated direct costs are relevant. These problems are described in Chapter 26. Other decisions are longer-range and involve the whole business or a major segment of it. For these decisions full costs are relevant. They are discussed in Chapter 27.

GENERAL OBSERVATIONS ON MANAGEMENT ACCOUNTING

Before getting into the details, we here make some general observations about the nature and use of management accounting information. These should be kept in mind throughout the rest of the book.

Different Numbers for Different Purposes

Mathematics has definitions that are valid under a wide variety of circumstances. Such is not the case with most accounting definitions. Each of the several purposes previously described requires a different accounting approach. Since these different numbers may superficially resemble one another, a person not familiar with them may easily become confused or frustrated.

The most common source of confusion is the word *cost*. In management accounting there are historical costs, standard costs, overhead costs, variable costs, differential costs, marginal costs, opportunity costs, direct costs, estimated costs, full costs, and other kinds of costs. Some of these terms are synonyms; others are almost but not quite synonyms; still others, although not synonyms at all, are used by some people as if they were.

Accounting numbers should always be discussed in terms of the particular problem that they are intended to help solve rather than in any abstract sense. A statement that "the cost of such-and-such is $100" literally has no meaning unless those who hear this statement understand clearly which of the several possible concepts of cost was intended.

Accounting Numbers Are Approximations

As is the case with any measurement, an accounting number is an approximation rather than a precisely accurate amount. Most of the data used in the physical sciences are also measurements. Like scientists and engineers, users of accounting information must acquire an understanding of the degree of approximation present in the data. Consider, for example, the concept of temperature. With the proper instruments the human body's temperature is easily measured to a tenth of a degree, but the sun's temperature is measurable only with an accuracy of 100 degrees or so. Although these measurements differ widely in their precision, each is useful for a particular purpose.

Similarly, some accounting numbers (such as the amount of cash on hand) may be accurate within very narrow limits, whereas others are only rough approximations. The degree of approximation is especially high in the case of numbers used for planning purposes, because these are always estimates of what will happen in the future.

Working with Incomplete Data

No one could reasonably ask students to solve a mathematics problem without furnishing them all the needed information. In a management problem, on the other hand, one almost never has exactly the information one would like to have. The person struggling with the problem usually can think of additional information that, if available, would be helpful. Conversely, there are many decision-making situations in which pages of numbers are available but only a small portion is truly relevant to the problem at hand and perhaps none of them is quite what one needs to solve it.

That problems must be solved, however, is a fact of life. Management decisions must be made and the decision often cannot be delayed until all pertinent information is available. We do the best we can with what we have and then move on to the next problem.

On the other hand, a decision should not be made if a vital, obtainable piece of evidence is missing. Deciding whether or not to act on the available evidence is one of the most difficult parts of the whole decision process. As Wallace B. Donham put it: "The art of business is the art of making irrevocable decisions on the basis of inadequate information."

Accounting Evidence Is Only Partial Evidence

Few, if any, management problems can be solved solely by the collection and analysis of numbers. Usually, there are important factors that cannot be, or have not been, reduced to quantitative terms. For example, consider how the performance of a baseball or softball player is judged. Detailed records are kept on each player's times at bat, walks, hits, strikeouts, putouts, stolen bases, and so on. Nevertheless, when a decision must be made as to whether Player A is better than Player B, the manager of the team knows better than to rely completely on this numerical information. Such factors as how well a player gets along with teammates, ability to hit in crucial situations, and other unmeasurable characteristics must also be taken into account.

Most organizations are much more complicated than baseball or softball teams. The "game" of business goes on all day, every day, rather than a finite number of times a year (162, in the case of major league baseball), and business results are not expressed by the number of games won and lost. Business measurements are therefore much more difficult and less precise than sports statistics.

Some people act as if most problems can be completely solved by numerical analysis. At the other extreme are those who believe that intuition is the sure guide to a sound decision and therefore pay no attention to numbers. Although the correct attitude is clearly somewhere between these extremes, there is no way to describing precisely where it is. The essential difficulty has been well summed up by G. K. Chesterton:

> The real trouble with this world of ours is not that it is an unreasonable world, nor even that it is a reasonable one. The commonest kind of trouble is that it is nearly reasonable, but not quite. Life is not an illogicality; yet it is a trap for logicians. It looks just a little more mathematical and regular than it is; its exactitude is obvious, but its inexactitude is hidden; its wildness lies in wait.

People, Not Numbers, Get Things Done

An obvious fact about organizations is that they consist of human beings. Anything that an organization accomplishes is the result of human actions. Although numbers can assist the people in an organization in various ways, the numbers by themselves accomplish nothing. But numbers don't talk back; they give the appearance of being definite and precise. It is a comforting illusion to imagine that the construction of a set of numbers is the same as acting on a real problem.

A management accounting system may be well designed and carefully operated, but the system is of no use to management unless it results in *action* by human beings. For instance, three companies may use exactly the same system with entirely different results. In one company the system may be *useless* because management never acts on the information collected and the organization has become aware of this fact. In the second company the system may be *helpful* because management uses the information as a general guide for planning, implementation, and control and has educated the organization to use it in the same spirit. In the third company, the system may be worse than useless. It may be *damaging* because management overemphasizes the importance of the numbers and therefore takes unwise actions.

SUMMARY

Accounting is one type of information. The total amount of information available to a manager includes nonquantitative as well as quantitative elements. The quantitative elements include both monetary and nonmonetary amounts. Accounting is primarily monetary but includes related nonmonetary data.

Most accounting information, in terms of quantity of data, is operating information. This operating information provides the raw data for financial statements. Essentially, these statements are summaries to meet the needs of investors and other outside parties. They are also used by managers inside the organization.

As contrasted with financial reporting, management accounting is optional rather than required; is a means to an end rather than an end in itself; is used by a relatively small group of known individuals with known information needs rather than by outside parties whose needs must be presumed; has three sets of constructs rather than one; is not governed by GAAP; has more emphasis on the future; includes more nonmonetary information; has less emphasis on precision; involves more frequent reports, which are issued on a more timely basis; and does not expose the company to lawsuits by users of the reports. Nevertheless, the two types of accounting have much in common.

A management accounting system provides historical and estimated information on full costs (and components of full cost) structured by responsibility centers to support the measurement and control purposes of management accounting information. The information used for alternative choice decisions consists of estimates that are relevant to the specific alternatives being considered. These estimates cannot be obtained directly from the management accounting system.

In solving management accounting problems, keep in mind that certain terms, principally *cost,* are defined differently depending on the purpose; that accounting numbers are approximations; that they rarely provide exactly the information needed; that much more than accounting information is needed in the solution of a problem; and that people, not numbers, get things done.

Cases

Upon returning to civilian life after several years in the Navy, Sarah Bates sought a small business that she might buy. Being a thrifty person with no dependents, she had built up a fair amount of savings, the accumulation of which had been aided by the fact that she had seen considerable duty in areas where there had been nothing to buy.

Bates finally located a small boatyard for sale in a town on the coast of Maine where she had spent many summers. The proprietor was getting along in years and wished to retire. He was offering the yard for sale at what Bates believed to be a fair starting price that could probably be worked down to a very reasonable figure through negotiation.

It is not necessary here to go into the details of investigation and negotiation. Bates bought the yard. The business being somewhat larger than she could finance alone, she had borrowed the additional funds required from a friend, giving a mortgage on the property as security.

Bates realized the need for adequate accounting records if she was to manage the business successfully. The records on hand were for cash receipts and disbursements only. Actual balance sheets and profit and loss statements that had been prepared for the former owner for tax purposes were also

available. A person who was a reasonably capable bookkeeper and general office factotum had been inherited with the business.

Having had a course in accounting in college, Bates felt capable of using cost and financial information with some intelligence, but did not feel capable of initiating a suitable accounting system. Knowing that you, an old friend of hers, have been studying such matters, she has asked your advice as to what kind of accounting records should be kept and what kind of financial and cost information should be developed to control operations and to make proper charges to customers for services rendered. In addition to the information above, she has told you the following facts about the business.

One of the properties of the business was a large shed for the winter storage of boats. Being the most suitable building in the locality for such storage, there was great demand for space in it on the part of owners of expensive boats among the summer people.

There was plenty of empty land on the shorefront for outdoor storage. In most cases where space was rented for this purpose, the yard was also hired to haul the boats in on equipment that it had for the purpose.

In the spring and from time to time during other seasons, there was a goodly amount of business available in painting and repair work on boats.

There was a large-sized work shed containing woodworking tools and space in

*Copyright © by the President and Fellows of Harvard College. Harvard Business School case 149-003.

which to construct about six boats up to 40 feet in length at one time. Larger boats could be built outside when the weather was suitable, but Bates did not expect to get many, if any, orders for such craft. She did, however, expect to have from one to six boats up to 40 feet in length in construction at all times, some for local fishermen and some for summer people.

The property included a good-sized wharf and float, a store for the sale of marine hardware and supplies, and gasoline pumps. There being no yacht club in the town, the summer people who were boating-minded tended to gather around this wharf and store. Bates intended to encourage this and to add fishing tackle, sporting goods, and refreshments to the items handled by the store.

Question

What would you tell Bates concerning her accounting needs?

16

The Behavior of Costs

Understanding **cost-volume relationships**—how costs behave as the level of activity changes—is necessary for understanding the various uses of management accounting information described in later chapters. Accordingly, this chapter presents the concepts of fixed and variable costs as well as step-function costs. Cost behavior information can be combined with revenue information to develop a profitgraph, which this chapter discusses along with the related concept of contribution.

RELATION OF COSTS TO VOLUME

If an entity significantly increases the amount of goods or services it produces, then the amount of resources required to produce this higher volume should also increase: that is, higher volume causes higher costs. In many instances, however, the percentage increase in costs is *less than* the percentage increase in volume. To understand how this happens, it is necessary to understand the concepts of variable and fixed costs.

Variable and Fixed Costs

Variable costs are items of cost that vary, *in total,* directly and proportionately with volume. Thus, if volume increases 10 percent, the total amount of variable cost also increases by 10 percent. A common example of a variable cost item is materials cost.

Example. This table shows the total variable cost of cathode ray tubes used in producing computer monitors:

Number of Monitors	Cost per Monitor	Total Variable Cost
1	$24	$ 24
2	24	48
10	24	240
100	24	2,400
200	24	4,800

Note two things in this example. First, the volume measure (more broadly, the measure of the *level of activity*) is specified. In this case, volume is measured as the number of monitors produced. When labeling a cost as variable, the activity level with which the cost item varies must be clear. Second, the total cost is variable because the cost *per unit of volume* remains constant: $24 per monitor in the example. To avoid confusion, remember that the term *variable cost* refers to costs whose *total* varies proportionately with volume.

Other examples of variable costs include the cost of powering equipment (variable with the number of hours the equipment is on), stationery and postage costs (variable with the number of letters written), salespersons' commissions (variable with the number of sales dollars generated), and vehicle fuel costs (variable with the number of miles traveled).

Fixed costs are items of cost that, in total, do not vary at all with volume. Building rent, property taxes, and management salaries are examples. These costs may increase with time, but they do not vary because of changes in the level of activity within a specified period of time. Because of inflation, a restaurant's rent for next year may be higher than it is this year; but within this year, the rent is unaffected by the day-to-day changes in the restaurant's volume (number of customers).

Because the amount of a fixed cost is constant in total, the amount of fixed cost *per unit of activity* decreases as volume increases (and conversely, fixed cost per unit increases as volume decreases). For example, if a salaried sales clerk is paid $300 a week and waits on 400 customers in a certain week, then the cost per customer is $0.75 (= $300 ÷ 400). If in the following week the same clerk waits on 500 customers, then the cost per customer that week is $0.60 (= $300 ÷ 500). It becomes clear from the example that when volume increases, the cost per customer decreases. Note that for a fixed cost item, the cost per unit is always an *average* cost; that is, the total fixed cost is averaged over (divided by) the number of units of volume.

Although the term *fixed cost* may imply that the amount of cost cannot be changed, the term itself refers only to items of cost that do not change with changes in volume. Fixed costs may change for other reasons, such as a deliberate management decision to change them. The term *nonvariable* is

EXHIBIT 16–1
THREE TYPES OF COST BEHAVIOR

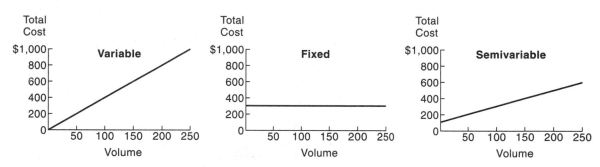

therefore more appropriate than *fixed;* but we use fixed cost because it is more commonly used.

> **Example.** Property protection costs, such as paying security guards, are ordinarily fixed costs because these costs do not vary with changes in volume. Property protection costs will increase, however, if management decides to upgrade the level of protection. Alternatively, costs will decrease if management decides to reduce the level of protection.

Semivariable costs are those costs that include a combination of variable cost and fixed cost items. (In this context, the prefix *semi* means partly; it does not mean exactly half.) The total amount of a semivariable cost item varies in the same direction as, but *less than proportionately* with, changes in volume. If volume increases by 10 percent, the total amount of a semivariable cost will increase by less than 10 percent. Semivariable costs are also called *semifixed, partly variable,* or *mixed* costs.

The cost of operating an automobile is semivariable with respect to the number of miles driven: gasoline, oil, tires, and servicing costs are variable, whereas insurance and registration fees are fixed. In most manufacturing firms, electricity costs are semivariable with the volume of goods produced: the cost of powering production equipment is variable, whereas the cost of lighting the premises is fixed.

Cost-Volume Diagrams

The relationship between costs and volume can be displayed in a **cost-volume (C-V) diagram.** Illustration 16–1 shows diagrams of total costs versus volume for the three patterns of cost behavior described above. Because each cost-volume relationship in the illustration is a straight line, each can be described by the equation $y = mx + b$, where y is the cost at a volume of x; m is the rate of cost change per unit of volume change, or the slope; and b is the vertical intercept, which represents the fixed cost component.

Rather than using the above general mathematical notation for a straight line, the following notation is easier to remember for C-V diagrams:

ILLUSTRATION 16–2
RELATION OF TOTAL COSTS TO VOLUME

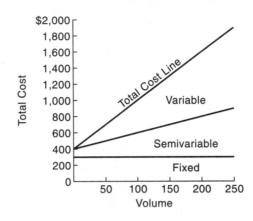

$$TC = TFC + (UVC * X)$$

where

TC = Total cost
TFC = Total fixed cost (per time period)
UVC = Unit variable cost (per unit of volume)
X = Volume

The equations for the three cost lines in Illustration 16–1 are:

A. Variable cost line: $TC = \$4 * X$
B. Fixed cost line: $TC = \$300$
C. Semivariable cost line: $TC = \$100 + (\$2 * X)$

Illustration 16–2 gives a generalized picture of cost behavior. This illustration was constructed simply by combining (i.e., graphically adding) the three separate elements shown in Illustration 16–1. Thus, the fixed cost is $300 for a period of time, regardless of the volume in that period. The variable cost is $4 per unit of volume, which means that the *total* variable cost in a period varies proportionately with volume. The semivariable cost has a fixed element of $100 per period of time and a variable element of $2 per unit of volume.

Since a semivariable cost can be split into fixed and variable components, the behavior of total costs can be described in terms of only two components: a *fixed* component, which is a total amount per period, and a *variable* component, which is an amount per unit of volume. In Illustration 16–2 the fixed amount is $400 per period (= $300 + $100) and the variable amount is $6 per unit of volume (= $4 + $2). Thus, the equation of the total cost line is $TC = \$400 + (\$6 * X)$. For example, if X = 200 units, $TC = \$400 + (\$6 * 200) = \$400 + \$1,200 = \$1,600$. Note in this equation that the

ILLUSTRATION 16–3
RELATION OF UNIT COSTS TO VOLUME

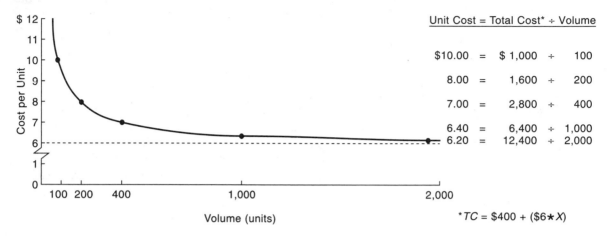

Unit Cost = Total Cost* ÷ Volume

$10.00	=	$ 1,000	÷	100
8.00	=	1,600	÷	200
7.00	=	2,800	÷	400
6.40	=	6,400	÷	1,000
6.20	=	12,400	÷	2,000

*$TC = \$400 + (\$6 * X)$

semivariable cost has disappeared as a separate item, part of it being combined with the variable cost and the remainder being combined with the fixed cost. This combination can be made for any semivariable cost item that is expressed as a fixed dollar amount per period plus a rate per unit of volume—that is, any item for which there is a linear relationship between cost and volume. From this point on, we usually shall consider only the fixed and variable components of cost.

Relation to Unit Costs

The average cost per unit is simply total cost divided by volume. We emphasize again that the cost per unit of volume behaves quite differently than does total cost. As volume goes up, total cost remains constant for a fixed cost item, whereas the total increases for variable or semivariable cost items because additional volume causes additional variable costs to be incurred. By contrast, average unit cost remains constant for a variable cost item, whereas the per-unit cost for fixed and semivariable costs decreases as volume increases (because fixed cost per unit decreases as the fixed costs are averaged over increasing volumes).

Illustration 16–3 shows the relation of unit cost to volume; the graph is based on the total cost considered earlier: $TC = \$400 + (\$6 * X)$. Note how the unit cost decreases as the $400 fixed cost is averaged over increasing volumes. As volume increases without limit, the unit cost will approach $6, the unit variable cost; this is because the average fixed cost per unit approaches zero as volume increases without limit.

Realizing that unit costs are affected by volume is more than being aware of a mathematical fact: it is an important managerial insight. Unit costs play an important role in many decisions, including product pricing decisions. If someone says, "Our cost of producing and selling Product X is $15 per unit," the question should immediately be raised, "At what volume is our unit cost $15?" Unit costs are averages; therefore, a unit cost amount is meaningful only in the context of the volume over which the total costs were averaged in calculating the unit cost.

Inherent Conditions

Every C-V diagram (and its equation) is based on certain inherent conditions. They include (1) a range of volume, (2) the length of the time period, and (3) the environment, each of which is described below. In many cases these are not stated explicitly. (This was the case in our use of the unqualified word *variable* in the preceding section.) Failing to recognize these conditions can cause serious misunderstandings, which we describe in later sections.

Relevant Range. Illustrations 16–1 and 16–2 imply that costs move along a straight line through the entire range of volume, from zero to whatever number is at the far right of the diagram. This implication is not realistic. For example, at zero volume (i.e., when facilities are not operating at all), management decisions may cause costs to be considerably lower than the $400 fixed costs shown in Illustration 16–2. Also, when volume gets so high that a company requires a second shift, costs may behave quite differently from how they behave under one-shift operations. Even within the limits of a single shift, costs usually will behave differently when the facilities are very busy from the way they behave under low-volume operations.

In short, a single straight line gives a good approximation of the behavior of costs *only within a certain range of volume.* This range is referred to as the **relevant range** because it is the range that is relevant for the situation being analyzed.

Illustration 16–4 shows the same cost pattern as Illustration 16–2, and indicates the relevant range by the shaded area extending from 100 units to 200 units. Although the cost line extends back to zero, this does not imply that costs actually will behave according to the line at volumes below 100 units. Rather, the cost line is extended leftward solely as a means of identifying the fixed component of total costs *within the relevant range.* The fixed component (i.e., $400 per period) is the amount of cost indicated by the point where the total cost line intercepts the vertical axis. Similarly, the total cost line should not be used for volumes above the upper limit of the relevant range (200 units in the illustration).

Relevant Time Period. The amount of variable cost depends on the time period over which cost behavior is being estimated. If the time period is only one day, few costs are variable. A certain number of employees are at work on that day, and in most companies all, or almost all, of them will remain on the job and will get paid for the entire day regardless of volume fluctuations within that day. The cost of materials and some supplies will

ILLUSTRATION 16–4
DESIGNATION OF RELEVANT RANGE

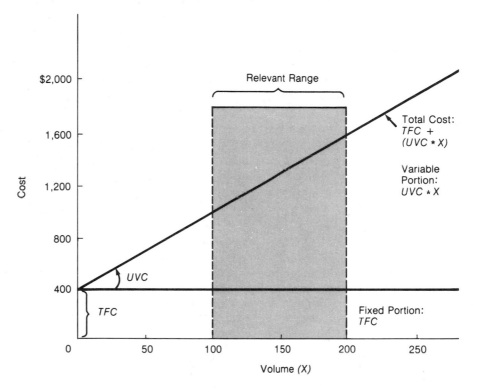

vary with production volume that day, and changes in operating time for equipment may affect power consumption, but that is about all.

If the time period is a month, more costs become variable. In particular, the size of the work force can be varied according to the volume of activity planned for the month. Consumption of some other items, such as certain utilities costs, may also vary with the activity level for a month.

With a one-year time period, many more costs are variable. In deciding on the budget for a year, management typically decides on changes in the amount of many overhead costs according to its estimate of the volume for the year. This is true not only for the number of employees in many administrative and support activities, but also for such expenses as advertising, sales promotion, and (within limits) research and development. In some instances even occupancy costs can be varied by changing the square footage of the facilities that are used.

One cost element that is not variable, even with a one-year horizon, is the cadre of top managers (e.g., there must be a plant manager if the plant is operated at all and, at the headquarters level, a president and vice presidents of operations, marketing, and finance). Also, certain base levels of items such as utilities remain fixed: for example, irrespective of other activity levels, a company must provide heat and light for the managers' offices, as well as support ongoing minimal levels of activities such as security, maintenance, housekeeping, and groundskeeping that cannot be avoided if operations are conducted at all. Finally, depreciation expense is not variable; but it is a sunk cost (as opposed to a cash outflow), and even it can be reduced by disposing of depreciable assets.

The relevant time period should always be specified. In many cost analyses the time period is the variability within a year. This period is appropriate when the cost numbers are being used to aid such decisions as whether to accept an order at lower than normal price, how much to allow as quantity discounts, or whether to pay overtime rather than to add a shift. Erroneous conclusions result, however, when one assumes that this one-year period is applicable to *all* analyses of cost behavior.

> **Example.** In the trial that decided the amount of profit that Polaroid Corporation lost over the 10-year period in which Eastman Kodak Corporation infringed on Polaroid's instant photography patents, the Polaroid expert witness claimed that the variable portion of nonmanufacturing costs was only 14 percent of sales revenue. This estimate was based on the relationship between nonmanufacturing costs and revenue *within* each year. The Kodak expert witness argued that variability should be judged on the basis of how costs as a percentage of revenue varied on an *annual basis* for the ten years of the period. Considering each year as the unit of measurement, variable nonmanufacturing costs ranged from 29 percent to 39 percent of sales revenue, the average for the ten years being 34 percent.
>
> The court accepted the argument that variable nonmanufacturing costs were approximately 34 percent of revenue. This increased the nonmanufacturing cost on which Polaroid's claim was based, and reduced its claimed profit by hundreds of millions of dollars.[1]

Environment. The C-V diagram shows only how costs vary with volume. Costs in a period may change as a result of many influences in the economic environment: changes in wage rates, fringe benefits, and material prices as well as changes arising from technological changes in production processes. If any of these changes is significant, then the C-V diagram does not properly estimate what costs will be in a given period.

Linear Assumption

The C-V diagram assumes that costs change with volume along a *straight* line. This **linear assumption** about the cost-volume relationship often is not valid. For example, some cost functions are curved. In practice, however, segments of the curve can be adequately approximated by straight line

---

[1] *Polaroid Corporation* vs. *Eastman Kodak Company,* U.S. District Court, District of Massachusetts, 1989, C.A. 76-1634-MA.

ILLUSTRATION 16–5
DIAGRAM OF A STEP-FUNCTION COST

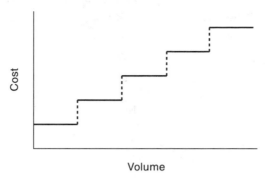

segments, each with its own relevant range. More common than these **curvelinear costs** are step-function costs.

Step-Function Costs. Some items of costs may vary in steps; such a **step-function cost** is shown in Illustration 16–5. Step-function costs are incurred when resources are used in discrete "chunks," such as when one supervisor is added for every additional ten nonsupervisory employees.

Because they are people-intensive, service organizations and administrative and support functions of all organizations experience step-function costs. When a person is added to a service or support activity, its costs step up (increase) by the wages and fringes of that additional employee. At the same time, adding that person has increased the *capacity* of the activity to handle more volume. In the diagram in Illustration 16–5, the height of a stair step ("riser") indicates the cost of adding this increment of capacity, and the step's width ("tread") shows how much additional volume of that activity can be serviced by this additional increment of capacity.

> **Example.** A certain automobile repair facility is equipped with eight service bays. It presently employs only five technicians on a salaried basis. If a sixth technician is added, labor costs for the facility will step up by the amount of this person's salary and fringes, and the capacity to handle about 40 additional hours per week of automobile service volume will be added.

Linear Approximations. Underlying step-function costs are more prevalent than C-V diagrams may reflect. If a step-function's "risers" are low and "treads" are narrow—that is, if each chunk of additional resource is relatively small and the additional capacity that can be served by each one is also small—then the step-function can be approximated by a variable cost line with no important loss of accuracy. On the other hand, if it is believed that during the relevant time period the volume for a specific step-function cost will remain within the relevant range for a *single* stair step (tread), then the cost is appropriately treated as a fixed cost for that time period. Thus, although quite common in practice, step-function costs are often "hidden" in C-V diagrams as either variable or fixed costs.

Estimating the Cost-Volume Relationship

Any of several methods may be used to estimate the cost-volume relationship, that is, to arrive at the total fixed cost and the unit variable cost in the equation:

$$TC = TFC + (UVC * X)$$

The following list is arranged in order from the method that requires the most judgment to the one that depends most heavily on statistical analysis.

1. Judgment. Use judgment in deciding how each item, or category, of cost will vary with volume and what the amount of fixed costs will be. This method is appropriate when the results will be used to estimate costs in a situation in which historical data are not relevant, such as a proposal to introduce a new product made with a new process. It is also used when employing a more expensive or time-consuming method is not worthwhile. The reliability of the results, of course, depends on the experience and skill of the estimator. This approach is also called the **account-by-account method** because the analyst considers each account in the cost structure and judges whether the costs in that account are variable, fixed, or semivariable.

2. High-Low Method. Estimate total costs at each of two volume levels, which establishes two points on the line. This is called the high-low method because one of the volumes selected is likely to be quite high and the other quite low. The upper and lower limits of the relevant range are often selected for this purpose. Then proceed as follows:

a. Subtract total cost at the lower volume from total cost at the higher volume and subtract the number of units at the lower volume from the number of units at the higher volume.

b. Divide the difference in cost by the difference in volume; this gives *UVC,* the amount by which total cost changes with a change of one unit of volume (i.e., the *slope* of the C-V line).

c. Multiply either of the volumes by *UVC* and subtract the result from the total cost at that volume, thus removing the variable component and leaving the fixed component, *TFC* (i.e., the *vertical intercept*).

A variation of this method is to estimate total costs at one volume and then estimate how costs will change with a unit increase from this volume; that is, estimate one point on the line and then estimate its slope (*UVC*). *TFC* can then be found by subtraction, as described above.

3. Scatter Diagram. Make a diagram in which actual costs recorded in past periods are plotted (on the vertical axis) against the volume levels in those periods (on the horizontal axis). Data on costs and volumes for each of the preceding several months might be used for this purpose. Draw a line that best fits these observations. Refer to Illustration 16–6 for an example of this type of diagram. The line of best fit is drawn by visual inspection of the plotted points. The *TFC* and *UVC* values are then determined by reading the values for any two points on the line and using the high-low method described above.

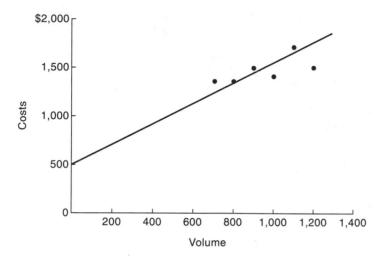

Months	Costs	Volume
July	$1,400	1,000
August	1,700	1,100
September	1,500	900
October	1,300	800
November	1,500	1,200
December	1,300	700

4. Linear Regression. Fit a line to the observations by the statistical technique called the **method of least squares,** or **linear regression.** This procedure gives the *TFC* and *UVC* values directly. Many statistical and spreadsheet programs and hand-held calculators can perform linear regression calculations. In this method it is advisable to analyze each historical data point (that is, each cost-volume pair in each prior time period) before performing the linear regression in order to eliminate any clearly atypical observations—called *outliers.* For example, if a strike caused unusually high labor costs in a given period, then this data point might be eliminated.

In deciding on a method, the general rule is to use as much relevant information as is available, subject to limitations of time and cost in performing the analysis. A judgmental analysis can be done quickly and inexpensively. At the other extreme, statistical methods require collecting comparable data for a large enough number of prior periods to make the results statistically significant. However, statistical methods are preferable if the data are valid and relevant.[2]

Problems with Statistical Estimates. Estimating C-V relationships by means of a scatter diagram or linear regression is a common practice, but the results can be misleading. In the first place, this technique shows, at best, what the relationship between costs and volumes *was* in the past, whereas managers usually are interested in what the relationship *will be* in the future. The future is not necessarily a mirror of the past. Also, the

[2] In one study of companies' use of C-V diagrams, only 13 percent of the respondents preferred linear regression over judgment in analyzing cost behavior. See Roy A. Anderson and Harry R. Biederman, "Using Cost-Volume-Profit Charts," *The Controller's Handbook* (Homewood, Ill.: Dow Jones-Irwin, 1978), chap. 6.

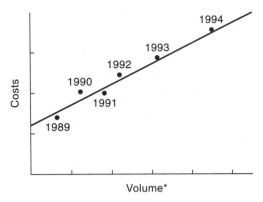

ILLUSTRATION 16–7
SCATTER DIAGRAM SHOWING DRIFT

Volume*

*As measured by sales revenue.

relationship we seek is that prevailing under a *single set of operating conditions,* whereas each point on a scatter diagram may represent changes in factors other than the two being studied (cost and volume).

Illustration 16–7 shows a common source of difficulty. In this scatter diagram, volume is represented by sales revenue, as is often the case. Each dot is located by plotting the costs for one year on the *y*-axis and the sales revenue for that year on the *x*-axis. The dots lie along a well-defined path, which is indicated by the straight line. However, this line may *not* indicate a relationship between costs and volume. It may instead indicate nothing more than the tendency for revenues *and* costs to increase over the past six years because of inflationary factors. If this is the case, then the line shows the trend, or **drift,** of costs *through time,* not the relationship between cost and volume *at a given time.* Any scatter diagram (1) in which volume is measured in *revenue* dollars (rather than in physical units or some other nonmonetary measure, as in our previous diagrams) and (2) that covers a period of years in which revenues were generally increasing each year, is likely to have this characteristic. The longer the period covered and/or the higher the inflation rate, the more unreliable the diagram becomes.

Even if the volume is measured in *constant* dollars (i.e., dollars of a given purchasing power) or physical units, regression analysis can lead to misleading inferences. Consider a cost element that behaves as a step function, and assume that the organization's activity level has been increasing each year from 1990 to 1994, as in Illustration 16–8. Within a given year, the cost may have been fixed; that is, actual cost was on one of the stair steps of the diagram. (This phenomenon occurs in organizations that make personnel additions at the start of the fiscal year, e.g., university faculties.) But if regression analysis were applied to the five annual cost amounts, the

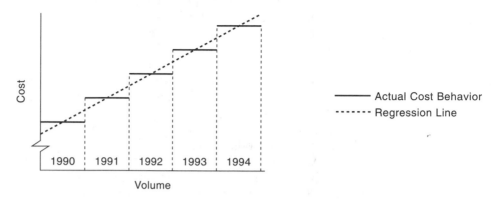

ILLUSTRATION 16–8
MISLEADING INFERENCE FROM REGRESSION ANALYSIS

resulting C-V line would make the cost *appear* to be semivariable *within* a one-year time horizon. Thus, great care must be taken not to draw short-run cost behavior inferences from a regression analysis of long-run data.

Illustration 16–8 also illustrates the notion mentioned earlier whereby costs that are fixed in the short run may not be fixed from a longer-run perspective. In fact, some people refer to costs with this pattern of behavior as **long-term variable costs**.

Measures of Volume

So far most of our C-V diagrams have described a single-product organization for which aggregate volume can be measured by the number of units produced.[3] In the more common case of an organization that produces several products, it is unlikely that the number of units produced can provide a reliable measure of activity because some products cost more per unit than others. Therefore, these organizations must use other measures of volume. Among the "common denominator" volume measures used in practice are labor-hours, labor dollars, machine-hours, homogeneous quantity units such as tons or barrels, and sales value (i.e., the revenues that will be generated by the items produced). Presumably, a certain measure is selected because it most closely reflects the conditions that *cause* costs to change.

In selecting a volume measure, two basic questions must be answered: (1) Should the measure be based on inputs or on outputs? (2) Should the measure be expressed in terms of money amounts, or in terms of nonmonetary quantities? Each of these questions is discussed below.

---

[3]In case the reader began her or his studies in this book with Part 2, we again explain our use of the word *product*. We use *product* to refer to the outputs of an organization, whether those outputs are tangible *goods* or intangible *services*. Similarly, the verb *produce* and the noun *production* can refer either to the manufacture of goods or to the provision of services.

Input versus Output Measures.   **Input measures** relate to the *resources used* in a responsibility center. Examples include labor-hours worked, labor cost, machine-hours operated, kilowatt-hours of electricity consumed, or pounds of materials used. **Output measures** relate to the *goods and services* that flow out of the center.

For C-V diagrams that show the relationship between manufacturing costs and volume, an input measure such as labor-hours or machine-hours may be a good measure of volume because many elements of manufacturing costs tend to vary more closely with input factors than with output. Other costs, such as inspection and shipping costs, might vary more closely with the quantity of goods produced (that is, with output).

A C-V diagram for a retail store or other merchandising organization normally uses sales revenues, an output measure, as the volume measure. Because the largest cost in such an organization is its cost of goods sold, that cost tends to have a fairly constant percentage relationship with sales revenues for any given type of merchandising firm. Similarly, in a state's motor vehicle registration offices, the primary variable cost is for application forms and similar supplies; the cost of these varies with the number of applications processed, which is an output factor.

Monetary versus Nonmonetary Measures.   A volume measure expressed in nonmonetary quantities, such as labor-hours or tons, is often better than one expressed in dollars, because a nonmonetary measure is unaffected by changes in prices. A wage increase would cause labor costs to increase even if there were no actual increase in the volume of activity. If volume is measured in terms of labor dollars, such a measure could be misleading. On the other hand, if price changes are likely to affect both labor costs and other costs to the same degree, the use of labor cost as the measure of volume in a C-V diagram for total costs may be a means of allowing implicitly for the effect of these price changes.

Choice of a Measure.   These considerations must be tempered by practicality. Total labor costs are often available in the accounting system without extra calculation, whereas the computation of total labor-hours or machine-hours may require additional work. Also, since the volume measure for analytical purposes is often (but not always) the same as that used in allocating indirect production costs (production overhead) to products for the purpose of valuing inventories in financial accounting, the appropriateness of the measure for the latter purpose must also be taken into account.

In general, the volume measure chosen should be related to the activity that *causes* the cost to be incurred. The more items of cost that are combined in the total cost function, the more difficult it is to relate the *causality* of the mixture of costs to a single activity measure.

This difficulty in identifying a single activity measure amidst many different items of cost is particularly troublesome if the mixture includes step-function costs. For example, it is possible for a manufacturing firm to increase the number of different style numbers or models offered without causing its overall volume, measured as number of units, to increase correspondingly. This product proliferation creates increased work for support activities such as design engineering, production scheduling, purchasing, and parts administration to the extent that each of these functions may need to add one or more persons to handle its increased workload. For each of these functions, it is the specific function's increased level of activity, not a change in overall volume, that creates the need to add additional capacity in the form of additional employees. For example, the appropriate volume measure for the parts administration function is the number of parts to be administered, not the quantity of these parts that the factory is producing. A C-V diagram can have only one axis for volume. If the diagram tries to encompass too broad a range of activities, then this mixture is likely to hide underlying step-function costs, each of which should have its own unique measure of volume.

Also, the appropriateness of a particular measure may change over time. For example, as a factory becomes more highly automated, machine-hours tends to become a more valid volume measure than the traditionally used labor-hours or labor dollars because increased use of the automated equipment causes increases in the factory's variable and step-function costs.

THE PROFITGRAPH

The C-V diagram in Illustration 16–4 can be expanded into another useful diagram, called the **profitgraph** (or **cost-volume-profit graph** or **C-V-P graph**), simply by adding a revenue line to it. A profitgraph shows the expected relationship between total costs and revenue at various volumes.[4] A profitgraph can be constructed either for the business as a whole or for some segment of the business such as a product, a product line, or a division.

On a profitgraph, the measure of volume may be the number of units produced and sold, or it may be dollars of sales revenue. We have already stated the formula for the cost line: $TC = TFC + (UVC * X)$. Revenue is plotted on the profitgraph on the assumption of a constant selling price per unit. That assumption results in a linear revenue graph whose slope is the selling price per unit. If volume is measured as units of product sold and is designated by the variable X and if the unit selling price is designated as UR (unit revenue), then the total revenue, TR, equals the unit selling price (UR) times the number of units of volume (X). That is, $TR = UR * X$. (For example, if the unit selling price is $8.50, the total revenue from the sale of 200 units will be $1,700.)

A profitgraph showing these relationships is shown in Illustration 16–9. Although not shown explicitly on the diagram, it should be understood that the relationships are expected to hold only within the relevant volume range.

---

[4]This graph is also called a **break-even chart,** but that label has the unfortunate connotation that the objective of a business is merely to break even.

ILLUSTRATION 16–9
PROFITGRAPH

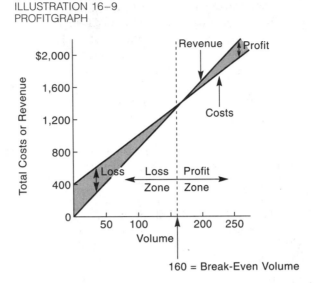

160 = Break-Even Volume

The profitgraph is a useful device for analyzing the overall profit characteristics of a business. To illustrate such an analysis, assume the following situation, which is the same as that shown in previous diagrams:

Fixed costs (*TFC*).........................	$400 per period
Variable costs (*UVC*)......................	$6 per unit
Selling price (*UR*).........................	$8.50 per unit

For simplicity, we shall assume that the company makes only one product.

Break-Even Volume

At the **break-even volume,** total costs equal total revenue. This is simply a mathematical fact. The break-even point is of little practical interest in a profitable company because the company focuses on the profit region, which should be considerably above the break-even volume. At lower than break-even volumes, a loss is expected; at higher volumes, a profit is expected. The amount of loss or profit expected at any volume is the vertical distance between the points on the total cost and revenue lines at that volume. The break-even volume is computed as follows:

Since revenue (*TR*) at any volume (*X*) is	$TR = UR * X$
And cost (*TC*) at any volume (*X*) is	$TC = TFC + (UVC * X)$
And since at the break-even volume, costs = revenue, or	$TR = TC$
Then the break-even volume is the volume at which	$UR * X = TFC + (UVC * X)$

If we let *X* equal the break-even volume, then for the above situation we have:

$$\$8.50 * X = \$400 + (\$6 * X)$$
$$X = 160 \text{ units}$$

At the break-even volume of 160 units, revenue equals 160 units at $8.50 per unit, which is $1,360; and total costs equal $400 + 160 units at $6 per unit, which is also $1,360.

The equation for the break-even volume, X, can also be stated in the following form:

$$X = \frac{TFC}{UR - UVC}$$

To state this equation in words, it says that the break-even volume can be found by dividing the fixed costs (*TFC*) by the difference between selling price per unit (*UR*) and variable cost per unit (*UVC*).

Operating Leverage

Using the same relationships as in Illustration 16–9, we can demonstrate how the *average* profit per unit changes with volume. For example, at 200 units, revenue is $1,700, costs are $400 + ($6 * 200) = $1,600, and profit is $100. For the 200 units, this is an average profit of $0.50 per unit. At 250 units, revenue is $2,125, costs are $1,900, and profit is $225, for an average profit of $0.90 per unit. This increase in per-unit profit is caused by the phenomenon described earlier in this chapter: unit cost decreases as volume increases. That is, as volume increases, average per-unit cost decreases because the average *fixed* cost of each unit decreases. This phenomenon is referred to loosely as "spreading the fixed costs over a higher volume" or more formally as **operating leverage.**

To understand why the term *leverage* is used, consider again the examples in the preceding paragraph. When volume is 200 units, profit is $100. But when volume goes up by 50 units to 250 units, an increase of *25* percent, the profit goes up by $125 to $225, an increase of *125* percent. In this particular example, then, the leverage factor was five: profit went up five times as much as volume. Of course, leverage works both ways—which is why businesses become so concerned about volume decreases of only a few percentage points.

Contribution

Although profit per unit is different at each volume, another number is constant for all volumes within the relevant range. This number is called the **unit contribution, unit contribution margin,** or **marginal income.** It is the difference between the unit selling price and the *variable* cost per unit.

In our example the unit contribution is $2.50 (= $8.50 – $6.00) per unit. Because this number is a constant, it is an extremely useful way of expressing the relationship between revenue and cost at any volume. For each change of one unit of volume, profit will change by $2.50. Starting at the lower end of the relevant range, each additional unit of volume increases profit by the amount of unit contribution.

We can use the above notation to express these relationships, adding the symbol I for total income or profit:

$$I = (UR - UVC) * X - TFC$$

In word form, this equation says that total income at any volume is unit contribution ($UR - UVC$) times volume, minus fixed cost. In the above example, at a volume of 250 units,

$$(UR - UVC) * X - TFC = I$$
$$(\$8.50 - \$6.00) * 250 - \$400 = \$225$$

In words, the contribution of $2.50 per unit times 250 units, minus the fixed cost of $400, gives total income of $225. Stated another way, if the unit contribution is $2.50 per unit and fixed costs are $400 per period, then 160 units must be sold before enough contribution will be earned to recover fixed costs. After that, a profit of $2.50 per unit will be earned. The break-even formula can now be expressed as:

$$\text{Break-even volume} = \frac{\text{Fixed costs}}{\text{Unit contribution}}$$

Break-even volume can also be stated in terms of *revenues* rather than physical units. In words, the formula is:

$$\text{Break-even volume} = \frac{\text{Fixed costs}}{\text{Contribution percent}}$$

The denominator is contribution as a percent of revenues. The more complete name for this is the **contribution margin percentage.** In the example, this is $2.50 ÷ $8.50 = 29.4 percent; that is, each dollar of revenue will produce 29.4 cents of contribution. Thus, the break-even volume is $400 ÷ 0.294 = $1,360, which is equivalent to the earlier break-even volume of 160 units at $8.50 per unit.

Understanding the Contribution Concept.   The concept of contribution is an important one in business, and merely defining contribution may not adequately convey the concept or why the difference between revenue and variable cost is called *contribution.* Illustration 16–10 helps the reader develop a clear understanding of the contribution concept.

Each "spurt" labeled UR represents the revenue from the sale of one unit of product. Part of the revenue proceeds from the sale of each unit must be used for its variable costs; these are the UVC spurts shown as outflows. What remains from each unit's revenue after providing for its variable cost is the unit contribution, depicted by the spurts labeled C. The size of the fixed cost "pot" into which the unit contributions are flowing represents the amount of the fixed costs of the period. If the period's unit contributions just fill the fixed cost pot, then break-even operations have been achieved. Note that if the size (capacity) of the fixed cost pot is divided by the size of

ILLUSTRATION 16–10
SCHEMATIC OF CONTRIBUTION

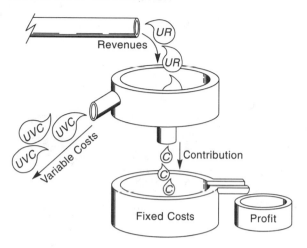

each unit contribution spurt, then the result will be how many unit contribution spurts are needed to just fill the pot—that is, the break-even volume. (If the capacity of the pot is 400 and each contribution spurt is of size 2.5, then 400 ÷ 2.5 = 160 spurts will just fill the pot.) Finally, once the fixed cost pot is filled, any additional contribution overflows into the profit pot. But no overflow occurs (that is, no profit is earned) until the fixed cost pot is first filled.

We hope that this intuitive approach helps reinforce what contribution is: it is contribution *first* to fixed costs and *then* (above break-even volume) to profit. The schematic can also help one understand such things as the impact on break-even volume if fixed costs decrease, if unit contribution increases, and so on. Inelegant as it is, the schematic is really a simple model of the economics of a business.

However, one should realize that in many instances the schematic may be *deceptively* simple. Marketing tactics intended to increase volume and hence produce more contribution may also *increase* the size of the so-called "fixed" cost pot, particularly if the volume-increasing actions cause certain step-function costs to increase.

> **Example.** Awixa Company, which makes machined metal parts, was incurring fixed costs associated with its idle production capacity. It did not expect to be able to use this idle capacity unless it changed its marketing tactics. To generate more volume and contribution, it instructed its sales force to tell customers it was willing to make variations of its existing products. The tactic worked and many orders—most for relatively few units—were written for product variations. After one year sales volume increased only slightly while profits had actually decreased. Closer analysis revealed that (1) some of the "new" orders were actually customers substituting customized variations

ILLUSTRATION 16–11
CONTRIBUTION PROFITGRAPH

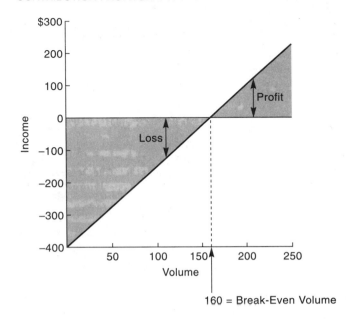

160 = Break-Even Volume

for the standard products that they formerly ordered and (2) the change in marketing tactics had increased the costs of several support departments (especially the order processing and machine setup departments), which had needed to add people to handle the additional work created by the large number of small, specialized orders. The cost increases had more than offset the contribution from the additional sales volume.

In the example, overall volume had not increased very much, but significant changes in product variety and product mix created increases in various *step-function* costs. The company had not recognized these increases because they had thought of all costs as being either fixed or variable with respect to *overall volume.*

Contribution Profitgraphs. If using the unit contribution concept over a range of volume is valid, it is possible to construct another useful form of profitgraph, which is shown in Illustration 16–11. In this profitgraph the vertical axis shows income. Note that the income line (1) has a value of zero at 160 units, the break-even volume; (2) has a slope of $2.50 per unit of volume, the unit contribution;[5] and (3) shows a loss of $400 at zero volume (because $400 is the amount of fixed cost, which will have no contribution to offset it at zero volume).

---

[5]For example, as volume goes from 160 to 200 units, income goes from $0 to $100; slope = $\Delta y \div \Delta x = \$100 \div 40$ units = $2.50 per unit.

Cash versus Accrual Profitgraphs

The revenue and cost numbers used in profitgraphs and break-even calculations may be either cash-basis or accrual-basis amounts. The choice in a break-even analysis depends on whether the analyst is interested in determining (1) the volume at which cash inflows from sales equal related cash outlays for operating costs or (2) the volume at which reported revenue equals the related expenses. Although revenue and cash inflows from sales (i.e., collections) tend to be about equal in a given time period, the noncash nature of *depreciation* will cause the period's reported fixed expenses to be larger than the related cash outflows. Thus, when using a profitgraph, it is important to know whether the underlying numbers are cash flows or accrual-basis amounts.

For profitgraphs to be meaningful on a cash basis, one must assume that the period's sales volume and production volume (both expressed in physical units) are equal. For example, suppose that May sales were 200 units but that May production output was 250 units. It is not meaningful to call May's profit the difference between (1) the cash receipts from 200 units and (2) the cash costs of producing 250 units plus May's cash selling and administrative costs, because the company produced 50 units for inventory and the cash costs of these units were not associated with May's sales. Hence, the profitgraph implicitly assumes sales volume and production volume equality for cash-basis numbers. However, with accrual accounting's matching concept, if 200 units are sold, then only 200 units' costs are charged as the related expense (i.e., costs of goods sold is based on 200 units), and the costs of the other 50 units are held in the asset account, Finished Goods Inventory. Thus, one need not assume production and sales volume equality for an accrual-basis profitgraph to be meaningful, provided one remembers to interpret total cost as the period's *cost of goods sold* plus selling and administrative costs, rather than the period's *production costs* plus selling and administrative costs.

Using the Profitgraph

Improving Profit Performance. These cost-volume-profit (C-V-P) relationships suggest that a useful way of studying the basic profit characteristics of a business is to focus not on the profit per unit (which is different at every volume) but rather on the total fixed costs and the contribution margin. In these terms there are four basic ways in which the profit of a business that makes a single product can be increased:

1. Increase selling price per unit (UR).
2. Decrease variable cost per unit (UVC).
3. Decrease fixed costs (TFC).
4. Increase volume (X).[6]

---

[6]Before reading the numerical example that follows, the reader might, as a test of understanding of the contribution concept, visualize the impact of each of these four changes in terms of the schematic in Illustration 16–10.

The separate effects of each of these possibilities are shown in the following calculations and in the contribution profitgraphs displayed in Illustration 16–12. Each starts from the assumed present situation: selling price $8.50 per unit, variable cost $6 per unit, fixed costs $400 per period, volume 200 units, and hence a profit of ($2.50 * 200) − $400 = $100. The effect of a 10 percent change in each profit-determining factor would be:

| | Effect on: | | New | Income |
Factor	Revenue	Costs	Income	Increase*
A. Increase selling price by 10%	$+170	$ 0	$270	170%
B. Decrease variable cost by 10%	0	−120	220	120
C. Decrease fixed costs by 10%	0	−40	140	40
D. Increase volume by 10%	+170	+120	150	50

*Increase over present income of $100.

If instead of varying each factor separately we look at some of the interrelationships among them, we can calculate, for example, that a 34 percent (i.e., $136) increase in fixed costs could be offset either by an 8 percent increase in selling price, a 27 percent increase in volume, or an 11 percent decrease in variable costs.

The foregoing calculations assume that each of the factors is independent of the others, a situation that is rarely the case in the real world. An increase in selling price, for example, is often accompanied by a decrease in volume. Therefore, it is essential to study changes in the factors together rather than separately.

Margin of Safety.   Another calculation made from a profitgraph is the **margin of safety.** This is the amount or ratio by which the current volume exceeds the break-even volume. Assuming current volume is 200 units, the margin of safety in our illustrative situation is 40 units (= 200 − 160 break-even volume), or 20 percent of current volume. Sales volume can decrease by 20 percent before a loss is incurred, other factors remaining equal.

Several Products

The C-V-P relationships described above apply to businesses that produce only a single product. In a business that produces several products, the C-V-P relationships also hold if each product has approximately the same contribution margin percentage. A profitgraph could be constructed for such a company by using sales revenue, rather than units, as the measure of volume. In such a business, each dollar of sales revenue produces approximately the same amount of contribution as every other dollar of sales revenue, so the fact that there are multiple products becomes essentially irrelevant. (For example, if a shoe store has a contribution margin percentage of 40 percent, the store manager sees no difference between selling one

ILLUSTRATION 16–12
EFFECT OF 10 PERCENT CHANGE IN PROFIT FACTORS

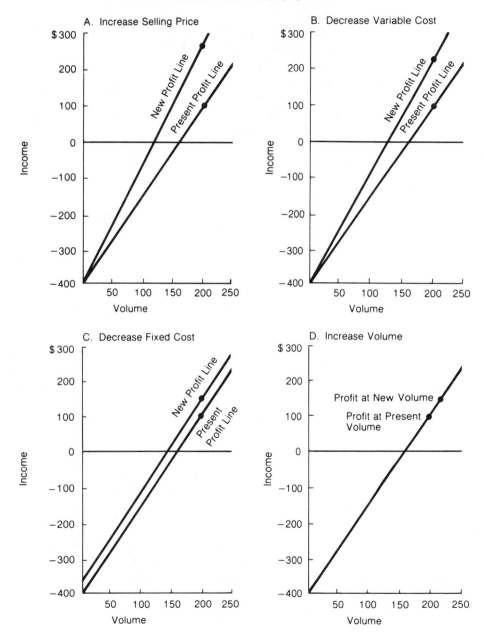

pair of $100 shoes or two pairs of $50 shoes, because $40 contribution will be generated in either instance.)

If, however, the business produces several products and they have different contribution margin percentages, then the depiction of a valid C-V-P relationship is more complicated. If the **product mix** (the relative proportion of each product's sales to the total) remains relatively constant, then a single profitgraph is still valid. It is based on the *weighted-average* unit contribution for all products rather than the individual unit contribution of any product.

Changes in the product mix affect profits in a way that cannot be revealed by the type of profitgraph described above. For example, even if sales revenue does not change from one period to the next, profits will increase if in the latter period the proportion of products that have a high contribution margin percentage is greater than it was in the first period.

When products have different unit contributions and when the product mix changes, one approach to C-V-P analysis is to treat each product as a separate entity and to construct a profitgraph for that entity, just as we did for the business as a whole. This method requires that all costs of the business be allocated to individual products, using the approaches that we will describe in Chapter 18. The break-even point on such a profitgraph is the volume at which the total contribution of that product recovers that product's equitable share of the company's total fixed costs.

Other Influences on Costs

C-V diagrams and profitgraphs show only what total costs are expected to be at various levels of volume. For example, such diagrams will show that the total variable cost of 200 units is double the variable cost of 100 units. There are many reasons, other than the level of volume, why the costs in one period are different from those in another period. Some of these reasons are described here:

1. Changes in input prices. One of the most important causes of changes in a C-V diagram is that the prices of input factors change. Inflation is a persistent and probably permanent phenomenon. Wage rates, salaries, material costs, and costs of services all go up. A C-V diagram can be misleading if it is not adjusted for the effect of these changes.

2. The rate at which volume changes. Rapid changes in volume are more difficult for personnel to adjust to than are moderate changes in volume. Therefore, the more rapid the change in volume, the more likely it is that costs will depart from the straight-line cost-volume pattern.

3. The direction of change in volume. When volume is increasing, costs tend to lag behind the straight-line relationship, either because the organization is unable to hire the additional workers that are assumed in the cost line or because supervisors try to get by without adding more costs. Similarly, when volume is decreasing, there is a reluctance to lay off workers and to shrink other elements of cost. This also causes a lag.

4. The duration of change in volume. A temporary change of volume in either direction tends to affect costs less than a change that lasts a long time, for much the same reasons as were given in the preceding paragraph.

5. Prior knowledge of the change. If managers have adequate advance notice of a change in volume, they can plan for it. Actual costs therefore are more likely to remain close to the C-V line than is the case when the change in volume is unexpected.

6. Productivity. The C-V diagram assumes a certain level of productivity in the use of resources. As the level of productivity changes, the cost changes. Overall productivity in the United States has fluctuated in recent years (after increasing at a rate of 3.1 percent per year between 1948 and 1967); labor costs have fluctuated correspondingly (in constant dollar terms).

7. Management discretion. Some cost items change because management has decided that they *should* change. Some companies, for example, have relatively large headquarters staffs, while others have small ones. The size of these staffs, and hence the costs associated with them, can vary within fairly wide limits, depending on management's judgment as to optimum size. Such types of cost are called **discretionary costs.** They are discussed in more detail in Chapter 23.

For these and other reasons, it is not possible to predict the total costs of an organization in a certain period simply by predicting the volume for that period and then determining the costs at that volume by reading a C-V diagram. Nevertheless, the effect of volume on costs and profits is so important that the C-V diagram and profitgraph are very useful tools in analysis. In using them, it is important to temper interpretation of relationships they depict by estimating the influence of other factors and being aware of the existence of "hidden" step-function costs.

Learning Curves. Studies have shown that the reduction in unit production cost associated with increased productivity has, in many situations, a characteristic pattern that can be estimated with reasonable accuracy. This pattern is called the **learning curve,** or **experience curve.** It is described in the Appendix to this chapter.

SUMMARY

Understanding cost behavior is basic to further studying management accounting. Total variable costs change in direct proportion with volume, whereas unit variable cost is a constant. Total fixed costs do not vary with volume, but unit fixed cost decreases as volume increases. Semivariable costs can be decomposed into a variable cost and a fixed cost component.

The level of volume has an important effect on costs. The effect can be depicted in a C-V diagram or, if the relationship is approximately linear, by the equation $TC = TFC + (UVC * X)$. The diagram and the equation state that the total costs (TC) at any volume are the sum of the fixed costs (TFC) plus the product of the unit variable costs (UVC) times the number of units (X). These relationships hold only within a certain range of volume, the relevant range, for a relevant time period, and for a given set of environmental conditions.

Step-function costs occur when a significant "chunk" of cost must be incurred to create an additional increment of capacity. Depending on the height of the step, its relevant range of volume, and the relevant time period, in some instances it is possible to approximate these costs as variable costs and, in other instances, as fixed costs.

When a revenue line is superimposed on a C-V diagram, the diagram becomes a profitgraph. The profitgraph shows the relationship between revenue and costs (and hence the profit or loss) at any volume within the relevant range. A special case shown on the profitgraph is the break-even volume, which can be calculated by dividing fixed costs by the unit contribution (unit price minus unit variable costs). The profitgraph can also be used to analyze the probable consequences of various proposals to change the basic relationships depicted therein. Since profit is affected by factors other than volume, however, the profitgraph does not tell the whole story.

APPENDIX: LEARNING CURVES

In many situations productivity increases as a function of the *cumulative* volume of output of a product. The aircraft industry was the first to reveal this phenomenon by discovering that certain costs tend to decrease, per unit, in a predictable pattern as the workers and their supervisors become more familiar with the work; as the work flow, tooling, and methods improve; as less materials get wasted and rework is minimized; as fewer skilled workers need to be used; and so on. The decreasing costs are a function of the learning process, which results (in part) in requiring fewer labor-hours to produce a unit of product as more units of the same product are completed. Also, output tends to increase as equipment is "fine-tuned." It should be noted, however, that every cost element does not necessarily decrease. For instance, material costs often are not subject to the learning process, except to the extent that they may decrease because waste is decreased or less expensive substitute materials are discovered.

Research in a number of industries has demonstrated a regular pattern to this cost reduction and that this is likely to be a constant percentage reduction in average unit cost when *cumulative* production doubles. For example, an 80 percent learning curve means that if the average unit cost is $50 when production has reached 10,000 units, cumulative average unit cost will decline to $40 per unit (= $50 * 0.80) when production cumulates to 20,000 units. (Cumulative average cost is the total cost to date divided by the total number of units produced to date.) Such a relationship is a straight line when plotted on log-log graph paper.[7]

> **Example.**   Assume a company introduced product A in 1984 and makes 10,000 units a year, that the costs of product A were subject to an 80 percent learning curve, and that the total cost for the 10,000 units made in 1984 was $500,000. The average unit cost in 1984 therefore was $50.
>
> In 1985 the company made an additional 10,000 units. If the 80 percent learning curve held, cumulative average unit cost of the 20,000 total units would be 80 percent of $50, or $40. The total cost of the 20,000 units would be $800,000 (= 20,000 * $40), the costs for 1985 would be $300,000 (= $800,000 − $500,000 costs of 1984), and the unit cost for 1985's production would be $30 (= $300,000 ÷ 10,000), a $20 decrease from 1984.

Carrying the example into later years gives a much less dramatic decline. For example, by the end of 1993, 100,000 units would have been produced. Thus, the 10,000 units produced in 1994 would represent only a 10 percent increase in the cumulative quantity, and the unit cost in that year would decrease by less than $1. In more detail:

Years since Introduction	Cumulative Quantity	Cumulative Average Unit Cost	Unit Cost for Increment	Average Annual Decrease
1	10,000	$50.00	$50.00	—
2	20,000	40.00	30.00	$20.00
4	40,000	32.00	24.00	3.00
8	80,000	25.60	19.20	1.20
16	160,000	20.48	15.36	0.48

Because of the learning phenomenon, historical unit costs tend to be higher than future costs in terms of constant dollars. This is especially the case with *new* products, because the learning phenomenon has relatively little effect on the costs of products that have been manufactured for many years. Such products are said to be "near the bottom of the learning curve."

This characteristic decline in average unit cost does not happen automatically. Rather, it depends on *management efforts* to increase efficiency. It is important, therefore, to exploit the learning potential and for management

---

[7]The learning-curve formula is $Y_i = ai^k$, where i = cumulative units produced, Y_i = cumulative average unit cost of i units, $a = Y_1$ (cost of the first unit), and k is a parameter determined by the rate of learning (e.g., for an 80 percent learning curve, $k = -0.3219$). Expressed in logarithms, the formula becomes $\log Y_i = \log a + (k * \log i)$; hence, the linearity when graphed on log-log paper.

to realize that costs as depicted on a C-V diagram are probably too high if cumulative volume has increased significantly since the diagram was prepared.

Although originally limited to production costs, learning curve analysis in recent years has been found to be applicable to advertising costs, marketing costs, product development costs, certain general and administrative costs, and the total costs of operating an entire organization.[8]

---

[8]The learning curve described here is called the "Wright curve" after its inventor. An alternative called the "Crawford curve" is also used. For a description, see Diane D. Pattison and Charles J. Teplitz, "Are Learning Curves Still Relevant?" *Management Accounting,* February 1989, pp. 37–40.

Cases

CASE 16–1 Jackson Thomas

Jackson Thomas was supervisor for an assembly department in Rogers Electronics Company. In recent weeks, Thomas had become convinced that a certain component, number J-42, could be produced more efficiently if certain changes were made in assembly methods. Thomas had described this proposal to the company's industrial engineer, but the engineer had quickly dismissed Thomas's ideas—mainly, Thomas thought, because the engineer had not thought of them first.

Thomas had frequently thought of starting a business and felt that the ability to produce the J-42 component at a lower cost might provide this opportunity. Rogers's purchasing agent assured Thomas that Rogers would be willing to buy J-42s from Thomas if the price were 10–15 percent below Rogers's current cost of $5.20 per unit. Working at home, Thomas experimented with the new methods, which were based on the use of a new fixture to aid in assembling each J-42. This experimentation seemed successful, so Thomas proceeded to prepare some estimates for large-scale J-42 production. Thomas determined the following:

1. A local toolmaker would make the new fixtures for a price of $1,575 each. One fixture would be needed for each assembly worker.

2. Assembly workers were readily available, on either a full-time or part-time basis, at a wage of $11.75 per hour. Thomas felt that another 20 percent of wages would be necessary for fringe benefits. Thomas estimated that on the average (including rest breaks), a worker could assemble, test, and pack 15 units of the J-42 per hour.

3. Purchased components for the J-42 should cost about $2.68 per unit over the next year. Shipping supplies and delivery costs would amount to approximately $0.16 per unit.

4. Suitable space was available for assembly operations at a rental of $1,900 per month. A 12-month lease was required.

5. Assembly tables, stools, and other necessary equipment would cost about $945 per assembly worker.

6. Thomas, as general manager, would receive a salary of $6,300 per month.

7. A combination office manager-bookkeeper was available for a salary of $2,200 per month.

8. Miscellaneous costs, including maintenance, supplies, and utilities, were expected to average about $1,500 per month.

9. Rogers Electronics would purchase between 400,000 and 525,000 units of J-42 a year, with 450,000 being Rogers's purchasing agent's "best guess." However, Thomas would have to commit to a price of $4.45 per unit for the next 12 months.

Thomas showed these estimates to a friend who was a cost analyst in another electronics firm. This friend said that all of the estimates appeared reasonable, but told Thomas that in addition to the required investment in fixtures and equipment, about $220,000 would be needed to finance accounts receivable and inventories. The friend also advised buying enough fixtures and other equipment to enable producing the maximum estimated volume (525,000 units per year) on a one-shift basis (assuming 2,000 labor-hours per assembler per year). Thomas thought this was good advice.

Questions

1. What are Thomas's expected variable costs per unit? Fixed costs per month? What would the total costs per year of Thomas's business be if volume were 400,000 units? 450,000 units? 525,000 units? (Limit yourself to cash costs; ignore depreciation of fixtures and

equipment. Also, disregard any interest costs Thomas might incur on borrowed funds.)

2. What is the average cost per unit of J-42 at each of these three volumes?

3. Reanswer Questions 1 and 2 assuming that (a) Thomas wanted to guarantee assembly workers 2,000 hours of pay per year; (b) enough workers would be hired to assemble 450,000 units a year; (c) these workers could work overtime at a cost (including fringes) of $21.15 per hour; and (d) no additional fixed costs would be incurred if overtime were needed. (Do not use these assumptions for Question 4.)

4. Reanswer Questions 1 and 2, now including depreciation as an expense. Assume the fixtures and other equipment have a useful life of six years, and that straight-line depreciation will be used.

5. Do you think Jackson Thomas should resign from Rogers Electronics and establish the proposed enterprise?

CASE 16–2   Hospital Supply, Inc.

Hospital Supply, Inc., produced hydraulic hoists that were used by hospitals to move bedridden patients. The costs of manufacturing and marketing hydraulic hoists at the company's normal volume of 3,000 units per month are shown in Exhibit 1.

Questions

The following questions refer only to the data given in Exhibit 1. Unless otherwise stated, assume there is no connection between the situations described in the questions; treat each independently. Unless otherwise stated, assume a regular selling price of $4,350 per unit. Ignore income taxes and other costs not mentioned in Exhibit 1 or in a question itself.

1. What is the break-even volume in units? In sales dollars?

2. Market research estimates that monthly volume could increase to 3,500 units, which is well within hoist production capacity limitations, if the price were cut from $4,350 to $3,850 per unit. Assuming the cost behavior patterns implied by the data in Exhibit 1 are correct, would you recommend that this action be taken? What would be the impact on monthly sales, costs, and income?

3. On March 1 a contract offer is made to Hospital Supply by the federal government to supply 500 units to Veterans Administration hospitals for delivery by March 31. Because of an unusually large number of rush orders from their regular customers, Hospital Supply plans to produce 4,000 units during March, which will use all available capacity. If the government order is accepted, 500 units normally sold to regular customers would be lost

EXHIBIT 1
COSTS PER UNIT FOR HYDRAULIC HOISTS

Unit manufacturing costs:

Variable materials	$550	
Variable labor.	825	
Variable overhead.	420	
Fixed overhead	660	
Total unit manufacturing costs		$2,455

Unit marketing costs:

Variable.	275	
Fixed	770	
Total unit marketing costs		1,045
Total unit costs		$3,500

to a competitor. The contract given by the government would reimburse the government's share of March production costs, plus pay a fixed fee (profit) of $275,000. (There would be no variable marketing costs incurred on the government's units.) What impact would accepting the government contract have on March income?

4. Hospital Supply has an opportunity to enter a foreign market in which price competition is keen. An attraction of the foreign market is that demand there is greatest when demand in the domestic market is quite low; thus, idle production facilities could be used without affecting domestic business.

An order for 1,000 units is being sought at a below-normal price in order to enter this market. Shipping costs for this order will amount to $410 per unit, while total costs of obtaining the contract (marketing costs) will be $22,000. Domestic business would be unaffected by this order. What is the minimum unit price Hospital Supply should consider for this order of 1,000 units?

5. An inventory of 200 units of an obsolete model of the hoist remains in the stockroom. These must be sold through regular channels at reduced prices or the inventory will soon be valueless. What is the minimum price that would be acceptable in selling these units?

6. A proposal is received from an outside contractor who will make 1,000 hydraulic hoist units per month and ship them directly to Hospital Supply's customers as orders are received from Hospital Supply's sales force. Hospital Supply's fixed marketing costs would be unaffected, but its variable marketing costs would be cut by 20 percent (to $220 per unit) for these 1,000 units produced by the contractor. Hospital Supply's plant would operate at two-thirds of its normal level, and total fixed manufacturing costs would be cut by 30 percent (to $1,386,000). What in-house unit cost should be used to compare with the quotation received from the supplier? Should the proposal be accepted for a price (i.e., payment to the contractor) of $2,475 per unit?

7. Assume the same facts as above in Question 6 except that the idle facilities would be used to produce 800 modified hydraulic hoists per month for use in hospital operating rooms. These modified hoists could be sold for $4,950 each, while the variable manufacturing costs would be $3,025 per unit. Variable marketing costs would be $550 per unit. Fixed marketing and manufacturing costs would be unchanged whether the original 3,000 regular hoists were manufactured or the mix of 2,000 regular hoists plus 800 modified hoists was produced. What is the maximum purchase price per unit that Hospital Supply should be willing to pay the outside contractor? Should the proposal be accepted for a price of $2,475 per unit to the contractor?

CASE 16–3 Bill French*

Bill French picked up the phone and called his boss, Wes Davidson, controller of Duo-Products Corporation. "Wes, I'm all set for the meeting this afternoon. I've put together a set of break-even statements that should really make people sit up and take notice—and I think they'll be able to understand them, too." After a brief conversation, French concluded the call and turned to his charts for one last checkout before the meeting.

French had been hired six months earlier as a staff accountant. He was directly responsible to Davidson and had been doing routine types of analytical work. French was a business school graduate and was considered by his associates to be quite capable and unusually conscientious. It was this latter characteristic that had apparently caused him to "rub some of the working folks the wrong way," as one of his coworkers put it. French was well aware of his capabilities and took advantage of every opportunity that arose to try to educate those around him. Davidson's invitation for French to attend an informal manager's meeting had come as a surprise to others in the accounting group. However, when French requested permission to make a presentation of some break-even data, Davidson acquiesced. Duo-Products had not been making use of this type of analysis in its planning procedures.

Basically, what French had done was to determine the level at which the company must operate in order to break even. As he put it,

The company must be able at least to sell a sufficient volume of goods so that it will cover all the variable costs of producing and selling the goods. Further, it will not make a profit unless it covers the fixed costs as well. The level of operation at which total costs are just covered is the break-even volume. This should be the lower limit in all our planning.

The accounting records had provided the following information that French used in constructing his chart:

Plant capacity—2 million units per year
Past year's level of operations—1.5 million units
Average unit selling price—$7.20
Total fixed costs—$2,970,000
Average unit variable cost—$4.50

From this information French observed that each unit contributed $2.70 to fixed costs after covering its variable costs. Given total fixed costs of $2,970,000, he calculated that 1,100,000 units must be sold in order to break even. He verified this conclusion by calculating the dollar sales volume that was required to break even. Since the variable costs per unit were 62.5 percent of the selling price, French reasoned that 37.5 percent of every sales dollar was left available to cover fixed costs. Thus, fixed costs of $2,970,000 required sales of $7,920,000 in order to break even.

When he constructed a break-even chart, his conclusions were further verified. The chart also made it clear that the firm was operating at a fair margin above break-even, and that the pretax profits accruing (at the rate of 37.5 percent of every sales dollar over break even) increased rapidly as volume increased (see Exhibit 1).

*Copyright © by the President and Fellows of Harvard College. Harvard Business School case 104-039.

EXHIBIT 1
BREAK-EVEN CHART—TOTAL BUSINESS

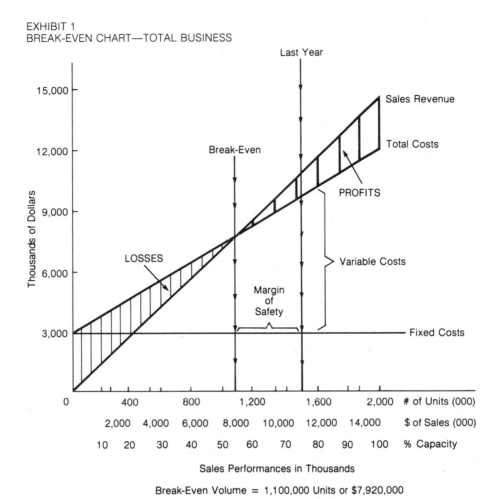

Break-Even Volume = 1,100,000 Units or $7,920,000

Shortly after lunch, French and Davidson left for the meeting. Several representatives of the manufacturing departments were present, as well as the general sales manager, two assistant sales managers, the purchasing officer, and two people from the product engineering office. Davidson introduced French to the few people whom he had not already met, and then the meeting got under way. French's presentation was the last item on the agenda. In due time the controller introduced French, explaining his interest in cost control and analysis.

French had prepared copies of his chart and supporting calculations for everyone at the meeting. He described carefully what he had done and explained how the chart pointed to a profitable year, dependent on meeting the sales volume that had been maintained in the past. It soon became apparent that some of the participants had known in advance what French planned to discuss; they had come prepared to challenge him and soon had taken control of the meeting. The following exchange ensued (see Exhibit 2 for a list of participants and their titles):

John Cooper: You know, Bill, I'm really concerned that you haven't allowed for our planned changes in volume next year. It seems to me that you should have allowed for the sales department's guess that we'll boost unit sales by 20 percent. We'll be pushing 90 percent of capacity then. It sure seems that this would make quite a difference in your figuring.

Bill French: That might be true, but as you can see, all you have to do is read the cost and profit relationship right off the chart for the new volume. Let's see—at a million eight-hundred-thousand units we'd . . .

Fred Williams: Wait a minute, now! If you're going to talk in terms of 90 percent of capacity, and it looks like that's what it will be, you had better note that we'll be shelling out some more for the plant. We've already got approval on investments that will boost fixed costs by at least $60,000 a month. And that may not be all. We may call it 90 percent of plant capacity, but there are a lot of places where we're just full up and we can't pull things up any tighter.

John Cooper: Fred is right, but I'm not finished on this bit about volume changes. According to the information that I've got here—and it came from your office—I'm not sure that your break-even chart can really be used even if there were to be no changes next year. It looks to me like you've got average figures that don't allow for the fact that we're dealing with three basic products. Your report on each product line's costs last year (see Exhibit 3) makes it pretty clear that the "average" is way out of line. How would the break-even point look if we took this on an individual product basis?

Bill French: Well, I'm not sure. It seems to me that there is only one break-even point for the firm. Whether we take it product by product or in total, we've got to hit that point. I'll be glad to check for you if you want, but . . .

Ray Bradshaw: Guess I may as well get in on this one, Bill. If you're going to do anything with individual products, you ought to know that we're looking for a big shift in our product mix. The "A" line is really losing out, and I imagine that we'll be lucky to hold two-thirds of its volume next year. Wouldn't you buy that, Arnie? (Agreement from the general sales manager.) That's not too bad, though, because we expect that we should pick up the 200,000 that we lose, plus about a quarter million units more, in "C" production. We don't see anything that shows much of a change in "B". That's been solid for years and shouldn't change much now.

Arnie Winetki: Bradshaw's called it about as we figure it, but there's something else here. We've talked about our pricing on "C" enough, and now I'm really going to push our side of it. Ray's estimate of maybe half a million units—450,000 I guess it was—increase on "C" for next year is on the basis of doubling the price with no change in cost. We've been priced so low on this item that it's been a crime—we've got to raise it for two reasons. First, for our reputation: the price is out of line with other products in its class and is completely inconsistent with our quality reputation. Second, if we don't raise the price, we'll be swamped, and we can't handle it. You heard what Williams said about capacity. The way the whole "C" field is exploding, we'll have to deal with another half-million units in unsatisfied orders if we don't jack the price up. We can't afford to expand that much for this product.

EXHIBIT 3
PRODUCT CLASS COST ANALYSIS
Normal Year

	Aggregate	"A"	"B"	"C"
Sales at full capacity (units)	2,000,000			
Actual sales volume (units)	1,500,000	600,000	400,000	500,000
Unit sales price	$ 7.20	$ 10.00	$ 9.00	$ 2.40
Total sales revenue	10,800,000	6,000,000	3,600,000	1,200,000
Variable cost per unit	4.50	7.50	3.75	1.50
Total variable cost	6,750,000	4,500,000	1,500,000	750,000
Fixed costs	2,970,000	960,000	1,560,000	450,000
Profit	1,080,000	540,000	540,000	0
Ratios:				
Variable cost to sales	0.625	0.75	0.42	0.625
Unit contribution to sales	0.375	0.25	0.58	0.375
Utilization of capacity	75%	30%	20%	25%

At this point, Anne Fraser walked toward the front of the room from where she had been standing near the rear door. The discussion broke for a minute, and she took advantage of the lull to interject a few comments.

Anne Fraser: This certainly has been a helpful discussion. As long as you're going to try to get all the things together for next year, let's see what I can add to help you:

Number One: Let's remember that everything that shows in the profit area here on Bill's chart is divided almost evenly between the government and us. Now, for last year we can read a profit of about $900,000. That's right; but we were left with half of that, and then paid out dividends of $300,000 to the stockholders. Since we've got an anniversary year coming up, we'd like to put out a special dividend of about 50 percent extra. We ought to retain $150,000 in the business, too. This means that we'd like to hit $600,000 profit *after* taxes.

Number Two: From where I sit, it looks as if we're going to have negotiations with the union again, and this time it's likely to cost us. All the indications are—and this isn't public—that we may have to meet demands that will boost our production costs—what do you call them here, Bill—variable costs—by 10 percent across the board. This may kill the bonus-dividend plans, but we've got to hold the line on past profits. This

means that we can give that much to the union only if we can make it in added revenues. I guess you'd say that that raises your break-even point, Bill—and for that one I'd consider the company's profit to be a fixed cost.

Number Three: Maybe this is the time to think about switching our product emphasis. Arnie may know better than I which of the products is more profitable. You check me out on this Arnie—and it might be a good idea for you and Bill to get together on this one, too. These figures that I have (Exhibit 3) make it look like the percentage contribution on line "A" is the lowest of the bunch. If we're losing volume there as rapidly as you sales folks say, and if we're as hard pressed for space as Fred has indicated, maybe we'd be better off grabbing some of that big demand for "C" by shifting some of the assets from "A" to "C".

Wes Davidson: Thanks, Anne. I sort of figured that we'd wind up here as soon as Bill brought out his charts. This is an approach that we've barely touched on, but, as you can see, you've all got ideas that have to be made to fit here somewhere. Let me suggest this: Bill, you rework your chart and try to bring into it some of the points that were made here today. I'll see if I can summarize what everyone seems to be looking for.

First of all, I have the idea that your presentation is based on a rather important series of assumptions. Most of the questions that were raised were really about those assumptions. It might help us all if you try to set the assumptions down in black and white so that we can see just how they influence the analysis.

Then, I think that John would like to see the unit sales increase factored in, and he'd also like to see whether there's any difference if you base the calculations on an analysis of individual product lines. Also, as Ray suggested, since the product mix is bound to change, why not see how things look if the shift materializes as he has forecast? Arnie would like to see the influence of a price increase in the "C" line; Fred looks toward an increase in fixed manufacturing costs of $60,000 a month; and Anne has suggested that we should consider taxes, dividends, expected union demands, and the question of product emphasis.

I think that ties it all together. Let's hold off on our next meeting until Bill has time to work some more on this.

With that, the meeting disbanded. French and Davidson headed back to their offices and French, in a tone of concern, asked Davidson, "Why didn't you warn me about the hornet's nest I was walking into?"

"Bill, you didn't ask!"

Questions

1. What are the assumptions implicit in Bill French's determination of his company's break-even point?

2. On the basis of French's revised information, what does next year look like:
   a. What is the break-even point?
   b. What level of operations must be achieved to pay the extra dividend, ignoring union demands?
   c. What level of operations must be achieved to meet the union demands, ignoring bonus dividends?
   d. What level of operations must be achieved to meet both dividends and expected union requirements?

3. Can the break-even analysis help the company decide whether to alter the existing product emphasis? What can the company afford to invest for additional "C" capacity?

4. Calculate *each* of the three products' break-even points using the data in Exhibit 3. Why is the *sum* of these three volumes not equal to the 1,100,000 units aggregate break-even volume?

5. Is this type of analysis of any value? For what can it be used?

CASE 16–4   Azienda Vinicola Italiana*

Azienda Vinicola Italiana produced and bottled wines. A large percentage of its sales were of special table wine. Most of its customers, located in the principal Italian cities, were served through local representatives. Its prices were in line with those of competitors.

In 1993, the firm sold 704,000 liters[1] of wine in 871,850 bottles. In recent years, de-

mand had been increasing, and the firm had approached the limit of its productive capacity, which was estimated to be 900,000 bottles a year.

The production process was not complicated, since the firm did not buy grapes but rather bought either mosto[2] or bulk wine.

---

*Copyright © by IPSOA (Turino).

[1]One liter is slightly more than one U.S. liquid quart.

[2]Mosto is the juice of grapes before the fermentation process takes place. The fermentation process takes about one month. During this process, carbon dioxide develops and the sugar is converted into alcohol. Therefore, mosto is an unstable product, and wine is a stable product.

EXHIBIT 1

Income Statement
For 1993 in Lire
(000 omitted)

Sales		1,921,370
Costs:		
Labor	357,136	
Raw materials	602,272	
Auxiliary materials	393,514	
General manufacturing expenses	52,744	1,405,666
Gross margin		515,704
General administrative expenses	184,196	
Depreciation	115,940	
Interest	82,500	
Advertising	86,900	469,536
Net income		46,168

This policy had the disadvantage that the firm could not assure itself of a consistently high-quality product. Moreover, it was estimated that if grapes were purchased, the price of raw material would be reduced by about Lit.[3] 110 per bottle. On the other hand, the purchase and installation of equipment needed for pressing grapes would require an additional investment of about Lit. 550 million. No significant increase in labor costs was anticipated under such a practice.

In the production department, there were 20 employees who worked a total of about 40,000 hours in 1993, and whose average wage per hour, including fringe benefits, was Lit. 8,000. The administrative manager was of the opinion that 40 percent of this labor expense should be considered as being fixed, while the remainder could be considered as varying proportionately with production volume.

In 1993, production had required 700,000 liters of mosto and bulk wine, purchased at a total cost of Lit. 602,272,000. The average cost incurred for auxiliary materials (bottles,

stoppers, neckbands, labels, and so forth) was about Lit. 450 per bottle.

The income statement for 1993 is shown in Exhibit 1.

The administrative manager wished to reorganize the firm in order to exploit its productive capability to the utmost and, above all, to increase the net profit, which the owners did not consider satisfactory. They were of the opinion that a net profit of 8 or 9 percent of sales could be realized.

As a basis upon which to make decisions, the administrative manager intended to use charts of costs and revenues that he had seen other firms use and that he considered helpful. The first step in this graphic analysis was a study of costs, separating fixed costs from variable costs. For that purpose, he examined the income statements of preceding years and came to the conclusion that the figures for 1993 were representative. He also noticed that the different types of wine had been sold in more or less the same relative proportions each year, despite large fluctuations in the total volume of business, and this fact confirmed his belief that the figures for 1993 were representative. He therefore prepared the following analysis (in thousands of lire):

---

[3]In 1993, 1,000 Italian lire (abbreviated "Lit.") equaled approximately U.S. $0.60.

Fixed costs:	
40% of labor cost.....................	142,854
Staff salaries	118,196
General manufacturing expenses........	52,744
General administrative expenses	66,000
Advertising expenses	86,900
Interest............................	82,500
Depreciation	115,940
	665,134

Variable costs:	
60% of labor cost.....................	214,282
Raw materials	602,272
Auxiliary materials	393,514
	1,210,068

The administrative manager assumed a maximum capacity of 900,000 bottles a year. At current prices he estimated this would produce sales revenue of Lit. 1,980 million.

With the present structure of costs and revenue, the profits resulting from an annual production of 900,000 bottles would be small. The administrative manager decided,

therefore, to try to discover a way to change costs and revenue so as to obtain a profit of Lit. 176 million a year, which would be almost 9 percent of sales of Lit 1,980 million.

Questions

1. Accepting the distribution between fixed and variable elements as estimated by the administrative manager, prepare a chart of costs and revenues. Determine the volume of production at which the firm reaches its break-even point and the profit at capacity operation.

2. Draw three other charts, each constructed so that a production of 900,000 bottles will produce a profit of Lit. 176 million, one in which selling price is assumed to increase, another in which fixed costs are assumed to decrease, and a third in which variable costs are assumed to decrease. What are the break-even points in each of these situations?

3. What are the most likely alternatives to consider so as to achieve a profit of Lit. 176 million?

CASE 16–5 Morrin Aircraft Company*

On several occasions since late 1991, Morrin Aircraft Company had received contracts from airlines for MA-900 passenger aircraft. In March 1994, Tom Scott, one of the buyers for Morrin, was trying to decide on a fair price to offer the Pierce Company, a subcontractor, for the manufacture of metal containers used for passenger luggage and other cargo. These enclosed containers were loaded and unloaded in an airline's luggage or cargo area at an airport. They essentially eliminated manual handling of goods at the point where the airplane was parked. In addition to permitting quicker loading/unloading of the plane itself, the containers eliminated damage to goods caused by inclement weather and resulted in more efficient usage of a plane's cargo hold.

The containers, made of a special lightweight alloy, required some difficult machining operations. Because the containers were put on or taken off aircraft by using special equipment, and since each airplane's cargo hold was equipped with special tracks to accommodate the containers, it was crucial that they be made exactly to Morrin's dimensions and other specifications.

Pierce had been manufacturing these containers for Morrin since December 1991, at which time its bid of $3,036[1] per container for the 120 containers then required was the lowest of the several bids considered. With each new order for the MA-900 that Morrin received, Scott had successfully negotiated new contracts for the manufacture of the containers with Ken White, a Pierce sales engineer. During this period, Pierce continued to meet all quality standards and delivery schedules.

On each successive contract after the original one signed in December 1991, Scott had applied an 80 percent learning curve to the price of the previous order, excluding the cost of raw material and also excluding profit. Scott assumed that the tooling cost incurred by Pierce Company in manufacturing the containers was amortized over the cost of the original contract, and therefore he made no allowance for tooling cost in estimating the price of subsequent contracts. Although it appeared to Scott that White was not familiar with the use of learning curves in purchase contracting, White agreed to manufacture the containers at the prices quoted by Scott. As a result, that price paid per unit for the containers was lowered on each successive contract. Pierce's production of containers was essentially continuous over this time period. (Application of the learning curve would not be valid if production were not reasonably continuous.)

In making his calculations of the price to offer Pierce after the first contract had been fulfilled, Scott had to rely on his own estimates of raw material price, tooling cost, and Pierce's profit. Scott knew from his previous experiences with Pierce that the company would refuse to reveal its cost and profit figures. Because of his past experience in purchasing and the use of the learning curve, however, Scott was confident that his estimates were fairly accurate. Morrin's own labor-hour records showed that an 80 percent curve was appropriate for the production of similar containers for another airplane made in the 1980s, and this led Scott to conclude that the same 80 percent curve was applicable to the Pierce Company. Breaking down the original bid of $3,036 per container, Scott estimated that profit was around $276, which was 10 percent of total cost, and that raw material costs were about $960 per unit. He estimated that Pierce's tooling cost was about $43,200 and that this had probably been amortized over the 120 containers ordered under the first contract.

In order to set up his 80 percent curve to find the cumulative average price on which he could base his future price offers, Scott made these calculations:

Original price per container		$3,036
Less: Profit at 10% of cost	$276	
Tooling cost on first order: $43,200 ÷ 120 units	360	
Raw material cost per unit	960	
Items not subject to learning curve		1,596
Costs subject to learning curve		$1,440

[1]All monetary amounts in this case are stated in constant dollars, i.e., dollars of equivalent purchasing power.

The adjusted cost of $1,440 per container for 120 units was plotted on log-log graph paper (see Exhibit 1). Scott then took double

EXHIBIT 1
EIGHTY PERCENT LEARNING CURVE
MA-900 Cargo Containers

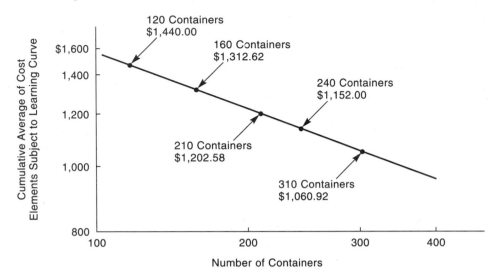

the quantity of the original order (or 240 units) and 80 percent of the unit cost ($1,152) and plotted his second point on the log-log graph paper. Through these two points he drew a straight line.

When Morrin required 40 more containers, Scott looked at his graph to find the new cumulative average of cost elements subject to learning for the total quantity of the old and new orders, 160 containers. The new cumulative average cost was $1,312.62 per container (see Exhibit 1). Using this information, Scott calculated:

160 units at $1,312.62 per unit average for cost elements subject to learning curve........................	$210,019
Less: 120 units purchased at $1,440 per unit average for cost elements subject to learning curve	172,800
Total price to be paid on new order for cost elements subject to learning curve........................	$ 37,219

The new average price per container to be paid on the new order for cost elements subject to learning was $37,219 ÷ 40 containers, or $930.48. To this $930.48, Scott added back the cost items not subject to the curve that previously had been subtracted:

Cost elements subject to learning curve..................	$ 930.48
Plus: Raw material	960.00
Average price per unit before profit.....................	1,890.48
Plus: Profit at 10% of cost..............................	189.05
Total price per unit on the new order...............	$2,079.53

Scott believed this figure of $2,079.53 per container was appropriate to use in his negotiations with White, who finally, but grudgingly, accepted this figure.

In subsequent negotiations, the prices Scott offered Pierce Company on successive contracts for the containers became lower and lower. White became more emphatic in his objections and warned Scott that "this learning curve business is going too far." However, each time Scott asked to see Pierce's cost data to justify some other price, White would give the same answer: "Our cost data are none of your business!"

On February 2, 1994, about one month before the final delivery of the latest order, which had been contracted for in November 1993, White complained that Pierce had experienced an unusually large increase in material cost that added $48 to the cost per container. Furthermore, White stated that modifications in the design of the containers since the original contract had increased the raw material cost per unit by another $72. White stated that because of these increased costs and the low $1,992 per unit price paid by Morrin for the currently produced containers, he was quite skeptical as to whether his company would take on any further contracts for containers, especially since at that time it could get all the business it wanted. He went on to say that his company was "sick and tired of producing containers at a loss for Morrin and having to make up these losses out of contracts with other companies." Though Scott believed that the raw material cost increases mentioned by White were correct, he did not have any way of appraising the validity of White's statements about Pierce's losing money on this contract with Morrin.

Two weeks after this conference between Scott and White, Morrin received aircraft orders that would require 100 more containers. Again Scott was confronted with the task of securing more containers. From December 1991 to March 1994, Pierce would have pro-duced 210 containers. Over this period, the price paid for the containers had decreased from $3,036 per unit on the first order to $1,992 per unit on the current order contracted for in November 1993 and scheduled for completion within the next two weeks. The total price of the 210 units *for the cost elements subject to the learning curve* was $252,542. This sum compared to $302,400 that would have been paid on 210 containers for these same cost elements if the learning curve had not been applied. A further saving to Morrin was realized because the profit that Pierce received per unit was a fixed percentage of cost. Thus, with the lower calculated cost per unit based on the learning curve, the profit to Pierce was cut correspondingly.

Scott realized that it was important to continue dealing with Pierce for the additional 100 containers. He recalled that in 1991 the Pierce Company's first bid of $3,036 per unit was the lowest of the several bids submitted; the next lowest bid at that time was $3,264. If Pierce refused to accept any more orders, dealing with a new subcontractor would probably result in a substantial increase in price. Scott estimated that the lowest price for which he could currently purchase containers from another subcontractor would be in the neighborhood of $3,360 per unit (including the amortized cost, over 100 units, of new tooling). Furthermore, Scott considered Pierce an excellent source of supply because it produced a satisfactory product and always met its delivery schedule.

On the other hand, Scott knew that the validity of the learning curve had been widely accepted in the aircraft industry and that it was especially applicable to the manufacture of items such as the containers, for which direct labor was a major cost component. Furthermore, it was his job as a purchasing agent for Morrin to get as low a price as possible commensurate with a satisfactory product.

Scott had an appointment with White the next day, at which time they would open negotiations for the 100 additional containers. Scott knew that White would suggest a substantial upward revision in the price.

Questions

1. If he used the 80 percent learning curve, what price would Mr. Scott calculate for the new order of 100 containers?

2. What price should Mr. Scott use as a basis for his negotiations?

3. What is the highest price that the Morrin Aircraft Company should pay to the Pierce Company for the containers?

4. What are the implications of the use of learning curves in purchase contracting to both the prime contractor and the subcontractor?

5. In what situations would the use of the learning curve in purchase contracting not be appropriate?

17

Full Costs and Their Uses

This is the first of four chapters that describe the construction and use of full cost information—the type of management accounting information used for many cost measurement purposes. It is discussed first because financial accounting (the subject of Part 1 of this book) uses full cost information; full cost accounting thus provides a bridge between financial and management accounting. Moreover, the earliest management accounting systems focused on the collection and reporting of full cost information.

Apart from its use in financial accounting, full cost accounting information is useful to managers. The most important use is to help set selling prices for goods and services, including prices set by contract as the sum of full costs plus a specified profit.

This chapter introduces full cost concepts and describes generally how full costs are recorded in a cost accounting system. It also discusses the uses of full cost information. How direct and indirect costs are measured for the costing of products and how this information can be analyzed to aid in controlling costs are described in more detail in subsequent chapters.

COST CONCEPTS

Cost is the most slippery word in accounting; it is used for many different notions. If someone says, without elaboration, "The cost of a widget is $1.80," it is impossible to understand exactly what is meant. The word *cost* becomes more meaningful when preceded by a modifier, making phrases such as direct cost, full cost, opportunity cost, differential cost, and so on. But even these phrases do not convey a clear meaning unless the context in which they are used is clearly understood.

General Definition

To understand **cost,** we begin with a broad definition: *Cost is a measurement, in monetary terms, of the amount of resources used for some purpose.* This definition includes three important ideas. First and most basic is the notion that cost measures the *use of resources.* The cost elements of producing a tangible good or intangible service are physical quantities of material, hours of labor service, and quantities of other resources. Cost measures how many, or how much, of these resources were used. The second idea is that cost measurements are expressed in *monetary terms.* Money provides a common denominator that permits the amounts of individual resources, each measured according to its own scale, to be combined so that the total amount of all resources used can be determined. Five pounds of material and one hour of labor cannot be added together to produce a meaningful total; but if the amounts are converted to money at, say, $2 per pound for material and $17 per hour for labor, they can be added to produce a total cost of $27. Third, cost measurement always relates to a *purpose.* These purposes include products, departments, projects, or any other thing or activity for which a monetary measurement of resources used is desired.

Cost Object

Cost object[1] is the technical name for the product, project, organizational unit, or other activity or purpose for which costs are measured. (Some people prefer **cost objective.**) In each instance the cost object must be carefully stated and clearly understood. In a blue-jeans factory, for example, the manufacture of a batch comprised of four dozen pairs of Style 607 jeans may be one cost object, the manufacture of one batch of Style 608 jeans may be another, and the manufacture *and sale* of a batch of Style 607 jeans may be still another.

A cost object can be defined as broadly or as narrowly as one wishes. At one extreme all the jeans manufactured in a jeans factory in a given time period could be considered as a single cost object. But if such a broad definition were used, differences in the resources used for the various styles of jeans would not be measured. At the other extreme each individual pair of jeans manufactured could be considered as a single cost object. But if such a narrow definition were used, the amount of recordkeeping involved in measuring costs would be tremendous. As it happens, many jeans

---

[1]"Allocation of Service and Administrative Costs," *IMA Statement Number 4B* (June 1985).

factories use a *batch* of a single style and material as the unit of costing. Although different sizes of jeans use slightly different amounts of materials, usually the cost object definition does not differentiate among sizes of the same material. For example, one batch of Style 703 corduroy jeans, waist 32"/inseam 31", would not be a different cost object from one batch of Style 703 corduroy, waist 34"/inseam 32".

Similarly, in a service organization a variety of cost object definitions is possible. In a hospital, for example, any of the following could be cost objects: the hospital as a whole, the nursing staff, the X-ray department, the emergency room, the personnel office, the cardiovascular ward, treatment of a type of disease, care of an individual patient, the performance of a certain battery of blood tests, and so on.

Full Cost

Full cost means all the resources used for a cost object. In some circumstances full cost is easily measured. If Ms. Chen pays $35 for a pair of jeans at a store, $35 is the full cost of the pair of jeans to Ms. Chen because she used $35 of her resources to acquire the pair of jeans.

But suppose we ask: What was the full cost of *producing* the pair of jeans? This is a much more difficult question. A jeans factory may make thousands of pairs of jeans a month. Some are plain while others have intricate pocket stitching; some are made of denim whereas others are made of other material. Clearly, for these different styles of jeans different amounts of resources are used; they have different costs.

Direct and Indirect Costs

The various items of cost can be divided into two categories: direct costs and indirect costs. *The full cost of a cost object is the sum of its direct costs plus a fair share of applicable indirect costs.*

The **direct costs** of a cost object are items of costs that are specifically *traced to,* or *caused by,* that cost object. Denim used in manufacturing a batch of jeans is a direct cost of that batch of jeans, and so are the earnings of the employees who worked directly in making that batch of jeans.

Indirect costs are elements of costs that are associated with, or caused by, two or more cost objects *jointly* but that are not directly traced to each of them individually. The nature of an indirect cost is such that it is not possible, or at least not feasible, to measure *directly* how much of the cost is attributable to a single cost object. Examples of indirect costs of a batch of jeans include the factory manager's salary and insurance on the factory building and equipment.

In the example above, the cost object was explicitly stated as being a batch of jeans. If the cost object were instead specified to be the factory where the jeans are produced, then the factory manager's salary and the insurance costs are *direct* costs of that cost object. This illustrates that the terms *direct* and *indirect* are meaningful only in the context of a specified cost object.

Although obviously the cost elements directly traced to a cost object are a part of its cost, it is *not* obvious that some fraction of the elements of indirect cost are part of the cost. One can actually see the denim in a pair of jeans, and labor services obviously were involved in fashioning this denim into jeans. Thus, there is no doubt about counting such material and labor as part of the cost of the jeans. But what is the connection between, say, the salary of the purchasing agent (who buys denim and other materials) and the cost of the jeans? The purchasing agent did not work on the jeans; the purchasing office may not even be in the building where the jeans were made.

The basic rationale is that indirect costs are caused jointly by the several cost objects; to argue otherwise would be to assert that indirect costs are sheer waste. For example, the purchasing agent's salary is not traceable to specific batches of jeans; but without the purchasing agent, there would be no materials on hand from which to make the jeans. Thus, some fraction of the purchasing agent's salary—along with other indirect costs—must be part of the total cost of each batch of jeans.

These comments also apply to cost objects other than the manufacture of goods. The full cost of occupancy of a hotel room includes a fair share of the costs of the hotel lobby and registration desk. The full cost of a university accounting course includes a fair share of the school's administrative, secretarial, maintenance, and utilities costs. We shall defer until later the question of how the fair share of indirect costs applicable to each cost object is measured.

Applicable Accounting Principles

The cost concept and the matching concept generally govern the measurement of the costs applicable to an accounting period and to the products produced in that period. These concepts and the principles related to them do not, however, give much guidance as to how total product costs are to be assigned to individual products or groups of products. They permit any "systematic and rational" method of doing this.

In 1971 Congress created the Cost Accounting Standards Board (CASB), which published 19 cost accounting standards (a term synonymous with "principles"). Although the CASB's authority initially included only the measurement of full costs on defense contracts, all government agencies are now required to adhere to its pronouncements, and many companies also follow them.[2] This is because the problems of measuring the full cost of defense contracts are much the same as the problems of measuring full costs in other situations. In 1980 the CASB was legislated out of existence, but it was reactivated in 1989.

The Institute of Management Accountants (IMA) issues *Statements on Management Accounting,* several of which deal with full cost accounting.

---

[2]CASB standards apply to any negotiated federal contract or subcontract in excess of $500,000 and to any contractor having a total of $10 million or more in federal contracts, regardless of the individual contracts' size.

ILLUSTRATION 17–1
ELEMENTS OF PRODUCT COST

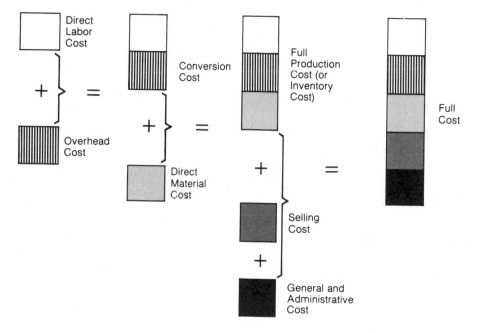

These statements are advisory in nature; no organization is required to follow them. Nevertheless, the IMA expects that the guidelines will gain widespread support, both because of the credibility of the committee of experienced accountants and professors that issues the statements and the rigor taken by that committee in developing the *Statement* guidelines.

Elements of Product Cost

The most common cost object of interest in a business is a **product.** This can be either a tangible good, such as a batch of jeans, or a service, such as a repair job on an automobile. The system that accumulates and reports the costs of product cost objects is called a **product costing system.** Elements of product cost are either material, labor, or services. In a product costing system these elements are customarily recorded in certain categories, shown in Illustration 17–1.

Direct Material Cost. "The quantities of material that can be specifically identified with a cost object in an economically feasible manner, priced at the unit price of direct material" are the **direct material** cost of a cost object.[3] These materials, often called **raw materials** or just **materials,** are to be distinguished from **supplies,** or **indirect materials,** which are materials used in the production process but not directly traced to individual

_____

[3]"Definition and Measurement of Direct Material Cost," *IMA Statement Number 4E* (June 1986).

products. Examples of supplies include lubricating oil for factory machinery and spices in a restaurant's kitchen.

Direct Labor Cost. "The labor quantities that can be specifically identified with a cost object in an economically feasible manner, priced at a unit price of direct labor" are the **direct labor** cost of a cost object.[4] The earnings of workers who assemble parts into a finished good or operate machines in its production are direct labor costs of the product. The cost of a technician's time spent repairing an automobile is a direct cost of the repair job.[5]

Other Direct Costs. Conceptually, any cost traced to a single product is a direct cost of that product. Energy costs, for example, are direct costs of manufacturing energy-intensive products such as glass, and services purchased from an outside company are direct costs if they are identifiable with a single product. However, most companies classify only direct material and direct labor costs as direct production costs. For simplicity we shall assume that these are the only direct costs of a product.

Overhead Cost. All indirect production costs—all production costs other than direct costs—are included in **overhead cost.**[6] One element of overhead is indirect labor: the earnings of employees who do not work directly on a single product but whose efforts are related to the overall process of production. Examples include supervisors, janitors, materials handlers, stockroom personnel, inspectors, and crane and forklift operators. Another element of overhead is indirect material costs, described above. Overhead also includes such items as heat, light, power, maintenance, depreciation, taxes, and insurance related to assets used in the production process.

Conversion Cost. The sum of direct labor cost and overhead cost is **conversion cost.** It includes all production costs needed to convert direct materials into finished goods. As factories become automated, direct material costs tend to become a much more significant cost element than direct labor; at the same time the distinction between direct labor and indirect labor becomes blurred. As a result, some companies no longer distinguish between direct labor and overhead cost; instead, the single category of conversion cost is used.

Full Production Cost. The sum of direct material cost and conversion cost is **full production cost.** In a manufacturing firm full production cost often is called **inventory cost** because this is the cost at which completed goods are carried as inventory and the amount that is reported as cost of sales when the goods are sold. The cost at which goods are carried in

---

[4]"Definition and Measurement of Direct Labor Cost," *IMA Statement Number 4C* (June 1985).

[5]The term **prime cost** is defined as the sum of direct material cost and direct labor cost. Although the term is falling into disuse, we mention it here for completeness.

[6]**Indirect production cost** is a more precise term than overhead, but the latter is more commonly used. Other terms meaning the same thing include **factory overhead** and **burden** (which is falling into disuse).

inventory includes neither distribution nor selling costs, nor those general and administrative costs that are unrelated to production operations. In a manufacturing firm full production cost includes *only* the costs that are incurred "within the four factory walls."

In financial accounting these full production costs that flow through inventory accounts are called **product costs** to distinguish them from *period costs,* which do not flow through inventory accounts but rather are charged as expenses of the period in which they are incurred. The term *inventory cost* is more descriptive of full production costs than *product cost* because the full cost of a product cost object also includes nonmanufacturing costs such as the cost of selling the product. Nevertheless, referring to inventory costs as product costs is well established in practice.

Nonproduction Costs. **Nonproduction costs** (also called **period costs**) are all costs incurred in an organization other than inventory costs. These include selling costs, research and development costs, general and administrative costs, and interest costs. In a company's income statement, many of these costs are reported as a lump sum under the single caption, Selling, general, and administrative expense (informally called SG&A by many businesspersons).

In a manufacturing firm selling costs include both **marketing** (order-getting) costs and **logistics** (order-filling) costs. The distinction between the two types of selling cost is that marketing costs are incurred *before* a sales order is received whereas logistics costs are incurred *after* the goods have been produced. Marketing costs include market research, advertising, point-of-sale promotions, and salespersons' compensation and travel costs. Logistics costs include warehousing and delivery costs as well as the recordkeeping costs associated with processing an order.

General and administrative costs include the costs of service and staff units (such as the human resource management and public relations departments) and general corporate costs, including the compensation of top management and donations to charitable organizations. Interest costs are the costs of using borrowed funds. In most companies no attempt is made to associate interest costs with specific products. Research and development (R&D) costs are the costs associated with efforts to find new or improved products or production processes.[7]

Full Cost. The **full cost** of a product is simply the sum of all the cost elements described above. Thus, full product cost includes both inventory (full production) cost and nonproduction cost. However, in practice, many accountants use the term *full cost* to mean only full *production* cost. This is another example of the lack of precision in practitioners' use of cost-related

---

[7]As described in Part 1, generally accepted accounting principles (GAAP) require that research and development costs be reported as a separate item. Also, under certain specialized conditions, part of a period's interest costs may be capitalized as part of the cost of a long-lived asset (see Chapter 7).

terms and another reason why one must "look beyond the label" to be certain what the user of a term really means.

PRODUCT COSTING SYSTEMS

At this point we shall describe the essentials of a common type of product costing system that is used to measure full production costs and to assign them to goods in a manufacturing company. Cost accounting systems in manufacturing firms tend to be more complex than those in other types of organizations. Thus, a knowledge of product costing in a manufacturing company is also useful in understanding cost accounting systems in merchandising and service organizations.

In Chapter 6 we described the product cost accounting process in overall terms. The description here merely provides more detail on the flows discussed there. Nevertheless, we are now interested in product costing not only to understand how amounts for inventories on the balance sheet and cost of sales on the income statement are measured, but also as necessary background for understanding in later chapters how managers can use product cost data in making a variety of decisions.

Account Flowchart

An **account flowchart** is helpful in understanding the flow of costs through a cost accounting system. Such a flowchart depicts the accounts used in a system, shown in T account form, with arrows indicating the flow of amounts from one account to another.

Most of the accounts on a cost accounting flowchart are either asset accounts or expense accounts. A characteristic of both asset and expense accounts is that increases are shown on the debit (left-hand) side and decreases are shown on the credit (right-hand) side. An arrow on a flowchart indicates a transfer "from" one account "to" another account, signifying that the first account is being decreased and the second is being increased. It follows that the typical arrow on a flowchart leads from the credit side of one account to the debit side of another. These flows represent events that happen during the production process. Besides the arrows designating flow, other lines indicate entries for certain external transactions associated with the production process: for example, the transaction for the acquisition of materials from an outside vendor, which is a debit to Materials Inventory and a credit to Accounts Payable or Cash.

Illustration 17–2 shows the flowchart concept and the essential cost flows in a manufacturing company. This flowchart contains a hypothetical set of figures for a month's operations in Marker Pen Company, a small company that manufactures and sells felt-tip pens. The flowchart is divided into three sections: (1) *acquisition*, containing the accounts related to the acquisition of resources; (2) *production*, containing the accounts related to the production process; and (3) *sale*, the accounts related to the sale of products.

ILLUSTRATION 17–2
ACCOUNT FLOWCHART OF MARKER PEN COMPANY
($000)

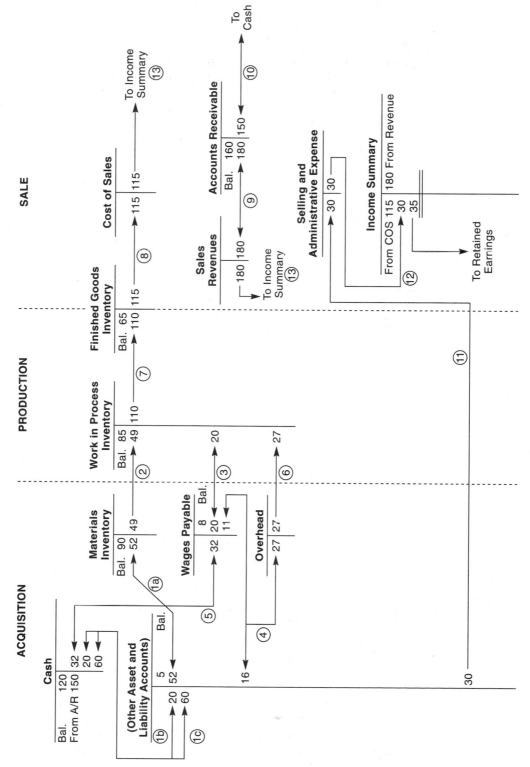

Note: Circled numbers refer to events and journal entries described in the text.

The following explains the cycle of operations depicted on the flowchart (each journal entry described should be traced to Illustration 17–2):

1. During the month $52,000 of materials were purchased on open account, $20,000 of various other assets were purchased for cash, and $60,000 of accounts payable were paid. The journal entries recording these transactions are as follows:

```
a. Materials Inventory.............................. 52,000
       Accounts Payable.............................          52,000

b. (Other Asset and Liability Accounts) .............. 20,000
       Cash.........................................          20,000

c. Accounts Payable ............................... 60,000
       Cash.........................................          60,000
```

2. During the month direct materials costing $49,000 (principally felt tips, plastic, ink, and wicks) were withdrawn from inventory and sent to the factory to be converted into pens. This decrease in Materials Inventory and increase in Work in Process Inventory is recorded:

```
Work in Process Inventory.......................... 49,000
       Materials Inventory.............................          49,000
```

3. During the month direct labor employees converted this material into pens. The $20,000 that they earned adds to the amount of Work in Process Inventory, and the resulting liability increases Wages Payable, as recorded in the following journal entry:

```
Work in Process Inventory.......................... 20,000
       Wages Payable ...................................          20,000
```

4. Overhead (indirect production) costs amounting to $27,000 were incurred during the month. Of the total $10,600 was documented by current invoices for such things as rent, electricity, and telephone bills, so the offsetting credits were to Accounts Payable. Indirect labor and supervision costs were $11,000, with the offsetting credit to Wages Payable. The remaining $5,400 represented depreciation on factory assets. All of these items are here summed up in the general account, Overhead, but in practice they are usually recorded in separate indirect cost accounts, one for each type of cost. The journal entry is:

```
Overhead .......................................... 27,000
       Wages Payable ...................................          11,000
       (Other Asset and Liability Accounts) .............          16,000
```

5. Factory employees (direct and indirect) were paid $32,000 cash. This decreased the liability account, Wages Payable, and also decreased Cash. (The payment of wages also involves FICA taxes, withholding taxes, and other complications, which have been omitted from this introductory diagram.) The journal entry is:

Wages Payable	32,000	
Cash		32,000

6.   Since the overhead costs incurred during the month are a part of the cost of the pens worked on during that month, at month-end the total overhead cost incurred is transferred to Work in Process Inventory, as in the following journal entry:

Work in Process Inventory	27,000	
Overhead		27,000

This $27,000 credit to Overhead reduces that account's balance to zero. The Overhead account is called a **clearing account** because the month's accumulated overhead costs are "cleared out" of this account at the end of each month. Also, note that the actual indirect production costs were first debited to this Overhead account (entry 4). Such debits to Overhead may take place several times during the month as overhead costs are incurred. The month-end credit clearing entry then transferred those costs from their temporary repository in Overhead and applied them to Work in Process Inventory along with the direct material and direct labor costs. (We stress understanding the nature of the Overhead clearing account at this point because our experience has shown that such an understanding now minimizes difficulties encountered later on with more complicated aspects of overhead accounting.)

7.   Pens whose total cost was $110,000 were completed during the month and transferred to Finished Goods Inventory. This resulted in a decrease in Work in Process Inventory, as recorded in the following journal entry:

Finished Goods Inventory	110,000	
Work in Process Inventory		110,000

8.   Pens with a cost of $115,000 were sold during the month. These pens were removed from inventory and shipped to customers. On the accounting records this is reflected by a credit to Finished Goods Inventory and a debit to Cost of Sales,[8] as in the following journal entry:

Cost of Sales	115,000	
Finished Goods Inventory		115,000

9.   For these same pens, sales revenue of $180,000 was earned; this is recorded in the accounts as a credit to Sales Revenue and a debit to Accounts Receivable. Note that the Sales Revenue credit described here and the Cost of Sales debit described in entry 8 related to the *same* pens. The

---

[8]As noted in Chapter 6, some manufacturing companies use the term *Cost of Goods Sold* rather than *Cost of Sales*.

difference between the balances in the Sales Revenue and Cost of Sales accounts, which is $65,000, therefore represents the gross margin earned on pens sold during the month. The journal entry for the sales transaction is:

```
Accounts Receivable ...............................  180,000
     Sales Revenue...................................             180,000
```

10. Accounts receivable collected during the month amounted to $150,000. Some of these collections were for sales made in the current month, but most were for sales made in previous months. The journal entry is:

```
Cash...............................................  150,000
     Accounts Receivable.............................             150,000
```

11. During the month $30,000 of selling and administrative (period) expenses were incurred. These are recorded in the following journal entry:

```
Selling and Administrative Expense.................   30,000
     (Other Asset and Liability Accounts) .............             30,000
```

12. Since S&A expenses are always applicable to the current period, the Selling and Administrative Expense account is closed to the Income Summary account, as in the following journal entry:

```
Income Summary ...................................   30,000
     Selling and Administrative Expense...............             30,000
```

13. The balances in the Sales Revenue and Cost of Sales accounts are also closed to Income Summary. The $35,000 balance in Income Summary then reflects the pretax income for the period. (To simplify the example, income taxes and certain nonoperating and financial items normally appearing on income statements have been excluded.) These closing journal entries are:

```
Sales Revenue ......................................  180,000
     Income Summary ...............................             180,000

Income Summary ...................................  115,000
     Cost of Sales ......................................             115,000
```

Strictly speaking, the product costing system ends with entry 8. The other entries are given in order to show the complete set of transactions for the company. The income statement for the Marker Pen Company is shown in Illustration 17–3.

Chapter 18 will further describe product costing systems, including the details of measuring the direct costs of products and of assigning products their fair share of indirect costs. Before becoming familiar with those aspects of product costing, however, we shall consider full cost information for cost objects other than tangible goods.

ILLUSTRATION 17–3

MARKER PEN COMPANY
Income Statement
For the Month of _____

Sales	$180,000
Cost of sales	115,000
Gross margin	65,000
Selling and administrative expense	30,000
Income (before income taxes)	$ 35,000

NONMANUFACTURING COSTS

Until the last three or four decades, most cost accounting systems dealt solely with measuring the costs of manufactured goods. This was probably because these costs must be measured in order to obtain the amounts for Work in Process Inventory and Finished Goods Inventory on the balance sheet and the amount for Cost of Sales on the income statement. Other costs are reported as expenses on the income statement in aggregate amounts; hence, there was no need to assign them to specific cost objects for external financial reporting purposes.

In more recent years cost accounting systems have been expanded to include other types of cost. For industrial firms these include the selling, general, and administrative costs mentioned earlier. Instead of treating such costs as broad categories, cost systems can treat them as more specific cost objects. For example, each marketing function—advertising, personal selling, market research, and so on—can be a cost object. Some of these can be subdivided into still smaller cost objects. For example, personal selling costs can be categorized by customer, industry, geographical region, or even individual field salesperson; each such category is a cost object.

In whatever manner these cost objects are defined by a company, the guiding principle remains the same: the full cost of a cost object is the sum of its direct costs plus an equitable share of indirect costs. For example, if the cost object is an individual field salesperson, the direct costs include the person's salary (or commissions) and fringes, travel expenses, and costs of entertaining clients. The indirect costs include the salary of the district sales manager and the costs of operating the district sales office that provides support services to the field salesperson. The principles for making the indirect cost assignment are the same as those for assigning indirect costs to products (described in Chapter 18).

Merchandising Companies

In drugstores, department stores, supermarkets, and other merchandising companies, cost of sales is essentially the merchant's invoice cost of the goods sold. These companies therefore need only a very simple cost accounting system to find the cost of sales. They do, however, use full cost information for other purposes, a principal one being to measure the profitability of various selling departments within the company. Each selling department is a cost object.

Service Organizations

In the United States more people are employed by service organizations (including government agencies) than by manufacturing firms. The same general approach used in measuring the cost of tangible goods is applicable to measuring the cost of services they provide.

In some service organizations it is appropriate to treat the services provided to a specific client as a "job" and to establish a cost object for each job. For example, automobile repair shops accumulate on a **job cost record** the costs incurred for each car that they service. This cost record includes direct costs, such as for repair parts and technicians' labor, and a share of the indirect costs of the repair shop, such as the shop supervisor's salary, occupancy costs (heat, light, rent, and so on), and depreciation of shop equipment. This cost record is, in effect, a work in process inventory account for that particular job, which is a cost object. Cost accounting in firms providing legal, architectural, engineering, and consulting services also uses a job cost record for each job or project worked on by the firm. Similarly, hospital and medical clinic accounting systems treat each patient as a cost object, establishing a job cost record for the services the patient is provided. Chapter 18 discusses in more detail the principles of **job costing;** these apply to both manufacturing and service organizations.

In other cases a service organization does not establish a cost record for each job. For example, in a hospital laboratory, a separate cost record is not established for each individual blood analysis performed. Instead, to determine the cost of such a blood test, an averaging process is used. First, the direct costs of performing these tests are identified; these are the costs of the lab technicians' time and the specialized supplies they use to perform the tests. Second, since the lab performs other tests in addition to blood tests, the cost of the laboratory supervisor, lab occupancy costs, and similar general costs are indirect costs of the various types of tests performed. Thus, a share of these indirect costs is assigned to the blood test cost object. Finally, a count is kept of the number of blood tests performed. For a given time period, the full cost of the blood test cost object divided by the number of tests performed gives the average per-unit cost of a blood test. This approach is called **process costing** and is described further in Chapter 18.

Nonprofit Organizations

A **nonprofit organization** is an organization whose primary objective is something other than earning a profit. Most nonprofit organizations provide services rather than manufacture tangible goods. Health-care, educational, performing arts, and membership organizations are predominantly nonprofit organizations. Government organizations are nonprofit organizations.

The cost accounting practices of nonprofit organizations are similar to those of profit-oriented organizations. Both nonprofit and profit-oriented organizations use resources; and in both cases the problem of cost measurement is to identify the amount of resources used for each of the various cost objects that the organization has. However, accounting systems in some nonprofit organizations, particularly government organizations, differ from those in profit-oriented companies. Describing these differences is beyond the scope of this book, but, in general, they do not affect the way in which cost information is accumulated.

For parts of their operations, some nonprofit organizations use cost systems already described. For example, a hospital gift shop is, in effect, a merchandising company; and accounting for client-specific services such as hospital care or blood tests, described above, is conceptually the same whether the hospital is a profit-seeking or nonprofit organization.

Many nonprofit organizations' operations, however, do not involve client-specific transactions. Rather, the operations take the form of goal-oriented sets of activities called **programs** that make services available to the organization's membership or to the general public. For example, a public library lends books through its circulation department, has a periodicals reading room, provides a reference service, and has a special children's section. Each of these related activities constitutes a program of the library and can be treated as a cost object. The full cost of each program is the sum of its direct costs and a fair share of the library's indirect costs, such as heat, lighting, and general maintenance and upkeep.

USES OF FULL COST

Some of the uses management makes of information on full costs are in (1) financial reporting; (2) analysis of profitability; (3) answering the question, "What did it cost?"; (4) arriving at prices in regulated industries; and (5) normal pricing.

Financial Reporting

We have already described how full production cost is the basis for reporting work in process inventory and finished goods inventory on the balance sheet, and cost of sales on the income statement. When a company constructs a building, a machine, or some other fixed asset for its own use, the amount recorded in the accounts and reported on the balance sheet is the asset's full cost.

Cost accounting information is also used to measure the income of the principal segments of the business. As pointed out in Chapter 14, the Financial Accounting Standards Board (FASB) requires that shareholder annual reports of large companies report revenues, operating profit, and identifiable asset amounts for each significant business segment.

Until recently, companies were permitted considerable latitude in deciding how to measure cost of sales for determining their taxable income. The Tax Reform Act of 1986 substantially reduced this latitude. Essentially, the act requires companies to measure cost of goods sold as the full production cost of those goods.

Analysis of Profitability

Chapter 13 discussed ratios and other techniques useful in analyzing the profitability of an *entire* business. Cost accounting makes it possible to make similar analyses of individual *parts* of a business, such as an individual product, product line (a family of related products), plant, division, sales territory, or any other subdivision of the company that is of interest. Using the principles of cost accounting, the direct costs and an appropriate share of the indirect costs of a part can be determined. If the part does not earn a reasonable profit—or if the revenue generated by this part does not exceed these costs by an amount representing a reasonable return on assets employed—there is an indication that something is wrong.

What Did It Cost?

The problem of measuring the cost of something arises in many contexts: What was the cost of eliminating pollution in a certain river? What did the last presidential election cost? What was the cost of police protection last year in City X? What did it cost the U.S. Postal Service to send a letter from Chicago to San Francisco? What was the cost of operating a school cafeteria? What was the cost of a certain research project? These questions are usually answered by measuring the full cost of the cost object.

Cost-Type Contracts.   Full costs are used in contracts in which one party has agreed to buy goods or services from another party at a price based on cost. There are tens of billions of dollars of such contracts annually. Because of the variations in methods of measuring cost, the method to be used in the contract must be spelled out in some detail so as to avoid misunderstanding.

Setting Regulated Prices

Many prices are set not by the forces of the marketplace but by regulatory agencies. These include prices for residential utilities (electricity, gas, water, sewer, and local telephone service), cable television, postal service, insurance premiums, and many others. In each of these cases, the regulatory agency (the Federal Communications Commission, state public utility and insurance commissions, and so on) allows a price equal to full cost plus an allowance for profit. In most cases the regulatory agency provides a manual (sometimes several hundred pages long) spelling out in great detail how full costs are to be measured.

Product Pricing

Differentiated Products and Commodities.   A **differentiated product** is a product that consumers prefer over competing products. The product may be differentiated because of its own characteristics, because consumers are persuaded by advertising, because of warranty or credit terms, or other characteristics. Other, undifferentiated, products are **commodities.** Examples are agricultural products, generic drugs (as contrasted with patented proprietary drugs), minerals, many timber and paper products, and a host of other products that consumers buy without paying attention to the manufacturer or brand name. Some services, such as drive-through oil changes and photocopying, are commodities.

For our purpose the significance of the distinction is that cost measurements are used in arriving at the price of differentiated products, but not the price of commodities. For commodities the selling price is found in the marketplace; the producer sells at this price, or not at all. Essentially, the producer of a commodity succeeds by producing at a lower cost than competitors. Although not used for pricing, cost measurements are used by commodity producers in attempting to reduce costs and, if costs cannot be reduced sufficiently to make a commodity product profitable, in deciding whether to continue offering the product.

Normal Pricing.   As was discussed in Chapter 13, a principal economic objective of a business is to earn a satisfactory return on its investment—on the assets that it uses. In order to earn a satisfactory return, revenues from the sale of goods and services must be large enough both (1) to recover all costs and (2) to earn a profit that provides a satisfactory return on investment. The business will prosper if *for all its products combined,* total sales revenues exceed total costs by a sufficiently large amount. But selling prices must be set separately for each product. How can this be done for *each* product so that a satisfactory profit is earned for *all* products?

The answer is that each product should bear a *fair share* of the total costs of the business. We can expand this statement to say that in general the selling price of a product should be high enough (1) to recover its direct costs, (2) to recover a fair share of all applicable indirect costs, and (3) to yield a satisfactory profit. Such a price is a **normal price.**[9]

The foregoing is a statement of *general tendency* rather than a prescription for setting the selling price for each and every product. In fact, the selling price of a given product usually is not set simply by ascertaining the full cost and profit components and then adding them up. Often, for example, prices are set by estimating the perceived value of a product from the buyer's standpoint. Nevertheless, the measurement of the cost of a product marks a starting point in an analysis of what the actual selling price should be.

Profit Component of Price.   The fact that an objective of a profit-oriented business is to earn a satisfactory return on assets employed suggests that the

---

[9]Some people question whether full costs are widely used as a basis for pricing. In a survey of large industrial companies, 85 percent reported that they do use full cost pricing. (Source: V. Govindarajan and Robert N. Anthony, "How Firms Use Cost Data in Pricing Decisions," *Management Accounting,* July 1983, pp. 30–36.)

profit component of a product's price should be related to the *amount* of assets employed in making the product. Nevertheless, it is common pricing practice to relate the profit component to costs rather than to assets. In some situations it is easy to establish a profit margin expressed as a percentage of cost in such a way that the resulting selling price will give a satisfactory return on assets employed. In general, this is the case when all products have approximately the same unit cost and/or when the assets employed by products vary proportionately with their cost.

> **Example.** A retail shoe store decides that a satisfactory profit is a 15 percent return (before income taxes) on its investment. If its total investment in inventory, accounts receivable, and other assets is estimated to be $600,000, then its profit must be $600,000 * 15 percent = $90,000 for the year. If its total operating costs excluding the cost of the shoes are estimated to be $210,000, then its selling price must be such that the gross margin above the costs of the shoes amounts to $210,000 + $90,000 = $300,000. If the store expects to sell shoes that cost $900,000 in total, then total sales revenue must be $1,200,000 in order to obtain this $300,000.
>
> The store can obtain the desired $300,000 by setting a selling price that is 33⅓ percent above the cost of the shoes ($1,200,000 ÷ $900,000 = 133⅓ percent). If the expected sales volume were realized, this pricing policy would generate revenue of $1,200,000 for the year, of which $900,000 would go for the cost of the shoes, $210,000 for operating costs, and $90,000 for profit. Shoe store owners customarily describe such a set of numbers as demonstrating a profit of 7.5 percent on sales (= $90,000 ÷ $1,200,000). More important, it is a return of 15 percent on assets employed (= $90,000 ÷ $600,000).

Although setting the profit margin as a percentage of costs or of selling price works satisfactorily if the assets employed for each product are proportionate to the costs of each product, it breaks down if this condition does not exist. As described in Chapter 13, companies with a relatively low asset turnover require a relatively high profit margin, as a percentage of costs or of selling price, in order to earn a satisfactory return on assets employed.

Assigning assets employed to products involves essentially the same techniques as assigning costs to products. Until fairly recently, it was widely believed that the accounting effort required to assign assets employed to products was so great and the results so unreliable that the effort was not worthwhile. Now, however, it is recognized that practical ways of doing this are not so difficult as had been thought.

Time and Material Pricing. In this method of setting prices, one pricing rate is established for direct labor and a separate pricing rate for direct material. Each of these rates is constructed so that it includes allowances for indirect costs and for profit. This method of pricing is used in repair shops (e.g., for automobile and television repairs), printing shops, and similar types of service establishments. It is also used by many professional persons and organizations, including physicians, lawyers, engineers, ski instructors, consultants of various types, and public accounting firms.

In time and material pricing the *time* component is expressed as a labor rate per hour, which is calculated as the sum of (1) direct salary and fringe benefit costs of the employee; (2) an equitable share of all indirect costs, except those related to material; and (3) an allowance for profit. In professional-service firms this rate is usually called a **billing rate.** The material component of the price includes a **material loading** that is added to the invoice cost of materials used on the job. This loading consists of an allowance for material-handling costs and storage costs plus an allowance for profit.

Nonprofit Organizations. In nonprofit organizations the same pricing practices as those described above are appropriate, with one exception. Since a nonprofit organization has no shareholder equity, it does not need to earn a profit as a return on this investment. Nevertheless, most nonprofit organizations do need a small margin above full costs to provide a safety allowance for unforeseen contingencies and to pay for the cost of holding current assets (which usually is not counted as an element of product cost).

Adjusting Costs to Prices. Pricing, quite naturally, is usually thought of as the process of setting selling prices. In some situations, however, the process works in reverse: the selling price that is believed to be the best from the standpoint of competitive strategy is taken as a given; the problem then is to determine how much cost the company can afford to incur if it is to earn a satisfactory profit at the given price. This approach is called **target costing.** In the apparel business, for example, it is customary to use retail "price points": $19.95, $29.95, $39.95, and so on. The manufacturer designs individual garments to fit one of these price points. In order to ensure that the manufacturer makes a satisfactory profit on a garment, the retail selling price is taken as a given, the retailer's normal gross margin is deducted to arrive at the manufacturer's selling price, and then the manufacturer's normal gross margin is subtracted. The remainder is how much the manufacturer can afford to spend on cloth, labor, and other elements of production cost. Target costing has been used by Japanese firms for automobiles and consumer electronics products, among others.[10]

Contribution Pricing. In the situations described above the company makes pricing decisions using information on full costs as a first approximation. There are other situations in which individual products may be sold at a loss—that is, at a price below full costs. Even though these products are sold at a loss, under certain conditions they may increase the company's total profit. These are special situations, and they require special cost constructions. The approach, called **contribution pricing,** is described in Chapter 26.

Importance of Timely Cost Data. Whatever the basis of pricing— including following a market price—the relevant cost data are current costs

---

[10]See Toshiro Hiromoto, "Another Hidden Edge—Japanese Management Accounting," *Harvard Business Review* (July–August 1988).

and estimates of near-term future costs. However, the cost system data may not report current costs. This is especially true in inflationary times. This is not to say that companies are always willing or able to pass these increases on to their customers in the form of higher prices. It is important, though, for management to know that costs have increased, so that price increases can at least be considered. Every year hundreds of businesses (most of them small) go bankrupt because their managers did not know the current costs of producing the firms' goods or services and hence set inadequate prices.

SUMMARY

Cost measures the monetary amount of resources used for some purpose. The purpose is called a cost object. The cost objects in a manufacturing company are its products, organization units, projects, and any activity for which cost information is desired.

Full cost means all the resources used for a cost object. Full cost is the sum of (1) the cost object's direct costs (the costs that are directly traced to it) and (2) a fair share of the indirect costs (those costs incurred jointly for several cost objects). A cost accounting system routinely collects costs and assigns them to cost objects. A T account flowchart of a cost accounting system is helpful in understanding how the system works.

Cost accounting systems are well developed for tangible goods. In recent years the same principles have increasingly been applied to services and to selling and administrative activities in both profit-seeking and nonprofit organizations. Full cost information for goods and services is used in financial reporting, in analyzing the profitability of parts of a business, in answering the question, "What did it cost?," as a basis for setting regulated prices, and as a first approximation in deciding on selling prices of differentiated products.

Cases

CASE 17–1   Delaney Motors*

Frank Delaney owned and operated Delaney Motors, a General Motors automobile dealership in Ohio. Its operations consisted of new-car sales, used-car sales, parts sales, vehicle lease and rentals, vehicle service, and automobile body repairing and repainting. The dealership was profitable, earning almost 5 percent on sales, but the reported profit on the body shop operation seemed low to Mr. Delaney. Consequently, he engaged a consultant to study the body shop operation and make recommendations.

As background for his study, the consultant took Mr. Delaney's data for the most recent year and made certain adjustments, shown in Exhibit 1. He explained them in the following paragraphs taken from his report:

> Most semivariable costs contain a significant portion of common costs. For example, the accountant performs many common services in order to maintain the corporate structure (e.g., preparing and filing the dealer's tax returns). The attorneys and the owner also spend much of their time providing general services.
>
> Although many of the expenses would not be significantly reduced if the owner

sold certain departments, each department benefits from these expenses, and thus should be allocated a portion of these costs. The body shop, for example, should pay its proportionate share of accountant's fees relating to the preparation and filing of the dealership's income tax returns.

Telephone expenses and the fixed costs could properly be allocated to the departments if the necessary documentation were available. Since it is not, other cost allocation methods must be considered.

A potentially controversial issue involves the owner's salary. The body shop manager could claim that because he exercises no control over the owner's salary, this cost should not be charged to his department. The owner puts his time and name in all aspects of the business, however, and his salary should be allocated accordingly. Furthermore, industry data show that owners' salaries tend to vary with sales volume.

Semivariable costs can be allocated to operating departments in several ways, thereby better appraising departmental and managerial performance. These bases include units of production, machine-hours, material costs, sales dollars, direct labor costs, and direct labor-hours. Valid cost allocation bases reliably relate semivariable costs to the basis used for the allocation. Because the operating departments produce heterogeneous products that require dissimilar materials and machines (the new-car and used-car departments probably use no machines), the first three allocation bases—units of production, machine-hours, and material costs—clearly are inappropriate.

*This case is based on material in Alan Reinstein, "Improving Cost Allocation for Auto Dealers," *Management Accounting*, June 1982, pp. 52–57. Used by permission.

EXHIBIT 1
ANALYSIS OF BODY SHOP PROFITABILITY

Line

1	Sales: body shop.......................................	$306,652
2	Gross profit: body shop	91,107
3	Gross profit percentage (line 2 ÷ line 1)	29.7%

Analysis of semivariable costs

4	Legal and auditing (body shop)..........................	0
5	Owner's salary (body shop)..............................	0
6	Telephone and telegraph (body shop).....................	839
7	Total body shop semivariable costs.......................	839
8	Legal and auditing (company)	2,113
9	Owner's salary (company)...............................	21,600
10	Telephone and telegraph (company)......................	21,676
11	Total company semivariable costs	45,389
12	Body shop percentage (line 7 ÷ line 11)..................	1.85%
13	Body shop employees as percent of total (5/23)............	21.7%
14	Revised body shop semivariable costs (line 11 * line 13).....	9,867
15	Increase in body shop semivariable costs (line 14 − line 7) ..	9,028

Analysis of fixed costs

16	Body shop fixed costs, as now allocated	6,106
17	Total company fixed costs	28,815
18	Body shop percentage (line 16 ÷ line 17)..................	23.65%
19	Revised body shop fixed costs (20% of line 17).............	5,163
20	Decrease in body shop fixed costs (line 19 − line 16)	(943)

Summary of findings

21	Net increase in costs (line 15 − line 20)....................	8,085
22	Unrevised body shop profit	9,009
23	Revised body shop profit (line 22 − line 21)	924
24	Unrevised profit to sales (line 22 ÷ line 1).................	2.94%
25	Revised profit to sales (line 23 ÷ line 1)...................	0.30%

		Other Dealers		
		No. 9	*No. 6*	*No. 3*
1	Sales, body shop	$363,662	$505,025	$681,201
3	Gross profit percent............	32.9%	30.0%	30.6%
14	Body shop, semivariable*.......	9,547	13,913	18,177
19	Body shop, fixed*.............	12,767	11,134	12,233
22	Body shop profit, unrevised	4,453	26,338	56,401
23	Body shop profit (loss)*........	(8,190)	19,386	36,650
24	Unrevised percent profit to sales	1.22%	5.22%	8.28%
25	Revised percent profit to sales*..	(2.25)%	3.84%	5.38%

*Revised, as described in text.

Sales dollars also are an invalid cost allocation basis. For example, the cost of sales ratio on a $9,000 new automobile usually exceeds the cost of sales ratio for a $1,000 body shop repair, thereby implying an unequal allocation basis.

Direct labor costs do constitute a valid cost allocation basis in companies in which semivariable costs are labor related (i.e., the operations are predominantly manual) and hourly rates among and within departments are fairly uniform. But because the dealership's semivariable costs are not labor related and the hourly rates are usually not uniform, direct labor costs do not constitute a competent activity basis for your company.

Direct labor-hours will provide an acceptable cost allocation base. Although some semivariable costs do not vary directly with direct labor-hours, such as legal and audit fees, in the interest of practicality and because the other methods clearly are not acceptable, allocating semivariable costs based on direct labor-hours appears to be the most viable alternative.

Your financial statements list the number of direct and indirect employees in each department but fail to disclose the number of departmental hours worked. It is assumed that all direct employees work approximately the same number of hours per week. The number of direct laborers consequently becomes the cost allocation base for semivariable costs. As discussed later, fixed costs are allocated based on the ratio of departmental square footage to total dealer square footage, adjusted by a weighting factor.

Calculations

A summary of selected data extracted from your financial statements is shown in Exhibit 1.

The body shop's and dealership's semivariable costs are shown in lines 7 and 11, respectively. Semivariable cost allocations are based upon direct labor-hours, assuming that each employee works the same number of hours per week. In line 13 the number of body shop employees performing the direct labor work is divided by the total number of employees for the entire dealership. Based on this method, the increase in semivariable costs, as seen in line 15, shows that you have underallocated overhead to the body shop manager, whose bonus includes a portion of his department's profit. The cost accounting system therefore should be changed to more accurately reflect each department's use of dealership resources.

Fixed costs for the body shop and the dealership are summarized in lines 16 and 17. The quotient of these two amounts appears in line 18. In line 19 the revised allocation of fixed costs is shown. Many GM dealers allocate fixed costs to the body shop based on the ratio of body shop square footage to dealer's total square footage. This allocation base accurately allocates fixed building costs but fails to account for the various machinery, equipment, furniture, and fixtures located throughout the dealership.

To allocate these fixed costs more properly, "weights," similar to those developed by Volkswagen, should be used.[1] Volkswagen dealers multiply the square footage of each dealership segment by a value factor to weight the proper distribution of fixed costs. For example, used vehicles and body shop weights are 2.4 and 1.0, respectively. Assuming that these weights also apply to you, you should reduce your allocation to the body shop to 20 percent. Line 19 thus represents this 20 percent balance of the dealership's fixed costs.

Lines 21 through 25 summarize the findings. The revised cost allocations decrease the body shop's profits from 2.94 percent of sales to 0.30 percent of sales.

The consultant had collected data similar to that shown in Exhibit 1 for 11 other dealerships. Summary data for three of these

---

[1]Volkswagen Dealers' Accounting and Management Procedures Manual, *Distribution of Occupancy Expenses,* pp. K80–K81.

are shown at the bottom of Exhibit 1. They are arranged in order of the body shop profit percentage (line 25): Dealer No. 3 had the third highest percentage, Dealer No. 6 was in the middle, and Dealer No. 9 was third from the bottom.

The consultant pointed out that the body shop was even less profitable than Mr. Delaney had thought, and he suggested that Mr. Delaney consider selling it, leasing it to another party, increasing prices, or, if the body shop demand was thought to be elastic, lowering prices. He pointed out that selling or leasing the body shop would permit Mr. Delaney to devote more time to other areas of the dealership.

Mr. Delaney considered this recommendation, but he was by no means sure that profitability should be the major consideration. He felt that the dealership had an obligation to provide high-quality body shop work to its customers, and that a lessee might provide below-standard service. He was not sure that prices could be raised, but asked the consultant to find out more about the prices charged by competitive dealers before making a judgment on this.

Questions

1. Comment on the consultant's adjustments made in Exhibit 1. Do you agree with each of them? If not, can you suggest better methods of making the adjustments for the stated purpose?

2. Assuming Mr. Delaney decides to keep the body shop, and the consultant reports that it is feasible to raise prices, should Mr. Delaney do so? If he does, what general guide can you suggest as to how much prices should be increased?

3. What action should Mr. Delaney take?

CASE 17–2 Lipman Bottle Company*

In November 1982 Robert Lipman, vice president of Lipman Bottle Company, was wondering what pricing strategy he should recommend to his father. Located in Albany, New York, Lipman Bottle began operations as a bottle distributor in 1909. Distributors maintain a close working relationship with several major bottle manufacturers (e.g., Owens-Illinois). In return for acting as a sales representative, distributors receive a discount of 5–8 percent off regular prices. This permits distributors to charge users of bottles the same price as if a purchase were made directly from the manufacturer.

Typically, distributors maintain a warehouse with an inventory of commonly used bottles and closures. For special or large orders, distributors arrange for an order to be shipped directly from the manufacturer to the distributor's customer. The manufacturer bills the distributor at factory price less 5–8 percent, and the distributor bills the user at factory price. The advantages for the manufacturer are that a smaller sales force is required and that the distributor will service accounts too small to be served by one manufacturer. The advantages to the user are that the distributor can provide immediate delivery of many items, can offer the advantage of greater buying power, and can serve as an expert who is familiar with bottles and closures from many manufacturers.

EXHIBIT 1

LIPMAN BOTTLE COMPANY
Income Statement—Printing Operations
10 Months Ended October 31, 1982

		Variable with Machine-Hours	Variable with No. of Passes	Fixed
Sales revenues	$379,880			
Expenses:				
Payroll	216,258	$161,258		$ 55,000
Supplies	12,458		$12,458	
Factory expense	20,389	10,389	5,000	5,000
Machine parts	4,457		4,457	
Depreciation	22,505	17,505		5,000
Rent	23,770			23,770
Heat, light, and power	20,897		18,897	2,000
Health insurance	19,176	14,000		5,176
Miscellaneous	7,933	7,933		
Insurance	14,541	10,000		4,541
Payroll tax	17,793	13,000		4,793
Advertising	1,664			1,664
Total expenses	381,841*	$234,085	$40,812	$106,944
Profit (loss)	$ (1,961)			
Total machine-hours (including setup)		16,000		
Variable cost per machine-hour		$14.63		
Total passes			15,500,000	
Cost per thousand passes			$2.63	

*Scrap costs are not included in the printing department expenses.

In the past 20 years the growing use of plastics had increased business for bottle distributors for at least two reasons. First, the choice of bottles had expanded greatly, making expert advice more valuable. The growing variety of caps, lids, and spray pumps handled by distributors had had a similar effect. A second reason was that distributors began specializing in printing labels directly onto plastic bottles. For many users it was convenient to have both purchasing and printing of plastic bottles handled by one vendor.

The Firm. In 1981 Lipman had total sales of $6.2 million, with $500,000 from printing operations. Although the printing operation was only marginally profitable, that service was considered essential for ob-taining the more profitable bottle sales. While he realized that printing should not be viewed solely in terms of its profits, Mr. Lipman felt that the firm was offering a valuable service and should price that service to earn a reasonable return.

Last year printing sales were $500,000, and we made $30,000. This year, with the economy worse, we'll sell $450,000 and about break even (Exhibit 1). We have capacity for $1 million. I'm not sure what to do. We're the leading firm in Albany; there is another firm here, about half our size. There's also a new small firm causing trouble with price cutting. Our main competitor has begun to cut prices as well. I hate to, but I have to do the same thing. What worries me is that I don't really know what

EXHIBIT 2
PRINTING PRICES CHARGED BY INDUSTRY LEADERS
Price per Thousand (M) Bottles
At Various Order Quantities

Bottle Size (oz.)	Order Quantity					
	Under 10M	10M	25M	50M	100M	250M
	One Separation					
0–4.9	40.45	31.80	24.40	21.20	20.25	18.20
5–9.9	47.00	36.60	27.90	24.10	23.40	20.80
10–14.9	59.00	46.00	35.30	30.80	29.00	26.10
15–23.9	68.80	53.20	41.00	35.60	34.10	30.50
24–32.9	72.40	56.80	43.10	37.90	36.10	32.20
	Two Separations					
0–4.9	94.00	72.10	55.70	48.60	46.50	42.40
5–9.9	106.00	82.60	63.40	55.40	52.50	47.30
10–14.9	132.00	103.00	78.90	69.00	66.10	59.15
15–23.9	158.60	122.80	94.60	82.80	79.00	70.50
24–32.9	162.20	125.60	96.10	84.10	80.40	71.40

my prices should be, or which prices to cut. We can charge a little more than the large bottle manufacturers, but not much.

Albany is still a good market even with the competition. There is some price cutting, but I know we can keep our market share. The market here, though, is primarily to industrial users. The real market is New York–New Jersey. That's where the cosmetics and pharmaceutical manufacturers are located. If we could get a couple of shampoo bottles, we'd really grow.

Pricing. The bottle printing industry consists of two primary types of printers aside from distributors. Bottle manufacturers provide printing as a service to customers who purchase their plastic bottles. Price lists are published for printing, with the cost of scrap bottles included in the price. Discounts from list prices are unusual.

The second class of printers is custom decorating houses. Price lists are rarely published, although custom pricing is similar to price lists published by bottle manufacturers,

adjusted for difficulty of design. Small discounts, however, are widespread. Since printing is normally done on bottles supplied by the customer, the printer is not responsible for scrap costs, but does not receive a commission on sale of bottles.

Lipman had far more printing capacity than needed to print bottles that the firm sold. Thus, Lipman both published a price list for simple designs and acted as a custom decorating house with special pricing. As shown in Exhibit 2, the price list of a major bottle manufacturer, prices are influenced by three factors:

A. *Bottle size* (capacity in fluid ounces). Bottles are loaded onto a chuck, then rotated while a silk screen moves horizontally to print directly onto the plastic bottle. Since larger bottles take longer to print and require more warehouse space, prices increase as bottle size increases.

B. *Quantity.* Each run requires setup time to load ink and a silk screen onto a machine and to set the machine to accept a bottle. In addition, there may be a slight learning effect with each bottle. Thus, cost per bottle decreases as quantity increases.

C. *Separations.* "Separations" means the number of individual impressions required to print a single bottle. When round bottles are printed, they are rotated horizontally in place in the printing machine. A silk screen with the image to be printed is positioned above the bottle and slides horizontally, synchronized to move at the same speed as the surface of the bottle. Because it rotates 360°, a round bottle can be printed front and back in a single machine cycle; i.e., this is a one-separation or single "pass" operation. However, two-sided bottles (commonly called ovals) cannot rotate and thus, generally, only one side can be printed per pass. Printing both front and back of an oval usually requires the entire lot of bottles to be loaded and unloaded twice—one pass per side, or a total of two separations. When decorating a bottle in multiple colors, the artwork must be separated into its color components and a separate screen prepared for each color. To decorate a round bottle in three colors, for example, requires three separate screens and three passes, whereas oval bottles require one screen and one pass per color, per side (a total of six separations, for a three-colored oval).

Operations. The Lipman graphics department included a camera and a developing lab for producing silk screens for printing. Since customers were charged separately for these services, that department was close to a break-even operation.

Production operations consisted of 10 printing machines and 8 drying ovens. Bottles were loaded onto a machine for printing, then placed on a conveyor that carried those bottles through a drying oven. Two extra printing machines were available so that they could be rolled to the setup area and prepared for a new job. This permitted greater utilization of costly ovens and the space they occupied.

Eight of the machines were semiautomatic. Each bottle had to be loaded into the machine and unloaded onto the dryer belt by hand. Ovals, as described above, had to be printed on one side, allowed to dry, then reloaded for printing on the reverse side. However, one machine had an automatic feature for oval bottles. An operator still had to load and unload that machine manually, but ovals could be printed on both sides before being unloaded into the drying oven. The remaining machine was fully automatic. One operator loaded bottles into a feed hopper, while a second operator observed the printing operations for quality. Oval bottles could be printed on both sides in a single machine cycle and were automatically unloaded into the drying oven.

The Problem. Mr. Lipman asked Thomas Shull, a consultant, to review the firm's pricing policy:

> We publish a price list for simple jobs printed on our bottles. Since we earn a commission on the bottles, prices aren't all that important for printing. However, I'm not sure that the industry pricing is correct. Prices decrease with order size and increase with bottle size. I think that the decrease in price with order size is reasonable, since we don't have to search for more business to keep our shop full if we have large orders. Bottle size pricing doesn't seem quite right, however. It does take longer to print a large bottle than a small one, but the difference isn't all that great. Maybe the price differential shouldn't be as large as it is.
>
> A second factor is the new automatic machines that print both sides of an oval without reloading. Most of our competitors

EXHIBIT 3
SCRAP AND SHIPPING COSTS

| | | One Separation | Two Separations | | |
| | | | Cost of Scrap | | |
Size	Cost of 1,000 Bottles	Cost of 2 Percent Lost Bottles (scrap)	Cost of 4 Percent Lost Bottles (scrap)	Loss of 2 Percent of Printing*	Total Cost of Scrap
0–1 oz....	$ 70	$1.40	$2.80	$0.50	$3.30
1¼–4.......	84	1.68	3.36	0.50	3.86
5–6.......	94	1.88	3.76	0.50	4.26
7–10......	116	2.32	4.64	0.50	5.14
11–12......	125	2.50	5.00	0.50	5.50
13–16......	130	2.60	5.20	0.50	5.70
17–32......	145	2.90	5.80	0.50	6.30

Cost of Shipping to New York–New Jersey Area

Size	Bottles per Truckload	Cost per 1,000 Bottles†
0–1 oz................	1,040,000	$ 1.06
1¼–4..................	280,000	3.93
5–6..................	190,000	5.79
7–10.................	145,000	7.59
11–12.................	120,000	9.17
13 16........	86,000	12.79
17–32................	42,000	26.19

*Preliminary estimate of printing costs is $25 per thousand.
†Estimated cost per truckload is $1,100.

use semiautomatic machines. Maybe we shouldn't be charging as much for ovals with the new machines.

The final problem is our custom decorating. We are trying to expand in the New York–New Jersey area, and almost all of the business we might get would be custom decorating. We would have no commissions on bottles, so our profit would be entirely from printing. We would also have to pay freight.

I would like to see our published price list revised to reflect our costs. However, I don't want it to vary greatly from the ones published by major manufacturers. I would also like to know variable cost for bidding on custom decorating. That won't be published, since I have to adjust each price for difficulty of the order; but I'll use the cost list as a guide. Finally, I'd like costs adjusted

for transportation to New York–New Jersey. My goal is to earn 30 percent on sales before tax when we're at capacity.

Before preparing price lists, Mr. Shull, Mr. Lipman, and the operations manager agreed that the scrap and shipping costs in Exhibit 3, and the operating information in Exhibit 4, would be used in pricing calculations.

Questions

1. Calculate the variable costs per thousand bottles for one-separation rounds, two-separation rounds, and two-separation ovals, assuming that all ovals are printed on the machine with the automatic feature for ovals. Do one set of calculations for the Albany area (scrap included) and another for New York–New Jersey (freight included, but not scrap).

EXHIBIT 4
OPERATING INFORMATION

1. Cost per hour of setup time and of operating time are approximately equal.
2. Setup time for a job is approximately two hours per separation.
3. Average operating time for one-separation jobs on semiautomatic machines is approximately 0.95 hour per 1,000 bottles, regardless of quantity. Sizes 0–1 ounce and 17–32 ounces are approximately 5 percent slower than average (1.0 hour per 1,000), while all other sizes are approximately 5 percent faster than average (0.9 hour per 1,000).
4. Average operating time for two-separation jobs on semiautomatic machines is approximately 1.1 hours per 1,000 passes (2.2 hours per 1,000 bottles), regardless of quantity. Sizes 0–1 ounce and 17–32 ounces are approximately 10 percent slower than average (1.2 hours per 1,000 passes, 2.4 hours per 1,000 bottles), and other sizes 10 percent faster (1.0 hour per 1,000 passes, 2.0 hours per 1,000 bottles).
5. Average operating times for ovals on the semiautomatic machine with automatic feature for ovals is approximately 0.80 hour per 1,000 passes (1.6 hours per 1,000 bottles), regardless of quantity. Sizes 0–1 ounce and 17–32 ounces are approximately 10 percent slower than average (0.88 hour per 1,000 passes, 1.76 hours per 1,000 bottles), while all other sizes are approximately 10 percent faster than average (0.72 hour per 1,000 passes, 1.44 hours per 1,000 bottles).
6. The fully automatic machine is approximately twice as fast on rounds as the semiautomatic machines and approximately twice as fast on ovals as the semiautomatic machine with automatic feature for ovals. However, two people are required to operate the machine and it is approximately twice as costly to operate. Thus, this machine can be ignored for costing purposes.

To keep the number of calculations you need to do within reason, consider only two bottle size ranges—0–1 ounce and 17–32 ounces—and only two order quantity ranges—5,000–9,999 and 100,000–249,999. (Together with the two sales areas, this results in 24 combinations for which to calculate variable costs.)

2. Prepare a suggested price list for the Albany area. Consider only one-separation rounds and two-separation rounds or ovals, and only the two sizes and order quantities described in Question 1. How did Mr. Lipman's goal of a 30 percent margin (at capacity) affect your price recommendations?

3. Which products should the company attempt to sell in New York–New Jersey? Explain.

18

Additional Aspects of Product Costing Systems

This chapter describes the two general types of product cost accounting: job order costing and process costing. Also discussed are the measurement of direct material and direct labor costs, along with the techniques for allocating to a product its fair share of indirect costs. This discussion describes, in effect, how to determine the numbers that flow through a cost accounting system (such as the one diagrammed in Illustration 17–2). Also described is a more detailed approach to indirect cost allocation—activity-based costing. As in the preceding chapter, these systems and techniques are illustrated in a manufacturing setting, in part because it is easier to visualize tangible products. However, the concepts and techniques also apply to nonmanufacturing settings.

JOB ORDER COSTING AND PROCESS COSTING

Production Processes

The production processes employed by companies can be thought of in terms of four classifications: unit production, batch production, assembly-line production, and process production. In **unit production,** the focus of activity is a physically identifiable job, such as producing a large turbine generator, building a custom-designed house, or performing a consulting job for a client. In **batch** (or **lot**) **production,** a batch of identical items (for example, 100 fuel injectors) moves in stages from one factory workstation to

599

ILLUSTRATION 18–1
SPECTRUM OF PRODUCTION PROCESSES

| Unit Production | Batch Production | Assembly-Line Production | Process Production |

the next. In **assembly-line production,** the jobs are separately identifiable but tend to be similar (or identical) to one another, such as assembling Pontiac Grand-Ams, Compaq computers, and Whirlpool refrigerators. In **process production,** outputs are not identifiable as individual units of product until late in the production process; examples are found in the petroleum, chemical, milling, steel, distillery, forest products, and glass container industries.

As with many classification schemes, the lines between these categories are not clear-cut. Rather, any production process falls somewhere on a continuum, or spectrum, with "pure" unit production operations (called **job shops**) at one end, "pure" process operations at the other end, and batch and assembly-line operations falling somewhere in between. (See Illustration 18–1.)

Averaging

One key purpose of a product costing system in any of these production settings is to arrive at the full production cost for *one unit* of product. Achieving this purpose can be complicated. Some costs are incurred at a fairly uniform level throughout the year (e.g., supervisory salaries), whereas production volume may fluctuate from month to month. How are fixed costs to be assigned on an ongoing basis to individual units of product? Similarly, for some direct labor costs, it is not feasible to track the cost to a specific unit of product. On an automobile assembly line, for example, a worker may have a minute or less to perform the designated task on a specific vehicle; obviously, there is not enough time for the worker to record the vehicle identification number and task starting and ending times necessary to charge that worker's actual time to that specific vehicle.

Product costing systems deal with these complications by *averaging* some total cost items to arrive at unit cost amounts. It is important to recognize where in the system such averaging takes place.

Basic Types of System

In accounting there are two basic types of product costing systems: job order systems and process systems. Organizations that operate according to unit production and batch production ordinarily use job order cost systems, whereas assembly-line and process production operations use process cost systems. Each system has its own general characteristics (described sepa-

ILLUSTRATION 18-2
JOB COST RECORD

Product: Item 607					Job No. 2270
Date started: 3/28		Date completed: 4/12			
Units started: 100		Units completed: 100			

		Costs			
Week Ending	Dept. No.	Direct Material	Direct Labor	Overhead	Cumulative Cost
March 31	12	$642.00	$108.00	$108.00	$ 858.00
April 7	12		222.00	222.00	1,302.00
7	16		200.00	160.00	1,662.00
14	16		250.00	200.00	2,112.00
Total		$642.00	$780.00	$690.00	$2,112.00
Unit cost		$ 6.42	$ 7.80	$ 6.90	$ 21.12

rately below). In practice, however, a given system may have some characteristics of a job order system and other characteristics of a process system, especially if production operations fall somewhere near the center of the spectrum.

Essentially, a **job order cost system** (or simply **job cost system**) collects costs for *each physically identifiable job* or unit of product as it moves through the production process, regardless of the accounting period in which the work is done. A **process cost system** collects costs for *all* of the products worked on *during an accounting period* and determines unit costs *by averaging* the total costs over the total number of units worked on.

Job Order Costing

The job in a job order cost system may consist of a single unit (e.g., a turbine or a house), or it may consist of a batch of identical items covered by a single production order (e.g., 10,000 copies of a book or 12 dozen style 885 blouses). Each job is given an identification number, and its costs are collected on a **job cost record** set up for that number. Costs are recorded as the job moves through the various steps in the production process; these steps usually correspond to separate departments. Anyone who has had an automobile repaired has seen such a record, except that the amounts that the customer sees have been converted from costs to retail prices.

A job cost record for a manufactured item is shown in Illustration 18-2. The direct material costs are entered based on the total costs from an itemized materials requisition bearing the Job No. 2270. The direct labor costs are entered based on employee time records charging time to Job No. 2270. The overhead costs are charged using departmental rates, the development of which is described later in this chapter. From inspection of the job cost record, one can see that the overhead rate for Department 12 was 100 percent of direct labor costs and the rate for Department 16 was 80 percent. Note that because the cost object—Job No. 2270—included 100 units of item 607, finding the cost of *one* unit requires averaging the total job costs over the 100 units in the batch; this averaging is shown at the bottom of the job cost record.

The sum of all the costs charged to job cost records during an accounting period is the basis for the entries debiting Work in Process (WIP) Inventory and crediting Materials Inventory, Wages Payable, and Overhead accounts (i.e., entries 2, 3, and 6 in Illustration 17–2). When each job is completed, the total cost recorded on the job cost record is the basis for the entry transferring the product from WIP Inventory to Finished Goods Inventory (entry 7), and this same cost is the basis for the entry transferring the product from Finished Goods Inventory to Cost of Sales when the product is sold (entry 8). The total cost recorded on all job cost records for jobs that are still in process as of the end of an accounting period therefore equals the total of the WIP Inventory account at that time.

Some companies, such as professional service firms and repair shops, have no inventory of finished goods. When a job is completed and billed to the client, Cost of Sales is debited and WIP Inventory (sometimes called Jobs in Process) is credited. (In professional service firms, the name Cost of Services is sometimes used, rather than Cost of Sales.)

Process Costing

In a process cost system, all production costs for an accounting period (e.g., one month) are collected in the WIP Inventory account. These costs are *not* identified with specific units or batches of product. A record of the number of units worked on during the period is also maintained. Dividing total costs by the number of units produced gives the average cost per unit. This cost per unit becomes the basis for calculating the dollar amount of the entries that record the transfer from WIP Inventory to Finished Goods Inventory and the subsequent transfer from Finished Goods Inventory to Cost of Sales.

Equivalent Production. Assigning a cost to the partially completed products in WIP Inventory at the end of an accounting period presents a special problem in process costing. These partially completed units cannot be accounted for as if they cost as much as completed units, because only a fraction of their total cost has so far been incurred. Thus, the partially completed units and the completed units must be converted to a common base. This base is called an **equivalent unit of production**—that is, the equivalent of one *completed* unit.

To convert the number of partially completed products into their equivalence in terms of completed units, it is often assumed that units in process at the end of the period are 50 percent complete. Thus, in order to calculate the number of equivalent units produced for the period, (1) each unit completed and transferred out to finished goods is given a weight of one, (2) each unit in process at the end of the period is given a weight of one-half, and (3) these two amounts are added to arrive at the period's equivalent units of production.[1]

Finding the equivalent units of production allows one to find the average cost per equivalent unit by adding the cost of beginning WIP inventory to the production costs of the period and then dividing that sum by the equivalent units of production.

> **Example.** Illustration 18–3 shows how to make this calculation. In a certain factory, production costs incurred in May amounted to $60,600. On May 1 the WIP inventory was valued at a cost of $12,000. During May, 2,450 completed units were transferred from WIP inventory to finished goods inventory. On May 31, 550 equivalent units (1,100 half-completed units) were in WIP inventory. Thus, during May, 3,000 (= 2,450 + 550) equivalent units were produced, as is shown in part B of Illustration 18–3. This means that May's production activities were equivalent to the amount of work that would be needed to start work on and completely produce 3,000 finished units.
>
> Note how the procedures shown in part C assign the $72,600 sum of beginning WIP inventory and May production costs to Finished Goods Inventory and ending WIP Inventory. First, the average cost per equivalent unit is calculated. Then this amount ($24.20) is used to value the equivalent units transferred to finished goods inventory ($59,290) and the partially completed units in ending WIP inventory ($13,310).[2]

Direct Material Cost. The explanation given in the preceding example applies to *conversion cost,* the sum of direct labor cost and overhead. Direct *material* cost may be treated differently, depending on when material enters the production process. Material added evenly throughout the process could reasonably be costed along with the conversion costs by use of the 50

---

[1]It would be more precise to estimate the actual stage of completion of each partially completed unit, but this involves more effort. At the other extreme, some companies disregard the units in process and show no WIP Inventory account. If the work in process inventory is small or if it remains relatively constant in size, no serious error is introduced.

[2]The method used in Illustration 18–3, formally called the **weighted-average process costing method,** is widely used because of its simplicity. Part of that simplicity derives from a fact the reader may have already noted: the partially completed units in *beginning* WIP inventory are ignored in calculating the equivalent units produced. Implicitly, the method assumes that all of these units were completed and transferred to finished goods during the period and that the other units completed and transferred during the period were also started in that period. Because this is what in fact happens in many companies, this assumption usually creates no significant errors. However, a more complicated approach, the **FIFO** (first-in, first-out) **process costing method,** can be used if the errors would be significant. The FIFO method is described in advanced cost accounting texts.

ILLUSTRATION 18–3
EQUIVALENT PRODUCTION CALCULATIONS

A. Assumed Situation

	Units	Cost
Beginning WIP inventory	—	$12,000
Production	—	60,000
Transferred to finished goods inventory	2,450	?
Ending WIP inventory	1,100	?

B. Calculation of Equivalent Units of Production

$$\frac{\text{Equivalent units}}{\text{of production}} = \frac{\text{Units}}{\text{transferred}} + \frac{\text{Equivalent units}}{\text{in ending WIP}}$$

$$3,000 \quad = \quad 2,450 \quad + \quad (0.50 * 1,100)$$

C. Calculation of Cost

$$\text{Unit cost} = \frac{\text{Beginning WIP} + \text{Production costs}}{\text{Equivalent units of production}}$$

$$= \frac{\$12,000 + \$60,600}{3,000 \text{ units}} = \$24.20$$

Work in Process Inventory

Balance, May 1	12,000	To Finished Goods Inventory (2,450 units @ $24.20)	59,290
		Balance, May 31 (550 units	
May production costs	60,600	@ $24.20)	13,310
	72,600		72,600
Balance, May 31	13,310		

---

percent assumption described above. If, as often is the case, all the materials for a unit are issued at the *beginning* of the production process, then the calculations for materials are done first, treating the units in ending WIP inventory as being 100 percent complete as regards their materials content.

Example. Refer again to Illustration 18–3. For purposes of materials calculations, the equivalent units of production for May equal the sum of the 2,450 units that were transferred out of WIP plus the 1,100 units that were on hand May 31 (each with a weight of one for materials), a total of 3,550 equivalent units. The materials cost in beginning WIP Inventory would be added to the costs of materials issued in May, and this sum would then be divided by the 3,550 units equivalent production to arrive at the average material cost per equivalent unit. This unit cost would be multiplied by 2,450 to get the materials component of the goods transferred out and by 1,100 to get the materials cost of the ending WIP inventory. Finally, these materials calculations are combined with those for conversion costs (as in Illustration 18–3) to arrive at the total amounts for transfers to Finished Goods Inventory and month-end WIP Inventory.

Choice of a System

In most situations the nature of the production process indicates whether a job order cost system or a process cost system is more appropriate. Nevertheless, since a process cost system requires less recordkeeping than a job cost system, there is a tendency to use it even though the products manufactured are not entirely alike. Thus, a manufacturer of children's shoes may use a process cost system despite some differences in cost among the various sizes, styles, and colors of shoes manufactured. By contrast, manufacturers of men's or women's shoes usually employ a job cost system because the differences among the costs of the various styles are so significant that a process cost system would not provide adequate product cost information.

Remember that in a process cost system, the unit costs are *averages* derived from the total costs of the period. As a result, differences in the costs of individual products are not revealed. Thus, if there are important reasons for keeping track of the cost differences between one product and another or between one production lot and another of the same type of product, then a job order cost system is more appropriate. For example, a company would use a job cost system if the customer paid for the specific item, production order, or services on the basis of cost (as is often the case in repair shops, printing shops, consulting firms, hospitals, and other job shop operations). Also, a job cost system makes it possible to examine actual costs on specific jobs; this may help in locating trouble spots and in pricing similar jobs in the future. In a process cost system, costs cannot be traced to specific units or batches. Moreover, as production processes become more automated there is a tendency to shift the collection of conversion costs (i.e., direct labor and overhead) from a job cost basis to a process cost basis.

For our purposes there is no need to study differences in the detailed records required for the two types of systems. Both systems are essentially devices for collecting full production costs. Either furnishes the information required for the accounting entries shown in Illustration 17–2.

Variations in Practice

Because the product costing system outlined in Illustration 17–2 is a schematic representation of underlying structures, it will seldom be precisely duplicated in actual practice. Organizations build on the basic structure by adding accounts that collect the data in more detail, so as to meet their particular needs for information. A company may, for example, set up several Materials Inventory accounts, each one covering a different type of material, instead of a single account. Alternatively, the Materials Inventory account may be a control account, controlling dozens of individual subsidiary accounts. Another common variation is to have several Work in Process accounts, one for each main department or cost center in the organization. Such a system is essentially like that shown in Illustration 17–2, except that work is transferred from one department to another. The finished goods of one department become, in effect, the raw material of the next department.

Backflush Accounting. At the opposite extreme, some companies do not use any WIP inventory accounts. They charge the cost of material used directly to Finished Goods Inventory on the basis of bills of material that show how much material should have been used for each unit of finished product. They similarly charge all conversion costs directly to Finished Goods Inventory. This simple approach is called **backflush accounting.**[3]

MEASUREMENT OF DIRECT COSTS

As defined in Chapter 17, an item of cost is direct with respect to a specified cost object if it is traced to that cost object or if only that cost object caused the cost to be incurred. Also, to treat a cost item as direct, it must be feasible to measure the amount of resource that was used for the specified cost object.[4] If the causal relationship for an item of cost applies to two or more cost objects, the cost item is indirect with respect to these cost objects.

In this chapter the cost objects we are interested in are products—goods and services. For these cost objects, direct costs are those directly caused by the production of the specified products. For other types of cost objects, the word *direct* could refer to quite different items of cost. Thus, the salary of a department supervisor is a direct cost of the department that this person manages; but it is an indirect cost of the products produced in that department, because no exclusive causal relationship exists between any single product and the supervisor's salary.

The two principal types of direct product costs are direct labor cost and direct material cost. We will discuss them in the context of a job order cost system, but similar considerations are relevant in a process cost system.

Direct Labor Cost

The measurement of direct labor cost has two aspects: (1) measuring the *quantity* of labor time expended and (2) ascertaining the *price* per unit of labor time.

Measuring the quantity of labor time is relatively easy. A daily timecard or comparable record is usually kept for each direct worker. On it, a record

---

[3]This method can lead to inaccuracies if the company does not have small WIP inventories due to rapid conversion cycle time. For further discussion, see Richard V. Calvasina et al., "Beware the New Accounting Myths," *Management Accounting,* December 1989, pp. 41–45.

[4]Cost Accounting Standards Board, *Restatement of Operating Policies, Procedures, and Objectives* (May 1977), p. 6. This source also uses a "benefit" criterion; but it is unnecessary.

is made of the time the worker spends on each job or, if direct workers are paid a piece rate, the number of pieces completed. These timecards are used to measure labor costs and also as a basis for payroll computations.[5] Problems arise concerning the treatment of idle time, personal time, over-time, and so on, but these problems are beyond the scope of this introductory description.

It is conceptually more difficult to decide on the best way to price these labor times than it is to measure the quantity of time. Many companies have a simple solution: they price direct labor at the amounts actually earned by the employees concerned (so much an hour if employees are paid on a day-rate or hourly-rate basis; so much a piece if they are paid on a piece-rate basis). There may be either a separate labor rate for each employee or an average labor rate for all the direct labor employees in a department or of a given skill classification. For example, public accounting firms typically use an average labor rate for each of several job categories—staff assistant, senior, manager, and so on—when charging labor costs to jobs, even though there is variation in the actual rates paid employees in any given category.

Example.   Assume that four departments work on a certain job and that the time worked in each department (as shown by the timecards) and the labor rates are as indicated below. From this information, the total direct labor cost of the job can be determined:

Department	Direct Labor-Hours on Job	Hourly Labor Rate	Direct Labor Cost
A	20	$16.00	$ 320.00
B	3	15.50	46.50
C	6	17.80	106.80
D	40	17.00	680.00
Total direct labor cost of job			$1,153.30

Some companies add **labor-related costs** to the basic wage rate. They reason that each hour of labor effort costs the company not only the wages earned by the employee but also the FICA taxes, paid holiday and vacation time, pension contributions, and other fringe benefits paid by the employer.[6] The company must pay these labor-related benefits; they are caused by the fact that the employee works and they are therefore part of the real cost of using the employee's services.[7] This argument is conceptually valid.

---

[5]Timecards once were manually kept, but many now are electronic records created at special terminals that can read bar codes for the employee ID, job number, and so on.

[6]But *not* the *employee's* FICA contribution. This is a deduction from the employee's earnings; it is therefore not a cost to the company (see Chapter 10).

[7]The complete list of labor related costs in a fairly typical company includes pension cost, Federal Insurance Contributions Act (FICA), Federal Unemployment Tax Act (FUTA), state unemployment tax, medical insurance, dental insurance, long-term disability insurance, group life insurance, travel and accident insurance, disability income recovery, profit-sharing

A few companies even include a share of the costs of the personnel department and employee welfare programs as a part of direct labor cost. Although using such a higher labor price gives a more accurate picture of direct labor costs, it also involves additional recordkeeping. Many companies do not believe the gain in accuracy is worthwhile and thus treat labor-related costs as part of overhead.[8]

Direct Material Cost

The measurement of direct material cost also has the same two aspects: the *quantity* of material used and the *price* per unit of quantity. The quantity is usually determined from requisitions that are used to order material out of the stockroom and into production. The problem of pricing this material is similar to that for pricing direct labor. Material may be priced solely at its purchase or invoice cost, or there may be added some or all of the following **material-related costs:** inward freight, inspection costs, moving costs, purchasing department costs, and interest and space charges associated with holding material in inventory.

As was the case with labor costs, it is conceptually desirable to include these material-related items as part of material cost. To do so, however, may involve more recordkeeping than a company believes worthwhile. Many companies therefore treat material-related costs as part of overhead.[9]

The measurement of direct material costs is also affected by the assumption made about the flow of inventory costs (LIFO, FIFO, or average cost). Chapter 6 discussed the effect of these alternative flow assumptions.

Direct versus Variable Cost

Much confusion exists in practice between the meaning of *direct cost* and *variable cost.* This confusion occurs because if the cost object is a product (as in the above discussion), many costs that are direct to the product are also variable with the production volume of the product. Because material costs and the costs of production employees (as opposed to the costs of these employees' supervisors) are both direct costs of a product, and because in total these direct material costs (almost always) and direct labor costs (often) are also variable with the volume of that product, people tend to use the words *direct* and *variable* interchangeably. Similarly, *indirect* and *fixed* are often used incorrectly when referring to cost, as though they were synonyms.

The two sets of terms are based on very different concepts. The direct/indirect cost dichotomy relates to the *traceability* of costs to specific cost

---

bonus, employee stock ownership plan (ESOP), and perhaps even legal insurance. These costs average 40 percent or more of wages.

[8]For example, a study made by the Cost Accounting Standards Board (CASB) reported that 84 percent of the respondents treated health insurance and pension costs applicable to direct labor as overhead costs. See CASB, *Progress Report to the Congress* (1977), p. 38.

[9]The CASB study cited in the preceding footnote reported that whereas 52 percent of the respondents treated inward freight as part of direct material cost, only 36 percent accounted for incoming-material inspection costs as direct. Only 43 percent treated cash discounts as a reduction in direct material cost; the others treated these discounts as a reduction in overhead.

objects; the variable/fixed cost dichotomy relates to the *behavior* of costs as volume fluctuates. In a sense, cost traceability is an accountant's concept, whereas cost behavior is an economist's concept—although both concepts are important in management accounting. Because the common usage of these terms does not always coincide correctly with the underlying concepts, one must be careful not to infer that the user of the terms is necessarily using them precisely.

ALLOCATION OF INDIRECT COSTS

Distinction between Direct and Indirect Costs
For a given cost object, it is conceptually desirable to classify a given item of cost as direct rather than indirect. This is because an item of direct cost is assigned directly to the cost object, whereas the assignment of indirect costs to cost objects is a more roundabout and usually less accurate process. Nevertheless, the category of indirect costs does, and must, exist.

Costs are not traced directly to a product (the cost object for a product costing system) for one of three reasons: (1) It is *impossible* to do so, as in the case of a factory superintendent's salary. (2) It is *not feasible* to do so, because the recordkeeping required for such a direct tracing would cost too much. (For example, the thread and copper rivets used on a pair of jeans cost only a few pennies, and it is not worthwhile to trace them to each batch of jeans. They are therefore classified as indirect materials.) (3) Management *chooses* not to do so. Many companies classify certain items of costs as indirect simply because it has become customary in the industry to do so. (This is true of the cost of fringe benefits related to direct labor, mentioned above.)

Problems arise in attempting to define the precise line between items of cost that are directly caused by a product, and other costs. For instance, a cost may be *caused* by a product even though it is not incurred at the same time as the product is being made.

> **Example.** In a certain week, Sara Clark, a drafter in an architectural firm, was originally scheduled to spend 25 hours on project A and 15 hours on project B. As it happened, project A, which had to be done first, required 35 hours of her time. Consequently, Ms. Clark worked 50 hours during the week: 35 regular hours on A, 5 regular hours on B, and 10 weekend hours (at 50 percent premium) on B. The overtime premium should be charged to project A because it was A, not B, that caused Ms. Clark to work on the weekend.

Moreover, there are differences of opinion as to how close the causal relationship between the cost and a cost object must be in order to classify a cost item as direct. Many production operations, such as automated production, assembly lines, and refineries and other continuous flow operations, require a basic work force no matter what output is produced. Some would argue that the cost of this "core" work force constitutes a cost required for operation of the facility in general, much like heat and light, and that it is therefore an overhead cost. Although some companies continue to treat such costs as direct labor, as manufacturing becomes increasingly automated more companies classify these "core" labor costs as overhead.[10] In fact, some companies have entirely eliminated the direct labor category, combining overhead and labor costs into a single *conversion cost* category.

Nature of Allocation

The full cost of a cost object includes, in addition to its direct costs, a *fair share* of the indirect costs that were incurred for several cost objects, of which the cost object in question is one. Thus, the cost of an automobile repair job includes a fair share of all the indirect costs (i.e., the overhead costs) in the repair shop. The "fair share" idea sounds vague, and it is. But it is the only way of approaching the problem of measuring the indirect costs of a cost object.

What is a fair share? Probably the best way to think about this is in terms of what proportions of the indirect costs are *caused by* each of the various cost objects. For example, a job that requires the use of relatively expensive equipment (with attendant relatively high costs for depreciation, maintenance, insurance, and property taxes) causes more overhead costs than a job that requires the same number of direct labor-hours but can be performed using only hand tools. Thus, in an automobile repair shop three hours of labor spent performing an engine tune-up and front wheel alignment causes more overhead than three hours spent waxing the car. Similarly, a job requiring three hours of a worker's time causes more overhead than a job requiring only half as much of that worker's time. It is also apparent that for a given time period (such as a month), all of the jobs performed collectively caused, in some sense, all of the period's costs, whether those costs are ultimately classified as direct or indirect with respect to each job cost object.

From the above line of reasoning, it follows that (1) all items of production cost should be assigned to cost objects and (2) to the extent that the causal relationship can be determined, the amount assigned to an individual cost object should be related to the amount of indirect cost caused by that cost object.

The process of assigning indirect costs to individual cost objects is called **allocation.** The verb *to allocate* means "to assign indirect costs to individual cost objects." Indirect costs are allocated to products by means of an **overhead rate** (also called an **absorption rate,** an **allocation rate,** or a **burden rate**). Usually this rate is established annually, prior to the beginning of the accounting year. The method of calculating overhead rates is described below.

Note the distinction between *assign* and *allocate.* All costs are assigned to cost objects. Some costs, such as direct material, are assigned directly, whereas those not directly assigned are allocated. (A few accountants use

---

[10]In these circumstances, the labor cost is also *fixed;* yet some companies continue routinely to classify all of their direct labor costs as being variable with production volume.

attribute in the same way we use *assign*.) If we could alter long-standing accounting vocabulary usage traditions, we would say that direct costs are *directly charged* to a cost object and that indirect costs are *allocated*.[11]

Cost Centers

A **cost center** is a cost object for which costs of one or more related functions or activities are accumulated. Marker Pen Company, for example, has a department that manufactures wicks. The wick department is an example of a cost center; the costs incurred in that department are for the function or activity of manufacturing wicks for pens.

In a product costing system, items of cost are first accumulated in cost centers and then assigned to products. For this reason a cost center is often called an **intermediate cost object** to distinguish it from a product, which is a **final cost object.**

Cost Centers versus Responsibility Centers. Recall from Chapter 15 that a responsibility center is an organization unit headed by a manager. The wick department in the pen factory is a responsibility center; it is also a cost center. Indeed, most responsibility centers are also cost centers.

Not all cost centers are responsibility centers, however. The printing department in a company may operate a number of printing presses of different sizes and capabilities. Each printing press may be a cost center even though only the whole printing department is a responsibility center. Conversely, when the goods flowing through a factory are essentially similar, an entire factory may be treated as a single cost center, even though the factory consists of several responsibility centers each headed by a supervisor.

Production and Service Cost Centers. Cost centers are of two types: production cost centers and service cost centers. A **production cost center** either (1) produces a product or a component of a product or (2) performs a distinct step or task of such production. The barrel, wick, and assembly departments in the pen factory are production cost centers. A metal parts manufacturer's heat treating department, which performs its task on every part requiring heat treating, is a production cost center. The individual printing presses mentioned above are also production cost centers. Each selling department in a store is, in essence, a production cost center.

All other cost centers are **service cost centers.** They provide services to production cost centers, to other service cost centers, or for the benefit of the organization as a whole. The maintenance department and the general factory office are examples. Not all service cost centers are identifiable organization units, however. Some organizations, for example, have an **occupancy** cost center, in which are accumulated all the costs associated

---

[11]Unfortunately, the Cost Accounting Standards Board defines "allocate" to mean *assign* as used here (and as used in practice generally). The CASB therefore has no term for costs that are assigned indirectly.

with the physical premises, including rent or depreciation, property taxes, insurance, and utilities costs.

Service cost centers are often called **indirect cost pools** or **overhead pools.** The term *pool* conveys the idea that they are repositories in which indirect costs are accumulated. The costs subsequently flow out of these pools to other cost centers.

Calculating Overhead Rates

Calculating an overhead rate for a cost center is only possible after a series of steps in which total overhead costs are assigned to the production cost centers. Illustration 18–4 is a diagram of the allocation procedure; the situation is that of the Marker Pen Company factory, which consists of three production cost centers and two service cost centers. The production cost centers are the barrel, wick, and assembly departments. One of the service cost centers is the maintenance cost center, and the other is for the general factory administration activities. (Realistically, many companies would have more service cost centers than this; we are trying to keep the illustration simple because the procedure itself is quite complicated.)

Direct material and labor costs are assigned directly to product cost objects by the techniques described earlier in this chapter. The allocation of overhead costs to product (final) cost objects involves three steps:

1. All overhead costs for an accounting period are assigned to the service and production cost centers, which are intermediate cost objects. This flow is shown in part A of Illustration 18–4.

2. The total cost accumulated in each service cost center is reassigned to production cost centers (part B).

3. The total overhead costs accumulated in each production cost center, including the reassigned service center costs, are allocated to the products that pass through the production cost center (part C).

What follows is a detailed description of these three steps.

1. Initial Assignment to Cost Centers.   The first step in the allocation of overhead costs is to assign to the cost centers all items of indirect production cost for the period, treating each cost center as a cost object. There are two substeps to this assignment respectively corresponding to costs that are direct and indirect to the cost centers. First, any cost item that can be uniquely associated with a cost center is directly charged to that center. For example, supervision costs are directly assigned to the specific cost centers in which the supervisors work. Similarly, depreciation on machinery and equipment is directly assigned to the cost centers in which the specific depreciable assets are located. Second, overhead costs that benefit several cost centers jointly are allocated to those centers. For example, the costs of lighting and heating the production facilities and the rent on these facilities are assigned to the various cost centers based on the proportion of the

ILLUSTRATION 18–4
ALLOCATING OVERHEAD COSTS TO PRODUCTS

A. Initial Assignment to Cost Centers

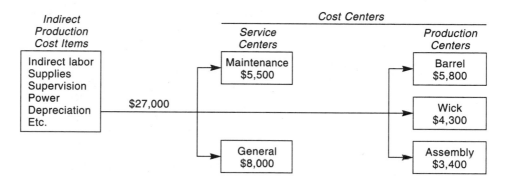

B. Reassignment of Service Center Costs to Production Centers

C. Allocation to Products

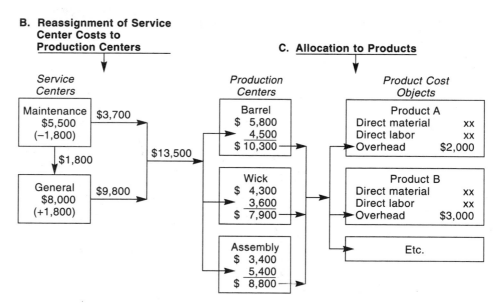

facilities' total square footage occupied by each cost center. That is, a cost center occupying 10 percent of the total space will be allocated 10 percent of these occupancy costs. Similarly, the cost of the plant nurse's office is allocated to the five cost centers based on their proportionate headcount.

Note from the preceding description that these overhead cost items are assigned to the cost centers *one cost item at a time,* and that for the items that are allocated to the centers, different bases of allocation may be used for different items (e.g., square footage and headcount). That is, the total overhead costs are *not* simply added and then this total distributed to the centers. When this item-by-item assignment process is completed, the sum

ILLUSTRATION 18–5
CALCULATING OVERHEAD RATES

Cost Item	Total	Service Centers		Production Centers		
		Maintenance	General	Barrel	Wick	Assembly
		A. Initial Assignment to Cost Centers:				
Supervision.	$ 8,400	$ 1,050	$ 0	$ 2,750	$2,400	$2,200
Depreciation.	5,400	750	1,600	1,650	900	500
(All other)	13,200	3,700	6,400	1,400	1,000	700
Subtotals.	27,000	5,500	8,000	5,800	4,300	3,400
		B. Reassignment of Service Center Costs:				
Maintenance		(5,500)*	1,800	2,200	1,000	500
General.			(9,800)	2,300	2,600	4,900
Indirect cost. . . .	$27,000	$ 0	$ 0	$10,300	$7,900	$8,800
		C. Calculation of Overhead Rates:				
Direct labor-hours.	4,000			900	1,100	2,000
Overhead rate per direct labor-hour				$11.44	$7.18	$4.40

*Parentheses indicate subtraction.

of the overhead costs assigned to all the cost centers equals the total overhead cost for the period.

Part A of Illustration 18–5 shows how the $27,000 of overhead costs were initially assigned to the production and service cost centers. (For simplicity, details are shown for only two overhead cost items and the rest are lumped together as "All other.") For example, of the $8,400 of supervision cost, a relatively small amount was assigned to the maintenance cost center (because one of the maintenance workers spends only a portion of her time supervising the department), zero was assigned to the general cost center (because all of the labor costs of this combination of several administrative functions, including the plant manager, are included in "All other"), $2,750 was assigned to the barrel department, $2,400 to the wick department, and $2,200 to the assembly department.

2. Reassignment of Service Center Costs. The second step in the allocation of overhead costs is to reassign the total cost accumulated in each service cost center so that eventually all overhead costs are assigned to the production cost centers. Some service center costs are assigned directly to the cost centers that receive the service.[12] Maintenance department costs,

---

[12]Recall that the words *direct* and *indirect* must always relate to a cost object. When one speaks of indirect production costs (that is, factory overhead), it is understood that the cost objects are products. But a cost item that is indirect with respect to a product (a final cost object) may be direct with respect to a cost center (an intermediate cost object). Thus, it is not

for example, may be assigned to the various cost centers on the basis of the number of hours of maintenance service performed for each one. On the other hand, some service center costs must be allocated to the other cost centers. In the illustration, the general cost center costs have been allocated to the three production centers in proportion to those centers' direct labor-hours; for example, the assembly department was charged half of these costs ($9,800 ÷ 2 = $4,900) because its direct labor-hours were half of the factory's total (2,000 ÷ 4,000 = 0.50).

Step-Down Order. In Illustration 18–5 part of the cost of the maintenance cost center is charged to the general cost center. Conceivably, part of the cost of the general cost center should be charged to the maintenance cost center, and this creates a problem. Whenever there are a number of service cost centers, the interrelationships among them could theoretically lead to a long series of distributions, redistributions, and re-redistributions.[13] In practice, however, these redistributions are usually avoided by allocating the service center costs in a prescribed order, which is called the **step-down order.**

There are no hard-and-fast rules for determining this step-down order. In general, organizations first allocate either (1) the costs of the service center that provides the most services to other cost centers or (2) the costs of the service center that receives the fewest services from other service centers. In the illustration the prescribed order is maintenance first and general second; this is because maintenance provides considerably more services to the general service center than it receives from the general service center. No additional cost is assigned to a service cost center after its costs have been assigned to the other cost centers.

Some organizations do not feel that the improved precision in costing they attain by using a step-down procedure is sufficient to warrant the added complications of the procedure. These organizations simply assign each service center's costs to production centers, ignoring any services provided by one service center to another service center. This approach is called the **direct method** of service center cost allocation.

3. Allocation of Overhead Costs to Products. Having collected all the overhead costs in production cost centers, the third and final step is to allocate these costs to the products worked on in these cost centers. In a process cost system this is easy. The total number of equivalent units of production for the month is determined by the method described previously, and the total overhead cost is divided by the number of equivalent units. This gives the overhead cost per unit for each product.

---

inconsistent to speak of directly assigning a plant overhead item to a cost center, or to directly assigning costs from a service cost center to a production cost center.

[13]Techniques of matrix algebra are sometimes used to perform this series of distributions and redistributions. This is called the **reciprocal services method** of allocation; it is described in advanced cost accounting texts.

In a job cost system, however, the procedure is more complicated. The various jobs worked on in the production center are of different sizes and complexities and therefore should bear different amounts of overhead cost. To the extent feasible, overhead costs should be so allocated to jobs that each job bears its fair share of the total overhead cost of the cost center. In order to do this, it is necessary to calculate an overhead rate.

An overhead rate assigns costs to products based on some activity (or volume) measure. The choice of that measure for a given production cost center is discussed below. After choosing the appropriate measure, one can calculate the overhead rate for that production cost center by dividing the center's total overhead cost for the period by its total amount of activity during that period.

> **Example.** Continuing with the example in Illustration 18–5, Marker Pen has chosen direct labor-hours (DLH) as the activity (volume) measure for the allocation of overhead costs to products in each of its three production cost centers. In the barrel department the DLH for the month totaled 900. Dividing the $10,300 total overhead cost by the 900 DLH volume gives an overhead rate of $11.44 per DLH for the barrel department. The other two production cost center's rates are calculated in the same manner.

Usually, there is only one overhead rate for each production cost center. Thus, although overhead and service center costs are assigned to production cost centers by a variety of methods (each reflecting the causal relationship for a particular cost item), the total amount of indirect cost for a production cost center is ordinarily allocated to products by a single overhead rate.

The overhead cost for each product that passes through the production cost center is calculated by multiplying the cost center's overhead rate by the number of activity units accumulated for that product.

> **Example.** Refer again to Illustration 18–5. Suppose that a certain batch of pens, Job No. 307, required 10 DLH in the barrel department, 15 DLH in the wick department, and 35 DLH in assembly. Its total overhead cost would be calculated as follows:

Cost Center	DLH	Overhead Rate	Overhead Cost
Barrel............................	10	$11.44	$114.40
Wick............................	15	7.18	107.70
Assembly	35	4.40	154.00
Total overhead cost of Job No. 307			$376.10

It is said that Job No. 307 had $376.10 of overhead costs *allocated* to it, or *applied* to it, or *absorbed* by it. (Any of these three terms may be used in practice.)

Cost Drivers (Allocation Bases)

By definition, the indirect costs of a cost object must be allocated to it. The activity or volume measure used in an overhead rate has traditionally been called the **allocation basis**. More recently, the term **cost driver** has come into usage because it more strongly connotes that the allocation basis should represent the force that drives (i.e., causes) the indirect costs to be incurred. (The related term **driver rate** may also be used instead of allocation rate or overhead rate.) The basis of allocation should correspond as closely as feasible to the basic criterion given above: it should express a *causal relationship* between the cost being allocated and the object to which it is being allocated.

The Marker Pen example provided several illustrations of this concept. Heat, light, and rent costs were allocated to the various cost centers based on square footage because the amount of area occupied drives the total amount of occupancy costs that must be incurred. For example, if the factory space were doubled, the total occupancy costs presumably would approximately double. The cost of the plant nurse's office was driven by the number of employees to be served, so headcount was the appropriate basis to use in assigning this cost to the various cost centers. Maintenance costs were driven by the number of maintenance hours of work performed.

If the costs assigned to a cost center represent a mixture of activities, then the choice of an appropriate cost driver is much less clear-cut. For example, the $10,300 of overhead cost to be assigned to products from the barrel department cost center includes a mixture of occupancy, supervision, depreciation, maintenance, general factory administration, and still other overhead costs. As a result, no clear answer emerges when one asks, "What is the driver of all of the overhead costs for the barrel department?" The response, "All of the products passing through that department drive its overhead costs" is true, but not very helpful in arriving at a specific allocation basis. As a result, most companies fall back on the traditional direct-labor drivers, DLH or DL$, even if the department is not labor intensive. Some companies use direct labor as the driver in their labor-intensive production cost centers and machine-hours in their equipment-intensive ones. Recently, a small number of companies have begun using two rates for a given production cost center, one for the center's labor-related overhead and the other for its machine-related overhead.[14]

The dozens of alternative cost drivers that are used to allocate costs either to cost centers or to products can be grouped into the following principal categories:

---

[14]Strictly speaking, this approach does not in fact use two overhead rates for a given production *cost center*. Rather, with this approach a given production *department*, instead of being treated as one intermediate cost object, is further subdivided into two cost centers (or cost pools), one for the department's labor-related overhead, the other for its machine-related overhead. Then each of these smaller cost pools uses its own volume measure. Although these two cost pools are separate cost centers, their costs apply to the same production cost *department*, which is a responsibility center. This is another illustration of the fact that a cost center is not necessarily a responsibility center.

1. Payroll related. The employer's share of social security taxes, health insurance, and other fringe benefits may be allocated on the basis of the total labor costs. Alternatively, as mentioned above, fringe benefit costs for direct workers may enter into the calculation of direct labor costs; if so, they will not appear as overhead costs at all.

2. Headcount related. Human resource department costs and other costs associated with the number of employees rather than with the amount that they are paid may be allocated on the basis of number of employees (headcount).

3. Material related. This category of cost typically includes the costs of purchasing and receiving materials, including counting, weighing, or inspecting them. These costs may be allocated on the basis of either the quantity or the cost of direct material used in production cost centers. Alternatively, they may be excluded from the cost center overhead costs and instead assigned to products as part of their material cost. For example, if the material-related cost rate is 10 percent of direct material cost, then a product with $5 direct material cost will have this cost "grossed up" to $5.50 so as to include the material-related costs.

4. Space related. Some items of cost are associated with the space that the cost center occupies, and they are allocated to cost centers on the basis of the relative floor area or cubic space of the cost centers. These are also called **facility related** costs.

5. Transaction related. Some costs are caused by the number of times some activity is performed rather than by the value of the goods or services associated with the activity. For example, the cost of preparing a purchase order is unaffected by the dollar amount of the items on the order, and the cost of scheduling a job is the same whether it is a large job or a small one. Such drivers are also called **activity related.** If the activity is performed once for each batch of product that is processed—such as preparing a set of production documents for a job, scheduling the job, setting up a piece of equipment, or inspecting one item from each batch produced—the driver is called a **batch-level driver.**

6. Product related. Some costs are caused by the existence of the product itself. Examples include engineering change order costs for a product, the cost of tools and dies that are used only for a single product, and the cost of maintaining product-related documents such as drawings, bills of material, and production routings.

7. Overall drivers. As mentioned above, if the pool of costs to be allocated includes a mixture of activities, then a clear-cut causally related driver is difficult to identify. In these instances, a broad, overall measure such as DLH, DL$, machine-hours, material cost, prime cost (direct material plus direct labor), or number of units is used. Because the choice of such a driver often is made only after the failure to find a driver that more clearly reflects a clear-cut causal relationship, some people refer to these as **default drivers.** Note that these drivers all have something in common: any of them will assign twice as much cost to two units of product as to one unit. This is because two units have twice as much direct-labor content, machine time, direct material, or prime costs as does one unit. Drivers with this characteristic are therefore called **unit-level drivers.**

Plantwide Overhead Rate. Many companies, although having a number of production departments, use the same overhead rate for all of them. This **plantwide overhead rate** is calculated by dividing total plant overhead costs by an overall activity measure, usually DLH or DL$. This is the simplest possible way to allocate overhead to products; it involves none of the complications illustrated in the Marker Pen example because there is only one cost center in the product costing system—the entire plant.[15]

Predetermined Overhead Rates

The preceding description of the accumulation of overhead costs in cost centers and their eventual allocation to products followed the same chronological order as that used for the accounting for direct material and direct labor. That is, first the amount of cost for the month was ascertained, and then this amount was subsequently assigned to products. This approach was used for teaching purposes; it is the easiest way of relating the flow of overhead costs to the physical activities of the production process.

A better way of allocating overhead costs in most situations is to establish *in advance,* usually once a year, an overhead rate for each production cost center and then use these **predetermined overhead rates** throughout the year. We shall limit the discussion of predetermined overhead rates to a job cost system, but similar considerations apply to a process cost system.

Why Overhead Rates Are Predetermined. Calculating an estimated annual overhead rate in advance is preferable to computing an actual rate at the end of each month for the following three reasons:

1. Overhead rates computed monthly would be unduly affected by conditions peculiar to that month. Some overhead costs change from month to month; heating costs, for example, are higher in the winter than in the summer. Also, volume may change from month to month because of vacation periods, holidays, seasonal demand for a company's product, and so on. Either of these phenomena can cause the actual overhead rate to fluctuate from month to month. But it is not useful to report, for example, that pens manufactured in August, a month when the plant was closed for a two-week vacation period, cost considerably more than identical pens made in September. Product costs would be misleading if the overhead costs assigned to products were affected by these fluctuations.

2. The use of a predetermined overhead rate permits product costs to be

---

[15]A survey of 298 manufacturing plants found that 41 percent of them used a plantwide overhead rate. Source: Keith V. Smith and Charlene Sullivan, "Survey of Cost Management Systems in Manufacturing," *Working Paper 90-5-1,* Purdue University, Krannert School of Management (May 1990).

calculated more promptly. Direct material and direct labor costs can be assigned to products as soon as the material requisitions and time records are available. If, however, overhead rates were calculated only at the end of each month, overhead costs could not be assigned to products until after all the information on overhead costs for the month had been assembled. With the use of a predetermined overhead rate, overhead costs can be allocated to products at the same time that direct costs are assigned to them.

3. Calculation of an overhead rate once a year requires less effort than going through the same calculation every month.

Procedure for Establishing Predetermined Rates

The calculation to establish predetermined overhead rates follows exactly the same three steps as described above for allocating overhead costs to products, except that the numbers used represent what the activity levels and costs are *estimated to be* during the coming year rather than what they *actually were*.

Flexible Overhead Budget. In many companies this estimate is made in the form of a **flexible** (or **variable**) **overhead budget** that is prepared for each production cost center. Such a budget shows what overhead costs are expected to be at various volumes (i.e., activity levels). Since some overhead cost elements are fixed and others are variable or semivariable, total overhead costs will be different at each volume level. As will be explained in later chapters, the flexible overhead budget is an important tool for cost control.

Illustration 18–6 is a flexible budget for total monthly overhead costs in the barrel department of the pen company, using direct labor-hours (DLH) as the volume measure. As suggested by this illustration, the budget can be presented either in tabular form or in graphic (C-V diagram) form. The column headed 900 DLH is similar to the column for the barrel department in Illustration 18–5, except that the earlier illustration showed *actual* overhead costs totaling $10,300 for a volume of 900 DLH whereas Illustration 18–6 shows *budgeted* amounts for this volume. The other columns show budgeted amounts for several different DLH levels. The procedures for developing each column of Illustration 18–6 are the same as those described for Illustration 18–5, except that again the costs here are estimates rather than actual amounts.

Analysis of the budget estimates in Illustration 18–6 will reveal that supervision is a fixed cost (at $2,750 per month), as are depreciation ($1,650 per month) and allocated general costs ($2,300 per month). The mixture of costs labeled "All other" is semivariable (at $400 per month plus $1.20 per DLH); this mixture includes, among other things, supplies and power for manufacturing equipment, which are variable with production volume. Similarly, the maintenance costs are semivariable (at $1,700 per month plus $0.60 per DLH). Thus, within this range of volume, total budgeted overhead costs are expected to vary according to the equation, $TC = \$8,800 + (\$1.80 * DLH)$.

ILLUSTRATION 18–6
FLEXIBLE OVERHEAD BUDGET

MARKER PEN COMPANY
Barrel Department

Costs	Volume (DLH)			
	800	900	1,000	1,100
Supervision.	$ 2,750	$ 2,750	$ 2,750	$ 2,750
Depreciation.	1,650	1,650	1,650	1,650
(All other)	1,360	1,480	1,600	1,720
Subtotal.	5,760	5,880	6,000	6,120
Maintenance service center	2,180	2,240	2,300	2,360
General service center	2,300	2,300	2,300	2,300
Total overhead.	$10,240	$10,420	$10,600	$10,780

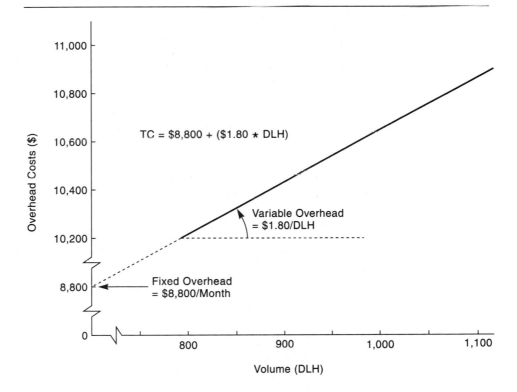

Estimating Volume. The second step in establishing the predetermined overhead rate is to estimate the *average* level of activity in each production cost center during the coming year. This involves first estimating the volume of the factory as a whole for the coming year and then converting this estimate into a volume estimate for each production cost center. In Marker Pen Company, it is estimated that in the coming year the factory will operate at 75 percent of capacity. When the factory operates at this level, the barrel department's average volume is 1,000 DLH per month. This is called the *standard volume* and is further discussed below.

Overhead Rate. The final step is to calculate each production cost center's overhead rate. This is simply the center's budgeted overhead costs at standard volume, divided by that standard volume. For the barrel department, this is $10,600 ÷ 1,000 DLH = $10.60 per DLH. Note that because of the presence of fixed costs in the flexible budget, the higher the standard volume, the lower the overhead rate. For example, if standard volume were only 800 DLH, the rate would be $12.80 per DLH (= $10,240 ÷ 800); at a standard volume of 1,100 DLH, the rate would be $9.80 per DLH.

Also note that once standard volume is estimated, all the budgeted cost data for volumes other than the standard volume are irrelevant *for purposes of calculating the overhead rate.* The rate remains the same for the entire year even if volume fluctuates from month to month. If the rate were changed every month to correspond precisely to that month's volume, then a primary reason for using predetermined rates—to avoid misleading month-to-month product-cost fluctuations—would be lost. The other columns in the table are useful, however, for monthly overhead *cost control* purposes. In exactly the same manner as was previously illustrated for actual overhead rates, the annual rate (once determined) is used to assign overhead costs to products passing through the cost center.

Standard Volume. The most uncertain part of the process of establishing predetermined overhead rates is estimating what the average monthly level of activity will be. This amount is called the **standard volume,** or **normal volume.** In most companies monthly standard volume is one-twelfth of the total volume anticipated for the coming year. Some companies use instead one-twelfth of the average annual volume expected over several years into the future.

As noted above, the estimate of volume has a significant influence on overhead rates. Many items of overhead cost are fixed costs. To take the extreme case, if *all* overhead costs were fixed, the overhead rate would vary inversely with the level of volume estimated for the forthcoming year. To the extent that not all overhead costs are fixed, changes in overhead rates associated with changes in the estimate of volume are not as severe, but they are nevertheless significant in most situations. Therefore, careful attention must be given to making the best possible estimate of volume when calculating predetermined overhead rates.

Example. A papermaking machine is a large, expensive machine that either runs at capacity or doesn't run at all. Its depreciation, the costs associated with the building in which it is housed, and most other items of overhead cost are unaffected by how many hours a year the machine operates. Assume that these overhead costs are estimated to be $1 million a year and are entirely fixed; that is, they are estimated to be $1 million regardless of how many hours the machine operates during the year. If the measure of activity used in establishing the overhead rate is machine-hours, the overhead rates shown below would apply for the various estimates of machine-hours to be operated during the year:

Cost	Number of Machine-Hours	Overhead Rate (per machine-hour)
$1,000,000	2,000	$500
1,000,000	4,000	250
1,000,000	6,000	167

The effect of the volume estimate on the amount of overhead cost assigned to products during the year is therefore great. Indeed, in a situation like this, in which fixed overhead costs are large relative to total costs (including direct labor and direct material), the accounted cost of the product may be affected more by the estimate of annual volume than by any other single factor.

The important point to remember is that the predetermined overhead rate will be relatively low if the estimated volume of activity is relatively high, because the same amount of fixed cost will be averaged over a larger number of units.

Underabsorbed and Overabsorbed Overhead

When a predetermined overhead rate is used, the amount of overhead costs allocated to products in a given month is likely to differ from the amount of overhead costs actually incurred in that month. This is because the actual overhead costs assigned to the cost center in the month and/or the actual activity level for the month are likely to be different from the estimates used when the predetermined overhead rate was calculated. If the amount of overhead cost absorbed by products exceeds the amount actually incurred, overhead is said to be **overabsorbed;** if the amount is less, overhead costs are **underabsorbed** (or **unabsorbed**). For cost control purposes, underabsorbed and overabsorbed overhead can be subdivided into spending and volume components, as we discuss in Chapter 20.

For simplicity, no account for overabsorbed or underabsorbed overhead was shown in the cost accounting flowchart given in Illustration 17–2. Such an account is labeled an **overhead variance** account. An entry to Overhead Variance is generated whenever the Overhead clearing account is closed. Since the debit side of Overhead cumulates *actual* overhead costs incurred and the credit side cumulates amounts *absorbed* into Work in Process, the entry closing Overhead and transferring the balance to Overhead Variance will be the difference between the period's actual and absorbed overhead costs. If actual overhead costs were more than the absorbed costs, then costs were underabsorbed and the entry to Overhead Variance will be a debit. If actual costs were less than the absorbed costs, then costs were overabsorbed and the entry to Overhead Variance will be a credit.

Example. If actual production overhead costs (debits to Overhead) were $28,000 but only $27,000 was applied to products on the basis of the overhead rates (credits to Overhead), then the Overhead clearing account would have a $1,000 debit balance, reflecting $1,000 underabsorbed costs. The entry to close Overhead and transfer its balance to Overhead Variance would be:

Overhead Variance.................................... 1,000
    Overhead (clearing account) 1,000

The details underlying this entry will be described in the next chapter.

The overhead variance occurs solely because a *predetermined* overhead rate is used to absorb costs into Work in Process. There is no overhead variance when after-the-fact overhead rates are used, because such rates are based on actual costs and actual volumes rather than on estimates.

Activity-Based Costing

In many companies the cost system that performs the allocations described above was designed many years ago when production operations were labor-intensive and overhead costs were relatively low. The system's primary purpose was to provide the inventory and cost of goods sold amounts for financial reporting purposes. To the surprise of many nonaccountants, there is no GAAP requirement that *individual* products be accurately costed; rather, the requirement is only that *in the aggregate* the inventory and cost of goods sold amounts not be materially misstated. This requirement usually can be met by the simple plantwide overhead rate approach described earlier. However, if the plant has diversity in the form of multiple production processes, different technologies (e.g., some labor-intensive, some machine-intensive), or variation in batch size or setup times, then this approach may give inaccurate overhead cost allocations at the *individual product* level, overcosting some products and undercosting others. Such potential inaccuracies may be significant in those companies that, as a result of decades of gradual shifting from labor-intensive to capital-intensive operations, today have overhead costs amounting to half or more of their total production costs. A simplified example will illustrate this phenomenon.

> **Example.** Boncam Company makes two similar products, A and B, with the characteristics shown below. They make the products in sequential batches on the same machine; that is, they make a batch of A, then a batch of B, and then they repeat the cycle. A machine setup must be made each time there is a changeover from one product to the other. For simplicity, all overhead costs other than setup costs are ignored.

	Prime Cost	DLH per Unit	Batch Size (units)	Setup Cost per Batch
Product A	$20	1	5	$110
Product B	20	1	50	110

If the company uses DLH as the cost driver for assigning overhead to products, then the volume of this driver for one cycle will be 55 DLH. This gives an overhead rate of $4 per DLH (= $220 ÷ 55 DLH). Since either product has one DLH of labor content per unit, this results in $4 of overhead being assigned to each unit, giving a full production cost of $24 per unit for either A or B. Thus, the system signals that these products consume identical amounts of resources per unit produced.

Now suppose as an alternative that Boncam charged setup costs to each specific batch. The overhead for A now becomes $22 per unit (= $110 ÷ 5 units) and $2.20 per unit for B. This results in full production cost of $42 per unit for A and $22.20 for B. There no longer is an inaccurate indication that a unit of either product consumes the same amount of resources.

Note that even though the two approaches result in significantly different unit costs, both treat *aggregate* costs accurately. For a cycle of 55 units of product, the DLH overhead allocation approach assigns total production costs of $1,320 (= 55 * $24). The second approach assigns the same amount: (5 * $42) + (50 * $22.20) = $210 + $1,110 = $1,320.

Whereas the example focuses on what happens if there is variation in setup costs per batch, other sources of diversity or variation can result in similar inaccuracies. For instance, assume that a company has an equipment-intensive machining department with high overhead costs (because of power, depreciation, maintenance, and so on) and a labor-intensive assembly department with relatively low overhead costs (because fringes are treated as part of direct labor cost and relatively little equipment is used). Use of a plantwide rate based on direct labor will result in overcharging those products having relatively high labor content and relatively little machine-hour content. Using a plantwide rate based on machine-hours might improve costing accuracy because machine-hours is a more significant driver of plantwide overhead costs than is labor-hours. Nevertheless, using machine-hours as the driver would only reverse the effect: products having relatively high labor content would now be *under*charged. For example, if a product were assembled entirely from purchased parts, it would be assigned no overhead at all by the machine-hours driver.

Some companies have addressed this latter problem by creating separate cost centers for machining and assembly, using machine-hours as the driver in machining and a direct-labor driver in assembly. While this is significantly better than using a plantwide rate or using the same driver for both cost centers, it does not address the batch size diversity problem illustrated in the Boncam Company example.

Cross Subsidies

Both of the above examples illustrate the fact that if the overhead cost structure is quite complex and diverse and a simple overhead allocation approach is used, then some products' costs will be understated and others' costs will be overstated. That is, a simple overhead approach applied to a diverse cost structure will "average away" the cost implications of the diversity at the individual product level, as the example with batch-size diversity clearly illustrated. When this phenomenon occurs, the costing system is said to be creating **cross subsidies**. In the Boncam Company example, using DLH as the allocation basis, the large-batch product was subsidizing the product made in small batches. In the second example, using a direct-labor driver would result in subsidizing machine-intensive products with labor-intensive ones; and the direction of the cross subsidies would reverse if machine-hours were used as the driver.

If a cost system meets GAAP requirements, what difference does it make if it creates such cross subsidies? The answer would be "None" *if* cost data for individual products were never used in decision making. However, pricing decisions (described in Chapter 17) and a variety of alternative choice decisions (described in Chapter 26) draw on cost information at the individual product level. If there are significant inaccuracies in these product-specific data, then some incorrect decisions may be made.

Activity-Based Costing Concepts

Recently, an approach that minimizes such cross-subsidization has been developed; it is called **activity-based costing** (or simply **ABC**).[16] While a detailed description of ABC is beyond the scope of this introductory text, its fundamentals can be described.

ABC is not dramatically different from traditional overhead costing in its overall concepts. Both approaches involve a "flow down" of costs from a total overhead cost "bucket" (represented by the first box in part A of Illustration 18–4) through intermediate cost objects (cost centers or cost pools) to the final product cost objects. The key differences between many companies' traditional systems and ABC overhead costing are in the details of this overall flow-down approach. More specifically:

1.   In ABC many more service center cost pools are created than has traditionally been the case. The new name given these pools is **activities** or **activity centers.** For example, whereas a traditional system may treat the production engineering support department as one service cost center, the ABC approach would subdivide this further into the various support activities that are performed by the department—layout analysis, process improvement, preparation of product routings, tool design, establishing time standards, new equipment justification, and so on. If a company's overhead is a major portion of its production costs, and if its support activities collectively account for half or more of that overhead, then it can create a larger number of support activity cost pools and still have each pool contain a significant amount of costs to be assigned.

2.   In traditional costing, service center costs are usually allocated to production cost centers; thus, these support costs are assigned to products as a portion of a production cost center's overhead rate (as in Illustrations

---

[16]Of the many articles on ABC that have appeared in the last few years, the most informative have been written by Professors Robin Cooper and Robert Kaplan and have appeared in *Harvard Business Review, Management Accounting,* and *Journal of Cost Management.* For an earlier description of a similar approach, see George J. Staubus, *Activity Costing and Input-Output Accounting,* Homewood, Ill.: Richard D. Irwin, Inc., 1971.

ILLUSTRATION 18-7
ABC OVERHEAD ASSIGNMENT

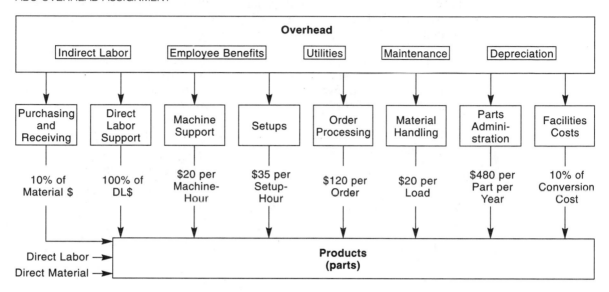

18-4 and 18-5). In ABC the possibility is left open that a support activity's costs should be assigned directly to products without flowing such costs through a production cost center. Thus, for example, setup costs might be explicitly charged to a batch of products rather than indirectly charged as a portion of the overhead rate of the production cost center where the setup was performed.

3.   Traditional costing uses *unit-level drivers* (most commonly, direct labor-hours or direct labor dollars) to make the final assignment of overhead costs from a production cost center to a product. For a given product, this makes the total overhead assigned to it by the various production centers through which it passes directly proportional to the number of units produced. In addition to unit-level drivers, the ABC approach uses batch-level and product-level drivers, particularly for certain support activities.

Illustration 18-7 shows how the ABC approach was applied in a plant making machined parts on semiautomated equipment.[17] The plant did not perform secondary operations on the parts, such as heat-treating, nor did it assemble these parts into more complex products. Because the plant's production operations had so little process diversity, a traditional system typically would have used a plantwide overhead rate. This plantwide rate would be $45 per machine-hour. With ABC, eight different activities were created; each of these is a cost pool with its own cost driver and driver rate. Note the variety of drivers that are employed: the traditional unit-level drivers—material costs, DL$, and machine-hours; three batch-level drivers—

---

[17]For more details see "John Deere Component Works (A)," Harvard Business School case 9-187-107. (Our illustration rounds some of the actual case's numbers.)

setup hours, orders processed, and loads moved; a product-level driver—
number of unique part numbers; and an overall driver for facility-level
costs—conversion costs. The following example illustrates how traditional
costing and ABC would apply to a specific part.

Example. Part R339 is supplied to only one customer, who buys 12,000
units per year. The part is produced once a month in batch size 1,000; each
such batch constitutes one production order to be processed. The setup time
per batch is 3 hours, and there are two material movements per batch. The
part's direct costs per unit are $0.20 for materials and $0.05 for labor. A
1,000-unit batch consumes 10 machine-hours of processing time (i.e., 0.01
machine-hour per unit).

Question: What are the annual production costs of part R339?

Traditional approach: Using a plantwide overhead rate of $45 per machine
hour, the cost of one unit would be:

Direct materials	$0.20	
Direct labor	0.05	
Overhead (0.01 mach.-hr. * $45)	0.45	
Total cost per unit	$0.70	
Annual cost (12,000 * $0.70)		$8,400

ABC approach: The unit-level, batch-level, product-level, and facilities-
level costs are separately identified in determining the annual cost:

Unit-level costs:		
Direct materials	$0.20	
Purchasing/receiving (10% of DM$)...............	0.02	
Direct labor	0.05	
Labor support (100% of DL$)....................	0.05	
Machine support (0.01 mach.-hr. * $20)	0.20	
Total per unit	$0.52	
Annual cost for 12,000 units......................		$ 6,240
Batch-level costs:		
Setup (3 hrs. * $35).............................	$105	
Order processing	120	
Material handling (2 loads * $20).................	40	
Total per batch	$265	
Annual cost for 12 batches		3,180
Product-level costs:		
Parts administration (per year)....................		480
Annual subtotal		9,900
Facilities-level allocation*.............................		726
Total annual cost		$10,626
Cost per unit ($10,626 ÷ 12,000).................	$0.89	

*This allocation was calculated as 10 percent of conversion cost, which
the company defined to be all of the costs in the annual subtotal except
direct materials and purchasing/receiving. Backing out those two amounts,
the annual conversion cost for 12,000 units made in 12 batches is $9,900 −
12,000 * ($0.20 + $0.02) = $7,260; 10 percent of this amount is $726.

In comparing the two approaches, note that the traditional approach calculates the unit cost first and then arrives at the total annual cost by multiplying this unit cost by the annual volume. Thus, once the $0.70 unit cost is calculated, the indicated total cost of any annual quantity can quickly be calculated by multiplying that quantity by $0.70; for example, $7,000 for an annual quantity of 10,000 units. Also note that the calculation of unit and total annual costs would not be affected by changed assumptions as to batch size (and hence, number of batches per year), setup time, or number of material movements required per batch. The traditional approach signals that average resource consumption per unit of product is totally independent of the product's annual volume or the size of the batches in which the product is made. Such a signal can mislead the company into thinking that specialized products made in small batches and sold at the same unit price as higher-volume standardized products are just as profitable on a per-unit basis, when in fact this is seldom the case.

By contrast, the ABC approach first calculates an annual total cost for the given quantity and number of batches and then arrives at the per-unit cost in the final step by averaging this total over the annual quantity. Thus, unlike the traditional approach where the per-unit amount was unaffected by changes in annual quantity and batch size, the ABC approach does signal that batch size and annual quantity affect resource consumption and hence affect per-unit costs. For the particular combination of volume and batch size assumed in the illustration, the ABC unit cost was 27 percent higher than the cost indicated by a plantwide overhead rate approach. This is a significant difference if the company is pricing such parts based on their full production costs.

The company represented in Illustration 18–7 in fact sought much of its business by bidding against similar producers on specialized parts to be made for specific customers (as opposed to producing more generic catalog items). It did not adopt ABC until its management became puzzled by the results of their bidding: even though its semiautomated equipment was ideally suited for large jobs, the company was consistently losing bids for high-volume, large batch-size products while consistently winning the lower-volume, small batch-size jobs. The company's bids had been based on numbers in a cost system that was creating cross subsidies by undercosting smaller-volume jobs and overcosting the large ones, a system that indicated that annual quantity and batch size had no impact on unit costs. When the company added a margin to the unit cost from this system, the resultant bid price was an unwitting *attempt* to establish such subsidies in the marketplace. But in competitive markets, this cross-subsidization will not happen. Thus, the company's bids on higher-volume parts were uncompetitively high, whereas its bids on the lower-volume items constituted a real bargain. When it began basing its bids on costs calculated using the ABC approach, it began winning some of the high-volume work (and stopped winning much of the low-volume work for which its equipment was not well-suited).

ABC Models.   In the description of activity-based costing, we have been careful to refer to it as an *approach* rather than as a *system.* The term *costing system* implies that routine transactions are processed by the system, as exemplified by the flowchart in Illustration 17–2, and that the system routinely provides the numbers for inventory and cost of sales that are needed in financial reporting. With very few exceptions, this is not the case with activity-based costing. Rather, virtually all companies adopting the ABC approach have done so in the form of a cost estimating *model* that resides on a personal computer at a specific plant. This model is not linked with the cost system that the company has traditionally used across all of its plants. In fact, because there is no such linkage, the traditional cost system is still used for financial reporting purposes. The ABC model, on the other hand, is employed on an "as-needed" basis to provide estimates of costs that are used in product profitability analysis (discussed in Chapter 24) and in making pricing decisions, make-or-buy decisions, and other decisions to be described in Chapter 26. We do not point this out as a criticism of ABC; rather, we are clarifying the fact that, to date, ABC has been used as a cost estimating tool rather than as a cost accounting system. Our prediction is that this will continue to be the case, as it will likely continue to be more economical to maintain a relatively simple companywide cost system and PC-based cost models at those sites where such a model will be used frequently than it will be to develop a far more elaborate, activity-based companywide cost system.

Activity-Based Management.   Those companies that have built ABC models generally have found the model-building process itself to be valuable. In modeling its operations, the company has realized that it is not very efficient at providing certain support services and it therefore looks for ways to improve these functions. The cost driver rates in Illustration 18–7 provide examples: Why should it cost $120 to process an order if companies like Lands' End and L.L. Bean can process their customers' orders for a small fraction of this amount? Why should it cost $20 to move a load of parts from one location in the factory to another when one can get a multi-mile taxi ride for the same amount? Is there not some way to administer a single part number for less than $480 per year? Recognizing that ABC models are thus useful in process analysis and continuous improvement initiatives, some consulting firms have coined the term **activity-based management (ABM).** This is really just another name for the process of finding ways to perform tasks "better, faster, and cheaper," which is also called *total quality management, quality function deployment, process improvement,* or *reengineering.* The point is that ABM is not ABC; rather, an ABC model can, along with giving more accurate product costs, provide activity cost data that are useful in continuous improvement efforts, whatever name may be applied to these efforts.

SUMMARY

There are two main types of product costing systems. With job order costing, costs are accumulated separately for each individual item or for a batch of similar items. With process costing, costs are accumulated for all units together and then divided between completed units (in finished goods inventory) and partially completed units (in ending work in process inventory) according to some reasonable assumption as to their stage of completion at the end of the period.

Measurement of direct material costs and direct labor costs involves measuring both a resource quantity and a price per unit of resource. The unit price measurement aspect is more difficult because of the question of how to handle material-related costs such as inventory holding cost and labor-related costs such as fringe benefits.

Items of cost are indirect either because it is not possible to assign them directly, because it is not worthwhile to do so, or because the management chooses not to do so. Overhead costs are allocated to products by means of an overhead rate. This rate is usually calculated prior to the beginning of the accounting year because the use of such a predetermined rate results in more meaningful and timely product costs with less accounting effort. The overhead rate is used to allocate overhead costs to the products that pass through the production cost center. The number of units of activity required for each product multiplied by the overhead rate gives the total amount of overhead cost absorbed by that product.

Flexible budgets are used to describe the information needed to calculate a predetermined overhead rate. Although only one point in the flexible budget—the estimated costs at standard volume—is used in calculating the rate, the rest of the budget is useful for cost control purposes.

If a simple overhead costing approach is applied to a complex overhead cost structure, the resulting allocated costs may not be accurate at the individual product level. Activity-based cost models are intended to address this problem. They provide data on an as-needed basis, rather than replace the existing cost system. Building the model can also lead to useful process improvement insights.

Cases

CASE 18-1   Problems in Full Cost Accounting

A.   Westland Company

Westland Company makes two products, A and B. At the beginning of October, account balances were:

Raw material*	$20,000
Work in process	0
Finished goods	0
Wages payable	0

*Composed of 1,000 lbs. of X @ $12 and 2,000 lbs. of Y @ $4.

Overhead is allocated to products at a rate of $12 per direct labor-hour. During October, the following transactions took place:

1. 750 pounds of raw material X were issued for production of 1,000 units of product A.

2. 375 direct labor-hours at an average hourly rate of $15 were used in manufacturing product A.

3. 900 pounds of raw material Y were issued for production of product A.

4. 1,000 pounds of raw material Y were issued for the manufacture of 2,000 units of product B.

5. 300 direct labor-hours at an average hourly rate of $15 were incurred in manufacturing product B.

6. 2,000 pounds of raw material X were purchased at a cost of $12.50 per pound.

7. 1,000 pounds of raw material Y were purchased at a cost of $3.90 per pound.

8. 500 pounds of raw material X were issued for production of product B.

9. 800 units of product A and 1,500 units of product B were completed. The incomplete units of product A had required 70 hours of direct labor; the incomplete units of product B had required 50 hours.

10. Actual overhead expenses totaled $8,100.

Westland used the FIFO inventory accounting method.

Questions

1. Prepare T accounts and indicate how each of the above transactions flows through the accounting system.

2. If 600 units of product A and 1,000 units of product B were sold during October, what are the amounts for October cost of sales and month-end finished goods?

B.   Campfire Outfitters Company

Campfire Outfitters Company produces backpacks, tents, and sleeping bags. Each is produced in a separate production center. The company also has a purchasing department, which buys nylon, goose down, aluminum tubing, and other items, and a small engineering department, which also does R&D and quality control work. Major items of production overhead expense are rent, heating, electricity, indirect labor, and supplies. Rent costs are allocated to cost centers on the basis of square footage; heating costs, on the basis of cubic feet. Electricity is charged to cost centers on the basis of metered usage; indirect labor and supplies are also charged on the basis of actual usage. The costs of purchasing and engineering are allocated to the three production departments on the basis of direct labor-hours.

For March, preliminary figures showed the following:

	Cost Centers				
	Purchasing	Engineering	Backpacks	Tents	Sleeping Bags
Square feet......................	450	650	800	1,100	1,000
Cubic feet.......................	3,600	5,200	7,200	9,900	9,100
Electricity	$75	$125	$250	$200	$150
Indirect labor....................	$1,600	$3,200	$700	$700	$750
Supplies	$225	$375	$125	$75	$100
Direct labor-hours................			625	875	1,000

Rent expense was $6,000; heating costs were $700.

Question

Calculate the overhead rate per direct labor-hour for each production cost center in March.

C. Brainerd Company

Brainerd Company does custom information retrieval and report preparation for a variety of clients. There are two production cost centers: Information Retrieval and Report Writing. Supporting service cost centers are Data Processing and Library Services. Brainerd Company does not attempt to charge costs for Data Processing and Library Services to projects according to actual use of these services, but rather, at month-end allocates these costs to Information Retrieval and Report Writing according to the number of direct labor-hours spent on projects in those two production centers. Then each project is charged an amount per direct labor-hour for each production cost center's overhead.

Indirect costs are primarily rent, utilities, and labor. Rent and utilities are allocated to the four cost centers according to square footage of office space; indirect labor is as-signed to each department as incurred. Information Retrieval and Report Writing each occupy 4,000 square feet, Data Processing occupies 1,500 square feet, and Library Services occupies 6,500 square feet.

The following transactions took place in September:

1. $1,200 (80 hours) of direct information retrieval labor were incurred for project A.

2. $375 (25 hours) of direct information retrieval labor were incurred for project B.

3. $2,400 (160 hours) of direct information retrieval labor were incurred for project C.

4. $300 (20 hours) of direct report preparation labor were incurred for project A.

5. $150 (10 hours) of direct report preparation labor were incurred for project B.

6. $750 (50 hours) of direct report preparation labor were incurred for project C.

7. $20,000 rent expense.

8. $6,800 indirect Data Processing labor expense.

9. $2,900 indirect Library Services labor expense.

10. $750 indirect Information Retrieval labor expense.

11. $1,200 utilities expense.

12. $1,900 other Data Processing expense.

13. $250 other Library Services expense.

Questions

1. Determine the amount of direct costs for each project during September.
2. Calculate indirect costs for each of the production and service departments for September.
3. Calculate the rates at which indirect costs should be allocated to each project for each of the two production departments.
4. Determine the full costs of each of the three projects carried out in September.
5. Assuming that projects A, B, and C are typical, does Brainerd Company need to use two production cost centers rather than a companywide costing rate? Explain.

D. Copymat Company

Copymat Company is a small copying company that specializes in electrostatic copying. It is located in a small college town, so the amount of work varies considerably with the seasons. On the last Sunday afternoon in June, the company made 1,300 copies. Only one person worked Sunday afternoons; this person cost $8 an hour for the four hours Copymat was open on Sunday.

The cost of paper averages 0.7 cent per copy; other supplies and electricity cost about 0.4 cent per copy. Other monthly operating costs are:

Rent	$1,200
Equipment rental	900
Manager's salary	2,000
Advertising	500
Other	400

Volume over the year totals four million copies. There are 7,280 direct labor-hours worked per year at an average cost of $8 an hour.

Questions

1. Calculate the total variable cost of the copying jobs done on the last Sunday in June.
2. Calculate the total labor cost of these jobs.
3. Suggest a way to assign labor and indirect costs to the cost of a copy made on that Sunday, and defend your suggestion.
4. Determine the full cost of one copy on the last Sunday in June, using the costing method you suggested for the preceding question.
5. Determine the average *annual* full cost of one copy.
6. Copymat charges five cents per copy. Should they stay open on Sunday afternoons if the above situation is typical? (Assume the copy center is open 50 Sunday afternoons per year.)

CASE 18–2 Huron Automotive Company

Sandy Bond, a recent business school graduate who had recently been employed by Huron Automotive Company, was asked by Huron's president to review the company's present cost accounting procedures. In outlining this project to Bond, the president had expressed three concerns about the present system: (1) its adequacy for purposes of cost control, (2) its accuracy in arriving at the true cost of products, and (3) its usefulness in providing data to judge supervisors' performance.

Huron Automotive was a relatively small supplier of selected vehicle parts to the large automobile and truck companies. Huron competed on a price basis with larger suppliers that were long-established in the market. Huron had competed successfully in the past by focusing on parts that, relative to the industry, were of small volume and hence did not permit Huron's competitors to take advantage of economies of scale. For example, Huron produced certain parts required only by "off-the-road" equipment such as front loaders.

Bond began the cost accounting study in Huron's carburetor and fuel injector (CFI) division, which accounted for about 40 percent of Huron's sales. This division contained five production departments: casting and stamping, grinding, machining, custom work, and assembly. The casting and stamping department produced cases, valves, and certain other parts. The grinding department prepared these parts for further machining and precision ground those parts requiring close tolerances. The machining department performed all necessary machining operations on standard products, whereas the custom work department performed part of the machining and certain other operations on custom products, which usually were replacement carburetors for antique cars or other highly specialized applications. The assembly department assembled and tested all products, both standard and custom.

Thus, custom products passed through all five departments and standard products passed through all departments except custom work. Spare parts produced for inventory went through only the first three departments. Both standard and custom products were produced to order; there were no inventories of completed carburetors or fuel injectors.

Bond's investigation showed that with the exception of materials costs, all product costing was done based on a single, plantwide, direct labor hourly rate. This rate included both direct labor and factory overhead costs. Each batch of products was assigned its labor and overhead cost by having workers charge their time to the job number assigned to the batch, and then multiplying the total hours charged to the job number by the hourly rate. Exhibit 1 shows how the July hourly rate of $55.96 was calculated.

It seemed to Bond that because the average labor skill level varied from department to department, each department should have its own hourly costing rate. With this approach, time would be charged to each batch by department; then the hours charged by a department would be multiplied by that department's costing rate to arrive at a departmental labor and overhead cost for the batch; and finally these departmental labor and overhead costs would be added (along with materials cost) to obtain the cost of a batch.

Bond decided to see what impact this approach would have on product costs. The division's accountant pointed out to Bond that labor hours and payroll costs were already traceable to departments. Also, some overhead items, such as departmental supervisors' salaries and equipment depreciation, could be charged directly to the relevant department. However, many other overhead items, including heat, electricity, property taxes, and insurance, would need to be allocated to each department if the new approach were implemented. Accordingly, Bond determined a reasonable allocation basis for each of these joint costs (e.g., cubic feet of space occupied as the basis of allocating heating costs), and then used these bases to recast July's costs on a departmental basis. Bond then calculated hourly rates for each department, as shown in Exhibit 2.

In order to have some concrete numbers to show the president, Bond decided to apply the proposed approach to three CFI division

EXHIBIT 1
CALCULATION OF PLANTWIDE LABOR AND
OVERHEAD HOURLY RATE
Month of July

	Dollars	Hours
Labor:		
Casting/stamping	$ 54,604	2,528
Grinding	38,520	2,140
Machining.	191,876	7,675
Custom work	81,664	3,712
Assembly	291,784	15,357
Total labor.	658,448	31,412
Overhead	1,099,323	
Total labor and overhead	$1,757,771	

$$\text{Hourly rate} = \frac{\$1,757,771}{31,412} = \$55.96 \text{ per hour}$$

(= $20.96 labor + $35.00 overhead)

EXHIBIT 2
PROPOSED DEPARTMENTAL LABOR AND OVERHEAD HOURLY RATES

Department	Labor Rate per Hour	Overhead per Hour	Total Cost per Hour
Casting/stamping	$21.60	$31.37	$52.97
Grinding	18.00	30.14	48.14
Machining.	25.00	62.52	87.52
Custom work	22.00	40.48	62.48
Assembly	19.00	21.19	40.19

activities: production of model CS-29 fuel injectors (CFI's best-selling product), production of spare parts for inventory, and work done by the division for other Huron divisions. Exhibit 3 summarizes the hourly requirements of these activities by department. Bond then costed these three activities using both the July plantwide rate and the pro forma July departmental rates.

Upon seeing Bond's numbers, the president noted that there was a large difference in the indicated cost of CS-29 injectors as calculated under the present and proposed methods. The present method was therefore probably leading to incorrect inferences about the profitability of each product, the president surmised. The impact of the proposed method on spare parts inventory valuation was similarly noted. The president therefore was leaning toward adopting the new method, but told Bond that the departmental supervisors should be consulted before any change was made.

Bond's explanation of the proposal to the supervisors prompted strong opposition from some of them. The supervisors of the outside departments for which the CFI division did work each month felt it would be

EXHIBIT 3
DIRECT LABOR-HOUR DISTRIBUTION FOR THREE CARBURETOR DIVISION
ACTIVITIES

Department	CS-29 Injectors (per batch of 100)	Spare Parts for Inventory (per typical month)	Work for Other Divisions (per typical month)
Casting/stamping	21 hrs.	304 hrs.	674 hrs.
Grinding	12	270	540
Machining.	58	1,115	2,158
Custom work	—	—	—
Assembly	35	—	—
Total	126 hrs.	1,689 hrs.	3,372 hrs.

unfair to increase their costs by increasing charges from the CFI division. One of them stated:

> The CFI division handles our department's overflow machining work when we're at capacity. I can't control costs in the CFI division, but if they increase their charges, I'll never be able to meet my department's cost budget. They're already charging us more than we can do the work for in our own department, if we had enough capacity, and you're proposing to charge us still more!

Also opposed was the production manager of the CFI division:

> I've got enough to do getting good quality output to our customers on time, without getting involved in more paperwork! What's more, my department supervisors haven't got time to become bookkeepers, either. We're already charging all of the division's production costs to products and work for other departments; why do we need this extra complication?

The company's sales manager also did not favor the proposal, telling Bond:

> We already have trouble being competitive with the big companies in our industry. If we start playing games with our costing system, then we'll have to start changing our prices. You're new here, so perhaps you don't realize that we have to carry some

low-profit—or even loss—items in order to sell the more profitable ones. As far as I'm concerned, if a product *line* is showing an adequate profit, I'm not hung up about cost variations among items *within* the line.

The strongest criticism of Bond's proposed new system came from Huron's director of financial planning:

> Departmentalizing the costing rate may be a good idea, but I'm not sure you're attacking the main problem. How can we do anything with these cost estimates when you change the rates every month? When volume is rising, all of our products make money, no matter which system you use. But when overall volume is falling, some products begin to show losses even though their own sales continue to hold up. I don't know whether they're really losing money or whether they just can't carry a full share of the costs of idle capacity. I don't see how your system is going to help me answer that question.

Faced with all these arguments, Bond decided to make some more calculations before going back to the president. First, Bond asked the industrial engineering department to estimate the monthly volume at which each of the five production departments typically operated over the course of a year (normal volume). Then Bond assembled a

EXHIBIT 4
DEPARTMENTAL OVERHEAD RATES BASED ON NORMAL VOLUME

	Normal Volume (DLH)	Normal Overhead Cost*	Overhead per Direct Labor-Hour
Casting/stamping	2,500	$ 78,800	$31.52
Grinding	2,400	69,000	28.75
Machining.	8,000	492,000	61.50
Custom work	3,600	147,820	41.06
Assembly	17,500	352,450	20.14
Total.	34,000	$1,140,070	$33.53

*Estimated overhead cost if each department operates at its normal volume.

new set of overhead cost estimates and recalculated the proposed overhead rates, as shown in Exhibit 4. Finally, Bond recalculated the labor and overhead costs of a 100-unit lot of model CS-29 injectors and of a typical month's spare parts production and work for other divisions, based on the "normalized" departmental rates.

When Bond circulated these new calculations, the production manager of the CFI division was even more perturbed that before:

> That's even worse! Now you're piling paperwork on paperwork! And on top of everything, we won't be able to charge out all of our costs. What am I supposed to do with the costs in machining and assembly if I can't charge them to products or spare parts or the work we do for other divisions?

When Bond reported the various managers' opposition to the president, the president replied:

> You're not telling me anything that I haven't already heard from unsolicited phone calls from several supervisors the last few days. I don't want to cram anything down their throats—but I'm still not satisfied our current system is adequate. Sandy, what do you think we should do?

Questions

1. Using the data in the exhibits, determine the cost of a 100-unit batch of model CS-29, a month's spare parts, and a month's work done for other divisions under the present method, Bond's first proposal, and Bond's revised proposal.

2. Are the cost differences among the methods significant? What causes these differences?

3. Suppose that Huron purchased a new machine costing $400,000 for the custom work department. Its expected useful life is five years. This machine would reduce machining time and result in higher quality custom carburetors. As a result, the department's direct labor-hours would be reduced by 30 percent, and this extra labor would be transferred to departments outside the carburetor division. About 10 percent of the custom work department's overhead is variable with respect to direct labor-hours. Using July's data:

   a. Calculate the plantwide hourly rate (present method) if the new machine were acquired. Then calculate indicated costs for the custom work department in July, using both this new plantwide rate and the former $55.96 rate.

   b. Calculate the hourly rate for the custom work department only (first proposed method), assuming the machine were acquired and the first proposed costing procedure were adopted. Then calculate indicated costs for the custom work department in July, using both this new rate and the former $62.48 rate.

   c. Under the present costing procedures, what is the impact on the indicated costs of custom products if the new machine is acquired? What is this impact if the first proposed costing procedure is used? What inference do you then draw concerning the usefulness of the present and proposed methods?

4. Assume that producing a batch of 100 model CS-29 injectors requires 126 hours, distributed by department as shown in Exhibit 3, and $4,200 worth of materials. Huron sells these carburetors for $113 each. Should the CS-29 price be increased? Should the CS-29 be dropped from the product line? (Answer using both the present and the first proposed costing methods).

5. Assume that Huron also offers a model CS-30 that is identical to a CS-29 in all important aspects, including price, but is preferred for some applications because of certain design features. Because of the CS-30's relatively low sales volume, Huron buys certain major components for the CS-30 rather than making them in-house. The total cost of materials and purchased parts for 100 units of model CS-30 is $8,000; the labor required per 100 units is 12, 7, 17, and 35 hours, respectively, in the casting/stamping, grinding, machining, and assembly departments. If a customer ordered 100 units and said that either model CS-29 or CS-30 would be acceptable, which model should Huron ship? Why? (Answer using only the first proposed costing method and the assumptions regarding CS-29 from Question 4.)

6. What benefits, if any, do you see to Huron if either proposed costing method is adopted? Consider this question from the standpoint of (a) product pricing, (b) cost control, (c) inventory valuation, (d) charges to outside departments, (e) judging departmental performance, and (f) diagnostic uses of cost data. What do you conclude Huron should do regarding their costing procedures?

CASE 18–3   Rosemont Hill Health Center*

In March 1993, Florence Mitchell, administrator of the Rosemont Hill Health Center (RHHC), expressed concern about RHHC's cost accounting system. The extensive funding RHHC had received during its early years was decreasing, and Ms. Mitchell wanted to prepare the center to be self-sufficient, but she lacked critical cost information.

At a meeting with Robert Simi, RHHC's new accountant, Ms. Mitchell outlined the principal issues:

> First of all, our deficit is increasing. We obviously have to reverse this trend if we're going to become solvent. But to do that, we have to know where our costs are incurred. That leads to the second problem: we don't know the cost of each of the services we offer. Although our patients receive a variety of services, we charge everyone the same per visit fee.

Ms. Mitchell provided a further motivation for analyzing RHHC's costs: federal and local funding was available for family planning and mental health programs, but to qualify, RHHC would need a precise calculation of cost per visit in these departments. Likewise, to receive third-party reimbursement for patient visits, RHHC's fee schedule had to be reasonably related to costs.

Background. RHHC was established in 1975 by a consortium of community groups. Situated in Roxbury, an inner-city residential neighborhood of Boston, the center was intended to provide comprehensive health care to residents of Roxbury and neighboring communities. Eighteen years after its inception, RHHC maintained strong ties with the community groups responsible for its

*Copyright © by the President and Fellows of Harvard College. Harvard Business School case 178-189.

EXHIBIT 1

ROSEMONT HILL HEALTH CENTER
Income Statement
For the Year Ended December 31, 1992

Revenue from patient fees		$1,085,700
Other revenue		28,600
Total revenues		1,114,300
Expenses:		
Program services	$745,000	
Utilities.	32,000	
Laboratory	81,000	
General and administrative.	293,000	
Total expenses		1,151,000
Surplus (deficit).		$ (36,700)

---

development and for its subsequent acceptance in Roxbury.

Funding for RHHC was initially provided by the federal government as part of the Department of Health and Human Services' attempt to equalize health care in the United States. When these operating funds were depleted in 1991, the city of Boston supplemented RHHC's income with a small three-year grant. Because Ms. Mitchell realized that government support could not continue indefinitely, she intended to make the center self-sufficient as soon as possible. RHHC's 1992 income statement is shown in Exhibit 1.

RHHC was composed of eight departments: pediatrics, adult medicine, family planning, nursing, mental health, social services, dental, and community health. In addition, the center had a laboratory and medical records department. Community health, which had been designed by RHHC's clients, was a multidisciplinary department providing a link between the health and social services at RHHC and the schools and city services of the community. The department was staffed by a part-time speech pathologist, a part-time learning specialist, and a full-time nutritionist. In total, RHHC had 22 paid employees and a volunteer staff of 6–10 students who were acquiring clinical and managerial experience.

The Existing Information System. RHHC's previous accountant had established a cost system to determine the fee charged to patients. According to this method, shown in Exhibit 2, the fee was derived from the average yearly cost of one patient visit. The accountant would first determine the direct cost of each department. He would then add overhead costs, such as administration or rent and utilities, to the total cost of all the departments to determine the center's total costs. Finally, he would divide that total by the year's number of patient visits. Increased by an anticipated inflation figure for the following year (approximately 6 to 8 percent), this number became the charge per patient visit for the subsequent year.

In reviewing this method with Mr. Simi, Ms. Mitchell explained the problems she perceived. She said that although she realized this was not a precise method of determining charges for patients, the center's charge had to be held at a reasonable level to keep the health services accessible to as

EXHIBIT 2
EXPENSES AND PATIENT VISITS* FOR 1992, BY DEPARTMENT

Department	Number of Patient Visits	Expenses		
		Salaries†	Other‡	Total
Pediatrics	5,000	$ 64,000	$ 26,000	$ 90,000
Family planning	10,000	16,000	48,000	64,000
Adult medicine	2,100	96,000	51,000	147,000
Nursing	4,000	87,000	19,000	106,000
Mental health	1,400	48,000	26,000	74,000
Social services	1,500	94,000	26,000	120,000
Community health	2,500	16,000	32,000	48,000
Dental	6,400	64,000	32,000	96,000
Subtotal	32,900	485,000	260,000	745,000
Administration		121,000	6,000	127,000
Rent			115,000	115,000
Utilities			32,000	32,000
Laboratory work		52,000	29,000	81,000
Cleaning			19,000	19,000
Recordkeeping		22,000	10,000	32,000
Total		$680,000	$471,000	$1,151,000

Number of patient visits	32,900
Average cost per visit ($1,151,000 ÷ 32,900)	$35.00

*Patient visits rounded to nearest 100; expenses rounded to nearest $1,000.
†Includes fringe benefits.
‡Materials, supplies, contracted services, depreciation, and other nonpersonnel expenses.

many community residents as possible. Additionally, she anticipated complications in determining the cost per patient visit for each of RHHC's departments:

> You have to consider that our overhead costs, such as administration and rent, have to be included in the cost per patient visit. That's easy to do when we have a single overall cost, but I'm not certain how to go about it when determining costs on a departmental basis. Furthermore, it's important to point out that some of our departments provide services to others—nursing, for example. There are three nurses in that department, all earning the same salary. But one works exclusively for adult medicine, and another divides her time evenly between family planning and pediatrics. Only the third spends his entire time in the nursing department seeing patients who don't need

a physician, although he occasionally refers patients to physicians. In the social services department, the situation is more complicated. We have two MSW's (Masters in Social Work), each earning $35,000 a year, and one bachelor's degree social worker earning $24,000. The two MSW's yearly see about 1,500 patients who need general social work counseling, but they also spend about 50 percent of their time in other departments. The BA social worker cuts pretty evenly across all departments except dental, of course, where we don't need social work assistance.

Mr. Simi added further dimensions to the problems:

> I've spent most of my time so far trying to get a handle on allocating these overhead costs to the departments. It's not an easy job,

EXHIBIT 3
FLOOR SPACE AND LABORATORY USAGE, BY DEPARTMENT*

Department	Floor Space (sq. ft.)	Laboratory Usage (hrs./yr.)
Pediatrics	1,000	1,000
Family planning	1,300	200
Adult medicine	1,800	2,400
Nursing	300	100
Mental health	1,000	—
Social services	500	—
Community health	1,100	100
Dental	1,000	200
Administration	500	—
Recordkeeping	300	—
Laboratory	1,200	—
Total	10,000	4,000

*All amounts are rounded to the nearest 100.

you know. Administration, for example, seems to help everyone out equally, yet I suppose we might say more administrative time is spent on the departments where we pay more salaries. Rent, on the other hand, is pretty easy: that can be done on a square-foot basis. We could classify utilities according to usage if we had meters to measure electricity, phone usage, and so forth; but because we don't, we have to do that on a square-foot basis as well. This applies to cleaning too, I guess. It seems to me that recordkeeping can be allocated on the basis of the number of records, and each department generates one record per patient visit.

Laboratory work is the most confusing. Some departments don't use the laboratory at all, while others use the laboratory regularly. I guess the fairest would be to charge for laboratory work on an hourly basis. Since there are two people in the laboratory, each working 2,000 hours a year, the charge per hour would be about $13. But this is a bit unfair, since the laboratory also uses supplies, space, and administrative time. So we should include those other costs in the laboratory hourly rate. Thus, the process is confusing and I haven't really decided how

to sort it out. However, I have prepared totals for floor space and laboratory usage (Exhibit 3).

The Future

As Ms. Mitchell looked toward the remainder of 1993, she decided to calculate a precise cost figure for each department. RHHC was growing, and she estimated that total patient volume would increase by about 10 percent during 1993, spread evenly over each department. She anticipated that costs would increase by about 8 percent. She asked Mr. Simi to prepare a step-down analysis for 1992 so that they would know RHHC's costs for each department. She planned to use this information to assist her in determining patient fees for the remainder of 1993.

Questions

1. Using an appropriate step-down procedure to allocate service center costs to production centers, determine the total 1992 costs and cost per visit for each production center.

2. What does your analysis suggest about how the center should charge its patients for services?

CASE 18–4   Siemens Electric Motor Works (A)*

Ten years ago our electric motor business was in real trouble. Low labor rates allowed the Eastern Bloc countries to sell standard motors at prices we were unable to match. We had become the high-cost producer in the industry. Consequently, we decided to change our strategy and become a specialty motor producer. Once we adopted our new strategy, we discovered that while our existing cost system was adequate for costing standard motors, it was giving us inaccurate information when we used it to cost specialty motors.

—*Mr. Karl-Heinz Lottes—Director of Business Operations, EMW*

Siemens Corporation.   Headquartered in Munich, Siemens AG, a producer of electrical and electronic products, was one of the world's largest corporations. Revenues totaled 51 billion deutschmarks (DM) in 1987, with roughly half this amount representing sales outside of the Federal Republic of Germany. The Siemens organization was split into seven major groups and five corporate divisions. The largest group, Energy and Automation, accounted for 24 percent of total revenues. Low wattage alternating current (A/C) motors were produced at the Electric Motor Works (EMW), which was part of the Manufacturing Industries Division of the Energy and Automation Group. High wattage motors were produced at another facility.

The Electric Motor Works.   Located in the small town of Bad Neustadt, the original Siemens EMW plant was built in 1937 to manufacture refrigerator motors for "Volks-

kuhlschraenke" (people's refrigerators). Less than a year later, Mr. Siemens decided to halt the production of refrigerator motors and began to produce electric motors for other applications. At the end of World War II, the Bad Neustadt plant was the only Siemens factory in West Germany capable of producing electric motors. All the other Siemens production facilities had been completely destroyed or seized by Eastern Bloc countries. After an aggressive rebuilding program, Bad Neudstadt emerged as the firm's primary producer of electric motors.

Through the 1970s, EMW produced about 200 different types of standard motors, at a total annual volume of about 230,000 motors. Standard motors accounted for 80 percent of sales volume—the remaining 20 percent were customized motors. The production process was characterized by relatively long runs of a single type of motor. Because identical motors were used by a wide range of customers, standard motors were inventoried and shipped as orders were received. Production of standard A/C motors was extremely competitive. The key to success was to reduce costs so that the firm could price aggressively while making a profit. Despite a major expansion and automation program begun in 1974, by the early 1980s it had become obvious that the lower labor rates of the Eastern Bloc competitors gave them an insurmountable cost advantage.

Change in Strategy.   An extensive study of EMW's production capabilities and the market for electric motors indicated that EMW was in a position to become a profitable producer of low-volume, customized A/C motors. To help implement this strategy, the Bad Neustadt plant was enlarged and

---

*Copyright © by the President and Fellows of Harvard College. Harvard Business School case 189-089.

dedicated to the manufacture of A/C motors with power ratings ranging from 0.06 to 18.5 kilowatts. These motors supported a number of applications including automation engineering, machine tools, plastic processing, and paper and printing machines.

For the new strategy to succeed, EMW needed to be able to manufacture efficiently a large variety of motors in small production runs. Between 1985 and 1988, EMW spent DM50 million a year to replace almost every machine on the shop floor and thereby create a production environment that could support its new strategy.

By 1987, the production process was highly automated with numerically controlled machines, flexible machining centers, and robotically fed production processes used throughout the factory. Large-volume common components were manufactured using the appropriate automated equipment, whereas very low-volume components might be made in manual processes. Where possible, flexible manufacturing was used to produce small-volume specialty components. While a normal annual production volume for common components might be 100,000 units, a single component could have up to 10,000 custom variations that might have to be produced one at a time.

To design a custom motor, modifications were made to a standard motor design. The process involved determining where standard components could not be used. These standard components were replaced by custom components that provided the functionality required by the customer.

By 1987, the EMW strategy seemed to be successful. Of a total of 65,625 orders accepted, 90 percent were for custom motors. A total of 630,000 motors was produced (see Exhibit 1). Including all customized variations, Siemens EMW produced about 10,000 unique products that collectively required 30,000 different special components.

Change in the Calculation of Product Costs. Beginning in 1926, EMW had used a product costing system. This system assigned material and labor costs directly to the products and divided overhead costs into three categories: material related, production related, and support related. Material-related overhead included costs associated with material acquisition, and was allocated to products based on their direct materials cost. Production-related overhead was directly traced into production cost centers, and was allocated to products using either direct labor-hours or machine-hours, but not both. For more manually intensive machine classes, direct labor-hours was used; for machines whose operation required few direct labor-hours, machine-hours was used. In 1987, EMW used 600 cost centers, one per machine type. Support-related overhead was allocated to products based on the sum of direct material and direct labor costs, material overhead, and production overhead. The breakdown of each cost category as a percent of total costs was as follows:

	Percent of Total Costs	Burden Rate
Direct material	29%	
Direct labor	10	
Material overhead	2	5.7% of material cost
Production overhead	33	(600 different rates)
Support-related overhead	26	35.4% of manufacturing cost

EXHIBIT 1
DISTRIBUTION OF ORDERS ACCEPTED FOR PRODUCTION IN 1987

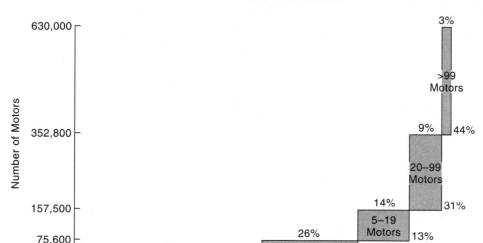

Two years after the change in strategy, problems with the traditional cost system became apparent. Management's concern with the traditional cost system was its inability to capture the relation between the increased support costs and the change in product mix. Under the traditional system, support costs were allocated to each motor based on its consumption of direct materials, direct labor, and either direct labor-hours or machine-hours. Management felt that most support costs were more closely related to the number of orders received or the number of internal factory orders for the customized components required by a specific model of motor.

As shown in Exhibit 1, 74 percent of the orders accepted for production by EMW after the change in strategy were for fewer than five motors. This simultaneous increase in the number of orders and reduction in the average number of motors per order increased the load on the production support

departments. An analysis of the way work was generated by orders in the shipping and handling, order processing, technical analysis of incoming orders, billing, and product costing departments indicated that the same resources were required to process an order for one motor as an order for 100 units of that motor.

The increase in the number of products with special options similarly caused the production scheduling, purchasing, packaging, product development, and design departments to expand. An analysis of the way work was generated by special components in these departments indicated that it was not the total number of special components produced, but the number of different special components (i.e., unique part numbers) in each motor design that determined the work load. For example, processing an order of 50 units of a custom motor with a design requiring 10 special components per unit generated the same amount of work as processing an

EXHIBIT 2
1987 RECONCILIATION
TRADITIONAL COST SYSTEM TO PROCESS-ORIENTED SYSTEM
(thousands)

	Traditional	Transferred	Process-Oriented
Material.................................	DM105,000		DM105,000
Material overhead.........................	6,000		6,000
Labor....................................	36,000		36,000
Labor or machine overhead.................	120,000		120,000
Manufacturing cost........................	267,000 (74%)*		267,000 (74%)
Engineering costs.........................	12,000	DM(6,300)	5,700
Tooling costs.............................	22,500	0	22,500
Administrative costs......................	60,000	(27,000)	33,000
Support-related cost*.....................	94,500 (26%)	(33,300) (9%)	61,200 (17%)
Customer order-processing.................		13,800	13,800
Special components processing.............		19,500	19,500
Total cost	DM361,500	DM 0	DM361,500

*Percent of total cost.

order of only one unit of a custom motor also requiring 10 special components. For either order, 10 special components had to be processed. In 1987, EMW processed 65,625 customer orders. The motors produced to fill these orders required that 325,000 different batches of special components be processed. In total, over a million units of special components were produced in 1987.

An extensive study was undertaken to identify the support costs that management believed were driven by processing customer orders and processing internal factory orders for special components. Part of each of the following departments' costs was allocated to two new overhead cost pools:

Costs Related to Customer Order Processing
Billing
Order Receiving
Product Costing and Bidding
Shipping

Costs Related to Processing Orders for Special Components
Inventory Handling
Product Costing and Bidding
Product Development
Purchasing
Receiving
Scheduling and Production Control
Technical Analysis of Incoming Orders

Once these costs were identified they were removed from the former support-related cost pool and assigned to two new cost pools. Exhibit 2 illustrates the formation of the two process-oriented cost pools for 1987. The first column presents total costs grouped by traditional costing system definitions. To move to process-oriented costing (PRO-KASTA[1]), DM6.3 million was removed from

[1]PROKASTA is an abbreviation for PROzessorientierte KAlkulation für STAffelkosten, which translated means Process Oriented Calculation for Cost Schedule.

EXHIBIT 3
UNIT COSTS FOR FIVE MOTOR MODELS (DM)
Modified Cost System

	A	B	C	D	E
Cost of Base Motor (before assignments from two new cost pools)	304.0	304.0	304.0	304.0	304.0
Cost of All Special Components* (before assignments from two new cost pools)	39.6	79.2	118.8	198.0	396.0
No. of Different Types of Special Components per Motor	1	2	3	5	10

Assumptions:	Base Motor Cost	Special Components Cost
Materials	90	12.0
Material overhead	5	0.7
Direct labor	35	4.5
Manufacturing overhead	117	15.0
Manufacturing cost	247	32.2
Support-related overhead (modified)	57	7.4
Unit cost (before assignments from two new cost pools)	304	39.6

*For illustrative purposes, each different special component is assumed to cost DM39.6 per unit.

the engineering costs and DM27 million from administrative costs; these DM33.3 million of costs were then assigned to the new cost pools, DM13.8 million to order-processing costs and DM19.5 million to special components costs.

With process-oriented costing, the cost of the base motor from which the customized product was derived and the cost of each custom component was calculated using the traditional cost system but with the new, smaller support-related cost pool (see Exhibit 3). The two new cost elements (customer order and special component order processing) were then added.

Effect of the Modified Cost System. In 1987, EMW received close to DM1 billion in orders, but accepted only DM450 million. Production volume ran at 115 percent of rated capacity. The product cost information generated by the redesigned system played

an integral role in helping EMW managers determine which orders were profitable and should be accepted.

Mr. Karl-Heinz Lottes, Director of Business Operations, commented on the role of the new cost system in helping to establish the new strategy:

> Without the redesigned system, our new strategy would have failed. With the information generated by the process-oriented cost system we can identify those orders we want to accept. While some orders we lose to competitors, most we turn down because they are not profitable. Anyone who wants to understand the importance of the PROKASTA system simply has to look at the costs of some typical orders under the traditional system and PROKASTA.

Questions

1. Consider the five illustrative motor models in Exhibit 3. Under the former (traditional)

system, what would the full cost of fulfilling an order for *one unit* of each model have been? What would have been the *average cost per unit* of each model if 10 units were ordered? 20 units? 100 units? What do your results suggest about the shortcomings of the old system with the new strategy?

2. Repeat the Question 1 calculations using the modified (PROKASTA) system. Have the shortcomings in the traditional system been addressed?

3. How significant are the differences in the average cost per unit between the modified system and the traditional system? (Respond by examining the ratio of modified to traditional cost for each of the twenty model-type/order-quantity combinations.)

4. Siemens's former cost system had 602 cost pools; the modified system added only two additional pools, through which a relatively small portion of overhead (DM33.3 million out of DM220.5 million total overhead) was assigned. Explain why such an apparently modest elaboration of an already complex cost system significantly changed the costs of certain model/quantity combinations.

5. Suggest how Siemens could further improve its system while at the same time *reducing* the total number of cost pools well below 604.

19

Standard Costs, Variable Costing Systems, Quality Costs, and Joint Costs

This chapter continues the discussion of product costing systems. Most of it deals with standard cost systems, which are product costing systems based on estimates of what costs should have been incurred rather than on actual costs. Also described are variable costing systems, an alternative to full cost product costing systems; the identification of so-called quality costs; and two complicated problems in full costing: the costing of joint products and by-products.

STANDARD COSTS

A **standard cost** is a measure of how much an item of cost *should be,* as contrasted with a record of how much it actually was. The term **budgeted cost** applies to the same definition. In practice, standard cost is used to describe what the cost of *one unit of product* should be whereas budgeted cost is used to describe what the *total cost* of many units or of a time period should be. A **standard cost system** is a product costing system that records standard costs either in addition to or instead of actual costs.

Standard Cost Sheet

In a standard cost system a **standard cost sheet** is developed for each product. This sheet is analogous to a recipe in that it includes a list of the "ingredients" of the product and describes the steps necessary to convert

ILLUSTRATION 19–1
STANDARD COST SHEET

Bill of Materials:

Item	Standard Quantity	Standard Price	Total Cost
Material X	120 sq. in.	$ 0.05	$ 6.00
Part Y	6 each	2.50	15.00
Component Z	1 each	24.50	24.50
Total materials			$45.50

Conversion Operations:

Description	Standard Time	Standard Rate	Total Cost
Form material X	0.06 hour	$12.50	$ 7.50
Attach parts Y	0.20	12.50	2.50
Join with Z	0.05	9.00	0.45
Test and pack	0.15	9.00	1.35
Total labor	1.00 hour		11.80
Production overhead @ $17.70 per direct labor-hour*			17.70
Total standard unit cost			$75.00

* The overhead rate is based on variable overhead costs of $7.70 per direct labor-hour (DLH) plus fixed overhead of $10,000 per month at a standard monthly volume of 1,000 DLH (I.e., annual standard volume is 12,000 DLH). Monthly budgeted overhead costs at standard volume are thus $10,000 + ($7.70 * 1,000) = $17,700; averaged over (divided by) 1,000 DLH, this equals $17.70 per DLH.

the ingredients into a finished item. A hypothetical standard cost sheet is shown in Illustration 19–1.

The formal name for the cost sheet's ingredients list is a **bill of materials.** It shows the *standard quantity* of each item of material input needed to make one unit of output—that is, one unit of the product. These standard quantities are then converted to monetary amounts by multiplying each material's standard quantity by the *standard price* per unit of that input. The sum of these amounts is the standard direct material cost for the product.

The formal name for the cost sheet's conversion operations is a **labor routing** (or simply **routing**). To determine the standard cost of the direct labor input to the product, a procedure like that for direct material is followed. The various labor operations required to make the item are listed, and a *standard time* is determined for each one. Then these standard times are multiplied by *standard rates* to convert them to monetary amounts. The sum of these amounts for all of the operations is the product's standard direct labor cost.

Overhead is included in the standard cost sheet by applying a predetermined overhead rate to some standard activity measure, such as standard direct labor-hours or standard direct labor dollars. In machine-intensive

operations the standard cost sheet will show standard machine times, and the overhead rate can be applied to these standard machine-hour amounts rather than to a labor amount.

In companies with automated manufacturing processes, direct labor costs may amount to as little as 5 percent of total production costs. Many such companies have decided that it is not worthwhile to treat direct labor as a separate category; they combine it with overhead costs, giving a single rate for standard conversion costs.

The sum of the standard costs of the inputs—direct material, direct labor, and overhead—is the standard cost of one unit of output. This standard unit cost is used as the basis for accounting entries involving finished goods inventory and cost of sales, as will be described below. Elements of the standard cost are also used in the budgeting process. For example, if 1,000 units of product X with a standard material cost of $45.50 per unit are to be produced in November, then the materials cost budget for that month will be $45,500. (Budgeting is described in more detail in Chapter 24.) The standard product cost is also used by many companies in making normal pricing decisions.

| **Account Flowchart** | Illustration 19–2 shows the account flowchart for Marker Pen Company's system (described in Chapter 17), converted to a standard cost basis. It is the same as the actual cost system shown in Illustration 17–2 except that four **variance accounts** have been added. The standard costs for a period and the costs actually incurred are usually different, and variance accounts are a repository for these differences. |

As an illustration of the variance concept, assume that the standard direct labor costs of all the operations performed during a month totaled $17,000. Then Work in Process (WIP) Inventory would be debited for $17,000. If actual direct labor costs for the month were $20,000, the credit to the liability account, Wages Payable, must be $20,000. The $3,000 difference between the actual and standard amounts would be debited to the Labor Variance account.

Standard costs represent what the cost *should* be. Therefore, if actual costs are higher than standard costs, the variance is said to be unfavorable. **Unfavorable variances** appear as *debits* in variance accounts. Similarly, if actual costs are below standard, the variance is a **favorable variance** and appears as a *credit* in a variance account.

Entries in Illustration 19–2 are for the same transactions and are numbered the same as the entries on Illustration 17–2. The entries in which standard costs are introduced are as follows:

Entry 1. Purchase of materials: A credit (favorable) material price variance of $2,000 is created because the actual cost of the quantity of materials received was $52,000 whereas the standard cost of this quantity of materials was $54,000. The actual cost was the actual quantity received times the

ILLUSTRATION 19-2
STANDARD COST SYSTEM FLOWCHART FOR MARKER PEN COMPANY
($000)

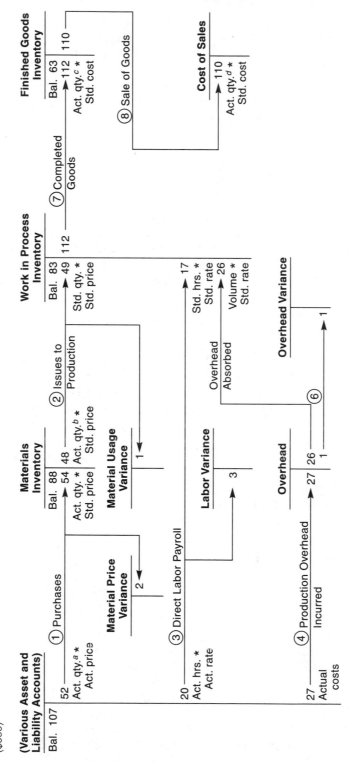

Note: Circled numbers refer to events described in Chapter 17 (Illustration 17-2 and related text).
[a] Quantity = Amount received.
[b] Quantity = Amount issued.
[c] Quantity = Number of completed units.
[d] Quantity = Number of units sold.

actual price paid per unit of material whereas Materials Inventory was debited for the actual quantity received times the *standard* unit price. Both amounts are based on the quantity received; thus, the variance occurs solely because the standard and actual unit *prices* of material were different. Thus, the **materials price variance** is calculated as follows:

$$\begin{aligned}\text{Materials price variance} &= (\text{Actual quantity} * \text{Standard price}) \\ &\quad - (\text{Actual quantity} * \text{Actual price}) \\ &= (\text{Standard price} - \text{Actual price}) * \text{Actual quantity} \\ &= \Delta\text{Price} * \text{Actual quantity}\end{aligned}$$

where ΔPrice stands for the difference between the standard and actual prices per unit of material.

Entry 2. Usage of materials: The standard materials cost of pens processed was $49,000 because the standard quantity of materials (the quantity that *should* have been issued) times the standard price per unit of material input was $49,000. However, the materials *actually* issued during the month had a standard cost of only $48,000 (actual quantity issued times standard price per unit of material). Note that both amounts are based on standard prices; thus, the $1,000 credit (favorable) difference between these two amounts occurs solely because the standard and actual quantities of materials issued were different. Thus, the **materials usage variance** is calculated as follows:

$$\begin{aligned}\text{Materials usage variance} &= (\text{Standard quantity} * \text{Standard price}) \\ &\quad - (\textit{Actual quantity} * \textit{Standard price}) \\ &= (\text{Standard price} - \text{Actual price}) * \text{Actual quantity} \\ &= \Delta\text{Quantity} * \text{Standard price}\end{aligned}$$

where ΔQuantity stands for the difference between the standard quantity and the actual quantity of materials issued.

Entry 3. Direct labor: Explained above. The actual labor cost was the actual hours multiplied by actual rates whereas Work in Process Inventory was debited for standard hours (the number of hours that *should* have been worked) multiplied by standard labor rates. Thus, the $3,000 debit (unfavorable) labor variance occurs because of a difference between standard and actual *times* (hours) and/or a difference between standard and actual labor *rates.* The $3,000 variance mixes the time and rate causes of the variance. In the next chapter decomposing this labor variance into a time component and a rate component will be described.[1]

---

[1]Some companies design their system so that the labor rate and time variances are isolated in separate variance accounts. This approach requires establishing a Direct Labor clearing account that has entries made to it analogous to those made to Materials Inventory. First, labor amounts are debited to Direct Labor based on actual times and *standard* rates; since the corresponding credit to Wages Payable is based on actual times and *actual* rates, there may be a difference. This difference is **labor rate variance,** and is debited or credited to an account with that name. Then a credit entry is made to Direct Labor to "issue" the labor to WIP; since this credit is also based on *actual* times and standard rates, but the debit to WIP is based on

Entry 6. Overhead: Indirect production costs applied to products by means of standard (predetermined) overhead rates were $26,000; that is, $26,000 of overhead cost was absorbed. Actual factory overhead costs incurred were $27,000, resulting in a debit (unfavorable) overhead variance of $1,000. (This variance also can be decomposed into pieces that relate to its two distinct causes: volume and spending. This analysis will be described in the next chapter.)

Entries 7 and 8. Finished goods: The calculation of the standard cost per unit of output (finished product) was described above. When goods are completed, the actual quantity of goods transferred from work in process to finished goods inventory is multiplied by the standard unit cost to arrive at the amount for the credit and debit entries. For example, if the standard unit cost for a pen is $0.20 and 560,000 pens are completed, then Work in Process Inventory is credited for $112,000 (= 560,000 * $0.20), and Finished Goods Inventory is debited for $112,000, as in entry 7. Similarly, if 550,000 pens are sold, Finished Goods Inventory is credited for $110,000 (= 550,000 * $0.20), and Cost of Sales is debited for $110,000, as in entry 8. No variances are associated with these entries.

Overhead Clearing Account.   As mentioned in Chapter 17, understanding the nature of the Overhead clearing account reduces problems in understanding detailed overhead variances in the next chapter. Recall that this is called a *clearing account* because it contains costs that are to be cleared, or transferred, to other accounts. During the month each time an actual overhead cost is incurred, the appropriate asset or liability account is credited, and the Overhead account is debited. For example, the production manager's monthly salary would be recorded as follows:

```
Overhead (clearing account) ........................ 3,000
    Wages payable ..................................     3,000
```

Thus, the debit side of the Overhead account can be thought of as an adding machine tape that is accumulating the month's *actual* overhead costs.

The credit side of the Overhead account shows the amount of overhead *absorbed* by (allocated to) products during the month. For example, if the assembly department's annual predetermined overhead rate is $4.40 per DLH (as developed in Chapter 18), and in a given month the labor content of the department's production was 2,000 standard DLH, then $8,800 (= 2,000 * $4.40) of overhead would be absorbed by this entry:

```
Work in Process Inventory .......................... 8,800
    Overhead (clearing account) ....................     8,800
```

---

standard times and standard rates, the **labor time variance** is isolated in the same manner that the material usage variance was. (Since the debits and credits to Direct Labor are exactly the same, the account is automatically cleared; it is just a gimmick that enables isolating these two variances in the accounts.)

Similar entries would be made to absorb overhead for the barrel and wick departments. In Illustration 19–2 the sum of these three departmental overhead absorption entries is $26,000.

Since most companies use predetermined overhead rates, excepting rarely by sheer coincidence the month's actual overhead costs (Overhead debits) will not exactly equal the amount of overhead absorbed (Overhead credits). Any balance remaining in Overhead is closed periodically (usually monthly) to Overhead Variance. In the illustration this is a debit (unfavorable) variance of $1,000 because actual overhead was $27,000 whereas only $26,000 was absorbed into Work in Process Inventory. Thus, it can be seen that a debit entry to Overhead Variance means that the period's actual overhead costs were underabsorbed (actual greater than absorbed) whereas a credit to Overhead Variance occurs when actual overhead costs are overabsorbed (absorbed greater than actual).

In summary, the only mechanical difference between the accounts in a standard cost system and those in an actual cost system is that the former has variance accounts. Whenever one part of a transaction is at standard cost and the other part is at actual cost, variance accounts are necessarily introduced.

Disposition of Variances. In a standard cost system production cost variances represent the amount by which the goods produced in an accounting period have been "miscosted" by the standard costs. Conceptually, to correct these costs and convert them back to actual costs, the output of the period's production efforts should first be "traced" to partially completed goods (WIP Inventory), completed but unsold goods (Finished Goods Inventory), and goods both made and sold during the period (Cost of Sales). Then the production variances should be allocated proportionately among these accounts. This procedure is consistent with the matching concept of financial accounting, which states that product costs should appear on the income statement in the period when an item is *sold* rather than the period in which it was produced.

As a practical matter, however, this disposition of production cost variances is difficult to accomplish, since the tracing of output is a nontrivial exercise. More importantly, management wants variances reported as promptly as practicable to minimize the time lag between a variance's occurrence and the subsequent managerial investigation. Therefore, for *management* accounting purposes variances are usually treated as period costs (as expenses of the month in which they were incurred). This is accomplished by closing the variance accounts each month, either to Cost of Sales or directly to Income Summary.[2]

---

[2]For external financial statements and income tax purposes, the conceptually correct treatment governs. Nevertheless, the expedient method of treating these production variances as period costs is acceptable *if* this method does not result in inventory and cost of sales amounts that are materially different from the amounts reached by the conceptually correct method.

Variations in the Standard Cost Idea

In the system shown in Illustration 19–2, standard costs were introduced when materials entered Materials Inventory and when material, labor, and overhead were debited to WIP Inventory. This is common practice, but standard costs can also be introduced at other points. For example, instead of debiting Materials Inventory at actual quantity received times standard unit prices, some companies carry materials at actual cost (i.e., actual quantity times actual unit price) and make the conversion to standard cost when the materials are issued for use in production. In such a system there would be no material price variance account, and the material variance account would combine both the price and the usage components of the variance.

Some companies do not use standard costs for all elements of cost. They may, for example, use standard direct labor costs, but actual direct material costs; or they may do the reverse. The choice depends on the advantages obtainable in the particular situation. Regardless of these variations, the essential points are that (1) in a standard cost system some or all of the elements of cost are recorded in at least one of the inventory accounts at standard rather than at actual cost, and (2) at whatever point a shift from actual to standard is made, a variance account is generated.

Terminology Ambiguities

As explained above, a total cost for material, labor, or overhead is obtained by multiplying a quantity (or volume) times a unit price (or rate). Either the quantity or the price or both can be an actual amount or a standard amount. Thus, there are four possible multiplications involved in determining a total cost:

1. Actual quantity * Actual unit price.
2. Actual quantity * Standard unit price.
3. Standard quantity * Actual unit price.
4. Standard quantity * Standard unit price.

Clearly the first total is an actual amount, and the fourth is a standard amount. But what about the second and third totals? In practice, they also are usually referred to as standard amounts even though they are not standard in the same sense as the fourth. Thus, when one hears, for example, that material costs are debited to Work in Process at standard, one must check further to determine whether the term *standard* is being used in the second, third, or fourth sense described above.

Uses of Standard Costs

A standard cost system may be used for any or all of several reasons: (1) It provides a basis for controlling performance. (2) It provides cost information useful for certain types of decisions. (3) It may provide a more rational measurement of inventory amounts and of cost of sales. (4) It may reduce the cost of recordkeeping.

Control. A good starting point in the control of managers' performance is to look at what the managers' departments actually did compared to what they should have done. Standard costs provide a basis for such comparisons, as will be discussed in detail in Chapter 20.

> **Example.** If the standard direct material cost for all the jeans manufactured in a month was $243,107 and if the actual cost of the direct material used on those jeans was $268,539, clearly direct material costs were $25,432 higher than they should have been. Without some standard there is no starting point for examining the appropriateness of the $268,539 actual direct material cost.

Decision Making. Standard costs are often used as a basis for arriving at normal selling prices or price bids, as described in Chapter 17. Standard direct costs are also often the best available approximation of the relevant differential costs in making some alternative choice decisions, as discussed in Chapters 26 and 27.

More Rational Costs. A standard cost system eliminates an undesirable quirk in the accounting system. It records the *same* costs for *physically identical* units of a product whereas an actual cost system may record different costs for physically identical units. For example, the actual direct labor cost of each batch of a given style of jeans could be different, depending on such factors as whether the employees who worked on the jeans had a relatively high wage rate because of long seniority. The jeans themselves, however, are physically the same. Realistically, there is no good reason for carrying one pair of the same jeans in inventory at one cost and another pair at a different amount or for charging cost of sales at different amounts. In a standard cost system all jeans of the same style would be carried in inventory and charged to cost of sales at the same unit cost.

Recordkeeping Savings. A standard cost system may appear to require more recordkeeping than an actual cost system because of the addition of standard costs to the system. In fact, however, use of standard costs may reduce the effort required to operate the system because all the individual material requisitions for a month can be totaled and posted as a single credit to Materials Inventory. Instead of making separate entries for direct material cost on each job cost sheet, one amount, the standard unit material cost, is all that is needed. Neither is there any need for workers to keep track of the time they spend on individual batches. All that is needed is one amount—the predetermined standard direct labor cost.

Often, a company uses a standard cost system because it would not be feasible to collect the actual costs for each unit or batch of product. For example, automobile manufacturers do not collect the actual cost of each car they assemble. The assembly line moves through each workstation at the rate of approximately one car per minute. If each worker had to record the time spent on each vehicle, the line would have to be slowed down just to allow for this substantial recordkeeping effort.

The amount of recordkeeping required for finished goods inventory and cost of sales is also considerably reduced. Since all units of the same product are assigned the same cost, the complications disappear that are involved in keeping track of costs according to a last-in, first-out (LIFO), first-in, first-out (FIFO), or average cost assumption (as described in Chapter

6). For example, if 12,000 pairs of jeans are sold by a blue-jean manufacturer in May, using a standard cost system to determine the cost of sales entry, the accountant need not be concerned about the actual cost of the various batches of inventoried jeans from which the shipments were made. The cost of sales total is simply the sum of the amounts obtained by multiplying the number of pairs shipped of each style of jeans times that style's standard unit cost.

Additional effort is involved in one aspect of a standard cost system: determining the individual standards. In many situations the effort required to do this is not great. The determination of standard unit *quantities* is done only occasionally. Once a standard quantity has been determined, it is used for months or even years without change. Only a change in a product's design or production methods or a significant "learning effect" (described in Chapter 16) requires changing unit quantities. However, the *price* component of a standard cost usually is updated annually or more often to reflect the impact of inflation and other factors on material prices and labor rates. Updating prices requires much less effort than redetermining standard quantities. When a new predetermined overhead rate is set for each cost center the overhead component of standard costs is also revised, usually annually. This overhead rate revision would be done in most companies whether or not they used a standard cost system for direct materials and direct labor.

An illustration of some of the procedural details of a standard cost system is shown in Appendix A to this chapter.

VARIABLE COSTING SYSTEMS

The cost accounting systems described above are called **full cost,** or **absorption cost, systems** because the full costs of producing goods or services are absorbed by (i.e., assigned to) those products. Generally accepted accounting principles (GAAP) and tax regulations both require that work in process and finished goods inventories be stated at approximately full production cost. This agrees with the financial accounting concept that assets are measured at cost.

Nevertheless, for management accounting purposes some companies state inventories only at *variable* production costs—material, direct labor, and variable overhead—and treat fixed overhead costs as expenses of the period in which these costs were incurred. Conceptually, these fixed costs are regarded as the costs of *maintaining capacity* during the period rather than as *product* (i.e., inventoriable) costs.[3]

Thus, a **variable costing system** by definition is one that treats only variable production costs as inventoriable product costs and treats fixed production costs as period costs. It is also commonly—but incorrectly—

---

[3]General Electric Company aptly calls these fixed capacity costs "readiness to serve" costs.

called a **direct costing system.**[4] Like full costing, a variable costing system can be based either on actual costs or standard costs.

Comparison of Absorption and Variable Costing

Advocates of variable costing feel that it has the following advantages over absorption costing systems:

1. In variable costing no fixed overhead costs are charged to individual units of product, so no overhead rate for the fixed component of overhead costs need be used in the cost accounting system. As shown earlier, this calculation can be complicated. In particular, it requires an estimate of standard volume; if only variable overhead costs are charged to products this is not necessary because variable overhead can then be accounted for in the same manner as variable material and direct labor costs. (Although an overhead rate to absorb both fixed and variable overhead costs is needed for financial accounting and income tax calculations, an approximation calculated only at year-end usually suffices.)

2. The overhead variance in a full costing system is made up of two components. One component—the **overhead spending variance**—is caused by actual overhead costs differing from the costs called for by the flexible overhead budget. The other, caused by actual production volume differing from the standard volume that was used to calculate the predetermined overhead rate, is the **overhead volume variance.** (Calculation of these two components of the overhead variance is described in Chapter 20.) By contrast the overhead variance in a variable costing system is purely a spending variance. Some managers feel that full costing's overhead *volume* variance is not useful information and that it causes confusion among those not sophisticated in cost accounting. Variable costing avoids this confusion.

3. Variable costing systems separate variable and fixed production costs. This separation is useful for control purposes because it is natural to control variable cost items on a cost-per-unit basis but to control fixed cost items on a total-cost-per-period basis. This separation is also useful for the differential analyses discussed in detail in Chapters 26 and 27 and for doing the break-even calculations described in Chapter 16. (It is possible to make this same separation in an absorption system by identifying the variable and fixed components of the total overhead rate, as will be demonstrated below.)

4. With variable costing reported monthly income is related directly to the month's sales volume. With absorption costing reported monthly income is affected by both the month's sales volume and its production volume. That is, a change in the physical size of finished goods inventory,

---

[4]If the cost object is a unit of a product, then direct costs generally include only material and direct labor; variable costs include both of these *plus* variable overhead. Therefore, the correct name for the system we are discussing is *variable* costing. However, the first article on this subject (by Jonathan Harris in the January 15, 1936, issue of the *N.A.C.A. Bulletin*) repeatedly referred to these variable costs as *direct* costs; thus, the misnomer, "direct costing system," was established in practice.

which always occurs when there is an imbalance between production and sales volumes, also affects the period's reported income. Under absorption costing, for example, sales may increase from one month to the next while reported income decreases. Because it is reasonable to expect that income should fluctuate with sales volume—the higher the volume, the higher the profit—this advantage of variable costing is an important one.[5]

Illustration 19–3 compares absorption and variable costing systems. The illustration is based on these assumptions:

Beginning inventory, period 1	0 units
Standard and actual production volume	100 units per period
Sales volume, period 1	80 units @ $50
Sales volume, period 2	120 units @ $50
Standard variable costs ($15 prime costs + $5 variable overhead)	$20 per unit
Budgeted fixed production overhead	$1,000 per period

Standard full production cost:

$$\underbrace{\$20}_{\text{Variable}} + \underbrace{\frac{\$1,000}{100 \text{ units}}}_{\text{Average Fixed}} \quad \text{. . . . .} \quad \$30 \text{ per unit}$$

Selling and administrative costs (all fixed)	$1,400 per period

From the illustration note that in period 1 when there was an inventory buildup because production volume exceeded sales volume by 20 units, absorption costing reported a *higher* income than did variable costing. On the other hand, when sales volume exceeded production volume in period 2, absorption costing reported a *lower* income than did variable costing. Combining the two periods, sales and production volumes were equal (at 200 units for the combined periods), and both systems reported the *same* income ($1,200 for the combined periods).

As shown in Illustration 19–3 (and as we will prove in Appendix B of this chapter), the following relationships always hold:

1. If the period's sales volume (in physical units) is *equal* to production volume, both systems report the *same* income.

2. If the period's sales volume *exceeds* production volume (there is a decrease in the physical size of finished goods inventory), then absorption costing reports a *lower* income than does variable costing.

3. If the period's sales volume is *less than* production volume (there is an increase in the physical size of finished goods inventory), then absorption costing reports a *higher* income than does variable costing.

---

[5]As we shall explain in the next chapter, absorption costing can be modified to make monthly income a function of the month's sales volume, but not of its production volume, by *not* closing the monthly overhead volume variance to the monthly income statement. This will also rectify the confusion mentioned in the second point above. Thus, variable costing is not the only remedy to these two problems.

ILLUSTRATION 19–3
COMPARISON OF ABSORPTION AND VARIABLE COSTING

Income Statement
Period 1

	Absorption Costing (Unit cost = $30)	Variable Costing (Unit cost = $20)
Sales (80 units @ $50).....................	$4,000	$4,000
Cost of goods sold:		
Beginning inventory	$ 0	$ 0
Cost of goods produced (100 units)........	3,000	2,000
Available for sale	3,000	2,000
Less: Ending inventory (20 units)	600	400
Cost of goods sold (80 units)...........	2,400	1,600
Gross margin.............................	1,600	2,400
Less: Period costs:		
Production overhead	—	1,000
Selling and administrative................	1,400	1,400
Total period costs....................	1,400	2,400
Income before taxes	$ 200	$ 0

Income reconciliation between the two methods: Inventory increased by 20 units * $10 per unit absorbed fixed overhead costs = $200 greater income with absorption costing because $200 of fixed overhead costs were capitalized in inventory.

Income Statement
Period 2

	Absorption Costing (Unit cost = $30)	Variable Costing (Unit cost = $20)
Sales (120 units @ $50).....................	$6,000	$6,000
Cost of goods sold:		
Beginning inventory (20 units).............	$ 600	$ 400
Cost of goods produced (100 units)........	2,000	2,000
Available for sale (120 units)	3,600	2,400
Less: Ending inventory	0	0
Cost of goods sold (120 units)...........	3,600	2,400
Gross margin.............................	2,400	3,600
Less: Period costs:		
Production overhead	—	1,000
Selling and administrtive.................	1,400	1,400
Total period costs....................	1,400	2,400
Income before taxes	$1,000	$1,200

Income reconciliation between the two methods: Inventory decreased by 20 units * $10 per unit absorbed fixed overhead costs = $200 lower income with absorption costing. This results from the "release" from inventory of $200 of fixed overhead costs actually incurred in period 1 but deferred until the goods were sold in period 2.

As is demonstrated in the income reconciliations of the illustration, these differences in reported income between the two approaches are explained by the fact that absorption accounting *capitalizes* (defers) fixed production overhead costs in the inventory asset accounts until the period in which the products are sold, whereas variable costing *expenses* these fixed costs as they are incurred.

> **Example.** As an extreme example assume the plant in Illustration 19–3 was operated in period 3, but the company sold *zero* units during this third period. Before taking account of selling and administrative costs, absorption costing will report *zero* income whereas variable costing will report a $1,000 loss. Under absorption costing all of the period 3 fixed overhead cost will be deferred until the goods produced in period 3 are sold—when these fixed costs will be released from inventory and charged to cost of goods sold at the rate of $10 per unit sold (along with the variable costs of $20 per unit). With variable costing only the variable costs are held in inventory; the $1,000 period 3 fixed overhead costs are an expense of that period, and only the $20 per unit variable cost will be released from inventory in later periods when the goods produced in period 3 are actually sold.

Overhead Rates in the Two Systems. As Illustration 19–3 indicates, the accounting for overhead costs in a standard variable costing system is essentially the same as the accounting for direct material and direct labor costs because all three costs are variable.[6] However, the overhead rate in an absorption costing system is, in effect, the sum of two rates: one to absorb the *variable* overhead costs and the other to charge each unit of activity with its fair share of *fixed* overhead costs. The variable overhead rate is relatively easy to determine. In Illustration 18–6 it is simply the slope of the flexible overhead budget line ($1.80 per DLH in that example). The fixed overhead absorption rate cannot be determined, however, without first estimating the standard volume over which the fixed overhead costs are to be averaged; in Illustration 18–6 this is $8,800 fixed costs ÷ 1,000 DLH standard volume, or $8.80 per DLH. Note that the sum of these two pieces of the absorption rate ($1.80 + $8.80 = $10.60) is indeed the full cost overhead rate we calculated from Illustration 18–6. (Illustration 19–1 provides another example: the $17.70 rate is the sum of a variable overhead rate of $7.70 per DLH and a fixed overhead rate of $10,000 ÷ 1,000 DLH = $10 per DLH.)

It is sometimes useful to think of the full cost overhead absorption rate as the sum of these two individual components, one related to budgeted variable overhead costs per unit of volume, the other to the *average* budgeted fixed overhead costs per unit. In particular, remember (again using Illustration 18–6 numbers) that one additional DLH is expected to cause the company to incur $1.80 more total overhead costs. But one more DLH is *not*

---

[6]As noted in Chapter 17, companies with a high degree of automation may treat some or all direct labor as a fixed cost.

expected to increase actual fixed overhead costs by $8.80; it will only cause $8.80 more fixed overhead to be *absorbed* into WIP Inventory. Avoiding the potential confusion between a volume change's effect on *actual* overhead costs versus its effect on *absorbed* overhead costs is one of the advantages mentioned by variable costing advocates.

Why Use Full Costing?

Surveys consistently indicate that despite its purported advantages, variable costing is used by only a very small minority of companies in their routine management accounting systems.[7] Probably the most important reason is senior management's concern that variable costing may lead decision makers to focus excessively on contribution margin and not enough on the management of nonvariable costs. As companies automate their operations, a tendency for the cost structure to shift away from variable costs towards fixed and step-function costs occurs. The large contribution margins reported by variable costing under such circumstances may, it is feared, lead decision makers to believe the business is more profitable than is actually the case. Similarly, variable costing balance sheets show inventories at amounts much lower than reported to shareholders, and any shift in the cost structure toward nonvariable costs magnifies the understatement. When senior management is emphasizing inventory reduction initiatives, they are concerned that these lower reported inventory amounts will tend to undermine such efforts.

There are additional reasons that may explain the lack of enthusiasm for variable costing in practice. For one, although it is conceptually easy to distinguish between fixed and variable costs, in practice it may be difficult to identify separately the variable costs as products flow from one department to another. Decomposition of semivariable costs into their fixed and variable components may be particularly difficult, as may be deciding whether to treat step-function costs as variable or fixed. Moreover, most companies need full costs for at least some of the various purposes, principally product pricing, described in Chapter 17. Finally, variable costing cannot be used for financial reporting and income tax accounting, and most companies prefer not to use a system for management accounting purposes that is inconsistent with that required for financial reporting.

In any event the "either-or" tone of most discussions about variable costing versus absorption costing is somewhat misleading. If a company sets its annual overhead rate using the flexible overhead budget procedure described in Chapter 18—if it decomposes total overhead costs into variable and fixed components—it can quite readily prepare management reports in

---

[7]For example, a survey of 298 manufacturing plants found that only 3 percent of them did not apply fixed overhead costs to products. Source: Keith V. Smith and Charlene Sullivan, "Survey of Cost Management Systems in Manufacturing," *Working Paper 90-5-1,* Purdue University, Krannert School of Management (May 1990).

ILLUSTRATION 19–4
FULL COST INFORMATION IN COMPARATIVE FORMATS

Conventional Absorption Costing Format		*Variable Costing/Contribution Margin Format*	
Revenues (1,000 units @ $100)	$100,000	Revenues (1,000 units @ $100)	$100,000
Cost of sales (1,000 units @ $75)*	75,000	Variable costs (1,000 units @ $70)‡	70,000
Gross margin	25,000	Contribution margin	30,000
Selling and administrative†	16,000	Fixed costs:	
Income	$ 9,000	Production§	10,000
		Selling and administrative	11,000
			21,000
		Income	$ 9,000

*Made up of $65 variable cost ($45.50 materials, $11.80 direct labor, $7.70 variable overhead) plus $10 per unit average fixed production overhead cost, as detailed in Illustration 19–1.

†Made up of variable costs equal to 5 percent of revenues plus $11,000 fixed costs.

‡$65 per unit variable production cost plus $5 (=$100 * 5 percent) variable selling and administrative cost.

§For a "pure" variable costing report, this should be the period's *actual* fixed production costs. For a report that will always give the same income as conventional full costing, this amont should be the *sales* volume times the standard fixed overhead cost per unit, plus the period's overhead spending variance.

either the conventional full cost format or in the contribution margin format preferred by variable costing's advocates. An example is shown in Illustration 19–4.

In the illustration a conventional absorption costing income statement is shown on the left-hand side. The reader has seen many such statements while studying financial accounting. Note that the full cost from Illustration 19–1 ($75) is the basis of the cost of sales calculation. For the statement on the right-hand side, the variable overhead cost per unit is added to the variable material and direct labor costs to determine the total variable production cost per unit ($65). To this is added the unit variable selling and administrative cost ($5) to arrive at the total variable cost per unit ($70). This amount is multiplied by the period's sales volume to arrive at the period's total variable costs ($70,000), which are subtracted from revenues to give contribution margin ($30,000). The fixed costs, both those related to production activities and those related to selling and administrative activities, are subtracted from contribution margin to give income ($9,000).

Thus, a company that segregates its fixed and variable costs can "have its cake and eat it too." The absorption costing income statement can be used for those analyses and decisions where clear visibility of gross margin and selling and administrative costs is important. The alternative format can be used for those short-term decisions, such as contribution pricing, that require the visibility of contribution margin. At the same time the company need not distort its balance sheet in management accounting reports by showing a significant asset, inventory, at only a fraction of its total (full) cost.

QUALITY COSTS

As part of their total quality management initiatives, many companies have attempted to make more explicit the **quality costs** or **costs of quality** they incur. These include any costs in excess of those that would have been incurred if a good were manufactured or a service provided exactly right the first time. These costs typically are categorized into four groups, described below.

Prevention costs are the costs associated with preventing defects and other quality problems. (These costs are sometimes labeled *quality prevention costs*—conveying an inaccurate and unfortunate connotation.) They include supplier education and certification[8], product redesign, process improvements, and other efforts aimed at preventing problems from occurring in the first place. These are "good" quality costs to incur because they represent activities that often significantly reduce costs in the other three categories.

Quality appraisal (or **detection**) **costs** include inspection, testing, and other activities designed to find problems *before* a good is delivered. (Formerly, these activities often were labeled "quality control" efforts.) In the case of services, such activities usually involve checking processes, because the output of these processes—an intangible service—is usually difficult to inspect before it is provided to the customer. (Sometimes a third party observes the delivery of the service; this is a form of inspection, but it takes place *as* the service is provided.)

Internal failure costs include scrap, rework, and other activities to "make things right" *before* a good is delivered. These costs are incurred as a result of the appraisal activities. They may exist for some services—for example, a tax return with errors can be reworked before it is given to the customer, but for personal services, internal failure costs cannot be identified since such a service cannot be scrapped or reworked before it is provided to the customer.

External failure costs are the costs of "making things right" when a quality problem has occurred *after* the product has been delivered to the customer. This category includes refunds, warranty costs (both repairs and replacements), product liability costs, and the cost of repeating a service that was not performed properly the first time. The most important external failure cost is not readily measurable—the cost of lost future business that results from dissatisfied customers "bad-mouthing" the organization that delivered the poor-quality good or service.

Unlike product costs, these costs of quality often are estimates based on special studies rather than the output of routine accounting systems. However, the fact that estimates are used does not diminish the usefulness

---

[8]A "certified" supplier is one whose processes have been examined by the customer and judged to produce output of such consistently high quality that the customer does not need to inspect any incoming goods from the supplier.

of identifying such costs. In some cases thinking about these categories has led to improvements in a company's routine product costing system. For example, some companies formerly treated most internal failure costs as an overhead item that got allocated to all products, irrespective of which specific products were causing them. These companies now charge such costs to the specific product that caused them to be incurred.

JOINT PRODUCTS AND BY-PRODUCTS

Two difficult costing problems that occur in some industries are the costing of joint products and by-products. These problems are discussed below.

Joint-Product Costing

Joint products are two or more dissimilar end products that are produced from a single batch of raw material or by a single production process. A classic example is the variety of end products made from a steer. These include hides, many different cuts of meat, frozen meat dishes, pet food, fertilizers, and a variety of chemicals. Other obvious examples can be found in oil refining and timber processing.

In the production process the raw material is treated as a single unit up to a certain point—the **split-off point.** Beyond the split-off point separate end products are identified, and costs are accumulated for each of these end products during subsequent stages of the production process. For example, up to the point at which the steer is slaughtered and dressed, the costs of feed, grazing, transportation, and other items are accumulated for the steer as a whole. At that point these costs must be divided among the many end products made from the steer. The problem of joint-product costing is to find some reasonable basis for allocating to each of the joint products the costs incurred up to the split-off point.

This problem is essentially the same as that of allocating indirect costs to cost centers. In both cases the objective is to assign a fair share of the joint or common costs to the separate end products, and in neither case can the results be an entirely accurate measure of the actual costs.

Sales Value Method. One common basis is to allocate joint costs in proportion to the sales value of the end products minus the separate processing and marketing costs estimated to be incurred for each end product beyond the split-off point. If the selling price is based on cost, the sales value method involves a certain amount of circular reasoning; but there may be no better alternative. If gasoline sells for twice the price of kerosene, it is reasonable that gasoline should bear twice as much of the joint costs.

> **Example.** In June, Kruse Company produced 200 units of product A and 300 units of product B, having sales values of $2,000 ($10 per unit of A) and $6,000 ($20 per unit of B), respectively. Joint production costs up to the split-off point were $3,000. Beyond the split-off point $600 of additional

production and marketing costs are incurred for A and $1,500 for B. With the sales value method the $3,000 joint costs are allocated as follows:

Joint Products	(1) Sales Value	(2) Costs Beyond Split-Off	(1) – (2)	Calculation	Joint Costs Allocated to Each Product
A.........	$2,000	$ 600	$1,400	(14/59) * $3,000 =	$ 712
B.........	6,000	1,500	4,500	(45/59) * 3,000 =	2,288
			$5,900		

Unit costs would then be calculated as follows:

	Product A	Product B
Joint costs	$712 ÷ 200 = $3.56	$2,288 ÷ 300 = $ 7.63
Costs beyond split-off	600 : 200 = 3.00	1,500 ÷ 300 = 5.00
Unit cost	$6.56	$12.63

Weight Method.   Another basis of apportionment is weight: the joint costs are divided in proportion to the weight of the joint material in the several end products. In the case of the steer, the weight method implicitly assumes that the hamburger is as valuable as the sirloin steak, which is unrealistic. But in other situations the assumption that costs are related to weight might be reasonable. In any event the amount of cost charged to each end product must be recognized as resulting from a judgmental decision and, hence, as not entirely accurate.

Having allocated joint costs to products at the split-off point, the measurement of costs *beyond* this point is done in the usual manner. Each product is a separate cost object, and the additional material, labor, and overhead costs of completing the finished product are assigned to it.

By-Product Costing

By-products are a special kind of joint product. If management wishes to manufacture products A and B in some predetermined proportion or to make as much of each end product as possible from a given quantity of raw material, then these products are ordinary joint products. By contrast, if management's objective is to make as much of product A as possible but some quantity of product B inevitably emerges from the process, then product A is a main product and product B is a by-product. The intention is to make as much of the main product and as little of the by-product as possible.

As management's intention changes, the classification changes. For example, early in the 20th century, kerosene was the main product made from crude oil. Subsequently, with the growth in consumption of gasoline, kerosene became a by-product. Currently, kerosene has become a main product again because it is an important component of jet engine fuel.

A by-product is usually costed so that *zero profit* is reported for it. That is, it is charged with joint costs equal to its sales revenue less any costs incurred beyond the split-off point. Consequently, all profits are attributed to the main product. In the preceding example if A were regarded as a by-product rather than a joint product, it would be charged with $1,400 of the $3,000 joint costs, thus reducing A's profit to zero. Arithmetically, this approach is equivalent to initially charging all costs to the main product and then crediting any by-product sales to the main product's costs.

ACCURACY OF COSTS

From the description given in this and the preceding two chapters, it should be apparent that the costs of a cost object cannot be measured with complete accuracy if some items of cost are indirect, as is usually the case. Two equally well-informed and competent accountants can arrive at different costs for the same product or other cost object. These differences arise from differing judgments on, among others, the following matters.

Judgment Calls   1. *Capital, product, and period costs.* In Chapter 14 we showed how the judgment as to whether a given item of cost should be classified as a capital cost, a product cost, or a period cost affects both the measurement of costs and the measurement of net income for a period.

2. *Measurement of direct costs.* If Company A classifies only the wages of direct workers as direct labor but Company B includes labor-related costs, Company A's direct labor costs will be less than Company B's. Since labor-related costs may amount to 40 percent or more of wages, this difference can be substantial.

3. *Distinction between direct and indirect costs.* In the above example the labor-related costs that Company A excluded from direct costs were part of its indirect (overhead) costs. Although a share of these overhead costs is allocated to products, the allocation process is such that a different amount may be allocated to a given product than would be the case if the item were treated as a direct cost. (For example, if machine-hours were used as the overhead driver, the amount of labor-related costs assigned to a given product could be quite different.)

4. *Alternative allocation methods.* Many judgments must be made in deciding how overhead cost items are allocated to both service and production cost centers, and how the costs of service centers are assigned to production centers.

5. *Choice of an activity measure.* The amount of overhead allocated to a product is affected by the measure of activity (volume) used in the overhead rate. Measuring volume in terms of direct labor-hours, for example, may give

different results than measuring it in terms of direct labor dollars or machine-hours.

6. *Estimate of volume.* As illustrated in Chapter 18, the estimate of standard volume used in arriving at the predetermined overhead rate can have a significant influence on the per-unit overhead charge.

7. *Definition of cost center.* How cost centers are defined significantly influences the amount of overhead allocated to a product. In some manufacturing companies each important machine is a cost center. At the other extreme the entire plant may be a single cost center, giving rise to a plantwide overhead rate. A number of choices fall between these two extremes. In general, the more narrow the definition of a cost center, the more equitable is the resulting amount of indirect cost allocated to the product. On the other hand, it is also true that the more narrow the definition of the cost centers, the more cost centers there will be, and more work will therefore be required to compute and apply separate overhead rates.

Tendencies toward Uniformity

Because of the above factors and others, no one can measure precisely the actual amount of resources used in producing a good or service when indirect costs are involved. Nevertheless, there are forces tending toward uniformity of method. Most important, a company usually employs the same practices throughout the company for measuring full costs. Consequently, comparisons of the costs of various products can validly be made. Furthermore, there tends to be a similarity of costing practices within an industry, and this facilitates cost comparisons within that industry.

COST SYSTEM DESIGN CHOICES

The various aspects of costing systems described in this and the preceding two chapters make clear that an organization faces many choices in designing a costing system. Should it be a job order or a process system? An actual cost or standard cost system? If an actual cost system, should an after-the-fact actual overhead rate or a predetermined overhead rate be used? If a standard cost system, at what point in the system should the shift from actual costs to standard costs be made? Should an absorption costing income statement or contribution margin format be used? Should "pure" variable costing (with balance sheet inventories valued at variable cost) be used instead of, or in addition to, absorption costing? How many cost centers should be defined? How should volume be measured in each of them? What is the appropriate step-down order for allocating the costs of service centers to production cost centers? Should labor-related and material-related costs be treated as direct costs or as a part of overhead costs? Should the system be kept simple and supplemented by an activity-based costing model to provide more accurate product cost estimates for decision-making purposes?

Clearly all of these questions (and more) need to be answered in designing an appropriate cost system. Moreover, with the increasing diversity of organizations' activities and production technologies, the questions must be answered several times, once for each segment of an organization's operations. This is true not only of diversified corporations but also of many other organizations. For example, a cost system for a hospital's gift shop differs from that for its cafeteria, and both of these differ from the system on which patient billing is based. Thus, one of today's management accountant's jobs—designing these systems in conjunction with senior management—is far more complex than was the case when cost accounting was in its infancy.

SUMMARY

The essential idea of a standard cost accounting system is that costs and inventory amounts are recorded at what costs *should* be rather than what they actually are. At some point in the flow of costs through the system, there is a shift from actual costs to standard costs. Wherever this occurs, a variance develops. This can be as early as the receipt of materials (in which case the variance is a material price variance) or as late as the movement of finished products from the production facilities to finished goods inventory.

Variable costing systems treat only variable production costs as product (inventoriable) costs, and treat fixed production overhead costs as an expense of the period in which these costs are incurred. Variable costing, which may have certain advantages for internal (management) accounting in some companies, is not widely used in practice, probably because its advantages can be obtained in other ways without understating inventory on the balance sheet or risking a lack of adequate attention to the management of nonvariable costs.

Many companies find it useful to identify their costs of quality, further categorizing such costs as relating to problem prevention, quality appraisal, internal failures, and external failures.

When joint-product costs or by-product costs are involved, costs up to the split-off point must be divided among the several cost objectives in some equitable fashion.

Although it is impossible to measure full costs with complete accuracy whenever indirect costs are involved, such measures are useful, especially if the costing practices are comparable within a company or an industry.

APPENDIX A: STANDARD COSTING ILLUSTRATION

As an illustration of some of the procedural details of a standard cost system, we describe the system of the Black Meter Company (the disguised name of an actual company).

Black Meter Company manufactures water meters in a wide range of sizes. The water meter installed in most homes is an example of its product. The meters consist of a hard rubber piston that is put in motion by the flow of water past it, a gear train that reduces this motion and registers it on a dial, and two heavy bronze castings bolted together around the measuring device.

The company has several production departments. The castings and many interior parts of meters are cast in the foundry and then, based on size, are sent to one of the three machining departments. Some of the mechanical parts are sent to a subassembly department where they are assembled into gear trains. Other parts go directly to the meter assembly department. Several other departments provide service to the production departments.

System Overview

Because the company ships meters to customers as soon as the meters are completed, its Finished Goods Inventory account reflects primarily repair parts, not complete meters. It also has Materials Inventory and WIP Inventory accounts, and uses a standard full cost system. Standard costs are established for each element of direct labor, direct material, and production overhead.

During the month actual costs are accumulated: material is purchased, the earnings of workers are recorded, and production overhead items (such as utilities) are purchased. These entries are made at actual cost. Elements of cost, however, are debited to WIP Inventory at predetermined *standard* costs. Since actual costs differ from standard costs, variance accounts are necessary.

Establishing Standard Costs

A standard unit cost is established for every type of material that is purchased. This is done annually by adjusting the current standard price for any market changes expected for the following year. For example, if the current price of a certain grade of phosphor bronze is $1.12 a pound and no change is predicted, its standard cost for the next year will be $1.12 per pound.

Standard hourly rates for direct labor and overhead are also determined annually. These rates are used to assign costs to products according to the number of standard direct labor-hours incurred in the manufacture of each product. This is done on a departmental basis because each department is a cost center. For each production department the accountants start with data on the actual direct labor payroll, including fringe benefits, and the number of direct labor-hours worked in each of the past few years. The departmental supervisors advise what adjustments should be made to take account of future conditions. Thus, an amount for total labor cost and an amount for hours worked at normal levels of activity are derived. Dividing the payroll amount by the normal number of hours yields a standard direct labor rate per standard direct labor-hour for each department.

Overhead costs for a production department include overhead costs incurred in that department plus an allocated portion of the costs of service departments. Estimates are made of these amounts for each production

ILLUSTRATION 19–5
STANDARD LABOR AND OVERHEAD RATES
Partial Listing

Department Number	Department Name	Rate per Hour		
		Labor	Overhead	Total
120A	Foundry—molding	$18.00	$31.50	$49.50
120B	Foundry—grinding and snagging	16.00	24.00	40.00
122	Small parts manufacture	16.50	26.40	42.90
123	Interior parts manufacture	15.50	24.80	40.30
130	Train, register, and interior assembly . . .	14.00	17.50	31.50
131	Small meter assembly	15.00	18.75	33.75

ILLUSTRATION 19–6
FOUNDRY STANDARD COST

FOUNDRY STANDARD COST						
Drawing No.: D-2408		Part:	5/8" HF Chamber Rings	Material Cost:		101.92
				Pattern Cost:		15.00
Material:		Phosphor Bronze #806 100 pcs., 91.0 lbs. at $1.12				
Oper. No.	Operations and Tools	Prod. Center	Machine	Std. Hours per 100 Pcs.	Std. Rate per Hour	Total
1	Mold	120 A	Match Plate	1.76	49.50	87.12
2	Grind	120 B	Wheel	0.45	40.00	18.00
3	Snag	120 B	Bench	0.68	40.00	27.20
	Total					249.24

department at normal volume. These estimated total overhead costs are divided by the standard number of direct labor-hours for each producing department (the same number that had been used in calculating the standard labor rate) to arrive at an overhead rate per standard direct labor-hour. Illustration 19–5 gives these rates relevant to later illustrations in this example.

Standard Cost Sheets. These standard hourly costing rates, which include both direct labor and overhead, are used to develop a standard cost for each type of meter. Illustrations 19–6, 19–7, and 19–8 give examples of these calculations. The examples show the development of the standard cost of a 100-unit batch of 5/8-inch HF meters.

Illustration 19–6 shows the calculation for a 5/8-inch chamber ring that is manufactured in the foundry and is one component of the 5/8-inch HF

ILLUSTRATION 19–7
PARTS DEPARTMENT STANDARD COST

PARTS DEPARTMENT STANDARD COST						
Drawing No.: X-2408	Part: 5/8" HF Chamber Ring				Material Cost:	
Plating: H.T. & E.T.	Material: Bronze 100 pcs., 89 lbs.				249.24	
Oper. No.	Operations and Tools	Prod. Center	Machine	Std. Hours per 100 Pcs.	Std. Rate per Hour	Total
1	Broach outlet #734	122	P.P.	0.75	42.90	32.18
2	Finish tap-plate bore and face	123	Heald	0.55	40.30	22.17
	Drill 6 holes	123	Drill	0.93	40.30	37.48
3	C-sink 3 holes tap-plate side	123	Drill	0.47	40.30	18.94
	Tap 3 holes tap-plate side	123	Heskins	0.17	40.30	6.85
4	Rough and Finish inside and outside	123	Heald	5.00	40.30	201.50
	C-sink 3 holes on bottom	123	Drill	0.20	40.30	8.06
5	Tap 3 holes on bottom	123	Drill	0.30	40.30	12.09
	Spline inside	123	Spliner	0.47	40.30	18.94
6	Spline outside	123	Miller	0.50	40.30	20.15
	Dress	123	Bench	5.80	40.30	233.74
	Total					861.34

meter. As is the case with most parts, costs are calculated for a lot size of 100 units. The chamber rings are cast from bronze that has a standard cost of $1.12 a pound. Since the standard quantity of bronze required for 100 pieces is 91 pounds, the standard material cost is $2.12 * 91 = $101.92, as shown in the "Material Cost" box. Black Meter's industrial engineering department determined the 91-pound standard quantity. The standard cost of the pattern used in the casting, $15.00, is also entered.

To apply the standard direct labor and overhead rates to any part, it is necessary to have the standard direct labor-hours for the operations involved in making that part. These are obtained from time studies performed by the industrial engineering department and are entered in the fifth column of the foundry standard cost sheet. The standard time to mold 100 chamber rings is 1.76 direct labor-hours, to grind them 0.45 hour, and to snag them 0.68 hour.

In the sixth column of the foundry form is recorded the combined standard direct labor and overhead rate per standard direct labor-hour for

ILLUSTRATION 19–8
ASSEMBLY DEPARTMENT STANDARD COST

ASSEMBLY DEPARTMENT STANDARD COST						
Drawing No.: 2735		*Assembly:* 5/8" HF ET FB				
Parts of Assembly		*Cost*	*Parts of Assembly*			*Cost*
X-2408 Chamber Ring		861.34	K-5030 5/8" HF Dur. Bolt (6)			90.00
K-2414 Chamber Top Plate		247.20	K-4630 5/8" HF ac Nut		(6)	30.00
K-2418 Chamber Bot. Plate		227.73	K-5068 5/8" HF Washers		(6)	24.00
K-2465 Disc Piston Assem.		448.47	2782 Chamber Pin			11.12
2761 Top Case		968.35	6172 Misc. Train Conn.			40.41
X-2770 Bottom Case		284.60	K-2776 Casing Gasket			18.45
3209 5/8" Closed Train		1,135.29	2779 Casing Strainer			39.45
			2412 5/8" HF Sand Plate			28.38

Oper. No.	*Operations and Tools*	*Prod. Center*	*Machine*	*Std. Hours per 100 Pcs.*	*Std. Rate per Hour*	*Total*
1	Assem. Disc Interior	130	Bench	7.5	31.50	236.25
2	Assem. Train and Strainer to Case	131	Bench	4.6	33.75	155.25
3	Assem. Int. and Bottom to Meter	131	Bench	5.6	33.75	189.00
	Total					5,035.29

the operation. For example, Illustration 19–5 shows the labor and overhead rate for molding in Department 120A as $49.50 per standard direct labor-hour; this amount appears on Illustration 19–6 as the standard rate per hour for the molding operation. It is multiplied by the standard direct labor time of 1.76 hours to give a standard cost of labor and overhead of $87.12. The other two foundry operations follow the same procedure. The total standard foundry cost of 100 chamber rings is $249.24.

Illustration 19–7 accumulates additional standard costs for these 100 chamber rings as they pass through the parts manufacture department. They enter the parts department at the standard cost of $249.24, the same cost at which they left the foundry. After the operations listed on Illustration 19–7 have been performed on them, they become finished chamber rings. These operations have increased the standard cost to $861.34.

Similar standard cost sheets are prepared for each of the other components of the 5/8-inch meter. As shown in Illustration 19–8, these parts are assembled into complete meters. In each of these assembly operations, standard costs are added; the total standard cost of 100 meters is $5,035.29.

Standard costs are calculated in the same manner for all the meters that Black Meter manufactures.

ILLUSTRATION 19–9
JOB TIME CARD

Mach. No.	Prod. Center 130	Quantity Ordered 3,000		Order Number 21•86572		Clock No. 337
Part Name 5/8" O. Trains, # 3209						
Prev. Quantity Finished 0	Oper. No. 9	Operation Name Finish Assembly				Name B. Harris
Quantity Finished 2,400	Std. Hours Per 100 1.75	Std. Hours 42|00	Std. Rate 14|00	Standard Labor 588|00		
Stop Sept. 20 40.0		Actual Hours 40|0	D.W. Rate 14|25	Earnings 570|00		
Start Sept. 16 00.0		Foreman R.H.L.		Gain or (Loss) 18|00		

Accounting Entries

All direct material, direct labor, and overhead costs are debited to WIP Inventory at standard costs. Actual costs are collected in total for the period by department, but no actual costs are collected for individual batches of meters.

Material. As soon as any material is received, the standard cost of that material is written on the vendor's invoice. Each purchase is then journalized: credit the actual cost of the material to Accounts Payable, debit Materials Inventory for the standard cost, and debit or credit the difference to a Material Price Variance account. When material is issued for use in production, the quantity is the standard amount (e.g., 91 pounds in the example shown in Illustration 19–6), and the entry crediting Materials Inventory and debiting WIP Inventory is made at the standard cost (e.g., $101.92 in the example shown in Illustration 19–6).

A physical inventory is taken every six months (at the end of June and December) and is valued at standard cost. Any difference between this amount and the balance as shown in the Materials Inventory account is debited or credited to a Material Usage Variance account.

Labor. The job time card is the basic document for recording direct labor costs. Each production employee fills out such a card for each order on which he or she works during a week. The time card reproduced as Illustration 19–9 shows that B. Harris worked all week on one order. On the time card Harris records the quantity finished, the actual hours worked, and the standard hours. A payroll clerk enters each employee's hourly rate and the standard direct labor rate for that department, then extends the actual and standard direct labor cost of the work completed.

ILLUSTRATION 19–10
COPY OF SALES INVOICE

Village of Vernon, Water Dept.
Attn: E.J. Blackburn, Mayor
Vernon, NY 13476

Qty	Description	Unit Price	Total
10	5/8" x 3/4" Model HF Meters SG SH ET FB & 3/4"	72.00	720.00
1	Change Gear #46X	9.50	9.50
			729.50

Ship gear by UPS   Meters   503.53
                        Parts   4.75

By totaling all the time cards the payroll clerk obtains the actual wages earned by each employee in each department and also the total standard labor cost of the work done in each department. These amounts are the basis for an entry that credits Wages Payable for the actual amount and debits WIP Inventory for the standard amount of direct labor. The variance is recorded in a Direct Labor Variance account.

Overhead.   For each department the standard direct labor-hours worked is multiplied by the overhead rate for that department (as obtained from Illustration 19–5). This gives the amount of absorbed overhead cost for each department for that month. These amounts are credited to the Overhead clearing account and debited to WIP Inventory. During the month actual manufacturing overhead costs have been accumulated and debited to the Overhead clearing account. The overhead variance is this account's month-end balance, which is the difference between the actual overhead costs and the absorbed overhead cost. This is debited or credited to the Overhead Variance account.

When these transactions have been recorded, all material, direct labor, and overhead have been charged into the WIP Inventory account at standard cost, and the variance accounts have been debited or credited for the difference between actual and standard. These variance accounts are then closed to the income statement each month.

Sales and Cost of Sales

A copy of each sales invoice is sent to the office, where a clerk enters the standard cost of the items sold (see Illustration 19–10). At the end of the month, the figures on these duplicate invoices are totaled to get amounts for sales revenue and for the standard cost of goods sold. The standard cost

ILLUSTRATION 19–11

BLACK MEIER COMPANY
Income Statement
For the Month of June

Net sales.		$3,426,949
Less: Cost of sales at standard cost	$2,379,142	
Variances (detailed below)	(15,321)	2,363,821
Gross margin.		1,063,128
Selling expense.	263,426	
General and administrative expense	507,255	770,681
Income before income taxes		292,447
Income taxes.		105,281
Net income.		$ 187,166

Variances

	Debit	Credit
Favorable variances:		
Material price.		$ 79,059
Unfavorable variances:		
Material usage.	$24,227	
Direct labor	16,429	
Overhead	23,082	(63,738)
Net variance.		$ 15,321

---

is a credit to Inventory and a debit to Cost of Sales. The total sales amount is a credit to Sales and a debit to Accounts Receivable. When this is completed, the accounting department can prepare the monthly income statement (see Illustration 19–11). Note, incidentally, that although the net amount of the variance on this income statement is relatively small, there are sizable detailed variances that tend to offset one another. Management investigates these variances and takes action when warranted.

APPENDIX B: ABSORPTION VERSUS VARIABLE COSTING'S IMPACT ON INCOME

This Appendix proves the three statements made in this chapter about the effects of absorption costing and variable costing on reported income. In Illustration 19–3 we saw that both systems treat revenues, variable costs, and selling and administrative costs in the same way. Hence, our proof can focus on the difference in the two systems' treatment of fixed production overhead costs.

Let:

S = Sales volume, in units
P = Production volume, in units
F = Fixed production overhead costs per period

With absorption costing the amount of fixed overhead charged to the income statement is $(F/P) * S$, where F/P is the *fixed* cost absorption rate. Variable costing charges F. The difference in these amounts is:

$$\underbrace{\left(\frac{F}{P} * S\right)}_{\text{Absorption}} \quad - \quad \underbrace{F}_{\text{Variable}} \quad = \underbrace{\frac{F}{P} * (S - P)}_{\text{Difference}}$$

Using this formula, let us now consider each of the three cases mentioned in the chapter:

Case 1. *No change in finished goods inventory: $S = P$.* In this case $S - P = 0$, so the difference in fixed overhead cost charged to the income statement is zero. Thus, income is the *same* under both methods.

Case 2. *Decrease in finished goods inventory: $S > P$.* Now $S - P > 0$, so the difference in fixed overhead charges is positive. Thus, absorption costing charges *more* fixed overhead cost to income than does variable costing, so absorption costing reports *lower* income than does variable costing.

Case 3. *Increase in finished goods inventory: $S < P$.* In this case $S - P < 0$, so the difference is negative. That is, absorption costing charges *less* fixed overhead cost to income and therefore results in *higher* reported income than does variable costing.

Note also that these calculations demonstrate the fourth feature of variable costing that was stated in the text: variable costing income is *not* a function of period's production volume (P), because the income statement is charged with F dollars of fixed overhead regardless of P; absorption costing income *is* affected by P because the period's income statement is charged with $(F/P) * S$ fixed overhead costs. In particular, for a given sales volume, S, absorption costing income can be increased by increasing *production* volume, P, since the fixed overhead expense term, $(F/P) * S$, gets smaller as P increases. In other words, a company (or responsibility center within a company) can increase reported income under absorption costing by building up finished goods inventory. This is called "increasing profit by selling overhead to inventory."[9]

---

[9]The above proof assumes a constant level of production, as in Illustration 19–3. Without this assumption but presuming that predetermined overhead rates are used, the proof becomes more complex, owing to overhead volume variances, which are not explained until Chapter 20. If the period's overhead volume variance is closed to the income statements (as is common practice for *management* accounting monthly or quarterly income statements), the conclusions still hold. For the reader wanting to prove this after studying Chapter 20, let r = the predetermined *fixed* overhead rate. Then the overhead volume variance is $F - (P * r)$, and absorption costing charges the period's income with $(S * r) + F - (P * r)$ fixed overhead costs. Variable costing still charges F. The difference becomes $(S * r) + F - (P * r) - F = r * (S - P)$, and the arguments in cases 1, 2, and 3 above still hold.

Cases

CASE 19–1 Bennett Body Company*

Ralph Kern, controller of Bennett Body Company, received a memorandum from Paul Bennett, the company's president, suggesting that Kern review an attached magazine article and comment on it at the next executive committee meeting. The article described the Conley Corporation's cost accounting system. Bennett Body was a custom manufacturer of truck bodies. Occasionally, a customer would reorder an exact duplicate of an earlier body, but most of the time some modifications caused changes in design and hence in cost.

The Conley System. Kern learned from the article that Conley also manufactured truck bodies but that these were of standard design. Conley had 12 models that it produced in quantities based on management's estimates of demand. In December of each year, a plan, or budget, for the following year's operations was agreed on, which included estimates of costs and profits as well as of sales volume.

Included in this budget were department-by-department estimated costs for each of the 12 models of truck bodies. These costs were determined by totaling estimated labor at an expected wage rate, estimated materials at an expected cost per unit, and an allocation for overhead that was based on the proportion of

estimated total overhead costs to estimated total direct labor dollars. The sum of the labor, materials, and overhead estimates for each model became the standard cost of the model.

No attempt was made in Conley's accounts to record the actual costs of each model. Costs were accumulated for each of the four direct production departments and for several service departments. Labor costs were easily obtainable from payroll records, since all employees assigned to a production department were classified as direct labor for that department. Material sent to the department was charged to it on the basis of signed requisition slips. Overhead costs were charged to the department on the basis of the same percentage of direct labor as that used in determining the standard cost.

Since Conley's management also knew how many truck bodies of each model were worked on by each department monthly, the total standard costs for each department could easily be calculated by multiplying the quantity of that model produced by its standard cost. As the year progressed, management watched closely the difference between the departmental actual cost and standard cost.

As each truck body was completed, its cost was added to finished goods inventory at the standard cost figure. When the truck body was sold, the standard cost became the

*Copyright © by the President and Fellows of Harvard College. Harvard Business School case 161-001.

EXHIBIT 1
SUMMARY OF COSTS, DEPARTMENT 4, NOVEMBER

	Number of Bodies	Material		Labor		Overhead	
		Per Unit	Total	Per Unit	Total	Per Unit	Total
Model 101	10	$1,415	$14,150	$2,079	$20,790	$2,079	$20,790
109	8	1,890	15,120	1,656	13,248	1,656	13,248
113	11	2,885	31,735	1,984	21,824	1,984	21,824
154	20	895	17,900	1,832	36,640	1,832	36,640
Total standard	49		$78,905		$92,502		$92,502
Actual costs			83,738		94,026		94,026
Variances			$–4,833		$–1,524		$–1,524

cost of sales figure. This system of cost recording avoided the necessity of accumulating detailed actual costs on each specific body that was built; yet the company could estimate, reasonably well, the costs of its products. Moreover, management believed that the differences between actual and standard cost provided a revealing insight into cost fluctuations that eventually should lead to better cost control. An illustrative tabulation of the costs for Department 4 is shown in Exhibit 1. No incomplete work remained in this department either at the beginning or at the end of the month.

The Bennett System. Because almost every truck body that Bennett built was in some respect unique, costs were accumulated by individual jobs. When a job was started, it received a code number, and costs for the job were collected weekly under that code number. When materials used for a particular job were issued to the workers, a record of the quantities issued was obtained on a requisition form. The quantity of a given material—so many units, board feet, linear feet, pounds, and so on—was multiplied by its purchase cost per unit to arrive at the actual cost of material used. Maintenance of cumulative records of these withdrawals by code number made the total material cost of each job easy to determine.

Likewise, all labor costs of making a particular truck body were recorded. If a worker moved from job to job, a record was made of the worker's time spent on each job, and the worker's weekly wages were divided among these jobs in proportion to the amount of time spent on each. Throughout the shop, the time of any person working on anything directly related to an order—Job No. 437, for example—was ultimately converted to a dollar cost and charged to that job.

Finally, Bennett's overhead costs that could not be directly associated with a particular job were allocated among all jobs on the proportional basis of direct labor-hours involved. Thus, if in some month 135 direct labor-hours were spent on Job No. 437, and this was 5 percent of the 2,700 direct labor-hours spent on all jobs at Bennett that month, then Job No. 437 received 5 percent of all the overhead cost—supplies, salaries, depreciation, and so forth—for that month.

Under this system, Bennett's management knew at the end of each month what each body job in process cost to date. They could also determine total factory cost and therefore gross profit at the completion of each job.

The note that Mr. Bennett attached to the magazine article read:

Ralph:

Please review the system of cost accounting described in this article with the view of possible applications to our company. Aside from the overall comparison, I am interested particularly in your opinion on:
1. Costs of paperwork and recordkeeping, as compared with our system.
2. Possible reasons for cost differences between the actual and standard costs under Conley's system.
3. How you think Conley develops the standard cost of factory overhead for a particular model for the purpose of preparing the budget.
4. Whether you think that we should change our period for determining the overhead allocation rate from monthly to annually. If so, why?
5. Which system is better from the standpoint of controlling costs?

These are just a few questions which might be helpful in your overall analysis. I would like to discuss this question at the next executive committee meeting.
Thank you.

Paul Bennett

Questions

1. As Mr. Kern, what would you be prepared to say in response to Mr. Bennett's memorandum?

2. How, if at all, should Bennett modify its present system?

CASE 19–2   Black Meter Company

Refer to the description of Black Meter's cost accounting system in Appendix A and consider the following:

1. Trace through the cost accounting procedures described so that you are able to show how the numbers in each illustration are derived from, and/or help derive, the other illustrations.

2. Try to imagine what an actual cost system for Black Meter would look like. How would it compare with the standard cost system in terms of:

   a. Recordkeeping effort required?
   b. Usefulness of cost information to Black Meter's management?

3. Develop a flowchart for Black Meter's system similar to the one in Illustration 19–2. Do not use dollar amounts, but indicate flows between accounts and show whether entries are at standard or actual costs. In what respects, if any, do these two flowcharts differ?

4. Suppose that the direct labor rates for Departments 120A and 131 were each

increased by $1.00 per hour. What effect would these changes have on the succeeding illustrations and on the total standard cost of 100 ⅝-inch HF meters?

5. As a consultant to Black Meter Company's controller, what would be your evaluation of the present system?

CASE 19–3　Amurath Company

Amurath Company produced one item, product X, which was produced from raw materials A and B. Amurath used a standard cost system. In Amurath's system all debits to Work in Process were made at standard amounts, i.e., standard quantities at standard prices. As of November 1 all inventory accounts had zero balances. The following transactions occurred in November:

1. 1,000 pounds of raw material A were purchased for $14 per pound and put into inventory at the standard price of $13.53 per pound.

2. 600 pounds of raw material B were purchased for $25.51 per pound and put into inventory at the standard price of $25.90 per pound.

3. 700 pounds of raw material A were issued to production. The standard quantity of material for the units begun was 670 pounds.

4. 285 pounds of raw material B were issued to production. The standard quantity for the units begun was 300 pounds.

5. 500 pounds of raw material A were purchased for $13.30 per pound.

6. 615 pounds of raw material A were issued to production to begin units that at standard required 600 pounds.

7. 250 pounds of raw material B were issued to production to begin units for which the standard amount was 240 pounds.

8. 1,175 hours of direct labor at $14.66 were used in the manufacture of product X. The work that was accomplished called for a standard 1,100 hours at $14.86.

9. Overhead costs of $11,520 were incurred. Overhead was charged to Work in Process at a rate of $10.92 per standard direct labor-hour.

10. 900 units of product X at a standard full cost of $51.56 each were completed in November.

11. 800 units of product X were sold for $57,280.

Questions

1. Set up T accounts and post all of the above transactions.

2. What was Amurath Company's gross margin for November? In answering this question, please state and defend your treatment of the variances that were generated by November production operations.

CASE 19–4　Nemad Company

Nemad Company decided to adopt a standard cost system. The production manager wanted to set standards to use during the next year for the production of selector lever assemblies. Each assembly contained eight slotted levers made of steel. Due to the high tolerances required, an average of 10 percent of the levers cut do not meet specifications and must be discarded. The steel lever stock cost was $0.45 per piece at the end of this year; each lever required one piece of stock.

The workweek for production workers at the Nemad Company was 40 hours. Included in this time were two daily 15-minute breaks. Management estimated that over the course of a year, an average worker would spend 15 percent of his or her nominal working time waiting for tools, for machine set-ups, and for necessary interruptions of work. Time-study observations indicated that a worker could make a selector lever assembly in 12 minutes. Management estimated that workers under observation for time-study produce at about 90 percent of their normal rate. The average pay for production workers was $18 per hour.

Inflation was expected to increase production costs at a rate of about 4 percent for the next year. Production volume was level throughout the year.

Question

What should be the direct material and direct labor standards for the manufacture of one selector lever assembly for next year?

CASE 19-5 Brisson Company

Brisson Company made radio antennas, which were sold through auto supply stores and mail-order catalogs. These antennas were used by vehicle owners to replace antennas that had been vandalized or had otherwise become ineffective. Brisson made two models: the F-100 was used for fender mounting, and the S-100 was used for side mounting (e.g., on truck cabs).

Brisson used a standard cost system, which included these standards per dozen antennas:

	F-100	S-100
Materials:		
Chrome-plated tubing	$12.37	$11.25
Cable and plug	10.80	10.80
Mounting device	6.63	8.43
	29.80	30.48
Direct labor (@ $12 per hour)	18.00	18.00
Overhead (@ 125% of direct labor)	22.50	22.50
Total cost per dozen	$70.30	$70.98

Materials were debited to Materials Inventory at standard cost upon receipt, any difference between the standard amount and actual invoice price being entered in the Material Price Variance account. Credits to Materials Inventory reflected the actual quantities issued, costed at standard price per unit. All debits to Work in Process Inventory were based on standard quantities and standard prices or rates. Credits to Work in Process Inventory, debits to Finished Goods Inventory, and credits to Cost of Sales were all based on the $70.30 and $70.98 full standard production costs shown above. Variance accounts were closed to the Income Summary account at the end of the month.

The following descriptions relate to April operations:

1. On April 1 balance sheet account balances were as follows:

	Dr.	Cr.
Materials Inventory	$ 50,250	
Work in Process Inventory	75,600	
Finished Goods Inventory	155,400	
All other assets	325,500	
Accounts Payable		$104,700
Wages Payable		6,150
All other liabilities		47,250
Shareholders' Equity		448,650
Total	$606,750	$606,750

2. During April Brisson received materials for 2,500 dozen F-100 antennas and 1,000 dozen S-100 antennas. The invoice amounts totaled $103,535.

3. During April Brisson paid $102,300 worth of accounts payable. It collected $192,000 due from its customers. (Both Cash and Accounts Receivables are included in "All other assets" in the above account list.)

4. The stockroom issued materials during April for 3,200 dozen F-100 antennas and 700 dozen S-100 antennas, consistent with the planned production for the month. Stockroom requisitions also included issues of materials in excess of quantities needed to produce these 3,900 dozen antennas. These issues were to replace parts that had been bent or broken during the production process and were as follows: 100 dozen F-100 tubes, 20 dozen S-100 tubes, 45 dozen cables and plugs, 20 dozen F-100 mounting devices, and 4 dozen S-100 mounting devices. The original parts issued that these extra issues replaced were all thrown into the trash bin because they had no significant scrap value.

5. Direct labor cost incurred in April was $72,300. Indirect labor cost was $40,500. Wages paid were $116,700. (Ignore social security taxes and fringe benefits.)

6. Actual production overhead costs (excluding indirect labor) in April totaled $55,800. Of this amount, $37,500 was credited to Accounts Payable and the rest to various asset accounts (included above in "All other assets").

7. Selling and administrative expenses in April were $78,750; this same amount was credited to various asset accounts.

8. April's standard cost sheets showed the following standard costs for antennas worked on during the month: direct labor, $79,200, and overhead, $99,000.

9. During April 3,000 dozen F-100 antennas and 800 dozen S-100 antennas were delivered to the finished goods storage area; work on some of these goods had been started during March.

10. April sales were $271,250 for 2,400 dozen F-100 antennas and $103,900 for 900 dozen S-100 antennas. The offsetting entries were to accounts receivable (included in "All other assets").

Questions

1. Set up T accounts, post beginning balances, and then record the above transactions. Adjust and close the accounts, determine April's income (ignore income taxes), and close this income to Shareholders' Equity. Do not create any balance sheet T accounts not listed above.

2. Prepare the April income statement (again, disregarding income taxes). Why is your number for April income only an approximation?

3. Prepare a balance sheet as of April 30.

CASE 19–6 Landau Company

In early August, Terry Silver, the new marketing vice president of Landau Company, was studying the July income statement. Silver found the statement puzzling: July's sales had increased significantly over June's, yet income was lower in July than in June. Silver was certain that margins on Landau's products had not narrowed in July and therefore felt that there must be some mistake in the July statement.

When Silver asked the company's chief accountant, Meredith Wilcox, for an explanation, Wilcox stated that production in July was well below standard volume because of employee vacations. This had caused overhead to be underabsorbed, and a large unfavorable volume variance had been generated, which more than offset the added gross margin from the sales increase. It was company policy to charge all variances to the monthly income statement, and these production volume variances would all wash out by year's end, Wilcox had said.

Silver, who knew little about accounting, found this explanation to be "incomprehensible. With all the people in your department, I don't understand why you can't produce an income statement that reflects the economics of our business. In the company that I left to come here, if sales went up, profits went up. I don't see why that shouldn't be the case here, too."

As Wilcox left Silver's office, a presentation at a recent Institute of Management Accountants meeting came to Wilcox's mind. At that meeting the controller of Winjum Company had described that firm's variable costing system, which charged fixed overhead to income as a period expense and treated only variable production costs as inventoriable

product costs. Winjum's controller had stressed that, other things being equal, variable costing caused income to move with sales only, rather than being affected by both sales and production volume as was the case with full absorption costing systems.

Wilcox decided to recast the June and July income statements and balance sheets using variable costing. (The income statements as recast and as originally prepared, and the related inventory and retained earnings impacts, are shown in Exhibit 1.) Wilcox then showed these statements to Terry Silver, who responded, "Now that's more like it! I *knew* July was a better month for us than June, and your new 'variable costing' statements reflect that. Tell your boss [Landau's controller] that at the next meeting of the executive committee I'm going to suggest we change to this new method."

At the next executive committee meeting, Silver proposed adoption of variable costing for Landau's monthly internal income statements. The controller also supported this change, saying that it would eliminate the time-consuming efforts of allocating fixed overhead to individual products. These allocations had only led to arguments between product managers and the accounting staff. The controller added that since variable costing segregated the costs of materials, direct labor, and variable overhead from fixed overhead costs, management's cost control efforts would be enhanced.

Silver also felt that the margin figures provided by the new approach would be more useful than the present ones for comparing the profitability of individual products. To illustrate the point, Silver had worked out an example. With full costing, two products in Landau's line, numbers 129 and 243, would appear as follows:

Product	Standard Production Cost	Selling Price	Unit Margin	Margin Percent
129	$2.54	$4.34	$1.80	41.5
243	3.05	5.89	2.84	48.2

Thus, product 243 would appear to be the more desirable one to sell. But on the proposed basis, the numbers were as follows:

Product	Standard Production Cost	Selling Price	Unit Margin	Margin Percent
129	$1.38	$4.34	$2.96	68.2
243	2.37	5.89	3.52	59.8

EXHIBIT 1
EFFECTS OF VARIABLE COSTING

Income Statements
June and July

	June		July	
	Full Costing	Variable Costing	Full Costing	Variable Costing
Sales revenues	$865,428	$865,428	$931,710	$931,710
Cost of sales at standard	484,640	337,517	521,758	363,367
Standard gross margin	380,788	527,911	409,952	568,343
Production cost variances:*				
Labor	(16,259)	(16,259)	(11,814)	(11,814)
Material	12,416	12,416	8,972	8,972
Overhead volume	1,730	—	(63,779)	—
Overhead spending	3,604	3,604	2,832	2,832
Actual gross margin	382,279	527,672	346,163	568,333
Fixed production overhead	—	192,883	—	192,883
Selling and administrative	301,250	301,250	310,351	310,351
Income before taxes	$ 81,029	$ 33,539	$ 35,812	$ 65,099

*Parentheses denote unfavorable (debit) variances.

Impact on Inventories and Retained Earnings

The only asset account affected by the difference in accounting method was Inventories; on the liabilities and owners' equity side, only Retained Earnings was affected. (There was no tax liability impact since variable costing was not permitted for income tax reporting purposes.)

	As of June 30		As of July 31	
	Full Costing	Variable Costing	Full Costing	Variable Costing
Inventories	$1,680,291	$1,170,203	$1,583,817	$1,103,016
Retained earnings	3,112,980	2,602,892	3,131,602	2,650,801

According to Silver, these numbers made it clear that product 129 was the more profitable of the two.

At this point, the treasurer spoke up. "If we use this new approach, the next thing we know you marketing types will be selling at your usual markup over *variable* costs. How are we going to pay the fixed costs *then*? Besides, in my 38 years of experience, it's the lack of control over long-run costs that can bankrupt a company. I'm opposed to any proposal that causes us to take a myopic view of costs."

The president also had some concerns, having further considered the proposal. "In the first place, if I add together the June and July pretax profit under each of these methods, I get almost $117,000 with the present method, but only $99,000 under the proposed method. While I'd be happy to lower our reported profits from the standpoints of relations with our employee union and income taxes, I don't think it's a good idea as far as our owners and bankers are concerned. And I share Jamie's [the treasurer's] concern about controlling long-run costs. I think we should defer a decision on this matter until we fully understand all of the implications."

Questions

1. Critique the various pros and cons of the variable costing proposal that were presented in the meeting. What arguments would you add?

2. Should Landau adopt variable costing for its monthly income statements?

CASE 19–7 Craik Veneer Company*

The sales manager of Craik Veneer Company received an offer from Groton Company to buy one million feet per month of sound "backs" of 1/24-inch birch veneer[1] at $20 per thousand surface feet. The sales manager wanted to accept the offer, but the production manager argued that it should not be accepted because the cost of production was at least $24 per thousand feet and probably more.

Craik manufactured rotary-cut birch veneer from high-grade logs bought in Vermont. Selected sections called *blocks* were cut out of those logs, the length of the block varying from 84 inches to 98 inches. These blocks, as cut for the lathe, cost an average of $440 per thousand board feet. A thousand board feet, log measure, was an amount of logs which, being sawed, would produce a thousand board feet of lumber. (A board foot is 1 square foot 1 inch thick.) After being cut, the blocks were put in vats filled with hot water and left there for 24 to 48 hours until the entire log was heated through.

Manufacturing Process. In the rotary veneer process a block was put in a lathe that had a heavy frame, guide bars, and pressure bars where a knife longer than the block was brought against its side so that it cut off a thin slice of wood the entire length of the block. The process was similar to unrolling a large roll of paper held on a horizontal shaft. The process could be controlled with skillful operation, so it would produce veneer of uniform thickness. Craik produced principally 1/24-inch veneer, and for the purposes of this case it may be assumed that all of its product was 1/24-inch.

*Copyright © by the President and Fellows of Harvard College. Harvard Business School case 154-002.

[1] *Veneer* is a term applied to thin leaves or layers of wood. Generally, veneer is made of valuable wood and is laid over a core of inferior wood.

The sheet of veneer from the lathe, for instance from a 98-inch block, was brought onto a clipping table approximately 60 feet long. This table had rubber belts on its upper surface that moved the veneer along to the clipper. At this point the veneer was like a long sheet of paper moving along the table, the veneer being 98 inches along the grain. The clipper was a long knife extending entirely across the table. The clipper operator was one of the most highly skilled workers in the plant.

Constantly inspecting the sheet of veneer, the operator first took one cut to get a straight edge. If the next section of the sheet was of high quality, the operator advanced the sheet not over 3 feet 8 inches, depending on customers' requirements. If the sheet showed a defect within 3 feet 8 inches, the operator made the cut just short of the defect. A worker called the "off bearer" piled these sheets on a hand truck reserved for high-grade or "face" veneer. If the defect was a knot, the clipper operator then advanced the sheet enough to clear the knot and took another cut, making a piece of waste possibly 3 inches wide. If the operator decided that a section of the sheet was not of face quality, it was cut off for "backs," either 3 feet 8 inches or in lesser widths. Backs were put on another hand truck.

The clipper operator thus separated the whole sheet of veneer into faces, backs, and waste. The faces consisted of pieces of veneer 98 inches long along the grain and anywhere from 6 inches to 3 feet 8 inches wide. The sound backs were of the same size. The waste went to a chipper and was then burned. The term *faces* came from the fact that these veneer sheets were substantially perfect and could be used on the exposed parts of furniture or on the best face of plywood.[2] The backs had minor defects and

were so called because they were used on the back of plywood panels. The quality required for faces was established by specifications of the industry. The dividing line between sound backs and waste was similarly established. Craik had a reputation for using high-grade logs and for producing a high grade of veneer both on faces and backs.

Groton Company's Offer.   Groton Company's product design department had developed two new lines of furniture, one in blond modern and one in colonial, in which the table tops, dresser tops and panels, drawer fronts, and other exposed parts were of birch veneer over lower-grade birch or poplar cores, with table legs, dresser frames, and so on, of solid birch. Groton's people knew that while all sheets of backs contained defects, 50 to 60 percent of the area of backs as produced by Craik were of face quality. They had discovered that by buying backs 84 inches to 98 inches long, they could cut clear face-quality veneer into lengths that would match their use requirements: enough 54-inch lengths for their longest dresser tops and enough of other lengths down to 14-inch drawer fronts. The remainder of the veneer that was not of face quality could be used for such purposes as making plywood for drawer bottoms. The methods developed in the product design department had been tested by cutting up several carloads of backs bought from Craik and by the manufacture and sale of the furniture.

On the basis of this experience, Groton Company offered Craik $20 per thousand feet for 1 million feet per month of sound backs in $1/24$-inch birch veneer for the next 12 months.

Cost Information.   Craik cut an average of 12,000 board feet of logs a day in one eight-hour shift. With the high quality of logs it bought, it got a yield of 18,000 surface feet of $1/24$-inch veneer per 1,000 board feet cut; this graded on the average 50 percent faces and 50 percent backs.

Labor and factory overhead costs together averaged $24 per thousand surface feet of

---

[2]Veneer is a single thin sheet of wood. Plywood consists of several sheets (three, five, or nine) glued together with the grain of alternate courses at right angles to add to the strength.

veneer; selling costs averaged $4. Both the cost of the blocks and operating costs for the heating, lathe turning, and clipping operations were joint costs; backs had to be produced in order to get the faces. The remaining operations in drying, a slight amount of reclipping, storing, and shipping were in a sense separate costs as the operations were done on backs separately, although with the same equipment. The labor and factory overhead costs through clipping averaged $20.25 per 1,000 surface feet of veneer; those for drying and later operations, $3.75.

The selling price for ¹⁄₂₄-inch birch faces 84 inches to 98 inches long was $88 per thousand surface feet. Face veneer 84 inches to 98 inches had a high price because it could be used on large surfaces, such as flush birch doors that require lengths up to 8 feet. The veneer shorter in length along the grain, made from recutting backs, had a somewhat lower price because it could not be used for these purposes. Unlike faces, the price of backs fluctuated widely. Sometimes Craik could get $25 per thousand feet, but the insistence of the production manager on $25 had led to the accumulation of a heavy inventory of backs. Faces were easy to sell and were shipped as fast as they were produced.

More effort was required to sell backs than to sell faces, although both were sold to the same customers by the same sales force. Sometimes buyers of faces were required to take a percentage of backs in order to get a carload of faces. For these reasons Groton's offer was attractive to the sales manager.

Discussion of Offer. When the production manager was first informed by the sales manager of the offer of $20 per thousand surface feet, the production manager contended that "Your salespersons are so lazy, they would give veneer away if nobody watched them." The production manager went on to say:

> If a birch block cost $440 per thousand and we get 18,000 feet of ¹⁄₂₄-inch-thick veneer from every thousand board feet of the block, the cost of the block to be allocated to a thousand feet of veneer, whether backs or faces, is $440 divided by 18,000 feet, or about $24.44 per thousand feet. Simple arithmetic proves that selling backs at $20 per thousand doesn't even pay for the material, let alone labor and overhead.

The sales manager countered that this argument was fallacious:

> Allocating the cost of the block to the veneer in this manner implies that backs are as valuable as faces, which is not the case. The $24.44 material figure for a thousand feet of veneer that you get is merely an average of the value of faces and backs. The material for faces is worth considerably more per thousand feet than this figure; the material for backs is worth considerably less.

The sales manager suggested that the proper procedure was to allocate the cost of the block to faces and backs in proportion to the amounts for which the products were sold. Using this method, the ratio that the revenue of one of the two grades of veneer bore to the revenue received from both grades of veneer would be applied to the total cost of the block, the result representing the cost to be allocated to that particular grade. To illustrate this method, assume a block of a thousand board feet cost $440, and the selling prices and quantities of faces and backs are as shown in the following table:

Grade	¹⁄₂₄-Inch Veneer in Feet	Sales Revenue per 1,000 Feet	Net Value	Percent of Total	Cost Applicable to Each
Faces	9,000	$88	$792	81.5	$358.52
Backs	9,000	20	180	18.5	81.48
	18,000		$972	100.0	$440.00

The material cost applicable to each product, then, per thousand feet of ¼-inch veneer would be $358.52/9,000 feet * 1,000 feet, or $39.84 for faces; and $81.48/9,000 feet * 1,000 feet, or $9.05 for backs.

The production manager again argued that this did not represent the true material cost, which was the same for both products, and added:

> Under your method the material cost allocated to either faces or backs would be a function of their relative selling prices. If the selling price of faces fell from $88 per thousand to $44 per thousand and the price of backs remained the same, you would then charge much more material cost to backs, and much less to faces. Your method of allocating cost doesn't make sense.

The sales manager at this point said:

> OK, if you don't think that method is justified, then let's treat backs as a by-product. I think you'll agree that we would prefer to be making faces all the time, yet we can't. As long as we manufacture faces, we're going to produce backs as an undesirable consequence. Now if we consider backs as a by-product, we can charge all block costs to faces. The net proceeds from the sale of backs, after allowing for all conversion, selling, and administrative expenses, can be credited to the raw material cost of faces. All profits and losses of the business would be borne by the main·product.

The production manager, however, pointed out again that the cost of material allocated to faces would still be a function of the selling price of backs and, furthermore, there would be some difficulty in trying to value inventories at the end of an accounting period. Any profits arising from the sale of backs would be hidden, since they would be included in the credit to faces. "It is impor-

tant to determine the profit or loss being realized on the sale of backs so we can establish a firm sales policy," the production manager asserted.

Because of their inability to resolve this question, the production manager and the sales manager consulted Craik's president, who in turn asked the controller to examine the cost situation to determine whether the $20 per thousand surface feet of ¼-inch backs would result in a profit or not.

Questions

1. As controller, what method of allocating raw material costs would you recommend? What similarities and differences would be encountered in allocating labor and overhead costs as compared to material costs?

2. Should the sales manager accept Groton's $20 per thousand feet offer for the ¼-inch backs?

3. If a group of blocks containing 1,000 board feet costs $450, what would be the cost applicable to faces and backs under each of the methods of allocating costs described in the case, and other methods that you may devise, if the following conditions existed:

    a. The current market price of ¼-inch faces is $88 per thousand feet; ¼-inch backs are currently selling at $22 per thousand.

    b. 10,000 feet of ¼-inch faces and 8,000 feet of ¼-inch backs were produced from a group of blocks.

    c. Factory labor and overhead cost averaged $24 per thousand feet of veneer ($20.25 for operations through clipping and $3.75 for drying and later operations). Selling costs averaged $4 per thousand feet of veneer. If backs were not manufactured (i.e., if they were treated the same as waste), labor, overhead, and selling costs amounting to roughly $5 per thousand feet of backs might be saved.

20

Production Cost Variances

The preceding three chapters focused on the nature, collection, and measurement of management accounting information. This is the first of five chapters that deal with the use of that information by management in controlling the organization. This chapter and Chapter 21 describe the calculation and use of variances. Chapters 22–25 deal with the use of responsibility accounting information in the management control process.

As was seen in the preceding chapter, a standard cost system generates variances—differences between actual costs and standard costs. These variances provide important information for management. This chapter describes techniques for analyzing production cost variances in a way that provides managers with useful insights in controlling the performance of the production function.

DIRECT MATERIAL AND LABOR VARIANCES

Direct Material Variances

A standard cost represents what the cost should be. The standard direct material cost of *one unit* of product (i.e., one unit of output) is found by multiplying the quantity of material (input) that should be needed for producing one unit of output times the price that should be paid per unit of material input (e.g., 9 pounds per unit of output at $4 per pound = $36 per unit of output). The *total* standard direct material cost for an *accounting period* is the standard material cost per unit of output multiplied by the number of units produced in that period (e.g., if 100 units are produced, the total standard material cost is $3,600). This total standard material cost ($3,600) can also be calculated by multiplying the total standard quantity of material (900 pounds) by the standard cost per unit of material ($4 per pound). The total standard quantity of 900 pounds is 100 units produced times 9 pounds per unit.

Similarly, the *actual* direct material cost of one unit of output is the actual quantity of material input used in producing that unit times the actual price paid per unit of material. The total actual direct material cost for a period is the sum of these actual costs for all the units produced in the period.

The difference between the total standard material cost and the total actual material cost of the goods *actually produced* is the **direct material cost variance.** That means direct material variances are based on the actual output quantity of a period; planned or budgeted output levels play no part in the analysis. Because both the standard and actual material cost totals were computed by multiplying a physical input quantity (e.g., 900 pounds) by a price per unit of input (e.g., $4 per pound), it is possible to decompose the total material cost variance into a quantity component and a price component. Specifically, these components are as follows:

1. The fact that the actual quantity of material used for the output produced differed from the standard quantity causes the **material usage variance** (also the **yield variance** or simply the **quantity variance**).

2. The fact that the actual price of each unit of material input differed from the standard price causes the **material price variance.**

The algebraic sum of these two variances is the total material variance—that is, the difference between total actual direct material costs for the period and total standard direct material costs. If the company's standard cost system includes only one account for material variance, this sum is the amount that would appear in that account.[1]

Favorable and Unfavorable Variances. If actual cost is lower than standard cost, the variance is said to be *favorable;* if the reverse, the variance is said to be *unfavorable.* As explained in Chapter 19, favorable variances appear as credits in variance accounts whereas unfavorable variances are debits in variance accounts. We shall use these adjectives in the description that follows. However, it should be recognized that "favorable" in this sense does not necessarily mean that performance was good; it means only that actual costs were lower than standard costs. The interpretation of these variances, once they have been identified, is discussed later.

---

[1]As pointed out in Chapter 19, some companies' standard cost systems have two material variance accounts. Such systems identify the material price variance when the material is received into materials inventory. When this is done, the material price variance is based on the quantity of materials *received* during the period rather than the quantity that was *used* during the period. In these systems the material usage variance is developed when materials are issued to production, as shown in Illustration 19–2.

Formulas. The commonly used rules for finding the two direct material variances are as follows:

1. The material *usage* variance is the difference between total standard quantity and total actual quantity of material input, with each total quantity priced at the *standard* price per unit of material. Both total quantities are based on the number of units of output actually produced.

2. The material *price* variance is the difference between the standard price and the actual price per unit of material input, multiplied by the *actual* quantity of material used.

Using the symbol Δ (delta) to stand for the difference between an actual amount and a standard amount, these rules can be stated as:

$$\text{Usage variance} = \Delta\text{Quantity} * \text{Standard price}$$
$$\text{Price variance} = \Delta\text{Price} * \text{Actual quantity}$$

Example. Each unit of product X is supposed to require 9 pounds of direct material costing $4 per pound. In March 100 units of X were made, and their production consumed 825 pounds of material costing $5 per pound. The total amounts for materials are calculated as follows:

	Unit Price		Physical Quantity		Total Cost
Standard.....................	$ 4	*	900*	=	$3,600
Actual	5	*	825	=	4,125
Difference (Δ)	$(1)		75		$ 525 U†

* 100 units produced ∧ 9 pounds per unit.
† U = Unfavorable; F = Favorable.

Applying the above rules, the $525 U total material variance can be decomposed as follows:

ΔQuantity	*	Standard price	=	Usage variance
75	*	$4	=	300 F
ΔPrice	*	Actual quantity	=	Price variance
$(1)	*	825	=	$825 U

Note that the algebraic sum of the price and usage variances is the net, or total, variance ($300 F + $825 U = $525 U).

Graphic Aids. Many people find their first exposure to variance formulas to be somewhat perplexing. We therefore present two graphic aids that should help in understanding the formulas.

The three columns in Illustration 20–1 reflect (1) how much cost should have been incurred for materials, based on a *standard* physical amount of material per unit of product output, a standard price for each unit of material input, and the actual quantity of output produced (the column labeled *SQSP*); (2) how much cost should have been incurred for the quantity of material that was *actually* used (*AQSP*); and (3) how much cost was actually incurred for the material actually used (*AQAP*).

ILLUSTRATION 20–1
DIAGRAM OF DIRECT MATERIAL VARIANCES

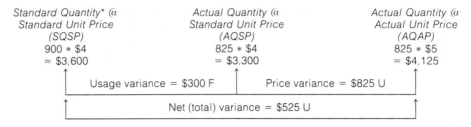

Standard Quantity* @	*Actual Quantity @*	*Actual Quantity @*
Standard Unit Price	*Standard Unit Price*	*Actual Unit Price*
(SQSP)	*(AQSP)*	*(AQAP)*
900 * $4	825 * $4	825 * $5
= $3,600	= $3,300	= $4,125

Usage variance = $300 F   Price variance = $825 U

Net (total) variance = $525 U

* Standard quantity for the *actual* volume; that is, the quantity that should have been used to produce the *actual* output.

ILLUSTRATION 20–2
GEOMETRIC DEPICTION OF DIRECT MATERIAL VARIANCE

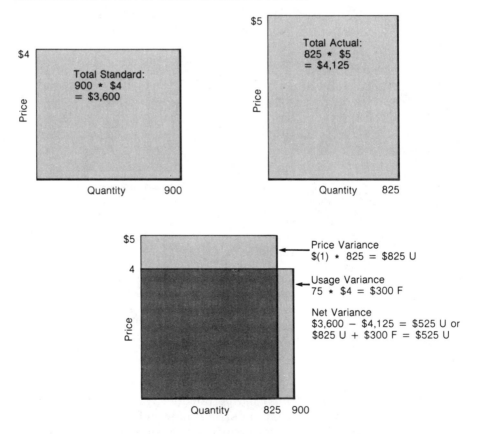

Illustration 20–2 depicts the material variance components geometrically. The variance components are the areas where the total standard cost rectangle and total actual cost rectangle do *not* coincide.

ILLUSTRATION 20–3
DIAGRAM OF A JOINT VARIANCE

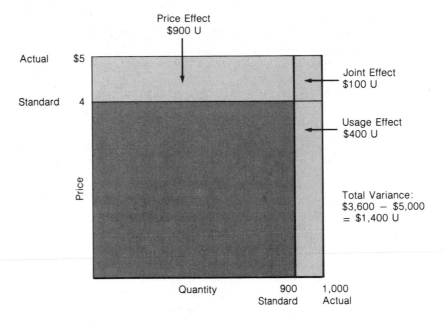

In both illustrations the usage variance is favorable because a lesser quantity of material was used than was allowed by the standard. The price variance is unfavorable because the actual price per unit of material was higher than was allowed by the standard.

Uses of the Variances. The separation of the direct material net variance into its price and usage components facilitates management's analysis and control of material costs. The price variance often is the responsibility of the purchasing department whereas the usage variance is the responsibility of the department that uses the material. But the fact that these two material variances can be separated does not mean they are necessarily independent. For example, investigation of a favorable price variance may reveal that substandard quality material bought at a discount price caused abnormal spoilage in production operations, as reflected in an unfavorable usage variance. In this case the price variance is not favorable in any literal sense, and the purchasing department, not a production department, has caused the usage variance.

Joint Variance. Illustration 20–2 clearly shows the nature of the two direct material variances when one of them is favorable and the other unfavorable. The situation is less clear, however, when *both* variances are favorable or when *both* are unfavorable. Illustration 20–3 shows the nature of the difficulty. It is based on the same assumptions as the earlier example, except that now we assume that 1,000 pounds of material were actually consumed (instead of 825 pounds).

In this situation the $1,400 U variance arose partly because the actual price per unit of material input exceeded standard by $1 and partly because the input quantity actually used exceeded standard by 100 pounds. *At least* $900 U is a price variance because $1 per pound over the standard price was paid for the 900 pounds that should have been used. Similarly, *at least* $400 U is a usage variance because the 100 extra pounds at the standard $4 price would have cost $400. There remains a $100 U (= $1,400 U – $900 U – $400 U) variance to be explained, however. As shown in the upper-right corner of Illustration 20–3, this $100 results from the *combination* of off-standard per unit price and off-standard usage.

This **joint variance** is not usually reported separately. The rules stated above assign this $100 as part of the price variance. The rationale is that it is the purchasing agent's job to buy materials at the standard price, even though the quantity required may exceed standard.

Direct Labor Variances

Direct labor variances are analyzed the same as direct material variances. The standard direct labor cost of one unit of output is the standard labor input time (usually expressed in hours) that should be spent producing that unit of output multiplied by a standard rate per unit of time (e.g., standard earnings per hour). If workers are paid on a piece-rate basis, the standard labor cost per unit of product is simply the piece rate or rates for producing that unit. Total standard direct labor cost of an accounting period is the standard labor cost per unit of output multiplied by the number of units of output produced in that period. Actual labor costs per unit of output or per accounting period are calculated similarly.

The variance between total actual and total standard direct labor costs can be decomposed into two components: (1) a **labor efficiency variance** (also called the **quantity variance** or the **usage variance**), caused by the fact that the actual input time differed from the standard time, and (2) a **labor rate variance** (or **labor price variance**), caused by the fact that actual hourly rates or actual piece rates differed from standard rates.

The formulas for decomposing the net labor variance into these two components are parallel to the formulas for direct material variances:

$$\text{Efficiency variance} = \Delta\text{Time} * \text{Standard rate}$$
$$\text{Rate variance} = \Delta\text{Rate} * \text{Actual time}$$

Example.   Product Y has a standard time of 9 hours per unit at a standard rate of $4 per hour. In April 100 units of Y were produced, with an expenditure of 825 labor-hours costing $5 per hour. Thus, total actual direct labor cost was $4,125 (= 825 hours * $5), whereas the total standard cost was $3,600 (= 100 units * 9 hours per unit * $4 per hour). The net variance is $525 U, which is decomposed as follows:

$$\Delta\text{Time} * \text{Standard rate} = \text{Efficiency variance}$$
$$75 \quad * \quad \$4 \quad = \quad \$300\ F$$
$$\Delta\text{Rate} * \text{Actual time} = \text{Rate variance}$$
$$\$(1) \quad * \quad 825 \quad = \quad \$825\ U$$

Illustrations 20–1 and 20–2 also apply to this example: just change the word *material* to *labor, quantity* to *time, price* to *rate,* and *usage* to *efficiency.*

Interpretation of the Direct Labor Variances.   The reason for decomposing the total direct labor variance is that the labor rate variance is evaluated differently from the labor efficiency variance. The rate variance may arise because of a change in wage rates for which the supervisors in charge of the production responsibility centers cannot be held responsible. On the other hand, the supervisors may be held entirely responsible for the efficiency variance because they should control the number of hours that direct workers spent on the production for the period.

A valid distinction between the rate variance and the efficiency variance cannot be made in all cases; many situations occur in which the two factors are interdependent. For example, a supervisor may find it possible to complete the work in less than the standard time by using workers who earn a higher than standard rate, and be perfectly justified in doing so. Even so, the use of the technique described may lead to a better understanding of what actually happened.

OVERHEAD VARIANCES

Recall from Chapter 18 that in assigning overhead costs to products most cost systems use a predetermined overhead rate. This rate is calculated by dividing the estimated production activity level (normal or standard volume) into the total overhead costs estimated to be incurred at that volume. The estimated amount of cost at various volumes can be shown in a flexible overhead budget,[2] as was described in Chapter 18. Such a flexible budget usually can be adequately represented by a straight line, as in part A of Illustration 20–4. The equation for this line is $TC = TFC + (UVC * X)$. In the context of overhead budgeting, the symbols in this equation mean the following:

$$TC = \text{Total overhead cost}$$
$$TFC = \text{Total fixed overhead cost per period}$$
$$UVC = \text{Variable overhead cost per unit}$$
$$X = \text{Production volume, in units}[3]$$

The overhead rate, R, is the average overhead cost per unit at the *standard* volume. It therefore is found by dividing the total overhead costs at standard volume by the number of units (S) represented by that volume:

---

[2]The words *standard* and *budget* both connote estimates of what costs *should* be. In practice, standard is used with *per-unit* cost amounts whereas budget is used with *total* amounts; for example, "The standard labor cost of product Z is $10 per unit," or "The labor cost budget for 50 units of Z is $500."

[3]Production volume can also be measured in terms of such activity measures as direct labor-hours, direct labor dollars, or machine-hours. Measuring volume as units of output in these examples simply makes it easier to visualize the situation being illustrated.

$$R = \frac{TFC + (UVC * S)}{S}$$

Example. Assume that budgeted fixed overhead costs are $500, budgeted variable overhead costs are $1 per unit, and standard volume is 1,000 units. Then the overhead rate is $1.50 per unit, calculated as follows:

$$R = \frac{\$500 + (\$1 * 1,000)}{1,000} = \$1.50$$

Note that this rate is the sum of the variable overhead per unit, $1, and the *average fixed* overhead per unit at standard volume, $0.50 (= $500 ÷ 1,000). The overhead rate will always be the sum of these two components.

The **overhead variance** (or **net overhead variance**) is the difference between the overhead costs actually incurred and the overhead costs absorbed by (charged to) production in the WIP Inventory account. As was diagrammed in Illustration 19–2 and explained in the related text, actual overhead costs are debited to the Overhead clearing account, and absorbed overhead costs are credited to that account. The overhead variance is found by closing the balance in the Overhead clearing account to the Overhead Variance account (entry 6 in Illustration 19–2). The resulting amount that appears in the Overhead Variance account is the net overhead variance.

This net variance can be decomposed into two elements: (1) a **production volume variance** and (2) a **spending variance.** The production volume variance is caused by actual production volume being different from the standard volume used in calculating the predetermined overhead rate. The overhead spending variance is caused by actual overhead costs being different from the amount allowed by the flexible overhead budget. Each of these is further explained below.

ILLUSTRATION 20–4
BEHAVIOR AND ABSORPTION OF OVERHEAD COST

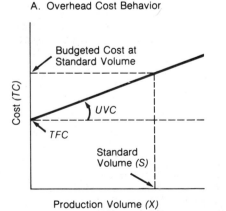

A. Overhead Cost Behavior

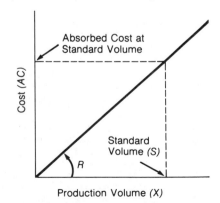

B. Overhead Cost Absorption

Production Volume Variance

Each unit of output produced will be charged with overhead costs at the predetermined rate. The amount of overhead *absorbed* by the units produced is therefore the overhead rate times the number of units actually produced. Algebraically, $AC = R * X$, in which the symbols have these meanings:

$$AC = \text{Total absorbed overhead cost}$$
$$R = \text{Overhead rate}$$
$$X = \text{Volume, in units}$$

Graphically, the total amount absorbed at any volume is a straight line, starting at zero and with the slope R, as shown in part B of Illustration 20−4. However, since the *budgeted* costs at any volume behave in the fashion indicated in part A of Illustration 20−4, *budgeted costs and absorbed costs will be equal only at the standard volume.*

Example. Using the relationships assumed above, the budgeted and absorbed costs at various volumes will be:

Actual Volume (X)	Budgeted $500 + ($1 * X)	Absorbed $1.50 * X	Difference
800	$1,300	$1,200	$−100
900	1,400	1,350	−50
1,000	1,500	1,500	0
1,100	1,600	1,650	+50
1,200	1,700	1,800	+100

Note from the example that at any volume below the standard volume, the amount of overhead costs absorbed is less than the budgeted cost at that volume. At these volumes budgeted costs are said to be **underabsorbed** (or **unabsorbed**). Conversely, at any volume higher than the standard volume, budgeted overhead costs will be **overabsorbed.** Underabsorption variance is unfavorable and overabsorption is favorable. This difference between budgeted and absorbed costs is caused solely by the fact that actual volume is different from the standard volume (the volume used in arriving at the predetermined overhead rate). That is why it is called a production *volume* variance. Note that the production volume variance is in no way related to the amount of *actual* costs incurred.

The standard volume used in calculating the predetermined overhead rate usually is the volume expected during the course of the year. Therefore, standard monthly volume is simply one-twelfth the standard annual volume. Thus, when results for a given month are being analyzed, one should expect to see a volume variance for that month unless the month's volume coincidentally was exactly the same as one-twelfth of the year's standard volume. Because of seasonal and other short-term influences, for a month's actual volume to be exactly equal to one-twelfth the annual standard volume is indeed a coincidence.

ILLUSTRATION 20–5
BUDGETED, ABSORBED, AND ACTUAL OVERHEAD COSTS

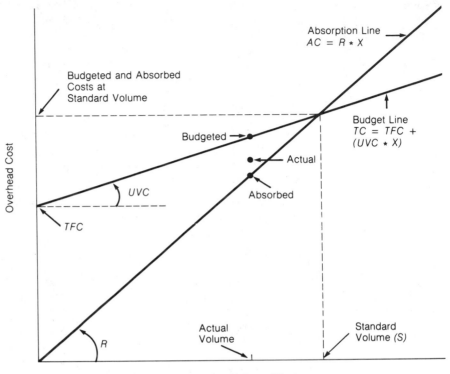

Illustration 20–5 shows graphically the relationship between budgeted and absorbed overhead costs at various volumes. It was constructed by merging the two diagrams in Illustration 20–4. The point labeled actual volume is to the left of the standard volume (*S*), indicating that volume in the month illustrated is lower than the standard volume. Consequently, there was an unfavorable production volume variance in that month. Its amount is the budgeted overhead for the *actual* volume minus the amount absorbed.

Spending Variance

The **spending variance** is equal to the budgeted overhead costs for the period's *actual* level of volume minus the period's actual overhead costs. In the diagram the spending variance is favorable because actual costs are below the budgeted amount. When actual costs are above budget, the variance is unfavorable.

The spending variance for overhead costs has the same significance as the *sum* of the usage and price variances (i.e., the *net variance*) for direct material cost and direct labor cost. Indeed, it is possible to decompose the spending variance for some overhead items, such as electricity and supplies, into usage and price components in the same manner as was described for direct cost variances. For example, because of the importance of energy costs, a variance in electricity spending may be decomposed into a variance caused by a difference between budgeted and actual prices per kilowatt-hour and a variance caused by the difference between actual and budgeted kilowatt-hour usage. The price component is noncontrollable, whereas the usage component is controllable. Ordinarily, however, the overhead spending variance is examined on an item-by-item basis without further decomposition of an item.

A Caution. To master the overhead variance calculations described in the next section, it is important to understand fully the different meanings of the two lines in Illustration 20–5. The flexible budget line shows the *expected* relationship between volume and actual overhead costs. Amounts on this flexible budget line are *not* the basis of the credit to the Overhead clearing account. This credit entry is for the amount of cost *absorbed*. The absorption line therefore shows the relationship between production volume and the credit to the Overhead clearing account (and accompanying debit to WIP Inventory). Note that the absorption line *looks* just like a graph of purely variable costs; but as the flexible budget line indicates, actual overhead costs are expected to be semivariable—to have *both* fixed and variable cost elements making up the total.

Both the flexible budget and overhead absorption lines are based on *production* volume. The period's *sales* volume plays no role in the accounting for production overhead costs nor for direct material and direct labor costs. (Although this statement may seem obvious, some students seem to forget it when applying the overhead variance formulas in practice.)

Calculation of Overhead Variances

The net overhead variance is the algebraic sum of the volume variance and the spending variance. To understand how each variance is calculated, refer again to Illustration 20–5. The situation illustrated in that diagram is one in which (1) actual production volume is below standard volume, and (2) actual costs are below the budgeted costs for the actual volume but higher than absorbed costs. Note that budgeted costs are the amount of costs budgeted for the production volume level actually attained in the period. They are the amount that would have been budgeted had it been known ahead of time exactly what the actual volume would be. The following relationships hold:

1. *Net overhead variance* is equal to absorbed costs minus actual costs. In Illustration 20–5 the variance is unfavorable. As stated above, the net overhead variance is also the algebraic sum of the volume variance and the spending variance.

ILLUSTRATION 20–6
DIAGRAM OF OVERHEAD VARIANCES

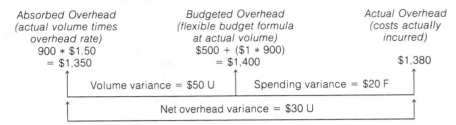

Absorbed Overhead (actual volume times overhead rate)	Budgeted Overhead (flexible budget formula at actual volume)	Actual Overhead (costs actually incurred)
900 * $1.50 = $1,350	$500 + ($1 * 900) = $1,400	$1,380

Volume variance = $50 U   Spending variance = $20 F

Net overhead variance = $30 U

2. *Production volume variance* is equal to absorbed costs minus budgeted costs. In Illustration 20–5 this variance is unfavorable. Remember, both the absorbed and budgeted cost amounts are based on the period's *actual* production volume.

3. *Spending variance* is equal to budgeted costs minus actual costs. In Illustration 20–5 this variance is favorable.

> **Example.** Assume the following conditions: actual volume in an accounting period is 900 units of product; actual overhead costs are $1,380. The flexible budget formula is $500 fixed overhead per period plus $1 variable overhead per unit of product; the standard volume is 1,000 units per period. Hence, the absorption rate is [$500 + ($1 * 1,000)] ÷ 1,000 = $1.50 per unit of product.
>
> Based on these assumptions, the following calculations apply:

$$
\begin{aligned}
\text{Budgeted cost at actual volume} &= \$500 + (\$1 * 900) = \$1,400 \\
\text{Absorbed cost at actual volume} &= \$1.50 * 900 = \$1,350 \\
\text{Net variance} = \text{Absorbed} - \text{Actual} &= \$1,350 - \$1,380 = \$30 \text{ U} \\
\text{Volume variance} = \text{Absorbed} - \text{Budgeted} &= \$1,350 - \$1,400 = \$50 \text{ U} \\
\text{Spending variance} = \text{Budgeted} - \text{Actual} &= \$1,400 - \$1,380 = \$20 \text{ F}
\end{aligned}
$$

This analysis is shown in diagram form in Illustration 20–6.

Although not obvious, the production volume variance is also equal to the *fixed* portion of the overhead rate multiplied by the difference between actual volume and standard volume. (This is proven in Appendix A to this chapter.) For the example the fixed portion of the overhead rate is $500 ÷ 1,000 = $0.50; actual minus standard volume is 900 − 1,000 = −100 units. Thus the volume variance is $0.50 * (−100) = $50 U. The importance of being aware of this version of the formula is that it emphasizes the facts that (1) a volume variance will exist whenever actual and standard volumes for a period differ, and (2) the volume variance shows the amount of underabsorbed or overabsorbed budgeted *fixed* costs. Thus, if all overhead costs were variable with respect to production volume, the production volume variance would not arise.

Use of the Overhead Variances. Generally, production managers are held responsible for the spending variance in their responsibility centers.

The fact that the spending variance calculation is based on the budgeted amount at *actual* volume means that the manager cannot reasonably claim that the spending variance is caused by a difference between the month's standard and actual volumes. Because the flexible budget cannot take account of all the noncontrollable factors that affect costs, however, there may be a reasonable explanation for the spending variance in some overhead items, particularly for *allocated costs* such as rent, insurance, and property taxes. The existence of an unfavorable variance is therefore not, by itself, grounds for criticizing performance. Rather, it is a signal that investigation and explanation are required.

In appraising spending performance one should look behind the total spending variance and examine the individual overhead items of which it consists. The total budgeted cost is the sum of the budgeted amounts for each of the separate items of cost. A spending variance can and should be developed for each important item; it is the difference between the actual cost incurred and the budget allowance for that item. Attention should be focused on significant spending variances for individual *controllable* elements of overhead costs.

For a time period of one month, the production volume variance is not useful for control purposes. All it shows is how much overhead cost was underabsorbed (or overabsorbed) because the month's volume was below (or above) the standard volume built into the overhead rate. As mentioned above, the time horizon for this standard volume is one year, and there ordinarily is no expectation that a given month's volume should equal one-twelfth the annual standard volume. Thus, there is no expectation that the production volume variance for one month should be zero. Rather, the expectation is that over the course of a year, the unfavorable variances from those months with below-standard volume and the favorable ones from months having above-standard volume will net out to zero.

In this regard it is important not to confuse monthly standard volume with a month's *planned* volume.[4] A company generally plans its level of activity on a monthly basis, expecting various factors such as seasonality (as in the toy industry) and holiday or vacation periods to result in month-to-month volume fluctuations. The sum of the 12 monthly planned volumes is the annual planned volume, which generally is then used as the annual standard (or normal) volume for calculating the predetermined overhead rate. Thus, the monthly standard volume is simply the average of the 12 planned monthly volumes. Whereas a difference between monthly standard volume and a month's actual volume is expected, a difference between a month's *planned* volume and its actual volume generally warrants investgation.

---

[4]The confusion is understandable, since *planned* and *standard* do mean the same thing in certain other management accounting contexts. The confusion would be lessened if the term *normal volume* were always used instead of standard volume; but the latter term is more common in practice, and hence we use it in this text.

The production department manager may be responsible for such deviations; for example, the failure to obtain the planned volume of output may result from an inability to keep products moving through the department at the proper speed, or production quality problems may have hurt sales volume. Alternatively, someone outside the department may be responsible: the month's planned volume may not have been attained because the sales department was unable to obtain the planned volume of orders; because some earlier department in the manufacturing process failed to deliver materials, components, or subassemblies as they were needed; or because vendors did not deliver items when needed. But it is not this difference between a month's planned and actual volumes that is the basis of calculating the overhead volume variance; hence, the volume variance is not useful for control purposes on a monthly basis.

Idle Capacity Costs. The fixed costs of a production department (or of most any other activity) can be thought of as being incurred in order to maintain a certain level of capacity—a "readiness to serve" (as General Electric Company calls it). If the capacity is not fully utilized, some fixed costs are, in a sense, being wasted. For example, if the fixed costs of a department are $100,000 per month and only 75 percent of the capacity is utilized in a given month, then that month's idle capacity costs are $25,000.

We just explained why the production volume variance is not useful for control purposes on a monthly basis. However, the alternative formula for production volume variance given above (fixed overhead rate times difference between actual and standard volume) provides a means for calculating a volume variance that is useful—one that identifies a cost center's idle capacity costs. Instead of defining monthly normal volume as one-twelfth of the annual volume actually expected to be attained, it is defined to be the volume at *practical capacity*. (Practical capacity is less than theoretical capacity in that it takes account of down-time for maintenance, holidays, and the like.) Then, the **idle capacity variance** is defined to be the ratio, fixed costs divided by practical capacity, multiplied by the difference between actual volume and practical capacity. This variance will be zero for any period in which the cost center operates at practical capacity; below that level of activity, the variance will be negative. A negative variance indicates the amount of fixed cost that was "wasted" because capacity was underutilized.

Because this alternative definition of normal volume is expected to result in an unfavorable volume variance (unless the company expects to operate at practical capacity throughout the year), it is not appropriately used for inventory valuation purposes. However, it does result in a product cost number that may be more useful for pricing purposes than the traditional number based on standard volume. With the traditional approach if volume falls, the average fixed cost per unit goes up. If full product cost data are used in pricing (as they frequently are, particularly in businesses that bid for work), there is a danger that prices will be increased as volume is falling, thus exacerbating any downward trend in volume. This risk is eliminated if the idle capacity costs are segregated in a variance account rather than being routinely assigned to products through the usual overhead absorption procedure.

Although management usually expects capacity in any department to be underutilized at times during the year, chronic excess capacity generally becomes a matter of concern. The existence of chronic excess capacity suggests two alternative courses of action: (1) put the capacity to profitable use or (2) reduce the capacity and hence reduce the associated fixed costs. (Recall that many so-called fixed costs in a department are actually step-function costs, so there are opportunities to reduce capacity that do not entail a major downsizing.) Segregating and highlighting excess capacity costs rather than "hiding" them in cost of the products using the rest of the capacity is more likely to force consideration of these two courses of action. Accordingly, we suggest that the idle capacity variance be reported to marketing managers, not just production managers.

Overhead "Efficiency" Variance. In some instances the net overhead variance can be decomposed into three (rather than two) elements, one of which is usually called an overhead "efficiency" variance. Such a variance arises only in one fairly unusual type of standard cost accounting system. It is described in Appendix B at the end of this chapter.

SUMMARY

A variance is the difference between a standard cost and an actual cost. A standard cost system generates production cost variances related to direct material cost, direct labor cost, and overhead cost. The direct material variance can be decomposed into usage and price components, and the direct labor variance can be divided into efficiency and rate components. However, these variance components may be interdependent. The overhead variance can be separated into production volume and spending components.

The purpose of decomposing variances into these components is to facilitate managers' analysis of actual results. Responsibility for a variance component is assigned to a specific responsibility center. The terms *favorable* and *unfavorable* should be used with care; they denote the algebraic sign of a variance, not value judgments of a manager's performance. Unlike the overhead spending variance, the overhead production volume variance is not useful for monthly control purposes; but it can be modified to become a useful idle capacity cost variance.

APPENDIX A: FIXED COSTS AND THE OVERHEAD VOLUME VARIANCE

The volume variance arises solely because of the presence of *fixed* production costs. We shall explain this fact in this Appendix.

ILLUSTRATION 20–7
DIAGRAM OF OVERHEAD VARIANCES

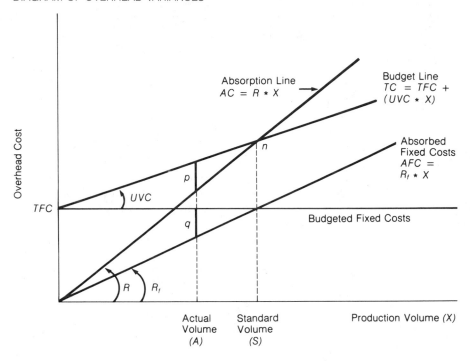

As a simple intuitive "proof," consider line segment p in Illustration 20–7. By definition the length of this segment is the volume variance (difference between absorbed and budgeted overhead at actual volume). Now imagine a gradual change in the overhead cost structure, such that budgeted costs at standard volume remain the same (point n), but the fixed cost portion (TFC) gradually diminishes. Note what happens to p as TFC approaches zero: p also approaches zero. At the limit ($TFC = 0$) the absorption and budget lines coincide, and there is no volume variance. (This is why there is no volume variance with a variable costing system: fixed costs are ignored for absorption purposes, so the budget and absorption lines are the same, both representing solely variable costs.) Thus, were there no fixed overhead costs, there would be no volume variance.

A more rigorous proof first involves realizing that the overhead rate (R in Illustration 20–7, the slope of the absorption line) is the sum of the variable overhead cost per unit of volume (UVC) and a rate that absorbs the fixed costs. This second rate is fixed costs, TFC, divided by standard volume, S; geometrically it is the slope, R_f, of the line labeled "absorbed fixed costs." It is easily demonstrated that, in fact, $R = R_f + UVC$:

$$R = \frac{\text{Budgeted cost at } S}{\text{Standard volume } (S)} = \frac{TFC + (UVC * S)}{S} = \frac{TFC}{S} + UVC = R_f + UVC$$

Now by definition, if actual volume is A, then:

$$\text{Volume variance} = \text{Absorbed cost at } A - \text{Budgeted cost at } A$$
$$p \quad = \quad (R * A) \quad - [TFC + (UVC * A)]$$

We want to prove that q, which is the difference between budgeted and absorbed *fixed* costs, is equal to p:

$$q = \text{Absorbed fixed cost at } A - \text{Budgeted fixed cost at } A$$
$$= \quad (R_f * A) \quad - TFC$$
$$= \quad (R - UVC) * A \quad - TFC$$
$$= (R * A) - [TFC + (UVC * A)]$$
$$= p = \text{Volume variance}$$

Thus, volume variance arises solely from the underabsorption or overabsorption of budgeted *fixed* costs.

The above also suggests the quick, alternative way to calculate the overhead volume variance mentioned in the text. Note that at standard volume (S), absorbed fixed costs, $R_f * S$, exactly equal budgeted fixed costs, *TFC*. Then:

$$q = (R_f * A) - TFC = (R_f * A) - (R_f * S) = R_f * (A - S)$$

In words volume variance equals the *fixed* cost absorption rate times the difference between actual and standard volumes. Volume variance is unfavorable if $A < S$, and favorable if $A > S$.

APPENDIX B: THREE-PART OVERHEAD VARIANCE ANALYSIS

In some companies a production department's overhead is absorbed into WIP Inventory on the basis of a measure of *output* (e.g., *standard* direct labor-hours "allowed" or "earned" for the goods actually produced), but the overhead budget used for evaluating the department manager's overhead spending performance is based on *input* (e.g., *actual* direct labor-hours worked). The rationale for this budgeting procedure is that many overhead costs are caused by the actual level of input factors, not by some "theoretical" level representing what inputs *should* have been for the output produced.

> **Example.** In the welding department of the Staton Company, each direct labor-hour worked costs the firm $3 for fringe benefits. In May 500 direct labor-hours were worked by the welders, although the welding work *accomplished* should (at standard times) have required only 460 hours. Although the budget for fringe benefits *would* have been $1,380 (= 460 * $3) if the welding work had been performed in the standard time, in fact 500 hours were worked, so the appropriate fringe benefit budget is $1,500; that is, 500 labor-hours would be expected to cause $1,500 fringe benefit costs.

In companies where overhead is absorbed into WIP Inventory based on outputs produced but input volume is used for overhead budgeting, the usual overhead spending variance described in the text can be decomposed into two pieces:

$$\begin{array}{ccc} \text{Spending} \\ \text{variance} \end{array} = \begin{array}{c} \text{Budgeted overhead} \\ \text{at input volume} \end{array} - \begin{array}{c} \text{Actual} \\ \text{overhead} \end{array}$$

$$\begin{array}{ccc} \text{Efficiency} \\ \text{variance} \end{array} = \begin{array}{c} \text{Budgeted overhead} \\ \text{at output volume} \end{array} - \begin{array}{c} \text{Budgeted overhead} \\ \text{at input volume} \end{array}$$

To illustrate, assume all the same facts as were used in Illustration 20–6, and add these assumptions:

· Volume is measured in direct labor-hours (rather than units of product).

· Each unit has a standard direct labor time of 1.0 hour.

· Only 860 direct labor-hours were actually worked in producing the 900 units of product.

Then the three-part overhead variance analysis becomes that shown in Illustration 20–8.

Note from the illustration that the so-called overhead "efficiency" variance has nothing to do with *overhead* efficiency; rather, it is the result of *labor* efficiency. It shows how much the flexible overhead budget changed because actual and budgeted labor costs were not the same.

Also remember that this three-part analysis is applicable only if overhead is absorbed into WIP Inventory on the basis of *output.* If, instead, overhead is absorbed (debited) into WIP Inventory based on actual *input* volume (e.g., actual direct labor dollars) but goods are transferred from WIP Inventory to Finished Goods Inventory at standard unit costs (including standard overhead per unit), then the overhead efficiency variance is "buried" in WIP Inventory. It will remain buried there until a physical inventory is taken and costed at standard to establish a new beginning balance for WIP Inventory. This physical inventory results in an adjustment to WIP Inventory, and the overhead efficiency variance is part of this adjustment (along with pilferage, accounting errors, and—if labor and material were debited to WIP Inventory at actual but credited at standard—material and labor variances).

ILLUSTRATION 20–8
THREE-PART OVERHEAD VARIANCE ANALYSIS

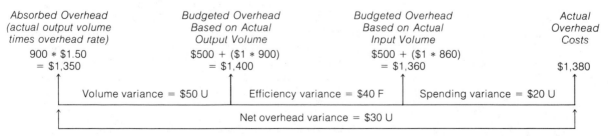

Cases

CASE 20–1   Problems in Variance Analysis

Alpha Company

Alpha Company calculates material and labor cost variances monthly. For May the following data apply to its two products:

(Relates to Alpha Company)

	Standard Material per Unit	Standard Labor per Unit	Units Produced in May
Product 1	9 lbs.	7.5 hrs.	600
Product 2	11	9.0	700

Actual usage in May was 14,000 pounds of materials and 10,000 labor-hours.

Questions

1. Calculate the material usage variance in pounds and the labor efficiency variance in hours.

2. If the standard materials price is $40 per pound and the standard labor rate is $16 per hours, restate the variances in monetary terms.

Beta Company

Beta Company produces two products, A and B, each of which uses materials X and Y. The following unit standard costs apply:

(Relates to Beta Company)

	Material X	Material Y	Direct Labor
Product A	4 lbs. @ $15	1 lb. @ $9.50	⅕ hr. @ $18
Product B	6 lbs. @ $15	2 lbs. @ $9.50	⅓ hr. @ $18

During November 4,200 units of A and 3,600 units of B were produced. Also, 39,000 pounds of X were purchased at $14.40, and 11,000 pounds of Y were purchased at $9.70; all of these materials (but no other materials) were used for the month's production. This production required 2,025 direct labor-hours at $17.50.

Questions

1. Calculate the material price and usage variances for the month.
2. Calculate the labor rate and efficiency variances for the month.

3. How would your answers to Questions 1 and 2 change if you had been told that November's *planned* production activity was 4,000 units of A and 4,000 units of B?
4. How would your answers to Questions 1 and 2 change if you had been told that November's sales were 4,000 units of A and 3,500 units of B?

Gamma Company

Gamma Company makes one product, which passes through two production operations. Under normal conditions, 150 pounds of raw material are required to make 100 units of product; all of the materials for a unit are issued to and used in operation 1. In operation 1 standard output is eight partially completed units per direct labor-hour, with a standard wage rate of $18 per hour. In operation 2, standard labor time is 12.5 hours per 100 units, at a standard wage rate of $19.80. Normal volume is 550,000 units per month. In March, output was 479,000 units, and 732,864 pounds of raw material were consumed. No spoilage occurred in operation 2. Since the production cycle is very short, there was no beginning or ending work in process inventory. March direct labor-hours and costs were as follows:

	Direct Labor	
	Hours	Costs
Operation 1	60,354	$1,101,461
Operation 2	58,438	1,153,566

Questions

1. Prepare an analysis of direct labor in March for Gamma's two operations.

2. Suppose that in operation 1, standard labor performance was expressed as 12 pounds of raw material processed per direct labor-hour (rather than eight partially completed units per direct labor-hour). Assume that the off-standard raw material yield in March was caused by the purchasing agent's buying raw materials of an off-standard quality. How, if at all, would this change your analysis of direct labor costs for March?

Delta Company

Delta Company's flexible budget formula for overhead costs is $120,000 per month fixed costs plus $36 per unit variable costs. Standard volume is 5,000 units a month. Actual overhead costs for May were $365,000, and output was 6,000 units.

Questions

Determine the following:

1. Budgeted overhead at standard volume.
2. Overhead absorption rate.
3. Overhead costs absorbed in May.
4. May's overhead production volume variance.
5. May's overhead spending variance.
6. May's net overhead variance.

Epsilon Company

Epsilon Company's expected volume for the year was 360,000 units. At this volume, planned annual overhead costs were $432,000 variable overhead and $180,000 nonvariable overhead. In March, output was 25,000 units and actual overhead expense was $42,400. Determine for March (a) the overhead flexible budget formula, (b) standard overhead per unit of output, and (c) the overhead variances.

Zeta Company

Zeta Company absorbed overhead at the rate of 65 cents per direct labor dollar. According to Zeta's flexible budget for overhead, for a direct labor payroll of $21,000, overhead should be $13,850; and overhead should be $15,250 for a payroll of $25,000. What is the budget formula? If actual overhead costs turned out to be $13,650 and $16,000, respectively, at these two volumes, what would be the overhead volume, spending, and net variances? What is Zeta's standard volume?

Eta Company

In June, Eta Company's overhead volume variance was $0 and its spending variance was $3,000 unfavorable; actual overhead expense was $35,000 for an output of 800 tons. In July, overhead expense was $30,000 and output was 600 tons; spending variance was

$0. In August, output was 900 tons and actual overhead expense was $34,500. What was July's volume variance? What was the budget amount for August? How much overhead was absorbed in August? What were the August overhead variances?

Theta Company

Department 12 of the Theta Company manufactured rivets and no other products. All rivets were identical. The company used a standard cost system plus a variable budget for overhead expense. Standard unit overhead cost was determined by dividing budgeted costs at an expected average volume by the number of rivets (in thousands) which that volume level represented.

Certain cost information is shown in the following table, and you are requested to fill in the blank spaces. The clue to determining the expected average volume can be found by a close analysis of the relationships among the figures given for allocated service and general overhead.

	Actual Cost, August	Standard Charge per 1,000 Rivets	Total Standard Cost, August	Overhead Budget, August	Overhead Budget Formula
Direct labor..........................	$ 34,000	$12.00	$ ____	Not used	
Direct material	62,300	20.00	60,000	Not used	
Department direct overhead expense.....	25,000	____	____	$28,000	$16,000 per month plus $4.00 per thous. rivets
Allocated service and general overhead..........................	14,000	4.00	12,000	16,000	$16,000 per month
Total	$136,100	$ ____	$ ____	$44,000	

Questions

1. How many rivets were produced in August?
2. What was the expected average volume (in terms of rivet output) at which the standard unit overhead charge was determined?
3. Fill in the blanks in the table.
4. Explain as much of the difference between total actual costs and total standard costs as you can on the basis of the information given.

Iota Company

Iota Company uses a standard cost system. One month's data for one of the company's products are given below:

1. Standard pounds of material in finished product: 3 pounds per unit.
2. Standard direct material cost: $3.50 per pound.
3. Standard hours of direct labor time: 1 hour per unit.
4. Standard direct labor cost: $8 per hour.
5. Materials purchased and received (12,000 pounds): $41,520.
6. Materials used: 11,000 pounds.
7. Direct labor cost incurred (3,840 hours): $28,416.
8. Actual production: 3,500 units.

9. Overhead budget formula: $18,000 per month plus $2.70 per direct labor-hour.

10. Overhead incurred: $26,374.

11. Standard volume: 4,000 direct labor-hours.

Questions

1. Compute the material usage and price variances.

2. Compute the labor efficiency and rate variances.

3. Compute the overhead volume and spending variances.

CASE 20–2 SunAir Boat Builders, Inc.*

Located in New Hampshire, SunAir Boat Builders served boaters with a small, lightweight fiberglass sailboat capable of being carried on a car roof. Though the firm could hardly be considered as one of the nation's industrial giants, its burgeoning business had required it to institute a formal system of cost control. Jan Larson, SunAir's president, explained:

> Our seasonal demand, as opposed to a need for regular, level production, means that we must keep a good line of credit at the bank. Modern cost control and inventory valuation procedures enhance our credibility with the bankers and, more importantly, have enabled us to improve our operations. Our supervisors have realized the value of good cost accounting, and the main office has, in turn, become much more aware of problems in the barn.

SunAir's manufacturing and warehouse facilities consisted of three historic barns converted to make 11-foot "Silver Streak" sailboats. The company's plans included the addition of 15- and 18-foot sailboats to its present line. Longer-term plans called for adding additional sizes and styles in the hope of becoming a major factor in the regional boat market.

The "Silver Streak" was an open-cockpit, day sailer sporting a mainsail and small jib on a 17-foot, telescoping aluminum mast. It was ideally suited to the many small lakes and ponds of the region, and after three years it had become quite popular. It was priced at $2,265 complete.

Manufacturing consisted basically of three processes: molding, finishing, and assembly. The molding department mixed all ingredients to make the fiberglass hull, performed the actual molding, and removed the hull from the mold. Finishing included hand additions to the hull for running and standing rigging, reinforcement of the mast and tiller steps, and general sanding of rough spots. Assembly consisted of the attachment of cleats, turnbuckles, drain plugs, tiller, and so forth, and the inspection of the boat with mast, halyards, and sails in place. The assembly department also prepared the boat for storage or shipment.

Mixing and molding fiberglass hulls, while manually simple, required a great deal of expertise, or "eyeball," as it was known in the trade. Addition of too much or too little catalyst, use of too much or too little heat, or failure to allow proper time for curing could each cause a hull to be discarded. Conversely, spending too much time on adjustments to mixing or molding equipment or on "personalized" supervision of each hull could cause severe underproduction prob-

---

*Copyright © by the President and Fellows of Harvard College. Harvard Business School case 172-052.

lems. Once a batch of fiberglass was mixed there was no time to waste being overcautious or it was likely to "freeze" in its kettle.

With such a situation, and the company's announced intent of expanding its product line, it became obvious that a standard cost system would be necessary to help control costs and to provide some reference for supervisors' performance.

Randy Kern, the molding department supervisor, and Bill Schmidt, SunAir's accountant, agreed after lengthy discussion to the following standard costs:

Materials—Glass cloth—120 sq. ft.	@ $ 2.00	=	$240.00
—Glass mix — 40 lbs.	@ $ 3.75	=	150.00
Direct labor—Mixing — 0.5 hr.	@ $20.25	=	10.12
—Molding — 1.0 hr.	@ $20.25	=	20.25
Indirect costs—Absorb at $24.30 per hull*		=	24.30
Total cost to mold hull		=	$444.67

*The normal volume of operations for overhead derivation purposes was assumed to be 450 hulls per month. The estimated monthly indirect cost equation was: Budget = $9.72 * hulls + $6,561.

Analysis of Operations. After several additional months of operations, Bill Schmidt expressed his disappointment about the apparent lack of attention being paid to the standard costs. The molders tended to have a cautious outlook toward mixing too little or "cooking" too long. No one wanted to end up throwing away a partial hull because there was too little glass mix.

In reviewing the most recent month's production results, Schmidt noted the following actual costs for production of 430 hulls:

Materials:	
Purchased	60,000 sq. ft. glass cloth @ $1.80
	20,000 lbs. glass mix @ $4.09
Used	54,000 sq. ft. glass cloth
	19,000 lbs. glass mix
Direct labor:	Mixing 210 hrs. @ $21.37
	Molding 480 hrs. @ $20.25
Overhead:	Incurred $11,140

Before proceeding with further analysis, Schmidt called Kern to arrange a discussion of variances. He also told Jan Larson, "Maybe we should look into an automated molding operation. Although I haven't finished my analysis, it looks like there will be unfavorable variances again. Kern insists that the standards are reasonable, then never meets them!"

Larson seemed disturbed and answered, "Well, some variances are inevitable. Why don't you analyze them in some meaningful manner and discuss your ideas with Kern, who is an expert in molding whose opinion I respect. Then the two of you meet with me to discuss the whole matter."

Questions

1. Determine the molding department's direct cost variances and overhead variances. Why do you think they occurred?

2. Do you think SunAir's standards are meaningful? How would you improve them?

3. Assume that the month's actual and standard production costs for items *other than* molding hulls amounted to $914.33 per boat, and that 430 boats were sold. Prepare a statement of budgeted and actual gross margin for the month, assuming planned sales of 450 boats.

CASE 20–3   Medi-Exam Health Services, Inc.

Medi-Exam Health Services, Inc. (MEHS), located in a major metropolitan area, provides annual physical screening examinations, including a routine physical, EKG, and blood and urine tests. MEHS's clients are companies offering annual physicals for their employees, but which are too small to warrant having a full-time medical staff of their own to provide this service. MEHS has its own portable equipment, which it moves from client to client so the examinations can be done at the customer's facilities. MEHS also has its own central laboratory for obtaining test results. A standard examination is priced at $160 per patient.

While conducting examinations for Peterson Electronics Company, Dr. James Molloy, one of the owners of MEHS, began talking with Peterson's head of financial planning. The patient told Dr. Molloy how Peterson used a profitgraph to help indicate the approximate profit the firm could expect to earn at various levels of output.

At the next meeting with MEHS's accountant, Jane Mattick, Dr. Molloy asked if such a technique would be useful for MEHS. Ms. Mattick said she would draw up a profitgraph for 500 physicals, a normal month's number of examinations. Her chart appears in Exhibit 1.

On September 1 Dr. Molloy learned that 310 physical examinations had been billed in August. Using the chart, he determined that profit should be approximately $6,000 for August. On September 8 Dr. Molloy received a copy of the income statement for August, showing a book profit of $10,000 (Exhibit 2).

Although he was pleasantly surprised by these results, Dr. Molloy was curious as to why the pretax profit was approximately 70 percent higher than he had expected, based on the profitgraph.

EXHIBIT 1
MEDI-EXAM HEALTH SERVICES PROFITGRAPH

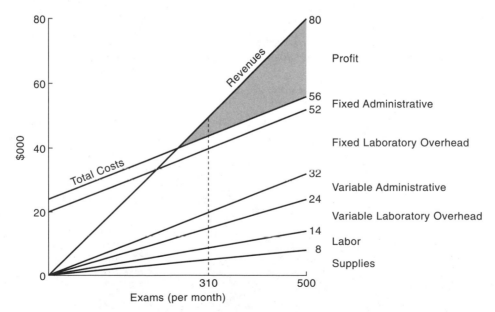

EXHIBIT 2

MEDI-EXAM HEALTH SERVICES, INC.
Income Statement
For August

Revenues (310 examinations billed)		$49,200
Expenses:		
Standard cost of services billed	$27,280	
Variances:		
Volume (debit)	1,600	
All other (debit)	1,120	
Administrative expenses	9,200	39,200
Profit (before income taxes)		$10,000

Questions

1. Compute the monthly break-even volume for Medi-Exam Health Services.

2. Compute the exact profit indicated by the profitgraph for a volume of 310 examinations.

3. Determine the number of examinations *performed* (as opposed to billed) in August.

4. Reconcile the profit just computed with the August book profit of $10,000.

CASE 20–4 Cotter Company, Inc.*

In preparing its annual profit plan, the management of Cotter Company, Inc., realized that its sales were subject to monthly seasonal variations. Nevertheless, management expected that for the year as a whole the sales volume (in units) would equal the production volume, and profit before taxes would total $240,000, as shown below:

	Annual Budget	
	Amount	Percent of Sales
Sales	$2,400,000	100
Standard cost of sales:		
Prime costs	960,000	40
Production overhead	840,000	35
Total standard cost	1,800,000	75
Gross margin	600,000	25
Selling and general expenses	360,000	15
Income before taxes	$ 240,000	10

---

*Copyright © by the President and Fellows of Harvard College. Harvard Business School case 168-005.

Management defined *prime costs* as those costs for labor and materials that were strictly variable with the quantity of production. The production overhead included both fixed and variable costs; management's estimate was that within a range around planned sales volume of plus or minus $750,000 per year, variable production overhead would be equal to 25 percent of prime costs. Thus, the total production overhead budgeted for the year consisted of $240,000 of variable costs (25 percent of $960,000) and $600,000 of fixed costs. All of the selling and general

expenses were fixed, except for commissions on sales equal to 5 percent of the selling price.

Sam Cotter, the president of the company, approved the budget, stating that, "A profit of $20,000 a month isn't bad for a little company in this business." During January, however, sales suffered the normal seasonal dips, and production was also cut back. The result, which came as some surprise to the president, was that January showed a loss of $7,000.

COTTER COMPANY, INC.
Operating Statement
January

Sales		$140,000
Standard cost of sales.		105,000
Standard gross margin		35,000
	Favorable or	
Manufacturing variances.	(Unfavorable):	
Prime cost variances	$ (3,500)	
Production overhead:		
Spending variance	1,000	
Volume variance	(12,500)	(15,000)
Actual gross margin.		20,000
Selling and general expenses		27,000
Loss before taxes		$ (7,000)

Questions

1. Explain, as best you can with the data available, why the January profit was $27,000 less than the average monthly profit expected by the president.

2. At what level of monthly volume does Cotter expect to earn exactly zero profit? (Hint: For simplicity, assume that Cotter makes only one product, which has a selling price of $1 per unit.)

3. What was Cotter's January production volume? (Use the hint from Question 2.)

4. How much did finished goods inventory change in January?

5. What were actual production overhead costs in January?

6. Continuing to use the assumption in Question 2's hint, assume further that Cotter's standard prime production costs per unit are as follows: materials, 2.5 pounds at 10 cents per pound; labor, 1 minute at $9 per hour. In January, 390,000 pounds of materials were used, at a cost of 9 cents per pound. Total direct labor costs were $28,400 for 2,500 hours. Calculate the four detailed prime cost variances.

CASE 20–5   Lupton Company

Lupton Company manufactured two products, for simplicity called here A and B. Lupton used a standard cost system; were a flowchart of this system prepared, it would be identical to the flowchart shown in Illustration 19–2. Thus, the price and usage components of the raw materials variance were captured in the accounts. However, decomposing the labor and production overhead variances required "outside-the-accounts" calculations, which Lupton's management performed on an ad hoc basis rather than routinely. Standards were used without change for the entire calendar year. All monthly variances were closed to the monthly income statement.

The company had hired a student majoring in business administration as a summer employee. In early June, when the May income statement became available, the production manager asked this student to make a detailed analysis of the April and May results (see Exhibit 1). As guidance to the student, as well as to calibrate the student's accounting expertise, the production manager had prepared a list of questions to answer:

EXHIBIT 1

LUPTON COMPANY
Gross Margin Statements
For April and May

	April		May	
Sales revenues		$738,000		$553,500
Cost of sales at standard:				
Materials.	$196,800		$147,600	
Direct labor	184,500		123,000	
Overhead	147,600	528,900	98,400	369,000
Gross margin at standard.		209,100		184,500
Production variances:				
Materials price.	(2,460)		(7,380)	
Materials usage.	(1,230)		(3,690)	
Labor.	(1,230)		(4,920)	
Overhead	(55,360)	(60,280)	(18,460)	(34,450)
Actual gross margin.		$148,820		$150,000

Supplementary Data

1. Debits to Work in Process for materials related to product A totaled $35,055 and $31,365 in April and May, respectively. For product B materials, these debits totaled $1,845 and $79,335, respectively.
2. The direct labor debited to Work in Process in *March* was $135,300. Budgeted production overhead for *March* was $102,090.
3. April's and May's actual production overhead costs were equal.
4. May's actual production overhead costs were equal to the budgeted overhead at standard volume.
5. Product A's standard material cost per unit was $12.30; its full standard cost was $45.51.

1. In April and May, did we spend more for our production operations than would be expected, assuming our standard costs represent reasonable expectations? (Answer without considering the supplementary data in Exhibit 1.)

2. If actual production overhead costs were the same both months, what could have caused the decrease in unfavorable overhead variance for May?

3. Was April's production level above or below standard volume (which is $123,000 direct labor dollars per month for every month)? (Answer without considering the supplementary data in Exhibit 1.)

4. Was May's production level higher or lower than April's? Was it above or below standard volume? (Answer without considering the supplementary data in Exhibit 1.)

5. The percentage decrease in total standard gross margin from April to May was less than the percentage decrease in total sales revenues. What could account for this?

6. In May, the actual purchase price per pound of one of our raw materials decreased. In view of this, how could there have been an increase in the unfavorable materials price variance?

7. Some of this lower-priced raw material was put into production in May. What items on the May gross margin statement were affected by this?

8. Some of this lower-priced raw material was included in products that were *sold* in May. How did this affect amounts on the May gross margin statement?

9. Although our standard volume is expressed in terms of direct labor dollars per month, I can't remember whether we absorb overhead on the basis of direct labor dollars or material dollars. Can you figure out which basis we use?

10. What is the standard direct labor cost per unit of product A?

11. Given the information in supplementary data item 1, could performance with respect to total material usage actually have improved from April to May?

12. Was the *combined* dollar balance in Work in Process and Finished Goods higher or lower at the end of May than it was at the end of April?

13. Did the proportion of product A sold increase from April to May?

14. Given the information in the supplementary data items, what was May's overhead spending variance?

15. What was the overhead production volume variance in May?

16. What was the overhead production volume variance in April?

17. What was the overhead spending variance in April?

Question

Answer, with complete yet concise responses, the production manager's 17 questions.

CASE 20–6   C. F. Church Manufacturing Company*

C. F. Church Manufacturing Company was established in 1898 for the purpose of manufacturing toilet seats. The manufacturing process was quite simple. First, the seats were shaped out of wood at a branch plant. They were then shipped to the main plant, where they underwent the particular finishing processes required. Some units were sprayed with paint, but the best seats were coated with cellulose nitrate sheeting. After the

*Copyright © by the President and Fellows of Harvard College. Harvard Business School case 147-001.

EXHIBIT 1

ASSEMBLY ORDER № 6291 Coated				REQUISITION № 6291 Hinges – Screws – Bumpers				REQUISITION № 6291 Cartons – Fillers			
Date August	Plate No. 2000			Date August				Date August			
Shipping Order No.				DESCRIPTION	QUANTITY			DESCRIPTION	QUANTITY		
Work Order No.	Quantity 100			Hinges 2,000	100			Cartons 25	100		
Seals 2,000 - 917								Fillers	200		
Covers 2,000 - 917				Screws ¾ × 7				800			
				Screws ⅝ × 7				214	100		
Hinges 2,000				1¼ × 8	400			105			
				Brass Ferrules	200			Blocks			
Special Instructions				Bar Bumpers	200						
				Tack Bumpers	200						
				Delivered by				Delivered by			
					UNIT COST*	AMOUNT	✓		UNIT COST*	AMOUNT	✓
				Hinges				Cartons			
FOR COST DEPT. ONLY	UNIT COST†	AMOUNT	✓	Screws				Filler No. 1			
Material	5 51	551 00		Screws				No. 105			
Labor	92	92 00		Ferrules				No. 800			
Burden	1 90	190 00		Bar Bumpers				No. 214			
Total Cost	8 33	833 00		Tack Bumpers				Blocks			

* These were actual amounts on a LIFO basis.
† These were standard amounts (see Exhibit 4).

seats were coated, the rough edges were filled and the seats were sanded, buffed, and polished. Finally, hinges and rubber bumpers were added, and the seats were packed for shipment. Most operations were performed by hand with the aid of small machines, such as paint spray guns and buffing wheels.

1. Accounting

Collection of Material and Labor Cost. A major part of the work required in the cost system was the accumulation of data on actual and standard costs. The procedure used for materials was as follows. When an order for a particular style was started through the factory, the supervisor of the department that performed the first operation received a manufacturing order. On the basis of this order, the supervisor filled out a stores requisition slip for the necessary materials. Items listed on this requisition subsequently were priced by entering their purchase cost on the requisition on a LIFO basis. (Since raw material was purchased infrequently in large contract lots, this procedure was not difficult.) When seats were ready to

be assembled and packed, the assembly department supervisor made out an assembly order (Exhibit 1). This included a requisition for hinges, screws, bumpers, cartons, and fillers, which were also costed at LIFO. The totals of the requisition slips for the month served as the basis for credits to the respective materials inventory accounts and a debit to Work in Process for the cost of material put into process.

The direct labor debit to Work in Process was equally straightforward. Daily, each production employee made out a time and production report (Exhibit 2) on which he or she recorded the factory order number, the operation, the time spent on each operation, and the number of pieces that he or she had finished. A clerk in the payroll department entered the correct piece rate or hourly rate and made the proper extension. The total of the direct labor thus computed provided the credit to the Accrued Wages account and the debit (for direct labor) to Work in Process.

Flexible Overhead Budget (Annual). The debit to Work in Process for production overhead was based on estimates made annually of the relation of monthly overhead expenses

EXHIBIT 2

FORM C-STR7918				C.F. CHURCH MFG. CO. Time and Production			Date *August* —		
Employee No. *3/3*		Name							
Order No.	Oper. No.	TIME			Labor or Piece Rate	No. Pieces	Cost		✓
		Started	Finished	Elapsed					
2068	31	7:20	12:00	4.7	3.40	550	18	70	
2068	31	1:00	4:20	3.3	3.40	400	13	60	
							32	30	

to direct labor costs for each department. These estimates were made so that, for each department, a schedule of standard overhead expenses at varying possible rates of capacity utilization, i.e., a flexible budget, was available. Exhibit 3 illustrates such a budget for the coating department, Department No. 3.

The process used to prepare these departmental flexible overhead budgets was as follows:

1. Determine 100 percent capacity of each department in terms of direct labor-hours and direct labor dollars by theoretically loading each unit of productive machinery and equipment with the number of workers required to operate it, together with the necessary productive employees on floor or benchwork. Consider, however, the normal sales volume of different types of products and limitations as to type of equipment in any one department that affect the capacity of the plant as a whole. For example, output might be limited to the capacity of the coating and spraying departments.

2. Establish monthly overhead expense allowances for each department, considering four general classifications: indirect labor, indirect supplies, fixed charges, and charges from nonproductive (i.e., service) departments.

3. Base allowance for indirect labor and indirect supplies on the past year's experience, making adjustments if necessary for changes in wage rates and the prices of supplies. Compute these projections first for the 100 percent capacity determined above, and from this point use a sliding or graduated scale for the lower percentages of capacity. Give due recognition to the fact that some of these costs do not vary at all with production, that others vary in the same ratio as production, and that others, although not fixed, do not move proportionately with the rate of actual plant activity.

4. Prorate power expense according to the number of horsepower hours used and metered in the respective departments; water expense (after consideration is given to any special demands for water in particular departments) according to the number of employees; insurance, taxes, and depreciation with reference to the net book value of buildings and equipment. Charge directly to the department involved specific insurance that definitely can be assigned to an

EXHIBIT 3   FLEXIBLE OVERHEAD BUDGET, DEPARTMENT NO. 3 (COATING)

	100%	95%	90%	85%	80%	75%	70%	65%	60%	50%	40%
Indirect labor:											
01 Supervision	775.00	775.00	775.00	775.00	775.00	775.00	775.00	775.00	775.00	775.00	775.00
08 General labor	625.00	595.00	565.00	535.00	505.00	470.00	440.00	405.00	375.00	315.00	250.00
10 Idle and lost time											
11 Guaranteed rate cost	375.00	356.00	338.00	319.00	300.00	281.00	263.00	244.00	225.00	188.00	150.00
16 Overtime bonus	100.00	100.00	95.00	95.00	90.00	85.00	80.00	75.00	50.00	25.00	25.00
19 Repairs and maint.	175.00	175.00	165.00	165.00	160.00	160.00	160.00	150.00	150.00	100.00	100.00
Total indirect labor	2,050.00	2,001.00	1,938.00	1,889.00	1,830.00	1,771.00	1,718.00	1,649.00	1,575.00	1,403.00	1,300.00
Indirect supplies:											
31 Repairs and maint.	25.00	25.00	25.00	25.00	25.00	20.00	20.00	20.00	15.00	15.00	10.00
35 Acetone and isotone	1,625.00	1,545.00	1,465.00	1,385.00	1,305.00	1,220.00	1,140.00	1,055.00	975.00	815.00	650.00
37 Sandpaper and sandbelts	11.00	10.00	10.00	9.00	9.00	8.00	8.00	7.00	7.00	5.00	4.00
38 Glue and cement	775.00	736.00	700.00	660.00	620.00	580.00	540.00	500.00	465.00	385.00	310.00
41 Consumable supplies	125.00	120.00	112.00	106.00	100.00	94.00	88.00	81.00	75.00	63.00	50.00
42 Loose and hand tools	50.00	48.00	45.00	43.00	40.00	38.00	35.00	33.00	30.00	25.00	20.00
46 Miscellaneous	15.00	14.00	14.00	13.00	12.00	11.00	10.00	9.00	9.00	7.00	6.00
Total indirect supplies	2,626.00	2,498.00	2,371.00	2,241.00	2,111.00	1,971.00	1,841.00	1,705.00	1,576.00	1,315.00	1,050.00
Fixed charges:											
65 Insurance—bldgs. and equip.	21.58	21.58	21.53	21.58	21.58	21.58	21.58	21.58	21.58	21.58	21.58
66 Insurance—L. and C.	161.00	153.00	145.00	137.00	129.00	121.00	113.00	105.00	97.00	80.00	64.00
68 Power	27.00	26.00	24.00	23.00	22.00	21.00	19.00	18.00	16.00	14.00	11.00
69 Water	17.25	17.25	17.25	17.25	17.25	17.25	17.25	17.25	17.25	17.25	17.25
70 Taxes—city and town	28.68	28.68	28.68	28.68	28.68	28.68	28.68	28.68	28.68	28.68	28.68
71 Taxes—social security	530.00	504.00	477.00	450.00	424.00	398.00	371.00	345.00	318.00	265.00	212.00
72 Depreciation	81.25	81.25	81.25	81.25	81.25	81.25	81.25	81.25	81.25	81.25	81.25
73 Provision for vacations	725.40	725.40	725.40	725.40	725.40	725.40	725.40	725.40	725.40	725.40	725.40
78 Group insurance	112.70	112.70	112.70	112.70	112.70	112.70	112.70	112.70	112.70	112.70	112.70
80 Pensions	420.36	420.36	420.36	420.36	420.36	420.36	420.36	420.36	420.36	420.36	420.36
Total fixed charges	2,125.22	2,090.22	2,053.22	2,017.22	1,982.22	1,947.22	1,910.22	1,875.22	1,838.22	1,766.22	1,694.22
Total dept. expense	6,801.22	6,589.22	6,362.22	6,147.22	5,923.22	5,689.22	5,469.22	5,229.22	4,989.22	4,484.22	4,044.22
Charges from other depts.	9,435.37	9,333.33	9,240.12	9,140.56	9,040.03	8,945.27	8,826.90	8,751.83	8,630.42	8,440.11	8,235.38
Total overhead expense	16,236.59	15,922.55	15,602.34	15,287.78	14,963.25	14,634.49	14,296.12	13,981.05	13,619.64	12,924.33	12,279.60
Direct labor dollars	9,375.00	8,906.00	8,437.00	7,969.00	7,500.00	7,031.00	6,562.00	6,094.00	5,625.00	4,687.00	3,750.00
Overhead rate	173%	179%	185%	192%	200%	208%	218%	229%	242%	276%	327%

individual department, such as insurance on trucks in the shipping department or boiler indemnity for the steam department.

5. Distribute the total expense of nonproductive departments such as steam, general plant, shipping, and plant administration to the productive departments on the most logical basis: steam according to floor area, general plant and plant administration according to direct labor-hours, and shipping according to direct labor dollars. The estimated cost of defective work for the whole plant was distributed to operating departments on the basis of the expected distribution of direct labor dollars. This item of expense was included in the total of charges from other departments, shown at the bottom of Exhibit 3.

6. Revise the flexible overhead budgets during the year only for unexpected increases or decreases in wage rates or indirect material costs or an important change in the manufacturing processes.

Standard Overhead Rate. After a department's flexible overhead budget was prepared, executives estimated the average monthly percentage of capacity utilization expected in that department during the coming year. The standard overhead rate was the rate shown in Exhibit 3 for the estimated percentage of capacity. For example, it was estimated that during the year the coating department would operate at an average of 80 percent of capacity. The standard overhead rate for the coating department was therefore 200 percent of direct labor, as shown at the bottom of the 80 percent column in Exhibit 3. The other columns in Exhibit 3 were used for control purposes, as described below.

Actual Overhead Costs (Monthly). Actual overhead costs incurred during the month were debited to the Overhead clearing account in the general ledger and to an appropriate detail account in an overhead subsidiary ledger. There was a detail account for each item listed in Exhibit 3 (supervision, general labor, and so forth) in each department. Service department and other overhead costs were allocated to the producing departments. At the end of the month, the amount of absorbed overhead was calculated by multiplying the overhead rate for each department by the actual direct labor cost of the department for the month. In the coating department, for example, the actual direct labor for August was $5,915.60, and this multiplied by 200 percent gave $11,831.20, the absorbed overhead. (Note that the rate used was the overhead rate determined annually, *not* the overhead rate under the column in Exhibit 3 that relates to the actual volume of the current month.)

The absorbed overhead for all departments was debited to Work in Process and credited to the Overhead clearing account. Any balance remaining in the Overhead account (i.e., the net overhead variance) was then closed to Cost of Goods Sold. In August, for example, actual overhead was $45,914.98, absorbed overhead was $45,904.44, so $10.54 was debited to Cost of Goods Sold.

Standard Product Costs. Deliveries from work in process to finished goods were recorded by completion in the factory of the assembly order (Exhibit 1). On the lower left corner of that form there was space for the cost department to fill in the standard cost per unit and the total amount of standard cost for the order, and the total of these standard costs entries for a month was credited to Work in Process and debited to Finished Goods Inventory.

The standard costs per unit mentioned in the previous paragraph were prepared for each product in the form illustrated in Exhibit 4. Because the lines on the standard cost sheets were arranged by successive op-

EXHIBIT 4

Standard Cost				
Date January 1			Plate No. 2000	
Description	Material	Labor	Overhead	Total
Receive woodwork	1.17	0.004	0.008	1.182
Insp. and hand sand		0.012	0.024	1.218
Bottom coat	0.542	0.038	0.076	1.874
Trim T.B. and O.F. seats		0.011	0.022	1.907
Sand edges T.B.C.F. out		0.003	0.008	1.918
Sand edges T.B.C.F. in		0.003	0.008	1.929
Inspect		0.012	0.024	1.965
Top coat	0.543	0.079	0.158	2.745
Shave		0.010	0.020	2.775
Sand edges—upright belt		0.005	0.014	2.794
Sand seats and covers		0.039	0.107	2.940
Inspect and file		0.015	0.030	2.985
Dope		0.004	0.008	2.997
Buff seats and covers		0.108	0.208	3.313
Inspect		0.012	0.024	3.349
Buff repairs		0.044	0.085	3.478
Trademark		0.007	0.014	3.499
Drilling		0.004	0.008	3.511
Total seat	2.255	0.410	0.846	3.511
Total cover no.	1.983	0.399	0.826	3.208
Total seat and cover	4.238	0.809	1.672	6.719
Assemble		0.032	0.064	6.815
Cleanup polish		0.033	0.066	6.914
Seal end of carton		0.006	0.012	6.932
Inspect and wrap		0.034	0.068	7.034
Seat, label, and pack		0.010	0.020	7.064
Bar bumpers	0.043			7.107
Tack bumpers	0.019			7.126
Screws 1¼-8	0.047			7.173
Hinge	1.04			8.213
Carton and filler 2—No. 1	0.125			8.338
Total cost	5.512	0.924	1.902	8.338

erations, they showed the cumulative cost of a product at the completion of every operation as well as the final cost at which the product was delivered to finished goods inventory. For each operation and for the total cost there was a breakdown that showed separately the standard costs of materials, labor, and overhead. The method of arriving at these costs is described below.

Standard materials costs consisted of a predetermined physical amount per unit priced at the expected purchase price for each classification of raw stock or of finished parts stock. Standard labor costs for the various piece-rate operations were simply the current piece rates; in the case of daywork operations, they were the quotients obtained by dividing the daywork rate by an estimated attainable average output. Standard overhead costs were found by multiplying the departmental overhead rates selected for the year by the standard labor costs for the operations concerned. For example, the standard cost sheet for a style calling for a coated finish might show a standard labor charge of $0.079 for an operation in the coating department. As indicated above, operations in the coating department for the year were estimated to be at 80 percent of capacity, which for the coating department meant an overhead rate of 200 percent of direct labor. Thus, the standard overhead cost for the coating operation with a labor charge of $0.079 was set at 200 percent of this amount, or $0.158.

These standard product costs were used to price deliveries into finished goods, to cost work in process physical inventories, and to transfer production between accounts. Once the standard costs were prepared, it was expected that they would remain constant for the year, unless there was a significant and unanticipated change in material costs, labor rates, or the departmental overhead costs.

Variances. At the end of each month, a physical inventory of raw materials, supplies, work in process, and finished goods was taken. For this inventory, raw materials and supplies were priced on the basis of LIFO purchase cost, and work in process and finished goods were priced according to the standard cost sheets described above. The difference between the inventory thus determined and the book balance of each inventory account was closed into Cost of Goods Sold. The most important of these differences was for work in process inventory.

A work in process statement (Exhibit 5) was prepared each month. This report showed the beginning inventory at standard cost, plus actual direct materials, actual labor, and actual absorbed overhead added during the period in each department. From this total cost figure, there were subtracted the actual deliveries to finished goods as indicated on the completed assembly orders, plus defects and less products transferred from finished goods back to work in process for reworking, all costed at standard cost.

The resulting book value of work in process was compared with the figure obtained by valuing, at standard, the results of the physical inventory ($80,959.69). Any difference indicated by this comparison constituted the variance of actual cost from standard and was closed to Cost of Goods Sold. The physical inventory balance at standard constituted the debit to Work in Process at the beginning of the next month. If this work in process variance was large, its causes were investigated and action was taken accordingly.

A descriptive summary of the inventory accounts is given in Exhibit 6.

2. Control of Overhead Expenses.

Budgeted Overhead Expenses. The company used the departmental flexible overhead budgets to set targets for the supervisors who were responsible for incurring expenses. A knowledge of the actual amount of direct labor for each productive department made it a simple matter to determine which column of figures to use as the benchmark for evaluating the spending performance of each supervisor. For example, the coating department (Exhibit 3) might be expected to operate, on the *average*, at 80 percent of capacity; but in any one month the actual operations might vary considerably from this average. Thus, if direct labor dropped to $7,031, the supervisor would be expected to spend only $580 for glue and cement rather than the $620 allowable at the average operating level.

Comparison of Actual and Budget. The departmental comparisons of the actual overhead expenses, by accounts, with the appropriate budgeted allowance for that volume, are illustrated in the departmental budget sheet, Exhibit 7. The August budgeted expense figures for the coating department are based upon an output level of 65 percent of capacity. This figure was arrived at by com-

EXHIBIT 5

Work in Process		
Period Ending __August__		Order No. __GENERAL__

	Detail	Amount
	Balance from Last Period		158,597.19
	DIRECT MATERIALS		76,338.21
Dept. No.	DIRECT LABOR		
1	Varnish		
2	Spray	2,990.25	
3	Coating	5,915.60	
4	Filing	998.83	
5	Sanding	1,637.53	
6	Buffing and Polishing	6,175.78	
8	Assembling and Packing	4,788.60	
	Total Direct Labor		22,506.59
	OVERHEAD		
1	Varnish		
2	Spray	6,180.50	
3	Coating	11,831.20	
4	Filing	1,937.73	
5	Sanding	4,489.05	
6	Buffing and Polishing	11,888.76	
8	Assembling and Packing	9,577.20	
10	Shipping	———	
	Total Overhead		45,904.44
	TOTAL COST		303,346.43
	Less Deliveries		222,386.74
	BALANCE IN PROCESS at Std. Cost		80,959.69

Deliveries at Std. Cost								
Date		Amount	Date		Amount	Date		Amount
8/31	Deliv.	220,876.63						
	Variance	1,259.07						
	Defective	251.04						
	Net	222,386.74						

paring the actual direct labor expense for the month, amounting to $5,915.60, to the closest corresponding direct labor expense, $6,094, which is under the 65 percent column shown on Exhibit 3. (Exhibit 7 is a standard form, and only those lines that are pertinent to the operations of the coating department are filled in on the example shown.)

Exhibit 7 also reported two items over which the supervisor had no control. Other

EXHIBIT 6   SUMMARY OF ENTRIES TO INVENTORY ACCOUNTS
August

Raw Materials
(Several accounts according to nature of material)

Debit	Credit
$151,204 Balance	$76,318.21 Requisitions, priced at last-in, first-out cost (debit to Work in Process).
$343,640.19 Purchases at invoice cost (credit to Accounts Payable).	$138.32 Adjustment to physical inventory (Dr. or Cr.).
$1,101.67 Materials salvaged from returned goods (credit to Cost of Goods Sold).	

A physical inventory of all raw materials was taken each month and the difference between inventory and book balance written off to Cost of Goods Sold.

Work in Process

Debit	Credit
$158,597.19 Balance	$220,894.24 Deliveries to finished goods at standard costs (debit to Finished Goods).
$76,318.21 Direct materials from requisitions priced at last-in, first-out cost (credit to Raw Materials).	$251.04 Defective work, from defective work order (debit to Overhead).
$22,506.59 Direct labor from payroll summary (credit to Accrued Wages).	$1,259.07 Adjustment to physical inventory (Dr. or Cr.).
$20.00 Materials purchased not usually carried in inventory (credit to Accounts Payable).	
$17.61 Transfers from finished goods for reworking or alteration, at standard cost (credit to Finished Goods).	
$45,904.44 Absorbed overhead from overhead summary sheet (credit to Overhead).	

Finished Goods

Debit	Credit
$429,682.73 Balance	$400,954.09 Shipments at standard costs (debit to Cost of Goods Sold).
$220,894.24 Deliveries to finished goods at standard costs (credit to Work in Process).	$17.61 Transfers to work in process for reworking or alteration at standard cost (debit to Work in Process).

A physical inventory was taken of all work in process every month. This was priced and totaled according to standard costs at last operation performed; the difference between the inventory and balance in the Work in Process account, representing the cost variation, was written off to Cost of Goods Sold.

EXHIBIT 7

C.F. CHURCH MFG. CO. HOLYOKE Analysis of Overhead Expenses			
DEPARTMENT __#3 Coating__		MONTH __August__	
	Budget	Actual Expense	(Over) or Under Actual
INDIRECT LABOR			
01 Supervision	775.00	756.00	19.00
04 Truck Drivers and Helpers			
06 Shipping			
08 General Labor	405.00	171.22	233.78
09 Repair and Rework			
10 Idle and Lost Time		1.77	(1.77)
11 Guaranteed Rate Cost	244.00	28.14	215.86
16 Overtime Bonus	75.00	32.98	42.02
19 Repairs and Maint.	150.00	38.26	111.74
17 Vacations		46.00	(46.00)
21 Paid Holidays			
Total	1,649.00	1,074.37	574.63
INDIRECT SUPPLIES			
31 Repairs and Maint.	20.00	360.18	(340.18)
33 Repairs and Maint., Trucks			
35 Acetone and Isotone	1,055.00	739.48	315.52
36 Buffing Compounds and Buffs			
37 Sandpaper and Sandbelts	7.00	9.60	(2.60)
39 Labels, Tape, etc., Glue and Cement	500.00	734.71	(234.71)
40 Shipping Cartons			
41 Consumable Supplies	81.00	55.54	25.46
42 Loose and Hand Tools	33.00	13.55	19.45
46 Miscellaneous	9.00	7.51	1.49
Total	1,705.00	1,920.57	(215.57)
OTHER OVERHEAD EXPENSES			
Insurance, Power, Taxes, Social Security, Depreciation, Group Insurance, and Pension	1,875.22	1,472.46	402.76
DEFECTIVE WORK (memo)	600.00	251.04	348.96
DIRECT LABOR	6,094.00	5,915.60	178.40

overhead expenses showed the total amount of fixed charges allocated to the department on the basis of the percentage distributions described earlier. Defective work was the total amount of defective work budgeted ($600) and actual ($251.04) for the *entire plant*, and it bore no direct relation to the work done in the coating department. The amount allocated to each department for defective work was not shown on Exhibit 7 because the basis of allocation was consid-

ered too arbitrary. The amounts for both other overhead expenses and for defective work were shown in the analysis of overhead expenses principally as a matter of information for the supervisor. They were not considered as being controllable by the supervisor.

Each month the accounting department prepared Exhibit 8, summarizing the actual, budgeted, and absorbed overhead costs for each operating department. The amount shown as actual expense was obtained by

EXHIBIT 8
OVERHEAD SUMMARY AND STATISTICS

Plant—Holyoke   Period Ending—August 31

Dept. No.	Description	Direct Labor	Actual Expense	Budgeted Expense	(Loss) or Gain on Budget	Absorbed Expense	Over- or (Under-) absorbed
1							
2	Spray	2,990.25	6,464.64	7,103.64	639.00	6,180.50	(284.14)
3	Coating	5,915.60	12,829.53	13,981.05	1,151.52	11,831.20	(998.33)
4	Filing	998.83	2,590.83	2,190.20	(400.63)	1,937.73	(653.10)
5	Sanding	1,637.53	3,907.74	5,243.47	1,335.73	4,489.05	581.31
6	Buffing	6,175.78	11,275.76	10,750.25	(525.51)	11,888.76	613.00
7							
8	Assemble and pack	4,788.60	8,846.48	8,998.58	152.10	9,577.20	730.73
	Total plant	22,506.59	45,914.98	48,267.19	2,352.21	45,904.44	(10.54)

adding the charges from other departments to the other overhead items shown in Exhibit 7 (excluding defective work). The budgeted expense was the total overhead for each department as shown on the flexible overhead budget (Exhibit 3 for the coating department) at the applicable level of operations (65 percent for the coating department in August).

The amount of absorbed expense was computed by applying the annual overhead rate to the direct labor in each productive department, as explained in the preceding section.

In the opinion of the management, the entries in the column headed (loss) or gain on budget could be considered a measure of the effectiveness of departmental supervision, whereas the amount over- or (under-) absorbed was influenced both by efficiency and by the volume of production.

The departmental overhead budget constituted the point of real control over expenditures. At the end of each month, the factory manager met with the cost accountant and the supervisors to discuss spending. At these meetings the supervisors were encouraged to discuss their performance as indicated by the budget report. When the system was first installed, the cost accountant did most of the talking, but with increasing familiarity with the costs for which they were responsible, each supervisor gradually became "cost conscious," and after a short time each supervisor knew approximately what the monthly performance would be, even before seeing the budget comparison report.

The supervisor in charge of the coating department was particularly interested in controlling the overhead costs under his jurisdiction. During the first week of September, he received the analysis of overhead expenses for August (Exhibit 7), and he checked all the items carefully to learn if there were any costs out of line with his expectations for that month. He copied the August figures onto a sheet (Exhibit 9) on which he had previously summarized the figures for recent months (except for July, which included a vacation shutdown). After he felt that he had a good idea of his cost position, he arranged for a meeting with the factory manager and the cost accountant to review the situation with them.

EXHIBIT 9
SUMMARY OF PERFORMANCE IN THE COATING DEPARTMENT

	April		May		June		August	
	Actual	(Over) or Under	Actual	(Over) or Under	Actual	(Over) or Under	Actual	(Over) or Under
Indirect labor:								
01 Supervision.................	811	(36)	782	(7)	756	19	756	19
08 General labor	654	(119)	558	(23)	418	22	171	234
10 Idle and lost time	—	—	—	—	—	—	2	(2)
11 Guaranteed rate cost	313	6	154	165	50	213	28	216
16 Overtime bonus	63	32	45	50	37	43	33	42
19 Repairs and maint...........	89	76	30	135	35	125	38	112
17 Vacations	—	—	—	—	—	—	46	(46)
Total	1,930	(41)	1,569	320	1,296	422	1,074	575
Indirect supplies:								
31 Repairs and maint...........	5	20	85	(60)	176	(156)	360	(340)
35 Acetone and isotone..........	1,300	85	1,134	251	1,031	109	739	316
37 Sandpaper and sandbelts	10	(1)	14	(5)	5	3	10	(3)
39 Labels, tape, glue, and cement..	575	85	462	199	182	358	735	(235)
41 Consumable supplies..........	66	40	116	(10)	48	40	56	25
42 Loose and hand tools..........	37	6	14	29	10	25	14	19
46 Miscellaneous...............	27	(14)	9	3	9	1	8	1
Total	2,020	221	1,834	407	1,461	380	1,922	(217)
Other overhead: Insurance, power, taxes, social security, deprec., group insur., pension	1,456	561	2,014	3	1,836	74	1,472	403
Defective work (memo)	391	209	656	(56)	594	6	251	349
Direct labor	7,812	157	8,024	(55)	6,599	(36)	5,916	178

Questions

1. What are the major purposes of the standards developed by the company?

2. How does the company develop standard overhead rates? How often do you think they should be changed?

3. What steps are involved in the development of the standard cost sheet (Exhibit 4)? How accurate do you judge the figures to be?

4. Try to explain fully the basis of each entry in Exhibit 6. In particular, what are the possible causes of the $138.32 credit to Raw Materials and the $1,259.07 credit to Work in Process labeled "adjustment to physical inventory" in Exhibit 6?

5. Reconcile the amounts in Exhibit 5 with the entries shown in Exhibit 6.

6. Explain so as to distinguish them clearly from one another, the figures $12,829.53, $13,981.05, and $11,831.20 shown for the coating department on Exhibit 8.

7. If you were the plant manager, what evaluation would you make of the performance of the coating department supervisor in controlling the department's overhead costs? About which items in Exhibits 7 and 9 would you be likely to question the supervisor?

8. How many dollars of the coating department variances reported in Exhibit 8 are attributable to "charges from other departments"? Of what significance are these variances to (a) the coating department and (b) the service departments that created these charges? Should they be included in the overhead summary and statistics report?

21

Analyzing Other Variances

This chapter completes the discussion of variance analysis by extending the description of production cost variances in Chapter 20 to variances for other elements on the income statement. The techniques described in these two chapters decompose the total difference between budgeted net income and actual net income into the factors that caused this difference, and they show how much of the total difference related to each of these factors.

There are two other types of variances: marketing variances and general and administrative variances. The marketing variances can be further decomposed into those factors associated with gross margin and those associated with selling expenses. A complete analysis of a sample income statement illustrating all types of variance is shown. Based on such an analysis, management can ask relevant questions about the causes of the variances and take appropriate action based on the answers to these questions.

OVERVIEW OF THE ANALYTICAL PROCESS

The Need for Variance Analysis   Management wants to know not only *what* the amounts of the differences between actual and planned results were but also, and more important, *why* these variances occurred. In a given organization, the techniques used to analyze variances depend on management's judgment as to how useful the

731

results are likely to be. Some organizations do not use any formal techniques; others use only a few of those described here; still others use even more sophisticated techniques. There are no prescribed criteria beyond the general rule that any technique should provide information worth more than the costs involved in developing it.

We shall refer to the data with which actual performance is being compared as the *budgeted* data because (as will be further discussed in Chapter 24) a carefully prepared budget is usually the best indication of what performance should be. The same techniques can be used to analyze actual performance in terms of any other basis of comparison, such as performance in some prior period or in some other responsibility center. Although our principal focus is in analyzing the performance of responsibility centers in a business company, the same general approach can be used for analyzing any situation in which inputs are used to produce outputs.

Types of Variances

In Chapters 19 and 20, we used the term **variance** for a difference between actual and standard production costs. We shall now broaden its meaning to include the difference between the actual amount and the budgeted amount of *any* revenue or cost item or of margin (gross margin or contribution margin).

An **unfavorable variance** is one that makes actual net income lower than budgeted net income. Thus, an unfavorable revenue variance occurs when actual revenue is *less* than budgeted revenue, but an unfavorable cost variance occurs when actual cost is *higher* than budgeted cost. A **favorable variance** makes actual net income higher than budgeted net income. If actual revenue is above budget or actual cost is below budget, a favorable variance occurs.

As we have emphasized before, the words *favorable* and *unfavorable* do not necessarily connote value judgments about managerial performance. For example, a purchasing agent might create a favorable material price variance by purchasing substandard materials, which probably is not a good thing for the company. Also, many variances are uncontrollable by a company's managers (e.g., an increase in electricity cost per kilowatt-hour) and so do not connote either good or poor management performance. Thus, unfavorable and favorable indicate *only the algebraic impact* of a variance on net income. As in Chapter 20, these terms are abbreviated here as U and F, respectively.

In looking at a business as a whole, attention ultimately is directed to the "bottom line," or the amount of net income. (In this discussion, we exclude nonoperating items, extraordinary items, and income taxes and focus on *operating income*.) If a certain company's budgeted operating income for April was $82,000 and actual operating income was only $78,000, the $4,000 U variance indicates that something went wrong in April. It does not, however, indicate *what* went wrong. In order to take effective action, management needs to identify the variances in specific items that together explain the total unfavorable variance.

Variance items can be grouped into three categories, each of which corresponds roughly to an area of responsibility within a company:

1. Marketing variances, which are the responsibility of the marketing organization.

2. Production cost variances, which are the responsibility of the production organization.

3. Other variances (general and administrative expenses, nonoperating items, and so on), which are the responsibility of top management and its staff units.

This categorization, together with more detailed subdivisions, is depicted in Illustration 21–1. This variance "tree" serves to remind us that whatever the specific variance we are calculating, the overriding objective is to explain why budgeted and actual *net income* differed.

MARKETING VARIANCES

The objectives of the typical marketing organization include (1) generating its budgeted gross margin and (2) doing so within the spending limits described in its expense budget.[1] Analysis of its success in meeting these objectives requires the calculation of marketing expense variances and gross margin variances.

Expense Variances

Most marketing expense variance components are easy to calculate: for each item of marketing expense, actual costs are subtracted from the budgeted amount. For example, if the year's advertising budget was $750,000 but actual advertising costs were $800,000, then clearly there was a $50,000 unfavorable variance. What is *not* easy is determining whether there was sufficient justification for overspending the advertising budget. This is because the "right" amount to spend for advertising, as for most marketing expenses, is a matter of judgment.

Gross Margin Variances

Gross margin is the difference between sales revenue and cost of sales. Total sales revenue is the sum of the multiplications of each product's sales

---

[1]Many marketers view their overall goal as generating budgeted *revenues*. This, however, is too narrow a view of marketing's actual impact on a company's profitability.

ILLUSTRATION 21–1
OVERVIEW OF VARIANCE ANALYSIS

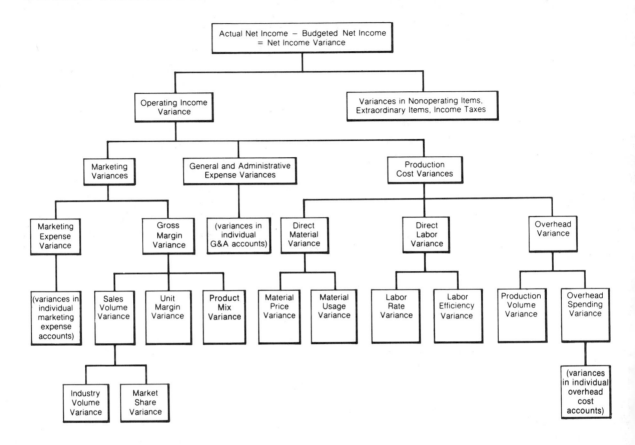

volume (in physical units) times its unit selling price. Similarly, total cost of sales is the sum of the multiplications of each product's sales volume times its unit production cost (i.e., the amount credited to Finished Goods Inventory and debited to Cost of Sales when goods are sold). In most instances the marketing department is responsible for the products' sales volumes and unit selling prices but not for their unit production costs. Accordingly, when calculating **gross margin variances**, *cost* per unit should be a *standard* amount. Following this procedure prevents differences between actual and standard unit costs, which are *production* variances, from clouding the picture of the variances for which the marketing organization can reasonably be held accountable.

The total gross margin variance is the difference between actual and budgeted total gross margin (both based on *standard* unit production costs). For example:

	Actual	Budgeted	Difference (Δ)
Unit gross margin	$11*	$10†	$1
Volume, in units	900	1,000	(100)
Gross margin	$9,900	$10,000	
Gross margin variance..................	$100 U		

* Based on $33 actual selling price and $22 standard unit cost.
† Based on $32 budgeted selling price and $22 standard unit cost.

Why Work with Margins? Before illustrating how this gross margin variance can be decomposed into several elements, we should first explain why it is more useful to work with gross margins than to deal separately with revenues and cost of sales. First, consider this table:

	Unit Amount*	Budget Units	Budget Total	Actual Units	Actual Total	Variance
Sales revenue...............	$25	1,000	$25,000	800	$20,000	$5,000 U
Cost of sales...............	15	1,000	15,000	800	12,000	3,000 F
Gross margin	$10	1,000	$10,000	800	$ 8,000	$2,000 U

* Budgeted and actual

Since budgeted and actual unit margins were the same ($10 per unit), the $2,000 unfavorable gross margin variance clearly was caused by the 200-unit shortfall in sales volume. The $5,000 U revenue variance, however, overstates the *income* impact of this shortfall, because it was partially offset by the related $3,000 F cost of sales variance. The real impact of the lower volume was the net of these two amounts, which is the $2,000 U variance in gross margin. This $2,000 is the appropriate amount about which to question the marketing group, for it is their job to generate gross margin, the spread between sales revenue and cost of sales.

Types of Gross Margin Variances. The gross margin variance can be decomposed into three components:

1. The *unit margin variance,* which arises because the actual gross margin per unit was different from the budgeted gross margin.

2. The *sales volume variance,* which arises because the actual sales volume, in units, was different from the budgeted sales volume.

3. The *product mix variance,* which arises because some products had higher unit margins than others and the actual product mix (i.e., the actual proportions of products sold) was different from the budgeted mix.

We shall first describe how to isolate the unit margin and sales volume variances. In order to defer the description of the mix variance, which is considerably more complicated, we shall assume in these calculations that the company has a single product.

Unit Margin and Sales Volume Variances. The $100 U gross margin variance ($9,900 − $10,000) calculated in the earlier example is explainable in terms of a $1 variance in unit margin (in this case, caused by a change in the unit selling price) and a 100-unit variance in sales volume. One can see that (1) the higher unit margin increased gross margin by $900 ($1 per unit for each of the 900 units sold) and (2) the 100-unit volume shortfall would have decreased gross margin by $1,000 (100 units at $10) *if* the per unit margin had been as planned. Using Δ (delta) to denote the difference between an actual and a budgeted amount, this intuitive derivation can be formalized as follows:

ΔUnit margin	*	Actual volume	=	Unit margin variance
$1	*	900	=	$900 F
ΔVolume	*	Budgeted unit margin	=	Sales volume variance
(100)	*	$10	=	$1,000 U
Actual gross margin	−	Budgeted gross margin	=	Net gross margin variance
$9,900	−	$10,000	=	$100 U

Note that these formulas are set up so that favorable variances will be algebraically positive and unfavorable variances will be algebraically negative. However, it is easier—and a better test of understanding—to use common sense rather than memorizing formulas to determine whether a variance is favorable or unfavorable.

Graphic Aids. The graphic aids that were presented in Illustrations 20−1 and 20−2 can be easily adapted to apply to gross margin variances. Illustration 21−2 (adapted from Illustration 20−1) shows that in decomposing the total margin variance into its volume and unit margin components, we in effect create a hypothetical "after-the-fact" margin budget based on *actual* volume but *budgeted* unit margin. This is the middle column in Illustration 21−2, labeled *AVBM*. The sales volume variance is the differ-

ILLUSTRATION 21−2
DIAGRAM OF GROSS MARGIN VARIANCES

Budgeted Volume at Budgeted Margin (BVBM)	*Actual Volume at Budgeted Margin* (AVBM)	*Actual Volume at Actual Margin* (AVAM)
1,000 * $10 = $10,000	900 * $10 = $9,000	900 * $11 = $9,900

Sales volume variance = $1,000 U ↑ | Unit margin variance = $900 F

Net (total) variance = $100 U

ence between the original margin budget, *BVBM,* and this hypothetical budget. The unit margin variance is the difference between total actual gross margin (again, based on actual volume and actual unit price but on *standard* unit cost), *AVAM,* and the hypothetical budget, *AVBM.*

Selling Price Variance. Let *AP* and *BP* stand, respectively, for actual unit selling price and budgeted unit selling price, and *AC* and *BC* for actual unit cost and budgeted standard unit cost. Then, the unit margin variance, which is actual minus budgeted margin (*AM* – *BM*), equals (*AP* – *AC*) – (*BP* – *BC*). If actual standard unit cost turns out to be equal to the budgeted standard cost (*AC* = *BC*) during the period, then the unit margin variance formula simplifies to *AM* – *BM* = *AP* – *BP*. That is, if *AC* = *BC*, the unit margin variance is caused solely by a difference between actual and budgeted selling price per unit. Many companies use the same standard unit costs during the year as were used in preparing that year's budget, thus making *AC* = *BC*. In such companies the unit margin variance is called the **selling price variance.** This name, although descriptive in a situation where *AC* = *BC*, obscures the fact that it is unit margin, not just unit selling price, with which the marketing organization should be concerned.

On the other hand, in periods of rapid inflation it is not unusual to increase both standard unit costs and selling prices one or more times during a year. If during the period both the standard unit cost *and* the selling price were increased by equal amounts, thus passing unit cost increases through to customers, then the budgeted and actual unit margins would be the same, and there would be *zero* unit margin variance. This signals that the marketing organization was taking the expected action: increasing prices to maintain the spread between selling price and unit cost. In this case the price increase does not result in a favorable margin variance that might misleadingly appear to reflect better-than-expected performance by the marketing organization.

Further Decomposition of Variances. It is sometimes possible to break down the margin variances even further. Because these variances are usually the most important causes of changes in net income, such breakdowns are often worthwhile. The volume variance can be subdivided if data are available on total sales of a product by all companies. From these data a company can compute its **market share**—that is, the percentage of its sales to total industry sales. Variances caused by changes in total industry sales reflect general economic conditions, whereas variations caused by changes in market share are the responsibility of the company's own marketing organization. The formulas for this decomposition of sales volume variance into **industry volume variance** and **market share variance** components are:

$$\begin{array}{c} \text{Industry} \\ \text{volume variance} \end{array} = \begin{array}{c} \Delta\text{Industry} \\ \text{volume} \end{array} * \begin{array}{c} \text{Budgeted} \\ \text{market share} \end{array} * \begin{array}{c} \text{Budgeted} \\ \text{unit margin} \end{array}$$

$$\begin{array}{c} \text{Market} \\ \text{share variance} \end{array} = \begin{array}{c} \Delta\text{Market} \\ \text{share} \end{array} * \begin{array}{c} \text{Actual} \\ \text{industry volume} \end{array} * \begin{array}{c} \text{Budgeted} \\ \text{unit margin} \end{array}$$

Similarly, it is sometimes possible to decompose the unit margin variance into that portion attributable to general price movements and that attributable to the company's own pricing tactics.

In multiproduct companies, margin variance analyses are performed for each product line and, in some instances, for individual products within a line. It is also possible to subdivide margin variances by different responsibility centers, such as a firm's district sales offices.

Product Mix Variance. When a company sells several products having different unit gross margins, the mix (relative proportions) of high-margin and low-margin products sold influences the total gross margin. The difference in gross margin caused by the difference between the mix assumed in the budget and the actual mix sold is the **product mix variance.** This variance did not show up in the preceding examples because we assumed the company had only one product. Neither would it show up in a multiproduct situation if the actual and budgeted unit margins used in the variance formulas were the *weighted average* of those for all products, that is, the various products' unit margins weighted by their relative proportions in the product mix.[2]

Calculating the Mix Variance. The portion of the mix variance attributable to each product is calculated from the difference between the actual quantity sold and that product's *budgeted proportion;* that is, the quantity that would have been sold if that product's sales had been the budgeted percentage of actual sales volume. The mix variance is the sum of these amounts for all products.

The calculations of all three margin variances are shown in Illustration 21−3. The assumed situation is similar to that in Illustration 21−2 except that we now assume that the company makes three products, each having a different unit margin. The budget indicated that 30 percent of total sales (in physical units) would be in product A, which has a relatively low unit margin, and 30 percent would be in product C, which has a relatively high unit margin. In the period, actual sales (in units) of the low-margin product A were only 20 percent of the total, and actual sales of the high-margin product C were 40 percent of the total. The actual mix was thus "richer" than planned; this produced a favorable mix variance of $180.

Note that the approach in Illustration 21−3 is similar to Illustration 21−2, except that in 21−3 we create *two* hypothetical after-the-fact margin budgets. One is based on what the volume of each product would have been had the actual total volume been distributed among the products in the budgeted mix proportions. The other is based on actual mix. If we work only with the budgeted and actual *average* unit margins of $10 and $11, respectively (shown in part A of 21−3), Illustration 21−2 can be applied to this multiproduct situation. But if we look at products individually (as in

---

[2]Although perhaps not obvious to nonmathematicians, if one divides the total gross margin by the total number of units sold, the resulting average is in fact a weighted average.

ILLUSTRATION 21–3
MARGIN VARIANCES FOR MULTIPLE PRODUCTS

A. Assumed Situation

Product	Budget Volume Percent	Budget Volume Units	Budget Margin Unit	Budget Margin Total	Actual Volume Percent	Actual Volume Units	Actual Margin Unit	Actual Margin Total
A	30	300	$ 9.00	$ 2,700	20	180	$ 9.50	$1,710
B	40	400	10.00	4,000	40	360	11.00	3,960
C	30	300	11.00	3,300	40	360	11.75	4,230
Total	100	1,000	$10.00*	$10,000	100	900	$11.00*	$9,900

* These are averages derived from total volume and total margin: $10,000 ÷ 1,000 = $10.00; $9,900 ÷ 900 = $11.00.

B. Variance Calculations

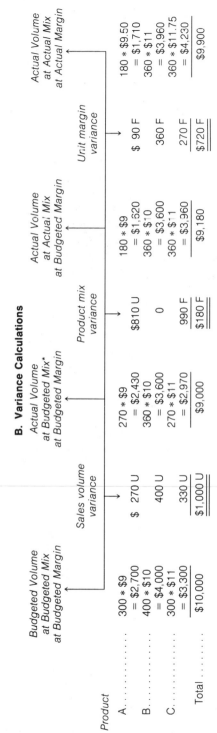

Product	Budgeted Volume at Budgeted Mix at Budgeted Margin	Actual Volume at Budgeted Mix* at Budgeted Margin	Actual Volume at Actual Mix at Budgeted Margin	Actual Volume at Actual Mix at Actual Margin
A	300 * $9 = $2,700	270 * $9 = $2,430	180 * $9 = $1,620	180 * $9.50 = $1,710
B	400 * $10 = $4,000	360 * $10 = $3,600	360 * $10 = $3,600	360 * $11 = $3,960
C	300 * $11 = $3,300	270 * $11 = $2,970	360 * $11 = $3,960	360 * $11.75 = $4,230
Total	$10,000	$9,000	$9,180	$9,900

Sales volume variance:
- A: $ 270 U
- B: 400 U
- C: 330 U
- Total: $1,000 U

Product mix variance:
- A: $810 U
- B: 0
- C: 990 F
- Total: $180 F

Unit margin variance:
- A: $ 90 F
- B: 360 F
- C: 270 F
- Total: $720 F

* Budgeted volume percentage for each product applied to total actual volume (e.g., 30 percent * 900 = 270 for product A).

739

21–3), the $900 F unit margin variance in 21–2 is shown to be the sum of a $720 F unit margin variance and a $180 F mix variance.[3]

Other Uses of the Mix Concept. The mix concept is often used in analyzing gross margin variances. It is important to know to what extent the total variance was caused by changes in the "richness" of the sales mix. The mix concept has wider applicability, however. In general, it is possible to develop a mix variance whenever a cost or revenue item is broken down into components and the components have different unit prices (or labor rates). When a price variance is computed by use of an average price, we do not know whether the variance is caused by a true difference in prices or by a change in the proportion of the elements that make up the total—that is, by a change in mix.

For instance, instead of using the total number of direct labor-hours and the *average* hourly labor rate in calculating the direct labor cost variances, we could use the number of direct labor-hours in each skill category and the hourly rate for that skill category. We can then develop a labor mix variance. Similarly, in cases where raw materials are blended into a composite material, we can calculate a materials mix variance. Generally, in situations where there are multiple inputs (e.g., material types, labor skill categories) or multiple outputs (e.g., several products), a price or unit margin variance calculated using average prices or margins can be decomposed into a "true" price or unit margin variance and a mix variance.

Some chemical companies, and other companies whose manufacturing process consists primarily of blending several raw materials into a finished product, compute a materials mix variance. Most companies do not compute materials mix or labor mix variances, however. In some instances, the "recipes" for the blend do not permit any variation in the mix; or perhaps union work rules preclude the occurrence of a labor mix variance. Even when such variances may occur, many companies have decided that the additional information is not worth the cost of calculating it.

Other Approaches. In the above analysis we have assumed the company uses a standard full cost system, and cost of sales is therefore stated at full standard production cost. This, in fact, is by far the most common approach, since most companies want to explain the gross margin variance by means of the same accounting conventions as they use in their shareholder income statements. However, other approaches are possible. If the

---

[3] A short-cut formula for calculating total product mix variance is:

$$\left(\begin{matrix} \text{Average budgeted margin} \\ \text{at actual mix} \end{matrix} - \begin{matrix} \text{Average budgeted margin} \\ \text{at budgeted mix} \end{matrix} \right) * \text{Actual volume}$$

In the example, the average budgeted margin at actual mix is $(180 * \$9) + (360 * \$10) + (360 * \$11) \div 900 = \$10.20$. Therefore, mix variance = $(\$10.20 - \$10.00) * 900 = \$180$ F. However, this short-cut formula does not reveal each product's portion of the mix variance, which many companies find to be useful information. For this reason also, we have not presented the "one-line" formulas for the total unit margin and sales volume variances in a multiproduct situation.

company uses a variable costing system, cost of sales will include only the variable production costs, which will lead to some differences in the analysis of variances. (These differences are illustrated in the Appendix to this chapter.) At the other extreme, if the company treats the factory as a profit center, goods will be transferred to the marketing department at an amount that includes an element for profit, and this also will affect the analysis.

PRODUCTION COST VARIANCES

Because of their close relationship with standard cost systems (Chapter 19), production cost variances were described in Chapter 20. At this point, we shall review one aspect of production cost variances that many people find especially difficult.

Using the formulas presented in Chapter 20, variances can be calculated for each of the three elements of production cost: direct labor, direct material, and production overhead. When calculating these variances it is necessary to understand clearly what is meant by the "budgeted" amounts in production cost variance formulas because the concept of a production cost budget differs from that of a gross margin budget.

Correct Volume Measures

The overall goal in variance analysis is to explain the difference between actual and budgeted net income. Actual net income is a function of actual sales volume, and budgeted net income is dependent upon budgeted sales volume. Thus, the formula for gross margin sales volume variance appropriately was based on the difference between these actual and budgeted *sales* volumes.

The analysis of production variances makes no use of sales volumes. The only relevant volume is the *production* volume, and a difference between actual and standard (or normal) production volume generates only one variance: the overhead volume variance.[4] No volume variance arises from a difference between the period's actual and planned production volumes for direct material or direct labor costs. This is because these production costs are capitalized in inventory accounts as incurred, and they do not impact the income statement until the period in which the goods are sold. Thus, for a given level of actual sales volume, if production volume is greater than was planned, the additional direct material and direct labor costs are reflected in an inventory (asset) buildup, not on the income statement. (A

---

[4]As explained in Chapter 20, although the standard volume is usually the same as the planned (or budgeted) volume for a time horizon of one year, this is not true for shorter time periods such as one month; thus, except by coincidence, monthly standard volume is not the same as a month's planned volume. Therefore, a monthly overhead volume variance is not caused by the difference between the month's actual and *planned* volumes, but rather by the difference between the month's actual volume and *standard* (or *normal*) volume.

similar statement applies when actual production volume is less than was planned.)

For this reason, when calculating material and labor cost variances as part of an analysis of income variance, the budgeted production volume is essentially an irrelevant number. Rather, we want to compare *what material and labor costs actually were with what these costs should have been for the actual volume of goods produced.* Thus, in material and labor cost variance formulas, "actual cost" means actual cost at actual volume, and "budgeted cost" (or "standard cost") means standard costs for the *actual* volume. In other words, for purposes of material and labor cost variance analysis, the budgeted cost amount is developed *after the fact,* based on the known actual production volume rather than on either the planned or standard (normal) production volume.

To illustrate the irrelevance of planned production volume in an analysis of material and labor cost variances, consider this example:

	Month of August	
	Budget	Actual
Production volume, in units.............	500	600
Direct materials cost, per unit	$10.00	$10.00
Direct materials cost, total	$5,000	$6,000

In an important sense there is no direct materials variance here. The amount that should have been spent for direct materials for the 600 units produced in August was $10 per unit, or $6,000 total; and $6,000 *was* the actual direct materials cost. The $1,000 difference between budgeted and actual total direct materials cost reflects only the fact that, for whatever reason, 100 more units were produced than had originally been planned. In particular, this $1,000 difference does not suggest poor performance relative to the usage of materials.

Knowing the reasons why production volume was 100 units above plan *is* important. But the fact that it was 100 units higher (and the direct materials cost was $1,000 greater) than if the original production plan had been followed gives us no useful insights for explaining net income variance or for raising questions about management performance. Specifically, if the company's August net income variance was $12,000 U, *no part* of this $12,000 variance is accounted for by the $1,000 difference between actual direct materials cost and the original materials budget.[5] In summary:

- The gross margin sales volume variance results from a difference between budgeted and actual *sales* volume.

---

[5]Some authors refer to this $1,000 difference, caused solely by a difference between planned and actual production volumes, as a "production volume variance" or "budget adjustment variance." In our view, these labels are misleading, since this difference is *not* a component of overall net income variance.

- The overhead volume variance, which results from a difference between standard and actual *production* volume, relates solely to overhead costs (and, as explained in Chapter 20, is not useful for control purposes in any event).
- There is no volume variance for direct material costs or direct labor costs.

OTHER VARIANCES

Conceptually, the total variance in items of general and administrative expenses and in some nonoperating items could be decomposed into volume and spending components, as production overhead costs were treated. This is not usually done, however. Instead, the differences between actual and budgeted amounts are simply listed. For most of these items, the expectation is that the budgeted amounts will be adhered to regardless of volume fluctuations. Isolation of a volume variance under these circumstances would not be appropriate.

Certain nonoperating items, such as extraordinary items, income taxes, and foreign currency translation adjustments, may also cause a net income variance. At the responsibility center level, such items generally are not included in the income statement, so they do not create any variance in pretax operating income. At whatever level in the corporation nonoperating items are included in the income statement, it is possible to analyze any variance in these items. In some instances a variance in income tax expense is decomposed into a rate component (if the budgeted and actual tax rates differ) and a "quantity" component (if the budgeted and actual pretax income differ).

COMPLETE ANALYSIS

As a way of summarizing the techniques described in Chapter 20 and in this chapter, the complete analysis of a simple situation is shown in Illustration 21–4. The income statement (part A) shows a variance of $413 U between the month's actual and budgeted income. (For simplicity all amounts except unit costs and margins are in thousands; thus, a volume of 200 means 200,000 units, and $413 means $413,000.) The question is, What accounts for this $413 variance? The answer is given in part B, which decomposes the total variance into elements. The remainder of the illustration shows how each of these elements was found.

Marketing Variances

The first step in the computation is to analyze the difference between budgeted and actual gross margins. This part of the analysis is shown in part C. The analysis reflects these facts (not shown in the illustration): (1) both the budgeted cost of sales and the actual *standard* unit cost of sales were $15.40, and (2) the budgeted selling price was $18.90 per unit, and the actual price was $20.30 per unit. Thus, the budgeted unit margin was $3.50 and the actual unit margin was $4.90.

ILLUSTRATION 21–4
COMPUTATION OF VARIANCES
($000 except unit costs and unit margins)

A. Income Statement
Month of November

	Budget	Actual	Variance
Sales	$3,780	$3,857	
Less: Standard cost of sales	3,080	2,926	
Gross margin at standard cost	700	931	$231 F
Production variances	0	574	574 U
Gross margin	700	357	343 U
Selling, general, and administrative expense	280	350	70 U
Income before taxes	$ 420	$ 7	$413 U

B. Summary of Variances

Unit margin	$ 266 F
Sales volume	35 U
Net margin	231 F
Material price	112 U
Material usage	28 F
Labor rate	56 U
Labor efficiency	168 U
Overhead production volume	105 U
Overhead spending	161 U
Net production	574 U
Selling, general, and administrative	70 U
Income variance	$413 U

C. Gross Margin Variances

Underlying data:	Sales (units)	Unit Margin	Total Margin
Budget	200	$3.50	$ 700
Actual	190	4.90	931
Net margin variance			$231 F

Computation of Margin Variances

(1) *Unit margin variance:*

$$\Delta\text{Unit margin} * \text{Actual units} = \text{Unit margin variance}$$
$$\$1.40 \quad * \quad 190 \quad = \quad \$266 \text{ F}$$

(2) *Sales volume variance:*

$$\Delta\text{Volume} * \text{Budgeted unit margin} = \text{Sales volume variance}$$
$$(10) \quad * \quad \$3.50 \quad = \quad \$35 \text{ U}$$

(continued)

   The unit margin variance is determined by multiplying the actual sales quantities for each product by the difference between actual and budgeted unit margins. (For brevity's sake, a mix variance is not shown.) The sales volume variance is the loss or gain in gross margin that results from a

ILLUSTRATION 21–4 *(concluded)*

D. Production Cost Variances

Underlying Cost Data

Item	Standard	Actual
Production volume	200 units*	170 units
Direct material	2 lbs./unit * $1.40/lb.	320 lbs. * $1.75 = $560
Direct labor	0.4 hr./unit * $14.00/hr.	80 hrs. * $14.70 = $1,176
Overhead	$700 per mo. + $3.50 per unit	$1,456

Computation of Cost Variances

(1) *Material price variance:*

$$\Delta\text{Price} * \text{Actual quantity} = \text{Material price variance}$$
$$(\$0.35) * \qquad 320 \qquad = \qquad \$112\text{ U}$$

(2) *Material usage variance:*

$$\Delta\text{Quantity} * \text{Standard price} = \text{Material usage variance}$$
$$20\dagger \qquad * \qquad \$1.40 \qquad = \qquad \$28\text{ F}$$

(3) *Labor rate variance:*

$$\Delta\text{Rate} * \text{Actual hours} = \text{Labor rate variance}$$
$$(\$0.70) * \qquad 80 \qquad = \qquad \$56\text{TU}$$

(4) *Labor efficiency variance:*

$$\Delta\text{Hours} * \text{Standard rate} = \text{Labor efficiency variance}$$
$$(12\ddagger) \qquad * \qquad \$14.00 \qquad = \qquad \$168\text{ U}$$

(5) *Overhead production volume variance:*

Absorbed overhead: 170 units * $7 per unit§	$1,190
Budgeted overhead: $700 + ($3.50 * 170 units)	1,295
Overhead production volume variance	$ 105 U

(6) *Overhead spending variance:*

Budgeted overhead (as above)	$1,295
Actual overhead	1,456
Overhead spending variance	$ 161 U

---

* Based on annual standard volume of 2,400 units.
† 170 units at 2 lbs per unit standard minus 320 lbs. actual.
‡ 170 units at 0.4 hour per unit standard minus 80 hours actual.
§ Annual overhead rate = [$8,400 + ($3.50 * 2,400 units)] ÷ 2,400 units = $7 per unit.

difference between actual and budgeted sales volume. The algebraic sum of the unit margin variance ($266 F) and the sales volume variance ($35 U) is the $231 F shown as the net variance in gross margin on the income statement. Note that margin variances are favorable when actual is greater than budget, which of course is the opposite situation from cost variances.

Although the separate accounts making up the "selling, general, and administrative expense" category are not detailed in Illustration 21–4, those accounts related to marketing activities would be isolated in practice, and budgeted versus actual amounts would be calculated. These marketing-related variances would then be added to the gross margin variances to arrive at the total marketing variance.

Production Cost Variances

Next, we turn to an analysis of the production cost variances. Note that actual production volume (170 units, as shown in part D) is less than actual sales volume (190 units), the difference being inventory that is carried at standard cost. Note also that the monthly standard volume of 200 units is irrelevant to the calculation of direct material and direct labor variances. The fact that the actual and standard volumes are different does signal that there will be an overhead volume variance in November. Carrying the inventory at standard cost means that expense variances are treated as period costs (for management accounting purposes) and charged directly to cost of sales during the period in which they occur. The labor, material, and production overhead variances described in Chapter 20 are calculated in part D. Their algebraic sum equals the $574 U net production cost variance noted on the income statement.[6]

An examination of variances in general and administrative expense items completes the analysis of the income variance. This is not shown. It would consist of an analysis of the amount of, and reasons for, differences between the budgeted amount and the actual amount for each significant item of general and administrative expense.

Uses of Variances

Analyzing the difference between actual and budgeted income involves many detailed calculations of individual variances. It is easy to get so involved in these details that one loses sight of the purpose of variance analysis, which is to identify the various *causes* of the overall income variance. Decomposing income variances into elements makes it possible to assign these elements to individual managers.

The assignment of variance elements to managers raises questions about performance, but variance calculations themselves do not explain performance. Although an unfavorable variance means that actual income is lower than planned, that is all that label connotes. It does *not* necessarily mean that a manager performed poorly. Similarly, favorable variances do not necessarily imply good performance.

> **Example.** For December, the machining department of Apex Valve Company had a $7,000 U spending variance in its maintenance account (one of the production overhead accounts). Investigation revealed that the department's manager had spent $8,000 in December for an unanticipated overhaul of a machine. Without the overhaul, the variance would have been $1,000 F. However, the maintenance department had advised the machining department's manager that the machine would be worn beyond repair in six months without the overhaul, requiring a replacement machine costing $70,000. After understanding the situation, the factory manager praised the machining department manager for exercising good judgment in authorizing the overhaul.

---

[6]As explained in Chapter 20, if the overhead rate were calculated using *practical capacity* as the definition of normal volume, then the overhead volume variance would reflect idle capacity costs. This variance, although created by the production costing system, may be regarded as a responsibility of the marketing organization.

As this example indicates, managers may receive incorrect and unfair signals about their performance if their superiors automatically draw performance inferences from variance reports rather than investigating the causes of the variances.

Another natural—but unwise—tendency is for managers to pay far closer attention to unfavorable variances than to favorable ones. In many organizations one hears comments to the effect that "our managers only have to explain things when they go off base," that is, when there are unfavorable variances on their reports. The example above illustrates the problems inherent in failing to investigate favorable variances. The variance would have been $1,000 F without the overhaul, yet the decision not to overhaul the machine would have been a poor one.

When investigating variances, it is important to distinguish between those that are *controllable* by a responsibility center's manager and those that are noncontrollable. Although both types of variances are helpful in explaining the *center's economic* performance, the focus when evaluating the *center manager's* performance should be on the controllable variances. (The concept of controllable cost is described in more depth in Chapter 23.)

The example also illustrates a possible cause of any variance: the budgeted amounts may have been based on assumed conditions that differed from those that actually prevailed. In the example, the overhaul was not anticipated when the budget was prepared. Thus, variances often reflect managers' forecasting fallibilities rather than their operating management weaknesses.

In summary, variances can be very useful in signaling possible managerial strengths or shortcomings. But automatically equating the terms *favorable* to good performance and *unfavorable* to poor performance can sometimes lead to unjustified appraisal judgments by superiors and can thereby demoralize subordinate managers and create resentment on their part.

SUMMARY

The difference between budgeted and actual net income can be decomposed into a number of variances, for each of which management needs to understand the cause. These variances are grouped into three categories: production (described in Chapter 20), marketing, and general and administrative.

The marketing variances are of two types: gross margin and selling expenses. Although some people focus on the sales revenue variance, the gross margin variance components are likely to be more meaningful. One of these components, the mix variance, is difficult to calculate, but it is important in many situations.

Variance numbers raise questions that require management's investigation. The numbers do not by themselves indicate what action, if any, needs to be taken. In particular, it is important to distinguish between variances that are controllable by the manager and those that are not.

APPENDIX: VARIANCES WITH VARIABLE COSTING

In variable costing, fixed production overhead costs are treated as period costs rather than product costs. This leads to two differences in a variable costing variance analysis compared with an absorption (full) costing analysis: (1) the margin variances will relate to contribution margin rather than gross margin, and (2) there will be no production overhead volume variance (as was proven in Appendix A to Chapter 20).

Margin Analysis

To illustrate contribution margin variance analysis, consider the information given in part D of Illustration 21–4. The standard *variable* cost of sales is $11.90 per unit ($2.80 for direct material, $5.60 for direct labor, and $3.50 for variable overhead). This $11.90 variable cost is $3.50 less than the $15.40 standard full cost because the standard *fixed* overhead per unit was $3.50.[7] Thus, the budgeted unit contribution margin is $7.00 (i.e., $3.50 higher than the budgeted gross margin) and the actual unit contribution margin is $8.40 (= $4.90 actual gross margin + $3.50). Thus, we have:

$$Budgeted\ margin\ =\ \$7.00 * 200\ units\ =\ \$1,400$$
$$Actual\ margin\ =\ \$8.40 * 190\ units\ =\ \underline{1,596}$$
$$Net\ margin\ variance\ =\ \$1,596 - \$1,400\ =\ \$\ \ 196\ F$$

$$\Delta Unit\ margin\ *\ \ \ \ Actual\ units\ \ \ \ =\ \ Unit\ margin\ variance$$
$$\$1.40\ \ \ \ \ *\ \ \ \ \ \ \ \ \ \ 190\ \ \ \ \ \ \ \ \ \ =\ \ \ \ \ \ \ \ \$266\ F$$

$$\Delta Volume\ \ \ *\ Budgeted\ unit\ margin\ =\ Sales\ volume\ variance$$
$$(1)\ \ \ \ \ *\ \ \ \ \ \ \ \$7.00\ \ \ \ \ \ \ \ =\ \ \ \ \ \ \ \ \ \$70\ U$$

Note that the unit margin variance calculated above, $266 F, is the same as that calculated using gross margin (Illustration 21–4, part C). The $35 F difference in the net margin variances between full costing and variable costing ($231 F – $196 F = $35 F) is thus accounted for by the difference in the two approaches' sales volume variances ($35 U – $70 U = $35 F). This difference in sales volume variance occurs because of the $3.50 per unit fixed production overhead that is not included in the unit contribution margin: the Δvolume of 10 units times this $3.50 per unit difference between unit gross margin and unit contribution margin equals the $35 difference in the sales volume variances of the two approaches.

Other Variances

There is no difference between full costing and variable costing systems' reported direct material and direct labor variances, because these are

---

[7]In variable costing, the cost of sales may include variable selling, general, and administrative costs as well as variable production costs. In this example we are assuming for simplicity that all S, G & A costs are fixed.

variable cost items.[8] Whereas full costing will report both a production overhead spending variance and volume variance, variable costing will report only the spending variance. This spending variance will be the same ($161 U) under either approach, although a variable costing system is more likely to decompose this spending variance into variable cost and fixed cost components. In variable costing, the variable overhead spending variance is part of the total contribution margin variance, whereas the fixed overhead spending variance is part of the total period cost spending variance. Because selling, general, and administrative expenses are treated as period costs under either variable or full costing, the variances in these items will be the same in both systems.

Reconciliation of Income Variance

As shown in Illustration 21–4, full costing reported an income variance of $413 U. If variable costing had been used with the assumptions in that illustration, budgeted income would have been $1,120, and actual income $777, thus giving an income variance of $343 U. (As an exercise, the reader may wish to confirm these amounts.) The difference in the two approaches' income variances is therefore $70 U (= $413 U − $343 U). The $70 more unfavorable income variance under full costing is accounted for by the net of two items: (1) $35 more favorable sales volume variance with full costing (explained above) and (2) the $105 U overhead production volume variance reported by full costing but not by variable costing.

---

[8]As pointed out earlier, some highly automated companies no longer treat direct labor cost as being variable with production volume.

Cases

CASE 21–1 Campar Industries, Inc.

Campar Industries, Inc., was a multidivisional firm whose several divisions competed in different countries. This case deals with variance analysis problems in several of the divisions.

Alpha Division

In its annual profit budget, Alpha Division budgeted product A's sales volume at 24,000 units. Product A's budgeted price was $72 per unit; its standard cost was $43 per unit. Actual sales of product A turned out to be $1,658,250 for a volume of 22,000 units.

Question

Determine Alpha Division's gross margin variances.

Beta Division

Beta Division makes three products. Last month's budgeted and actual sales and margins for these products were as follows:

	Budget		Actual	
	Unit Sales	Unit Margin	Unit Sales	Unit Margin
Product 1	3,200	$12.00	2,850	$12.24
Product 2	1,700	15.60	2,500	15.10
Product 3	5,100	10.80	4,250	10.56
	10,000	$12.00	9,600	$12.241

Question

Determine the gross margin mix, selling price, and sales volume variances. Calculate the net gross margin variance directly, then as a check see if it equals the sum of the three variance components you calculated individually.

Gamma Division

Gamma Division makes a product for which the standard raw materials cost per 100 pounds of finished product is as follows:

60 lbs.	of material X @ $1.69/lb.	$101.40
40 lbs.	of material Y @ $2.34/lb.	93.60
100 lbs.	of materials with total cost	$195.00

Because materials were not supposed to be spoiled during production, these standards included no waste allowance.

During June, actual raw materials usage and costs were:

Material X: Used	5,500 lbs.	@	$1.69/lb.	=	$ 9,295
Material Y: Used	4,500 lbs.	@	$2.53/lb.	=	11,385
	10,000 lbs.				$20,680

Actual finished product: 9,900 lbs.

Question

Calculate the raw materials variances for June, referring back to Chapter 20 if necessary. *Note:* This problem contains a raw materials mix variance, analogous to the gross margin mix variance described in this chapter.

Delta Division

Delta Division makes two products, A and B. Both products use the same raw materials and are produced in the same factory by the same work force. In preparing its annual statement of budgeted gross margin, Delta's management used the following assumptions:

(Relates to Delta Division)		
	Products	
	A	B
Sales (units)	1,900	3,100
Unit selling price	$300.00	$185.00
Standard unit costs:		
Raw materials (@ $1.80/lb.)	$72.00	$54.00
Direct labor (@ $25.00/hr.)	$62.50	$37.50
Overhead (@ 120% of DL$)	$75.00	$45.00
Other production standards:		
Production volume (units)	1,900	3,100
Overhead budget: $0.80 per DL$ plus $94,000 fixed		
Overhead absorption: Based on *actual* DL$		

The year's actual results were as follows:

1. 1,750 units of A were sold for a total of $533,750.

2. 3,250 units of B were sold for a total of $601,250.

3. Production totaled 1,800 units of A and 3,300 units of B.

4. 180,000 pounds of raw materials were purchased and used; their total cost was $330,480.

5. 9,450 hours of direct labor were worked at a total cost of $233,880.

6. Actual overhead costs were $320,000.

Questions

1. Do as detailed an analysis of variances as the data given permit.

2. Prepare a summary statement for presentation to Delta's top management showing the year's budgeted and actual gross margin and an explanation of the difference between them.

CASE 21–2 Darius Company

Darius Company's operating budget for October had anticipated pretax operating income of $75,000. Drew Mackenzie, Darius's general manager, was therefore very disappointed when, in early November, Darius's controller gave Mackenzie a report showing that only $3,000 of operating income had been earned in October (see Exhibit 1). Mackenzie requested that the controller prepare an analysis of the $72,000 unfavorable operating income variance as soon as possible.

EXHIBIT 1

DARIUS COMPANY
Income Statement and Variances
For the Month of October
($000)

	Budget	Actual	Variance
Sales	$1,080	$1,064	
Standard cost of goods sold	960	912	
Standard gross margin	120	152	$ 32 F
Production variances	—	(94)	94 U
Actual gross margin	120	58	62 U
Selling and administrative	45	55	10 U
Operating income	$ 75	$ 3	$72 U

The October budget had incorporated the standards and budgets that are given below along with actual data.

Marketing. Budgeted sales had been 200,000 units (10 percent market share) at a unit margin of $0.60. Actual sales were 190,000 units (9.25 percent market share) at a unit margin of $0.80. Selling expenses had been budgeted at $12,000 fixed costs for the month; $14,120 was actually incurred.

Production. The standard production volume used for overhead absorption purposes was 200,000 units per month. October's budgeted production volume used in developing the annual operating budget had been 205,000 units, but actual October pro-

duction volume turned out to be only 180,000 units. Darius's only product had a standard unit cost of $4.80, comprised of $0.60 direct material cost (4 pounds at $0.15 per pound), $2.70 direct labor cost (0.3 hour at $9.00 per hour), and $1.50 overhead ($0.75 of which was budgeted variable overhead). In October, 700,000 pounds of material were purchased for $126,000 and used in production; 56,944 direct labor-hours costing $523,880 were used; and overhead costs of $308,120 were incurred.

Question

Prepare as detailed an explanation as possible of the October $72,000 unfavorable income variance.

CASE 21–3 Dallas Consulting Group*

"I just don't understand why you're worried about analyzing our profit variance," said Dave Lundberg to his partner, Adam Dixon. Both Lundberg and Dixon were part-

___
*Copyright © by the President and Fellows of Harvard College. Harvard Business School case 180-172.

ners in the Dallas Consulting Group (DCG). "Look, we made $120,000 more profit than we expected in 1993 (see Exhibit 1). That's great as far as I am concerned," continued Lundberg. Adam Dixon agreed to come up with data that would help sort out the causes of DCG's $120,000 profit variance.

EXHIBIT 1
1993 BUDGET AND ACTUAL RESULTS
(thousands)

	Budget	Actual	Variance
Revenues	$2,550	$2,670	$120
Expenses:			
Salaries	1,850	1,850	—
Income	$ 700	$ 820	$120

EXHIBIT 2
DETAIL OF REVENUE CALCULATIONS

Service*	Hours	Rate	Amount
Budget:			
A	6,000	$125	$ 750,000
B	9,000	200	1,800,000
	15,000		$2,550,000
Actual:			
A	2,000	$135	$ 270,000
B	12,000	200	2,400,000
	14,000		$2,670,000

*Service A = time-motion studies.
Service B = consulting for production operations.

DCG was a professional services partnership of three established consultants who specialize in cost reduction through the use of time-motion studies and through the streamlining of production operations by optimizing physical layout, manpower, and so on. In both of these areas, DCG consultants spent a great deal of time studying customers' operations.

The three partners each received fixed salaries that represented the largest portion of operating expenses. All three were professors, and each used his or her university office for DCG business. DCG itself had only a post office box. All other DCG employees, primarily graduate students at the university, were also paid fixed salaries. No other significant operating costs were incurred by the partnership.

Revenues consisted solely of professional fees charged to customers for the two different types of services DCG offered. Charges were based on the number of hours actually worked on a job. Thus, an increase in the actual number of hours worked on a job would cause a corresponding increase in revenue. Since all salaries were fixed, however, DCG's total operating expenses would not change.

Following the conversation with Lundberg, Dixon gathered the data summarized in Exhibit 2. He took the data with him to Lundberg's office and said, "I think I can identify several reasons for our increased profits. First of all, we raised the price for time-motion studies to $135 per hour. Also, if you remember, we originally estimated that the 10 consulting firms in the Dallas area would probably average about 15,000 hours of work each in 1993, so the total industry volume in Dallas would be 150,000 hours. However, a check with all of the local consulting firms indicates that the actual total consulting market must have been around 112,000 hours."

"This is indeed interesting, Adam," replied Lundberg. "This new data leads me to believe that there are several causes for our increased profits, some of which may have been negative.... Do you think you could quantify the effects of these factors in terms of dollars?"

Question

Use your knowledge of profit variance analysis to quantify the performance of DCG for 1993 and explain the significance of each variance to Mr. Lundberg.

CASE 21–4 Woodside Products, Inc.

Phil Brooks, president of Woodside Products, Inc., called Marilyn Mynar into his office one morning in early July 1993. Ms. Mynar was a business major in college and was employed by Woodside during her college summer vacation.

"Marilyn," Brooks began, "I've just received the preliminary financial statements for our 1993 fiscal year, which ended June 30. Both our board of directors and our shareholders will want, and deserve, an explanation of why our pretax income was virtually unchanged even though revenues were up by $363,000. The accountant is tied up working with our outside CPA on the annual audit, so I thought you could do the necessary analysis. What I'd like is as much of a detailed explanation of the $1,954 profit increase as you can glean from these data [Exhibit 1]. I'd also like you to draft a statement for the next board meeting that explains the same $1,954 profit increase, but in a fairly intuitive, summary way. Of course, that doesn't mean 'don't use any numbers' "!

EXHIBIT 1

Operating Results
For the Years Ended June 30

1992		1993
$8,283,750	Sales revenues	$8,646,750
4,846,875	Cost of sales	5,255,388
3,436,875	Gross margin	3,391,362
2,086,810	Selling and administrative costs	2,039,343
$1,350,065	Income before taxes	$1,352,019

Other 1992 Data

1. Sales = 88,125 units @ $94.
2. Cost of sales = 88,125 units @ $55.
3. Selling and administrative costs were $4.42 per unit variable selling cost plus $1,697,298 fixed S&A.
4. Production volume and sales volume were equal.
5. Production costs per unit were:

Materials	$20.00	(8 lbs. @ $2.50)
Direct labor	12.00	(0.75 hr. @ $16.00)
Variable overhead	4.00	(per unit)
Fixed overhead	19.00	(based on long-term std. volume of 88,125 units)
	$55.00	

Other 1993 Data

1. Sales = 82,350 units @ $105.
2. Cost of sales includes 1993 production cost variances.
3. Selling and administrative costs were $4.70 per unit variable selling cost plus $1,652,298 fixed S&A.
4. Production volume was 81,100 units; standard volume was 88,125 units.
5. 626,200 pounds of material @ $2.90 were consumed by production.
6. 64,860 direct labor-hours were worked @ $16.80.
7. Actual variable overhead costs were $359,500.

Question

Prepare the detailed analysis of the $1,954 profit increase from fiscal 1992 to fiscal 1993 and draft an explanation for Woodside's board of directors, as requested by Phil Brooks. For the board's report, you may make any reasonable conjectures you wish as to what caused the variances you have calculated. For both years, assume that inventory was valued at $55 per unit. Assume also that none of the members of the board of directors has expertise in accounting calculations or terminology.

22

Control: The Management Control Environment

In this and the next three chapters we describe the nature of the management control process and the use of accounting information in that process. This chapter describes the environment in which management control takes place: the organization, the rules and procedures governing its work, the organization's culture, and the organization's external environment.

Management control focuses on organization units called responsibility centers. There are four types of responsibility centers that can be used, depending on the individual situation—revenue centers, expense centers, profit centers, and investment centers. Profit centers and investment centers may require the use of transfer pricing, which this chapter also addresses.

MANAGEMENT CONTROL

An organization has goals; it wants to accomplish certain things. It also has strategies for attaining these goals, which are developed through an activity called **strategy formulation.** Strategy formulation is not a systematic activity because strategies change whenever a new opportunity to achieve the goals—or a new threat to attaining the goals—is perceived, and opportunities and threats do not appear according to a regular schedule.

Essentially, the management control process takes the goals and strategies as given and seeks to assure that the strategies are implemented by the organization. Formally, **management control** is defined as the process by which managers influence members of the organization to implement the organization's strategies efficiently and effectively.

The word *control* suggests activities that ensure the work of the organization proceeds as planned, which is certainly part of the management control function. However, management control also involves planning, which is deciding what should be done. The organization will not know how to implement strategies unless plans are developed that indicate the best way of doing so.

These plans have essentially two parts: (1) a statement of objectives, which are the results that the managers should achieve in order to implement strategies, and (2) the resources required in order to attain these objectives. (The words *goals* and *objectives* are often used interchangeably. We use **goals** for broad, usually nonquantitative, long-run plans relating to the organization as a whole, and **objectives** for more specific, often quantitative, shorter-run plans for individual responsibility centers.)

Moreover, managers do not always seek *planned* results. If there is a better way than the one indicated in the plan, managers ordinarily should employ that better way. Therefore, the statement that management control seeks to assure *desired* results is more realistic than a reference to planned results.

With respect to a machine or other mechanical process, we can say that the process is either "in control" or "out of control"; that is, either the machine is doing what it is supposed to be doing, or it is not. In an organization, such a dichotomy is not appropriate. An organization is rarely "out of control"; rather, its *degree* of control lies somewhere along a continuum ranging from excellent to poor.

Management control is a process (described in the succeeding three chapters) that takes place in an environment. This chapter discusses some of the important characteristics associated with this environment.

THE ENVIRONMENT

Four facets of the management control environment discussed in this section are as follows: the nature of organizations; rules, guidelines, and procedures that govern the actions of the organization's members; the organization's culture; and the external environment.

The Nature of Organizations

A building with its equipment is not an organization. Rather, it is the people who work in the building that constitute the organization. A crowd walking down a street is not an organization, nor are the spectators at a football game when they are behaving as individual spectators. But the cheering section at a game is an organization; its members work together under the direction of the cheerleaders. An organization is a group of human beings who work together for one or more purposes. These purposes are called *goals.*

Management.   An organization has one or more leaders. Except in rare circumstances, a group of people can work together to accomplish the organization's goals only if they are led. These leaders are called **managers** or, collectively, **the management.** An organization's managers perform many important tasks, among these are the following:

· Deciding what the organization's goals should be.

· Deciding on the objectives that should be achieved in order to move toward these goals.

· Communicating these goals and objectives to members of the organization.

· Deciding on the tasks that are to be performed in order to achieve these objectives and on the resources that are to be used in carrying out these tasks.

· Ensuring that the activities of the various organizational parts are coordinated.

· Matching individuals to tasks for which they are suited.

· Motivating these individuals to carry out their tasks.

· Observing how well these individuals are performing their tasks.

· Taking corrective action when the need arises.

Just as the leader of a cheering section performs these functions, so too does the chief executive officer of General Electric Company.

Organization Hierarchy.   A manager can supervise only a limited number of subordinates. (Old Testament writers put this number at 10.) It follows that an organization of substantial size must have several layers of managers in the organization structure. Authority runs from the top unit down through the successive layers. Such an arrangement is called an **organization hierarchy.**

The formal relationships among the various managers can be diagrammed in an **organization chart.** Illustration 22–1 shows a partial organization chart. A number of organization units report to the chief executive officer (CEO). Some of these are **line units**; that is, their activities are directly associated with achieving the objectives of the organization. They produce and market goods or services. Others are **staff units,** which exist to provide various support services to other units and to the chief executive officer. The principal line units are called *divisions* in the illustration. Each division contains a number of *departments,* and within each department are a number of *sections.* Different companies and nonbusiness organizations use different names for these layers of organization units. Also, in some companies, the chairman of the board is the chief executive officer and the president is the chief operating officer (COO).

ILLUSTRATION 22–1
PARTIAL ORGANIZATION CHART

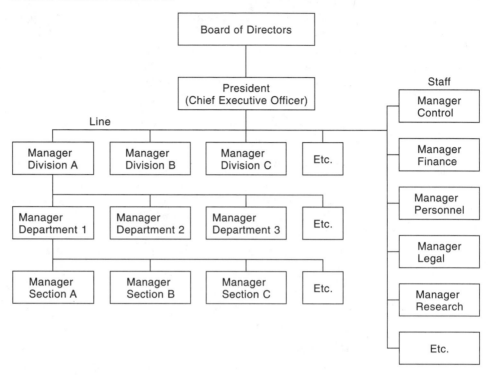

Responsibility Centers. All the units in Illustration 22–1 are **organization units.** Thus, Section A of Department 1 of Division A is an organization unit. Division A itself, including all of its departments and sections, is also an organization unit. Each of these units is headed by a manager who is responsible for the work done by the unit; each unit therefore is called a **responsibility center.** Managers are responsible in the sense that they are held accountable for the activities of their organization units. These activities include not only the work done within the responsibility center but also its relationships with the external environment (described below). Each of the four types of responsibility centers is described in a later section.

Rules, Guidelines, and Procedures

An organization has a set of rules, guidelines, and procedures that influence the way its members behave. Some of these controls are written; others are less formal. They vary, depending in part on the size, complexity, and other characteristics of the organization and in part on the wishes of the organization's senior management. These rules, guidelines, and procedures exist until the organization changes them. Typically, such change comes slowly.

Some of these controls are physical: security guards, computer passwords, and the like. Others are written in manuals, memoranda, or other documents. Still others are based on the oral instructions of managers. Some may even involve nonverbal communication, such as the appropriate mode of office attire: since the boss wears casual clothes, you do too. An important set of rules is the written and unwritten rules relating to the rewards the organization offers for good performance or the penalties for substandard performance and prohibited activities.

Culture

Each organization has its own culture, with norms of behavior that are derived in part from tradition, in part from external influences (such as the norms of the community and of labor unions), and in part from the attitudes of senior management and the board of directors. Cultural factors are unwritten, and they are therefore difficult to identify. Nevertheless, they are important. For example, they explain why one entity has much better actual control than another, although both have adequate formal management control systems.

An important aspect of culture is the attitude of senior management, particularly on the part of the chief executive officer and the chairman[1] of the board, toward control. This has an important influence on the organization's control environment. Some top managers prefer tight controls; others prefer loose controls. Either can work well in appropriate circumstances.

External Environment

The external environment of an organization includes everything that is outside of the organization itself, including customers, suppliers, competitors, the community, regulatory agencies, and others. The organization is continually involved in a two-way interaction with its external environment.

The nature of the environment in which an organization operates affects the nature of its management control system. Differences in environmental influences on the organization can be summarized in one word: uncertainty. In an organization having relatively certain revenues and whose technology is not subject to rapid change (e.g., pulp-making), management control is considerably different from management control in an organization that operates in a fiercely competitive marketplace and whose products must be changed frequently in order to take advantage of new technological breakthroughs (e.g., computers).

---

[1]The authors fully realize that the position of chairman of the board may be held by a woman. We use the term *chairman* because it is almost universally used in business practice irrespective of the position holder's gender (unlike in some universities and other nonprofit organizations, where the titles *chairperson, chair,* and *chairwoman* are also used).

ILLUSTRATION 22–2
NATURE OF A RESPONSIBILITY CENTER

A. Analogy to a Generating Plant

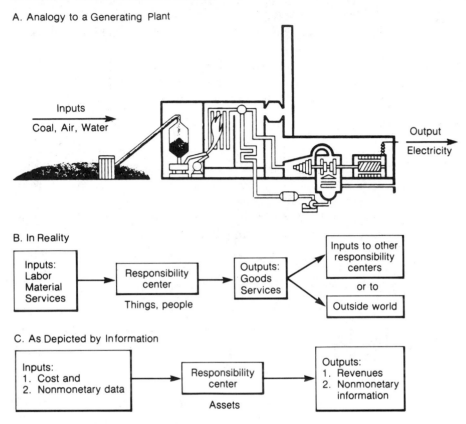

B. In Reality

Inputs:
Labor
Material
Services → Responsibility center → Outputs: Goods Services → Inputs to other responsibility centers / or to / Outside world

Things, people

C. As Depicted by Information

Inputs:
1. Cost and
2. Nonmonetary data → Responsibility center → Outputs:
1. Revenues
2. Nonmonetary information

Assets

An organization that operates in a relatively uncertain environment relies more on the *informal* judgment of its managers than on its formal management control system. Also, managers at all levels in such an organization need prompt, accurate information about what is going on in the outside world.

RESPONSIBILITY CENTERS

Illustration 22–2 provides a basis for describing the nature of responsibility centers. The top section depicts an electricity generating plant, which in some important respects is analogous to a responsibility center. Like a responsibility center, the plant (1) uses *inputs* to (2) do *work,* which (3) results in *outputs.* In the case of the generating plant, the inputs are coal, water, and air, which the plant combines to do the work of turning a turbine connected to a generator rotor. The outputs are kilowatts of electricity.

Inputs and Outputs

As shown in part B of Illustration 22–2, a responsibility center also has inputs: physical quantities of material, hours of various types of labor, and a variety of services. Usually, both current and noncurrent assets are also required. The responsibility center performs work with these resources. As a result of this work, it produces outputs: goods (if tangible) or services (if intangible). These products go either to other responsibility centers within the organization or to customers in the outside world.

Part C of the illustration shows information about these inputs, assets, and outputs. Although the resources used to produce outputs are mostly nonmonetary things such as pounds of material and hours of labor, for purposes of management control these things must be measured with a monetary common denominator so that the physically unlike elements of resources can be combined. The monetary measure of the resources used in a responsibility center is *cost.* In addition to cost information, nonaccounting information on such matters as the physical quantity of material used, its quality, and the skill level of the work force is also useful.

If the outputs of a responsibility center are sold to an outside customer, accounting measures these outputs in terms of revenue. If, however, goods or services are transferred to other responsibility centers within the organization, the measure of output may be either a monetary measure, such as the cost of the goods or services transferred, or a nonmonetary measure, such as the number of units of output.

Responsibility Accounting

Responsibility center managers need information about what has taken place in their respective areas of responsibility. In addition to historical information about inputs (cost) and outputs, managers also need information about planned *future* inputs and outputs. The management accounting construct that deals with both planned and actual accounting information about the inputs and outputs of a responsibility center is called **responsibility accounting.** Responsibility accounting involves a continuous flow of information that corresponds to the continuous flow of inputs into, and outputs from, an organization's responsibility centers.

Contrast with Full Cost Accounting. An essential characteristic of responsibility accounting is that it focuses on responsibility centers. Full cost accounting focuses on goods and services (formally called *products*) rather than on responsibility centers. This difference in focus is what distinguishes responsibility accounting from full cost accounting. In making this distinction we do not mean to imply that product cost accounting and responsibility accounting are two separate accounting systems. In fact, they are two related parts of the management accounting system.

It is common for a given responsibility center in an organization to perform work related to several products. For example, the Ford Taurus and Mercury Sable automobiles (products) are assembled in the same plants (responsibility centers). In each responsibility center, different inputs are

ILLUSTRATION 22–3
CONTRAST BETWEEN FULL COSTS AND RESPONSIBILITY COSTS

A. Full Product Costs

Cost element:	Total	Product X	Product Y
Direct material..	$20,000	$14,000	$ 6,000
Direct labor	13,000	8,000	5,000
Indirect production....................................	9,620	5,920	3,700
Selling and administration..........................	5,500	3,645	1,855
Total costs	$48,120	$31,565	$16,555

B. Responsibility Costs

	Total	Departments (Responsibility Centers) 1	2	3	4
Cost element:					
Direct material..............	$20,000	$16,000	$ 4,000		
Direct labor	13,000	4,000	9,000		
Supervision.................	4,240	800	1,200	$ 840	$1,400
Other labor costs	6,970	1,500	170	2,200	3,100
Supplies	1,290	660	330	100	200
Other costs	2,620	880	440	500	800
Total costs	$48,120	$23,840	$15,140	$3,640	$5,500

C. In Matrix Format

Department	Product X	Product Y	Responsibility Costs
1	16,496	7,344	$23,840
2	9,184	5,956	15,140
3	2,240	1,400	3,640
4	3,645	1,855	5,500
Product Costs	$31,565	$16,555	$48,120

consumed in order to produce the center's output; these inputs are called **cost elements** (or, sometimes, **line items**). That is, there are three different dimensions of cost information, each of which answers a different question: (1) Where was the cost incurred (responsibility center dimension)? (2) For what output was the cost incurred (product dimension)? (3) What type of resource was used (cost element dimension)?

Illustration 22–3 shows how these three dimensions of cost information typically appear in an organization's cost reporting system. For simplicity, it is assumed that this is a manufacturing company with only four departments: 1 and 2 are the production departments, fabrication and assembly; department 3 provides all production support functions; and department 4 performs all selling and administrative activities. Part A of the illustration shows the full costs of the organization's two products for a one-month period, and the details of the cost elements that make up these full costs. Note that it is impossible to identify from the part A information what costs the managers of Departments 1, 2, and 3 were individually responsible for. In particular, the costs of Department 3 have been allocated first to the two production departments and then, through their overhead rates, to the two products; hence, Department 3 costs are a portion of the amount shown as each product's production overhead costs.

By contrast, responsibility accounting identifies the amount of costs that each of the four departmental managers is responsible for, as shown in part B of the illustration. Note that part B, however, does not show the costs of the two products. Both types of information are needed. Note also that the total product costs ($48,120) are equal to the total responsibility costs. The two parts are different arrangements of the same underlying data.

Full product costs and responsibility costs, then, are two different ways of "slicing the same pie." This is depicted in part C of Illustration 22–3, which summarizes the cost data in a matrix format to show both product costs and responsibility costs, without including the cost element details. If cost information in the cells of the matrix is added across a *row,* the total is responsibility accounting data, which is useful for management control purposes. If this information is instead added down a *column,* the total is product cost information, which is useful for pricing decisions and product profitability evaluation.

In addition to the department managers, some organizations have *product managers* who are responsible for the product costs in the columns of the matrix (as well as for their products' revenues). Such organizations are called *matrix organizations,* and in them both the columns and rows of part C represent responsibility centers.

Effectiveness and Efficiency

The performance of a responsibility center manager can be measured in terms of the effectiveness and efficiency of the work of the responsibility center. **Effectiveness** means how well the responsibility center does its job—that is, the extent to which it produces the intended or expected results. **Efficiency** is used in its engineering sense—that is, the amount of output per unit of input. An efficient operation either produces a given quantity of outputs with a minimum consumption of inputs or produces the largest possible outputs from a given quantity of inputs.

Effectiveness is always related to the organization's objectives. Efficiency, per se, is not. An efficient responsibility center is one that does whatever it does with the lowest consumption of resources. However, if what it does (i.e., its output) is an inadequate contribution to the accomplishment of the organization's objectives, then it is ineffective.

Example. If a department responsible for processing incoming sales orders does so at a low cost per order processed, it is efficient. If, however, the department is slow in answering customer queries about the status of orders, thus antagonizing customers to the point where they take their business elsewhere, the department is ineffective.

Stated informally, then, efficiency means "doing things right," whereas effectiveness means "doing the right things."

In many responsibility centers a measure of efficiency can be developed that relates actual costs to a number that expresses what costs *should* be for a given amount of output (that is, to a standard or budget). Such a measure can be a useful indication, but never a perfect measure, of efficiency for at least two reasons: (1) recorded costs are not a precisely accurate measure of resources consumed, and (2) standards are, at best, only approximate measures of what resource consumption ideally should have been in the circumstances prevailing.

A responsibility center should be both effective *and* efficient; it is not a case of one or the other. In some situations both effectiveness and efficiency can be encompassed within a single measure. For example, in profit-oriented organizations, profit measures the combined result of effectiveness and efficiency. When an overall measure does not exist, classifying the various performance measures used as relating either to effectiveness (e.g., warranty claims per 1,000 units sold) or efficiency (e.g., labor-hours per unit produced) is useful.

TYPES OF RESPONSIBILITY CENTERS

As previously noted, an important business goal is to earn a satisfactory return on investment (ROI). Return on investment is the ratio:

$$\text{ROI} = \frac{\text{Revenues} - \text{Expenses}}{\text{Investment}}$$

The three elements of this ratio lead to definitions of the types of responsibility centers important in management control systems. These are (1) revenue centers, (2) expense centers, (3) profit centers, and (4) investment centers.

Revenue Centers

If a responsibility center manager is held accountable for the outputs of the center as measured in monetary terms (revenues) but is not responsible for the costs of the goods or services that the center sells, then the responsibility center is a **revenue center.** Many companies treat regional sales offices as revenue centers. In retailing companies, it is customary to treat each selling department as a revenue center.

A sales organization treated as a revenue center usually has the additional responsibility for controlling its selling expenses (travel, advertising, point-of-purchase displays, and so on). Therefore, revenue centers are often expense centers as well. However, a revenue center manager is not responsible for the center's major cost item—its cost of goods and services sold. Thus, subtracting just the selling expenses for which the manager is responsible from the center's revenues does not result in a very meaningful number, and certainly does not measure the center's profit.

Expense Centers

If the control system measures the expenses (i.e., the costs) incurred by a responsibility center but does not measure its outputs in terms of revenues, then the responsibility center is called an **expense center.** Every responsibility center has outputs; that is, it does something. In many cases, however, measuring these outputs in terms of revenues is neither feasible nor necessary. For example, it would be extremely difficult to measure the monetary value of the accounting or legal department's outputs. Although measuring the revenue value of the outputs of an individual production department generally is relatively easy to do, there is no reason for doing so if the responsibility of the department manager is to produce a stated *quantity* of outputs at the lowest feasible cost. For these reasons, most individual production departments and most staff units are expense centers.

Expense centers are not quite the same as cost centers. Recall from Chapter 18 that a cost center (or cost pool) is a device used in a full cost accounting system to collect costs that are subsequently to be charged to cost objects. In a given company most but not all cost centers are also expense centers. However, a cost center such as "Occupancy" is not a responsibility center at all and, hence, is not an expense center.

Standard Cost Centers. A special type of expense center in which standard costs have been set for many of its cost elements is called a **standard cost center.** Actual performance is measured by the *variances* between its actual costs and these standards (as was described in Chapter 20). Because standard cost systems are used in operations having a high degree of task repetition, such operations are also the settings for standard cost centers. Examples include all kinds of assembly-line operations, fast-food restaurants, blood-testing laboratories, and automobile service facilities. By contrast, most production support and corporate staff departments are not standard cost centers.

Profit Centers

Revenue is a monetary measure of outputs; expense (or cost) is a monetary measure of inputs, or resources consumed. Profit is the difference between revenue and expense. If performance in a responsibility center is measured in terms of the difference between (1) the revenues it earns and (2) the expenses it incurs, the responsibility center is a **profit center.**

In financial accounting, revenue is recognized only when it is realized by a sale to an outside customer. By contrast, in responsibility accounting, revenue measures the outputs of a responsibility center in a given accounting period *whether or not the company realizes the revenue in that period.* Thus, a factory is a profit center if it "sells" its output to the sales department and records the revenue and cost of such sales. Likewise, a service department, such as the corporate training department, may "sell" its services to the responsibility centers that receive these services. These "sales" generate revenues for the service department. Since the difference between sales revenues and the cost of these sales is profit, the service department is a profit center if both of these elements are measured.[2]

A given responsibility center is a profit center only if management *decides* to measure that center's outputs in terms of revenues. Revenues for a company as a whole are automatically generated when the company makes sales to the outside world. By contrast, revenues for an internal organization unit are recognized only if management decides that it is a good idea to do so. No accounting principle *requires* that revenues be measured for individual responsibility centers within a company. In recent years many companies in their total quality management programs have been emphasizing that "every department has customers: some have external customers, others have internal customers." To reinforce this philosophy, many departments that formerly were expense centers have been converted to profit centers. With some ingenuity, practically any expense center could be turned into a profit center because some way of putting a selling price on the output of most responsibility centers can be found. The question is whether there are sufficient benefits in doing so.

Advantages of Profit Centers.   A profit center resembles a business in miniature. Like a separate company, it has an income statement that shows revenues, expenses, and profit. Most of the decisions made by the profit center manager affect the numbers on this income statement. The income statement for a profit center, therefore, is a basic management control document. Because their performance is measured by profit, the managers of profit centers are motivated to make decisions about inputs and outputs that will increase the profit reported for their profit centers. Since they act somewhat as they would if they were running their own businesses, the profit center is a good training ground for general management responsibility. The use of the profit center concept is one of the important tools that has made possible the decentralization of profit responsibility in large companies.

Criteria for Profit Centers.   In deciding whether to treat a responsibility center as a profit center, the following points are relevant:

1.   Using the profit center idea involves extra recordkeeping. The profit center itself has the extra work of measuring output in revenue terms; the

---

[2]In some such service centers, the prices for the center's services are set with the intent of recovering exactly the costs of the services—that is, breaking even. Even though the goal is to earn zero profit, the center is still a profit center because it is responsible for both its revenues and expenses. In fact, a profit center can even have a negative profit goal, indicating that its budgeted costs exceed its budgeted revenues.

responsibility centers that receive its outputs have the work of recording the cost of goods or services received.

2. If the manager of a responsibility center has little authority to decide on the quantity and quality of its outputs or on the relation of output to costs, then a profit center is usually of little use as a control device. This does not imply that the manager of a profit center must have *complete* control over outputs and inputs; few, if any, managers have such complete authority.

3. When senior management requires responsibility centers to use a service furnished by another responsibility center, the service usually is furnished at no charge, and the service unit therefore is not a profit center. For example, if senior management requires internal audits, the audited units usually are not asked to pay for the cost of the internal auditing service, and the internal auditing unit therefore is not a profit center.

4. If outputs are fairly homogeneous (e.g., cement), a nonmonetary measure of output (e.g., tons of cement produced) may be adequate, and no substantial advantage may be gained in converting these outputs to a monetary measure of revenue.

5. To the extent that the profit center technique puts managers in business for themselves, it promotes a spirit of competition. In many situations, competition provides a powerful incentive for good management. In other situations, however, where organization units should cooperate closely with one another, the profit center device may generate excessive friction between profit centers, to the detriment of the company's overall welfare. Also, it may generate too much interest in short-run profits to the detriment of long-run results.

Transfer Prices   A **transfer price** measures the value of products (i.e., goods or services) furnished by a profit center to other responsibility centers within a company. It is to be contrasted with a *market price,* which measures exchanges between a company and its outside customers. Internal exchanges that are measured by transfer prices result in (1) *revenue* for the responsibility center furnishing (i.e., selling) the product and (2) *cost* for the responsibility center receiving (i.e., buying) the product. Whenever a company has profit centers, transfer prices usually are required. There are two general types of transfer prices: the market-based price and the cost-based price.

Market-Based Transfer Prices. If a market price for the product exists, a **market-based transfer price** is usually preferable to a cost-based price. The buying responsibility center should ordinarily not be expected to pay more internally than it would have to pay if it purchased from an outside vendor, nor should the selling center ordinarily be entitled to more revenue than it could obtain by selling to an outside customer. If the market price is abnormal, as when an outside vendor sets a low "distress" price in order to use temporarily idle capacity, then such temporary aberrations are ordinarily disregarded in arriving at transfer prices. The market price may be adjusted downward to reflect the fact that credit costs (e.g., bad debt losses) and possibly certain selling costs are not incurred in an internal exchange. This downward adjustment, usually only a few percentage points, assures that the buying center is not indifferent between buying within the company or on the outside.

Market-based prices, where available, are widely used.[3] They have the benefit of being reasonably objective rather than a function of the relative negotiating skills of the selling and buying profit center managers. Also, many companies expect their profit centurs to deal with one another almost literally "at arm's length" as independent businesses, and market-based prices add to the realism of this business relationship. In practice, however, the "true" market price is sometimes not clear, because different suppliers may set different prices on essentially identical items. A clearly stated policy (e.g., "the lowest available price, after consideration of supplier reliability and other factors such as warranty, delivery, and credit terms") or an arbitration mechanism (described below) is needed to deal with these market-price ambiguities.

Cost-Based Transfer Prices. In a great many situations, no reliable market price exists for use as a basis for the transfer price. In these situations a **cost-based transfer price** is used. If feasible, the cost should be a *standard* cost. If it is an actual cost, the selling responsibility center has little incentive to control efficiency, because any cost increases will be automatically passed on to the buying center in the transfer price.

Senior management may specify the method of computing cost and the amount of profit to be included in the transfer price in order to lessen the chance of arguments. To avoid disputes, any policy statement as to how costs and profit are to be computed must be thorough and carefully worded. In particular, short-term per-unit costs may be different from longer-term costs. There can also be questions as to whether all of the cost elements normally included in the seller's definition of full cost should be included in the definition of cost used to determine internal prices. Also,

---

[3]Based on a survey of 239 large companies, Richard F. Vancil, in *Decentralization: Managerial Ambiguity by Design* (New York: Financial Executives Research Foundation, 1979), p. 180, reported the prevalence of various transfer-pricing policies as follows:

Basis of Transfer Price	Percent
Market price	31
Negotiation	22
Full cost plus profit	17
Full cost	25
Variable costs	5
	100

disputes—or at least resentment on the part of the buyer—may occur if market conditions have squeezed the seller's outside profit margins to a lower level than that specified in the policy statement.[4]

Negotiation and Arbitration.   Because of the potential areas for disagreement in both market-based and cost-based transfer pricing, such prices are sometimes negotiated between buyer and seller rather than being set by reference to outside prices or by a formula applied to the seller's costs. Also, the seller is sometimes willing to depart from the normal company transfer price policy. For example, the selling responsibility center may be willing to sell below the normal market price rather than lose the business, which could happen if the buying responsibility center took advantage of a temporarily low outside price. In such circumstances, the two parties negotiate a deal.

If either responsibility center manager lacks complete freedom to act or the parties have unequal bargaining powers, these negotiations will not always lead to an equitable result. The prospective buying center may not have **sourcing freedom**—the power of threatening to take its business elsewhere—or the prospective seller may not have the power of refusing to do the work. When such conditions exist, there usually needs to be an arbitration mechanism to settle transfer pricing disputes. Such negotiations and arbitration can be very time consuming.

> **Example.**   A U.S.-based automobile company decided to market a car in the United States that would be manufactured in one of the company's European plants. It took almost one full year for the European manufacturing profit center and the U.S. marketing profit center to reach agreement on the transfer price.

Risk of Suboptimization.   Usually, profit centers are not, in fact, legally independent business entities. (When they are legally separate, they have the same parent.) When they engage in transactions among themselves, there is sometimes the risk that a decision that will increase a given profit center's reported income will not increase the *total* company's income. This **risk of suboptimization** may exist when the selling profit center's normal transfer price is higher than its short-run costs, which is almost always the case.

> **Example.**   Division B buys component X from Division A. Division B uses this component in product Y. The current transfer price for X, which includes full costs plus a profit margin, is $50. Division B's *variable* cost of product Y, including the $50 for component X, is $150 per unit (i.e., $100 of variable cost

---

[4]If the buying and selling responsibility centers are located in different countries (e.g., G.M. selling items made in one of its U.S. parts plants to one of its European assembly plants), then the laws of either country may impact how the transfer price is set. The intent of the laws is to limit the extent to which profits can be shifted from a high-tax country to a low-tax country by manipulating the transfer price. Further discussion of these laws is beyond the scope of this introductory text.

is added by B's production and selling operations). Both divisions currently have considerable excess capacity. This has led Division B to consider temporarily contribution pricing (described in Chapter 26) product Y. Division B has the opportunity, without spoiling the market, to sell 1,000 units of Y to a new customer on a one-time basis for $145 per unit. Since this is less than B's $150 per unit variable cost, B rejects this opportunity.

However, it happens that A's variable cost for component X is only $20 per unit, making the *company's* variable cost for product Y only $120 per unit ($20 variable cost in A plus $100 in B). Thus, the company could earn a contribution of $25 per unit (= $145 price – $120 variable costs) on the deal that B has turned down. Adherence to the established transfer prices has therefore led to suboptimization for the company as a whole and for each division.

This example of suboptimization probably is found more often in textbooks than in practice. Since it is in the self-interest of both managers that the sale be made to the outside customer at a below-normal price, the sensible course of action is for them to get together and negotiate a mutually agreeable transfer price. This price would be higher than the selling division's variable cost but lower than its normal transfer price. In effect, the contribution margin from the transaction would be divided fairly between the two divisions.

Multiple Criteria.   Companies seek many things in their transfer pricing policies: objectivity, realism, fairness to all parties involved, a minimum of time spent in negotiating and arbitrating, and minimum risk of suboptimization. They also want the prices eventually to result in measured profits that reflect the "true" economics of each of the profit centers involved. For example, if Division A sells to Division B on an ongoing basis, corporate management does not want Division B to look more profitable than it really is solely because unrealistically low transfer prices result in profit arbitrarily being shifted from A to B. (Such a hidden subsidy could lead to a decision to increase investment in Division B when in fact the expansion is not warranted.) These various criteria, particularly realism versus risk of suboptimization, often conflict. Not surprisingly, therefore, one frequently hears profit center managers express dissatisfaction with the particular transfer pricing approach used in their company.

Investment Centers

An **investment center** is a responsibility center in which the manager is held responsible for the use of assets as well as for profit.[5] It is, therefore, the ultimate extension of the responsibility idea. In an investment center the manager is expected to earn a satisfactory return on the assets employed in the responsibility center.

---

[5]Note that in an investment center, both profit *and* assets are measured. Many companies refer to both their profit centers and their investment centers as "profit centers."

Many companies use a ratio of profit to investment to measure an investment center's return on investment. Return on assets (profit divided by total assets) and return on "net assets" or invested capital (profit divided by assets net of certain or all current liabilities) are commonly used, in part because these ROI measures correspond to ratios calculated for the company as a whole by outside securities analysts. Other companies measure an investment center's **residual income** (also more recently called **economic value added** or **EVA**), which is defined as profit (before interest expense) minus a capital charge. The capital charge is calculated by applying a rate to the investment in the center's assets or net assets.[6]

> **Example.** Division Z of ABC Corporation is an investment center. In 19x1 the division's profit was $150,000 (net of interest expense of $30,000), and the division employed $1,000,000 of assets. For purposes of calculating residual income, ABC levies a 10 percent capital charge on assets employed. Division Z's ROI and residual income for the year would be calculated as follows:

$$\text{ROI} = \frac{\text{Profit}}{\text{Investment}} = \frac{\$150,000}{\$1,000,000} = 15 \text{ percent}$$

$$\text{Residual income} = \text{Preinterest profit} - (\text{Capital charge} * \text{Investment})$$
$$= \$180,000 - (0.10 * \$1,000,000) = \$80,000$$

Residual income is conceptually superior to ROI as a performance measure. Suppose the Division Z manager in the example above could increase profits by $12,000 a year by making an investment of $100,000. Because the 12 percent (= $12,000 ÷ $100,000) return on this investment is less than the 15 percent average return the division is already earning, the manager may shy away from making this investment. However, if the incremental capital cost rate is truly 10 percent, the investment would increase corporate "wealth" by the amount of additional annual residual income the investment would produce: $12,000 − (0.10 * $100,000) = $2,000.

Despite its conceptual advantage, many companies do not use residual income as an investment center measure, for two reasons. First, ROI percentages are ratios that can be used to compare investment centers of differing sizes, whereas residual income is an absolute dollar amount that is a function of the investment center's size. Second, a company's residual income is an internal figure that is not reported to shareholders and other outsiders.

---

[6]In a survey of the *Fortune* 1,000 largest U.S. industrial firms, James S. Reece and William R. Cool found that of those companies having investment centers, 65 percent used only an ROI measure, 2 percent used only residual income, 28 percent used both ROI and residual income, and the remaining 5 percent either used some other method or did not disclose their method. (See "Measuring Investment Center Performance," *Harvard Business Review,* May–June 1978.) A more recent study reported that the use of residual income had increased to 36 percent. (Source: Vijay Govindarajan, "Profit Center Measurement: An Empirical Study," Working Paper, Amos Tuck School of Business Administration, Dartmouth College, 1994.)

Whether ROI or residual income is used, the measurement of assets employed—the *investment base*—poses many difficult problems. For example, consider cash. The cash balance of the company is a safety valve, or buffer, protecting the company against short-run fluctuations in funds requirements. Compared with an independent company, an investment center needs relatively little cash because it can obtain funds from headquarters on short notice. Part of the headquarters cash balance therefore exists for the financial protection of the investment centers and can logically be allocated to them as part of their capital employed. This cash can be allocated to investment centers in any of several ways.

Similar problems arise with respect to each type of asset that the investment center uses. Valuation of plant and equipment is especially controversial: options include gross book value, net book value, and replacement cost. A discussion of these problems is outside the scope of this introductory treatment. For our present purpose, we need only state that many problems exist and that there is much disagreement as to the best solution. Despite these difficulties, a growing number of companies find it useful to create investment centers.[7]

The investment center approach is normally used only for a relatively "free-standing" product division—that is, a division that both produces and markets a line of goods or a set of services and significantly influences its own level of assets. This approach has the effect of "putting managers in business for themselves" to an even greater extent than does the profit center. Reports on performance show not only the amount of profit that the investment center has earned, which is the case with reports for a profit center, but also relates the profit to the amount of assets used in generating it (either through an ROI measure or residual income). This is obviously a more encompassing report on performance than a report that does not take into account the assets employed. On the other hand, the possible disadvantages mentioned above for profit centers exist in a magnified form in investment centers.

Two Misconceptions.   Some people think that the principal reason for using the investment center approach is to enhance control over *all* assets. This is not the case. Most companies exercise control over fixed assets via the capital investment procedures described in Chapter 27. This control precludes a responsibility center manager from unilaterally making large investments in fixed assets. Rather, the investment center approach primarily directs managers' attention to the *current* assets under their day-to-day control, particularly inventories and receivables.

Second, many companies monitor the ROI or residual income of their profit centers to see if the company is continuing to earn a satisfactory

---

[7]Govindarajan's 1994 survey (see footnote 6) found that 93 percent of the *Fortune* 1,000 companies had two or more profit centers. Companies considerably smaller than these 1,000 have also adopted the investment center measurement approach.

return on the capital tied up in those units. This measurement process *does not* make those units investment centers. Such a unit is an investment center only if its *manager is held accountable* for the ROI or residual income of the unit.

Nonmonetary Measures

The fact that each responsibility center is treated as either a revenue, expense, profit, or investment center does not mean that only monetary measures are used in monitoring its performance. Virtually all responsibility centers have important nonfinancial objectives: the quality of their goods or services, employee morale, and so on. Particularly in expense centers such as staff units, these nonmonetary factors may be more important than monetary measures. Many companies employ, in addition to their monetary control systems, formal systems for establishing and measuring nonmonetary factors. Such systems are frequently called **management by objectives (MBO) systems;** they are described in Chapter 24.

SUMMARY

An organization consists of responsibility centers. Management control involves the planning and control of these centers' activities so they make the desired contributions toward achieving the organization's objectives. The management control environment includes the nature of the organization; its rules, guidelines, and procedures; its culture; and its external environment.

Responsibility centers use inputs and assets to produce outputs. Responsibility accounting focuses on planned and actual amounts for responsibility center inputs and outputs. It is to be contrasted with full cost accounting, which focuses on products rather than on responsibility centers.

There are four types of responsibility centers: revenue centers, in which outputs are measured in monetary terms; expense centers, in which inputs are measured in monetary terms; profit centers, in which both inputs and outputs are measured in monetary terms; and investment centers, in which both profits and assets employed are measured and related to each other. In profit centers and investment centers, a transfer price is used to measure products furnished to other responsibility centers. Nonmonetary measures are also important in all types of responsibility centers.

Cases

CASE 22–1   Shuman Automobiles, Inc.*

Clark Shuman, owner and general manager of an automobile dealership, was nearing retirement and wanted to begin relinquishing his personal control over the business's operations. (See Exhibit 1 for current financial statements.) The reputation he had established in the community led him to believe that the recent growth in his business would continue. His long-standing policy of emphasizing new-car sales as the principal business of the dealership had paid off, in Shuman's opinion. This, combined with close attention to customer relations so that a substantial amount of repeat business was generated, had increased the company's sales to a new high level. Therefore, he wanted to make organizational changes to cope with the new situation, especially given his desire to withdraw from any day-to-day managerial responsibilities.

Accordingly, Shuman divided up the business into three departments: new-car sales, used-car sales, and the service department. He then appointed three of his most trusted employees managers of the new departments: Janet Moyer, new-car sales; Paul Fiedler, used-car sales: and Nate Bianci, ser-

vice department. All of these people had been with the dealership for several years.

Each manager was told to run her or his department as if it were an independent business. In order to give the new managers an incentive, their remuneration was to be calculated as a straight percentage of their department's gross profit.

Soon after taking over as manager of new-car sales, Janet Moyer had to settle upon the amount to offer a particular customer who wanted to trade his old car as a part of the purchase price of a new one with a list price of $14,400. Before closing the sale, Moyer had to decide the amount she would offer the customer for the trade-in value of the old car. She knew that if no trade-in were involved, she would deduct about 8 percent from the list price of this model new car to be competitive with several other dealers in the area. However, she also wanted to make sure that she did not lose out on the sale by offering too low a trade-in allowance.

During her conversation with the customer, it had become apparent that the customer had an inflated view of the worth of his old car, a far from uncommon event. In this case, it probably meant that Moyer had to be prepared to make some sacrifices to close the sale. The new car had been in stock for some time, and the model was not selling

*Copyright © by the President and Fellows of Harvard College. Harvard Business School case 177-033.

EXHIBIT 1

SHUMAN AUTOMOBILES, INC.
Income Statement
For the Year Ended December 31

Sales of new cars............................			$6,879,371
Cost of new-car sales*......................	$6,221,522		
Sales remuneration.........................	137,470		6,358,992
			520,379
Allowances on trade†			154,140
New-car gross profit........................			366,239
Sales of used cars		3,052,253	
Cost of used-car sales*.....................	$2,623,100		
Sales remuneration.........................	92,815		
		2,715,915	
		336,338	
Allowances on trade†		56,010	
Used-car gross profit.......................			280,328
			646,567
Service sales to customers..................		980,722	
Cost of work*..............................		726,461	
		254,261	
Service work on reconditioning:			
Charge	238,183		
Cost*...................................	245,915	(7,732)	
Service work gross profit....................			246,529
Dealership gross profit			893,096
General and administrative expenses			345,078
Income before taxes			$ 548,018

*These amounts include all costs assignable directly to the department, but exclude allocated general
dealership overhead.
†Allowances on trade represent the excess of amounts allowed on cars taken in trade over their
appraised value.

very well, so she was rather anxious to make the sale if this could be done profitably.

In order to establish the trade-in value of the car, the used-car manager, Fiedler, accompanied Moyer and the customer out to the parking lot to examine the car. In the course of his appraisal, Fiedler estimated the car would require reconditioning work costing about $840, after which the car would retail for about $7,100. On a wholesale basis, he could either buy or sell such a car, after reconditioning, for about $6,100. The retail automobile dealer's handbook of used-car prices, the "Blue Book," gave a cash buying price range of $5,500 to $5,800 for the trade-in model in good condition. This range represented the distribution of cash prices paid by automobile dealers for the model of car in the area in the past month. Fiedler estimated that he could get about $5,000 for the car "as is" (that is, without any work being done to it) at next week's regional used car auction.

The new-car department manager had the right to buy any trade-in at any price she thought appropriate, but then it was her responsibility to dispose of the car. She had the alternative of either trying to persuade the used-car manager to take over the car and accepting the used-car manager's appraisal price, or she herself could sell the car through wholesale channels or at auction. Whatever course Moyer adopted, it was her primary responsibility to make a profit for the dealership on the new cars she sold, without affecting her performance through excessive allowances on trade-ins. This primary goal, Moyer said, had to be "balanced against the need to satisfy the customers and move the new cars out of inventory—and there is only a narrow line between allowing enough on a used car and allowing too much."

After weighing all these factors, with particular emphasis on the personality of the customer, Moyer decided to allow $6,500 for the used car, provided the customer agreed to pay the list price for the new car. After a certain amount of haggling, during which the customer came down from a higher figure and Moyer came up from a lower one, the $6,500 allowance was agreed upon. The necessary papers were signed, and the customer drove off.

Moyer returned to the office and explained the situation to Joanne Brunner, who had recently joined the dealership as accountant. After listening with interest to Moyer's explanation of the sale, Brunner set about recording the sale in the accounting records of the business. As soon as she saw that the new car had been purchased from the manufacturer for $12,240, she was uncertain as to the value she should place on the trade-in vehicle. Since the new car's list price was $14,400 and it had cost $12,240, Brunner reasoned that the gross margin on the new-car sale was $2,160. Yet Moyer had allowed $6,500 for the old car, which needed $840 of repairs and could be sold retail for $7,100 or wholesale for $6,100. Did this mean that the

new-car sale involved a loss? Brunner was not at all sure she knew the answer to this question. Also, she was uncertain about the value she should place on the used car for inventory valuation purposes. Brunner decided that she would put down a valuation of $6,500, and then await instructions from her superiors.

When Fiedler, the used-car manager, found out what Brunner had done, he stated forcefully that he would not accept $6,500 as the valuation of the used car. He commented as follows:

> My used-car department has to get rid of that used car, unless Janet (Moyer) agrees to take it over herself. I would certainly never have allowed the customer $6,500 for that old tub. I wouldn't have given anymore than $5,260, which is the wholesale price less the cost of repairs. My department has to make a profit too, you know. My own income depends on the gross profit I show on the sale of used cars, and I won't stand for having my income hurt because Janet is too generous toward her customers!

Brunner replied that she had not meant to cause trouble but had simply recorded the car at what seemed to be its cost of acquisition, because she had been taught that this was the best accounting practice. Whatever response Fiedler was about to make to this comment was cut off by the arrival of Clark Shuman, the general manager, and Nate Bianci, the service department manager. Shuman picked up the phone and called Janet Moyer, asking her to come over right away.

"All right, Nate," said Shuman, "now that we are all here, would you tell them what you just told me?"

Bianci said, "Clark, the trouble is with this trade-in. Janet and Paul were right in thinking that the repairs they thought necessary would cost about $840. Unfortunately, they failed to notice that the rear axle is cracked; it will have to be replaced before we

EXHIBIT 2

SHUMAN AUTOMOBILES, INC.
Analysis of Service Department Expenses
For the Year Ended December 31

	Customer Jobs	Reconditioning Jobs	Total
Number of jobs	3,780	468	4,248
Direct labor	$302,116	$ 98,820	$ 400,936
Supplies	103,966	32,755	136,721
Department overhead	84,592	27,670	112,262
	490,674	159,245	649,919
Parts	235,787	86,670	322,457
	726,461	245,915	972,376
Charges made for jobs to customers or other departments	980,722	238,183	1,218,905
Gross profit (loss)	254,261	(7,732)	246,529
General overhead proportion			140,868
Departmental profit for the year			$ 105,661

can retail the car. This will probably use up parts and labor costing about $640.

"Beside this," Bianci continued, "there is another thing that is bothering me a good deal more. Under the accounting system we've been using, I can't charge as much on an internal job as I would for the same job performed for an outside customer. As you can see from my department statement (Exhibit 2), I lost almost $8,000 on internal work last year. On a reconditioning job like this, which costs out at $1,480, I don't even break even. If I did work costing $1,480 for an outside customer, I would be able to charge about $2,000 for the job. The Blue Book gives a range of $1,960 to $2,040 for the work this car needs, and I have always aimed for about the middle of the Blue Book range.[1] That would give my department a gross profit of $520, and my own income is now based on

that gross profit. Since a large proportion of the work of my department is the reconditioning of trade-ins for resale, I figure that I should be able to make the same charge for repairing a trade-in as I would get for an outside repair job."

Fiedler and Moyer both started to talk at once at this point. Fiedler managed to edge out Moyer: "This axle business is unfortunate, all right; but it's very hard to spot a cracked axle. Nate is likely to be just as lucky the other way next time. He has to take the rough with the smooth. It's up to him to get the cars ready for me to sell."

Moyer, after agreeing that the failure to spot the axle was unfortunate, added: "This error is hardly my fault, however. Anyway, it's ridiculous that the service department should make a profit on jobs it does for the rest of the dealership. The company can't make money when its left hand sells to its right."

At this point, Clark Shuman was getting a little confused about the situation. He thought there was a little truth in everything that had been said, but he was not sure how

---

[1] In addition to the monthly Blue Book for used-car prices, there was a monthly Blue Book that gave the range of charges for various classes of repair work, based on the actual charges made and reported by vehicle repair shops in the area.

much. It was evident to him that some action was called for, both to sort out the present problem and to prevent its recurrence. He instructed Ms. Brunner, the accountant, to "work out how much we are really going to make on this whole deal," and then retired to his office to consider how best to get his managers to make a profit for the dealership.

A week after the events described above, Clark Shuman was still far from sure what action to take to motivate his managers to make a profit for the business. During the week, Bianci had reported to him that the repairs to the used car had cost $1,594, of which $741 represented the cost of those repairs that had been spotted at the time of purchase, and the remaining $853 the cost of supplying and fitting a replacement for the cracked axle. To support his own case for a higher allowance on reconditioning jobs, Bianci had looked through the duplicate customer invoices over the last few months and had found examples of similar (but not identical) work to that which had been done on the trade-in car. The amounts of these invoices averaged $2,042, and the average of the costs assigned to these jobs was $1,512. (General overhead was not assigned to individual jobs.) In addition, Bianci had obtained from Ms. Brunner the cost analysis shown in Exhibit 2. Bianci told Shuman that this was a fairly typical distribution of the service department's expenses.

Questions

1. Suppose the new-car deal is consummated, with the repaired used car being retailed for $7,100, the repairs costing Shuman $1,594. Assume that all sales personnel are on salary (no commissions) and that general overhead costs are fixed. What is the dealership incremental gross profit on the total transaction (i.e., new and repaired-used cars sold)?

2. Assume each department (new, used, service) is treated as a profit center, as described in the case. Also assume in *a–c* that it is known with certainty *beforehand* that the repairs will cost $1,594.

   a. In your opinion, at what value should this trade-in (*unrepaired*) be transferred from the new-car department to the used-car department? Why?

   b. In your opinion, how much should the service department be able to charge the used-car department for the repairs on this trade-in car? Why?

   c. Given your responses to *a* and *b*, what will be each department's incremental gross profit on this deal?

3. Is there a strategy in this instance that would give the dealership more profit than the one assumed above (i.e., repairing and retailing this trade-in used car)? Explain. In answering *this* question, assume the service department operates at capacity.

4. Do you feel the three-profit-center approach is appropriate for Shuman? If so, explain why, including an explanation of how this is better than other specific alternatives. If not, propose a better alternative and explain why it is better than three profit centers and any other alternatives you have considered.

CASE 22–2   Birch Paper Company*

"If I were to price these boxes any lower than $480 a gross," said James Brunner, manager of Birch Paper Company's Thompson Division, "I'd be countermanding my order of last month for our sales force to stop shaving their bids and to bid full cost quotations. I've been trying for weeks to improve the quality of our business. If I turn around

*Copyright © by the President and Fellows of Harvard College. Harvard Business School case 158-001.

now and accept this job at $430 or anything less than $480, I'll be tearing down this program I've been working so hard to build up. The division can't show a profit by putting in bids that don't even cover a fair share of overhead costs, let alone give us a profit."

Birch Paper Company was a medium-sized, vertically integrated paper company, producing white and kraft papers and paperboard. A portion of its paperboard output was converted into corrugated boxes by the Thompson Division, which also printed and colored the outside surface of the boxes. Including Thompson, the company had four producing divisions and a timberland division, which supplied part of the company's pulp requirements.

For several years each division had been judged on the basis of its profit and return on investment. Top management had been working to gain effective results from a policy of decentralizing responsibility for all decisions except those relating to overall company policy. Top management felt that the concept of decentralization had been successfully applied and that the company's profits and competitive position had definitely improved.

Early in the year, the Northern Division designed a special retail display box for one of its finished papers in conjunction with the Thompson Division, which was equipped to make the box. Thompson's package design and development staff spent several months perfecting the design, production methods, and materials that were to be used; because of the unusual color and shape, these were far from standard. According to an informal agreement between the two divisions, Thompson was reimbursed by Northern only for the out-of-pocket cost of its design and development work.

When the specifications were all prepared, the Northern Division asked for bids on the box from the Thompson Division and from two outside companies, West Paper Company and Erie Papers, Inc. Birch's division

managers normally were free to buy from whichever supplier they wished, and even on sales within the company, divisions were expected to meet the going market price if they wanted the business.

At this time the profit margins of converters such as the Thompson Division were being squeezed. Thompson, like many other similar converters, bought its board, liner, or paper and printed, cut, and shaped it into boxes. Though it bought most of its materials from other Birch divisions, most of Thompson's sales were to outside customers. If Thompson got the order from Northern, it probably would buy its linerboard and corrugating medium from the Southern Division of Birch. The walls of a corrugated box consist of outside and inside sheets of linerboard sandwiching the corrugating medium.

About 70 percent of Thompson's out-of-pocket cost of $400 a gross for the order represented the cost of linerboard and corrugating medium. Though Southern had been running below capacity and had excess inventory, it quoted the market price, which had not weakened as a result of the oversupply. Its out-of-pocket costs on liner and corrugating medium were about 60 percent of selling price.

The Northern Division received bids on the boxes of $480 a gross from the Thompson Division, $430 a gross from West Paper, and $432 a gross from Erie Papers. Erie offered to buy from Birch the outside linerboard with the special printing already on it, but would supply its own inside liner and corrugating medium. The outside liner would be supplied by the Southern Division at a price equivalent to $90 per gross of boxes, and would be printed for $30 a gross by the Thompson Division. Of the $30, about $25 would be out-of-pocket costs.

Since this situation appeared to be a little unusual, William Kenton, manager of the Northern Division, discussed the wide discrepancy of bids with Birch's marketing vice president. He told the marketing vice president, "We sell in a very competitive market, where higher costs cannot be passed on. How can we be expected to show a decent profit and return on investment if we have to buy our supplies at more than 10 percent over the going market?"

Knowing that Brunner had on occasion in the past few months been unable to operate the Thompson Division at capacity, the marketing vice president thought it odd that Brunner would add the full 20 percent overhead and profit charge to his out-of-pocket costs. When asked about this over the telephone, Brunner's answer was the statement that appears at the beginning of this case. Brunner went on to say that having done the design and developmental work on the box at only out-of-pocket cost, he felt entitled to a normal markup on the production of the box itself.

The vice president thought about the cost structures of the various divisions. He remembered a comment the controller had made to the effect that costs that were variable for one division could be largely fixed for the company as a whole. He knew that in the absence of specific orders from top management, Kenton would accept the lowest bid, namely, that of West Paper for $430. However, it would be possible for top management to order the acceptance of another bid if the situation warranted such action. And though the volume represented by the transactions in question was less than 5 percent of the volume of any of the divisions involved, other transactions could conceivably raise similar problems later.

Questions

1. What are the additional costs to Birch Paper Company if Northern buys the boxes from West or Erie, rather than from Thompson?

2. Does the present system motivate Mr. Brunner in such a way that actions he takes in the best interests of the Thompson Division are also in the best interests of the Birch Paper Company? Explain.

3. What should the marketing vice president do?

CASE 22–3   Enager Industries, Inc.

I don't get it. I've got a new product proposal that can't help but make money, and top management turns thumbs down. No matter how we price this new item, we expect it to make $130,000 pretax. That would contribute 14 cents per share to our earnings after taxes, which is nearly as much as the 15-cent earnings-per-share increase in 1987 that the president made such a big thing about in the shareholders' annual report. It just doesn't make sense for the president to be touting e.p.s. while his subordinates are rejecting profitable projects like this one.

The frustrated speaker was Sarah McNeil, product development manager of the Consumer Products Division of Enager Indus-tries, Inc. Enager was a relatively young company, which had grown rapidly to its 1987 sales level of over $74 million. (See Exhibits 1–3 for financial data for 1986 and 1987.)

Enager had three divisions, Consumer Products, Industrial Products, and Professional Services, each of which accounted for about one third of Enager's total sales. Consumer Products, the oldest of the three divisions, designed, manufactured, and marketed a line of houseware items, primarily for use in the kitchen. The Industrial Products Division built one-of-a-kind machine tools to customer specifications; i.e., it was a large "job shop," with the typical job taking sev-

EXHIBIT 1

ENAGER INDUSTRIES, INC.
Income Statements
For 1986 and 1987
(thousands of dollars, except earnings per share figures)

	Year Ended December 31	
	1986	*1987*
Sales	$70,731	$74,225
Cost of sales	54,109	56,257
Gross margin	16,622	17,968
Other expenses:		
Development	4,032	4,008
Selling and general	6,507	6,846
Interest	994	1,376
Total	11,533	12,230
Income before taxes	5,089	5,738
Income tax expense	2,036	2,295
Net income	$ 3,053	$ 3,443
Earnings per share (500,000 and 550,000 shares outstanding in 1986 and 1987, respectively)	$6.11	$6.26

eral months to complete. The Professional Services Division, the newest of the three, had been added to Enager by acquiring a large firm that provided land planning, landscape architecture, structural architecture, and consulting engineering services. This division had grown rapidly, in part because of its capability to perform environmental impact studies.

Because of the differing nature of their activities, each division was treated as an essentially independent company. There were only a few corporate-level managers and staff people, whose job was to coordinate the activities of the three divisions. One aspect of this coordination was that all new project proposals requiring investment in excess of $500,000 had to be reviewed by the corporate vice president of finance, Henry Hubbard. It was Hubbard who had recently rejected McNeil's new product proposal, the essentials of which are shown in Exhibit 4.

Performance Evaluation. Prior to 1986, each division had been treated as a profit center, with annual division profit budgets negotiated between the president and the respective division general managers. In 1985, Enager's president, Carl Randall, had become concerned about high interest rates and their impact on the company's profitability. At the urging of Henry Hubbard, Randall had decided to begin treating each division as an investment center so as to be able to relate each division's profit to the assets the division used to generate its profits.

Starting in 1986, each division was measured based on its return on assets, which was defined as the division's net income divided by its total assets. Net income for a division was calculated by taking the division's "direct income before taxes" and then subtracting the division's share of corporate administrative expenses (allocated on the basis of divisional revenues) and its share of

EXHIBIT 2

ENAGER INDUSTRIES, INC.
Balance Sheets
For 1986 and 1987
(thousands of dollars)

	As of December 31	
	1986	*1987*
Assets		
Current assets:		
Cash and temporary investments	$ 1,404	$ 1,469
Accounts receivable	13,688	15,607
Inventories	22,162	25,467
Total current assets	37,254	42,543
Plant and equipment:		
Original cost	37,326	45,736
Accumulated depreciation	12,691	15,979
Net	24,635	29,757
Investments and other assets	2,143	3,119
Total assets	$64,032	$75,419
Liabilities and Owners' Equity		
Current liabilities:		
Accounts payable	$ 9,720	$12,286
Taxes payable	1,210	1,045
Current portion of long-term debt	—	1,634
Total current liabilities	10,930	14,965
Deferred income taxes	559	985
Long-term debt	12,622	15,448
Total liabilities	24,111	31,398
Common stock	17,368	19,512
Retained earnings	22,553	24,509
Total owners' equity	39,921	44,021
Total liabilities and owners' equity	$64,032	$75,419

income tax expense (the tax rate applied to the division's "direct income before taxes" after subtraction of the allocated corporate administrative expenses). Although Hubbard realized there were other ways to define a division's income, he and the president preferred this method since "it made the sum of the [divisional] parts equal to the [corporate] whole."

Similarly, Enager's total assets were subdivided among the three divisions. Since each division operated in physically separate facilities, it was easy to attribute most assets, including receivables, to specific divisions. The corporate-office assets, including the centrally controlled cash account, were allocated to the divisions on the basis of divisional revenues. All fixed assets were recorded at their balance sheet values, that is, original cost less accumulated straight-line depreciation. Thus, the sum of the divisional assets was equal to the amount shown on the

EXHIBIT 3
RATIO ANALYSIS FOR 1986 AND 1987

	1986	1987
Net income ÷ Sales	4.3%	4.6%
Gross margin ÷ Sales	23.5%	24.2%
Development expenses ÷ Sales	5.7%	5.4%
Selling and general ÷ Sales	9.2%	9.2%
Interest ÷ Sales	1.4%	1.9%
Asset turnover*	1.10x	0.98x
Current ratio	3.41	2.84
Quick ratio	1.38	1.14
Days' cash*	7.9	7.9
Days' receivables*	70.6	76.7
Days' inventories*	149.5	165.2
EBIT ÷ Assets*	9.5%	9.4%
Return on invested capital*,†,‡	6.9%	7.0%
Return on owners' equity*	7.6%	7.8%
Net income ÷ Assets*,§	4.8%	4.6%
Debt/capitalization*	24.0%	28.0%

*Ratio based on year-end balance sheet amount, not annual average amount.
†Invested capital includes current portion of long-term debt, excludes deferred taxes.
‡Adjusted for interest expense add-back.
§Not adjusted for add-back of interest; if adjusted, 1986 and 1987 ROA are both 5.7 percent.

corporate balance sheet ($75,419,000 as of December 31, 1987).

In 1985 Enager had as its return on year-end assets (net income divided by total assets) a rate of 4.5 percent. According to Hubbard, this corresponded to a "gross return" of 9.3 percent; he defined gross return as equal to earnings *before* interest *and* taxes (EBIT) divided by assets. Hubbard felt that a company like Enager should have a gross EBIT return on assets of at least 12 percent, especially given the interest rates the corporation had paid on its recent borrowings. He therefore instructed each division manager that the division was to try to earn a gross return of 12 percent in 1986 and 1987. In order to help pull the return up to this level, Hubbard decided that new investment proposals would have to show a return of at least 15 percent in order to be approved.

1986–1987 Results. Hubbard and Randall were moderately pleased with 1986's results. The year was a particularly difficult one for some of Enager's competitors, yet Enager had managed to increase its return on assets from 4.5 percent to 4.8 percent, and its gross return from 9.3 percent to 9.5 percent. The Professional Services Division easily exceeded the 12 percent gross return target; Consumer Products' gross return on assets was 8 percent; but Industrial Products' return was only 5.5 percent.

At the end of 1986, the president put pressure on the general manager of the Industrial Products Division to improve its return on investment, suggesting that this division was not "carrying its share of the load." The division manager had taken exception to this comment, saying the division could get a higher return "if we had a lot of old machines the way Consumer Products does." The president had responded that he did not understand the relevance of the division manager's remark, adding, "I don't see why the return on an old asset should be higher than that on a new asset, just because the old one cost less."

EXHIBIT 4
FINANCIAL DATA FROM NEW PRODUCT PROPOSAL

1. Projected asset investment:*

Cash	$ 50,000
Accounts receivable	150,000
Inventories	300,000
Plant and equipment†	500,000
Total	$1,000,000

2. Cost data:

Variable cost per unit	$3.00
Differential fixed costs (per year)‡	$170,000

3. Price/market estimates (per year):

Unit Price	Unit Sales	Break-even Volume
$6.00	100,000 units	56,667 units
7.00	75,000	42,500
8.00	60,000	34,000

*Assumes 100,000 units' sales.
†Annual capacity of 120,000 units.
‡Includes straight-line depreciation on new plant and equipment.

The 1987 results both disappointed and puzzled Carl Randall. Return on assets fell from 4.8 percent to 4.6 percent, and gross return dropped from 9.5 percent to 9.4 percent. At the same time, return on sales (net income divided by sales) rose from 4.3 percent to 4.6 percent, and return on owners' equity also increased, from 7.6 percent to 7.8 percent. These results prompted Randall to say the following to Hubbard:

You know, Henry, I've been a marketer most of my career, but until recently I thought I understood the notion of return on investment. Now I see in 1987 our profit margin was up and our earnings per share were up; yet two of your return on investment figures were down while return on owners' equity went up. I just don't understand these discrepancies.

Moreover, there seems to be a lot more tension among our managers the last two years. The general manager of Professional Services seems to be doing a good job, and she seems pleased with the praise I've given her. But the general manager of Industrial Prod-

ucts seems cool toward me every time we meet. And last week, when I was eating lunch with the division manager at Consumer Products, the product development manager came over to our table and expressed her frustration about your rejecting a new product proposal of hers the other day.

I'm wondering if I should follow up on the idea that Karen Kraus in HRM brought back from the organization development workshop she attended over at the university. She thinks we ought to have a one-day off-site "retreat" of all the corporate and divisional managers to talk over this entire return on investment matter.

Questions

1. Why was McNeil's new product proposal rejected? Should it have been? Explain.

2. Evaluate the manner in which Randall and Hubbard have implemented their investment center concept. What pitfalls did they apparently not anticipate?

3. What, if anything, should Randall do now with regard to his investment center measurement approach?

CASE 22–4 Piedmont University

When Hugh Scott was inaugurated as the 12th president of Piedmont University in 1991, the university was experiencing a financial crisis. For several years enrollments had been declining and costs had been increasing. The resulting deficit had been made up by using the principal of "quasi-endowment" funds. For true endowment funds, only the income could be used for operating purposes; the principal legally could not be used. Quasi-endowment funds had been accumulated out of earlier years' surpluses with the intention that only the income on these funds would be used for operating purposes; however, there was no legal prohibition on the use of the principal. The quasi-endowment funds were nearly exhausted.

Scott immediately instituted measures to turn the financial situation around. He raised tuition, froze faculty and staff hirings, and curtailed operating costs. Although he had come from another university and was therefore viewed with some skepticism by the Piedmont faculty, Scott was a persuasive person, and the faculty and trustees generally agreed with his actions. In the year ended June 30, 1993, there was a small operating surplus.

In 1993, Scott was approached by Neil Malcolm, a Piedmont alumnus and partner of a local management consulting firm. Malcolm volunteered to examine the situation and make recommendations for permanent measures to maintain the university's financial health. Scott accepted this offer.

Malcolm spent about half of his time at Piedmont for the next several months and had many conversations with Scott, other administrative officers, and trustees. Early in 1994 he submitted his report. It recommended increased recruiting and fundraising

activities, but its most important and controversial recommendation was that the university be reorganized into a set a profit centers.

At that time the principal means of financial control was an annual expenditure budget submitted by the deans of each of the schools and the administrative heads of support departments. After a dean or department head discussed a budget with the president and financial vice president, it was usually approved with only minor modifications. There was a general understanding that each school would live within the faculty size and salary numbers in its approved budget, but not much stress was placed on adhering to the other items.

Malcolm proposed that in the future the deans and other administrators submit budgets covering both the revenues and the expenditures for their activities. The proposal also involved some shift in responsibilities, and new procedures for crediting revenues to the profit centers that earned them and charging expenditures to the profit centers responsible for them. He made rough estimates of the resulting revenues and expenditures of each profit center using 1993 numbers; these are given in Exhibit 1.

Several discussions about the proposal were held in the University Council, which consisted of the president, academic deans, provost, and financial vice president. Although there was support for the general idea, there was disagreement on some of the specifics, as described below.

Central Administrative Costs. Currently, no university-wide administrative costs were charged to academic departments. The proposal was that these costs would be allocated to profit centers in proportion to the relative costs of each. The graduate school deans regarded this as unfair. Many costs incurred

EXHIBIT 1
ROUGH ESTIMATES OF 1993 IMPACT OF THE PROPOSALS
(millions of dollars)

Profit Center	Revenues	Expenditures
Undergraduate liberal arts school	$ 42.0	$ 40.9
Graduate liberal arts school	7.8	16.1
Business school	21.4	17.2
Engineering school	23.8	24.2
Law school	9.4	9.1
Theological school	1.7	4.8
Unallocated revenue*	7.0	—
Total, academic	$113.1	$112.3
Other		
Central administration	$ 14.1	$ 14.1
Athletics	3.6	3.6
Computers	4.8	4.8
Central maintenance	8.0	8.0
Library	4.8	4.8

*Unrestricted gifts and endowment revenue, to be allocated by the president.

by the administration were in fact closely related to the undergraduate school. Furthermore, they did not like the idea of being held responsible for an allocated cost that they could not control.

Gifts and Endowment. The revenue from annual gifts would be reduced by the cost of fund-raising activities. The net amount of annual gifts plus endowment income (except gifts and income from endowment designated for a specified school) would be allocated by the president according to his decision as to the needs of each school, subject to the approval of the Board of Trustees. The deans thought this was giving the president too much authority. They did not have a specific alternative, but thought that some way of reducing the president's discretionary powers should be developed.

Athletics. Piedmont's athletic teams did not generate enough revenue to cover the costs of operating the athletic department. The proposal was to make this department self-sufficient by charging fees to students who participated in intramural sports or who used the swimming pool, tennis courts, gymnasium, and other facilities as individuals. Although there was no strong opposition, some felt that this would involve student dissatisfaction, as well as much new paperwork.

Maintenance. Each school had a maintenance department that was responsible for housekeeping in its section of the campus and for minor maintenance jobs. Sizable jobs were performed at the school's request by a central maintenance department. The proposal was that in the future the central maintenance department would charge schools and other profit centers for the work they did at the actual cost of this work, including both direct and overhead costs. The dean of the business school said that this would be acceptable provided that profit centers were authorized to have maintenance work done by an outside contractor if its price was lower than that charged by the maintenance department. Malcolm explained that he had discussed this possibility with the head of maintenance, who opposed it on the grounds that outside contractors could not be held accountable for the high quality standards that Piedmont required.

Computers. Currently, the principal mainframe computers and related equipment were located in and supervised by the engineering school. Students and faculty members could use them as they wished, subject to an informal check on overuse by people in the computer rooms. About one-fourth of the capacity of these computers was used for administrative work. A few departmental mainframe computers and hundreds of microcomputers and word processors were located throughout the university, but there was no central record of how many there were.

The proposal was that each user of the engineering school computers would be charged a fee based on usage. The fee would recover the full cost of the equipment, including overhead. Each school would be responsible for regulating the amount of cost that could be incurred by its faculty and students so that the total cost did not exceed the approved item in the school's budget. (The mainframe computers had software that easily attributed the cost to each user.) Several deans objected to this plan. They pointed out that neither students nor faculty understood the potential value of computers and that they wanted to encourage computer usage as a significant part of the educational and research experience. A charge would have the opposite effect, they maintained.

Library. The university library was the main repository of books and other material, and there were small libraries in each of the schools. The proposal was that each student

and faculty member who used the university library would be charged a fee, either on an annual basis, or on some basis related to the time spent in the library or the number of books withdrawn. (The library had a secure entrance at which a guard was stationed, so a record of who used it could be obtained without too much difficulty.) There was some dissatisfaction with the amount of paperwork that such a plan would require, but it was not regarded as being as important as some of the other items.

Cross Registration. Currently, students enrolled at one school could take courses at another school without charge. The proposal was that the school at which a course was taken would be reimbursed by the school in which the student was enrolled. The amount charged would be the total semester tuition of the school at which the course was taken, divided by the number of courses that a student normally would take in a semester, with adjustments for variations in credit hours.

Questions

1. How should each of the issues described above be resolved?
2. Do you see other problems with the introduction of profit centers? If so, how would you deal with them?
3. What are the alternatives to a profit center approach?
4. Assuming that most of the issues could be resolved to your satisfaction, would you recommend that the profit center idea be adopted, or is there an alternative that you would prefer?

23

Control: The Management
Control Process

The preceding chapter discussed factors in an organization's environment that affect management control. In this and the next two chapters, we describe how the management control system works—the management control *process.* This chapter describes the principal steps in the process, the characteristics of accounting information used in the process, and behavioral aspects of management control.

PHASES OF MANAGEMENT CONTROL

Much of the management control process involves informal communication and interactions. Informal communication occurs by means of memoranda, meetings, conversations, and even by such signals as facial expressions. Although these informal activities are of great importance, they defy a systematic description. Besides these informal activities, most organizations also have a formal management control system consisting of the following phases, each of which is described briefly below and in more detail in succeeding chapters:

1. Strategic planning.
2. Budgeting.
3. Measurement and reporting.
4. Evaluation.

ILLUSTRATION 23–1
PHASES OF MANAGEMENT CONTROL

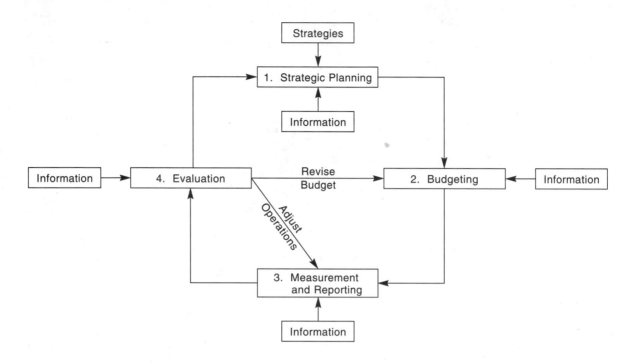

As shown in Illustration 23–1, each of these phases leads to the next. They recur in a regular cycle, constituting a "closed loop."

Strategic Planning

Strategic planning is the process of deciding on the programs the organization will undertake and the approximate amount of resources to be allocated to each program. (Some organizations call this step **programming** or **long-range planning**.) **Programs** are the principal activities the organization has decided to undertake to *implement* the strategies chosen in the strategy formulation process. Program decisions, therefore, take an organization's strategies as a given.

In a profit-oriented company each principal product or product line is a program. There are also various research and development (R&D) programs (some aimed at improving existing products or processes, others searching for marketable new products), human resource development programs, public relations programs, and so on. In some organizations program decisions are made informally; in others a formal planning system is used.

Budgeting

Strategic planning is a planning process; so is budgeting. An essential difference between strategic planning and budgeting is that strategic planning looks forward several years into the future whereas budgeting focuses on the next year. A **budget** is a plan expressed in quantitative, usually monetary, terms that covers a specified period of time, usually one year. Most organizations have a budget.

In preparing a budget, each program is translated into terms that correspond to the responsibility of those managers who have been charged with executing the program or some part of it. Thus, although plans are originally made in terms of individual *programs,* the plans are translated into terms of *responsibility centers* in the budgeting process. The process of developing a budget is essentially one of negotiations between managers of responsibility centers and their superiors. The end product is an approved statement of the revenues expected during the budget year and of the resources to be used in each responsibility center for achieving the objectives of the organization. (Chapter 24 describes both strategic planning and budgeting in further detail.)

Measurement and Reporting

During the period of actual operations, records are kept of resources actually consumed (i.e., costs) and of revenues actually earned. These records are structured so that cost and revenue data are classified both by programs (i.e., by products, R&D projects, and the like) and by responsibility centers. Data classified according to programs are used as a basis for future strategic planning, and data classified by responsibility centers are used to measure the performance of responsibility center managers. For the latter purpose, data on actual results are reported in such a way that they can be compared with the budget so that variances can be calculated. (Techniques for calculating variances were described in Chapters 20 and 21.)

The management control system communicates both accounting and nonaccounting information to managers throughout the organization. Some of the nonaccounting information is generated within the organization, and some of it describes what is happening in the external environment. This information, which keeps managers informed and helps to ensure that the work done by the separate responsibility centers is coordinated, is conveyed in the form of reports.

Reports are also used as a basis for control. Essentially, control reports are derived from an analysis that compares actual performance with planned (budgeted) performance and attempts to explain the difference (variance). (Control reports are discussed in Chapter 25.)

Task Control. Much of the information about operations is a summary of the detailed operating information generated in the course of performing specific tasks, such as producing a specific job order or entering customers' orders in the order-processing system. The system used to control these specific tasks is called **task control.** Techniques for controlling a variety of tasks are well developed and, with the widespread use of computers, increasingly automatic. A discussion of task control techniques is outside the scope of this book.

Evaluation

Based on these formal control reports, in conjunction with personal observations and other informally communicated information, managers evaluate what, if any, action should be taken. As indicated in Illustration 23–1, three types of response ("feedback loops") are possible. First, current operations may be adjusted in some way. For example, the purchasing agent may be instructed to locate a new source of supply for a material whose substandard quality is creating large unfavorable material usage variances. Second, operating budgets may be revised. For example, an unexpected, lengthy truckers' strike may have caused plant shutdowns, with the result that both expense and revenue budgets need revision in order to be realistic under the new circumstances. Third, programs may need to be revised or eliminated. For example, a product may be discontinued because its profits are judged to be too small relative to the investment required to support the product.

ACCOUNTING INFORMATION USED IN MANAGEMENT CONTROL

Full cost accounting information (described in Chapters 17–19) is used in the management control process as an aid in making program decisions. In preparing budgets and in measuring performance, the accounting information is structured by responsibility centers, and when so structured is called **responsibility accounting.** Responsibility accounting is necessary because control can be exercised only through the managers of responsibility centers.

In explaining the nature and use of responsibility accounting information, we need to introduce two new ways of classifying costs: (1) as controllable or noncontrollable and (2) as engineered, discretionary, or committed.

Controllable Costs

An item of cost is a **controllable cost** if the amount assigned to a responsibility center is significantly influenced by the actions of the manager of the responsibility center. Otherwise, it is noncontrollable. There are two important aspects of this definition: (1) it refers to a specific responsibility center, and (2) it suggests that controllability results from a *significant* influence rather than from a *complete* influence.

The word *controllable* must be used in the context of a specific responsibility center rather than as an innate characteristic of a given cost item. When an organization is viewed as a complete entity, *every* item of cost is controllable: someone, somewhere in the organization, can take actions that influence it. In the extreme case costs for any segment of the organization can be reduced to zero by closing down that segment; costs incurred in producing a good or service can be changed by purchasing that good or service from an outside supplier; and so on. Thus, the important question is not what costs are controllable in general but rather what costs are controllable in a specific responsibility center because it is these costs on which the management control system must focus.

Controllable refers to a significant rather than a complete influence because only in rare cases does one manager have complete control over *all* the factors that influence any item of cost. The influence that the manager of a department has over its labor costs may actually be quite limited: wage rates may be established by the human resources department or by union negotiations; the amount of labor required for a unit of activity in the department (e.g., assembling one unit of a product) may have been determined by someone outside the department who specified the detailed steps of the process; and the level of activity (i.e., volume) of the department may be influenced by the actions of other departments, such as the sales group or some earlier department in the production process. Nevertheless, department managers usually have a significant influence on the amount of labor cost incurred in their own departments. They have some control over the amount of workers' idle time, the speed and efficiency with which work is done, whether labor-saving equipment is acquired, and other factors that affect labor costs.

Direct material and labor costs in a given production responsibility center are usually controllable. Some elements of overhead cost are controllable by the responsibility center to which the costs are assigned, but others are not. Indirect labor, supplies, and power consumption are usually controllable. So are service centers' charges that are based on services *actually rendered.* However, an *allocated* cost is not controllable by the responsibility center to which the allocation is made. The amount of cost allocated depends on the amount of costs incurred in the service center and the formula used to make the allocation rather than on the actions of the manager of the responsibility center receiving the allocation. This is the case unless the cost is actually a direct cost that is allocated only for convenience, as in the case of social security taxes on direct labor.

Controllable Contrasted with Direct Costs. The cost items in a responsibility center may be classified as either direct or indirect with respect to that center. Indirect costs are allocated to the responsibility center and are therefore not controllable by it, as explained above. All controllable costs are therefore direct costs. Not all direct costs are controllable, however.

> **Example.** Depreciation on major departmental equipment is a direct cost of the department. Nevertheless, the depreciation charge is often noncontrollable by the departmental supervisor, who may have no authority to acquire or dispose of expensive equipment. The rental charge for rented premises is another example of a direct but noncontrollable cost.

Controllable Contrasted with Variable Costs. Neither are controllable costs necessarily the same as variable costs—those costs that vary proportionately with the level of activity (volume). Some costs (such as supervision, heat, light, and journal subscriptions) may be unaffected by volume, but they are nevertheless controllable. Conversely, although most variable costs are controllable, that is not always the case. In some situations the cost of raw material and parts, whose consumption varies directly with volume, may be entirely outside the influence of the departmental manager.

> **Example.** In an automobile assembly plant one automobile requires an engine, a body, seats, and so on, and the plant manager can do nothing about it. Moreover, the plant manager cannot choose the source of these inputs; most of them come from other divisions of the automobile company. The manager is responsible for not damaging or wasting these items, but not for the main flow of the items.

Direct labor, usually thought of as an obvious example of a controllable cost, may be noncontrollable in certain types of responsibility centers. Situations of this type must be examined very carefully, however, because supervisors tend to argue that more costs are noncontrollable than actually is the case to avoid being held responsible for them.

> **Example.** If an assembly line has 20 work stations and cannot be operated unless it is staffed by 20 persons of specified skills having specified wage rates, direct labor cost on that assembly line may be noncontrollable. Nevertheless, the assumption that such costs are noncontrollable may be open to challenge: it may be possible to find ways to do the job with 19 persons, or with 20 persons who have a lower average skill classification and hence have lower wage rates.

Cultural norms may also affect controllability. For example, with some recent exceptions, managers in most large Japanese companies cannot lay off employees because these companies provide their workers with career employment. However, the manager can have the employee transferred to another responsibility center, thus saving some labor cost in the manager's department (but not for the company overall). Labor contract work rules can also affect controllability in unionized departments.

As described in Chapter 16, controllability also depends on the length of the time period used for planning budgeted performance and measuring actual performance. Because performance in many responsibility centers is measured monthly, controllability in these circumstances is implicitly taken to refer to costs that are controllable during a month. (Of course, some costs, such as materials waste, are controllable within a much shorter time horizon.)

Converting Noncontrollable Costs to Controllable Costs. A noncontrollable item of cost can be converted to a controllable cost in either of two related ways: (1) by changing the basis of cost assignment from an allocation to a direct assignment or (2) by changing the locus of responsibility for decisions—that is, decentralization.

Changing the Basis of Cost Assignment. As noted above, allocated costs are noncontrollable by the manager of the responsibility center to which they are allocated. Many costs allocated to responsibility centers could be converted to controllable costs simply by assigning the cost so that the amount of costs assigned is influenced by actions taken by the responsibility center's manager.

> **Example.** If all electricity coming into a large building is measured by a single meter, there is no way of measuring the actual electrical consumption of each department in the building. The electrical cost is therefore necessarily allocated to each department and is noncontrollable. However, electricity cost can be changed to a controllable cost for the several departments in the building by installing meters in each department so that each department's actual consumption of electricity is measured.

Services that a responsibility center receives from service units can be converted from allocated to controllable costs by assigning the cost of services to the benefiting responsibility centers on some basis that measures the amount of services actually rendered.

> **Example.** If maintenance department costs are charged to production responsibility centers as a part of an overhead rate, they are noncontrollable. But if a responsibility center is charged on the basis of an hourly rate for each hour that a maintenance employee works there and if the head of the responsibility center can influence the requests for maintenance work, then maintenance is a controllable element of the cost of the center. When costs are assigned in this fashion, the amount is the transfer price that was described in Chapter 22.

Practically any item of indirect cost conceivably could be converted to a direct and controllable cost. For some (such as charging the president's salary on the basis of the amount of her or his time spent on the problems of various parts of the business), however, the effort involved in doing so clearly is not worthwhile. There are nevertheless a great many unexploited opportunities in many organizations to convert noncontrollable costs to controllable costs.

The same principle applies to costs that are actually incurred in responsibility centers but are not assigned to the responsibility centers at all, even on an allocated basis. Under these circumstances the materials or services are "free" insofar as the heads of the responsibility centers are concerned. Since these managers do not have to "pay" for these services (as part of the costs for which they are held responsible), they are unlikely to be concerned about careful use of these materials or services.

> **Example.** For many years New York City did not charge residents for the amount of water that they used. When water meters were installed and residents were required to pay for their own use of water, the total quantity of water used in the city decreased by a sizable amount.

Decentralization. Changing the locus of responsibility for cost incurrence is another way to convert noncontrollable costs to controllable costs. Although the most important decisions affecting costs are made at or near the top of an organization, the further removed these decisions are from where resources are actually used, the less responsive the decisions may be to conditions currently existing at that place. An organization in which managers at the top make a relatively high proportion of decisions is said to be **centralized;** one in which lower-level managers make relatively more decisions is said to be **decentralized.**

A decentralized organization is one in which a relatively large portion of total costs is controllable in the lower-level responsibility centers. Many organizations have found that if they have a good management control system, senior management can safely delegate responsibility for many decisions to lower-level managers, thus using to advantage the knowledge and judgment of these people who are more intimately familiar with current conditions at their level.

Reporting Noncontrollable Costs. In responsibility center performance reports, controllable costs should be clearly separated from noncontrollable costs. Some people argue that the separation of controllable from noncontrollable costs is not enough. They insist that noncontrollable costs should not even be reported. Actually, there may be good reasons for reporting the noncontrollable costs assigned to a responsibility center. One reason is that senior management may want the manager of the responsibility center to be concerned about such costs, the expectation being that this concern may indirectly lead to better cost control.

> **Example.** The control report of a production department may list an allocated portion of the cost of the human resource management (HRM) department, even though the supervisor of the production department has no direct responsibility for HRM department costs. Such a practice can be justified on the grounds that the supervisor will refrain from making unnecessary requests of the HRM department if made to feel some responsibility for its costs, or may in various ways put pressure on the manager of the HRM department to exercise good cost control. The control report should be formatted, however, to distinguish clearly between this noncontrollable cost and the controllable costs.

Another reason for reporting noncontrollable costs in responsibility centers is that if managers are made aware of the total amount of costs incurred in operating their centers, they may have a better understanding of how much other parts of the organization contribute to their operations. This is particularly important for profit and investment centers whose managers have authority to set selling prices: the responsibility center's revenues must recover all of the costs incurred in producing its goods and services, including support costs incurred in various service centers and its share of the costs of corporate headquarters activities.

Engineered, Discretionary, and Committed Costs

Another classification of costs useful in management control is that among (1) engineered, (2) discretionary, and (3) committed costs. Although both engineered and discretionary costs are controllable, the approach to the control of one is different from that of the other. Committed costs are not controllable in the short run, but they are controllable in the long run.

Engineered Costs. Items of cost for which the right or proper amount of cost that should be incurred can be estimated are **engineered costs.** Direct material cost is the clearest example. Given the specifications for a product, engineers can determine within reasonably close limits the physical quantities of materials that should be used for each unit of product. The total amount of direct material costs that should be incurred can then be estimated by translating these input quantities into money by means of a standard price for each type of material. The result is the standard material cost per unit of product. This standard unit cost can then be multiplied by the number of units of output to be produced in the period to arrive at the budgeted total amount of direct material cost for the period.

Since production engineering is not an exact science and prices of materials cannot be perfectly forecasted, the standard amount per unit of output is not necessarily *precisely* the amount that should be spent. But the estimates usually can be made with enough precision that there is relatively little basis for disagreement. In particular, there can be no doubt that there is a direct relationship between volume (i.e., units of output) and costs; two units require double the amount of material that one unit requires. Similarly, in most situations, direct labor costs are engineered costs. Standard cost centers, by their very nature, have a high proportion of engineered costs. (In fact, they are sometimes called *engineered cost centers.*)

Discretionary Costs. Items of cost whose amount can be varied at the discretion of the manager of the responsibility center are **discretionary costs.** (They are also called **programmed costs** or **managed costs.**) The amount of a discretionary cost can be whatever management wants it to be, within wide limits. Unlike engineered costs, there is no analytical way of deciding what the "right" amount of a discretionary cost should be. How much should be spent for research and development (R&D), advertising, public relations, employees' parties, donations, or for the accounting department are matters of *judgment,* not engineering studies. In most companies the discretionary cost category includes all R&D activities, all general and administrative activities, most marketing activities, and many items of indirect production cost.

Although there is no "right" total amount for a discretionary cost item, valid standards may be developed for controlling some of the detailed activities included within it.

> **Example.** Although no one knows the optimum amount that should be spent for the accounting function as a whole, it is nevertheless possible to measure the performance of individual clerks in the accounting department in terms of number of postings or number of invoices prepared per hour.

Similarly, although we cannot know the "right" amount of total travel expense, we can set standards for the amount that should be spent per day or per mile.

Furthermore, new developments in management accounting result in a gradual shift of items from the discretionary cost category to the engineered cost category. Several companies have recently started to use what they believe to be valid techniques for determining the "right" amount that they should spend on advertising in order to achieve their sales objectives, or the "right" number of sales personnel.

Discretionary Cost Relationships.   One must be aware of *spurious relationships* in the area of discretionary costs. The decision as to how much should be spent for a discretionary cost item may take several forms, such as (1) spend the same amount as last year, (2) spend x percent of sales, or (3) spend y dollars plus x percent of sales. These three decision rules or policies result in historical spending patterns that, when plotted against volume, have the same superficial appearance as the patterns of engineered cost: fixed, variable, or semivariable, respectively. These relationships, however, are fundamentally different from those observed for engineered costs. For engineered variable costs the pattern is inevitable: an increase in volume *causes* the amount of cost to increase. For discretionary costs the relationship exists only because of a management policy and can be changed simply by changing the policy.

> **Example.**   A company may have decided that R&D costs should be 3 percent of sales revenue. There can be no scientific reason for such a decision, for no one knows the optimum amount that should be spent for R&D. In all probability such a rule exists because management thinks that this is what the company can afford to spend. In this company there will be a linear relationship between sales volume and R&D costs. This is not a cause-and-effect relationship, however, and there is no inherent reason why future R&D costs should conform to the historical pattern.

Another example of a potentially misleading cost-volume relationship is marketing costs, which include the costs of the selling organization, advertising, sales promotion, and so on. These costs may vary with sales volume, but the relationship is the reverse of that for production costs: marketing cost is the independent variable, and sales volume is the dependent variable. Marketing costs vary not in response to sales volume but rather in *anticipation of* sales volume, according to decisions made by management.[1] They are therefore discretionary costs.

If management has a policy of spending more for marketing activities when sales volume is high, then a scatter diagram of the relationship between marketing costs and sales volume will *appear* the same as the diagrams for the relationship between production costs and production

---

[1]Exceptions are salespersons' commissions and other payments related to sales revenue. These items are caused by, and vary directly with, sales revenue. Also, as pointed out in Chapter 17, marketing costs should be distinguished from logistics, or order-filling, costs. Logistics costs are essentially as controllable as production costs.

volume. The two diagrams should be interpreted quite differently, however. The production cost diagram indicates that production cost *necessarily* increases as volume increases, whereas the selling cost diagram shows either that selling cost has been *permitted* to increase with increases in volume or that the higher costs have *caused* the higher volume. Further, subject to some qualifications, it may be said that for total production costs the lower they are, the better, whereas low marketing costs may reflect inadequate selling effort. The "right" level of marketing costs is a judgment made by management.

Committed Costs. Items of cost that are the inevitable consequences of commitments previously made are **committed costs** (also called **sunk costs**). Depreciation is an example: once an entity has purchased a building or a piece of equipment, there is an inevitable depreciation charge so long as the asset continues to be owned or until it is fully depreciated. Salaries of managers who have employment contracts also are committed costs.

In the short run committed costs are noncontrollable. They can be changed only by changing the commitment—for example, by disposing of the building or equipment whose depreciation is being recorded. Committed costs may or may not be direct costs for a given responsibility center.

BEHAVIORAL ASPECTS OF MANAGEMENT CONTROL

The management control process involves human beings, from those in the lowest responsibility center of the organizational hierarchy up to and including each member of senior management. The management control process consists in part of inducing these human beings to take those actions that will help attain the organization's goals and to refrain from taking actions inconsistent with them. Although an accumulation of the costs of producing a particular product is useful for some senior management purposes, management cannot literally control a product or the costs of producing it. What management does—or attempts to do—is influence the actions of the *people* responsible for incurring these costs. The discipline that studies the behavior of people in organizations is called **social psychology.** This discipline, rather than economics, provides the underlying principles that are relevant in the control process. We shall note briefly some aspects of behavior essential to an understanding of this process.

Behavior of Participants

Each person in an organization is called a **participant.** People become participants (join an organization) because they believe that by doing so they can achieve their *personal* goals. After they have become members, their decision to contribute to the work of the organization is also based on their perception that this will help them achieve their personal goals.

Needs. An individual's behavior in an organization (and elsewhere) is motivated by his or her *needs.* These needs cause various objects or outcomes to be attractive to that person. One categorization of needs, based on Abraham Maslow's work, is the following:

Extrinsic needs:

1. "Existence" needs, including oxygen, food, shelter, and sex.
2. A security need.
3. A social need.
4. A need for esteem and reputation.
5. A need for self-control and independence.

Intrinsic needs:

6. Needs for competence, achievement, and self-realization.

The first five kinds of needs, called **extrinsic needs,** can be satisfied by outcomes external to the person: for example, food, money, or praise from a colleague. The sixth category, however, can be satisfied only by outcomes persons "give" to themselves; these needs are called **intrinsic needs.**

People seek both intrinsic and extrinsic need satisfaction. Research indicates that existence and security needs must be satisfied before higher-order needs (i.e., categories 3–6) come into play. Also, once a given need is satisfied, people cease seeking outcomes relevant to that need; thus, a satisfied need is not a motivator. The exception to this is the sixth category. Competence, achievement, and self-realization needs are never fully satisfied; once self-realization begins to take place, it continues to be a strong motivator.

Some outcomes satisfy several needs. The best example is compensation, which for many people satisfies existence, security, and esteem needs. But it is difficult to generalize about how outcomes will motivate or satisfy members of an organization because different persons assign different degrees of importance to the various needs. A job that is dull to one person is satisfying to another.

> **Example.** In one automobile plant a number of workers quit more interesting and challenging jobs in favor of routine work on the assembly line. To these people the higher pay on the assembly line (an extrinsic reward) was more important than the potentially greater intrinsic rewards in their former jobs.

An individual's needs are also influenced by background, culture, education, and type of job (e.g., managerial versus nonmanagerial). Furthermore, a given person's needs will be different at different times.

Motivation

Given the complexity of their needs, how do people behave in order to satisfy them? One approach to this question is provided by the **expectancy theory** of motivation. This theory states that the motivation to engage in a given behavior is determined by (1) a person's beliefs or "expectancies" about what outcomes are likely to result from that behavior, and (2) the attractiveness the person attaches to those outcomes as a result of the outcomes' ability to satisfy her or his needs.

> **Example.** A person who has a high need for achievement and who is not a good player of card games will probably not join a bridge club whose members are skilled card players. However, another person, no better at playing bridge than the first, might be motivated to join because of a high need for social contacts. The first person has a low expectancy that playing bridge with the club's members will satisfy the need for achievement whereas the second person feels there is a good chance that affiliating with the group will help satisfy his or her social need. A third person, who is a superb bridge player and is somewhat introverted, may decline an invitation to join the bridge club because neither winning more bridge games nor socializing with the other players is an attractive outcome.

Expectancy theory seems to be a useful way of trying to understand motivation. Nevertheless, more research needs to be done for us to have better insights into persons' behavior in organizations.

Research indicates that motivation is weakest when a person perceives a goal (i.e., need fulfillment) as being either unattainable or too easily attainable. Motivation is strongest when there is roughly a 50–50 chance of achieving a goal. This is particularly relevant to the budgeting phase of the management control process, as will be discussed in the next chapter.

Incentives

Individuals are influenced by both positive and negative incentives. A **positive incentive** (also called a **reward**) is an outcome that results in increased need satisfaction. A **negative incentive** (also called a **punishment** or a **deprivation**) is an outcome that results in decreased need satisfaction. People join organizations in order to receive rewards that they cannot obtain without joining. Organizations dispense rewards to participants who perform in agreed-upon ways. Research on incentives tends to support the following statements:

1. Senior management's attitude toward the management control system can itself be a powerful incentive. If senior management signals by its actions that it regards the management control system as important, other managers will react positively. If senior management pays little attention to the system, other managers also are likely to pay relatively little attention to it.

2. Individuals tend to be more strongly motivated by the potential to earn rewards than by the fear of punishment.

3. What constitutes a reward is situational. For example, money is not a status factor in some cultures, and promotion to management is not always regarded as a status factor (e.g., in universities).

4. Monetary compensation is an important means of satisfying certain needs; but beyond the subsistence level, the amount of compensation is not necessarily as important as nonmonetary rewards. Nevertheless, the amount of a person's earnings is often important indirectly, as an indication of how

her or his achievement and ability are regarded. A person receiving $50,000 a year may be disgruntled if a colleague of perceived equal ability receives $51,000 a year.

5.   Intrinsic motivation depends on persons' receiving reports (written or oral) about their performance. Without such feedback, people are unlikely to obtain a feeling of achievement or self-realization.

6.   The optimal frequency of feedback is related to the *time span of discretion* of the task, the time between performance of the task and when inadequate performance is detectable. At lower levels in the organization, this span may be only hours; for senior management it may be a year or more.

7.   The effectiveness of incentives diminishes rapidly as the time elapsed between an action and administration of the reward or punishment begins to exceed the time span of discretion.

8.   People tend to accept feedback about their performance more willingly and to use it more constructively when it is presented in a manner that they regard as objective—or without personal bias.

9.   Beyond a certain point adding more incentives (which adds more pressure) for improved performance accomplishes nothing. This optimum point is far below the maximum amount of pressure that conceivably could be exerted. The coach who says, "Don't press; don't try too hard," is applying this principle.

Types of Incentives.   Incentives need not be monetary nor even formal. In some situations a quite simple device can be effective.

> **Example.**   In the Army when a parachute is packed for future use by the paratroops, the person doing the packing must attach a tag with his or her name to the parachute pack. At random times a pack is selected from inventory and given to the person who packed it—who then must jump from an airplane, using that parachute. This simple technique results in excellent quality in the packers' work.

For managers a more formal incentive occurs when compensation is related by formula to their responsibility centers' performance; that is, when bonuses are based on a comparison of planned and actual results. In view of the importance that many people attach to monetary compensation, this is a strong incentive indeed. In some cases it is too strong: managers may engage in unethical behavior to earn a substantial reward when they believe the planned result is not otherwise attainable. Thus, a bonus plan is most successful when there is general agreement that the basis of measurement is fair.

Negative incentives include not receiving a bonus (where there is a bonus system and the employee is eligible); not receiving a pay increase or receiving a smaller one than peer employees receive; not being promoted (when thinking one is a candidate for promotion); and, in more extreme cases, pay cuts, demotions, suspensions, and termination. As this partial list indicates, punishments often take the form of not receiving a reward rather than explicit penalties such as demotions.

Rewards and punishments are highly personalized. For example, management might feel it is punishing an employee by not promoting this person to an available higher-level job. But the employee who feels undeserving of the promotion or does not have a high need for achievement may not perceive lack of a promotion as a punishment. Similarly, a person receiving a $25,000 bonus may not be satisfied if this person feels a $35,000 bonus is deserved, even though senior management views the $25,000 bonus as a handsome reward. Because individuals differ in their needs and in their reactions to incentives, adapting application of the management control system to the personalities and attitudes of the individuals supervised is a difficult challenge for any manager.

Focus on Line Managers. Since subordinates are responsible to their superiors, they should receive praise, criticism, and other forms of incentives from their superiors. Staff people should not be directly involved in these motivation activities (except with respect to control of the staff organization itself). Line managers are the focal points in management control. Staff people collect, summarize, and present information that is useful to managers in the management control process. There may be many such staff people; indeed, the controller's department is often the largest staff department in an organization. However, the significant decisions and control actions are the responsibility of the line managers, not the staff.

Goal Congruence

Because an organization does not have a mind of its own, it cannot literally have goals. The organizational goals that we have referred to are actually the goals of top management and the board of directors. Senior management wants these organizational goals to be attained, but other participants have their own personal goals that *they* want to achieve. These personal goals are the satisfaction of their needs. In other words, participants act in their own self-interest.

The difference between organizational goals and personal goals suggests the principal criterion for the design of the management control system: it should be designed such that *the actions it leads people to take in accordance with their perceived self-interest are actions that are also in the best interest of the organization.* In the language of social psychology, the system should encourage **goal congruence.** It should be structured so that the goals of participants, so far as feasible, are consistent with the goals of the organization as a whole.

Perfect goal congruence does not exist; but as a minimum, the system should not encourage the individual to act *against* the best interests of the organization. For example, if the management control system signals that the emphasis should be only on reducing costs and if a manager responds by reducing costs at the expense of adequate quality, the manager has been motivated but in the wrong direction. It is therefore important when evaluating any practice used in a management control system to ask two separate questions:

1. What action does it motivate people to take in their own perceived self-interest?
2. Is this action in the best interests of the organization?

Agency Theory.   In recent years some researchers have formalized the goal congruence concept in an approach called **agency theory.** Whereas goal congruence refers to relationships between the overall organization and a manager (or other employee) or between a superior and subordinate, agency theory describes such relationships in terms of *contracts* between a *principal* and an *agent* acting on behalf of the principal. Although this approach has provided a useful framework for academic research, thus far it has been too theoretical to be of use to practitioners in designing management control systems.

An Example: The Data Processing Department

To illustrate how management control practices affect managers' behavior, consider the problem of controlling information processing costs in a company that has a central data processing department that provides services to other responsibility centers. These services may include production of various reports or the use of the computer in analyzing various problems. There are many methods of charging computer costs to the responsibility centers that use computer services, and each conveys a different message to the operating managers and to the data processing manager. Thus, each method motivates these managers differently.

At one extreme no charge at all might be made. If the computer is offered as a free service, operating managers are encouraged to explore the possibility of using the computer for work that was formerly done manually or for special analyses that otherwise would not be undertaken. This practice is often used when a company has substantial excess computer capacity and wants to promote its use. This method also signals that the data processing manager is responsible for decisions regarding computer usage. If the demand for this no-cost (to the user) computer work becomes greater than the computer capacity, the data processing manager rations the available capacity among the uses that she or he considers to be most important.

Another possibility is to make no charge for recurring reports prepared by the computer but to charge for special analyses. This provides an incentive for shifting recurring data processing to the computer but motivates the operating manager to consider whether elaborate studies of special problems are worth their cost.

As still another alternative, the total data processing costs might be allocated to all responsibility centers as a part of allocated general overhead costs. The amount allocated to a responsibility center would be based on its relative size. Since the cost is allocated, it is not controllable by responsibility center managers. This method would, however, make these managers aware of the magnitude of computer costs and could lead them to raise questions about the efficiency of the computer operation.

Another possibility is to charge a transfer price that is either related to prices charged by outside computer service organizations or is built up from full cost plus a profit margin. (Many time-sharing systems use this approach.) This motivates responsibility center managers to decide whether each computer application is worth its cost. The manager might also be permitted to use an outside computer service if the outside service charged a lower price. This would motivate the data processing manager to operate the computer center efficiently so that its prices would be equal to, or less than, outside prices.

As a variation, computer work done at night might be charged for at a lower rate than work done in the daytime. This would motivate users to decide whether the unattractiveness of using the computer after regular working hours is offset by the lower price. It thus tends to spread the workload over the entire 24-hour period.

Each of these methods of handling data processing costs motivates the managers involved—both the manager of data processing and the managers of the other responsibility centers—to act differently. The best method is the one that motivates them to act as senior management *wants* them to act. Any of those methods described, or others, can be best under a certain set of circumstances.[2]

The above example indicates the considerations that are important in structuring responsibility accounting information. These considerations are basically different from those involved in full cost accounting where the purpose is to measure the amount of resources used for producing goods or services. Full cost accounting is not influenced by behavioral considerations, but in responsibility accounting behavioral considerations are dominant.

Cooperation and Conflict

The appearance of an organization chart implies that the way in which organizational goals are attained is that the highest-level manager makes a decision and communicates that decision down through the organizational hierarchy; then, managers at lower levels of the organization proceed to implement it. It should now be apparent that this is *not* the way in which an organization actually functions.

What actually happens is that each subordinate reacts to the instructions of his or her superior in accordance with how those instructions affect the

---

[2]As an exercise the reader might think through analogous approaches that a company could use to control some other centralized service function, for example, its corporate training center that provides educational seminars and programs to the various parts of the company.

subordinate's personal needs. Because there is usually more than one responsibility center involved in implementing a given plan, the interactions between these centers' managers also affect what actually happens. For example, the manager of the maintenance department is supposed to ensure that the maintenance needs of the operating departments are satisfied. If there is friction between the maintenance manager and an operating manager, the needs of that operating manager's department may be slighted. For these and many other reasons, *conflict* exists within organizations.

At the same time, the work of the organization will not get done unless its participants work together with a certain amount of harmony. Thus, there is also *cooperation* in organizations. Participants realize that unless there is a reasonable amount of cooperation, the organization will dissolve and they will then be unable to satisfy *any* of the needs that motivated them to join the organization in the first place.

An organization attempts to maintain an appropriate balance between conflict and cooperation. Some conflict is not only inevitable, it is desirable. Conflict that results in part from the competition among participants for promotion or other forms of need satisfaction is, within limits, healthy. A certain amount of cooperation is also obviously essential. But if undue emphasis is placed on engendering cooperative attitudes, some participants may be denied the opportunity of satisfying their intrinsic needs for competence, achievement, and self-realization.

Other Types of Control

The accounting system used in management control is a *formal* system; that is, it has reports that can be described and observed. By contrast there are two *informal* types of control that influence the behavior of an organization's participants. **Social controls** are informal in nature but can be very influential. These controls take the form of **group norms,** which relate to such things as appropriate attire (e.g., managers not wearing jeans at work) or level of personal productivity (e.g., chastising a "rate buster" who makes others in the group appear inefficient by comparison). **Self controls** relate to an individual's motivation and personal values. When an employee takes pride in performing work of a high quality, even though the organization or peer group may be pressuring this person to work faster and not be so concerned about quality, he or she is exercising a level of self control that overrides the social and formal controls.

SUMMARY

The four phases of the management control process cycle are strategic planning, budgeting, measurement and reporting, and evaluation. Each of these phases leads to the next. There are also feedback loops from evaluation to the other phases.

In the strategic planning process full costs are relevant. In the other management control phases the budgeted and actual amounts are reported by responsibility centers, which is a different way of structuring management accounting information than that used in full cost accounting. Responsibility accounting cost concepts include the notions of controllable, engineered, discretionary, and committed costs. Controllable costs are items of cost whose amounts can be significantly influenced by actions of the manager of a responsibility center. Engineered costs are those for which the "right" amount to be incurred can be estimated, whereas discretionary cost amounts are a function of managerial judgment. Committed costs are noncontrollable in the short run.

In the management control process behavioral considerations are as important as economic considerations. In particular, the motivational impact of various practices needs to be considered. This is a difficult matter, for individuals have different needs and even a given person's needs change over time. The objective of management control system design should be to achieve goal congruence, the harmony between actions managers take in their perceived self-interest, and actions in the best interest of the organization.

Cases

CASE 23–1 Tru-Fit Parts, Inc.

Tru-Fit Parts, Inc., manufactured a variety of parts for use in automobiles, trucks, buses, and farm equipment. These parts fell into three major groupings: ignition parts, transmission parts, and engine parts. Tru-Fit's parts were sold both to original-equipment manufacturers (the "OEM" market) and to wholesalers, who constituted the first link in the channel of distribution for replacement parts (the "aftermarket" or "AM").

As shown in Exhibit 1, Tru-Fit had a manufacturing division for each of its three product groupings. Each of these divisions, which were treated as investment centers for management control purposes, was responsible not only for manufacturing parts but also for selling its parts in the OEM market. Also, each manufacturing division sold parts to the fourth division, AM Marketing. This division was solely responsible for marketing all Tru-Fit parts to AM wholesalers. It operated several company-owned warehouses in the United

EXHIBIT 1
PARTIAL ORGANIZATION CHART

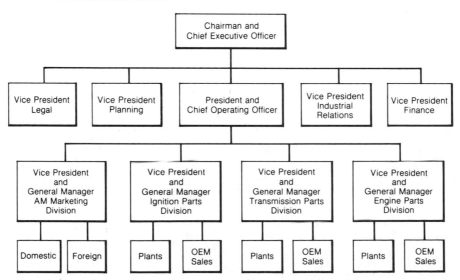

States and overseas. AM Marketing was also treated as an investment center.

Before elimination of intracompany sales, the sum of the four divisions' sales was about $1 billion a year. Of this, approximately $260 million was attributable to the Ignition Parts Division, $200 million to the Transmission Parts Division, $180 million to the Engine Parts Division, and $360 million to AM Marketing. After elimination of intracompany sales from the manufacturing divisions to AM Marketing, outside sales constituted almost one-third of the manufacturing divisions' volume. Top management's goal was to increase to 50 percent the AM portion of outside sales from the present level of 45 percent.

Within each manufacturing division each plant also was treated as an investment center. OEM sales were credited to the plants, which maintained finished goods inventories; shipments to OEM customers were made directly from the plants. A plant's ROI target was based on budgeted profit (including allocations of division and corporate overhead and an imputed income tax) divided by actual beginning-of-year "net assets" (defined to be total assets less current liabilities). Actual ROI was actual profit divided by actual beginning-of-year assets.

The reason that the profit figure included allocated overheads and taxes was so that the figure would correspond to the manner in which profit was calculated for shareholder reporting purposes. According to top management this gave a plant manager a clearer perspective of the plant's contributions to the corporate "bottom line."

Beginning-of-year net assets was used because added investment in a given year might result in little, if any, incremental profit in that year, but rather would increase later years' profits. Top management felt that such investments might not be proposed if investment center managers were penalized

(in the form of lower ROI) in the first year of the new investment. Because the investment base for the year was "frozen" at the beginning-of-year level, maximizing profits during the year was equivalent to maximizing ROI. (AM Marketing's ROI was measured in the same manner as was the plants' ROI.)

The OEM sales department in each manufacturing division was responsible for working with OEM company engineers to develop innovative and cost-effective new parts and for servicing customer accounts for parts already being supplied the OEM by Tru-Fit. Each of these OEM sales departments was treated as a revenue center. Because of the differing nature of OEM and AM marketing, top management did not want to consolidate AM and OEM activities in a single organization. Even OEM marketing was not consolidated, because each division's OEM marketers tended to work with different people within a given customer's organization. Moreover, two of the three manufacturing divisions had been independent companies before being acquired by Tru-Fit, and so there was a tradition of their doing their own OEM marketing.

According to Tru-Fit executives, the factors critical to success in the OEM market were (1) the ability to design innovative and dependable parts that met the customer's performance and weight specifications; (2) meeting OEM delivery requirements so that the OEM company could minimize its own inventories; and (3) controlling costs, since the market was very price-competitive. In the AM market, availability was by far the most important factor, followed by quality and price.

Approximately 50 Tru-Fit line managers and staff group heads participated in an incentive bonus plan, which worked as follows. First, the size of the corporatewide bonus pool was established; its size was related by a formula to corporate earnings per share. Each participant in the bonus plan had a certain number of "standard bonus points"; the higher the participant was in the organizational hierarchy, the more standard points he or she had. The total of these points for all participants was divided into the bonus pool to arrive at a standard dollar award per point. Then this amount was multiplied by the participant's number of standard points to arrive at the participant's "standard bonus." This standard award could be varied upward or downward as much as 25 percent at the discretion of the participant's superiors.

In the case of a plant manager, the standard award was also adjusted by a formula that related percent of standard award to the plant's profit variance. For example, if the plant's actual profit for the year exceeded its budgeted profit by 5 percent, the plant manager's bonus was raised from 100 percent of standard to 110 percent of standard. In making this bonus adjustment, the plant's actual profit was adjusted for any favorable or unfavorable gross margin variance caused by sales volume to the AM Marketing division being higher or lower than budgeted. For example, if all of a plant's favorable profit variance were attributable to a favorable gross margin volume variance on sales to AM Marketing, the plant manager's bonus would not be raised above 100 percent of standard. Similarly, the plant manager would not be penalized if AM Marketing actually purchased less from the plant than the amount that had been estimated by AM Marketing when the plant's annual profit budget had been prepared.

In general, top management was satisfied with the present performance measurement scheme. In discussions with the casewriter, however, they mentioned three areas of concern.

First, there always seemed to be a few disputes over transfer prices from the manufacturing divisions to AM Marketing. Whenever possible, transfers were made at outside OEM market prices. In the case of a part sold as an OEM part several years earlier, the former OEM market price was adjusted upward for inflation to arrive at the AM transfer price; this procedure caused virtually no disputes. The problems occurred when the part being transferred was strictly an AM part— one that had never been sold by Tru-Fit in the OEM market and for which there was neither a current OEM outside market price nor a former OEM market price that could be adjusted upward for inflation. Usually, such transfer price issues were resolved by the two divisions involved, but occasionally the corporate controller was asked to arbitrate a dispute.

Second, top management felt that the manufacturing divisions too often tended to treat AM Marketing as a "captive customer." For example, it was felt that when AM Marketing and an outside OEM customer were placing competing demands on a plant, the plant usually favored the OEM customer, because the OEM customer could take its business elsewhere whereas AM Marketing could not. (Management was not willing to let AM Marketing sell a competitor's product, feeling this would reflect adversely on the overall image of the company.)

Third, top management felt that both AM Marketing and the three manufacturing divisions carried excessive inventories most of the year. The controller said, "Thank goodness we have a generous Christmas vacation policy here; at least the inventories get down to a reasonable level at year-end when our production volume is low because of employee holiday vacations."

Questions

1. What would you recommend to top management regarding the three problems they have identified?

2. Are there any matters not mentioned by top management that you feel are problematical?

CASE 23-2   American Steel Corporation*

"I'm no expert in high finance," said Pat Harbrock, manager of the Denver branch of the Warehouse Sales Division of American Steel Corporation, in April 1994. "So it didn't occur to me that I might be better off if my new warehouse were leased instead of owned. But I was talking to Len Dorfmann over in Omaha the other day and he said that he's getting a lot better return on investment in his district because he's in a leased facility. I'm sure that the incentive compensation plan you put in last year is fair, but I didn't know whether it adjusted automatically for the difference between owning and leasing, and I just thought I'd raise the question. There's still time to try to find someone to take over my construction contract and then lease the building back to me when it's finished if you think that's what ought to be done."

American Steel Corporation was an integrated steel producer with annual sales in 1993 of about $4.5 billion. Operating the Warehouse Sales Division reflected a strategy of "downstream" vertical integration. This division was an autonomous unit that operated 21 field warehouses throughout the United States. These warehouses primarily served customers, such as smaller construction firms and metal fabricators, that did not wish to maintain their own inventories of metal shapes. Each warehouse also had equipment to cut or bend its products to meet a customer's specific needs. Total 1993 sales of the division were about $225 million, of which approximately half represented steel products (rod, bar, wire, tube, sheet, and plate) purchased from American Steel's Mill Products Division. The balance of the volume in the Warehouse Sales Division was for copper, brass, and aluminum products purchased from large producers of those metals. The Warehouse Sales Division competed with other producer-owned warehouses as well as with independently owned warehouses. American's warehouses purchased their steel products from the Mill Products Division at the same prices charged to independently owned metal supply warehouses.

In mid-1992 Lou Debbink had been appointed general manager of the Warehouse Sales Division, having previously spent 12 years in the sales function of the Mill Products Division. His appointment reflected, in part, disappointment in the performance of the Warehouse Sales Division. Debbink was given full authority for the operations of the division and was charged by top management with the responsibility to "make the division grow, both in sales volume and ROI [return on investment]," subject only to approval of the division's annual profit plan and proposed capital expenditures by corporate headquarters.

Prior to Debbink's appointment as its general manager, the division had been operated in a centralized manner from its St. Louis headquarters: all purchase orders had been issued by division headquarters, and most other operating decisions at any particular warehouse had required prior divisional approval. Debbink decided to decentralize the management of the division by making each branch warehouse manager responsible for the division's activities in his or her geographic area. In most cases these managers had worked in the metal supply warehouse business all of their careers; many of them

---

*Copyright © by the President and Fellows of Harvard College. Harvard Business School case 110-066.

had previously held lower-level positions in the American Steel warehouse of which they were now manager.

New Incentive Plan. In Debbink's opinion, one of the key features of the new decentralization policy was an incentive compensation plan that was announced in late 1992 to become effective on January 1, 1993. The description of the plan as presented to the branch managers is reproduced in Exhibits 1, 2, and 3. Monthly operating statements had been prepared for each warehouse for many years; thus, implementing the new plan required only the preparation of balance sheets for each warehouse. Two major asset categories, inventories and fixed assets (buildings and equipment), were easily attributed to specific locations. Accounts receivable were billed and collected by the corporate headquarters accounting department, but an investment in receivables equal to 35 days' sales (the average collection period for the division) was charged to each warehouse. Finally, a small cash fund deposited in a local bank was recorded as an asset of each branch; this account was used to pay various locally incurred expenses. No current or long-term liabilities were recorded on the balance sheets at either the divisional or branch level; thus, the "balance sheets" were actually just statements of assets.

Debbink had held a meeting of the warehouse branch managers in December 1992 for the purpose of presenting the new plan. At this meeting he said:

> Dale Andrews [division sales manager] and I have spent a lot of time during the last few months working out the details of this plan. Our objective was to devise a fair way to compensate those branch managers who do a superior job of improving the performance in their regions. First, we reviewed our salary structure and made a few adjustments so that no branch manager would feel that we weren't paying a competitive salary. Next,

we worked out a simple growth incentive to recognize that one part of our job is simply to sell steel, although we didn't re strict it to steel alone. But more importantly, we've got to improve the profit performance of this division. We established 12 percent as the return on investment floor representing average performance. As you know, we won't even do that well for 1992, but our 1993 budget shows that we'll earn about 12 percent before taxes.

> Thus, in 1993 we expect about half the branches to be below 12 percent—and earn no ROI bonus—while the other half will be the ones who really carry the weight. This plan will pay a bonus to all managers who help the division increase its average rate of return. We also decided on a sliding-scale arrangement for those above 12 percent, trying to recognize that the manager who makes a 20 percent return on a $10 million investment is doing as good a job as one who makes a 40 percent return on only $2 million.

> Finally, we put a $50,000 limit on the ROI portion of the bonus because we feel it shouldn't exceed 50 percent of salary. But we can always make salary adjustments in those cases where the bonus plan doesn't seem to adequately compensate a manager for that branch's performance.

The Denver Issue. After the telephone call in April 1994 from Pat Harbrock (quoted in the opening paragraph of this case), Debbink called Andrews in and related the question that Harbrock had raised. "We knew we probably had some bugs to work out in this system," Andrews responded. "Let me review the Denver situation and we'll discuss it tomorrow."

The next day, Andrews and Debbink met again. Andrews summarized the Denver problem as follows:

> As you know, Pat Harbrock is planning a big expansion in Denver. Pat's been limping along in an old, multistory building with an inadequate variety of inventory; as a result,

EXHIBIT 1
NEW BRANCH MANAGERS' COMPENSATION PLAN

I. **Objectives**

The Warehouse Sales Division has three major objectives:

A. To operate the Division and its branches at a profit
B. To utilize efficiently the assets of the Division
C. To grow

This compensation plan is a combination of base salary and incentive earnings. Incentive earnings will be paid to those managers who contribute to the achievement of these objectives and in proportion to their individual performance.

II. **Compensation Plan Components**

There are three components of this plan:

A. **Base Salary**

Base salary ranges are determined for the most part on dollar sales volume of the districts in the prior year. The higher the sales volume, the higher the range for which the manager becomes eligible. The profitability of dollar sales or increases in dollar sales is also an important consideration. Actual salaries will be established by the Division's general manager, and the salary ranges will be reviewed periodically in order to keep them competitive with those of other companies in the metal supply warehouse business.

B. **Growth Incentive**

If the district earns a pretax income for the calendar year, the manager will earn $500 for every $100,000 of increased sales over the prior year (i.e., 0.50 percent of any sales increase). Proportionate amounts will be paid for greater or lesser growth.

C. **Return on Investment Incentive**

In this feature of the plan, an incentive will be paid in relation to the size of investment and return on investment. The manager will be paid in direct proportion to the effective use of the assets placed at his or her disposal. The main emphasis of this portion of the plan is on increasing ROI at any level of investment, high or low.

III. **Limitations on ROI Incentive**

A. No incentive will be paid to a manager whose branch earns less than 12 percent pretax ROI.
B. No increase in incentive payment will be made for performance in excess of 50 percent pretax ROI.
C. No payment will be made in excess of $50,000, regardless of ROI performance.

IV. **Calculations of ROI Incentive**

Exhibit 2 is a graphic presentation of this portion of the incentive. Since all possible levels of investment and ROI cannot be detailed on the graph, exact incentive figures cannot be determined therefrom. The exact amount of an incentive can be determined from Exhibit 3 using the following procedure:

Example   Investment = $8,265,500
ROI = 14.7%

Step 1: Subtract the next lowest multiple of $500,000 from the investment and divide the remainder by $500,000. The result is a percentage:

$8,265,500 − $8,000,000 = $265,500
$265,500 ÷ $500,000 = 0.531

Step 2: In the 1% column of Exhibit 3 take the difference between the next highest and next lowest investment:

Investment	1% Col.
$8,000,000	$1,060
8,500,000	1,088
Difference	$ 28

Step 3: Multiply the result of Step 2 by the result of Step 1 and add to the 1% column figure for the next lowest investment:

$28 * 0.531 = $14.87 + $1,060 = $1,074.87

Step 4: Multiply the result of Step 3 by the actual ROI percentage:

$1,074.87 * 14.7 = $15,801

EXHIBIT 2

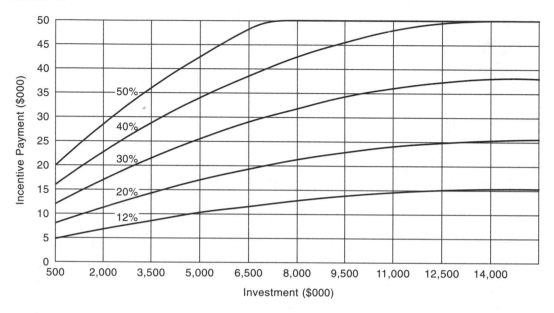

Denver's sales actually declined last year. About a year ago Pat worked up an RFE [Request for Expenditure] for a new warehouse that we approved here and sent to corporate. It was approved by headquarters last fall, the contract was let, and it's supposed to be completed by the end of this year. I pulled out a page of the RFE that summarizes the financial story [see Exhibit 4]. Pat forecasts nearly tripling Denver's sales volume over the next eight years, and the project will pay out in a little over six years.

Here [Exhibit 5] is a summary of the incentive compensation calculations for Denver that I worked up after I talked to you yesterday. Harbrock had a very high ROI last year and received one of the biggest bonuses we paid. Against that background, I next worked up a projection of what the 1995 bonus will be assuming the new facility is on-line by the start of 1995. As you can see, the ROI will drop from 43.3 percent to only 17.4 percent; and even on the bigger investment the expected 1995 bonus will go down substantially.

Finally, I pulled out the file on New Orleans where we're leasing the new warehouse that was completed a few months ago. Our lease there is a so-called net lease, which means that we pay the insurance, taxes, maintenance, and so forth just as if we owned it. The lease runs for 20 years with renewal options at reduced rates for two additional ten-year periods. Assuming that we could get a similar deal for Denver, and taking into account the different land and building costs at the two locations, I estimate that the lease expense at Denver during the first 20 years would be about $370,000 per year. Pushing that through the bonus formula for Denver's projected 1995 operations shows an ROI of 20.8 percent, and Pat's 1995 bonus would be virtually the same as if the building were owned.

EXHIBIT 3
SCHEDULE OF INCENTIVE PAYMENTS

Investment (thousands)	ROI Percent					
	1%*	12%	20%	30%	40%	50%
$ 500	$ 400	$ 4,800	$ 8,000	$12,000	$16,000	$20,000
1,000	458	5,496	9,160	13,740	18,320	22,900
1,500	514	6,168	10,280	15,420	20,560	25,700
2,000	568	6,816	11,360	17,040	22,720	28,400
2,500	620	7,440	12,400	18,600	24,800	31,000
3,000	670	8,040	13,400	20,100	26,800	33,500
3,500	718	8,616	14,360	21,540	28,720	35,900
4,000	764	9,168	15,280	22,920	30,560	38,200
4,500	808	9,696	16,160	24,240	32,320	40,400
5,000	850	10,200	17,000	25,500	34,000	42,500
5,500	890	10,680	17,800	26,700	35,600	44,500
6,000	928	11,136	18,560	27,840	37,120	46,400
6,500	964	11,568	19,280	28,920	38,560	48,200
7,000	998	11,976	19,960	29,940	39,920	49,900
7,500	1,030	12,360	20,600	30,900	41,200	50,000
8,000	1,060	12,720	21,200	31,800	42,400	50,000
8,500	1,088	13,056	21,760	32,640	43,520	50,000
9,000	1,114	13,368	22,280	33,420	44,560	50,000
9,500	1,138	13,656	22,760	34,140	45,520	50,000
10,000	1,160	13,920	23,200	34,800	46,400	50,000
10,500	1,180	14,160	23,600	35,400	47,200	50,000
11,000	1,198	14,376	23,960	35,940	47,920	50,000
11,500	1,214	14,568	24,280	36,420	48,560	50,000
12,000	1,228	14,736	24,560	36,840	49,120	50,000
12,500	1,240	14,880	24,800	37,200	49,600	50,000
13,000	1,250	15,000	25,000	37,500	50,000	50,000
13,500	1,258	15,096	25,160	37,740	50,000	50,000
14,000	1,264	15,168	25,280	37,920	50,000	50,000
14,500	1,268	15,216	25,360	38,040	50,000	50,000
15,000	1,270	15,240	25,400	38,100	50,000	50,000

"On balance, therefore," Andrews concluded, "there's not a significant difference in the bonus payment between owning and leasing; and in either event Pat will be taking a substantial cut in incentive compensation."

Questions

1. What role should the new investment center incentive plan play in decisions such as Denver's lease-versus-own issue?

2. Evaluate in depth the new incentive system. How, if at all, would you modify it?

EXHIBIT 4
EXCERPT FROM DENVER BRANCH RFE

Incremental Sales, Expenses, and Net Income Due to New Facility
(thousands of dollars)

	Base Year Ending 12/31/94	Year 1	Year 2	Year 3	Year 4	Increment by end of: Year 5	Year 6	Year 7	Year 8
Sales revenue	12,300	1,565.0	3,015.0	6,080.0	9,495.0	12,565.0	16,630.0	19,635.0	22,670.0
Gross margin	3,065	235.0	452.3	912.0	1,424.3	1,884.8	2,494.5	2,945.3	3,400.5
Expenses excl. deprec.	965	441.0	507.7	648.7	805.8	947.0	1,134.0	1,272.2	1,411.8
Pretax income before depreciation	2,100	(206.0)	(55.4)	263.3	618.5	937.8	1,360.5	1,673.1	1,988.7
Additional mill profit		78.3	150.8	304.0	474.8	628.3	831.5	981.8	1,133.5
Pretax income before deprec., including mill profit		(127.7)	95.4	567.3	1,093.3	1,566.1	2,192.0	2,654.9	3,122.2
Relocation write-off		250.0							
Pretax income before deprec.		(377.7)	95.4	567.3	1,093.3	1,566.1	2,192.0	2,654.9	3,122.2
Depreciation		97.6	97.6	97.6	97.6	97.6	97.6	97.6	97.6
Pretax income		(475.3)	(2.2)	469.7	995.7	1,468.5	2,094.4	2,557.3	3,024.6
Tax expense (credit) @ 40%		(190.1)	(0.9)	187.9	398.3	587.4	837.8	1,022.9	1,209.8
Net income		(285.2)	(1.3)	281.8	597.4	881.1	1,256.6	1,534.4	1,814.8
Add back deprec./relocation		347.6	97.6	97.6	97.6	97.6	97.6	97.6	97.6
Annual return of funds		62.4	96.3	379.4	695.0	978.7	1,354.2	1,632.0	1,912.4

Total return over 8 yrs. 7,110

Capital expenditures required:
Land	300
Building	2,600
Equipment	1,060
Relocation expense	250
Total	4,210

Payback period.................. 6.4 years

EXHIBIT 5
ROI AND INCENTIVE COMPENSATION CALCULATIONS
Denver Branch Warehouse

($000)	Warehouse Sales Divn. 1993 Actual	Denver Branch		
		1993 Actual	1995 Projected	
			Own	Lease
End-of-year investment:				
Land	$ 5,150	$ 125.2	$ 300.0	—
Buildings (net)	13,951	326.4	2,535.0	—
Equipment (net)	2,722	32.1	961.4	$ 961.4
Total noncurrent	21,823	483.7	3,796.4	961.4
Cash fund	1,383	50.3	60.0	60.0
Accounts receivable	22,518	1,548.9	1,386.5	1,386.5
Inventories	55,296	2,850.8	3,466.3	3,466.3
Total end-of-year investment	101,020	4,933.7	8,709.2	5,874.2
Beginning-of-year investment	99,796	5,295.1	8,326.0	5,426.0
Average annual investment	$100,408	$5,114.4	$8,517.6	$5,650.1
Pretax income before depreciation	$ 14,223	$2,280.5	$1,644.0	$1,644.0
Depreciation expense	1,070	66.0	163.6	98.6
Lease expense	841	—	—	370.4
Pretax income	$ 12,312	$2,214.5	$1,480.4	$1,175.0
Return on investment	12.3%	43.3%	17.4%	20.8%
Incentive Compensation:				
Sales increase (decrease) (000)		$(870.0)	$1,565	$1,565
Bonus @ $500 per $100,000		—	7,825	7,825
ROI bonus calculation:				
Base investment (000)		$5,000	$8,500	$5,500
Value from 1% column, Exh. 3		$850	$1,088	$890
Difference to next base		$40	$26	$38
Interpolated portion		$9.15	$0.92	$11.41
Total value per percentage point		$859.15	$1,088.92	$901.41
ROI bonus		$37,201	$18,947	$18,749
Total incentive compensation		$37,201	$26,772	$26,574

Assumptions used for 1995 Denver projections:
1. Old facility sold at end of 1994; proceeds remitted to corporate headquarters.
2. Straight-line depreciation on new facility: building, 40 yrs.; equipment, various lives.
3. Year-end investment in receivables and inventories will be 10% and 25% of annual sales, respectively, consistent with the 1993 overall Division average.
4. Pretax income taken from RFE [Exhibit 4] as $2,100 (1994) less $206 first-year decline less $250 relocation write-off. Additional mill profit of $78.3 does not appear on divisional books and was used only at corporate headquarters for capital expenditure evaluation purposes.

CASE 23–3 Empire Glass Company*

Organization. Empire Glass Company was a publicly held container and packaging company. It was organized into several major product divisions, each headed by a vice president who reported to the company's executive vice president, Landon McGregor. The Glass Products Division, the focus of this case, was responsible for manufacturing and selling glass food and beverage bottles.

McGregor's corporate staff included three financial department heads—the controller, chief accountant, and treasurer. The controller's department consisted of only two people—James Walker and his assistant, Ellen Newell. The market research and labor relations departments also reported in a staff capacity to McGregor.

All the product divisions were organized along similar lines. Reporting to each division vice president were staff members in the customer service and product research areas. Reporting in a line capacity to each vice president were general managers of manufacturing and of marketing who were responsible for all of the division's manufacturing and marketing activities. Each of these executives was assisted by a small staff of specialists. Exhibit 1 presents an organization chart of top management and of the Glass Products Division's management group. All corporate and divisional managers and staff were located in British City, Canada. Exhibit 2 shows the typical organization structure of a plant within the Glass Products Division.

Products and Technology. Glass Products operated seven plants in Canada. Food jars constituted their largest product group, including jars for products like catsup, mayonnaise, jams, pickles, and instant coffee. Beer and soft-drink bottles were also produced in large quantities. A great variety of containers for wines, liquors, drugs, cosmetics, and chemicals were produced in smaller quantities. Most of the thousands of different products, varying in size, shape, color, and decoration, were produced to order. The typical lead time between a customer's order and shipment from the plant was two to three weeks.

The principal raw materials were sand, soda ash, and lime. The first manufacturing step was to melt batches of these materials. The molten mass was then passed into automatic or semiautomatic machines, which filled molds with the molten glass and blew the glass into the desired shape. The ware then went through an automatic annealing oven, where it was cooled slowly under carefully controlled conditions. If the glass was to be coated on the exterior to increase its resistance to abrasion and scratches, this coating was applied at the oven. Any decorating (such as a trademark or other design) was then added, the product inspected again, and the finished goods packed in corrugated containers.

Quality inspection was critical. If the melt in the furnace was not completely free from bubbles and stones, or if the fabricating machinery was slightly out of adjustment or molds were worn, the rejection rate was very high. Although a number of machines were used in the inspection process, including electric eyes, much of the inspection was still visual.

EXHIBIT 1
TOP MANAGEMENT AND GLASS PRODUCTS MANAGEMENT

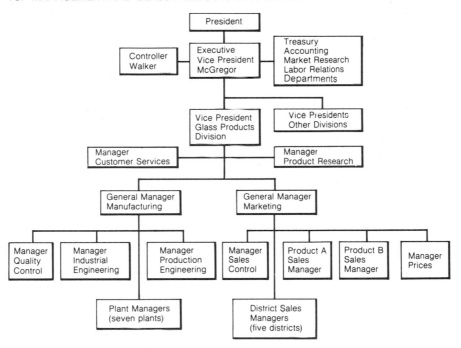

Although glass bottles had been machine molded at relatively high speed for over 75 years, Glass Products spent substantial sums each year to modernize its equipment. These improvements had greatly increased the speed of operations and had substantially reduced the visual inspection and manual handling of glassware.

Most of the jobs were relatively unskilled and highly repetitive, giving the worker little control over work methods or pace. The moldmakers who made and repaired the molds, the machine repairpersons, and those who made the equipment setup changes between different products were considered to be the highest classes of skilled workers. Wages were relatively high in the industry, in part because the plants were noisy and hot. Production employees belonged to two national unions, and bargaining was conducted

on a national basis. Output standards were established for all jobs, but no bonus was paid to hourly workers for exceeding standard.

Marketing. Over the years Glass Products' sales had grown at a slightly faster rate than had the total glass container market. Until the late 1950s the division had charged a premium for most of its products, which were of better quality than competitive products. Subsequently, however, the competitive products' quality had improved, and it now matched the division's quality level, but competitors had retained their former price structure. Consequently, Glass Products had been forced to lower its prices to meet its competitors' prices. According to one division executive:

Currently, price competition is not severe, particularly among the two or three larger

EXHIBIT 2
TYPICAL PLANT ORGANIZATION—GLASS PRODUCTS DIVISION

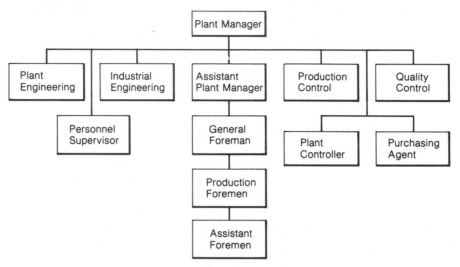

companies that dominate the glass bottle industry. Most of our competition is with respect to product quality and customer service . . . In fact, our biggest competitive threat is from containers other than glass.

Transportation costs limited each plant's market primarily to its immediate vicinity. Although some of the customers were large and bought in huge quantities, many were relatively small.

Budgetary Control System

James Walker, Empire Glass Company controller for over 15 years, described the company's budgetary control system:

"To understand the role of the budgetary control system, you must first understand our management philosophy. We have a divisional organization based on broad product categories. Divisional activities are coordinated by the executive vice president, and the head office group provides a policy and review function for him. Within broad policy limits we operate on a decentralized basis; each of the divisions performs the full man-

agement job that normally would be inherent in any independent company. The only exceptions are the head office group's sole responsibilities for sources of funds and labor relations with bargaining units that cross division lines.

"Given this form of organization, the budget is the principal management tool used by head office to coordinate the efforts of the various segments of the company toward a common goal. Certainly, in our case the budget is much more than a narrow statistical accounting device."

Sales Budget. "As early as May 15 of the year preceding the budget year, top management asks each of the division vice presidents to submit preliminary reports stating what they think the division's capital requirements, sales, and income will be during the next budget year. In addition, top management wants to learn the division vice president's general feelings toward the trends in these items over the two years following the upcoming budget year. At this stage head office is not interested in much detail but rather in a forecast based on the operating executives' practical feel for the market. Since all divisions plan their capital requirements at least five years in advance and had made predictions of the forthcoming budget year's market when the budget estimates were prepared last year, these preliminary estimates of next year's conditions and requirements are far from wild guesses."

After the opinions of the division vice presidents are in, the market research staff goes to work. They develop a formal statement of the marketing climate in detail for the forthcoming budget year and in general terms for the subsequent two years. Once these general factors have been assessed, a sales forecast is constructed for the company and for each division. Consideration is given to the relationship of the general economic climate to our customers' needs and Empire's share of each market. Explicitly stated are basic assumptions as to price, weather conditions, introduction of new products, gains or losses in particular accounts, forward buying, new manufacturing plants, industry growth trends, packaging trends, inventory carryovers, and developments in alternative packaging. This review of all the relevant factors is followed for each of our product lines, regardless of its size and importance. The completed forecasts of the market research group are then forwarded to the divisions for review, criticism, and adjustments.

"The primary goal of the head office group in developing these sales forecasts is to assure uniformity among the divisions with respect to the basic assumptions on business conditions, pricing, and the treatment of possible emergencies. Also, we provide a yardstick that assures us the company's overall sales forecast will be reasonable and attainable.

"The division top management then goes back to the district managers and asks them what they expect to do in the way of sales during the budget year. Head office and the divisional staffs will give the district managers as much guidance as they request, but it is the sole responsibility of each district

manager to come up with the district's sales budget.

"After the district sales managers' budgets are received by divisional management, they are consolidated and reviewed by the marketing general manager, who may suggest revisions. District managers know little of what's happening outside their territories, but at headquarters we can estimate the size of the whole market for, say, beer, and the market share of each of our customers. That's where the market research forecasts come in handy. Let me emphasize, however, that nothing is changed in the district manager's budget unless he or she agrees. Then, once the budget is approved, nobody is relieved of responsibility without top-management approval. Also, no arbitrary changes are made in the approved budgets without the concurrence of all the people responsible for the budget.

"Next, we go through the same procedure at the division and headquarters levels. We continue to repeat the process until everyone agrees that the sales budgets are sound. Then, each level of management takes responsibility for its particular portion of the budget. These sales budgets then become fixed objectives.

"I would say a division has four general objectives in mind in reviewing its sales budget:

1. A review of the division's competitive position, including plans for improving that position.

2. An evaluation of its efforts either to gain a larger share of the market or to offset competitors' activities.

3. A consideration of the need to expand facilities to improve the division's products or introduce new products.

4. A review and development of plans to improve product quality, delivery methods, and service."

Manufacturing Budgets. "Once the division vice presidents, executive vice president, and president have given final approval to the sales budget, we make a sales budget for each plant by breaking down the division sales budget according to the plants from which the goods will be shipped. These plant sales budgets are then further broken down on a monthly basis by price, volume, and product end use.

"With this information available the plants then budget their contribution margin, fixed expenses, and income before taxes. Contribution margin is the difference between the fixed sales dollar budget and variable manufacturing costs. Income is the difference between contribution and fixed costs. It is the plant manager's responsibility to meet this budgeted *profit* figure, even if actual dollar sales drop below the budgeted level.

"Given the plant's sales budget, it is up to the plant manager to determine the fixed overhead and variable costs—at standard—that the plant will need to incur so as to meet the demands of the sales budget. In my opinion requiring the plant managers to make their own plans is one of the most valuable things associated with the budget system. Each plant manager divides the preparation of the overall plant budget among the plant's various departments.

"First, the departments spell out the program in terms of the physical requirements, such as tons of raw material, and then the plans are priced at standard cost. The plant industrial engineering department is responsible for developing engineered cost standards. This phase of the budget also includes budgeted cost reductions, budgeted unfavorable variances from standards, and certain budgeted programmed fixed costs in the manufacturing area, such as service labor. The industrial engineer prepares this phase of the budget in conjunction with departmental line supervision.

"Before each plant sends its budget in to British City, a group of us from head office goes out to visit each plant. In the case of Glass Products, Ellen Newell, assistant controller, and I, along with representatives of the division's manufacturing staffs, visit each of the division's plants. Let me stress this point: We do not go on these trips to pass judgment on the plant's proposed budget. Rather, we go with two purposes in mind. First, we wish to acquaint ourselves with the thinking behind the figures that each plant manager will send in to British City. This is helpful because when we eventually review these budgets with top management—the president and executive vice president—we will have to answer questions about the budgets, and we will know the answers. Second, the review is a way of giving guidance to the plant managers as to whether or not they are in line with what the company needs to make in the way of profits.

"Of course, when we make our field reviews, we do not know what each of the other plants is planning. Therefore, we explain to the plant managers that while their budget may look good now, when we put all the plants together in a consolidated budget, the plant managers may have to make some changes because the projected profit is not high enough. When this happens, we tell the plant managers that it is not their programs that are unsound. The problem is that the company cannot afford the programs. I think it is very important that the plant managers have a chance to tell their story. Also, it gives them the feeling that we at headquarters are not living in an ivory tower.

"These plant visits are spread over a three-week period, and we spend about half a day at each plant. The plant managers are free to bring to these meetings any of their supervisors they wish. During the visit we discuss the budget primarily. However, if I have time I like to wander through the plant and see how things are going. Also, I go over in great detail the property replacement and maintenance budget with the plant engineer.

"About September 1 the plant budgets come into British City and the accounting department consolidates them. Then, the division vice presidents review their respective division budgets to see if they are reasonable in terms of what the vice president thinks the corporate management wants. If the vice president is not satisfied with the consolidated plant budgets, the various plants within the division will be asked to trim their budgeted costs.

"When the division vice presidents and the executive vice president are satisfied, they will send their budgets to the president. He may accept the division budgets at this point. If he doesn't, he will specify the areas to be reexamined by division and, if necessary, by plant. The final budget is approved at our December board of directors meeting."

Comparison of Actual and Standard Performance. "At the end of the sixth business day after the close of the month, each plant faxes certain operating variances to the head office, which we put together on what we call the variance analysis sheet. Within a half-hour after the last plant report comes through, variance analysis sheets for the divisions and plants are compiled. On the morning of the seventh business day, these reports are on the desks of top management. The variance analysis sheet highlights the variances in what we consider to be critical areas. Receiving this report as soon as we do helps us at head office to take timely action. Let me emphasize, however, we do not accept the excuse that plant managers have to go to the end of the month to know what happened during the month. They have to be on top of these particular items daily.

"When the actual results come into the head office, we go over them on the basis of exception; we only look at the unfavorable variances. We believe this has a good effect on morale. The plant managers don't have to explain everything they do. They have to explain only where they go off base. In par-

ticular, we pay close attention to the net sales, contribution margin, and the plant's ability to meet its standard manufacturing cost. When analyzing sales, we look closely at price and mix changes, which are the sales group's responsibility.

"All this information is summarized on a form known as the Profit Planning and Control Report No. 1 (see Exhibit 3). This document is backed up by a number of supporting documents (see Exhibit 4). The plant PPCR No. 1 and the month-end trial balance showing both actual and budget figures are received in British City at the close of the eighth business day after the end of the month. These two very important reports, along with the supporting reports (PPCR No. 2—PPCR No. 11), are then consolidated by the accounting department to show the results of operations by division and company. The consolidated reports are distributed the next day.

"In connection with the fixed cost items, we want to know whether the plants carried out their planned programs. If they have not, we want to know why. Also, we want to know if they have carried out these programs at the cost they said they would.

"To me the three most important items on PPCR No.1 are the P/V ratio, actual plant income, and percent return on capital employed. At the plant level, capital employed includes inventories at standard variable cost plus the replacement value of fixed assets. We use replacement value because it puts plants having disparate fixed asset original acquisition costs on an equal footing. At the division level accounts receivable also are included in capital employed.

"In addition to these reports, at the beginning of each month, the plant managers prepare current estimates for the upcoming month and quarter on forms similar to the variance analysis sheets. Since our budget is based on known programs, the value of this current estimate is that it gets the plant

EXHIBIT 3
PROFIT PLANNING AND CONTROL REPORT NO. 1

MONTH				YEAR TO DATE		
Income Gain (+) or Loss (−) From					Income Gain (+) or Loss (−) From	
Prev. Year	Budget	Actual		Actual	Budget	Prev. Year
			Gross Sales to Customers			
			Discounts & Allowances			
			Net Sales to Customers			
%	%		% Gain (+)/Loss (−)		%	%
			DOLLAR VOLUME GAIN (+)/ LOSS (−) DUE TO:			
			Sales Price			
			Sales Volume			
			Trade Mix			
			Std. Variable Cost of Sales			
			Contribution Margin			
			CONTRIB. MARGIN GAIN (+)/ LOSS (−) DUE TO:			
			Profit Volume Ratio (P/V)*			
			Dollar Volume			
%	%	%	Profit Volume Ratio (P/V)*		%	%
			Budgeted Fixed Mfg. Cost			
			Fixed Manufacturing Cost-Transfers			
			Plant Income (standard)			
%	%	%	% of Net Sales		%	%
%	%	%	% Mfg. Efficiency		%	%
			Manufacturing Variances			
			Methods Improvements			
			Other Revisions of Standards			
			Material Price Changes			
			Division Special Projects			
			Company Special Projects			
			New Plant Expense			
			Other Plant Expenses			
			Income on Seconds			
			Plant Income (actual)			
%	%		% Gain (+)/Loss (−)		%	%
%	%	%	% of Net Sales		%	%
			CAPITAL EMPLOYED			
			Total Capital Employed			
%	%	%	% Return		%	%
			Turnover Rate			

_____　　_____　　_____　19 ____
　　Plant　　　　　　Division　　　　　　Month

* The P/V ratio was defined to be: $\dfrac{\text{Price} - \text{Variable cost}}{\text{Price}}$

EXHIBIT 4
BRIEF DESCRIPTION OF PPCR NO. 2—PPCR NO. 11

Report	Individual Plant Reports Description
PPCR No. 2	Manufacturing expense: Plant materials, labor, and variable overhead incurred. Detail of actual figures compared with budget and previous year's figures for year to date and current month.
PPCR No. 3	Plant expense: Plant fixed expenses incurred. Details of actual figures compared with budget and previous year's figures for year to date and current month.
PPCR No. 4	Analysis of sales and income: Plant operating gains and losses due to changes in sales revenue, contribution margins, and other sources of income. Details of actual figures compared with budget and previous year's figures for year to date and current month.
PPCR No. 5	Plant control statement: Analysis of plant raw material gains and losses, spoilage costs, and cost reduction programs. Actual figures compared with budget figures for current month and year to date.
PPCR No. 6	Comparison of sales by plant and product groups: Plant sales dollars, contribution margin, and P/V ratios broken down by end product use (i.e., soft drinks, beer). Compares actual figures with budgeted figures for year to date and current month.

Report	Division Summary Reports Description
PPCR No. 7	Comparative plant performance, sales, and income: Gross sales and income figures by plants. Actual figures compared with budget figures for year to date and current month.
PPCR No. 8	Comparative plant performance, total plant expenses: Contribution margin, total fixed costs, manufacturing efficiency, other plant expenses, and P/V ratios by plants. Actual figures compared with budgeted and previous year's figures for current month and year to date.
PPCR No. 9	Manufacturing efficiency: Analysis of gains and losses by plant in areas of materials, spoilage, supplies, and labor. Current month and year-to-date actuals reported in total dollars and as a percentage of budget.
PPCR No. 10	Inventory: Comparison of actual and budget inventory figures by major inventory accounts and plants.
PPCR No. 11	Status of capital expenditures: Analysis of the status of capital expenditures by plants, months, and relative to budget.

people to look again at their programs. Hopefully, they will realize that they cannot run their plants just on a day-to-day basis.

"If we see a sore spot coming up, or if the plant manager draws our attention to a potential trouble area, we may ask that daily reports concerning this item be sent to division top management. In addition, the division top management may send a division staff specialist—say, a quality control expert—to the plant concerned. The division staff members can make recommendations, but it is up to the plant manager to accept or reject these recommendations. Of course, it is well known throughout the company that we expect the plant managers to accept gracefully the help of the head office and division staffs."

Sales-Manufacturing Relations. "If a sales decline occurs during the early part of the year and if the plant managers can convince us that the change is permanent, we may revise the plant profit budgets to reflect these new circumstances. However, if toward the end of the year actual sales suddenly drop below budget, we don't have much time to change the budget plans. What we do is ask the plant managers to go back over their budgets with their staffs and see where reduction of expense programs will do the least harm. Specifically, we ask them to consider what they may be able to eliminate this year or delay until next year.

"I believe it was Confucius who said: 'We make plans so we have plans to discard.' Nevertheless, I think it is wise to make plans, even if you have to discard them. Having plans makes it a lot easier to figure out what to do when sales fall off from the budgeted level. The understanding of operations that comes from preparing the budget removes a lot of the potential chaos that might arise if we were under pressure to meet a stated profit goal and sales declined quickly and unexpectedly at year-end, just as they did last year. In these circumstances we don't try to ram anything down the plant managers' throats. We ask them to tell us where they can reasonably expect to cut costs below the budgeted level.

Whenever a problem arises at a plant between sales and production, the local people are supposed to solve the problem themselves. Take rush orders, for example: a customer's purchasing agent may insist on an immediate delivery that would disrupt the production schedule and adversely affect costs. The production group can make recommendations as to alternative ways to take care of the problem, but it's the sales manager's responsibility to get the product to the customer. The sales force are supposed to know their customers well enough to judge whether or not the customer really needs the product. If the sales manager says the customer needs the product, that ends the matter. As far as we are concerned, the customer's wants are primary; our company is a case where sales wags the rest of the dog. Of course, if the change in the sales program involves a major plant expense that is out of line with the budget, then the matter is passed up to division top management for a decision.

"The sales department has responsibility for revenue variances related to product price, sales mix, and volume. They do not have responsibility for plant operations or profit. However, it is understood that the sales group will cooperate with the plant people whenever possible."

Motivation. "There are various ways in which we motivate the plant managers to meet their profit goals. First of all, we only promote capable people. Also, an incentive program has been established that provides substantial bonuses if plant managers achieve or exceed their profit goals. In addition, each month we put together a bar chart that shows, by division and plant, their ranking with respect to manufacturing efficiency.[1] We feel the plant managers are fully responsible for variable manufacturing costs,

---

[1]Manufacturing efficiency percent =
$$\frac{\text{Total standard variable manufacturing costs}}{\text{Total actual variable manufacturing costs}} * 100$$

since all manufacturing standards have to be approved by plant managers.

"Most of the plant managers give wide publicity to these bar charts. The efficiency measure itself is perhaps a little unfair in some respects when you are comparing one plant with another. Somewhat different mixes of products are run through different plants. These require different setups, and so forth, that have an important impact on the position of a plant. However, in general, the efficiency rating is a good indication of the quality of the plant managers and their supervisors.

"Also, a number of plants run competitions within the plants that reward department heads based on their relative standing with respect to a certain cost item. The plant managers, their staffs, and employees have great pride in their plants.

"The number one item now stressed at the plant level is quality. The market situation is such that in order to make sales you have to meet the market price and exceed the market quality. By quality I mean not only the physical characteristics of the product but also delivery schedules. The company employee publications' message is that if the company is to be profitable it must produce high-quality items at a reasonable cost. This is necessary so that the plants can meet their obligation to produce the maximum profits for the company in the prevailing circumstances."

The Future. "An essential part of the budgetary control system is planning. We have developed a philosophy that we must begin our plans where the work is done—in the line organization and out in the field. Perhaps in the future we can avoid or cut back some of the budget preparation steps

and start putting together our sales budget later than May 15. However, I doubt if we will change the basic philosophy. Frankly, I doubt if the line managers would want any major change in the system; they are very jealous of the management prerogatives the system gives them.

"It is very important that we manage the budget. We have to be continually on guard against its managing us. Sometimes, the plants lose sight of this fact. They continually have to be made conscious of the necessity of having the sales volume to make a profit. And when sales fall off and their programs are reduced, they do not always appear to see the justification for budget cuts—although I suspect they see more justification for these cuts than they will admit. It is this human side of the budget to which we have to pay more attention in the future."

Questions

1. Compare the descriptive material in this case with the diagram in Illustration 23–1. What aspects of the management control cycle are *not* explicitly described in the case?

2. Trace through Empire's profit budgeting process, beginning on May 15. For each step:
   a. Relate the information flow to Exhibits 1 and 2.
   b. Try to visualize who is involved and what "game playing" may occur.
   c. Speculate as to why Empire includes this step in the process (as opposed to some more expeditious method). Then evaluate Empire's budgeting process.

3. Comment on the strong points and weak points of Empire's management control system. Be sure to consider the question of whether the plants should be held responsible for profits and return on capital employed (ROI).

24

Strategic Planning
and Budgeting

This chapter describes the two principal types of planning activities that are part of the management control process. One, called strategic planning, is the process of making decisions on upcoming major programs. It involves formulating long-range plans. The other, called budgeting, is the process of planning the activities of the organization's responsibility centers for the next period, usually the next year. We deal primarily with what managers and others do in the course of preparing and using budgets, which is the *managerial* aspect of budgeting, rather than with how budget numbers are calculated and assembled, which is the *technical* aspect of budgeting.

Strategic Planning

The purpose of management control is to *implement* an organization's strategies. The process of identifying, evaluating, and deciding on these strategies is called **strategy formulation.** Although the strategy formulation process is sometimes referred to as a system, it is not in fact systematic. It is important to reconsider strategies whenever there is a need to do so: an opportunity to capitalize on new technology, a change in consumer preferences, a threat from a new competitor, and so on. Because the occurrence of such events is unpredictable, strategy formulation cannot be a systematic process carried out according to a predetermined schedule.

The systematic part of an organization's planning and control activities starts with **strategic planning** (sometimes called **programming** or **long-range planning**). Strategic planning is the process of deciding on the programs the organization will undertake to implement its strategies and on the approximate amount of resources to be allocated to each program. There are three main parts to the strategic planning process: (1) reviewing ongoing programs, (2) considering proposals for new programs, and (3) coordinating programs by means of a formal strategic planning system.[1]

Ongoing Programs

Most activities the typical organization will undertake in the next few years are similar to those already in progress. If a company currently manufactures and sells 20 lines of packaged foods, it probably will handle almost all of those lines next year and the year after. However, it is dangerous to be complacent about these ongoing programs. Consumers' needs and tastes change; competitive conditions change; production methods change. It is important for a company to recognize the implications of these changes and to adapt accordingly. Thus, there must be a systematic, thorough way of reviewing each of the existing programs to anticipate new conditions and decide upon appropriate actions.

If a company does not undertake systematic program review on a regular basis, it may quickly see a need to do so when it experiences a decline in profitability. In the recession that began in 1989, many companies had to undertake a crash **downsizing** program to eliminate costs that had been permitted to get out of line in the preceding years of prosperity. Some companies reduced their number of employees by 10–15 percent, or even more, in this manner. Such downsizing has continued into the 1990s.

Zero-Base Review. A systematic way of making an analysis of ongoing programs is called a **zero-base review.** It gets this name because, in deciding on the costs that are appropriate for a program, the cost estimates are built up "from scratch"—from zero. (This contrasts with taking the current level of costs as a starting point, as is customary in the budgeting process.) Such reviews are useful for major programs to overcome the natural tendency toward complacency and inertia. They are also useful for expense centers having a high proportion of discretionary costs, such as the legal and personnel departments and, indeed, most staff activities. Because a zero-base review is time-consuming and upsetting to the normal functioning of the responsibility center, it cannot be effectively conducted every year for every program and every expense center. An effective zero-base review

---

[1]Some companies use the term *strategic planning* to refer to the combination of activities that we have separately identified as strategy formulation and strategic planning (or programming or long-range planning). However, more commonly, a company's so-called strategic planning or long-range planning system takes the formulated strategies as a given and begins with the systematic program evaluation and coordination activities that we have labeled strategic planning.

involves *thoroughly* reviewing each part of the whole organization every three to five years.[2]

Making a zero-base review of an expense center involves asking basic questions about each significant activity of the center, such as:

1. Should this activity continue to be performed at all?

2. Is too much being done? Too little?

3. Should it be done internally, or should it be contracted to an outside firm (the familiar "make-or-buy" question)?

4. Is there a more efficient way of obtaining the desired results?

5. How much should it cost?

In the last few years this same basic activity analysis approach has been popularized under new names, including **process analysis, process reengineering,** and **activity-based management.** (In Japan, a similar analytical approach is called **functional analysis.**)

Making a zero-base review of a product line entails asking basic questions about the demand for the product, the nature of the competition, the marketing strategy, the production strategy, and so on. Among other indicators of performance, a zero-base review evaluates the product line's return on assets employed and market share.

Zero-base reviews are particularly appropriate in government agencies and other nonprofit organizations, which tend to have high proportions of discretionary costs. Without such reviews, a program an agency established to address some societal need may still be in place years later when the need has subsided or even disappeared. For this reason, legislatures subject certain programs to **sunset laws,** which require that a zero-base review be conducted after a specified number of years.

Activity-Based Costing. As was described in Chapter 18, activity-based costing involves more accurate allocations of joint (indirect) costs to cost objects than usually result when broad-based overhead rates are used. Although that description related to manufacturing overhead, the same approach can be used in assigning any indirect cost to the various cost objects that jointly cause the cost to be incurred. In particular, ABC concepts can be used in arriving at the full cost of a product line or other program of interest. Examining the costs (resource consumption) of the various activities required to implement the program and then applying these activity-

---

[2]There are references in the literature to **zero-base budgeting.** This term implies that such reviews should be made *annually* for all programs, as a part of the annual budgeting process. A good zero-base review, however, requires far more time than is normally available during the preparation of the annual budget. In 1978 President Carter instituted annual zero-base budgeting in the federal government, with much attendant fanfare. This practice was abandoned in 1981 (with much less publicity) because the Reagan administration concluded it "had proved cumbersome ... and hadn't achieved significant results in holding down federal government spending." (Source: *The Wall Street Journal,* August 10, 1981.)

based costs to the demands a program places on each of these activities ("activity consumption") yields full cost figures. The approach may be used either in performing zero-base reviews of ongoing programs or in evaluating new program proposals (described in the next section).

In using ABC in product profitability analyses, some companies have found that products that appeared profitable with costs assigned to them by a traditional product costing system are in fact unprofitable. These tend to be products that are made in small volumes and that involve a relatively large amount of batch-level and product-level support costs. Because product costing systems generally assign all overhead costs using unit-level drivers, these support costs get underallocated to these low-volume, support-intensive products, thus resulting in an understatement of their full cost and an overstatement of their profit. Such a revelation causes the company to consider ways to simplify (or "rationalize" or "deproliferate") its product lines in order to reduce support costs, and to reevaluate its pricing structure to be sure that customers for these low-volume, support-intensive products are not getting a "free ride."

Proposed New Programs

Within the boundaries of the agreed-upon strategies, management should be alert to the need for proposed new programs, either to counter a threat to existing operations or to take advantage of new opportunities. Management analyzes these proposals whenever the need or the opportunity comes to its attention. In business such proposals usually involve new capital investments, and the appropriate analytical techniques are therefore those described in Chapter 27, which deals specifically with this topic.

Whether or not new capital investment is involved, special attention must be given to whether a new program will increase step-function costs in the various departments that will play a role in implementing the program. As mentioned in Chapter 16, sometimes such costs are mistakenly labeled "fixed," resulting in an understatement of the impact a new program will have on the organization's total costs.

Benefit/Cost Analysis. Revenue is a measure of the output of a profit-oriented organization. Nonprofit organizations also have outputs, but many cannot measure their outputs in monetary terms. Similarly, the outputs of many units within a profit-oriented company cannot be expressed as revenue. In these situations, analysis of a new program proposal based on its estimated profit or return on investment is not possible. Sometimes, it is possible to use a similar approach by comparing the costs of a program with some measure of the benefits that are expected as a consequence of incurring these costs. This approach is called a **benefit/cost analysis.**

Benefit/cost analysis is widely used for analyzing programs in nonprofit organizations. Profit-oriented companies also use benefit/cost analysis for analyzing such program proposals as spending more money to improve safety conditions, to reduce pollution, to improve the company's reputation with the public, or to provide better information to management. Zero-base reviews also usually require extensive use of this approach.

The cost estimates in a benefit/cost analysis are usually straightforward. The difficult part of the analysis is estimating the value of the benefits. In the many situations in which no meaningful estimate of the quantitative amount of benefits can be made, the anticipated benefits are carefully described in words. Then, the decision maker must answer the question: Are the perceived benefits worth *at least* the estimated cost? For example, "If $85,000 is added to the costs of the city park summer recreation program, will the increased output (benefits) of the program be worth at least $85,000?" The answer to this question is necessarily judgmental, but the judgment can be aided by a careful estimate of the program's costs and a careful assessment of the likely benefits.

Formal Strategic Planning Systems

Every organization should review its ongoing programs and make decisions on proposed new programs. Although many do this informally, most large companies have a formal system in which the financial and other consequences of these programs are projected for a number of years in the future. Such a projection is called a **long-range plan.** It shows revenues, costs, and other information for individual programs for a number of years ahead—usually 5 years but possibly as few as 2 or 3 (in the case of companies in very dynamic industries such as electronics and multimedia).

Usually the strategic planning process begins several months prior to the start of the annual budgeting process. Formal strategic planning begins after senior management has analyzed the need for changes in basic goals and strategies. These are disseminated to the operating managers, who then prepare tentative programs, following the guidelines set forth by senior management. Next, these proposed programs are discussed at length with senior management, and out of these discussions emerges a set of programs for the whole company. These approved programs provide the guidelines for preparing the annual budget.

BUDGETING

A **budget** is a plan expressed in quantitative, usually monetary, terms covering a specified period of time, usually one year. Practically all companies, except some of the smallest, prepare budgets. Many companies refer to their annual budget as a **profit plan,** since it shows the planned activities that the company expects to undertake in its responsibility centers in order to obtain its profit goal. Almost all nonprofit organizations also prepare budgets.

Uses of the Budget

The budget serves as:

1. An aid in making and coordinating short-range plans.
2. A device for communicating these plans to the various responsibility center managers.

3. A way of motivating managers to achieve their responsibility centers' goals.

4. A benchmark for controlling ongoing activities.

5. A basis for evaluating the performance of responsibility centers and their managers.

6. A means of educating managers.

Planning. Major planning decisions are usually made in the strategic planning activity, and the process of developing the budget is essentially a refinement of these plans. Managers must consider how conditions in the future may change and what steps they should take to get ready for these changed conditions.

Furthermore, each responsibility center affects and is affected by the work of other responsibility centers. The budgetary process helps *coordinate* these separate activities to ensure that all parts of the organization are in balance with one another. Most important, production plans must be coordinated with marketing plans to ensure that the production processes are geared up to produce the planned sales volume. Similarly, cash management plans (e.g., plans for short-term borrowing or for short-term investment of excess funds) must be based on projected inflows from sales and outflows for operating costs.

Communication. Management's plans will not be carried out (except by coincidence) unless the organization understands what the plans are. These plans include such specific things as how many goods and services are to be produced; what methods, people, and equipment are to be used; how much material is to be purchased; and what selling prices are to be. The organization also needs to be aware of policies and constraints to which it is expected to adhere. Examples of these kinds of information include the maximum amounts that may be spent for advertising, maintenance, and administrative costs; wage rates and hours of work; and desired quality levels. The approved budget is the most useful device for communicating quantitative information concerning these plans and limitations.

Motivation. If the atmosphere is right, the budgeting process can also be a powerful force in motivating managers to work toward the objectives of their responsibility centers and, hence, the goals of the overall organization. Such an atmosphere cannot exist unless responsibility center managers have been told what is expected of their responsibility centers. Motivation will be greatest when these managers have played an active role in the development of their budgets, as described later in this chapter.

Control. As described in Chapter 22, management control's purpose is to attain desired results. A budget is a statement of the results desired as of the time the budget was prepared. A carefully prepared budget is the best possible standard against which to compare actual performance. This is because it incorporates the estimated effect of all variables that were foreseen when the budget was being prepared.

Until fairly recently, the general practice was to compare current results with results for last month or for the same period a year ago; this is still the basic means of comparison in some organizations. But such a historical standard has the fundamental weakness that it does not take account of changes either in the underlying forces at work or in the planned programs for the current year. A comparison of actual performance with budgeted performance provides a "red flag"; it directs attention to areas where action may be needed. An analysis of the variance between actual and budgeted results may (1) help identify a problem area that needs attention, (2) reveal an exploitable opportunity not predicted in the budgeting process, or (3) reveal that the original budget was unrealistic in some way.

Evaluation. Monthly variances from budgets are used for control purposes *during* the year. The comparison of actual and budgeted results for the *entire* year is frequently a major factor in the year-end evaluation of each responsibility center and its manager. Some companies calculate a manager's bonus as a predetermined percentage of the net favorable variance in his or her responsibility center.

Education. Although many companies do not explicitly recognize it as such, budget preparation is an educational tool. Budgets serve to educate managers about the detailed workings of their responsibility centers and the interrelationships of their centers with other centers in the organization. This is particularly true for a person who has been newly appointed to the position of responsibility center manager. Any person who has attempted preparation of an annual budget for personal financial affairs can appreciate the educational nature of this process.

Multiple-Use Complications. Because the budget serves multiple purposes, budget preparation can be a complicated process. One problem is that managers may introduce *bias* when preparing their portion of the budget. For example, some expense center managers propose expense budgets that are somewhat higher than senior management's "best guess" as to the amount of costs actually required to carry out the center's planned activities. They do this to protect themselves against uncertainties that may result in unfavorable variances that would look bad in the evaluation phase of the management control cycle. However, the corporate treasurer needs realistic (unbiased) numbers for cash flow planning purposes.

This raises difficult questions: Should there be, in effect, two sets of budget numbers? Should a company evaluate a manager based on the realistic amount or the inflated amount? Rather than accepting the bias by having two sets of numbers, most companies try to design checks and balances into the budget preparation process that are intended to eliminate—or at least substantially reduce—the amount of bias in the budget numbers. One important device for eliminating bias is budget negotiation, described later in this chapter.

The Master Budget

Although we have referred to "the" budget, the complete *budget package* in an organization includes several items, each of which is also referred to as a budget. We shall therefore refer to the total package as the **master budget.** Illustration 24–1 shows the components of this package in a typical company. The three principal parts of the master budget are:

1. An **operating budget,** showing planned operations for the coming year, including revenues, expenses, and changes in inventory and other working capital items.
2. A **cash budget,** showing the anticipated sources and uses of cash in that year.
3. A **capital expenditure budget,** showing planned changes in property, plant, and equipment.

We shall describe first the nature of the operating budget and the steps involved in its preparation, then the cash budget and the capital expenditure budget. Another document, the **budgeted balance sheet,** is derived directly from the other budgets and is therefore not described separately.

THE OPERATING BUDGET

The operating budget sets forth the first-year slice of the long-range plan in terms of the responsibility centers obligated for implementing the plan. The long-range plan is structured in terms of programs, whereas a given responsibility center's activities cut across a number of programs. As a statement of the performance expected for each responsibility center manager, the operating budget is an excellent control device because comparing it with actual performance can provide a basis for assessment. Each manager is responsible for preparing those parts of the operating budget that correspond to her or his sphere of responsibility.

Responsibility budgets are broken down into **cost elements**—for example, labor, materials, supplies, maintenance, supervision, and utilities. Such a breakdown is useful both as a guide to spending and as a basis for identifying the areas of inadequate performance if actual spending differs from the budgeted amounts.

Project Budgets

Some organizations work on defined projects. The producer of a motion picture or a television special has a budget for that particular project, and exercises control in terms of that budget. This is also the case in the construction of major capital assets: buildings, roads, aircraft, ships, and the like. The manager of the project may use personnel and other resources from various functional departments in the organization. If so, the project budget contains amounts that are also reported in the budgets for the functional responsibility centers.

ILLUSTRATION 24–1
MASTER BUDGET COMPONENTS

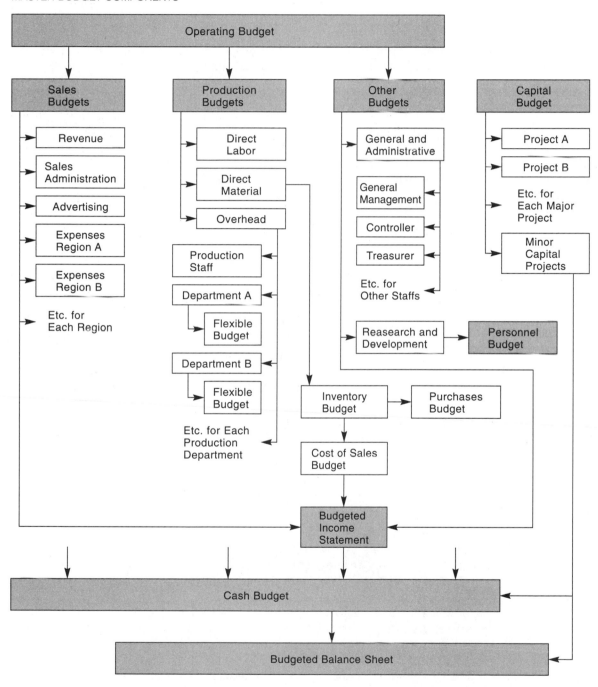

If personnel from functional departments are assigned temporarily to a project, they have two bosses, the project manager and the manager of their functional department. Such a practice results in a **matrix organization.** Because of dual lines of authority and responsibility, the control of a matrix organization is complicated. In budget preparation it is important that the project budgets be consistent with the budgets of the functional departments that will be supplying resources to the projects.

Flexible (Variable) Budgets

If the total costs in a responsibility center are expected to vary with changes in volume, as is the case with most standard cost centers, the responsibility budget may be in the form of a **flexible budget,** or **variable budget.** Such a budget shows the planned behavior of costs at various volume levels. It is appropriately used in responsibility centers with a high proportion of engineered costs, because additional volume causes additional cost in such centers. (The use of flexible budgets for production overhead costs was described in Chapter 18.) The flexible budget is usually expressed in terms of a cost-volume relationship—that is, a fixed amount for a specified time period plus a variable amount per unit of volume. In structuring such a budget, care must be taken that the time period is clear, that volume is correctly defined, and that step-function costs have been treated appropriately (as discussed in Chapter 16).

When there is a flexible budget, the costs at *one* volume level are used as part of the master budget. That volume level is the planned level of operations for the budget period; for an annual budget, this is usually the same as the *standard* (*normal*) *volume* used for setting predetermined overhead rates (as described in Chapter 18). Budgeted costs at other volume levels are used in the evaluation phase of the management control cycle, at which time actual costs are compared with the budgeted costs corresponding to the actual volume level that was experienced.

Management by Objectives

The foregoing description of budgets emphasized monetary information because such information is incorporated in an accounting system. Accounting information alone cannot provide an adequate benchmark for the performance of a responsibility center, however. At best, it measures profitability; and although profitability is one important goal in a profit-oriented company, it is by no means the only goal. In nonprofit organizations and in expense centers in profit-oriented companies, profit is not a goal at all. Furthermore, the income reported for a profit center measures only short-run performance. It shows the results of the manager's decisions on *current* profits but tells nothing about actions the manager may have taken that influence *future* profits.

As a way of overcoming these inadequacies, many organizations supplement the monetary accounting information with other information about the results of the manager's actions. A system that does this is called a **management by objectives (MBO) system.** It gets this name because the system states specific objectives that the responsibility center manager is expected to achieve during the period covered by the budget. These objectives are analogous to the revenues, expenses, and profit amounts in financial budgets. This approach is especially useful in expense centers for which comparisons of actual cost versus budgeted cost are of limited usefulness in evaluating performance.

For example, an organization may expect a sales manager to open three new sales offices next year, an engineering manager to develop a new training program, or a production manager to take certain steps in reducing the rate of defects. Such actions often cause the incurrence of additional expenses in the current period, which reduces current profits. But these actions are expected to lead to improved profitability in future periods or to the attainment of other company goals. MBO helps ensure that these actions are not foregone in an attempt to improve short-term cost performance.

Lee Iacocca describes his use of MBO at Ford Motor Company and later at Chrysler Corporation as follows:

> Over the years, I've regularly asked my key people—and I've had them ask *their* key people, and so on down the line—a few basic questions: "What are your objectives for the next 90 days? What are your plans, your priorities, your hopes? And how do you go about achieving them?"
>
> [This] quarterly review system makes employees accountable to *themselves.* Not only does it force each manager to consider his [or her] own goals, but it's also an effective way to remind people not to lose sight of their dreams.[3]

Experience with MBO in businesses has shown that it improves results in those responsibility centers where monetary measures are not felt to be useful indicators of performance. Without MBO, there is a tendency in such areas not to measure results at all. For MBO to be successful, however, it must be actively supported by senior management and carefully integrated with other aspects of the management control system. In some companies MBO has proven ineffective because it was implemented by the human resource management department and was not integrated with the management control system administered by the controller's department. MBO should be an integral part of the management control system, not a separate system.

At the profit or investment center level, MBO seems more appropriate for new endeavors than for mature ones. If a division is formed to enter a business that is new to the company, nonfinancial objectives such as developing channels of distribution and building market share are dominant in the division's early years. But as the division matures, financial objectives such as return on investment or net cash flow generated become more important.

---

[3]Lee Iacocca, *Iacocca, An Autobiography* (New York: Bantam Books, 1984), p. 47.

PREPARING THE OPERATING BUDGET

Budget preparation can be studied both as a technical process and as a managerial process. From a technical standpoint, one studies the mechanics of the system, the procedures for assembling the budget data, and budget formats. The procedures are similar to those described in Part 1 of this book for recording actual transactions, and the end result of the calculations and summarizations is a set of financial statements—a balance sheet, income statement, and cash flow statement—identical in format with those resulting from the accounting process that records historical events. The principal difference is that the budget amounts reflect planned future activities rather than data on what has happened in the past. We shall focus here on the preparation of an operating budget as a *managerial* process.

Organization for Budget Preparation

A **budget committee,** consisting of several members of the senior management group, usually guides the work of preparing the budget. This committee recommends to the chief executive officer (CEO) the general guidelines that the organization is to follow. After the CEO's approval of these guidelines, the budget committee disseminates them to the various responsibility centers and then coordinates the separate budgets prepared by those centers. The committee resolves any differences among the centers' budgets and then submits the final budget to the CEO and board of directors for approval. (In a small company that has no budget committee, this work is done by the CEO or by the CEO's immediate subordinate.) Budgeting instructions go down through the regular chain of command, and the budget comes back up for successive reviews and approvals through the same channels. The line organization makes decisions about the budget, and the CEO gives final approval, subject to ratification by the board of directors.

The line organization is usually assisted in its budget preparations by a staff unit headed by the **budget director.** As a staff person, the budget director's functions are to disseminate instructions about budget preparation mechanics (the forms and how to fill them out), to provide past performance data useful in preparing the budget, to make computations based on decisions reached by the line organization, to assemble the budget numbers, and to ensure that all managers submit their portions of the budget on time. The accounting staff at various levels in the organization assist the budget director.

The budget staff may do a very large share of the budget work. It is not the crucial part, however, because the line organization always makes the significant decisions. Once the line organization members have reached an agreement on such matters as labor productivity and wage rates, for example, the budget staff can calculate the detailed amounts for labor costs by products and by responsibility centers. This is a considerable job of computation, but it is based entirely on the decisions of the line managers.

The budget staff, which is usually a unit of the controller's department, is like a telephone company: it operates an important communication system.

It is responsible for the speed, accuracy, and clarity with which messages flow through the system, but it does not decide on the *content* of the messages themselves.

Budget Timetable

Most organizations prepare budgets once a year, covering the upcoming fiscal year. They usually make separate budget estimates for each month or each quarter within the year. Some organizations initially estimate data by months only for the next three months or the next six months, with the balance of the year being shown by quarters. With this approach, a detailed budget by months is prepared shortly before the beginning of each new quarter.

Some organizations follow the practice of preparing a new budget every quarter, but for a full year ahead. Every three months, the budget amounts for the quarter just completed are dropped, the amounts for the succeeding three quarters are revised if necessary, and budget amounts for the fourth succeeding quarter are added. This is called a **rolling budget.**

Most components of a company's operating budget are affected by decisions or estimates made in constructing other components (see Illustration 24–1). Nearly all components are affected by the planned sales volume; the purchases budget is affected by planned production volume and decisions as to materials inventory levels; and so on. Thus, there has to be a carefully worked out timetable specifying the order in which the several parts of the operating budget are developed and the time when each must be completed. In general, this timetable covers the following steps:

1. Setting planning guidelines.
2. Preparing the sales budget.
3. Initial preparation of other budget components.
4. Negotiation to agree on final plans for each component.
5. Coordination and review of the components.
6. Final approval.
7. Distribution of the approved budget.

In a typical organization, the elapsed time for the whole budget preparation process is approximately three months, with the most hectic part (steps 4, 5, and 6 above) requiring approximately one month. A very small business may go through the whole process in one day.

Setting Planning Guidelines

The budget preparation process is *not* the mechanism through which most major program decisions are made. Rather, it involves detailed planning by responsibility centers to implement the broader program plans that have already been decided upon in the strategic planning process. When budget preparation begins, a great many decisions affecting the budget year already have been made. The amount and character of available facilities dictates the maximum level of operations. If an expansion of facilities is to take place during the budget year, the decision would ordinarily have been made a year or more previously because of the time required to construct buildings and to acquire and install equipment. If a new product is to be introduced, considerable time would have already been spent prior to the budget year on product development, testing, design, and initial promotional work. Thus, the budget is not a brand new creation; it is built within the context of ongoing operations and newly approved programs.

If the organization has a formal long-range plan, this plan provides a starting point in preparing the budget. If there is no long-range plan, senior management establishes policies and guidelines that are to govern budget preparation. These guidelines vary greatly in content in different organizations. At one extreme, there may be only a brief general statement such as, "Assume that industry volume next year will be 5 percent higher than the current year." More commonly, detailed information and guidance are given on such matters as projected economic conditions, allowance to be made for price increases and wage increases, changes in the product line, changes in the scale of operations, allowable number of personnel promotions, and anticipated productivity gains. In addition, detailed instructions are issued as to what information is required from each responsibility center and how this information is to be recorded on the budget documents.

Preparing the Sales Budget

The amount of sales and the product mix (i.e., the proportion of total sales represented by each product) govern the level and general character of a company's operations. Thus, because it affects most of the other plans, a sales plan must be made early in the budget preparation process.

The sales *budget* is different from a sales *forecast,* which is merely a passive prediction of some uncontrollable outcome (e.g., one forecasts the weather, one does not budget it). By contrast, a budget carries with it a *commitment* by the responsibility center manager to take those actions necessary to attain the desired results. For example, this may be the sales forecast: "With the present amount of sales effort, we expect sales to run at about the same level as they are currently." By contrast, the sales budget may show a commitment to a substantial increase in sales, reflecting management's intention to add sales personnel, to increase advertising and sales promotion, or to add or redesign products.

At the same time a company is preparing the sales budget, it should also be preparing a selling expense budget that reflects the size and nature of the marketing efforts that are intended to generate the budgeted sales revenue. However, in this early stage, it may suffice to show the main elements of selling expense, with such details as the expenses of operating field selling offices left until the next step.

In almost all companies the sales budget is the most difficult plan to make. This is because a company's sales revenue depends on the actions of its customers, which are not subject to the direct control of management. In contrast, the amounts of cost incurred are determined primarily by actions of the company itself (except for the prices of certain input factors) and therefore can be planned with more confidence.

Basically, there are two ways of making estimates as a basis for the sales budget:

1. Make a *statistical forecast* on the basis of a mathematical analysis of general business conditions, market conditions, product growth curves, and the like.

2. Make a *judgmental estimate* by collecting the opinions of executives and salespersons. In some companies, sales personnel are asked to estimate the sales of each product to each of their customers; in others, regional managers estimate total sales in their regions: in still others, the field organization does not participate in the estimating process.

Both the statistical and the judgmental methods have advantages and weaknesses. Studies indicate that the majority of large corporations use a combination of both methods, although a minority rely solely on judgment. Many companies have concluded that the use of sophisticated techniques— regression analysis, input-output analysis, and econometric models—does not produce more accurate forecasts than "naive" methods, including judgment and simple extrapolation from past results.[4]

Another sales budgeting approach is to buy a forecast of industry sales that has been prepared by professional economists using sophisticated mathematical models. The company must then forecast its own *market share* and apply this to the industry forecast to arrive at a sales budget. Other companies use test markets to refine their estimates of sales of *new* products, but this has the potential problem of giving other firms more time to develop their own competitive new products.

Some companies negotiate revenue budgets at various levels in the sales organization. For example, salespersons may negotiate sales targets with their district sales manager. In cases where such negotiations take place, the comments below on negotiating expense budgets also apply.

Initial Preparation of Other Budget Components

The budget guidelines prepared by senior management, together with the sales budget, are disseminated down through the successive levels in the organization. Managers at each level may add other, more detailed information for the guidance of their subordinates. When these guidelines arrive at

---

[4]A careful analysis of the relative accuracy of various methods has been conducted in one large company that spent $5.5 million annually on sales forecasting efforts. The company found that forecasts based on both quantitative methods and management judgment were as accurate as strictly quantitative forecasts and were more useful to management. See Kenton B. Walker and Craig E. Bain, "Sales Volume Forecasting: A Comparison of Management, Statistical, and Combined Approaches," *Journal of Management Accounting Research*, Fall 1989, pp. 119–35.

the lowest responsibility centers, their managers prepare proposed budgets for the items within their sphere of responsibility, working within the constraints specified in the guidelines.

In expense centers the proposed budgets reflect the managers' judgment (perhaps with bias) as to the amounts of resources required to carry out their centers' functions effectively. These amounts may have been tentatively agreed upon in a previous zero-base review. Alternatively (and more commonly), the manager focuses on how the coming year's activities will differ from the current year's and then adjusts the current year's budget amounts for these differences plus increased salaries and other inflationary impacts. This approach is called **incremental budgeting.**

Standard cost centers review current standards for input quantities (e.g., labor-hours, pounds of material) for the various products to determine their ongoing applicability. These standards may be adjusted downward for learning-curve effects (described in Chapter 16) or for significant antici- pated changes in production processes that will increase productivity. Next year's unit material prices and labor rates are also estimated. Together, the quantity and price (or rate) standards determine the budgeted direct cost for each unit of product. These per-unit amounts are then multiplied by the budgeted production volumes for the various products to arrive at total budgeted costs for direct material and direct labor. The budgeted indirect costs are then added to arrive at the center's total budgeted costs. As previously mentioned, some companies prepare flexible budgets for their standard cost centers in order to facilitate subsequent analysis of actual versus budgeted performance and also to let managers know in advance how their costs are expected to change with changes in volume.

Negotiation

Now comes the crucial (from a control standpoint) stage in the process: negotiations between the managers who prepared the budgets and their superiors.[5] The value of the budget as a plan of what is to happen, as a motivating device, and as a standard against which actual performance will be measured depends largely on whether and how skillfully this negotiation is conducted. Numerous studies have shown that participation in standard setting enhances most subordinates' motivation to achieve the objectives. It is important that subordinates feel that their participation is meaningful and that the negotiation is not a sham.

A number of studies have also shown that the budget is most effective as a motivating device when it represents a "tight" (challenging) but attainable target. The objective that is too tight is rejected by the subordinate as too difficult; one that is too loose does not challenge the manager or satisfy

---

[5]In a perceptive study, G. H. Hofstede describes this process as a game. See *The Game of Budget Control* (Assen, the Netherlands: Van Gorcum & Co., N.V., 1968). A negotiation is a game, in the formal sense, as the reader who has participated in budget negotiations can appreciate.

that manager's need for achievement. The subordinate and superior therefore seek to arrive at a desirable middle ground.

The negotiating process applies principally to revenues and to items of discretionary cost. If engineered costs have been properly analyzed, there is little room for differences of opinion about them. Committed costs, by definition, are not subject to negotiation so long as the commitment remains in force.

Slack. Few machines and no organizations operate at 100 percent efficiency. Human beings will not exert maximum effort hour after hour and day after day, and no reasonable manager expects them to do so. Also, there is a great deal of waste motion, miscommunication, and duplication of effort in any organization. For all these reasons, there is **slack**—that is, a difference between the potential output and actual output—in an organization. The actual amount of slack cannot be measured. A certain amount of it is desirable; otherwise, the organization would be viewed as a "pressure cooker" and not an attractive place in which to work. The problem is to keep slack within reasonable bounds. This is a primary objective of the negotiating process.

Negotiating Tactics. As did the subordinate, the superior usually must take the current level of expense as the starting point in negotiations, modifying this according to his or her perception of how satisfactory the current level is. The superior does not have enough time during the budget review to reexamine each of the detailed elements of expense so as to ensure that the subordinate's estimates are optimum. One way of addressing the problem of slack is to make an arbitrary cut—say, 5 percent—in the budget estimates. But this has the weakness of any arbitrary action: it affects efficient and inefficient managers alike. Furthermore, if managers know that an arbitrary cut is going to be made, they can counter it by padding their original estimates by a corresponding amount.

More reasonable tactics are available for keeping costs in line during the negotiating process. The superior should require a full explanation of any proposed cost increases and attempt to find reasons why costs may be expected to decrease. Such reasons might include a decrease in the workload of the responsibility center or an increase in productivity resulting from the installation of new equipment or a new method. (The superior recognizes that these prospective decreases may not be voluntarily disclosed by the subordinate.) Questions may be raised as to why certain competitors in the industry appear to be more efficient than the subordinate's responsibility center.

For their part, subordinates defend their estimates. They justify proposed cost increases by explaining the underlying causes, such as additional work they are expected to do, the effect of inflation, the need for better-quality output, and so on.

The Commitment. The end product of the negotiation process is an agreement that represents a *commitment* by each party, the subordinate and the superior. As previously mentioned, this commitment differentiates a budget from a forecast. By agreeing to the budget estimates, the subordinate says to the superior, in effect: "I can and will operate my responsibility center in accordance with the plan described in this budget." By approving the budget estimates, the superior says to the subordinate, in effect: "If you operate your responsibility center in accordance with this plan, you will do what we consider to be a good job." Both of these statements contain the implicit qualification of "subject to adjustment for unanticipated changes in circumstances." Both parties recognize that actual events (such as changes in price levels and general business conditions) may not correspond to those assumed when the budget was prepared and that these changes may affect the budget plans. In judging whether the commitment is, in fact, being accomplished as the year progresses, management must take such changes into account.

The nature of the commitment, both as to individual items of expense and as to the total expense of the responsibility center, may be one of three types:

1. A *ceiling*—"Not more than $X should be spent for books and periodicals."

2. A *floor*—"At least $Y should be spent for employee training."

3. A *guide*—"Approximately $Z may be spent for overtime."

Often individual items are not explicitly identified as being in one of these three categories, but it is obviously important that the two parties have a clear understanding as to which item belongs in which category.

Coordination and Review

The negotiation process is repeated at successively higher levels of responsibility centers in the organizational hierarchy, up to the very top. Negotiations at higher levels may, of course, result in changes in the detailed budgets agreed to at lower levels. If these changes are significant, the budget is recycled back down the organizational hierarchy for revision. However, if the budget process is well understood and well conducted by those who participate in it, such recycling ordinarily is not necessary. In the successive stages of negotiation, the manager who has the role of superior at one level becomes the subordinate at the next higher level. Since managers are well aware of this fact, they are strongly motivated to negotiate budgets with their subordinates that can be defended successfully with their superiors. If a superior demonstrates that a proposed budget is too loose, this reflects adversely on the subordinate's ability as a manager and as a negotiator.

As the individual budgets move up the organizational hierarchy in the negotiation and review process, they are also examined in relationship to one another. This examination may reveal aspects of the plan that are out of balance. If so, some of these budgets may need to be changed. The individual responsibility center budgets may also reveal the need to change amounts in the program plans, and these changes may in turn disclose that parts of the overall plan appear to be out of balance. Various summary documents, including the budgeted income statement, the budgeted balance sheet, and the cash flow budget, are also prepared during this step.

Final Approval and Distribution

Just prior to the beginning of the budget year, the proposed budget is submitted to senior management for approval. If the guidelines have been properly set and adhered to and if significant issues that arise during the budgeting process are brought to senior management for resolution, the proposed budget should contain no great surprises. Approval is by no means perfunctory, however, for it signifies the official agreement of senior management to the proposed plans for the year. The chief executive officer therefore usually spends considerable time discussing the budget with immediate subordinates. After the CEO approves the budget, it is submitted to the board of directors for final ratification.

The components of the approved budget are then transmitted down through the organization to the appropriate responsibility centers. Each center's approved budget constitutes authority to carry out the plans specified therein.

Revisions

The budget incorporates certain assumptions as to conditions that will prevail during the budget year. Actual conditions will never be exactly the same as those assumed, and the differences may be significant. The question then arises: Should the budget be revised to reflect what is now known about current conditions? There is considerable difference of opinion on this question.

Those who favor budget revision point out that the budget is supposed to reflect the plan in accordance with which the organization is operating and that when the plan has to be altered because of changing conditions, the budget should reflect these changes. If the budget is not revised, they maintain, it is no longer realistic and loses its potential to motivate managers.

The opponents of revising the budget argue that the revision process not only is time-consuming but also may obscure the objectives that the organization originally intended to achieve and the reasons for departures from these objectives. In particular, a revision may reflect the manager's skill in negotiating a change rather than reflecting an actual change in the underlying assumed conditions. Since revisions for spurious reasons stretch the credibility of the budget, critics refer to such a revised budget as a **rubber baseline.** Many organizations, therefore, do not revise their budgets during the year; instead, they take account of changes in conditions when they analyze the difference between actual and budgeted performance. An equitable analysis of variance should preclude motivation problems, these people argue.

Some companies solve this problem by having two budgets: a baseline budget set at the beginning of the year, and a current budget (also called a *current outlook* or *updated budget*) reflecting the best current estimate of revenue and expenses. A comparison of actual performance with the baseline performance shows the extent of deviation from the original plan. A comparison of the current budget with the baseline budget shows how much of this deviation is attributable to changes in current conditions from those originally assumed.

Variations in Practice

The preceding is a general description of the budget process. Some organizations treat the process more casually than is implied in the above description. A few organizations formulate their budgets in a process that is essentially the reverse of that described. Instead of having budget estimates originate at the lowest responsibility centers, the budget is prepared by a high-level staff, approved by senior management, and then transmitted down through the organization. This **imposed budget,** or **top-down budget,** is a less effective motivating device because standards set by others are less likely to be understood and more likely to be seen as difficult or unfair.

Merchandising Companies.   Retail stores and other merchandising companies employ a budgeting process that is somewhat simpler than that described above. This is because they do not face the complexities of preparing a production budget and coordinating it with a sales budget. Each responsibility center (including selling departments and support functions) does, of course, prepare an expense budget, and the selling departments also prepare sales budgets.

Instead of preparing a monthly budget showing the goods to be purchased for inventory, retail store buyers generally use the **open-to-buy procedure.** Buyers are given a dollar limit for the sum of goods on hand and on order at any time, and they must govern their purchases so that they do not exceed this limit. For example, if the sporting goods buyer has an open-to-buy of $200,000, and $170,000 of sporting goods are on hand or on order, additional orders totaling up to $30,000 may be placed.

Nonprofit Organizations.   The budgeting process in most nonprofit organizations is even more important than in a profit-oriented company. This is because the profit measure for a business provides guidance as to what actions not contemplated by the budget should be taken during the year, whereas managers of nonprofit organizations must conform their actions to mandates imposed by their governing bodies. These mandates are set forth in the approved budget. Municipal, state, and federal government bodies are prohibited by law from exceeding the budgeted amounts.

Budgeting in nonprofit organizations is very much like budgeting in a business. The organization has programs that it conducts, and the annual budget is the first-year slice of the longer-range program plans. For example, the programs for a community health care center might include nutrition, mental health, dental care, pediatrics, prenatal care, drug abuse, and general medicine; the annual budget would allocate human and other resources to the responsibility centers that will carry out the activities of these programs over the next year.

THE CASH BUDGET

The operating budget is usually prepared in terms of revenues and expenses. For financial planning purposes, it must be translated into terms of cash inflows (receipts) and cash outflows (disbursements). This translation results in the **cash budget.** The financial manager uses the cash budget to make plans to ensure that the organization has enough, but not too much, cash on hand during the year ahead.

There are two approaches to the preparation of a cash budget:

1. Start with the budgeted balance sheet and income statement and adjust the amounts thereon to derive the planned sources and uses of cash. This procedure is substantially the same as that described for preparation of the cash flow statement in Chapter 11, except that the data are estimates of the future rather than historical. The procedure is therefore not described here.

2. Analyze those plans having cash flow implications and directly estimate each of the inflows and outflows of cash. An example of this approach is shown in Illustration 24–2. Some points about this technique are briefly described here.

Collection of accounts receivable is estimated by applying a "lag" factor to estimated sales. This factor may be based simply on the assumption that the cash from this month's sales will be collected next month. Or there may be a more elaborate assumption—for example, that 10 percent of this month's sales will be collected this month, 60 percent next month, 20 percent in the third month, 9 percent in the fourth month, and the remaining 1 percent will never be collected.

The estimated amount and timing of *materials purchases* is obtained from the materials purchases budget and is translated into cash outlays by applying a lag factor for the ordinary time interval between receipt of the material and payment of the invoice.

Most other operating expenses are taken directly from the expense budget, since the timing of cash outlays is likely to correspond closely to the incurrence of the expense. Depreciation and other items of expense not requiring cash disbursements are excluded. Capital expenditures are also shown as outlays, with amounts taken from the capital expenditure budget.

The bottom section of Illustration 24–2 shows how cash plans are made. The company desires a minimum cash balance of about $150,000 as a cushion against unforeseen needs. From the budgeted cash receipts and cash disbursements, a calculation is made of whether the budgeted cash balance exceeds or falls below this minimum. In January, the budgeted cash

ILLUSTRATION 24–2
CASH BUDGET
($000)

	January	February	March	April	May	Totals for Year
Gross shipments.	1,200	1,987	2,063	1,387	2,363	21,000
Cash balance beginning of month.	375	396	152	150	157	375
Add: Cash receipts:						
Collections of accounts receivable	1,380	1,350	1,605	1,635	1,680	19,305
Miscellaneous receipts.	66	81	70	105	105	1,050
Total receipts.	1,446	1,431	1,675	1,740	1,785	20,355
Total cash available.	1,821	1,827	1,827	1,890	1,942	20,730
Less: Cash disbursements:						
Operating expenses	810	915	1,035	885	975	10,730
Materials purchases	503	570	1,050	600	607	7,140
Taxes.		60	412	13		1,310
Equipment purchases.					100	100
Dividends	112			135		517
Pension contribution		210				247
Total disbursements.	1,425	1,755	2,497	1,633	1,682	20,044
Cash balance (deficiency) end of month before bank loans (repayments).	396	72	(670)	257	260	686
Bank loans (repayments)		80	820	(100)	(100)	0
Cash balance end of month.	396	152	150	157	160	686

balance exceeds the minimum. In February, the budget indicates a balance of only $72,000. Consequently, plans are made to borrow $80,000 to bring the balance to the desired level. The lower portion of the cash budget therefore shows the company's short-term financing plans.

THE CAPITAL EXPENDITURE BUDGET

The **capital expenditure budget** is essentially a list of what management believes to be worthwhile projects for the acquisition of new facilities and equipment. This budget shows the estimated cost of each project and the timing of the related expenditures.

Project Proposals

Proposals for capital investment projects may originate anywhere in the organization. The capital expenditure budget is usually prepared separately from the operating budget. In many companies it is prepared at a different time and cleared through a capital appropriations committee that is separate from the budget committee.

In the capital expenditure budget, individual projects are often classified by purpose, such as:

1. Cost reduction and replacement.
2. Expansion and improvement of existing product lines.
3. New products.
4. Health, safety, and/or pollution control.
5. Other.

Proposals in the first two categories usually are amenable to an economic analysis. Techniques for making such an analysis are described in Chapter 27. Some new-product proposals can also be substantiated by an economic analysis, although the estimate of sales of the new product is essentially a guess in many situations. Proposals in the other categories usually cannot be quantified sufficiently to make an economic analysis feasible.

As proposals for capital expenditures come up through the organization, they are screened at various levels. Only the sufficiently attractive ones flow up to the top and appear in the final capital expenditure budget. Estimated cash outlays are shown by years or by quarters, so that the cash required in each time period can be determined. At the final review meeting, which is usually at the board of directors level, not only are the individual projects discussed, but the total amount requested in the budget is compared with estimated funds available. Some apparently worthwhile projects may not be approved, simply because not enough funds are available to finance them all.

Authorization

Approval of the capital budget usually means approval of the projects *in principle* but does not constitute final authority to proceed with them. For this authority, a specific **authorization request** is prepared for the project, spelling out the proposal in more detail, perhaps with firm price quotations on the new assets. Depending on their size and character, these authorization requests are approved at various levels in the organization. For example, each supervisor may be authorized to buy tools or other equipment items costing not more than $250 each, provided the total for the year does not exceed $5,000. At the other extreme, all projects costing more than $100,000 and all projects for new products, whatever their cost, may require approval of the board of directors. In between, there is a scale of amounts that determines at which echelon of the organization projects may be authorized.

Follow Up

Some companies use **post-completion audits** to follow up on capital expenditures. These include checks on the spending itself and also an appraisal of how well the estimates of cost and revenue actually turned out. In a few companies there is tight linkage between the cost savings estimated in a capital expenditure request and operating budget figures for the periods of projected savings. Such linkage, like post-completion audits, is aimed at motivating managers to make realistic savings estimates in their capital budgeting requests. Because managers may take satisfaction from controlling a larger asset base or having the "latest and greatest" equipment in their departments, proposals tend to be biased if the company has no such checks and balances in its capital budgeting procedures.

SUMMARY

Organizations make two main types of plans: (1) strategic (or long-range) plans, which usually cover several future years and are focused on major programs, and (2) budgets, which are usually annual plans structured by responsibility centers. Budgets are used as a device for making and coordinating plans, for communicating these plans to those responsible for carrying them out, for motivating managers at all levels, as a benchmark for controlling ongoing activities, as a standard with which actual performance subsequently can be compared, and as a means of educating managers.

The operating budget is prepared within the context of basic policies and plans that have already been decided upon in the strategic planning process. The principal steps in the budgeting process are (1) dissemination of guidelines stating the overall plans and policies and other assumptions and constraints that are to be observed in the preparation of budget estimates; (2) preparation of the sales budget; (3) preparation of other estimates by the managers of responsibility centers, assisted but not dominated by the budget staff; (4) negotiation of an agreed-upon budget between subordinate and superior, which gives rise to a bilateral commitment by these parties; (5) coordination and review as these initial plans move up the organizational chain of command; (6) approval by senior management and the board of directors; and (7) dissemination of the approved budget back down through the organization.

The cash budget translates revenues and expenses into cash inflows and outflows, thus facilitating financial planning.

The capital expenditure budget is a list of worthwhile projects for the acquisition of new long-lived assets. These projects are often classified by their purpose; not all of them are amenable to an economic analysis. Approval of the capital expenditure budget constitutes only approval in principle; a subsequent authorization is usually required before work on the project can begin.

Cases

In January, a meeting was held in the office of the mayor of Oakmont to discuss a proposed municipal parking facility. The participants included the mayor, the traffic commissioner, the administrator of Oakmont's Downtown Parking Authority, the city planner, and the finance director. The purpose of the meeting was to consider a report by Richard Stockton, executive assistant to the Parking Authority's administrator, concerning estimated costs and revenues for the proposed facility.

Mr. Stockton's opening statement was as follows:

"As you know, the mayor proposed two months ago that we construct a multilevel parking garage on Elm Street. At that time, he asked the Parking Authority to assemble pertinent information for consideration at our meeting today. I would like to summarize our findings.

"The Elm Street site is owned by the city. It is presently occupied by the remains of the old Embassy Cinema, which was gutted by fire last June. The proprietors of the Embassy have since used the insurance proceeds to open a new theater in the suburbs; their lease of the city-owned land on which the Embassy was built expired last month.

"We estimate that it would cost approximately $80,000 to demolish the old Embassy. A building contractor has estimated that a

multilevel structure, with space for 800 cars, could be built on the site at a cost of about $4 million. The useful life of the garage would be around 40 years.

"The city could finance construction of the garage through the sale of bonds. The finance director has informed me that we could probably float an issue of 20-year tax-exempts at 5 percent interest. Redemption would commence after three years, with one seventeenth of the original number of bonds being called in each succeeding year.

"A parking management firm has already contacted us with a proposal to operate the garage for the city. They would require a management fee of $60,000 per year. Their proposal involves attendant parking, and they estimate that their costs, exclusive of the fee, would amount to $480,000 per year. Of this amount, $350,000 would be personnel costs; the remainder would include utilities, mechanical maintenance, insurance, and so forth. Any gross revenues in excess of $540,000 per year would be shared 90 percent by the city and 10 percent by the management firm. If total annual revenues are less than $540,000, the city would have to pay the difference.

"I suggest we offer a management contract for bid, with renegotiations for every three years. The city would derive additional income of around $100,000 per year by renting the ground floor of the structure as retail space. It's rather difficult for the Parking Authority to estimate revenues from the

---

*Written by G. M. Taylor and Prof. R. F. Vancil. Used by permission.

garage because, as you know, our operations to date have been confined to fringe-area parking lots. However, we conducted a survey at a private parking garage only three blocks from the Elm Street site; perhaps that information will be helpful.

"This private garage is open every day from 7 A.M. until midnight. Their rate schedule is as follows: $1.50 for the first hour; $1 for the second hour; and 50 cents for each subsequent hour, with a maximum rate of $4 per day. Their capacity is 400 spaces. Our survey indicated that during business hours 75 percent of their spaces were occupied by 'all-day parkers'—cars whose drivers and passengers work downtown. In addition, roughly 400 cars use the garage each weekday with an average stay of three hours. We did not take a survey on Saturday or Sunday, but the proprietor indicated that the garage is usually about 75 percent utilized by short-term parkers on Saturdays until 6 P.M., when the department stores close; the average stay is about two hours. There's a lull until about 7 P.M., when the moviegoers start coming in; he says the garage is almost full from 8 P.M. until closing time at midnight. Sundays are usually very quiet until the evening, when he estimates that his garage is 60 percent utilized from 6 P.M. until midnight.

"In addition to this survey, we studied a report issued by the City College economics department last year. This report estimated that we now have approximately 50,000 cars entering the central business district (CBD) every day from Monday through Saturday. Based on correlations with other cities of comparable size, the economists calculated that we need 30,000 parking spaces in the CBD. This agrees quite well with a block-by-block estimate made by the Traffic Commissioner's office last year, which indicated a total parking need in the CBD of 29,000 spaces. Right now we have 22,000 spaces in the CBD. Of these, 5 percent are curb spaces

(half of which are metered, with a two-hour maximum limit of 50 cents), 65 percent are in open lots, and 30 percent are in privately owned and operated garages.

"Another study indicated that 60 percent of all auto passengers entering the CBD on a weekday were on their way to work; 20 percent were shoppers; and 20 percent were businesspeople making calls. The average number of people per car was 1.75. Unfortunately, we have not had time to use the data mentioned thus far to work up estimates of the revenues to be expected from the proposed garage.

"The Elm Street site is strategically located in the heart of the CBD, near the major department stores and office buildings. It is five blocks from one of the access ramps to the new crosstown freeway that we expect will be open to traffic next year, and only three blocks from the Music Center that the mayor dedicated last week. As we all know, the parking situation in that section of town has steadily worsened over the last few years, with no immediate prospect of improvement. The demand for parking is clearly there, and the Parking Authority therefore recommends that we go ahead and build the garage."

The mayor thanked Mr. Stockton for his report and asked for comments. The following discussion took place:

Finance director: I'm all in favor of relieving parking congestion downtown, but I think we have to consider alternative uses of the Elm Street site. For example, the city could sell that site to a private developer for at least $2 million. The site could support an office building from which the city would derive property taxes of around $400,000 per year at present rates. The office building would almost certainly incorporate an underground parking garage for the use of the tenants, and therefore we would not only improve our tax base and increase revenues but also increase the availability of parking at no cost to the city. Besides, an office building on that site would serve to improve the amenity of downtown. A multilevel garage built above ground, on the other hand, would reduce the amenity of the area.

Planning director: I'm not sure I agree completely with the finance director. Within a certain range we can increase the value of downtown land by judicious provision of parking. Adequate, efficient parking facilities will encourage more intensive use of downtown traffic generators such as shops, offices, and places of entertainment, thus enhancing land values. A garage contained within an office building might, as the finance director suggests, provide more spaces, but I suspect these would be occupied almost exclusively by workers in the building and thus would not increase the total available supply. I think long-term parking downtown should be discouraged by the city. We should attempt to encourage short-term parking—particularly among shoppers—in an effort to counteract the growth of business in the suburbs and the consequent stagnation of retail outlets downtown. The rate structure in effect at the privately operated garage quoted by Mr. Stockton clearly favors the long-term parker. I believe that if the city constructs a garage on the Elm Street site, we should devise a rate structure that favors the short-term parker. People who work downtown should be encouraged to use our mass transit system.

Finance director: I'm glad you mentioned mass transit because this raises another issue. As you know, our subways are presently not used to capacity and are running at a substantial annual deficit that is borne by the city. We have just spent millions of dollars on the new subway station under the Music Center. Why build a city garage only three blocks away that will still further increase the subway system's deficit? Each person who drives downtown instead of taking the subway represents a loss of one dollar (the average round trip fare) to the subway system. I have read a report stating that approximately two-thirds of all persons entering the CBD by car would

still have made the trip by subway if they had not been able to use their cars.

Mayor: On the other hand, I think shoppers prefer to drive rather than take the subway, particularly if they intend to make substantial purchases. No one likes to take the subway burdened down by packages and shopping bags. You know, the Downtown Merchants Association has informed me that they estimate that each new parking space in the CBD generates on average an additional $20,000 in annual retail sales. That represents substantial extra profit to retailers; I think retailing after-tax profits average about 3 percent of gross sales. Besides, the city treasury benefits directly from our 3 percent sales tax.

Traffic commissioner: But what about some of the other costs of increasing parking downtown and therefore, presumably, the number of cars entering the CBD? I'm thinking of such costs as the increased wear and tear on city streets, the additional congestion produced with consequent delays and frustration for the drivers, impeding the movement of city vehicles, noise, air pollution, and so on. How do we weigh these costs in coming to a decision?

Parking administrator: I don't think we can make a decision at this meeting. I suggest that Dick Stockton be asked to prepare an analysis of the proposed garage along the lines of the following questions:

1. Using the information presented at this discussion, should the city of Oakmont construct the proposed garage?
2. What rates should be charged?
3. What additional information, if any, should be obtained before we make a final decision?

Mayor: I agree. Dick, can you let us have your answers to these questions in time for consideration at our meeting next month?

Question

How should Mr. Stockton respond to the three questions raised by the parking administrator?

CASE 24–2   Società Rigazio*

Società Rigazio manufactured a wide variety of metal products for industrial users in Italy and other European countries. Its head office was located in Milan, and its mills in northern Italy provided about 80 percent of the company's production volume. The remaining 20 percent was produced by two subsidiaries, one in Lyon, France, and the other in Linz, Austria, both serving local markets exclusively through their own sales organizations.

Until recently, the methods used by the Milan headquarters to review subsidiary operations were highly informal. The managing director of each subsidiary visited Milan twice a year, in October and April, to review the subsidiary's performance and discuss its plans for the future. At other times, the managing director would call or visit Milan to report on current developments or to request funds for specified purposes. These latter requests were usually submitted as a group, however, as part of the October meeting in Milan. By and large, if sales showed an increase over those of the previous year and if local profit margins did not decline, the directors in Milan were satisfied and did nothing to interfere with the subsidiary managers' freedom to manage the businesses as they saw fit.

Last year, Società Rigazio found itself, for the first time in 12 years, with falling sales volume, excess production capacity, rising costs, and a shortage of funds to finance new investments. In analyzing this situation, the Milan top management decided that one thing that was needed was a more detailed system of cost control in its mills, including

flexible budgets for the overhead costs of each factory.

The Lyon mill was selected as a "pilot plant" for the development of the new system. Because the Lyon mill produced a wide variety of products in many production departments, it was not possible to prepare a single flexible budget for the entire mill. In fact, Gino Spreafico, the company's controller, found that the work done in most of the production departments was so varied that useful cost/volume relationships could not even be developed on a departmental basis. He began, therefore, by dividing many of the departments into cost centers so that a valid single measure of work performed could be found for each one. Thus, a department with both automatic and hand-fed cutting machines might be divided into two cost centers, each with a group of highly similar machines doing approximately the same kind of work.

The establishment of the cost centers did not change the responsibility pattern in the factory. Each department had a foreman who reported to one of two production supervisors; the latter were responsible directly to Jean Forclas, the plant manager. Each foreman continued to be responsible for the operations of all the cost centers in his or her department. In some cases, a cost center embraced an entire department, but most departments contained between two and five cost centers.

Once he had completed this task, Spreafico turned to the development of flexible budgets. For each cost center he selected the measure or measures of volume that seemed most closely related to cost (e.g., machine-hours) and decided what volume was normal for that cost center (e.g., 1,000 machine-

*Copyright © by IMEDE.

hours per month). The budget allowance at the normal level of operations was to be used later as an element of standard product costs, but the budget allowance against which the foremen's performance was to be judged each month was to be the allowance for the volume actually achieved during that particular month.

Under the new system, a detailed report of overhead cost variances would be prepared in Lyon for the foreman in charge of a particular cost center and for his or her immediate superior, the production supervisor. A summary report, giving the total overhead variance for each cost center, would be sent to the plant manager and to Jacques Duclos, the managing director of Rigazio France, S. A., Lyon. The Milan top management would not receive copies of any of these reports but would receive a monthly profit and loss summary, with comments explaining major deviations from the subsidiary's planned profit for the period.

The preparation of the budget formulas had progressed far enough by midyear to persuade Spreafico to try them out on the September cost data. A meeting of top management was then scheduled in Milan to discuss the new system on the basis of the September reports. Duclos and Forclas flew to Milan to attend this meeting, accompanied by the controller of Rigazio France and a production supervisor responsible for some 30 cost centers in the Lyon factory.

Enrico Montevani, Società Rigazio's managing director, opened the meeting by asking Spreafico to explain how the budget allowances were prepared. Spreafico began by saying that the new system was just in its trial stages and that many changes would undoubtedly be necessary before everyone was satisfied with it. "We started with the idea that the standard had to be adjusted each month to reflect the actual volume of production," he continued, "even though that might mean that we would tell the factory they were doing all right when in fact they had large amounts of underabsorbed overhead. In that case, the problem would be that we had failed to provide enough volume to keep the plant busy, and you can't blame the foremen for that. When you have fixed costs, you just can't use a single standard cost per hour or per ton or per unit, because that would be too high when we're operating near capacity and too low when we're underutilized. Our problem, then, was to find out how overhead cost varies with volume so that we could get more accurate budget allowances for overhead costs at different production volumes.

"To get answers to this question, we first made some preliminary estimates at headquarters, based on historical data in the accounting records both here and in Lyon. We used data on wage rates and purchase prices from the personnel and purchasing departments to adjust our data to current conditions. Whenever we could, we used a mathematical formula known as 'least squares regression' to get an accurate measure of cost variability in relation to changing volume, but sometimes we just had to use our judgment and decide whether to classify a cost as fixed or variable. I might add that in picking our formulas we tried various measures of volume and generally took the one that seemed to match up most closely with cost. In some cost centers we actually used two different measures of volume, such as direct labor-hours and product tonnage, and based some of our budget allowances on one and some on the other. These estimates were then discussed with Jean Forclas and his people at Lyon, and the revised budget formulas were incorporated in a computer program for use in monthly report preparation.

EXHIBIT 1
OVERHEAD COST SUMMARY—COST CENTER 2122
September (in francs)

	Standard Allowance at Normal Volume (500 DLH, * 25 tons)	Budgeted at Actual Volume (430 DLH, 23 tons)	Actual, Month of September	Over (Under) Budget
Supervision...............	1,440	1,440	1,164	(276)
Indirect labor..............	12,000	10,880	12,874	1,994
Waiting time.............	840	722	1,422	700
Hourly wage guarantee..........	560	482	240	(242)
Payroll taxes, etc............	12,852	11,282	11,990	708
Materials and supplies..........	1,200	1,032	1,124	92
Tools	6,000	5,160	5,104	(56)
Maintenance	12,800	12,288	15,008	2,720
Scrap loss	16,880	15,530	19,650	4,120
Allocated costs	42,080	42,080	42,436	356
Total.............	106,652	100,896	111,012	10,116
Per ton................	4,266.08	4,386.78	4,826.60	439.82

*DLH = direct labor-hour.

"Although you have a complete set of the cost center reports, perhaps we might focus on the one for cost center 2122 [Exhibit 1]. You can see that we have used two measures of volume in this cost center, direct labor-hours and product tonnage. During September, we were operating at less than standard volume, which meant that we had to reduce the budget allowance to 100,896 francs, which averaged out at 4,387 francs per ton. Our actual costs were almost exactly 10 percent higher than this, giving us an overall unfavorable performance variance of 10,116 francs, or 440 francs per ton.

"I know that Jacques Duclos and Jean Forclas will want to comment on this, but I'll be glad to answer any questions that any of you may have. Incidentally, I have brought along some extra copies of the formulas I used in figuring the September overhead allowances for cost center 2122, just in case you'd like to look them over" (Exhibit 2).

Questions

1. Do you agree with Spreafico that 4,386.78 francs per ton (see Exhibit 1) is a more meaningful standard for cost control than the "normal" cost of 4,266.08 francs? Explain.

2. Comment on the variances in Exhibit 1. Which of these are likely to be controllable by the foreman? What do you think the production supervisor should have done on the basis of this report?

3. What changes, if any, would you make in the format of this report or to the basis on which the budget allowances are computed?

4. In developing the budget allowances, did Spreafico make any mistakes that you think he could have avoided? Does his system contain any features that you particularly like?

EXHIBIT 2
FLEXIBLE OVERHEAD BUDGET FORMULA—COST CENTER 2122
(in francs)

	Allowance Factors		
	Fixed Amount Per Month	Variable Rate	Remarks
Supervision..........................	1,440	—	Percent of foreman's time spent in cost center
Indirect labor	4,000	16.00/DLH*	—
Waiting time..........................	—	1.68/DLH	Wages of direct labor workers for time spent waiting for work
Hourly wage guarantee...............	—	1.12/DLH	Supplement to wages of workers paid by the piece to give them guaranteed minimum hourly wage
Payroll taxes, etc.....................	1,632	22.44/DLH	Payroll taxes and allowances at 30 percent of total payroll, including direct labor payroll†
Materials and supplies................	—	2.40/DLH	—
Tools	—	12.00/DLH	—
Maintenance	6,400	256.00/ton	Actual maintenance hours used at predetermined rate per hour, plus maintenance materials used
Scrap loss	—	675.22/ton	Actual scrap multiplied by difference between materials cost and estimated scrap value per ton
Allocated costs	42,080	—	Actual cost per month, allocated on basis of floor space occupied

*DLH = direct labor-hour.
†Budgeted direct labor at standard volume, 500 hours at 56 francs per hour; actual direct labor cost for September was 24,424 francs.

CASE 24–3 Whiz Calculator Company*

In August, Bernard Riesman was named president of the Whiz Calculator Company. Riesman had been with the company for five years, and for the preceding two years had been vice president of manufacturing. Shortly after taking over his new position, Riesman held a series of conferences with the controller in which the subject of discussion was budgetary control. The new president thought that the existing method of planning and controlling selling costs was unsatisfactory, and he requested the controller to devise a system that would provide better control over these costs.

Whiz Calculator manufactured electronic calculators and subnotebook and laptop computers, which it sold through branch offices to wholesalers and retailers, as well as

* Copyright © by the President and Fellows of Harvard College. Harvard Business School case 174-051.

directly to government and industrial users. Most of the products carried the Whiz brand name, which was nationally advertised. The company was one of the largest in the industry.

Under the procedure then being used, selling expenses were budgeted on a "fixed" or "appropriation" basis. Each October, the accounting department sent branch managers and other managers in charge of selling departments a detailed record of the actual expenses of their departments for the preceding year and for the current year to date. Guided by this record, by estimates of the upcoming year's sales, and by their own judgment, these department heads drew up and submitted estimates of the expenses of their departments for the upcoming year. The estimates made by the branch managers were then sent to the sales manager, who was in charge of all branch sales. He determined whether or not they were reasonable and cleared up any questionable items by discussion. Upon approval by the sales manager, the estimates of branch expenses were submitted to the general manager of marketing, Paula Melmed, who was responsible for all selling, promotional, and warehousing activities.

Melmed discussed these figures and the expense estimates furnished by the other department heads with the managers concerned, and after differences were reconciled, she combined the estimates of all the selling departments into a selling expense budget. This budget was submitted to the budget committee for final approval. For control purposes, the annual budget was divided into 12 equal amounts, and actual expenses were compared each month with the budgeted figures. Exhibit 1 shows the form in which these monthly comparisons were made.

Riesman believed that there were two important weaknesses in this method of setting the selling expense budget. First, it was impossible for anyone to ascertain with any certainty the reasonableness of the estimates made by the various department heads. Clearly, the expenses of the preceding year did not constitute adequate standards against which these expense estimates could be judged, since selling conditions were never the same in two different years. One obvious cause of variation in selling expenses was the variation in the "job to be done," as defined in the sales revenue budget.

Second, selling conditions often changed substantially after the budget was adopted, but there was no provision for making the proper corresponding changes in the selling expense budget. Neither was there a logical basis for relating selling expenses to the actual sales volume obtained or to any other measure of sales effort. Riesman believed that it was reasonable to expect that sales expenses would increase, though not proportionately, if actual sales volume were greater than the forecasted volume; but he felt that with the existing method of control, it was impossible to determine how large the increase in expenses should be.

As a means of overcoming these weaknesses, the president suggested the possibility of setting selling cost budget standards on a fixed and variable basis, a method similar to the flexible budget technique used in the control of manufacturing expenses. The controller agreed that this manner of approach seemed to offer the most feasible solution, and he therefore undertook a study of selling expenses to devise a method of setting reasonable standards. Over a period of several years, the accounting department had made many analyses of selling costs, the results of which had been used for allocating costs to products, customers, and territories, and in assisting in the solution of certain special problems, such as determining how large an individual order had to be in order to be profitable. Many of the data accumulated for

EXHIBIT 1
BUDGET REPORT CURRENTLY USED

	Branch Sales and Expense Performance				
Month: August		Branch A		Mgr.: C. K. Patel	
	This Month				
	Budget†	Actual	Over* Under	Percent of Sales	Over* Under Year to Date
Net sales	605,000	509,000	96,000		109,262*
Manager's salary	4,875	4,875	—	0.96	—
Office salaries	2,825	2,790	35	0.55	2,367
Sales force compensation	30,250	25,450	4,800	5.00	5,463*
Travel expense	6,670	6,098	572	1.20	1,579*
Stationery, office supplies	2,030	1,736	294	0.34	562
Postage	450	511	61*	0.10	33
Light and heat	260	170	90	0.03	293
Subscriptions and dues	150	112	38	0.02	41
Donations	200	—	200	0.00	205
Advertising expense (local)	5,650	5,265	385	1.03	2,800*
Social security taxes	2,905	2,533	372	0.50	358*
Rental	1,900	1,900	—	0.37	—
Depreciation	1,485	1,485	—	0.29	—
Other branch expense	4,975	4,731	244	0.93	385*
Total	64,625	57,656	6,969	11.33	7,084*

† One-twelfth of annual budget.

these purposes were helpful in the controller's current study.

The controller was convinced that the fixed portion of selling expenses—the portion independent of any fluctuation in sales volume—could be established by determining the amount of expenses that had to be incurred at the minimum sales volume at which the company was likely to operate. He therefore asked Paula Melmed to suggest a minimum volume figure and the amount of expenses that would have to be incurred at this volume. A staff assistant studied the company's sales records over several business cycles, the long-term outlook for sales, and sales trends of other companies in the industry. From the report prepared by this assistant, Melmed concluded that sales vol-

ume would not drop below 65 percent of current factory capacity.

Melmed then attempted to determine the selling expenses that would be incurred at the minimum volume. With the help of her assistant, she worked out a hypothetical selling organization that in her opinion would be required to sell merchandise equivalent to 65 percent of factory capacity, complete as to the number of persons needed to staff each branch office and the other selling departments, including the advertising, merchandising, and sales administration departments. Using current salary and commission figures, the assistant calculated the amount required to pay salaries for such an organization. Melmed also estimated the other expenses, such as advertising, branch office

EXHIBIT 2
BUDGET FOR "OTHER BRANCH EXPENSE," BRANCH A

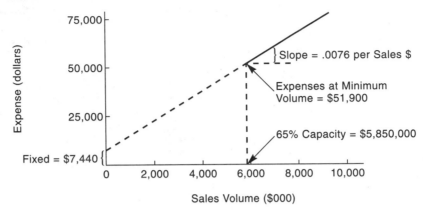

upkeep, supplies, and travel, that would be incurred by each branch and staff department at the minimum sales volume.

The controller decided that the variable portion of the selling expense standard should be expressed as a certain amount per sales dollar. He realized that the use of the sales dollar as a measuring stick had certain disadvantages in that it would not reflect such important influences in costs as order size, selling difficulty of certain territories, changes in buyer psychology, and so on. The sales dollar, however, was the measuring stick most convenient to use, the only figure readily available from the records then being kept, and also a figure that everyone concerned thoroughly understood. The controller believed that a budget that varied with sales would certainly be better than a budget that did not vary at all. He planned to devise a more accurate measure of causes of variation in selling expenses after he had an opportunity to study the nature of these factors over a long period of time.

As a basis for setting the variable expense standards, the controller used linear regression to determine a series of equations that correlated actual annual expenditures for the principal groups of expense items for several preceding years with annual sales volume. Using these equations, which showed to what extent these items had fluctuated with sales volume in the past, and modifying them in accordance with his own judgment as to future conditions, the controller determined a rate of variation (i.e., slope) for the variable portion of each item of selling expense. The controller thought that after the new system had been tested in practice, it would be possible to refine these rates, perhaps by the use of a technique analogous to the time-study technique that was employed to determine certain expense standards in the factory.

At this point the controller had both a rate of variation and one point (i.e., at 65 percent capacity) on a selling expense graph for each expense item. He was therefore able to determine a final equation for each item. Graphically, this was equivalent to drawing a line through the known point with the slope represented by the rate of variation. The height of this line at zero volume represented the fixed portion of the selling expense formula. The diagram in Exhibit 2 illustrates the procedure, although

EXHIBIT 3
BUDGET REPORT PROPOSED BY CONTROLLER

Expense Budget Report	Budget Factors		This Month			Branch: A Manager: C. K. Patel Month: August
						Year to Date
	Fixed	Variable	Flexible Budget	Actual	Over* Under	Over* Under
Net sales			509,000	509,000		
Manager's salary	4,875	—	4,875	4,875	—	†
Office salaries	271	0.0041	2,358	2,790	432*	
Sales force compensation	—	0.0500	25,450	25,450	—	
Travel expense	1,108	0.0087	5,536	6,098	562*	
Stationery, office supplies	550	0.0026	1,873	1,736	137	
Postage	92	0.0006	397	511	114*	
Light and heat	260	—	260	170	90	
Subscriptions and dues	10	0.0005	265	112	153	
Donations	32	0.0003	185	—	185	
Advertising expense (local)	68	0.0100	5,158	5,265	107*	
Social security taxes	394	0.0041	2,481	2,533	52*	
Rental	1,900	—	1,900	1,900	—	
Depreciation	1,485	—	1,485	1,485	—	
Other branch expense	620	0.0076	4,488	4,731	243*	
Total	11,665	0.0885	56,711	57,656	945*	

† The controller had not recalculated budgets for previous months, and figures were therefore not available for this column.

the actual computations were mathematical rather than graphical.

The selling expense budget for the coming year was determined by adding the new standards for the various fixed components and the indicated flexible allowances for the year's estimated sales volume. This budget was submitted to the budget committee, which studied the fixed amounts and the variable rates underlying the final figures, making only minor changes before passing final approval.

The controller planned to issue reports each month showing actual expenses for each department compared with budgeted expenses. The variable portion of the budget allowances would be adjusted to correspond to the actual volume of sales obtained during the month. Exhibit 3 shows the budget report that he planned to send to branch managers.

One sales executive privately belittled the controller's proposal. "Anyone in the selling game knows that sometimes customers fall all over each other in their hurry to buy, and other times, no matter what we do, they won't even nibble. It's a waste of time to make fancy formulas for selling cost budgets under conditions like that."

Questions

1. From the information given in Exhibits 1 and 3, determine, insofar as you can, whether each item of expense is (a) nonvariable, (b) partly variable with sales volume, (c) variable with sales volume, or (d) variable with some other factors.

2. What bearing do your conclusions in Question 1 have on the type of budget that is most appropriate?

3. If a variable budget is used, should dollar sales be used as the measure of volume?

4. Which report tells you more about Branch A's performance in August, Exhibit 1 or Exhibit 3?

5. Should the proposed sales expense budget system be adopted? Explain.

6. (Optional—requires calculator or spreadsheet software with linear regression routine.) Consider the following five-year time series of annual sales and some element of annual branch selling expense:

Year	Sales ($000)	Expenses ($)
1	5,238	48,764
2	5,694	53,549
3	6,189	58,135
4	6,728	62,351
5	7,313	68,349

Find the least-squares linear regression equation that relates annual expense to annual sales. Describe how this equation can be used to determine a flexible budget for the expense on a *monthly* basis.

CASE 24–4 Midwest Ice Cream Company (A)*

Frank Roberts, marketing vice president of Midwest Ice Cream Company, was pleased when he saw the final earnings statement for the company for last year. He knew that it had been a good year for Midwest, but he hadn't expected a large, favorable operating income variance. Only two years ago, the company had installed a new financial planning and control system; last year was the first one for which figures comparing budgeted and actual results were available.

Midwest's Planning and Control System. The following description of the financial planning and control system is taken from an internal company operating manual.

THE PLANNING FUNCTION

The starting point in making a profit plan is separating costs into fixed and variable categories. Some costs are purely variable and will require an additional amount with each increase in volume level. The manager has little control over this type of cost other than to avoid waste. The accountant can determine the variable manufacturing cost per unit for any given product or package by using current prices and yield records. Variable marketing cost is based on the allowable rate, for example, 6 cents per gallon for advertising. Costs that are not purely variable are classified as fixed, but they, too, will vary if significant changes in volume occur. There will be varying degrees of sensitivity to volume changes among these costs, ranging from a point just short of purely variable to an extremely fixed type of expense that has no relationship to volume.

The reason for differentiating between fixed and variable costs is because a variable cost requires no decision as to when to add or take off a unit of cost; it is dictated by volume. Fixed costs, on the other hand, require a management decision to increase or decrease the cost. Sugar is an example of a purely variable cost; only the yield can be controlled. Route salespersons' salaries are an example of a fixed cost that is fairly

---

* Copyright © by the President and Fellows of Harvard College. Harvard Business School case 175-070.

STEP 1

ESTABLISH STANDARDS FOR SELLING PRICE, VARIABLE EXPENSES, AND MARGINAL
CONTRIBUTION PER GALLON*

| | Regular | | | Premium |
| | One-Gallon Paper Container | One-Gallon Plastic Container | Two-Gallon Paper Container | One-Gallon Plastic Container |
Item				
Dairy ingredients	0.53	0.53	0.53	0.79
Sugar	0.15	0.15	0.15	0.15
Flavorings	0.10	0.10	0.105	0.12
Production	0.10	0.16	0.125	0.16
Warehouse	0.06	0.08	0.07	0.08
Transportation	0.02	0.025	0.02	0.025
Total manufacturing	0.96	1.045	1.00	1.325
Advertising	0.06	0.06	0.06	0.06
Delivery	0.04	0.04	0.04	0.04
Total marketing	0.10	0.10	0.10	0.10
Total variable costs	1.06	1.145	1.10	1.425
Selling price	1.50	1.70	1.45	2.40
Marginal contribution/gallon before packaging	0.44	0.555	0.35	0.975
Packaging	0.10	0.25	0.085	0.25
Marginal contribution/gallon	0.34	0.305	0.265	0.725

*In practice, a standard cost is developed for each flavor in order to recognize differing ingredients
costs.

sensitive to volume, but not purely variable. As volume changes, pressure will be felt to increase or decrease this expense, but management must make the decision; the change in cost level is not automatic. Depreciation charges for plant are an example of a relatively fixed cost in that large increases in volume can usually be realized before this type of cost is pressured to change.

We shall now explain and illustrate each of the four steps in the profit planning process. (The numbers in the tables illustrating each step are not intended to be realistic.)

The first step is to develop a unit standard cost for each element of variable cost by product and package size. Examples of four different products and/or packages are shown in Step 1. The accountant can do this by using current prices and yield records for material costs and current allowance rates for marketing costs. Advertising is the only cost element

not fitting the explanation of a variable cost given in the preceding paragraph. Advertising costs are set by management decision rather than being an "automatic" cost item like sugar. In this sense, advertising is just like route salespersons' expense. However, management has decided that the advertising allowance is equal to 6 cents per gallon for the actual number of gallons sold. This management decision, therefore, has transformed advertising into a variable expense.

After the unit variable cost has been developed, this amount is subtracted from the selling price to arrive at marginal contribution per unit. At any level of volume, it is easy to determine the contribution that should be generated to cover fixed costs and provide profits. This will be illustrated in Step 4.

Step 2 is perhaps the most critical of all because all plans are built around the sales

STEP 2
ICE CREAM SALES FORECAST IN GALLONS

	January	February		December	Total
One-gallon paper	100,000	100,000	. . .	100,000	1,200,000
One-gallon plastic	50,000	50,000	. . .	50,000	600,000
Two-gallon paper	225,000	225,000	. . .	225,000	2,700,000
One-gallon premium	120,000	120,000	. . .	120,000	1,440,000
Total	495,000	495,000	. . .	495,000	5,940,000

STEP 3
BUDGETED FIXED EXPENSES

	January	February		December	Total
Manufacturing expense:					
Labor	7,333	7,333	. . .	7,333	88,000
Equipment repair	3,333	3,333	. . .	3,333	40,000
Depreciation	6,667	6,667	. . .	6,667	80,000
Taxes	3,333	3,333	. . .	3,333	40,000
Total	20,667	20,667	. . .	20,667	248,000
Delivery expense:					
Salaries—general	10,000	10,000	. . .	10,000	120,000
Salaries—drivers	10,667	10,667	. . .	10,667	128,000
Helpers	10,667	10,667	. . .	10,667	128,000
Supplies	667	667	. . .	667	8,000
Total	32,000	32,000	. . .	32,000	384,000
Administrative expense:					
Salaries	5,167	5,167	. . .	5,167	62,000
Insurance	1,667	1,667	. . .	1,667	20,000
Taxes	1,667	1,667	. . .	1,667	20,000
Depreciation	833	833	. . .	833	10,000
Total	9,333	9,333	. . .	9,333	112,000
Selling expense:					
Repairs	2,667	2,667	. . .	2,667	32,000
Gasoline	5,000	5,000	. . .	5,000	60,000
Salaries	5,000	5,000	. . .	5,000	60,000
Total	12,667	12,667	. . .	12,667	152,000

forecast. Much thought should be given to forecasting a realistic sales level and product mix. Consideration should be given to the number of days in a given period, as well as to the number of Fridays and Mondays, as these are two of the heaviest days and will make a difference in the sales forecast. Other factors that should be considered are (1) the general economic conditions in the marketing area, (2) weather, (3) anticipated promotions, and (4) competition.

Step 3 involves setting fixed cost budgets based on management's judgment as to the need in light of the sales forecast. It is here that good planning makes for a profitable operation. The number of routes needed for

STEP 4
THE PROFIT PLAN

	Marginal Contri- bution (see Step 1)	Gallons Sold/ Month	Contribution			
			January	February	December	Total
One-gallon paper	0.34	100,000	$ 34,000	$ 34,000 . . .	$ 34,000	$ 408,000
One-gallon plastic.	0.305	50,000	15,250	15,250 . . .	15,250	183,000
Two-gallon paper	0.265	225,000	59,625	59,625 . . .	59,625	715,500
One-gallon premium.	0.725	120,000	87,000	87,000 . . .	87,000	1,044,000
Total contribution.			195,875	195,875 . . .	195,875	2,350,500
Fixed costs (see Step 3):						
Manufacturing			20,667	20,667 . . .	20,667	248,000
Delivery.			32,000	32,000 . . .	32,000	384,000
Administrative			9,333	9,333 . . .	9,333	112,000
Selling			12,667	12,667 . . .	12,667	152,000
Total fixed costs			74,667	74,667 . . .	74,667	896,000
Operating profit.			121,208	121,208 . . .	121,208	1,454,500
Income tax.			48,483	48,483 . . .	48,483	581,800
Net profit.			$ 72,725	$ 72,725 . . .	$ 72,725	$ 872,700

both winter and summer volume is planned. The level of manufacturing payroll is set.[1] Insurance and taxes are budgeted, and so on. After Step 4 has been performed, it may be necessary to return to Step 3 and make adjustments to some of the costs that are discretionary in nature.

Step 4 is the profit plan itself. By combining the marginal contributions developed in Step 1 with the Step 2 sales forecast, we arrive at a total marginal contribution by month. Subtracting the fixed costs budgeted in Step 3, we have operating profit. If this profit figure is not sufficient, then a new evaluation should be made of the fixed costs developed in Step 3.

---

[1]Because this system is based on a one-year time frame, manufacturing labor is considered to be a fixed cost. The level of the manufacturing work force is not really variable unless a time frame longer than one year is adopted.

THE CONTROL FUNCTION

To illustrate the control system, we will take the month of January and assume sales for the month to be 520,000 gallons, as shown in Exhibit A. From Step 2 we see that 495,000 gallons had been forecasted. When we apply our marginal contribution per unit for each product and package, we find that the 520,000 gallons have produced $6,125 less standard contribution than the 495,000 gallons would have produced at the forecasted mix. So even though there has been a nice increase in sales volume, the mix has been unfavorable. The $6,125 represents the difference between standard contribution at forecasted volume and standard contribution at actual volume. It is thus due to differences in volume and product mix. The impact of each of these two factors is shown at the bottom of Exhibit A.

Exhibit B shows a typical departmental budget sheet comparing actual cost of goods

EXHIBIT A

Contribution Analysis
January

	Actual Gallon Sales	Standard Contribution per Gallon	Total Standard Contribution
One-gallon paper	90,000	0.34	$ 30,600
One-gallon plastic.	95,000	0.305	28,975
Two-gallon paper	245,000	0.265	64,925
One-gallon premium.	90,000	0.725	65,250
Total.	520,000		189,750
Forecast (Step 2) 495,000 gallons			
Forcasted contribution (at 495,000 gallons)			195,875
Over (under) forecast.			$ (6,125)

	Planned	Actual
Gallons	495,000	520,000
Contribution	$195,875	$189,750
Average per gallon.	$0.3957	$0.3649
Difference.		$0.0308U

Variance due to volume:
25,000 gallons * $0.3957   = $ 9,892 F

Variance due to mix:
$0.0308 * 520,000 gallons   =   16,017 U

Total variance   = $ 6,125 U

EXHIBIT B

Manufacturing Cost of Goods Sold
January

Month			Year to Date	
Actual	Budget		Actual	Budget
312,744	299,000	Dairy ingredients		
82,304	78,000	Sugar		
56,290	55,025	Flavorings		
38,770	37,350	Warehouse		
70,300	69,225	Production		
11,514	11,325	Transportation		
571,922	549,925	Subtotal, variable		
7,305	7,333	Labor		
4,065	3,333	Equipment repair		
6,667	6,667	Depreciation		
3,333	3,333	Taxes		
21,370	20,667	Subtotal, fixed		
593,292	570,592	Total		

with budgeted costs. A sheet is issued for each department so the person responsible for a particular area of the business can see which items are in line with the budget and which need attention. In our example, there is an unfavorable operating variance of $22,700. You should note that the budget for variable cost items has been adjusted to reflect *actual* volume, thereby eliminating cost variances that are due strictly to the difference between planned and actual volume.

Since the level of fixed costs is independent of volume anyway, it is not necessary to adjust the budget for these items for volume differences. The original budget for fixed cost items is still appropriate. The totals for each department are carried forward to an earnings statement, Exhibit C. We have assumed all other departments' actual costs and budgeted costs are in line, so the only operating variance is the one for manufacturing. This variance added to the sales volume and mix variance of $6,125 results in an overall unfavorable variance from the original plan of $28,825, as shown at the bottom of Exhibit C.

The illustration here has been on a monthly basis, but there is no need to wait until the end of the month to see what is

EXHIBIT C

Earnings Statement January				
Month			Year to Date	
Actual	Budget		Actual	Budget
867,750	867,750	Total ice cream sales		
593,292	570,592	Mfg. cost of goods sold		
52,800	52,800	Delivery expense		
31,200	31,200	Advertising expense		
76,075	76,075	Packaging expense		
12,667	12,667	Selling expense		
9,333	9,333	Administrative expense		
775,367	752,667	Total expense		
92,383	115,083	Profit or (loss)		
36,953	—	Provision for income taxes		
55,430	—	Net profit or (loss)		

Actual profit before taxes 92,383 (1)
Original profit forecast (Step 4) 121,208 (2)
Revised profit forecast based on actual volume 115,083 (3)

$$\text{Variance due to volume and mix (unfavorable)} = \overset{(2)}{121{,}208} - \overset{(3)}{115{,}083} = 6{,}125 \text{ U}$$

$$\text{Variance due to operations (unfavorable)} = \overset{(3)}{115{,}083} - \overset{(1)}{92{,}383} = \underline{22{,}700 \text{ U}}$$

$$\text{Total variance} = \overset{(2)}{121{,}208} - \overset{(1)}{92{,}383} = \underline{28{,}825 \text{ U}}$$

happening. Each week, sales can be multiplied by the contribution margins to see how much standard contribution has been generated. This can be compared to one-fourth of the monthly forecasted contribution to see if volume and mix are in line with forecast. Neither is it necessary to wait until the end of the month to see if expenses are in line. Weekly reports of such items as production costs or sugar can be made, comparing budget with actual. By combining the variances as shown on weekly reports and adjusting the forecasted profit figure, an approximate profit figure can be had long before the books are closed and monthly statements issued. More important, action can be taken to correct an undesirable situation much sooner.

Questions

1. Explain in as much detail as possible where *all* the numbers for Steps 1–4 would come from. (You will need to use your imagination; the case does not describe all details of the profit planning process.)

2. Explain the difference between a month's planned profit as shown in Step 4 and a month's budgeted profit as shown in Exhibit C. Why would Midwest want to have *two* target profit amounts for a given month? (Hint: Study the variance calculations at the bottom of Exhibit C.)

3. Evaluate Midwest's budgeting and control processes.

CASE 24–5 Reading Manufacturing Company*

In July 1994 Richard Berks, treasurer of Reading Manufacturing Company, was reviewing the firm's working capital position. It was his custom to calculate working capital needs for the next six months in January and July of each year and to formulate plans for meeting such needs.

Reading Manufacturing Company, which had been founded in 1982, operated a machine shop. The company had originally made custom manufacturing tooling for nearby companies. In 1989, a newly designed industrial fastening machine was introduced by the company.

Operating losses and poor financial management had kept the company in financial difficulty during the greater part of its early history. In the spring of 1990, this situation came to the attention of Mr. Berks, a businessman who specialized in rehabilitating financially weak concerns. He analyzed the company and found that it employed a number of skilled machinists and possessed good equipment suitable for precision work. He was also impressed by prospects for the company's fastening machine, which was far superior to competitive products. As a result of his analysis, he concluded that with competent management, the company could be operated profitably. Berks approached the stockholding group, and an agreement was worked out whereby Berks became, in effect, head of the company. For his efforts, he was to receive a fixed salary plus a percentage of profits.

During the next few years, Berks concentrated on obtaining fixed-price Army contracts for the manufacture of precision equipment. Because of rigid economies he instituted, these contracts proved highly profitable. These profits and Berks's skillful

*Copyright © by the President and Fellows of Harvard College. Harvard Business School case 175-297.

EXHIBIT 1

READING MANUFACTURING COMPANY
Balance Sheets

	Dec. 31, 1992	Dec. 31, 1993	June 30, 1994
Assets			
Current assets:			
Cash	$ 124,627	$ 154,234	$266,429
Accounts receivable, net	461,827	283,997	200,547
Inventory	436,934	326,554	—
Raw material	—	—	126,086
Work in process	—	—	63,706
Prepaid expenses	6,960	11,318	3,120
Total current assets	1,030,348	776,103	659,888
Fixed assets:			
Plant and equipment, at cost	446,467	452,669	458,650
Less: Accumulated depreciation	139,526	191,194	193,510
Plant and equipment, net	306,941	261,475	265,140
Total assets	$1,337,289	$1,037,578	$925,028
Liabilities and Shareholders' Equity			
Current liabilities:			
Accounts payable	$ 265,613	$ 146,445	$ 87,034
Accrued liabilities	92,083	17,626	40,859
Taxes payable	220,838	289,850	161,573*
Total current liabilities	578,534	453,921	289,466
Long-term liabilities	343,968		
Shareholders' equity:			
Common stock	364,800	364,800	364,800
Retained earnings	49,987	218,857	270,762
Total liabilities and shareholders' equity	$1,337,289	$1,037,578	$925,028

*Payable as follows: $61,083 on September 15, 1994, and December 15, 1994; $9,852 on March 15, 1995, June 15, 1995, September 15, 1995, and December 15, 1995.

financial management soon rehabilitated the company. By the end of 1992, the deficit accumulated during the years of unprofitable operations had been eliminated. (Financial statements for 1992, 1993, and the first half of 1994, appear in Exhibits 1 and 2.)

When the Army contracts were completed and no follow-on work with the Army could be obtained, Berks took steps to curtail overhead expenses, but he retained the company's skilled machinists. Berks concentrated on promoting the company's industrial fastening machine, demand for which was good. Monthly shipments during the first half of 1994 averaged about 75 units priced at $1,900 each. More units could have been sold and shipped, but Berks did not wish to risk overextending the company while conditions were so unsettled.

Early in May, the company received an invitation to bid on an Army contract for the manufacture of 301 specialized field trailers. Berks thought that a good profit could be made on the trailers, so he decided to submit a bid. His first bid of $6,900 a unit was rejected, but a second bid of $5,900 was

EXHIBIT 2

READING MANUFACTURING COMPANY
Income Statements

	Twelve Months Ending 12/31/92	Twelve Months Ending 12/31/93	Six Months Ending 6/30/94
Sales, net	$2,715,725	$3,183,120	$834,874
Cost of sales:			
Material	350,861	931,824	208,128
Direct labor	1,117,114	823,277	146,678
Depreciation	62,544	51,667	31,123
Factory overhead	507,283	460,224	196,934
Total cost of sales	2,037,802	2,266,992	582,863
Gross margin	677,923	916,128	252,011
Less: Operating expense:			
Shipping expense	91,786	56,506	2,256
Selling expense	100,243	71,808	—
Administrative expense	302,717	415,680	141,840
Total operating expense	494,746	543,994	144,096
Net operating income	183,177	372,134	107,915
Other charges	2,957	5,002	—
Income before taxes	180,220	367,132	107,915
Tax expense	63,077	183,566	37,770
Net income	$ 117,143	$ 183,566	$ 70,145

accepted. One "prototype" trailer was to be produced during August for the purpose of testing production methods. It was to be retained at the plant but invoiced on September 1 at $5,900. This unit was to be manufactured from materials on hand. Direct labor for this unit was estimated at $4,800. The lessons learned making the first unit were expected to enable the company to start trailer production at full scale about September 1. Production was expected to be maintained at a fairly constant rate until November 30. Delivery of the trailers was to start the first week in October and was to be made at the rate of 100 units a month during October, November, and December.

Estimated per unit direct costs of producing the trailer were as follows: labor, $2,323; material, $1,229. In addition to the estimated

direct labor cost of $2,323 per unit, Berks estimated that the buildup of the additional labor force needed for trailer production would require some $24,000 in extra wage expense during August. Similarly, some $28,800 of additional wage expense was budgeted for December so as to permit less abrupt reduction of the work force upon completion of the contract. Virtually all of the $28,800 would be paid out in the first three weeks of December.

To ensure against delays in delivery, Berks intended to keep a minimum of one month's supply of raw material on hand at all times during the production period. Work in process inventory for trailer production was expected to average $192,000 during the period of full-scale production. The great majority of the company's purchases were made on

EXHIBIT 3
TENTATIVE SCHEDULE OF PURCHASES
July–December 1994

	July	Aug.	Sept.	Oct.	Nov.	Dec.
Raw material (fasteners)	—	$ 19,142	$ 28,800	$ 28,800	$28,800	$28,800
Raw material (trailers)	—	122,900	122,900	122,900	—	—
Special tools (trailers)	—	19,200	—	—	—	—
Total	—	$161,242	$151,700	$151,700	$28,800	$28,000
Replacement machinery	$48,000 (uncertain date)					

terms of amount due within 30 days ("net/30") after the purchased items were received, and invoices were paid promptly when due. Wages were paid weekly.[1] The production process from raw material to finish product was estimated to take a month. The Army would accept shipments in lots of 25 units, and payment would be received about 60 days after shipment.

Estimated per unit direct costs of producing the fastening machine were as follows: materials, $384; labor, $346. A minimum inventory of a three months' supply of raw material was currently considered necessary because of unsettled conditions. Work in process inventory for fastening machine production was expected to continue at the present level. All current inventory was usable. The length of the production process was four weeks. Units were shipped as soon as produced, and terms of sale were net/30. The company had a backlog of orders for 350 machines. Production and shipments, however, were expected to continue at the rate of about 75 units a month through the first quarter of 1995.

Monthly indirect expenses were currently running as follows: depreciation, $5,180; other factory overhead, $33,600; and admin-

istration, $22,560. Tooling for the Army contract started in July. During July and August, tooling expenses and experimental manufacture of the prototype were expected to increase factory overhead by about $11,520 a month. Starting in September, when full-scale production of the trailers was to begin, factory overhead was expected to become about $43,200 a month until the end of November. Administration expense was expected to increase to about $28,800 a month from September 1 to the end of December.

The Army contract had made necessary the purchase of $19,200 of special tools. Delivery of these tools was expected in August; it was to be paid for COD. Upon completion of the contract, these tools would be scrapped. An additional $48,000 would also have to be spent for the replacement of old machinery that appeared to be nearing the end of its useful life. There was no way of knowing, however, when this machinery would finally break down. Berks was confident that he could find replacement equipment within a few days in the event of an emergency.

Berks worked out a tentative purchase schedule for the various material requirements (Exhibit 3). It shows the amounts of purchases in the months that the purchased items were expected to be received by Reading.

---

[1]There were four paydays in July, five in August, four each in September and October, five in November, and four in December.

The company maintained a small deposit account with a local bank and kept the remainder of its cash in an account with the Fourth National Bank, a medium-sized bank with a legal loan limit of $1,500,000. Berks had discussed the company's prospects in general terms with the bank's officers on a number of occasions, but he had never requested a loan.

Berks considered the current cash balance of almost $266,500 to be in excess of operating needs. He was willing to reduce cash to a minimum of $48,000. No dividend payments were scheduled for the rest of 1994.

It was Berks's policy not to plan more than six months in advance, since he believed it was impossible to predict with any accuracy what was going to happen for a longer period. The company's plans for the first half of 1995 would be made in the light of conditions as they developed and of the company's prospective financial condition at the end of 1994.

Questions

1. Set up a worksheet, with columns for each of the next six months (July–December 1994), and develop a schedule of monthly cash inflows and outflows. In preparing this schedule, assume the following:

a. All accounts receivable as of June 30, 1994, are collected in July, and all June 30, 1994, accounts payable are paid in July.

b. Work in process inventories, prepaid expenses, and accrued liabilities will remain constant at their June 30, 1994, levels.

c. The $48,000 machine will be purchased in July 1994.

Remembering Berks's desire to have a minimum cash balance of $48,000, what does your schedule reveal about Reading's borrowing needs over the next six months?

2. Use the data from the case and from your cash flow worksheet to prepare a budgeted income statement for the six months ending December 31, 1994; a projected balance sheet as of December 31, 1994; and a budgeted cash flow statement for the six months ending December 31, 1994. Assume a tax rate of 40 percent and ignore interest on any new borrowings that will be needed during these six months. Assume the old machine replaced in July had originally cost $32,000, was fully depreciated, and had no residual value. For preparing these three statements, you will probably find it useful to draw up T accounts for each balance sheet and income statement account, and post six-month totals from your cash flow worksheet (appropriately adjusted to the accrual basis) to these accounts.

25

Reporting and Evaluation

The first section of this chapter describes the various reports on actual performance provided to management, focusing principally on the monthly report that compares actual performance with some standard, preferably the budget described in the preceding chapter. The second section describes how managers use these reports to identify areas requiring investigation, and how they conduct the investigation and take action. The final section describes incentive compensation plans based on managers' performance.

CONTROL REPORTS

Key Success Factors

In all organizations and in most responsibility centers within them, a limited number of factors must be watched closely because they are crucial to achieving the objectives of the organization or the responsibility center. These are called **key success factors,** and quantitative measures related to them are called **key indicators.** These factors can shift quickly and unpredictably; when they do, they have a significant effect on performance. The number of such performance-affecting variables is small, usually no more than five in a given responsibility center. The reporting system should be designed so that particular attention is paid to them.

> **Example.** A consultant states that to know how well she is doing financially, she needs to keep track of only three key indicators: (1) billed hours (the

number of hours charged daily to client projects), (2) the ratio of accounts receivable to monthly billings (as an indication of whether client bills are being paid promptly), and (3) the ratio of expenses to revenues.

As a general rule, a key success factor has these characteristics:

· It has an *important* impact on performance of the responsibility center.
· It is *volatile*—it can change quickly, often for reasons not controllable by the manager.
· If a change does occur, *prompt action* should be taken.
· The change can be *measured* by a related key indicator.

Key success factors affect profit, but profit is not itself a key success factor; rather, it is the accountant's measure of overall economic success. Control of production costs is often a key success factor, particularly for companies competing in commodity industries; but in industries having large gross margins, such as cosmetics, cost control is not a key success factor. (This does not mean that such a company can afford to be wasteful, but rather that cost control is not a "make-or-break" activity.) In service industries like hotels and airlines, capacity utilization (measured as occupancy rate or load factor) is a key success factor because there is no way to "inventory" idle capacity (an empty room or seat) and sell it at a later date (whereas manufacturing capacity can be inventoried in the form of finished goods to be sold at some later date).

Types of Management Reports

Three types of reports are prepared for the use of managers: information reports, economic performance reports, and managerial performance (control) reports. Although our emphasis is on the third type, we touch on the other two types briefly because they are important parts of the total communications that managers receive.

Information reports are designed to tell management what is going on. Each reader studies these reports to detect whether or not something has happened that requires investigation. If nothing significant is noted, which is often the case, the report is put aside without action. If something does strike the reader's attention, an inquiry or an action is initiated. The information on these reports may come from the accounting system; it may also come from a wide variety of other sources and include such external information as news summaries, stock prices, information from industry trade associations, and economic data published by the government.

Performance Reports.   There are two general types of reports about the performance of a responsibility center. One type deals with its performance as an economic entity. A conventional income statement prepared for a profit center is one such **economic performance report,** and the net income shown is a basic measure of economic performance. Economic performance reports are derived from conventional accounting information, including full cost accounting. The other type of performance report focuses on the performance of the manager of the responsibility center. This **managerial performance report** is usually referred to as a **control report.** Control reports are prepared from responsibility accounting information. Essentially they report how well the manager did compared with some standard of what the manager was expected to do. The principal difference between economic performance and managerial performance reports is that the latter, if properly designed, exclude noncontrollable items from the measures that will be used as a basis of evaluating the manager.

The control report may show that a profit center manager is doing an excellent job, considering the circumstances. But if the profit center is not producing a satisfactory profit, action may be required regardless of this fact. There are therefore two different ways in which the performance of a responsibility center is judged. The control report focuses on the manager's responsibility for actual performance that corresponds to the commitment made during the budget preparation process. Behavioral considerations are important in the use of this report. The economic performance report focuses on an analysis of the responsibility center as an economic entity. For example, if an investment center manufactures and markets a certain line of products, the economic performance report is used in evaluating whether this center's profitability is sufficient to warrant the company's continued investment in that particular market segment or whether the invested funds should be redeployed elsewhere. (This sort of economic analysis led General Electric to sell its small appliance business to Black & Decker and its consumer electronics business to Thompson Electronics, for example.) The following discussion is limited to control reports.

Period of Control Reports

The proper **control period**—or the period of time covered by one report—is the shortest period of time in which management can usefully intervene and in which significant changes in performance have occurred or are likely to occur. This period varies for various items. For key success factors it is more frequent than for other items. A *flash report* is issued immediately if a significant change has occurred in a key success factor or if an unexpected, important event of any type has occurred. This report may be issued in real time; as soon as it happens, an event, such as malfunction of a crucial machine, may be brought to management's attention by computers programmed for this purpose. *Daily reports* may be issued for important and volatile items, such as new orders booked. *Monthly reports* on overall performance are common, although in some relatively stable businesses, these reports are issued only quarterly. We shall focus on monthly reports (including the annual report, which typically is not substantially different from the monthly report for the twelfth month).

The report period also varies with the level in the organization. The same type of event is reported more frequently at lower levels in the organization than at higher levels; managers at lower levels are expected to deal with the problem without waiting for instructions from their superiors.

The other aspect of report timing is the *interval* that elapses between the end of the period covered by the report and the issuance of the report itself. For monthly reports the interval should be less than a week. To meet such a deadline, it may be necessary to make approximations of certain "actual" amounts for which exact information is not available. Such approximations are worthwhile because an approximately accurate report provided promptly is far preferable to a precisely accurate report that is received so long after the event that no effective action can be taken.

Contents of Control Reports

The essential purpose of a control report is to compare actual performance in a responsibility center with what performance should have been under the *circumstances prevailing* so that reasons for the difference between actual and expected performance are identified and, if feasible, quantified. It follows that three kinds of information are conveyed in such reports: (1) information on what performance actually was; (2) information on what performance should have been; and (3) reasons for the difference between actual and expected performance. This suggests three essential characteristics of good control reports:

1. Reports should be related to personal responsibility.
2. Actual performance should be compared with the best available standard.
3. Significant information should be highlighted.

As a basis for discussing these points, we shall use the set of control reports shown in Illustration 25–1.

Focus on Personal Responsibility. In Chapters 22 and 23 we emphasized **responsibility accounting,** the type of management accounting information that classifies costs and revenues according to the centers responsible for incurring the costs and generating the revenues. Responsibility accounting therefore provides information that meets the criterion that control reports should be related to personal responsibility.

Responsibility accounting also classifies the costs assigned to each responsibility center as controllable or noncontrollable within it. In many companies control reports show only controllable costs; in others reports also contain noncontrollable costs for information purposes. In Illustration 25–1 only controllable costs are reported. For the drill press department these are direct labor and controllable overhead. Direct material cost is not included because neither the quantity nor the price of material used is controllable by the department manager. The drill press manager is responsible, however, for repair and rework costs of defective material or products, and this item of controllable cost does appear on the report.

ILLUSTRATION 25–1
PACKAGE OF CONTROL REPORTS

A. First-Level (Lowest) Report

Drill press department (supervisor)	Actual		Variance*	
	June	Year to Date	June	Year to Date
Output:				
Standard direct labor-hours	1,620	8,120	170	802
Direct labor cost:				
Amount.	$ 27,020	$ 154,980	$ 2,520	$ 7,980
Efficiency variance			4,354	12,649
Rate variance.			(1,834)	(4,669)
Controllable overhead:				
Setup costs	8,309	50,568	(1,855)	630
Repair and rework.	3,640	20,412	1,260	637
Overtime premium.	3,388	19,236	(525)	(3,710)
Supplies.	1,505	9,156	(847)	(2,688)
Small tools.	1,820	10,647	1,120	(574)
Other	4,508	27,216	637	1,365
Total overhead.	$ 23,170	$ 137,235	$ (210)	$ (4,340)

B. Second-Level Report

Production department cost summary (general superintendent)	Actual		Variance	
	June	Year to Date	June	Year to Date
Direct labor:				
Drill press	$ 27,020	$ 154,980	$ 2,520	$ 7,980
Lathe	36,680	222,320	3,780	10,920

Total direct labor	$189,840	$1,133,790	$21,140	$ 35,910
Controllable overhead:				
Office.	$ 13,720	$ 86,100	$ (805)	$ (4,725)
Drill press	23,170	137,235	(210)	(4,340)
Lathe	21,805	126,595	630	(945)
Punch press.	40,180	235,445	(455)	(4,480)
Plating	13,055	68,565	(1,225)	5,775
Heat treating	22,365	126,105	1,470	245
Assembly.	37,380	250,915	(4,375)	(9,660)
Total overhead.	$171,675	$1,030,960	$ (4,970)	$(18,130)

* Variances in parentheses are unfavorable.

ILLUSTRATION 25–1
(concluded)

C. Third-Level Report				
Factory cost summary (vice president of production)	*Actual*		*(Over) or under Budget*	
	June	*Year to Date*	*June*	*Year to Date*
Controllable overhead:				
Vice president's office..........	$ 14,770	$ 84,210	$ (2,205)	$ 245
General superintendent.........	171,675	1,030,960	(4,970)	(18,130)
Production control.............	8,645	52,990	(875)	(1,470)
Purchasing...................	8,260	49,315	665	525
Maintenance	25,130	132,720	(1,645)	1,715
Tool room....................	28,840	176,225	1,120	(2,240)
Inspection	15,715	95,760	1,260	(1,120)
Receiving, shipping, stores	25,410	160,755	(490)	(5,110)
Total overhead	$298,445	$1,782,935	$ (7,140)	$(25,585)
Direct labor	$189,840	$1,133,790	$21,140	$ 35,910

Selection of a Standard. A report that contains information *just* on actual performance is virtually useless for control purposes; it becomes useful only when actual performance is compared with some standard. (Without the standard the report is an information report rather than a control report.) Standards used in control reports are of three types: (1) predetermined standards, or budgets, (2) historical standards, and (3) external standards.

If carefully prepared, **predetermined standards (budgets)** are the best formal standard. The validity of such standards depends largely on how much care went into their development. Budget numbers arrived at in a slipshod manner obviously will not provide a reliable basis for comparison.

Historical standards are records of past actual performance. Results for the current month may be compared with results for last month or with results for the same month a year ago. This type of standard has two potentially serious weaknesses: (1) conditions may have changed between the two periods in a way that invalidates the comparison, and (2) when managers are measured against their own past record, there may be no way of knowing whether the prior period's performance was acceptable in the first place.

External standards are standards derived from the performance of other responsibility centers. The performance of one branch sales office may be compared with the performance of other branch sales offices. If conditions in these responsibility centers are similar, such a comparison may provide a useful basis for judging performance. In recent years some companies have used the performance of responsibility centers in other companies as a standard; this approach is called **benchmarking.** The standards employed in benchmarking are usually nonmonetary standards, such as defect rates or length of time to respond to a customer complaint.

Highlighting Significant Information.   The problem of designing a good set of control reports has changed drastically since the advent of the computer. When data had to be processed manually, care was needed to limit the quantity of information in reports because the cost of preparing them was relatively high. By contrast, a computer can print more figures in a minute than a manager can assimilate in a day. Thus, the current problem is to decide on the *right type* of information that should be given to management so as to avoid "information overload."

Individual cost and revenue elements, therefore, should be reported only when they are likely to be significant. The significance of an item is not necessarily proportional to its size. Management may be interested in a cost item of relatively small amount if this item is a discretionary cost that warrants close attention, such as travel expense. Management is similarly interested if costs incurred for a relatively small item may be symptomatic of a larger problem—for example, spoilage or rework costs, which may indicate quality control problems.

A management control system should operate on the **exception principle.** That is, a control report should focus management's attention on the relatively small number of items in which actual performance is significantly different from the standard. Little or no attention needs to be given to the relatively large number of situations where performance is satisfactory.

No control system makes a perfect distinction between the situations that warrant management attention and those that do not. For example, although those items for which there is a significant unfavorable variance are usually flagged for further investigation, such an investigation may reveal that the variance was entirely justified. Conversely, even though the variance is zero or favorable, an unsatisfactory situation may exist.

> **Example.**   When the general superintendent reads the production department cost summary report (part B of Illustration 25–1), no attention is called to the overhead performance of the drill press department in June because its actual costs were only $210 in excess of standard, an insignificant amount (less than 1 percent variance). We can observe from the details of drill press performance in part A, however, that setup costs, overtime premium, and supplies are considerably in excess of standard, and these excesses may indicate that problems do exist.

Note that Illustration 25–1 does not show the budgeted amounts but only the differences between actual and budget. Many control reports have three columns: (1) actual, (2) standard (or budget), and (3) variance. The standard column is not really necessary because the user of the report can determine each standard amount by adding the actual and the variance.

Illustration 25–2 shows a control report for the refrigerator division of an appliance company (which the company calls a "segment"). The report is prepared using the contribution margin format described in Chapter 19: the company uses a cost system that values inventory at full costs, but which keeps variable and fixed costs segregated so that income statements can be prepared in this format. Because this is a control report (as opposed to an economic performance report), costs deemed noncontrollable by the division manager, such as allocated headquarters costs, are excluded; but fixed expenses direct to the division are included because the division manager can significantly influence them. Note that the report includes information on orders received and order backlog, which are regarded as key indicators. The report also contains a revised budget, labeled current forecast; as was discussed in Chapter 24, this updates, but does not replace, the original plan. Also reported are sales volume and product mix variances because profits are particularly sensitive to these two factors. The division is an investment center; thus, in the lower-right corner its return on assets is reported. Note that this is done in a way that reminds the manager of the formula (described in Chapter 13) that states that ROA equals asset turnover times profit margin percentage (return on sales); improving either of these parameters will increase ROA.

Use of Control Reports

A general question can be raised about a comparison between actual and expected performance: Of what use is it? Managers' performance can be measured only *after* they have performed—when the work has already been done and no subsequent action by anyone can change what has been done. Of what value, therefore, are reports on past performance? There are two answers to this question.

First, if people know in advance that their performance is going to be measured, reported, and judged, they tend to act differently than if they had believed that no one was going to check up on them. Second, even though it is impossible to alter an event that has already happened, an analysis of how people have performed in the past may indicate ways of obtaining better performance in the future; such analysis leads to *learning*. Corrective action taken by people themselves is important; the system should "help people to help themselves." Action by the superior is also necessary; such action ranges in severity from giving verbal criticism or praise, to suggesting specific means of improving future performance, to the extremes of dismissing or promoting a person.

Feedback. In engineering the process called *feedback* refers to circuits that are arranged so that information about a device's current performance is fed back in such a way that the future performance of that device may be changed. A thermostat is a feedback device. If the temperature of a room drops below a prescribed level, the thermostat senses that information and activates the furnace. In an engineering diagram the circuitry and associated control apparatus is called a *feedback loop.*

ILLUSTRATION 25–2

REPORT OF SEGMENT CONTRIBUTION
For the Period Ending April 30
Refrigeration Division
(dollars in thousands)

Month	Gross Sales Over (Under)	Gross Sales Actual Plan*	Std Profit Contrib. Amount Over (Under)	Std Profit Contrib. Amount Actual Plan*	Std Profit Contrib. Percent Sales Over (Under)	Std Profit Contrib. Percent Sales Actual Plan*	Segment Expense Variances Actual	Direct Fixed Expenses Plan	Segment Contrib. Over (Under)	Segment Contrib. Actual Plan*	Segment Contrib. Last Year	Orders Received This Year	Orders Received Last Year	Order Backlog This Year	Order Backlog Last Year	Month
Jan	(231)	1,266	(89)	328	(2.0)	25.9	(15)	429	(104)	(116)		371	601	1,315	749	Jan
Feb	(102)	1,830	(41)	490	(0.8)	26.8	2	444	(39)	48		972	1,100	1,511	1,269	Feb
Mar	(10)	2,609	(4)	749	(0.1)	28.7	(26)	438	(30)	285		1,241	1,301	1,427	527	Mar
Apr	(45)	2,331	(16)	683	(0.1)	29.3	(13)	450	(29)	220		622	727	1,311	608	Apr
May		1,860*		489*		26.3*		414		75*			711		371	May
Jun		2,193*		645*		29.4*		327		318*			1,921		1,006	Jun
Jul		2,109*		591*		28.0*		423		168*			1,875		1,137	Jul
Aug		2,145*		618*		28.8*		420		198*			992		1,192	Aug
Sep		2,508*		708*		28.2*		435		273*			1,176		1,187	Sep
Oct		1,932*		534*		27.6*		432		102*			1,483		1,369	Oct
Nov		1,419*		417*		29.4*		408		9*			1,519		908	Nov
Dec		1,290*		318*		29.3*		432		(54)*			1,633		1,579	Dec

	Gross Sales Over (Under)	Gross Sales Actual Plan*	Amount Over (Under)	Amount Actual Plan*	Percent Over (Under)	Percent Actual Plan*	Seg. Exp. Var. Actual	Direct Fixed Exp. Plan	Seg. Contrib. Over (Under)	Seg. Contrib. Actual Plan*	Orders Received This Year	Orders Received Last Year
Year to Date	(388)	8,036	(150)	2,250	(0.5)	28.0	(52)	1,761	(202)	437	3,206	3,729
Original Plan		23,880		6,780		28.4		5,052		1,728		
Current Forecast		23,492		6,630		28.2	(52)	5,052		1,526		

Sales Volume and Mix Variances	This Month	Year to Date
Planned Profit Contribution	669	2,400
Sales Volume Variance	(14)	(110)
Sales Mix Variance	(2)	(40)
Actual Profit Contribution	683	2,250

Return on Assets		Original Plan	Current Forecast
Average Segment Assets		14,431	14,140
Capital Turnover		1.65	1.66
Return on Sales	*	7.2%	6.5%
Return on Assets Employed	=	11.9%	10.8%

( ) Indicates unfavorable variance or loss.

885

Control reports are feedback devices, but they are only one part of the feedback loop. Unlike the thermostat, which acts automatically in response to information about temperature, a control report does not by itself cause a change in performance. A change results only when *managers* take actions that lead to change. Thus, in management control the feedback loop requires the control report *plus* management action.

Steps in the Control Process

The control process consists of three steps: (1) *identify* areas that require investigation, (2) *investigate* these areas to ascertain whether action is warranted, and (3) *act* when investigation indicates the need for action.

Identification.   The control report is useful only in the first step in the process. It suggests areas that *appear* to need investigation. The variances described in Chapters 20 and 21 are designed to call attention to such areas. The manager's superior interprets the variances in the light of her or his own knowledge about conditions in the responsibility center. The superior may have already learned, from conversations or personal observation, that there is an adequate explanation for the variance or may have observed the need for corrective action before the report was issued. Some managers say that an essential characteristic of a good management control system is that reports should contain no surprises. By this they mean that managers of responsibility centers should inform their superiors as soon as significant events occur and should institute the necessary action immediately. If this is done, important information will already have been communicated informally to the superior prior to receipt of the formal report.

In examining the report, the superior attempts to judge both the efficiency and the effectiveness of the responsibility center. To do this, information on outputs is needed. Control reports for standard cost centers usually contain reliable output information. But in many other responsibility centers, output cannot be expressed in quantitative terms; this is the case with most staff departments of a company and also generally with nonprofit organizations. In these cases the report shows, at best, whether the manager of the responsibility center spent the amount that was planned to be spent. It does not show what was accomplished—the center's effectiveness. The reader of the report must therefore form a judgment as to the manager's effectiveness by other means, usually by conversations with those who are familiar with the work done or by personal observation.

For all types of responsibility centers, the evaluating manager must also distinguish between items of engineered cost and items of discretionary cost. With respect to engineered costs, the general rule is: "The lower they are, the better," consistent with quality and safety standards. With respect to discretionary costs, however, good performance often consists of spending the amount agreed on. Spending too little may be as bad as, or worse than, spending too much. A production manager can easily reduce current costs by skimping on maintenance; a marketing manager can reduce advertising expenditures; the president may eliminate a research project. None of these actions may be in the overall long-run best interest of the company, although all of them result in lower costs on the current short-run reports of performance.

Superiors must also remember that a variance is meaningful only if it is derived from a valid standard. Even a standard cost may not be an accurate estimate of what costs should have been for either or both of two reasons: (1) the standard was not set properly, or, (2) although set properly in the light of conditions existing at the time, those conditions have changed so that the standard has become obsolete. An essential first step in the analysis of a variance, therefore, is an examination of the validity of the standard.

In summary, the proper interpretation of a control report involves much more than a look at the size of the variances. In order to determine what, if any, investigation should be made, managers bring to bear all their experience regarding the work of the responsibility centers, all the information they have obtained from informal sources, and their intuitive judgment or "feel" for what needs attention.

Investigation. Usually, an investigation of possible significant areas takes the form of a conversation between the head of a responsibility center and his or her superior. In this conversation the superior probes to determine whether further action is warranted. More often than not, it is agreed that special circumstances not anticipated in the budget have arisen that account for the variance. If the changed circumstances are noncontrollable, this may be the explanation for an unfavorable variance, and the responsibility center manager therefore cannot be justifiably criticized. Corrective action may nevertheless be required because the unfavorable variance indicates that the company's overall profit is going to be less than planned.

Another possible explanation of an unfavorable variance is some unexpected, random occurrence, such as a machine breakdown. The superior should be less concerned about these random events than about tendencies that are likely to continue in the future unless corrected. Thus, there is particular interest in variances that persist for several months, especially if they increase in magnitude from one month to the next. The superior wants to find out what the underlying causes of these trends are and how they can be corrected.

Action. Based on investigation, the superior decides whether further action is required. The superior and the manager should agree on the steps that will be taken to remedy the unsatisfactory conditions. Equally important, if investigation reveals that performance has been good, a "pat on the back" is appropriate.

Of course, frequently no action at all is indicated. The superior judges that performance is satisfactory, and that is that. The superior should be particularly careful not to overly emphasize short-run performance. An inherent characteristic of management control systems is that they tend to focus on short-run rather than long-run performance. Thus, if too much emphasis is placed on results as shown in current control reports, long-run profitability may be hurt.

Reporting and Continuous Improvement

In recent years many companies have instituted initiatives called **total quality management** that involve attempting to enhance on an ongoing basis the effectiveness and efficiency of every aspect of the business. Not surprisingly, such **continuous improvement** efforts have produced better results when there was an explicit attempt made to measure and report the results being achieved.

Continuous improvement efforts usually are focused on activities at lower levels in the organization and involve nonmanagerial employees as well as the department manager. Most of the nonmanagerial employees are not accustomed to working with monetary control reports, and even the manager may rely more on personal observation and monitoring activities in terms of physical quantities than on reading control reports. In these circumstances visual displays in the form of charts and graphs are often the most effective type of control "report." The display should track progress on the key indicators that relate to the department's key success factors, and it should be visible to all of the department's employees.[1]

A few companies have concluded that using standard costs and variance reporting for performance evaluation in lower-level responsibility centers hampers, rather than enhances, continuous improvement efforts.[2] Such a decision is based on two observations relating to the *behavioral* aspects of variance reporting. First, experience shows that in most companies managers focus their investigation almost exclusively on unfavorable variances and often ignore favorable ones. Yet analysis of favorable variances may provide as many insights into how to improve operations as analysis of unfavorable ones. Second, in many instances people stop trying to improve once they reach the standard. They feel that if they continue to improve, the standard will just be made tougher the following year, or they feel that they should "save" any further ideas on how to improve until the next time an unfavorable variance needs to be addressed.

Companies not using their standard cost system for lower-level performance reporting use the nonmonetary chart or graph approach described above. In some cases they may not even set specific targets for the key indicators being tracked, but rather just exhort employees to "keep doing better." For example, rather than stating that "the target for the third quarter is to reduce the defect rate to 1 part in 1,000," the goal is stated as "strive for zero defects."

---

[1]IBM Corporation used this approach in the division that won the Malcolm Baldrige Award. Each department identified five key variables and tracked progress on them on a clearly visible chart. This was called the "five up on the wall" approach.

[2]These companies do not abandon their standard cost *systems;* they continue to use these systems for the other purposes described in Chapter 19, and they continue to use variance reporting in higher-level responsibility centers.

INCENTIVE COMPENSATION

As was stressed in Chapter 23, compensation can be a powerful motivating device. Many companies therefore reward profit center and investment center managers with a bonus based on their performance. A study of the pay and bonuses received by 14,000 managers over the period 1981–85 (totaling 70,824 observations from 219 organizations) found that, on average, bonuses were 20 percent of base pay. However, there were substantial differences among organizations, even those in the same industry.[3]

Typically, bonuses are based on a measure of annual performance. In some companies it is measured quarterly; in others there are long-run performance bonus plans covering a period of three to five years. Managers at higher levels usually receive a higher percentage of their compensation in the form of bonuses than do managers at lower levels, and the time horizon for at least a portion of the performance bonus is longer at higher levels.

Most bonus plans have both a quantitative aspect and a judgmental aspect; the bonus is based in part on the control report described earlier in this chapter, and in part on the superior's judgment as to the manager's performance. This judgment is applied to unmeasurable aspects of performance, such as whether the manager took some action that improved this year's measured results but that will be harmful to the company in the future. Few bonuses are based purely on a mechanical calculation employing data in the accounting report.[4]

Any of the many ways of measuring performance described in this book may be used in the quantitative measurements: income before taxes and extraordinary items, net income, return on assets employed, residual income (or EVA), and so on. Income before taxes and extraordinary items is perhaps the most common measure for profit centers and higher-level responsibility centers.

SUMMARY

Reports may be classified as information reports, economic performance reports, or managerial performance (control) reports. We focused on control reports, especially those prepared monthly for performance in a responsibility center. These reports compare actual performance with some standard. The best type of standard is a predetermined standard, or budget, but historical standards and comparisons with other responsibility centers are also used. Reports are designed to highlight significant information, especially information relating to key success factors.

---

[3]Barry Gerhart and George T. Milkovich, "Organizational Differences in Managerial Compensation and Financial Performance," *Academy of Management Journal,* December 1990, pp. 663–91.

[4]For a thorough description of bonus plans, see Kenneth A. Merchant, *Rewarding Results: Measuring Profit Center Managers* (Boston: Harvard Business School Press, 1989).

A report, by itself, does no more than identify the possible existence of a situation requiring management attention; variances are developed that do this. The next step is to investigate and the final step is to act, if action is warranted. Action should not be taken without an investigation because factors not revealed in the report may be the cause of the reported result.

Incentive compensation plans are based in part on the performance reported in control reports, but the amount of compensation is also influenced by the superior's judgment as to the manager's performance.

Cases

CASE 25-1 Crompton, Ltd.*

In 10 years Crompton, Ltd., had achieved noteworthy success in penetrating the highly competitive British abrasive products industry. Located in Sheffield, England, its factory employed more than 300 people, manufacturing grinding wheels for sale to steel converters and cutlery manufacturers in the Sheffield area.

From the time the company started in business, John Lucas, the factory manager, had controlled factory operations primarily by direct personal supervision. Because he had been so familiar with operations, he had known which departments were having difficulties and what they were doing to cope with them. He had worked very closely with the departmental supervisors and they, in turn, had never been afraid to call on him for help and advice.

With the growth of the company, this arrangement became more and more difficult. Lucas had to rely more and more on the individual supervisors to inform him of problems they were having, and he was quite sure that some of them, particularly the newer ones, were not as effective as they should have been. Unfortunately, he had no evidence on which to decide which departments needed attention. With this in mind, he asked Lou Field, a local accountant, to draw up a system of monthly reports that would supplement the knowledge that he would continue to gain by direct observation.

In the production of grinding wheels, abrasive grain was mixed with a bonding material according to the customer's requirements; molded in either a hot or a cold press, depending on the kind of bond; baked in a kiln; fitted with a bushing to take a motor spindle; "trued" to take off rough edges; shaped specially if needed; tested for balance and ability to withstand high speeds; and finally packed and shipped to the customer.

After several weeks of study and discussion with Crompton factory personnel, Field proposed that a report in the form illustrated in Exhibit 1 be prepared for each of the 18 production centers in the factory. One copy of the report would go to the supervisor in charge of that production center; a second copy would go to Lucas.

Field explained that the objective had been to produce a simple report, with as few figures as possible. Accordingly, the report had been limited to the following four items:

1. Gross production.
2. Rejection rate.
3. Net production per labor-hour.
4. Direct labor cost.

Gross production was measured by the total "list price" of the products passing through the department. Field considered using some other indicator of production volume, such as the total number of units or

EXHIBIT 1
HOT PRESS DEPARTMENT OPERATION REPORT, NOVEMBER*

	Gross Production (£)[†]	Rejections (percent)	Net Production per Labor-Hour (£/hr.)	Direct Labor (£)
November (4 weeks)	521,368	6.35	388.6	12,920
October (4 weeks)	332,408	10.48	344.8	9,264
September (5 weeks).	485,440	10.78	430.6	9,332
August (2 weeks)	125,134	9.10	281.2	3,516
July (4 weeks)	317,830	13.41	337.4	8,954
January–June (26 weeks)	2,224,404	8.90	311.6	64,366
Last fiscal year (52 weeks).	3,073,368	11.14	224.2	99,248

*Each "month" consists of either four of five full weeks, except August when the factory is closed for two weeks. A "year" consists of 52 weeks (50 working weeks plus two vacation weeks); approximately one year in every five, a calendar year includes 53 payroll dates, and that "year" consists of 53 weeks.
[†]£ = pounds, the British monetary unit.

total weight of the output, but rejected all these because the output varied so widely in size and complexity. The "list price" was a stabilized amount for each wheel, established several years earlier and unchanged since that time. Actual customer prices were set each year by multiplying the list price by a percentage (e.g., 145 percent) which management felt was "right" for the current market.

Rejections occurred in all production departments, although the majority were discovered in the testing department. At a weekly conference the plant superintendent determined the source of the defect and allocated responsibility accordingly. Rejections were quoted as a percentage of gross production handled.

Net production per labor-hour was gross production, minus rejects, all measured at list prices, divided by the number of direct labor-hours.

Direct labor costs were the actual direct labor-hours for the month multiplied by the actual wage rates paid individual workers during the month, including any premium payments for overtime hours. Departmental supervisors were responsible for scheduling

work in their departments and thus were expected to keep overtime premiums to the lowest level consistent with their delivery commitments.

Each report provided three sets of figures with which the most recent month's record could be compared: (1) the four immediately preceding months, separately for each month; (2) the six months prior to that, as semiannual totals; and (3) the most recent complete fiscal year, as annual totals. Thus, the November figures could be compared with those for October, September, August, and July; for January–June; and for the 12 months January–December of the preceding fiscal year.

Finally, Field suggested that the departments could be compared with each other to determine which were the most productive, which were showing the most improvement, and which seemed to need Lucas's attention the most.

Questions

1. In what ways does Exhibit 1 differ from the financial accounting reports you have studied?

2. What did Lucas mean by "control information"? Why did he need it?

3. What suggestions would you make for improving Exhibit 1 so as to be more useful to Lucas?

CASE 25-2   Midwest Ice Cream Company (B)*

Two years ago Midwest Ice Cream Company installed a financial planning and control system. (See Midwest Ice Cream Company (A) for details of this system.) In January, after receiving the previous year's operating results, Jim Peterson, president of Midwest, had asked Frank Roberts, marketing vice president, to make a short presentation at the next board of directors meeting commenting on the major reasons for the favorable operating income variance of $71,700. He asked him to draft his presentation in the next few days so that the two of them could go over it before the board meet-

ing. Peterson wanted to illustrate to the board how an analysis of profit variance could highlight those areas needing management attention as well as those deserving a pat on the back.

The Annual Profit Plan. Following the four-step approach outlined in Case 24-4, the management group of Midwest Ice Cream prepared the previous year's profit plan. The timetable they followed is shown in Exhibit 1.

The budget preparation procedures for last year constituted the first time the company had taken a formalized approach to profit

EXHIBIT 1
BUDGET PREPARATION TIMETABLE

		October (weeks)				November (weeks)			
		1	2	3	4	1	2	3	4
I	Variable cost standards		X						
II-A	Sales forecast		X						
II-B	Approval of sales forecast			X					
III-A	Preliminary payroll budget			X					
III-B	Preliminary budget for other operating expenses			X					
III-C	Approval of payroll budget and other expenses budget				X				
IV-A	Preliminary profit plan					X			
IV-B	Approval of profit plan						X		
IV-C	Board of directors meeting							X	

* Copyright © by the President and Fellows of Harvard College. Harvard Business School case 175-070.

planning. Accordingly, the company had not wanted to get too sophisticated in its first attempt at budgeting. Thus, the budget figures were based on current operations at that time, adjusted only for expected inflation.

Based on an anticipated overall ice cream market of about 11,440,000 gallons in their marketing area and a market share of 50 percent, Midwest had forecasted overall gallon sales of 5,720,329 for the year. A summary of the profit plan is shown in Exhibit 2.

Actual Results. By the spring of last year, it had become clear that the year's sales volume was going to be higher than forecast.

In fact, Midwest's actual sales for the year totaled 5,968,366 gallons, an increase of about 248,000 gallons over budget. Market research data indicated that the total ice cream market in Midwest's marketing area was 12,180,000 gallons, as opposed to the forecast of about 11,440,000 gallons. The revised profit plan for the year, based on actual volume, is shown in Exhibit 3.

The fixed costs in the revised profit plan are the same as before, $1,945,900. The variable costs, however, have been adjusted to reflect a volume level of 5,968,366 gallons instead of 5,720,329 gallons, thereby eliminating wide cost variances due strictly to the

EXHIBIT 2
ANNUAL PROFIT PLAN

	Standard Contribution Margin/Gallon	Forecasted Gallon Sales	Forecasted Contribution Margin
Vanilla	$0.4329	2,409,854	$1,043,200
Chocolate	0.4535	2,009,061	911,100
Walnut	0.5713	48,883	28,000
Buttercrunch	0.4771	262,185	125,000
Cherry Swirl	0.5153	204,774	105,500
Strawberry	0.4683	628,560	294,400
Pecan Chip	0.5359	157,012	84,100
Total	$0.4530	5,720,329	$2,591,300

Breakdown of Budgeted Total Expenses

	Variable	Fixed	Total
Manufacturing	$5,888,100	$ 612,800	$6,500,900
Delivery	187,300	516,300	703,600
Advertising*	553,200	—	553,200
Selling	—	368,800	368,800
Administrative	—	448,000	448,000
Total	$6,628,600	$1,945,900	$8,574,500

* The advertising allowance was 6 percent of sales dollars.

Recap:	
Sales	$ 9,219,900
Variable cost of sales	6,628,600
Contribution margin	2,591,300
Fixed costs	1,945,900
Income from operations	$ 645,400

EXHIBIT 3
REVISED PROFIT PLAN
Budgeted Profit at Actual Volume

	Standard Contribution Margin/Gallon	Actual Gallon Sales	Forecasted Contribution Margin
Vanilla....................................	$0.4329	2,458,212	$1,064,200
Chocolate	0.4535	2,018,525	915,400
Walnut	0.5713	50,124	28,600
Buttercrunch............................	0.4771	268,839	128,300
Cherry Swirl.............................	0.5153	261,240	134,600
Strawberry...............................	0.4683	747,049	349,800
Pecan Chip..............................	0.5359	164,377	88,100
Total	$0.4539	5,968,366	$2,709,000

Breakdown of Budgeted Total Expenses

	Variable	Fixed	Total
Manufacturing...........................	$6,113,100	$ 612,800	$6,750,900
Delivery	244,500	516,300	760,800
Advertising	578,700	—	578,700
Selling	—	368,800	368,800
Administrative...........................	—	448,000	448,000
Total	$6,936,300	$1,945,900	$8,882,200

Recap:	
Sales	$ 9,645,300
Variable cost of sales..................	6,936,300
Contribution margin	2,709,000
Fixed costs..........................	1,945,900
Income from operations.................	$ 763,100

difference between planned volume and actual volume. Assume, for example, that cartons are budgeted at 4 cents per gallon. If the forecast volume is 10,000 gallons, the carton budget is $400. If actual sales are only 8,000 gallons but $350 worth of cartons are used, it is misleading to say that there is a favorable variance of $50. The variance is unfavorable by $30, but this only shows up if the budget is adjusted to actual volume:

Carton allowance	= $0.04 per gallon
Forecast volume	= 10,000 gallons
Actual volume	= 8,000 gallons
Variance (based on forecast volume)	= $400 − $350 = $50 Favorable
Variance (based on actual volume)	= $320 − $350 = $30 Unfavorable

For costs that are highly volume-dependent, variances therefore should be based on a budget that reflects the volume of operation actually attained. Since the level of fixed

EXHIBIT 4

	Earnings Statement Year Ended December 31			

Month			Year to Date	
Actual	Budget		Actual	Budget
		Sales—net	$9,657,300	$9,645,300
		Manufacturing cost of goods sold—Schedule A–2*	6,824,900	6,725,900
		Delivery—Schedule A–3	706,800	760,800
		Advertising—Schedule A–4	607,700	578,700
		Selling—Schedule A–5	362,800	368,800
		Administrative—Schedule A–7	438,000	448,000
		Total expenses	8,940,200	8,882,200
		Income from operations	717,100	763,100
		Other income—Schedule A–8	12,500	12,500
		Other expense—Schedule A–9	6,000	6,000
		Income before taxes	723,600	769,600
		Provision for income taxes	289,440	
		Net earnings	$ 434,160	

	Analysis of Variance from Forecasted Operating Income		

Month			Year to Date
		1. Actual income from operations	$717,100
		2. Budgeted profit at forecasted volume	645,400
		3. Budgeted profit at actual volume	763,100
		Variance due to sales volume—[(3) minus (2)]	117,700 F
		Variance due to operations—[(1) minus (3)]	46,000 U
		Total variance—[(1) minus (2)]	$ 71,700 F

*Schedules A–3 through A–9 have not been included in this case. Schedule A–2 is reproduced as Exhibit 5.

costs is independent of volume anyway, it is not necessary to adjust the budget for fixed cost items.

Exhibit 4 is the year's earnings statement. (The monthly figures for December have been excluded for purposes of this case.) Exhibit 5 is the detailed expense breakdown for the manufacturing department. (The detailed expense breakdowns for the other de-

partments have been excluded for purposes of this case.)

Analysis of Profit Variance. Three days after Jim Peterson asked Frank Roberts to pull together a presentation for the board of directors analyzing the previous year's profit variance, Roberts came into Peterson's office to review his first draft. He showed Peterson the following schedule:

Favorable variance due to sales:		
Volume	$117,700 F	
Price*...	12,000 F	$129,700 F
Unfavorable variance due to operations:		
Manufacturing	99,000 U	
Delivery...	54,000 F	
Advertising..	29,000 U	
Selling..	6,000 F	
Administration	10,000 F	58,000 U
Net variance—favorable		$ 71,700 F

*This price variance is the difference between the standard sales value of the gallons actually sold and the actual sales revenues ($9,657,300 − $9,645,300).

EXHIBIT 5

Manufacturing Cost of Goods Sold
Year Ended December 31

Month				Year to Date	
Actual	Budget			Actual	Budget
		Variable Costs			
		Dairy ingredients		$3,679,900	$3,648,500
		Milk price variance		57,300	—
		Sugar		599,900	596,800
		Sugar price variance		23,400	—
		Flavoring (including fruits and nuts)		946,800	982,100
		Cartons		567,200	566,900
		Plastic wrap		28,700	29,800
		Additives		235,000	251,000
		Supplies		31,000	35,000
		Miscellaneous		3,000	3,000
		Subtotal		6,172,200	6,113,100
		Fixed Costs			
		Labor–cartonizing and freezing		425,200	390,800
		Labor–other		41,800	46,000
		Repairs		32,200	25,000
		Depreciation		81,000	81,000
		Electricity and water		41,500	40,000
		Miscellenous		1,500	30,000
		Spoilage		29,500	—
		Subtotal		652,700	612,800
		Total		$6,824,900	$6,725,900

Roberts said that he planned to give each member of the board a copy of this schedule and then to comment briefly on each item. Peterson said he thought the schedule was okay as far as it went, but that it just didn't highlight things in a manner that indicated what corrective actions should be taken this year or what really had caused the favorable overall variance. He suggested that Roberts try to break down the sales volume variance into the part attributable to sales mix, the part attributable to market share shifts, and the part actually attributable to volume changes. He also suggested breaking down the manufacturing variance to indicate what actions are called for this year to correct the unfavorable variance. How much of the total was due to price differences versus quantity differences, for example? Finally, he suggested that Roberts call on John Vance, the controller, if he needed help in the mechanics of breaking out these different variances.

As Roberts returned to his office he considered Peterson's suggestion of getting Vance involved in revising the schedule to be presented to the board. Roberts did not want to consult Vance unless it was absolutely necessary because Vance always went overboard on the technical aspects of any accounting problem. Roberts couldn't imagine a quicker way to put the board members to sleep than to throw one of Vance's number-filled, six-page memos at them. "Peterson specifically wants a nontechnical presentation for the board," Roberts thought to himself, "and that rules out John Vance. Besides, you don't have to be a CPA to focus in on the key variance areas from a general management viewpoint."

Questions

1. Review the variance analysis in Exhibit 4, being certain you understand it. This is the same idea as in Exhibit C of Midwest Ice Cream Company (A).

2. Calculate the gross margin mix variance, using the approach shown in the lower portion of Exhibit A of the (A) case. Then calculate a detailed (i.e., flavor-by-flavor) mix variance, using the approach illustrated in part B of text Illustration 21–3. For what purposes would the detailed analysis be more useful than the aggregate mix variance calculation?

3. How would you modify Frank Roberts's variance analysis before explaining the $71,700 F profit variance to the board of directors?

4. Considering both this case and Midwest Ice Cream Company (A), evaluate the company's new budgetary control system.

CASE 25–3   Thomas J. Lipton, Inc. (A)*

In early September 1980 Don Logan was contemplating the poor reception given to the latest changes in product-line profit statements and the measures by which product-line financial performance was evaluated. As Associate Director of Financial Analysis for Thomas J. Lipton, Inc., Mr. Logan had been the main advocate for the changes. Now he was responsible for ensuring a smooth transition to the new system.

Mr. Logan's involvement in revising the financial statements began in June 1980 when he proposed that product-line profit-and-loss statements (P&Ls) should be adjusted for inflation. In addition, he proposed that certain corporate expenses be allocated to individual products and that product-line P&Ls contain a capital charge for the fixed assets and working capital employed by product lines. He felt that the proposed P&Ls would measure the real flow of resources associated with each product line, giving a more meaningful assessment of the line's

*Copyright © by the Darden Graduate Business School Foundation, Charlottesville, VA..

profitability and leading to better decisions by product managers. Allocating assets among product lines would also allow them to be evaluated on the basis of inflation-adjusted return on investment rather than the less informative return on sales. Lipton's senior management agreed with the proposed changes and decided that 1981 would be a trial year for the new P&Ls.

After working with his staff through the summer implementing the new system, Mr. Logan realized that many of the product managers, whose performance would be measured by the new system, did not understand it. Some of them questioned the principles involved; others wondered how the new system would affect their particular products. The product managers' concerns caused Mr. Logan to reconsider the entire situation.

Food Processing Industry. The food processing industry in 1980 was mature and very competitive. During the 1970s demand for food had remained constant and consumers had become more cost conscious. Due to limited opportunities for expanding existing product lines and the risks associated with introducing new products, acquisitions represented a relatively safe means of growing and diversifying. During the 1970s many food companies pursued policies of acquisition. As the industry became more concentrated, smaller firms found it harder to compete.

The size and performance of the major U.S. food companies varied significantly. In 1979 the industry leader was Beatrice Foods with $7.5 billion in sales, followed by Kraft with $6.5 billion. Consolidated Foods was the fastest growing, having achieved a 17 percent compound annual sales growth rate between 1974 and 1979. Quaker Oats was recognized as the earnings growth leader after registering a five-year average annual earnings growth rate of 28 percent. The

undisputed industry leader in financial performance was Kellogg. In 1979 it ranked number one in return on investment (20.3 percent), return on sales (8.5 percent), and return on equity (25.2 percent). By comparison the average return on equity for food companies over the previous five years was 14.7 percent, and ROE for all industries was 13.8 percent.

The Company. Thomas J. Lipton, Inc., was established in 1915 as a tea importing firm by Sir Thomas Lipton, a flamboyant multimillionaire tea merchant. After his death in 1931, a holding company owned by the Anglo-Dutch corporation Unilever N.V. purchased the company from his estate. By 1980 Lipton was a diversified food company with 1979 sales of $698 million, which ranked number 357 on the Fortune 500. Although Lipton's sales and profits had increased steadily over the last 28 years, it only ranked 19th in sales among U.S. food companies in 1979.

Lipton's stable of products consisted of both products developed internally and those that had been obtained through acquisition. The 30 product lines were divided into three operating divisions: Beverage, Food, and General Management. Lipton brands were among the leaders in tea, soup, and salad dressing markets. Despite diversification, a few of Lipton's product lines continued to generate the bulk of the company's revenues. Lipton was the dominant supplier of tea to the retail trade in the United States, and tea continued to account for over 40 percent of Lipton's revenues.

Of Lipton's 25 brands or product lines, 11 had sales under $10 million, 10 had sales between $10 million and $50 million, and 4 had sales in excess of $50 million. Ten had shown sales increases in 1979, six had been stable, and nine had experienced sales decreases. These 1979 sales results reflected trends in which some products' sales were growing rapidly, some were stable, and others were declining.

Within the industry, Lipton had positioned itself in the growing market for convenience and instant foods. Looking toward the future, Lipton's marketing strategy was to strengthen the position of its tea business and other segments in which the company held a dominant position. For product lines that were profitable but whose growth prospects were limited, Lipton's objective was to maintain sales at their present level. Lipton also sought to develop new products in high-growth segments of the food industry. Its long-term marketing objective was to continue to broaden its base through internal growth and acquisition.

Lipton had a very good relationship with Unilever, its parent company. In 1979, Lipton had one of the best financial performance records of any Unilever subsidiary. Consequently, Unilever did not maintain tight control over Lipton's day-to-day operations. Biannually, Lipton and Unilever would agree to a basic strategic plan and determine projected profits and growth rates.

For the future, Lipton had several financial and operating objectives. In 1979, sales had been projected to continue to grow by 10½ percent per year and the after-tax profit margin to improve to 6 percent. Another objective was to achieve a 15 percent after-tax return on average invested capital, where invested capital was defined as total assets minus current liabilities. By mid-1980, it looked as if Lipton would do better than the 1979 projections.

Other important financial objectives revolved around Lipton's current and potential cash needs. Lipton wished to maintain its AA bond rating in order to minimize borrowing costs and maximize future borrowing flexibility. It was important that Lipton continue to generate cash from operations. Lipton's intention was to maintain a dividend payout ratio comparable to other major food companies. The remaining cash could be used to fund operations or make acquisitions; but since the equity market was closed to Lipton, all growth had to be financed from retained earnings or by borrowing.

Financial Performance Measurement. Until 1975 the primary measure that Lipton's management used to evaluate its corporate performance was after-tax return on sales (ROS). However, around 1974 the ROS measure began to fall into disfavor because it did not measure whether Lipton was receiving an adequate return on investment. In 1975 Lipton's management therefore began to use after-tax return on average invested capital (ATRIC). A problem with the use of ATRIC was that it was only calculated for the whole company, since assets and current liabilities had never been accurately broken down by product line.

The basic measure of product-line financial performance used by Lipton's management was called trading profit. Exhibit 1 shows the format used in 1979 for calculating product-line trading profit. Product lines and product-line managers were evaluated on the basis of trading profit, delivered profit, profit as a percent of sales, and growth in unit volume. Thus the format for product-line P&Ls seemed to match the information needs of a marketing-oriented manager.

Although internally Lipton did not adjust its financial measures for the effects of inflation, it was required to do this on the reports it sent to Unilever. Unilever's extensive worldwide operations and subsidiaries had forced the parent company to cope with and understand inflation in the 1940s and 1950s. Hence, in the late 1970s Unilever evaluated Lipton's overall financial performance on the basis of three inflation-adjusted measures:

- Ratio of net sales to average gross capital employed (capital turnover).

EXHIBIT 1
P&L FORMAT USED IN 1979

Sales volume		*xxx cases*
Net sales revenues		**$xxx**
Variable cost of sales:		
Manufacturing	$xxx	
Freight	xxx	
Public warehousing	xxx	
Total variable cost of sales		xxx
Variable profit contribution		**xxx**
Nonvariable cost of sales:		
Manufacturing	xxx	
Plant warehousing	xxx	
Other	xxx	
Total nonvariable cost of sales		xxx
Delivered profit		**xxx**
Direct marketing expenses:		
Advertising	xxx	
Sales promotion	xxx	
Direct marketing services	xxx	
Marketing write-offs	xxx	
Product group	xxx	
Direct selling	xxx	
Total direct marketing expense		xxx
Direct profit contribution		**xxx**
Indirect expenses:		
Indirect selling	xxx	
Indirect marketing services	xxx	
Technical research	xxx	
Administrative	xxx	
Total indirect expense		xxx
New product development charge		xxx
Trading profit		**$xxx**

- Trading profit before tax as a percent of net sales (return on sales).
- After-tax return on average gross capital employed (return on capital).

In these three measures both profits and assets were adjusted to account for the effect of inflation on fixed assets. On the corporate P&L depreciation expense was calculated on the basis of the current replacement value (CRV) for fixed assets. On the balance sheet the net book value of fixed assets was stated as gross CRV less accumulated CRV depreciation. Gross capital employed equaled net CRV of fixed assets plus working capital. Exhibit 2 shows an example of these calculations.

In the late 1970s the ATRIC measure that Lipton's management used internally began to receive criticism because it was not adjusted for inflation, and increasing U.S. inflation had begun to alter its usefulness. Inflation increased nominal profits even with no change in unit volume. In addition, invested capital was determined by historical costs, which did not reflect the cost of replacing fixed assets. Inflated profits and understated assets meant that the real ATRIC was much

EXHIBIT 2
INFLATION-ADJUSTED MEASURE OF FINANCIAL PERFORMANCE

	Historical Cost	CRV Cost
Sales	$100	$100
Cost of goods sold	70	70
Adjustment for CRV depreciation	—	10
Trading profit before tax	30	20
Taxes	15	15
Profit after tax	$ 15	$ 5
Average gross fixed assets	$135	$200
Accumulated depreciation	70	125
Average net fixed assets	65	75
Average working capital	15	15
Average gross capital employed	$ 80	$ 90
Sales/Average gross capital employed	1.25	1.11
Trading profit before tax/Net sales	$30/$100 = 30%	$20/$100 = 20%
Profit after tax/Average gross capital employed	$15/$80 = 18.8%	$5/$90 = 5.6%

lower than the reported ATRIC. The company's overall performance appeared to be improving even though in real terms that was not necessarily the case.

In May 1979 Mr. Logan had several conversations with Robert Sims, Manager of Marketing Financial Analysis, about the way in which financial performance of product lines was being stated. Though the two men did not agree on a specific format, they did agree on some general objectives. One was that the current format needed change; another was that the product managers needed a clearer understanding of the financial constraints and framework within which they operated. The two men also agreed that it might take two or three years to get people to really listen, and therefore a three-year timetable was appropriate for full implementation of the education and changes necessary.

The following spring Mr. Logan had occasion to discuss some of his thoughts in a presentation to the management group. At that time he focused particularly on the need to conserve cash, and ways in which a capital charge and some sort of inflation adjustment could clarify the picture. To his surprise Lipton's president said right away that he thought it was a good idea and asked for a recommended financial reporting format.

Since both Mr. Logan and Mr. Sims saw the development of a proper reporting format as an evolutionary and educational process, the thought of presenting a recommended format within a few weeks was a little disturbing. Both men felt that whatever they presented would be subject to continuing review and modification over the next couple of years.

In thinking about the next steps, Mr. Logan reviewed the product-line P&Ls for 1979 and concluded that there were three weaknesses in the present method of calculating product-line profits. First, he recognized that inflation had distorted product-line P&Ls. Increased product-line revenue and profits did not necessarily indicate improved performance. Furthermore, inflation increased the costs of replacing fixed assets. Historical cost depreciation did not accurately reflect the

EXHIBIT 3
CORPORATE OI&D ITEMS APPLICABLE TO PRODUCT LINES

Benefits to Brands	*Costs to Brands*
Discount on purchases[1]	Profit-sharing costs[8]
T.J.L. media[2]	Sundry expenses
Operations income[3]	
Inventory revaluations[4]	
Overabsorption of fixed overhead[5]	
Tax benefit of donations[6]	
Commodity profits[7]	

Explanations:
1. Prompt payment discounts received by central purchasing were to be distributed.
2. T.J.L. media—A centralized department handled media purchases and the savings of about 6 percent of advertising expense were to be distributed in proportion to advertising.
3. Operations income was income received from auxiliary operations, such as sales of computer time or billing services.
4. Inventory revaluations occurred when the standard cost of inventory increased from one accounting period to the next. This was usually small but at times had been a significant amount.
5. Overabsorption of fixed overhead occurred if actual production volume was higher than the planned level.
6. The tax benefit of donations resulted from occasional gifts-in-kind to charitable organizations.
7. Commodity profits resulted from centralized commodity transactions.
8. Profit-sharing costs resulted from a system in which Lipton distributed to employees a part of earnings above a certain level, that level being defined in terms of a rate of return on shareholders' equity. The amount each employee received was based on salary level. The amount of profit-sharing to be borne by each brand would be based either on the brand's profitability or on its share of total salaries. It had not been decided which base was more appropriate.

cost of replacing those assets in the future. Thus, in an inflationary environment nominal profits gave misleading information as to the ability of a product line to operate as a going concern in the future.

Second, the cost of using working capital and fixed assets did not appear on product-line P&Ls. Therefore, trading profit did not reflect the cost of all funds invested in a particular brand. Mr. Logan thought that failure to allocate that expense encouraged product managers to increase working capital balances more than was really necessary.

The third problem observed by Mr. Logan was that many product expenses were not allocated or, if so, were improperly allocated among product lines. The unallocated corporate other income and deductions (OI&D) account contained many items that applied to individual product lines. (Exhibit 3 lists corporate OI&D items that applied to product lines.) Other allocation problems centered on the new-product development charge and on manufacturing and corporate overhead. The former was allocated to established products on the basis of profits. Mr.

EXHIBIT 4
PROPOSED 1981 P&L FORMAT

Net sales revenues	$ xxx
Variable cost of sales*	xxx
Variable profit contribution	xxx
Nonvariable cost of sales*	xxx
Delivered profit	xxx
Direct marketing expenses*	xxx
Direct profit contribution	xxx
Indirect expenses*	xxx
New-product development charge	xxx
Trading profit	xxx
Less: CRV depreciation adjustment	(xxx)
Less: Working capital charge	(xxx)
Less: Fixed asset charge†	(xxx)
Add back: New-product development charge	xxx
Less: OI&D costs	(xxx)
Plus: OI&D benefits	xxx
Economic profit	$ xxx

* Details same as in Exhibit 1.
† The fixed asset charge was calculated by multiplying a percentage rate times the net CRV
of the assets (i.e., current replacement value less accumulated CRV depreciation).

Logan thought it should not be charged to established products. The latter was allocated to product lines on the basis of planned production, which often differed significantly from actual production. Manufacturing overhead was part of nonvariable cost of sales and corporate overhead was part of administrative expense. Mr. Logan thought the effect of these allocation policies was to distort the relative financial performance of product lines and make it difficult to interpret year-to-year changes in product-line performance. Mr. Logan concluded that product-line P&Ls did not reflect the true contribution of each product to the corporation as a whole. Furthermore, he felt it was no longer possible to conclude with any reliability how well each product manager had performed in his or her job.

Having studied the problem, Mr. Logan decided that the time was ripe for revising the method of calculating product-line prof-itability. All of the changes would be instituted simultaneously during 1981 so that the resulting figures would measure what he would call the product line's "economic profit." He recommended that four items be added to the 1981 product-line P&Ls to arrive at economic profit. Trading profit would be calculated in its present form, but below that, changes would be made to reflect the costs of continuing to operate each product line. The specific changes were (1) a deduction to reflect the difference between CRV depreciation and historical cost depreciation, (2) an interest charge for capital employed by a product line, (3) elimination of the new-product development charge, and (4) inclusion of previously unallocated corporate OI&D items. Exhibit 4 shows the proposed P&L format for 1981. Mr. Logan thought that economic profit would be a measure of the true economic earnings generated by a product. If it was positive then real wealth would

EXHIBIT 5
PRODUCT LINE X P&L 1980 DATA RECAST IN PROPOSED FORMAT

Net sales revenues	$30,274
Historical cost trading profit	$ 4,526
Less: CRV depreciation adjustment	(547)
Less: Working capital charge	(2,416)
Less: Fixed asset charge	(2,821)
Add back: New-product development charge	244
OI&D items (net)	148
Economic profit (loss)	$ (866)

Source: Disguised figures based on a Marketing Financial Analysis staff presentation.

have been created for Lipton and for Unilever.

He also thought that economic profit would provide information that would enable senior managers to make better decisions. He noted that the difference between economic profit and trading profit could point out particular long-term problems or advantages associated with particular product lines that were not apparent by just looking at trading profit. He believed that in the long run Lipton would want to focus its financial resources on those product lines that showed a positive economic profit.

Mr. Logan also thought that economic profit would induce product managers to make decisions beneficial to the corporation as a whole. Explicitly charging for working capital would eliminate the incentive to increase working capital balances unnecessarily. Allocating brand-related OI&D income and expenses would increase product managers' awareness of these items. By evaluating managers on an inflation-adjusted basis, the product managers would be evaluated on the same basis as Unilever judged Lipton. In short, product managers would face the same economic environment as the firm when making decisions.

Mr. Logan believed that there were real advantages to using economic profit as the basis for measuring product performance. In summary he concluded that it: (1) reflected the existence of inflation and high interest rates, (2) created a consistency between Lipton's internal P&Ls and those used by Unilever to evaluate Lipton, (3) provided a more accurate allocation of product-line expenses, (4) forced product managers to focus on the strengths and weaknesses of their product lines, and (5) indicated to upper management what areas of the business deserved more attention.

Indeed, preliminary analysis showed that the economic profit approach would give a far different "snapshot" of product-line performance from that shown by historical profit. Exhibit 5 shows the difference between trading profit and economic profit for one of the product lines. Whereas trading profit was positive, the economic profit of this line was negative.

Financial Analysis Viewpoint. In a presentation to his staff, Mr. Sims stated:

The main thrust of all this change is to communicate to the product managers that business conditions in the 1980s are going to make it tougher. Lipton is smaller than many other food companies, and therefore we need to be more efficient, better marketers, and more careful with our capital. It doesn't make sense to disguise the profitability of certain products. We need to eliminate all those distortions to know where our profits are coming from. This will enable us to take strategic actions on some of our "problem" products.

Mr. Logan followed by explaining:

For too long, product managers have proceeded along thinking our capital costs are free. It has taken me a long time to convince them that there can be a big difference between reported income and "real" income. I think we've finally come up with a financial performance measure that will work on the brand level. The keys are to build flexibility into the system and find an equitable way to motivate product managers. I view this as an opportunity to mold product managers into well-rounded businesspersons, aware of all aspects of the business, financial as well as marketing.

Product Manager Concerns. Management approval for both the new P&L format and the change in performance measurement was secured by early August 1980. Soon thereafter, Mr. Logan and other members of the Marketing Financial Analysis section made presentations to the product managers. Although many product managers agreed that a change was necessary, their immediate reactions were fear and suspicion. Mr. Logan inferred from the managers' questions that the underlying financial concepts were not understood. He realized that product managers would have to be taught how economic profit was derived and how its components could be managed so that financial goals could be met. Product managers' cooperation was essential if the change were to be successful.

In early September Mr. Logan sat at his desk and mulled over the entire situation. He realized that certain details of the system needed to be resolved. He had to decide on a percentage rate for the capital charge and whether different rates should be assessed against fixed assets and working capital. He

also knew that an incentive system would have to be designed to motivate the product managers. He wondered what the best way was to educate the product managers and whether there should be different performance standards for each product line. Finally, he was concerned that the new performance measurement system might have some unforeseen consequences, motivating product managers to take actions detrimental to the long-term health of their brands.

His concentration was broken by a knock at the door. Michael Hirst, a product manager, walked in, appearing very troubled.

Don, do you realize you're making me build inflation into my prices so I can cover these additional costs? I'll be priced right out of the market. It also looks like I'm going to be penalized because my brand is capital-intensive, and I'm going to be responsible for fixed manufacturing costs that I have no control over. I won't even know when I've done a good job. How will I be compared to other product managers? If I cut down on my working capital balance, that's going to hurt my service level. What should I target for, anyway? I hope you can tell me in a few weeks what I'll be charged for interest. And when the new brand P&Ls come out, I hope you can tell me what actions I'll need to take to improve my performance.

Later that afternoon, Mr. Logan became involved in a similar discussion with John Dobson, another product manager.

You know, Don, I still don't see what's wrong with excluding OI&D from the brand P&Ls, and I'm still having trouble grasping this CRV depreciation. Why should I start charging now to cover the cost of an asset I will need in 15 years after I just bought one last year? My trading profit shows I made a profit last year, but your figures say a negative economic profit resulted. That doesn't make sense to me. If I have negative economic profit several years in a row, what does that mean? Am I pricing high enough? If so, will future funds be diverted away from me? Right now, I'm keeping my prices low so I can grab market share. This makes my economic profit low, but don't you think I should be compensated for contributing to the growth and diversification of the firm?

The last remark concerned an aspect of performance measurement about which Mr. Logan had been thinking for some time. In fact, he had already discussed with several people the need to reflect real growth in some sort of measure. So far he had not found a satisfactory way to put a dollar value on growth, nor did he see how one could distinguish between growth in a rising economy and growth in recessionary times.

The Need for a Decision. Mr. Logan was now at the "point of no return." Lipton management had committed itself to the economic profit approach for at least 1981–82. He wanted it to be accepted by everyone because he believed it was conceptually cor-rect, especially in an inflationary environment. At the same time, he knew many of the misunderstandings and key details of the plan needed clarification. He was already considering additional enhancements to the system. He decided to call Kate Williams, a member of the Marketing Financial Analysis staff, and assign her to the project.

> Kate, I want you to undertake a complete analysis of the entire decision process that has transpired over the last nine months and determine what is the best way to handle the product managers. Also, I want to know if you feel the economic profit approach is the best performance measurement available and, if so, what additional enhancements will be necessary. I expect your recommendation within a month.

Question

Undertake the analysis and evaluation that Mr. Logan has assigned Ms. Williams.

26

Short-Run Alternative Choice Decisions

This chapter begins a discussion of the third use of management accounting information—making alternative choice decisions. In such problems, the manager seeks to choose the best one of several alternative courses of action. The quantitative analysis of these alternatives focuses on the differences in their costs (and sometimes also differences in their revenues and assets employed). This chapter introduces the construct of differential costs and contrasts it with the full cost construct that was discussed in Chapters 17–19. This chapter also describes the use of differential costs (and differential revenues) in the analysis of several types of problems, each having a relatively short time horizon. Alternative choice problems involving longer time horizons and differential assets are discussed in Chapter 27.

THE DIFFERENTIAL CONCEPT

Cost Constructions for Various Purposes

Chapters 17–19 discussed the measurement of full costs, one type of cost construction. In this chapter we introduce a second main type of cost construction, called *differential costs*. Some people have difficulty accepting the idea that there is more than one type of cost construction. They say, "When I pay a company $280 for a suit, the suit surely cost me $280. How could the cost be anything else?" It is appropriate, therefore, that we establish three points: (1) *cost* has more than one meaning; (2) differences in cost constructions relate to the *purpose* for which the cost information is to be used; and (3) unless these differences are understood, serious mistakes can be made. To explain these points, consider the following case:

> **Example.** A company manufactures and sells desks. According to its cost accounting records, the full cost of making and marketing a certain desk is $500. Suppose that a customer offered to buy such a desk for $450. If the company considered that the only relevant cost for this desk was the $500 full cost, it would of course refuse the order. Its revenue would be only $450, and its costs would be $500; therefore, the management would conclude that the company would incur a loss of $50 on the order.
>
> But it might well be that the additional *out-of-pocket* costs of making and selling this one desk—the lumber and other material, the earnings of the cabinetmaker who worked on the desk, and the commission to the salesperson—would be only $350. The other items making up the $500 *full* cost were items of cost that would not be affected by this one order. The management might therefore decide to accept this order at $450. If it did, the company's costs would increase by $350, its revenue would increase by $450, and its income would increase by the difference, $100. Thus, the company would be $100 better off by accepting this order than by refusing it. Evidently, the company in this example could make the wrong decision if the management relied on the full cost information.

In this example we used both $500 and $350 as measures of the cost of the desk. These numbers represent two types of cost constructions, each of which is used for a different purpose. The $500 measures the full cost of the desk, which is the cost used for the purposes described in Chapter 17. The $350 is another type of cost construction and it is used for other purposes, one of which is to decide, under certain circumstances, whether to sell an item at a price below the item's full cost. This latter type of cost construction is differential cost.

Differential Costs and Revenues

More formally, **differential costs** are costs that are different under one set of conditions than they would be under another.[1] Differential costs always relate to a specific situation. In the previous example, the differential cost of the desk was $350. Under another set of circumstances—for example, if a similar problem arose several days later—the differential costs might be something other than $350. The differential cost to the *buyer* of the desk was $450; the buyer incurred a cost of $450 that would not have been incurred if the desk had not been purchased.

The differential concept also applies to revenues. **Differential revenues** are those that are different under one set of conditions than they would be

---

[1]Differential costs are also called **relevant costs.** This term is not descriptive, because all types of cost constructions are relevant for certain purposes.

under another. In the desk example the differential revenue of the desk manufacturer was $450; if it accepted the order for the desk, its revenue would differ by $450 from what revenue would have been if it did not accept the order.

Contrasts with Full Costs

There are three important differences between full costs and differential costs.

1. Nature of the Cost.   The full cost of a product or other cost object is the sum of its direct costs plus a fair share of applicable indirect costs. Differential costs include only those elements of cost that are different under a certain set of conditions. This is the most important distinction between full costs and differential costs.

In the example of the desk given above, the volume, or output, of the desk manufacturer would be higher by one desk if it accepted the order compared with what volume would have been if it did not accept the order. The proposal under consideration therefore had an effect on volume as well as on costs. This is the case with a great many problems involving differential costs. A thorough understanding of the cost behavior concepts discussed in Chapter 16 is therefore a prerequisite for the analysis of many differential accounting problems.

2. Source of Data.   Information on full costs is taken directly from a company's cost accounting system. That system is designed to measure and report full costs on a regular basis. There is no comparable system for collecting differential costs. The appropriate items that constitute differential costs are assembled to meet the analytical requirements of a specific problem.

Since the cost items that are differential in a given problem depend on the nature of that specific problem, it is not possible to identify items of differential cost in the accounting system and to collect these costs on a regular basis. Instead, the accounting system may be designed so that it can furnish the raw data that are useful in *estimating* the differential costs for a specific problem. Ideally, an accounting system should be designed so that it separately identifies items of variable cost, step-function cost, and fixed costs, making it clear to what measure of volume or "cost driver" each of the variable and step-function costs relates. For example, raw materials cost relates to production volume, whereas selling commissions relate to sales volume.

In practice, relatively few companies' routine accounting systems meet this ideal. It is an unusual system that explicitly identifies step-function costs as a separate category, and many systems do not even make a distinction between fixed and variable costs. Rather than elaborating their cost *systems,* some companies build activity-based cost *models* to aid in making the cost estimates that are needed in alternative choice decisions.[2]

Whatever the source of cost data, recall from Chapter 16 that any cost behavior classification depends on the relevant time period that is assumed. The previous statements about the desk assume a time period of one month; that is, an item of cost is variable if the month's total amount of that cost changes proportionately with the month's volume change. This is a common assumption in classifying costs as being variable.

3. Historical Cost. The full cost accounting system collects historical costs; that is, it measures what the costs *were*. For some purposes, such as setting prices, these historical costs are adjusted to reflect the estimated impact of future conditions. But for other purposes, such as financial reporting, the historical costs are used without change. *Differential costs always relate to the future.* They are intended to show what the costs *will be* if a certain course of action is adopted in the future, rather than show what costs were in the past.

CONTRIBUTION ANALYSIS

In calculating break-even volume (Chapter 16), the notion of unit contribution was introduced. This section extends this notion to a technique called **contribution analysis.** We do so both because contribution analysis is an important tool in analyzing differential costs and because, in explaining the technique, we can clarify the relationships among, and differences between, variable costs, fixed costs, direct costs, indirect costs, full costs, and differential costs.

Contribution analysis focuses on what is called the contribution margin. The **contribution margin** for a company (or for a product line, division, or other segment of a company) is the difference between its total revenues and its total variable costs.[3] Illustration 26–1 contrasts the conventional income statement for a laundry and dry-cleaning company, with the same data rearranged so as to measure the contribution margin for each of its two services. Analysis of the underlying records shows that of the $42,000 total revenues in June, $32,400 was earned on dry-cleaning work and $9,600 on

---

[2]Although these activity-based cost models are sometimes referred to as activity-based cost systems, most are not, in fact, cost systems. The models are usually limited in scope (e.g., one plant), reside only on a local personal computer, and are not capable of recording sales and production transactions on a routine basis. Rather, the models are updated periodically, usually only once or twice a year, which is adequate for their use in cost estimating.

[3]We use the term *contribution margin* for the difference between total revenues and total variable costs, and we use **unit contribution** or **marginal income** for the difference per unit. The more complete term, **unit contribution margin,** is also used in practice instead of unit contribution.

ILLUSTRATION 26–1
CONTRAST BETWEEN CONVENTIONAL AND CONTRIBUTION MARGIN INCOME
STATEMENTS

A. Income Statement—Conventional Basis
Month of June

Revenues		$42,000
Expenses:		
Salaries and wages	$19,800	
Supplies	10,800	
Heat, light, and power	2,400	
Advertising	1,200	
Rent	4,200	
Depreciation on equipment	4,800	
Other (telephone, insurance, etc.)	1,800	
Total expense		45,000
Income (loss)		$ (3,000)

B. Income Statement—Contribution Margin Basis
Month of June

	Dry Cleaning		Laundry	
Revenues		$32,400		$9,600
Variable expenses:				
Wages	$7,800		$4,200	
Supplies	9,000		1,800	
Power	1,500		300	
Total variable expenses		18,300		6,300
Contribution margin		14,100		3,300
Direct fixed expenses:				
Depreciation on equipment		3,600		1,200
Contribution to indirect expenses		10,500		2,100
			$12,600	
Total contribution				
Indirect fixed expenses:				
Salaries	$7,800			
Heat and light	600			
Advertising	1,200			
Rent	4,200			
Other	1,800			
Total indirect fixed expenses		15,600		
Income (loss)		$(3,000)		

laundry. The expense items[4] on the income statement were analyzed to determine which amounts were variable and, of these, how much was

---

[4] Since this is an income statement, amounts deducted from revenues are called expenses. As pointed out in Chapter 3, expenses are one type of cost (i.e., the costs that are applicable to the current accounting period). Thus, although the description in this chapter uses the broader term, *costs,* it applies equally well to that type of cost labeled *expense.*

attributable to dry cleaning and how much to laundry. Of the total amount of $19,800 for salaries and wages, $7,800 of wages was a variable expense of dry cleaning, and $4,200 was a variable expense of laundry. The remaining $7,800 of salaries was a fixed expense applicable to the business as a whole. The other variable expenses were found to be supplies and power. The total amount of variable expense was $18,300 for dry cleaning and $6,300 for laundry.

The contribution margin, which is the difference between revenues and total variable expenses, was therefore $14,100 for dry cleaning and $3,300 for laundry.

In addition to variable expenses, dry cleaning had $3,600 of direct fixed expense; this was the depreciation on the dry-cleaning equipment. Laundry had $1,200 of direct fixed expenses. Subtracting these direct but fixed expenses from the contribution margin shows how much each service contributed to the indirect fixed costs of the business. These amounts were $10,500 for dry cleaning and $2,100 for laundry, a total of $12,600. Since the total of the indirect fixed costs was $15,600, this contribution was not large enough to produce income for the month. The difference was the loss of $3,000.

Types of Cost

We shall use the numbers in Illustration 26–1 to review the types of costs previously discussed:

- *Variable costs* (here expenses) were $18,300 for dry cleaning and $6,300 for laundry. They were variable because they varied proportionately with the volume of dry cleaning and laundry done.

- *Fixed costs* were the $4,800 of depreciation on equipment plus the $15,600 of indirect fixed expenses, a total of $20,400.

- *Direct costs* of the dry-cleaning service (cost object) included its variable costs ($18,300) and also its direct fixed costs (the $3,600 depreciation on dry-cleaning equipment). The total direct cost of the dry-cleaning service was therefore $21,900. It was direct because it included all costs that were traced directly to the dry-cleaning cost object. It was higher than the dry-cleaning variable costs because it also included the direct fixed costs.

- *Indirect costs* were those amounts (totaling $15,600) that were not traced directly either to the dry-cleaning cost object or to the laundry cost object.

- *Full costs* are not shown in the analysis. In order to obtain the full costs of each of the two cost objects, it would be necessary to allocate the $15,600 of indirect costs to dry cleaning and to laundry on some equitable basis.

This list does not include differential costs, because they cannot be identified in general. Rather, they must always be related to a specific alternative choice problem.

Example. Suppose that the management is considering certain actions intended to increase the volume of dry-cleaning work and it asks how increased volume will affect income. In this situation the differential costs are the variable costs (and the revenue is, of course, differential revenue). Each additional dollar of dry-cleaning business is expected to add 44 cents to profit, the percentage of contribution margin to sales revenues ($14,100 ÷ $32,400 = 44 percent).

The message conveyed by the contribution analysis statement differs from the message conveyed by the conventional income statement. The income statement indicates that the business operated at a loss. If the indirect expenses were allocated to the two services in proportion, say, to their variable expenses, each of the two services would also show a loss:

	Total	Dry Cleaning	Laundry
Contribution to indirect expenses	$12,600	$10,500	$ 2,100
Allocated indirect expenses	15,600	11,605	3,995
Income (loss)	$ (3,000)	$ (1,105)	$(1,895)

From these numbers, someone might conclude that one or the other of these services should be discontinued in order to reduce losses. By contrast, the contribution analysis shows that each of the services made a contribution to indirect fixed costs and that the total loss of the business would therefore not be reduced by discontinuing either of them. Later in this chapter we discuss this type of analysis.

ALTERNATIVE CHOICE PROBLEMS

In an **alternative choice problem,** two or more alternative courses of action are specified, and the manager chooses the one that he or she believes to be the best.[5] In many alternative choice problems, the choice is made on a strictly judgmental basis. That is, there is no systematic attempt to define, measure, and assess the advantages and disadvantages of each alternative. Persons who make judgmental decisions may do so simply because they are not aware of any other way of making up their minds, or they may do so because the problem is one in which a systematic attempt to assess alternatives is too difficult, too expensive, or simply not possible. No mathematical formula will help solve a problem in which the attitudes of the individuals involved or organizational politics are dominant factors. Nor is there any point in trying to make calculations if the available information is so sketchy or inaccurate that the results would be completely unreliable.

---

[5]In a broad sense, *all* management decisions involve a choice among alternatives. The problems discussed here are those in which the alternatives are clearly specified.

In many other situations, however, it is useful to reduce at least some of the potential consequences of each alternative to a quantitative basis and to weigh these consequences in a systematic manner. In this and the next chapter, we discuss techniques for making such an analysis.

Objectives

In an alternative choice problem, the manager seeks the alternative most likely to accomplish the objectives of the organization. When investors furnish equity capital to a profit-oriented business, they do so in the expectation of earning a return—a profit—on their investments. This return is received in the form of some combination of dividend revenue and capital gains. This idea leads to the statement that the objective of a company is to *maximize the value of the shareholders' investment* (or, as it is sometimes stated, to maximize shareholder wealth).

There are practical problems with using this concept in decision making, however. For one, in the case of publicly traded shares, the market value of the shareholders' investment may change literally by the minute. Second, in most instances it is not possible to estimate how much a specific decision will affect the price of the company's shares. Finally, the decision maker seldom knows which one out of many alternative courses of action will produce a *maximum* outcome, and some actions that could increase value are ethically unacceptable. As a result of these problems, in practice an internal (not market) performance measure is used—*return on investment (ROI)*—and the business objective is stated as earning a *satisfactory* (as opposed to maximum) return on investment.

Satisfactory ROI is important, but it is by no means the only objective of a business. In many practical problems, personal satisfaction, friendship, community responsibilities, or other considerations may be much more important than ROI. The company may also have other measurable objectives, such as maintenance of its market position, stabilization of employment, or increasing reported earnings per share. When these considerations are dominant, the solution to the problem cannot be reached by the techniques discussed here. The most these techniques can do is show the effect on ROI of seeking some other objective.

Thus, the decision maker seeks *a* course of action that will produce a satisfactory ROI. Of two alternative solutions to a problem, the manager will choose the one likely to yield the *greater* ROI, provided this is consistent with other objectives. If the amount of investment is unaffected by the decision, then the preferred alternative is the one resulting in the higher profit. If neither investment nor revenues are affected by the choices, then the preferred alternative is the one with the lower cost.

The return-on-investment criterion is not ordinarily used in nonprofit organizations. In these organizations the objective is to provide services of acceptable quality at the lowest possible cost. Nevertheless, the techniques for analyzing alternative choice problems in nonprofit organizations are essentially the same as those applicable to profit-oriented organizations.

The preferred alternative is the one expected to provide the desired amount of services at the lower cost.

Steps in the Analysis

The analysis of most alternative choice problems involves the following steps:

1. Define the problem.
2. Select possible alternative solutions.
3. For each selected alternative, measure and evaluate those consequences that can be expressed in quantitative terms.
4. Identify those consequences that cannot be expressed in quantitative terms and evaluate them against each other and against the measured consequences.
5. Reach a decision.

We shall focus primarily on information that can be expressed in quantitative terms. Thus, we are interested primarily in step 3 of the above list. We will briefly mention the other steps.

Steps 1 and 2: Define the Problem and Alternative Solutions. Unless the problem is clearly and precisely defined, quantitative amounts that are relevant to its solution cannot be determined. In many situations the definition of the problem may be the most difficult part of the whole process. Moreover, even after the problem has been identified, the possible alternative solutions to it may not be obvious.

> **Example.** A manager is considering a proposal to buy a certain machine to produce an item that is now being produced manually. At first glance there appear to be two alternatives: (a) continue to make the item by manual methods or (b) buy the new machine. Actually, however, several additional alternatives should be considered: (c) buy a machine other than the one proposed, (d) improve the present manual method, or even (e) eliminate the production operation altogether and buy the item from an outside source. Some thought should be given to these other possibilities before attention is focused too closely on the original proposal.

The more alternatives that are considered, the more complex the analysis becomes. For this reason, having identified all the possible alternatives, the analyst should eliminate on a judgmental basis those that are clearly unattractive, leaving only a few for detailed analysis.

In most problems one alternative is to continue what is now being done—that is, to reject a proposed change. This *status quo* alternative, called the **base case,** is used as a benchmark against which other alternatives are measured.

Step 3: Measure the Quantitative Factors. Usually, many advantages and disadvantages are associated with each alternative. The decision maker's task is to evaluate each relevant factor and to decide, on balance, which alternative has the largest net advantage. If the factors, or variables, are expressed solely in words, such an evaluation is an exceedingly difficult task.

> **Example.**   Consider the statement: "A proposed production process will save labor, but it will result in increased power consumption and require additional insurance protection." Such a statement provides no way of weighing the relative importance of the saving in labor against the increased power and insurance costs. If, by contrast, the statement is: "The proposed process will save $1,000 in labor, but power costs will increase by $200 and insurance costs will increase by $100," the net effect of these three factors can easily be determined; that is, $1,000 − ($200 + $100) indicates a net advantage of $700 for the proposed process.

The above example demonstrates the reason for expressing as many factors as possible in quantitative terms: once this is done, one can find the net effect of these factors simply by addition and subtraction.

Step 4: Evaluate the Unmeasured Factors.   For most problems there are important factors that are not measurable. The final decision must take into account both measurable and unmeasurable differences between the alternatives. The process of weighing the relative importance of these unmeasured factors, both as compared with one another and as compared with the net advantage or disadvantage of the measured factors, is a judgmental process.

It is easy to overlook the importance of these unmeasured factors. The numerical calculations for the measured factors often require hard work and result in a number that appears to be definite and precise. Yet all the factors that influence the final number may be collectively less important than a simple factor that cannot be measured. For example, many persons could meet their transportation needs less expensively by using taxis and buses rather than by operating an automobile; but they nevertheless own a car for reasons of prestige, convenience, or other factors that cannot be measured quantitatively.

To the extent that calculations can be made, it is possible to express as a single number the net effect of many factors that bear on the decision. The calculations therefore reduce the number of factors that must be considered separately in the final judgment process that leads to the decision. That is, they narrow the area within which judgment must be exercised. Rarely, if ever, do they eliminate the necessity for this crucial judgment process.

Step 5: Reach a Decision.   After the first attempt to identify, evaluate, and weigh the factors, the decision maker has two choices: (1) seek additional information or (2) make a decision and act on it. Many decisions could be improved by obtaining additional information, and that is usually possible. However, obtaining the additional information always involves effort (which means cost); more important, it involves delay. There comes a point, therefore, when the manager concludes that it is better to act than to defer a decision until more data have been collected.

DIFFERENTIAL COSTS

Earlier in this chapter we introduced the type of cost construction called differential costs. Since differential costs are normally used in analyzing alternative choice problems, we now discuss them in more depth.

If some alternative to the base case, or status quo, is proposed, differential costs are those that will be different under the proposed alternative than they are in the base case. Items of cost that will be unaffected by the proposal are not differential and can be disregarded. The terms **out-of-pocket costs** and **avoidable costs** are used generally to mean the same thing as differential cost. No general category of costs can be labeled differential; differential costs always relate to the specific alternatives being analyzed.

> **Example.** A company is considering buying Part No. 101 from an outside supplier instead of manufacturing the part. The base case (case 1) is to continue manufacturing Part No. 101, and the alternative (or case 2) is to purchase it from the outside supplier. All revenue items, selling and administrative expenses, and production costs other than those directly associated with the manufacture of Part No. 101 will probably be unaffected by the decision. If so, there is no need to consider them. Items of differential cost could be as follows:

	If Part No. 101 Is Manufactured (base case)	If Part No. 101 Is Purchased (case 2)	Difference −	Difference +
Direct material	$ 570	$ 0	$ 570	
Purchased parts	0	1,700		$ 1,700
Direct labor	600	0	600	
Power	70	0	70	
Other costs	150	0	150	
Total	$1,390	$1,700	$1,390	$ 1,700
				−1,390
Net differential cost				$ 310

Since costs would be increased by $310 if Part No. 101 were purchased, the indication is that the proposal to purchase Part No. 101 should be rejected.

Mechanics of the Calculation

There is no prescribed format for comparing the differential costs of several alternatives. The arrangement should be that which is most convenient and which most clearly sets forth the facts to the decision maker.

> **Example.** For the problem described in the preceding example, the same result can be obtained with somewhat less effort by finding the net differences between the alternatives:

Purchase price of Part No. 101		$ 1,700
Costs saved by not manufacturing Part No. 101:		
Direct material	$570	
Direct labor	600	
Power	70	
Other costs	150	
Total costs saved		−1,390
Net disadvantage in purchasing		$ 310

Unaffected Costs. Cost items unaffected by the decision are not differential and may be disregarded. Nevertheless, a listing of some or all of these unaffected costs may be useful, especially if more than two alternatives are being compared. If this is done, the unaffected costs must be treated in exactly the same way under each of the alternatives. The net difference between the costs of any two alternatives, which is the result sought, is not changed by adding equal amounts to the cost of each alternative.

    Example. Part No. 101 is a component of product A. It may be convenient to list each of the items of cost and the revenue of product A for each of the alternatives, as in Illustration 26–2. The difference in profit is the same $310 arrived at in the earlier examples, because the proposal to purchase Part No. 101 affected neither product A's revenue nor product A's costs beyond the effects already listed.

    The calculation in Illustration 26–2 requires somewhat more effort than those in the preceding examples, but it may be easier to understand. Also,

ILLUSTRATION 26–2
CALCULATION OF DIFFERENTIAL PROFIT

	Profit on Product A			
	Base Case		**Purchase of Part No. 101**	
Revenue		$10,000		$10,000
Costs:				
Direct material	$1,570		$1,000	
Purchased parts	0		1,700	
Direct labor	3,000		2,400	
Power	200		130	
Other costs	1,450		1,300	
Occupancy costs	800		800	
General and administrative	2,000		2,000	
Total costs		9,020		9,330
Profit		980		670
		−670 ←		
Differential profit of base case		$ 310		

the practice of listing each item of cost and revenue may help to ensure that no items of differential cost are overlooked.

Danger of Using Full Cost.   The full costs that are measured in a full cost accounting system may be misleading in alternative-choice problems. In particular, when estimating differential costs, items of cost that are *allocated* to products should be viewed with skepticism. For example, a company may allocate production overhead costs to products as 150 percent of direct labor costs. But this does *not* mean that if direct labor costs are decreased by $600, there will be a corresponding decrease of $900 in overhead costs. Overhead costs may not decrease at all, they may decrease but by an amount less than $900, or they may even increase due to an increased procurement and inspection workload resulting from the purchase of Part No. 101. In order to estimate what will actually happen to overhead costs, one must go behind the overhead rate and analyze what will happen to the various elements of overhead cost.

> **Example.**   The full costs of product A shown in Illustration 26–2 included $800 for occupancy costs and $2,000 for general and administrative costs. Occupancy cost is the cost of the building in which product A is manufactured, and the $800 represents the share of total occupancy cost allocated to product A. If Part No. 101 (one part in product A) is purchased, the floor space in which Part No. 101 is now manufactured no longer would be required. It does not necessarily follow, however, that occupancy costs would thereby be reduced. The costs of rent, heat, light, and other items of occupancy cost might not be changed at all by the decision to purchase Part No. 101. Unless the actual amount of occupancy cost were changed—that is, unless some occupancy costs would be avoided—this item of cost is not differential.
>
> Similarly, general and administrative costs of the whole company probably would be unaffected by a decision to purchase Part No. 101. Unless the actual amount of these costs would be affected, they are not differential.

Fringe Benefits.   Labor costs are an important item of cost in many decisions. The real cost of labor is significantly higher than the actual amount of wages earned. It includes such items as the employer's share of social security taxes; insurance, medical, and pension plans; vacation and holiday pay; and other fringe benefits. It is typical in the United States for these benefits to amount to about 40 percent of wages earned. In estimating differential labor costs, fringe benefits usually should be taken into account.

Opportunity Costs.   Opportunity cost is a measure of the value that is lost or sacrificed when the choice of one course of action requires giving up an alternative course of action. Opportunity costs are not costs in the usual sense of the word; that is, they are not associated with cash outlays. Rather, an opportunity cost is *income* (profit) forgone, or given up, which has the same downward impact on net income as a cost incurred.

> **Examples.**   If the floor space required to make Part No. 101 can be used for some other profit-producing purpose, then the sacrifice involved in using this

space for Part No. 101 is an opportunity cost of making that part. This cost is measured by the income that would be sacrificed if the floor space is instead used for Part No. 101; this income is not the same as the allocated occupancy cost. If the floor space used for Part No. 101 could be used to manufacture another item that could be sold for a profit of $400, the $400 then becomes a cost of continuing to manufacture Part No. 101.

An attorney has more work available to her than she can accept; that is, she is working "at capacity." She bills clients $125 an hour for her services. She also does four hours a week volunteer legal work for a local nonprofit organization. The opportunity cost to her of this volunteer work is $500 a week (4 hours $*$ $125), the amount of the billings (income) she forgoes in order to do the volunteer work.

Opportunity costs are not measured in accounting records, and they are not relevant in many alternative choice problems. They are significant, however, in situations where resources are *constrained* (i.e., limited), as in the above case of the attorney. In such situations, a decision to undertake a certain activity precludes performing some other activity. In general, if accepting an alternative requires devoting to that alternative any facilities or other resources that otherwise could be used for some other income-producing purpose, then there is an opportunity cost. This cost is measured by the income that would have been earned had the resources been devoted to the other purpose.

By their very nature, opportunity costs are "iffy." In most situations, it is extremely difficult to estimate what, if any, additional profit could be earned if the resources in question were devoted to some other use.

Other Terminology

The term *differential costs* does not necessarily have the same meaning as the term *variable costs.* Variable costs are those that vary proportionately with changes in the volume of output. By contrast, differential costs are always related to specific alternatives that are being analyzed. If, in a specific problem, the alternatives involve operating at different volumes within the relevant range of a cost-volume diagram, then differential costs may well be the same as variable costs. Depending on the problem, however, the differential costs may include nonvariable items. A proposal to change the number of security guards and their duties, for example, involves no elements of variable cost. A proposal to discontinue a product usually involves some differential fixed costs and step-function costs as well as the differential variable costs.

Marginal cost is a term used in economics for what accountants call variable costs. The marginal cost of a product is the cost of producing one additional unit of that product. Thus, marginal costs may be the same as differential costs in those problems in which an alternative under consideration involves changing the volume of output. **Incremental cost** and **relevant cost** are terms that usually mean the same thing as differential cost, as are the above-mentioned terms, *out-of-pocket cost* and *avoidable cost.*

**Estimates of
Future Costs**

Because the alternatives under consideration always relate to the future, differential costs are always estimates of future costs. Nevertheless, in many instances, the best information about future costs is derived from an analysis of historical costs. One can easily lose sight of the fact that historical costs, as such, are irrelevant. Historical costs may be a useful guide as to what costs are likely to be in the future, but using them as a guide is basically different from using them as if they were factual statements of what the future costs are going to be.

Except where future costs are determined by long-term contractual arrangements, differential costs necessarily are estimates. Usually, they cannot be close estimates. An estimated labor saving of $50,000 a year for five years, for example, implies assumptions as to future wage rates, future fringe benefits, future labor productivity, future activity levels (volumes), and other factors that cannot be known with certainty. Consequently, carrying computations of cost estimates to several decimal places ordinarily serves no purpose. In fact, there is a danger of being misled by the illusion of precision that such calculations give.

Sunk Costs

A **sunk cost** is a cost that has already been incurred and therefore cannot be changed by any decision currently being considered. All historical costs (for example, the book value of depreciable assets) are sunk costs. Since it exists because of actions taken in the past, a sunk cost is *not* a differential cost. No decision made today can change what has already happened. Decisions made now can affect only what will happen in the future.

The book value of plant and equipment and the related depreciation expense can cause difficulty in the analysis of alternative choice problems. It is sometimes argued that when a proposed alternative involves disposal of an existing machine, the depreciation on that machine will no longer be a cost and this saving in depreciation expense should therefore be taken into account as an advantage of the proposed alternative. This is not true. The argument overlooks the fact that the book value of the machine will sooner or later be recorded as an expense, regardless of whether the proposed alternative is adopted. If the alternative is *not* adopted, depreciation on the machine will continue. If the alternative *is* adopted, the remaining book value will be written off when the machine is disposed of. In either case, the total amount of cost is the same, so the book value is not a differential cost.

> **Example.** Assume that Part No. 101 from the previous examples is now manufactured on a certain machine and that depreciation of $1,000 on this machine is one of the items of "other costs" in Illustration 26–2. The machine was purchased six years ago for $10,000; since depreciation has been recorded at $1,000 a year, a total of $6,000 has been recorded to date. The machine therefore has a net book value of $4,000. The machine has zero scrap value.
>
> It is sometimes argued that the calculation in Illustration 26–2 neglects the $1,000 annual saving in depreciation costs that will occur if the machine is disposed of and that purchasing Part No. 101 is therefore the preferable

alternative. (If the cost of purchasing Part No. 101 is reduced by $1,000, then the profit of this alternative becomes $1,670, which is $690 greater than the $980 profit for the base case.) This is a fallacious argument. If the machine is scrapped, its book value must be written off, and this amount exactly equals the total depreciation charge over the machine's remaining life. Thus, there is no differential cost associated with the book value of the existing machine.

The irrelevance of sunk costs is demonstrated in Illustration 26–3 by comparison of two income statements for the complete time periods of the remaining life of the machine. One shows the results of operations if Part No. 101 is purchased and the machine is scrapped. The other shows the results if Part No. 101 continues to be made on the machine. Illustration 26–3 shows that over the four-year period, the differential profit favoring the base case is $1,240. This is $310 per year, the same amount shown in Illustration 26–2.

The cost of a depreciable asset is supposed to be written off over its useful life. If a machine is scrapped, its useful life obviously has come to an end. If its total cost has not been written off by that time, one knows by hindsight that an estimating error has been made: if the machine's useful life and residual value had been correctly estimated when it was acquired, then the net book value of the machine would be zero when it is scrapped. Because this error was made in the past, no current decision can change it.

If the machine had a *disposal value,* this fact would be relevant because the machine's sale would then bring in additional cash. If the *income tax effect* of writing off the loss on disposal were different from the tax effect of writing off depreciation over the four-year period, the effect of taxes would

ILLUSTRATION 26–3
IRRELEVANCE OF SUNK COSTS

	Profit on Product A (total for four years)	
	Base Case	Purchase of Part No. 101
Revenue	$40,000	$40,000
Costs, other than machine	$32,080*	$33,320†
Depreciation.	4,000	0
Loss on disposal of machine	0	4,000
Total costs	36,080	37,320
Profit	3,920	$ 2,680
	–2,680 ◄	
Differential profit of base case, four years.	$ 1,240	
Annual differential profit ($1,240 ÷ 4).	$ 310‡	

*($9,020 – $1,000) * 4 years.
†($9,330 – $1,000) * 4 years.
‡Same amount as in Illustration 26–2.

be relevant. (The method of allowing for this tax effect will be discussed in Chapter 27.) The book value of the machine itself, however, is not relevant.

Importance of the Time Span

The question of what costs are differential depends to a great extent on the time span of the problem. If the proposal is to make literally only one additional unit of an item, only the direct material costs may be differential. The work could conceivably be done without any differential labor costs if workers were paid on a daily basis and had some idle time. At the other extreme, if the proposal involves a commitment to produce an item over the foreseeable future, almost all items of production costs would be differential.

In general, the longer the time span of the proposal, the more items of cost that are differential. In the very long run, *all* costs are differential. Thus, in very long-run problems, differential costs include the same elements as full costs because one must consider even the replacement of buildings and equipment, which are sunk costs in the short run. By contrast, in many short-run problems, relatively few cost items are subject to change by a management decision.

Example: Operating an Automobile

To illustrate that the cost elements that are differential in an alternative choice problem vary with the nature of the problem, consider the relevant costs for various decisions that may be made about owning and operating an automobile. A study made by Runzheimer International and published by the American Automobile Association gives the national average cost in 1994 of operating a 1994 six-cylinder Ford Taurus four-door sedan (equipped with standard accessories—radio, automatic transmission, power brakes, power steering, and air conditioning) as follows:

	Average per Mile
Variable costs:	
Gasoline and oil	5.6¢
Maintenance	2.5
Tires	1.1
Total variable costs	9.2¢

	Amount per Year
Fixed costs:	
Insurance	$ 697
License, registration, taxes	204
Depreciation	2,988
Total fixed costs	$3,889

Assume that these costs are valid estimates of future costs (which actually is not the case because of inflation). What are the differential costs in each of the circumstances cited below?

1. You own a car like the one described above and have it registered. You are thinking about making a trip of 1,000 miles. What are the differential costs?

    Answer: The differential costs are 9.2 cents a mile times the estimated mileage of the trip. A trip of 1,000 miles therefore has a differential cost of $92. The fixed costs are not relevant since they will continue whether or not the trip is made.

2. You own a car but have not registered it. You are considering whether to register it for next year or to use alternative forms of transportation that you estimate will cost $3,400. If you register the car, you expect to drive it 10,000 miles during the year. Should you register it?

    Answer: The differential costs are the insurance and fees of $901 plus 9.2 cents a mile times the 10,000 miles you expect to travel by car, a total of $1,821. The $901 has become a cost because it is affected by the decision about registration. If alternative transportation will cost $3,400, you are well advised to register the car.

3. You do not own a car but are considering the purchase of the car described above. If your estimate is that you will drive 10,000 miles per year for five years and that alternative transportation will cost $3,400 per year should you do so?

    Answer: The differential costs are $3,889 a year plus 9.2 cents a mile times the 10,000 miles you expect to travel per year: $3,889 + $920 = $4,809. If alternative transportation will cost $3,400 a year, you are well advised to use alternative transportation (disregarding noneconomic considerations).[6]

Each of the above answers is, of course, an oversimplification because it omits nonquantitative factors and relies on averages. In an actual problem, the person would need data that more closely approximated the costs of her or his own automobile.

TYPES OF ALTERNATIVE CHOICE PROBLEMS

As noted earlier, a dominant objective of a business is to earn a satisfactory return on investment (ROI). Three basic elements—costs, revenue, and investment—are involved in a company's ROI:

$$ROI = \frac{Revenues - Costs}{Investment}$$

---

[6]Since this question has a multi-year time horizon, the present value analytical approach described in Chapter 27 should be used in answering it. Although the conclusion stated here is correct, the analysis would differ if such present value techniques were used.

Although the general approach to all alternative choice problems is similar, it is useful to discuss three subcategories separately: problems that involve only the cost element (discussed in the next section), problems including both revenue and cost elements (discussed in the latter part of this chapter), and problems that involve investment as well as revenues and costs (discussed in Chapter 27).

Problems Involving Costs

Alternative choice problems involving only costs have several general characteristics: The base case is the status quo, and an alternative to the base case is proposed. If the alternative is estimated to have lower differential costs than the base case, it is accepted (assuming nonquantitative factors do not offset this cost advantage). If there are several alternatives, the one with the lowest differential cost is accepted. Problems of this type are often called **trade-off problems** because one type of cost is traded off for another. Some examples are mentioned here.

Methods Change. The alternative being proposed is the adoption of some new method of performing an activity. If the differential costs of the proposed method are significantly lower than those of the present method, the method should be adopted (unless offsetting nonquantitative considerations are present).

Operations Planning. In a manufacturing plant that has a variety of machines, or in a chemical processing plant, several routes for scheduling products through the plant are possible. The route with the lowest differential costs is preferred. Similar planning problems exist in nonmanufacturing settings: for example, deciding which of several warehouses should ship appliances to each of the retailers selling these appliances, or deciding which group of architects should be assigned to work on a new project.

Other production decisions can be analyzed in terms of differential costs. One example is deciding whether to use one shift plus overtime or to add a second shift. Another is deciding, when demand is low, whether to operate temporarily at a low volume or to shut down until operations at normal volume are again economical.

Make or Buy. Among the most common types of alternative choice problems are **make-or-buy problems.** At any given time, an organization performs certain activities with its own resources, and it pays outside firms to perform certain other activities. It constantly seeks to improve the balance between these two types of activities by asking: Should we contract with some outside party to perform some function that we are now performing ourselves, or should we ourselves perform some activity that we now pay an outside party to do? A make-or-buy analysis can be made for practically any activity that the organization performs or that it might perform. At one extreme is the analysis of producing individual parts, illustrated above. At the other extreme, a company may consider whether to contract with an outside manufacturer to produce the whole product. For example, some companies that sell computers buy the completed product from other manufacturers and simply attach their own brand name; other companies (including the largest, IBM) manufacture some of their component parts, buy others, and assemble the finished computer.

As the example given in Illustration 26–2 shows, the cost of the outside service (the "buy" alternative) usually is easy to estimate. The more difficult problem is to find the differential costs of the "make" alternative because of the short-run nondifferential nature of many of the cost items.

Order Quantity.   When replenishing inventory of an item involves setup costs that are incurred only once for each batch produced (or ordering costs for each batch ordered from a supplier), the question arises of how many units should be made (ordered) in one batch. If the demand is predictable and if sales are reasonably steady throughout the year, the optimum quantity to produce (order) at one time—the **economic order quantity (EOQ)**—is arrived at by considering the trade-off between two offsetting costs: setup (ordering) costs, whose total decreases with increasing batch size, and inventory carrying costs, which increase in total as batch size increases. The relevant costs are differential costs. Details on EOQ analysis are given in the Appendix at the end of this chapter.

Problems Involving Both Revenues and Costs

In the second class of alternative choice problems, the proposal being studied affects both costs and revenues. Insofar as the quantitative factors are concerned, the best alternative is the one with the largest difference between differential revenue and differential cost, that is, the alternative with the most **differential income** or **differential profit.** Some problems of this type are described briefly here.

Supply/Demand/Price Analysis.   In general, the lower the selling price of a product, the greater the quantity that will be sold. This relationship between a product's selling price and the quantity sold is called its **demand schedule,** or **demand curve.** As the quantity sold increases by one unit, the *total* cost of making the product increases by the variable cost of that one additional unit. Since fixed costs do not change, total costs increase less than proportionately with increases in demand. This semivariable relationship between total production costs and volume is called the product's **supply schedule,** or **supply curve;** it looks like the C-V diagram in Illustration 16–4, which assumes that step-function costs remain constant within the relevant range.

The supply schedule usually can be estimated with a reasonable degree of accuracy. If the demand schedule also can be estimated, then the optimum selling price can be determined. This optimum price is found by estimating the total revenues and total variable costs for various quantities sold and selecting the selling price that yields the greatest total contribution.

Example.   Assume that fixed costs for a product are $20,000 per month and that variable costs are $100 per unit. The supply/demand analysis is given in the following table:

	Unit Selling Price	Unit Variable Cost	Unit Contri- bution	Estimated Quantity Sold	Total Contri- bution	Fixed Costs	Profit
$300	$100	$200	125	$25,000	$20,000	$ 5,000
250	100	150	200	30,000	20,000	10,000
200*	100	100	310	31,000	20,000	11,000
150	100	50	450	22,500	20,000	2,500
125	100	25	550	13,750	20,000	(6,250)

*Preferred alternative.

Clearly, $200 is the best selling price: at that price the profit of $11,000 is more than the profit at either a higher or lower price. Since the fixed costs are a constant, they could be eliminated from the calculation; that is, the same decision can be reached by choosing the price that yields the greatest total contribution.

Such an analysis is feasible only if the demand schedule can be estimated. In most situations there is no reliable way of estimating how many units will be sold at various selling prices; this type of analysis cannot be used in such circumstances. Instead, the selling price is arrived at by adding a profit margin to the full cost of the product (as described in Chapter 17), or it is set by competitive market forces. Also, the analysis is more complicated if some step-function costs will change between the lowest and highest sales volumes being considered.

Contribution Pricing. Although full cost is the normal basis for setting selling prices and a company must recover its full costs or eventually go out of business, differential costs and revenues are appropriately used in some pricing situations. In normal times, a company may refuse to take orders at prices that are not high enough to yield a satisfactory profit. But if times are bad, such orders may be accepted if the differential revenue obtained from them exceeds the differential costs of filling the order. The company is better off to receive some revenue above its differential costs than to receive nothing at all. These off-price orders make some contribution to fixed costs and profit. Such a selling price is therefore called a **contribution price** to distinguish it from a normal price.

The practice of selling surplus quantities of a product in a selected marketing area at a price below full costs, called **dumping,** is another version of the contribution idea. However, dumping may violate the Robinson-Patman Amendment in domestic markets and generally is prohibited by trade agreements in foreign markets.

It is difficult to generalize about the circumstances that determine whether full costs or differential costs are the appropriate approach to setting prices. Even in normal times, an opportunity may be accepted to make some contribution to profit by using temporarily idle facilities. Conversely, even when current sales volume is low, the contribution concept may be rejected on the grounds that the low price may "spoil the market"; that is, other customers will demand the lower price, or competitors may drop their prices. (With deregulation of fares in the airline industry, many air carriers painfully learned the meaning of spoiling the market with contribution-based discount fares.) Also, perhaps more sales can in fact be obtained at normal profit margins if the marketing organization works harder or is more creative.

Discontinuing a Product.   If the selling price of a product is below its full cost, then conventional accounting reports will indicate that the product is being sold at a loss. This fact may lead some people to recommend that the product be discontinued, an action that may make the company worse off rather than better off. If there is excess production capacity, retaining a product that makes some contribution to fixed overhead and profit is better than not having the product at all. Only if the product's total contribution is less than the *differential* fixed and step-function costs that could be saved by dropping the product will the company be better off doing so. An analysis of differential revenues and differential costs is the proper approach to problems of this type.

Adding Services.   A company can add to its income by finding additional ways of using idle capacity in its assets, if the differential revenue from these uses exceeds the differential costs of providing them. For this reason, a chain of fast-food restaurants may add breakfast items to its menu and open four hours earlier each day; a grocery store may decide to remain open on Sundays; and a hotel may offer special rates on weekends when volume is low. In all these situations, differential costs rather than full costs are relevant.

When analyzing such problems, one must take care to ensure that the differential revenue is truly differential and does not represent a diversion from normal revenue. For example, a grocery store will not earn additional income by staying open Sundays if the revenue earned on Sunday comes from customers who would otherwise have shopped at that store on some other day of the week. Similarly, care must be taken to ensure that the so-called fixed costs are truly fixed, as opposed to being step-function costs that could be reduced if the capacity-filling initiative were not undertaken. For example, it might be better for an airline to drop a flight, or even a route, than to try to attract a few more passengers with discounted fares. Thus, in addition to considering ways to use the idle capacity, the company should consider the savings that would result if it eliminated the excess capacity.

Sale versus Further Processing.   Many companies, particularly those that manufacture a variety of finished products from basic raw materials, must address the problem of whether to sell a product that has reached a certain stage in the production process or do additional work on it. Meat packers, for example, can sell an entire carcass of beef, they can continue to process the carcass into various cuts, or they can go even further and make frozen dinners out of some of the cuts. The decision requires an analysis of the differential revenues and costs.

Let us designate the alternative of selling the product at a certain stage as case 1 and that of processing it further as case 2. The case 2 product, having received more processing than the case 1 product, presumably can be sold at a higher price. But the case 2 product also involves processing costs (and possibly marketing costs) not incurred in case 1. If the differential revenue in case 2 (i.e., the difference between the case 2 revenue and the case 1 revenue) exceeds the additional processing and marketing costs, then case 2 is preferred. The important point to note is that the analysis may disregard all costs up to the point in the production process where this decision is made. These costs are incurred whether or not additional processing takes place and therefore are not differential.

Other Marketing Tactics.   The same analytical approach can be used for a number of other marketing problems. Examples include deciding which customers are worth soliciting by sales personnel and how often the salesperson should call on each customer; whether to open additional warehouses or, conversely, whether to consolidate existing warehouses; whether to improve the reliability of a product in order to reduce the number of maintenance calls; the minimum size of customer order that will be accepted; and whether to put more meat in each hamburger and increase its price.

Differential Investment

Chapter 27 discusses alternative choice decisions that affect the amount of funds committed to investments in *noncurrent* assets; the analytical approach to these problems is more complicated than the one described in this chapter for short-run decisions. However, both short-run and long-term decisions may lead to changes in the entity's investment in *current* assets, particularly accounts receivable and inventories. For example, a decision to lower the price of some product below its full cost in order to increase its unit sales volume may cause related increases in receivables and inventories.

When a decision does impact the level of current assets, the cost of *holding* these differential assets should be built into the analysis. For receivables, the holding cost rate used is typically equal to the sum of the short-term interest rate (since, if the customer had paid cash, the seller could invest the funds short term or reduce short-term debt) plus the cost of bad debts. Sometimes a billing and collection cost is also included. For inventories, there tends to be great variation in the holding cost rate used, ranging from a low of around 10 percent (representing primarily financing costs) to a high of 30–35 percent (the higher rates also including such inventory-related costs as ordering, handling, storage, pilferage, and insurance). To the extent that a portion of the differential inventories are financed by differential, interest-free accounts payable, there is a partial offset of the differential financing costs.

Example. One of Devin Company's product-line managers has proposed increasing the line's sales volume and profit over the next 12 months by simultaneously liberalizing the credit terms to certain major customers and reducing prices on several items in the line. The estimated impact of the proposal on current assets is an accounts receivable increase of $450,000 and an inventory increase of $200,000 throughout the 12-month period. The company estimates its accounts receivable and inventory holding cost rates to be 10 percent and 25 percent, respectively. The analysis of the proposal should therefore include differential costs of $95,000 (= $450,000 * .10 + $200,000 * .25) for holding these differential current assets.

Sensitivity Analysis

All types of alternative choice problems involve making assumptions and estimates about the future. When analyzing a particular problem, it is important to make note of each of these assumptions. For example, "I assumed that selling and administrative costs would not be differential between the two alternatives," or "I assumed an inflation rate of 5 percent for the next 10 years." But it is equally important not to get bogged down in worrying about whether the assumption made was the best assumption that could have been made. In particular, cost estimates often do not need to be refined, because the initial analysis so overwhelmingly favors one alternative that such refinement could not possibly change the conclusion.

After doing an analysis with the first set of assumptions, it is often useful—particularly when it comes time to sell the results of the analysis to others—to redo the analysis several times using different assumptions. Because its purpose is to determine how sensitive the initial conclusion was to the initial assumptions, this is called a **sensitivity analysis.** If a small change in, say, the estimate of future labor costs changes the initial conclusion, then we say that the problem is sensitive to labor costs. With spreadsheet programs for personal computers, these "what-if?" sensitivity analyses often can be performed in a few minutes. (The Appendix to this chapter contains more details on sensitivity analysis.)

The "Just One" Fallacy

When one considers the impact on costs of a specific activity, it is possible to take a perspective that is too narrowly or near-term focused and, as a result, to underestimate the differential costs. For example, what is the differential cost for a large grocery store to service one additional customer per hour (excluding the cost of the goods that the customer purchases)? Looked at narrowly, the answer probably is that the differential cost is essentially zero—no more than the cost of a few additional inches of cash register tape and power to run the checkout conveyor belt for a few additional seconds. The store likely has enough capacity to handle one more customer per hour without adding any personnel or other resources. However, the store would not be able to service 100 additional customers per hour without adding resources: additional checkout clerks and baggers,

ILLUSTRATION 26–4
ANALYTICAL TREATMENT OF STEP-FUNCTION COSTS

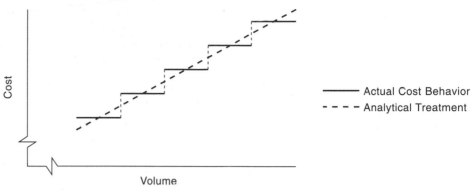

other personnel such as another butcher, produce person, or shelf stocker, and maybe even additional grocery carts or another checkout lane. Thus, there definitely is a differential cost associated with 100 additional customers per hour. This suggests a paradox: the differential cost of each additional customer per hour is zero, yet the differential cost of 100 additional customers is not zero. How can this be? Is not 100 times zero equal to zero?

We call this paradox the **"just one" fallacy.** If one thinks about the underlying cause of the paradox, it is the existence of *step-function costs* in the cost structure. As described in Chapter 16, many resources (such as checkout clerks) are added in discrete "chunks," each one resulting in an increment of capacity that can handle a certain additional volume of activity (customers, in this example). An increase in volume of *just one* unit does not require the addition of capacity; but a *series of increases* of one unit will cumulate to the point where another chunk of capacity—another step-up in costs—will be required to service the *collective* additional volume.

How does one deal with this phenomenon in an analysis of differential costs? The treatment of maintenance costs in the earlier automobile operating cost example illustrates the correct approach. Although no *cash* outlays may be made for maintenance on a specific trip, these costs should nevertheless be treated as differential since each additional trip causes these costs to be incurred sooner than if the trip were not made. The mileage-based step-function costs associated with having routine maintenance performed are treated as though they were *variable* costs, as suggested by Illustration 26–4. It would not be reasonable that most trips be charged nothing for maintenance costs incurred, say, every 3,000 miles, nor would it be reasonable to charge only the one specific trip that caused the odometer to exceed a multiple of 3,000 miles (e.g., 21,000 miles) with all of these costs. In effect, then, each "chunk" of step-function cost is averaged over the additional units of volume (here, miles; earlier, grocery store customers) that will be served by this additional increment of resources.

As suggested in Chapter 16, some companies have not recognized how costs that may appear not to be differential when a *single* decision is focussed on are nevertheless differential when a broader and longer-term perspective is taken. For example, some companies with excess manufacturing capacity have accepted numerous small incremental orders at reduced prices on the rationale that "the fixed costs stay fixed, so any contribution from an incremental order falls right to the bottom line as profit." Yet, having accepted many such orders, these companies find that their overall profits have not increased because their "fixed" costs have increased. What is happening is this: the *collective* additional orders have placed enough additional demands on various support activities—order processing, production scheduling, setting up equipment, material handling, and so on—that capacity has needed to be added to these activities, causing a step-up in their costs (just as in the grocery store example). These step-function costs were treated as fixed and nondifferential in the analysis of the profitability of each incremental order, when in fact they should have been treated as though they were variable because *collectively* all of the additional orders have created differential step-function costs.

In sum, one must be cautious when analyzing the differential costs of a narrowly specified alternative—attract *just one more* customer; sell *just this one* product on a contribution pricing basis; and so on. Costs that are not differential with an increase of literally "just one" do become differential when the incremental volume of activity is larger, as it is when the "just one" rationale gets used repeatedly in a given time period.

This phenomenon is also symmetrical in the sense that it also holds for *reductions* in levels of activity. For example, it is commonly argued that if a company drops a product it is selling at a price below full cost, the company will be worse off because the product's contribution to fixed costs will be lost. While true for just one product, this is not generally true if a number of marginal products are dropped. In fact, some companies have discovered that they can increase their profits by *decreasing* the number of smaller orders they accept or by pruning small-volume products from their product lines, because these decisions result in step-function cost reductions that more than offset the lost contribution margin.

SOME PRACTICAL POINTERS

In attacking specific problems, the following points may be helpful:

1. Use imagination in choosing the alternatives to be considered but don't select so many that you bog down before you begin. A fine but crucial line divides the alternative that is a "stroke of genius" and the alternative that is a "hare-brained idea."

2.   Don't yield to the natural temptation to give too much weight to the factors that can be reduced to numbers, even though the numbers have the appearance of being definite and precise.

3.   On the other hand, don't slight the numbers because they are "merely" approximations. A reasonable approximation is much better than nothing at all.

4.   Often, it is easier to work with total costs rather than with unit costs. Unit cost is a fraction:

$$\text{Unit cost} = \frac{\text{Total cost}}{\text{Number of units}}$$

Changes in either the numerator or the denominator result in changes in unit costs. Taking one of these changes into account and overlooking the other produces an error.

5.   There is a tendency to underestimate the cost of doing something new, because all the consequences may not be foreseen.

6.   The *number* of arguments is irrelevant in an alternative choice problem. A dozen reasons may be, and often are, advanced against trying out something new; but all these reasons put together may not be so strong as a single argument in favor of the proposal.

7.   Be realistic about the margin of error in any calculation involving the future. Precise conclusions cannot be drawn from rough estimates, nor is an answer necessarily valid just because you spent a long time calculating it.

8.   Despite uncertainties, you should make a decision if you have as much information as you can obtain at reasonable cost and within a reasonable time. Postponing action is the same as deciding to perpetuate the existing situation, which may be the worst possible decision.

9.   Show clearly the assumptions you made and the results of a sensitivity analysis, so that others going over your work can substitute their own judgmental assumptions if they wish.

10.   Do not expect that everyone will agree with your conclusion simply because it is supported with carefully worked-out numbers. Think about how you can sell your conclusion to those who must act on it.

SUMMARY

Differential costs and revenues are those that are different under one set of conditions than they would be under another set. Differential costs always relate to a specified set of future conditions. Variable costs are an important category of differential costs in situations where changes in volume are involved. But fixed costs and step-function costs also are differential in many alternative choice problems.

When an alternative choice problem involves changes in costs but not in revenue or investment, the best solution is the one with the lowest differential costs, insofar as cost information bears on the solution. Although historical costs may provide a useful guide to what costs will be in the future, we are always interested in future costs, never in historical costs for their own sake. In particular, sunk costs are irrelevant. Also, allocated costs must be analyzed with care to see if they are differential. The longer the time span involved, the more costs are differential.

When the problem involves both cost and revenue considerations, differential revenues as well as differential costs must be estimated. The best alternative is the one having the largest differential profit.

Differential costs and revenues rarely provide the answer to any business problem, but they facilitate comparisons and narrow the area within which judgment must be applied in order to reach a sound decision.

APPENDIX: USEFUL DECISION MODELS

A model is a statement, usually in mathematical terms, of the relationships among variables in a specified set of circumstances. The contribution-basis income statement for the laundry and dry-cleaning business illustrated in this chapter is a model. The relationships shown therein were (Laundry revenues – Laundry direct costs) + (Dry-cleaning revenues – Dry cleaning direct costs) – Indirect costs = Income. More complicated models are useful in certain types of alternative choice problems. Some of these, along with related mathematical techniques, are described here.

Economic Order Quantity

Under certain circumstances, the economic order quantity to purchase, or the economic batch size to produce in a manufacturing process, can be estimated by considering the relationship between ordering costs (or setup costs) and inventory carrying costs. The nature of the problem is indicated in Illustration 26–5, which shows how two alternative policies for an item with annual sales of 1,200 units, occurring at an even rate of 100 per month, affect inventory levels and the number of setups. Part A shows that if the entire 1,200 units were manufactured in one batch, only one setup a year would be necessary; but inventory carrying costs would be high since the inventory would start with 1,200 units and would average 600 units over the year.[7] By contrast, as shown in part B, the manufacture of four batches of 300 units each (i.e., one batch each quarter) would involve four times as much setup cost but a relatively low inventory carrying cost since there would be an average of only 150 units in inventory at any one time.

---

[7]Inventory is 1,200 units immediately after the batch has been manufactured and declines to zero a year later. Assuming that the decline is at a roughly even rate throughout the year, the average inventory for the year is one-half the sum of the beginning plus ending inventories; thus: ½ * (1,200 + 0) = 600.

ILLUSTRATION 26–5
DIFFERENT PRACTICES REGARDING SIZE OF ORDERS
(OR NUMBER OF SETUPS)

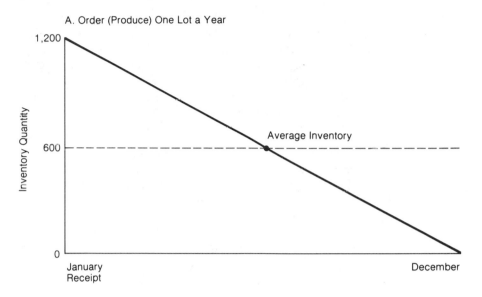

A. Order (Produce) One Lot a Year

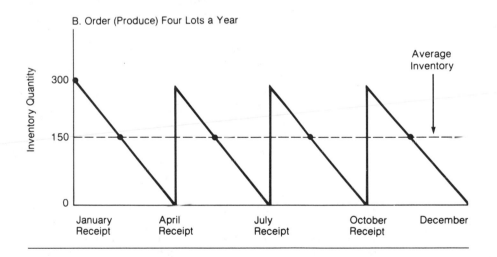

B. Order (Produce) Four Lots a Year

Thus, there is a trade-off between setup costs and inventory carrying cost. The objective is to minimize the sum of these two costs. This sum can be expressed algebraically as:

$$T = \left(S * \frac{R}{Q}\right) + \left(\frac{Q}{2} * C * K\right)$$

where

R = Annual requirements (in units).

C = Production cost per unit (or price per unit if purchasing from an outside vendor).

S = Cost of one setup (or, if bought outside, cost of preparing an order and processing the vendor's invoice).

Q = Order quantity (number of units in one batch).

K = Cost of carrying one unit in inventory for one year, expressed as a percentage of C.

The first term in the equation represents total setup costs: R/Q setups will be required per year at a cost of $$S$ each. The second term is the carrying cost. The *average* number of units in inventory will be $Q/2$. Each unit represents an investment of $$C$. The annual carrying cost of *one* unit is K percent of C, so the *total* carrying cost is $C * K$ times the average inventory. Using calculus, it can be proven that T is minimized at one value of Q. This value is the economic order quantity:

$$EOQ = \sqrt{\frac{2 * S * R}{C * K}}$$

Example.   The following amounts are estimated for a certain item:

Setup cost (S)	$300
Annual requirements (R)	1,200 units
Production cost (C)	$10 per unit
Carrying charge (R)	20%

Therefore:

$$EOQ = \sqrt{\frac{2 * \$300 * 1,200}{\$10 * 0.2}}$$
$$= \sqrt{360,000} = 600 \text{ units}$$

Since 1,200 units are required per year, there must be $1,200 \div 600 = 2$ batches manufactured per year. If the item were purchased rather than produced in-house, only a few words change: setup cost becomes ordering cost, and production cost becomes the purchase price per unit.

The costs used in this equation are differential costs. The differential setup costs include the extra labor costs (including fringe benefits) and any differential overhead costs associated with making a setup. The differential inventory carrying charge includes financing costs, inventory insurance, the costs associated with warehouse occupancy, inventory handling, shrinkage, and obsolescence—that is, all costs that are expected to be variable with the amount of inventory on hand. Making these cost estimates is quite difficult in practice.[8]

In recent years much attention has been devoted to changing scheduling and setup practices so as to reduce the level of inventory and cost per setup. The **just-in-time (JIT) inventory control** approach schedules deliveries of purchased parts so they arrive at the factory just before they are needed. Also, production is scheduled (and plants are laid out) so that work in process inventory at various workstations is kept to a minimum. The introduction of computer-controlled equipment makes it possible to shift from one job to another with relatively low changeover costs. Both of these developments tend to reduce the economic order quantity substantially.

Expected Value   All the numbers used in alternative choice problems are estimates of what will happen in the future. In the text examples we used *single-value* or *point* estimates. That is, each estimate was a single number representing someone's best estimate as to what differential costs or revenues would be. Some companies use estimates in the form of probability distributions rather than single numbers. Instead of stating, "I think sales of item X will be $100,000 if the proposed alternative is adopted," the estimator develops a range of possibilities, together with an estimate of the probability that each will occur. These separate possibilities are weighted by the probabilities. The sum of these weighted amounts is called the **expected value** of the probability distribution:

(a) Possible Sales Volume	(b) Estimated Probability		(a) * (b) Weighted Amount
$ 60,000.	0.1		$ 6,000
80,000.	0.1		8,000
100,000.	0.4		40,000
120,000.	0.2		24,000
140,000.	0.2		28,000
	1.0	Expected value:	$106,000

[8]Conceptually, fixed production costs should be excluded from the equation for T; that is, C should be variable production cost, not full production cost, because fixed costs for the year are independent of the batch size. Although these fixed costs are capitalized in inventory with a full (absorption) cost system, and accounting inventory valuation at full cost is therefore dependent on Q, the *actual pattern of cash flows* for fixed production costs is not altered by the batch-size decision. On the other hand, the pattern of cash outflows for materials, labor, and variable overhead is affected by Q. Nevertheless, in practice, companies tend to use full production cost for C. First, this number is readily available from the usual full cost accounting system. Second, inventory carrying cost per unit of product is $C * K$. If C is variable production cost for items manufactured in-house but full cost plus a manufacturer's profit for similar items purchased from outside manufacturers, then the carrying cost on a purchased item appears to be much higher than for a similar item made in-house. This discrepancy is rejected as counterintuitive by many managers.

The probability 0.1 opposite $60,000 means that there is estimated to be 1 chance in 10 that sales will be $60,000. The sum of the probabilities must always add to 1.0 because the estimates must include all possible outcomes. Although sales conceivably could be any amount between zero and an extremely high number, estimators cannot be expected to assign probabilities to each of a long list of possibilities. Therefore, they work only with a few numbers that are intended to be representative of the complete distribution. A group of five possibilities (as in the example above) is common, and the use of only three—"pessimistic," "most likely," and "optimistic"—is also common.

The expected value of $106,000 would be used as the best estimate of differential revenue. If a single-value estimate rather than an expected value were used, it would be $100,000 because this is the outcome with the highest probability. The $106,000 expected value is a better estimate of sales because it incorporates the whole probability distribution.

People in business do not find it easy to develop estimates in the form of probability distributions. But if they can do so, the validity of the estimates can be greatly increased.

Sensitivity Analysis

This chapter described the concept and purpose of a sensitivity analysis. One specific technique is to vary each estimate in turn by a given percentage (say, 10 percent) and determine what effect the variation in that item has on the final results. If the effect is large, the result is *sensitive* to that item.

In a more sophisticated approach called the **Monte Carlo method**,[9] a probability distribution is developed for each variable in the problem (industry sales growth, market share, variable costs per unit, and so on). A value is randomly selected from each distribution, and the values thus selected are then used to calculate the economic outcome of the problem for that particular set of variable values. This procedure is repeated 1,000 times, and the results of these 1,000 "trials" are then ordered from the "best" to the "worst" outcome. This ordering gives a probability distribution of possible outcomes. If this distribution is tight (i.e., there is a narrow range between the best and worst outcomes), then the problem is assumed to be relatively insensitive to the estimate used for any particular variable. If the range of outcomes is wide, then the decision involves considerable risk as to what the actual economic outcome will be. This risk could easily remain hidden if only single-value estimates were used in analyzing the problem.

Decision Tree Analysis

One characteristic of the problems described in this chapter is that a single decision had to be made and estimated revenues would be earned and estimated costs would be incurred as a consequence of that decision. In

---

[9] For an excellent nontechnical description of this technique, see David Hertz, "Risk Analysis in Capital Investment," *Harvard Business Review,* September–October 1979.

another class of problems, a series of decisions must be made, at various time intervals, with each decision influenced by the information available at the time it is made. An analytical tool that is useful for such problems is the **decision tree.**

In its simplest form a decision tree is a diagram that shows several decisions, or *acts,* and the possible consequences of each act; these consequences are called *events.* In a more elaborate form, the probabilities and the revenues or costs of each event's outcomes are estimated, and these are combined to give an expected value for the event.

Since a decision tree is particularly useful in depicting a complicated series of decisions, any brief illustration is somewhat artificial. Nevertheless, the decision tree shown in Illustration 26−6 will suffice to show how the technique works.

The assumed situation is this. A company is considering whether to develop and market a new product. Development costs are estimated to be $100,000. There is a 0.7 probability that the development effort will be successful—that is, that the product developed will work (perform its intended function). If the product works, it will be produced and marketed. There are two production processes available. An old process costs $50,000 differential fixed costs plus $2 variable cost per unit. A new process, employing more equipment and less labor, costs $100,000 differential fixed costs and $1 per unit. The process must be chosen *before* any sales are known. Following are the estimates of various levels of success:

a. If the product is a *big success* (probability 0.4), 100,000 units will be sold at $6 each, for a total of $600,000. Production costs using the old process will be $50,000 + (100,000 * $2) = $250,000, giving income of $250,000 (after subtracting the $100,000 development cost from the total revenue). If the new process is used, production costs will be $100,000 + (100,000 * $1) = $200,000, and income will be $300,000.

b. If the product is a *moderate success* (probability 0.4), 50,000 units will be sold at the $6 price. Either old or new process production costs will be $150,000, giving income (net of development costs) of $50,000.

c. If the product is a *failure* (probability 0.2), only 5,000 units will be sold at $6 each. Production will cost $60,000 using the old process or $105,000 using the new process, giving losses of $130,000 and $175,000, respectively.

To decide (1) whether or not to develop the product and (2) *if* the product works, whether to use the old or new process, the decision tree must be "collapsed," or "folded back," using these rules:

1. Replace each event "node" with the expected value of that event's outcomes.

2. At each act "node," choose the act with the highest expected value.

These expected values (EVs) are shown in Illustration 26−6. For example, *if* the product is developed, *if* it works, and *if* management chooses to use the old process, then the EV of the three possible sales outcomes is

ILLUSTRATION 26–6
DECISION TREE ANALYSIS

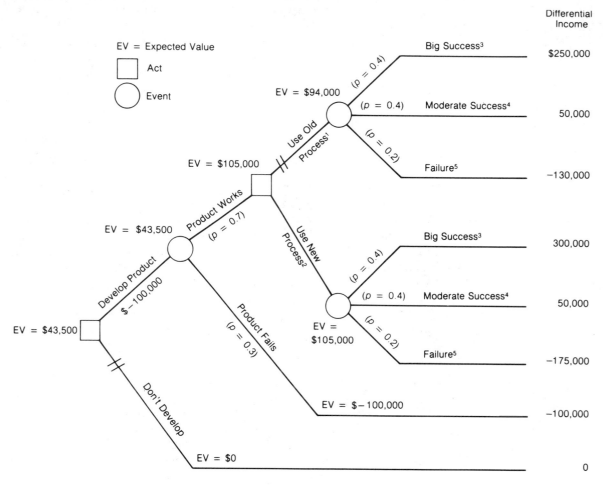

Notes:
  [1] Old process costs $50,000 plus $2 per unit.
  [2] New process costs $100,000 plus $1 per unit.
  [3] Big success is 100,000 units @ $6 = $600,000 revenues.
  [4] Moderate success is 50,000 units @ $6 = $300,000 revenues.
  [5] Failure is 5,000 units @ $6 = $30,000 revenues.

(0.4 * $250,000) + (0.4 * $50,000) + (0.2 * $−130,000) = $94,000. Similarly, if the developed product works, using the *new* process has an EV of $105,000. Therefore, *if* the product is successfully developed, management should use the new process. In the illustration, this is shown by "chopping off" (with the double hash mark) the branch labeled "Use Old Process."

If the development is undertaken, either the product will work, with an EV of $105,000, or it will fail, with a loss of $100,000. (Following a product failure, the probability of this loss is 1.0, so the EV is $–100,000.) Thus, the expected value of the decision to undertake development is (0.7 * $105,000) + (0.3 * $–100,000) = $43,500; but the EV of not developing the product (which is the base case) is $0. Therefore, the development effort should be undertaken, as indicated by chopping off the "Don't Develop" branch. In sum, the *optimal* strategy—that is, the sequence of decisions having the highest EV—is to develop the product and, if development succeeds, to use the new production process. That strategy has an EV of $43,500.

This does not mean, however, that the ultimate outcome is guaranteed to be differential income of $43,500. In fact, *none* of the possible outcomes results in $43,500 income, as can be seen by looking at the decision tree endpoint values. Rather it means that based on the estimates that have been made in considering this decision, management should gamble and go ahead with the development, because the *expected* payoff from this gamble is positive and the payoff if the gamble is not taken will be zero.

Linear Programming

In the situations described thus far, the available resources are implicitly assumed to be adequate to carry out whichever alternative is selected. However, in some situations this assumption is not valid. For example, a machine has only a certain amount of capacity; if that capacity is used by one product, it cannot be used for another. Similarly, a factory building has room for only so many machines. In these situations, there are *constraints* on the uses of resources.

Linear programming is a model for solving problems that involve several constraints. In it, a series of mathematical statements is developed. The first, called the *objective function,* is the quantity to be optimized. This is usually a formula for differential costs, which the model will minimize, or one for differential income, which is to be maximized. The other statements express the constraints of the situation.

> **Example.** A company makes two products, each of which is worked on in two departments. Department 1 has a capacity of 500 labor-hours per week; Department 2, 600 labor-hours. The labor requirements of each product in each department are:

	Labor-Hours per Unit	
	Product A	Product B
Department 1............	5.0	2.5
Department 2...........	3.0	5.0

As many units of B as can be made can also be sold, but a maximum of 90 units of A can be sold per week. The unit contribution (i.e., unit price minus unit variable costs) is $2 for A and $2.50 for B. How many units of each should be made in order to maximize total contribution?

The problem can be expressed mathematically as follows:
Maximize: $C = 2A + 2.5B$ (maximize contribution, the objective function)
Subject to: $5A + 2.5B \leq 500$ (Department 1 capacity constraint)
$\qquad\quad 3A + \quad 5B \leq 600$ (Department 2 capacity constraint)
$\qquad\qquad\qquad A \leq 90$ (Product A sales constraint)
$\qquad\quad A \geq 0, B \geq 0$ (A negative number of units cannot be made)

In words, the above says: find the number of units of A and B that should be made each week so as to maximize total contribution margin, where contribution is $2 per unit for A and $2.50 per unit for B, subject to the constraint that a unit of A requires 5 hours in Department 1 and a unit of B requires 2.5 hours there, and only 500 hours per week are available in Department 1; and so forth.

This situation can be illustrated graphically as in Illustration 26–7. One can see from the table above that Department 2 could make 200 units of A if it worked only on A, or 120 units of B if it worked only on B. In Illustration 26–7, the line between these two extremes, labeled Department 2 Capacity Constraint, shows all of the possible A–B product combinations that would use up all of Department 2's available capacity of 600 hours. The other lines are drawn in the same manner.

The shaded area in the illustration, bounded by the axes and the three constraint lines, is called the *feasible set* because any A–B product mix combination in that area can be produced and sold whereas combinations outside that area are infeasible. The optimum A–B combination must lie on the "northeast" boundary of the feasible set, because any point inside that boundary does not use up all the available manufacturing capacity and/or A sales "capacity" and hence does not maximize contribution, as more units could be made and sold. It is also true, but not intuitively obvious, that the optimum A–B combination lies at a *vertex* of that boundary—that is, at either point *w, x, y,* or *z.*

What a linear programming computer program does, in effect, is calculate the contribution, *C,* at each vertex of the feasible set boundary and identify the point that gives the highest contribution. Of course, for more realistic problems (such as determining the least costly delivery routes for a fleet of trucks or determining the most profitable mix of petroleum products to be refined from a quantity of crude oil), tens or even hundreds of mathematical statements are involved, and the problem cannot be solved manually. Computers can and do solve such problems rapidly.

Shadow Prices. As part of the solution to a linear programming problem, the computer program also calculates a **shadow price** (also called **opportunity cost**) for each constrained resource—that is, for each resource

ILLUSTRATION 26–7
LINEAR PROGRAMMING GRAPHICAL SOLUTION

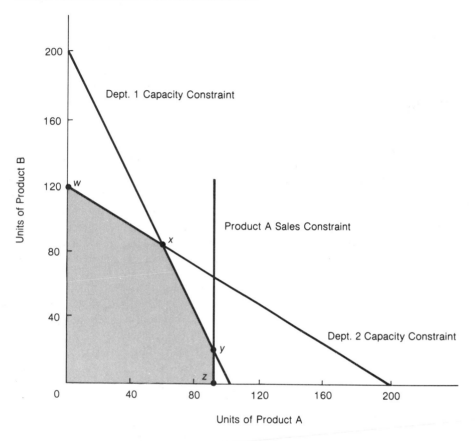

that is completely utilized at the optimum solution. For example, if the optimum solution involves using all of Department 2's capacity, the shadow price for this capacity would indicate the amount by which contribution would increase if the capacity could be increased by 1 hour (to 601 hours). This shadow price would be the maximum amount the company should be willing to spend to add a unit of capacity (i.e., 1 labor-hour per week) in Department 2.

Cases

CASE 26–1 Import Distributors, Inc.

Import Distributors, Inc. (IDI), imported appliances and distributed them to retail appliance stores in the Rocky Mountain states. IDI carried three broad lines of merchandise: audio equipment (tuners, tape decks, CD players, etc.), television equipment (including videotape recorders), and kitchen appliances (refrigerators, freezers, and stoves that were more compact than U.S. models). Each line accounted for about one-third of total IDI sales revenues. Although each line was referred to by IDI managers as a "department," until 1994 the company did not prepare departmental income statements.

In late 1993 departmental accounts were set up in anticipation of preparing quarterly income statements by department starting in 1994. In early April of 1994, the first such statements were distributed to the management group. Although in the first quarter of 1994 IDI had earned net income amounting to 4.3 percent of sales, the television department had shown a gross margin that was much too small to cover the department's operating expenses (see Exhibit 1).

The television department's poor showing prompted the company's accountant to suggest that perhaps the department should

EXHIBIT 1

Television Department Income Statement
For the First 3 Months of 1994

		Percent
Net sales revenues	$1,612,403	100.0
Cost of sales	1,422,473	88.2
Gross margin	189,930	11.8
Operating expenses:		
Personnel expenses (Note 1)	10,140	
Department manager's office	12,393	
Rent (Note 2)	50,107	
Inventory, taxes, and insurance	37,274	
Utilities (Note 3)	3,006	
Delivery costs (Note 4)	32,248	
Sales commissions (Note 5)	80,621	
Administrative costs (Note 6)	40,310	
Inventory financing charge (Note 7)	23,708	
Total operating expenses	289,807	18.0
Income taxes (credit)	(34,957)	(2.2)
Net income (loss)	$ (64,920)	(4.0)

EXHIBIT 1 *Continued*

Notes:
1. These were warehouse personnel. Although merchandise in the warehouse was arranged by department, these personnel performed tasks for all three departments on any given day.
2. Allocated to departments on the basis of square footage utilized. IDI had a five-year noncancelable lease for the facilities.
3. Allocated to departments on the basis of square footage utilized.
4. Allocated on the basis of sales dollars. A delivery from IDI to a retail store typically included merchandise from all three departments.
5. Salespersons were paid on a straight commission basis; each one sold all three lines.
6. Allocated on the basis of sales dollars.
7. An accounting entry that was not limited solely to the cost of financing inventory; assessed on average inventory in order to motivate department managers not to carry excessive stocks. This charge tended to be about three times the company's actual out-of-pocket interest costs.

be discontinued. "This is exactly why I proposed that we prepare departmental statements—to see if each department is carrying its fair share of the load," the accountant explained. This suggestion led to much discussion among the management group, particularly concerning two issues: First, was the first quarter of the year representative enough of longer-term results to consider discontinuing the television department? And second, would discontinuing television equipment cause a drop in sales in the other two departments? One manager, however, stated that "even if the quarter was typical and other sales wouldn't be hurt, I'm still not convinced we'd be better off dropping our television line."

Question

What action should be taken with regard to the television department?

CASE 26–2   Forner Carpet Company

Forner Carpet Company produced high-grade carpeting materials for use in automobiles and recreational vans. Forner's products were sold to finishers, who cut and bound the material so that it would fit perfectly in the passenger compartment or cargo area (e.g., automobile trunk) of a specific model vehicle. These finishers also made carpet floor mats. Some of these finishers were captive operations of major automobile assembly divisions, particularly those that assembled the "top of the line" cars that included high-grade carpeting; other finishers concentrated on the replacement and van customizing markets.

Late in 1993, the marketing manager and the chief accountant of Forner met to decide on the list price for carpet number L-42. It was industry practice to announce prices just prior to the January–June and July–December "seasons." Over the years, companies in the industry had adhered to their announced prices throughout a six-month season unless significant unexpected changes in costs occurred.

Forner was the largest company in its segment of the automobile carpet industry; its 1993 sales had been over $40 million. Forner's salespersons were on a salary basis, and each one sold the entire product line. Most of Forner's competitors were smaller than Forner; accordingly, they usually awaited Forner's price announcement before setting their own selling prices.

Carpet L-42 had an especially dense nap; as a result, making it required a special machine, and it was produced in a department whose equipment could not be used to produce Forner's other carpets. Effective January 1, 1993, Forner had raised its price on this carpet from $3.95 to $4.75 per square yard. This had been done in order to bring L-42's margin up to that of the other carpets in the line. Although Forner was financially sound, it expected a large funds need in the next few years for equipment replacement and possible diversification. The 1993 price increase was one of several decisions made in order to provide funds for these plans.

Forner's competitors, however, had held their 1993 prices at $3.95 on carpets competitive with L-42. As shown in Exhibit 1, which includes estimates of industry volume on these carpets, Forner's price increase had apparently resulted in a loss of market share. The marketing manager, Kim Gurskis, estimated that the industry would sell about 630,000 square yards of these carpets in the first half of the 1994. Gurskis was sure Forner could sell 150,000 yards if it dropped the price of L-42 back to $3.95. But if Forner held its price at $4.75, Gurskis feared a further erosion in Forner's share. However, because some customers felt that L-42 was superior to competitive products, Gurskis felt that Forner could sell at least 75,000 yards at the $4.75 price.

During their discussion, Gurskis and the chief accountant, Brooks Coleman, identified two other aspects of the pricing decision. Coleman wondered whether competitors would announce a further price decrease if Forner dropped back to $3.95. Gurskis felt it was unlikely that competitors would price below $3.95 because none of them was more efficient than Forner, and there were rumors that several of them were in poor financial condition. Coleman's other concern was whether a decision relating to carpet L-42

EXHIBIT 1
CARPET L-42: PRICES AND PRODUCTION, 1991–1993

Selling Season*	Production Volume (square yards)		Price (per square yard)	
	Industry Total	Forner Carpet	Most Competitors	Forner Carpet
1991–1	549,000	192,000	$4.75	$4.75
1991–2	517,500	181,000	4.75	4.75
1992–1	387,000	135,500	3.95	3.95
1992–2	427,500	149,500	3.95	3.95
1993–1	450,000	135,000	3.95	4.75
1993–2	562,500	112,500	3.95	4.75

* 199x–1 means the first 6 months of 199x; 199x–2 means the second six months of 199x.

EXHIBIT 2
ESTIMATED COST PER SQUARE YARD OF CARPET L-42 AT VARIOUS PRODUCTION VOLUMES
First Six Months of 1994

	Volume (square yards)					
	50,000	75,000	100,000	125,000	150,000	175,000
Raw materials	$0.520	$0.520	$0.520	$0.520	$0.520	$0.520
Materials spoilage	0.052	0.051	0.049	0.049	0.051	0.052
Direct labor	1.026	0.989	0.979	0.962	0.975	0.997
Department overhead:						
Direct*	0.568	0.544	0.524	0.520	0.520	0.520
Indirect†	1.240	0.827	0.620	0.496	0.413	0.354
General overhead‡	0.308	0.297	0.294	0.289	0.293	0.299
Factory cost.	3.714	3.228	2.986	2.836	2.772	2.742
Selling and administrative§	1.671	1.453	1.344	1.276	1.247	1.234
Total cost	$5.385	$4.681	$4.330	$4.112	$4.019	$3.976

* Materials handlers, supplies, repairs, power, fringe benefits.
† Supervision, equipment depreciation, heat, and light.
‡ 30 percent of direct labor.
§ 45 percent of factory cost.

would have any impact on the sales of Forner's other carpets. Gurskis was convinced that since L-42 was a specialized item, there was no interdependence between its sales and those of other carpets in the line.

Exhibit 2 contains cost estimates that Coleman had prepared for various volumes of L-42. These estimates represented Coleman's best guesses as to costs during the first six months of 1994, based on past cost experience and anticipated inflation.

Questions

1. What was the relationship (if any) between the L-42 pricing decision and the company's future need for capital funds?

2. Assuming no other prices are to be considered, should Forner price L-42 at $3.95 or $4.75?

3. If Forner's competitors hold their prices at $3.95, how many square yards of L-42 would Forner need to sell at a price of $4.75 in order to earn the same profit as selling 150,000 square yards at a price of $3.95?

4. What additional information would you wish to have before making this pricing decision? (Despite the absence of this information, still answer Question 2!)

5. With hindsight, was the decision to raise the price in 1993 a good one?

CASE 26–3 **Hanson Manufacturing Company***

In February 1993 Herbert Wessling was appointed general manager by Paul Hanson,

president of Hanson Manufacturing Company. Wessling, age 56, had wide executive experience in manufacturing products similar to those of the Hanson Company. The appointment of Wessling resulted from management problems arising from the death of

EXHIBIT 1

HANSON MANUFACTURING COMPANY
Income Statement
For Year Ending December 31, 1992

Gross sales		$40,690,234
Cash discounts		622,482
Net sales		40,067,752
Cost of sales		25,002,386
Gross margin		15,065,366
Less: Selling expense	$7,058,834	
General administration	2,504,597	
Depreciation	5,216,410	14,779,841
Operating income		285,525
Other income		78,113
Income before interest		363,638
Less: Interest expense		555,719
Income (loss)		$ (192,081)

Richard Hanson, founder and, until his death in early 1992, president of the company. Paul Hanson had only four years' experience with the company, and in early 1993 was 34 years old. His father had hoped to train Paul over a 10-year period, but the father's untimely death had cut short this seasoning period. The younger Hanson became president after his father's death, and had exercised full control until he hired Mr. Wessling.

Paul Hanson knew that he had made several poor decisions during 1992 and that the morale of the organization had suffered, apparently through lack of confidence in him. When he received the 1992 income statement (Exhibit 1), the loss of almost $200,000 during a relatively good year for the industry convinced him that he needed help. He attracted Mr. Wessling from a competitor by offering a stock option incentive in addition to salary, knowing that Wessling wanted to acquire financial security for his retirement. The two men came to a clear understanding that Wessling, as general manager, had full authority to execute any changes he desired. In addition, Wessling would explain the rea-

sons for his decisions to Mr. Hanson and thereby train him for successful leadership upon Wessling's retirement.

Hanson Manufacturing Company made only three industrial products, 101, 102, and 103, in its single plant. These were sold by the company sales force for use in the processes of other manufacturers. All of the sales force, on a salary basis, sold the three products but in varying proportions. Hanson sold throughout New England, where it was one of eight companies with similar products. Several of its competitors were larger and manufactured a larger variety of products. The dominant company was Samra Company, which operated a plant in Hanson's market area. Customarily, Samra announced prices, and the other producers followed suit.

Price cutting was rare; the only variance from quoted selling prices took the form of cash discounts. In the past, attempts at price cutting had followed a consistent pattern: all competitors met the price reduction, and the industry as a whole sold about the same quantity but at the lower prices. This contin-

EXHIBIT 2
ANALYSIS OF PROFIT AND LOSS BY PRODUCT
Year Ended December 31, 1992

	Product 101		Product 102		Product 103		Total
	Thou-sands	$ per Cwt.	Thou-sands	$ per Cwt.	Thou-sands	$ per Cwt.	Thou-sands
Rent	450	0.2111	450	0.4370	600	0.6079	1,500
Property taxes	300	0.1407	145	0.1408	139	0.1408	583
Property insurance	286	0.1341	138	0.1340	132	0.1337	556
Compensation insurance	599	0.2809	284	0.2758	317	0.3212	1,200
Direct labor	4,964	2.3281	2,341	2.2736	2,640	2.6748	9,945
Indirect labor	1,693	0.7940	814	0.7906	883	0.8947	3,390
Power	86	0.0403	96	0.0932	116	0.1175	298
Light and heat	43	0.0202	43	0.0418	58	0.0588	144
Building service	29	0.0136	29	0.0282	39	0.0395	97
Materials	2,935	1.3765	1,809	1.7569	1,862	1.8866	6,606
Supplies	201	0.0943	183	0.1777	135	0.1368	519
Repairs	68	0.0319	57	0.0554	39	0.0395	164
Total production cost	11,654	5.4657	6,388	6.2040	6,960	7.0519	25,002
Selling expense	3,496	1.6396	1,758	1.7074	1,805	1.8288	7,059
General administration	1,241	0.5820	624	0.6060	640	0.6484	2,505
Depreciation	2,169	1.0173	1,643	1.5957	1,404	1.4225	5,216
Interest	201	0.0943	153	0.1486	202	0.2047	556
Total cost	18,761	8.7989	10,566	10.2617	11,011	11.1563	40,338
Less other income	39	0.0183	20	0.0194	19	0.0193	78
	18,722	8.7806	10,546	10.2423	10,992	11.1371	40,260
Sales (net)	19,847	9.3083	9,978	9.6906	10,243	10.3782	40,068
Profit (loss)	1,125	0.5276	(568)	(0.5516)	(749)	(0.7589)	(192)
Unit sales (cwt.)	2,132,191		1,029,654		986,974		
Quoted selling price	$9.41		$9.91		$10.56		
Cash discounts taken, percent of selling price	1.08%		2.21%		1.72%		

Note: Figures may not add exactly because of rounding.

ued until Samra, with its strong financial position, again stabilized the situation following a general recognition of the failure of price cutting. Furthermore, because sales were to industrial buyers and the products of different manufacturers were similar, Hanson was convinced it could not unilaterally raise prices without suffering volume declines.

During 1992, Hanson's share of industry sales was 12 percent for type 101, 8 percent for 102, and 10 percent for 103. The industrywide quoted selling prices were $9.41, $9.91, and $10.56, respectively.

Wessling, upon taking office in February 1993, decided against immediate major changes. Rather, he chose to analyze 1992 operations and to wait for results of the first half of 1993. He instructed the accounting department to provide detailed expenses and earnings statements by products for 1992 (see Exhibit 2). In addition, he requested an explanation of the nature of the costs including their expected future behavior (see Exhibit 3).

To familiarize Paul Hanson with his methods, Wessling sent copies of these exhibits to

EXHIBIT 3
ACCOUNTING DEPARTMENT'S COMMENTARY ON
COSTS

Direct labor: Variable. Nonunion shop at going
community rates. No abnormal demands foreseen. It
may be assumed that direct labor dollars is an
adequate measure of capacity utilization.

Compensation insurance: Variable. Nine percent of
direct and indirect labor is a good estimate.

Materials: Variable. Exhibit 2 figures are accurate.
Includes waste allowances.

Power: Variable. Rates are fixed.

Supplies: Variable. Exhibit 2 figures are accurate.

Repairs: Variable. Varies as volume changes within
normal operating range. Lower and upper limits are
fixed.

*General administration, selling expense, indirect labor,
interest:* Almost nonvariable. Can be changed by
management decision.

Cash discount: Almost nonvariable. Average cash
discounts taken are consistent from year to year.
Percentages in Exhibit 2 are accurate.

Light and heat: Almost nonvariable. Heat varies only with
fuel cost changes. Light is a fixed item regardless of
level of production.

Property taxes: Almost nonvariable. Under the lease
terms, Hanson Company pays the taxes; assessed
valuation has been constant; the rate has risen slowly.
Any change in the near future will be small and
independent of production volume.

Rent: Nonvariable. Lease has five years to run.

Building service: Nonvariable. At normal business level,
variances are small.

Property insurance: Nonvariable. Three-year policy with
fixed premium.

Depreciation: Nonvariable. Fixed-dollar total.

Hanson, and they discussed them. Hanson
stated that he thought product 103 should be
dropped immediately as it would be impossible to lower expenses on product 103 as
much as 76 cents per hundredweight (cwt.).
In addition, he stressed the need for economies on product 102.

Wessling relied on the authority arrangement Mr. Hanson had agreed to earlier and
continued production of the three products.
For control purposes, he had the accounting
department prepare monthly statements

using as standard costs the actual costs per
cwt. from the 1992 profit and loss statement
(Exhibit 2). These monthly statements were
his basis for making minor marketing and
production changes during the spring of
1993. Late in July 1993, Wessling received
from the accounting department the six
months' statement of cumulative standard
costs including variances of actual costs from
standard (see Exhibit 4). They showed that
the first half of 1993 was a profitable period.

During the latter half of 1993, the sales of
the entire industry weakened. Even though
Hanson retained its share of the market, its
profit for the last six months was small. In
January 1994, Samra announced a price reduction on product 101 from $9.41 to $8.47
per cwt. This created an immediate pricing
problem for its competitors. Wessling forecast that if Hanson Company held to the
$9.41 price during the first six months of
1994, their unit sales would be 750,000 cwt.
He felt that if they dropped their price to
$8.47 per cwt., the six months' volume
would be 1,000,000 cwt. Wessling knew that
competing managements anticipated a further decline in activity. He thought a general
decline in prices was quite probable.

The accounting department reported that
the standard costs in use would probably
apply during the first half of 1994, with two
exceptions: materials and supplies would be
about 5 percent above standard, and light
and heat would decrease about 3 percent.

Wessling and Hanson discussed the product 101 pricing problem. Hanson observed
that especially with the anticipated increase
in materials and supplies costs, a sales price
of $8.47 would be below cost. He therefore
wanted the $9.41 to be continued since he
felt the company could not be profitable
while selling a key product below cost.

Questions

1. If the company had dropped product 103 as of
    January 1, 1993, what effect would that action

EXHIBIT 4
PROFIT AND LOSS BY PRODUCT, AT STANDARD
Showing Variances from January 1 to June 30, 1993

Item	Product 101 Standard per Cwt.	Total at Standard	Product 102 Standard per Cwt.	Total at Standard	Product 103 Standard per Cwt.	Total at Standard	Total Standard (thousands)	Total Actual (thousands)	Variances
Rent	0.2111	210	0.4370	311	0.6079	305	826	750	+ 76
Property taxes	0.1407	140	0.1408	100	0.1408	71	311	303	+ 8
Property insurance	0.1341	134	0.1340	95	0.1337	67	296	278	+ 18
Compensation insurance	0.2809	280	0.2758	196	0.3212	161	637	633	+ 4
Direct labor	2.3281	2,321	2.2736	1,619	2.6748	1,341	5,281	5,308	− 27
Indirect labor	0.7940	792	0.7906	563	0.8947	448	1,803	1,721	+ 82
Power	0.0403	40	0.0932	66	0.1175	59	165	170	− 5
Light and heat	0.0202	20	0.0418	30	0.0588	29	79	83	− 4
Building service	0.0136	14	0.0282	20	0.0395	20	54	50	+ 4
Materials	1.3765	1,372	1.7569	1,251	1.8866	946	3,569	3,544	+ 25
Supplies	0.0943	94	0.1777	127	0.1368	69	290	290	—
Repairs	0.0319	32	0.0554	39	0.0395	20	91	88	+ 3
Total production cost	5.4657	5,449	6.2040	4,418	7.0519	3,535	13,402	13,218	+184
Selling expense	1.6396	1,634	1.7074	1,216	1.8288	917	3,767	3,706	+ 61
General administration	0.5820	580	0.6060	432	0.6484	325	1,337	1,378	− 41
Depreciation	1.0173	1,014	1.5957	1,136	1.4225	713	2,863	2,681	+182
Interest	0.0943	94	0.1486	106	0.2047	103	303	290	+ 13
Total cost	8.7989	8,771	10.2617	7,307	11.1563	5,592	21,672	21,273	+399
Less other income	0.0183	18	0.0194	14	0.0193	10	42	42	—
	8.7806	8,753	10.2423	7,294	11.1371	5,583	21,630	21,231	+399
Actual sales (net)	9.3083	9,279	9.6906	6,901	10.3782	5,202	21,382	21,382	—
Profit or loss	0.5276	526	(0.5516)	(393)	(0.7589)	(380)	(248)	151	+399
Unit sales (cwt.)	996,859		712,102		501,276				

Note: Figures may not add exactly because of rounding.

have had on the $151,000 profit for the first six months of 1993?

2. In January 1994, should the company reduce the price of product 101 from $9.41 to $8.47?

3. What is Hanson's most profitable product?

4. What appears to have caused the return to profitable operations in the first six months of 1993?

CASE 26–4 Liquid Chemical Company*

Liquid Chemical Company manufactured and sold a range of high-grade products

---

*Copyright © by the University of Bristol (Great Britain).

throughout Great Britain. Many of these products required careful packing, and the company had always made a feature of the special properties of the containers used. They had a special patented lining, made from a material known as GHL, and the firm operated a department especially to maintain its containers in good condition and to make new ones to replace those that were beyond repair.

Dale Walsh, the general manager, had suspected for some time that the firm might save money and get equally good service by buying its containers from an outside source. After careful inquiries, he approached a firm specializing in container production, Packages, Ltd., and asked for a quotation. At the same time he asked Paul Dyer, his chief accountant, to give him an up-to-date statement of the cost of operating the container department.

Within a few days, the quotation from Packages, Ltd., came in. The firm was prepared to supply all the new containers required—at that time running at the rate of 3,000 a year—for £300,000[1] a year, the contract to run for a guaranteed term of five years and thereafter to be renewable from year to year. If the required number of containers increased, the contract price would be increased proportionally. Additionally, and irrespective of whether the above contract was entered into or not, Packages, Ltd., would undertake to carry out purely maintenance work on containers, short of replacement, for a sum of £90,000 a year, on the same contract terms.

Walsh compared these figures with the cost figures prepared by Dyer, covering a year's operations of the container department, as shown in the accompanying table.

	£	£
Materials		178,360
Labor		126,000
Department overhead:		
Manager's salary	20,300	
Rent	11,480	
Depreciation of machinery	38,220	
Maintenance of machinery	9,170	
Other expenses	40,120	
		119,290
		423,650
Proportion of general administrative overhead		57,330
Total cost of department for year		480,980

Walsh's conclusion was that no time should be lost in closing the department and in entering into the contracts offered by Packages, Ltd. However, he felt bound to give the manager of the department, Sean Duffy, an opportunity to question this conclusion before he acted on it. He therefore called him in and put the facts before him, at the same time making it clear that Duffy's own position was not in jeopardy; for even if his department were closed, there was another managerial position shortly becoming vacant to which he could be moved without loss of pay or prospects.

---

[1]At the time of this case, one British pound (£) was worth about $1.50.

Duffy asked for time to think the matter over. The next morning, he asked to speak to Walsh again and said he thought there were a number of considerations that ought to be borne in mind before his department was closed. "For instance," he said, "what will you do with the machinery? It cost £300,000 four years ago, but you'd be lucky if you got £50,000 for it now, even though it's good for another five years or so. And then there's the stock of GHL we bought a year ago. That cost us £255,000, and at the rate we're using it now, it'll last us another four years or so. We used up about one-fifth of it last year. Dyer's figure of £178,360 for materials probably includes about £51,000 for GHL. But it'll be tricky stuff to handle if we don't use it up. We bought it for £1,275 a ton, and you couldn't buy it today for less than £1,450. But you wouldn't have more than £1,100 a ton left if you sold it, after you'd covered all the handling expenses."

Walsh thought that Dyer ought to be present during this discussion. He called him in and put Duffy's points to him. "I don't much like all this conjecture," Dyer said. "I think my figures are pretty conclusive. Besides, if we are going to have all this talk about 'what will happen if,' don't forget the problem of space we're faced with. We're paying £21,840 a year in rent for warehouse space a couple of miles away. If we closed Duffy's department, we'd have all the storage space we need without renting."

"That's a good point," said Walsh, "but I'm a bit worried about the workers if we close the department. I don't think we can find room for any of them elsewhere in the firm. I could see whether Packages can take any of them. But some of them are getting on. There are Walters and Hines, for example. They've been with us since they left school 40 years ago. I'd feel bound to give them a small pension—£4,000 a year each, say."

Duffy showed some relief at this. "But I still don't like Dyer's figures," he said. "What about this £57,330 for general administrative overhead? You surely don't expect to sack anyone in the general office if I'm closed, do you?" "Probably not," said Dyer, "but someone has to pay for these costs. We can't ignore them when we look at an individual department, because if we do that with each department in turn, we shall finish up by convincing ourselves that directors, accountants, clerks, stationery, and the like don't have to be paid for. And they do, believe me."

"Well, I think we've thrashed this out pretty fully," said Walsh, "but I've been turning over in my mind the possibility of perhaps keeping on the maintenance work ourselves. What are your views on that, Duffy?"

"I don't know," said Duffy, "but it's worth looking into. We shouldn't need any machinery for that, and I could hand the supervision over to a foreman. You'd save £5,500 a year there, say. You'd only need about one-third of the workers, but you could keep on the oldest. You wouldn't save any space here or at the rented warehouse, so I suppose the rent would be the same. I shouldn't think the other expenses would be more than £16,500 a year," "What about materials?" asked Walsh. "We use about 10 percent of them on container maintenance," Duffy replied.

"Well, I've told Packages, Ltd., that I'd let them know my decision within a week," said Walsh. "I'll let you know what I decide to do before I write to them."

Questions

1. Identify the four alternatives implicit in the case.
2. Using cash flow as the criterion, which alternative is the most attractive?
3. What, if any, additional information do you think is necessary in order to make a sound decision?

CASE 26–5   Baldwin Bicycle Company

In May 1989 Suzanne Leister, marketing vice president of Baldwin Bicycle Company, was mulling over the discussion she had had the previous day with Karl Knott, a buyer from Hi-Valu Stores, Inc. Hi-Valu operated a chain of discount department stores in the Northwest. Hi-Valu's sales volume had grown to the extent that it was beginning to add "house-brand" (also called "private-label") merchandise to the product lines of several of its departments. Mr. Knott, Hi-Valu's buyer for sporting goods, had approached Ms. Leister about the possibility of Baldwin's producing bicycles for Hi-Valu. The bicycles would bear the name "Challenger," which Hi-Valu planned to use for all of its house-brand sporting goods.

Baldwin had been making bicycles for almost 40 years. In 1989 the company's line included 10 models, ranging from a small beginner's model with training wheels to a deluxe 12-speed adult's model. Sales were currently at an annual rate of about $10 million. (The company's 1988 financial statements appear in Exhibit 1.) Most of Baldwin's sales were through independently owned toy stores and bicycle shops. Baldwin had never before distributed its products through department store chains of any type. Ms. Leister felt that Baldwin bicycles had the

EXHIBIT 1
FINANCIAL STATEMENTS
(thousands of dollars)

BALDWIN BICYCLE COMPANY
Balance Sheet
As of December 31, 1988

Assets		*Liabilities and Owners' Equity*	
Cash	$ 342	Current liabilities	$3,478
Accounts receivable	1,359	Noncurrent liabilities	1,512
Inventories	2,756	Total liabilities	4,990
Plant and equipment (net)	3,635	Owners' equity	3,102
	$ 8,092		$8,092

Income Statement
For the Year Ended December 31, 1988

Sales revenues	$10,872
Cost of sales	8,045
Gross margin	2,827
Other expenses	2,354
Income before taxes	473
Income tax expense	218
Net income	$ 255

image of being above average in quality and price, but not a "top of the line" product.

Hi-Valu's proposal to Baldwin had features that made it quite different from Baldwin's normal way of doing business. First, it was very important to Hi-Valu to have ready access to a large inventory of bicycles, because Hi-Valu had had great difficulty in predicting bicycle sales, both by store and by month. Hi-Valu wanted to carry these inventories in its regional warehouses, but did not want title on a bicycle to pass from Baldwin to Hi-Valu until the bicycle was shipped from one of its regional warehouses to a specific Hi-Valu store. At that point, Hi-Valu would regard the bicycle as having been purchased from Baldwin, and would pay for it within 30 days. However, Hi-Valu would agree to take title to any bicycle that had been in one of its warehouses for four months, again paying for it within 30 days. Mr. Knott estimated that on average, a bike would remain in a Hi-Valu regional warehouse for two months.

Second, Hi-Valu wanted to sell its Challenger bicycles at lower prices than the name-brand bicycles it carried, and yet still earn approximately the same dollar gross margin on each bicycle sold—the rationale being that Challenger bike sales would take away from the sales of the name-brand bikes. Thus, Hi-Valu wanted to purchase bikes from Baldwin at lower prices than the wholesale prices of comparable bikes sold through Baldwin's usual channels.

Finally, Hi-Valu wanted the Challenger bike to be somewhat different in appearance from Baldwin's other bikes. While the frame and mechanical components could be the same as used on current Baldwin models, the fenders, seats, and handlebars would need to be somewhat different, and the tires would have to have the name "Challenger" molded into their sidewalls. Also, the bicycles would have to be packed in boxes printed with the Hi-Valu and Challenger names. Ms. Leister

thought that possibly these requirements would increase Baldwin's purchasing, inventorying, and production costs over and above the added costs that would be incurred for a comparable increase in volume for Baldwin's regular products.

On the positive side, Ms. Leister was acutely aware that the "bicycle boom" had flattened out, and this plus a poor economy had caused Baldwin's sales volume to fall the past two years. As a result, Baldwin currently was operating its plant at about 75 percent of one-shift capacity. Thus, the added volume from Hi-Valu's purchases could possibly be very attractive. If agreement could be reached on prices, Hi-Valu would sign a contract guaranteeing to Baldwin that Hi-Valu would buy its house-brand bicycles only from Baldwin for a three-year period. The contract would then be automatically extended on year-to-year basis, unless one party gave the other at least six-months' notice that it did not wish to extend the contract.

Suzanne Leister realized she needed to do some preliminary financial analysis of this proposal before having any further discussions with Karl Knott. She had written on a pad the information she had gathered to use in her initial analysis; this information is summarized in Exhibit 2 on page 958.

Questions

1. What is the expected added profit from the Challenger line?
2. What is the expected impact of cannibalization of existing sales?
3. What costs will be incurred on a one-time basis only?
4. What are the additional assets and related carrying costs?
5. What is the overall impact on the company in terms of (a) profits, (b) return on sales, (c) return on assets, and (d) return on equity?
6. What are the strategic risks and rewards?
7. What should the company do? Why?

EXHIBIT 2
DATA PERTINENT TO HI-VALU PROPOSAL
Notes taken by Suzanne Leister

---

1. *Estimated first-year costs of producing Challenger bicycles* (average unit costs, assuming a constant mix of models):

Materials.................................	$39.80*
Direct labor	19.60
Overhead (@ 125% of direct labor)	24.50†
	$83.90

> * Includes items specific to models for Hi-Valu, not used in our standard models.
> †Accountant says about 40 percent of total production overhead cost is variable; 125 percent of DL$ rate is based on volume of 100,000 bicycles per year.

2. *One-time added costs* of preparing drawings and/or arranging sources for fenders, seats, handlebars, tires, and shipping boxes that differ from those used in our standard models; approximately $5,000 (based on estimated two person-months of effort at $2,500 per month).

3. *Unit price and annual volume:* Hi-Valu estimates it will need 25,000 bikes a year and proposes to pay us (based on the assumed mix of models) an average of $92.29 per bike for the first year. Contract to contain an inflation escalation clause such that price will increase in proportion to inflation-caused increases in costs shown in item 1, above; thus, the $92.29 and $83.90 figures are, in effect, "constant-dollar" amounts. Knott intimated that there was very little, if any, negotiating leeway in the $92.29 proposed initial price.

4. *Asset-related costs* (annual variable costs, as percent of dollar value of assets):

Pretax cost of funds (to finance receivables or inventories) .	11.5
Recordkeeping costs (for receivables or inventories).......	2.0
Inventory insurance	0.6
State property tax on inventory	0.7
Inventory-handling labor and equipment..................	6.0
Pilferage, obsolescence, damage, etc...................	2.2

5. *Assumptions for Challenger-related added inventories* (average over the year):

   Materials: two months' supply.
   Work in process: 1,000 bikes, half completed (but all materials for them issued).
   Finished goods: 500 bikes (awaiting next carload-lot shipment to a Hi-Valu warehouse).

6. *Impact on our regular sales:* Some customers comparison shop for bikes, and many of them are likely to recognize a Challenger bike as a good value when compared with a similar bike (either ours or a competitor's) at a higher price in a nonchain toy or bicycle store. In 1988, we sold 98,791 bikes. My best guess is that our sales over the next three years will be about 100,000 bikes a year if we forgo the Hi-Valu deal. If we accept it, I think we'll lose about 3,000 units of our regular sales volume a year, since our retail distribution is quite strong in Hi-Valu's market regions. These estimates do not include the possibility that a few of our current dealers might drop our line if they find out we're making bikes for Hi-Valu.

CASE 26-6 Trammel Snowmobile Company*

Trammel Snowmobile Company produced two models of snowmobiles, which are small, open vehicles with powered drive tracks that will operate on snow-covered terrain. The company had four departments: body fabrication, engine production, model S assembly, and model V assembly. Monthly production capacity in these departments was as follows:

	Model S	Model V
Body fabrication	25,000	35,000
Engine production	33,333	16,667
Model S assembly	22,500	—
Model V assembly	—	15,000

For example, if only model S snowmobiles were to be produced, the body department could make 25,000 bodies a month and the engine department could produce 33,333 engines a month. Equivalently, if the body department capacity is expressed as being 25,000 body units, then each model S body requires one unit of capacity, and each model V body requires only five-sevenths of a unit of capacity. Similarly, it can be said that each model S engine uses up one of the 33,333 units of capacity in the engine department, whereas a model V engine requires 2 units of engine department capacity. These capacity relationships are shown in Exhibit 1.

Exhibit 2 shows prices and cost data for each model. At present, Trammel was able to sell as many snowmobiles as it could pro-duce. In recent months, production (and, therefore, sales) had been 3,333 model S and 15,000 model V. This product mix used up all of the capacity in the engine department and the model V assembly department, but did not require the other two departments to operate at capacity.

It was not clear to Trammel's management group that the current product mix was the best one. This was a matter of concern because of the company's poor profit showing in recent months. In an executive committee meeting called to discuss the matter, the sales manager offered the opinion that company profits would increase if the model S were dropped and resources were devoted exclusively to the model V. "When you subtract our selling costs, which average nearly 5 percent of sales, model S doesn't even show a profit. You can't lose money on each model S and then make it up on volume!"

The controller, on the other hand, said that the present product mix appeared to be the best one. "No matter how you look at it, we should make as many model V as we can: it has the larger gross margin per unit, the larger per unit excess of revenues over out-of-pocket costs, and the larger per unit absorption of overhead costs. But we would have excess capacity in the engine department if we didn't make *any* model S; so we should make all the units of V we can, plus enough units of S to get the engine department up to capacity too."

The production manager added another possibility: "I know that the Bryant Engine Company is hungry for work—one of my friends who works there just got laid off. If we could provide them with our list of engine components suppliers and a set of

---

* This case is adapted from an example used by Robert Dorfman in "Mathematical or 'Linear' Programming: A Nonmathematical Exposition," *American Economic Review,* December 1953.

EXHIBIT 1
DIAGRAM OF FEASIBLE PRODUCT MIXES

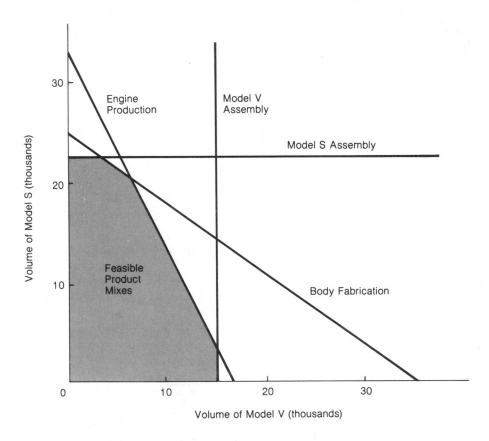

drawings, they could produce engines for model S snowmobiles; then we could use up more of our body and model S assembly capacities." The sales manager responded, "I don't see the merit in that idea. Bryant will surely charge us more than our own costs of making an engine, and that will just give us a bigger loss on each model S, after subtracting selling costs from its gross margin."

Questions

1. Given the present capacity constraints, what is the most profitable product mix for Trammel? (Assume nonproduction costs are the same for any mix that causes the plant to operate at full capacity.)

2. What is the most that Trammel could pay Bryant for a model S engine without reducing Trammel's profits?

3. Should Trammel consider purchasing completed model V engines from an outside supplier? If so, what is the most Trammel could pay for such engines without reducing its profits?

4. Subsequent to the events described in the case, Trammel's management was contacted by a consulting industrial engineer, who claimed that she could advise the company on how to increase the effective capacity in its two assembly departments without having to make any significant additional investment in the departments. Her fee for this advice was very high, so Trammel's management wanted

EXHIBIT 2
PER UNIT GROSS MARGIN DATA

	Model S		Model V	
Selling price		$1,750		$2,240
Production costs:				
Materials:				
Body	267		333	
Engine	461		423	
Assembly	80	808	118	874
Direct labor:				
Body	84		60	
Engine	143		286	
Assembly	63	290	63	409
Overhead:*				
Body	168		120	
Engine	286		572	
Assembly	126	580	126	818
Total		1,678		2,101
Gross margin		$ 72		$ 139

* Approximately 40 percent of these per-unit overhead amounts were costs that varied with volume. Thus, at the present production mix (3,333 model S and 15,000 model V), total overhead costs were about $14,203,000, of which about $5,681,000 was variable.

to know how much this added capacity would be worth before buying her services. How much would Trammel's optimal monthly profit increase if it had one more unit of model S assembly capacity? One more unit of model V assembly capacity? How, if at all, do your answers change if Trammel can buy engines from an outside supplier at an attractive price?

CASE 26–7   Gentle Electric Company*

Robert Edison, general manager of Gentle Electric Company (GEC), was contemplating several recent developments in the power transformer market. Mr. Edison was concerned because in its production of control units for passenger and freight elevators, GEC used five large transformers each working

day of the month. (GEC operated on a 20-day per month schedule.) For several years, the transformers had been produced in only two locations in the United States, one in New England and the other on the West Coast. Luckily for GEC, the New England producer was located several miles away and offered free delivery to GEC within hours.

Several months earlier, Mr. Edison had compiled the following information about the transformers:

*Copyright © by the President and Fellows of Harvard College. Harvard Business School case 672-038.

Information		Source of Information
Total annual usage	1,200 units	Purchasing
Requisitions per year	48 times (weekly)	Purchasing
Units per requisition	25 units	Purchasing
Inventory carrying cost	20%	Controller
Weight per unit	500 lbs.	Shipping and receiving
Cost of unloading	$0.10 per cwt.	Warehouse manager
Clerical cost per requisition	$10	Purchasing
Expediting cost per requisition	$15	Shipping and receiving
Warehouse capacity	200 units	Warehouse manager
Outside warehouse costs	$12 per unit per year*	Warehouse manager

*There is existing space in the warehouse for 200 units. Additional space must be leased for a year. Thus, if an order of more than 200 units arrives, part of it must be stored in leased space.

Several months after compiling this information, Mr. Edison was informed by his purchasing agent that GEC's local supplier had followed its West Coast competitor in announcing a new price structure:

Units per Order	Unit Price*
First 100	$500
Next 100	490
Each unit over 200	475

*For example, an order of 210 units would cost 100($500) +100($490) + 10($475) = $103,750.

Just recently, GEC's local supplier announced that it was discontinuing production of transformers, forcing GEC to deal with the West Coast supplier whose prices are the same as the local supplier except that they are FOB, California. The traffic department informed Mr. Edison that the transportation cost per hundred-weight is $6 for carload lots of 50,000 pounds. The LCL (less than carload) rate is $10 per hundredweight. The replenishment cycle will normally take one week.

Mr. Edison wonders what effects these new developments will have on its cost structure for transformer purchases.

Questions

1. The optimal value of Q shown in the text minimizes the function:

$$T = (R * C) + \left(S * \frac{R}{Q}\right) * \left(\frac{Q}{2} * C * K\right)$$

The first term in this function is annual acquisition costs; the second is annual ordering (or setup) costs; and the third is annual inventory holding costs.

a.   Be sure you understand what each term represents and how it was derived. Try to make explicit the assumptions that are built into the model (i.e., formula).

b.   If you remember calculus, prove that the formula for *EOQ* given in the text's section on economic order quantity in fact minimizes *T*.

2. Assume the original transformer price was $500 per unit. Was Gentle Electric initially replenishing its inventory in the most economical way? (Assume all requisitions are subject to both clerical and expediting costs.)

3. When Gentle Electric was offered a volume discount, which costs were affected? What happened to EOQ?

4. What should be Gentle Electric's ordering rule when it begins to deal with the West Coast firm?

Hint: For 3 and 4, there are discontinuities in the total annual cost function, *T* (acquisition costs plus ordering costs plus holding costs). You will need to develop a "customized" formula for Gentle Electric's annual costs for each smooth segment of the total cost curve.

CASE 26-8   Warren Agency*

Thaddeus Warren operated a real estate agency that specialized in finding buyers for commercial properties. Warren was approached one day by a prospective client who had three properties that she wished to sell. The client indicated the prices she wished to receive for these properties as follows:

Property	Price
A	$100,000
B	200,000
C	400,000

Warren would receive a commission of 4 percent on any of the properties he was able to sell.

The client laid down the following conditions: "Mr. Warren, you have to sell A first. If you can't sell it within a month, the entire deal is off—no commission and no chance to sell B or C. If you sell A within a month, then I'll give you the commission on A and the option of (a) stopping at this point, or (b) selling either B or C next under the same conditions (i.e., sell within a month or no commission on the second property and no chance to sell the third property). If you succeed in selling the first two properties, you will also have the option of selling the third."

After the client had left, Warren proceeded to analyze the proposal that had been made to him to determine whether or not to accept it. He figured his selling costs and his chances of selling each property at the prices set by the client to be as given in the following table:

Property	Selling Costs	Warren's Assessment of Probability of Sale
A	$3,200	0.7
B	800	0.6
C	1,600	0.5

He believed that sale of a particular property would not make it any more or less likely that the two remaining properties could be sold. Selling costs would have to be incurred whether or not a particular property was sold but could be avoided by deciding not to attempt to sell the property.

Since property A would have to be sold before any further action could be taken, Warren prepared the following table in an attempt to determine whether or not to accept property A:

Outcome	Probability	Act Accept	Refuse
A sold	0.7	$ 800	$0
A not sold	0.3	−3,200	0
Expected value:		$ −400	$0

Thus, accepting A would be unprofitable looked at by itself. Warren was not very happy with this conclusion, however, because he reasoned that success in selling A would entitle him to offer either B or C, and it looked as if either of these properties would result in an expected profit. He felt that somehow or other the value of this opportunity should be taken into consideration.

Questions

1. Develop a decision tree for Warren's problem. (Hint: The tree will have 11 end points.)

---

*Copyright © by the President and Fellows of Harvard College. Harvard Business School case 106-036.

2. Based on the decision tree analysis, what should Warren do?

3. Suppose that before any of the properties is listed, another realtor approaches Warren and offers to buy from Warren the rights to this deal (i.e., with all of the conditions that were stipulated by the client). For what amount should Warren be willing to sell these rights?

27

Longer-Run Decisions: Capital Budgeting

Chapter 26 discussed types of alternative choice problems with a relatively short time horizon. Such short-run decisions do not commit, or lock in, the organization to a certain course of action over a considerable period in the future. Similarly, they usually do not significantly affect the amount of funds that must be invested in the organization. In this chapter we extend the discussion of alternative choice decisions to those that involve relatively long-term differential investments of capital. Such problems are called **capital investment problems;** they are also commonly called **capital budgeting problems** because a capital budget is a list of the capital investment projects that an organization has decided to carry out.

In these problems differential costs and revenues are treated the same as in Chapter 26; the only difference is that the longer time horizon of capital budgeting problems magnifies the problems of estimating these cost and revenue items. However, the long-term investment aspect of capital budgeting problems leads to a more complicated analytical approach. It is important that these complications be mastered because capital budgeting decisions *do* lock in the organization to a course of action for several, perhaps many, future years.

NATURE OF THE PROBLEM

When an organization purchases a long-lived asset, it makes an investment similar to that made by a bank when it lends money. The essential

965

characteristic of both types of transactions is that cash is committed today in the expectation of recovering that cash plus some additional cash in the future: the investor commits cash today with the expectation of receiving a return *of* the investment as well as a return *on* the investment.

In the case of the bank loan, the return of investment is the repayment of the principal and the return on investment is the inflow of interest payments received over the life of the loan. In the case of the long-lived asset, both the return of investment and the return on investment are in the form of *cash earnings* generated by use of the asset. If, over the life of the investment, the inflows of cash earnings exceed the initial investment outlays, then we know that the original investment was recovered (return of investment) and that some profit was earned (positive return on investment). Thus, an **investment** is the purchase of an expected future stream of cash inflows.

When an organization considers whether or not to purchase a new long-lived asset, the essential question is whether the future cash inflows are likely to be large enough to warrant making the investment. The problems discussed in this chapter all have this general form: A certain amount is proposed for investment now in the expectation that the investment will generate a stream of cash inflows in future years; are the anticipated future cash inflows large enough to justify investing funds in the proposal? Some illustrative problems are described here:

Replacement.   Shall we replace existing equipment with more efficient equipment? The future expected cash inflows on this investment are the cost savings resulting from lower operating costs, or the profits from additional volume produced by the new equipment, or both.

Expansion.   Shall we build or otherwise acquire a new facility? The future expected cash inflows on this investment are the cash profits from the goods and services produced in the new facility.

Cost Reduction.   Shall we buy equipment to perform an operation now done manually? That is, shall we spend money in order to save money? The expected future cash inflows on this investment are savings resulting from lower operating costs.

Choice of Equipment.   Which of several proposed items of equipment shall we purchase for a given purpose? The choice often turns on which item is expected to give the largest return on the investment made in it.

New Product.   Should a new product be added to the line? The choice turns on whether the expected cash inflows from the sale of the new product are large enough to warrant the investment in equipment, working capital, and the costs required to make and introduce the product.

General Approach   All these problems involve two quite dissimilar types of amounts. First, there is the investment, which is usually made in a lump sum at the beginning of the project. Although not literally made today, it is made at a specific point in time that for analytical purposes is called "today," or **Time Zero.** Second, there is a stream of cash inflows expected to result from this investment over a period of future years.

These two types of amounts cannot be compared directly with one another because they occur at different times. To make a valid comparison, we must bring the amounts involved to equivalent values at the same point in time. The most convenient point is at Time Zero. We need not adjust the amount of the investment since it is already stated at its Time Zero (present) value. We need only to convert the stream of future cash inflows to their present value equivalents so that we can then compare them directly with the amount of the investment.[1]

Net Present Value.   To do this, we multiply the cash inflow for each year by the present value of $1 for that year at the appropriate rate of return (Appendix Table A, three pages prior to the Index). This process is called **discounting** the cash inflows. The rate at which the cash inflows are discounted is called the **required rate of return,** the **discount rate,** or the **hurdle rate.** The difference between the present value of the cash inflows and the amount of investment is called the **net present value (NPV).** If the NPV is a nonnegative amount, the proposal is acceptable.

> **Example.**   A proposed investment of $1,000 is expected to produce cash inflows of $625 per year for each of the next two years. The required rate of return is 14 percent. The present value of the cash inflows can be compared with the present value of the investment as follows:

	Year	Amount	Discount Factor (Table A)	Total Present Value
Cash inflow.....................	1	$ 625	0.877	$ 548
Cash inflow.....................	2	625	0.769	481
Present values of cash inflows....				1,029
Less: Investment..............	0	1,000	1.000	1,000
Net present value				$ 29

The proposed investment is acceptable.

The decision rule given above is a general rule, and some qualifications to it will be discussed later.

Return on Investment

So far, we have shown how the net present value can be calculated if the investment, cash inflows, and the required rate of return are given. It is

---

[1]If the reader is not familiar with the concept of present value, the Appendix to Chapter 8 (up to the section titled Calculating Bond Yields) should be read before continuing with this chapter.

useful to look at the situation from another viewpoint: How can the rate of return be calculated when the investment and the cash inflows are given?

Consider a bank loan. Assume that a bank lends $25,000 and receives interest payments of $2,500 at the end of each year for five years, with the $25,000 loan principal being repaid at the end of the fifth year. It is correct to say that the bank earned a return of 10 percent on its investment of $25,000. The return percentage is found by dividing the annual cash inflow by the amount of investment that was outstanding (i.e., unrecovered) during the year. In this case the amount of loan outstanding each year was $25,000 and the cash inflow was $2,500 in each year, so the rate of return was $2,500 ÷ $25,000 = 10 percent.

If, however, a bank lends $25,000 and is repaid $6,595 at the end of each year for five years, the problem of finding the return is more complicated. In this case only part of each year's $6,595 cash inflow represents the return *on* investment, and the remainder is a repayment of the principal (return *of* investment). This is the same loan that was used in the Kinnear Company example in the Appendix to Chapter 8. As was demonstrated there, this loan also has a return of 10 percent, in the same sense as did the loan described in the preceding paragraph: the $6,595 annual payments will recover the $25,000 loan investment and in addition will provide a return of 10 percent of the amount of *unrecovered* investment (principal still outstanding) each year. The fact that the return is 10 percent is demonstrated in Illustration 8–1. Of the $6,595 repaid in the first year, $2,500, or 10 percent of the $25,000 then outstanding, is the return; the $4,095 remainder of the payment reduces the principal down to $20,905. In the second year $2,091 is a return of 10 percent on the $20,905 of principal then outstanding, and the $4,504 remainder reduces the principal to $16,401. And so on.

As seen in the above example, when an investment involves annual interest payments with the full amount of the investment being recovered in a lump sum at the end of the investment's life, the computation of the return is simple. But when the annual payments combine both principal and interest, the computation is more complicated. Some investment problems are of the simple type. For example, if a business buys land for $25,000, rents it for $2,500 a year for five years, and then sells it for $25,000 at the end of five years, the return is 10 percent. Many capital investment decisions, on the other hand, relate to depreciable assets, which characteristically have little or no resale value at the end of their useful life. The cash inflows must therefore be large enough for the investor both to recover the investment itself during its life and also to earn a satisfactory return on the amount not yet recovered, just as in the situation shown in Illustration 8–1.

Stream of Cash Inflows.   The cash inflows on most capital investments are a series of amounts received over several future years. Calculating the present value of a series, or stream, of cash inflows was explained in the

Appendix to Chapter 8. Recall that for a *level* stream (i.e., equal annual inflows), the factors in Appendix Table B can be used.

Table A and Table B are often used in combination, as shown in the next example. This example also demonstrates that the return on investment for the business renting its land, mentioned above, is indeed 10 percent.

> **Example.** A proposed investment of $25,000 is expected to generate annual cash inflows of $2,500 a year for the next five years, with the $25,000 to be recovered in a lump sum at the end of the fifth year. Is this proposal acceptable if the required rate of return is 10 percent?
>
> As shown by the following calculation, the cash inflows discounted at 10 percent have a present value of $25,000, which is equal to the original investment. Thus, the investment's return is 10 percent, and it is therefore acceptable.

Year	Inflow	10 Percent Discount Factor	Present Value
1–5	$2,500/yr.	3.791 (Table B)	$ 9,478
End of 5	$25,000	0.621 (Table A)	15,525
Total present value			$25,003*

* Would be $20,000 if discount factors included more decimal places.

Other Compounding Assumptions. Tables A and B are constructed on the assumption that cash inflows are received once a year, on the last day of the year. For many problems this is not a realistic assumption because cash in the form of increased revenues or lower costs is likely to flow in throughout the year. Nevertheless, annual tables are customarily used in capital investment problems on the grounds that (1) they are easier to understand than tables constructed on other assumptions, such as monthly or continuous compounding, and (2) they are good enough, considering the inevitable margin of error in the basic estimates.

Annual tables *understate* the present value of cash inflows if these inflows are, in fact, received throughout the year rather than entirely on the last day of the year. Tables are available showing the present values of earnings flows that occur quarterly, monthly, or even continuously.

> **Example.** The table on the next page illustrates the degree to which annual tables understate the present value of inflows received during the year. The numbers in the table show the ratio of the present value of periodic, within-the-year receipts to the present value of an equal annual total received at the end of one year. For example, the table shows that if the discount rate is 10 percent and cash inflows are received continuously, then the use of a PV table that assumes year-end inflows will understate the present value of the inflows by 4.7 percent.

Frequency	Discount Rates			
of Inflow	6 Percent	10 Percent	15 Percent	25 Percent
Semiannually	1.014	1.023	1.032	1.049
Monthly	1.026	1.043	1.062	1.096
Continuously	1.029	1.047	1.068	1.106

ESTIMATING THE VARIABLES

We now discuss how to estimate each of the five elements involved in capital investment calculations. These are:

1. Required rate of return.
2. Economic life (number of years for which cash inflows are anticipated).
3. Amount of cash inflow in each year.
4. Amount of investment.
5. Terminal value.

Required Rate of Return

Two alternative ways of arriving at the required rate of return—trial and error, and cost of capital—will be described here.

Trial and Error. Recall that the higher the required rate of return, the lower the present value of the cash inflows. It follows that the higher the required rate of return, the fewer the investment proposals that will have cash inflows whose present value exceeds the amount of the investment. Thus, if a given rate results in the rejection of many proposed investments that management intuitively feels are acceptable, or if not enough proposals are being sent to senior management for final approval, the indication is that this rate is too high. Conversely, if a given rate results in senior management's receiving a flood of project proposals, the indication is that the rate is too low. As a starting point in this trial-and-error process, a company may select a rate that other companies in the same industry use.

Cost of Capital. In economic theory the required rate of return should be equal to the company's **cost of capital.** This is the cost of debt capital plus the cost of equity capital, weighted by the relative amount of each in the company's capital structure.

Example. Assume a company in which the cost of debt capital (e.g., bonds) is 5 percent, the cost of equity capital (e.g., common stock) is 15 percent, 30 percent of the total capital is debt, and 70 percent of capital is equity. The cost of capital is calculated as follows:

Type	Capital Cost	Weight	Weighted Cost
Debt (bonds)....................	5%	0.3	1.5%
Equity (stock)....................	15	0.7	10.5
Total.........................		1.0	12.0%

Thus, the cost of capital is 12.0 percent.

In the example the 5 percent used as the cost of debt capital may appear to be low. It is low because it has been adjusted for the income tax effect of debt financing. Since interest on debt is a tax-deductible expense, each additional dollar of interest expense ultimately costs the company only $0.60 (assuming a tax rate of 40 percent) because income taxes are reduced by $0.40 for each additional interest dollar. For reasons to be explained, capital investment calculations should be made on an aftertax basis, so the rate of return should be an aftertax rate.

The problem with the cost-of-capital approach is that, although the cost of debt is usually known within narrow limits, the cost of equity is difficult to estimate. Conceptually, the cost of equity capital is the rate of return that equity investors expect to earn on their investment in the company's stock. These expectations are reflected in the stock's market price. Unfortunately, getting from the concept of the cost of equity to a specific number can be a difficult trip. Some companies use the **capital asset pricing model (CAPM)** to make the estimate. This method, the use of which requires that the company's shares be publicly traded, is described in finance texts. Suffice it to say here that the cost of equity capital is an estimate, and, unless the company's stock is actively traded, the estimate is quite imprecise.[2]

Selection of a Rate. Most companies use a judgmental approach in establishing the required rate of return. Either they experiment with various rates by the trial-and-error method described above, or they judgmentally settle upon a rate because they feel elaborate calculations are likely to be fruitless.

The required rate of return selected by the methods described above applies to investment proposals of *average* risk. (Average here refers to the risk of all of the firm's existing investments considered as a whole.) In general, the return demanded for an investment varies directly with the investment's risk. Thus, the required return for an individual investment

---

[2]For regulated public utilities the cost of equity capital is treated as a cost that a utility is allowed to recover, along with operating costs and interest, through the rates the utility charges its customers. In rate hearings conducted by public utility commissions, the cost of equity is always an issue, with each side's expert witnesses supporting different numbers as being correct.

project of greater-than-average risk should be higher than the average rate of return on all projects. Conversely, a project with below-average risk should have a lower required rate.

Effect of Nondiscretionary Projects.   Some investments are made to meet environmental, health, and safety requirements or to enhance employee wellness and satisfaction rather than based on an analysis of their profitability. These are often classified as **necessity projects.** Examples include pollution-control equipment, installation of devices to protect employees from injury, and in-company day-care and recreational facilities. These investments use capital but provide no readily identifiable cash inflows. Thus, if the other, profit-enhancing discretionary investments had a net present value of zero when discounted at the cost of capital, the company would not recover all of its capital costs. The discretionary projects not only must stand on their own feet but also must carry the capital-cost burden of the nondiscretionary (i.e., necessity) projects. For this reason many companies use a required rate of return that is higher than the cost of capital.

> **Example.**   Zelph Company typically has $10 million invested in capital projects, 20 percent of which represents necessity projects. If Zelph's cost of capital is 12 percent, its capital projects must earn $1.2 million per year in addition to recovering the amount invested. The $8 million of discretionary projects must therefore earn 15 percent, not 12 percent (because $8 million ∗ 0.15 = $1.2 million). Even the 15 percent is an understatement, because the $2 million capital invested in the necessity projects must also be recovered.

Economic Life   The **economic life of an investment** is the number of years over which cash inflows are expected as a consequence of making the investment. Even though cash inflows may be expected for an indefinitely long period, the economic life is usually set at a specified maximum number of years, such as 10, 15, or 20. This maximum is often shorter than the life actually anticipated both because of the uncertainty of cash inflow estimates for distant years and because the present value of cash inflows for distant years is so low that the amount of these cash inflows has no significant effect on the calculation. For example, at a discount rate of 12 percent, a $1 cash inflow in year 21 has a present value of only 9.3 cents.

The end of the period selected for the economic life is called the **investment horizon,** which suggests that beyond this time cash inflows are not visible. Economic life can rarely be estimated exactly. Nevertheless, it is important that the best possible estimate be made, for the economic life has a significant effect on the calculations.

When a proposed project involves the purchase of equipment, the economic life of the investment corresponds to the estimated service life of the equipment *to the user.* When thinking about the life of equipment, there is a tendency to consider primarily its *physical life*—the number of years until the equipment wears out. Although the physical life is an upper limit, in most cases the economic life of the equipment is considerably shorter than its physical life. The primary reason is that technological progress makes equipment obsolete and the investment in the equipment will cease to earn a return when it is replaced by even better equipment. (Computers provide an extreme example.)

The economic life also ends when the entity ceases to make profitable use of the equipment. This can happen because the operation performed by the equipment is made unnecessary by a change in style or process, because the market for the product made with the equipment has vanished, or because the entity decides (for whatever reason) to discontinue the product.

The key question is: Over what period of time is the investment likely to generate cash inflows for *this* entity? When the investment no longer produces cash inflows, its economic life has ended. In view of the uncertainties associated with the operation of an organization, most managers are conservative in estimating what the economic life of a proposed investment will be.

Cash Inflows
The earnings from an investment are the additional amounts of *cash* expected to flow in as a consequence of making the investment as compared with what the cash inflows would be if the investment were not made. The *differential* concept emphasized in the preceding chapter is therefore equally applicable here, and the discussion in that chapter should carefully be kept in mind in estimating cash inflows for the type of problem now being considered. In particular, recall that the focus is on *cash* inflows. Accounting numbers based on the accrual concept are not necessarily relevant.

Consider, for example, a proposal to replace existing equipment with better equipment. What are the cash inflows associated with this proposal? First, the existing equipment must still be usable. If it no longer works, there is no alternative and hence no analytical problem; it *must* be replaced. The comparison, therefore, is between (1) continuing to use the existing equipment (the base case) and (2) investing in the proposed equipment. The existing equipment has certain labor, material, power, repair, and other costs associated with its future operation. If the new equipment is proposed as a means of reducing costs, there will be different, lower costs associated with its use. The difference between these two amounts of cost is the cash inflow anticipated if the new equipment is acquired. (Note that in this example, the differential cash inflow is really a reduction in cash outflows.)

If the proposed equipment is not a replacement but instead increases productive capacity, the differential income from the higher sales volume is a cash inflow anticipated from the use of the proposed equipment. This differential income is the difference between the added sales revenue and the additional costs required to produce that sales revenue. These differential costs include any material, labor, selling costs, or other costs that would not be incurred if the increased volume were not produced and sold.

Often a project's cash flows can be analyzed with an implicit base case of the *status quo,* but this is not always a valid approach. For example, if a company chooses not to invest in more modern equipment, it may loose market position to competitors who are investing in such equipment. In this instance the base case will involve a worsening of present results rather than a level continuation of them. Thus, the cash flow analysis of the investment must be done carefully to ensure that the differential flows in fact reflect the difference between a "better future" (if the investment is made) and a "deteriorating past" (if it is not made).

Inflation. If inflation is expected to continue in future years, the purchasing power of a $1 cash inflow decreases as the length of time until the inflow will be received increases. The question arises as to whether future inflows should therefore be restated in terms of current (*Time Zero*) purchasing power before discounting them. In general, the answer is no. This is because the discount rate already includes an inflation component: the discount rate is higher if inflation is expected than the rate would be if there were no expectations of future inflation. The rate is higher either because (1) management intentionally increases the rate to account for future inflation or (2) because the company's cost of capital reflects the financial markets' inflation expectations (e.g., bond interest rates are higher in inflationary periods than in periods of stable prices).[3]

Depreciation

Depreciation on the proposed equipment is *not* an item of differential cost. In capital investment problems we are analyzing *cash* flows. The cash flow associated with acquisition of equipment is an *outflow* at Time Zero. This cash outflow is the amount of the investment against which the present value of the expected future cash inflows is compared. Because of the matching concept, accrual accounting capitalizes this initial cost as an asset and then uses a depreciation method to charge this cost systematically to the periods in which the asset is used. Recall that the accounting entry to record depreciation (dr. Depreciation Expense, cr. Accumulated Depreciation) has no impact on cash. Not only do these depreciation entries not affect cash; to treat them as outflows would result in double-counting the cost of the equipment in the present value analysis.

Depreciation on the existing equipment is likewise not relevant because the book value of existing equipment represents a sunk cost. For the reason explained in the preceding chapter, sunk costs should be disregarded.

Income Tax Impact. For alternative choice problems in which no investment is involved, aftertax income is 60 percent of pretax income,

---

[3] If the cash flows being discounted *are* expressed in constant-dollar terms, it is important that the discount rate not include an element for inflation (or an *inflation premium,* as it is called in some finance texts). Otherwise the cash flows would be doubly discounted for inflation, and the net present value would be understated.

assuming a tax rate of 40 percent.[4] Thus, if a proposed cost-reduction method is estimated to save $10,000 a year pretax, it will save $6,000 a year after tax. Although $6,000 is obviously not as welcome as $10,000 would be, the proposed cost-reduction method would increase income; in the absence of arguments to the contrary, the decision should be made to adopt it. This is the case with *all* the alternative choice problems discussed in the preceding chapter: if the proposal is acceptable on a pretax basis, it is also acceptable on an aftertax basis.

When depreciable assets are involved in a proposal, however, the situation is quite different. In proposals of this type, there is no simple relationship between pretax cash inflows and aftertax cash inflows. This is the case because, although depreciation is not a factor in estimates of operating cash flows, it *does* affect the calculation of taxable income; thus, it affects cash outflows because it affects the amount of tax payments. Because depreciation offsets part of what would otherwise be additional taxable income, it is called a *tax shield*. Depreciation "shields" the pretax cash inflows from the full impact of income taxes.

To calculate the *aftertax* cash inflows, we must take account of this **depreciation tax shield**. At the same time, for the reasons given above we must be careful not to permit the amount of depreciation itself to enter into the calculation of cash flows. Illustration 27–1 shows a net present value calculation including the tax shield.

ILLUSTRATION 27–1
CALCULATION OF NET PRESENT VALUE WITH TAX SHIELD

Assumed situation: A proposed machine costs $10,000 and will provide estimated pretax cash inflows of $3,500 per year for five years. The required rate of return is 12 percent, the tax rate is 40 percent, and straight-line depreciation is used.

	Taxable Income Calcuation	Present Value Calculation
Annual pretax cash inflow	$3,500	$ 3,500
Less: Additional depreciation	2,000	
Differential taxable income	1,500	
Differential income tax ($1,500 * 40%)		–600
Aftertax annual cash inflow		2,900
Present value of $2,900 over 5 years (factor = 3.605)		10,779
Less: Investment		10,000
Net present value		$ 779

The proposal is acceptable.

---

[4]As of 1994, the effective federal tax rate on corporations with $18.3 million or more taxable income was 35 percent. (The other extreme of the graduated rate structure was a 15 percent rate for companies earning up to $50,000 pretax.) In examples in this book, we use a 40 percent tax rate because (*a*) it makes illustrative calculations simpler to understand than would using 35 percent and (*b*) many corporations pay state and/or local taxes on income that raise their overall rate to around 40 percent.

Accelerated Depreciation.   For simplicity the example in Illustration 27–1 assumed straight-line depreciation. In fact, most companies use accelerated depreciation[5] in calculating taxable income because it increases the present value of the depreciation tax shield. Because accelerated depreciation results in nonlevel amounts of taxable income from year to year, Table B (which assumes a level flow each year) cannot be used in calculating present values. Instead, one must compute the aftertax income each year and find the present value of each annual amount by using Table A.

Differential Depreciation.   If the proposed asset is to replace an asset that has not been fully depreciated for tax purposes, then the tax shield is based on only the *differential depreciation*—the difference between depreciation on the present asset and that on the new one. If the new asset is purchased, the old one will presumably be disposed of, so its depreciation will no longer provide a tax shield to the operating cash flows. In this case the present value of the tax shield of the remaining depreciation on the old asset must be calculated (usually year by year), and this amount must be subtracted from the present value of the depreciation tax shield on the proposed asset.

Tax Effect of Interest.   Interest actually paid (as distinguished from imputed interest) is an allowable expense for income tax purposes. Therefore, if interest costs will be increased as a result of the investment, it can be argued that interest provides a tax shield similar to depreciation and that its impact should be estimated by the same method as for depreciation. Customarily, however, interest is *not* included anywhere in the calculations of either cash inflows or taxes. This is because the calculation of the required rate of return includes an allowance for the tax effect of interest: the estimate of the cost of debt is the aftertax cost of debt.

In problems where the method of financing is an integral part of the proposal, the tax shield provided by interest may appropriately be considered. In these problems the rate of return in the calculation is a return on the part of the investment that was financed by the shareholders' equity, not a return on the total funds committed to the investment.

> **Example.**   A company is considering an investment in a parcel of real estate and intends to finance 70 percent of the investment by a mortgage loan on the property. It may wish to focus attention on the return on its own funds, the remaining 30 percent. In this case it is appropriate to include in the calculation both the interest on the mortgage loan and the effect of this interest on taxable income. The rationale is that these debt funds—the mortgage—would not have been available to the company were it not investing in the real estate.[6]

---

[5]Since 1981 U.S. tax laws have used the term *accelerated cost recovery* rather than accelerated depreciation.

[6]Technically, this recognition of the tax effect of interest also assumes that the project-related debt (the mortgage loan, in the example) will not increase the perceived overall riskiness of the company and hence will not cause an increase in its overall cost of capital.

Investment   The investment is the amount of funds an entity risks if it accepts an investment proposal. The relevant investment costs are the *differential* costs—the cash outlays that will be made if the project is undertaken but that will not be made if it is not undertaken. The cost of the asset itself, any shipping and installation costs, and costs of training employees in the use of the new asset are examples of differential investment costs. These outlays are part of the investment, even though some of them may not be capitalized (treated as assets) in the accounting records.

Existing Assets.   If the purchase of a new asset results in the sale of an asset, the net proceeds from the sale reduce the amount of the differential investment. In other words, the differential investment represents the total amount of *additional* funds that must be committed to the investment project. The net proceeds from the existing asset are its selling price less any costs incurred in selling it and in dismantling and removing it, and adjusted for any income tax effects (described below).

Investments in Working Capital.   Although our examples of investments have thus far been fixed assets, an investment actually is the commitment, or long-term locking up, of funds in *any* type of asset. Thus, investments include long-term commitments of funds to finance additional inventories, receivables, and other current assets. In particular, if new equipment is acquired to produce a new product, additional funds will probably be required for inventories, accounts receivable, and increased cash needs. Part of this increase in current assets may be financed by increased accounts payable; the remainder of the financing must come from permanent capital. This additional working capital is as much a part of the Time Zero differential investment as is the capital required to finance the equipment itself.[7]

Deferred Investments.   Many projects involve a single commitment of funds at one moment of time, which we have called Time Zero. For some projects, on the other hand, the commitments are spread over a considerable period of time. The construction of a new facility may require disbursements over several years, or a proposal may involve the construction of one unit of a facility now and a second unit several years later. To make the present value calculations, these investments must be brought to a common point in time. This is done by the application of discount rates to the amounts of cash outflow involved. In general, the appropriate rate depends on the uncertainty that the investment will be made; the lower the uncertainty, the lower the rate. Thus, if the commitment is a definite one, the discount rate may be equivalent to the interest rate on high-grade bonds (which also represent a definite commitment). If, however, the future

---

[7]In the preceding chapter the differential investment in current assets was assumed to be for a *short* term; thus, it was assumed that short-term debt rather than permanent capital would be used to finance differential current assets. The cost of this short-term debt is one element of the differential holding costs that were described in that chapter.

investments will be made only if earnings materialize, then the rate can be the required rate of return.

Investment Tax Credit.   At times, under specified conditions, income tax regulations permit a company to take an **investment tax credit (ITC)** when it purchases new machinery, equipment, and certain other types of depreciable assets. In the tax law in effect until 1986, a company that bought a new machine for $100,000 could subtract 10 percent of that amount, or $10,000, from its current tax obligation. This was a direct reduction of $10,000 in the net investment, so the effective cash cost of the machine was only 90 percent of the invoice amount. The Tax Reform Act of 1986 eliminated the investment tax credit for equipment placed in service on or after January 1, 1986.[8]

Capital Gains and Losses.   When existing equipment is replaced by new equipment, the transaction may give rise to either a gain or loss, depending on whether the amount realized from the sale of the existing equipment is greater or less than its net book value. (If the new equipment is "of a like kind" to the equipment to be replaced, no gain or loss is recognized for tax purposes.) The Tax Reform Act of 1986 eliminated the previous years' different tax treatment of these so-called **capital gains and losses**; any such gain or loss is now taxed at the company's ordinary income tax rate. When existing assets are disposed of, the relevant amount by which the new investment is reduced is the *net* proceeds of the sale—the sale proceeds adjusted for the tax impact associated with the disposal. The adjustment will be downward if there is a gain, since the gain will create an additional tax outflow. Conversely, a loss will result in an upward adjustment of the sale proceeds.

Terminal Value   A project may have a value at the end of its time horizon. This **terminal value** is a cash inflow at that time.[9] In the analysis of the project, the *discounted* amount of the terminal value is added to the present value of the other cash inflows. Several types of terminal value are described in the following paragraphs.

---

[8]Note that the treatment of the tax credit for capital investment analysis purposes is independent of whether the company uses the flow-through method or the deferral method of accounting for the credit in its financial statements because we are interested solely in when the ITC reduces the cash outflow for tax payments. The 1986 tax act's repeal of the ITC does not constitute the first time that Congress has eliminated the ITC. It is thus possible that the ITC will be reinstated prior to publication of the next edition of this book, which is why we describe it here. In 1993 the Senate passed a tax bill that included reinstatement of the ITC, but the House bill did not include it, and it was eliminated in the conference committee that rationalized the conflicting bills.

[9]In some instances there is an additional *outlay* at the end of the project horizon. A notable example is the cost of decommissioning a nuclear power plant, which is hundreds of millions of dollars.

Residual Value. A proposed asset may have a **residual value** (i.e., salvage or resale value) at the end of its economic life. In many cases the estimated residual value is so small and occurs so far in the future that it has no significant effect on the decision. Moreover, any salvage or resale value realized may be approximately offset by removal and dismantling costs. In situations where the estimated residual value is significant, the net residual value (after removal costs and any tax effect from a capital gain or loss) is viewed as a cash inflow at the time of disposal and is discounted along with the other cash inflows.

Acquisitions and New Products. If one company acquires another, it usually expects its investment in the acquired company to produce a stream of cash inflows for an indefinitely long period. This may also be true with an investment in development of a new product. However, the estimates of cash inflows in later years are so speculative that many companies arbitrarily set the economic life of such a project at 10 years (5 in some companies).

After economic life is set, there is the problem of estimating terminal value. One approach to this problem is to assume that the acquired company or the new product is sold to another party on the assumed terminal date. Since the new buyer would be buying a stream of future cash inflows, the price could be arrived at by estimating the value of these cash flows, perhaps by applying a multiple to the cash flows of the terminal year. This selling price is then discounted, using the appropriate factor from Table A.

Working Capital. Often, the terminal value of investments in current assets is reasonably assumed to be approximately the same as the amount of the initial investment in them. That is, it is assumed that at the end of the project, these items can be liquidated at their original cost. (This cost can be adjusted upward if inflation is expected to increase the investment in working capital over the life of the project.) The amount of terminal current assets, net of any related accounts payable settlements, is treated as a cash inflow in the last year of the project, and its present value is found by discounting that amount at the required rate of return.

Nonmonetary Considerations

The quantitative analysis involved in a capital investment proposal does not provide the complete solution to the problem because it encompasses only those elements that can be reduced to numbers. As was true for the short-term alternative choice problems in the preceding chapter, a full consideration of the problem involves evaluating the *nonmonetary* factors.

Many investments are undertaken without a calculation of net present value. The necessity projects described earlier are a major example. For some of these, no economic analysis is necessary; if an unsafe condition is found, it must be corrected regardless of the cost. For many capital expenditure proposals in the research/development and general/administrative areas, no reliable estimate of increased revenues or decreased costs can be made, so the approach described here is not feasible.[10]

Even if the proposal is amenable to a quantitative analysis, the result is, at most, a guide to the decision maker. Other factors must be considered in arriving at the final decision, and in some cases their importance overwhelms the quantitative analysis. Among these factors are the following:

- The person proposing the project wants it to be approved, and therefore may give optimistic estimates of the numbers. Unless the person has a prior "track record" of such bias, it is difficult to detect.

- The *status quo* alternative may be incorrectly stated. For example, it may implicitly be assumed that if a proposal for a new process is rejected, the sales of the products made with the existing process will continue as is. However, failure to make the investment may cause the company's market position to deteriorate: competitors are making such investments, and the resulting better quality or customer responsiveness will cause the company's sales to decline if it does not make similar investments.

- Training costs and start-up costs associated with some new technology may be included in their entirety in the first proposal that will benefit from them, when in fact these costs will benefit similar follow-on projects in the future. This causes a negative bias in the analysis of the initial project and may suggest postponing investments that are in fact needed to remain competitive.

- On the other hand, a project proposal may have its scope—and hence its costs—understated in order to stay below the investment threshold where board of directors approval is required. This "foot-in-the-door" tactic often involves one or more follow-on proposals needed to complete the original proposal's partial solution.

- The proposal may overlook increases in "hidden" costs (usually step-function costs) that will result from the increased workload the project will create in various support departments. (The "just one" paradox described in the preceding chapter applies to capital investment proposals as well.)

In sum, the techniques described in this chapter are by no means the whole story of capital budgeting decisions. They are, however, the only part of the story that can be described as a definite procedure; the remainder generally is learned only through experience.

---

[10]Based on a survey of 100 large industrial companies, Thomas Klammer et al. reported that only 45 percent of respondents used discounting techniques for general and administrative costs, and only 8 percent used these techniques for "social expenditures." See "Capital Budgeting Practices—A Survey of Corporate Use," *Journal of Management Accounting Research,* Fall 1991, pp. 120–21.

Summary of the Analytical Process

Following is a summary of the previous presentation of the steps involved in using the **net present value method** in analyzing a proposed investment:

1. Select a required rate of return. This rate applies to projects deemed to be of average risk and may be adjusted for a specific proposal whose risk is felt to be above or below average.

2. Estimate the economic life of the proposed project.

3. Estimate the differential cash inflows for each year during the economic life, being careful that the base case is properly defined and quantified.

4. Find the net investment, which includes the additional outlays made at Time Zero, less the proceeds (adjusted for tax effects) from disposal of existing equipment and the investment tax credit, if any.

5. Estimate the terminal values at the end of the economic life, including the residual value of equipment and current assets that will be liquidated.

6. Find the present value of all the inflows identified in steps 3 and 5 by discounting them at the required rate of return, using Table A (for single annual amounts) or Table B (for a series of equal annual flows).

7. Find the net present value by subtracting the net investment from the present value of the inflows. If the net present value is zero or positive, decide that the proposal is acceptable insofar as the monetary factors are concerned.

8. Taking into account the nonmonetary factors, reach a final decision. (This part of the process is at least as important as all the other parts put together, but there is no way of generalizing about it.)

As an aid to visualizing the relationships in a proposed investment, it is often useful to use a diagram of the flows similar to that shown in Illustration 27–2.

OTHER METHODS OF ANALYSIS

So far, we have limited the discussion of techniques for analyzing capital investment proposals to the net present value (NPV) method. We shall now describe three alternative ways of analyzing a proposed capital investment: (1) the internal rate of return method, (2) the payback method, and (3) the unadjusted return on investment method.

Internal Rate of Return Method

When the NPV method is used, the required rate of return must be selected in advance of making the calculations because this rate is used to discount the cash inflows in each year. As already pointed out, the choice of an appropriate rate of return is a difficult matter. The **internal rate of return (IRR) method** avoids this difficulty. It computes the rate of return that equates the present value of the cash inflows with the present value of the

ILLUSTRATION 27–2
CASH FLOW DIAGRAM

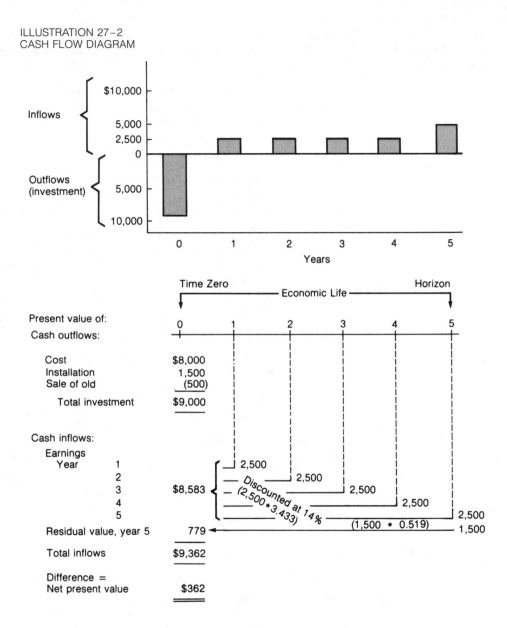

investment—the rate that makes the NPV equal zero. This rate is called the **internal rate of return,** or the **discounted cash flow (DCF) rate of return.** (The IRR method is sometimes called the **DCF method.**)

If the management is satisfied with the internal rate of return, then the project is acceptable. If the IRR is not high enough, then the project is unacceptable. In deciding what rate of return is high enough, the same considerations apply as those in selecting a required rate of return.

Level Inflows.   If the cash inflows are level (the same amount each year), the computation is simple. It will be illustrated by a proposed $1,200 investment with estimated cash inflow of $400 a year for four years. The procedure is as follows:

1. Divide the investment, $1,200, by the annual inflow, $400. The result, 3.0, is called the **investment/inflow ratio.**

2. Look across the four-year row of Table B. The column in which the figure closest to 3.0 appears shows the approximate rate of return. Since the closest figure is 3.037 in the 12 percent column, the return is approximately 12 percent.

3. If management is satisfied with a return of approximately 12 percent, then it should accept this project (aside from qualitative considerations). If it requires a higher return, it should reject the project.

The number 3.0 in the above example is simply the ratio of the investment to the annual cash inflows. Each number in Table B shows the ratio of the present value of a stream of cash inflows to an investment of $1 made today, for various combinations of rates of return and numbers of years. The number 3.0 opposite any combination of year and rate of return means that the present value of a stream of inflows of $1 a year for that number of years discounted at that rate is $3. The present value of a stream of inflows of $400 a year is in the same ratio; therefore, it is $400 times 3, or $1,200. If the number is more than 3.0, as is the case with 3.037 in the example above, then the return is correspondingly more than 12 percent.

In using Table B in this method, it is usually necessary to interpolate—to estimate the location of a number that lies between two numbers in the table. There is no need to be precise about these interpolations because the final result can be no better than the basic data, which are ordinarily only rough estimates. A quick interpolation made visually is usually as good as the accuracy of the data warrants.

Uneven Inflows.   If cash inflows are not the same in each year, the IRR must be found by trial and error. The cash inflows for each year are listed, and various discount rates are applied to these amounts until a rate is found that makes their total present value equal to the present value of the investment. This rate is the internal rate of return. This trial-and-error process can be quite tedious if the computations were made manually; in practice, computer programs and calculators perform the calculations quickly.

Payback Method

The number referred to above as the investment/inflow ratio is also called the **payback period** because it is the number of years over which the investment outlay will be recovered (paid back) from the cash inflows *if* the estimates turn out to be correct. That is, the project will "pay for itself" in this number of years. If a machine costs $1,200 and generates cash inflows of $400 a year, it has a payback of three years.

The **payback method** is often used as a quick but crude method for appraising proposed investments. If the payback period is equal to, or only slightly less than, the economic life of the project, then the proposal is clearly unacceptable. If the payback period is considerably less than the economic life, then the project begins to look attractive.

If several investment proposals have the same general characteristics, then the payback period can be used as a valid way of screening out the unacceptable proposals. For example, if a company finds that equipment ordinarily has a life of 10 years and if it requires a return of at least 15 percent, then the company may specify that new equipment will be considered for purchase only if it has a payback period of five years or less. This is because Table B shows that a payback period of five years is equivalent to a return of approximately 15 percent if the life is 10 years.

The danger of using payback as a criterion is that it gives no consideration to differences in the length of the estimated economic lives of various projects. There may be a tendency to conclude that the shorter the payback period, the better the project. However, a project with a long payback may actually be better than a project with a short payback if it will produce cash inflows for a much longer period of time. Also, the payback method makes no distinction between projects whose entire investment is made at Time Zero and those for which the investment is incurred over a period of several years.

Discounted Payback Method.   A more useful and more valid form of the payback method is the **discounted payback method.** In this method the present value of each year's cash inflows is found, and these are cumulated year by year until they equal or exceed the amount of investment. The year in which this happens is the **discounted payback period.** A discounted payback of five years means that the total cash inflows over a five-year period will be large enough to recover the investment *and* to provide the required return on investment. If the decision maker believes that the economic life will be at least this long, then the proposal is acceptable.

Unadjusted Return on Investment Method

The **unadjusted return on investment method** computes the net income expected to be earned from the project each year, in accordance with the principles of accrual accounting, including a provision for depreciation expense. The unadjusted return on investment is found by dividing the annual net income either by the amount of the investment or by one-half the amount of investment. (One-half of the investment is used on the premise that over the entire life of the project, an average of one-half the initial investment is outstanding because the investment is at its full amount at Time Zero and shrinks gradually to nothing by its terminal year.) This method is also referred to as the **accounting rate of return method.**

Since depreciation expense in accrual accounting provides, in a sense, for the recovery of the cost of a depreciable asset, one might suppose that the return on an investment could be found by relating the investment to its accrual accounting income after depreciation; but such is not the case. Earlier, we showed that an investment of $1,200 with cash inflows of $400 a year for four years has a return of 12 percent. In the unadjusted return method the calculation would be as follows (ignoring taxes):

Gross earnings	$400
Less depreciation (¼ of $1,200)	300
Net income	$100

Dividing net income ($100) by the investment ($1,200) gives an indicated return of 8⅓ percent. But we know this result is incorrect: the true return is 12 percent. If we divide the $100 net income by one-half the investment ($600), the result is 16⅔ percent, which is also incorrect.

This error arises because the unadjusted return method makes no adjustment for the differences in present values of the inflows of the various years. It treats each year's inflows as if they were as valuable as those of every other year whereas the prospect of an inflow of $400 next year is actually more attractive than the prospect of an inflow of $400 two years from now, and the latter $400 is more attractive than the prospect of an inflow of $400 three years from now.

The unadjusted return method, based on the *gross* amount of the investment, will always *understate* the true return. The shorter the time period involved, the more serious is the understatement. If the return is computed by using *one-half* the investment, the result is always an *overstatement* of the true return. A method that does not consider the time value of money cannot produce an accurate result.

Multiple Decision Criteria

Despite the conceptual superiority of the methods that involve discounting, surveys show that the payback and unadjusted return methods are also widely used in practice. Surveys also show that most companies use two or more methods in their investment proposal analyses—and the larger the company's annual capital budget, the greater the variety of techniques used.[11]

Several factors explain the use of decision criteria that do not involve discounting. First, some corporate managers tend to be concerned about the

[11]Klammer et al. (see footnote 10) report that for expansion projects 87 percent of the firms used the results of a discounting technique as their primary quantitative criterion. Of these about two-thirds used IRR and one-third used NPV as the primary technique. Most firms used more than one technique.

short-run impact a proposed project would have on corporate profitability as reported in the published financial statements. Thus, a project acceptable according to the NPV criterion may be rejected because it will reduce the company's reported net income and accounting return on investment (ROI) in the first year or two of the project. If management believes that the accounting ROI is used by securities analysts in evaluating a company's securities, management may use the unadjusted return method as one of its decision criteria.

The manager of a profit center may have similar concerns. If the manager feels that his or her career advancement is related to near-term profitability of the profit center, then a proposal that would have an adverse short-run impact on those profits may never be submitted to corporate headquarters. This is particularly likely to happen if the manager has incentive compensation tied to the profit center's short-term profitability. In this regard one must remember that *people* generate capital budgeting proposals; these proposals do not magically materialize on their own.

Another factor explaining why projects that have an acceptable NPV or IRR are sometimes rejected (or not even proposed) is managers' **risk aversion.** Although a given proposal may constitute an acceptable "gamble" from an overall company point of view, a manager may fear being penalized if the project does not work out as anticipated.[12]

Risk aversion probably explains the widespread use, despite its conceptual flaws, of the payback criterion. If project A has an estimated IRR of 20 percent and a payback of eight years whereas project B's estimated IRR is 15 percent and its payback is three years, the profit center manager may well prefer project B. Project A's time horizon is long, increasing the uncertainty of the estimates made in calculating its IRR. Moreover, it will be a number of years until it is known for sure whether A was a good investment. By eight years from now, the manager hopes to have been promoted at least once, and some unknown successor will reap most of project A's benefits. But project B can make the manager look good in the near term and help him or her to be promoted.

In sum, factors other than the true economic return (i.e., IRR) of a project greatly—and legitimately—influence whether a project is approved and even whether the project is formally proposed to top management.

PREFERENCE PROBLEMS

There are two classes of investment problems: screening problems and preference problems. In a **screening problem** the question is whether or not

---

[12]Many studies have demonstrated that most people (with the notable exception of compulsive gamblers) are risk averse. One elegant study has even concluded that bumble bees are risk averse! (See Leslie A. Real, "Animal Choice Behavior and the Evolution of Cognitive Architecture," *Science,* August 30, 1991, pp. 980–86.)

to accept a proposed investment. The discussion so far has been limited to this class of problem. Many individual proposals come to management's attention; by the techniques described above, those that are worthwhile can be screened out from the others.

In **preference problems** (also called **ranking,** or **capital rationing problems**), a more difficult question is asked: Of a number of proposals, each of which has an adequate return, how do they rank in terms of preference? If not all the proposals can be accepted, which ones are preferable? The decision may merely involve a choice between two competing proposals, or it may require that a series of proposals be ranked in order of their attractiveness. Such a ranking of projects is necessary when there are more worthwhile proposals than funds available to finance them, which is often the case.

Criteria for Preference Problems

Both the IRR and NPV methods are used for preference problems. If the internal rate of return method is used, the preference rule is as follows: the higher the IRR, the better the project. A project with a return of 20 percent is said to be preferable to a project with a return of 18 percent, *provided that the projects are of equal risk.* If the projects entail different degrees of risk, then judgment must be used to decide how much higher the IRR of the more risky project should be.

If the net present value method is used, the present value of the cash inflows of one project cannot be compared directly with the present value of the cash inflows of another unless the investments are of the same size. Most people would agree that a $1,000 investment that produced cash inflows with a present value of $2,000 is better than a $1,000,000 investment that produces cash inflows with a present value of $1,001,000, even though they each have an NPV of $1,000. In order to compare two proposals under the NPV method, therefore, we must relate the size of the discounted cash inflows to the amount of money risked. This is done simply by dividing the present value of the cash inflows by the amount of investment, to give a ratio that is called the **profitability index.** Thus, a project with an NPV of zero has a profitability index of 1.0. The preference rule is: the higher the profitability index, the better the project.

Comparison of Preference Rules

Conceptually, the profitability index is superior to the internal rate of return as a device for ranking projects. One reason is that higher discount rates will have been used in discounting the cash flows of more risky projects; thus, no judgmental adjustment of the profitability index ranking must be made. (Of course, deciding how much higher a discount rate to use was judgmental.) Also, the IRR method will not always give the correct preference between two projects with difference lives or with different patterns of earnings.

Example.   Proposal A involves an investment of $1,000 and a cash inflow of $1,200 received at the end of one year; its IRR is 20 percent. Proposal B involves an investment of $1,000 and cash inflows of $305 a year for five years; its IRR is only 16 percent. But proposal A is *not necessarily* preferable to proposal B. Proposal A is preferable only if the company can expect to earn a high return during the following four years on some other project in which the funds released from A at the end of the first year are reinvested. Otherwise, proposal B, which earns 16 percent over the whole five-year period, is preferable.

The incorrect signal illustrated in this example is not present in the profitability index method. Assuming a discount rate of 12 percent, the two proposals described above would be analyzed as follows:

Proposal	(a) Cash Inflow	(b) Discount Factor	(c) Present Value (a) * (b)	(d) Investment	Index (c) ÷ (d)
A	$1,200 – 1yr.	0.893	$1,072	$1,000	1.07
B	305 – 5yrs.	3.605	1,100	1,000	1.10

The profitability index signals that proposal B is better than proposal A. This is, in fact, the case if the company can expect to reinvest the money released from proposal A so as to earn no more than 12 percent on it. In most comparisons, however, IRR and the profitability index give the same relative ranking.

Although the profitability index method is conceptually superior to the IRR method and also easier to calculate (since there is no trial-and-error computation), the IRR method is widely used in practice—for two reasons. First, the profitability index method requires that the required rate of return be established before the calculations are made. But many analysts prefer to work from the other direction—to find the IRR and then see how it compares with their idea of the rate of return that is appropriate in view of the risks involved. Second, the profitability index is an abstract number that is difficult to explain, whereas the IRR is similar to interest rates and earnings rates with which every manager is familiar.

NONPROFIT ORGANIZATIONS

Nonprofit organizations make decisions involving the acquisition of capital assets, and their analytical techniques are essentially the same as those described above for profit-oriented companies.

The capital required for an investment in plant or equipment is obtained from either debt or equity capital or some combination of both. The cost of borrowed funds usually is easily measured. Equity capital is obtained either from past operations that have generated revenues in excess of expenses or from donors. If not invested in the project being analyzed, equity capital can be invested in other assets providing a return (e.g., certificates of deposit). The return on those alternative investments, adjusted for differences in risk, is the required rate of return.

In most respects estimates of cash inflows and outflows are the same in nonprofit organizations as for those described above. These organizations do not pay income taxes, so that part of the calculation is unnecessary. If the organization is reimbursed for services it performs (as is the case with hospitals and with university research contracts), then the proposal's effect on the calculation of the reimbursement amount must be taken into account. The net present value method is usually preferable to the internal rate of return method. The payback method and unadjusted return methods have the same weaknesses in nonprofit organizations as described above.

SUMMARY

A capital investment problem is essentially one of determining whether the anticipated cash inflows from a proposed project are sufficiently attractive to warrant risking the investment of funds in the project.

In the net present value method the basic decision rule is that a proposal is acceptable if the present value of the cash inflows expected to be derived from it equals or exceeds the present value of the investment. To use this rule, one must estimate (1) the required rate of return, (2) the economic life, (3) the amount of cash inflow in each year, (4) the amount of investment, and (5) the terminal value.

The internal rate of return method finds the rate of return that equates the present value of cash inflows to the present value of the investment—the rate that gives the project an NPV of zero. The simple payback method finds the number of years of cash inflows that are required to equal the amount of investment. The discounted payback method finds the number of years required for the discounted cash inflows to equal the initial investment. The unadjusted return on investment method computes a project's net income according to the principles of accrual accounting and expresses this profit as a percentage of either the initial investment or the average investment. The simple payback and unadjusted return methods are conceptually weak because they ignore the time value of money.

In preference problems the task is to rank two or more investment proposals in order of their desirability. The profitability index—the ratio of the present value of cash inflows to the investment—is the most valid way of making such a ranking.

The foregoing are monetary considerations. Nonmonetary considerations are often as important as the monetary considerations and in some cases are so important that no economic analysis is worthwhile. In some instances a manager's aversion to risk may cause a project with an acceptable return to be rejected or not even proposed.

Cases

CASE 27–1 Sinclair Company

A. Equipment Replacement

Sinclair Company is considering the purchase of new equipment to perform operations currently being performed on different, less efficient equipment. The purchase price is $250,000, delivered and installed.

A Sinclair production engineer estimates that the new equipment will produce savings of $72,000 in labor and other direct costs annually, as compared with the present equipment. She estimates the proposed equipment's economic life at five years, with zero salvage value. The present equipment is in good working order and will last, physically, for at least five more years.

The company can borrow money at 9 percent, although it would not plan to negotiate a loan specifically for the purchase of this equipment. The company requires a return of at least 15 percent before taxes on an investment of this type. Taxes are to be disregarded.

Questions

1. Assuming the present equipment has zero book value and zero salvage value, should the company buy the proposed equipment?

2. Assuming the present equipment is being depreciated at a straight-line rate of 10 percent, that it has a book value of $135,000 (cost, $225,000; accumulated depreciation, $90,000), and has zero net salvage value today, should the company buy the proposed equipment?

3. Assuming the present equipment has a book value of $135,000 and a salvage value today of $75,000 and that if retained for 5 more years its salvage value will be zero, should the company buy the proposed equipment?

4. Assume the new equipment will save only $37,500 a year, but that its economic life is expected to be 10 years. If other conditions are as described in (1) above, should the company buy the proposed equipment?

B. Replacement Following Earlier Replacement

Sinclair Company decided to purchase the equipment described in Part A (hereafter called "model A" equipment). Two years later, even better equipment (called "model B") comes on the market and makes the other equipment completely obsolete, with no resale value. The model B equipment costs $500,000 delivered and installed, but it is expected to result in annual savings of $160,000 over the cost of operating the model A equipment. The economic life of model B is estimated to be 5 years. Taxes are to be disregarded.

Questions

1. What action should the company take?

2. If the company decides to purchase the model B equipment, a mistake has been made somewhere, because good equipment, bought only two years previously, is being scrapped. How did this mistake come about?

C. Effect of Income Taxes

Assume that Sinclair Company expects to pay income taxes of 40 percent and that a loss on the sale or disposal of equipment is treated as a capital loss resulting in a tax saving of 28 percent of the loss. Sinclair uses an 8 percent discount rate for analyses performed on an aftertax basis. Depreciation of the new equipment for tax purposes is computed using the accelerated cost recovery system (ACRS) allowances; assume that these allowances were 35, 26, 15, 12, and 12 percent for years 1 to 5, respectively. The new equipment qualifies for a 5 percent investment tax credit, which will not reduce the cost basis of the asset for calculating ACRS depreciation for tax purposes.

Questions

1. Should the company buy the equipment if the facts are otherwise the same as those described in Part A (1)?

2. If the facts are otherwise the same as those described in Part A (2)?

3. If the facts are otherwise the same as those described in Part B?

D. Change in Earnings Pattern

Assume that the savings are expected to be $79,500 in each of the first three years and $60,750 in each of the next two years, other conditions remaining as described in Part A (1).

Questions

1. What action should the company take?

2. Why is the result here different from that in Part A (1)?

3. What effect would the inclusion of income taxes, as in Part C, have on your recommendation? (You are not expected to perform any more calculations in answering this question.)

CASE 27-2 Dhahran Roads*

As Christopher Eldon reread the telex, he was delighted that the nearly endless conversations with the Transportation Ministry of the Kingdom of Saudi Arabia were finally coming to a close. For several years Cummins, Epley, and Mayo (CEM), a U.S.-based construction contractor, had been looking for an appropriate project to serve as the basis for launching a Saudi subsidiary. As Senior Vice President for International Operations, Mr. Eldon had responsibility for developing new markets and had been personally involved in the Saudi undertaking. It now appeared that his efforts were about to pay off.

CEM had been selected as the prime contractor for a 168 million riyals[1] project. The project involved the reconstruction and upgrading of the highway network linking the several terminals of the Dhahran airport and connecting the entire complex with the city. This was the type of project on which CEM had established its international reputation for being a leading major construction contractor. Unfortunately, the total cost of the project was estimated to be 146 million riyals and, as a result, the 168 million riyals value provided only a 15 percent return. This was below the 18 percent hurdle rate required by

---

*Copyright © by the Darden Graduate Business School Foundation, Charlottesville, VA.

[1]The unit of currency in Saudi Arabia is the Saudi riyal (SR). In 1982, the exchange rate was approximately SR 1 = $0.29.

CEM for projects of this nature. On the other hand, it seemed a small cost to pay in order to establish a foothold in the booming Saudi construction market.

The telex requested from Mr. Eldon a response to the project proposal within a week. The wording of the contract would then be finalized in the subsequent weeks and the contract signed by mid-January 1983.

The Project. The terms of the proposed contract offered to CEM by the Ministry of Transportation contained several provisions:

- The ministry would advance to CEM 15 percent of the total value of the contract. The advance would be paid at the signing of the contract.

- If work progressed on schedule, CEM could bill the Ministry as milestones were reached in accordance with the following schedule:

1983	SR 12,000,000
1984	39,000,000
1985	39,000,000
1986	39,000,000
1987	39,000,000

- The Ministry would pay 80 percent of each bill received. Payment would of course be subject to a satisfactory inspection of the site by the Ministry. The 20 percent deduction would be withheld for (*a*) the recovery of the advance payment (15 percent) and (*b*) the accumulation of a retention fund (5 percent).

- Half of the retention would be reimbursed at the time of completion (end of 1987). The second half would be repaid at the end of 1988 provided that the roads did not show any flaws in their first year of use.

During the past several months, the CEM engineering department had inspected the site, confirmed the surveyings, and reviewed the drawings that had been provided by the Ministry. In the opinion of the Vice President of Engineering, the project presented no unusual challenges. It was very similar to several CEM projects in other countries that were now nearly complete and that had moved ahead without difficulty. For CEM to proceed, equipment would have to be ordered immediately so that it would be available in the fourth quarter of 1983 when earth moving would commence. The cost of the equipment would be 38 million riyals. Seventy-five percent of the cost would have to be paid upon placement of the order, the balance due on delivery. At the end of the project, the equipment would have no salvage value. The engineering department estimated that the cost of completing the project (not including the equipment) would be 108 million riyals. Eight million would be expended in 1983 for preliminary site work. The project would then proceed at a steady pace, costing approximately 25 million riyals per year for the following four years.

The project would be managed by one of CEM's experienced project managers, Matt Joseph. Mr. Joseph had just completed a major waterworks project in East Africa and was noted for strong engineering skills and tight cost control.

The contract would be signed by Saudi CEM, the Saudi Arabian subsidiary of CEM. Saudi CEM had been established in 1982 by Royal Decree upon the recommendation of the Ministry of Commerce and the approval of the Council of Ministers (the required procedure for the formation of a corporation in the Kingdom). The formation had been executed in anticipation of potential contracts such as the road system for the Dhahran airport. CEM represented 50 percent of the ownership of Saudi CEM; the other 50 percent was held by Saudi nationals. In Saudi Arabia corporate income taxes are paid only on that fraction of the earnings that is apportioned to the foreign interests in Saudi entities. As a result, the tax liability for the contract would be based on half the earnings (CEM's portion of the ownership) and would be assessed at the Kingdom's corporate tax rate of 45 percent. The taxes would be due at the completion of the project and would be paid by Saudi CEM.

Questions

1. What do you recommend regarding the project?
2. How sensitive is your recommendation to the assumptions you made in your base-case analysis? (This question is best explored by developing a spreadsheet model for the problem.)

CASE 27–3 Rock Creek Golf Club*

Rock Creek Golf Club (RCGC) was a public golf course, owned by a private corporation. In January the club's manager, Lee Jeffries, was faced with a decision involving replacement of the club's fleet of 40 battery-powered golf carts. The old carts had been purchased five years ago, and had to be replaced. They were fully depreciated; RCGC had been offered $200 cash for each of them.

Jeffries had been approached by two salespersons, each of whom could supply RCGC with 40 new gasoline-powered carts. The first salesperson, called here simply A, would sell RCGC the carts for $2,240 each. Their expected salvage value at the end of five years was $240 each.

Salesperson B proposed to lease the same model carts to RCGC for $500 per cart per year, payable at the end of the year for five years. At the end of five years, the carts would have to be returned to B's company. The lease could be canceled at the end of any year, provided 90 days' notice was given.

In either case, out-of-pocket operating costs were expected to be $420 per cart per year, and annual revenue from renting the carts to golfers was expected to be $84,000 for the fleet.

Although untrained in accounting, Jeffries calculated the number of years until the carts would "pay for themselves" if purchased outright, and found this to be less than two years, even ignoring the salvage value. Jeffries also noted that if the carts were leased, the five-year lease payments would total $2,500 per cart, which was more than the $2,240 purchase price; and if the carts were leased, RCGC would not receive the salvage proceeds at the end of five years. Therefore, it seemed clear to Jeffries that the carts should be purchased rather than leased.

When Jeffries proposed this purchase at the next board of directors meeting, one of the directors objected to the simplicity of Jeffries' analysis. The director had said, "Even ignoring inflation, spending $2,240 now may not be a better deal than spending five chunks of $500 over the next five years. If we buy the carts, we'll probably have to borrow the funds at 8 percent interest cost. Of course, our effective interest cost is less than this, since for every dollar of interest

*Adapted from an example used by Gordon B. Harwood and Roger H. Hermanson in "Lease-or-Buy Decisions," *Journal of Accountancy*, September 1976, pp. 83–87; © American Institute of Certified Public Accountants.

expense we report to the IRS we save 34 cents in taxes. But the lease payments would also be tax deductible, so it's still not clear to me which is the better alternative. There's a sharp new person in my company's accounting department; let's not make a decision until I can ask her to do some further analysis for us."

Questions

1. Assume that in order to purchase the carts, RCGC would have to borrow $89,600 at 8 percent interest for five years, repayable in five equal year-end installments. Prepare an amortization schedule for this loan, showing how much of each year's payment is for interest and how much is applied to repay principal. (Round the amounts for each year to the nearest dollar.)

2. Assume that salesperson B's company also would be willing to sell the carts outright at $2,240 per cart. Given the proposed lease terms, and assuming the lease is outstanding for five years, what interest rate is implicit in the lease? (Ignore tax impacts to the leasing company when calculating this implicit rate.) Why is this implicit rate different from the 8 percent that RCGC may have to pay to borrow the funds needed to purchase the carts?

3. Should RCGC buy the carts from A, or lease them from B? (Assume that if the carts are purchased, RCGC will use accelerated depreciation for income tax purposes, based on an estimated life of five years and an estimated residual value of $240 per cart. The accelerated depreciation percentages for years 1–5, respectively, are 35 percent, 26 percent, 15.6 percent, 11.7 percent, and 11.7 percent.)

4. Assume arbitrarily that purchasing the carts has an NPV that is $4,000 higher than the NPV of leasing them. (This is an arbitrary difference for purposes of this question and is not to be used as a "check figure" for your earlier calculations.) How much would B have to reduce the proposed annual lease payment to make leasing as attractive as purchasing the cart?

CASE 27–4   KLS Steel Company*

Headquartered in Milwaukee, KLS Steel Company is one of the larger regional steel service centers in the Midwest. KLS maintains warehouses in 15 medium-sized cities in the Midwest. Local firms purchase steel from these warehouses, rather than directly from steel producers, for a variety of reasons. Since service centers are able to buy in carload quantities, freight costs are often lower for a service center. Also, by purchasing for a large number of customers, a service center is able to obtain quantity discounts. Thus, the price to the user may be no higher than if the user were to purchase directly from a steel producer. At the same time, the user is able to reduce its steel inventories, since delivery time is often far shorter from a service center than from a steel producer.

As an additional incentive for their customers, steel service centers often provide special services, such as heat treating, cutting to length, and light assembly. A special service that KLS provides is cold-drawn steel (CDS). That service is performed in the Milwaukee warehouse for all 15 KLS warehouses. To cold-draw steel, one end of a steel bar is tapered, or pointed. The pointed end is then passed through a die (a block of hardened steel with a tapered hole through the center). On the other side of the die, a set of steel jaws grasps the pointed end of the bar and a heavy steel chain attached to the jaws pulls (or draws) the remainder of the steel bar through the die. That process compresses the steel slightly to provide more uniform qualities and to provide a smoother surface on the bar. Bars are then processed on a straightener, since the drawing process often puts a slight twist or bend in a bar. Finally, bars are cut to length on a saw. Although KLS owns other saws, one saw is required for the CDS department. In addition, an overhead crane is required specifically for that department. Several additional pieces of equipment are also used primarily by the CDS department.

The CDS department is of some concern to KLS's president:

> The previous president bought most of the drawing equipment from a bankrupt firm in 1957. We could just as easily purchase cold-drawn steel from firms who specialize in that process. There is no real reason for us to provide the service, other than that we own the equipment. Since we have the equipment, we may as well stay in the business. We process about 17,000 tons a year. Although the CDS charge is based on a number of factors, on average we charge about $180 a ton for the service. If we eliminated our CDS department, we would buy CDS from a specialty producer and then resell it. We would make about $5 a ton, after tax, if we used an outside supplier. That is reasonably close to what we do in-house (see Exhibit 1). If we tried to sell our equipment, I know that we wouldn't get much more than $100,000 (after tax), so the department is performing reasonably well.

> The problem is that some of the equipment is getting old. The crane, which was purchased in 1958, is still in pretty good shape. However, the draw bench and the straightener were originally purchased in the 1930s. The draw bench uses too much electricity, and scrap cost is too high. Both the draw bench and the straightener are often broken, and repair costs keep increasing. Even though the saw is only 15 years old and is still in good shape, newer ones

are faster. The draw bench may be a good investment since a new one would save quite a bit on repairs and would also save on scrap and electricity. We can analyze the other equipment later.

> We use discounted cash flow analysis to evaluate all corporate investments and expect to earn 10 percent, after tax, on the investment. I've had our accountants and engineers put together an estimate of operating costs for both the new and the old draw bench (Exhibit 2). I expect no real changes in our operations. Sales, adjusted for inflation, will probably stay at the 1987 level. I would expect our costs to go up at about the same rate as inflation, except for repair costs on the equipment. Exhibit 2 shows all amounts in 1987 dollars, since the 10 percent goal is in addition to inflation.

> I'm concerned about one other thing. I have a friend at a consulting firm in Boston. She claims that you shouldn't invest in businesses where you have a low market share and low growth. That is clearly the case with our CDS department, but if an investment in that department has a greater discounted cash flow than an investment in other departments, it seems to me we have

---

EXHIBIT 1

KLS STEEL COMPANY
CDS Department Income Statement
Year Ended December 31, 1987

Service revenues*	$3,083,000
Cost of sales†	2,665,000
Selling, general, and administrative	238,000
Income before taxes	180,000
Income taxes	90,000
Net income	$ 90,000

* Does not include revenues from the price of the "raw" steel that undergoes the cold-drawing process.

† Includes straight-line depreciation of $4,000 per year. All equipment will be fully depreciated in five years. The draw bench is already fully depreciated. Does not include "raw" steel cost, except for scrap losses.

EXHIBIT 2
DRAW BENCH PROPOSAL
(all amounts in 1987 dollars)

	1987	1/1/88	1988	1989	1990
Operating expense:					
1. Current equipment..................................	288,000		290,000	350,000*	288,000
2. New draw bench			202,000	204,000	206,000
3. Savings (1 – 2).....................................			88,000	146,000	82,000
4. Less: Depreciation (DDB)†.........................			100,000	80,000	64,000
5. Net savings before tax (3 – 4)			(12,000)	66,000	18,000
6. State and federal tax (50%)........................			6,000	(33,000)	(9,000)
7. Investment tax credit...............................			50,000	—	—
8. Net change in income (5 + 6 + 7)			44,000	33,000	9,000
9. Add: Depreciation			100,000	80,000	64,000
10. Add: Increase in salvage value‡.....................			—	—	—
11. Cash flow (8 + 9 + 10)			144,000	113,000	73,000
Investment, net of trade-in...........................		500,000			
NPV (10%)..		59,203			
IRR		12.99%			

*Includes equipment overhaul and additional production overtime needed because of overhaul. All overhaul costs are expensed in the year in which they are incurred.
†Zero salvage value, double-declining-balance depreciation will be used for both income tax and financial reporting purposes.
‡Salvage value in 1997, aftertax, is estimated to be:

	New Draw Bench	Old Draw Bench
Draw bench........................	$ 85,000	$10,000
Remaining equipment	40,000	40,000
Total........................	$125,000	$50,000

to invest in the CDS department. I asked her about that, but she seemed to think that discounted cash flow didn't work for such businesses.

Questions

1. Should KLS purchase the new draw bench?
2. Evaluate the consultant's comment.

CASE 27–5 Climax Shipping Company*

The controller of the Climax Shipping Company, located near Pittsburgh, was preparing a report for the executive committee

_____
* Copyright © by the President and Fellows of Harvard College. Harvard Business School case 154-015.

regarding the feasibility of repairing one of the company's steam riverboats or of replacing the steamboat with a new diesel-powered boat.

Climax was engaged mainly in the transportation of coal from nearby mines to steel mills, public utilities, and other industries in

EXHIBIT 2 *(concluded)*
DRAW BENCH PROPOSAL
(all amounts in 1987 dollars)

1991	1992	1993	1994	1995	1996	1997
300,000	355,000*	290,000	304,000	360,000*	292,000	308,000
208,000	210,000	212,000	250,000*	210,000	212,000	214,000
92,000	145,000	78,000	54,000	150,000	80,000	94,000
51,200	40,960	32,770	32,770	32,770	32,770	32,760
40,800	104,040	45,230	21,230	117,230	47,230	61,240
(20,400)	(52,020)	(22,615)	(10,615)	(58,615)	(23,615)	(30,620)
—	—	—	—	—	—	—
20,400	52,020	22,615	10,615	58,615	23,615	30,620
51,200	40,960	32,770	32,770	32,770	32,770	32,760
—	—	—	—	—	—	75,000
71,600	92,980	55,385	43,385	91,385	56,385	138,380

the Pittsburgh area. The company's steamboats also, on occasion, carried cargoes to places as far away as New Orleans. The boats owned by Climax were all steam-powered, and were between 15 and 30 years old.

The steamboat the controller was concerned about, the Cynthia, was 23 years old and required immediate rehabilitation or replacement. It was estimated that the Cynthia had a useful life of another 20 years provided that adequate repairs and maintenance were made. Whereas the book value of the Cynthia was $165,900, it was believed that she would bring somewhat less than this amount, possibly around $105,000, if she were to be sold. The total of immediate rehabilitation costs for the Cynthia was estimated to be $483,000. It was estimated that these general rehabilitation expenditures would extend the useful life of the Cynthia for about 20 years.

New spare parts from another boat, which had been retired recently, were available for use in the rehabilitation of the Cynthia. An estimate of their fair value, if used on the Cynthia, was $182,700, which was their book value. Use of these parts would, in effect, decrease the immediate rehabilitation

costs from $483,000 to $300,300. It was believed that if these parts were sold on the market, they would bring only around $126,000. They could not be used on any of the other Climax steamboats.

Currently, the Cynthia was operated by a 20-member crew. Annual operating costs for this crew would be approximately as follows:

Wages and fringes.....................	$488,400
Commissary supplies....................	64,760
Repairs and maintenance................	102,500
Fuel and lubricants....................	147,200
Misc. service and supplies.............	50,400
Total.............................	$853,260

It was estimated that the cost of dismantling and scrapping the Cynthia at the end of her useful life after the overhaul would be offset by the value of the scrap and used parts taken off the boat.

An alternative to rehabilitating the steamboat was the purchase of a diesel-powered boat. Quapelle Company, a local boat manufacturer, quoted the price of $1,365,000 for a diesel boat. An additional $315,000 for a basic parts inventory would be necessary to service a diesel boat, and such an inventory would be sufficient to service up to three diesel boats. If four or more diesels were purchased, however, it was estimated that additional spare parts inventory would be necessary.

The useful life of a diesel-powered boat was estimated to be 25 years, at the end of which time the boat either would be scrapped or would be completely rehabilitated at a cost approximating that of a new boat. The controller did not contemplate the possibility of diesel engine replacement during the 25-year life, since information from other companies having limited experience with diesel-powered riverboats did not indicate that such costs needed to be anticipated. But a general overhaul of the engines, costing at current prices $250,000, would be expected every 10 years.

One of the features Quapelle pointed out was the 12 percent increase in average speed of diesel-powered boats over the steamboats. The controller discounted this feature, however, because the short runs and lock-to-lock operations involved in local river shipping would prohibit the diesel boats from taking advantage of their greater speed. There was little opportunity for passing, and diesel-powered boats would have to wait in turn at each lock for the slower steamboats. The controller felt it would be many years, if at all, before diesel boats displaced the slower steamboats.

After consulting Quapelle and other companies operating diesel-powered boats, the controller estimated that the annual operating costs of a diesel-powered boat would total $657,880, broken down as follows:

Wages and fringes, crew of 13	$342,170
Commissary supplies	42,080
Repairs and maintenance*	91,140
Fuel and lubricants	120,960
Extra stern repairs	8,400
Misc. service and supplies	53,130
Total	$657,880

* Excluding possible major overhaul of diesel engines.

Although the controller had not considered the matter, you may assume that at the end of the 20th year the diesel boat would have a realizable value of $140,000, and the remaining inventory of parts would have a book and realizable value of $157,500.

The controller was also concerned about a city smoke ordinance that would take effect in two years. To comply with the ordinance, all hand-fired steamboats had to be converted to stoker firing. Several of the Climax steam boats were already stoker-fired; the Cynthia, however, was hand-fired. The additional cost of converting the Cynthia to stoker firing was estimated to be $168,000, provided it was done at the same time as the general rehabilitation. This $168,000 included the cost of stokers and extra hull conversion and was not included in the $483,000 rehabilitation figure.

The controller also knew that if $483,000 were spent presently in rehabilitating the Cynthia and it was found out later that no relief, or only temporary relief for one or two years, was to be granted under the smoke ordinance, the cost of converting to stoker firing would no longer be $168,000, but around $290,000. The higher cost would be due to rebuilding, which would not be necessary if the Cynthia was converted to stoker firing at the time of her general rehabilitation.

Conversion would reduce the crew from 20 to 18, with the following details:

Wages and fringes	$445,700
Commissary supplies	58,300
Repairs and maintenance*	102,500
Fuel and lubricants*	147,200
Misc. service and supplies*	50,400
Total	$804,100

* These costs would be the same for a crew of 20 or 18.

All of the operating data the controller had collected pertaining to crew expenses were based on a two-shift, 12-hour working day, which was standard on local riverboats. He had been informed, however, that the union representing crew members wanted a change to a three-shift, eight-hour day. If the union insisted on an eight-hour day, accommodations on board the steamers or the diesels would have to be enlarged. The controller was perturbed by this fact because he knew the diesels could readily be converted to accommodate three crews whereas steamers could not.

How strongly the union would insist on the change and when it would be put into effect, if ever, were questions for which the controller could get no satisfactory answers. He believed that the union might have a difficult time in getting acceptance of its demands for three eight-hour shifts on steamers, since it would be very difficult, if not impossible, to convert the steamers to hold a larger crew because of space limitations. The controller thought that the union might succeed in getting its demands accepted, however, in the case of diesel-powered boats. One of the diesel boats currently operating in the Pittsburgh area had accommodations for three crews, although it was still operating on a two-shift basis. The diesel boats that Quapelle offered to build for Climax could be fitted to accommodate three crews at no additional cost.

Another factor the controller was considering was alternative uses of funds. Climax had sufficient funds to buy four diesel-powered boats; however, there were alternative uses for these funds. The other projects management was considering had an estimated return of at least 10 percent after taxes. The income tax rate at the time was 45 percent.

As a further inducement to secure a contract to build a diesel boat, Quapelle offered to lease a diesel boat to Climax. The lease terms offered called for year-end annual payments of $222,235 for 15 years. At the end of 15 years, when Quapelle had in effect recovered the value of the boat, it would charge a nominal rental of $11,760 a year. Title to the boat would continue to remain in the hands of Quapelle. Climax would incur all costs of operating and maintaining the boat, including general overhaul every 10 years, and would still need to invest $315,000 in a basic spare parts inventory.

Questions

1. If management chooses to rehabilitate the Cynthia, should the stoker conversion be done immediately or delayed for two years? (For simplicity, assume straight-line depreciation in all of your analyses. Also, assume that no investment tax credit was in effect at the time.)

2. If Climax acquires the diesel-powered boat, should they buy it or lease it?

3. Which alternative would you recommend?

4. (Optional) What is the effective interest rate on the 15year Quapelle lease?

28

Management Accounting
System Design

When a person looks at a photograph or a painting, the eye takes in the total picture and conveys it to the brain. Even at a first glance the relationships among the parts of the picture can be perceived. By contrast a book must be read a page at a time, and only when one has finished the book can the total "picture" described in the book be perceived. In this chapter we will briefly review some of the topics and concepts of management accounting to help tie together the various parts of the total picture. This review will serve as the basis for a discussion of some key elements in the design of a management accounting system.

TYPES OF ACCOUNTING INFORMATION

Part 1 of this book emphasized financial accounting information, which is prepared in accordance with generally accepted accounting principles (GAAP) and reported to shareholders and other interested outside parties. Unlike financial accounting, which is built around the single basic equation, Assets = Liabilities + Owners' Equity, management accounting has three principal purposes, each of which requires a different cost construct.

Two of these three purposes are measurement and control; information used for these purposes is taken directly from the management accounting system. For the measurement purpose the system collects the full cost of cost objects; for the control purpose it collects costs incurred in responsibility centers. The third purpose of management accounting is to aid in the solution of alternative choice problems. Data used for this purpose are not found directly in the management accounting system because the relevant data vary with the nature of the specific alternative choice problem being analyzed. (Although these comments refer to costs, they are also applicable to revenues and balance sheet items.)

Measurement

Cost is a measurement, in monetary terms, of the amount of resources used for some purpose, called a cost object. The full cost of a cost object is the sum of its direct costs and a fair share of its applicable indirect costs. The most pervasive cost objects in a company are the goods and services it produces and sells, and companies operate cost accounting systems to collect these product costs on a routine basis. Generally, these systems account for the full costs of a product, although a small minority of companies use variable costing systems. The full cost principle can be used to measure the full cost of any activity of interest (e.g., the organization's training programs), not just product costs. Full costs are used in financial reporting to measure inventories and the related cost of sales. Full costs are used in management accounting to arrive at normal prices and regulated rates and to analyze the economic performance of business segments and the profitability of the products these segments produce and sell.

Control

The management accounting system is also structured so that it collects costs by responsibility centers, which are organization units headed by managers who are held accountable for these units' performance. This part of the system is used for control. For this purpose the system has data on planned inputs and outputs and also on actual inputs and outputs. In the management control process, managers compare these planned and actual amounts, identify the source of the significant variances, investigate their causes, and take appropriate actions. Behavioral considerations are at least as important as accounting considerations in this process.

Alternative Choice Problems

In finding the preferable alternative in an alternative choice problem, the analyst considers costs that are different under one set of conditions than they would be under another. These amounts are differential costs. (The analysis may also consider differential revenues and assets.) In shorter-run problems a contribution analysis is appropriate; longer-run problems, called capital budgeting problems, usually involve estimating the present values of revenue inflows and cost outflows. Relevant data for analyzing an alternative choice problem are not identified as such in the accounting system because the data depend on the nature of the specific problem. Much judgment must be exercised in these analyses; for example, costs that are not differential in the short run may be differential in the longer run.

The reader is asked at this point to refer back to Illustration 15–3, which summarizes the distinct uses of the different types of management accounting information—and which should seem far less vague now than when first encountered.

Relative Importance	Each of the three cost constructs is useful for one of the three purposes, as indicated in Illustration 15–3, but it may not be relevant for another purpose, and indeed may be misleading if used for that purpose. An attempt to determine their relative importance is pointless; an organization needs all three.

In particular, a classroom environment may foster a tendency to overemphasize the importance of alternative choice problems because the identification of differential costs is intellectually challenging, and these decisions have important consequences (especially the "big bucks" capital investment problems). Nevertheless, in most organizations these differential cost problems arise far less frequently than decisions involving the use of full cost information. For example, a selling price must be arrived at for every product. In profit-seeking organizations the profitability of these products, along with that of the business units that produce and market them, is (or at least should be) analyzed routinely. All organizations need to measure costs incurred in responsibility centers as a foundation of the management control process.

COST CATEGORIES

In discussing both financial and management accounting, we have introduced a number of different categories of *cost*. Different concepts underlie the various adjectives used to modify that slippery term. The following review may help clarify the distinctions among eight of the various ways of categorizing costs.

1. Accounting Treatment.   When a cost is incurred, it is treated either (1) as a reduction in retained earnings (i.e., an expense), in which case we say the cost has been *expensed,* or (2) as an asset, in which case the cost is said to have been *capitalized.* Costs that are expensed as they are incurred are called **period costs.** Capitalized costs include not only the cost of plant and equipment and of materials and supplies inventories, but also the cost of work in process and finished goods inventories. These latter two are **product costs.** In accord with the matching concept, product costs are expensed when the product is sold.

2. Traceability to a Cost Object.   Costs that are traced to, or caused by, a single cost object are **direct costs** of that cost object. Costs associated with two or more cost objects jointly are **indirect costs** of those cost objects. The

full cost of a cost object is the sum of its direct costs and its fair share of indirect costs.

The terms *direct cost* and *indirect cost* are meaningless in isolation; they must be related to a specified cost object. For example, a plant manager's salary is a direct cost of the plant but an indirect cost of each product made in the plant (unless the plant makes only one product). Indirect production costs are frequently called **production overhead, factory overhead,** or (less descriptively) simply **overhead costs.**

3. Cost Element.   The adjective modifying cost may indicate the **cost element** for which the cost was incurred. Examples include materials cost, direct labor cost, interest cost, selling cost, and so on.

4. Behavior with Respect to Volume.   An item of cost whose total amount varies proportionately with volume is called a **variable cost.** The clearest example is materials cost in a production setting. A cost item whose total does not vary at all with volume is called a **nonvariable,** or **fixed, cost.** Some costs vary in the same direction as, but less than proportionately with, volume; these are **semivariable costs.** They can be decomposed into their fixed and variable cost components. Still other costs increase in "chunks" as capacity is added to an activity; these are **step-function costs.** Remember that in describing cost behavior with respect to volume, a relevant range is stated (or at least implied). Also, a time period must be stated (or implied); a cost that is fixed with respect to volume in a one-week period may be variable with respect to volume for a year.

5. Time Perspective.   Many cost data are for economic events that have already transpired; these are **historical costs,** or **actual costs.** However, for many uses—particularly in management accounting—the relevant data are *future costs.* Estimated future costs may take the form of **standard costs** (usually per-unit amounts) or **budgets** (usually amounts per time period).

6. Degree of Managerial Influence.   If a responsibility center manager can significantly influence the amount of an item of cost, that item is said to be a **controllable cost;** otherwise, it is **noncontrollable** (by that manager). Note that this cost concept refers to a specific manager. Responsibility center costs not controllable by the center's manager presumably are controllable by someone else in the organization.

7. Ability to Budget "Right" Amounts.   If the "right," or "proper," amount to spend for some activity can be predetermined, then that cost item is an **engineered cost.** Direct materials cost in a production setting is the clearest example. If, on the other hand, the proper amount to spend is a matter of judgment, the item is a **discretionary cost** (sometimes called a **programmed,** or **managed, cost**). A cost that is the inevitable consequence of some past decision can be budgeted with certainty; this is a **committed cost** (for example, rent that was established in a 5-year lease signed last year). Another type of committed cost is a **sunk cost** (an example is depreciation).

8. Changeability with Respect to Specified Conditions.   Costs that are different under one set of conditions than they would be under another set

ILLUSTRATION 28–1
SUMMARY OF TYPES OF COST

Full Costs	*Responsibility Costs*	*Differential Costs*
Direct: Costs traced to a single cost object.	Costs incurred in responsibility centers.	Costs that would be different if a proposed alternative were adopted. Construction depends on nature of the specific problem.
Indirect: Not traced; an equitable portion is allocated to the cost object.		
Full: Direct costs + Indirect costs.	**Controllable:** Manager can exercise significant (but not necessarily complete) influence.	
	Noncontrollable: Other costs, including committed and allocated costs.	**Variable:** Costs that vary proportionately with volume.
Capitalized: Asset to be amorized over future periods.		**Fixed:** Costs that do not vary with volume.
Product: Direct + Indirect production cost of a product.	**Engineered:** "Right" amount can be estimated.	**Semivariable:** Costs that vary with volume, but less than proportionately. Can be decomposed into variable and fixed components.
Period: Expense of current period	**Discretionary:** Amount subject to manager's discretion; agreed on in budget process.	
	Committed: Will not change in the short run (a type of fixed cost).	**Step-function:** Costs that increase in discrete "chunks" as capacity is added to an activity.*
Full costs are either historical costs or estimated future costs.	Responsibility costs are either historical costs or estimated future costs.	Differential costs are always estimated future costs.

*An understanding of variable, fixed, semivariable, and step-function cost behavior is important for *all three* purposes of management accounting but is particularly important in analyzing alternative choice problems.

are called **differential costs** (or **incremental costs** or **avoidable costs**). The notion of differential costs is meaningful only for a specified problem. That is, two or more alternative situations (one of which may be the status quo) must be specified in order for differential costs to be calculated.

These eight ways of categorizing costs are not all-inclusive. Even though we used almost 30 different cost terms in describing those eight categories, we did not mention replacement costs, opportunity costs, imputed costs, marginal costs, or several other kinds of costs. However, the person who understands the differences among these eight categorizations—and some of the distinctions are quite subtle—is in a good position to think and communicate clearly about whatever costs may be involved in a particular report or problem analysis. Illustration 28–1 summarizes a number of these cost distinctions.

DESIGNING THE MANAGEMENT ACCOUNTING SYSTEM

To conclude our summary of management accounting, we will highlight some of the desirable characteristics of management accounting systems that we have mentioned in previous chapters. As we have already stressed, the system should fit with other organizational characteristics, including goals and objectives, nature of the goods and services produced, organization structure, and the level of sophistication that managers have in using management accounting information. Thus, all of the considerations we mention below will not necessarily apply to a given organization.

Accounting Database

As we have seen in both Part 1 and Part 2 of this book, accounting information does not just magically materialize when it is needed. The raw data must be "captured" from various **source documents.** These documents include vendor invoices, employee time cards and other personnel-related records, customer billing and payment records, and so forth. Increasingly, the raw data are entered into the accounts by scanners or other automatic devices. These raw data constitute the organization's **operating information,** which is recorded using double-entry recordkeeping procedures in the organization's **accounts.** The complete set of these accounts, called the **chart of accounts,** determines the structure of the organization's accounting database.

Level of Detail

A major design issue in management accounting is how detailed the chart of accounts should be. For financial accounting purposes not much detail is required. For example, solely for financial accounting purposes all sales could be credited to a single Sales Revenue account and debited either to Cash or Accounts Receivable. However, this would make it difficult to perform an analysis of sales by product line, profit center, sales district, or individual customer.

The types of analysis managers want performed on a more-or-less routine basis determine the amount of detail in the chart of accounts. In effect, the chart of accounts design question is: For each item of cost (or revenue or assets), how many "ID tags" do we want to "tie onto" that item?

> **Example.** On June 5 a department of the Farnsworth Company used $1,000 worth of materials for a product it was making that day. Any of the following questions might be asked concerning this event:
>
> 1. What *specific* materials were used?
> 2. What was the *product line* to which the product belonged?
> 3. In which *department* were the materials used?

The first question relates to a more detailed *cost element* description, the second to a *program* description, the third to a *responsibility center* description. Answering each of these three questions requires "hanging a separate ID tag" on the item of cost.

More formally, answering all three implies that the chart of accounts should include as one detailed account, "Material X Used in Product Y in Department Z." If Farnsworth Company uses 100 raw materials for 20 products that are made in 10 responsibility centers, this could require as many as *20,000* (= 100 * 20 * 10) detailed accounts, all relating only to a *single* general category, the materials component of work in process inventory.

In the above example if the company wants to report product and responsibility center data on a routine basis, then the account structure must incorporate the second and third ID tags. If, in addition, it routinely wants to know how many dollars worth of material X is used throughout the company (as opposed to all kinds of material used collectively), the first ID tag is necessary. Many organizations *do* want detailed information on all three of these dimensions, so the example does not exaggerate how many detailed account "building blocks" larger organizations actually have. Fortunately, computers have the ability to find, manipulate, and aggregate these building blocks quickly.

The accounting database can be further elaborated if an organization wants to segregate fixed and variable cost elements. (Remember that semi-variable costs also can be decomposed into fixed and variable components, and, if the time period is explicit, step-function costs can be approximated by either a variable or a fixed cost.) This elaboration might be appropriate if the organization performed many short-run differential cost analyses or if it wanted to prepare internal income statements in a contribution margin format. A still further elaboration would occur if the organization wanted the account structure to identify costs as to whether or not they are controllable in the responsibility center in which they are incurred (or to which they are charged).

There are no formulas to determine the "right" level of detail in the account structure. Here, as with other system design issues, management must exercise judgment in making the omnipresent "value of information" benefit/cost trade-off because, to date, the theoretical field of **information economics** has provided little practical help in making such decisions. It does seem to be true, however, that more organizations feel they suffer from having too little detail in the accounting database than too much. In many instances long-standing charts of accounts were not reviewed when the organization computerized its accounting database. Although the need for more detail is recognized today, the costs of rewriting all of the computer programs to accommodate more detail may be viewed as prohibitive. On the other hand, there are examples of unnecessarily costly systems, whose designers concerned themselves with providing information for any conceivable analysis rather than just for those that are more or less routinely performed.

Cost Accounting Systems

An organization faces many choices when designing its cost accounting system. Those choices include job costing versus process costing, actual costs versus standard costs, volume measures, and several other choices that were listed in the final section of Chapter 19. Many organizations' activities are sufficiently diverse that, in effect, several cost accounting systems must be designed for a given organization. However, there should be one integrated accounting database underlying the several systems because each system in essence simply aggregates account building blocks in a different way.

Differential Analyses. The design of a cost accounting system also affects the ease with which certain differential accounting analyses can be performed. However, by definition, the ad hoc nature of these analyses means that there can be no such thing as a differential costing *system*. Moreover, differential costs are future costs. Although data in the cost accounting system can aid in estimating the relevant differential costs for a particular alternative choice problem, strictly speaking, historical costs themselves are not relevant in differential analyses.

Management Control Systems

Whereas the availability of detailed accounting database information may be crucial to support full cost and differential accounting analyses, behavioral considerations are at least as important as responsibility accounting information in the management control process. Every existing or proposed practice in the management control system must be held up to the **goal congruence** test by considering these questions:

1. What action will it motivate managers to take in their own perceived self-interest?
2. Will this action be in the best interests of the organization?

Organizations sometimes fail to consider these questions, particularly when establishing policies for such things as how transfer prices will be set or for the specifics of measuring the return on investment (ROI) of various investment centers. This neglect often results in a procedure's having unintended consequences, which in hindsight do not really seem all that surprising.

> **Example.** In measuring an investment center's ROI, most companies include fixed assets in the investment base at net book value—original cost less accumulated depreciation. With foresight one can see that, other things being equal, this practice will cause an investment center's ROI "automatically" to increase each year because the investment base (denominator of the ROI fraction) becomes smaller due to each year's addition to accumulated depreciation.
>
> Some companies blame this ROI measurement scheme for their investment center managers' lack of motivation to propose modernization projects. Such a scheme normally causes ROI to decrease if a significant new project is

undertaken. The investment center managers may not be convinced that their superiors will later recognize the underlying reason for their investment centers' *apparent* ROI performance deterioration. In fact, a gradually rising ROI might indicate that the investment center's productive capability is deteriorating. In any case senior management is responsible for deciding on how ROI is to be measured. If there are unintended consequences from a particular approach, senior management—*not* the investment center manager—is to blame.

Another common mistake in management control is for superiors to assume, without investigation, that unfavorable variances imply poor managerial performance. Managerial morale can suffer tremendously if managers receive edicts from on high to correct unfavorable variances, without having the opportunity to discuss the causes of the variances with their superiors. Managers also resent a tendency in most organizations for superiors to pay a great deal of attention to unfavorable variances while remaining essentially silent with respect to favorable variances.

These problems are not shortcomings of the control system design per se but rather are matters of managerial *style.* To repeat, in the management control process, *behavioral* considerations are at least as important as accounting considerations. Thus, a conceptually sound management control system design will not be effective if managers feel that their superiors are using responsibility accounting information in an arbitrary or unfair way.

Cases

CASE 28–1 Amtrak Auto Ferry Service*

In July 1983 Don Hagarty, Director of Financial Planning for Amtrak, was asked by the Vice President for Corporate Planning to do a financial analysis of a proposed auto ferry service. The estimates of required capital expenditures and projections for annual revenues had been made by others, and he was fairly confident that they were appropriate. Hagarty's main concern was the development of the right costs to apply to the decision. In doing similar studies, the financial planning group usually relied on Amtrak's cost simulation model to identify the relevant costs. Recently, however, the model's method of classifying costs had become the subject of considerable debate and was therefore being carefully reviewed. Hagarty thought that the financial evaluation of the proposed auto ferry service, in addition to being an important decision in itself, would provide a good project to use for testing the present method of determining relevant costs and for evaluating some current proposals for improving the costing procedures.

Background. The National Railroad Passenger Corporation (Amtrak) was created on October 30, 1970, to revive the intercity passenger train industry. Operations began on May 1, 1971, with trains connecting 21 city pairs. At the time Amtrak did not own any track, stations, terminals, yards, or repair facilities and was thus totally dependent on other railroads for its existence.

As originally envisioned, Amtrak would require several years of federal subsidies before becoming a profitable operation. Throughout the 1970s the system expanded and new service was introduced. The oil crisis of 1973, which produced long lines at gas stations, also stimulated new interest in passenger trains. With the Amtrak Improvement Act of 1973, Congress attempted to make Amtrak permanent. Throughout its existence Amtrak had been acquiring engines and cars, and in 1976 it began acquiring track in the Northeast Corridor (Washington, D.C., to Boston). Then Congress adopted the Amtrak Improvement Act of 1978 and the Amtrak Reorganization Act of 1979. These acts reduced the route system by 15 percent and mandated certain operating goals for the corporation. Chief among these were a 50 percent improvement in on-time performance within three years, a systemwide average speed of 55 miles per hour, and a stipulation that Amtrak cover 44 percent of operating expenses through fares by the end of fiscal 1982 and 50 percent by 1985.

Although by 1983 Amtrak had not reached the desired 55 mph average speed, it had exceeded its on-time performance goal and had reached the 50 percent revenue/cost ratio three years ahead of the original schedule. Amtrak's 1982 business plan focused on improving the 50 percent revenue/cost ratio

---

and achieving an internal goal of covering all short-term avoidable costs from the farebox by 1985. Amtrak had recently begun revenue enhancement activities related to passenger rail service. For example, management was trying to make more efficient use of Amtrak's substantial real estate assets by marketing air rights over its stations in Chicago, Philadelphia, and Washington. The company had also recently entered into a long-term agreement with MCI Communications giving MCI the rights to lay fiber optics cables along track in the Northeast Corridor.

Current Situation. As part of the cost reduction efforts, Amtrak developed a computerized Cost Simulation Modeling System (CSMS). The most common types of decisions analyzed by CSMS were (1) the addition or deletion of a route, (2) increases or decreases in train frequency, and (3) changes in train "consist" (i.e., configuration of cars and engines). The model could also be used for route-by-route profitability comparisons and for less frequently occurring decisions such as the cost of adding mail service on a particular route. The CSMS was used at Amtrak's headquarters, and an effort was underway to encourage its use at the operating level where day-to-day cost reductions could be achieved.

As originally developed, CSMS focused on the notion of short-term avoidable costs; its function was to identify those costs that could be avoided if a route or service were to be discontinued. For example, to evaluate the decision of whether to drop a particular route, CSMS would produce an estimate of the costs that could be avoided if that decision were made, such as the cost of on-board service labor, materials, and fuel as well as some common costs that could be avoided if the route were dropped.

The concept of avoidable costs became embedded in legislation on Amtrak. In one instance route criteria were stated in terms of the ratio of short-term avoidable loss per passenger mile. In another instance the amount of compensation for certain state-subsidized routes was also related to the difference between forecasted revenue and short-term avoidable costs.

Over the years the forecasts made by CSMS had received some criticism. Estimates of direct costs such as on-board service labor or fuel were not questioned as much as those costs that were indirect. Running maintenance of equipment, for example, was considered to be 80 percent avoidable; it was allocated to a route on the basis of car miles or trips. Included in this expense were cleaning, inspection, and unscheduled repairs. This work was mostly done at the end of a route by a facility that handled equipment used on several routes. When a change was proposed, it was hard for the maintenance department to see that it would have much of a change in costs if only a small part of the facility's responsibility were affected. Furthermore, as one manager put it, "cars taken off one route usually end up on another route anyway."

The Cost System Review. In 1982 Amtrak initiated a study of the underlying cost concepts used in the cost model. Some of the issues addressed in that study were as follows:

1. How should the concept of short-run versus long-run be defined? How can the difference be estimated? Which is the most useful definition for the decisions Amtrak makes?

2. Linkages among activities affect costs. If a station serves two routes and one is to be eliminated, the station will have to remain operating. If both routes are cut, the station can be closed. What should be the avoidable cost of that station for each route?

3. Most of Amtrak's cars were now new and hence required low maintenance. What

cost should be included: the current maintenance cost or some sort of long-term average?

4. How should the concept of fixed and variable costs be incorporated into Amtrak's cost framework?

5. The model was designed to forecast avoidable costs for proposed changes. In considering a route's actual cost experience for a period of time, is there such a thing as actual avoidable costs?

The study's main conclusion was that the current three-way split of costs should be changed to six categories. The following diagram illustrates how the new arrangement would look:

Existing Cost Model

Short-term avoidable costs	
Other costs	
Capital costs	

Proposed Classification

	Operating	Capital
Differential costs: Traceable costs		
Common variable costs		
Residual costs		

The proposed categories emphasized the definition of differential costs, which are those costs that would change when a proposed decision was implemented. The residual costs were those that would not change. The borderline between the two categories would depend on the nature of the decision.

The differential costs were further divided into the traceable and common variable classifications. Traceable costs were those costs that would change immediately and directly.

Their change would be quite evident in the field. In the case of adding or dropping a route, costs for fuel usage and on-board service, for example, would be traceable differential costs.

Common variable costs differed from traceable costs in one or both of two ways:

1. They would be the allocated costs such as maintenance, which is allocated by car miles or trips. Though considered differential, they could not be specifically traced to a route or car.

2. They would be costs that included a short-term discretionary element. Maintenance could be postponed, but eventually the costs would be incurred.

Changes in common variable costs would not necessarily be immediate and would not be as evident in the field.

It was also concluded that capital costs could be differential or residual and that differential capital costs could be traceable or common variable. The latter situation would arise when facilities were shared.

Exhibit 1 presents a listing of Amtrak cost categories, together with the percent currently considered differential or "short-term avoidable" and a tentatively proposed classification using the new scheme.

Auto Ferry Service. In mid-1983 Amtrak was considering the establishment of an auto ferry service between Newark, New Jersey, and Sanford, Florida. The concept was to be modeled after Auto-Train, a company that had built its reputation hauling passengers and their cars between Washington, D.C., and Florida.

Auto-Train's pitch had been simple: Instead of driving, why not eat, sleep, and watch movies on a train while your car travels with you? The company got off to a blazing start in the early 70s, with revenues growing from $2 million to $30 million in its first five years of operation. Overzealous

EXHIBIT 1
AMTRAK COST CATEGORIES

Cost Category (1)	Relative Magnitude (percent of 1983 budget) (2)	Percent Differential (3)		Decision: Change in		
		On NEC†	Off NEC	Route (4)	Frequency (5)	Consist (6)
Transportation:						
Train and engine crews.......	17.9	100	100	T	T	
Diesel fuel.................	11.1	100	100	T	T	T
Electric power..............		100	100			
Other direct	1.1	100	100	C	C	
Mainline operations	0.8	0	100	C*	C*	
Yard operations.............	1.9	0	100	C*	C*	C*
Transportation overhead	0.1	0	100			
Joint facilities...............	0.9					
Incentives...................	0.1	0	0			
Avoidable RR expense	1.0	17.3	77.4			
Locomotive maintenance:						
Running repairs..............	5.1	80	80	C*	C*	
Heavy repairs	—	0	0	C*	C*	
Overhead	0.5	43.4	43.4			
Car maintenance:						
Running repairs..............	14.8	80	80	C*	C*	C*
Heavy repairs	—	0	0	C*	C*	C*
Overhead	3.0	43.4	43.4			
Maintenance of way:						
Track and signals............	2.5	40	100	C	C	C
Facilities and buildings	0.2	0	100			
Overhead	—	0	0			
Onboard service:						
Labor......................	7.1	100	100	T	T	T
Supplies	2.8	100	100	T	T	T
Commissary.................	0.1	5	5	C	C	C
Crew base	—	5	5			
Station services:						
Station services..............	3.2			C*	C*	C*
Support.....................	—	0	0			
Marketing:						
Sales and marketing	0.7	10	10			
Reservations and information..	5.9	100	100	C	C	C
General support:						
Revenue accounting	0.4	40	40			
Information services..........	0.8	20	20			
Support.....................	—	0	0			
Taxes and insurance:						
Taxes......................	0.3	0	0			
Insurance	0.3	10	10			
Depreciation:						
General and administration....	—	0	0			
Interest	—	0	0			
Other......................	17.8	0	0			

† NEC = Northeast Corridor.

Explanation:
Column 1 Cost categories used in the cost model.
Column 2 Size of cost categories as a percent of total short-term avoidable costs forecasted for 1983.
Column 3 Of the cost in each category, the percent of the total forecasted cost that was considered short-term avoidable. Fewer of the costs in the Northeast Corridor were considered avoidable because the facilities there were mostly owned by Amtrak. In other areas these facilities-related costs were based on service contracts with other railroads.
Column 4, 5, 6 T = traceable; C = common; * = a step function would be appropriate in the model. These were classifications growing out of the Amtrak cost study.

expansion and a series of derailments around 1976, however, left Auto-Train in serious financial straits. Revenue and earnings growth flattened as the company cut back service and took on more debt. Finally, in September 1980 when a desperately needed loan fell through, Auto-Train was forced to declare bankruptcy. It was never a lack of passengers that plagued Auto-Train—the trains ran nearly full until the end.

Amtrak hoped to avoid Auto-Train's strategic and financial errors, but wanted to capitalize on the potentially large market for a similar service. The proposed auto ferry service would differ from Auto-Train primarily in that service would begin at Newark rather than at Lorton, Virginia, which had been Auto-Train's terminus. Customers would still be able to get on and off at Lorton. Like Auto-Train, Amtrak hoped to create a friendly, relaxed atmosphere including late-night movies and an on-board musician. Amtrak's revenue forecast of $34 million per year was based partly on Auto-Train's experience and partly on current market conditions and the capacity offered.

The proposed consist for the auto ferry service included the following cars on peak demand days:

1 E-60 electric locomotive

2 P-30 locomotives

7 Amfleet II coaches

2 dome coaches

1 lounge

2 buffet/table cars

1 table car

7 sleepers

20 tri-level auto carriers (12-auto capacity)

3 bi-level auto carriers (8-auto capacity)

Three full sets of equipment plus one back-up set would be required for a daily frequency. The auto rack cars were to be those previously leased to Auto-Train that were already equipped with the high-speed trucks and automobile fastening systems required for this type of operation. These cars would require some rehabilitation as a result of being out of service for over two years.

The facilities at Lorton and Sanford were to be purchased or leased from their current owners whereas the Newark facility would have to be added to the existing passenger station. The Lorton and Sanford facilities were in disrepair and would require considerable rehabilitation. Primary car maintenance would be conducted at Sanford and turnaround servicing at Newark. The investment in facilities and rack cars was estimated at $6 million.

In its initial analysis Amtrak projected annual operating costs of $34 million. The figure was intended to reflect the incremental cost of this type of service on Amtrak operations. Wherever possible, costs were identified at precise levels of personnel assigned, rates payable, and equipment overhead. Because the Newark–Washington portion of the route was owned by Amtrak, there was some question as to whether certain costs incurred in the NEC (Northeast Corridor) should be allocated to the auto ferry service or should be considered a "free good." Because Amtrak did not own any track between Lorton and Sanford, many of the operating functions would be contracted out to two railroads: the Richmond, Fredericksburg & Potomac and the Seaboard Coast Line. These costs would be charged to Amtrak on the basis of actual trips, train miles, or car miles, or in some cases on the basis of actual costs incurred.

Exhibit 2 gives Don Hagarty's initial estimates of annual incremental costs for the proposed auto ferry service. As shown on the exhibit, most of the costs reflected the existing definition of short-term avoidable costs. These figures were generated by the cost model after the specific characteristics and

EXHIBIT 2
ESTIMATED INCREMENTAL COSTS FOR AUTO FERRY SERVICE

Costs marked with an asterisk (*) were not normally considered short-term avoidable costs in the operation of the cost model. However, they were included here as incremental costs for this particular decision. In item 10, 10 percent of total sales and marketing expense was normally considered short-term avoidable and was allocated to a route on the basis of $0.20 per passenger. That 10 percent was largely made up of credit card and travel agency commissions. Figures that follow are thousands of dollars.

1. Train and engine crew:

	NEC	$ 545
	Non-NEC	2,174
		$2,719

Calculation on the basis of the specific contracts we have with the RF&P (Washington–Richmond) and SCL (Richmond–Sanford) for non-NEC costs, based on a five-man train crew per district. North of Washington, projected annual costs were used for the Amtrak crew.

2. Fuel and electric power: $4,455

Specific estimates based on route, consist, and engines to be used.

3. Transportation:

	NEC	$ 351*
	Non-NEC	1,307
		$1,658

Comprises mainline operations, yard operations, and transportation overhead. Mainline operations include direct labor and material costs of train and crew dispatching, drawbridge operations, and clearing wrecks. Yard operations include payroll and other direct costs related to directing the movement of trains and switching trains within yards. Transportation overhead includes payroll and other expenses related to the management and supervision of train operations, highway vehicle operations, and track inspection.

The non-NEC figure is based on the terms of contracts with carrying railroads. The NEC figure is an allocation based on ratios (e.g., cost per train trip) for existing trains.

4. Locomotive and car maintenance:

	Running	$5,531
	Heavy	1,720*
	Overhead	770
		$8,021

Comprises "short-term avoidable" portion (80 percent) of running repairs on engines and cars, direct labor and material portion of heavy repairs, and variable overhead applicable to equipment maintenance at 43.4 percent of total maintenance overhead. Dollar estimates were based on estimated current total cost and projected system activity. Running maintenance includes inspection, servicing, cleaning, and running repairs for locomotives and passenger cars. Heavy maintenance represents direct costs of programmed repairs, e.g., intermediate and heavy overhauls. Overhead includes all costs related to maintenance of equipment, management, supervision, clerical and office staffs, and shop overhead.

5. On-board service labor: $3,160, staffed as follows:

Position	Peak Total
Train manager	1
Entertainer	1
Sleeping car attendants	7
Dining car attendants	12
Lounge car attendants	2
	23

Costs calculated based on average man-year salaries and fringe benefits for various positions.

6. On-board service supplies: $1,517

Calculated using an expectation that supplies would be 62 percent of projected on-board service revenue.

7. Railroad performance payments: $1,070*

Computed using historical RF&P and SCL on-time performance and rates for appropriate segments.

EXHIBIT 2 *(concluded)*

---

8. Maintenance of way: NEC $ 81*
                         Non-NEC   <u>323</u>
                                    $404

Represents all direct labor and material costs related to maintenance of roadway, track, road crossings, tunnels, bridges, trestles, and culverts. For the NEC, the figure quoted represents the variable portion (40 percent) of total costs distributed to specific trains using a rate per unit mile. The non-NEC maintenance of way costs are strictly variable contract rates with the RF&P and SCL.

9. Stations: Direct (Sanford and Lorton) $547
                    Allocated (Newark)   <u>92*</u>
                                                     $639

Direct station costs represent the staffing requirements at each of the three stations as follows:

Position	Total
Station supervisor	1
Lead ticket clerk	1
Ticket clerks	2
Redcap/receptionists	<u>4</u>
	8

Since the auto ferry service will bring the total number of trains being served at Newark from 18 to 20, the two auto ferry service trains will absorb 10 percent of total station costs. The Lorton and Sanford stations will be dedicated to auto ferry service and will have no shared costs.

10. Sales and marketing: $2,740*

Comprised of advertising ($1,600) plus credit card commissions and travel agency commissions computed at the appropriate percentage applied to projected sales through credit cards and travel agents.

11. Reservations: $1,469

Assumed that an auto ferry service reservation would take 1.5 times the average time to make an Amtrak reservation. Allocated systemwide reservation bureau costs with an assumption that such costs are 85 percent variable. This does not include any allocation of the cost of the centralized computer reservation system, which is assumed to be fixed.

12. General Support: $1,820*

Comprises the service's share of remaining overhead believed to be to some degree variable over the long term: revenue accounting, information services, common facilities, stations, commissaries, crew bases, and field and corporate support overhead.

13. Insurance: $3,353*

Includes policy premiums, automobile damage liability, and self-insurance for passengers allocated on the basis of passenger miles and for employees and third parties on the basis of car miles.

14. Automobile loading/unloading: $471

Assumes part-time nonunion labor paid at minimum wage and staffed as follows at each location:

Position	Total
Foremen	2
Drivers—1st shift	16
Drivers—2nd shift	<u>16</u>
	34

15. Lease of facilities: $444

Estimated annual cost to lease facilities at Sanford and Lorton.

Total cost: $33,940

route of the train were entered. In a few cases, such as for car loading personnel, the specific projected costs were used.

Some of the costs shown in Exhibit 2 were considered by Hagarty to be incremental even though they would not be included in the short-term avoidable classification. These are marked on the exhibit by an asterisk (*) and their nature is described.

In reviewing his cost estimates shown in Exhibit 2, Hagarty wondered if he had included too many items as incremental or perhaps left some out. Furthermore, he knew that whatever costs were included would have to be explained and defended. He wanted to be able to do that in a way that laid the foundations for explanation of other cost analyses and provided a clear framework for use by the operating and marketing segments of the organization.

Questions

1. Respond to the five issues raised in the section titled "The Cost System Review."

2. Evaluate the financial desirability of instituting the auto ferry service.

CASE 28–2 Uncle Grumps Toys*

One morning John Worby, President of Uncle Grumps Toys, sat down with Anne McMullen, Executive Vice President, to discuss year-end performance evaluations of the management group. These discussions were important because the company had traditionally given managers a sizable bonus based on their evaluation. To the extent that it was possible, John and Anne preferred to base their evaluation on objective measures of performance with an emphasis on achievement of budgeted goals.

The budget process began in late August, and by mid-November the management team supplied the board of directors with a complete budget outlining monthly sales estimates, production cost estimates, and capital spending requirements. The directors then discussed the implications of the budget and, upon acceptance, authorized it. The firm's progress throughout the year was monitored against this budget every six months at the board meetings, which were held on the fifteenth of January and July. At the January meeting the board also voted on the management bonuses for the prior year.

Uncle Grumps Toys was a Boston-based company that manufactured a very successful line of foam rubber toys called "Uncle Grumps." These were cuddly Hobbit-like dolls with large noses, a discerning smile, and enormous feet, which sold for $20 wholesale. From the moment of introduction, they had been a runaway success. Plans to expand the line were on the drawing board, and a smaller baby version was to be introduced in the spring of 1988.

The business was highly seasonal with over half of the sales occurring from mid-August to early November. This was followed by a two-month trough before birthday and occasional gift sales picked up again. Sales were then fairly static until the next Christmas rush began. Budgeted sales for 1987 were $40 million with a standard gross margin, on full production cost, of 24 percent.

Management had decided that even though sales were highly seasonal, production would be level throughout the year. This

---

*An abridged version of McMullen and Worby (A), Copyright © by the President and Fellows of Harvard College. Harvard Business School case 179-197.

enabled Uncle Grumps Toys to stabilize employment and to sell a greater number of toys during the Christmas period than would have been possible if a shift approach had been used. Current production was at full capacity using one shift a day, five days a week. In 1986 sales were considerably greater than expectation and had almost resulted in orders being rejected due to a lack of inventory. In fact, by year-end only 44,000 toys were left in stock.

John and Anne decided to discuss the production manager's performance first. The production manager, Holly Frost, had been with the firm for just over a year, and this was to be her first bonus. John and Anne admired Holly and felt she had been very innovative and had substantially improved the production process. One improvement, introduced at the beginning of the third quarter, resulted in the average material content of each toy being reduced from 5 lbs. to 4.5 lbs., a substantial savings.

In measuring Holly's managerial performance, John and Anne felt that some adjustment was necessary because 1987 had been a rather turbulent year. The factory had been closed from February 5 to March 4 (20 working days) due to "The Great Blizzard of '87," and then the factory roof collapsed under the weight of three feet of snow. During this period employees did not work but were given half pay.

To make up for lost production, a four-hour Saturday morning shift was introduced from March 7 until the end of the year. Employees were paid time-and-a-half for this work. Additional overtime was required in the fourth quarter when the sales department managed to gain a $750,000 order from a catalog sales company for an extra 50,000 toys. The order was placed in the middle of October and, along with other orders, required that overtime be increased to 16 hours per weekend, at time-and-a-half, for six weekends (this includes the Saturday morning time already planned). Sales for 1987 were 2,094,000 units.

John and Anne started with the budgeted and actual figures reported in Exhibit 1. The company had not implemented a standard cost system. Because unit costs were relatively stable, direct materials were tracked in pounds, direct labor in hours, and actual usage was compared with budget. Before they could adequately judge Holly's performance, however, John and Anne decided they needed additional information. John spoke with the materials inventory clerk and came back with an inventory listing (Exhibit 2) and a reminder that the company used FIFO inventory costing. Anne spoke with the payroll clerk and was given a summary of quarterly payroll listings (Exhibit 3).

Looking at the pile of information they had collected, John and Anne settled down to the process of evaluating Holly's performance. After several hours John and Anne took a break. They felt they had made progress but still were not certain that they knew how Holly had performed.

Over coffee Anne remarked to John, "Well, now we have a lot of facts but it's not clear to me how we can use them to analyze Holly's performance."

"I have the same concern," replied John. "There are so many numbers and only some are relevant to Holly."

"I know, but which ones? That's the question."

"That's first on the agenda when we finish coffee. But there is something else bothering me and that is a comment Holly made about those catalog sales," said John.

"What was that?" asked Anne.

"Well, Holly thinks we lost money on the deal because we sold them to the catalog company below cost."

"Didn't you explain to her about contribution analysis?" asked Anne.

"Well, yes, but she said she understood that, and we were still losing out. Unfortunately, she was called away before she could explain to me what she meant."

EXHIBIT 1
QUARTERLY PRODUCTION REPORT
(all figures in thousands)

| | Quarterly Budget | Quarterly Actuals | | | | Total 1987 |
		1	2	3	4	
Variable Costs:						
Raw materials	$1,800*	$1,410	$1,775	$2,190	$1,880	$ 7,255
Direct labor	3,848†	3,205	4,406	4,466	5,453	17,530
Indirect labor	300	250	350	356	410	1,366
Supplies	75	50	100	50	90	290
Power	375	270	420	410	450	1,550
Fixed Costs:						
Repairs and maintenance	300	130	120	500	280	1,030
Depreciation	700	700	700	700	700	2,800
Insurance	250	252	231	260	260	1,003
	$7,648	$6,267	$8,102	$8,932	$9,523	$32,824
Units produced	500	350	550	550	600	2,050

*Budget based on 5 lbs./toy.
†Budget based on 0.962 hr./toy.

EXHIBIT 2
SUMMARY OF RAW MATERIAL INVENTORY MOVEMENTS
(all figures in thousands)

Opening balance (Dec. 6, 1986)	718 lbs.	$ 500
Purchases (Dec. 6, 1986–Dec. 4, 1987)	10,000	7,255
Usage (Dec. 6, 1986–Dec. 4, 1987)	(9,570)	(6,891)
Closing balance (December 4, 1987)	1,148	$ 864

EXHIBIT 3
SUMMARY OF DIRECT LABOR EXPENSES
(all figures in thousands, except employees)

	Average Number of Employees	Regular Hours	Overtime Hours	Cost†
13 weeks ending 3/6/87	960	494*	0	$ 3,205
13 weeks ending 6/5/87	970	500	52	4,406
13 weeks ending 9/4/87	980	505	54	4,466
13 weeks ending 12/4/87	990	510	135	5,453
Total		2,009	241	$17,530

*Includes the 153,000 hours when the factory was closed for 20 days, during which time employees received half pay.
†Holly was responsible for negotiating all labor contracts.

Questions

1. How well did Holly Frost perform as production manager in 1987? Explain.

2. Was the special deal made with the catalog company a good idea? Explain.

APPENDIX TABLES

TABLE A
PRESENT VALUE OF $1 RECEIVED N YEARS HENCE

Years Hence	1%	2%	4%	6%	8%	10%	12%	14%	15%	16%	18%	20%	22%	24%	25%	26%	28%	30%	35%	40%	45%	50%
1	0.990	0.980	0.962	0.943	0.926	0.909	0.893	0.877	0.870	0.862	0.847	0.833	0.820	0.806	0.800	0.794	0.781	0.769	0.741	0.714	0.690	0.667
2	0.980	0.961	0.925	0.890	0.857	0.826	0.797	0.769	0.756	0.743	0.718	0.694	0.672	0.650	0.640	0.630	0.610	0.592	0.549	0.510	0.476	0.444
3	0.971	0.942	0.889	0.840	0.794	0.751	0.712	0.675	0.658	0.641	0.609	0.579	0.551	0.524	0.512	0.500	0.477	0.455	0.406	0.364	0.328	0.296
4	0.961	0.924	0.855	0.792	0.735	0.683	0.636	0.592	0.572	0.552	0.516	0.482	0.451	0.423	0.410	0.397	0.373	0.350	0.301	0.260	0.226	0.198
5	0.951	0.906	0.822	0.747	0.681	0.621	0.567	0.519	0.497	0.476	0.437	0.402	0.370	0.341	0.328	0.315	0.291	0.269	0.223	0.186	0.156	0.132
6	0.942	0.888	0.790	0.705	0.630	0.564	0.507	0.456	0.432	0.410	0.370	0.335	0.303	0.275	0.262	0.250	0.227	0.207	0.165	0.133	0.108	0.088
7	0.933	0.871	0.760	0.665	0.583	0.513	0.452	0.400	0.376	0.354	0.314	0.279	0.249	0.222	0.210	0.198	0.178	0.159	0.122	0.095	0.074	0.059
8	0.923	0.853	0.731	0.627	0.540	0.467	0.404	0.351	0.327	0.305	0.266	0.233	0.204	0.179	0.168	0.157	0.139	0.123	0.091	0.068	0.051	0.039
9	0.914	0.837	0.703	0.592	0.500	0.424	0.361	0.308	0.284	0.263	0.225	0.194	0.167	0.144	0.134	0.125	0.108	0.094	0.067	0.048	0.035	0.026
10	0.905	0.820	0.676	0.558	0.463	0.386	0.322	0.270	0.247	0.227	0.191	0.162	0.137	0.116	0.107	0.099	0.085	0.073	0.050	0.035	0.024	0.017
11	0.896	0.804	0.650	0.527	0.429	0.350	0.287	0.237	0.215	0.195	0.162	0.135	0.112	0.094	0.086	0.079	0.066	0.056	0.037	0.025	0.017	0.012
12	0.887	0.788	0.625	0.497	0.397	0.319	0.257	0.208	0.187	0.168	0.137	0.112	0.092	0.076	0.069	0.062	0.052	0.043	0.027	0.018	0.012	0.008
13	0.879	0.773	0.601	0.469	0.368	0.290	0.229	0.182	0.163	0.145	0.116	0.093	0.075	0.061	0.055	0.050	0.040	0.033	0.020	0.013	0.008	0.005
14	0.870	0.758	0.577	0.442	0.340	0.263	0.205	0.160	0.141	0.125	0.099	0.078	0.062	0.049	0.044	0.039	0.032	0.025	0.015	0.009	0.006	0.003
15	0.861	0.743	0.555	0.417	0.315	0.239	0.183	0.140	0.123	0.108	0.084	0.065	0.051	0.040	0.035	0.031	0.025	0.020	0.011	0.006	0.004	0.002
16	0.853	0.728	0.534	0.394	0.292	0.218	0.163	0.123	0.107	0.093	0.071	0.054	0.042	0.032	0.028	0.025	0.019	0.015	0.008	0.005	0.003	0.002
17	0.844	0.714	0.513	0.371	0.270	0.198	0.146	0.108	0.093	0.080	0.060	0.045	0.034	0.026	0.023	0.020	0.015	0.012	0.006	0.003	0.002	0.001
18	0.836	0.700	0.494	0.350	0.250	0.180	0.130	0.095	0.081	0.069	0.051	0.038	0.028	0.021	0.018	0.016	0.012	0.009	0.005	0.002	0.001	0.001
19	0.828	0.686	0.475	0.331	0.232	0.164	0.116	0.083	0.070	0.060	0.043	0.031	0.023	0.017	0.014	0.012	0.009	0.007	0.003	0.002	0.001	
20	0.820	0.673	0.456	0.312	0.215	0.149	0.104	0.073	0.061	0.051	0.037	0.026	0.019	0.014	0.012	0.010	0.007	0.005	0.002	0.001	0.001	
21	0.811	0.660	0.439	0.294	0.199	0.135	0.093	0.064	0.053	0.044	0.031	0.022	0.015	0.011	0.009	0.008	0.006	0.004	0.002	0.001		
22	0.803	0.647	0.422	0.278	0.184	0.123	0.083	0.056	0.046	0.038	0.026	0.018	0.013	0.009	0.007	0.006	0.004	0.003	0.001	0.001		
23	0.795	0.634	0.406	0.262	0.170	0.112	0.074	0.049	0.040	0.033	0.022	0.015	0.010	0.007	0.006	0.005	0.003	0.002	0.001			
24	0.788	0.622	0.390	0.247	0.158	0.102	0.066	0.043	0.035	0.028	0.019	0.013	0.008	0.006	0.005	0.004	0.003	0.002	0.001			
25	0.780	0.610	0.375	0.233	0.146	0.092	0.059	0.038	0.030	0.024	0.016	0.010	0.007	0.005	0.004	0.003	0.002	0.001	0.001			
26	0.772	0.598	0.361	0.220	0.135	0.084	0.053	0.033	0.026	0.021	0.014	0.009	0.006	0.004	0.003	0.002	0.002	0.001				
27	0.764	0.586	0.347	0.207	0.125	0.076	0.047	0.029	0.023	0.018	0.011	0.007	0.005	0.003	0.002	0.002	0.001	0.001				
28	0.757	0.574	0.333	0.196	0.116	0.069	0.042	0.026	0.020	0.016	0.010	0.006	0.004	0.002	0.002	0.002	0.001	0.001				
29	0.749	0.563	0.321	0.185	0.107	0.063	0.037	0.022	0.017	0.014	0.008	0.005	0.003	0.002	0.002	0.001	0.001	0.001				
30	0.742	0.552	0.308	0.174	0.099	0.057	0.033	0.020	0.015	0.012	0.007	0.004	0.003	0.001	0.001	0.001	0.001	0.001				
40	0.672	0.453	0.208	0.097	0.046	0.022	0.011	0.005	0.004	0.003	0.001	0.001										
50	0.608	0.372	0.141	0.054	0.021	0.009	0.003	0.001	0.001	0.001												

TABLE B
PRESENT VALUE OF $1 RECEIVED ANNUALLY FOR N YEARS

Years (N)	1%	2%	4%	6%	8%	10%	12%	14%	15%	16%	18%	20%	22%	24%	25%	26%	28%	30%	35%	40%	45%	50%
1	0.990	0.980	0.562	0.943	0.926	0.909	0.893	0.877	0.870	0.862	0.847	0.833	0.820	0.806	0.800	0.794	0.781	0.769	0.741	0.714	0.690	0.667
2	1.970	1.942	1.886	1.833	1.783	1.736	1.690	1.647	1.626	1.605	1.566	1.528	1.492	1.457	1.440	1.424	1.392	1.361	1.289	1.224	1.165	1.111
3	2.941	2.884	2.775	2.673	2.577	2.487	2.402	2.322	2.283	2.246	2.174	2.106	2.042	1.981	1.952	1.953	1.868	1.816	1.696	1.589	1.493	1.407
4	3.902	3.808	3.630	3.465	3.312	3.170	3.037	2.914	2.855	2.798	2.690	2.589	2.494	2.404	2.362	2.320	2.241	2.166	1.997	1.849	1.720	1.605
5	4.853	4.713	4.452	4.212	3.993	3.791	3.605	3.433	3.352	3.274	3.127	2.991	2.864	2.745	2.689	2.635	2.532	2.436	2.220	2.035	1.876	1.737
6	5.795	5.601	5.242	4.917	4.623	4.355	4.111	3.889	3.784	3.685	3.498	3.326	3.167	3.020	2.951	2.885	2.759	2.643	2.385	2.168	1.983	1.824
7	6.728	6.472	6.002	5.582	5.206	4.868	4.564	4.288	4.160	4.039	3.812	3.605	3.416	3.242	3.161	3.083	2.937	2.802	2.508	2.263	2.057	1.883
8	7.652	7.325	6.733	6.210	5.747	5.335	4.968	4.639	4.487	4.344	4.078	3.837	3.619	3.421	3.329	3.241	3.076	2.925	2.598	2.331	2.108	1.922
9	8.566	8.162	7.435	6.802	6.247	5.759	5.328	4.946	4.772	4.607	4.303	4.031	3.786	3.566	3.463	3.366	3.184	3.019	2.665	2.379	2.144	1.948
10	9.471	8.983	8.111	7.360	6.710	6.145	5.650	5.216	5.019	4.833	4.494	4.192	3.923	3.682	3.571	3.465	3.269	3.092	2.715	2.414	2.168	1.965
11	10.368	9.787	8.760	7.887	7.139	6.495	5.937	5.453	5.234	5.029	4.656	4.327	4.035	3.776	3.656	3.544	3.335	3.147	2.752	2.438	2.185	1.977
12	11.255	10.575	9.385	8.384	7.536	6.814	6.194	5.660	5.421	5.197	4.793	4.439	4.127	3.851	3.725	3.606	3.387	3.190	2.779	2.456	2.196	1.985
13	12.134	11.343	9.986	8.853	7.904	7.103	6.424	5.842	5.583	5.342	4.910	4.533	4.203	3.912	3.780	3.656	3.427	3.223	2.799	2.468	2.204	1.990
14	13.004	12.106	10.563	9.295	8.244	7.367	6.628	6.002	5.724	5.468	5.008	4.611	4.265	3.962	3.824	3.695	3.459	3.249	2.814	2.477	2.210	1.993
15	13.865	12.849	11.118	9.712	8.559	7.606	6.811	6.142	5.847	5.575	5.092	4.675	4.315	4.001	3.859	3.726	3.483	3.268	2.825	2.484	2.214	1.995
16	14.718	13.578	11.652	10.106	8.851	7.824	6.974	6.265	5.954	5.669	5.162	4.730	4.357	4.033	3.887	3.751	3.503	3.283	2.834	2.489	2.216	1.997
17	15.562	14.292	12.166	10.477	9.122	8.022	7.120	6.373	6.047	5.749	5.222	4.775	4.391	4.059	3.910	3.771	3.518	3.295	2.840	2.492	2.218	1.998
18	16.398	14.992	12.659	10.828	9.372	8.201	7.250	6.467	6.128	5.818	5.273	4.812	4.419	4.080	3.928	3.786	3.529	3.304	2.844	2.494	2.219	1.999
19	17.226	15.678	13.134	11.158	9.604	8.365	7.366	6.550	6.198	5.877	5.316	4.844	4.442	4.097	3.942	3.799	3.539	3.311	2.848	2.496	2.220	1.999
20	18.046	16.351	13.590	11.470	9.818	8.514	7.469	6.623	6.259	5.929	5.353	4.870	4.460	4.110	3.954	3.808	3.546	3.316	2.850	2.497	2.221	1.999
21	18.857	17.011	14.029	11.764	10.017	8.649	7.562	6.687	6.312	5.973	5.384	4.891	4.476	4.121	3.963	3.816	3.551	3.320	2.852	2.498	2.221	2.000
22	19.660	17.658	14.451	12.042	10.201	8.772	7.645	6.743	6.359	6.011	5.410	4.909	4.488	4.130	3.970	3.822	3.556	3.323	2.853	2.498	2.222	2.000
23	20.456	18.292	14.857	12.303	10.371	8.883	7.718	6.792	6.399	6.044	5.432	4.925	4.499	4.137	3.976	3.827	3.559	3.325	2.854	2.499	2.222	2.000
24	21.243	18.914	15.247	12.550	10.529	8.985	7.784	6.835	6.434	6.073	5.451	4.937	4.507	4.143	3.981	3.831	3.562	3.327	2.855	2.499	2.222	2.000
25	22.023	19.523	15.622	12.783	10.675	9.077	7.843	6.873	6.464	6.097	5.467	4.948	4.514	4.147	3.985	3.834	3.564	3.329	2.856	2.499	2.222	2.000
26	22.795	20.121	15.983	13.003	10.810	9.161	7.896	6.906	6.491	6.118	5.480	4.956	4.520	4.151	3.988	3.837	3.566	3.330	2.856	2.500	2.222	2.000
27	23.560	20.707	16.330	13.211	10.935	9.237	7.943	6.935	6.514	6.136	5.492	4.964	4.524	4.154	3.990	3.839	3.567	3.331	2.856	2.500	2.222	2.000
28	24.316	21.281	16.663	13.406	11.051	9.307	7.984	6.961	6.534	6.152	5.502	4.970	4.528	4.157	3.992	3.840	3.568	3.331	2.857	2.500	2.222	2.000
29	25.066	21.844	16.984	13.591	11.158	9.370	8.022	6.983	6.551	6.166	5.510	4.975	4.531	4.159	3.994	3.841	3.569	3.332	2.857	2.500	2.222	2.000
30	25.808	22.396	17.292	13.765	11.258	9.427	8.055	7.003	6.566	6.177	5.517	4.979	4.534	4.160	3.995	3.842	3.569	3.332	2.857	2.500	2.222	2.000
40	32.835	27.355	19.793	15.046	11.925	9.779	8.244	7.105	6.642	6.234	5.548	4.997	4.544	4.166	3.999	3.846	3.571	3.333	2.857	2.500	2.222	2.000
50	39.196	31.424	21.482	15.762	12.234	9.915	8.304	7.133	6.661	6.246	5.554	4.999	4.545	4.167	4.000	3.846	3.571	3.333	2.857	2.500	2.222	2.000

Index

Cost concepts—*Cont.*
  misconceptions about, 465–66
  nonmanufacturing costs, 581–83
  product costing systems, 576–81
  uses of full cost, 583–88
Cost constrictions, 909–10
Cost drivers, 617–19
Cost elements, 764, 838, 1004
Cost method, for treasury stock, 288
Cost object, 570–71, 1003–4
  full cost, 610
  indirect cost calculation, 609–30
  intermediate versus final, 611
Cost of capital, 970–71
Cost of goods manufactured, 173–74
Cost of goods sold, 72
  current, 184
  inventory costing methods, 178–86
  manufacturing company, 170–77
  merchandising companies, 163–70
Cost of quality, 665–66
Cost of sales, 71–72
  merchandising company, 163–70
  service companies, 177–78
  in standard cost system, 676–77
  by types of company, 162
Cost recovery method of revenue recognition, 134
Cost reduction, in capital budgeting, 966
Cost-reimbursement contract, 132–33
Costs; *see also* Differential costs; Fixed costs; Full cost accounting; *and* Variable costs
  accuracy of, 668–69
  adjusting to prices, 587
  alternative choice problems, 1002–3
  controllable, 794–98
  control of, 1002
  curvelinear, 535
  definition, 27, 61
  differential, 909–12, 919–26
  direct and indirect, 518, 571–72
  direct versus variable, 608–9
  discretionary, 551, 799–801
  drift of, 538
  engineered, 799
  full, 571
  general definition, 570
  judgment calls, 668–69

Costs—*Cont.*
  and learning curve, 551, 552–54
  in management accounting, 521
  meaning of, 569–70
  measurement, 1002
  noncontrollable, 796–98
  not associated with future revenue, 62–63
  pension plans, 312–13
  of production, 573–75
  reasons for variation, 550–51
  relevant to volume, 527–41
  research and development, 234
  in responsibility centers, 519–20
  semivariable, 529
  step-function, 535
  types of, 914–15, 1003–5
  unaffected, 920–21
  unexpired, 475
Cost-type contracts, 584
Cost-volume diagram, 529–31, 539–41
  linear assumption, 534–35
  relation to unit costs, 531–32
  relevant range, 532
  relevant time period, 532–34
Cost-volume-profitgraph; *see* Profitgraphs
Cost-volume relationship, 536–39
Cotter Company, Inc., case, 715–16
Coupon rate, 255
Covenants, 253
Coverage ratio, 378
Craik Veneer Company, case, 687–89
Crawford curve, 554 n
Credit card sales, 140–41
Credit side, 95–96
Criteria, 14–15
Crompton, Ltd., case, 981–93
Cross subsidies, 625–26
Culture of organizations, 761
Cumulative preferred stock, 285
Current assets, 35–36
Current cost accounting, 332–33
Current cost of goods sold, 184
Current liabilities, 38, 252, 260–61
Current outlook, 850
Current rate method, 329
Current ratio, 42, 148–49
Current yield, 270
Curvelinear costs, 535

D

Daily reports, 879
Dallas Consulting Group, case, 752–53

Darius, 12
Darius Company, case, 751–52
Data processing, 116
Data processing department, 806–7
Days' cash, 149–50
Days' inventory in hand, 187–88
Days' payables ratio, 431
Days' receivables, 150–51
Debenture, 254
Debit and credit, 95–96
  equality, 115
Debit-balance accounts, 101
Debit side, 95–96
Debt capital, 261
  compared to equity capital, 295–96
  definition, 252–53
  types, 253–54
Debt/capitalization ratio, 263
Debt/equity ratio, 262–63
Debt ratios, 261–63
Debt transactions, on cash flow worksheet, 375–76
Decentralization, 798
Decision making, 6–7
  centralized versus decentralized, 798
  with standard cost system, 657
Decision models
  decision tree analysis, 940–43
  economic order quantity, 936–39
  expected value, 939–40
  linear programming, 943–45
  Monte Carlo method, 940
  sensitivity analysis, 940
Decision tree analysis, 940–43
Declining balance depreciation method, 214
Default
  bonds, 253
  mortgage, 254
Default drivers, 618–19
Deferral method of financial reporting, 226
Deferred charges, 64
  intangible assets, 233
Deferred compensation, 348
Deferred income tax liability, 320–21
Deferred Investment, 977–78
Deferred revenues, 38
Deferred tax assets, 322–23
Deferred taxes, 317–19
  on cash flow statement, 364
  as liability, 261